Capital Punishment
and the
Judicial Process

Capital Punishment and the Judicial Process

THIRD EDITION

Randall Coyne
FRANK ELKOURI AND EDNA ASPER ELKOURI PROFESSOR OF LAW
UNIVERSITY OF OKLAHOMA COLLEGE OF LAW

Lyn Entzeroth
ASSOCIATE PROFESSOR OF LAW
UNIVERSITY OF TULSA COLLEGE OF LAW

CAROLINA ACADEMIC PRESS
Durham, North Carolina

ISBN 1-59460-272-7
LCCN 2006927463

Carolina Academic Press
700 Kent Street
Durham, North Carolina 27701
Telephone (919) 489-7486
Fax (919) 493-5668
www.cap-press.com

Printed in the United States of America

Summary of Contents

Table of Contents

Table of Cases

References are to page numbers. Principal cases are in italics.

Table of Prisoners

List of Web Addresses

http://www.aclu.org/death-penalty (American Civil Liberties Union).

http://www.capdefnet.org (Capital Defense Network).

http://www.criminaljustice.org (National Association of Criminal Defense Lawyers).

http://www.deathpenaltyinfo.org (Death Penalty Information Center).

http://www.deathpenaltyinfo.org.Innocentlist.html.

http://www.fbi.gov/ucr/ucr.htm (Federal Bureau of Investigation Uniform Crime Reports).

http://www.gallup.com/indicators/inddeath_pen.asp (polling information).

http://www.icj-cij.org.

http://www.icj-cij/org/icwww/idocket/igus/igusframe.htm.

http://www.justice.policy.net/jreport/finrep/PDF (Liebman Report).

httppp://www.law.columbia.edu/instructionalservices/liebman (A Broken System: Error Rates in Capital Cases, 1973-1995).

http://www.lawschool.cornell.edu/library/death (Cornell Law School Death Penalty Project).

http://www.mvfr.org (Murder Victims' Families for Reconciliation).

http://www.newsobserver.com.

http://www.ojp.usdoj.gov/bjs/cp.htm (Bureau of Justice Statistics on Capital Punishment).

http://www.onu.edu/faculty/streib/femdeath.htm (females and the death penalty).

http://www.probono.net (American Bar Association Death Penalty Representation Project).

http://www.prodeathpenalty.com (articles, news stories, legislative developments).

http://www.SoundPortraits.org.

http://www.usdoj.gov/dag/pubdoc/dpsurvey.html (tables and reports on use of the federal death penalty).

Preface to the Third Edition

Since the second edition of the casebook, the United States Supreme Court has decided several key death penalty cases, including *Roper v. Simmons*, *Atkins v. Virginia*, and *Ring v. Arizona*, which have had a significant impact on how the death penalty may be imposed. In addition, we have seen state moratoriums on the use of the death penalty and the potential application of international law in cases involving foreign nationals charged with capital offenses in the United States. These judicial, political and legislative changes in the field of capital punishment convinced us to provide a third edition incorporating the new decisions and initiatives. It is my hope that this third edition will continue to provide comprehensive and up-to-date material on many of the topics that arise when the state seeks to impose the penalty of death.

On a more personal note, since Randy invited me to collaborate on the first edition of the casebook, I have been lucky enough to serve as a law clerk to Oklahoma Court of Criminal Appeals Judge Charles Chapel, United States Magistrate Judge Bana Roberts, and now to teach law at the University of Tulsa College of Law. My clerking experiences exposed me to many aspects and issues in capital punishment, state direct appeal and post-conviction procedure, and federal habeas corpus litigation. I was most grateful for the opportunity share that experience by means of this casebook. More recently, I have had the opportunity to teach a course on capital punishment, which has helped me think about these areas of the law not only from a scholarly standpoint or from the view point of a practitioner, but to consider these issues from the perspective of a law teacher and how to best convey the material to law students. It is my hope that these experiences have been useful in the preparation of this third edition in which we continue to try to improve and enhance the casebook.

Of course, this third edition benefits tremendously from the suggestions, comments and assistance of many people. My students in the capital punishment class I teach at the University of Tulsa College of Law provided me with insights, perspectives, patience - and even a fair amount of humor - as we worked our way through the various topics covered in this book. As always, my students gave me far more than I, or this casebook, could ever give to them. To all of them, I am indebted.

My research assistants, Nicholas Haugan, E.J. Rouse, and Velia Lopez, provided wonderful research assistance and advice. I also appreciate the support Dean Robert Bukin has given me as I worked on the third edition.

LSE

Completing the third edition of *Capital Punishment and the Judicial Process* is particularly gratifying considering that in 1993, the three preeminent casebook publishers—Little, Brown, West Publishing, and Michie—declined to publish our manuscript because they believed that there wasn't a sufficient market for such a book. Our wonderful publisher, Carolina Academic Press, disagreed. Thirteen years and three editions later, classes in the death penalty are being taught in law schools throughout the United States and *two* casebooks now compete in a market once rumored not to exist.

Since publication of the second edition, the federal government, as expected, resumed executions. My former client, Timothy McVeigh, was the first to die, followed by Juan Raul Garza and Louis Jones, Jr. McVeigh's co-conspirator Terry Nichols, who had been sentenced to life without parole in federal proceedings, again avoided a death sentence in state court proceedings when an Oklahoma jury also sentenced him to LWOP. Similarly, Zacarias Moussaoui — the only person convicted in connection with the September 11, 2001 terrorist attacks on America — taunted his victims and demanded to be executed, only to be sentenced to LWOP.

As in earlier editions, this revision would not have been possible without the able assistance of numerous friends. The thoughtful suggestions of Professor Sanjay K. Chhablani and Professor Jeffrey Kirchmeier have greatly improved our work. Two colleagues who have helped us stay current on death penalty developments and who deserve special thanks are Professor Peter Krug and Larry Laneer. Victoria Gillispie and Cory King provided outstanding research assistance. Lyn and I also owe a great debt to the University of Oklahoma support staff. Supervisor Dawn Tomlins, along with Melissa Adamson and Misty Akins, provided first-rate secretarial support.

RTC

Preface to the Second Edition

Since the first edition of these materials was published in 1994, the grim landscape of capital punishment has changed significantly, both within the United States and throughout the world. New York reinstated capital punishment in 1995, becoming the 38th death penalty jurisdiction in the United States. In 1994, Congress expanded the federal death penalty when it passed the Violent Crime Control and Law Enforcement Act. A significant portion of that legislation, the Federal Death Penalty Act of 1994 (FDPA), remedied the constitutional defects in the federal death penalty sentencing scheme identified by the Supreme Court in its 1972 decision, *Furman v. Georgia*. The Supreme Court upheld the FDPA in 1999 and upheld the military death penalty in 1996. As a result, thirty-six states, along with the United States military and the federal government, now have valid, enforceable death penalty statutes.

Between 1976, when the Supreme Court approved a group of modern death penalty statutes in *Gregg v. Georgia*, and the end of 1993, 226 prisoners were executed in the United States, an average of 12.5 executions per year. Between 1994, when the first edition of this book was published, and May 2001, when the second edition manuscript was sent to the publisher, another 488 prisoners were put to death in various states, an average of more than 60 executions per year. During that same seven and one-half year period, a number of states which had not executed anyone since before 1972 resumed executions. Those states include Colorado, Idaho, Kentucky, Maryland, Ohio, Oregon, Pennsylvania, and Tennessee. If the federal government succeeds in carrying out the expected execution of convicted Oklahoma City bomber Timothy McVeigh in 2001, he may become the first federal prisoner put to death since Victor Feguer was hung in Kansas in 1963. If Mr. McVeigh succeeds in postponing his execution, that dubious honor will likely fall to Juan Garza.

A statistically significant component of the surge in executions nationwide has been the increasing willingness of states to execute female prisoners. Until Texas put to death Karla Faye Tucker in 1998, no woman had been executed during the modern era of capital punishment since 1984, when Velma Barfield died by lethal execution in North Carolina's death chamber. Since Tucker's execution, five other female prisoners have been executed. Florida executed Judi Buenoano in 1998; Texas executed Betty Lou Beets in 2000; Arkansas executed Christina Riggs in 2000; and during the first five months of 2001, Oklahoma executed Wanda Jean Allen and Marilyn Plantz. With passage of the Anti-Terrorism and Effective Death Penalty Act in 1996—a law which restricts capital prisoners' ability to obtain relief in federal habeas corpus, and which imposes for the first time filing deadlines on habeas petitions—the execution rate will likely continue to soar.

Notwithstanding the United States' resolute retention and trenchant defense of capital punishment, there are signs that support for the death penalty is eroding. The American Bar Association's 1997 resolution that there be a moratorium on the imposition and enforcement of the death penalty has ignited a nationwide moratorium movement. Moratorium efforts have been energized by a variety of developments. Chief among these is the publication in 2000 of Professor James S. Liebman's Columbia Law School study, "A Broken System: Error Rates in Capital Cases," which reveals that serious mistakes were made in fully two-thirds of all capital cases examined. Consistent with Professor Liebman's study, the Death Penalty Information Center reports 95 wrongful convictions in death penalty cases since 1976.

A growing number of states have banned the execution of mentally retarded defendants. As this edition goes to press, bills banning the execution of mentally retarded defendants await the governors' signatures in Florida, Missouri and Texas. If these bills become law, the total number of jurisdictions banning such executions will rise to 17. Regardless, the Supreme Court appears poised to reconsider the constitutionality of the death penalty as applied to mentally retarded persons next term in *McCarver v. North Carolina*.

South Africa's abolition of capital punishment in 1997 is perhaps the most startling international development since publication of the first edition. Amnesty International reports that more than half the countries worldwide have now abolished the death penalty in law or practice. Other international developments include the Canadian Supreme Court's 2001 decision in *Burns v. United States*, holding that Canada will not extradite to the United States murder defendants without assurances that the death penalty will not be sought.

In order to reflect these profound developments, the second edition is forty percent longer than the first. This new edition, we hope, is greatly improved, thanks primarily to the critical comments and suggestions of professors and students who used the first edition. At the suggestion of Professor George Thomas (Rutgers), the Supreme Court opinions now include the original divisions into parts and subparts, to assist readers in figuring out the voting patterns in splintered decisions. Professors Linda E. Carter (McGeorge) and Jeffrey L. Kirchmeier (CUNY) provided much-needed constructive criticism. Virtually all of their suggestions have been taken to heart.

On a more personal note, we hope that the second edition has been enriched as well through our recent professional experiences. Co-author Lyn S. Entzeroth left her position with the Oklahoma Court of Criminal Appeals in 1999 to undertake her current position as law clerk to United States Magistrate Judge Bana Roberts. As a result, she has been immersed in the minefields of federal habeas litigation. Co-author Randall Coyne spent two years working as trial counsel for Timothy McVeigh, convicted of the 1995 Oklahoma City bombing which claimed 168 lives.

A small army of University of Oklahoma law students, paid and unpaid, helped the authors research and massage these materials into their final form. They deserve and hereby officially receive our deepest thanks: Greg Andrews, Carey Bertrand, Kim Bump, Deresa Gray, Darren Reece, Jodi Velasco, James Warner and Kelly Wehling.

Peter Krug, Larry Laneer and Robert Ravitz also provided tremendous help and encouragement with the second edition. The patience and understanding of Magistrate Judge Bana Roberts and her chambers is greatly appreciated and aided enormously in the timely completion of the second edition.

We can't imagine receiving any better secretarial assistance than that provided by the University of Oklahoma's Secretarial Support Staff. Connie Hamm bore the brunt of our seemingly endless revisions, with good cheer and tireless professionalism.

Preface to First Edition

My arrival in Oklahoma as a new faculty member at the University of Oklahoma College of Law in 1990 coincided with that state's decision to resume executions after a twenty-four year moratorium. My decision to audit a death penalty class being offered by Mandy Welch, then of the Oklahoma Appellate Public Defender's Office, marked the beginning of a warm and lasting friendship. When Mandy became consumed by the final stages of litigation in the capital post- conviction appeals of Charles Troy Coleman, I agreed to take over the class. I have taught the course ever since. As there was no published text available, course materials consisted almost entirely of unedited photocopies of Supreme Court opinions. The project which culminated in this casebook began as a humble effort to improve the teaching materials for my students. After receiving generous encouragement from students, friends and colleagues, I resolved to publish the first law school casebook devoted entirely to capital punishment. Although I have had ample occasion to doubt the wisdom of that decision, I have never for a moment doubted the wisdom of engaging Lyn Entzeroth to be my coauthor. Lyn's considerable criminal law experience, both as former appellate public defender and more recently as law clerk to Judge Charles Chapel of the Oklahoma Court of Criminal Appeals, infused the project with an invaluable perspective: that of the practitioner.

Lyn and I are indebted to countless people for their support and assistance. Perhaps foremost are the many students whose critical comments and insights have enriched both my teaching and this casebook. Friends and colleagues who have been especially helpful include Kathie Anderson, Sandra Babcock, Dale A. Baich, Jack Boger, Scott W. Braden, Stephen B. Bright, David Bruck, Dick Burr, Jeffrey Coyne, André de Gruy, Richard C. Dieter, Frank Elkouri, James W. Ellis, Deirdre Enright, Michael Enright, Millard Farmer, Mary T. Hall, Rick Halperin, Enid Harlow, Scott Howe, George Kendall, Drew Kershen, Margery Koosed, Peter Krug, Fred A. Leuchter, Robert McGlasson, Patsy Morris, Michael Millman, Teresa L. Norris, Diann Y. Rust-Tierney, Clive Stafford Smith and Nick Trenticosta. Capable research assistance was provided by Brad Carson, Kimberley E. Chandler, Patrick J. Ehlers, Kathryn T. Evans, Pamela A. Meyers and Paul D. Quackenbush. Tireless, cheerful, professional support was provided by the unsung heroes in the typing pool of the University of Oklahoma College of Law: Eugenia Sams, Jacquie Wilkins, Robin Mize and Dawn Tomlins. It bears noting that Eden Harrington was no help whatsoever. Lyn and I dedicate this work to Marley B. Coyne, the wondrous result of an earlier collaboration.

Acknowledgments

Thanks to the following authors and copyright holders for permission to use their materials:

American Law Institute, Model Penal Code Section 210.6, Copyright 1985 by The American Law Institute. Reprinted with the permission of The American Law Institute.

Amnesty International, List of Abolitionist and Retentionist Countries, published by Amnesty International, 2001. Reprinted with permission.

Amnesty International, Open Letter to the President on the Death Penalty, January 1994. Reprinted with permission.

Andrews, Roberto, Just Kill the Bastards and Let God Sort It Out, 12 J. of Defective Thinkers 666 (2001). Reprinted with permission of the author's parole officer.

Baldus, David, et al., Racial Discrimination and the Death Penalty in the Post-*Furman* Era, 83 Cornell L. Rev. 1638 (1998). Reprinted with permission of the authors.

Baldus, David, George Woodworth and Charles Pulaski, Law and Statistics in Conflict: Reflections on McCleskey v. Kemp, Chapter 13, Handbook of Psychology and Law (1992). Reprinted with permission of the authors.

Baldus, David, George Woodworth et al., The Use of Peremptory Challenges in Capital Murder Trials: A Legal and Empirical Analysis, 3 U. Pa. J. Const. L. 3 (2001). Reprinted with permission of the authors.

Bedau, Hugo A., The Decline of Executive Clemency in Capital Cases, 18 N.Y.U. Rev. L. & Soc. Change 255 (1990-91). Reprinted with permission of the authors.

Bilionis, Louis D., Legitimating Death, 91 Mich. L. Rev. 1643 (1993). Reprinted with permission

Bright, Stephen, Counsel for the Poor: The Death Sentence Not for the Worst Crime but for the Worst Lawyer, 103 Yale L.J. 1835 (1994). Reprinted with permission of the author.

Bright, Stephen, Death by Lottery — Procedural Bar of Constitutional Claims in Capital Cases Due to Inadequate Representation of Indigent Defendants, 92 W. Va. L. Rev. 679 (1990). Reprinted with permission of the author.

Bruck, David I., Decisions of Death, December 12, 1983. Updated 2001. Reprinted with permission of the author.

Christian, Diane and Bruce Jackson, Death Row, Beacon Press (1980). Reprinted with permission of the authors.

Cochran, John K., Mitchell B. Chamlin & Mark Seth, Deterrence or Brutalization?: An Impact & Assessment of Oklahoma's Return to Capital Punishment, 32 Criminology 107 (1994). Reprinted with permission of the authors.

Coyne, Randall, Constitutional Rights Discarded as Many Pursue Grasso's Wish to Die, Oklahoma Gazette, May 6, 1993. Reprinted with permission of the author.

Coyne, Randall, Inflicting Payne on Oklahoma: The Use of Victim Impact Evidence During the Sentencing Phase of Capital Cases, 45 Okla. L. Rev. 589 (1992). Reprinted with permission of the author.

Dayan, Marshall, Using Mitigating Evidence in Jury Selection in Capital Trials, published in The Champion, July 1993. Reprinted with permission of the author.

Death Penalty Information Center, Millions Misspent: What Politicians Don't Say About the High Costs of the Death Penalty, October 1992. Reprinted with permission of the author.

Fong, Ivan K., Ineffective Assistance of Counsel at Capital Sentencing, 39 Stan. L. Rev. 461 (1987). Reprinted with permission of the author.

Friendly, Henry, Is Innocence Irrelevant? 38 U. Chi. L. Rev. 142 (1970). Reprinted with permission.

Goldstein, Richard, Queer on Death Row; In Murder Cases Being Gay Can Seal a Defendant's Fate, Village Voice, February 2001. Reprinted with permission of The Village Voice.

Goodpaster, Gary, The Trial for Life: Effective Assistance of Counsel in Death Penalty Cases, 58 N.Y.U. L. Rev. 299 (1983). Reprinted with permission of the New York University Law Review.

Granucci, Anthony F., Nor Cruel and Unusual Punishments Inflicted: The Original Meaning, 57 Cal. L. Rev. 839 (1969). Reprinted with permission of the author.

Greenberg, Jack, Against the American System of Capital Punishment, 99 Harv. L. Rev. 1670 (1976). Reprinted with permission of the author.

Howe, Scott W., Resolving the Conflict in the Capital Sentencing Cases, 26 Ga. L. Rev. 323 (1992). Reprinted with permission of the author.

Kahler, Kathryn, Courts Turn Their Backs on the Poor: Murder Defendants Often Assigned Inept Lawyers, Plain Dealer, June 10, 1990. Reprinted with permission.

Lane, J. Mark, "Is There Life Without Parole?": A Capital Defendant's Right to a Meaningful Alternative Sentence, 26 Loy. L. A. L. Rev. 327 (1993). Reprinted with permission of the author.

Kirchmeier, Jeffrey L., Aggravating and Mitigating Factors: The Paradox of Today's Arbitrary and Mandatory Capital Punishment Scheme, 6 Wm. & Mary Bill of Rights J. 345 (Spring 1998). Reprinted with permission of the author.

Kirchmeier, Jeffrey L., Drinks, Drugs and Drowsiness: The Constitutional Right to Effective Assistance of Counsel and the *Strickland* Prejudice Requirement, 75 Neb. L. Rev. 425 (1996). Reprinted with permission of the author.

Kirchmeier, Jeffrey L., Let's Make a Deal: Waiving the Eighth Amendment by Selecting a Cruel and Unusual Punishment, 32 Conn. L. Rev. 615 (Winter 2000). Reprinted with permission of the author.

Lay, Judge Donald P., The Writ of Habeas Corpus: A Complex Procedure for a Simple Process, 77 Minn. L. Rev. 1015 (1993). Reprinted with permission of the author.

Leuchter, Fred A., Lethal Injection Manual for the State of Missouri. Reprinted with permission of the author.

Liebman, James S. and Randy Hertz, Federal Habeas Corpus Practice and Procedure (3d ed. 1998) (Lexis Law Publishing). Reprinted with permission of the authors.

Liebman, James S., Federal Habeas Corpus Practice and Procedure, published by the Michie Company (1988). Reprinted with permission of the Michie Company.

Liebman, James S., The Overproduction of Death, 100 Colum. L. Rev. 2030 (2000). Reprinted with permission of the author.

Lungren, Daniel and Mark Krotoski, Public Policy Lessons from the Robert Alton Harris Case, originally published in 40 UCLA L. Rev. 295. Copyright 1992, The Regents of the University of California. All Rights Reserved. Reprinted with permission.

McCord, David, State Death Sentences for Felony Murder Accomplices Under the *Enmund* and *Tison* Standards, 32 Ariz. St. L.J. 843 (2000). Reprinted with permission of the author.

Olszewski, Lori, New Theory About What Makes a Murderer, San Francisco Chronicle, p. 1., and p. A12 col. l, copyright San Francisco Chronicle, reprinted by permission.

Rapaport, Elizabeth, The Death Penalty and Gender Discrimination, 25 L. & Soc'y Rev. 367 (1991). Reprinted with permission of the author.

Rapaport, Elizabeth, Equality of the Damned: The Execution of Women on the Cusp of the 21st Century, 26 Ohio N.U. L. Rev. 581 (2000). Reprinted with permission of the author.

Rapaport, Elizabeth, Some Questions About Gender and the Death Penalty, 20 Golden Gate U. L. Rev. 501 (1990). Reprinted with permission of the author.

Rosen, Richard A., Felony Murder and the Eighth Amendment Jurisprudence of Death, 31 B. C. L. Rev. 1103 (1990). Reprinted with permission of the author.

Stafford Smith, Clive A. and Remy Voisin Starns, Folly by Fiat: Pretending that Death Row Inmates Can Represent Themselves in State Capital Post-Conviction Proceedings, 45 Loy. L. Rev. 55 (1999). Reprinted with permission of the authors.

Stafford Smith, Clive A. and Anthony Paduano, Deathly Errors: Juror Misperceptions Concerning Parole in the Imposition of the Death Penalty, 18 Colum. Hum. Rts. L. Rev. 211 (1987). Reprinted with permission of the authors.

Stafford Smith, Clive A., An Englishman Abroad (1987). Reprinted with permission of the author.

Streib, Victor L., Death Penalty for Children: The American Experience with Capital Punishment for Crimes Committed While Under Age Eighteen, 36 Okla. L. Rev. 613 (1983). Reprinted with permission of the author.

Streib, Victor L., Death Penalty for Female Offenders, 58 U. Cin. L. Rev. 845 (1990). Reprinted with permission of the author.

Tabak, Ronald J. and Mark Lane, The Execution of Injustice: A Cost and Lack-of-Benefit Analysis of the Death Penalty, 23 Loy. L.A. L. Rev. 59 (1989). Reprinted with permission of the authors.

van den Haag, Ernest, The Ultimate Punishment: A Defense, 99 Harv. L. Rev. 1662 (1986). Reprinted with permission.

Weisberg, Jacob, This Is Your Death, The New Republic, July 1, 1992. Reprinted with permission.

Capital Punishment
and the
Judicial Process

Chapter 1

The Great Debate over Capital Punishment

A. Introduction

In 1922, Clarence Darrow wrote: "The question of capital punishment has been the subject of endless discussion and will probably never be settled so long as men believe in punishment. [Q]uestions of this sort, or perhaps of any sort, are not settled by reason; they are settled by prejudices and sentiments or by emotion. When they are settled they do not stay settled, for the emotions change as new stimuli are applied to the machine." This chapter does not attempt to settle the question of capital punishment. Rather, it contains readings designed to stimulate discussion of the broad moral, social, political, religious and constitutional issues raised by the death penalty.

Since 1972, when the Supreme Court temporarily halted executions nationwide in *Furman v. Georgia* (*infra* chapter 3), an average of 300 of the approximately 21,000 homicides committed in the United States each year have resulted in a sentence of death. Liebman, "The Overproduction of Death," 100 Colum. L. Rev. 2030, 2053 (2000). Each capital case, it seems, raises recurring issues over the efficacy, fairness and wisdom of retaining the death penalty. As one wag put it, capital punishment is "a penalty regarding the justice and expediency of which many worthy persons—including all the assassins—entertain grave misgivings." Ambrose Bierce, *The Devil's Dictionary* 14 (1911).

B. A Historical Summary

Capital punishment has been defined as "the execution of a criminal under death sentence imposed by competent public authority." Baker, *Worthy of Death* 9 (Moody Press 1973). Simply put, capital punishment penalizes those convicted of certain crimes by killing them. "Capital" derives from the Latin *caput* which the Romans used to refer variously to the head, the life, or the civil rights of an individual. "Capital" punishment, then, is the "chief," "principal" or "most extreme" penalty society can impose.

Since the beginnings of civilization, capital punishment has been used to penalize various forms of conduct. Although its precise origins are unknown, the roots of capital punishment lie in violent retaliation by members of a tribe or group against persons committing hostile acts towards group members. Scott, *The History of Capital Punishment* 1 (1950). Thus, death as a penalty may have its origins in private vengeance.

Gradually, as individuals ceded their personal prerogatives to a sovereign power, the authority to punish wrongdoing became part of the sovereign's "divine right" to rule. Capital punishment became a public function as the state assumed responsibility for redressing private wrongs.

The Babylonian Code of Hammurabi (c. 1750 B.C.) provided death as a penalty for twenty-five different offenses, including corruption by government officials, theft and the fraudulent sale of beer. Under the Old Testament, death was deemed the appropriate punishment for various offenses, including murder, adultery, blasphemy, homosexuality, bestiality, sorcery, witchcraft, and cursing a parent. Ancient Egyptian records indicate that criminals were sentenced to death as early as 1500 B.C. The Assyrian laws (c. 1500 B.C.) included provisions for capital punishment, although mutilation was more commonly imposed. Similarly, the Hittites' legal code (c. 1400 B.C.) recognized death as an appropriate sanction for a variety of offenses. In the fifth century B.C., Roman death penalty law consisted of the Twelve Tablets. Death sentences were carried out by such means as crucifixion, drowning, beating to death, burning alive, and impalement. In the seventh century B.C., the Athenian leader Draco fashioned a criminal code which prescribed the death penalty for most offenses. Baker, *Worthy of Death* 15 (Moody Press 1973); Flanders, *Capital Punishment* 4 (Facts on File, Inc. 1991).

During the reign of Henry II (1154–1189), English law first recognized that crime was more than a personal affair between the victim and the criminal. By 1500, English law recognized eight major capital offenses: treason, petty treason (killing of a husband by his wife), murder, larceny, robbery, burglary, rape, arson, and marrying a Jew. Various kings greatly expanded the list of capital offenses and the reign of Henry VIII was especially bloody. During his thirty-six years as king, 72,000 subjects were put to death, an average of 2000 subjects per year. Some common methods of execution at that time were boiling, burning at the stake, hanging, beheading, and drawing and quartering.

The more merciful Elizabeth I ordered an average of 800 executions per year. Krivosha, Copple & McDonough, "A Historical and Philosophical Look at the Death Penalty—Does it Serve Society's Needs?," 16 Creighton L. Rev. 1, 12 (1982–83). Shortly after 1800, England recognized more than 200 capital crimes, ranging from crimes against person and property to crimes against the public peace. The number of capital crimes in Britain continued to rise throughout the next two centuries. By the 1700s, 222 crimes were punishable by death in Britain, including stealing, cutting down a tree, and robbing a rabbit warren. Because of the severity of the death penalty, many juries would not convict defendants if the offense was not serious.

Although England clearly countenanced capital punishment, other European countries also embraced the death penalty. An example from France illustrates a method of execution fairly common throughout Europe. On March 2, 1757, Damiens the regicide was sentenced to die. The execution was to take place "before the main door of the Church of Paris." According to the death warrant, Damiens was to be "taken and conveyed in a cart, wearing nothing but a shirt, holding a torch of burning wax weighing two pounds"; then, "in the said cart, to the Place de Grève, where, on a scaffold that will be erected there, the flesh will be torn from his breasts, arms, thighs and calves with red-hot pincers, his right hand, holding the knife with which he committed the said parricide, burnt with sulphur, and, on those places where the flesh will be torn away, poured molten lead, boiling oil, burning resin, wax and sulphur melted together then his body drawn and quartered by four horses and his limbs and body consumed by fire, reduced to ashes and his ashes thrown to the winds." For a more graphic description of this execution, first published in the Amsterdam Gazette of April 1, 1757, see Foucault, *Discipline and Punish — The Birth of the Prison* 3 (Random House 1979).

Capital punishment was not as widespread in the American colonies. The earliest confirmed execution in the United States occurred in 1608 when George Kendall, an original councilor for the colony of Virginia, was convicted of spying for the Spanish. Kendall died by firing squad. In 1612, Virginia Governor Sir Thomas Dale enacted the Divine, Moral and Martial Laws, which provided the death penalty for even minor offenses such as stealing grapes, killing chickens, and trading with Indians.

The first American executed for murder was a pilgrim named John Billington who sailed to America on the Mayflower, settled in Virginia, and was hanged in 1630. The first woman executed in the United States, Jane Champion, was hanged in James City, Virginia in 1632. Female felons were thereafter burned to death until that execution method was repealed in 1790.

The first written expression of capital crimes known to exist in the United States was drafted by the Massachusetts Bay Colony in 1636. Citing various provisions of the Old Testament as support, "The Capitall Lawes of New-England" list the following crimes as punishable by death: idolatry, witchcraft, blasphemy, assault in sudden anger, sodomy, buggery, adultery, statutory rape, rape, manstealing, perjury in a capital trial, and rebellion. The New York Colony instituted the Duke's Laws of 1665. Under these laws, offenses such as striking one's mother or father, or denying the "true God," were punishable by death.

According to Professor Granucci, "There is no evidence to connect the cruel and unusual punishments clause with the 'Bloody Assize.'" Granucci, "'Nor Cruel and Unusual Punishments Inflicted:' The Original Meaning," 57 Calif. L. Rev. 839, 855 (1969). In September 1678, Titus Oates, a minister of the Church of England, proclaimed that a plot existed to assassinate King Charles II. Ultimately, with the assistance of Oates' testimony, fifteen Catholics were found guilty of treason and were executed. When the hysteria subsided, officials learned that Oates was an inveterate liar and the "Popish Plot" was a complete hoax. Accordingly, Oates was indicted on two counts of perjury and was tried before the King's Bench.

Oates was convicted, but spared death because perjury was no longer a capital offense in England. Nonetheless, he received stiff punishment. In addition to being defrocked and fined 2,000 marks, Oates was sentenced to life imprisonment, and was whipped and pilloried four times a year.

Although the colonies had fewer capital crimes than England, executions were anything but rare. Death penalty historian Watt Espy has documented more than 18,000 legal executions in the United States. *A Dismayed Historian of the Gallows*, The New York Times, Nov. 18, 1992. Espy's research has uncovered numerous executions which, judged by modern standards, appear sadistically cruel. One particularly merciless execution occurred in New Orleans in 1754. Five murderous mutineers were strapped naked to a wheel, their bodies stretched taut. Then, after each bone was broken by a sledge hammer, they were left to starve to death.

From the 1920s to the 1940s, there was a resurgence in the use of the death penalty. This was due, in part, to the writings of criminologists, who argued that the death penalty was a necessary social measure. In the United States, Americans were suffering through Prohibition and the Great Depression.

In 1924, Clarence Darrow, an ardent death penalty foe, represented Nathan Leopold and Richard Loeb, two young men charged with murdering a neighborhood child. Darrow's impassioned plea for mercy resulted in life sentences for both defendants and inspired abolitionists. That same year, the use of cyanide gas was introduced, as Nevada sought a more humane way of executing its inmates. Gee Jon was the first person executed by lethal gas. The state tried to pump cyanide gas into Jon's cell while he slept, but this proved impossible, and the gas chamber was constructed. A few years later, death penalty proponents cited the St. Valentine's Day Massacre (1929) and the Lindbergh baby kidnapping (1932) as justifications for expanding its use.

At least 14,000 executions occurred before 1930, when the federal government began keeping Bureau of Justice Statistics on legal executions. There were more executions in the 1930s than in any other decade in American history, an average of 167 per year. In 1930, there were 155 executions nationwide. In 1935, this number had increased to 199. By 1940, there was a slight decline in executions (160). When the United States entered World War II in 1941, the federal government and forty-two of the forty-eight states authorized capital punishment. Nonetheless, executions continued to decline. In 1945, 120 executions took place and in 1950, 119. In 1955, the number dropped to 81. In 1960, 49 executions took place. By 1965, executions had dropped to 15. By 1970, there were no executions in this country. U.S. Dep't of Justice, *Bureau of Justice Statistics Bulletin, Capital Punishment 1999.* For the most recent capital punishment statistics kept by the Justice Department, see http://www.ojp.usdoj.gov/bjs.

Note on Public Opinion Polls and Support for Capital Punishment

When asked in 2000, "What do you think should be the penalty for murder—the death penalty or life in prison with absolutely no possibility of parole?," 52% supported the death penalty, 37% supported life without parole, and 11% indicated no opinion. Also in 2000, CNN asked "Should death row convicts have a guaranteed right to DNA testing?" Ninety-two percent indicated that it was better to test than to execute someone wrongfully. Eight percent said that DNA testing should not be guaranteed ("No, that's what trials are for.").

According to a February 2001 Gallup Poll, two-thirds (67%) of Americans favored the death penalty in cases of murder. Gallup polling also showed that the overwhelming majority of Americans (91%) believed that, in the previous twenty years, a person had been wrongly convicted and sentenced to death.

The Bureau of Justice Statistics *Sourcebook of Criminal Justice Statistics 2002* reflects growing support for life without parole as an alternative to the death penalty. By 2001, the number of respondents favoring life without parole had climbed to 44%. Support for life without parole was stronger among black respondents (73%), respondents holding post-graduate degrees (62%), and those who identified themselves as Democrats (60%).

A Gallup report released in October 2005 revealed that only 64% of Americans favored the death penalty for a person convicted of murder. The last time the poll found a lower support was in 1978 when 62% favored the death penalty. This most recent poll result is consistent with Gallup Polls taken in October 2004 and 2003, both of which registered 64% support for the death penalty. The highest support level ever detected by Gallup was 80% in 1994. The lowest level of support ever detected by the poll was 42% in 1966. For full details on American public opinion about the death penalty see http://www.gallup.com/poll/indicators/inddeath_pen.asp

C. Selecting Those Deserving of Death

Decisions of Death[1]

David Bruck (Updated 2006)

There are 3,318 men and 55 women awaiting execution in the United States[2]. It's not easy to imagine how many people 3,373 is. If death row were really a row, it would stretch for more than 4 miles, cell after six-foot-wide cell. In each cell, one person, sitting, pacing, watching TV, sleeping, writing letters. Locked in their cells nearly twenty-four hours a day, the condemned communicate with each other by shouts, notes, and hand-held mirrors, all with a casual dexterity that handicapped people acquire over time. Occasionally there is a break in the din of shouted conversations—a silent cell, its inhabitant withdrawn into a cocoon of madness. That's what death row would look like. That's what, divided up among the prisons of thirty-eight states, it does look like.

… But in another sense, death row is very small. If every one of these 3,318 inmates were to be taken out of his or her cell tomorrow and gassed, electrocuted, hanged, shot, or injected, the total of convicted murderers imprisoned in this country would decline from some 134,600 (at last count) to 131,227—a reduction of a little over 2 percent. Huge as this country's death row population has become, it does not include—and has never included—more than a tiny fraction of those who are convicted of murder.

It falls to the judicial system of each of the thirty-eight states that retain capital punishment to cull the few who are to die from the many who are convicted of murder. This selection begins with the crime itself, as the community and the press react with outrage or with indifference, depending on the nature of the murder and the identity of the victim. With the arrest of a suspect, police and prosecutors must decide what charges to file, whether to seek the death penalty, and whether the defendant should be allowed to plea-bargain for his life. Most of these decisions can later be changed, so that at any point the defendant's chances of slipping through the death penalty net depend on chance: the inclinations and ambitions of the local prosecutor, the legal and political pressures which impel him to one course of action or another, and the skill or incompetence of the court-appointed defense counsel.

In the courtroom, the defendant may be spared or condemned by the countless vagaries of the trial by jury. There are counties in each state where the juries almost always impose death, and counties where they almost never do. There are hanging judges and lenient judges, and judges who go one way or the other depending on who the victim's family happens to be, or the defendant's family, or who is prosecuting the case, or who is defending it.

Thus at each stage between arrest and sentence, more and more defendants are winnowed out from the ranks of those facing possible execution. And even for those few who are condemned to die, there lies ahead a series of appeals which whittle down the number of condemned still further, sparing some and consigning others to death on the basis of appellate courts' judgments of the nuances of a trial judge's instructions to the jury, of whether the court-appointed defense lawyer had made the proper objections at

---

1. Original version published in The New Republic, Dec. 12, 1983.
2. Statistics are current as of April 2006. Death Row, U.S.A. (NAACP Legal Defense and Educational Fund, Inc.).

the proper moments during the trial, and so on. By the time the appeals process has run its course, almost every murder defendant who faced the possibility of execution when he was first arrested has by luck, justice, or favor evaded execution, and a mere handful are left to die.

The condemned man himself remembers the many points of his procession through the judicial system at which he might have been spared, but was not. He knows, too, from his years of waiting in prison, that most of those who committed crimes like his have evaded the execution that awaits him. So do the prosecutors who have pursued him through the court system, and the judges who have upheld his sentence. And so do the defense lawyers, the ones glimpsed on the TV news in the last hours, exhausted and overwrought for reasons that, given their client's crimes, must be hard for most people to fathom.

I am one of those lawyers, and I know the sense of horror that propels those last-minute appeals. It is closely related to the horror that violent crime awakens in all of us — the random kind of crime, the sniper in the tower or the gunman in the grocery store. The horror derives not from death, which comes to us all, but from death that is inflicted at random, for no reason, for being on the wrong subway platform or the wrong side of the street. Up close, that is what capital punishment is like. And that is what makes the state's inexorable, stalking pursuit of this or that particular person's life so chilling.

The lawyers who bring those eleventh-hour appeals know from their work how many murderers are spared, how few are sentenced to die, and how chance and race decide which will be which.

If one believes, as many do, that murderers deserve whatever punishment they get, then none of this should matter. But if the 3,373 now on death row throughout the United States had actually been selected by means of a lottery from the roughly 134,600 inmates now serving sentences for murder, most Americans, whatever their views on capital punishment as an abstract matter, would surely be appalled. This revulsion would be all the stronger if we limited the pool of those murderers facing execution by restricting it to blacks. Or if we sentenced people to die on the basis of the race of the *victim*, consigning to death only those — whatever their race — who have killed whites, and sparing those who have killed blacks.

The reason why our sense of justice rebels at such ideas is not hard to identify. Violent crime undermines the sense of order and shared moral values without which no society could exist. We punish people who commit such crimes in order to reaffirm our standards of right and wrong, and our belief that life in society can be orderly and trusting rather than fearful and chaotic. But if the punishment itself is administered chaotically or arbitrarily, it fails in its purpose and becomes, like the crime which triggered it, just another spectacle of the random infliction of suffering — all the more terrifying and demoralizing because this time the random killer is organized society itself, the same society on which we depend for stability and security in our daily lives. No matter how much the individual criminal thus selected for death may "deserve" his punishment, the manner of its imposition robs it of any possible value, and leaves us ashamed instead of reassured.

It was on precisely this basis the Supreme Court in *Furman v. Georgia* (*infra* chapter 3) struck down every death penalty law in the United States, and set aside the death sentences of more than six hundred death row inmates. *Furman* was decided by a single vote (all four Nixon appointees voting to uphold the death penalty laws), and though the five majority justices varied in their rationales, the dominant theme of their opinions was that the Constitution did not permit the execution of a capriciously selected handful out of all those convicted of capital crimes. For Justice Byron White and the rest of the *Furman* majority, years of reading the petitions of the condemned had simply revealed "no meaningful basis for distinguishing the few cases in which [death] is imposed from the many in which it is not." Justice Potter Stewart compared the country's capital sentencing methods to being struck by lightning, adding that "if any basis can be discerned for the selection of these few to be sentenced to die, it is on the constitutionally impermissible basis of race." Justice William O. Douglas summarized the issue by observing that the Constitution would never permit any law which stated

> that anyone making more than $50,000 would be exempt from the death penalty [nor] a law that in terms said that blacks, those that never went beyond the fifth grade in school, those who made less than $3,000 a year, or those who were unpopular or unstable would be the only people executed. *A law which in the overall view reaches that result in practice has no more sanctity than a law which in terms provides the same.* [Emphasis added.]

On the basis of these views, the Supreme Court in *Furman* set aside every death sentence before it, and effectively cleared off death row. Though *Furman v. Georgia* did not outlaw the death penalty as such, the Court's action came at a time when America appeared to have turned against capital punishment, and *Furman* seemed to climax a long and inexorable progression toward abolition. After *Furman*, Chief Justice Warren E. Burger, who had dissented from the Court's decision, predicted privately that there would never be another execution in the United States.

What happened instead was that the majority of state legislatures passed new death sentencing laws designed to satisfy the Supreme Court. By [April 2006], thirty-four years after *Furman*, there are roughly as many states with capital punishment laws on the books as there were in 1972.

In theory the capital sentencing statutes under which the 3,373 prisoners now on death row were condemned are very different from the death penalty laws in effect prior to 1972. Under the pre-*Furman* laws, the process of selection was simple: the jury decided whether the accused was guilty of murder, and if so, whether he should live or die. In most states, no separate sentencing hearing was held: jurors were supposed to determine both guilt and punishment at the same time, often without benefit of any information about the background or circumstances of the defendant whose life was in their hands. Jurors were also given no guidelines or standards with which to assess the relative gravity of the case before them, but were free to base their life-or-death decision on whatever attitudes or biases they happened to have carried with them into the jury room. These statutes provided few grounds for appeal and worked fast: as late as the 1950s, many prisoners were executed within a few weeks of their trials, and delays of more than a year or two were rare.

In contrast, the current crop of capital statutes have created complex, multi-tiered sentencing schemes based on lists of specified "aggravating" and "mitigating" factors which the jury is to consider in passing sentence. Sentencing now occurs at a separate hearing after guilt has been determined. The new statutes also provide for automatic appeal to the state supreme courts, usually with a requirement that the court determine whether each death sentence is excessive considering the defendant and the crime.

The first of these new statutes—from Georgia, Florida, and Texas—came before the Supreme Court for review in 1976. The new laws were different from one another in several respects—only Georgia's provided for case-by-case review of the appropriateness of each death sentence by the state supreme court; Florida's permitted the judge to sentence a defendant to death even where the jury had recommended a life sentence; and the Texas statute determined who was to be executed on the basis of the jury's answer to the semantically perplexing question of whether the evidence established "beyond a reasonable doubt" a "probability" that the defendant would commit acts of violence in the future. What these statutes all had in common, however, was some sort of criteria, however vague, to guide juries and judges in their life-or-death decisions, while permitting capital defendants a chance to present evidence to show why they should be spared. Henceforth—or so went the theory behind these new laws—death sentences could not be imposed randomly or on the basis of the race or social status of the defendant and the victim, but only on the basis of specific facts about the crime, such as whether the murder had been committed during a rape or a robbery, or whether it had been "especially heinous, atrocious and cruel" (in Florida), or "outrageously or wantonly vile, horrible or inhuman" (in Georgia).

After considering these statutes during the spring of 1976, the Supreme Court announced in *Gregg v. Georgia* (*infra* chapter 3) and two other cases that the new laws satisfied its concern, expressed in *Furman*, about the randomness and unfairness of the previous death sentencing systems. Of course, the Court had no actual evidence that these new laws were being applied any more equally or consistently than the ones struck down in *Furman*. But for that matter, the Court had not relied on factual evidence in *Furman*, either. Although social science research over the previous thirty years had consistently found the nation's use of capital punishment to be characterized by arbitrariness and racial discrimination, the decisive opinions of Justices White and Stewart in *Furman* cited none of this statistical evidence, but relied instead on the justices' own conclusions derived from years of experience with the appeals of the condemned. The *Furman* decision left the Court free to declare the problem solved later on. And four years later, in *Gregg v. Georgia*, that is what it did.

It may be, of course, that the Court's prediction in *Gregg* of a new era of fairness in capital sentencing was a sham, window dressing for what was in reality nothing more than a capitulation to the mounting public clamor for a resumption of executions. But if the justices sincerely believed that new legal guidelines and jury instructions would really solve the problems of arbitrariness and racial discrimination in death penalty cases, they were wrong.

It is impossible to predict how long the executions will continue.

In the meantime we will be the only country among all the Western industrial democracies which still executes its own citizens. Canada abolished capital punishment in 1976, as did France in 1981; England declined to bring back hanging in 1994. By contrast, our leading companions in the use of the death penalty as a judicial punishment for crime will be the governments of the former Soviet Union, Saudi Arabia, and Iran—a rogues' gallery of the most repressive and backward-looking regimes in the world.

It's no accident that democracies tend to abolish the death penalty while autocracies and totalitarian regimes tend to retain it. In his book, *The Death Penalty: A Debate*, John Conrad credits Tocqueville with the explanation for this, quoting from *Democracy in America*:

> When all the ranks of a community are nearly equal, as all men think and feel in nearly the same manner, each of them may judge in a moment the sensations of all the others: he casts a rapid glance upon himself, and that is enough.

> There is no wretchedness into which he cannot readily enter, and a secret in-
> stinct reveals to him its extent.... In democratic ages, men rarely sacrifice
> themselves for one another, but they display general compassion for the mem-
> bers of the human race. They inflict no useless ills, and they are happy to re-
> lieve the griefs of others when they can do so without much hurting them-
> selves; they are not disinterested, but they are humane.

Tocqueville went on to explain that his identification of America's democratic political culture as the root of the "singular mildness" of American penal practices was susceptible of an ironic proof:

> the cruelty with which Americans treated their black slaves. Restraint in pun-
> ishment, he wrote, extends as far as our sense of social equality, and no fur-
> ther: "the same man who is full of humanity toward his fellow creatures when
> they are at the same time his equals becomes insensible to their affliction as
> soon as that equality ceases."

In that passage, written [173] years ago, Tocqueville reveals to us why it is that the
death penalty—the practice of slowly bringing a fully conscious human face to face
with the prospect of his own extinction and then killing him—should characterize the
judicial systems of the least democratic and most repressive nations of the world. And it
reveals too why the vestiges of this institution in America should be so inextricably en-
tangled with the question of race. The gradual disappearance of the death penalty
throughout most of the democratic world certainly suggests that Tocqueville was right.
The day when Americans stop condemning people to death on the basis of race and inequality will be the day when we stop condemning anyone to death at all.

New Theory About What Makes a Murderer
Lori Olszewski, San Francisco Chronicle, August 12, 1993

When David Mason was 11, his mother dressed him in diapers and forced him to sit
on display in the family's front yard with his soiled underwear on his head. On other af-
ternoons, his parents beat him so severely with belts or spatulas that neighbors could
hear his screams. Mason, the death-row inmate who began life as an abused child,
shares that history with most of the men and women facing execution across the nation.
But an emerging body of research suggests that, in addition to being brutalized as children, an alarming number of the murderers on death row also may share a history of
head injuries that scar the brain.

Buried in the pages of arcane medical journals, the little known studies trace the dou-
ble-whammy of child abuse and possible neurological dysfunction. Some scientists say the
controversial findings are providing new clues about the source of the violence that lands
criminals on death row. "I have been looking at these issues for 30 years, and I believe there
is a biological basis for much violence," said Dr. Louis Jolyon West, professor of psychiatry
at the University of California at Los Angeles. West didn't always see it this way. In 1952, he
was one of the physicians at an Iowa state hanging who certified that a criminal swinging at
the end of the rope was indeed dead. "It didn't bother me, the idea of putting some
scoundrel to death. But as I studied the issue, the facts changed me," West said. "These are
not subjective evaluations, but scientifically based conclusions. Unless we address the root
causes of violence and take preventive measures, we will never get out of this mess."

The number of death row prisoners studied is small—no more than a few dozen—
but the similarities are compelling, especially when added to the anecdotal observations

of medical personnel who make a living assessing criminals. A study led by Dorothy Otnow Lewis, a professor of psychiatry at New York University School of Medicine, found that all 15 adult death row inmates who were studied had histories of severe head injury. Twelve of the 15 had evidence of neurological problems, ranging from blackouts to amnesia. Other findings suggest more subtle evidence of neurological damage among prisoners on death row. Some cannot perform simple tasks like skipping or touching their thumb to their fingers in sequence at a normal pace. Some have problems repeating a sequence of words. Doctors display brain X-rays—CAT scans and magnetic resonance images—in which the lesions on the criminals' brains are evident, even to a lay person. The psychiatrists and psychologists say these scars often cause problems in the parts of the brain, such as the frontal or temporal lobes, which affect judgment and the ability to control rage and other primitive emotions. They say impaired people may be more likely to explode in a fit of violence, especially if they were abused as children and carry around a frightening amount of repressed anger.

Opposing Viewpoint

The prosecutors who face the horror and pain left by the David Masons of the world see such studies as feeble excuses for heinous crimes. They say that the psychologists and psychiatrists are opponents of the death penalty or paid experts who are predisposed to find evidence that supports the side that pays their fees. "We see this argument (child abuse and brain injury) in case after case," said Dane Gillette, deputy state attorney general in charge of death penalty cases. "It has lost its viability as a defense or a mitigating circumstance through sheer repetition."

Mason's Denial

Despite the extensive evidence of abuse in his court file and eyewitness accounts, Mason now denies that he was abused, and he is fighting to keep his own execution on schedule for August 24.[3] In an interview last month, he said that child-abuse and head-injury defenses are overused. Many of those defense efforts are "a sham," he said, and they detract from the effectiveness of the defenses for those who need them, such as several mentally retarded inmates with him on death row. Prosecutors see the issue in terms of guilt or innocence as defined by the law. Why someone strangled an elderly woman on her pantry floor is not as important as ensuring that the criminal who took the life pays for the hellish deed. Said Gillette: "What it comes down to is: Does a bump on the head excuse someone from murder? I don't think so. You are still responsible for your behavior. I am not convinced the research has proven the connection between the bump and the violent act." The researchers believe "bump" is a poor way to characterize abuse and brain trauma far more profound than the usual childhood accidents of falling off a bike or tumbling down a few steps.

Study of Juveniles

The Lewis study, published in 1988, found that all of the 14 juveniles on death row in four states had a serious head injury as a result of battering or accidents. "Hit by truck at age 4—fractured skull," said one description. "Shot in right temple at age 16. Blow to head at age 8—amnesia for two weeks." Their cases, and the case files of other death row prisoners, provide stomach-wrenching documentation of the child abuse that molds violent criminals. For example, one of the juveniles who had fallen off a roof

---

3. David Mason died in California's gas chamber on August 24, 1993.

as a child also was placed on a hot stove by a caretaker and forced to participate in pornographic movies. Yet most victims of child abuse do not grow up to be murderers. Why not? "The difference is that the abused child who grows up to be violent is someone who has never been dealt a good card in life. They never met the teacher who made the difference or the kind neighbor," said Joan Carroll Cartwright, a psychologist who has evaluated a number of prisoners on San Quentin Prison's death row. But Lewis believes that the head injury factor, when combined with a history of brutal abuse, is the key. By impairing a person's judgment and ability to control impulsiveness, brain dysfunction makes it difficult for criminals to control their rage.

Some other respected psychiatrists say Lewis is overstating the connection between child abuse, head injuries and violence. Lewis, who has testified for serial killer Ted Bundy and other vilified criminals, is used to being alone on the unpopular side. "These are not the favorite patients of psychiatrists. They do not come into the office and they do not pay their bills," said Lewis. Lewis said the policy implications of her studies are clear. "Certainly, a civilized society does not kill mentally ill people," she said.

Some states do execute the mentally ill.... The legal issue in most states is not mental illness but competence, or whether someone is sufficiently coherent to form criminal intent. Still, experts say the research makes a compelling case that child abuse prevention must be incorporated into the nation's crime-fighting strategy with the same commitment as building prisons. But, said West, "politically, you can't sell prevention. The violence statistics in other countries are steady and ours are doubling. My personal belief is that the most important aspect is our failure to protect our children."

D. To Kill or Not to Kill ... For and Against the Death Penalty

The Ultimate Punishment: A Defense
Ernest van den Haag, 99 Harv. L. Rev. 1662 (1986).

In an average year about 20,000 homicides occur in the United States. Fewer than 300 convicted murderers are sentenced to death. But because no more than thirty murderers have been executed in any recent year, most convicts sentenced to death are likely to die of old age.[4] Nonetheless, the death penalty looms large in discussions: it raises important moral questions independent of the number of executions.

The death penalty is our harshest punishment.[5] It is irrevocable: it ends the existence of those punished, instead of temporarily imprisoning them. Further, although not intended to cause physical pain, execution is the only corporal punishment still applied to

---

4. Death row as a semipermanent residence is cruel, because convicts are denied the normal amenities of prison life. Thus, unless death row residents are integrated into the prison population, the continuing accumulation of convicts on death row should lead us to accelerate either the rate of executions or the rate of commutations. I find little objection to integration.

5. Some writers, for example, Cesare Bonesana, Marchese di Beccaria, have thought that life imprisonment is more severe. See C. Beccaria, Dei Delitti E Delle Pene 62–70 (1764). More recently, Jacques Barzun, has expressed this view. See Barzun, In Favor of Capital Punishment, in *The Death*

adults. These singular characteristics contribute to the perennial, impassioned controversy about capital punishment.

I. Distribution

Consideration of the justice, morality, or usefulness, of capital punishment is often conflated with objections to its alleged discriminatory or capricious distribution among the guilty. Wrongly so. If capital punishment is immoral in *se*, no distribution among the guilty could make it moral. If capital punishment is moral, no distribution would make it immoral. Improper distribution cannot affect the quality of what is distributed, be it punishments or rewards. Discriminatory or capricious distribution thus could not justify abolition of the death penalty. Further, maldistribution inheres no more in capital punishment than in any other punishment.

Maldistribution between the guilty and the innocent is, by definition, unjust. But the injustice does not lie in the nature of the punishment. Because of the finality of the death penalty, the most grievous maldistribution occurs when it is imposed upon the innocent. However, the frequent allegations of discrimination and capriciousness refer to maldistribution among the guilty and not to the punishment of the innocent.

Maldistribution of any punishment among those who deserve it is irrelevant to its justice or morality. Even if poor or black convicts guilty of capital offenses suffer capital punishment, and other convicts equally guilty of the same crimes do not, a more equal distribution, however desirable, would merely be more equal. It would not be more just to the convicts under sentence of death.

Punishments are imposed on persons, not on racial or economic groups. Guilt is personal. The only relevant question is: does the person to be executed deserve the punishment? Whether or not others who deserved the same punishment, whatever their economic or racial group, have avoided execution is irrelevant. If they have, the guilt of the executed convicts would not be diminished, nor would their punishment be less deserved. To put the issue starkly, if the death penalty were imposed on guilty blacks, but not on guilty whites, or, if it were imposed by a lottery among the guilty, this irrationally discriminatory or capricious distribution would neither make the penalty unjust, nor cause anyone to be unjustly punished, despite the undue impunity bestowed on others.

Equality, in short, seems morally less important than justice. And justice is independent of distributional inequalities. The ideal of equal justice demands that justice be equally distributed, not that it be replaced by equality. Justice requires that as many of the guilty as possible be punished, regardless of whether others have avoided punishment. To let these others escape the deserved punishment does not do justice to them, or to society. But it is not unjust to those who could not escape.

These moral considerations are not meant to deny that irrational discrimination, or capriciousness, would be inconsistent with constitutional requirements. But I am satisfied that the Supreme Court has in fact provided for adherence to the constitutional requirement of equality as much as is possible. Some inequality is indeed unavoidable as a

---

Penalty in America 154 (H. Bedau ed. 1964). However, the overwhelming majority of both abolitionists and of convicts under death sentence prefer life imprisonment to execution.

practical matter in any system.[6] But, *ultra posse nemo obligatur.* (Nobody is bound beyond ability.)[7]

Recent data reveal little direct racial discrimination in the sentencing of those arrested and convicted of murder.[8] The abrogation of the death penalty for rape has eliminated a major source of racial discrimination. Concededly, some discrimination based on the race of murder victims may exist; yet, this discrimination affects criminal victimizers in an unexpected way. Murderers of whites are thought more likely to be executed than murderers of blacks. Black victims, then, are less fully vindicated than white ones. However, because most black murderers kill blacks, black murderers are spared the death penalty more often than are white murderers. They fare better than most white murderers.[9] The motivation behind unequal distribution of the death penalty may well have been to discriminate against blacks, but the result has favored them. Maldistribution is thus a straw man for empirical as well as analytical reasons.

II. Miscarriages of Justice

In a recent survey Professors Hugo Adam Bedau and Michael Radelet found that 7000 persons were executed in the United States between 1900 and 1985 and that 25 were innocent of capital crimes.[10] Among the innocents they list Sacco and Vanzetti as well as Ethel and Julius Rosenberg. Although their data may be questionable, I do not doubt that, over a long enough period, miscarriages of justice will occur even in capital cases.

Despite precautions, nearly all human activities, such as trucking, lighting, or construction, cost the lives of some innocent bystanders. We do not give up these activities, because the advantages, moral or material, outweigh the unintended losses.[11] Analogously, for those who think the death penalty just, miscarriages of justice are offset by the moral benefits and the usefulness of doing justice. For those who think the death penalty unjust even when it does not miscarry, miscarriages can hardly be decisive.

III. Deterrence

Despite much recent work, there has been no conclusive statistical demonstration that the death penalty is a better deterrent than are alternative punishments. However, deterrence is less than decisive for either side. Most abolitionists acknowledge that they

---

6. The ideal of equality, unlike the ideal of retributive justice (which can be approximated separately in each instance), is clearly unattainable unless all guilty persons are apprehended, and thereafter tried, convicted and sentenced by the same court, at the same time. Unequal justice is the best we can do; it is still better than the injustice, equal or unequal, which occurs if, for the sake of equality, we deliberately allow some who could be punished to escape.

7. Equality, even without justice, may remain a strong psychological, and therefore political, demand. Yet Charles Black, by proving the inevitability of "caprice" (inequality), undermines his own constitutional argument, because it seems unlikely that the Constitution's fifth and fourteenth amendments were meant to authorize the death penalty only under unattainable conditions. *See* C. Black, *Capital Punishment: The Inevitability of Caprice and Mistake*(1974).

8. *See* Bureau of Justice Statistics, U.S. Dep't of Justice, Bulletin No. NCJ-98,399, Capital Punishment 1984, at 9 (1985); Johnson, The Executioner's Bias, Nat'l Rev., Nov. 15, 1985, at 44.

9. It barely need be said that any discrimination *against* (for example, black murderers of whites) must also be discrimination *for* (for example, black murderers of blacks).

10. Bedau & Radelet, *Miscarriages of Justice in Potentially Capital Cases* (1st draft, Oct. 1985) (on file at Harvard Law School Library).

11. An excessive number of trucking accidents or of miscarriages of justice could offset the benefits gained by trucking or the practice of doing justice. We are, however, far from this situation.

would continue to favor abolition even if the death penalty were shown to deter more murders than alternatives could deter. Abolitionists appear to value the life of a convicted murderer or, at least, his non-execution, more highly than they value the lives of the innocent victims who might be spared by deterring prospective murderers.

Deterrence is not altogether decisive for me either. I would favor retention of the death penalty as retribution even if it were shown that the threat of execution could not deter prospective murderers not already deterred by the threat of imprisonment.[12] Still, I believe the death penalty, because of its finality, is more feared than imprisonment, and deters some prospective murderers not deterred by the threat of imprisonment. Sparing the lives of even a few prospective victims by deterring their murderers is more important than preserving the lives of convicted murderers because of the possibility, or even the probability, that executing them would not deter others. Whereas the lives of the victims who might be saved are valuable, that of the murderer has only negative value, because of his crime. Surely the criminal law is meant to protect the lives of potential victims in preference to those of actual murderers.

Murder rates are determined by many factors; neither the severity nor the probability of the threatened sanction is always decisive. However, for the long run, I share the view of Sir James Fitzjames Stephen: "Some men, probably, abstain from murder because they fear that if they committed murder they would be hanged. Hundreds of thousands abstain from it because they regard it with horror. One great reason why they regard it with horror is that murderers are hanged." Penal sanctions are useful in the long run for the formation of the internal restraints so necessary to control crime. The severity and finality of the death penalty is appropriate to the seriousness and the finality of murder.[13]

IV. Incidental Issues: Cost, Relative Suffering, Brutalization

Many nondecisive issues are associated with capital punishment. Some believe that the monetary cost of appealing a capital sentence is excessive. Yet most comparisons of the cost of life imprisonment with the cost of execution, apart from their dubious relevance, are flawed at least by the implied assumption that life prisoners will generate no judicial costs during their imprisonment. At any rate, the actual monetary costs are trumped by the importance of doing justice.

Others insist that a person sentenced to death suffers more than his victim suffered, and that this (excess) suffering is undue according to the *lex talionis* (rule of retaliation). We cannot know whether the murderer on death row suffers more than his victim suffered; however, unlike the murderer, the victim deserved none of the suffering inflicted. Further, the limitations of the *lex talionis* were meant to restrain private vengeance, not the social retribution that has taken its place. Punishment—regardless of the motiva-

---

12. If executions were shown to increase the murder rate in the long run, I would favor abolition. Sparing the innocent victims who would be spared, *ex hypothesi*, by the nonexecution of murderers would be more important to me than the execution, however just, of murderers. But although there is a lively discussion of the subject, no serious evidence exists to support the hypothesis that executions produce a higher murder rate. *Cf.* Phillips, "The Deterrent Effect of Capital Punishment: New Evidence on an Old Controversy," 86 Am. J. Soc. 139 (1980) (arguing that murder rates drop immediately after executions of criminals).

13. *Weems v. United States*, 217 U.S. 349 (1910), suggests that penalties be proportionate to the seriousness of the crime—a common theme of the criminal law. Murder, therefore, demands more than life imprisonment, if, as I believe, it is a more serious crime than other crimes punished by life imprisonment. In modern times, our sensibility requires that the range of punishments be narrower than the range of crimes—but not so narrow as to exclude the death penalty.

tion—is not intended to revenge, offset, or compensate for the victim's suffering, or to be measured by it. Punishment is to vindicate the law and the social order undermined by the crime. This is why a kidnapper's penal confinement is not limited to the period for which he imprisoned his victim; nor is a burglar's confinement meant merely to offset the suffering or the harm he caused his victim; nor is it meant only to offset the advantage he gained.[14]

Another argument heard at least since Beccaria is that, by killing a murderer, we encourage, endorse, or legitimize unlawful killing. Yet, although all punishments are meant to be unpleasant, it is seldom argued that they legitimize the unlawful imposition of identical unpleasantness. Imprisonment is not thought to legitimize kidnapping; neither are fines thought to legitimize robbery. The difference between murder and execution, or between kidnapping and imprisonment, is that the first is unlawful and undeserved, the second a lawful and deserved punishment for an unlawful act. The physical similarities of the punishment to the crime are irrelevant. The relevant difference is not physical, but social.[15]

V. Justice, Excess, Degradation

We threaten punishments in order to deter crime. We impose them not only to make the threats credible but also as retribution (justice) for the crimes that were not deterred. Threats and punishments are necessary to deter and deterrence is a sufficient practical justification for them. Retribution is an independent moral justification.[16] Although penalties can be unwise, repulsive, or inappropriate, and those punished can be pitiable, in a sense the infliction of legal punishment on a guilty person cannot be unjust. By committing the crime, the criminal volunteered to assume the risk of receiving a legal punishment that he could have avoided by not committing the crime. The punishment he suffers is the punishment he voluntarily risked suffering and, therefore, it is no more unjust to him than any other event for which one knowingly volunteers to assume the risk. Thus, the death penalty cannot be unjust to the guilty criminal.[17]

---

14. Thus restitution (a civil liability) cannot satisfy the punitive purpose of penal sanctions, whether the purpose be retributive or deterrent.

15. Some abolitionists challenge: if the death penalty is just and serves as a deterrent, why not televise executions? The answer is simple. The death even of a murderer, however well-deserved, should not serve as public entertainment. It so served in earlier centuries. But in this respect our sensibility has changed for the better, I believe. Further, television unavoidably would trivialize executions, wedged in, as they would be, between game shows, situation comedies and the like. Finally, because televised executions would focus on the physical aspects of the punishment, rather than the nature of the crime and the suffering of the victim, a televised execution would present the murderer as the victim of the state. Far from communicating the moral significance of the execution, television would shift the focus to the pitiable fear of the murderer. We no longer place in cages those sentenced to imprisonment to expose them to public view. Why should we so expose those sentenced to execution?

16. See van den Haag, "Punishment as a Device for Controlling the Crime Rate," 33 Rutgers L. Rev. 706, 719 (1981) (explaining why the desire for retribution, although independent, would have to be satisfied even if deterrence were the only purpose of punishment.)

17. An explicit threat of punitive action is necessary to the justification of any legal punishment: *nulla poena sine lege* (no punishment without [preexisting] law). To be sufficiently justified, the threat must in turn have a rational and legitimate purpose. "Your money or your life" does not qualify; nor does the threat of an unjust law; nor, finally, does a threat that is altogether disproportionate to the importance of its purpose. In short, preannouncement legitimizes the threatened punishment only if the threat is warranted. But this leaves a very wide range of justified threats. Furthermore, the punished person is aware of the penalty for his actions and thus volunteers to take the risk even of an unjust punishment. His victim, however, did not volunteer to risk anything. The

There remain, however, two moral objections. The penalty may be regarded as always excessive as retribution and always morally degrading. To regard the death penalty as always excessive, one must believe that no crime—no matter how heinous—could possibly justify capital punishment. Such a belief can be neither corroborated nor refuted; it is an article of faith.

Alternatively, or concurrently, one may believe that everybody, the murderer no less than the victim, has an imprescriptible (natural?) right to life. The law therefore should not deprive anyone of life. I share Jeremy Bentham's view that any such "natural and imprescriptible rights" are "nonsense upon stilts."[18]

Justice Brennan has insisted that the death penalty is "uncivilized," "inhuman," inconsistent with "human dignity" and with "the sanctity of life," that it "treats members of the human race as nonhumans, as objects to be toyed with and discarded," that it is "uniquely degrading to human dignity" and "by its very nature, [involves] a denial of the executed person's humanity." Justice Brennan does not say why he thinks execution "uncivilized." Hitherto most civilizations have had the death penalty, although it has been discarded in Western Europe, where it is currently unfashionable probably because of its abuse by totalitarian regimes.

By "degrading," Justice Brennan seems to mean that execution degrades the executed convicts. Yet philosophers, such as Immanuel Kant and G.F.W. Hegel, have insisted that, when deserved, execution, far from degrading the executed convict, affirms his humanity by affirming his rationality and his responsibility for his actions. They thought that execution, when deserved, is required for the sake of the convict's dignity. (Does not life imprisonment violate human dignity more than execution, by keeping alive a prisoner deprived of all autonomy?)

Common sense indicates that it cannot be death—our common fate—that is inhuman. Therefore, Justice Brennan must mean that death degrades when it comes not as a natural or accidental event, but as a deliberate social imposition. The murderer learns through his punishment that his fellow men have found him unworthy of living; that because he has murdered, he is being expelled from the community of the living. This degradation is self-inflicted. By murdering, the murderer has so dehumanized himself that he cannot remain among the living. The social recognition of his self-degradation is the punitive essence of execution. To believe, as Justice Brennan appears to, that the degradation is inflicted by the execution reverses the direction of causality.

Execution of those who have committed heinous murders may deter only one murder per year. If it does, it seems quite warranted. It is also the only fitting retribution for murder I can think of.

Note

Consider the argument advanced by philosopher Walter Berns in his book, *For Capital Punishment*:

---

question whether any self-inflicted injury—such as a legal punishment—ever can be unjust to a person who knowingly risked it is a matter than requires more analysis than is possible here.

18. *The Works of Jeremy Bentham* 105 (J. Bowring ed. 1972). However, I would be more polite about prescriptible natural rights, which Bentham described as "simple nonsense." (It does not matter whether natural rights are called "moral" or "human" rights as they currently are by most writers.)

Capital punishment ... serves to remind us of the majesty of the moral order that is embodied in our law and of the terrible consequences of its breach.... The criminal law must possess a dignity far beyond that possessed by mere statutory enactment or utilitarian or self-interested calculations; the most powerful means we have to give it that dignity is to authorize it to impose the ultimate penalty. The criminal law must be made awful, by which I mean awe-inspiring or commanding "profound respect or reverential fear." It must remind us of the moral order by which alone we can live as human beings.

Against the American System of Capital Punishment

Jack Greenberg, 99 Harv. L. Rev. 1670 (1986).

Over and over, proponents of the death penalty insist that it is right and useful. In reply, abolitionists argue that it is morally flawed and cite studies to demonstrate its failure to deter. Were the subject not so grim and compelling, the exchanges would, by now, be tiresome.

Yet all too frequently, the debate has been off the mark. Death penalty proponents have assumed a system of capital punishment that simply does not exist: a system in which the penalty is inflicted on the most reprehensible criminals and meted out frequently enough both to deter and to perform the moral and utilitarian functions ascribed to retribution. Explicitly or implicitly, they assume a system in which certainly the worst criminals, Charles Manson or a putative killer of one's parent or child, for example, are executed in an evenhanded manner. But this idealized system is not the American system of capital punishment. Because of the goals that our criminal justice system must satisfy—deterring crime, punishing the guilty, acquitting the innocent, avoiding needless cruelty, treating citizens equally, and prohibiting oppression by the state—America simply does not have the kind of capital punishment system contemplated by death penalty partisans.

Indeed, the reality of American capital punishment is quite to the contrary. Since at least 1967, the death penalty has been inflicted only rarely, erratically, and often upon the least odious killers, while many of the most heinous criminals have escaped execution. Moreover, it has been employed almost exclusively in a few formerly slaveholding states, and there it has been used almost exclusively against killers of whites, not blacks, and never against white killers of blacks. This is the American system of capital punishment. It is this system, not some idealized one, that must be defended in any national debate on the death penalty. I submit that this system is deeply incompatible with the proclaimed objectives of death penalty proponents.

I. The American System of Capital Punishment

Here is how America's system of capital punishment really works today. Since 1967, the year in which the courts first began to grapple in earnest with death penalty issues, the death penalty has been frequently imposed but rarely enforced. Between 1967 and 1980, death sentences or convictions were reversed for 1899 of the 2402 people on death row, a reversal rate of nearly eighty percent. These reversals reflected, among other factors, a 1968 Supreme Court decision dealing with how juries should be chosen in capital cases, a 1972 decision declaring capital sentences unconstitutional partly because they were imposed arbitrarily and "freakishly," and a 1976 decision holding mandatory death sentences unconstitutional. Many death sentences were also invalidated on a wide variety of commonplace state-law grounds, such as hearsay rule violations or improper prosecutorial argument.

This judicial tendency to invalidate death penalties proved resistant to change. After 1972, in response to Supreme Court decisions, many states adopted new death penalty laws, and judges developed a clearer idea of the requirements that the Court had begun to enunciate a few years earlier. By 1979, the efforts of state legislatures finally paid off when John Spenkelink became the first person involuntarily executed since 1967. Nevertheless, from 1972 to 1980, the death penalty invalidation rate declined to "only" sixty percent. In contrast, ordinary noncapital convictions and sentences were almost invariably upheld.

Today, the death row population has grown to more than 1600 convicts. About 300 prisoners per year join this group, while about 100 per year leave death row, mainly by reason of judicial invalidations but also by execution and by death from other causes. Following Spenkelink's execution, some states began to put some of these convicted murderers to death. Five persons were executed involuntarily in 1983, twenty-one in 1984, and fourteen in 1985. Nevertheless, the number of actual executions seems to have reached a plateau. The average number of executions in the United States hovers at about twenty per year; as of March 1, only one person has been executed in 1986. Yet even if this number doubled, or increased fivefold, executions would not be numerous either in proportion to the nation's homicides (approximately 19,000 per year)[19] or to its death row population (over 1600).

One reason for the small number of executions is that the courts continue to upset capital convictions at an extraordinarily high rate, albeit not so high as earlier. Between January 1, 1982 and October 1, 1985, state supreme courts invalidated thirty-five percent of all capital judgments. State post-appellate process undid a few more. The federal district and appeals courts overturned another ten percent, and last Term the Supreme Court reversed three of the four capital sentences it reviewed. Altogether, about forty-five percent of capital judgments which were reviewed during this period were set aside by one court or another. One index of the vitality of litigation to reverse executions is that while legal attacks on capital punishment began as a coordinated effort by civil rights lawyers, they now come from a variety of segments of the bar.

States not only execute convicted killers rarely, but they do so erratically. Spenkelink's execution, the nation's first involuntary execution since 1967, did not augur well for new systems of guided discretion designed to produce evenhanded capital justice in which only the worst murderers would be executed. Spenkelink was a drifter who killed a traveling companion who had sexually abused him. The Assistant Attorney General of Florida in charge of capital cases described him as "probably the least obnoxious individual on death row in terms of the crime he committed."

The current round of invalidations highlights the erratic imposition of the death penalty. These invalidations have been based largely on grounds unrelated to the heinousness of the crime or the reprehensibility of the criminal. Thus, the most abhorrent perpetrators of the most execrable crimes have escaped the penalty on grounds wholly unrelated to moral desert—for example, because defense counsel, the prosecutor, or the judge acted ineffectively or improperly on some matter of evidence. By contrast, criminals far less detestable by any rational moral standard—like Spenkelink, "the least obnoxious individual on death row"—have gone to their deaths because their trials "went well." Of course, when errors occur in securing a death penalty, the sentence should be invalidated, particularly because "there is a significant constitutional

---

19. *See* Federal Bureau of Investigation, U.S. Dept. of Justice, Uniform Crime Reports, Crime in the United States 1984, at 6 (1985) (18,692 murders in 1984).

difference between the death penalty and lesser punishments." The corollary of this imperative is that the current system of capital punishment violates a central tenet of capital justice—that the most reprehensible criminals deserve execution and others deserve lesser sentences.

It is troubling as well that the current level of executions has been attained only by using expedited procedures that undermine confidence in the fairness of the death penalty process. Recent executions have occurred during a period in which some federal judges, frustrated with the slow pace of capital justice, have taken extraordinary measures to expedite capital cases in federal courts. For example, the Fifth Circuit has quickened habeas corpus appeals in capital cases by accelerating the dates of arguments and greatly compressing the time for briefing cases. Increasingly, the Supreme Court has encouraged this hurry-up justice. The Court has not only denied stay applications, but it has also vacated stays entered by lower courts in cases in which stays would have been routine in earlier times. In sum, the recent invalidation rate seems unlikely to change significantly, thereby perpetuating the current system of erratic and haphazard executions.

Of course, one major difference exists between the period 1982 to 1985 and earlier years: increasingly, the death penalty has been concentrated geographically, not applied evenly across the United States. In the most recent period, there were forty-three involuntary executions. Quite strikingly, all occurred in the states of the Old Confederacy. Thirty-four of the forty-three were in four states, and more than a quarter were in a single state, Florida, with thirteen. In all but four cases, the defendants killed white persons. In no case was a white executed for killing a black person.

Why are there so few executions? Convictions and sentences are reversed, cases move slowly, and states devote relatively meager resources to pursuing actual executions. Even Florida, which above all other states has shown that it can execute almost any death row inmate it wants to, has killed only 13 of 221 inmates since 1979, 12 since 1982. (It now has 233 convicts on death row.) Outside the former slave-holding states, more than half the states are now abolitionist either *de jure* (fourteen states) or *de facto* (five states have no one on death row). Moreover, past experience suggests that the execution level will not go very high. Before the 1967–76 moratorium, the number of executions exceeded fifty only once after 1957—fifty-six in 1960. At that time there were fewer abolitionist states and more capital crimes. This experience suggests that executions will not deplete the death row population.

The limited number of actual executions seems to me to reflect the very deep ambivalence that Americans feel about capital punishment. We are the only nation of the Western democratic world that has not abolished capital punishment.[20] By contrast, countries with whose dominant value systems we ordinarily disagree, like the Soviet Union, China, Iran, and South Africa, execute prisoners in great numbers.

II. The Failures of Capital Punishment

We have a system of capital punishment that results in infrequent, random, and erratic executions, one that is structured to inflict death neither on those who have com-

---

20. The European Convention of Human Rights has been amended to prohibit the death penalty in peace-time. *See* Protocol No. 6 to the Convention for the Protection of Human Rights and Fundamental Freedoms Concerning the Abolition of the Death Penalty, Apr. 28, 1983, Council of Europe, 22 I.L.M. 539. The consequence of the amendment is that parties to the treaty who ratify may not reinstitute the death penalty without repudiating the entire treaty, a move that would have undesirable political consequences.

mitted the worst offenses nor on defendants of the worst character. This is the "system"—if that is the right descriptive term—of capital punishment that must be defended by death penalty proponents. This system may not be justified by positing a particularly egregious killer like Charles Manson. Our commitment to the rule of law means that we need an acceptable general system of capital justice if we are to have one at all. However, the real American system of capital punishment clearly fails when measured against the most common justifications for the infliction of punishment, deterrence, and retribution.

If capital punishment can be a deterrent greater than life imprisonment at all, the American system is at best a feeble one. Studies by Thorsten Sellin showed no demonstrable deterrent effect of capital punishment even during its heyday. Today's death penalty, which is far less frequently used, geographically localized, and biased according to the race of the victim, cannot possibly upset that conclusion. The forty-three persons who were involuntarily executed from 1982 to 1985 were among a death row population of more than 1600 condemned to execution out of about 20,000 who committed non-negligent homicides per year. While forty-three percent of the victims were black, the death penalty is so administered that it overwhelmingly condemns and executes those who have killed whites.

Very little reason exists to believe that the present capital punishment system deters the conduct of others any more effectively than life imprisonment.[21] Potential killers who rationally weigh the odds of being killed themselves must conclude that the danger is nonexistent in most parts of the country and that in the South the danger is slight, particularly if the proposed victim is black. Moreover, the paradigm of this kind of murderer, the contract killer, is almost by definition a person who takes his chances like the soldier of fortune he is.[22]

But most killers do not engage in anything like a cost-benefit analysis. They are impulsive, and they kill impulsively. If capital punishment is to deter them, it can do so only indirectly: by impressing on potential killers a standard of right and wrong, a moral authority, an influence on their superegos that, notwithstanding mental disorder, would inhibit homicide. This conception of general deterrence seems deeply flawed because it rests upon a quite implausible conception of how this killer population internalizes social norms. Although not mentally disturbed enough to sustain insanity as a defense, they are often highly disturbed, of low intelligence, and addicted to drugs or alcohol. In any event, the message, if any, that the real American system of capital punishment sends to the psyches of would-be killers is quite limited: you may in a rare case be executed if you murder in the deepest South and kill a white person.[23]

---

21. In the sense of specific deterrence or incapacitation, of course, the forty-three who were put to death indeed have been deterred. But those serving life sentences in terms of years, of course, occasionally kill. That fact would not be accepted as grounds for having sentenced them to death in lieu of the original prison term. Recidivism by convicted murders and killings by prisoners generally are discussed in Bedau, "Recidivism, Parole, and Deterrence," in *The Death Penalty in America* at 173, and Wolfson, "The Deterrent Effect of the Death Penalty Upon Prison Murder," in *The Death Penalty in America* at 159, respectively. Wolfson concludes: "Given that the deterrent effect of the death penalty for prison homicide is to be seriously doubted, it is clear that management and physical changes in the prison would do more than any legislated legal sanction to reduce the number of prison murders." *Id.* at 172.

22. It might be argued that even the rare execution is dramatic and unduly publicized and consequently has great effect. Ironically, the slight increase in the number of executions in the past few years has robbed them of much dramatic effect.

23. As to an asserted salutary influence on the healthy mind, tending to cause it to shun lethal violence, one can only respond that no evidence has been offered. Religious, social, moral, and non-

The consequences of the real American system of capital justice are no more favorable as far as retribution is concerned. Retributive theories of criminal punishment draw support from several different moral theories that cannot be adequately elaborated here. While some of the grounds of retribution arguments resemble the conscience-building argument underlying general deterrence theory,[24] all retribution theories insist that seeking retribution constitutes a morally permissible use of governmental power. To retribution theorists, the death penalty makes a moral point: it holds up as an example worthy of the most severe condemnation one who has committed the most opprobrious crime.

As with many controversies over moral issues, these purely moral arguments may appear to end any real possibility for further discussion. For those who believe in them, they persuade, just as the moral counter-arguments persuade abolitionists. But discussion should not end at this point. Those who claim a moral justification for capital punishment must reconcile that belief with other moral considerations. To my mind, the moral force of any retribution argument is radically undercut by the hard facts of the actual American system of capital punishment. This system violates fundamental norms because it is haphazard, and because it is regionally and racially biased. To these moral flaws, I would add another: the minuscule number of executions nowadays cannot achieve the grand moral aims that are presupposed by a serious societal commitment to retribution.

Some retribution proponents argue that it is the pronouncement of several hundred death sentences followed by lengthy life imprisonment, not the actual imposition of a few executions, that satisfies the public's demand for retribution. Of course, the public has not said that it wants the death penalty as it exists—widely applicable but infrequently used. Nor, to the best of my knowledge, is there any solid empirical basis for such a claim. Like other statutes, death penalty laws are of general applicability, to be employed according to their terms.[25] Nothing in their language or legislative history authorizes the erratic, occasional, racially biased use of these laws. But my objections to this argument go much deeper. I find morally objectionable a system of many pronounced death sentences but few actual executions, a system in which race and region

---

capital legal requirements all teach us not to murder. If the death penalty were needed as an incremental influence to persuade noncriminals to abjure killing, there would be elevated murder rates in abolitionist states and nations; these have not been demonstrated.

24. The reply to this argument is the same as to the arguments that the death penalty deters by teaching not to kill. Retribution is also said to have another utilitarian by-product distinct from a Kantian eye-for-an-eye justification: it satisfies demands for vengeance, preventing retaliatory killing. Yet, during the period of no executions (1967–1977) and in the overwhelming number of states that have abolished the death penalty, have not sentenced anyone to death, or have not carried out executions, it is difficult to find an instance of vengeance killing, although during this time there have been perhaps 360,000 murders (about 20,000 per year for 18 years).

It is also argued that, particularly for those who have been close to the victim, who are members of his or her family, or who are fellow police officers, or for those members of the public who somehow feel an identification with the deceased, the death penalty provides personal satisfaction, repaying in some measure the loss they felt in the death of the victim. This hardly justifies the present system.

25. A few death penalty proponents say that the death penalty is the only way of "assuring" life imprisonment for the worst criminals. Recognizing that most death sentences have turned into interminable prison sentences, they say this is preferable to sentences of life imprisonment from which convicts may be released on parole. But human ingenuity can fashion a sentence of life without parole. The death sentence following extensive litigation, amounting to life sentence for most while executing only a few, is an inefficient way of achieving the purpose of life imprisonment. And again, this sort of life sentencing process is not what the death penalty laws contemplate.

are the only significant variables in determining who actually dies. My objection is not grounded in a theory that posits any special moral rights for the death row population. The decisive point is my understanding of the basic moral aspirations of American civilization, particularly its deep commitment to the rule of law. I cannot reconcile an erratic, racially and regionally biased system of executions with my understanding of the core values of our legal order.

Death penalty proponents may respond to this argument by saying that if there is not enough capital punishment, there should be more. If only killers of whites are being executed, then killers of blacks should be killed too; and if many sentences are being reversed, standards of review should be relaxed. In the meantime, they might urge, the death penalty should go on. But this argument is unavailing, because it seeks to change the terms of the debate in a fundamental way. It seeks to substitute an imaginary system for the real American system of capital punishment. If there were a different kind of system of death penalty administration in this country, or even a reasonable possibility that one might emerge, we could debate its implications. But any current debate over the death penalty cannot ignore the deep moral deficiencies of the present system.[26]

III. The Constitution and the Death Penalty

This debate about whether we should have a death penalty is a matter on which the Supreme Court is unlikely to have the last say now or in the near future. Yet, the Court's decisions have some relevance. The grounds that the Court has employed in striking down various forms of the death penalty resemble the arguments I have made. Freakishness was a ground for invalidating the death penalty as it was administered throughout the country in 1972. Rarity of use contributed to invalidation of the death penalty for rape and felony murder, and to invalidation of the mandatory death penalty. That constitutional law reflects moral concerns should not be strange: concepts of cruel and unusual punishment, due process, and equal protection express contemporary standards of decency.

Moreover, the whole development of the fourteenth amendment points to the existence of certain basic standards of decency and fairness from which no state or region can claim exemption. One such value is, of course, the racially neutral administration of justice. No one disputes that one of the fourteenth amendment's central designs was to secure the evenhanded administration of justice in the southern state courts and that the persistent failure to achieve that goal has been one of America's greatest tragedies. We cannot be blind to the fact that actual executions have taken place primarily in the South and in at least a racially suspect manner. In light of our constitutional history, the race-specific aspects of the death penalty in the South are profoundly unsettling.

Given the situation as I have described it, and as I believe it will continue so long as we have capital punishment, one could argue that the death penalty should be declared unconstitutional in all its forms. But the Court is unlikely to take that step soon. Only ten years have passed since the type of death statute now in use was upheld, and some states have had such laws for an even shorter period. Thirty-seven states have passed laws showing they want some sort of death penalty. Public opinion polls show that most Americans want capital punishment in some form. Having only recently invalidated one application of the death penalty in *Furman v. Georgia* in 1972, the Court is unlikely

---

26. Some death penalty proponents argue that the erratic quality of the capital sentencing system and its racial bias are characteristic of the criminal justice system generally. But while such a condition may or may not be tolerable when it results in imprisonment, it hardly justifies killing convicts.

soon to deal with the concept wholesale again. But, if the way capital punishment works does not change materially, I think that at some point the Court will declare the overall system to be cruel and unusual. If this prediction is correct—and it is at least arguably so—an additional moral factor enters the debate. Is it right to kill death row inmates during this period of experimentation? There is, of course, an element of bootstrapping to my argument: exercising further restraint in killing death-sentenced convicts reinforces arguments of freakishness and rarity of application. But unless one can assure a full and steady stream of executions, sufficient to do the jobs the death penalty proponents claim that it can do, there is further reason to kill no one at all.

E. The Debate over Deterrence and Retribution

1. Overview of Deterrence*

A major purpose of criminal punishment is to deter future criminal conduct. The deterrence theory assumes that a rational person will avoid criminal behavior if the *severity* of the punishment for that behavior and the perceived *certainty* of receiving the punishment combine to outweigh the benefits of the illegal conduct.

The deterrence achieved by using the death penalty must be examined in the context of the entire criminal justice system. For the death penalty to deter first-degree (or capital) murderers, the killer must know of the penalty's application to the crime and must believe that the certainty of punishment is sufficient to create an unacceptable risk. Without such awareness, the killer will probably not be deterred. One further factor must be considered when assessing a penalty's deterrent impact. Any deterrent value must be judged in the context of alternatives; if a lesser penalty achieves the same or a greater level of deterrence, no deterrent justification supports the enhanced punishment.

Possibly because deterrence is ingrained in our lives—for example, children are punished for violating the family rules—a majority of the public supports the death penalty because they consider it an effective deterrent. Supporters contend that death sentences and executions heighten the risk of punishment in a potential killer's mind. By threatening to take the killer's life, society "ups the ante" of killing another.

Studies of the deterrent effect of the death penalty have been conducted for several years, with varying results. As opponents of the death penalty argue, most of these studies have failed to produce evidence that the death penalty deters murderers more effectively than the threat of protracted imprisonment. Various reasons might explain this conclusion. First, the weight assigned to the enhanced severity is only marginal since the comparable punishment is, in most cases, life imprisonment without possibility of parole, or very long sentences. Second, the other key element in the deterrence theory, the perceived certainty of imposing the sentence, is rather low for most murders for a number of reasons: many crimes remain unsolved; the defendant may escape apprehension; evidence may be lacking or inadmissible; plea bargaining may enable the defendant to avoid capital punishment; the jury may acquit or not impose the penalty; and

---

* Adapted from Zimring & Laurence, Death Penalty, U.S. Dep't of Justice, Crime File Study Guide.

appeals and clemency petitions may delay or preclude execution. The actual probability that a murderer will receive a death sentence is quite low and the risk of being executed even smaller, about 1 per 1,000 killings in 1984. Even when the certainty of punishment is higher, many killers might refuse to believe they will be apprehended, let alone executed. Third, the assumption of rationality on which deterrence theories are based may not be valid for many killers.

Supporters of the death penalty make two principal arguments about deterrence: that common sense alone suggests that people fear death more than other punishments and that, when studies fail to resolve the issue, executions should continue on the assumption that a small saving of innocent lives will result.

It is worth noting that 10 of the 12 states without capital punishment have homicide rates below the national average. In a 2000 study, the New York Times found that during the previous 20 years, the homicide rate in states with the death penalty has been 48 percent to 101 percent higher than in states without the death penalty. Bonner & Fessenden, *States With No Death Penalty Share Lower Homicide Rates*, New York Times, p. 1, Sept. 22, 2000. According to the Times, North Dakota, which does not have the death penalty, had a homicide rate lower than South Dakota, a death penalty state. Similarly, Massachusetts, which abolished capital punishment in 1984, has a lower homicide rate (3.7 per 100,000) than Connecticut (4.9 per 100,000), a state with a small death row population. In West Virginia, a state that does not have the death penalty, the homicide rate was 30 percent below that of Virginia, a state with one of the highest execution rates in the country.

Over the past decade, a host of academic studies has examined the death penalty with mixed results. Several researchers claimed to have found no robust evidence of deterrence, while others claim to have uncovered compelling evidence to the contrary. In an effort to better understand the conflicting evidence, scholars from Yale Law School and the University of Pennsylvania published a thorough assessment of the statistical evidence, and reached the following conclusion:

"[T]he existing evidence for deterrence is surprisingly fragile, and even small changes in specifications yield dramatically different results. Our key insight is that the death penalty—at least as it has been implemented in the United States since *Gregg* ended the moratorium on executions—is applied so rarely that the number of homicides it can plausibly have caused or deterred cannot be reliably disentangled from the large year-to-year changes in the homicide rate caused by other factors. Our estimates suggest not just 'reasonable doubt' about whether there is any deterrent effect of the death penalty, but profound uncertainty. We are confident that the effects are not large, but we remain unsure even of whether they are positive or negative." Donohue & Wolfers, "Uses and Abuses of Empirical Evidence in the Death Penalty Debate," 58 Stan. L. Rev. 791, 793-94 (2005). For a discussion of the significant errors and flaws that seriously undermine the new social science claims that the death penalty acts as a deterrent, see Fagan, "Deterrence and the Death Penalty: Risk, Uncertainty, and Public Policy Choices," testimony presented to the Subcommittee on the Constitution, Civil Rights and Property Rights, Committee on the Judiciary, U.S. Senate, Feb. 1, 2006.

2. Brutalization

Some studies have shown that rather than diminish murder rates, executions have the opposite effect. The prospect that executions brutalize society—making its members more violent—is by no means a new theory. As Justice Brandeis, dissenting in *Olmstead v. United States*, 277 U.S. 438 (1928), stated, "Our government is the potent, the omnipresent teacher. For good or for ill, it teaches the whole people by example."

Brutalization may partially explain the case of Texas, which executed 17 people in 1993, more than it had executed in any year since 1938. Notwithstanding its vigorous enforcement of capital punishment, Texas' homicide rate in 1993 was 15.3 per 100,000. According to the Federal Bureau of Investigation, the national average was 9.8 per 100,000. See Verhovek, *With Practice, Texas is the Execution Leader*, New York Times, Sunday, Sept. 5, 1993, at 6E. In 2000, Texas executed 40 inmates, and between 1976 and April 2006, it executed 363 people. Although Texas has about seven percent of the nation's population, it is responsible for a large percentage of all executions since 1976.

A study by University of Oklahoma sociologists demonstrated a brutalization effect following that state's resumption of executions in 1990 after a 24-year lapse.

> Both the deterrence and brutalization hypotheses, albeit for different reasons, predict that the return to capital punishment will produce a change in the level of criminal homicides in the jurisdiction of interest. The former perspective assumes that potential offenders, including those who may be contemplating murder, rationally weigh the costs and benefits when deciding whether to engage in illegal behavior. Therefore, insofar as the gains associated with criminal homicide do not increase, the reimplementation of the death penalty is expected to influence some potential offenders to refrain from murder. Alternatively, the brutalization perspective suggests that state-sponsored killing, regardless of its political legitimacy, is likely to have a dehumanizing effect on the populace. As a result, the return to capital punishment is expected to weaken socially based inhibitions against the use of deadly force to settle disputes, thereby encouraging some segments of the population to kill in response to perceived wrongs and/or affronts to honor.

> ... [D]eterrence and brutalization processes are more likely to affect some types of criminal homicide than others. Specifically, we expect the deterrent effect of executions to be most evident in situations where the offender may anticipate the need for lethal force for the successful completion of another crime (Peterson and Bailey, 1991). Thus one would predict finding a deterrent effect primarily for felony murders, especially those which are death-eligible. Alternatively, one might expect a brutalization effect to be most pronounced in situations where the relational distance between offenders and victims already minimizes socially derived strictures against killing. That is, during stranger-related interactions involving affronts to honor the example set by the state is most likely to facilitate the use of deadly force to settle disputes.

> Contrary to the predictions of the deterrence hypothesis, we find no evidence that Oklahoma's reintroduction of execution produced a statistically significant decrease in the level of criminal homicides during the period under investigation. Regardless of the functional form specified for the model, the analyses show that the execution of Charles Troy Coleman [on September 10, 1990] had no effect on either total, total felony, stranger-felony, death-eligible felony, or robbery-felony homicides. Thus our findings are consistent with a growing body of research that typically fails to find a significant deterrent effect for the exercise of the death penalty (Peterson and Bailey, 1991).

> Our preliminary analyses, however, provide some evidence of a brutalization effect on stranger homicides. This interesting finding indicates that the

Coleman execution produced an abrupt and lasting increase in the level of stranger homicides in Oklahoma. Specifically, the results show that Coleman's execution led to an increase of approximately one additional stranger-related homicide incident per month.

We interpret these findings for stranger-related homicides as an indication that a return to the exercise of the death penalty weakens socially based inhibitions against the use of lethal force to settle disputes and thereby allows the offender to kill strangers who threaten the offender's sense of self or honor. Admittedly, this explanation could be viewed with some skepticism. After all, stranger-related homicide is a rather heterogeneous category encompassing various sorts of events, including felony murders. In recognition of this limitation, we further disaggregated the stranger homicide series and performed a number of supplementary intervention analyses.

In brief, we find that the Coleman execution produced null effects on both stranger-felony and stranger-robbery homicides. These results, however, should not be particularly surprising given that these two subcategories of stranger-related homicides are likely to be affected by instrumental concerns, as well as by the actors' social distance. More important, these supplementary analyses also reveal that the Coleman execution produced an abrupt and lasting increase in the level of both nonfelony and argument-related stranger homicides. Thus, in line with our initial speculation, it appears that the return to the death penalty, at least in Oklahoma, produces a brutalization effect in situations where prohibitions against killing are weakest and where the offender perceives having been wronged (i.e., nonfelony and argument-related stranger homicides).

Cochran, Chamlin and Seth, "Deterrence or Brutalization?: An Impact Assessment of Oklahoma's Return to Capital Punishment," 32 Criminology 107 (1994).

A more colorful description of a brutalization effect is provided in Rideau & Wikberg, *Life Sentences* 306–307 (Times Books 1992). There, a Swedish writer recounted the reaction of the crowd to a botched public execution.

A woman by the name of Johanne had been sentenced to die because she had been the mistress of her brother-in-law, and she was to be executed with the sword.... Master Anders Aalborg should perform the beheading. When the poor Johanne should die ... he bungled the first blow and merely cut a small ring into the neck so that the woman fell over and gave a pitiful scream; and thereafter he gave her five or six blows and still could not decapitate her. Then fear took hold of the executioner and he threw the sword of justice away, shouted in mortal fear "Mercy! Mercy!" and fled away. But the furious mob of people ... set out after him and he was beaten brutally and killed.

3. Publicizing Executions

Occasionally, public support for televising executions increases. Some capital punishment proponents favor publicizing executions in order to increase general deterrence. Some opponents of capital punishment favor publicizing executions because they agree with Albert Camus that "the man who enjoys his coffee while reading that justice is done would spit it out at the least detail." In his essay, "Reflections on the Guillotine" (Calmann-Lévy 1957), Camus states his position:

We all know that the great argument of those who defend capital punishment is the exemplary value of the punishment. Heads are cut off not only to punish but to intimidate, by a frightening example, any who might be tempted to imitate the guilty. Society is not taking revenge; it merely wants to forestall. It waves the head in the air so that potential murderers will see their fate and recoil from it....

... Society does not believe in what it says. If it really believed what it says, it would exhibit the heads. Society would give executions the benefit of the publicity it generally uses for national bond issues or new brands of drinks. But we know that executions in our country, instead of taking place publicly, are now perpetrated in prison courtyards before a limited number of specialists. We are less likely to know why and since when....

... If the penalty is intended to be exemplary, then, not only should the photographs be multiplied, but the machine should even be set on a platform in Place de la Concorde at two p.m., the entire population should be invited, and the ceremony should be put on television for those who couldn't attend. Either this must be done or else there must be no more talk of exemplary value. How can a furtive assassination committed at night in a prison courtyard be exemplary? At most, it serves the purpose of periodically informing the citizens that they will die if they happen to kill—a future that can be promised even to those who do not kill. For the penalty to be truly exemplary it must be frightening....

Instead of vaguely evoking a debt that someone this very morning paid society, would it not be a more effective example to remind each taxpayer in detail of what he may expect? Instead of saying: "If you kill, you will be imprisoned for months or years, torn between an impossible despair and a constantly renewed terror, until one morning we shall slip into your cell after removing our shoes the better to take you by surprise while you are sound asleep after the night's anguish. We shall fall on you, tie your hands behind your back, cut with scissors your shirt collar and your hair if need be. Perfectionists that we are, we shall bind your arms with a strap so that you are forced to stoop and your neck will be more accessible. Then we shall carry you, an assistant on each side supporting you by the arm, with your feet dragging behind through the corridors. Then, under a night sky, one of the executioners will finally seize you by the seat of your pants and throw you horizontally on a board while another will steady your head in the lunette and a third will let fall from a height of seven feet a hundred-and-twenty-pound blade that will slice off your head like a razor."

... Instead of boasting, with the pretentious thoughtlessness characteristic of us, of having invented this rapid and humane** method of killing condemned men, we should publish thousands of copies of the eyewitness accounts and medical reports describing the state of the body after the execution, to be read in schools and universities. Particularly suitable for this purpose is the recent report to the Academy of Medicine made by Doctors Piedelièvre and Fournier. Those courageous doctors, invited in the interest of science to examine the bod-

---

** According to the optimistic Dr. Guillotin, the condemned was not to feel anything; at most a "slight sensation of coldness on his neck."

ies of the guillotined after the execution, considered it their duty to sum up their dreadful observations: "If we may be permitted to give our opinion, such sights are frightfully painful. The blood flows from the blood vessels at the speed of the severed carotids, then it coagulates. The muscles contract and their fibrillation is stupefying; the intestines ripple and the heart moves irregularly, incompletely, fascinatingly. The mouth puckers at certain moments in a terrible pout. It is true that in that severed head the eyes are motionless with dilated pupils; fortunately they look at nothing and, if they are devoid of the cloudiness and opalescence of the corpse, they have no motion; their transparence belongs to life, but their fixity belongs to death. All this can last minutes, even hours, in sound specimens: death is not immediate.... Thus, every vital element survives decapitation. The doctor is left with this impression of a horrible experience, of a murderous vivisection, followed by a premature burial."

… An executioner's assistant (hence hardly suspect of indulging in romanticizing and sentimentality) describes in these terms what he was forced to see: "It was a madman undergoing a real attack of *delirium tremens* that we dropped under the blade. The head dies at once. But the body literally jumps about in the basket, straining on the cords. Twenty minutes later, at the cemetery, it is still quivering."

Jacob Weisberg's comments on televising executions, first published in the July 1, 1991 issue of The New Republic, follow:

Televised executions would mark the reversal of the process described in Louis P. Masur's *Rites of Execution* and Robert Johnson's *Death Work*, whereby executions have been removed further and further from the community that compels them. Through the eighteenth century, executions were atavistic spectacles performed in full public view. In the nineteenth [century] they were moved inside the prison yard and witnessed by only a few. In the twentieth century, executions moved deep inside the bowels of prisons, where they were performed ever more quickly and quietly to attract minimal notice. American death penalty opponents in the 1800s supported the abolition of public executions as a way-station to ending all executions. They thought that eliminating the grossest manifestations of public barbarism would inevitably lead to the end of capital punishment as an institution. The reform had the opposite effect, however. Invisible executions shocked the sensibilities of fewer people, and dampened the momentum of the reform movement.

Those abolitionists who now support televising executions have absorbed this historical lesson. They want to bring back the equivalent of public executions in order to shock the public into opposing all executions. They hope to accomplish with pictures what Arthur Koestler did with words in his 1955 tract *Reflections on Hanging*, the publication of which led to the abolition of the rope in Great Britain in 1969.

But advances in the art of killing may have deprived them of that tactic. The prospect of televised executions is likely to accelerate the trend away from grisly methods and toward ever more hermetic ways of dispatching wrongdoers. Had the KQED suit [requesting a court order requiring California to permit the gas chamber execution of Robert Alton Harris to be televised] been successful, Henry Schwarzschild, a retired ACLU death penalty expert, speculates that California would have responded by quickly joining the national trend toward lethal injection.

Michael Kroll of the Death Penalty Information Center objects to televising executions for exactly this reason. He argues that a video camera would capture only a "very antiseptic moment at the end of a very septic process." With the advent of death by the needle, execution itself is becoming so denatured and mechanistic as to be unshocking even to most live witnesses. This throws death penalty opponents back upon a less vivid, but more compelling case: that it is punishing people with death, not the manner in which they are killed, that is the true issue here; that capital punishment is to be opposed not simply because it is cruel, but because it is wrong.

Note

The ancient Romans clearly considered the death penalty to be a deterrent. Public executions of criminals by crucifixion, decapitation and burning were well-attended. Under Nero, victims were occasionally impaled and often were put to death in the arena. Baker, *Worthy of Death* 17 (Moody Press 1973).

One oft-cited example of the death penalty's lack of deterrent value involves the public executions on Tyburn Road in London. For more than 200 years, the Triple Tree, a triangular shaped gallows, stood at Tyburn. The unique configuration of the gallows enabled executioners to hang twenty-four people at a time—eight from each beam. History records that even as condemned prisoners were paraded from Newgate Prison to Tyburn—some having been sentenced to death for pickpocketing and thievery— pickpockets and thieves swarmed the parade route, working the crowd. See *The Triple Tree* 169 (Harrap London 1982).

In 2001, the execution of convicted Oklahoma City bomber Timothy McVeigh renewed debate over televising executions. The execution chamber at the federal prison in Terre Haute, Indiana has seats for ten victim witnesses. The 1995 bombing of the Oklahoma City federal building killed 168 people and injured hundreds more. To accommodate victims, McVeigh's execution was broadcast on a closed-circuit feed from Terre Haute to a secured facility in Oklahoma City. More than 250 victims expressed an interest in attending the broadcast and witnessing McVeigh's death. McVeigh did not oppose the broadcast and suggested that his execution be televised nationally, on a pay-per-view basis. For more on the Oklahoma City bombing cases and the McVeigh execution, see *infra* chapter 18.

4. Overview of Retribution[*]

The central justification of capital punishment is the need for society to express sufficient condemnation for heinous murderers. Supporters of the death penalty contend that the only proper societal response to the most vile murders is the most severe sanction possible. Thus, society should literally interpret the "eye for an eye" principle; when an individual takes a life, society's moral balance will remain upset until the killer's life is also taken.

Although death penalty opponents agree that some punishment, even a harsh one, should be imposed on offenders of society's norms, opponents do not agree that society

---

[*] Adapted from Zimring & Laurence, Death Penalty, U.S. Dep't of Justice, Crime File Study Guide.

can express its outrage with a vile crime only by inflicting a mortal punishment. Opponents further claim that society's goal of greater morality, rather than being advanced, is actually defeated when its expression of outrage for the taking of one life is the taking of another life. Indeed, opponents argue that the death penalty is, in some respects, more calculated and cold-blooded than many murders.

Though individuals must judge for themselves the proper role of retribution in criminal justice, the question is the same for everyone: At what point do we stop trying to match horrible criminal actions with horrible government actions? Taken to the extreme, a retribution theory might require the state to kill the offender in the exact same manner in which the victim was killed. Of course, this position is morally unacceptable to most people; our sense of outrage may be sufficiently expressed by less horrible forms of punishment. The key issue is whether any punishment short of killing offenders sufficiently expresses social condemnation of murder in modern America.

Notes and Question

1. In reinstating capital punishment in *Gregg v. Georgia* (*infra* chapter 3), the Court cited with approval the following language from *Furman v. Georgia* (*infra* chapter 3):

> The instinct for retribution is part of the nature of man, and channeling that instinct in the administration of criminal justice serves an important purpose.... When people begin to believe that organized society is unwilling or unable to impose upon criminal offenders the punishment they "deserve," then there are sown the seeds of anarchy. 408 U.S. 238, 308 (1972).

2. Consider the exchange between Justice Powell and Professor Anthony Amsterdam during oral argument in *Woodson v. North Carolina* (*infra* chapter 3).

> *Mr. Justice Powell:* Let me put a case to you. You've heard about Buchenwald, one of the camps in Germany in which thousands of Jewish citizens were exterminated.... If we had had jurisdiction over the commandant of Buchenwald, would you have thought capital punishment was an appropriate response to what that man or woman was responsible for?

> *Mr. Amsterdam:* We all have an instinct that says, "Kill him." ... But I think the answer to the question that your Honor is raising, ... [to] be consistent with the 8th Amendment to the Constitution ... my answer would be, "No."

Justice Powell persisted and asked about a man who might destroy New York City with a hydrogen bomb. Amsterdam's response was again "no."

3. In *Sumner v. Shuman*, 483 U.S. 66 (1987), the Court struck down the mandatory death penalty for an inmate who murders while serving a sentence of life without parole (LWOP). Justice Blackmun's majority opinion focused in part on whether a mandatory death sentence under those circumstances could be justified as necessary for either deterrence or retribution. According to the Court, the mandatory death penalty under those circumstances was "not necessary as a deterrent" since an inmate serving a life sentence is not ineligible for Nevada's death penalty if he is convicted of murder. Nor was a mandatory death penalty justified by Nevada's retributive interests. The Court rejected Nevada's argument that a mandatory death penalty for LWOP inmates convicted of murder was necessary because "there is no other available punishment for one already serving a sentence of life without possibility of parole." The Court recognized that

there are other sanctions less severe than execution that can be imposed even on a life-term inmate. An inmate's terms of confinement can be limited further, such as through a transfer to a more restrictive custody or correctional facility or deprivation of privileges or work or socialization.

Do you agree with the Court's assessment that LWOP inmates who murder can be adequately punished by further restricting their liberty or depriving them of privileges?

F. Other Issues in the Death Penalty Debate

1. Risk of Executing the Innocent

The specter of executing an innocent man haunts death penalty proponents and galvanizes death penalty opponents. Justice William Brennan observed: "Perhaps the bleakest fact of all is that the death penalty is imposed not only in a freakish and discriminatory manner, but also in some cases upon defendants who are actually innocent." Brennan, "Neither Victims Nor Executioners," 8 Notre Dame J. of Law, Ethics and Public Policy 1, 4 (1994).

As the Supreme Court has recognized, "Death is a different kind of punishment from any other which may be imposed." *Gardner v. Florida*, 430 U.S. 349, 357 (1977). What makes it different, of course, is its finality and irrevocability. Because of this, the Court has demanded that more reliable procedures be used in capital cases than are required in non-capital cases. *Beck v. Alabama*, 447 U.S. 625, 637–638 (1980).

Notwithstanding procedural and substantive safeguards designed to protect against mistakes, human error is inevitable. And in capital cases, human error can be fatal. As Justice Thurgood Marshall observed, "No matter how careful courts are, the possibility of perjured testimony, mistaken honest testimony and human error remain all too real. We have no way of judging how many innocent persons have been executed, but we can be certain that there were some." *Furman v. Georgia*, 408 U.S. 238, 367–368 (1972) (Marshall, J., concurring).

As early as 1987, one study identified more than 350 people in this century who have been erroneously convicted in the United States of crimes potentially punishable by death. Of these, 116 were sentenced to death and twenty-three were actually executed. Bedau & Radelet, "Miscarriages of Justice in Potentially Capital Cases," 40 Stan. L. Rev. 21, 36 (1987). See also Black, *Capital Punishment: The Inevitability of Caprice and Mistake* (W.W. Norton & Co. 1974). For more recent accounts of people wrongfully convicted of capital crimes, see Radelet, Bedau & Putnam, *In Spite of Innocence* (Northeastern University Press 1992) (chronicling the ordeals of 400 Americans wrongfully convicted of crimes punishable by death) and Scheck et al, *Actual Innocence: Five Days to Execution and Other Dispatches From the Wrongly Convicted* (2000).

A 1993 Staff Report issued by the House Judiciary Subcommittee on Civil and Constitutional Rights identified forty-eight people who were released from prison since 1973 after serving time on death row. "Innocence and the Death Penalty: Assessing the Danger of Mistaken Executions," 103rd Cong., 1st Sess., October 21, 1993. Noting that four former death row inmates were released during the first half of 1993 after their innocence became apparent, the Report concluded, "there is a real danger of innocent people being executed in the United States."

This conclusion is consistent with the observation that the 68 innocent individuals released from death row between 1973–1998 represent 1.2% of the 5,879 persons sentenced to death during that same period. See Gross, "Lost Lives: Miscarriages of Justice in Capital Cases," 61 Law & Contemp. Probs. 125, 128 n.13, 130 (1998).

According to the Death Penalty Information Center, between 1973 and March 2006, 123 innocent persons in 25 states were freed from death row. Florida has had more than its share of wrongfully convicted death row inmates. Florida leads the nation in death row exonerations. In Florida, 21 inmates have walked off death row—"in 3 cases within 16 hours of execution—after evidence emerged that they were wrongfully convicted. No state has released more condemned prisoners from death row." Freedberg, *Bush Rejects Idea of Death Penalty Ban*, St. Petersburg Times, Feb. 15, 2000, at 5B.

Not every innocent person lives to enjoy the fortuity of exoneration. As Justice Sandra Day O'Connor observed in 2001, "If statistics are any indication, the system may well be allowing some innocent defendants to be executed." Editorial, "Justice O'Connor on Executions," The New York Times, July 5, 2001. Consider Sonia Jacobs, who was eventually freed from death row because prosecutors suppressed exculpatory evidence, and lived long enough to be exonerated. Her boyfriend, convicted on virtually identical evidence, was executed by the time Jacobs prevailed on her appeal. Armstrong & Possley, *The Verdict: Dishonor*, Chicago Tribune, Jan. 10, 1999, at N1.

Nationwide, the average number of years served between being sentenced to death and exoneration was 9.2. The racial breakdown of those wrongfully convicted and exonerated prior to execution follows:

Black—62; White—48; Latino—12; Other—1.

See www.deathpenaltyinfo.org/Innocentlist.html (visited Mar. 15, 2006).

Error is not confined to the guilt phase of capital murder trials. Sentencing decisions are likewise vulnerable. As Justice Harlan observed in 1971:

> To identify before the fact those characteristics of criminal homicides which call for the death penalty, and to express these characteristics in language which can fairly be understood and applied by the sentencing authority, appear to be tasks which are beyond present human ability.

McGautha v. California, 402 U.S. 183, 204 (1971) (*infra* chapter 3).

As a practical matter, the number of innocent persons put to death since the 1972 *Furman* decision is anyone's guess. Confidence in the assertion that some innocent people have been executed is bolstered by the astonishing lack of confidence that state prosecutors exhibit in their own capital convictions by fighting tooth and nail to withhold DNA and other evidence that would verify the accuracy of capital convictions—if they are accurate. Liebman, "The Overproduction of Death," 100 Colum. L. Rev. 2030 (2000).

Nonetheless, death penalty supporters argue that the multi-level system of review and heightened scrutiny given to capital cases ensure that innocent people will not be executed. Skeptics counter that "if [innocent] men dodged the executioner, it was only because of luck and the dedication of the attorneys, reporters, family members and volunteers who labored to win their release. They survived despite the criminal justice system, not because of it. One must wonder how many others have not been so fortunate."

People v. Bull, 185 Ill.2d 179, 228 (1998) (Harrison, J., concurring in part and dissenting in part).

A smaller group maintains that the slight possibility of executing an innocent person is an acceptable price for maintaining a credible system of criminal justice. For example, Steven J. Markman and Paul G. Cassell have responded to objections about executing innocent persons by arguing that more persons are placed at risk from failures to execute. Markman & Cassell, "Protecting the Innocent: A Response to the Bedau-Radelet Study," 41 Stanford L. Rev. 121, 152–160 (1988) (purporting to refute the Bedau-Radelet study which identified twenty-three innocent executed defendants).

Excellent resources for tracking innocence in capital cases are: (1) http://www.justice.policy.net/jreport/finrep/PDF; and (2) http://www.deathpenaltyinfo.org//inn.html.

Note and Questions on Procedural Bar and Claims of Innocence

The case of Roy Clifton Swafford, resident of Florida's death row since 1985 for the 1982 rape and murder of Brenda Rucker, illustrates the potentially lethal intersection between rules requiring the prompt assertion of newly-discovered evidence and belatedly-discovered evidence of actual innocence.

"Swafford was convicted entirely on circumstantial evidence that placed him near the service station when the victim vanished and that linked him to the murder weapon, which he allegedly had disposed of in a restroom at an adult club being raided by the police. But the connection wasn't made until a year later, when one of Swafford's buddies, in jail on another charge, called the police to make a deal. He not only got out of jail, but also reaped a $10,000 reward.

"Witnesses disagreed, however, as to which restroom it was in which they had seen a man plant the gun, and it was less than certain that the man was Swafford. Moreover, one of the dancers testified that she and Swafford had been having sexual relations for three hours just before Rucker's abduction. Would he still have the energy and interest to kidnap and rape another woman? Not likely, but the jury suspended disbelief.

"Unknown to the defense, the police had investigated another strong suspect, one James Michael Walsh, who had been implicated by a buddy of his own, one Michael Lestz. Walsh, too, had been near the scene of a crime, supposedly with stolen guns, one of which was dumped at the same bar. Most suspiciously, Walsh had been conspicuously interested in pamphlets describing Rucker's murder, and he had a habit of burning sexual partners with cigarettes, just as someone had done to Rucker. But with Swafford in hand, the police wrote Walsh off.

"When [Swafford's defense lawyers] finally learned about Lestz after Swafford had come so close to execution that he was being prepared for the chair before a federal appeals court reprieved him they couldn't find him. Lestz had gone underground. He eventually filed for bankruptcy, and the tracing agency swiftly found him in Illinois, with [Swafford's] lawyers close behind. But it had taken more than two years, which is the [Florida] deadline for asserting newly discovered evidence." Martin Dyckman, *What's More Important than Righting a Wrong?*, St. Petersburg Times, April 28, 2002.

In a 4–3 decision released in April 2002, the Florida Supreme Court agreed with the trial judge that Swafford's attorneys had been too slow in tracking down a missing witness whose testimony might clear him, and upheld Swafford's death sentence. By failing to bring before the court within the two-year period mandated by Florida law strong evidence of actual innocence, Swafford was held to have procedurally defaulted on his claim and was barred from raising it in court.

A dissenting justice noted that Swafford's lawyers had undertaken "systematic and continuous efforts" to locate Lestz and Walsh, and failing to locate Lestz within the two-year limitation was simply a failure to accomplish the impossible. More important, the justice noted that if a new jury were permitted to hear Lestz's testimony, it "would probably produce an acquittal at trial."

What are the state's interests in enforcing its restrictions on the introduction of newly-discovered evidence? Should there be exceptions in capital cases, particularly where the evidence raises particularly troubling questions regarding the defendant's possible innocence?

Note and Questions on Wrongful Executions

Consider the following June 2003 news account:

"A British court overturned the conviction of a man hanged for murder 53 years ago after a confession by another man was found in police files. George Kelly was executed March 28, 1950, after being convicted in the shooting death of a Liverpool movie theater manager, Leonard Thomas, 44, during a burglary in March 1949. The confession wasn't presented at the trial or made available to Kelly's lawyer. Government lawyer Orlando Pownall declined to speculate why police failed to disclose the 1949 statement, and he said nearly everyone involved in the trial had died or could not be traced.

"The confession was found by an unidentified person who was interested in the case and read the police files. Kelly was 27 when he was hanged. Britain abolished the death penalty in 1965." *Hanged Man Has Conviction Overturned*, USA Today, June 11, 2003, p. 9A.

What relief, other than a posthumous pardon, should be available to Kelly's survivors? Is compensation appropriate under these circumstances? Assuming there is no statute of limitations for murder in the United Kingdom, should the person who confessed be pursued? If it could be proved that certain individuals in the police department or the prosecutor's office had knowledge of the confession and suppressed it—and are still alive—should they be prosecuted? Stripped of their pensions?

Note on DNA Exonerations

In recent years, the post-trial use of DNA to exonerate wrongfully convicted inmates has expanded. DNA played a substantial role in establishing the innocence of 10 of the 95 inmates released from death row between 1973–2001. Nonetheless, many prosecutors resist requirements to save biological samples and to make them available for DNA testing by convicted felons who claim they are innocent. For the most recent statistics, consult the website of the Death Penalty Information Center: http://www. deathpenaltyinfo.org/Innocentlist.html.

Earl Washington, a retarded man, was one of those exonerated by DNA testing. He confessed to virtually every unsolved sexual assault in Culpeper, Virginia. All charges, except one, were dismissed when it became clear that Washington could not have committed the crimes. He was successfully prosecuted and sentenced to die on the one charge that was not dropped: the rape and murder of a 5 foot 8-inch white woman. (Washington had confessed to killing, but not raping, a short black woman.)

Washington was arrested after having been awake all night drinking and was interrogated for two additional days. He willingly agreed to take police to the scene of the crime but took them to the wrong place. Washington showed no recognition of the actual murder scene until told by police that the crime had occurred there. When later asked why he told police that the victim was black, Washington answered: "I didn't see a picture of her in the newspaper when she got killed or nothing, [so] I just figured she was black."

The belated discovery that Washington could not have been the source of the semen and seminal fluid found on various articles of clothing and bedding at the crime scene led to Washington's release from death row after 11 years and to his formal exoneration after 18 years. Masters, *DNA Clears Inmate in 1982 Slaying*, Wash. Post, Oct. 3, 2001, at A1. Five years after Virginia's nationally recognized central crime laboratory botched DNA tests in Washington's case, a sharply critical independent audit of the lab forced a review of 150 DNA cases, including those involving some of the nearly two dozen inmates on Virginia's death row. Dao, *Lab's Errors Force Review of 150 DNA Cases*, The New York Times, May 7, 2005.

Kerry Max Cook landed on Texas' death row for the murder of Linda Jo Edwards, a 22-year-old woman who lived in his apartment complex. When Edwards was brutally raped, mutilated and murdered, suspicion initially focused on James Mayfield, a respected university librarian who had dated Edwards for years until the couple broke up a few weeks before her death. Mayfield denied killing Edwards, claimed he hadn't had sex with her in weeks and provided an alibi. Police then arrested Cook, a bisexual petty criminal whose fingerprint was found on Edwards' screen door.

Police then coerced an expert to testify—falsely, he admitted, years later—that Cook's fingerprint was less than 12 hours old. (The best forensic science has no way of determining the time a fingerprint was left at a crime scene.) A jailhouse snitch nicknamed "Shyster" testified that Cook had confessed to him. (Shyster later recanted.) Investigators then convinced an eyewitness to change her story from having seen Mayfield to having seen Cook in Edwards' apartment just before the killing. Cook was tried three times, sentenced to death three times, and his convictions were reversed three times due to procedural errors. Cook spent 20 years on death row, enduring repeated sexual abuse, before his fourth retrial ended with a plea bargain for time served.

Two years after convincing Cook to accept the plea bargain and gain his freedom, the prosecutor revealed that he had conducted DNA tests on Edwards' semen-stained clothes (which police had previously claimed had been lost before trial) and learned (1) that Cook could not have been the source of the semen (something the prosecutor evidently knew but did not disclose when he proposed the plea bargain); and (2) that the semen matched Mayfield's.

According to the Department of Justice, in a majority of cases in which DNA evidence ultimately exonerated a prisoner, the prosecution relied upon less conclusive forensic evidence that "narrowed the field of possibilities to include" the defendant, then bolstered the strength of the inconclusive evidence by calling experts to testify as to its "reliability and scientific strength." *Convicted by Juries, Exonerated by Science: Case Studies in the Use of DNA Evidence to Establish Innocence After Trial*, at 15 (U.S. Dep't of Justice 1996) (noting that 25% of the primary suspects in rape and rape-murder cases referred to the FBI for DNA testing between 1995 and 1998 were innocent).

Eddie Joe Lloyd, a mentally ill man, spent 17 years in prison after confessing to a rape and murder he did not commit. After being exonerated through DNA testing,

Lloyd said, "DNA is God's signature. God's signature is never a forgery, and his checks never bounce." Peters, *Wrongful Conviction Prompts Detroit Police to Videotape Certain Confessions*, The New York Times, April 11, 2006.

2. Error Rates in Capital Cases: The Liebman Study

Nearly all death sentences are reviewed on state direct appeal and, if affirmed, in a state post-conviction proceeding, and, if affirmed again, through a round of federal habeas corpus challenges. Professor James S. Liebman and a team of researchers completed a painstakingly thorough statistical study of capital cases between 1973 and 1995. Professor Liebman's conclusions follow.

> Remarkably, during the twenty-three-year period of our statistical study, 1973–1995, the result of this process [of appellate review] was the reversal by state direct appeal or state post-conviction courts of at least 47% of the capital judgments they reviewed, and federal habeas reversal of 40% of the capital judgments that survived state review. During the study period, that is, state courts (mainly) and federal courts reversed 68% — i.e., more than two of every three — of the capital judgments that were fully reviewed.

> This one-in-three figure, however, greatly overestimates the likelihood of execution, as is revealed by the statistical windows on the system. For example, the Justice Department's annual study of the death penalty reports the outcome, as of the study date, of death sentences imposed in each year since 1973. Consider the outcome of death sentences imposed in 1989. The cases of 103 of the 263 people sentenced to die that year had been resolved by the end of 1998. Among those 103 inmates, 78 (76%) had their capital judgments overturned by a state or federal court; only 13 (less than 13%) had been executed (compared to 9 who died of other causes). By this measure, for every one death row inmate whose case was finally reviewed during the nine-year period and who was executed, exactly six inmates had their cases overturned in the courts.

Liebman, "The Overproduction of Death," 100 Colum. L. Rev. 2030, 2053–56 (2000). Professor Liebman's study, "A Broken System: Error Rates in Capital Cases, 1973–1995" (2000), is available electronically at http://www.law.columbia.edu.instructionalservices/liebman/. An abridged version has been published as Liebman et al., "Capital Attrition: Error Rates in Capital Cases 1973–1995," 78 Tex. L. Rev. 1839 (2000).

What factors explain such a dramatic reversal rate in capital cases? Clearly, shoddy police work, ineffective defense counsel and prosecutorial misconduct contribute to injustice. Condemning the innocent is the most extreme example of a miscarriage of justice. But capital convictions can be wrong in many ways. Consider the variety of ways mistakes and capital cases result in wrongful death sentences.

> A [death penalty] conviction can be "wrong" in many ways. It might be excessive — for example, if the defendant is really guilty of second-degree murder but was convicted of first-degree murder; or the jury might have been right to conclude that the defendant committed the fatal act, but wrong to reject a defense of insanity or self-defense; or a conviction that is factually accurate might have been obtained in violation of the defendant's constitutional rights.

Gross, "Lost Lives: Miscarriages of Justice in Capital Cases," 61 Law & Contemp. Probs. 125, 129 (1998).

Professor James S. Liebman suggests still other ways in which a death sentence might be wrongful:

> —if the offense, although first degree murder, was not accompanied by the level of culpability or the kind of aggravating circumstance required by state law or the Eighth Amendment to make the offense death-eligible;

> —if mitigating circumstances outweigh aggravating circumstances, as the Court found, or at least suggested was the case in, e.g., *Parker v. Dugger*, 489 U.S. 308, 321–22 (1991) (concluding that nonstatutory mitigating circumstances may have been sufficient to outweigh aggravating circumstances and thus to rule out a capital sentence) (*infra* chapter 8) and *Eddings v. Oklahoma*, 455 U.S. 104, 113–14 (1981) (vacating a capital sentence because the trial judge improperly refused, as a matter of law, to consider what the Court thought was compelling mitigating evidence of defendant's abuse as a child) (*infra* chapter 5).

Liebman, "The Overproduction of Death," 100 Colum. L. Rev. 2083 at n.144 (2000).

For suggestions on how to prevent error in capital cases, see Liebman et al., "A Broken System, Part II: Why There Is So Much Error in Capital Cases, and What Can Be Done About It," Feb. 11, 2002 (executive summary).

3. Comparative Cost

Both proponents and opponents of capital punishment invoke cost considerations to support their positions. Some death penalty proponents assert that executing prisoners is cheaper than alternative punishments such as life imprisonment or life without parole. The notion of law-abiding taxpayers having to financially support convicted murderers for the rest of their lives is likely to influence jury deliberations. A juror weighing alternative punishments for capital murder might ask colloquially, "You mean we should provide free food, shelter and television to this killer?"

According to most death penalty opponents, the cost of capital punishment is far greater than the cost of warehousing inmates, even those serving sentences of life without parole. Because the Supreme Court has decreed that "death is a different kind of punishment from any other," *Gardner v. Florida*, 430 U.S. 349, 357 (1977), greater procedural safeguards are constitutionally required in capital cases. Ronald Tabak and Mark Lane, who have examined the cost added to the U.S. criminal justice system by capital punishment, state, "[w]hat this means in practical terms is very long, complex and extremely expensive litigation." Tabak & Lane, "The Execution of Injustice: A Cost and Lack-of-Benefit Analysis of the Death Penalty," 23 Loy. L.A. L. Rev. 59, 133 (1989).

> One must recognize, at the outset of this analysis, that the state must incur the enormous expenses of a capital trial whenever the death penalty is sought, no matter what the trial's outcome may be, even in the many cases where the defendant is found not guilty or is not sentenced to death. The enormous expense frequently can be avoided where the death penalty is not sought, because clearly guilty defendants often plead guilty when not facing the death penalty. But, if the state insists on seeking the death penalty, very few defendants will

plead guilty and agree to a death sentence, even when their guilt is clear, and some sort of trial usually occurs even when the defendant wants to be executed.

The added complexity and expense of capital trials begins well before trial. It is much more costly for both the prosecution and the defense to investigate death penalty cases for two reasons. First, the crime itself is likely to be investigated more thoroughly by both the prosecution (who must prove aggravating circumstances in order to seek the death penalty) and the defense (who must be prepared to argue the same issues). Second, because there is a separate penalty phase where any mitigating evidence may be presented, the defense should develop evidence, which the prosecution may endeavor to rebut, concerning the defendant's entire background — including childhood, mental and psychological conditions, family relations, employment history, prior arrests and convictions, medical history, and much more. This often entails the employment of social scientists, psychologists, psychiatrists, and various forensic experts, all of whom must be paid by the state in many instances. For example, in some situations the Constitution requires the state to pay for expert witnesses for the defense as well as the state.

Pretrial motions in capital cases are both more numerous and more complex than in other cases. Because there is a whole body of eighth amendment law relating specifically to death penalty cases, many more pretrial motions are required in a capital case. The process of voir dire should also be far more complex and lengthy in a capital case, where there are enhanced constitutional concerns regarding pretrial publicity, racial prejudice, and other areas of possible juror bias. Where pretrial publicity has affected potential jurors, the considerable additional costs of a change of venue may have to be incurred. Moreover, jurors should be asked a series of questions designed to determine whether they are excludable either because they could not impose the death penalty due to moral convictions, or because they would automatically impose the death penalty if guilt were found.

The inclusion of a separate sentencing phase in capital trials makes such trials longer than non-capital trials, quite apart from the additional complexities of pretrial proceedings and jury selection.

Not only are capital trials more lengthy and expensive, but, because the defendant's life is at stake, more retrials will likely be conducted. In some instances, one Supreme Court decision may mandate retrial of large segments — even the entire population — of the state's death row. These costs, both of the initial trial and the retrials, will be incurred even in the many cases where the jury does not return a death verdict upon retrial.

Additional areas of considerable expense are the constitutionally mandated appeals process and the often extensive collateral proceedings. The appeals process requires appointment of counsel where the defendant is indigent, which usually occurs. Of course, the state must always bear the cost of at least the prosecution's participation in all proceedings.

In addition to litigation *per se*, state clemency hearings entail further expense and complexities. Assuming these clemency hearings do not result in relief for a death row inmate, the state must then incur the cost of the execution itself.

Two other points, frequently ignored in the studies..., should also be considered. First, maintaining a death row, even in lamentably poor condition, is more expensive than keeping the same prisoners in other forms of custody—into which many death row inmates will go when their death sentences are overturned. Second, the extra costs of the capital punishment system are all incurred "up front" or within a few years, as compared to the savings from capital punishment, which do not arise, in the few cases where executions do occur, for a great many years. Hence, the savings from not having to incarcerate people following their executions must be discounted back to the present through the application of a discount rate reflecting the amount of interest which a dollar saved today could earn over the many years before the execution occurs.

Tabak & Lane, "The Execution of Injustice: A Cost and Lack-of-Benefit Analysis of the Death Penalty," 23 Loy. L.A. L. Rev. 59, 133–135 (1989).

An October 1992 report by the Death Penalty Information Center (DPIC) summarized its findings on the cost of capital punishment. The DPIC concluded that the cost of capital punishment is increasing and, because scarce financial resources are being diverted from more effective crime control measures, the public is actually less safe.

Across the country, police are being laid off, prisoners are being released early, the courts are clogged, and crime continues to rise. The economic recession has caused cutbacks in the backbone of the criminal justice system. In Florida, the budget crisis resulted in the early release of 3,000 prisoners. In Texas, prisoners are serving only 20% of their time and rearrests are common. Georgia is laying off 900 correctional personnel and New Jersey has had to dismiss 500 police officers. Yet these same states, and many others like them, are pouring millions of dollars into the death penalty with no resultant reduction in crime.

The exorbitant costs of capital punishment are actually making America less safe because badly needed financial and legal resources are being diverted from effective crime fighting strategies. Before the Los Angeles riots [which followed the acquittals of the police officers charged with beating Rodney King] for example, California had little money for innovations like community policing, but was managing to spend an extra $90 million per year on capital punishment. Texas, with over 300 people on death row, is spending an estimated $2.3 million per case, but its murder rate remains one of the highest in the country.

The death penalty is escaping the decisive cost-benefit analysis to which every other program is being put in times of austerity. Rather than being posed as a single, but costly, alternative in a spectrum of approaches to crime, the death penalty operates at the extremes of political rhetoric. Candidates use the death penalty as a facile solution to crime which allows them to distinguish themselves by the toughness of their position rather than its effectiveness.

The death penalty is much more expensive than its closest alternative—life imprisonment with no parole. Capital trials are longer and more expensive at every step than other murder trials. Pre-trial motions, expert witness investigations, jury selection, and the necessity for two trials—one on guilt and one on sentencing—make capital cases extremely costly, even before the appeals process begins. Guilty pleas are almost unheard of when the punishment is death. In addition, many of these trials result in a life sentence rather than the death penalty, so the state pays the cost of life imprisonment on top of the expensive trial.

The high price of the death penalty is often most keenly felt in those counties responsible for both the prosecution and defense of capital defendants. A single trial can mean near bankruptcy, tax increases, and the laying off of vital personnel. Trials costing a small county $100,000 from unbudgeted funds are common and some officials have even gone to jail in resisting payment.

Nevertheless, politicians from prosecutors to presidents choose symbol over substance in their support of the death penalty. Campaign rhetoric becomes legislative policy with no analysis of whether the expense will produce any good for the people. The death penalty, in short, has been given a free ride. The expansion of the death penalty in America is on a collision course with a shrinking budget for crime prevention. It is time for politicians and the public to give this costly punishment a hard look.

"Millions Misspent: What Politicians Don't Say About the High Costs of the Death Penalty," Death Penalty Information Center, October 1992, Executive Summary.

News stories tend to support the position of death penalty opponents. For example, the $2.3 million Texas taxpayers spend for each capital prosecution is three times the cost of incarcerating an inmate for forty years in a single cell in a maximum security prison. C. Hoppe, *Executions Cost Texas Millions*, The Dallas Morning News, March 8, 1992, at 1A.

Enforcing the death penalty costs Florida $51 million per year above and beyond what it would cost to punish all first-degree murderers with life without parole. Based on the 44 executions Florida has carried out since 1976, that state spent $24 million for each execution. Palm Beach Post, Jan. 4, 2000.

According to one report, abolishing capital punishment in California would save that state $90 million each year. Magnini, *Closing Death Row Would Save State $90 Million a Year*, The Sacramento Bee, March 28, 1988, at 1. In 2005, the New York Times reported that each of the first 11 executions in California cost a quarter of a billion dollars. For institutional reasons, the cost of housing death row inmates is three times that of the general population. Capital trials in California cost at least three times as much as non-capital trials. Semel, *The Death Penalty Doesn't Pay*, The Los Angeles Times, Jan. 13, 2006.

Kansas estimated that the annual cost of reinstating the death penalty would be $11.4 million. Kansas Legislative Research Dept. Memorandum, Feb. 11, 1987. Subsequently, Kansas found that the median death penalty case costs $1.26 million. The trial costs for death cases were about 16 times greater than for non-death cases ($508,000 per death case; $32,000 per non-death case). Appeal costs for death cases were 21 times greater. Performance Audit Report: Costs Incurred for Death Penalty Cases, State of Kansas, Dec. 2003.

New York estimated that reinstating the death penalty would cost $118 million each year. New York Department of Correctional Services study cited in Moran & Ellis: *Death Penalty: Luxury Item*, New York Newsday, June 14, 1989, at 60. Taxpayers in Suffolk County and New York state paid $2.5 million for the capital murder trial of Robert Shulman, who was sentenced to death in May 1999. The public cost of Shulman's sentence will continue to climb as he appeals his conviction and sentence. The New York Daily News estimated that the cost of pursuing the death penalty in that state could reach $238 million before the first condemned inmate is actually executed. N.Y. Daily News, Oct. 19, 1999.

In Washington state, Thurston County budgeted $346,000 in 1999 alone to seek a third death sentence for Mitchell Rupe, an inmate dying of liver disease. Rupe died in prison of liver failure, after his third capital jury failed to return a death sentence.

Ohio spent $1.5 million to kill Wilford Berry, a mentally retarded inmate who wanted to be executed. $18,147 was spent on overtime for prison employees and $2,250 was spent on overtime for state highway patrol officers at the time of the execution. Ohio spent $5,320 on a satellite truck so that the official announcement of Berry's execution could be instantly communicated to outside media. The lethal drugs used to kill Berry cost $88.42. Keeping Berry in prison for his entire life would have cost approximately half as much. Columbus Dispatch, Feb. 28, 1999.

Of course, tax dollars spent on capital cases are unavailable for other public purposes. For example, anticipated death penalty trial costs forced Okanogan County Commissioners in Washington state to delay pay increases for the county's 350 employees before approving a 2% increase, the smallest in years. They also decided not to replace 2 of the 4 public health nurses, ordered a halt on non-emergency travel, and put a hold on updating computers and county vehicles. Associated Press, Apr. 2, 1999.

Small counties in Georgia are reportedly going broke prosecuting death penalty cases. As one Long County Commissioner observed, "If you're spending $300,000 for a [death penalty] case, that's $300,000 that could be used for buying road equipment, paying salaries, the fire and sheriff's department.... If you have 2 or 3 of these [capital trials] in a row, that can put you in a million dollar hole. We're probably not too far removed from that. Long County had to rely on emergency state grants to keep government paychecks from bouncing."

Government employees aren't the only ones affected. Revenue losses in Louisiana prevented that state from paying private attorneys appointed to handle capital and other criminal cases for a year. The Advocate, Apr. 5, 1999. The extraordinary cost of capital cases prompted a Vinton County Ohio judge to inform prosecutors in 2002 that they could not seek the death penalty in the murder of a college student because the county's share of the defense costs would be too great. Liptak, *Citing Costs, Judge Rejects Death Penalty*, The New York Times, Aug. 18, 2002.

A U.S. General Accounting Office Report released in September 1989 suggested difficulties in drawing definitive conclusions about the cost of capital punishment.

> Federal data on the cost of implementing existing death penalty provisions are nonexistent. No one has been executed under federal statutes since 1963, and at the time of our review, no federal prisoners were on death row. Furthermore, as of September 1989, federal prosecutors have not sought to use the act's death penalty provisions.
>
> At the state level, cost data are limited. Of 37 states with death penalty laws, 34 had persons on death row. Few of these states have data on death penalty costs and, even when available, the data were incomplete.
>
> In recent years, studies, articles, and reports have been published on the costs associated with the death penalty at the state level. They have generally concluded that, contrary to what many people believe, death sentence cases cost more than nondeath sentence cases. However, we found these conclusions were not adequately supported. Most of the studies did not actually compare

death sentence cases with nondeath sentence cases, and some of the studies did not contain actual cost data. Further, even in cases where cost data were cited, these data were incomplete.

U.S. General Accounting Office, "Criminal Justice: Limited Data Available on Costs of Death Sentences," Sept. 1989.

The situation changed dramatically in 1993 with the publication of separate, comprehensive studies on the cost of capital and non-capital murder prosecutions in North Carolina and Maryland. According to the North Carolina study, North Carolina taxpayers pay $163,000 more to convict and execute an inmate than they do to convict a defendant and keep him in prison for 20 years. Cook & Slawson, *The Costs of Processing Murder Cases in North Carolina* 97 (May 1993). Considering the cost of prosecuting successful and unsuccessful death penalty cases, each execution in North Carolina cost approximately $2.16 million. *Id.* at 98–99. According to the study, the average cost of a bifurcated capital trial in North Carolina is $84,000. The average cost of a non-capital murder trial in North Carolina is $17,000. *Id.* at 2, 59. The study concluded: "The death penalty is usually justified on the basis that it offers public benefits in the form of greater deterrent and retributive value than life imprisonment. These benefits, if they exist, are not free, but rather come at a substantial cost to the public." *Id.* at 3–4.

Similarly, the 1993 Maryland study estimated that the cost of a fully-litigated capital case in that state was between $300,000 and $400,000. The Report of The Governor's Commission on the Death Penalty: An Analysis of Capital Punishment in Maryland: 1978 to 1993 xvii, Nov. 1993. A bifurcated trial and sentencing proceeding cost roughly $90,000; direct appeal cost $25,000; and state postconviction and federal habeas corpus cost $250,000. As of 1993, Maryland spent approximately $2 million each year on capital cases.

New York state's 1995 decision to reinstate capital punishment has proven to be costly. By March 31, 2001, the state's Division of Criminal Justice Services had reimbursed $5.1 million to counties across New York for the cost of prosecuting capital cases. As of April 30, 2002, New York had paid $68.4 million to lawyers representing 702 defendants charged with potentially capital crimes. Wholly apart from the costs associated with investigating, prosecuting and defending capital cases, the simple creation and maintenance of a constitutionally adequate death row facility cost New York taxpayers $1.3 million between 1995 and 2002. Perrotta, *Death Row Renovations Cost State $1.3 Million Since 1995*, New York Law Journal, Apr. 30, 2002.

Researcher Katherine Baicker of the Dartmouth College Economics Department completed a study which equated the impact of capital trials to natural disasters, in terms of economic impact on the budgets of county and state governments. (One obvious difference between capital trials and natural disasters, of course, is that counties and states receive federal aid in the event of floods, hurricanes, tornadoes and forest fires. No such federal assistance is available to help bankroll capital prosecutions conducted in state court.)

According to Baicker, in order for counties to absorb the "budget shocks" occasioned by the large expenditures associated with capital trials, county and state governments are forced to increase taxes and cut funding for other programs. Baicker's research demonstrates that the costs of capital trials "are borne in part by reducing expenditures on highways and police and in large part by increasing taxes." Each trial causes an increase in county spending of 1.8 percent and an increase in taxes of 1.6 percent. During the period 1982–1997, capital trials have caused an increase of more than $1.6 billion in both expenditures and revenues. Katherine Baicker, "How Safe is the Local Safety Net? Fiscal Distress, Public Spending, and the Budgetary Repercussions of Capital Convictions," Dartmouth College and NBER, Aug. 2001.

The capital prosecutions of the three men charged with the murder of James Byrd, Jr. in Jasper County, Texas substantiate Baicker's conclusions. In a case which attracted international attention, Byrd, a black, disabled, father of three, was decapitated when three white supremacists chained him to the back of their pickup truck and dragged him for three miles. Jasper County ran up a huge bill prosecuting Byrd's assailants. As of January 2002, the county spent $1.02 million, with other expenses expected. Two defendants were sentenced to death; a third received a life sentence. The strain on Jasper County's $10 million annual budget forced officials to increase property taxes 6.7% over two years to pay for the trials. County auditor Jonetta Nash said that only a massive flood that wiped out roads and bridges in the late 1970s came close to the fiscal impact of the trial. Gold, *Counties Struggle With High Cost of Prosecuting Death-Penalty Cases; Result is Often Higher Taxes, Less Spending on Services*, Wall Street Journal, Jan. 9, 2002.

In Oklahoma, state prosecutors decided to go forward in 2004 with a state prosecution following the federal prosecution and conviction of Oklahoma City bombing co-conspirator Terry Nichols. (In a separate federal trial, co-conspirator Timothy McVeigh had been sentenced to death. McVeigh was executed in 2001.) At the conclusion of his federal trial, Nichols had been sentenced to life without the possibility of parole and state prosecutors hoped to persuade an Oklahoma jury to sentence Nichols to death for his role in the terrorist plot which claimed 168 lives. Nichols' state defense cost $4.2 million, and it is likely that the prosecution costs were much higher. Hoberock, *Millions for Nichols' Defense*, Tulsa World, p. 1, Jan. 4, 2005. Although Nichols was convicted in state court of 161 murders, the state jury—like Nichols' federal jury—refused to sentence Nichols to death. As a result, Nichols was again sentenced to life without the possibility of parole. As might be expected, critics complained bitterly that state prosecutors wasted millions of taxpayer dollars in their futile quest to execute Nichols. On the other hand, one observer noted that "on a per-murdered victim basis," defense costs averaged $26,087 for each of the 161 murders. Other economies of scale were achieved, *inter alia*, in that 161 separate murder trials would require 1,932 jurors and 968 alternates. Camp, *A Bargain for the State*, Oklahoma Gazette, p. 8, Apr. 27, 2005.

A 1998 report from the Judicial Conference of the United States on the costs of the federal death penalty concluded that defense costs were about four times higher in cases where death was sought than in comparable cases where death was not sought. Prosecution costs in capital cases were found to be 67% higher than the defense costs, even excluding the investigative expenses incurred by law enforcement agencies. Federal Death Penalty Cases: Recommendations Concerning the Cost and Quality of Defense Representation (adopted by the Judicial Conference of the United States in 1998).

One certain way to reduce dramatically the cost of capital cases would be to restrict opportunities for death-sentenced individuals to appeal their convictions and sentences. China, for example, reportedly executes its condemned inmates soon after conviction. In what is more a symbolic gesture than an attempt to recover costs of capital punishment, the Chinese government then sends a bill to the family of the executee for the cost of the ammunition used in the execution. See *infra* chapter 19. See *infra* chapter 2 for a discussion of the cost of execution equipment and materials.

Due process is unquestionably expensive. This fact fuels repeated efforts to cut back on post-conviction remedies available to death row inmates. For an example of congressional action restricting death row inmates' access to habeas corpus, see the discussion of the Anti-terrorism and Effective Death Penalty Act in chapter 13, *infra*.

Note and Questions on Compensating the Wrongfully Condemned

On rare occasions, persons wrongfully convicted of capital crimes and sentenced to death receive financial compensation for their harrowing ordeals. In Illinois, Cook County reportedly agreed to pay $36 million to the Ford Heights Four, four men wrongfully convicted (two of whom were sentenced to death) for the 1978 murders of a suburban couple. Dennis Williams, another innocent man released from Illinois' death row was awarded $13 million. In Florida, the state legislature awarded $1 million to Freddie Pitts and Wilbert Lee in compensation for falsely incarcerating them on death row. Pitts and Lee spent 12 years on death row, including 10 years after the actual killer confessed to the crime in a statement which police suppressed. Kirk Bloodsworth received $300,000 from the Maryland legislature after DNA exonerated him of a rape and murder for which he spent two years on death row. Why do most innocent people released from death row fail to recover any damages? What should the standards be for compensating innocent persons condemned to death? Should prosecutors, police officers, defense lawyers, or judges be held accountable?

At least one innocent death row inmate—Frank Lee Smith of Florida—died awaiting execution, just months before being exonerated by DNA evidence. In December 2000, after spending 14 years on Florida's death row, Smith was finally cleared of the rape and murder of eight-year-old Shandra Whitehead. Two months earlier, Smith died in prison, just steps away from Florida's electric chair.

There were no eyewitnesses to the murder of Shandra Whitehead, and no physical evidence tied Smith to the crime. However, Chiquita Lowe and Gerald Davis—both 19—told prosecutors that they had spotted a scraggly-haired, delirious black man with a droopy eye in the neighborhood at the time of the crime. Shortly after the teenagers helped police develop a composite sketch of the man they saw, Lowe's family excitedly told her that the man in the sketch was standing outside their home, trying to sell them a television set. They urged her to call the police.

The man outside Lowe's house was Frank Lee Smith, 38, a former convict out on parole after serving 15 years in jail for manslaughter and a murder committed while he was a teenager. Based on Lowe's identification, Smith was arrested and charged with Whitehead's murder.

Although Chiquita Lowe was the star witness at Smith's trial, she began to have doubts even before she testified. She told investigative reporters, "When I went into the courtroom and seen [Smith], he was too skinny, too tall, and he did not have the droopy eye." She nonetheless confirmed her identification of Smith at his trial, despite her misgivings. She later said, "I was pressured by my family, people that's in my neighborhood, and the police officer. They kept telling me that I'm the only one that seen that man that night."

Soon after Florida scheduled Smith's execution, a defense investigator came across the name of Eddie Lee Mosley, a suspect in a number of rapes and murders of young black women that had occurred in Shandra Whitehead's neighborhood. Mosley was acquainted with Shandra. Her mother was his cousin. When the defense investigator showed Mosley's mug shot to Chiquita Lowe, she immediately recognized the man she saw the night of the murder. "I seen the man like I seen him yesterday. I seen the droopy eye, I see the look on his face and it just shook me up."

Smith's attorneys presented Lowe's sworn affidavit attesting to her incorrect identification to the Florida Supreme Court and were granted an evidentiary hearing. Florida authorities sought to discredit Lowe's new testimony by claiming that to have shown her Mosley's photo at the time of the murder. Despite having previously testified that Lowe had been shown two lineups, lead detective Richard Scheff—who was nominated for Deputy of the Month for solving the Whitehead case—now testified that there had been a third lineup that included Mosley. Lowe did not identify Mosley at that time, according to Scheff. The court denied Smith's motion for a new trial.

Defense lawyers filed several motions requesting DNA testing, all of which were denied by the state. Authorities agreed to test Smith's DNA posthumously, after Eddie Lee Mosley was linked through DNA tests to two other murders for which an innocent man had been convicted. The results of the DNA tests confirmed Eddie Lee Mosley—and not Frank Lee Smith—had raped and murdered Shandra Whitehead. "Requiem for Frank Lee Smith," Frontline, PBS, April 11, 2002.

Should the state be held responsible for the wrongful conviction of Smith? Should Smith's heirs be permitted to seek recovery? How would you calculate damages under the facts of this case? Should Scheff be held liable? Lowe? Under what circumstances?

Note on Hidden Human Costs of the Death Penalty

Psychological studies of the effects of the death penalty traditionally focus on social and societal ramifications, such as an execution's role in facilitating closure for a victim's family, or serving as a deterrent to would-be murderers. But what about the toll the death penalty exacts on those closest to executions? What price is paid by the prison wardens and guards who oversee the execution? What effect does witnessing the execution have on members of the press whose job it is to report on this aspect of our criminal justice system?

During a typical execution, more than 20 people will either serve as witnesses to the execution, or actually participate in carrying out the execution. In Texas, for example, the condemned is allowed five witnesses plus a spiritual advisor, the victims are allowed five witnesses, and there are five media witnesses. The execution tie down team consists of five prison guards, each of whom is responsible for strapping down a different part of the condemned prisoner's body. The prison warden and prison chaplain are always present in the death chamber and remain with the condemned until the execution is complete.

In the radio documentary, "Witness to an Execution," the warden, chaplain, and several guards from the Walls Unit in Huntsville, Texas, where executions are carried out, discussed their experiences participating in and witnessing executions. Several reporters who served as media witnesses to these executions were also interviewed.

Kenneth Dean, Major at the Walls Unit, has participated in and witnessed approximately 120 executions. He described his experience as a member of the tie down team.

"After all the straps are done they will look at you and they'll say 'Thank you'. And here you've just strapped them into the table. And they look at you in the eye and tell you 'Thank you for everything that you've done.' And, you know, that's kind of a weird feeling."

"It's kind of hard to explain what you actually feel, you know, when you talk to a man and you kind of get to know that person, and then you walk him out of a cell and you take him in there to the chamber and tie him down. And then a few minutes later he's … he's gone."

Leighanne Gideon, a former reporter for the *Huntsville Item,* witnessed 52 executions at the Huntsville Unit as a member of the press. She recounted her experiences in the witness room adjacent to the death chamber:

> "I was twenty-six years old when I witnessed my first execution. After the execution was over, I felt numb. I've seen family members collapse in there. I've seen them scream and wail. I've seen them beat the glass. You'll never hear another sound like a mother wailing whenever she is watching her son be executed. There's no other sound like it. It is just this horrendous wail. You can't get away from it. That wail surrounds the room. It's definitely something you won't ever forget."

Fred Allen, a member of the Walls Unit tie down team, participated in 120 executions before an emotional breakdown forced him to retire:

> "I was just working in the shop and all of a sudden something just triggered in me and I started shaking. And then I walked back into the house and my wife asked 'What's the matter?' and I said 'I don't feel good.' And tears—uncontrollable tears—was coming out of my eyes. And she said 'What's the matter?' And I said 'I just thought about that execution that I did two days ago, and everybody else's that I was involved with.' And what it was was something triggered within and it just—everybody—all of these executions all of a sudden all sprung forward."

Fred Allen retired after 16 years in the prison system. Three years after retiring, he said he can still see the eyes of the men he helped tie down.

> "Just like taking slides in a film projector and having a button and just pushing a button and just watching, over and over: him, him, him…. You see I can barely even talk because I'm thinking more and more of it. You know, there was just so many of 'em."

Jim Willett has overseen approximately 75 executions during the first two years he has served as Warden at the Walls Unit in Huntsville, Texas. He is present throughout the entire execution process, from retrieving the condemned from his cell to the moment the physician pronounces the time of death. He recognizes the emotional and sometimes even physical strain that participating in and witnessing an execution places on an individual.

> "The executions seem to affect all of us differently. Some get quiet and reflective after, others less so, but I have no doubt that it's disturbing for all of us. It always bothers you. It does me. I'll be retiring next year and to tell you the truth this is something I won't miss a bit. There are times when I'm standing there, watching those fluids start to flow, and wonder whether what we're doing here is right. It's something I'll be thinking about for the rest of my life."

"Witness to an Execution," Sound Portraits Productions (2000). Available at http://www.SoundPortraits.org.

4. Religion

Debate over the propriety of capital punishment often evokes heated argument along religious lines. Thomas Aquinas, the great theologian of the Middle Ages, supported the state's right to inflict the death penalty for certain crimes. Aquinas, *Summa Theologica*, pt. II-II, q. 64, art. 2,3. Similarly, Martin Luther ("Against the Murdering and Robbing Peasants," in *The Works of Martin Luther* (Muhlenberg 1931) 4:251) and Calvin (*Institutes*, IV. xx.10) agreed that death was an appropriate penalty for certain crimes. Conversely, Pope Leo I (fifth century) and Pope Nicholas I (ninth century) spoke out against the involvement of the church in capital punishment.

In the United States, where Christianity is the majority religion, discussion invariably begins with the Sixth Commandment's proscription, "Thou shalt not kill." Exodus 20:13. Death penalty proponents argue that violation of this commandment is righteously punished by death. Opponents counter that imposing death on one who murders violates the commandment.

General support for the death penalty is found in Genesis 9:6 ("Whoever sheds the blood of man, by man shall his blood be shed"). Carefully read, selected provisions of the Old Testament comprise a capital punishment code. For example, death was ordained for murder, kidnapping, and striking or cursing a parent. Exodus 21:12, 15, 16–17. Other capital offenses under Mosaic law include adultery (Leviticus 20:10); bestiality (Exodus 22:19); blasphemy (Leviticus 24:11–14, 16, 23); causing a woman to miscarry (Exodus 21:22, 23); disobedience to parents (Deuteronomy 21:18–21); disobedience of a court decision (Deuteronomy 17:8–12); incest (Leviticus 20:11–12, 14); offering human sacrifice (Leviticus 20:2–5); promoting false doctrines (Deuteronomy 13:1–10); rape of a betrothed virgin (Deuteronomy 22:23–27); sabbath desecration (Numbers 15:32–36); sacrificing to false gods (Exodus 22:20); sodomy (Leviticus 20:13); lack of chastity (Deuteronomy 22:20–21); and witchcraft (Exodus 22:18). One oft-cited provision appears to require strict proportionality: "Show no pity; life for life, eye for eye, tooth for tooth, hand for hand, foot for foot." Deuteronomy 19:21.

At least four methods of execution are expressly approved in the Old Testament: burning (Leviticus 20:14); hanging (Deuteronomy 21:22–23); stoning (Leviticus 20:2); and the sword (I Kings 2:25, 34, 46). Potential executioners include witnesses to the capital offense (Deuteronomy 13:6–10); the closest relative of the victim of the capital offense (Deuteronomy 19:11–12); and, in appropriate circumstances, the entire congregation (Numbers 15:32–36).

The Old Testament also provides for some limited measure of due process. According to Deuteronomy 17:6 and Numbers 35:30, no person shall be executed based on the testimony of fewer than two witnesses.

Mercy was not wholly lacking in the Old Testament. The first murder of record—Cain's slaying of his brother Abel—was not punished by death. Indeed, God himself spared Cain and protected him from retribution by placing a mark on him. Genesis 4:8–16. Despite having committed murder, Moses was not executed. Exodus 2:11–15. David likewise escaped execution, notwithstanding two capital offenses: adultery and murder. II Samuel 12:13.

The New Testament lends support to death penalty opponents. Deuteronomy's *lex talionis* ("an eye for an eye") is repudiated by Jesus himself. Jesus said, "Ye have heard that it hath been said, An eye for an eye and a tooth for a tooth: But I say unto you, That ye resist not evil: but whosoever shall smite thee on thy right cheek, turn to him the other also." Matthew 5:38–39.

Jesus's message of forgiveness is consistently repeated throughout the New Testament. For example, Jesus refused to require the death penalty for an offense punished by death under Mosaic law. Scribes and Pharisees placed before Jesus a woman caught in the very act of adultery, reminded him that the penalty was death by stoning, and asked his opinion as to appropriate punishment. Jesus replied, "He that is without sin among you, let him first cast a stone at her." Thus, without expressly condemning capital punishment, Jesus demanded that the woman's judges and executioners be sinless. John 8:1–11.

During the past thirty-five years, almost all of the nation's major religions have issued statements calling for an end to the death penalty. For example, in 1966, the Lutheran Church in America urged the abolition of capital punishment. Two years later, the National Council of Churches issued a statement calling for an end to the death penalty. In 1971, the Vatican announced its abolition of the death penalty. The following year, the United Methodist Church adopted a doctrine of social principles that included opposition to capital punishment. In 1983, Pope John Paul II became the first pontiff to speak out against the death penalty. Four years later, Pope John Paul II personally appealed for clemency for Paula R. Cooper, a young Indiana woman who faced execution for a murder she committed at age 15.

During March 1995, Pope John Paul II released an encyclical entitled "Evangelium Vitae" or "Gospel of Life." The document implores Roman Catholics worldwide to "resist crimes which no human law can claim to legitimize." Along with abortion and euthanasia, the death penalty, according to the Pope, contributes to a "culture of death" which "gives crimes against life a new and—if possible—even more sinister character." Justification for the death penalty is "very rare" if not "practically nonexistent." The Evangelium Vitae states:

> There is a growing tendency, both in the church and in civil society, to demand that [the death penalty] be applied in a very limited way or even that it be abolished completely.

In 1999, Pope John Paul II urged America's Roman Catholic population to extend the church's crusade to protect human life to include murderers on death row. Preaching before a crowd of 100,000 in St. Louis, the Pope called the death penalty "cruel and unnecessary," "even in the case of someone who has done great evil." "Modern society," according to John Paul II, "has the means of protecting itself, without definitively denying criminals the chance to reform." The New York Times, Jan. 28, 1999, p. A14.

A minority of conservative religious denominations steadfastly support the death penalty. Prominent among these are Mormons, Jehovah's Witnesses, and certain fundamentalist Christian and orthodox Jewish groups.

A resolution from the Southern Baptist Convention, held during June, 2000, follows:

RESOLUTION NO. 5 ON CAPITAL PUNISHMENT

WHEREAS, The Bible teaches that every human life has sacred value (Genesis 1:27) and forbids the taking of innocent human life (Exodus 20:13); and

WHEREAS, God has vested in the civil magistrate the responsibility of protecting the innocent and punishing the guilty (Romans 13:1–3); and

WHEREAS, We recognize that fallen human nature has made impossible a perfect judicial system; and

WHEREAS, God authorized capital punishment for murder after the Noahic Flood, validating its legitimacy in human society (Genesis 9:6); and

WHEREAS, God forbids personal revenge (Romans 12:19) and has established capital punishment as a just and appropriate means by which the civil magistrate may punish those guilty of capital crimes (Romans 13:4); and

WHEREAS, God requires proof of guilt before any punishment is administered (Deuteronomy 19:15–19); and

WHEREAS, God's instructions require a civil magistrate to judge all people equally under the law, regardless of class or status (Leviticus 19:15; Deuteronomy 1:17); and

WHEREAS, All people, including those guilty of capital crimes, are created in the image of God and should be treated with dignity (Genesis 1:27).

Therefore, be it RESOLVED, That the messengers to the Southern Baptist Convention, meeting in Orlando, Florida, June 13–14, 2000, support the fair and equitable use of capital punishment by civil magistrates as a legitimate form of punishment for those guilty of murder or treasonous acts that result in death; and

Be it further RESOLVED, That we urge that capital punishment be administered only when the pursuit of truth and justice result in clear and overwhelming evidence of guilt; and

Be it further RESOLVED, That because of our deep reverence for human life, our profound respect for the rights of individuals, and our respect for the law, we call for vigilance, justice, and equity in the criminal justice system; and

Be it further RESOLVED, That we urge that capital punishment be applied as justly and as fairly as possible without undue delay, without reference to the race, class, or status of the guilty; and

Be it further RESOLVED, That we call on civil magistrates to use humane means in administering capital punishment; and

Be it finally RESOLVED, That we commit ourselves to love, to pray for, and to minister the gospel to victims and perpetrators of crimes, realizing that only in Christ is there forgiveness of sin, reconciliation, emotional and spiritual healing, and the gift of eternal life.

Occasionally, politicians irreverently invoke religion in the public debate over the death penalty. The following remarks were made by New York politicians during that state's debate over reinstating capital punishment.

"Where would Christianity be if Jesus got eight to fifteen years with time off for good behavior?"—New York State Senator James H. Donovan

"If Senator Donovan can get resurrection into the death penalty, I might be willing to give it a second look."—New York Governor Hugh L. Carey

Jackson & Christian, *Death Row* vii (Beacon Press 1980).

5. The Moratorium Movement

Since the mid-1990s, the death penalty moratorium movement has been gaining momentum in the United States. Interestingly, the United States moratorium movement has caught the attention of the Canadian Supreme Court. Canada abolished the death penalty for all but a handful of military offenses in 1976, and in 1998, abolished the death penalty for all offenses. In *United States v. Burns*, 2001 S.C.C. 7 (2001), the Canadian Supreme Court held that the Canadian Minister of Justice was constitutionally bound to refuse to extradite to the United States murder suspects without first receiving assurances from the requesting authorities that the suspects would not be sentenced to death if convicted. For further discussion of *Burns*, see chapter 19, *infra*. In reaching its decision on extraditions, the Canadian Court took occasion to discuss the U.S. moratorium movement. An excerpt of this discussion in *Burns* is set forth below:

United States v. Burns
2001 S.C.C. 7 (2001)

… Concerns in the United States have been raised by such authoritative bodies as the American Bar Association which in 1997 recommended a moratorium on the death penalty throughout the United States because, as stated in an ABA press release in October 2000:

> The adequacy of legal representation of those charged with capital crimes is a major concern. Many death penalty states have no working public defender systems, and many simply assign lawyers at random from a general list. The defendant's life ends up entrusted to an often underqualified and overburdened lawyer who may have no experience with criminal law at all, let alone with death penalty cases.

> The U.S. Supreme Court and the Congress have dramatically restricted the ability of our federal courts to review petitions of inmates who claim their state death sentences were imposed in violation of the Constitution or federal law.

> Studies show racial bias and poverty continue to play too great a role in determining who is sentenced to death.

The ABA takes no position on the death penalty as such (except to oppose it in the case of juveniles and the mentally retarded). Its call for a moratorium has been echoed by local or state bars in California, Connecticut, Ohio, Virginia, Illinois, Louisiana, Massachusetts, New Jersey and Pennsylvania. The ABA reports that state or local bars in Florida, Kentucky, Missouri, Nebraska, North Carolina and Tennessee are also examining aspects of the death penalty controversy.

On August 4, 2000, the Board of Governors of the Washington State Bar Association, being the state seeking the extradition of the respondents, unanimously adopted a resolution to review the death penalty process. The Governor was urged to obtain a comprehensive report addressing the concerns of the American Bar Association as they apply to the imposition of the death penalty in the State of Washington. In particular, the Governor was asked to determine "[w]hether the reversal of capital cases from our state by the federal courts indicates any systemic problems regarding how the death penalty is being implemented in Washington State".

Other retentionist jurisdictions in the United States have also expressed recent disquiet about the conduct of capital cases, and the imposition and the carrying out of the death penalty. These include:

(i) Early last year Governor George Ryan of Illinois, a known retentionist, declared a moratorium on executions in that state … [because] Illinois [had] exonerated 13 death row inmates since 1977, one more than it actually executed. Governor Ryan said "I have grave concerns about our state's shameful record of convicting innocent people and putting them on death row". He remarked that he could not support a system that has come "so close to the ultimate nightmare, the state's taking of innocent life" (Governor Ryan Press Release, January 31, 2000).

(ii) The Illinois moratorium followed closely in the wake of a major study on wrongful convictions in death penalty cases by the Chicago Tribune newspaper, and a conference held at Northwestern University School of Law: see L.B. Bienen, "The Quality of Justice in Capital Cases: Illinois as a Case Study" (1998) 61 Law & Contemp. Probs. 193, at p. 213, fn. 103. The study examined the 285 death penalty cases that had occurred in Illinois since capital punishment was restored there. "The findings reveal a system so plagued by unprofessionalism, imprecision and bias that they have rendered the state's ultimate form of punishment its least credible" (Chicago Tribune, November 14, 1999, at p. C1).

(iii) One of the more significant exonerations in Illinois was the case of Anthony Porter who came within 48 hours of being executed for a crime he did not commit (Chicago Tribune, December 29, 2000, at p. 22N).

(iv) Both the New Hampshire House of Representatives and Senate voted to abolish the death penalty last year, although the measure was vetoed by the Governor. It is noteworthy that New Hampshire has not executed anyone since 1939 (New York Times, May 19, 2000, at p. 16, and May 20, 2000, at p. 16).

(v) In May 1999, the Nebraska legislature approved a bill that imposed a two-year moratorium on executions in that state and appropriated funds for a study of the issue. That initiative was vetoed by the Governor. However, the legislature unanimously overrode part of the veto so that the study could proceed.

(vi) Senator Russ Feingold of Wisconsin introduced a bill in Congress in April 2000 calling on the federal government and all states that impose the death penalty to suspend executions while a national commission reviews the administration of the death penalty.

(vii) On September 12, 2000, the United States Justice Department released a study of the death penalty under federal law. It was the first comprehensive review of the federal death penalty since it was reinstated in 1988. The data shows that federal prosecutors were almost twice as likely to recommend the death penalty for black defendants when the victim was non-black than when he or she was black. Moreover, a white defendant was almost twice as likely to be given a plea agreement whereby the prosecution agreed not to seek the death penalty. The study also revealed that 43 percent of the 183 cases in which the death penalty was sought came from 9 of the 94 federal judicial districts. This has led to concerns about racial and geographical disparity. The then Attorney General Janet Reno said that she was "sorely troubled" by the data and requested further studies (The New York Times, Sept. 12, 2000, at p. 17).

Foremost among the concerns of the American Bar Association, the Washington State Bar Association and other bodies who possess "hands-on" knowledge of the criminal justice system, is the possibility of wrongful convictions and the potential state killing of the innocent. It has been reported that 43 wrongfully convicted people have been freed in the United States as a result of work undertaken by The Innocence Project, a clinical law program started in 1992 at the Cardozo School of Law in New York. See, generally, B. Scheck, P. Neufeld, and J. Dwyer, Actual Innocence: Five Days to Execution and Other Dispatches from the Wrongly Convicted (2000). One of the authors, Peter Neufeld testified to the House of Representatives Committee on the Judiciary that

"DNA testing only helps correct conviction of the innocent in a narrow class of cases; most homicides do not involve biological evidence that can be determinative of guilt or innocence".

Finally, we should note the recent Columbia University study by Professor James Liebman and others which concludes that 2 out of 3 death penalty sentences in the United States were reversed on appeal: A Broken System: Error Rates in Capital Cases, 1973–1995 (June 12, 2000). The authors gathered and analyzed all of the available cases from the period of 1973 to 1995, the former being the year that states began to enact new death penalty statutes following the United States Supreme Court's decision in *Furman*, invalidating the existing regimes. Collection of the data for the study began in 1991.... In their executive summary, the authors report that "the overall rate of prejudicial error in the American capital punishment system was 68%." These errors were detected at one of three stages of appeal in the American legal system. The authors say that with "so many mistakes that it takes three judicial inspections to catch them" there must be "grave doubt about whether we do catch them all" (emphasis in original). The authors point out in footnote 81 that "[b]etween 1972 and the beginning of 1998, 68 people were released from death row on the grounds that their convictions were faulty, and there was too little evidence to retry the prisoner" and as of May 2000 "the number of inmates released from death row as factually or legally innocent apparently has risen to 87, including nine released in 1999 alone." For an abridged version of the Liebman study, see "Capital Attrition: Error Rates in Capital Cases, 1973–1995" (2000), 78 Tex. L. Rev. 1839.

It will of course be for the United States to sort out the present controversy surrounding death penalty cases in that country. We have referred to some of the reports and some of the data, but there is much more that has been said on all sides of the issue. Much of the evidence of wrongful convictions relates to individuals who were saved prior to execution, and can thus be presented as evidence of the system's capacity to correct errors. The widespread expressions of concern suggest there are significant problems, but they also demonstrate a determination to address the problems that do exist. Our purpose is not to draw conclusions on the merits of the various criticisms, but simply to note the scale and recent escalation of the controversy, particularly in some of the retentionist states, including the State of Washington....

Note on the American Bar Association's Call for a Moratorium on Executions

In February 1997, the American Bar Association passed a resolution by a vote of 280 to 119 as follows:

RECOMMENDATION

RESOLVED, that the American Bar Association calls upon each jurisdiction that imposes capital punishment not to carry out the death penalty until the jurisdiction implements policies and procedures that are consistent with the following longstanding American Bar Association policies intended to (1) ensure that death penalty cases are administered fairly and impartially, in accordance with due process, and (2) minimize the risk that innocent persons may be executed:

(i) Implementing ABA "Guidelines for the Appointment and Performance of Counsel in Death Penalty Cases" (adopted Feb. 1989) and Association policies intended to encourage competency of counsel in capital cases (adopted Feb. 1979, Feb. 1988, Feb. 1990, Aug. 1996);

(ii) Preserving, enhancing, and streamlining state and federal courts' authority and responsibility to exercise independent judgment on the merits of constitutional claims in state postconviction and federal *habeas corpus* proceedings (adopted Aug. 1982, Feb. 1990);

(iii) Striving to eliminate discrimination in capital sentencing on the basis of the race of either the victim or the defendant (adopted Aug. 1988, Aug. 1991); and

(iv) Preventing execution of mentally retarded persons (adopted Feb. 1989) and persons who were under the age of 18 at the time of their offenses (adopted Aug. 1983).

FURTHER RESOLVED, That in adopting this recommendation, apart from existing Association policies relating to offenders who are mentally retarded or under the age of 18 at the time of the commission of the offenses, the Association takes no position on the death penalty.

Coyne & Entzeroth, "Report Regarding Implementation of the American Bar Association's Recommendations and Resolutions Concerning the Death Penalty and Calling for a Moratorium on Executions," 4 Geo. J. on Fighting Poverty 3, 49 (1996).

Note on the Illinois Moratorium

On January 31, 2000, Illinois' Republican Governor George Ryan declared a moratorium on executions in that state because of concerns about a death penalty system "so fraught with error that it has come close to the ultimate nightmare." Prior to Governor Ryan's announcement, Illinois had released 13 condemned inmates from death row since 1977. During that same period, Illinois had executed 12 prisoners.

Governor Ryan created a 14-member Commission on Capital Punishment charged with reviewing Illinois' system of capital punishment to determine why the system repeatedly failed, resulting in the imposition of death sentences upon 13 innocent people. In addition the Commission was instructed to "examine ways of providing safeguards and making improvements in the way law enforcement and the criminal justice system carry out their responsibilities in the death penalty process." Finally, the Commission was directed to prepare a report providing comprehensive advice and recommendations to the Governor to ensure that the death penalty in Illinois is administered in a "just, fair and accurate" manner. Ill. Gov. George Ryan's Exec. Order No. 4 (2000) Creating the Commission on Capital Punishment.

The Commission issued its report in April 2002. Although a slight majority of commissioners favored abolition of the death penalty in Illinois, the report concentrated on ways to improve the administration of the death penalty rather than on the merits of capital punishment. Preamble to the Report of the Illinois Governor's Commission on Capital Punishment, April 2002, *reproduced in* Turow, "Ultimate Punishment," 119 *et seq.* (Farrar, Straus & Giroux) (2003). A summary of the Commission's specific recommendations follows:

A. Investigation

1. We recommend videotaping all questioning of a capital suspect conducted in a police facility, and repeating on tape, in the presence of the prospective defendant, any of his statement alleged to have been made elsewhere.

2. Recognizing an increasing body of scientific research relating to eyewitness identification, we propose a number of reforms regarding such testimony, including significant revisions in the procedures for conducting line-ups.

B. Eligibility for the Death Penalty

3. The Commission unanimously concluded that the current list of 20 factual circumstances under which a defendant is eligible for a death sentence should be eliminated in favor of a simpler and narrower group of eligibility criteria. A majority of the Commission agreed that the death penalty should be applied only in cases where the defendant has murdered two or more persons; or where the victim was either a police officer or a firefighter; or an officer or inmate of a correctional institution; or was murdered to obstruct the justice system; or was tortured in the course of the murder.

4. We also have recommended that the death penalty be barred in certain instances because of the character of the evidence or the defendant. We recommend that capital punishment not be available when a conviction is based solely upon the testimony of a single eyewitness, or of an in-custody informant, or of an uncorroborated accomplice, or when the defendant is mentally retarded.

C. Review of the Prosecutorial Decision to Seek the Death Penalty

5. In order to ensure uniform standards for the death penalty across the state, we recommend that a local state's attorney's decision to seek the death penalty be confirmed by a state-wide commission, comprised of the Attorney General, three prosecutors, and a retired judge.

D. Trial of Capital Cases

6. We have proposed a number of additional measures to augment the reforms already adopted by the Illinois Supreme Court to enhance the training of trial lawyers and judges in capital cases. Included are our suggestions for increased funding.

7. We have offered several recommendations aimed at intensifying the scrutiny of the testimony of in-custody informants, including recommending a pretrial hearing to determine the reliability of such testimony before it may be received in a capital trial.

8. To allow for future audits of the functioning of the capital punishment system, we also suggest that a designated array of information about the nature of the defendant and the crime be collected by the trial court.

E. Review

9. We recommend that when a jury determines that death is the appropriate sentence in a case, the trial judge, who has also heard the evidence, must concur with that determination, or else sentence the defendant to natural life.

10. We recommend that, as in several other states, the Illinois Supreme Court review each death sentence to ensure it is proportionate, that is, consider whether both the evidence and the offense warrant capital punishment in light of other death sentences imposed in the state.

Just three days before leaving office, Governor Ryan emptied Illinois' death row, commuting the death sentences of all 167 Illinois death row inmates. The vast majority (164) received sentences of life without parole. Ryan issued complete pardons to four death row inmates whose confessions had been beaten out of them. Thus, by Governor Ryan's count, since 1977, the Illinois criminal justice system had sentenced to death 17 innocent men. Of course, the spectre of innocent men awaiting execution is hardly new. At the time of the mass commutations occasioned by the 1972 *Furman* decision, at least four persons, ultimately exonerated, awaited execution. J. Marquart and J. Sorenson, "A National Study of *Furman*-Commuted Prisoners: Assessing the Threat to Society From Capital Offenders," reprinted in *The Death Penalty in America*, p. 164.

Chapter 2

Eighth Amendment Prohibition of Cruel and Unusual Punishment

A. Introduction to the Eighth Amendment

"Excessive bail shall not be required, nor excessive fines imposed, nor cruel and unusual punishments inflicted."—U.S. Const. amend. VIII.

The English Declaration of Rights, enacted December 16, 1689, stated that "excessive bail ought not be required, nor excessive fines imposed, nor cruel and unusual punishments inflicted." 1 W. & M., Sess. 2, c. 2. Similar language was included in Virginia's Constitution of 1776 and in the constitutions of Delaware, Maryland, New Hampshire, North Carolina, Massachusetts, Pennsylvania, and South Carolina. Likewise, the Northwest Ordinance, enacted under the Articles of Confederation, expressly prohibited cruel and unusual punishments.

Interpreting the precise meaning of the terms "cruel and unusual punishments" has proved an elusive goal of the judiciary. The Framers' failure to include such a restraint in the body of the Constitution was mentioned during debates of ratifying conventions in only two states (Massachusetts and Virginia). Unfortunately, there is scant evidence of the Framers' intent in including the Cruel and Unusual Punishments Clause among those restraints placed upon the new government in the Bill of Rights. What legislative history does exist provides minimal guidance. The debates in the First Congress on the adoption of the Bill of Rights contain only a brief discussion in the House of Representatives by two members who opposed the clause.

The original meaning of the Cruel and Unusual Punishments Clause continues to confound contemporary scholars. Some have argued that the inclusion of the Cruel and Unusual Punishments Clause in the English Declaration of Rights was in answer to the "Bloody Assize." The "Bloody Assize" describes the results of a special commission appointed by King James II to travel the circuit and try rebels associated with Monmouth's abortive rebellion. Mass plea bargaining ensued and word spread that those who agreed to plead guilty would not be executed. Because the penalty for treason at that time consisted of drawing the condemned man on a cart to the gallows, hanging him until half dead, cutting him down while still alive, disemboweling him and burning his bowels before him, and then beheading and quartering him, this was a particularly generous offer. In a matter of days, more than 500 trials were concluded. Those who unsuccessfully claimed their innocence were immediately executed. However, prosecutors did not keep their part of the bargain. After the commission disbanded, nearly 200 prisoners who had pleaded guilty were executed during the winter.

"Nor Cruel and Unusual Punishments Inflicted:" The Original Meaning

Anthony F. Granucci, 57 Calif. L. Rev. 839 (1969)

The Oates affair [*supra* chapter 1, p. 5] presented the only recorded contemporary uses of the terms "cruel and unusual" and "cruel and illegal." What does it explain about the original meaning of those words? It is clear that no prohibition on methods of punishment was intended. None of the punishments inflicted upon Oates amounts to torture. Life imprisonment is used widely today and probably would not be considered excessive in a case of perjury which had resulted in erroneous executions. Whipping did not constitute a cruel method of punishment in England at the time of Oates' conviction. It continued in use in England until 1948. As late as 1963 the Supreme Court of Delaware held that the imposition of 20 lashes for a robbery conviction was not cruel or unusual. While a fine of 2,000 marks may have been excessive and the defrocking of Oates unusual, neither was inherently cruel. In the context of the Oates' case, "cruel and unusual" seems to have meant a severe punishment[1] unauthorized by statute and not within the jurisdiction of the court to impose.[2]

This interpretation should not seem strange. In the seventeenth century, the word "cruel" had a less onerous meaning than it has today. In normal usage it simply meant severe or hard. The *Oxford English Dictionary* quotes as representative Jonathan Swift, who wrote in 1710, "I have got a cruel cold, and staid within all this day." Sir William Blackstone, discussing the problem of "punishments of unreasonable severity," uses the word "cruel" as a synonym for severe or excessive.

The English evidence shows that the cruel and unusual punishments clause of the Bill of Rights of 1689 was first, an objection to the imposition of punishments which were unauthorized by statute and outside the jurisdiction of the sentencing court, and second, a reiteration of the English policy against disproportionate penalties. Nevertheless, it is clear that the American framers read into the phrase [a prohibition against cruel *methods* of punishment.]

---

1. John Evelyn recorded in his diary some contemporary opinion on the whippings which Oates received.

"Oates, who had but two days before being pillored at several places, and whipped at the Carts tail from Newgate to Aldgate; was this day placed in a sledge (being not able to go by reason of his so late scourging) and dragged from prison to Tyburn, and whipped again all the way, which some thought to be very severe and extraordinary, but in case he were guilty of the perjuries, and so of the death of many innocents, as I fear he was, his punishment was but what he well deserved." 4 The Diary of John Evelyn 445 (E. DeBeer ed. 1955).

2. Some courts use an analogous standard today, holding that if a punishment is authorized by statute it cannot be "cruel and unusual." "[I]t is well settled that a sentence that falls within the terms of a valid statute cannot amount to a cruel and unusual punishment...." *Martin v. United States*, 317 F.2d 753, 755 (9th Cir. 1963).

Notes

1. Reverend Nathaniel Ward of Ipswich, Massachusetts drafted the first American law to prohibit cruel and unusual methods of punishment. In 1641, Ward's law was published as Clause 46 of *Body of Liberties*: "For bodily punishments we allow amongst us none that are inhumane, barbarous or cruel."

2. The Eighth Amendment's prohibition against cruel and unusual punishments has been made applicable to the states by operation of the Fourteenth Amendment. *Robinson v. California*, 370 U.S. 660 (1962). However, the amendment does not apply to the guilt phase of capital cases. Rather, Eighth Amendment issues arise only in the context of capital sentencing.

Excessive punishments are prohibited by the Eighth Amendment. In deciding whether a particular punishment is excessive, the Supreme Court measures the punishment against the crime for which it is imposed. If the Court finds that the punishment is "grossly disproportionate" to the crime, the penalty is struck down as unconstitutionally excessive. *Solem v. Helm*, 463 U.S. 277, 288 (1983). For cases and comment on proportionality as a limitation on punishment, see *infra* this chapter, page 61 *et seq.*

Alternatively, the Court may strike down a punishment as excessive if it does not make a measurable contribution to an acceptable penological goal. *Coker v. Georgia*, 433 U.S. 584, 592 (1977). Such punishments, according to the Court, are "nothing more than the purposeful and needless imposition of pain and suffering."

3. The prohibition against cruel and unusual punishments has been incorporated into the Uniform Code of Military Justice. Article 55 provides:

> Punishment by flogging, or by branding, marking, or tattooing on the body, or any other cruel or unusual punishment, may not be adjudged by any court-martial or inflicted upon any person subject to this chapter. The use of irons, single or double, except for the purpose of safe custody, is prohibited.

10 U.S.C. §855 (1956).

4. The use of capital punishment in the United States both preceded the adoption of the Eighth Amendment and continued unabated after ratification. One of the earliest recorded examples of a punishment being invalidated as cruel and unusual occurred in 1790. That year, the penalty of burning female felons was repealed by statute. 30 Geo. 3, c. 48 (1790). That same year, the Act of April 30, 1790, punished by death a number of offenses including murder, forgery, and counterfeiting. 1 Stat. 113-115 (First Cong., 2d Sess.). The following year, 1791, the first ten amendments to the United States Constitution (Bill of Rights) were ratified. Bear in mind that the Fifth and Fourteenth Amendments clearly countenance the death penalty. Both provide that no person shall be deprived "of life, liberty, or property, without due process of law."

B. Proportionality as a Limitation on Punishment

The proportionality principle is more easily stated than understood: The Constitution prohibits the infliction of grossly disproportionate punishments. In other words, to paraphrase Gilbert & Sullivan's *The Mikado* (1885), the punishment should fit the crime. Generally, the Court prefers to defer to the states' decisions regarding what constitutes non-excessive punishment.

Coker v. Georgia
433 U.S. 584 (1977)

Mr. Justice WHITE announced the judgment of the Court and filed an opinion in which Mr. Justice Stewart, Mr. Justice Blackmun, and Mr. Justice Stevens, joined.

Georgia Code Ann. §26-2001 (1972) provides that "(a) person convicted of rape shall be punished by death or by imprisonment for life, or by imprisonment for not less than one nor more than 20 years." Punishment is determined by a jury in a separate sentencing proceeding in which at least one of the statutory aggravating circumstances must be found before the death penalty may be imposed. Petitioner Anthony Ehrlich Coker was convicted of rape and sentenced to death. Both the conviction and the sentence were affirmed by the Georgia Supreme Court. Coker was granted a writ of certiorari, limited to the single claim, rejected by the Georgia court, that the punishment of death for rape violates the Eighth Amendment, which proscribes "cruel and unusual punishments" and which must be observed by the States as well as the Federal Government....

III

... We have concluded that a sentence of death is grossly disproportionate and excessive punishment for the crime of rape and is therefore forbidden by the Eighth Amendment as cruel and unusual punishment.

A

As advised by recent cases, we seek guidance in history and from the objective evidence of the country's present judgment concerning the acceptability of death as a penalty for rape of an adult woman. At no time in the last 50 years have a majority of the States authorized death as a punishment for rape. In 1925, 18 States, the District of Columbia, and the Federal Government authorized capital punishment for the rape of an adult female. By 1971 ... that number had declined, but not substantially, to 16 States plus the Federal Government. *Furman v. Georgia*, 408 U.S. 238 (1972), then invalidated most of the capital punishment statutes in this country, including the rape statutes, because, among other reasons, of the manner in which the death penalty was imposed and utilized under those laws.

With their death penalty statutes for the most part invalidated, the States were faced with the choice of enacting modified capital punishment laws in an attempt to satisfy the requirements of *Furman* or of being satisfied with life imprisonment as the ultimate punishment for any offense. Thirty-five States immediately reinstituted the death penalty for at least limited kinds of crime. This public judgment as to the acceptability of capital punishment, evidenced by the immediate, post-*Furman* legislative reaction in a large majority of the States, heavily influenced the Court to sustain the death penalty for murder in *Gregg v. Georgia*, 428 U.S. 153 (1976).

But if the "most marked indication of society's endorsement of the death penalty for murder is the legislative response to *Furman*," it should also be a telling datum that the public judgment with respect to rape, as reflected in the statutes providing the punishment for that crime, has been dramatically different. In reviving death penalty laws to satisfy *Furman*'s mandate, none of the States that had not previously authorized death for rape chose to include rape among capital felonies. Of the 16 States in which rape had been a capital offense, only three provided the death penalty for rape of an adult woman in their revised statutes — Georgia, North Carolina, and Louisiana. In the latter two States, the death penalty was mandatory for those found guilty, and those laws were invalidated by *Woodson v. Carolina*, 428 U.S. 280 (1976), and *Roberts v. Louisiana*, 428 U.S. 325 (1976). When Louisiana and North Carolina, responding to those decisions, again revised their capital punishment laws, they reenacted the death penalty for murder but not for rape; none of the seven other legislatures that to our knowledge have amended or replaced their death penalty statutes since July 2, 1976, including four States (in addition to Louisiana and North Carolina) that had authorized the death sentence for rape prior to 1972 and had reacted to *Furman* with mandatory statutes, included rape among the crimes for which death was an authorized punishment.

... It should be noted that Florida, Mississippi, and Tennessee also authorized the death penalty in some rape cases, but only where the victim was a child and the rapist an adult. The Tennessee statute has since been invalidated because the death sentence was mandatory. The upshot is that Georgia is the sole jurisdiction in the United States at the present time that authorizes a sentence of death when the rape victim is an adult woman, and only two other jurisdictions provide capital punishment when the victim is a child.

The current judgment with respect to the death penalty for rape is not wholly unanimous among state legislatures, but it obviously weighs very heavily on the side of rejecting capital punishment as a suitable penalty for raping an adult woman....

IV

These recent events evidencing the attitude of state legislatures and sentencing juries do not wholly determine this controversy, for the Constitution contemplates that in the end our own judgment will be brought to bear on the question of the acceptability of the death penalty under the Eighth Amendment. Nevertheless, the legislative rejection of capital punishment for rape strongly confirms our own judgment, which is that death is indeed a disproportionate penalty for the crime of raping an adult woman. We do not discount the seriousness of rape as a crime. It is highly reprehensible, both in a moral sense and in its almost total contempt for the personal integrity and autonomy of the female victim and for the latter's privilege of choosing those with whom intimate relationships are to be established. Short of homicide, it is the "ultimate violation of self." It is also a violent crime because it normally involves force, or the threat of force or intimidation, to overcome the will and the capacity of the victim to resist. Rape is very often accompanied by physical injury to the female and can also inflict mental and psychological damage. Because it undermines the community's sense of security, there is public injury as well.

Rape is without doubt deserving of serious punishment; but in terms of moral depravity and of the injury to the person and to the public, it does not compare with murder, which does involve the unjustified taking of human life. Although it may be accompanied by another crime, rape by definition does not include the death of or even the serious injury to another person. The murderer kills; the rapist, if no more than that, does not. Life is over for the victim of the murderer; for the rape victim, life may not be nearly so happy as it was, but it is not over and normally is not beyond repair. We have the abiding conviction that the death penalty, which "is unique in its severity and irrevocability," *Gregg v. Georgia*, 428 U.S. at 18, is an excessive penalty for the rapist who, as such, does not take human life.

This does not end the matter; for under Georgia law, death may not be imposed for any capital offense, including rape, unless the jury or judge finds one of the statutory aggravating circumstances and then elects to impose that sentence. For the rapist to be executed in Georgia, it must therefore be found not only that he committed rape but also that one or more of the following aggravating circumstances were present: (1) that the rape was committed by a person with a prior record of conviction for a capital felony; (2) that the rape was committed while the offender was engaged in the commission of another capital felony, or aggravated battery; or (3) the rape "was outrageously or wantonly vile, horrible or inhuman in that it involved torture, depravity of mind, or aggravated battery to the victim." Here, the first two of these aggravating circumstances were alleged and found by the jury.

Neither of these circumstances, nor both of them together, change our conclusion that the death sentence imposed on Coker is a disproportionate punishment for rape. Coker had prior convictions for capital felonies—rape, murder, and kidnaping—but these prior convictions do not change the fact that the instant crime being punished is a rape not involving the taking of life.

It is also true that the present rape occurred while Coker was committing armed robbery, a felony for which the Georgia statutes authorize the death penalty. But Coker was tried for the robbery offense as well as for rape and received a separate life sentence for this crime; the jury did not deem the robbery itself deserving of the death penalty, even though accompanied by the aggravating circumstance, which was stipulated, that Coker had been convicted of a prior capital crime.

We note finally that in Georgia a person commits murder when he unlawfully and with malice aforethought, either express or implied, causes the death of another human being. He also commits that crime when in the commission of a felony he causes the death of another human being, irrespective of malice. But even where the killing is deliberate, it is not punishable by death absent proof of aggravating circumstances. It is difficult to accept the notion, and we do not, that the rapist, with or without aggravating circumstances, should be punished more heavily than the deliberate killer as long as the rapist does not himself take the life of his victim. The judgment of the Georgia Supreme Court upholding the death sentence is reversed, and the case is remanded to that court for further proceedings not inconsistent with this opinion. So ordered.

Mr. Chief Justice BURGER, with whom Mr. Justice Rehnquist joins, dissenting.

… The clear implication of today's holding appears to be that the death penalty may be properly imposed only as to crimes resulting in death of the victim. This casts serious doubt upon the constitutional validity of statutes imposing the death penalty for a variety of conduct which, though dangerous, may not necessarily result in any immediate death, e.g., treason, airplane hijacking, and kidnaping. In that respect, today's holding does even more harm than is initially apparent. We cannot avoid taking judicial notice that crimes such as airplane hijacking, kidnaping, and mass terrorist activity constitute a serious and increasing danger to the safety of the public. It would be unfortunate indeed if the effect of today's holding were to inhibit States and the Federal Government from experimenting with various remedies including possibly imposition of the penalty of death to prevent and deter such crimes. Some sound observations, made only a few years ago, deserve repetition:

> Our task here, as must so frequently be emphasized and re-emphasized, is to pass upon the constitutionality of legislation that has been enacted and that is challenged. This is the sole task for judges. We should not allow our personal

preferences as to the wisdom of legislative and congressional action, or our distaste for such action, to guide our judicial decision in cases such as these. The temptations to cross that policy line are very great. In fact, as today's decision reveals, they are almost irresistible.

Whatever our individual views as to the wisdom of capital punishment, I cannot agree that it is constitutionally impermissible for a state legislature to make the "solemn judgment" to impose such penalty for the crime of rape. Accordingly, I would leave to the States the task of legislating in this area of the law.

Note

The Court has also found that the death penalty is disproportionate for kidnapping and rape where the victim is not killed, *Eberheart v. Georgia*, 433 U.S. 917 (1977) (per curiam), and is disproportionate for the crime of robbery where the victim is not killed. *Hooks v. Georgia*, 433 U.S. 917 (1977) (per curiam).

Note on Punishing Child Rape and Other Sex Crimes by Death

When the Supreme Court struck down the death penalty for rapists in *Coker v. Georgia*, *supra*, it was mindful of the fact that, of the 455 men executed for rape in America between 1930 and 1964, 405 were black. Almost all the executions took place in the South and almost all executees were convicted of raping white women.

Notwithstanding *Coker*, several jurisdictions, including Montana and Louisiana, retain statutes which provide the death penalty for rapists under certain circumstances. Three other states—Florida, South Carolina, and Oklahoma—have laws allowing the death penalty for certain sex crimes. For example, under Louisiana law persons convicted of the rape of a child under the age of 12 may be put to death. In August of 2003, a Louisiana jury sentenced to death Patrick O. Kennedy for raping an eight-year-old female relative. The rape victim was seriously injured and required surgery. Should Kennedy's death sentence survive review in the state court system, it may fall to the Supreme Court to determine whether *Coker*'s ban on executing rapists should be limited to rapes involving adult victims.

The last execution of a rapist in America took place in 1964. Liptak, *Louisiana Sentence Renews Debate on the Death Penalty*, The New York Times, Aug. 31, 2003. Indeed, since the Supreme Court reinstated the death penalty in 1976, no one has been executed for any offense that did not involve a criminal homicide. This is true, even though a number of states and the federal government authorize the death penalty for crimes not involving killing, including aircraft hijacking, espionage, kidnapping, treason, and large-scale drug trafficking.

Louisiana v. Wilson
Louisiana v. Bethley
685 So.2d 1063 (1996)

BLEICH, Justice.

We are called upon to determine the constitutionality of La. R.S. 14:42(C) as it authorizes the death penalty for offenders who rape a victim under the age of 12 years old. We find that R.S. 14:42(C) is constitutional.

FACTS AND PROCEDURAL HISTORY

On December 21, 1995, Anthony Wilson was charged by grand jury indictment with the aggravated rape of a five year old girl. He moved to quash the indictment, alleging that the crime of rape could never be punished with the death penalty. The trial court granted Wilson's motion to quash, resulting in this appeal by the State.

Patrick Dewayne Bethley was charged with raping three girls, one of whom was his daughter, between December 1, 1995, and January 10, 1996. The ages of the little girls at the time of the rape were five, seven, and nine. Furthermore, the State alleges that at the time of the alleged crimes, Bethley knew that he was HIV positive. Bethley filed a motion to quash urging the unconstitutionality of La. R.S. 14:42(C). The trial court granted Bethley's motion to quash. Although finding La. R.S. 14:42(C) would pass constitutional muster under the Eighth Amendment and the Equal Protection clause of the United States Constitution and Article I, § 20 of the Louisiana Constitution, the trial court held La. R.S. 14:42(C) unconstitutional because the class of death eligible defendants was not sufficiently limited. That ruling resulted in an appeal.

DISCUSSION

The thrust of both defendants' arguments is that the imposition of the death penalty for a crime not resulting in a death is "cruel and unusual punishment" and therefore unconstitutional under the Eight Amendment to the United States Constitution and Article I, § 20 of the Louisiana Constitution of 1974.

The phrase "cruel and unusual punishment" found in the Eighth Amendment and in Article I, § 20 takes its roots from the English Bill of Rights of 1689. Mun, Mandatory Life Sentence Without Parole Found Constitutionally Permissible For Cocaine Possession, 67 Wash. L.Rev. 713, 714 (1991). The English version of the phrase appears to prohibit punishments unauthorized by statute and beyond the jurisdiction of the court, as well as those disproportionate to the offense committed. However, the American drafters of the Eight Amendment were primarily concerned with proscribing "tortures" and other "barbarous" methods of punishment such as pillorying, decapitation, and drawing and quartering. Therefore, the American courts virtually ignored the Eighth Amendment since the barbaric practices proscribed had become obsolete.

Not until the nineteenth century did the Supreme Court recognize that the scope of the Eighth Amendment might be broader than originally thought and include the prohibition of disproportionately excessive sentences. See *Weems v. United States*, 217 U.S. 349 (1910). The years since *Weems* have seen a development of the Eighth Amendment's "cruel and unusual punishment" clause. As Chief Justice Warren said, "(t)he Amendment must draw its meaning from the evolving standards of decency that mark the maturing society." *Trop v. Dulles*, 356 U.S. 86, 101 (1958). Therefore, the Eighth Amendment bars not only those punishments that are barbaric but also those that are excessive.

A punishment is excessive and unconstitutional if it (1) makes no measurable contribution to acceptable goals of punishment and hence is nothing more that the purposeful and needless imposition of pain and suffering; or (2) is grossly out of proportion to the severity of the crime. *Gregg v. Georgia*, 428 U.S. 153 (1976).

EXCESSIVE PUNISHMENT ARGUMENT

The defendants' primary argument is that death is a disproportionate penalty for the crime of rape. The defendants' contention is based on *Coker v. Georgia*, 433 U.S. 584

(1977), decided by the Supreme Court in a plurality opinion. The *Coker* Court rejected capital punishment as a penalty for the rape of an adult woman saying: "Although rape deserves serious punishment, the death penalty, which is unique in its severity and irrevocability, is an excessive penalty for the rapist who, as such and as opposed to the murderer, does not take human life." The plurality took great pains in referring only to the rape of **adult women** throughout their opinion,[3] leaving open the question of the rape of a child. The defendants argue that the *Coker* findings cannot be limited to the rape of an adult. They contend the following words used by the Court would apply with equal force to the crime of statutory rape when no life is taken:

> "Rape is without doubt deserving of serious punishment; but in terms of moral depravity and of the injury to the person and to the public, it does not compare with murder, which does involve the unjustified taking of human life. Although it may be accompanied by another crime, rape by definition does not include the death or even the serious injury to another person. The murderer kills; the rapist, if no more than that, does not. Life is over for the victim of the murderer; for the rape victim, life may not be nearly so happy as it was, but it is not over and normally is not beyond repair. We have the abiding conviction that the death penalty, which is unique in its severity and irrevocability, ... is an excessive penalty for the rapist who, as such, does not take human life."[4]

---

3. The various justices, either in the plurality opinion, concurring opinion, or dissenting opinion, refer to "adult woman" fourteen times:

(1) Justice White, writing for the plurality, writes: "That question, with respect to rape of an **adult woman**, is now before us." *Coker, supra* at 592.

(2) Justice White: " ... we seek guidance ... concerning the acceptability of death as a penalty for rape of an **adult woman**." *Id.*, at 593.

(3) Justice White: " ... 4 of the 16 States did not take the mandatory course and also did not continue rape of an **adult woman** as a capital offense." *Id.*, at 595.

(4) Justice White: "The upshot is that Georgia is the sole jurisdiction ... that authorizes a sentence of death when the rape victim is an **adult woman**...." *Id.*, at 596.

(5) Justice White: " ... but it obviously weighs very heavily on the side of rejecting capital punishment as a suitable penalty for raping an **adult woman**." *Id.*, at 596.

(6) Justice White: " ... death is indeed a disproportionate penalty for the crime of raping an **adult woman**." *Id.*, at 597.

(7) Justice Powell, concurring in part and dissenting in part, writes: " ... ordinarily death is disproportionate punishment for the crime of raping an **adult woman**." *Id.*, at 601.

(8) Chief Justice Burger, in his dissent joined by Justice Rehnquist, writes: "Since the Court now invalidates the death penalty as a sanction for all rapes of **adults**...." *Id.*, at 611.

(9) Chief Justice Burger: "Georgia is the sole jurisdiction ... that authorizes a sentence of death when the rape victim is an **adult woman**." *Id.*, at 613.

(10) Chief Justice Burger: " ... Louisiana and North Carolina have enacted death penalty statutes for **adult rape**...." *Id.*, at 613.

(11) Chief Justice Burger: "Failure of more States to enact statutes imposing death for rape of an **adult woman**...." *Id.*, at 614.

(12) Chief Justice Burger: " ... Georgia has been the only State whose adult rape death penalty statute has not otherwise been invalidated...." *Id.*, at 615.

(13) Chief Justice Burger: " ... an appropriate punishment for the rape of an **adult woman**...." *Id.*, at 615.

(14) Chief Justice Burger: " ... rejecting capital punishment as a suitable penalty for raping an **adult woman**...." *Id.*.

4. The contention that the harm caused by a rapist is less serious than that caused by a murderer is apparently not subscribed to by all rape victims. In some cases women have preferred death to being raped or have preferred not to continue living after being raped. Karp, David J., *Coker v. Georgia: Disproportionate Punishment and the Death Penalty for Rape*, 78 Columbia L. Rev. 1714, 1720 (1978).

The *Coker* plurality further discusses rape as a serious crime, finding it "highly reprehensible, both in a moral sense and in its almost total contempt for the personal integrity and autonomy of the female victim. Short of homicide, it is the ultimate violation of self." These scathing descriptions of rape refer to the rape of an adult female. While the rape of an adult female is in itself reprehensible, the legislature has concluded that rape becomes much more detestable when the victim is a child.

La. R.S. 14:42(C) was amended by Acts 1995, No. 397, § 1 to allow for the death penalty when the victim of rape is under the age of twelve. Rape of a child less than twelve years of age is like no other crime. Since children cannot protect themselves, the State is given the responsibility to protect them. Children are a class of people that need special protection; they are particularly vulnerable since they are not mature enough nor capable of defending themselves. A "maturing society," through its legislature has recognized the degradation and devastation of child rape, and the permeation of harm resulting to victims of rape in this age category. The damage a child suffers as a result of rape is devastating to the child as well as to the community. As noted previously, in determining whether a penalty is excessive, the Supreme Court has declared that we should take into account the "evolving standards of decency", and in making this determination, the courts should not look to their own subjective conceptions, but should look instead to the conceptions of modern American society as reflected by objective evidence. As evidence of society's attitudes, we look to the judgment of the state legislators, who are representatives of society.

Louisiana's legislature determined a "standard of decency" by amending La. R.S. 14:42(C) to permit the death penalty in cases of aggravated rape when the victim is less than twelve, and deference must be given to that decision. The legislature alone determines what are punishable as crimes and the proscribed penalties. The legislature is not required to select the least severe penalty for the crime as long as the selected penalty is not cruelly inhumane or disproportionate to the offense. Furthermore, legislative enactments are presumed constitutional under both the Federal and the State Constitutions. The party challenging the constitutionality of a statute bears a heavy burden in proving the statute to be unconstitutional. This is true in part because the constitutional test is intertwined with an assessment of contemporary standards, and the decisions of the legislature are indicative of such standards.[6] "In a democratic society legislatures, not courts, are constituted to respond to the will and consequently the moral values of the people." *Furman v. Georgia*, 408 U.S. 238, 383 (1972) (Burger, C.J., dissenting). The courts must exercise caution in asserting their views over those of the people as announced through their elected representatives.

One of the most conservative and acceptable methods of determining the excessiveness of a penalty is to examine the statutes of the other states. The *Coker* Court summarized the last 50 years of the history of the death penalty, recognizing that just prior to the *Furman* decision in 1971, just 16 states plus the Federal Government authorized the death penalty for rape. Following *Furman*'s invalidation of most death penalty statutes,

---

6. Another body of people play a role in determining the contemporary standards of our society. That body is the juries who make the determination of whether a certain defendant deserves the death penalty for his particular crime. The *Coker* Court concluded that "in the vast majority of cases, at least 9 out of 10, juries have not imposed the death sentence [in rape cases]." However, in drawing this conclusion, the Court does not say whether these rape cases were the rape of an adult or of a child. Moreover, the reluctance of the juries to impose the death penalty may reflect the humane feeling that this most irrevocable of sanctions should be reserved for extreme cases.

35 states immediately reinstituted death penalty statutes; however, only 3 of the states which had previously included rape as a capital offense reinstated rape of an adult woman as a crime deserving of the death penalty, and none of the states that had not previously recognized the death penalty for rape included it among capital felonies. The three states reinstituting the death penalty for rape were Georgia, North Carolina, and Louisiana. North Carolina's and Louisiana's laws were subsequently invalidated since they mandated the death penalty for those offenders found guilty. *Woodson v. North Carolina*, 428 U.S. 280 (1976) and *Roberts v. Louisiana*, 428 U.S. 325 (1976). When Louisiana and North Carolina revised their statutes following the invalidation, they only permitted the death penalty for murder and not rape. Georgia's law permitting the death penalty for the rape of an adult woman was invalidated by *Coker*. The *Coker* Court used this data as an indication of society's failure to endorse the death penalty. However, this was with reference to adult women.

Louisiana is the only state that presently has a law in effect that provides for the death penalty for the rape of a child less than twelve. This fact, however, cannot be deemed determinative. The *Coker* Court pointed out in its discussion of the history of the death penalty that three states, Florida, Mississippi, and Tennessee authorized the death penalty in rape cases when the victim was a child and the offender was an adult. The Tennessee statute was invalidated in 1977 because the death sentence was mandatory. And as previously noted, Florida's and Mississippi's death penalty statutes were invalidated in 1981 and 1989 respectively. The Florida Supreme Court found the *Coker* analysis controlling in its invalidation of their statute, but the Mississippi Supreme Court invalidated the death penalty for the rape of a child without ever passing on the constitutionality of the law. Even though these states's statutes were subsequently invalidated, the simple fact that they enacted such statutes since the Furman decision may suggest the beginning of a trend and public opinion favoring such penalties—an evolution of a standard to deal with this heinous crime.

As Justice Powell wrote in his dissent in *Coker*:

> "Considerable uncertainty was introduced into this area of the law by this Court's *Furman* decision. A large number of States found their death penalty statutes invalidated; legislatures were left in serious doubt by the expressions vacillating between discretionary and mandatory death penalties, as to whether this Court would sustain any statute imposing death as a criminal sanction. Failure of more States to enact statutes imposing death for rape of an adult woman may thus reflect hasty legislative compromise occasioned by time pressures following Furman, a desire to wait on the experience of those States which did enact such statutes, or simply an accurate forecast of today's holding."

This reasoning applies as well to our analysis. Since *Coker*, only Florida's statute has been invalidated under its reasoning. Mississippi's statute and Tennessee's statute were invalidated for infirmities in the statute or sentencing schemes of their respective states. While Louisiana remains the sole jurisdiction with such a statute in effect, it does not do so without the suggestion of some trend or suggestion from several other states that their citizens desire the death penalty for such a heinous crime.

The *Coker* Court only took into account the recent past in considering what society deems to be cruel and unusual punishment. We cannot look solely at what the legislatures have refrained from doing under conditions of great uncertainty arising from the Supreme Court's "less than lucid holdings on the Eighth Amendment." The fact that Louisiana is presently the sole state allowing the death penalty for the rape of a child is not conclusive. There is no constitutional infirmity in a state's statute simply because that jurisdiction chose to be first. Statutes applied in one state can be carefully watched by other states so that the experience of the first state becomes available to all other states. That one State is "presently a minority does not, in my view, make [its] judgment less worthy of deference. Our concern for human life must not be confined to the guilty; a state legislature is not to be thought insensitive to human values because it acts firmly to protect the lives and related values of the innocent." The needs and standards of society change, and these changes are a result of experience and knowledge. If no state could pass a law without other states passing the same or similar law, new laws could never be passed. To make this the controlling factor leads only to absurd results. Some suggest that it has been over a year since Louisiana has amended its law to permit the death penalty for the rape of a child, and that no other state has followed suit. Since its enactment, the statute has been under constant scrutiny. It is quite possible that other states are awaiting the outcome of the challenges to the constitutionality of the subject statute before enacting their own.

CRIME WITHOUT DEATH

It has been argued that the death penalty should not be an option when the crime committed produces no death. The Supreme Court has held that the death penalty is an excessive penalty for a robber who does not take a human life. *Enmund v. Florida*, 458 U.S. 782 (1982). In *Enmund*, the defendant was the driver of the getaway car. His accomplices had robbed and shot two people. The shooter and Enmund were convicted of first degree murder and sentenced to death. The Supreme Court overturned Enmund's sentence of death holding that the Eighth Amendment does not permit the imposition of the death penalty of a defendant who aids and abets a felony in course of which murder is committed by others but who does not himself kill, attempt to kill, or intend that killing take place or that lethal force will be employed. The Court goes on to say that "we have no doubt that robbery is a serious crime deserving serious punishment. It is not, however, a crime 'so grievous an affront to humanity that the only adequate response may be the penalty of death.' " The Court focused on Enmund's conduct in determining the appropriateness of the death penalty. In *Enmund*, the defendant simply aided and abetted a robbery which, as the Court holds, is not deserving of the death penalty. However, La. R.S. 14:42(C) contemplates a defendant who rapes a child. The legislature has determined that this crime is deserving of the death penalty because of its deplorable nature, being a "grievous affront to humanity."

Justice O'Connor, joined by Chief Justice Burger, Justice Powell, and Justice Rehnquist, dissented in *Enmund* finding that the "death penalty is not disproportionate to the crime of felony murder, even though the defendant did not actually kill or intend to kill his victims." Justice O'Connor continues saying that the Court should not only consider contemporary standards in deciding if the death penalty is disproportionate to the crime, but should also consider the harm the defendant caused to the victim. Contemporary standards as defined by the legislature indicate that the harm inflicted upon a child when raped is tremendous. That child suffers physically as well as emotionally and mentally, especially since the overwhelming majority of offenders are family members. Louisiana courts have held that sex offenses against children cause untold psychological harm not only to the victim but also to generations to come.

"Common experience tells us that there is a vast difference in mental and physical maturity of an adolescent teenager ... and a pre-adolescent child ... It is well known that child abuse leaves lasting scars from generation to the next ...

such injury is inherent in the offense." *State v. Brown*, 660 So.2d 123, 126 (La.App. 2d Cir.1995).

" ... Aggravated rape inflicts mental and psychological damage to its victim and undermines the community sense of security. The physical trauma and indignities suffered by the young victim of this offense were of enormous magnitude ..." *State v. Polkey*, 529 So.2d 474 (La.App. 1 Cir.1988).

"... the child's tender age made her particularly vulnerable and capable of resisting ... considering acutely deleterious consequences of conduct on an eight-year-old child." *State v. Jackson*, 658 So.2d 722 (La.App. 2d Cir.1995).

Four of the nine justices of the Supreme Court find that the death penalty is permissible in situations when the defendant has neither killed or intended to kill anyone. The Court in *Coker* went even further in *Tison v. Arizona*, 481 U.S. 137 (1987), when it held that the death penalty is not disproportionate when the defendant plays a major part in a felony that results in murder, although the defendant did not actually commit the murder, and the defendant's mental state is only one of reckless indifference to life. The Court also declined to draw a clear line between crimes that warrant the death penalty and those that do not.

While the Eighth Amendment bars the death penalty for minor crimes under the concept of disproportionality, the crime of rape when the victim is under the age of twelve is certainly not a minor crime. The *Coker* Court recognized the possibility that the degree of harm caused by an offense could be measured not only by the injury to a particular victim but also by the resulting public injury. This implies that some offenses, in particular the rape of a child, might be so injurious to the public that death would not be disproportionate in relation to the crime for which it is imposed. "In part, capital punishment is an expression of society's moral outrage at particularly offensive conduct. This function may be unappealing to many, but it is essential in an ordered society that asks its citizens to rely on legal processes rather than self-help to vindicate their wrongs."

Thus, we conclude that given the appalling nature of the crime, the severity of the harm inflicted upon the victim, and the harm imposed on society, the death penalty is not an excessive penalty for the crime of rape when the victim is a child under the age of twelve years old....

GOALS OF PUNISHMENT

Two legitimate goals of punishment are retribution and deterrence. The defendants argue that the death sentence in the case of child rape fails to meet either of these goals. They say the imposition of the death penalty will have a chilling effect on the already inadequate reporting of this crime. Since arguably, most child abusers are family members, the victims and other family members are concerned about the legal, financial and emotional consequences of coming forward. According to defendants, permitting the death penalty for the crime will further decrease the reporting since no child wants to be responsible for the death of a family member. But what defendants fail to understand is that the child is not the one responsible. The child is the innocent victim. The offender is responsible for his own actions. The subject punishment is for the legislature to determine, not this Court.

Self-help is not permitted in our society, so there is a need for retribution in our criminal sanctions. The death penalty for rape of a child less than twelve years old would be a deterrence to the commission of that crime. There are a range of possible penalties for such a crime, but as Justice Burger notes in his dissent in *Coker*:

"We cannot know which among this range of possibilities is correct, but today's holding (finding the death penalty for rape of an adult woman to be unconstitutional) forecloses the very exploration we have said federalism was intended to offer."

While Louisiana is the only state that permits the death penalty for the rape of a child less than twelve, it is difficult to believe that it will remain alone in punishing rape by death if the years ahead demonstrate a drastic reduction in the incidence of child rape, an increase in cooperation by rape victims in the apprehension and prosecution of rapists, and a greater confidence in the role of law on the part of the people. This experience will be a consideration for this and other states' legislatures.

Our holding today permits the death penalty without a death actually occurring. In reaching this conclusion, we give great deference to our legislature's determination of the appropriateness of the penalty. This is not to say, however, that the legislature has free reign in proscribing penalties. They must still conform to the mandates of the Eighth Amendment and Article I, § 20 of the Louisiana Constitution, and they are still subject to judicial review by the courts. We hold only that in the case of the rape of a child under the age of twelve, the death penalty is not an excessive punishment nor is it susceptible of being applied arbitrarily and capriciously.

DECREE

For the reasons stated above, we find La. R.S. 14:42(C) to be constitutional. The motion to quash in each case is reversed and vacated. These cases are remanded to the respective trial courts.

CALOGERO, Chief Justice, dissenting.

No other State in the union imposes the death penalty for the aggravated rape of a child under twelve years of age. The reason for this, in my view, is that the statute fails constitutional scrutiny under the decisions of the United States Supreme Court in *Coker v. Georgia*, 433 U.S. 584 (1977), *Furman v. Georgia*, 408 U.S. 238 (1972), and *Gregg v. Georgia*, 428 U.S. 153 (1976). I therefore dissent and would hold R.S. 14:42(C) facially unconstitutional under the Eighth Amendment to the United States Constitution.

Solem v. Helm

463 U.S. 277 (1983)

Justice POWELL delivered the opinion of the Court.

The issue presented is whether the Eighth Amendment proscribes a life sentence without possibility of parole for a seventh nonviolent felony.

I

By 1975 the State of South Dakota had convicted respondent Jerry Helm of six nonviolent felonies. In 1964, 1966, and 1969 Helm was convicted of third-degree burglary. In 1972 he was convicted of obtaining money under false pretenses. In 1973 he was convicted of grand larceny. And in 1975 he was convicted of third-offense driving while intoxicated. The record contains no details about the circumstances of any of these offenses, except that they were all nonviolent, none was a crime against a person, and alcohol was a contributing factor in each case.

In 1979 Helm was charged with uttering a "no account" check for $100. The only details we have of the crime are those given by Helm to the state trial court:

> I was working in Sioux Falls, and got my check that day, was drinking and I ended up here in Rapid City with more money than I had when I started. I knew I'd done something I didn't know exactly what. If I would have known this, I would have picked the check up. I was drinking and didn't remember, stopped several places.

After offering this explanation, Helm pleaded guilty.

Ordinarily the maximum punishment for uttering a "no account" check would have been five years imprisonment in the state penitentiary and a $5,000 fine. As a result of his criminal record, however, Helm was subject to South Dakota's recidivist statute: "When a defendant has been convicted of at least three prior convictions [sic] in addition to the principal felony, the sentence for the principal felony shall be enhanced to the sentence for a Class 1 felony."

The maximum penalty for a "Class 1 felony" was life imprisonment in the state penitentiary and a $25,000 fine. Moreover, South Dakota law explicitly provides that parole is unavailable: "A person sentenced to life imprisonment is not eligible for parole by the board of pardons and paroles." The Governor is authorized to pardon prisoners, or to commute their sentences, but no other relief from sentence is available even to a rehabilitated prisoner.

Immediately after accepting Helm's guilty plea, the South Dakota Circuit Court sentenced Helm to life imprisonment. The court explained:

> I think you certainly earned this sentence and certainly proven that you're an habitual criminal and the record would indicate that you're beyond rehabilitation and that the only prudent thing to do is to lock you up for the rest of your natural life, so you won't have further victims of your crimes, just be coming back before Courts. You'll have plenty of time to think this one over.

We granted certiorari to consider the Eighth Amendment question presented by this case.

II

The Eighth Amendment declares: "Excessive bail shall not be required, nor excessive fines imposed, nor cruel and unusual punishments inflicted." The final clause prohibits not only barbaric punishments, but also sentences that are disproportionate to the crime committed.

A

The principle that a punishment should be proportionate to the crime is deeply rooted and frequently repeated in common-law jurisprudence. In 1215 three chapters of Magna Carta were devoted to the rule that "amercements"[6] may not be excessive. And the principle was repeated and extended in the First Statute of Westminster. These were not hollow guarantees, for the royal courts relied on them to invalidate disproportionate punishments. When prison sentences became the normal criminal sanctions, the common law recognized that these, too, must be proportional....

---

6. An amercement was similar to a modern-day fine. It was the most common criminal sanction in 13th century England.

B

The constitutional principle of proportionality has been recognized explicitly in this Court for almost a century. In the leading case of *Weems v. United States*, 217 U.S. 349 (1910), the defendant had been convicted of falsifying a public document and sentenced to 15 years of "cadena temporal," a form of imprisonment that included hard labor in chains and permanent civil disabilities. The Court noted "that it is a precept of justice that punishment for crime should be graduated and proportioned to offense," and held that the sentence violated the Eighth Amendment. The Court endorsed the principle of proportionality as a constitutional standard, and determined that the sentence before it was "cruel in its excess of imprisonment," as well as in its shackles and restrictions.

The Court next applied the principle to invalidate a criminal sentence in *Robinson v. California*, 370 U.S. 660 (1962). A 90-day sentence was found to be excessive for the crime of being "addicted to the use of narcotics." The Court explained that "imprisonment for ninety days is not, in the abstract, a punishment which is either cruel or unusual." Thus there was no question of an inherently barbaric punishment. "But the question cannot be considered in the abstract. Even one day in prison would be a cruel and unusual punishment for the 'crime' of having a common cold." ...

C

... [We] hold as a matter of principle that a criminal sentence must be proportionate to the crime for which the defendant has been convicted. Reviewing courts, of course, should grant substantial deference to the broad authority that legislatures necessarily possess in determining the types and limits of punishments for crimes, as well as to the discretion that trial courts possess in sentencing convicted criminals. But no penalty is *per se* constitutional. As the Court noted in *Robinson v. California*, a single day in prison may be unconstitutional in some circumstances.

III

A

When sentences are reviewed under the Eighth Amendment, courts should be guided by objective factors that our cases have recognized. First, we look to the gravity of the offense and the harshness of the penalty. In *Enmund* [*v. Florida*, 458 U.S. 782 (1982)], for example, the Court examined the circumstances of the defendant's crime in great detail. In *Coker* the Court considered the seriousness of the crime of rape, and compared it to other crimes, such as murder. In *Robinson* the emphasis was placed on the nature of the "crime." And in *Weems,* the Court's opinion commented in two separate places on the pettiness of the offense. Of course, a court must consider the severity of the penalty in deciding whether it is disproportionate.

Second, it may be helpful to compare the sentences imposed on other criminals in the same jurisdiction. If more serious crimes are subject to the same penalty, or to less serious penalties, that is some indication that the punishment at issue may be excessive. Thus in *Enmund* the Court noted that all of the other felony murderers on death row in Florida were more culpable than the petitioner there. The *Weems* Court identified an impressive list of more serious crimes that were subject to less serious penalties.

Third, courts may find it useful to compare the sentences imposed for commission of the same crime in other jurisdictions. In *Enmund* the Court conducted an extensive review of capital punishment statutes and determined that "only about a third of American jurisdictions would ever permit a defendant [such as Enmund] to be sentenced to die." Even in those jurisdictions, however, the death penalty was almost never imposed under similar circumstances. The Court's review of foreign law also supported its conclusion. The analysis in *Coker* was essentially the same. And in *Weems* the Court relied on the fact that, under federal law, a similar crime was punishable by only two years' imprisonment and a fine.

In sum, a court's proportionality analysis under the Eighth Amendment should be guided by objective criteria, including (i) the gravity of the offense and the harshness of the penalty; (ii) the sentences imposed on other criminals in the same jurisdiction; and (iii) the sentences imposed for commission of the same crime in other jurisdictions.

B

Application of these factors assumes that courts are competent to judge the gravity of an offense, at least on a relative scale. In a broad sense this assumption is justified, and courts traditionally have made these judgments—just as legislatures must make them in the first instance. Comparisons can be made in light of the harm caused or threatened to the victim or society, and the culpability of the offender....

There are other accepted principles that courts may apply in measuring the harm caused or threatened to the victim or society. The absolute magnitude of the crime may be relevant. Stealing a million dollars is viewed as more serious than stealing a hundred dollars—a point recognized in statutes distinguishing petty theft from grand theft. Few would dispute that a lesser included offense should not be punished more severely than the greater offense. Thus a court is justified in viewing assault with intent to murder as more serious than simple assault. It also is generally recognized that attempts are less serious than completed crimes. Similarly, an accessory after the fact should not be subject to a higher penalty than the principal.

Turning to the culpability of the offender, there are again clear distinctions that courts may recognize and apply. In *Enmund v. Florida*, 458 U.S. 782 (1982), the Court looked at the petitioner's lack of intent to kill in determining that he was less culpable than his accomplices. Most would agree that negligent conduct is less serious than intentional conduct. South Dakota, for example, ranks criminal acts in ascending order of seriousness as follows: negligent acts, reckless acts, knowing acts, intentional acts, and malicious acts. A court, of course, is entitled to look at a defendant's motive in committing a crime. Thus a murder may be viewed as more serious when committed pursuant to a contract.

This list is by no means exhaustive. It simply illustrates that there are generally accepted criteria for comparing the severity of different crimes on a broad scale, despite the difficulties courts face in attempting to draw distinctions between similar crimes....

IV

It remains to apply the analytical framework established by our prior decisions to the case before us. We first consider the relevant criteria, viewing Helm's sentence as life imprisonment without possibility of parole. We then consider the State's argument that the possibility of commutation is sufficient to save an otherwise unconstitutional sentence.

A

Helm's crime was "one of the most passive felonies a person could commit." It involved neither violence nor threat of violence to any person. The $100 face value of

Helm's "no account" check was not trivial, but neither was it a large amount. One hundred dollars was less than half the amount South Dakota required for a felonious theft. It is easy to see why such a crime is viewed by society as among the less serious offenses.

Helm, of course, was not charged simply with uttering a "no account" check, but also with being an habitual offender.[7] And a State is justified in punishing a recidivist more severely than it punishes a first offender. Helm's status, however, cannot be considered in the abstract. His prior offenses, although classified as felonies, were all relatively minor.[8] All were nonviolent and none was a crime against a person. Indeed, there was no minimum amount in either the burglary or the false pretenses statutes, and the minimum amount covered by the grand larceny statute was fairly small.

Helm's present sentence is life imprisonment without possibility of parole. Barring executive clemency, Helm will spend the rest of his life in the state penitentiary.... Helm's sentence is the most severe punishment that the State could have imposed on any criminal for any crime. Only capital punishment, a penalty not authorized in South Dakota when Helm was sentenced, exceeds it.

We next consider the sentences that could be imposed on other criminals in the same jurisdiction. When Helm was sentenced, a South Dakota court was required to impose a life sentence for murder, and was authorized to impose a life sentence for treason, first degree manslaughter, first degree arson, and kidnapping. No other crime was punishable so severely on the first offense. Attempted murder, placing an explosive device on an aircraft, and first degree rape, were only Class 2 felonies. Aggravated riot was only a Class 3 felony. Distribution of heroin, and aggravated assault, were only Class 4 felonies. Helm's habitual offender status complicates our analysis, but relevant comparisons are still possible. Under §22-7-7, the penalty for a second or third felony is increased by one class. Thus a life sentence was mandatory when a second or third conviction was for treason, first degree manslaughter, first degree arson, or kidnapping, and a life sentence would have been authorized when a second or third conviction was for such crimes as attempted murder, placing an explosive device on an aircraft, or first degree rape. Finally, §22-7-8, under which Helm was sentenced, authorized life imprisonment after three prior convictions, regardless of the crimes.

In sum, there were a handful of crimes that were necessarily punished by life imprisonment: murder, and, on a second or third offense, treason, first degree manslaughter, first degree arson, and kidnapping. There was a larger group for which life imprisonment was authorized in the discretion of the sentencing judge, including: treason, first degree manslaughter, first degree arson, and kidnapping; attempted murder, placing an explosive device on an aircraft, and first degree rape on a second or third offense; and any felony after three prior offenses. Finally, there was a large group of very serious offenses for which life imprisonment was not authorized, including a third offense of heroin dealing or aggravated assault.

---

7. We must focus on the principal felony—the felony that triggers the life sentence—since Helm already has paid the penalty for each of his prior offenses. But we recognize, of course, that Helm's prior convictions are relevant to the sentencing decision.

8. Helm, who was 36-years-old when he was sentenced, is not a professional criminal. The record indicates an addiction to alcohol, and a consequent difficulty in holding a job. His record involves no instance of violence of any kind. Incarcerating him for life without possibility of parole is unlikely to advance the goals of our criminal justice system in any substantial way. Neither Helm nor the State will have an incentive to pursue clearly needed treatment for his alcohol problem, or any other program of rehabilitation.

Criminals committing any of these offenses ordinarily would be thought more deserving of punishment than one uttering a "no account" check—even when the bad-check writer had already committed six minor felonies. Moreover, there is no indication in the record that any habitual offender other than Helm has ever been given the maximum sentence on the basis of comparable crimes. It is more likely that the possibility of life imprisonment under §22-7-8 generally is reserved for criminals such as fourth-time heroin dealers, while habitual bad-check writers receive more lenient treatment. In any event, Helm has been treated in the same manner as, or more severely than, criminals who have committed far more serious crimes.

Finally, we compare the sentences imposed for commission of the same crime in other jurisdictions. The Court of Appeals found that "Helm could have received a life sentence without parole for his offense in only one other state, Nevada," and we have no reason to doubt this finding. At the very least, therefore, it is clear that Helm could not have received such a severe sentence in 48 of the 50 States. But even under Nevada law, a life sentence without possibility of parole is merely authorized in these circumstances. We are not advised that any defendant such as Helm, whose prior offenses were so minor, actually has received the maximum penalty in Nevada. It appears that Helm was treated more severely than he would have been in any other State....

V

The Constitution requires us to examine Helm's sentence to determine if it is proportionate to his crime. Applying objective criteria, we find that Helm has received the penultimate sentence for relatively minor criminal conduct. He has been treated more harshly than other criminals in the State who have committed more serious crimes. He has been treated more harshly than he would have been in any other jurisdiction, with the possible exception of a single State. We conclude that his sentence is significantly disproportionate to his crime, and is therefore prohibited by the Eighth Amendment.

Harmelin v. Michigan
501 U.S. 957 (1991)

Justice SCALIA announced the judgment of the Court and delivered the opinion of the Court with respect to Part IV, and an opinion with respect to Parts I, II, and III in which the Chief Justice joins.

Petitioner was convicted of possessing 672 grams of cocaine and sentenced to a mandatory term of life in prison without possibility of parole....

Petitioner claims that his sentence is unconstitutionally "cruel and unusual" for two reasons. First, because it is "significantly disproportionate" to the crime he committed. Second, because the sentencing judge was statutorily required to impose it, without taking into account the particularized circumstances of the crime and of the criminal.... [Note that only Chief Justice Rehnquist joined Scalia's opinion in Parts I, II and III below.]

I

A

... *Solem v. Helm*, 463 U.S. 277 (1983), set aside under the Eighth Amendment, because it was disproportionate, a sentence of life imprisonment without possibility of parole, imposed under a South Dakota recividist statute for successive offenses that included three convictions of third-degree burglary, one of obtaining money by false pretenses, one of grand larceny, one of third-offense driving while intoxicated, and one of writing a "no account" check with intent to defraud. In the *Solem* account, *Weems v. United States*, 217 U.S. 349 (1910), no longer involved punishment of a "unique nature," but was the "leading case," exemplifying the "general principle of proportionality" which was "deeply rooted and frequently repeated in common-law jurisprudence," had been embodied in the English Bill of Rights "in language that was later adopted in the Eighth Amendment," and had been "recognized explicitly in this Court for almost a century." ... [W]e ... address[] anew, and in greater detail, the question whether the Eighth Amendment contains a proportionality guarantee—with particular attention to the background of the Eighth Amendment (which *Solem* discussed in only two pages) and to the understanding of the Eighth Amendment before the end of the 19th century (which *Solem* discussed not at all). We conclude from this examination that *Solem* was simply wrong; the Eighth Amendment contains no proportionality guarantee....

C

Perhaps the most persuasive evidence of what "cruel and unusual" [means] ... is found in early judicial constructions of the Eighth Amendment and its state counterparts. An early (perhaps the earliest) judicial construction of the Federal provision is illustrative. In *Barker v. People*, 20 Johns. (N.Y. Sup. Ct. 1823), aff'd, 3 Cow. 686 (N.Y. 1824), the defendant, upon conviction of challenging another to a duel, had been disenfranchised. Chief Justice Spencer assumed that the Eighth Amendment applied to the States, and in finding that it had not been violated considered the proportionality of the punishment irrelevant. "The disenfranchisement of a citizen," he said, "is not an unusual punishment; it was the consequence of treason, and of infamous crimes, and it was altogether discretionary in the legislature to extend that punishment to other offenses." Throughout the 19th century, state courts interpreting state constitutional provisions with identical or more expansive wording (i.e., "cruel or unusual") concluded that these provisions did not proscribe disproportionality but only certain modes of punishment. For example, in *Aldridge v. Commonwealth*, 4 Va. 447 (1824), the General Court of Virginia had occasion to interpret the cruel and unusual punishments clause that was the direct ancestor of our federal provision. In rejecting the defendant's claim that a sentence of so many as 39 stripes violated the Virginia Constitution, the court said:

> As to the ninth section of the Bill of Rights, denouncing cruel and unusual punishments, we have no notion that it has any bearing on this case. That provision was never designed to control the Legislative right to determine *ad libitum* upon the *adequacy* of punishment, but is merely applicable to the modes of punishment.... [T]he best heads and hearts of the land of our ancestors, had long and loudly declaimed against the wanton cruelty of many of the punishments practiced in other countries; and this section in the Bill of Rights was framed effectually to exclude these, so that no future Legislature, in a moment perhaps of great and general excitement, should be tempted to disgrace our Code by the introduction of any of those odious modes of punishment. 4 Va. at 449–450.

In the 19th century, judicial agreement that a "cruel and unusual" (or "cruel or unusual") provision did not constitute a proportionality requirement appears to have been universal. One case, late in the century, suggested in dictum, not a fullfledged proportionality principle, but at least the power of the courts to intervene "in very extreme cases, where the punishment proposed is so severe and out of proportion to the offense as to shock public sentiment and violate the judgment of reasonable people." *State v. Becker*, 3 S.D. 29, 51 N.W. 1018, 1022 (1892). That case, however, involved a constitutional provision proscribing all punishments that were merely "cruel." A few decisions early in the present century cited it (again in dictum) for the proposition that a sentence "so out of proportion to the offense ... as to 'shock public sentiment and violate the judgment of reasonable people'" would be "cruel and unusual."

II

We think it enough that those who framed and approved the Federal Constitution chose, for whatever reason, not to include within it the guarantee against disproportionate sentences that some State Constitutions contained. It is worth noting, however, that there was good reason for that choice—a reason that reinforces the necessity of overruling *Solem*. While there are relatively clear historical guidelines and accepted practices that enable judges to determine which *modes* of punishment are "cruel and unusual," *proportionality* does not lend itself to such analysis. Neither Congress nor any state legislature has ever set out with the objective of crafting a penalty that is "disproportionate," yet as some of the examples mentioned above indicate, many enacted dispositions seem to be so—because they were made for other times or other places, with different social attitudes, different criminal epidemics, different public fears, and different prevailing theories of penology. This is not to say that there are no absolutes; one can imagine extreme examples that no rational person, in no time or place, could accept. But for the same reason these examples are easy to decide, they are certain never to occur. The real function of a constitutional proportionality principle, if it exists, is to enable judges to evaluate a penalty that *some* assemblage of men and women *has* considered proportionate—and to say that it is not. For that real-world enterprise, the standards seem so inadequate that the proportionality principle becomes an invitation to imposition of subjective values.

This becomes clear, we think, from a consideration of the three factors that *Solem* found relevant to the proportionality determination: (1) the inherent gravity of the offense, (2) the sentences imposed for similarly grave offenses in the same jurisdiction, and (3) sentences imposed for the same crime in other jurisdictions. As to the first factor: Of course some offenses, involving violent harm to human beings, will always and everywhere be regarded as serious, but that is only half the equation. The issue is *what else* should be regarded to be *as serious* as these offenses, or even to be *more serious* than some of them. On that point, judging by the statutes that Americans have enacted, there is enormous variation—even within a given age, not to mention across the many generations ruled by the Bill of Rights. The State of Massachusetts punishes sodomy more severely than assault and battery, whereas in several States, sodomy is not unlawful at all. In Louisiana, one who assaults another with a dangerous weapon faces the same maximum prison term as one who removes a shopping basket "from the parking area or grounds of any store ... without authorization." A battery that results in "protracted and obvious disfigurement" merits imprisonment "for not more than five years," one half the maximum penalty for theft of livestock or an oilfield seismograph. We may think that the First Congress punished with clear disproportionality when it provided up to seven years in prison and up to $1,000 in fine for "cut[ting] off the ear or ears, ... cut[ting] out or disabl[ing] the tongue, ... put[ting] out an eye, ... cut[ting] off ... any limb or member of any person with intention ... to maim or disfigure," but provided the death penalty for "run[ning] away with [a] ship or vessel, or any goods or merchandise to the value of fifty dollars." But then perhaps the citizens of 1791 would think that today's Congress punishes with clear disproportionality when it sanctions "assault by ... wounding" with up to six months in prison, unauthorized reproduction of the "Smokey Bear" character or name with the same penalty, offering to barter a migratory bird with up to two years in prison, and purloining a "key suited to any lock adopted by the Post Office Department" with a prison term of up to 10 years. Perhaps both we and they would be right, but the point is that there are no textual or historical standards for saying so.

The difficulty of assessing gravity is demonstrated in the very context of the present case: Petitioner acknowledges that a mandatory life sentence might not be "grossly excessive" for possession of cocaine with intent to distribute. But surely whether it is a "grave" offense merely to possess a significant quantity of drugs—thereby facilitating distribution, subjecting the holder to the temptation of distribution, and raising the possibility of theft by others who might distribute—depends entirely upon how odious and socially threatening one believes drug use to be. Would it be "grossly excessive" to provide life imprisonment for "mere possession" of a certain quantity of heavy weaponry? If not, then the only issue is whether the possible dissemination of drugs can be as "grave" as the possible dissemination of heavy weapons. Who are we to say no? The Members of the Michigan Legislature, and not we, know the situation on the streets of Detroit.

The second factor suggested in *Solem* fails for the same reason. One cannot compare the sentences imposed by the jurisdiction for "similarly grave" offenses if there is no objective standard of gravity. Judges will be comparing what *they* consider comparable. Or, to put the same point differently: when it happens that two offenses judicially determined to be "similarly grave" receive significantly *dis*similar penalties, what follows is not that the harsher penalty is unconstitutional, but merely that the legislature does not share the judges' view that the offenses are similarly grave. Moreover, even if "similarly grave" crimes could be identified, the penalties for them would not necessarily be comparable, since there are many other justifications for a difference. For example, since deterrent effect depends not only upon the amount of the penalty but upon its certainty, crimes that are less grave but significantly more difficult to detect may warrant substantially higher penalties. Grave crimes of the sort that will not be deterred by penalty may warrant substantially lower penalties, as may grave crimes of the sort that are normally committed once-in-a-lifetime by otherwise law-abiding citizens who will not profit from rehabilitation. Whether these differences will occur, and to what extent, depends, of course, upon the weight the society accords to deterrence and rehabilitation, rather than retribution, as the objective of criminal punishment (which is an eminently legislative judgment). In fact, it becomes difficult even to speak intelligently of "proportionality," once deterrence and rehabilitation are given significant weight. Proportionality is inherently a retributive concept, and perfect proportionality is the talionic law.

As for the third factor mentioned by *Solem*—the character of the sentences imposed by other States for the same crime—it must be acknowledged that that can be applied with clarity and ease. The only difficulty is that it has no conceivable relevance to the Eighth Amendment. That a State is entitled to treat with stern disapproval an act that other States punish with the mildest of sanctions follows *a fortiori* from the undoubted fact that a State may criminalize an act that other States do not criminalize *at all*. Indeed, a State may criminalize an act that other States choose to *reward*—punishing, for example, the killing of endangered wild animals for which other States are offering a bounty. What greater disproportion could there be than that? "Absent a constitutionally imposed uniformity inimical to traditional notions of federalism, some State will always bear the distinction of treating particular offenders more severely than any other State." *Rummel*, 445 U.S. at 282. Diversity not only in policy, but in the means of implementing policy, is the very *raison d'etre* of our federal system. Though the different needs and concerns of other States may induce them to treat simple possession of 672 grams of cocaine as a relatively minor offense; nothing in the Constitution requires Michigan to follow suit. The Eighth Amendment is not a ratchet, whereby a temporary consensus on leniency for a particular crime fixes a permanent constitutional maximum, disabling the States from giving effect to altered beliefs and responding to changed social conditions....

III

The first holding of this Court unqualifiedly applying a requirement of proportionality to criminal penalties was issued 185 years after the Eighth Amendment was adopted.[9] In *Coker v. Georgia*, 433 U.S. 584 (1977), the Court held that, because of the disproportionality, it was a violation of the Cruel and Unusual Punishments Clause to impose capital punishment for rape of an adult woman. Four years later, in *Enmund v. Florida*, 458 U.S. 782 (1982), we held that it violates the Eighth Amendment, because of disproportionality, to impose the death penalty upon a participant in a felony that results in murder, without any inquiry into the participant's intent to kill. *Rummel v. Estelle*, 445 U.S. 263 (1980), treated this line of authority as an aspect of our death penalty jurisprudence, rather than a generalizable aspect of Eighth Amendment law. We think that is an accurate explanation, and we reassert it. Proportionality review is one of several respects in which we have held that "death is different," and have imposed protections that the Constitution nowhere else provides. We would leave it there, but will not extend it further....

IV

[After finding that the mandatory sentence of life without parole in this case did not violate the Eighth Amendment, the Court affirmed the judgment of the Michigan Court of Appeals.]

Justice WHITE, with whom Justice Blackmun and Justice Stevens join, dissenting.

The Eighth Amendment provides that "[e]xcessive bail shall not be required, nor excessive fines imposed, nor cruel and unusual punishments inflicted." Justice Scalia concludes that "the Eighth Amendment contains no proportionality guarantee." Accordingly, he says *Solem v. Helm*, 463 U.S. 277 (1983), "was simply wrong" in holding otherwise, as would be the Court's other cases interpreting the Amendment to contain a proportionality principle.... With all due respect, I dissent.

The language of the Amendment does not refer to proportionality in so many words, but it does forbid "excessive" fines, a restraint that suggests that a determination of excessiveness should be based at least in part on whether the fine imposed is disproportionate to the crime committed. Nor would it be unreasonable to conclude that it would

---

9. In *Robinson v. California*, 370 U.S. 660 (1962), the Court invalidated a 90-day prison sentence for the crime of being "addicted to the use of narcotics." The opinion does not cite *Weems* and rests upon the proposition that "[e]ven one day in prison would be a cruel and unusual punishment for the 'crime' of having a common cold." Despite the Court's statement to the contrary in *Solem v. Helm*, 463 U.S. 277, 287 (1983), there is no reason to believe that the decision was an application of the principle of proportionality.

be both cruel and unusual to punish overtime parking by life imprisonment, or, more generally, to impose any punishment that is grossly disproportionate to the offense for which the defendant has been convicted....

Contrary to Justice Scalia's suggestion, the *Solem* analysis has worked well in practice. Courts appear to have had little difficulty applying the analysis to a given sentence, and application of the test by numerous state and federal appellate courts has resulted in a mere handful of sentences being declared unconstitutional. Thus, it is clear that reviewing courts have not baldly substituted their own subjective moral values for those of the legislature. Instead, courts have demonstrated that they are "capable of applying the Eighth Amendment to disproportionate noncapital sentences with a high degree of sensitivity to principles of federalism and state autonomy." *Rummel*, 445 U.S. at 306. *Solem* is wholly consistent with this approach, and when properly applied, its analysis affords "substantial deference to the broad authority that legislatures necessarily possess in determining the types and limits of punishments for crimes, as well as to the discretion that trial courts possess in sentencing convicted criminals," and will only rarely result in a sentence failing constitutional muster. The fact that this is one of those rare instances is no reason to abandon the analysis....

Two dangers lurk in Justice Scalia's analysis. First, he provides no mechanism for addressing a situation such as that proposed in *Rummel*, in which a legislature makes overtime parking a felony punishable by life imprisonment. He concedes that "one can imagine extreme examples" — perhaps such as the one described in *Rummel* — "that no rational person, in no time or place, could accept," but attempts to offer reassurance by claiming that "for the same reason these examples are easy to decide, they are certain never to occur." This is cold comfort indeed, for absent a proportionality guarantee, there would be no basis for deciding such cases should they arise.

Second, as I have indicated, Justice Scalia's position that the Eighth Amendment addresses only modes or methods of punishment is quite inconsistent with our capital punishment cases, which do not outlaw death as a mode or method of punishment, but instead put limits on its application. If the concept of proportionality is downgraded in the Eighth Amendment calculus, much of this Court's capital penalty jurisprudence will rest on quicksand....

Note

Justice Kennedy, joined by Justices O'Connor and Souter, concurred in the result of *Harmelin*. However, while concurring in the result, these three justices found that although "the Eighth Amendment does not require strict proportionality between crime and sentence ... it forbids ... extreme sentences that are grossly disproportionate to the crime."

Michigan v. Bullock
Michigan v. Hasson
485 N.W.2d 866 (Mich. 1992)

CAVANAGH, Chief Justice.

We address in these consolidated cases ... the question whether Michigan's mandatory penalty of life in prison without possibility of parole, for possession of 650 grams or more of any mixture containing cocaine, is "cruel or unusual" under our state constitution.

On February 24, 1988, defendant Hasson traveled by air from Los Angeles to Lansing's Capital City Airport. He had a return ticket to Los Angeles on a flight scheduled to leave less than four hours after his arrival, yet he had checked two large suitcases. Acting on a tip from airline agents relayed through the Los Angeles police, the Michigan State Police met Hasson's flight. Before Hasson claimed his luggage, a police dog alerted officers to the presence of illegal drugs in both suitcases. The police observed Hasson deplane, retrieve his luggage, make a call from a public phone, and walk outside to the public driveway. After about thirty minutes, Hasson flagged down a car driven and owned by defendant Bullock. Bullock's seventeen-year-old grandson was a passenger in the car. Hasson placed his luggage in the trunk and got in the car, which began to pull away.

At that point, the police stopped the car and arrested all three occupants. The police, without attempting to obtain a warrant, then proceeded to search the entire car. They examined the glove compartment, Bullock's purse which she left in the car, and the luggage Hasson had placed in the trunk. They found traces of cocaine in the glove compartment and Bullock's purse, and over fifteen kilograms of cocaine in Hasson's luggage. This cocaine was admitted as evidence at trial over Hasson's and Bullock's objections, and both were convicted, in separate jury trials, of knowingly possessing 650 grams or more of cocaine. As mandated by ... statute ... both defendants were sentenced to life in prison without any possibility of parole....

We ... agreed to consider whether the mandatory penalty of life in prison without possibility of parole was invalid under either the federal or state constitutions. Following oral argument during the 1990–91 term, we ordered reargument this term to address the effect of the United States Supreme Court's intervening decision[ ] in ... *Harmelin v. Michigan*, 501 U.S. 957 (1991).

The United States Supreme Court, in *Harmelin v. Michigan*, rejected a challenge, brought under the "cruel and unusual punishments" clause of the Eighth Amendment of the United States Constitution, to Michigan's mandatory penalty of life in prison without possibility of parole for possession of 650 grams or more of a mixture containing cocaine. We address here a challenge to that penalty on the basis of [Michigan] Const. 1963, art. 1, §16, which is worded differently from,[10] and was ratified more than 171 years after, the Eighth Amendment.

While *Harmelin* is binding and authoritative for purposes of applying the United States Constitution, it is only persuasive authority for purposes of this Court's interpretation and application of the Michigan Constitution. This Court alone is the ultimate authority with regard to the meaning and application of Michigan law. In the case of a divided United States Supreme Court decision, we may in some cases find more persuasive, and choose to rely upon, the reasoning of the dissenting justices of that Court, and not the majority, for purposes of interpreting our own Michigan Constitution.

... We find ... at least three compelling reasons ... to interpret our state constitutional provision more broadly in these cases than the United States Supreme Court interpreted the Eighth Amendment in *Harmelin*.... Furthermore, we find that a proper interpretation of Const. 1963, art. 1, §16, in accordance with this Court's longstanding

---

10. U.S. Const., Am. VIII provides: "Excessive bail shall not be required, nor excessive fines imposed, nor cruel and unusual punishments inflicted." [Michigan] Const. 1963, art. 1, §16 provides: "Excessive bail shall not be required; excessive fines shall not be imposed; cruel or unusual punishment shall not be inflicted; nor shall witnesses be unreasonably detained."

precedent in this area, requires us to strike down the penalty at issue as unjustifiably disproportionate to the crime for which it is imposed, and therefore "cruel or unusual."

First, as we have already noted, the Michigan provision prohibits "cruel or unusual" punishments, while the Eighth Amendment bars only punishments that are both "cruel and unusual." This textual difference does not appear to be accidental or inadvertent. Language providing that "no cruel or unusual punishments shall be inflicted" was included in Article II of the Northwest Ordinance of 1787. Michigan's first Constitution, adopted in 1835, provided that "cruel and unjust punishments shall not be inflicted." The Constitution of 1850 provided that "cruel or unusual punishment shall not be inflicted...." Identical language was adopted as part of the 1908 and 1963 Constitutions.

This Court, in *People v. Lorentzen*, 387 Mich. 167, 194 N.W.2d 827 (1972), took specific note of this difference in phraseology and suggested that it might well lead to different results with regard to allegedly disproportionate prison terms. "The prohibition of punishment that is unusual but not necessarily cruel carries an implication that unusually excessive imprisonment is included in that prohibition." *Id.* at 172, 194 N.W. 2d at 827. As this Court noted in [*People v.*] *Collins*, [475 N.W.2d 684 (1991),] a "significant textual difference [ ] between parallel provisions of the state and federal constitutions" may constitute a "compelling reason" for a different and broader interpretation of the state provision.

Second, while two members of the *Harmelin* majority maintained that the historical circumstances and background of the adoption of the Eighth Amendment preclude the notion that the federal clause contains a "proportionality principle," such a conclusion cannot be reached with regard to the framing and adoption of the Michigan Constitution of 1963. Whatever the legal terms "cruel" and "unusual" were understood to mean in 1791 when the Eighth Amendment was ratified—or in 1689 when its antecedent, the English Bill of Rights, was adopted—by 1963 those words had been interpreted and understood by the United States Supreme Court and by this Court for more than half a century to include a prohibition on grossly disproportionate sentences ...

Finally, this Court, in interpreting Const. 1963, art. 1, §16, has long followed an approach more consistent with the reasoning of the *Harmelin* dissenters than with that of the *Harmelin* majority. Twenty years ago, in *People v. Lorentzen*, we struck down, under both the Eighth Amendment and Const. 1963, art. 1, §16, a mandatory minimum sentence of twenty years in prison (reducible to approximately ten years by earning "good time") for selling any amount of marijuana. Our analysis in *Lorentzen* foreshadowed in a striking manner the three-pronged test later adopted by the United States Supreme Court in *Solem v. Helm*, 463 U.S. 277 (1983).

Thus, *Lorentzen* noted the severity of the sentence imposed and the fact that it would apply to a marijuana sale by "a first offender high school student." *Lorentzen* then compared the penalty to those imposed for numerous other crimes in Michigan. *Lorentzen* further compared Michigan's penalty for selling marijuana to the penalties imposed for that offense by other states. Finally, *Lorentzen* applied a fourth criterion rooted in Michigan's legal traditions, and reflected in the provision for "indeterminate sentences" of Const. 1963, art. 4, §45: the goal of rehabilitation.

It is unclear, in the wake of *Harmelin*, whether *Lorentzen*'s or *Solem*'s analysis survives as a matter of federal constitutional law, and that need not concern us in any event. *Lorentzen*'s analysis, although relying in the alternative on the Eighth Amendment, was firmly and sufficiently rooted in Const. 1963, art. 1, §16. Indeed, we preceded our proportionality analysis in *Lorentzen* with a lengthy review of Michigan case law dating back to 1879. We believe the precedential weight of *Lorentzen* and its antecedents, as a matter of Michigan law, constitutes a very compelling reason not to reflexively follow the latest turn in the United States Supreme Court's Eighth Amendment analysis. We therefore continue to adhere, on the basis of the Michigan Constitution, to the analysis set forth in *Lorentzen* and later adopted in *Solem*.

Applying the *Lorentzen-Solem* analysis to these cases, we conclude, largely for the reasons stated by Justice White in his dissenting opinion in *Harmelin*, that the penalty at issue here is so grossly disproportionate as to be "cruel or unusual." The penalty is imposed for mere possession of cocaine, without any proof of intent to sell or distribute. The penalty would apply to a teenage first offender who acted merely as a courier. Indeed, on the basis of the information before this Court, it appears that prior to the offense giving rise to this case, defendant Bullock, a forty-eight-year-old grandmother, had never been convicted of any serious crime and had held a steady job as an autoworker for sixteen years.

It is true, as Justice Kennedy noted in *Harmelin*, that the collateral effects flowing even from mere possession of cocaine are terrible indeed. But conviction of the crime involved here does not require any proof that the defendant committed, aided, intended, or even contemplated any loss of life or other violent crime, or even any crime against property. As Justice White correctly noted in *Harmelin*, "[t]o be constitutionally proportionate, punishment must be tailored to a defendant's personal responsibility and moral guilt." While we emphatically do not minimize the gravity and reprehensibility of defendants' crime, it would be profoundly unfair to impute full personal responsibility and moral guilt to defendants for any and all collateral acts, unintended by them, which might have been later committed by others in connection with the seized cocaine. Persons who independently commit violent and other crimes in connection with illegal drugs can and should be held individually responsible by our criminal justice system.

… As Justice White noted in *Harmelin*, aside from manufacture, delivery, possession with intent to deliver, and possession of 650 grams or more of a substance containing cocaine or illegal narcotics, only first-degree murder—that is, "wilful, deliberate, and premeditated" murder, or murder committed in the course of certain serious felonies—is punishable in Michigan by mandatory life imprisonment without possibility of parole. The defendants in this case have been punished more severely than they could have been for second-degree murder, rape, mutilation, armed robbery, or other exceptionally grave and violent crimes.

Furthermore, as Justice White also noted, no other state in the nation imposes a penalty even remotely as severe as Michigan's for mere possession of 650 grams or more of cocaine. "Of the remaining 49 states, only Alabama provides for a mandatory sentence of life imprisonment without possibility of parole for a first-time drug offender, and then only when a defendant possesses ten kilograms or more of cocaine."

In sum, the only fair conclusion that can be reached regarding the penalty at issue is that it constitutes an unduly disproportionate response to the serious problems posed by drugs in our society. However understandable such a response may be, it is not consistent with our constitutional prohibition of "cruel or unusual punishment." The penalty is therefore unconstitutional on its face.

The proportionality principle inherent in Const. 1963, art. 1, §16, is not a simple, "bright-line" test, and the application of that test may, concededly, be analytically difficult and politically unpopular, especially where application of that principle requires us to override a democratically expressed judgment of the Legislature. The fact is, however, the people of Michigan, speaking through their constitution, have forbidden the imposition of cruel or unusual punishments, and we are duty-bound to devise a principled test by which to enforce that prohibition, and to apply that test to the cases that are brought before us. The very purpose of a constitution is to subject the passing judgments of temporary legislative or political majorities to the deeper, more profound judgment of the people reflected in the constitution, the enforcement of which is entrusted to our judgment.

For the reasons stated ... we strike down the sentences imposed on both defendants as "cruel or unusual" under Const. 1963, art. 1, §16.

The remaining question is what remedy to afford. In considering this question, we are guided by several factors. First, there are three aspects to the severity of the penalty at issue: (1) its length (life); (2) its mandatory character, i.e., the absence of individualized consideration for each defendant at the sentencing stage; and (3) the absence of any possibility of individualized parole consideration for each defendant. Second, our holding today is necessarily limited to the precise issue before us; we do not address today the validity of a hypothetical penalty lacking any of these three attributes. Third, the defendants at bar, in challenging this penalty, focused especially on the absence of the possibility of parole. Finally, our decision today necessarily invalidates the sentences of all defendants currently incarcerated under the same penalty, and for committing the same offense, as the defendants at bar.

We conclude that the most appropriate remedy under the circumstances is to ameliorate the no-parole feature of the penalty. We therefore strike down, with regard to these defendants and all others who have been sentenced under the same penalty and for the same offense, that portion of [the statute] denying such defendants the parole consideration otherwise available upon completion of ten calendar years of the sentence. Thus, each such defendant shall, upon serving ten calendar years of the sentence, become subject to the jurisdiction of the parole board and eligible for parole consideration in accordance with [Michigan law].

* * *

A deeply divided Supreme Court struggled to make sense of *Solem* and *Harmelin*'s Eighth Amendment jurisprudence in a pair cases raising constitutional challenges to California's recidivist sentencing law, adopted by the state's voters in a 1994 referendum. Split 5–4, the Court affirmed sentences of life without parole for at least 25 years for Gary Ewing, who stole three golf clubs from a pro shop, and life without parole for at least 50 years for Leandro Andrade, who stole nine videotapes worth $150 from two different Kmart stores.

Both men had previous convictions for a string of mostly minor property offenses that qualified as prior strikes under California's "three-strikes" law. At the time of the Court's ruling, more than 7,000 people were in California prisons serving sentences of at least 25 years under the law, including more than 300 whose "third strike" was a petty theft. A synopsis of the Justice O'Connor's opinion for the Court in *Lockyer v. Andrade*, 538 U.S. 63 (2003), follows.

Note: Lockyer v. Andrade, 538 U.S. 63 (2003)

California charged Leandro Andrade with two felony counts of petty theft with a prior conviction after he stole approximately $150 worth of videotapes from two different stores. Under California's three strikes law, any felony can constitute the third strike subjecting a defendant to a prison term of 25 years to life. The jury found Andrade guilty and then found that he had three prior convictions that qualified as serious or violent felonies under the three strikes regime. Because each of his petty theft convictions thus triggered a separate application of the three strikes law, the judge sentenced him to two consecutive terms of 25 years to life.

In affirming, the California Court of Appeal rejected his claim that his sentence violated the constitutional prohibition against cruel and unusual punishment. It found the *Solem v. Helm*, 463 U.S. 277, proportionality analysis questionable in light of *Harmelin v. Michigan*, 501 U.S. 957. It then compared the facts in Andrade's case to those in *Rummel v. Estelle*, 445 U.S. 263—in which the Supreme Court rejected a claim that a life sentence was grossly disproportionate to the felonies that formed the predicate for the sentence—and concluded that Andrade's sentence was not disproportionate. The California Supreme Court denied discretionary review.

The Federal District Court denied Andrade's subsequent habeas petition, but the Ninth Circuit granted him a certificate of appealability and reversed. Reviewing the case under the Antiterrorism and Effective Death Penalty Act of 1996 (AEDPA), the latter court held that an unreasonable application of clearly established federal law under 28 U.S.C. §2254(d)(1), occurs when there is clear error; concluded that both *Solem* and *Rummel* remain good law and are instructive in applying *Harmelin*; and found that the California Court of Appeal's disregard for *Solem* resulted in an unreasonable application of clearly established Supreme Court law and was irreconcilable with *Solem*, thus constituting clear error.

The U.S Supreme Court reversed, holding that the Ninth Circuit erred in ruling that the California Court of Appeal's decision was contrary to, or an unreasonable application of, this Court's clearly established law within the meaning of §2254(d)(1). Justice O'Connor's opinion for the Court was divided into three parts.

First, the AEDPA does not require a federal habeas court to adopt any one methodology in deciding the only question that matters under §2254(d)(1)—whether a state court decision is contrary to, or involved an unreasonable application of, clearly established federal law. In this case, this Court does not reach the question whether the state court erred, but focuses solely on whether habeas relief is barred by §2254(d)(1).

Second, the Supreme Court must first decide what constitutes such "clearly established" law. Andrade claimed that *Rummel*, *Solem*, and *Harmelin* clearly establish a principle that his sentence was so grossly disproportionate that it violated the Eighth Amendment. Under §2254(d)(1), "clearly established Federal law" is the governing legal principle or principles set forth by the Supreme Court at the time a state court renders its decision. The difficulty with Andrade's position is that the Court had not established a clear or consistent path for courts to follow in determining whether a particular sentence for a term of years can violate the Eighth Amendment. Indeed, according to Justice O'Connor's opinion, the only "clearly established" law emerging from the Court's jurisprudence in this area is that a gross disproportionality principle applies to such sentences. Because the Court's cases lack clarity regarding what factors may indicate gross disproportionality, the principle's precise contours are unclear, applicable only in the "exceedingly rare" and "extreme" case. *Harmelin*, (Kennedy, J., concurring in part and concurring in judgment).

Finally, the California Court of Appeal's decision was not "contrary to, or involved an unreasonable application of," the clearly established gross disproportionality principle. First, a decision is contrary to clearly established precedent if the state court applied a rule that contradicts the governing law set forth in this Court's cases or confronts facts that are materially indistinguishable from a Court decision and nevertheless arrives at a different result. *Williams v. Taylor*, 529 U.S. 362, 405–406. Andrade's sentence implicates factors relevant in both *Rummel* and *Solem*. Because *Harmelin* and *Solem* specifically stated that they did not overrule *Rummel*, it was not contrary to this Court's clearly established law for the state court to turn to *Rummel* in deciding whether the sentence was grossly disproportionate.

Also, the facts of Andrade's case fall in between *Solem* and *Rummel* but are not materially indistinguishable from either. Thus, the state court did not confront materially indistinguishable facts yet arrive at a different result. Second, under the "unreasonable application" clause, a federal habeas court may grant the writ if the state court identifies the correct governing legal principle but unreasonably applies it to the facts of the prisoner's case. *Williams v. Taylor*. The state court decision must be objectively unreasonable, not just incorrect or erroneous.

Finally, the Court concluded that the Ninth Circuit erred in defining "objectively unreasonable" to mean "clear error." While habeas relief can be based on an application of a governing legal principle to a set of facts different from those of the case in which the principle was announced, the governing legal principle here gives legislatures broad discretion to fashion a sentence that fits within the scope of the proportionality principle — the "precise contours" of which are "unclear." *Harmelin*. And it was not objectively unreasonable for the state court to conclude that these "contours" permitted an affirmance of Andrade's sentence. Cf., e.g., *Riggs v. California*, 525 U.S. 1114, 1115 (Stevens, J., dissenting from denial of certiorari).

Justice Souter was joined in dissent by Justices Stevens, Ginsburg and Breyer. His excerpted opinion follows.

"The application of the Eighth Amendment prohibition against cruel and unusual punishment to terms of years is articulated in the "clearly established" principle acknowledged by the Court: a sentence grossly disproportionate to the offense for which it is imposed is unconstitutional. *Harmelin v. Michigan*, 501 U.S. 957 (1991); *Solem v. Helm*, 463 U.S. 277 (1983); *Rummel v. Estelle*, 445 U.S. 263 (1980).... Andrade's sentence cannot survive Eighth Amendment review. His criminal history is less grave than Ewing's, and yet he received a prison term twice as long for a less serious triggering offense. To be sure, this is a habeas case and a prohibition couched in terms as general as gross disproportion necessarily leaves state courts with much leeway under the statutory criterion that conditions federal relief upon finding that a state court unreasonably applied clear law, see 28 U.S.C. §2254(d). This case nonetheless presents two independent reasons for holding that the disproportionality review by the state court was not only erroneous but unreasonable, entitling Andrade to relief. I respectfully dissent accordingly.

"The first reason is the holding in *Solem*, which happens to be our most recent effort at proportionality review of recidivist sentencing, the authority of which was not left in doubt by *Harmelin*. Although *Solem* is important for its instructions about applying objective proportionality analysis, the case is controlling here because it established a benchmark in applying the general principle. We specifically held that a sentence of life imprisonment without parole for uttering a $100 "no account" check was disproportionate to the crime, even though the defendant had committed six prior nonviolent felonies. In explaining our proportionality review, we contrasted the result with Rummel's on the ground that the life sentence there had included parole eligibility after 12 years, *Solem*.

"The facts here are on all fours with those of *Solem* and point to the same result. Andrade, like the defendant in *Solem,* was a repeat offender who committed theft of fairly trifling value, some $150, and their criminal records are comparable, including burglary (though Andrade's were residential), with no violent crimes or crimes against the person. The respective sentences, too, are strikingly alike. Although Andrade's petty thefts occurred on two separate occasions, his sentence can only be understood as punishment for the total amount he stole. The two thefts were separated by only two weeks; they involved the same victim; they apparently constituted parts of a single, continuing effort to finance drug sales; their seriousness is measured by the dollar value of the things taken; and the government charged both thefts in a single indictment. The state court accordingly spoke of his punishment collectively as well, carrying a 50-year minimum before parole eligibility, ("[W]e cannot say the sentence of 50 years to life at issue in this case is disproportionate"), and because Andrade was 37 years old when sentenced, the substantial 50-year period amounts to life without parole. The results under the Eighth Amendment should therefore be the same in each case. The only ways to reach a different conclusion are to reject the practical equivalence of a life sentence without parole and one with parole eligibility at 87, ("Andrade retains the possibility of parole"), or to discount the continuing authority of *Solem's* example, as the California court did, ("[T]he current validity of the *Solem* proportionality analysis is questionable"). The former is unrealistic; an 87-year-old man released after 50 years behind bars will have no real life left, if he survives to be released at all. And the latter, disparaging *Solem* as a point of reference on Eighth Amendment analysis, is wrong as a matter of law.

"The second reason that relief is required even under the §2254(d) unreasonable application standard rests on the alternative way of looking at Andrade's 50-year sentence as two separate 25-year applications of the three-strikes law, and construing the challenge here as going to the second, consecutive 25-year minimum term triggered by a petty theft. To understand why it is revealing to look at the sentence this way, it helps to recall the basic difficulty inherent in proportionality review. We require the comparison of offense and penalty to disclose a truly gross disproportionality before the constitutional limit is passed, in large part because we believe that legislatures are institutionally equipped with better judgment than courts in deciding what penalty is merited by particular behavior....

Whether or not one accepts the State's choice of penalogical policy as constitutionally sound, that policy cannot reasonably justify the imposition of a consecutive 25-year minimum for a second minor felony committed soon after the first triggering offense. Andrade did not somehow become twice as dangerous to society when he stole the second handful of videotapes; his dangerousness may justify treating one minor felony as serious and warranting long incapacitation, but a second such felony does not disclose greater danger warranting substantially longer incapacitation. Since the defendant's condition has not changed between the two closely related thefts, the incapacitation penalty is not open to the simple arithmetic of multiplying the punishment by two, without resulting in gross disproportion even under the State's chosen benchmark. Far from attempting a novel penal theory to justify doubling the sentence, the California Court of Appeal offered no comment at all as to the particular penal theory supporting such a punishment. Perhaps even more tellingly, no one could seriously argue that the second theft of videotapes provided any basis to think that Andrade would be so dangerous after 25 years, the date on which the consecutive sentence would begin to run, as to require at least 25 years more. I know of no jurisdiction that would add 25 years of imprisonment simply to reflect the fact that the two temporally related thefts took place on two separate occasions, and I am not surprised that California has found no such case, not even under its three-strikes law. In sum, the argument that repeating a trivial crime justifies doubling a 25-year minimum incapacitation sentence based on a threat to the public does not raise a seriously debatable point on which judgments might reasonably differ. The argument is irrational, and the state court's acceptance of it in response to a facially gross disproportion between triggering offense and penalty was unreasonable within the meaning of §2254(d).

"This is the rare sentence of demonstrable gross disproportionality, as the California Legislature may well have recognized when it specifically provided that a prosecutor may move to dismiss or strike a prior felony conviction "in the furtherance of justice." Cal.Penal Code Ann. §667(f)(2) (West 1999). In this case, the statutory safeguard failed, and the state court was left to ensure that the Eighth Amendment prohibition on grossly disproportionate sentences was met. If Andrade's sentence is not grossly disproportionate, the principle has no meaning. The California court's holding was an unreasonable application of clearly established precedent."

Notes

1. In "Reflections on the Guillotine," Albert Camus argued that capital punishment is never proportionate to the crime of murder.

> Let us leave aside the fact that the law of retaliation is inapplicable and that it would seem just as excessive to punish the incendiary by setting fire to his house as it would be insufficient to punish the thief by deducting from his bank account a sum equal to his theft. Let us admit that it is just and necessary to compensate for the murder of the victim by the death of the murderer. But beheading is not simply death. It is just as different, in essence, from the privation of life as a concentration camp is from prison. It is murder, to be sure, and one that arithmetically pays for the murder committed. But it adds to death a rule, a public premeditation known to the future victim, an organization, in short, which is in itself a source of moral sufferings more terrible than death. Hence there is no equivalence. Many laws consider a premeditated crime more serious than a crime of pure violence. But what then is capital punishment but the most premeditated of murders, to which no criminal's deed, however calculated it may be, can be compared? For there to be equivalence, the death penalty would have to punish a criminal who had warned his victim of the date at which he would inflict a horrible death on him and who, from that moment onward, had confined him at his mercy for months. Such a monster is not encountered in private life.

Camus, *Reflexions sur la peine Capitale* (Calmann-Levy 1957).

2. In 1994, spirited public debate in the United States focussed on whether 18-year-old Michael Fay, an American citizen, should be punished under Singapore's laws for vandalizing cars in that country. Fay confessed to spray-painting several vehicles in Singapore and was sentenced to receive six blows to his buttocks from a cane wielded by a martial arts expert. According to Fay's parents, the blows would leave Fay permanently scarred, both physically and psychologically. In the *Fay* case, Singapore sought to exercise its sovereign duty to impose on a United States citizen a punishment it routinely imposes on Singapore citizens. In a Dallas Morning News editorial, Harry Tatum wrote:

> We rail at nations that refuse to extradite brutal murderers to the United States because they don't allow capital punishment. We openly question

whether these violators will receive the penalties they deserve if they aren't tried here.

And then, when a young American teenager is sentenced to be flogged in another land, thousands of angry citizens call on our president and Singapore leaders to stop this brutality. We don't ask how many other young people have been beaten in Singapore for the same offense. It is Michael Fay we are concerned about because he's one of us.

The issue here is not whether Singapore has gone too far in its relentless quest for a crime-free city. The issue is whether the United States has the right to protest the caning of a U.S. citizen when it never argued against the application of the law to others who were punished in the same manner.

Tatum, *The Fate of Young Michael Fay*, The Dallas Morning News, Apr. 20, 1994.

In response to public outcry, President Clinton admonished the Singapore government that it would be a "mistake" to flog Fay. Shortly thereafter, Singapore reduced Fay's punishment to four blows. Fay was flogged on May 4, 1994 and his condition was reported as "satisfactory."

By October of 1994, Michael Fay was recovering from substance abuse in Minnesota. Fay was admitted to the Hazelden rehabilitation clinic after acknowledging that he had been regularly getting high by inhaling butane from pressurized cans. He blames the habit on the trauma of his caning in Singapore earlier that year for vandalizing cars — a crime he insists he did not commit. *Recovering, Michael Fay*, Time, Oct. 10, 1994.

In *Stanford v. Kentucky* (*infra*, chapter 5), the United States Supreme Court rejected the notion that evolving standards of decency are to be assessed by reference to the standards of foreign countries. ("We emphasize that it is *American* conceptions of decency that are dispositive, rejecting the contention of petitioners and their various *amici* that the sentencing practices of other countries are relevant....") Cf. *Roper v. Simmons, infra*, chapter 5.

3. As noted above, the same day the Court handed down *Lockyer v. Andrade*, it rejected a similar Eighth Amendment challenge in *Ewing v. California*, 538 U.S. 11 (2003). While on parole from a 9-year prison term, Gary Ewing walked into the pro shop of the El Segundo Golf Course in Los Angeles County. He walked out with three golf clubs, priced at $399 each, concealed in his pants leg. A shop employee, whose suspicions were aroused when he observed Ewing limp out of the pro shop, telephoned the police. The police arrested Ewing in the parking lot.

Because of prior convictions, Ewing — like Andrade — was subject to California's mandatory three strikes law and was sentenced to life, with no parole for at least 25 years. While many other states have versions of three-strikes laws, most require that the third offense be a violent or at least serious felony. Justice Breyer included an appendix to his dissenting opinion that analyzed how a defendant with Mr. Ewing's record would fare under the various state laws. He could have received no more than 10 years in 33 states, and 12 to 18 months in the federal system. Although in nine states Ewing could theoretically have received 25 years or more, Justice Breyer said that most of those states offered an earlier possibility of parole.

Do you think the majority in *Andrade* successfully reconciled *Solem* and *Harmelin*? Or are you persuaded by Justice Souter's dissenting observation regarding Andrade's sentence of 50 years for stealing nine videotapes worth about $150? According to Souter, "If Andrade's sentence is not grossly disproportionate, the principle has no meaning."

C. The Importance of State Constitutional Law

As *Michigan v. Bullock* demonstrates, state constitutional law plays a significant role in capital cases. Below, Professor Louis Bilionis challenges state judges to interpret their respective state constitutions independent of the Supreme Court's interpretation of the federal constitution.

Legitimating Death

Louis D. Bilionis, 91 Mich. L. Rev. 1643 (1993).

A. Critical Independent Assessments Under the State Constitution

Much has been written about the renaissance of state constitutional law, and lawyers everywhere now comprehend that the states are free to interpret their own constitutions to grant more rights and protections to individuals charged with crimes than the federal Constitution requires. Getting a state court to act with constitutional independence in a capital case is not, however, an easy feat to accomplish. On the one hand, there are craft-related obstacles. Rarely will the language used in the relevant state constitutional texts differ from the Eighth Amendment in ways material enough to invite, let alone compel, a fundamentally different interpretation; most state provisions simply prohibit, as does the Eighth Amendment, the imposition of "cruel and unusual punishments." Nor is there likely to be much precedent directly construing the state constitution that might bring a meaning to that text that is substantially broader than the federal. On the other hand, entrenched attitudes also conspire to retard the development of a state constitutional capital jurisprudence. State judges are not by predisposition a leftward leaning lot eager to bestow new rights upon murderers, and, in states where the judiciary is elected, some portion of the bench is apt to consider it a questionable career move to support more protections for killers than the U.S. Supreme Court says they have "a right to." In addition to these realistic if fairly crass considerations, there also exists a deeply ingrained tendency on the part of state jurists to regard the Supreme Court as the definitive expositor of all things constitutional. Given the sweeping, intricate web of death penalty law already woven by the Justices in Washington, state judges—mere mortal souls that they are—have trouble imagining there might be anything of constitutional magnitude remaining for them to contribute.

State jurists who think in this manner have surely overestimated the Supreme Court's capital jurisprudence. If the foregoing examination of balancing's role in capital cases makes nothing else clear, it demonstrates that the Supreme Court's death penalty jurisprudence leaves a potentially large constitutional void unfilled. Precisely because the Court balances, the rules it lays down do not coextend with the Eighth Amendment's normative content, do not exhaust the potential of those constitutional values, and do not ensure a normatively legitimate system of capital punishment. As Lawrence Sager would put it, "what the members of the federal tribunal have actually determined is that there are good reasons for stopping short of exhausting the content of the constitutional concept with which they are dealing," leaving in the process an "unenforced margin[ ] of underenforced norms." This constitutional vacuum exists in the death penalty area solely because the Supreme Court finds its own ability to implement constitutional norms constrained by institutional and structural limitations. The problem is the Court's grasp, not the reach of the underlying norms.

Therein lies the key to unleashing the potential of state constitutional law. Nature abhors a vacuum, and so too, in its own way, does our national constitutional environment. State constitutions are a force that can fill the void, adding a measure of enforcement to constitutional norms that the Supreme Court, because of its own limitations, cannot itself provide. Thus conceived, state constitutional law is not a liberal activist's ploy to *evade* the Supreme Court's Eighth Amendment doctrine, but in fact an integral means to *complement* the federal law.

The norms that the Supreme Court uses to address capital punishment's fundamental legitimacy are not exclusive to the federal Constitution. The principles of moral appropriateness, rational orderliness, and procedural fairness resonate as convincingly within the boundaries of a state as they do throughout the nation at large and thus can act as norms of state constitutional law that the state judiciary is obligated to enforce. In implementing these norms, a state court might well reserve the same right to balance that the U.S. Supreme Court reserves for itself, accommodating whatever relevant concerns might weigh against the fullest enforcement of the values in question. The important point, however, is that a state court will have to balance *for itself* because the concerns that are relevant to the exercise of state judicial power are not the same as those which are germane to federal action. Federal and state courts are different institutions differently positioned, facing different claims on the exercise of their powers and different restraining influences. The costs associated with the use of federal judicial power are one matter; the costs of using state judicial power to the same end can be quite another. It makes no sense, indeed it is unprincipled and irrational, for a state court uncritically to adopt as its own a balance struck by the U.S. Supreme Court. Depending on the circumstances, it is certainly possible for the federal balance and the state balance to tilt in the same direction. But this possibility cannot be confirmed until the state court balances the relevant considerations independently with intelligent awareness of the various differences.

To illustrate, imagine a jurist grappling with the application of capital punishment to mentally retarded offenders. Suppose, further, that study had led the judge to recognize that cases exist in which the severity of the offender's handicap render the death penalty an excessive and hence morally inappropriate punishment. What rule should the judge announce to implement the constitutional principle of moral appropriateness in these situations? One viable possibility would be to draw a line that categorically immunizes from the death penalty those offenders for whom it would most likely be excessive. But what are the costs of using judicial power in that way? The answer depends on where this hypothetical judge sits.

If the President appointed this judge to the Supreme Court, the proposed ruling's impact on federalism values and on the federal judiciary's effectiveness would weigh in her balancing. This justice might note that state legislatures and courts have not wholly ignored the mentally retarded offender's claim to constitutional protection; indeed, most states deal with the problem by having their capital sentencers consider the offender's mental retardation as a mitigating circumstance entitled to some, but not legally dispositive, weight in an overall sentencing calculus. Supplanting those state judgments in favor of broader protection might be desirable but inevitably would come at a price. Distanced from those state determinations, the Supreme Court justice usually cannot know how much, if any, reflection and deliberation went into them. Federalism protocol thus prescribes—until some contrary reason surfaces—that the Court treat expressions of state policy as the products of reasoned, good faith efforts to harmonize local wants with respect for constitutional principles. When the court overrides these dignified-by-hypothesis efforts, the authority of state institutions receives a direct hit, their enthusiasm for experimentation wanes, and the Court's own reservoir of good will dips. Moreover, these consequences are magnified if the Court's preferred rule is, as bright-line formulations sometimes are, open to easy criticism as inappropriately legislative in nature. How strongly these considerations figure in the final balance need not be of concern now, although readers familiar with *Penry v. Lynaugh* (*infra* chapter 5) know the decisive weight that the Supreme Court assigned to them. For our purposes, it is enough to identify them.

If the judge presides on the state supreme court and undertakes to evaluate the wisdom of the same rule under the state constitution, the countervailing considerations should look different for reasons entirely associated with the jurisdictional change. First and most obviously, any adverse institutional ramifications of granting greater protection to the mentally retarded offender are bound to be fewer in number and less daunting in magnitude simply because they will be confined to a single jurisdiction. State courts work in a relatively closed microcosm; rarely, and even then only if they really exert themselves, can they make state constitutional capital punishment law that does any appreciable violence to another state's institutions or impedes another state's freedom to experiment and meet local needs. Second, the court's close proximity to the affected system will allow it to give the potential institutional costs a finer appraisal and more accurate accounting. Unlike the Supreme Court, which must generalize across the nation, state judges enjoy an intimate familiarity with how policy and law are formulated at the state level, since they help produce the tapestry of constitutional, legislative, and judge-made law that constitutes the state's *corpus juris.* They know firsthand the roles of the various institutions of state government, their strengths and weaknesses, and the legal and customary relationships between them. State judges understand better than most the structure and operation of the state's criminal justice system. They need not indulge in speculative assumptions about the climate that produced the state's modern capital punishment enactments and the judicial constructions that have been placed upon them.

How might this potential advantage affect the judge's determination in the case of the mentally retarded offender? Depending upon the state in question, she might conclude that a more protective state constitutional rule would not impinge upon institutional prerogatives or principles of democratic self-governance in the way that a generalized conjecture might lead her to fear.

A close look might reveal, first, that the local practice of treating mental retardation as a mitigating circumstance in the sentencing decision does not represent a considered societal judgment *against* broader protection. Perhaps the practice originated in the post-*Furman* rush to get *some* capital sentencing law on the books that stood a chance of winning the Supreme Court's approval, or maybe it simply came about as a defensive reaction to *Lockett v. Ohio*'s dictate that all mitigating factors at the very least be put to the sentencer for its consideration. In either case, there is a substantial likelihood that neither the People nor any of their state institutions actually rejected greater protection for the mentally retarded offender's constitutional interest as an inordinate sacrifice of other state interests. Implementing the more protective rule, accordingly, would not signify a direct challenge to another department's judgment.

A decision to promulgate the more protective rule would curtail the legislature's freedom to respond differently to the problem in days to come. Rulings of genuinely constitutional dimension generally have that effect, but further inquiry by the state court could reveal good reasons for discounting its seriousness in this case. State laws, policies, traditions, and practices, for instance, may demonstrate an ambivalence about using the death penalty in the case of mentally retarded offenders that belies any claim that significant countervailing interests need debate in the political arena. The treatment of the mentally retarded in other contexts within and beyond the criminal justice system might fortify that conclusion. Furthermore, local sources also might provide a vocabulary the court could use in articulating the new, more protective state constitutional rule, ensuring a smoother integration of the rule into existing practice and blunting any charge that the court's standard lacks an acceptable foundation.

When considerations like the foregoing are present, they can swing the balance decisively in favor of broader judicial enforcement of the constitutional norm. So it was in *Fleming v. Zant*, [386 S.E.2d 339 (Ga. 1989),] a Georgia Supreme Court decision forbidding the death penalty for mentally retarded offenders under the state constitution. True, the case was especially easy because Georgia's legislature had recently passed a statute prospectively immunizing the mentally retarded from capital punishment. A different state court facing different local conditions should not follow *Fleming* uncritically, for the question might be considerably closer in its own jurisdiction. But, for the very same reason, it would be a mistake for that court to accept uncritically the balance struck by the U.S. Supreme Court in *Penry*. Independent judgment is necessary, and independent judgment is where state constitutional law begins.

There are signs that state court judges have started to think in these terms in death cases. In a textbook example of critical independent assessment, the Louisiana Supreme court held in *State v. Perry* (*infra*, chapter 5) that the state constitutional prohibition against cruel, excessive, or unusual punishment forbids the practice of forcibly medicating a defendant in order to make him sane enough to be executed. Pivotal to the case was the court's candid recognition that it need not, as a state court adjudicating under the state constitution, indulge in the kind of deferential assumptions that federalism principles might require if the case arose under the federal Constitution. From that premise, the court confidently concluded that the practice in question would infringe upon a "well-established norm," the moral prohibition against execution of a prisoner who has lost his sanity, without a hint of justification that this conclusion was founded upon local consensus or legislative pronouncement. Of similar import is the Colorado Supreme Court's decision in *People v. Young*, 814 P.2d 234 (Colo. 1991). There, the court relied upon its appreciation of the facts of local institutional life—to wit, a trial level sentencer's superiority over the legislature when it comes to rendering judgments about the moral correctness of the death penalty in specific factual settings—to invalidate legislation that required imposition of the death penalty upon a jury finding that aggravating and mitigating circumstances balance equally. Critical independent assessments have also been undertaken, with expectedly mixed results, in Tennessee, Indiana, New Jersey, and North Carolina.

I suspect that some hard-core death penalty supporters take a dim view of these developments, but believers in federalism should be pleased. The federal system is at its best when the states understand their independent obligation to heed and promote constitutional values. No governmental institution—federal or state; executive, legislative, or judicial—can singlehandedly ensure the full realization of constitutional values. The task requires tremendous power, much more than the American people have been willing to entrust in any single governmental body. That power has been diffused vertically and horizontally throughout the federal system to guard against its abuse—but not to prevent it from effectuating constitutional norms. When a state court grasps these basics and uses its power to supplement the enforcement of fundamental values pursuant to the state constitution, listen carefully to the objections and consider the source.

Note

Other articles which discuss the role of state constitutional law in death penalty cases include: Eastman, "The Progress of Our Maturing Society: An Analysis of State Sanctioned Violence," 39 Washburn L.J. 526 (2000); Twist, "The Debate Over Arizona's Death Penalty," 37-NOV Ariz. Att'y 26 (2000); Robinson, "Improving Process In Virginia Capital Cases," 12 Cap. Def. J. 363 (2000); Symposium, "Rights and Freedoms Under the State Constitution," 13 Touro L. Rev. 59 (1996). See *Lambert v. State, infra,* chapter 5.

D. Evolving Standards of Decency

Note: Trop v. Dulles, 356 U.S. 86 (1958)

In 1944, a private in the United States Army stationed in French Morocco escaped from a stockade at Casablanca where he was being held for a breach of discipline. Albert L. Trop had been gone for less than a day when he willingly surrendered to an officer while he was returning to his base. Following a court-martial, Trop was convicted of desertion and sentenced to three years of hard labor, forfeiture of all pay and allowances, and a dishonorable discharge. When Trop's application for a passport was denied in 1952, he learned that a federal statute had stripped him of his citizenship by reason of his conviction and dishonorable discharge for wartime desertion.

The United States Supreme Court granted certiorari to decide whether denationalization is a cruel and unusual punishment within the meaning of the Eighth Amendment. The Court summarily disposed of the proportionality question: "Since wartime desertion is punishable by death, there can be no argument that the penalty of denationalization is excessive in relation to the gravity of the offense." Nonetheless, the Court recognized a "principle of civilized treatment guaranteed by the Eighth Amendment" and measured Trop's penalty against that standard.

According to Chief Justice Warren's plurality opinion:

> At the outset, let us put to one side the death penalty as an index of the constitutional limit on punishment. Whatever the arguments may be against capital punishment, both on moral grounds and in terms of accomplishing the purposes of punishment—and they are forceful—the death penalty has been employed throughout our history, and, in a day when it is still widely accepted, it cannot be said to violate the constitutional concept of cruelty. But it is equally plain that the existence of the death penalty is not a license for the Government to devise any punishment short of death within the limit of its imagination.... The Court recognized in [*Weems v. United States,* 217 U.S. 349

(1910),] that the words of the [Eighth] Amendment are not precise and their scope is not static. The Amendment must draw its meaning from the evolving standards of decency that mark the progress of a maturing society.

Interpreting the Eighth Amendment in accordance with "evolving standards of decency," the Court held that "the use of denationalization as a punishment is barred by the Eighth Amendment." Critical to its holding was the Court's observation that "[t]he civilized nations of the world are in virtual unanimity that statelessness is not to be imposed as punishment for crime."

Notes and Questions

1. The English Declaration of Rights was enacted on December 16, 1689. The Bill of Rights—the first ten amendments to the United States Constitution—was ratified effective December 15, 1791. Although both documents prohibit "cruel and unusual punishments," some rather brutal criminal sanctions were regularly imposed, both in England and the colonies. Which of the following penalties would violate the Eighth Amendment as interpreted in accordance with "evolving standards of decency"? Branding? Maiming? Drowning? Burning to death? Ducking stool? Boiling to death? Pressing to death? Drawing and quartering? Beheading? Jougs (chaining someone to the church door by means of a locked, heavy iron collar)? Whipping? Stocks (subjecting to public ridicule a seated prisoner whose legs are locked securely between two interlocking pieces of wood)? Pillorying (subjecting to public ridicule a standing prisoner whose head and hands are secured between two interlocking pieces of wood)? For more detailed descriptions of these modes of punishment, see Andrews, *Old Time Punishments* (Dorsett Press 1991) and Earle, *Curious Punishments of Bygone Days* (Singing Tree Press 1968).

2. Given the *Trop* Court's emphasis on the practices and laws of the civilized nations of the world, should the death penalty be subject to invalidation on Eighth Amendment grounds if it can be shown that "all civilized nations" have either abolished capital punishment or refuse to impose it? What if it can be demonstrated that among Western nations the United States is the sole country to utilize the death penalty? For a more modern view of the Court's willingness to measure the death penalty laws in this country against the practices and laws of other nations, see *Thompson v. Oklahoma, Stanford v. Kentucky*, and *Roper v. Simmons, infra* chapter 5.

3. Does *Trop*'s holding suggest that denationalization is a punishment worse than death? While conceding that executing a wartime deserter is not an excessive punishment, the plurality nonetheless holds that stripping a wartime deserter's citizenship constitutes cruel and unusual punishment. Does this make sense? Perhaps the answer lies in the Court's characterization of denationalization: "There may be involved no physical mistreatment, no primitive torture. There is instead the total destruction of the individual's status in organized society. It is a form of punishment more primitive than torture, for it destroys for the individual the political existence that was centuries in the development."

4. In a footnote, the *Trop* Court discussed whether the word "unusual" has any qualitative meaning different from "cruel." Although the Court declared the answer to be "unclear," it noted, "If the word 'unusual' is to have any meaning apart from the word 'cruel,'... the meaning should be the ordinary one, signifying something different from that which is generally done." Measured by this standard, denationalization was "unusual" since it was never explicitly sanctioned by the government until 1940 and had never been tested against the Constitution until the *Trop* case.

5. Other decisions since 1976, which addressed the Eighth Amendment in the context of prison conditions lawsuits, demonstrate that the Court remains faithful to *Trop's* requirement that "evolving standards of decency" guide Eighth Amendment analysis. In *Hudson v. McMillian*, 503 U.S. 1 (1992), an inmate in a Louisiana prison sued his guards for a beating he received while shackled. While escorting Hudson to a "lockdown" area of the prison, guards punched and kicked him. Hudson successfully sued under 42 U.S.C. §1983 (the federal civil rights statute) and was awarded $800 in damages.

The Supreme Court held that force used by a prison guard need not cause "significant injury" to constitute cruel and unusual punishment. Writing for the majority, Justice O'Connor said, "We hold that whenever prison officials stand accused of using excessive physical force in violation of the Cruel and Unusual Punishments Clause, the core judicial inquiry is that set out in *Whitley* [*v. Albers*, 475 U.S. 312 (1986)]: whether force was applied in a good-faith effort to maintain or restore discipline, or maliciously and sadistically to cause harm." Although the extent of the injury suffered by a prisoner is not dispositive, it is relevant. And, while "contemporary standards of decency" inform Eighth Amendment analysis in this area, Justice O'Connor noted that society does not expect prisoners to live in comfort or to have unqualified access to health care. Consequently, deprivations in *those* areas must attain relatively high degrees of seriousness before they are actionable. On the other hand, "when prison officials maliciously and sadistically use force to cause harm, contemporary standards of decency always are violated ... whether or not significant injury is evident."

Justice Thomas, joined by Justice Scalia, dissented. Characterizing Hudson's injuries as minor (the trial judge found that Hudson had suffered bruises and swelling in the face, mouth and lip, loosened teeth, and a cracked dental plate), Justice Thomas observed, "surely prison was not a more congenial place in the early years of the Republic than it is today." Justice Thomas accused the majority of expanding the Cruel and Unusual Punishments Clause "beyond all bounds of history and precedent" and warned, "The Eighth Amendment is not, and should not be turned into, a National Code of Prison Regulation."

The following term, in *Helling v. McKinney*, 509 U.S. 25 (1993), the Court held that exposure to harmful amounts of secondhand cigarette smoke may sometimes violate a prison inmate's constitutional rights. In a 7–2 decision, the Court allowed William McKinney, a Nevada inmate, to pursue his claim that being forced to share a cell with an inmate who smoked five packs of cigarettes a day constituted cruel and unusual punishment. Writing for the Court, Justice White cautioned that, in order to prevail, the inmate "must show that he himself is being exposed to unreasonably high levels" of secondhand smoke. In addition, "the prisoner must show that the risk of which he complains is not one that today's society chooses to tolerate."

Justice Thomas, again joined by Justice Scalia, dissented. Justice Thomas complained that the Court had expanded the Eighth Amendment still further—this time to a prisoner's mere *risk* of injury.

6. In 1994, the United States Supreme Court heard a case brought by state prisoner Dee Farmer, a preoperative transsexual who projected feminine characteristics. Farmer was transferred to a penitentiary where he claimed he was beaten and raped. Farmer sued alleging that prison officials knew that the penitentiary had a history of inmate assaults and that Farmer would be particularly vulnerable to sexual attack. The lower courts rejected Farmer's suit because they believed prison officials lacked knowledge of the risk to Farmer because Farmer never expressed to them any concern for his safety.

The United States Supreme Court vacated and clarified the "deliberate indifference" standard for Eighth Amendment liability in *Farmer v. Brennan*, 511 U.S. 825 (1994). There, the Court held that an inmate alleging deliberate indifference to inmate health or safety must prove, by direct or circumstantial evidence, that prison officials knew that the inmate faced a substantial risk of serious harm and disregarded that risk by failing to take reasonable measures to abate it. Therefore, subjective recklessness, as it is understood in the criminal law, is the appropriate test for deliberate indifference. Whether prison officials had the requisite knowledge is a question of fact. Failure to alleviate a significant risk that prison officials should have perceived but did not perceive does not rise to the level of deliberate indifference.

Applying these principles to Farmer's case required a remand because the lower courts may have placed dispositive weight on the fact that Farmer never notified prison officials that he was in danger.

7. Perhaps the arguments regarding evolving standards of decency should be foreshadowed by this quote from Justice Benjamin N. Cardozo:

> I have faith ... that a century or less from now, our descendants will look back upon the penal system of today with the same surprise and horror that fill our own minds when we are told that only about a century ago 160 crimes were visited under English law with the punishment of death, and that in 1801 a child of 13 was hanged at Tyburn for the larceny of a spoon. Dark chapters are these in the history of law. We think of them with a shudder, and say to ourselves that we have risen to heights of mercy and of reason far removed from such enormities. The future may judge us less leniently than we choose to judge ourselves.

Cahn, *Confronting Injustice* 308 (Little, Brown & Co. 1966) (quoted in *Pope v. United States*, 373 F.2d 710, 740 n.4 (8th Cir. 1967)).

E. Modern Methods of Execution

1. Overview

Of the thirty-eight states with the death penalty, thirty-seven utilize lethal injection as the primary execution method. Nebraska is the only state that uses electrocution as its sole method of execution. Most states that utilize lethal injection have another method as "backup."

This Is Your Death

Jacob Weisberg, The New Republic, July 1, 1991

Thanks to the decision of a California district judge last week the American public has been spared the spectacle of criminals being executed on television. But the lawsuit, filed by KQED, the public television station in San Francisco, still served a useful function. It reminded people not only that the United States remains the only advanced democracy that executes criminals, but that it is the only country in the world with a grotesque array of execution techniques worth televising. A century ago Americans knew full well what it meant for the state to hang someone from the end of a rope. Today, thanks to the century-long search for a more "humane" method, we know little about the range of practices that would be featured on the execution channel.

[Hanging]

Of the five means of execution still extant in the United States, the oldest is hanging, which was nearly universal before 1900. The gallows was last used in Kansas in 1965 and remains an option in Delaware, Montana, and Washington State.[11] If a hanging were ever televised, viewers would see the blindfolded prisoner standing on a trap door with a rope fastened around his neck, the knot under his left ear. So long as he is hooded, it is impossible to know for how long after the trap door opens the victim suffers, or at what point he loses consciousness. But according to Harold Hillman, a British physiologist who has studied executions, the dangling person feels cervical pain, and probably suffers from an acute headache as well, a result of the rope closing off the veins of the neck.

In the opinion of Dr. Cornelius Rosse, the chairman of the Department of Anatomy at the University of Washington School of Medicine, the belief that fracture of the spinal cord causes instantaneous death is wrong in all but a small fraction of cases. The actual cause of death is strangulation or suffocation. In medical terms, the weight of the prisoner's body causes tearing of the cervical muscles, skin, and blood vessels. The upper cervical vertebrae are dislocated, and the spinal cord is separated from the brain, which causes death.

Clinton Duffy, the warden at San Quentin from 1942 to 1954, who participated in sixty hangings described his first thus:

> *The man hit bottom and I observed that he was fighting by pulling on the straps, wheezing, whistling, trying to get air, that blood was oozing through the black cap. I observed also that he urinated, defecated, and droppings fell on the floor, and the stench was terrible. I also saw witnesses pass out and have to be carried from the witness room. Some of them threw up.*

> *It took ten minutes for the condemned man to die. When he was taken down and the cap removed, "big hunks of flesh were torn off" the side of his face where the noose has been, "his eyes were popped," and his tongue was "swollen and hanging from his mouth." His face had also turned purple.*

The annals of Walla Walla State Penitentiary in Washington, which was seeking to hire an executioner in 1988 when Charles Campbell obtained a stay of execution, are filled with horror stories: prisoners partially decapitated by overlong drops, or pleading with hangmen to take them up and drop them again.

[Firing Squad]

Almost as rare as hanging—but still around—is the firing squad. Gary Gilmore, who was shot in Utah in 1977, was the last to die by this method, which remains an option only there and in Idaho. Gilmore was bound to a chair with leather straps across his waist and head, in front of an oval-shaped canvas wall. A black hood was pulled over his head. A doctor then located his heart with a stethoscope and pinned a circular white cloth target over it. Five shooters armed with .30-caliber rifles loaded with single rounds (one of them blank to spare the conscience of the executioners) stood in an enclosure twenty feet away. Each man aimed his rifle through a slot in the canvas and fired.

---

11. Washington State executed Westley A. Dodd by hanging on January 5, 1993. [Ed.]

Though shooting through the head at close range causes nearly instantaneous death, a prisoner subjected to a firing squad dies as a result of blood loss caused by rupture of the heart or a large blood vessel, or tearing of the lungs. The person shot loses consciousness when shock causes a fall in the supply of blood to the brain. If the shooters miss, by accident or intention, the prisoner bleeds to death slowly, as Elisio J. Mares did in Utah in 1951. It took Gilmore two minutes to die.

[**Electric Chair**]

It was to mitigate the barbarism of these primitive methods that New York introduced the electric chair in 1890 as a humane alternative. Eighty-three people have been electrocuted since the Supreme Court reinstated capital punishment in 1976, making the method the most common one now in use. It is probably the most gruesome to watch. After being led into the death chamber, the prisoner is strapped to the chair with belts that cross his chest, groin, legs, and arms. Two copper electrodes are then attached: one to his leg, a patch of which will have been shaved bare to reduce resistance to electricity, and another to his shaved head. The electrodes are either soaked in brine or treated with gel (Electro-Creme) to increase conductivity and reduce burning. The prisoner will also be wearing a diaper.

The executioner gives a first jolt of between 500 and 2,000 volts, which lasts for thirty seconds. Smoke usually comes out of the prisoner's leg and head. A doctor them examines him. If he's not dead, another jolt is applied. A third and fourth are given if needed to finish the job. It took five jolts to kill Ethel Rosenberg. In the grisly description of Justice Brennan:

> ... the prisoner's eyeballs sometimes pop out and rest on [his] cheeks. The prisoner often defecates, urinates, and vomits blood and drool. The body turns bright red as its temperature rises and the prisoner's flesh swells and his skin stretches to the point of breaking. Sometimes the prisoner catches on fire, particularly if [he] perspires excessively. Witnesses hear a loud and sustained sound like bacon frying and the sickly sweet smell of burning flesh permeates the chamber.

An electrocuted corpse is hot enough to blister if touched. Thus autopsy must be delayed while internal organs cool. According to Robert H. Kirschner, the deputy chief medical examiner of Cook County, Illinois, "The brain appears cooked in most cases."

There is some debate about what the electrocuted prisoner experiences before he dies, but most doctors I spoke to believe that he feels himself being burned to death and suffocating, since the shock causes respiratory paralysis as well as cardiac arrest. According to Hillman, "It must feel very similar to the medieval trial by ordeal of being dropped in boiling oil." Because the energy of the shock paralyzes the prisoner's muscles, he cannot cry out. "My mouth tasted like cold peanut butter. I felt a burning in my head and my left leg, and I jumped against the straps," Willie Francis, a 17-year-old who survived an attempted execution in 1946, is reported to have said. Francis was successfully executed a year later.

Though all methods of execution can be botched, electrocutions go wrong frequently and dramatically, in part because the equipment is old and hard to repair. At least five have gone awry since 1983. If the electrical current is too weak, the prisoner roasts to death slowly. An instance of this was the May 4, 1990, killing of Jesse Joseph Tafero in Florida. According to witnesses, when the executioner flipped the switch, flames and smoke came out of Tafero's head, which was covered by a mask and cap. Twelve-inch blue and orange flames sprouted from both sides of the mask. The power was stopped, and Tafero took several deep breaths. The superintendent ordered the executioner to halt the current, then try it again. And again.

The affidavits presented for an internal inquiry into what went wrong describe the bureaucratization of the death penalty brilliantly. In the words of one of the officials:

> ... while working in the Death Chamber, proceeding with the execution as scheduled, I received an indication from Mr. Barton to close my electric breaker. I then told the executioner to close his electric breaker. When the executioner completed the circuit, I noticed unusual fire and smoke coming from the inmate's headpiece. After several seconds, I received an indication to open the electrical breaker to stop the electrical flow. At this time, I noticed the body move as to be gasping for air. After several seconds, I received the indication to close the breaker the second time, which I did. Again, I noticed the unusual fire and smoke coming from the headpiece. After several seconds, I received the third indication to close the breaker, and again, the fire and smoke came from the headpiece ...

And so on. Apparently a synthetic sponge, soaked in brine, had been substituted for the natural one applied to Tafero's head. This reduced the flow of electricity to as little as one hundred volts, and ended up torturing the prisoner to death. According to the state prison medical director, Frank Kligo, who attended, it was "less than aesthetically attractive."

[Gas Chamber]

Advanced technology does not always make the death penalty less painful to undergo or more pleasant to watch. The gas chamber, which was invented by an army medical corps officer after World War I, was first introduced as a humane alternative to the electric chair in 1924 in Nevada. The original idea, which proved impracticable, was to surprise the prisoner by gassing him in his cell without prior warning. Seven states, including California, still use the gas chamber. The most recent fatality was Leo Edwards, a 36-year-old who was killed in Jackson County, Mississippi, in 1989.[12]

Had KQED won its suit, millions of viewers would have joined a dozen live witnesses in seeing Robert Alton Harris, who murdered two teenage boys in San Diego in 1978, led into a green, octagonal room in the basement of San Quentin Penitentiary. Inside the chamber are two identical metal chairs with perforated seats, marked "A" and "B." The twin chairs were last used in double execution in 1962. If Harris's execution goes ahead this year or next, two orderlies will fasten him into chair A, attaching straps across his upper and lower legs, arms, groin, and chest. They will also affix a long stethoscope to Harris's chest so that a doctor on the outside can pronounce death.

Beneath the chair is a bowl filled with sulfuric acid mixed with distilled water with a pound of sodium cyanide pellets suspended in a gauze bag just above. After the door is sealed, and when the warden gives the signal, an executioner in a separate room flicks a lever that releases the cyanide into the liquid. This causes a chemical reaction that releases hydrogen cyanide gas, which rises through the holes in the chair. Like most death row prisoners, Harris is likely to have been reduced to a state of passive acquiescence by his years on death row, and will probably follow the advice of the warden to breathe deeply as soon as he smells rotten eggs. As long as he holds his breath nothing will happen. But as soon as he inhales, according to the testimony of Duffy, the former warden,

---

12. On August 24, 1993, David Mason was executed in California's gas chamber. California has since switched to lethal injection. [Ed.]

Harris will lose consciousness in a few seconds. "At first there is evidence of extreme horror, pain, and strangling. The eyes pop. The skin turns purple and the victim begins to drool. It is a horrible sight," he testified.

In medical terms, victims of cyanide gas die from hypoxia, which means the cut-off of oxygen to the brain. The initial result of this is spasms, as in an epileptic seizure. Because of the straps, however, involuntary body movements are restrained. Seconds after he first inhales, Harris will feel himself unable to breathe, but will not lose consciousness immediately. "The person is unquestionably experiencing pain and extreme anxiety," according to Dr. Richard Traystman of Johns Hopkins. "The pain begins immediately and is felt in the arms, shoulders, back, and chest. The sensation is similar to the pain felt by a person during a heart attack, where essentially the heart is being deprived of oxygen." Traystman adds: "We would not use asphyxiation, by cyanide gas or by any other substance, in our laboratory to kill animals that have been used in experiments."

Harris will stop wriggling after ten or twelve minutes, and the doctor will pronounce him dead. An exhaust fan then sucks the poison air out of the chamber. Next the corpse is sprayed with ammonia, which neutralizes traces of the cyanide that may remain. After about half an hour, orderlies enter the chamber, wearing gas masks and rubber gloves. Their training manual advises them to ruffle the victim's hair to release any trapped cyanide gas before removing him.[13]

[Lethal Injection]

Thanks to these grotesqueries, states are increasingly turning to lethal injection. This method was imagined for decades (by Ronald Reagan, among others, when he was governor of California in 1973), but was technically invented in 1977 by Dr. Stanley Deutsch, who at the time chaired the Anesthesiology Department at Oklahoma University Medical School. In response to a call by an Oklahoma state senator for a cheaper alternative to repairing the state's derelict electric chair, Deutsch described a way to administer drugs through an intravenous drip so as to cause death rapidly and without pain. "Having been anesthetized on several occasions with ultra short-acting barbiturates and having administered these drugs for approximately 20 years, I can assure you that this is a rapid, pleasant way of producing unconsciousness," Deutsch wrote to state senator Bill Dawson in February 1977. The method was promptly adopted in Oklahoma, and is now either the exclusive method or an option in half of the thirty-six states with death penalty laws. It is becoming the method of choice around the country because it is easier on both the witnesses and the prisoner.

A recent injectee was Lawrence Lee Buxton, who was killed in Huntsville, Texas, on February 26, [1991]. Buxton was strapped to a hospital gurney, built with an extension panel for his left arm. Technicians stuck a catheter needle into Buxton's arm. Long tubes connected the needle through a hole in a cement block wall to several intravenous drips. The first, which was started immediately, dispensed harmless saline solution. Then, at the warden's signal, a curtain went up, which permitted the witnesses—reporters and friends of the soon-to-be deceased—to view the scene. Unlike some prisoners, Buxton did not have a long wait before the warden received a call from the governor's office, giving the final go-ahead.

According to Lawrence Egbert, an anesthesiologist at the University of Texas in Dallas who has campaigned against lethal injection as a perversion of medical practice, the

---

13. Robert Alton Harris died in California's gas chamber on April 21, 1992. [Ed.]

first drug administered was sodium thiopental, a common barbiturate used as an anesthetic, which puts patients quickly to sleep. A normal dose for a long operation is 1,000 milligrams; Buxton got twice that. As soon as he lost consciousness, the executioner administered pavulon, another common muscle relaxant used in heart surgery. The dose was 100 milligrams, ten times the usual, which stops the prisoner's breathing. This would have killed him in about ten minutes; to speed the process, an equal dose of potassium chloride was subsequently administered. This is another drug commonly used in bypass surgery that relaxes the heart and stops it pumping. It works in about ten seconds. All witnesses heard was the prisoner take a deep breath, then a gurgling noise as his tongue dropped back in his mouth. Watt Espy, who has compiled a list of 17,718 executions in America, from the early period of drownings, burnings, sawings-in-half, pressings-to-death, and even the crucifixions of two mutinous Continental Army soldiers, compares lethal injection to the way a devoted owner treats "a faithful dog he loved and cherished."

The only physical pain, if the killing is done correctly, "is the pain of the initial prick of the needle," according to Traystman. There are, however, some potential hitches. Since doctors are precluded by medical ethics from participating in executions except to pronounce death, the injections are often performed by incompetent or inexperienced technicians. If a death worker injects the drugs into muscle instead of a vein, or if the needle becomes clogged, extreme pain can result. This is what happened when James Autry was killed in 1984 in Texas. *Newsweek* reported that he "took at least ten minutes to die and throughout much of that time was conscious, moving about, and complaining of pain." Many prisoners have damaged veins from injecting drugs intravenously, and technicians sometimes struggle to find a serviceable one. When Texas executed Stephen Morin, a former heroin addict, orderlies prodded his arms with catheters for forty-one minutes. Being strapped to a table for a lengthy period while waiting to die is a form of psychological torture arguably worse than most physical kinds. This is demonstrated by the fact that mock executions, which cause no physical pain, are a common method of torture around the world. The agony comes not from the prospect of pain, but from the expectation of death.

Notes

1. Stephen Trombley's *The Execution Protocol: Inside America's Capital Punishment Industry* (Crown Publishers 1992) chronicles what procedures are followed and what precautions are taken when the state decides to take a life. For a sample of botched executions, see *id.* at 8–22.

2. Trombley's book reports that Fred A. Leuchter, a designer and manufacturer of execution equipment, has estimated the costs of various execution systems. At $30,000, Leuchter's modular lethal injection system is the least expensive piece of execution machinery. (The chemicals required for the execution cost between $600 and $700.) At the other end of the spectrum, Leuchter's gas chamber sells for approximately $300,000. (The cynanide required costs approximately $10 per execution.) An electric chair, Leuchter's preferred means of execution, sells for $35,000. (Leuchter estimates that the electricity required costs thirty-one cents per execution.) A gallows sells for $85,000. For states which have no execution machinery or which have not carried out executions in years, Leuchter manufactures an "Execution Trailer." At roughly $100,000, this mobile execution delivery system includes a lethal injection machine, a secure holding cell for the condemned inmate, and separate areas for the witnesses, chaplain, prison officials

and medical personnel. In addition to this equipment, Leuchter offers various services, including equipment certification, certified training, and execution support.

3. According to one author, punishments historically considered banned by the cruel and unusual punishments clause include burning at the stake, crucifixion, breaking on the wheel, the thumbscrew and, in certain circumstances, solitary confinement. Corwin, *Understanding the Constitution* 131 (1979). Several early decisions address the terms cruel and unusual. For example, in *State v. Borgstrom*, 69 Minn. 508 (1890), the court found that punishments which might properly be considered cruel included drowning, disemboweling, burning, boiling in oil, the pillory, and being sewn into a leather sack with a live dog, a cock, and an ape and being cast into the sea. In *James v. Commonwealth*, 12 Serg. & Rawle. 220 (1824), the court ordered a female defendant to be placed in a ducking stool and plunged three times into the water for the crime of being a common scold. The court stated that even though the punishment was "cruel, unusual, unnatural, and ludicrous,..., still, if it be the law of the land, the court must pronounce judgment for it."

2. Gas Chamber

Gray v. Lucas

710 F.2d 1048 (5th Cir. 1983)

Before POLITZ, TATE and HIGGINBOTHAM, Circuit Judges.

PER CURIAM: Jimmy Lee Gray, a Mississippi prisoner awaiting execution, appeals from the district court's order denying him habeas corpus relief. We affirm.

[Among his claims,] the petitioner Gray ... contends Mississippi's lethal-gas method of execution constitutes cruel and unusual punishment. Gray contends that he is entitled to an evidentiary hearing upon the factual issue whether Mississippi's method of execution by lethal gas offends eighth amendment guarantees because it involves the unnecessary and wanton infliction of pain, in the nature of torture and a lingering death.

He thus relies upon principles recently articulated by the Supreme Court in *Estelle v. Gamble*, 429 U.S. 97, 102–103 (1976):

> It suffices to note that the primary concern of the drafters was to proscribe "torture[s]" and other "barbar[ous]" methods of punishment. Accordingly, this Court first applied the Eighth Amendment by comparing challenged methods of execution to concededly inhuman techniques of punishment.

Our more recent cases, however, have held that the Amendment proscribes more than physically barbarous punishments. The Amendment embodies "broad and idealistic concepts of dignity, civilized standards, humanity, and decency...," against which we must evaluate penal measures. Thus, we have held repugnant to the Eighth Amendment punishments which are incompatible with "the evolving standards of decency that mark the progress of a maturing society," or which "involve the unnecessary and wanton infliction of pain."

The method of executing the death sentence in the state of Mississippi is governed by the Mississippi Code of Criminal Procedure, as follows:

> The manner of inflicting the punishment of death shall be by lethal gas, that is,
> by causing the person sentenced to suffer the death penalty to be placed in a

properly constructed gas chamber, and then causing said gas chamber to be filled with a lethal gas commonly used in the execution of persons sentenced to suffer the death penalty, and the person placed therein allowed to remain a sufficient length of time to cause death.

In support of this claim [that execution by means of lethal gas constitutes cruel and unusual punishment] Gray submits numerous affidavits, including three from individuals who have witnessed executions by lethal gas. Tad Dunbar, a television news anchorman, witnessed the 1979 Nevada execution of Jesse Walter Bishop by lethal gas. Dunbar attests that he was "shocked and horrified" that death came only after Bishop's protracted struggle with the lethal cyanide gas:

> When the cyanide gas reached him, he gasped, and convulsed strenuously. He stiffened. His head lurched back. His eyes widened, and he strained as much as the straps that held him to the chair would allow. He unquestionably appeared to be in pain.
>
> Periodically now, perhaps at thirty second intervals, he would convulse, alternately straining and relaxing in the chair. I noticed he had urinated. The convulsions continued for approximately ten more minutes, and you could see his chest expand, and then contract, trying to take in fresh air. These movements became weaker as the minutes ticked away. You could not tell when Bishop finally lost consciousness.
>
> According to prison officials, Bishop died at 12:21 a.m., approximately 12 minutes after the cyanide pellets had dropped in the chamber. Death was pronounced after the shade on our observation window had been drawn, though there was still some slight movement in the body.

Howard Brodie, National News artist for CBS news, witnessed California's 1967 execution of Aaron Mitchell by lethal cyanide gas. Brodie had previously witnessed four executions, but he recalled that Mitchell's was particularly horrible:

> The pellets of cyanide were released by mechanical controls, and dropped into an acid jar beneath the chair. The gas rose, and seemed to hit him immediately. Within the first minute Mitchell slumped down. I thought to myself how quickly cyanide really worked.
>
> Within 30 seconds he lifted his head upwards again. He raised his entire body, arching, tugging at his straps. Saliva was oozing from his mouth. His eyes open, he turned his head to the right. He gazed through my window. His fingers were tightly gripping his thumbs. His chest was visibly heaving in sickening agony. Then he tilted his head higher, and rolled his eyes upward. Then he slumped forward. Still his heart was beating. It continued for another several minutes.
>
> He was pronounced dead, twelve minutes after the pellets were released, by the doctor who could hear his heart through the stethoscope, die.

The Reverend Myer Tobey, S.J., witnessed four Maryland executions by lethal cyanide gas. Of the four, he remembered best the execution of Eddie Daniels in the late 1950's:

> In an instant, puffs of light white smoke began to rise. Daniels saw the smoke, and moved his head to try to avoid breathing it in. As the gas continued to rise he moved his head this way and that way, thrashing as much as his straps would allow still in an attempt to avoid breathing. He was like an animal

in a trap, with no escape, all the time being watched by his fellow humans in the windows that lined the chamber. He could steal only glimpses of me in his panic, but I continued to repeat "My Jesus I Love You," and he too would try to mouth it.

Then the convulsions began. His body strained as much as the straps would allow. He had inhaled the deadly gas, and it seemed as if every muscle in his body was straining in reaction. His eyes looked as if they were bulging, much as a choking man with a rope cutting off his windpipe. But he could get no air in the chamber.

Then his head dropped forward. The doctor in the observation room said that that was it for Daniels. This was within the first few minutes after the pellets had dropped. His head was down for several seconds. Then, as we had thought it was over, he again lifted his head in another convulsion. His eyes were open, he strained and he looked at me. I said one more time, automatically, "My Jesus I Love You." And he went with me, mouthing the prayer. He was still alive after those several minutes, and I was horrified. He was in great agony. Then he strained and began the words with me again. I knew he was conscious, this was not an automatic response of an unconscious man. But he did not finish. His head fell forward again.

There were several more convulsions after this, but his eyes were closed. I could not tell if he were conscious or not at that point. Then he stopped moving, approximately ten minutes after the gas began to rise, and was officially pronounced dead.

Gray also submits scientific and medical evidence suggesting that the method of inducing death by cyanide gas causes painful asphyxiation. Dr. Richard Traystman, Director of the Anesthesiology and Critical Care Medicine Research Laboratories at Johns Hopkins Medical School, explained in his affidavit how cyanide causes asphyxiation:

Very simply, cyanide gas blocks the utilization of the oxygen in the body's cells.... Gradually, depending on the rate and volume of inspiration, and on the concentration of the cyanide that is inhaled, the person exposed to cyanide gas will become anoxic. This is a condition defined by no oxygen. Death will follow through asphyxiation, when the heart and brain cease to receive oxygen.

The hypoxic state can continue for several minutes after the cyanide gas is released in the execution chamber. The person exposed to this gas remains conscious for a period of time, in some cases for several minutes, again depending on the rate and volume of the gas that is inhaled. During this time the person is unquestionably experiencing pain and extreme anxiety. The pain begins immediately, and is felt in the arms, shoulders, back, and chest. The sensation is similar to the pain felt by a person during a heart attack, where essentially, the heart is being deprived of oxygen. The severity of the pain varies directly with the diminishing oxygen reaching the tissues.

The agitation and anxiety a person experiences in the hypoxic state will stimulate the autonomic nervous system.... [The person] ... may begin to drool, urinate, defecate, or vomit. There will be muscular contractions. These responses can occur both while the person is conscious, or when he becomes unconscious.

When anoxia sets in, the brain remains alive for from two to five minutes. The heart will continue to beat for a period of time after that, perhaps five to seven minutes, or longer, though at a very low cardiac output. Death can occur ten to twelve minutes after the gas is released in the chamber.

Dr. Traystman concluded by stating that asphyxiation of animals for research purposes is disfavored in the scientific community. "We would not use asphyxiation, by cyanide gas or by any other substance, in our laboratory to kill animals that have been used in experiments—nor would most medical research laboratories in this country use it."

It is Gray's position that recent scientific evidence rebuts the fallacy, once commonly accepted, that death via lethal cyanide gas is painless. Gray submits that "[a] substantial body of authority now confirms that death by the administration of lethal gas is lingering, painful and terrifying, and involves substantial physical pain." While commentators have voiced this view, there has been as yet no thorough and definitive study on the precise issue Gray raises....

Gray argues strongly that he has produced a factual predicate clearly demonstrating that death by cyanide gas, causing asphyxiation at the cost of protracted pain over a period that may exceed seven minutes, may offend an indicated eighth amendment prohibition against the unnecessary and wanton infliction of pain. He contends that, therefore, he is entitled to an evidentiary hearing to prove the facts indicated in order to vindicate his constitutional claim in that regard.

Accepting Gray's proffered facts as proven, we ultimately conclude that they do not as a matter of law establish the eighth amendment claim asserted by him and, therefore, no evidentiary hearing is required. Traditional deaths by execution, such as by hanging, have always involved the possibility of pain and terror for the convicted person. Although contemporary notions of civilized conduct may indeed cause some reassessment of what degree or length is acceptable, we are not persuaded that under the present jurisprudential standards the showing made by Gray justifies this intermediate appellate court holding that, as a matter of law or fact, the pain and terror resulting from death by cyanide gas is so different in degree or nature from that resulting from other traditional modes of execution as to implicate the eighth amendment right.

... Having examined each of the contentions presented, we find no basis for federal habeas relief. Accordingly, the judgment of the district court is affirmed.

Gomez v. United States District Court
503 U.S. 653 (1992)

The Court of Appeals for the Ninth Circuit issued orders staying execution of a prisoner convicted of capital murder in state court. Application was made to vacate stay of execution. The Supreme Court held that the claim that execution by cyanide gas was cruel and unusual punishment was not required to be considered, as it had not been properly raised in earlier petitions for habeas corpus.

Orders staying executions vacated.

Justice STEVENS, with whom Justice Blackmun joins, dissenting.

In a time when the Court's jurisprudence concerning the imposition of the death penalty grows ever more complicated, Robert Alton Harris brings a simple claim. He argues that California's method of execution—exposure to cyanide gas—constitutes cruel and unusual punishment and therefore violates the Eighth and Fourteenth Amendments. In light of all that we know today about the extreme and unnecessary pain inflicted by execution by cyanide gas, and in light of the availability of more humane and less violent methods of execution, Harris' claim has merit. I would deny the State's application to vacate the stay imposed by the Court of Appeals and allow the courts below to hear and rule on Harris' claim.

Execution by cyanide gas is "in essence asphyxiation by suffocation or strangulation." As dozens of uncontroverted expert statements filed in this case illustrate, execution by cyanide gas is extremely and unnecessarily painful.

> "Following inhalation of cyanide gas, a person will first experience hypoxia, a condition defined as a lack of oxygen in the body. The hypoxic state can continue for several minutes after the cyanide gas is released in the execution chamber. During this time, a person will remain conscious and immediately may suffer extreme pain throughout his arms, shoulders, back, and chest. The sensation may be similar to pain felt by a person during a massive heart attack.

> "Execution by gas ... produces prolonged seizures, incontinence of stool and urine, salivation, vomiting, retching, ballistic writhing, flailing, twitching of extremities, [and] grimacing. This suffering lasts for 8 to 10 minutes, or longer."

Eyewitness descriptions of executions by cyanide gas lend depth to these clinical accounts. On April 6, 1992, Arizona executed Don Eugene Harding.

> "When the fumes enveloped Don's head he took a quick breath. A few seconds later he again looked in my direction. His face was red and contorted as if he were attempting to fight through tremendous pain. His mouth was pursed shut and his jaw was clenched tight. Don then took several more quick gulps of the fumes.

> "At this point Don's body started convulsing violently.... His face and body turned a deep red and the veins in his temple and neck began to bulge until I thought they might explode.

> "After about a minute Don's face leaned partially forward, but he was still conscious. Every few seconds he continued to gulp in. He was shuddering uncontrollably and his body was racked with spasms. His head continued to snap back. His hands were clenched.

> "After several more minutes, the most violent of the convulsions subsided. At this time the muscles along Don's left arm and back began twitching in a wavelike motion under his skin. Spittle drooled from his mouth.

> "Don did not stop moving for approximately eight minutes, and after that he continued to twitch and jerk for another minute. Approximately two minutes later, we were told by a prison official that the execution was complete.

> "Don Harding took ten minutes and thirty-one seconds to die."

The unnecessary cruelty of this method of execution convinced Arizona's Attorney General that the State should abandon execution by gas in favor of execution by lethal injection. His conclusion coincides with that of numerous medical, legal, and ethical experts.

The prohibition on cruel and unusual punishment "is not fastened to the obsolete, but may acquire meaning as public opinion becomes enlightened by a humane justice." *Weems v. United States*, 217 U.S. 349, 378 (1910). Accordingly, we have "interpreted th[e Eighth] Amendment 'in a flexible and dynamic manner.'" When the California statute requiring execution by cyanide gas was enacted in 1937, the gas chamber was considered a humane method of execution. Fifty-five years of history and moral development have superseded that judgment. The barbaric use of cyanide gas in the Holocaust, the development of cyanide agents as chemical weapons, our contemporary understanding of execution by lethal gas, and the development of less cruel methods of execution all demonstrate that execution by cyanide gas is unnecessarily cruel. "The traditional humanity of modern Anglo-American law forbids the infliction of unnecessary pain in the execution of the death sentence." *Louisiana v. Resweber*, 329 U.S. 459, 463 (1947) (opinion of Reed, J.).

Nowhere is this moral progress better demonstrated than in the decisions of the State legislatures. Of the 20 or so States to adopt new methods of execution since our ruling in *Gregg v. Georgia*, 428 U.S. 153 (1976), not a single State has chosen execution by lethal gas. Ten years ago, 10 States mandated execution by lethal gas; one by one, those States have abandoned that method as inhumane and torturous. Only California, Maryland, and Arizona currently mandate execution by gas.[14] Of the 168 persons executed in the United States since 1977, only 6 have been executed by lethal gas. We have frequently emphasized that "[t]he clearest and most reliable objective evidence of contemporary values is the legislation enacted by the country's legislatures." These "objective indicia that reflect the public attitude" toward execution by lethal gas clearly exhibit a nearly universal rejection of that means of execution. All of this leads me to conclude that execution by cyanide gas is both cruel and unusual, and that it violates contemporary standards of human decency.[15]

3. Electric Chair

Glass v. Louisiana

471 U.S. 1080 (1985)

On petition for writ of certiorari to the Supreme Court of Louisiana. April 29, 1985. The petition for a writ of certiorari is denied.

Justice BRENNAN, with whom Justice Marshall joins, dissenting from denial of certiorari.

The petitioner Jimmy L. Glass has been condemned to death by electrocution— "that is, causing to pass through the body of the person convicted a current of electricity of sufficient intensity to cause death, and the application and continuance of such current through the body of the person convicted until such person is dead." Glass contends that "electrocution causes the gratuitous infliction of unnecessary pain and suffering and does not comport with evolving standards of human dignity," and that this method of officially sponsored execution therefore violates the Eighth and Fourteenth Amendments. The Supreme Court of Louisiana held that this claim must summarily be rejected pursuant to "clearly established principles of law" and observed that, in any event, the claim is wholly lacking in medical or scientific merit.

---

14. As of 2006, California, Maryland and Arizona had switched to lethal injection as their primary method of execution. [Ed.]

15. In *Wilkerson v. Utah*, 99 U.S. 130, 135–136 (1878), we ruled that punishments of "unnecessary cruelty" violated the Eighth Amendment, citing the ancient practices of drawing and quartering and "public dissecting" as examples. Similarly in *In re Kemmler*, 136 U.S. 436, 446 (1890), we indicated that "burning at the stake, crucifixion, [and] breaking on the wheel" were as well cruel and unusual. To that list we might have added the garrotte, a device for execution by strangulation developed—and abandoned—centuries ago in Spain. See G. Scott, The History of Capital Punishment 159–160 (1950). To my mind, the gas chamber is nothing more than a chemical garrotte.

I adhere to my view that the death penalty is in all circumstances cruel and unusual punishment prohibited by the Eighth and Fourteenth Amendments, and would therefore grant certiorari and vacate Glass' death sentence in any event. One of the reasons I adhere to this view is my belief that the "physical and mental suffering" inherent in any method of execution is so "uniquely degrading to human dignity" that, when combined with the arbitrariness by which capital punishment is imposed, the trend of enlightened opinion, and the availability of less severe penological alternatives, the death penalty is always unconstitutional.

Even if I thought otherwise, however, I would vote to grant certiorari. Glass' petition presents an important and unsettling question that cuts to the very heart of the Eighth Amendment's Cruel and Unusual Punishments Clause—a question that demands measured judicial consideration. Of the 42 officially sponsored executions carried out since the Court's decision in *Gregg v. Georgia*, 428 U.S. 153 (1976), 31 have been by means of electrocution. And since *Gregg*, an ever-increasing number of condemned prisoners have contended that electrocution is a cruel and barbaric method of extinguishing human life, both per se and as compared with other available means of execution. As in this case, such claims have uniformly and summarily been rejected, typically on the strength of this Court's opinion in *In re Kemmler*, 136 U.S. 436 (1890), which authorized the State of New York to proceed with the first electrocution 95 years ago. *Kemmler*, however, was grounded on a number of constitutional premises that have long since been rejected and on factual assumptions that appear not to have withstood the test of experience. I believe the time has come to measure electrocution against well-established contemporary Eighth Amendment principles.

I

Electrocution as a means of killing criminals was first authorized by the New York Legislature in 1888, and resulted from a lengthy investigation to identify "the most humane and practical method known to modern science of carrying into effect the sentence of death in capital cases." In *In re Kemmler*, this Court rejected a constitutional attack on New York's statute by William Kemmler, who was scheduled to be the first person put to death by electrocution. The Court emphasized that, because the Eighth Amendment was not applicable to the States, "[t]he decision of the state courts sustaining the validity of the act under the state constitution is not reexaminable here." In dicta, the Court also followed a "historical" interpretation of the Cruel and Unusual Punishment Clause as it governed executions carried out by the Federal Government, suggesting that the constitutionality of a particular means of execution should be determined by reference to contemporary norms at the time the Bill of Rights was adopted. In addition, the Court approvingly observed that the state court had concluded that "it is within easy reach of electrical science at this day to so generate and apply to the person of the convict a current of electricity of such known and sufficient force as certainly to produce instantaneous, and, therefore, painless, death."

State and federal courts recurrently cite to *Kemmler* as having conclusively resolved that electrocution is a constitutional method of extinguishing life, and accordingly that further factual and legal consideration of the issue is unnecessary. But *Kemmler* clearly is antiquated authority. It is now well established that the Eighth Amendment applies to the States through the Fourteenth Amendment. *Robinson v. California*, 370 U.S. 660 (1962). Moreover, the Court long ago rejected *Kemmler's* "historical" interpretation of the Cruel and Unusual Punishments Clause, emphasizing instead that the prohibitions of the Clause are not "confine[d] ... to such penalties and punishment as were inflicted by the Stuarts." *Weems v. United States*, 217 U.S. 349, 372 (1910). This is because "[t]ime works changes, [and] brings into existence new conditions and purposes. Therefore a principle to be vital must be capable of wider application than the mischief which gave it birth." The Clause thus has an "expansive and vital character" that "draw[s] its meaning from the evolving standards of decency that mark the progress of a maturing society." Accordingly, Eighth Amendment claims must be evaluated "in the light of contemporary human knowledge," *Trop v. Dulles*, 356 U.S. 86 (1958), rather than in reliance on century-old factual premises that may no longer be accurate.

To be sure, legislative decisions concerning appropriate forms of punishment are entitled to considerable deference. But in common with all constitutional guarantees, "it is evident that legislative judgments alone cannot be determinative of Eighth Amendment standards since that Amendment was intended to safeguard individuals from the abuse of legislative power." "[T]he Constitution contemplates that in the end [a court's] own judgment will be brought to bear on the question of the acceptability" of a challenged punishment, guided by "objective factors to the maximum possible extent." Thus it is firmly within the "historic process of constitutional adjudication" for courts to consider, through a "discriminating evaluation" of all available evidence, whether a particular means of carrying out the death penalty is "barbaric" and unnecessary in light of currently available alternatives.

What are the objective factors by which courts should evaluate the constitutionality of a challenged method of punishment? First and foremost, the Eighth Amendment prohibits "the unnecessary and wanton infliction of pain." *Gregg v. Georgia*, 428 U.S. at 173. The Court has *never* accepted the proposition that notions of deterrence or retribution might legitimately be served through the infliction of pain beyond that which is minimally necessary to terminate an individual's life. Thus in explaining the obvious unconstitutionality of such ancient practices as disembowelling while alive, drawing and quartering, public dissection, burning alive at the stake, crucifixion, and breaking at the wheel, the Court has emphasized that the Eighth Amendment forbids "inhuman and barbarous" methods of execution that go at all beyond "the mere extinguishment of life" and cause "torture or a lingering death." It is beyond debate that the Amendment proscribes all forms of "unnecessary cruelty" that cause gratuitous "terror, pain, or disgrace." *Wilkerson v. Utah*, 99 U.S. 130, 135–136 (1879).

The Eighth Amendment's protection of "the dignity of man" extends beyond prohibiting the unnecessary infliction of pain when extinguishing life. Civilized standards, for example, require a minimization of physical violence during execution irrespective of the pain that such violence might inflict on the condemned. Similarly, basic notions of human dignity command that the State minimize "mutilation" and "distortion" of the condemned prisoner's body. These principles explain the Eighth Amendment's prohibition of such barbaric practices as drawing and quartering.

II

... There is considerable empirical evidence and eyewitness testimony ... which if correct would appear to demonstrate that electrocution violates every one of the principles set forth above. This evidence suggests that death by electrical current is extremely violent and inflicts pain and indignities far beyond the "mere extinguishment of life." Witnesses routinely report that, when the switch is thrown, the condemned prisoner "cringes," "leaps," and "'fights the straps with amazing strength.'" "The hands turn red, then white, and the cords of the neck stand out like steel bands." The prisoner's limbs, fingers, toes, and face are severely contorted. The force of the electrical current is so powerful[16] that the prisoner's eyeballs sometimes pop out and "rest on [his] cheeks."[17] The prisoner often defecates, urinates, and vomits blood and drool.

"The body turns bright red as its temperature rises," and the prisoner's "flesh swells and his skin stretches to the point of breaking." Sometimes the prisoner catches on fire, particularly "if [he] perspires excessively." Witnesses hear a loud and sustained sound "like bacon frying," and "the sickly sweet smell of burning flesh" permeates the chamber. This "smell of frying human flesh in the immediate neighborhood of the chair is sometimes bad enough to nauseate even the Press representatives who are present." In the meantime, the prisoner almost literally boils: "the temperature in the brain itself approaches the boiling point of water," and when the postelectrocution autopsy is performed "the liver is so hot that doctors have said that it cannot be touched by the human hand." The body frequently is badly burned and disfigured.

The violence of killing prisoners through electrical current is frequently explained away by the assumption that death in these circumstances is instantaneous and painless. This assumption, however, in fact "is open to serious question" and is "a matter of sharp conflict of expert opinion." Throughout the 20th century a number of distinguished electrical scientists and medical doctors have argued that the available evidence strongly suggests that electrocution causes unspeakable pain and suffering. Because "'[t]he current flows along a restricted path into the body, and destroys all the tissue confronted in this path ... [i]n the meantime the vital organs may be preserved; and pain, too great for us to imagine, is induced.... For the sufferer, time stands still; and this excruciating torture seems to last for an eternity.'" L.G.V. Rota, a renowned French electrical scientist, concluded after extensive research that

> "[i]n every case of electrocution, ... death inevitably supervenes but it may be very long, and above all, excruciatingly painful.... [T]he space of time before death supervenes varies according to the subject. Some have a greater physiological resistance than others. I do not believe that anyone killed by electrocution dies instantly, no matter how weak the subject may be. In certain cases death will not have come about even though the point of contact of the electrode with the body shows distinct burns. Thus, in particular cases, the condemned person may be alive and even conscious for several minutes without it being possible for a doctor to say whether the victim is dead or not.... This method of execution is a form of torture."

Although it is an open question whether and to what extent an individual feels pain upon electrocution, there can be no serious dispute that in numerous cases death is far from instantaneous. Whether because of shoddy technology and poorly trained personnel, or because of the inherent differences in the "physiological resistance" of condemned prisoners to electrical current, it is an inescapable fact that the 95-year history of electrocution in this country has been characterized by repeated failures swiftly to execute and the resulting need to send recurrent charges into condemned prisoners to ensure their deaths. The very first electrocution required multiple attempts before death resulted, and our cultural lore is filled with examples of attempted electrocutions that

---

16. "The force of the death-dealing blow the condemned prisoner receives is more easily understood when it is realized that this amount of electricity, transferred into mechanical power, would be equivalent to 884,400 foot-pounds per minutes, or enough electrical energy to light 800 lights in the average home.

17. In addition, the force of the current is so strong that it sometimes literally ruptures the prisoner's heart.

had to be restaged when it was discovered that the condemned "tenaciously clung to life."[18] Attending physicians routinely acknowledge that electrocutions must often be repeated in order to ensure death. It is difficult to imagine how such procedures constitute anything less than "death by installments" — "a form of torture [that] would rival that of burning at the stake."

This pattern of "death by installments" is by no means confined to bygone decades. Here is one eyewitness account of Alabama's electrocution of John Louis Evans on April 22, 1983:

"At 8:30 p.m. the first jolt of 1900 volts of electricity passed through Mr. Evans' body. It lasted thirty seconds. Sparks and flames erupted from the electrode tied to Mr. Evans' left leg. His body slammed against the straps holding him in the electric chair and his fist clenched permanently. The electrode apparently burst from the strap holding it in place. A large puff of grayish smoke and sparks poured out from under the hood that covered Mr. Evans' face. An overpowering stench of burnt flesh and clothing began pervading the witness room. Two doctors examined Mr. Evans and declared that he was not dead.

The electrode on the left leg was refastened. At 8:30 p.m. [sic] Mr. Evans was administered a second thirty second jolt of electricity. The stench of burning flesh was nauseating. More smoke emanated from his leg and head. Again, the doctors examined Mr. Evans. The doctors reported that his heart was still beating, and that he was still alive.

At that time, I asked the prison commissioner, who was communicating on an open telephone line to Governor George Wallace to grant clemency on the grounds that Mr. Evans was being subjected to cruel and unusual punishment. The request for clemency was denied.

At 8:40 p.m., a third charge of electricity, thirty seconds in duration, was passed through Mr. Evans' body. At 8:44, the doctors pronounced him dead. The execution of John Evans took fourteen minutes."

Similarly, this was the scene at Georgia's electrocution of Alpha Otis Stephens just last December 12th:

"The first charge of electricity administered today to Alpha Otis Stephens in Georgia's electric chair failed to kill him, and he struggled to breathe for eight minutes before a second charge carried out his death sentence for murdering a man who interrupted a burglary.

… A few seconds after a mask was placed over his head, the first charge was applied, causing his body to snap forward and his fists to clench.

His body slumped when the current stopped two minutes later, but shortly afterward witnesses saw him struggle to breathe. In the six minutes allowed for the body to cool before doctors could examine it, Mr. Stephens took about 23 breaths.

---

18. A noted instance of this phenomenon occurred when Ethel Rosenberg was electrocuted for treason: five consecutive attempts were required before she finally died. "After the fourth (shock) guards removed one of the two straps and the two doctors applied their stethoscopes. But they were not satisfied that she was dead. The executioner came to them from his switchboard in a small room 10 feet from the chair. 'Want another?' he asked. The doctors nodded. Guards replaced the straps and for the fifth time electricity was applied."

> At 12:26 A.M., two doctors examined him and said he was alive. A second two-minute charge was administered at 12:28 A.M."

Stephens "was just not a conductor" of electricity, a Georgia prison official said.

Thus there is considerable evidence suggesting—at the very least—that death by electrocution causes far more than the "mere extinguishment of life." This evidence, if correct, would raise a substantial question whether electrocution violates the Eighth Amendment in several respects. First, electrocution appears to inflict "unnecessary and wanton ... pain" and cruelty, and to cause "torture or a lingering death" in at least a significant number of cases. *Gregg v. Georgia*, 428 U.S. at 173. Second, the physical violence and mutilation that accompany this method of execution would seem to violate the basic "dignity of man." *Trop v. Dulles*, 356 U.S. at 100. Finally, even if electrocution does not invariably produce pain and indignities, the apparent century-long pattern of "abortive attempts" and lingering deaths suggests that this method of execution carries an unconstitutionally high risk of causing such atrocities. These features of electrocution seem so "inherent in [this] method of punishment" as to render it *per se* cruel and unusual and therefore forbidden by the Eighth Amendment.

Moreover, commentators and medical experts have urged that other currently available means of execution—particularly some forms of lethal gas and fast-acting barbiturates—accomplish the purpose of extinguishing life in a surer, swifter, less violent, and more humane manner. Several state legislatures have abandoned electrocution in favor of lethal injection for these very reasons; one of the architects of this change has emphasized that it resulted precisely from the recognition that the electric chair is "a barbaric torture device" and electrocution a "gruesome ritual." Other States have rejected electrocution in favor of the use of lethal gas.

For me, arguments about the "humanity" and "dignity" of any method of officially sponsored executions are a constitutional contradiction in terms. Moreover, there is significant evidence that executions by lethal gas—at least as administered in the gas chamber—and barbiturates—at least as administered through lethal injections—carry their own risks of pain, indignity, and prolonged suffering. But having concluded that the death penalty in the abstract is consistent with the "evolving standards of decency that mark the progress of a maturing society," courts cannot now avoid the Eighth Amendment's proscription of "the unnecessary and wanton infliction of pain" in carrying out that penalty simply by relying on 19th-century precedents that appear to have rested on inaccurate factual assumptions and that no longer embody the meaning of the Amendment. For the reasons set forth above, there is an ever-more urgent question whether electrocution in fact is a "humane" method for extinguishing human life or is, instead, nothing less than the contemporary technological equivalent of burning people at the stake.

Note

Glass v. Louisiana identifies William Kemmler as the first person put to death by electrocution in the United States. On August 6, 1890, Kemmler sat in New York's electric chair and died a gruesome death. According to an eyewitness account published in *The New York World* newspaper,

> The first execution by electrocution has been a horror. Doctors say the victim did not suffer. Only his maker knows if that is true. To the eye, it looked as though he were in convulsive agony. The current had been passing through his

body for 15 seconds when the electrode at the head was removed. Suddenly the breast heaved. There was a straining at the straps which bound him. A purplish foam covered the lips and was spattered over the leather head band. The man was alive.

Wardens, physicians, guards … everybody lost their wits. There was a startled cry for the current to be turned on again. Signals, only half understood, were given to those in the next room at the switchboard. When they knew what happened, they were prompt to act, and the switch-handle could be heard as it was pulled back and forth, breaking the deadly current into jets…. The rigor of death came on the instant. An odor of burning flesh and singed hair filled the room. For a moment, a blue flame played about the base of the victim's spine. This time the electricity flowed four minutes.

Kemmler was dead. Part of his brain had been baked hard. Some of the blood in his head had been turned to charcoal.

See generally Rideau & Wikberg, *Life Sentences* 283–303 (Times Books 1992).

4. Firing Squad

Notes and Questions

1. The first recorded execution by firing squad in this country occurred in 1608 when George Kendall, one of the original councilors for the colony of Virginia, was put to death. According to death penalty historian Watt Espy, Kendall was very unpopular among his fellow council members. William Reed, condemned to die by hanging for threatening and blaspheming the President of the Colony, begged the council for a reprieve, offering to testify that Kendall had plotted to betray his countrymen to the Spanish. The council pardoned Reed on condition that he both testify against Kendall and also serve as executioner. Gray & Stanley, *A Punishment in Search of a Crime* 48 (Avon Books 1989).

2. Weisberg's article, *This is Your Death*, discloses the common practice of issuing a blank round to one of the executioners to "spare the conscience" of all executioners. Assuming the executioners are trained marksmen, wouldn't each know from the recoil of his weapon whether he fired a live round?

3. Weisberg alludes to the botched execution by firing squad of Elisio Mares in Utah on September 10, 1951. According to Weisberg, because Mares was popular with prison staff all five marksmen aimed away from the target over Mares' heart. No single wound was fatal and Mares slowly bled to death.

4. The execution procedure in China usually guarantees instantaneous death. The prisoner's hands are tied behind his back and he is forced to kneel. A single bullet is then fired from a pistol at point-blank range into his head. See *infra* chapter 19. Should the United States follow China's example?

5. In *Wilkerson v. Utah*, 99 U.S. 130 (1879), the Court reviewed various military law treatises to demonstrate that under "the custom of war" shooting was a common method of inflicting the punishment of death. On that basis, the Court concluded:

Cruel and unusual punishments are forbidden by the Constitution, but the [military treatises] referred to are quite sufficient to show that the punishment of shooting as a mode of executing the death penalty for the crime of murder in the first degree is not included in that category, within the meaning of the [Eighth Amendment]. Soldiers convicted of desertion or other capital military offenses are in the great majority of cases sentenced to be shot, and the ceremony for such occasions is given in great fullness by the writers upon the subject of courts-martial. *Id.* at 134–135.

Does *Wilkerson* stand for the proposition that methods of execution, regardless of their brutality, will withstand Eighth Amendment challenge so long as they are commonly inflicted?

6. According to a 2003 New York Times article, three states—Utah, Idaho and Oklahoma—currently authorize execution by firing squad. Utah alone permits prisoners to choose between being shot to death by firing squad and being poisoned to death by lethal injection. Oklahoma allows execution by firing squad only if lethal injection and electrocution are ruled unconstitutional. Idaho permits execution by firing squad when lethal injection is found to be "impractical." So far, only Utah has had occasion to use a firing squad to execute.

Two of the first six prisoners executed in Utah after the 1976 Supreme Court decision reinstating capital punishment elected to die "in a hail of bullets from a team of state-sanctioned riflemen. The first was Gary Mark Gilmore, a career criminal turned murderer who, in 1977, became the first person in the nation put to death after the Supreme Court decision. The second was John Albert Taylor, who was executed in 1996 after raping and murdering a young girl."

A third condemned prisoner, Roberto Arguelles, selected firing squad as the means of carrying out his execution, scheduled for June 28, 2003. Mr. Arguelles, who pleaded guilty to the sexual assault and murders of three teenage girls and a 42-year-old woman in 1992, has expressed a desire to be executed, and has refused legal representation. He did not explain why he selected firing squad in lieu of lethal injection.

Soliciting sharpshooters, the Utah Corrections Department has appealed to law enforcement agencies located near the state prison and those located near the area where Mr. Arguelles committed his crimes to "submit names of responsible people" who might serve on the firing squad. According to Jack Ford, Utah Corrections Department spokesman, "It's standard practice." Janofsky, *Utah Officials Preparing for Another Firing Squad, to Be Used as Soon as Next Month*, New York Times, May 29, 2003 at A16.

5. Hanging

Notes

1. Several authors have written accounts of bungled hangings. "Andrew J. Palm, arch-foe of capital punishment ... tells of a repugnant case that occurred on August 1, 1884, in the Raymond Street jail, in Brooklyn. It involved the Negro killer, Alexander Jefferson, who had been convicted of the berserk murders of two persons, one an innocent bystander, when he fancied himself betrayed by his irresponsible mistress-sweetheart. With only a small group present at the hanging, the unhappy man came quivering and praying from his cell, strong in courage but frightened at the thought of a slow lingering death. He commented to the sheriff that he was not afraid to die, but that he

dreaded a possible blunder. He must have entertained a premonition because a blunder did occur. As Palm tells the hideous story of the hanging:

> He never flinched while he stood under the gallows. He even smiled at some acquaintances ... the sheriff wiped his brow and the hangman, Joe Levy, with the blow of an axe, cut the rope in his pen. The two weights, of 206 and 120 pounds, fell ... and Jefferson's body was raised about five feet in the air. It fell back limp when suddenly it began to writhe in agony. The movements at first were not violent, but presently the legs, which had not been pinioned, were drawn up toward the body, the knees reaching almost to the chin, while the arms were extended pleadingly towards the occupants of the balconies right and left. The man kicked furiously and moaned so piteously that a thrill of horror went through the audience. The sheriff was bewildered. His face turned pale and his eyes filled with tears. The hangman was called from his pen to witness his clumsy work. He looked at his struggling victim, but said he could do nothing for him. Jefferson freed his hands sufficiently and clutched the noose, but, being unable to loosen the rope, he tore the black cap from his face and stretched out his hand imploringly toward the audience. The appearance of his face was terrible. After eight minutes of agony, which must have been horrible, the contortions began to lessen, and finally ceased.

"One of the grimmest cases recorded was that of John Coffey, who was put to death on October 16, 1886, at Crawfordsville, Indiana. Quoting again from Palm, who in turn uses a newspaper as his source, we read:

> The execution ... yesterday was one of the most horrible affairs of its kind ever witnessed. When the drop fell, the rope broke and the body dropped to the ground. The neck was not broken, but the shock caused the blood to spurt from the wretched man's ears. He was carried back up the scaffold stairs, and, while the rope was being adjusted he regained consciousness and begged to have the cap removed and make another speech. This was refused and the drop fell again. The rope broke a second time, but the body was caught before it reached the ground. It was lifted up and held in place by deputy sheriffs while the noose was again adjusted, when the drop fell again. The rope held and Coffee was slowly strangled to death, dying in twelve minutes. The spectators were overcome with horror."

Teeters, *Hang By The Neck* 173–174, 177–178 (Charles C. Thomas Publisher 1967).

2. Until American states began restricting or abolishing public executions in the 1830s, hangings were well-attended. The last traditional public hanging under state law occurred in 1936 in Owensboro, Kentucky. A crowd of 10,000 witnesses gathered to watch Ramsey Bethea, a twenty-two year old black man, die for criminally assaulting a seventy-year-old woman. *10,000 See Hanging of Kentucky Negro*, The New York Times, Aug. 15, 1936, at 30.

3. Public hangings were especially popular in the South. Most of these hangings involved black defendants convicted of capital crimes, particularly the rape of white women. Even after nearly all states had laws requiring private executions, public hanging remained popular with lynch mobs. Again, the vast majority of persons hung were black. Of 4,743 reported lynchings between 1882 and 1968, Professor Drew Kershen[19]

---

19. In calculating these statistics, Professor Kershen drew upon the works of R. Zangrando, D. Grant, J. Chadbourn and J. Cutler. [Ed.]

calculates that 72.7% (3,446) involved black victims. Drew Kershen, "Lynch Law: The Ox Bow Incident," at 1 (unpublished 1993).

According to another scholar,

> [F]rom 1889 to 1899, on the average, one person was lynched every other day, and two out of three were black. In the first decade of the twentieth century, a person was lynched approximately every fourth day, and nine out of ten were black, a ratio of black over white that held into the 1930s. In the second decade, one person was lynched every five days, and in the third, one [e]very nine days. In the 1930s lynching declined significantly. Still, between 1889 and 1946, a year widely accepted as marking the era of lynching, almost 4,000 black[s] had been mobbed to their death.

Joel Williamson, *The Crucible of Race: Black-White Relations in the American South Since Emancipation* 117–118 (Oxford Univ. Press 1984).

Between 1885 and 1907, illegal lynchings outpaced legal executions in the United States. In 1892, twice as many people were lynched as were legally executed. *Id.* at 185. According to Professor Kershen, legal executions between 1881 and 1903 averaged 110 per year. Illegal lynchings during the same period averaged 147 per year. Kershen, "Lynch Law: The Ox Bow Incident," at 2–3.

4. In 1994, the United States Court of Appeals for the Ninth Circuit, sitting en banc, rejected a claim that execution by hanging was cruel and unusual punishment forbidden by the Eighth Amendment. *Campbell v. Wood*, 18 F.3d 662 (9th Cir. 1994). The majority opinion observed that only two states, Washington and Montana, provide for execution by hanging. Nonetheless, given that hanging was an acceptable means of execution when the Bill of Rights was adopted, the court found the difficult question to be "whether hanging comports with contemporary standards of decency."

Campbell had argued that *Coker* (*supra* this chapter) and *Enmund* (*infra* chapter 5) required that when the number of states exacting a given punishment dwindles, the punishment becomes unconstitutional. The court agreed that proportionality review entails a determination of contemporary standards of decency. However the court described its task as providing "methodology review … [which] focuses more heavily on objective evidence of the pain involved in the challenged method."

> We do not consider hanging to be cruel and unusual simply because it causes death or because there may be some pain associated with death. As used in the Constitution, "cruel" implies "something inhuman and barbarous, something more than the mere extinguishment of life." *In re Kemmler*, 136 U.S. 436 (1890). Campbell is entitled to an execution free only of "the unnecessary and wanton infliction of pain." *Gregg v. Georgia*, 428 U.S. 153 (1976).

During an evidentiary hearing, several pathologists had testified that there was no single "pathway" to death by hanging. Rather, several mechanisms may contribute to death: occlusion of blood vessels, reflexive cardiac arrest, occlusion of the airway and spinal cord damage. If the sole pathway to death was occlusion of the airway, the condemned inmate might remain conscious for more than a minute. On the other hand, several other pathways might lead to unconsciousness and death within 0 to 10 seconds.

The court carefully scrutinized Washington's method of hanging which derived from U.S. Army Regulation No. 633-15, Procedure for Military Executions (1959), but with two important modifications. First, Washington uses thicker rope than required to reduce the chances of partial or complete decapitation. Second and most important,

Washington's method provides for boiling and stretching the rope to remove elasticity, and for coating the rope with wax or oil so that it will slide easily. These procedures, per the court, guarantee that the kinetic energy caused by the drop will be quickly transferred to the neck structures, rather than simply being absorbed by the rope. In addition, treating the surface of the rope to reduce surface friction allows the rope to tighten about the neck—an important factor in causing rapid unconsciousness. Finally, by specifying that the knot should be positioned below the left ear, the procedure ensures that energy from the drop is transferred to the spinal structures and that the carotid and vertebral arteries will likely be occluded.

The court of appeals upheld the district court's finding that the risk of death by decapitation was negligible and that hanging according to the protocol did not involve lingering death, mutilation, or the unnecessary and wanton infliction of pain. Five judges dissented. Campbell was executed by hanging on May 27, 1994.

On the other hand, Mitchell Rupe, a 400-pound bank robber who shot two Olympia, Washington bank tellers to death during a 1981 robbery, persuaded a federal judge in 1994 that his weight created a grave risk of decapitation and therefore hanging him would constitute cruel and unusual punishment. At the time, hanging was the sole method of execution in Washington state. Rupe died from terminal liver disease inside a prison hospital on February 7, 2006.

6. Lethal Injection

Note and Questions: Heckler v. Chaney, 470 U.S. 821 (1985)

In a rather creative attempt to forestall executions, death row inmates in Oklahoma and Texas—both lethal injection states—petitioned the Food and Drug Administration (FDA) claiming that the use of certain drugs for human execution was the "unapproved use of an approved drug," prohibited under the federal Food, Drug, and Cosmetic Act (FDCA), 21 U.S.C. §301 et seq. Because these drugs were being used for a new purpose, the inmates claimed that the FDA was required to approve the drugs as "safe and effective" for human executions before they could be distributed in interstate commerce.

The inmates asked the FDA to (1) take enforcement actions against prison officials who were violating the FDCA; (2) require warning labels be affixed stating that the drugs were unapproved and unsafe for human execution; (3) send statements to drug manufacturers and prison officials stating that the drugs should not be used for human executions; and (4) order the recall of the drugs from various state prisons.

After the FDA refused to take the requested action, the inmates brought suit. On October 15, 1983, a federal appeals court panel ordered the FDA to weigh evidence that the drugs destined for use in lethal injections caused "tortuous pain." Ultimately, the United States Supreme Court in Heckler v. Chaney, 470 U.S. 821 (1985), held that the FDA's decision not to undertake enforcement action was within the agency's discretion and thus was not amenable to judicial review.

If the FDA were to exercise its discretion on behalf of Chaney and the other death row inmates, would it be an undue interference with a state's administration of its criminal justice system? Is it possible for a drug to be "unsafe for human execution" as the inmates alleged?

In 1982, Texas became the first state to execute by lethal injection. Texas' lethal injection execution protocol follows:

TEXAS DEPARTMENT OF CORRECTIONS PROCEDURES FOR THE EXECUTION OF INMATES SENTENCED TO DEATH

Male inmates sentenced to death will be housed at the Ellis Unit of the Texas Department of Corrections located approximately 16 miles northeast of Huntsville, Texas. Female inmates sentenced to death will be housed at the Mountain View Unit located in Gatesville, Texas. . . .

An inmate scheduled for execution shall be transported from the Ellis/Mountain View Unit to the Huntsville Unit prior to the scheduled execution. Transportation arrangements shall be known only to the unit Wardens involved, and no public announcement to either the exact time, method, or route of transfer shall be made. The Director's office and the Public Information Office will be notified immediately after the inmate arrives at the Huntsville Unit.

During transportation and after arrival at the Huntsville Unit, the inmates shall be constantly observed and supervised by security personnel.

The inmate may have the following visitors at the Huntsville Unit:

Department of Corrections Chaplain(s)

Minister(s)

Attorney(s)

Family member(s) and friend(s) on a list of approved visitors

All visits must be approved by the Warden. With the exception of Chaplains' visits, all visits will be terminated by 6 p.m. on the day immediately prior to the execution date. No media visits will be allowed at the Huntsville Unit.

The last meal will be served at approximately 6:30–7 p.m.

Prior to midnight, the inmate will shower and dress in clean clothes.

The Huntsville Unit Warden's Office will serve as the communications command post and only operations personnel will be allowed entry to this area. All other individuals, including witnesses to the execution, will assemble at approximately 11:45 p.m. in the lounge adjacent to the unit visiting room.

All necessary arrangements to carry out the execution shall be completed at a predetermined time. Shortly after midnight, the door will be unlocked, and the inmate will be removed from the holding cell.

The inmate will be taken from the cell area into the Death House and secured to a hospital gurney. A medically trained individual (not to be identified) shall insert an intravenous catheter into the condemned person's arm and cause a neutral saline solution to flow.

At a predetermined time, the witnesses shall be escorted to the Death House. Witnesses shall include:

Persons provided for in Vernon's Ann. C.C.P., Article 43.20.

Media — One Texas bureau representative designated by the Associated Press, one Texas bureau representative designated by the United Press International, one representative of the Huntsville Item, and one representative each from established separate rosters of the Texas print and broadcast media will be admitted to the execution chamber as witnesses, provided those designated agree to act as pool reporters for the remainder of the media present and to meet with all media representatives present immediately subsequent to the execution. No recording or transmitting devices, either audio or video, shall be permitted either in the unit or the execution chamber.

The Warden shall then allow the condemned person to make a last statement. Upon completion of the statement, if any, the Warden shall state, "We are ready." At this time, the designee(s) of the Director shall induce by syringe substance and/or substances necessary to cause death. This individual(s) shall be visually separated from the execution chamber by a wall and locked door, and shall also not be identified.

The Inmate will be pronounced dead. An inquest will be held by a Walker County Justice of the Peace. The physician, as well as any chaplain accompanying the inmate into the Death House, shall stand with any other witnesses present.

After the inmate is pronounced dead and the J.P.'s inquest is finished, the body shall be immediately removed from the Death House, taken to an awaiting ambulance, and delivered to a local funeral home. Arrangements for the body, to be concluded prior to the execution, shall be made per Vernon's Ann. C.C.P., Article 43.25.

The Director of the Department of Corrections in accordance with Article 42.23 shall return the death warrant and certificate with a statement of any such act and his proceedings endorsed thereon, together with a statement showing what disposition was made of the dead body of the convict, to the Clerk of the court in which the sentenced was passed.

Note on Evolution of Lethal Injection Machine

Although Texas leads the country in the number of executions by lethal injection, its procedures have been plagued by mishaps from the outset. In 1982, during the first lethal injection execution, Warden Jack Pursley reportedly mixed all three chemicals into a single syringe. Pursley's initial attempt to inject the deadly mixture into Charles Brooks failed because the chemicals had precipitated. Trombley, *The Execution Protocol: Inside America's Capital Punishment Industry* 74–75 (Crown Publishers 1992). As Jacob Weisberg reported in "This Is Your Death," *supra* page 99, misadventure marred the executions of James Autry and Stephen Morin. Similarly, the 1988 execution of Raymond Landry caused alarm when the intravenous line carrying the lethal chemicals burst, spraying the technicians and witnesses with the deadly drugs. (The IV tube was reinserted and Landry died after 24 minutes.) The following year, Stephen McCoy choked and heaved throughout his execution due to an incorrect mixture of lethal drugs. Texas' hapless experiences prompted New Jersey, another lethal injection state, to contact Fred Leuchter, an expert in execution machinery. New Jersey Department of Corrections officials asked Leuchter to invent a machine to minimize the risk of human error. Leuchter's lethal injection machine, designed to eliminate "execution glitches," was first used on January 6, 1989 for the execution of Missouri inmate George "Tiny" Mercer. Leuchter's invention is described next in the text.

Lethal Injection Manual for the State of Missouri

Fred A. Leuchter Associates, Inc.

THE DELIVERY MODULE

The Delivery Module consists of an eight inlet, one outlet stainless steel manifold containing two purge syringes filled with saline solution, two syringes filled with Sodium Pentathol, two syringes filled with Pancuronium Bromide, and two syringes filled with Potassium Chloride. The outlet is connected to a disposable intravenous administration set terminating in a needle tip and connected to a saline dispensing bag a short distance from the manifold. Additional hardware includes the cylinder matrix for supporting the syringe assembly, three electrical solenoids, three solenoid pull rods, six mechanical pull knobs, six connecting cables, six weight stop pins, six weighted pistons, six cylinders, and nine indicator lights. A total of eight disposable 60cc syringes are utilized in the system. During system makeready, all three solenoid pull rods are used, but only three of the six connecting cables, one for each set of two. The pull knobs are arranged in three pairs and both from each pair are pulled, one by each executioner, but only one from each pair is connected (either all odd or all even numbers). All manifold inlet connections are accomplished by luer lock fittings. The purge syringe back flow stop brackets and twelve piston spaces are also part of the The Delivery Module.

During makeready, the two saline syringes are used to bleed the system, the other syringes are installed, after filling, in the proper order, as assemblies, with the weighted piston, cylinder and piston stop pin. The cables are connected in the proper sequence and the solenoid pull rods inserted into the pistons. The Delivery Module shall be in the Execution Chamber.

PROCEDURE

It is suggested that the following procedure might be followed to facilitate a smooth execution. These dosages are established, although not recommended, through consultation with pharmaceutical manufacturers. We at Fred A. Leuchter Associates, Inc., not being pharmacologists, do not recommend, or in any way guarantee the efficacy of these chemicals or dosages, but simply communicate the recommendations of the manufacturers.

1. Pre-injection 10cc antihistamine, one half hour prior to execution.
2. Pre-injection 8cc 2% Sodium Pentathol (5 grams/250ml, Abbott Labs #6108-01) five minutes prior to transmittal of subject to death chamber.
3. Machine injection 15 cc Sodium Pentathol 2% Solution (as above) delivered over a ten second time period.
4. One minute wait.
5. Machine injection 15 cc Pancuronium Bromide (Pavulon, Organon Drug Co., 2ml/2mg/ml) over a ten second time period.
6. One minute wait.
7. Machine injection 15 cc Potassium Chloride (KCI Injectable solution).
8. Two minute wait.
9. Execution over.

DISCLAIMER

Fred A. Leuchter Associates, Inc. assumes no responsibility for the intended or actual use of this device.

Nelson v. Campbell

541 U.S. 637 (2004)

JUSTICE O'CONNOR delivered the opinion of the Court.

Three days before his scheduled execution by lethal injection, petitioner David Nelson filed a civil rights action in District Court, pursuant to 42 U.S.C. § 1983, alleging that the use of a "cut-down" procedure to access his veins would violate the Eighth Amendment. Petitioner, who had already filed one unsuccessful federal habeas application, sought a stay of execution so that the District Court could consider the merits of his constitutional claim. The question before us is whether § 1983 is an appropriate vehicle for petitioner's Eighth Amendment claim seeking a temporary stay and permanent injunctive relief. We answer that question in the affirmative, reverse the contrary judgment of the Eleventh Circuit, and remand the case for further proceedings consistent with this opinion.

I

Because the District Court dismissed the suit at the pleading stage, we assume the allegations in petitioner's complaint to be true. Petitioner was found guilty by a jury in 1979 of capital murder and sentenced to death. Following two resentencings, the Eleventh Circuit, on June 3, 2002, affirmed the District Court's denial of petitioner's first federal habeas petition challenging the most recent death sentence. *Nelson v. Alabama,* 292 F.3d 1291. Up until and at the time of that disposition, Alabama employed electrocution as its sole method of execution. On July 1, 2002, Alabama changed to lethal injection, though it still allowed inmates to opt for electrocution upon written notification within 30 days of the Alabama Supreme Court's entry of judgment or July 1, 2002, whichever is later. Ala. Code § 15-18-82.1 (Lexis Supp. 2003). Because he failed to make a timely request, petitioner waived his option to be executed by electrocution.

This Court denied petitioner's request for certiorari review of the Eleventh Circuit's decision on March 24, 2003. *Nelson v. Alabama,* 538 U.S. 926. Two weeks later, the Alabama Attorney General's office moved the Alabama Supreme Court to set an execution date. Petitioner responded by letter that he "had no plans to contest [the] motion," agreeing "that an execution date should be set promptly by the court in the immediate future." Hearing no objection, the Alabama Supreme Court, on September 3, 2003, set petitioner's execution for October 9, 2003.

Due to years of drug abuse, petitioner has severely compromised peripheral veins, which are inaccessible by standard techniques for gaining intravenous access, such as a needle. In August 2003, counsel for petitioner contacted Grantt Culliver, warden of Holman Correctional Facility where the execution was to take place, to discuss how petitioner's medical condition might impact the lethal injection procedure. Counsel specifically requested a copy of the State's written protocol for gaining venous access prior to execution, and asked that a privately retained or prison physician consult with petitioner about the procedure. The warden advised counsel that the State had such a protocol, but stated that he could not provide it to her. He nevertheless assured counsel that "medical personnel" would be present during the execution and that a prison physician would evaluate and speak with petitioner upon his arrival at Holman Correctional Facility.

Petitioner was transferred to Holman shortly after the Alabama Supreme Court set the execution date. Warden Culliver and a prison nurse met with and examined petitioner on September 10, 2003. Upon confirming that petitioner had compromised veins, Warden Culliver informed petitioner that prison personnel would cut a 0.5-inch incision in petitioner's arm and catheterize a vein 24 hours before the scheduled execution. At a second meeting on Friday, October 3, 2003, the warden dramatically altered the prognosis: prison personnel would now make a 2-inch incision in petitioner's arm or leg; the procedure would take place one hour before the scheduled execution; and only local anesthesia would be used. There was no assurance that a physician would perform or even be present for the procedure. Counsel immediately contacted the Alabama Department of Corrections Legal Department requesting a copy of the State's execution protocol. The legal department denied counsel's request.

The following Monday, three days before his scheduled execution, petitioner filed the present §1983 action alleging that the so-called "cut-down" procedure constituted cruel and unusual punishment and deliberate indifference to his serious medical needs in violation of the Eighth Amendment. Petitioner sought: a permanent injunction against use of the cut-down; a temporary stay of execution to allow the District Court to consider the merits of his claim; an order requiring respondents to furnish a copy of the protocol setting forth the medical procedures to be used to gain venous access; and an order directing respondents, in consultation with medical experts, to promulgate a venous access protocol that comports with contemporary standards of medical care. Appended to the complaint was an affidavit from Dr. Mark Heath, a board certified anesthesiologist and assistant professor at Columbia University College of Physicians and Surgeons, attesting that the cut-down is a dangerous and antiquated medical procedure to be performed only by a trained physician in a clinical environment with the patient under deep sedation. In light of safer and less-invasive contemporary means of venous access, Dr. Heath concluded that "there is no comprehensible reason for the State of Alabama to be planning to employ the cut-down procedure to obtain intravenous access, unless there exists an intent to render the procedure more painful and risky than it otherwise needs to be."

Respondents moved to dismiss the complaint for want of jurisdiction on the grounds that petitioner's §1983 claim and accompanying stay request were the "'functional equivalent'" of a second or successive habeas application subject to the gatekeeping provisions of 28 U.S.C. §2244(b). The District Court agreed and, because petitioner had not obtained authorization to file a second or successive application as required by §2244(b)(3), dismissed the complaint. A divided panel of the Eleventh Circuit affirmed. Relying on *Fugate v. Department of Corrections,* 301 F.3d 1287 (CA11 2002), in which the Eleventh Circuit had held that §1983 claims challenging the method of execution necessarily sound in habeas, the majority held that petitioner should have sought authorization to file a second or successive habeas application. The majority also concluded that, even were it to construe petitioner's appeal as a request for such authorization, it would nevertheless deny the request because petitioner could not show that, but for the purported Eighth Amendment violation, "'no reasonable factfinder would have found [him] guilty of the underlying offense.'" Thus, the Eleventh Circuit held that petitioner was without recourse to challenge the constitutionality of the cut-down procedure in Federal District Court. We granted certiorari and now reverse.

II

A.

Section 1983 authorizes a "suit in equity, or other proper proceeding for redress" against any person who, under color of state law, "subjects, or causes to be subjected, any citizen of the United States ... to the deprivation of any rights, privileges, or immunities secured by the Constitution." Petitioner's complaint states such a claim. Despite its literal applicability, however, § 1983 must yield to the more specific federal habeas statute, with its attendant procedural and exhaustion requirements, where an inmate seeks injunctive relief challenging the fact of his conviction or the duration of his sentence. See *Preiser v. Rodriguez*, 411 U.S. 475, 489 (1973). Such claims fall within the "core" of habeas corpus and are thus not cognizable when brought pursuant to § 1983. By contrast, constitutional claims that merely challenge the conditions of a prisoner's confinement, whether the inmate seeks monetary or injunctive relief, fall outside of that core and may be brought pursuant to § 1983 in the first instance. See *Muhammad v. Close*, 540 U.S. 749 (2004).

We have not yet had occasion to consider whether civil rights suits seeking to enjoin the use of a particular method of execution—*e.g.*, lethal injection or electrocution—fall within the core of federal habeas corpus or, rather, whether they are properly viewed as challenges to the conditions of a condemned inmate's death sentence. Neither the "conditions" nor the "fact or duration" label is particularly apt. A suit seeking to enjoin a particular means of effectuating a sentence of death does not directly call into question the "fact" or "validity" of the sentence itself—by simply altering its method of execution, the State can go forward with the sentence. Cf. *Weaver v. Graham*, 450 U.S. 24, 32–33, n. 17 (1981) (no *ex post facto* violation to change method of execution to more humane method). On the other hand, imposition of the death penalty presupposes a means of carrying it out. In a State such as Alabama, where the legislature has established lethal injection as the preferred method of execution, see Ala. Code § 15-18-82 (Lexis Supp. 2003) (lethal injection as default method), a constitutional challenge seeking to permanently enjoin the use of lethal injection may amount to a challenge to the fact of the sentence itself. A finding of unconstitutionality would require statutory amendment or variance, imposing significant costs on the State and the administration of its penal system. And while it makes little sense to talk of the "duration" of a death sentence, a State retains a significant interest in meting out a sentence of death in a timely fashion. See *Calderon v. Thompson*, 523 U.S. 538, 556–557 (1998); *In re Blodgett*, 502 U.S. 236, 238 (1992) (*per curiam*); *McCleskey v. Zant*, 499 U.S. 467, 491 (1991) ("The power of a State to pass laws means little if the State cannot enforce them").

We need not reach here the difficult question of how to categorize method-of-execution claims generally. Respondents at oral argument conceded that § 1983 would be an appropriate vehicle for an inmate who is not facing execution to bring a "deliberate indifference" challenge to the constitutionality of the cut-down procedure if used to gain venous access for purposes of providing medical treatment. We see no reason on the face of the complaint to treat petitioner's claim differently solely because he has been condemned to die.

Respondents counter that, because the cut-down is part of the execution procedure, petitioner's challenge is, in fact, a challenge to the fact of his execution. They offer the following argument: A challenge to the use of lethal injection as a method of execution sounds in habeas; venous access is a necessary prerequisite to, and thus an indispensable part of, any lethal injection procedure; therefore, a challenge to the State's means of achieving venous access must be brought in a federal habeas application. Even were we to accept as given respondents' premise that a challenge to lethal injection sounds in habeas, the conclusion does not follow. That venous access is a necessary prerequisite does not imply that a particular means of gaining such access is likewise necessary. Indeed, the gravamen of petitioner's entire claim is that use of the cut-down would be *gratuitous*. Merely labeling something as part of an execution procedure is insufficient to insulate it from a § 1983 attack.

If as a legal matter the cut-down were a statutorily mandated part of the lethal injection protocol, or if as a factual matter petitioner were unable or unwilling to concede acceptable alternatives for gaining venous access, respondents might have a stronger argument that success on the merits, coupled with injunctive relief, would call into question the death sentence itself. But petitioner has been careful throughout these proceedings, in his complaint and at oral argument, to assert that the cut-down, as well as the warden's refusal to provide reliable information regarding the cut-down protocol, are *wholly unnecessary* to gaining venous access. Petitioner has alleged alternatives that, if they had been used, would have allowed the State to proceed with the execution as scheduled. No Alabama statute requires use of the cut-down, see Ala. Code § 15-18-82 (Lexis Supp. 2003) (saying only that method of execution is lethal injection), and respondents have offered no duly-promulgated regulations to the contrary.

If on remand and after an evidentiary hearing the District Court concludes that use of the cut-down procedure as described in the complaint is necessary for administering the lethal injection, the District Court will need to address the broader question, left open here, of how to treat method-of-execution claims generally. An evidentiary hearing will in all likelihood be unnecessary, however, as the State now seems willing to implement petitioner's proposed alternatives.

We note that our holding here is consistent with our approach to civil rights damages actions, which, like method-of-execution challenges, fall at the margins of habeas. Although damages are not an available habeas remedy, we have previously concluded that a § 1983 suit for damages that would "necessarily imply" the invalidity of the fact of an inmate's conviction, or "necessarily imply" the invalidity of the length of an inmate's sentence, is not cognizable under § 1983 unless and until the inmate obtains favorable termination of a state, or federal habeas, challenge to his conviction or sentence. *Heck v. Humphrey*, 512 U.S. 477, 487 (1994); *Edwards v. Balisok*, 520 U.S. 641, 648 (1997). This "favorable termination" requirement is necessary to prevent inmates from doing indirectly through damages actions what they could not do directly by seeking injunctive relief—challenge the fact or duration of their confinement without complying with the procedural limitations of the federal habeas statute. Even so, we were careful in *Heck* to stress the importance of the term "necessarily." For instance, we acknowledged that an inmate could bring a challenge to the lawfulness of a search pursuant to § 1983 in the first instance, even if the search revealed evidence used to convict the inmate at trial, because success on the merits would not "*necessarily* imply that the plaintiff's conviction was unlawful." To hold otherwise would have cut off potentially valid damages actions as to which a plaintiff might never obtain favorable termination—suits that could otherwise have gone forward had the plaintiff not been convicted. In the present context, focusing attention on whether petitioner's challenge to the cut-down procedure would *necessarily* prevent Alabama from carrying out its execution both protects against the use of § 1983 to circumvent any limits imposed by the habeas statute and minimizes the extent to which the fact of a prisoner's imminent execution will require differential treatment of his otherwise cognizable § 1983 claims....

C.

Respondents argue that a decision to reverse the judgment of the Eleventh Circuit would open the floodgates to all manner of method-of-execution challenges, as well as last minute stay requests. But, because we do not here resolve the question of how to treat method-of-execution claims generally, our holding is extremely limited.

Moreover, as our previous decision in *Gomez v. United States Dist. Court for Northern Dist. of Cal.*, 503 U.S. 653 (1992) *(per curiam)*, makes clear, the mere fact that an inmate states a cognizable § 1983 claim does not warrant the entry of a stay as a matter of right. *Gomez* came to us on a motion by the State to vacate a stay entered by an en banc panel of the Court of Appeals for the Ninth Circuit that would have allowed the District Court time to consider the merits of a condemned inmate's last-minute § 1983 action challenging the constitutionality of California's use of the gas chamber. We left open the question whether the inmate's claim was cognizable under § 1983, but vacated the stay nonetheless. The inmate, Robert Alton Harris, who had already filed four unsuccessful federal habeas applications, waited until the 11th hour to file his challenge despite the fact that California's method of execution had been in place for years: "This claim could have been brought more than a decade ago. There is no good reason for this abusive delay, which has been compounded by last-minute attempts to manipulate the judicial process. A court may consider the last-minute nature of an application to stay execution in deciding whether to grant equitable relief."

A stay is an equitable remedy, and "equity must take into consideration the State's strong interest in proceeding with its judgment and ... attempts at manipulation." Thus, before granting a stay, a district court must consider not only the likelihood of success on the merits and the relative harms to the parties, but also the extent to which the inmate has delayed unnecessarily in bringing the claim. Given the State's significant interest in enforcing its criminal judgments, see *Blodgett*, 502 U.S., at 239; *McCleskey*, 499 U.S., at 491, there is a strong equitable presumption against the grant of a stay where a claim could have been brought at such a time as to allow consideration of the merits without requiring entry of a stay.

Finally, the ability to bring a § 1983 claim, rather than a habeas application, does not entirely free inmates from substantive or procedural limitations. The Prison Litigation Reform Act of 1995 (Act) imposes limits on the scope and duration of preliminary and permanent injunctive relief, including a requirement that, before issuing such relief, "[a] court shall give substantial weight to any adverse impact on ... the operation of a criminal justice system caused by the relief." 18 U.S.C. § 3626(a)(1); accord, § 3626(a)(2). It requires that inmates exhaust available state administrative remedies before bringing a § 1983 action challenging the conditions of their confinement. 42 U.S.C. § 1997e(a) ("No action shall be brought with respect to prison conditions under section 1983 of this title, or any other Federal law, by a prisoner confined in any jail, prison, or other correctional facility until such administrative remedies as are available are exhausted"). The Act mandates that a district court "shall," on its own motion, dismiss "any action brought with respect to prison conditions under section 1983 of this title ... if the court is satisfied that the action is frivolous, malicious, fails to state a claim upon which relief can be granted, or seeks monetary relief from a defendant who is immune from relief." § 1997e(c)(1). Indeed, if the claim is frivolous on its face, a district court may dismiss the suit before the plaintiff has exhausted his state remedies. § 1997e(c)(2).

For the reasons stated herein, the judgment of the Court of Appeals for the Eleventh Circuit is reversed, and the case is remanded for further proceedings consistent with this opinion.

Note on Eighth Amendment Challenges to the Use of Pavulon in Lethal Injections

Although the decision in *Nelson v. Campbell* marks the first time the Supreme Court has been willing to consider the constitutionality of the lethal injection procedure, Nelson is not the first death row inmate to challenge lethal injection under the Eighth Amendment. In 2003, death row inmates in Texas and Tennessee challenged the constitutionality of execution by lethal injection, arguing that the chemical pancuronium bromide (trade name Pavulon), utilized in the lethal injection processes of more than 30 states, can mask severe pain and its use therefore constitutes cruel and unusual punishment. Pavulon has been prescribed for use in executions since Oklahoma first adopted lethal injection as a method of execution in 1977. Pavulon paralyzes the skeletal muscles but has no effect on the brain or central nervous system. The result, critics believe, is that once Pavulon has been administered, the prisoner cannot speak or move, even if conscious and capable of feeling pain. Thus, they argue, Pavulon merely masks distress and suffering while the prisoner is left unable to speak or cry out while suffocating.

Death row inmate Abu-Ali Abdur'Rahman brought suit in Tennessee Chancery Court in June of 2003, arguing that the state's lethal injection protocol was adopted without proper review and that its use of the chemical Pavulon in the execution could cause a horrific and painful death if the first drug, sodium pentothal, did not render the prisoner completely unconscious. Although Abdur'Rahman's challenge was unsuccessful, the majority opinion, written by Davidson County Judge Ellen Hobbs Lyle, was nevertheless critical of the use of Pavulon in the execution procedure. Judge Lyle conceded there appeared to be no apparent purpose for using Pavulon in the state's lethal injection procedure. According to Judge Lyle's opinion:

> "The proof established that Tennessee's method is not state of the art. It was developed simply by copying the same method currently in use by some thirty other states.... Moreover, the method's use of Pavulon, a drug outlawed in Tennessee for euthanasia of pets, is arbitrary. The State failed to demonstrate any need whatsoever for the injection of Pavulon....

> "A significant part of the plaintiff's challenge to Tennessee's lethal injection method is the use of Pavulon. Dr. Heath, an assistant professor of clinical anesthesia at Columbia University ... testified that Pavulon is a neuromuscular blocking agent. Its effect is that it renders the muscles unable to contract but it does not affect the brain or the nerves.... Dr. Heath testified to what he termed the 'chemical veil' of Pavulon. He stated that Pavulon, because of its paralytic effect on the muscles, makes the patient look serene. The face muscles cannot move or contract or any muscles to show pain or suffering.

> "Testimony was also provided by Carol Weihrer who endured a surgery where Pavulon was administered and the anesthesia was not effective. Ms. Weihrer testified that she was able to hear, perceive and feel everything that was going on in her surgery. She was able to think. Torturously she was unable to move because of the effects of the Pavulon. She testified that she was attempting with all of her will to communicate that she was still conscious but that she was unable to because of the Pavulon.

> "Dr. Geiser, a professor of veterinary science at the University of Tennessee School of Agriculture, testified similarly to the effect of Pavulon on animals....

He testified that the use of Pavulon in euthanasia of animals has been outlawed in Tennessee and a number of other states. Dr. Geiser testified that Pavulon could potentially produce an inhumane situation with animals because it causes respiratory arrest without arrest of the central nervous system ... [and] the effect is like asphyxiation.

"Significantly, there was no proof from the State that the Pavulon is necessary to the lethal injection process.... The State's expert, Dr. Levy, on cross-examination, testified that he did not know of any legitimate purpose for the use of Pavulon in the Tennessee lethal injection process. He agreed that the injection of Pavulon without anesthesia would be a horrifying experience....

"Coupled with the testimony of the paralytic effect of Pavulon is that the State failed to provide any proof of the reason for its use in the lethal injection method. There was no testimony that the purpose of Pavulon in Tennessee's lethal injection method was to hasten death.... From this void of proof and in conjunction with the proof on the effects of Pavulon, the plaintiff argues that the reason Pavulon is used by the State is to mask or put a chemical veil over what death by lethal injection really looks like. The Pavulon gives a false impression of serenity to viewers, making punishment by death more palatable and acceptable to society.

"The plaintiff's chemical veil argument raises the age-old concern of a society conceived as colonists and schooled during maturing in the abuses of power by government. The chemical veil taps into every citizen's fear that the government manipulates the setting and gilds the lily, whether it be with reporting on the economy or election results, to orchestrate and manipulate public reaction.

"The proof before this Court did not demonstrate that the State, in creating Tennessee's lethal injection method, included use of Pavulon to create a chemical veil. Instead, the proof demonstrated that, if anything, Pavulon was included by the State out of ignorance and by just copying what other states do. In preparing the lethal injection method used by Tennessee, the proof revealed that the State did not consult physicians or pharmacologists. The State "copycatted," using what a majority of other states were doing, including the use of Pavulon.... Thus, the Court concludes that, while not offensive in constitutional terms, the state's use of Pavulon is 'gilding of the lily' or, stated in legal terms, arbitrary." *Abdur'Rahman v. Sundquist*, No. 02-2236 (Tenn. Chan. Ct. 20th Dist. June 2, 2003).

In a similar case, Texas death row inmate Kevin Zimmerman was granted a temporary stay of execution in December of 2003 by Justice Scalia. Zimmerman's attorney contended that the use of Pavulon served no legitimate purpose other than masking intense suffering during the execution, and thus violated the Eighth Amendment. Although Zimmerman's stay of execution was eventually dissolved by the full Supreme Court on January 21, 2004, Justices Stevens, Souter, Ginsburg and Breyer all voted in favor of upholding the stay of execution.

In January 2006, just minutes before his execution was to take place, Clarence Hill received a stay of execution from the U.S. Supreme Court. Hill had filed a civil rights claim alleging that Florida's lethal injection procedure relied on chemicals which could inflict severe and unnecessary pain. The Court granted certiorari to decide "whether, under this Court's decision in *Nelson*, a challenge to a particular protocol the State plans to use during the execution process constitutes a cognizable claim under 42 U.S.C. Sec. 1983?" *Hill v. Crosby*, No. 05-8794. The Court's ruling in *Hill* will be included in Coyne & Entzeroth, Supplement to Capital Punishment and the Judicial Process.

7. The Role of Physicians and Other Health Professionals

Notes and Questions

1. For physicians and other health professionals, participation in executions raises troubling issues of medical ethics. Since the formulation of the Hippocratic Oath during the fifth century B.C., the code of medical ethics has exalted the preservation of life and the cessation of pain above all other values. The oath provides:

> I will follow that method of treatment which, according to my ability and judgment, I consider for the benefit of my patients, and abstain from whatever is deleterious and mischievous. I will give no deadly medicine to anyone if asked, nor suggest any such counsel.

2. Which, if any, of the following medical procedures may a doctor perform consistent with the Hippocratic Oath?

A. Administer a pre-execution examination to determine mental and physical fitness for execution.

B. Order the drugs to be used for lethal injection.

C. Train the non-physician medical personnel who will prepare the syringes and administer the poison injection.

D. Prescribe sedatives to enable the condemned to face his execution calmly.

E. Prescribe medication to restore the inmate's sanity so that he may be executed.

F. Prepare the body of the condemned for execution (e.g., helping to locate a suitable vein for lethal injection or shaving hair so that electrodes may be efficiently attached to the body for electrocution).

G. Attend the execution as a medical witness.

H. Participate in the execution by supervising the procedure.

I. Examine the body of the condemned so that the execution can continue if the prisoner is not yet dead.

J. Examine the body of the condemned in order to certify that the penalty was carried out.

K. Perform an autopsy on the executed prisoner to determine the cause of death.

3. During its July 1980 annual meeting, the American Medical Association's House of Delegates adopted the following resolution:

> A physician, as a member of a profession dedicated to the preservation of life when there is hope of doing so, should not be a participant in a legally authorized execution. [However, a] physician may make a determination or certification of death as currently provided by law in any situation.

4. As of January 1, 2006, Texas had the second largest death row population in the United States (409 inmates). California's death row population at that time was 649. Since 1976, Texas has consistently led the nation in annual executions. In the year 2005, Texas put to death 19 inmates. Between 1977, when executions resumed in the United States, and March 20, 2006, Texas executed 360 inmates. The state with the second highest number of executions during this period is Virginia (94).

In 1982, Texas executed Charles Brooks, becoming the first state to execute by lethal injection. A Texas Medical Association policy then in effect provided, "A physician may be present at a chemical execution for the sole purpose of pronouncing death."

Dr. Ralph Gray, Medical Director for the Texas Department of Corrections, examined Mr. Brooks before the execution to determine whether Brooks' veins were large enough to accept the catheter needle used to deliver the lethal drugs. In addition, Dr. Gray supplied the lethal drugs and members of his staff were the medical technicians who administered the lethal injection. During the execution, Dr. Gray monitored Brooks' heartbeat through a stethoscope and at one point indicated that the execution should continue for a few more minutes.

A complaint filed with the local Texas county medical society charged that Dr. Gray's involvement in the execution violated the Texas Medical Association (TMA) policy. In February 1984, the society concluded that Dr. Gray had not participated in the execution in violation of the policy and that no breach of medical ethics had occurred. According to the society's opinion, the TMA policy "was intended to prohibit a physician's direct participation in an execution by lethal injection, such as by actual insertion of an intravenous catheter or actual introduction of the lethal agent(s)." *United States of America: The Death Penalty* 141–142 (Amnesty International 1987).

If the execution of Brooks was not justifiable homicide (authorized or commanded by law), would Dr. Gray's actions subject him to criminal liability to the same extent as the medical technicians who inserted the catheter and introduced the lethal drugs into Brooks' bloodstream?

5. See also Gawande, "When Law and Ethics Collide — Why Physicians Participate in Executions," 354 New England J. of Medicine 1221 (2006).

6. Note the serious dilemma created by requiring doctors to participate in executions. Doctors, dedicated to preserving life and nurturing health, may be prevented by their own ethical code from participating in executions. However, if doctors do not participate, and the execution is carried out by less competent personnel, the risk increases that the inmate will suffer needlessly. Ethical Opinion 2.06, authored by the American Medical Association's Council on Ethical and Judicial Affairs, provides in part: "An individual's opinion on capital punishment is the personal moral decision of the individual. A physician, as a member of a profession dedicated to preserving life when there is hope of doing so, should not be a participant in a legally authorized execution." Should this prohibition extend to a doctor's certification of death? If a doctor discovers that the inmate is not yet dead, wouldn't that lead to additional drugs being supplied to kill the inmate? What about a doctor who is called upon to certify that an inmate is psychiatrically fit to be executed? Although the ethical standard is nearly universal, it does not have the force and effect of law. Given that adherence to the rule is voluntary and no doctors have been reprimanded or stripped of their licenses for taking part in executions, does Ethical Opinion 2.06 matter?

7. In California, U.S. District Judge Jeremy Fogel ruled that the combination of drugs used to carry out lethal injections may constitute cruel and unusual punishment. Because he was troubled by the prospect that inmates may be conscious and subjected to excruciating pain once a paralyzing agent and then a heart-stopping drug are administered, Judge Fogel ordered California to change its lethal injection procedures before carrying out the February 21, 2006 scheduled execution of Michael Morales. Specifically, Judge Fogel directed that California select one of three options: a lethal injection of barbituates only (which might prolong the execution by as much as 45 minutes); having an anesthesiologist present at the execution to ensure that Morales was unconscious when the usual three-drug cocktail was administered; or a stay of execution pending a hearing. State officials selected the second option, and arranged for two anesthesiologists to be present at the execution. However, the two doctors refused to participate in the 12:01 a.m. execution after they learned that they would be expected to tell prison officials whether Morales needed more sedation or perhaps to order additional drugs to hasten Morales' death. Determined to proceed, state officials announced that they would switch to the first option—lethal injection using barbituates only. Judge Fogel agreed to the change, but only if a trained medical professional administered the lethal injection. Previously, California prison employees inserted the intravenous lines and the drugs were sent into the inmates bloodstream by a machine. State officials elected to postpone the execution indefinitely. Sahagun & Reiterman, *Execution of Killer-Rapist is Postponed After Doctors Walk Out*, The Los Angeles Times, Feb. 21, 2006.

8. Before earning national notoriety as a physician willing to assist terminally ill patients commit suicide, Dr. Jack Kevorkian proposed "that a prisoner condemned to death by due process of law be allowed to submit, by his own free choice, to medical experimentation under complete anaesthesia (at the time appointed for administering the penalty) as a form of execution in lieu of conventional methods prescribed by law." J. of Crim. Law, Criminology, and Police Science 50 (1959). What do you think of Dr. Kevorkian's proposal? Identify advantages and disadvantages. Does Kevorkian's suggestion differ from the practice of Nazis who during World War II conducted medical experiments on Jews and prisoners of war?

F. Death Penalty Jurisdictions and Racial Characteristics of Death Row Populations

According to the Death Penalty Information Center, thirty-eight jurisdictions had capital punishment statutes as of March 20, 2006. Of the thirty-eight jurisdictions with capital punishment statutes, six of these jurisdictions (Kansas, New Hampshire, New York, South Dakota, and the U.S. Military) have not had any executions since 1976. Thirteen jurisdictions did not have capital punishment statutes as of March 20, 2006. These are Alaska, District of Columbia, Hawaii, Iowa, Maine, Massachusetts, Michigan, Minnesota, North Dakota, Rhode Island, Vermont, West Virginia and Wisconsin.

Notes

1. For more information on race and the death penalty, see *infra* chapter 4.

2. The following statistics report the racial characteristics of death row inmates in these jurisdictions as of January 1, 2006:[20]

Race of Death Row Inmates (as of January 1, 2006)
NAACP Legal Defense Fund Statistics

State	Total	Black	White	Latino	Native Am.	Asian	Unk.
Alabama	190	94	94	2	0	0	0
Arizona	125	13	89	20	3	0	0
Arkansas	38	24	14	0	0	0	0
California	649	232	251	131	14	21	0
Colorado	2	1	0	1	0	0	0
Connecticut	8	3	3	2	0	0	0
Delaware	18	6	9	3	0	0	0
Florida	388	136	216	34	1	1	0
Georgia	109	51	54	3	0	1	0
Idaho	20	0	20	0	0	0	0
Illinois	10	3	5	2	0	0	0
Indiana	26	8	18	0	0	0	0
Kansas	8	3	5	0	0	0	0
Kentucky	37	8	28	1	0	0	0
Louisiana	85	54	28	2	0	1	0
Maryland	8	5	3	0	0	0	0
Mississippi	65	33	31	0	0	1	0
Missouri	53	22	31	0	0	0	0
Montana	4	0	4	0	0	0	0
Nebraska	10	1	6	3	0	0	0
Nevada	83	32	42	8	0	1	0
New Jersey	13	6	7	0	0	0	0
New Mexico	2	0	2	0	0	0	0
New York	1	1	0	0	0	0	0
N. Carolina	190	104	72	3	10	1	0
Ohio	196	98	91	3	2	2	0
Oklahoma	91	33	51	2	5	0	0
Oregon	33	3	26	2	1	0	1
Pennsylvania	231	140	71	18	0	2	0
S. Carolina	74	38	36	0	0	0	0
South Dakota	4	0	4	0	0	0	0
Tennessee	108	43	60	1	2	2	0
Texas	409	170	124	111	0	4	0
Utah	9	1	6	1	1	0	0
Virginia	22	12	10	0	0	0	0
Washington	10	4	6	0	0	0	0
Wyoming	2	0	2	0	0	0	0
U.S. Military	9	6	2	0	0	1	0
U.S. Gov't	40	23	16	0	1	0	0
Total	3380	1411	1537	353	40	38	1
		42%	45%	10%	1%	1%	.03%

---

20. Updated information is available at http://deathpenaltyinfo.org.

Distribution of Executions Throughout the Country Since 1976
(As of March 30, 2006)

State	Total	State	Total	State	Total
Texas	362	Ohio	20	Federal Gov.	3
Virginia	94	Indiana	17	Kentucky	2
Oklahoma	79	Delaware	14	Montana	2
Missouri	66	California	13	Oregon	2
Florida	60	Illinois	12	Connecticut	1
N. Carolina	41	Nevada	11	Colorado	1
Georgia	39	Mississippi	7	Idaho	1
S. Carolina	35	Utah	6	New Mexico	1
Alabama	34	Maryland	5	Tennessee	1
Louisiana	27	Washington	4	Wyoming	1
Arkansas	27	Nebraska	3		
Arizona	22	Pennsylvania	3		

3. Consider Professor Jeffrey Kirchmeier's analysis of an inmate's right to select a punishment which might violate the Eighth Amendment.

Let's Make a Deal: Waiving the Eighth Amendment by Selecting a Cruel and Unusual Punishment

Jeffrey L. Kirchmeier, 32 Conn. L. Rev. 615 (Winter 2000)

... [A] panel of the Ninth Circuit held in *LaGrand v. Stewart*, 173 F.3d 1144 (9th Cir. 1999), *rev'd*, 119 S.Ct. 1018 (1999), that a defendant's voluntary choice of lethal gas did not waive his claim that the use of lethal gas violates the Eighth Amendment. Arizona has a death penalty statute where lethal injection is the default method, and in *LaGrand*, the defendant had chosen lethal gas. The court noted that "the law of the circuit" is that "Eighth Amendment protections may not be waived, at least in the area of capital punishment." Thus, the court went on to address the defendant's challenge of lethal gas as an execution method, holding that lethal gas was a cruel and unusual punishment and enjoining the state of Arizona from executing Karl LaGrand by that method. Although the Ninth Circuit granted Karl LaGrand a stay of execution on the gas chamber issue, the Supreme Court subsequently vacated the stay without comment. [*Stewart v. (Karl) LaGrand*, 119 S. Ct. 1107 (1999).] Mr. LaGrand was allowed to change his execution method at the last minute, and he was executed by lethal injection.

Almost immediately, however, the issue arose again when Karl's brother, Walter, was scheduled to be executed, and he also chose lethal gas as his method of execution. After the Ninth Circuit court restrained and enjoined the State of Arizona from executing Walter by lethal gas, the Supreme Court granted the state's petition for writ of certiorari and vacated the injunction. [119 S. Ct. at 1020 (1999).] Thus, Walter LaGrand was executed in Arizona's gas chamber on March 3, 1999.

The following is the Supreme Court's complete analysis in *LaGrand* of whether a capital defendant may consent to be executed by an otherwise unconstitutional method of execution:

> By declaring his method of execution, picking lethal gas over the state's default form of execution — lethal injection — Walter LaGrand has waived any objection he might have to it. See e.g., *Johnson v. Zerbst*, 304 U.S. 458, 464 (1938). To hold otherwise, and to hold that Eighth Amendment protections cannot be

waived in the capital context, would create and apply a new procedural rule in violation of *Teague v. Lane*, 489 U.S. 288 (1989).

119 S. Ct. at 1020. Additionally, the Court found that the gas issue was procedurally defaulted because Walter LaGrand did not raise the issue on direct appeal....

IV. The Public Interest in the Eighth Amendment Ban on Cruel and Unusual Punishments Does not Permit Waiver by Individuals

There are three reasons why the Constitution does not allow defendants to waive the Eighth Amendment ban on cruel and unusual punishment.[217] First, the Supreme Court's own Eighth Amendment analysis indicates a strong societal interest in the ban on cruel and unusual punishments that should not be waived by one individual. Second, such Eighth Amendment waivers should not be permitted because they differ significantly from waivers of other constitutional rights since such Eighth Amendment waivers, unlike other constitutional waivers, provide no benefits and are a detriment to society. Third, allowing such waivers and allowing any punishment as a choice would lead to absurd results and deprive the Eighth Amendment of meaning.

A. Supreme Court Precedent Reveals a Societal Interest in the Eighth Amendment That Should Not Be Waived by an Individual

[T]he Court has consistently allowed certain constitutional rights to be waived by criminal defendants. Although the Court has held that certain constitutional rights may be waived by criminal defendants, it does not necessarily follow that a defendant may waive the right not to be subjected to a cruel and unusual punishment.... [I]n an execution volunteer case, *Lenhard v. Wolff*, [444 U.S. 807 (1979),] Justice Marshall wrote a dissent that questioned the constitutionality of Eighth Amendment waivers. Justice Marshall argued that the Eighth Amendment not only protects individuals, "it also expresses a fundamental interest of society in ensuring that state authority is not used to administer barbaric punishments." Therefore, he argued, society's interests in the ban on cruel and unusual punishments cannot be overridden by a defendant's waiver. Justices Brennan, Marshall, and White expressed similar concerns in *Whitmore v. Arkansas*, [495 U.S. 149, 171–76 (1990)].

The problem with this argument, however, is that society has an interest in all rights in the Bill of Rights being enforced, and Justice Marshall's argument could mean that defendants could not waive other rights, like the right to a jury trial. Actually, Justice Harlan made a similar argument in 1883 in *Hopt v. Utah*, [110 U.S. 574 (1884),] regarding the right of a defendant to be present at trial. In that case, Justice Harlan stated, "[that] which the law makes essential in proceedings involving the deprivation of life or liberty cannot be dispensed with, or affected by the consent of the accused." Since then, however, the Court has held in numerous cases that certain constitutional rights may be waived. This Article does not argue that all of those cases should be overruled; the question is whether this Eighth Amendment right differs from those other constitutional rights.

---

217. Initially, in considering waiver, there is an issue of whether a criminal defendant selecting certain punishments, such as the means of death, can ever really make a "knowing, voluntary and intelligent" waiver. The choice situation has an element of coercion, and many defendants may not be able to make such a "free" choice. For example, several studies indicate that a large proportion of capital defendants are brain damaged, mentally ill, mentally retarded and/or victims of childhood abuse. Such defendants may never be able to "knowingly, voluntarily and intelligently" make such a choice.

The Supreme Court's own Eighth Amendment analysis provides a significant reason why waiver should not apply in the context of the application of the Eighth Amendment to barbaric punishments. Unlike the analysis used regarding other rights, the Eighth Amendment analysis used by the Court to evaluate each punishment is based, in large part, on current societal standards, illustrating the public's interest in the Eighth Amendment.

As discussed above, the Supreme Court looks to both objective and subjective factors in determining whether a punishment violates the Eighth Amendment. In *Weems*, the Court looked at contemporary standards to strike down the punishment of hard and painful labor for document falsification.[229] There, the Court stated that the Eighth Amendment "may acquire meaning as public opinion becomes enlightened by a humane justice." In *Trop*, the Court struck down denationalization as a punishment in part because it was a rare form of punishment in today's "international community of democracies."[231] There, the Court said the Amendment "must draw its meaning from the evolving standards of decency that mark the progress of a maturing society." The Court has continued to rely upon objective societal standards as it has addressed the death penalty in cases beginning with *Furman* and *Gregg*. For example, in *Gregg*, a plurality stated that the cruel and unusual punishment clause requires courts to examine "objective indicia that reflect the public attitude toward a given sanction."[234] The same analysis has continued in subsequent cases, and the Justices continue to evaluate the "national consensus" from such indicators as legislative enactments and jury verdicts in interpreting the Eighth Amendment.

This reliance on objective factors in Eighth Amendment analysis creates a mandate from the Court that permitted punishments must reflect our contemporary society. The Court has indicated an overall community concern with the types of punishments society inflicts by using such terms as "public attitude," "national consensus," "human dignity," and "humane justice." Additionally, the use of the term "unusual" in the Eighth Amendment itself indicates a concern with punishments that are out of the ordinary from contemporary society. This requirement that the Eighth Amendment comply with today's world illustrates a societal interest beyond that of other rights whose main focus is on the protection of individuals. Thus, the Eighth Amendment is unique in that it protects the interests of contemporary society, and an individual should not be able to waive that protection from barbaric punishments.

The Eighth Amendment ban on cruel and unusual punishments has a societal base that is more comparable to some constitutional rights than to others. For example, First Amendment rights are society based, so the Court would likely hold that a criminal defendant could not waive First Amendment rights if a judge were to give the defendant the options of prison or attending the judge's church every week. Societal interests in the separation of church and state would prevent a defendant from electing to go to the judge's church even if the defendant "waived" the right to object by choosing that option over prison. Indeed, several courts have held that such sentences are unconstitutional.[245] The ban on cruel and unusual punishments, as well as the Establishment

---

229. *See Weems v. United States*, 217 U.S. 349, 378 (1910).

231. *Trop v. Dulles*, 356 U.S. 86, 102 (1958).

234. *Gregg v. Georgia*, 428 U.S. 153, 173 (1976).

245. *See Kerr v. Farney*, 95 F.3d 472 (7th Cir. 1996) (requiring an inmate to attend religion-based narcotics rehabilitation meetings violates the Establishment Clause of the First Amendment); *State v. Evans*, 796 P.2d 178, 179–80 (Kan. Ct. App. 1990) (holding that probation condition requiring church attendance at a specific church and 1,000 hours of maintenance at that church violated the Free Exercise Clause of the First Amendment); *State v. Morgan*, 459 So. 2d 6, 10 (La. Ct. App. 1984) (holding that a condition of probation that the defendant regularly attend an organized church of

Clause of the First Amendment, are unique because they help "define who we are as a nation." Here, however, such an analysis of every constitutional right is beyond the scope of this Article. For present purposes, it is enough to distinguish the Eighth Amendment right from other constitutional criminal rights where the Court does permit waiver. As discussed above, the Eighth Amendment right differs significantly from those other rights, and therefore, waiver should not be allowed in this context.

B. Eighth Amendment Waiver Differs from Other Constitutional Waivers

Not only does the Eighth Amendment ban on cruel and unusual punishments differ from other constitutional criminal rights under current Supreme Court cases, but as a practical matter, waiver of such Eighth Amendment rights differs significantly from the waiver of other criminal rights. Obviously, both types of rights are important, but the effects of these waivers differ in important ways.

The justification for disallowing waiver of constitutional rights applies with more force where the issue involves a barbaric punishment instead of a procedural violation. First, unlike the choice of punishment context, a defendant may benefit from waiving certain other rights, like the right to a jury trial. Further, society actually benefits by allowing defendants to waive their trial rights. As one commentator noted, plea-bargains play an important role in our criminal justice system, and, thus, "[i]t is waiver of rights that permits the system of criminal justice to work at all." Another commentator has argued that allowing waiver of Fourth, Fifth, and Sixth Amendment rights makes sense if one views waiver as not harming the people those rights were designed to protect. Thus, as a practical matter, waiver of other constitutional rights offers societal and individual benefits that are not present in the torturous punishment waiver context.[250]

In addition to the consideration of waiver benefits, another reason that waiver should not apply in the brutal punishment context is because such a waiver is more

---

his choice violates the Establishment Clause of the First Amendment); *Griffin v. Coughlin*, 673 N.E.2d 98, 111 (N.Y. 1996) (holding that prison's requirement that in order to qualify for a family reunion program the petitioner must participate in a treatment program that incorporates religious aspects violates the Establishment Clause of the First Amendment); *Taylor v. Commonwealth*, 38 S.E.2d 444, 448–49 (Va. 1946) (holding that a probation condition for delinquent boys requiring them to attend Sunday school and church violates the First Amendment); *cf. Warner v. Orange County Dep't of Probation*, 115 F.3d 1068, 1075 (2d Cir. 1995) (holding that a probation condition that the petitioner attend Alcoholics Anonymous violated the First Amendment establishment clause, but noting that the condition might be constitutional if the petitioner were given other options); *In re Quirk*, 705 So. 2d 172, 182 (La. 1997) (in a judiciary proceeding, noting that the law is not clear on the issue of whether a judge may make, or offer as an alternative, church attendance as a condition of probation).

250. One may argue that Gary Gilmore did not benefit from waiving his appeals because he may have obtained relief on appeal. However, arguably, a capital defendant whose execution is inevitable may benefit from a speedier execution to avoid the prolonged terror of waiting to be killed. *See Lackey v. Texas*, 514 U.S. 1045, 1045–47 (1995) (Stevens, J., memorandum respecting denial of certiorari) (discussing merits of argument that a prolonged stay on death row constitutes a cruel and unusual punishment); *In re Medley*, 134 U.S. 160, 172 (1890) (noting that "when a prisoner sentenced by a court to death is confined in the penitentiary awaiting the execution of the sentence, one of the most horrible feelings to which he can be subjected during that time is the uncertainty during the whole of it"). Of course, such a conclusion assumes that such a defendant would know when the execution is inevitable and is capable of making a knowing and voluntary waiver.

On the other hand, though a masochist might disagree, it is difficult to argue that one obtains any benefit from being tortured to death instead of being killed in a less painful way. Still, assuming surgical castration is an unconstitutional punishment, reasonable minds may disagree as to whether society benefits from providing the option of castration to repeat sex offenders.

detrimental to society than other constitutional criminal right waivers. Allowing a government to impose a particularly brutal punishment has a more substantial detrimental effect upon society than a defendant waiving his right to appeal or a right to an attorney. An individual who consents to have his house searched does not hurt society to the degree that a brutal punishment does.

The government's use of a brutal punishment, however, would harm society more greatly. There have been various studies that illustrate the harmful effects of even typical executions on the public, and there is evidence that executions can have a detrimental effect on society by actually increasing crime.[252] For example, historically, public executions had a harmful effect on the public, sometimes resulting in riots. By the late 1820s in the United States, essayists argued for private executions to replace public hangings. "Legislators, editors, ministers, and merchants decried public hangings as festivals of disorder that subverted morals, increased crimes, excited sympathy with the criminal, and wasted time." One writer stated that " 'a hundred persons are made worse, where one is made better by public execution."[256] Today, the general public is protected from the sight of executions.[257] Still, some people are still directly touched by executions, such as the judicial and executive decision-makers, the crime victim's family, the defendant's family, prison guards, reporters, lawyers, and the executioner.[258] The horrors of

---

252. "In 1980, two sociologists, William Bowers and Glenn Pierce, did a study going right back to 1907. They found that in New York, within a thirty-day period following every execution, between 1907 and 1963, there were two or three murders over and above the expected rate." Michael Kroll, The Write Stuff, in A Punishment in Search of a Crime 299, 302 (Ian Grey & Moira Stanley eds., 1989). George Bernard Shaw explained, "It is the deed that teaches, not the name we give it. Murder and capital punishment are not opposites that cancel one another, but similars that breed their kind." George Bernard Shaw, Man and Superman 232 (1903).

Albert Camus wrote about the guillotine:

Let us be frank about the penalty which can have no publicity, that intimidation which works only on respectable people, so long as they are respectable, which fascinates those who have ceased to be respectable and debases or deranges those who take part in it. It is a penalty, to be sure, a frightful torture, both physical and moral, but it provides no sure example except a demoralizing one. It punishes, but it forestalls nothing; indeed it may even arouse the impulse to murder.

Albert Camus, Reflections on the Guillotine, in Resistance, Rebellion and Death 174, 197 (Alfred A. Knoff, 1961). Camus also noted, "Statistics drawn up at the beginning of the century in England show that out of 250 who were hanged, 170 had previously attended one or more executions. And in 1886, out of 167 condemned men who had gone through the Bristol prison, 164 had witnessed at least one execution."

256. Another commentator wrote:

Executions in the times when they were universally public, were occasions for rioting, revelry and ribaldry, and seldom was the demeanour of the crowd decorous in the face of death. And seldom, too, did a public execution act as a deterrent. More often than not in the crowd would be friends of the criminal who had escaped by the merest accident being in his place and who, the very next day, would continue their criminal practices for which they had watched one of their number hang. In many accounts of the Tyburn and Newgate hangings one reads that pickpockets plied their trade busily among the crowd. It was considered the proper thing to be present at an important execution. John Laurence, A History of Capital Punishment 183 (1960).

257. "However many die, privacy is likely to remain the pre-eminent feature of executions. So powerful still is the belief that the public should be prevented from observing the execution, even television, which daily brings quivering images of sanitized death into the family room, is not permitted to broadcast the affair." Masur, at 162.

258. See, e.g., Edmund Brown, Public Justice, Private Mercy: A Governor's Education on Death Row 163 (1989). Former Governor Brown, who oversaw many executions, wrote:

[T]he longer I live, the larger loom those fifty-nine decisions about justice and mercy that

an especially torturous killing would affect those people. Further the public still reads and hears reports about executions, and if people were to read about a defendant being boiled in oil, there would probably be some detrimental societal effects. For example, Americans who read about the July 1999 electric chair execution of Allen Davis—where blood gushed from his mask and oozed through his chest strap—may think less of themselves and their government.

Such societal concerns about brutal punishments have been expressed by others. During a debate about capital punishment in the House of Lords in England, Lord Chancellor Gardiner stated:

> When we abolished the punishment for treason that you should be hanged, and then cut down while still alive, and then disembowelled while still alive, and then quartered, we did not abolish that punishment because we sympathized with traitors, but because we took the view that it was a punishment no longer consistent with our self respect.

The detriments of such Eighth Amendment waivers should be considered in the Court's Eighth Amendment analysis. As the Court has stated, "While the State has the power to punish, the [Eighth] Amendment stands to assure that the power be exercised within the limits of civilized standards."[259]

Thus, the difference between the waiver of the ban on cruel and unusual punishments and the waiver of other rights given to defendants by other constitutional amendments is that the waiver of those other rights, in general, provides a benefit to defendants and to society, so the constitution should allow such waivers. In the Eighth Amendment context, there is generally no benefit for defendants or society in allowing defendants to be punished in a cruel and unusual manner. In fact, such punishments would have a detrimental effect on society. Therefore, the Court should not permit waivers of such Eighth Amendment rights, as it does for other constitutional criminal rights.

C. Logic Dictates that Such Eighth Amendment Waivers Should Not Be Permitted

The problems with holding that a defendant may waive the ban on cruel and unusual punishments are best illustrated by some specific examples. If a rape defendant may waive his Eighth Amendment rights and be castrated in exchange for a lighter prison sentence, courts could allow thieves to have their hands chopped off and Peeping Toms to have their eyes gouged out. In order to raise some money for the state treasury and a victim's family, the government could pass a bill allowing capital defendants a monetary bonus if they choose—over lethal injection—public execution by guillotine in a coliseum before a paid audience.

Further, if, as the Court implies in *LaGrand*, *Johnson* permits Eighth Amendment waivers, then rape defendants, child defendants, and insane defendants could choose the death penalty even though the Court has held that it violates the Eighth Amendment to execute those categories of defendants. To go further, if the Court were to even-

---

I had to make as governor. They didn't make me feel godlike then: far from it; I felt just the opposite. It was an awesome, ultimate power over the lives of others that no person or government should have, or crave. And looking back over their names and files now, despite the horrible crimes and the catalog of human weaknesses they comprise, I realize that each decision took something out of me that nothing—not family or work or hope for the future—has ever been able to replace.

259. *Trop v. Dulles*, 356 U.S. 86, 100 (1958).

tually hold that the death penalty itself is a cruel and unusual punishment, defendants would still be able to choose that punishment as an option over prison. Perhaps a new Court TV show could be developed along the lines of the old Let's Make a Deal show, with defendants choosing among various punishment options, such as a one-year prison sentence or "what's behind Curtain Number Two." As long as defendants are given constitutional options, any punishment would be constitutional when reformed through the power of choice.

These absurd situations could result from the reasoning of the *LaGrand* opinion. Yet, it is difficult to believe that the Court would actually permit deals such as a minor consenting to being executed. The Court must draw the line somewhere and prevent some Eighth Amendment waivers. Because of the strong societal interests in preventing the use of barbaric punishments and because such Eighth Amendment waivers harm society, the Court should draw the line in a way that does not allow defendants to elect to be punished in a cruel and unusual manner.

Hopefully, we will continue to live in a society where such deals are not made. Yet, the purpose of the Constitution—and the Eighth Amendment in particular—is to guarantee that such punishments never occur in today's society. Because the Eighth Amendment protects societal interests regarding the method of execution, that protection cannot be waived by an individual.

V. CONCLUSION

The punishment choice issue has not come up very often, probably because once a defendant selects a punishment, that defendant is unlikely to challenge its constitutionality. In *LaGrand*, the issue apparently arose because the defendants chose the gas chamber so that they could raise the issue that it was a cruel and unusual punishment.[260] Perhaps the Court viewed this strategy as a lawyer tactic to delay the executions and thus, that may be why the Court disposed of the issue without much discussion. Yet, there are important societal interests at stake that the Court should address.

Perhaps nothing reflects a society more than the punishments it imposes on the most despised.[261] A review of world history illustrates the gradual development of society's views of appropriate punishments. In the United States, we believe that today we are more enlightened than our ancestors because we no longer permit punishments such as beheading, crucifixion, burning alive, starvation in dungeons, or "tearing to death by redhot pincers."[262] It is illogical to assume only that we are more enlightened than our predecessors but not that our descendants will likely be more enlightened than us. Thus, when evaluating the constitutionality of a punishment, the Court has made provisions for considering our development toward a more enlightened society.

---

260. See Associated Press, *German Citizen Is Put to Death in Gas Chamber*, Chi. Trib., March 4, 1999, at 5, available in LEXIS, News Library, Chtrib File ("Both brothers chose the gas chamber in hopes that courts would rule the method cruel and unusual and therefore unconstitutional.").

261. "The mood and temper of the public with regard to the treatment of crime and criminals is one of the most unfailing tests of the civilization of any country." Winston Churchill, 1910, quoted in Peter N. Walker, Punishment: An Illustrated History ii (1973).

262. Perhaps one of the more interesting punishments of ancient times was the Roman punishment for parricides. "They were thrown into the water in a sack, which contained also a dog, a cock, a viper and an ape. This superstitious form of punishment persisted, in some countries, into the Middle Ages." Under the implications of *LaGrand*, such a punishment would be constitutional as an option to prison.

The intimate relationship between the Eighth Amendment and our "evolving standards" and "public attitude" requires the Court to continue to recognize the societal interest in the ban on cruel and unusual punishments. The Eighth Amendment requires that the awesome power to punish is "exercised within the limits of civilized standards," and permitting waiver of the Eighth Amendment ban on cruel and unusual punishments would harm society and weaken the Eighth Amendment. As a district court judge stated, "What is at stake here is our collective right as a civilized people not to have cruel and unusual punishment inflicted in our name."

The Eighth Amendment protects the individual being punished, but it also protects the rest of American society and how we view ourselves and how the rest of the world views us. The Eighth Amendment bans cruel and unusual punishments, and that means that citizens of the United States have the right to live in a country that does not torture or maim its citizens. Therefore, if the Eighth Amendment is to have any meaning, the Court should strictly follow the demand that "nor cruel and unusual punishments [be] inflicted," even if a defendant desires such a punishment. It is our right.

Chapter 3

Early Constitutional Challenges to the Death Penalty

Legal challenges to the death penalty historically have been grounded in two constitutional provisions: the Eighth Amendment and the Fourteenth Amendment. The Eighth Amendment prohibits the infliction of "cruel and unusual punishments." According to the Fourteenth Amendment, no state may deprive a person of "life, liberty or property, without due process of law; nor deny to any person within its jurisdiction the equal protection of the laws."

When the Supreme Court heard arguments in *McGautha v. California*, 402 U.S. 183 (1971), virtually all states left to the unguided discretion of judge or jury the decision whether a particular defendant should receive the death penalty. McGautha challenged his death sentence on Fourteenth Amendment grounds, arguing that where death was a possible sanction, due process required that the decisionmaker's discretion be guided by concrete standards. The Court in 1971 rejected McGautha's Fourteenth Amendment challenge, but during the following term the Court agreed that vesting in the decisionmaker "untrammelled discretion" "to pronounce life or death" resulted in the imposition of cruel and unusual punishment under the Eighth Amendment. *Furman v. Georgia*, 408 U.S. 238 (1972) (*infra* this chapter). Four years later, in 1976, the Court upheld revised death penalty statutes which provided standards to guide the decisionmaker's discretion in choosing between life and death. *Gregg v. Georgia*, 428 U.S. 153 (1976) (*infra* this chapter).

A. Procedural Due Process

McGautha v. California
Crampton v. Ohio
402 U.S. 183 (1971)

Mr. Justice HARLAN delivered the opinion of the Court.

Petitioners McGautha and Crampton were convicted of murder in the first degree in the courts of California and Ohio respectively and sentenced to death pursuant to the statutes of those States. In each case the decision whether the defendant should live or die was left to the absolute discretion of the jury. In McGautha's case the jury, in accordance with California law, determined punishment in a separate proceeding following the trial on the issue of guilt. In Crampton's case, in accordance with Ohio law, the jury determined guilt and punishment after a single trial and in a single verdict. We granted certiorari in [both cases to address] the question whether [petition-ers'] constitutional rights were infringed by permitting the jury to impose the death penalty without any governing standards. For the reasons that follow, we find no con-stitutional infirmity in the conviction of either petitioner, and we affirm in both cases....

I

B

[In McGautha's case] [t]he jury was instructed [on the manner in which they were to impose the penalty of life or death] in the following language:

> In this part of the trial the law does not forbid you from being influenced by pity for the defendants and you may be governed by mere sentiment and sym-pathy for the defendants in arriving at a proper penalty in this case; however, the law does forbid you from being governed by mere conjecture, prejudice, public opinion or public feeling.
>
> The defendants in this case have been found guilty of the offense of murder in the first degree, and it is now your duty to determine which of the penalties provided by law should be imposed on each defendant for that offense. Now, in arriving at this determination you should consider all of the evidence re-ceived here in court presented by the People and defendants throughout the trial before this jury. You may also consider all of the evidence of the circum-stances surrounding the crime, of each defendant's background and history, and of the facts in aggravation or mitigation of the penalty which have been re-ceived here in court. However, it is not essential to your decision that you find mitigating circumstances on the one hand or evidence in aggravation of the of-fense on the other hand.
>
> ... Notwithstanding facts, if any, proved in mitigation or aggravation, in de-termining which punishment shall be inflicted, you are entirely free to act ac-cording to your own judgment, conscience, and absolute discretion. That ver-dict must express the individual opinion of each juror.
>
> Now, beyond prescribing the two alternative penalties [of life imprisonment or death], the law itself provides no standard for the guidance of the jury in the selection of the penalty, but, rather, commits the whole matter of determining which of the two penalties shall be fixed to the judgment, conscience, and ab-solute discretion of the jury. In the determination of that matter, if the jury does agree, it must be unanimous as to which of the two penalties is imposed.

... Late in the afternoon of August 25 the jury returned [a verdict] fixing McGautha's punishment at death....

C

... [In Crampton's case] [t]he jury was instructed that:

> If you find the defendant guilty of murder in the first degree, the punishment is death, unless you recommend mercy, in which event the punishment is im-prisonment in the penitentiary during life.

The jury was given no other instructions specifically addressed to the decision whether to recommend mercy, but was told in connection with its verdict generally:

You must not be influenced by any consideration of sympathy or prejudice. It is your duty to carefully weigh the evidence, to decide all disputed questions of fact, to apply the instructions of the court to your findings and to render your verdict accordingly. In fulfilling your duty, your efforts must be to arrive at a just verdict.

Consider all the evidence and make your finding with intelligence and impartiality, and without bias, sympathy, or prejudice, so that the State of Ohio and the defendant will feel that their case was fairly and impartially tried.

The jury deliberated for over four hours and returned a verdict of guilty, with no recommendation for mercy.

III

... [McGautha and Crampton claim] that the absence of standards to guide the jury's discretion on the punishment issue is constitutionally intolerable. To fit their arguments within a constitutional frame of reference petitioners contend that to leave the jury completely at large to impose or withhold the death penalty as it sees fit is fundamentally lawless and therefore violates the basic command of the Fourteenth Amendment that no State shall deprive a person of his life without due process of law. Despite the undeniable surface appeal of the proposition, we conclude that the courts below correctly rejected it.

A

[The Court initially recounted the history in both British and American jurisprudence of allowing jury discretion in setting the punishment of death. The Court noted that it] ... subsequently had occasion to pass on the correctness of instructions to the jury with respect to recommendations of mercy in *Andres v. United States*, 333 U.S. 740 (1948). The Court approved, as consistent with the governing statute, an instruction that: "This power (to recommend mercy) is conferred solely upon you and in this connection the Court can not extend or prescribe to you any definite rule defining the exercise of this power, but commits the entire matter of its exercise to your judgment." The case was reversed, however, on the ground that other instructions on the power to recommend mercy might have been interpreted by the jury as requiring them to return an unqualified verdict of guilty unless they unanimously agreed that mercy should be extended. The Court determined that the proper construction was to require a unanimous decision to withhold mercy as well, on the ground among others that the latter construction was "more consonant with the general humanitarian purpose of the statute." The only other significant discussion of standardless jury sentencing in capital cases in our decisions is found in *Witherspoon v. Illinois*, 391 U.S. 510 (1968). In reaching its conclusion that persons with conscientious scruples against the death penalty could not be automatically excluded from sentencing juries in capital cases, the Court relied heavily on the fact that such juries "do little more—and must do nothing less—than express the conscience of the community on the ultimate question of life or death." *Id.* at 519. The Court noted that "one of the most important functions any jury can perform in making such a selection is to maintain a link between contemporary community values and the penal system—a link without which the determination of punishment could hardly reflect 'the evolving standards of decency that mark the progress of a maturing society.'" The inner quotation is from the opinion of Mr. Chief Justice Warren for four members of the Court in *Trop v. Dulles*, 356 U.S. 86, 101 (1958).

In recent years academic and professional sources have suggested that jury sentencing discretion should be controlled by standards of some sort. The American Law Institute first published such a recommendation in 1959. Several States have enacted new criminal codes in the intervening 12 years, some adopting features of the Model Penal Code. Other States have modified their laws with respect to murder and the death penalty in other ways. None of these States have followed the Model Penal Code and adopted statutory criteria for imposition of the death penalty. In recent years, challenges to standardless jury sentencing have been presented to many state and federal appellate courts. No court has held the challenge good....

B

... [Further] [t]hose who have come to grips with the hard task of actually attempting to draft means of channeling capital sentencing discretion have confirmed the lesson taught by the history recounted above. To identify before the fact those characteristics of criminal homicides and their perpetrators which call for the death penalty, and to express these characteristics in language which can be fairly understood and applied by the sentencing authority, appear to be tasks which are beyond present human ability.

Thus the British Home Office, which before the recent abolition of capital punishment in that country had the responsibility for selecting the cases from England and Wales which should receive the benefit of the Royal Prerogative of Mercy, observed:

> The difficulty of defining by any statutory provision the types of murder which ought or ought not to be punished by death may be illustrated by reference to the many diverse considerations to which the Home Secretary has regard in deciding whether to recommend clemency. No simple formula can take account of the innumerable degrees of culpability, and no formula which fails to do so can claim to be just or satisfy public opinion.

The Royal Commission accepted this view, and although it recommended a change in British practice to provide for discretionary power in the jury to find "extenuating circumstances," that term was to be left undefined; "[t]he decision of the jury would be within their unfettered discretion and in no sense governed by the principles of law." The Commission went on to say, in substantial confirmation of the views of the Home Office:

> No formula is possible that would provide a reasonable criterion for the infinite variety of circumstances that may affect the gravity of the crime of murder. Discretionary judgment on the facts of each case is the only way in which they can be equitably distinguished. This conclusion is borne out by American experience: there the experiment of degrees of murder, introduced long ago, has had to be supplemented by giving to the courts a discretion that in effect supersedes it.

The draftsmen of the Model Penal Code expressly agreed with the conclusion of the Royal Commission that "the factors which determine whether the sentence of death is the appropriate penalty in particular cases are too complex to be compressed within the limits of a simple formula...." The draftsmen did think, however, "that it is within the realm of possibility to point to the main circumstances of aggravation and of mitigation that should be weighed and weighed against each other when they are presented in a concrete case." The circumstances the draftsmen selected were not intended to be exclusive. The Code provides simply that the sentencing authority should "take into account the aggravating and mitigating circumstances enumerated ... and any other facts that it deems relevant," and that the court should so instruct when the issue was submitted to the jury....

It is apparent that such criteria do not purport to provide more than the most minimal control over the sentencing authority's exercise of discretion. They do not purport to give an exhaustive list of the relevant considerations or the way in which they may be affected by the presence or absence of other circumstances. They do not even undertake to exclude constitutionally impermissible considerations. And, of course, they provide no protection against the jury determined to decide on whimsy or caprice. In short, they do no more than suggest some subjects for the jury to consider during its deliberations, and they bear witness to the intractable nature of the problem of "standards" which the history of capital punishment has from the beginning reflected. Thus, they indeed caution against this Court's undertaking to establish such standards itself, or to pronounce at large that standards in this realm are constitutionally required.

In light of history, experience, and the present limitations of human knowledge, we find it quite impossible to say that committing to the untrammeled discretion of the jury the power to pronounce life or death in capital cases is offensive to anything in the Constitution. The States are entitled to assume that jurors confronted with the truly awesome responsibility of decreeing death for a fellow human will act with due regard for the consequences of their decision and will consider a variety of factors, many of which will have been suggested by the evidence or by the arguments of defense counsel. For a court to attempt to catalog the appropriate factors in this elusive area could inhibit rather than expand the scope of consideration, for no list of circumstances would ever be really complete. The infinite variety of cases and facets to each case would make general standards either meaningless "boiler-plate" or a statement of the obvious that no jury would need....

Notes

1. McGautha's trial was conducted in two stages. After the jury decided the issue of McGautha's guilt, the same jury heard evidence and argument on the issue of punishment. Conversely, Crampton's guilt and punishment were determined at a single trial, where the jury deliberated about guilt and punishment simultaneously. Crampton argued that Ohio's system of unitary trials violated his Fifth Amendment privilege to be free from compelled self-incrimination. In Crampton's view, where guilt and punishment are determined by a jury at a single trial, the desire to address the jury on punishment unduly encourages waiver of the defendant's privilege to remain silent on the issue of guilt. The Court rejected Crampton's claim that bifurcated trials are constitutionally required in capital cases:

> ... It may well be, as the American Law Institute and the National Commission on Reform of Federal Criminal Laws have concluded, that bifurcated trials and criteria for jury sentencing discretion are superior means of dealing with capital cases if the death penalty is to be retained at all. But the Federal Constitution, which marks the limits of our authority in these cases, does not guarantee trial procedures that are the best of all worlds, or that accord with the most enlightened ideas of students of the infant science of criminology, or even those that measure up to the individual predilections of members of this Court. The Constitution requires no more than that trials be fairly conducted and that guaranteed rights of defendants be scrupulously respected. From a constitutional standpoint we cannot conclude that it is impermissible for a State to consider that the compassionate purposes of jury sentencing in capital cases are better served by having the issues of guilt and punishment determined in a

single trial than by focusing the jury's attention solely on punishment after the issue of guilt has been determined.

402 U.S. at 221.

2. On June 2, 1967, Luis Jose Monge was executed in Colorado's gas chamber. Soon thereafter, legal challenges to the constitutionality of capital punishment prompted a moratorium on executions. Because *McGautha* did not address the Eighth Amendment question — whether the death penalty constitutes cruel and unusual punishment — the moratorium remained in effect. Monge remained the last person legally executed in the United States until 1977, when Gary Gilmore died by firing squad in Utah.

B. Cruel and Unusual Punishment

In *McGautha*, the Court concluded that the Due Process Clause does not regulate capital sentencing procedures. During the more than 30 years since *McGautha*, the Court has repeatedly rejected that conclusion. Within a month of the *McGautha* decision, the Supreme Court granted certiorari in a group of three cases to decide whether "the imposition and carrying out of the death penalty [in these cases] constitute cruel and unusual punishment in violation of the Eighth and Fourteenth Amendments." All three cases involved black defendants, two of whom — Lucious Jackson and Elmer Branch — received death sentences for raping white women. The third defendant, William Furman, received his death sentence for murder. In each case, the jury had complete, unguided discretion to impose a sentence of life imprisonment or death.

By a vote of 5–4, the Supreme Court set aside all three death sentences in *Furman v. Georgia*, 408 U.S. 238 (1972). As a result of the decision, Jackson, Branch, Furman, and more than 600 other condemned persons then incarcerated on "death rows" throughout the country avoided execution. In striking down the death penalty laws of 39 states and various federal statutory provisions, the Court held that the imposition and infliction of the death penalty under arbitrarily and randomly administered systems in which juries are given unrestricted and unguided discretion to impose a sentence of life or death constitutes "cruel and unusual" punishment in violation of the Eighth and Fourteenth Amendments.

Although the judgment of the Court was announced in a terse *per curiam* opinion, all nine justices wrote separate opinions (consuming 119 pages of the Supreme Court Reporter) setting forth their disparate views on the subject. Collectively, the justices wrote more than 50,000 words, making *Furman* the longest collection of opinions ever. No justice in the five-member majority saw fit to join any of the others' opinions. Two members of the majority, Justices Brennan and Marshall, concluded that the death penalty was unconstitutional regardless of how it was administered. The other members of the majority, Justices Stewart, Douglas and White, agreed that the system of capital punishment then in existence was unconstitutional. However, these justices reserved judgment on whether capital punishment could be constitutionally administered under some other system.

Excerpts from the opinions of all nine justices follow.

Furman v. Georgia

408 U.S. 238 (1972)

Mr. Justice STEWART, concurring.

"[T]he death sentences now before us are the product of a legal system that brings them, I believe, within the very core of the Eighth Amendment's guarantee against cruel and unusual punishments, a guarantee applicable against the States through the Fourteenth Amendment. In the first place, it is clear that these sentences are 'cruel' in the sense that they excessively go beyond, not in degree but in kind, the punishments that the state legislatures have determined to be necessary. In the second place, it is equally clear that these sentences are 'unusual' in the sense that the penalty of death is infrequently imposed for murder, and that its imposition for rape is extraordinarily rare. I do not rest my conclusion upon these two propositions alone.

"These death sentences are cruel and unusual in the same way that being struck by lightning is cruel and unusual. For, of all the people convicted of rapes and murders in 1967 and 1968, many just as reprehensible as these, the petitioners are among a capriciously selected random handful upon whom the sentence of death has in fact been imposed. My concurring Brothers have demonstrated that, if any basis can be discerned for the selection of these few to be sentenced to die, it is the constitutionally impermissible basis of race. But racial discrimination has not been proved, and I put it to one side. I simply conclude that the Eighth and Fourteenth Amendments cannot tolerate the inflicting of a sentence of death under legal systems that permit this unique penalty to be so wantonly and so freakishly imposed."

Mr. Justice WHITE, concurring.

"The imposition and execution of the death penalty are obviously cruel in the dictionary sense. But the penalty has not been considered cruel and unusual punishment in the constitutional sense because it was thought justified by the social ends it was deemed to serve. At the moment that it ceases realistically to further these purposes, however, the emerging question is whether its imposition in such circumstances would violate the Eighth Amendment. It is my view that it would, for its imposition would then be the pointless and needless extinction of life with only marginal contributions to any discernable social or public purposes. A penalty with such negligible returns to the State would be patently excessive and cruel and unusual punishment violative of the Eighth Amendment.

"It is also my judgment that this point has been reached with respect to capital punishment as it is presently administered under statutes involved in these cases. Concededly, it is difficult to prove as a general proposition that capital punishment, however administered, more effectively serves the ends of the criminal law than does imprisonment. But however that may be, I cannot avoid the conclusion that as the statutes before us are now administered, the penalty is so infrequently imposed that the threat of execution is too attenuated to be of substantial service to criminal justice.

"... [P]ast and present legislative judgment with respect to the death penalty loses much of its force when viewed in light of the recurring practice of delegating sentencing authority to the jury and the fact that a jury, in its own discretion and without violating its trust or any statutory policy, may refuse to impose the death penalty no matter what the circumstance of the crime. Legislative 'policy' is thus necessarily defined not by what is legislatively authorized but by what juries and judges do in exercising the discretion so regularly conferred upon them. In my judgment what was done in these cases violated the Eighth Amendment."

Mr. Justice DOUGLAS, concurring.

"The words 'cruel and unusual' certainly include penalties that are barbaric. But the words, at least when read in light of the English proscription against selective and irregular use of penalties, suggest that it is 'cruel and unusual' to apply the death penalty— or any other penalty—selectively to minorities whose numbers are few, who are outcasts of society, and who are unpopular, but whom society is willing to see suffer though it would not countenance general application of the same penalty across the boards...."

"A law that stated that anyone making more than $50,000 would be exempt from the death penalty would plainly fall, as would a law that in terms said that Blacks, those who never went beyond the fifth grade in school, or those who make less than $3,000 a year, or those who were unpopular or unstable should be the only people executed. A law which in the overall view reaches that result in practice has no more sanctity than a law which in terms provides the same.

"... [T]hese discretionary statutes [at issue before the Court] are unconstitutional in their operation. They are pregnant with discrimination and discrimination is an ingredient not compatible with the idea of equal protection of the law that is implicit in the ban on 'cruel and unusual' punishments."

Mr. Justice BRENNAN, concurring.

Justice Brennan identified four principles "recognized in our cases and inherent in" the Eighth Amendment prohibition "sufficient to permit a judicial determination whether a challenged punishment does not comport with human dignity" and therefore is "cruel and unusual": (1) "a punishment must not be so severe as to be degrading to the dignity of human beings"; (2) the government "must not arbitrarily inflict a severe punishment"; (3) "a severe punishment must not be unacceptable to contemporary society"; and (4) "a severe punishment must not be excessive," *i.e.,* "unnecessary." Applying the first and "primary" principle, Justice Brennan concluded that capital punishment "involves by its very nature a denial of the executed person's humanity" and, in comparison to all other punishments, "is uniquely degrading to human dignity." "[W]ere it not that death is a punishment of longstanding usage and acceptance in this country," Justice Brennan "would not hesitate to hold, on that ground alone, that death is today a 'cruel and unusual punishment.' "

As to the second principle, Justice Brennan concluded, "When the punishment of death is inflicted in a trivial number of the cases in which it is legally available, the conclusion is virtually inescapable that it is being inflicted arbitrarily. Indeed, it smacks of little more than a lottery system."

Turning to his third principle, Justice Brennan stated, "The progressive decline in and the current rarity of the infliction of death demonstrate that our society seriously questions the appropriateness of this punishment today. The States point out that many legislatures authorize death as the punishment for certain crimes and that substantial segments of the public, as reflected in opinion polls and referendum votes, continue to support it. Yet the availability of this punishment through statutory authorization, as well as the polls and referenda, which amount simply to approval of that authorization, simply underscores the extent to which our society has in fact rejected this punishment. When an unusually severe punishment is authorized for wide-scale application but not, because of society's refusal, inflicted save in a few instance, the inference is compelling that there is a deep-seated reluctance to inflict it. Indeed, the likelihood is great that the punishment is tolerated only because of its disuse. The objective indicator of society's view of an unusually severe punishment is what society does with it. And today society will inflict death upon only a small sample of the eligible criminals. Rejection could hardly be more complete without becoming absolute. At the very least, I must conclude that contemporary society views this punishment with substantial doubt."

Finally, regarding the fourth principle, Justice Brennan stated, "we are not presented with the theoretical question whether under any imaginable circumstances the threat of death might be a greater deterrent to the commission of capital crimes than the threat of imprisonment. We are concerned with the practice of punishing criminals by death as it exists in the United States today. Proponents of this argument necessarily admit that its validity depends upon the existence of a system in which the punishment of death is invariably and swiftly imposed. Our system, of course, satisfies neither condition. A rational person contemplating a murder or rape is confronted not with the certainty of a speedy death, but with the slightest possibility that he will be executed in the distant future. The risk of death is remote and improbable; in contrast, the risk of long-term imprisonment is near and great. In short, whatever the speculative validity of the assumption that the threat of death is a superior deterrent, there is no reason to believe that as currently administered the punishment of death is necessary to deter the commission of capital crimes. Whatever might be the case were all or substantially all eligible criminals quickly put to death, unverifiable possibilities are an insufficient basis upon which to conclude that the threat of death today has any greater deterrent efficacy than the threat of imprisonment...."

"In sum, the punishment of death is inconsistent with all four principles: Death is an unusually severe and degrading punishment; there is a strong probability that it is inflicted arbitrarily; its rejection by contemporary society is virtually total; and there is no reason to believe that it serves any penal purpose more effectively than the less severe punishment of imprisonment. The function of these principles is to enable a court to determine whether a punishment comports with human dignity. Death, quite simply, does not."

Mr. Justice MARSHALL, concurring.

Justice Marshall concluded that the death penalty constitutes "cruel and unusual" punishment on two independent grounds: (1) "it is excessive and serves no valid legislative purpose," i.e., it is not a more effective deterrent than life imprisonment; and (2) "it is abhorrent to currently existing moral values."

"Punishment for the sake of retribution" is "not permissible under the Eighth Amendment.... At times a cry is heard that morality requires vengeance to evidence society's abhorrence of the act. But the Eighth Amendment is our insulation from our baser selves. The cruel and unusual language limits the avenues through which vengeance can be channeled. Were this not so, the language would be empty and a return to the rack and other tortures would be possible in a given case." Nor, "in light of the massive amount of evidence before us, [showing no correlation between the rate of murder or other capital crimes and the presence or absence of the death penalty, can capital punishment] be justified on the basis of its deterrent effect.... The statistical evidence is not convincing beyond all doubt, but, it is persuasive.... The point has now been reached at which deference to the legislatures is tantamount to abdication of our judicial roles as factfinders, judges and ultimate arbiters of the Constitution. We know that at some point the presumption of constitutionality accorded legislative acts gives way to a realistic assessment of those acts. This point comes when there is sufficient evidence available so that judges can determine not whether the legislature acted wisely, but whether it had any rational basis whatsoever for acting. We have this evidence before us now. There is no rational basis for concluding that capital punishment is not excessive. It therefore violates the Eighth Amendment.

"[W]hether or not a punishment is cruel or unusual depends, not on whether its mere mention 'shocks the conscience and sense of justice of the people,' but on whether people who were fully informed as to the purposes of the penalty and its liabilities would find the penalty shocking, unjust and unacceptable." Justice Marshall noted that "American citizens know almost nothing about capital punishment." According to Justice Marshall, knowledge of certain facts is "critical to an informed judgment on the morality of the death penalty"; "the death penalty is no more effective a deterrent than life imprisonment"; "convicted murderers are usually model prisoners, and ... almost always become model prisoners, and ... almost always become law-abiding citizens upon their release from prison"; "the costs of executing a capital offender exceed the costs of imprisoning him for life"; "no attempt is made in the sentencing process to ferret out likely recidivists for execution"; and "the death penalty may actually stimulate criminal activity." Moreover, "capital punishment is imposed discriminatorily against certain identifiable classes of people"; and "innocent people have been executed." Justice Marshall concluded: "Assuming knowledge of all the facts presently available regarding capital punishment, the average citizen would, in my opinion, find it shocking to his conscience and sense of justice. For this reason alone capital punishment cannot stand."

Chief Justice BURGER, dissenting.

According to the Chief Justice, these cases "turn[ ] on the single question whether capital punishment is 'cruel' in the constitutional sense. The term 'unusual' cannot be read as limiting the ban on 'cruel' punishments or as somehow expanding the meaning of the term 'cruel.'" Consequently, the Chief Justice was "unpersuaded by the facile argument that since capital punishment has always been cruel in the everyday sense of the word, and has become unusual due to decreased use, it is, therefore, now 'cruel and unusual.'"

The Chief Justice was equally unpersuaded by the argument that the death penalty was "excessive" or "unnecessary." Simply put, the Chief Justice found "no authority suggesting that the Eighth Amendment was intended to purge the law of its retributive elements" nor any basis for prohibiting "all punishments the States are unable to prove necessary to deter crime."

Chief Justice Burger lamented: "Only one year ago, in *McGautha v. California* (*supra* this chapter), the Court upheld the prevailing system of sentencing in capital cases." The *McGautha* Court found it "impossible to say that committing to the untrammeled discretion of the jury the power to pronounce life or death in capital cases is offensive to anything in the Constitution."

"Since the two pivotal concurring opinions turn on the assumption that the punishment of death is now meted out in a random and unpredictable manner, legislative bodies may seek to bring their laws into compliance with the Court's ruling by providing standards for juries and judges to follow in determining the sentence in capital cases or by more narrowly defining the crimes for which the penalty is to be imposed. If such standards can be devised or the crimes more meticulously defined, the result cannot be detrimental. However, Mr. Justice Harlan's opinion for the Court in *McGautha* convincingly demonstrates that all past efforts 'to identify before the fact' the cases in which the penalty is to be imposed have been 'uniformly unsuccessful.'...

"It seems remarkable to me that with our basic trust in lay jurors as the keystone in our system of criminal justice, it should now be suggested that we take the most sensitive and important of all decisions away from them. I could more easily be persuaded that mandatory sentences of death, without the intervening and ameliorating impact of jurors, are so arbitrary and doctrinaire that they violate the Constitution. The very infrequency of death penalties imposed by jurors attests to their cautious and discriminating reservation of that penalty for the most extreme cases. I had thought that nothing was clearer in history, as we noted in *McGautha* one year ago, than the American abhorrence of 'the common law rule imposing a mandatory death sentence on all convicted murderers.' [The change away from mandatory death sentences] was greeted by the Court as a humanizing development. I do not see how this history can be ignored and how it can be suggested that the Eighth Amendment demands the elimination of the most sensitive feature of the sentencing system."

Mr. Justice BLACKMUN, dissenting.

Although Justice Blackmun "personally rejoic[ed]" at the Court's result, he declared himself unable to accept it "as a matter of history, of law, or of constitutional pronouncement." Justice Blackmun agreed with the majority's assessment that the "cruel and unusual" punishment clause could not be confined to those punishments thought excessively cruel and barbarous at the time of the adoption of the Eighth Amendment. Instead, the clause "must draw its meaning from the evolving standards of decency that mark the progress of a maturing society" and may acquire new meaning "as public opinion becomes enlightened by a humane justice." However, Justice Blackmun took issue with "the suddenness of the Court's perception of progress in the human attitude since decisions of only a short while ago."

Justice Blackmun suggested that the issues raised by *Furman* are more suited to resolution by elected legislators. He cautioned: "We should not allow our personal preferences as to the wisdom of legislative and congressional action, or our distaste for such action, to guide our judicial decision in cases such as these." During the preceding decade, federal death penalty legislation dealing with presidential and congressional assassination and aircraft piracy had been overwhelmingly adopted. This fact, per Justice Blackmun, clearly demonstrates that "these elected representatives of the people — far more conscious of the temper of the times, of the maturing of society, and of the contemporary demands for man's dignity, than are we who sit cloistered on this Court — took it as settled that the death penalty then, as it always has been, was not in itself unconstitutional."

Mr. Justice POWELL, dissenting.

Justice Powell echoed Blackmun's dissent by characterizing the majority's ruling as "the very sort of judgment that the legislative branch is competent to make and for which the judiciary is ill-equipped. Throughout our history, Justices of this Court have emphasized the gravity of decisions invalidating legislative judgments, admonishing the nine men who sit on this bench of the duty of self-restraint, especially when called upon to apply the expansive due process and cruel and unusual punishment rubrics. I can recall no case in which, in the name of deciding constitutional questions, this Court has subordinated national and local democratic processes to such an extent....

"One must conclude, contrary to petitioners' submission, that the indicators most likely to reflect the public's view — legislative bodies, state referenda and the juries which have the actual responsibility—do not support the contention that evolving standards of decency require total abolition of capital punishment. Indeed, the weight of the evidence indicates that the public generally has not accepted either the morality or the social merit of the views so passionately advocated by the articulate spokesmen for abolition. But however one may assess the amorphous ebb and flow of public opinion generally on this volatile issue, this type of inquiry lies at the periphery—not the core—of the judicial process in constitutional cases. The assessment of popular opinion is essentially a legislative, not a judicial function....

"It is important to keep in focus the enormity of the step undertaken by the Court today. Not only does it invalidate hundreds of state and federal laws, it deprives those jurisdictions of the power to legislate with respect to capital punishment in the future, except in a manner consistent with the cloudily outlined views of those Justices who do not purport to undertake total abolition. Nothing short of an amendment to the United States Constitution can reverse the Court's judgment. Meanwhile, all flexibility is foreclosed. The normal democratic process, as well as the opportunities for the several States to respond to the will of their people expressed through ballot referenda (as in Massachusetts, Illinois, and Colorado), is now shut off....

"... It seems to me that the sweeping judicial action undertaken today reflects a basic lack of faith and confidence in the democratic process. Many may regret, as I do, the failure of some legislative bodies to address the capital punishment issue with greater frankness or effectiveness. Many might decry their failure either to abolish the penalty entirely or selectively, or to establish standards for its enforcement. But impatience with the slowness, and even the unresponsiveness, of legislatures is no justification for judicial intrusion upon their historic powers."

Mr. Justice REHNQUIST, dissenting.

"The task of judging constitutional cases imposed by Art. III cannot ... be avoided, but it must surely be approached with the deepest humility and genuine deference to legislative judgment. Today's decision to invalidate capital punishment is, I respectfully submit, significantly lacking in those attributes.

"I conclude that this decision holding unconstitutional capital punishment is not an act of judgment, but rather an act of will....

"A separate reason for deference to the legislative judgment is the consequence of human error on the part of the judiciary with respect to the constitutional issue before it. Human error there is bound to be, judges being men and women, and men and women being what they are. But an error in mistakenly sustaining the constitutionality of a particular enactment, while wrongfully depriving the individual of a right secured to him by the Constitution, nonetheless does so by simply letting stand a duly enacted law of a democratically chosen legislative body. The error resulting from a mistaken upholding of an individual's constitutional claim against the validity of a legislative enactment is a good deal more serious. For the result in such a case is not to leave standing a law duly enacted by a representative assembly, but to impose upon the Nation the judicial fiat of a majority of a court of judges whose connection with the popular will is remote at best."

Notes and Questions

1. The *Furman* Court stopped short of expressly overruling *McGautha*. In a footnote, the plurality in *Gregg v. Georgia*, 428 U.S. 153, 195 n.47 (1976), *infra* this chapter, attempted to reconcile *Furman* and *McGautha*:

In *McGautha v. California*, this Court held that the Due Process Clause of the Fourteenth Amendment did not require that a jury be provided with standards to guide its decision whether to recommend a sentence of life imprisonment or death or that the capital-sentencing proceeding be separated from the guilt-determination process. *McGautha* was not an Eighth Amendment decision, and to the extent it purported to deal with Eighth Amendment concerns, it must be read in light of the opinions in *Furman v. Georgia*. There the Court ruled that death sentences imposed under statutes that left juries with untrammeled discretion to impose or withhold the death penalty violated the Eighth and Fourteenth Amendments. While *Furman* did not overrule *McGautha*, it is clearly in substantial tension with a broad reading of *McGautha's* holding. In view of *Furman*, *McGautha* can be viewed rationally as a precedent only for the proposition that standardless jury sentencing procedures were not employed in the cases there before the Court so as to violate the Due Process Clause. We note that *McGautha's* assumption that it is not possible to devise standards to guide and regularize jury sentencing in capital cases has been undermined by subsequent experience. In view of that experience and the considerations set forth in the text, we adhere to *Furman's* determination that where the ultimate punishment of death is at issue a system of standardless jury discretion violates the Eighth and Fourteenth Amendments.

Did the Court successfully harmonize these cases?

2. Under *Furman*, a capital sentencing scheme which results in the arbitrary and capricious imposition of the death penalty is clearly unconstitutional. Should a court extend *Furman* by granting relief to an individual sentenced to death who is able to prove that the prosecutor's decision to charge her with a capital offense was arbitrary and capricious? If so, what relief should be granted? If not, why not?

3. Prior to *Furman*, the Court had invalidated only three punishments under the Cruel and Unusual Punishments Clause. *Weems v. United States*, 217 U.S. 349 (1910) (12 years in chains at hard and painful labor); *Trop v. Dulles*, 356 U.S. 86 (1958) (expatriation); and *Robinson v. California*, 370 U.S. 660 (1962) (imprisonment for narcotics addiction).

4. According to researchers, in 1972 there were 558 inmates on death row throughout the country (excluding Illinois) awaiting execution whose sentences were commuted as a result of *Furman*. Eighty-five percent (474) of these inmates were capital murderers. Fourteen percent (81) were rapists and one percent (4) were sentenced to death for armed robbery. Fifty-five percent (309) of these prisoners were black; forty-three percent (240) were white; one percent (8) were hispanic and one inmate was American Indian. The capital offenders were overwhelmingly male: only two women were on death row when *Furman* was decided. The median age of death row inmates was thirty-two years old. Marquart & Sorenson, "A National Study of the *Furman*-Commuted Inmates: Assessing the Threat to Society from Capital Offenders," 23 Loy. L.A. L. Rev. 5, 14 (1989).

C. Post-*Furman* Death Penalty Statutes

After *Furman*, a number of states, including Georgia, Florida, Texas, North Carolina and Louisiana, revised their death penalty statutes in an effort to satisfy the requirements of *Furman*. In 1976, the Court addressed the constitutionality of these death penalty statutes in a group of five consolidated states.

Oral argument from one of these cases, *Jurek v. Texas*, is excerpted below. Professor Anthony Amsterdam argued on behalf of Texas death row inmate Jerry Lane Jurek. Solicitor General Robert Bork argued on behalf of the United States government.

Oral Argument in *Jurek v. Texas*

Professor Amsterdam: First, that death sentences imposed pursuant to systems of arbitrary selectivity of this sort are unconstitutional under *Furman*. The square holding of the *Furman* decision, rightly conceded, compels that result. And, secondly, that apart from the specific holding in *Furman*, the death penalty as it is used or as it is proposed to be used today is an excessively cruel punishment when it is assessed against the history of this country's use of the punishment in this century. We are challenging in our second contention the forms of law under which it is now proposed to execute people in the United States.

Justice Stewart: I thought your second contention was broader, that the execution of a death sentence upon conviction in any state of a person of any crime is cruel and unusual punishment, no matter what the technique—whether it be electrocution or hanging or shooting or the gas chamber—and no matter how serious the offense, and no matter how completely a fair trial he may have been given. Now, isn't that your point?

Professor Amsterdam: That is precisely the second contention, yes. The first thing I want to note is that at the outset of a Texas capital trial, the jury is death-qualified; it's required to be death-qualified by statute, and it's required to be told prior to trial that the question of life or death is in issue.

The fact remains that the jury will know that their answers to the specific questions submitted at the penalty phase will determine whether the defendant is to be punished by death or life imprisonment. To say that the jury's answers would not be affected by their attitude toward the death penalty as a punishment for crime simply because they will not bring forth the ultimate verdict, simply because the law attaches death to the answer to factual questions, would be to disregard the obvious.

In this case, the evidence on which the jury solemnly decided that the defendant, that there was a probability that the defendant would commit criminal acts of violence that would constitute a continuing threat to society, that evidence consisted of: one, the fact that the defendant had committed a capital murder, which, of course, is true in all cases; and two, the one-line hearsay opinions of four local citizens in the community that the defendant's reputation for peace and good order was bad. The state's position was simple: the defendant is a reprobate; the defendant killed the daughter of a local peace officer; the defendant ought to die.

Justice Stewart: Doesn't your argument prove too much? In other words, in our system of adversary criminal justice, we have prosecutorial discretion; we have jury discretion, including jury nullification, as it's known; we have the practice of submitting to the jury the option of returning verdicts of lesser included offenses; we have appellate review; and we have the possibility of executive clemency. And that's true throughout our adversary system of justice. And if a person is sentenced to anything as the end product of that system, under your argument, his sentence, be it life imprisonment or five years imprisonment, is a cruel and unusual punishment because it's the product of this system. That's your argument, isn't it?

Professor Amsterdam: No.

Justice Stewart: And why not?

Professor Amsterdam: It is not. Our argument is essentially that death is different. If you don't accept the view that for constitutional purposes death is different, we lose this case, let me make that very clear. There is nothing that we argue in this case that will touch imprisonment, life imprisonment, any of those things.

Now, why do we say death is different? Our legal system as a whole has always treated death differently. We allow more peremptory challenges; we allow automatic appeals; we have different rules of harmless error; we have indictment requirements; unanimous verdict requirements in some jurisdictions, because death is different.

Death is factually different. Death is final. Death is irremediable. Death is unknowable; it goes beyond this world. It is a legislative decision to do something, and we know not what we do. Death is different because even if exactly the same discretionary procedures are used to decide issues of five years versus ten years, or life versus death, the result will be more arbitrary on the life or death choice.

[Solicitor General Robert Bork argued on behalf of the United States government.]

Solicitor General Bork: Mr. Chief Justice; may it please the Court. The United States appears as *amicus curiae* in these cases because the Congress has enacted and various presidents have signed into law statutes that permit capital punishment for various serious crimes. To begin with, we know as a fact that the men who framed the Eighth Amendment did not mean—did not intend as an original matter to outlaw capital punishment because, as has been mentioned, they prescribed the procedures that must be used in inflicting it in the Fifth Amendment. We know that the men who framed and ratified the Fourteenth Amendment did not intend to outlaw capital punishment, because they also discussed and framed the procedures which must be followed in inflicting it. So we know that as an original matter, as a matter of original intention, it is quite certain that the Eighth Amendment was not intended to bar the death penalty and that the Constitution contemplates its infliction.

I will suggest first that capital punishment is rationally related to legitimate legislative goals of the deterrence of crime and the expression of moral outrage among them; secondly, that capital punishment has not been shown to be inflicted on the basis of race, and that in any event, that question is irrelevant to the issue of the type of punishment; and thirdly, I will argue that capital punishment is not outlawed because the criminal justice system, which is mandated and permitted by the Constitution, has elements of discretion in it which are intended to be a safeguard of the system.

Justice Stewart: What if a state said for the most heinous kind of first-degree murders we are going to inflict breaking a man on the wheel and then disemboweling him while he is still alive and then burning him up: What would you say to that?

Solicitor General Bork: I would say that that practice is so out of step with modern morality and modern jurisprudence that the state cannot return to it. That kind of torture was precisely what the framers thought they were outlawing when they wrote the cruel and unusual punishments clause.

I would like to discuss the element of discretion, because that seems to me to be the crucial part of petitioners' counsel's argument. And the argument appears to be that the fact that at various stages in the criminal justice system people are entitled to make judgments renders the death penalty unconstitutional. I don't think there's any logic to that claim, and I don't think it's a constitutional proposition.

Counsel made it plain that he objects to every element of discretion in the system, not just jury discretion. He objects to them collectively and, if I understood him correctly yesterday, he objects—he would object to them singly. The power of an executive to exercise clemency alone would render—if that were the only element of discretion— would render the death penalty unconstitutional.

There is apparently no way, according to this argument, that anybody could devise a system of justice in which anybody used any judgment about the thing which could then inflict the death penalty. The system—the only system that would meet counsel's objections would be one that was so rigid and automatic and insensitive that it would be morally reprehensible, and then apparently it would meet the moral standards of the Constitution.

Counsel's real complaint is not that anybody is freakishly convicted and executed but, rather, that some murderers are freakishly spared and given life imprisonment. In other words, the fault in the system which makes it unconstitutional to inflict the death penalty is that it errs, if it errs at all, on the side of mercy and the side of safety, and that is what we are told makes it unconstitutional.

These arguments that are made against the death penalty could be made against any other form of punishment. There is not one of them that does not apply to life imprisonment. Now, the sole answer that counsel gives to this is that capital punishment is unique, it's different. Of course, it is different. Life imprisonment is different from a year in prison. Life imprisonment is different from a fine.

Capital punishment is also different in one other respect. It's different in that it deters more than any other punishment. There are some categories of criminals who cannot be deterred any other way. For example, a man serving life imprisonment—and he knows it is a real life term—has no incentive *not* to kill, and some of them have done so. A man who has committed an offense which carries life imprisonment, but has not yet been apprehended, has no incentive not to kill to escape or commit other crimes, except the prospect of a death penalty. So that, as the ultimate sanction, capital punishment is unique; it is different in the sense that it deters more and thereby saves more innocent lives; and it is unique in that it upholds the basic values of our society symbolically and internalizes them for us more than any other punishment.

Justice Powell: I have before me the 1973 report of the Federal Bureau of Investigation. It states that in 1968, 13,720 people were murdered in this country; in 1973, the latest year recorded in this report, 19,510 people were murdered—that's an increase of 42 percent. It is perfectly obvious from these figures that we need some way to deter the slaughter of Americans. I use the word "slaughter" because that word was used in connection with the disaster in Vietnam, in which 55,000 Americans were killed over a six-to-seven-year period. If the FBI figures are correct, there were more Americans killed in this country, murdered, than there were on the battlefields of Vietnam. Would you care to comment, elaborate, or state your views with respect to the deterrent effect, if any, of the death sentence?

Solicitor General Bork: Mr. Justice Powell, it seems to me that it cannot rationally be questioned that the death penalty has a deterrent effect. Mankind has always thought that throughout its history. We know it as a matter of common sense and common observation—we know that in all other aspects of human behavior, as you raise the cost and the risk, the amount of the activity goes down. I don't know why murder should be any different.

And I must say, at a time when international and domestic terrorism is going up, at a time when brutal murders are going up, it's an awesome responsibility to take from the states what they think is a necessary deterrent and save a few hundred guilty people and thereby probably condemn to death thousands of innocent people. That is truly an awesome responsibility.

This case is merely the latest in a continuing series seeking to obtain from this Court a political judgment that the opponents of capital punishment have been unable to obtain from the political branches of government. The United States asks that the constitutionality of the death penalty be upheld.

[Professor Amsterdam had reserved two minutes for rebuttal.]

Chief Justice Burger: Suppose over a period of time, six months or a year, the Gallup Poll and the Harris Poll and all the other polls that are conducted showed 90 percent of the people in this country in favor of capital punishment, 3 percent undecided, and the balance against it. Do you think that enters into the constitutionality appraisal?

Professor Amsterdam: No, Your Honor.

Chief Justice Burger: And the converse of that would be true?

Professor Amsterdam: I don't think that the plebiscites cut one way or the other.

Chief Justice Burger: Well, I got the impression from either what you said yesterday or this morning that in some way we have to evaluate the standards of the people of this country today in light of what people think.

Professor Amsterdam: I think that's true, but not as a matter of plebiscite.

I simply want to make two points very clear. First of all, to attack the death penalty on Eighth Amendment grounds is not to express sympathy for crime. It is not to express callousness with regard to victims. The death penalty may be the greatest obstacle to adequate enforcement of crime in this country today because it sops public conscience and makes you think we're doing something about serious crime instead of devising other methods of dealing with it.

Secondly, we are taxed in this case and have been throughout our Eighth Amendment presentation with the notion that it is we who are seeking to have this Court use subjective gut feelings, to be a superlegislature. That is not true. Our position is the only coherent analytic position on the Eighth Amendment. The Government says that the death penalty for jaywalking would be bad. Why? Because there is an emotional feeling that's being invited that that's too much. It can't be that it's a comparative test, such as Solicitor General Bork suggests. The Eighth Amendment was written to apply only to the federal government, not to the states; it couldn't be asking a comparative question.

We submit simply that our argument has a coherent Eighth Amendment base adequately and properly based on the facts; it accounts for the needs of law enforcement and protection of victims; and under that view, the death penalty is a violation of the Eighth Amendment.

Gregg v. Georgia
428 U.S. 153 (1976)

Judgment of the Court, and opinion of Mr. Justice Stewart, Mr. Justice Powell, and Mr. Justice Stevens, announced by Mr. Justice STEWART.

The issue in this case is whether the imposition of the sentence of death for the crime of murder under the law of Georgia violates the Eighth and Fourteenth Amendments.

I

The petitioner, Troy Gregg, was charged with committing armed robbery and murder. In accordance with Georgia procedure in capital cases, the trial was in two stages, a guilt stage and a sentencing stage. [During the first stage of the trial, the jury found Gregg guilty of two counts of armed robbery and two counts of murder.] ...

At the penalty stage, which took place before the same jury, neither the prosecutor nor the petitioner's lawyer offered any additional evidence. Both counsel, however, made lengthy arguments dealing generally with the propriety of capital punishment under the circumstances and with the weight of the evidence of guilt. The trial judge instructed the jury that it could recommend either a death sentence or a life prison sentence on each count. The judge further charged the jury that in determining what sentence was appropriate the jury was free to consider the facts and circumstances, if any, presented by the parties in mitigation or aggravation.

Finally, the judge instructed the jury that it "would not be authorized to consider (imposing) the penalty of death" unless it first found beyond a reasonable doubt one of these aggravating circumstances:

"One — That the offense of murder was committed while the offender was engaged in the commission of two other capital felonies, to-wit the armed robbery of the two murder victims.

"Two — That the offender committed the offense of murder for the purpose of receiving money and the automobile described in the indictment.

"Three — The offense of murder was outrageously and wantonly vile, horrible and inhuman, in that they [*sic*] involved the depravity of [the] mind of the defendant."

Finding the first and second of these circumstances, the jury returned verdicts of death on each count.

The Supreme Court of Georgia affirmed the convictions and the imposition of the death sentences for murder. After reviewing the trial transcript and the record, including the evidence, and comparing the evidence and sentence in similar cases in accordance with the requirements of Georgia law, the court concluded that, considering the nature of the crime and the defendant, the sentences of death had not resulted from prejudice or any other arbitrary factor and were not excessive or disproportionate to the penalty applied in similar cases. The death sentences imposed for armed robbery, however, were vacated on the grounds that the death penalty had rarely been imposed in Georgia for that offense and that the jury improperly considered the murders as aggravating circumstances for the robberies after having considered the armed robberies as aggravating circumstances for the murders.

We granted the petitioner's application for a writ of certiorari limited to his challenge to the imposition of the death sentences in this case as "cruel and unusual" punishment in violation of the Eighth and the Fourteenth Amendments....

III

We address initially the basic contention that the punishment of death for the crime of murder is, under all circumstances, "cruel and unusual" in violation of the Eighth and Fourteenth Amendments of the Constitution. In [due course] we will consider the sentence of death imposed under the Georgia statutes at issue in this case.

... [U]ntil *Furman v. Georgia*, 408 U.S. 238 (1972), the Court never confronted squarely the fundamental claim that the punishment of death always, regardless of the enormity of the offense or the procedure followed in imposing the sentence, is cruel and unusual punishment in violation of the Constitution. Although this issue was presented and addressed in *Furman*, it was not resolved by the Court. Four Justices would have held that capital punishment is not unconstitutional *per se*; two Justices would have reached the opposite conclusion; and three Justices, while agreeing that the statutes then before the Court were invalid as applied, left open the question whether such punishment may ever be imposed. We now hold that the punishment of death does not invariably violate the Constitution....

C

The imposition of the death penalty for the crime of murder has a long history of acceptance both in the United States and in England. The common-law rule imposed a mandatory death sentence on all convicted murderers. And the penalty continued to be used into the 20th century by most American States, although the breadth of the common-law rule was diminished, initially by narrowing the class of murders to be punished by death and subsequently by widespread adoption of laws expressly granting juries the discretion to recommend mercy....

Four years ago, the petitioners in *Furman* and its companion cases predicated their argument primarily upon the asserted proposition that standards of decency had evolved to the point where capital punishment no longer could be tolerated. The petitioners in those cases said, in effect, that the evolutionary process had come to an end, and that standards of decency required that the Eighth Amendment be construed finally as prohibiting capital punishment for any crime regardless of its depravity and impact on society....

The petitioners in the capital cases before the Court today renew the "standards of decency" argument, but developments during the four years since *Furman* have undercut substantially the assumptions upon which their argument rested. Despite the continuing debate, dating back to the 19th century, over the morality and utility of capital punishment, it is now evident that a large proportion of American society continues to regard it as an appropriate and necessary criminal sanction.

The most marked indication of society's endorsement of the death penalty for murder is the legislative response to *Furman*. The legislatures of at least 35 States have enacted new statutes that provide for the death penalty for at least some crimes that result in the death of another person. And the Congress of the United States, in 1974, enacted a statute providing the death penalty for aircraft piracy that results in death. These recently adopted statutes have attempted to address the concerns expressed by the Court in *Furman* primarily (i) by specifying the factors to be weighed and the procedures to be followed in deciding when to impose a capital sentence, or (ii) by making the death penalty mandatory for specified crimes. But all of the post-*Furman* statutes make clear that capital punishment itself has not been rejected by the elected representatives of the people....

... [H]owever, the Eighth Amendment demands more than that a challenged punishment be acceptable to contemporary society. The Court also must ask whether it comports with the basic concept of human dignity at the core of the Amendment. *Trop v. Dulles*, 356 U.S. at 100 (1958). Although we cannot "invalidate a category of penalties because we deem less severe penalties adequate to serve the ends of penology," the sanction imposed cannot be so totally without penological justification that it results in the gratuitous infliction of suffering.

The death penalty is said to serve two principal social purposes: retribution and deterrence of capital crimes by prospective offenders.[28]

In part, capital punishment is an expression of society's moral outrage at particularly offensive conduct. This function may be unappealing to many, but it is essential in an ordered society that asks its citizens to rely on legal processes rather than self-help to vindicate their wrongs.

The instinct for retribution is part of the nature of man, and channeling that instinct in the administration of criminal justice serves an important purpose in promoting the stability of a society governed by law. When people begin to believe that organized society is unwilling or unable to impose upon criminal offenders the punishment they "deserve," then there are sown the seeds of anarchy—of self-help, vigilante justice, and lynch law.

"Retribution is no longer the dominant objective of the criminal law," but neither is it a forbidden objective nor one inconsistent with our respect for the dignity of men. Indeed, the decision that capital punishment may be the appropriate sanction in extreme cases is an expression of the community's belief that certain crimes are themselves so grievous an affront to humanity that the only adequate response may be the penalty of death.

Statistical attempts to evaluate the worth of the death penalty as a deterrent to crimes by potential offenders have occasioned a great deal of debate. The results have been inconclusive....

Although some of the studies [on the deterrent effect of the death penalty] suggest that the death penalty may not function as a significantly greater deterrent than lesser penalties, there is no convincing empirical evidence either supporting or refuting this view. We may nevertheless assume safely that there are murderers, such as those who act in passion, for whom the threat of death has little or no deterrent effect. But for many others, the death penalty undoubtedly is a significant deterrent. There are carefully contemplated murders, such as murder for hire, where the possible penalty of death may well enter into the cold calculus that precedes the decision to act. And there are some categories of murder, such as murder by a life prisoner, where other sanctions may not be adequate.

The value of capital punishment as a deterrent of crime is a complex factual issue the resolution of which properly rests with the legislatures, which can evaluate the results of statistical studies in terms of their own local conditions and with a flexibility of approach that is not available to the courts. Indeed, many of the post-*Furman* statutes reflect just such a responsible effort to define those crimes and those criminals for which capital punishment is most probably an effective deterrent.

In sum, we cannot say that the judgment of the Georgia Legislature that capital punishment may be necessary in some cases is clearly wrong. Considerations of federalism, as well as respect for the ability of a legislature to evaluate, in terms of its particular State, the moral consensus concerning the death penalty and its social utility as a sanction, require us to conclude, in the absence of more convincing evidence, that the in-

---

28. Another purpose that has been discussed is the incapacitation of dangerous criminals and the consequent prevention of crimes that they may otherwise commit in the future.

fliction of death as a punishment for murder is not without justification and thus is not unconstitutionally severe.

Finally, we must consider whether the punishment of death is disproportionate in relation to the crime for which it is imposed. There is no question that death as a punishment is unique in its severity and irrevocability. When a defendant's life is at stake, the Court has been particularly sensitive to ensure that every safeguard is observed. But we are concerned here only with the imposition of capital punishment for the crime of murder, and when a life has been taken deliberately by the offender, we cannot say that the punishment is invariably disproportionate to the crime. It is an extreme sanction, suitable to the most extreme of crimes.

We hold that the death penalty is not a form of punishment that may never be imposed, regardless of the circumstances of the offense, regardless of the character of the offender, and regardless of the procedure followed in reaching the decision to impose it.

IV

We now consider whether Georgia may impose the death penalty on the petitioner in this case.

A

While *Furman* did not hold that the infliction of the death penalty *per se* violates the Constitution's ban on cruel and unusual punishments, it did recognize that the penalty of death is different in kind from any other punishment imposed under our system of criminal justice. Because of the uniqueness of the death penalty, *Furman* held that it could not be imposed under sentencing procedures that created a substantial risk that it would be inflicted in an arbitrary and capricious manner. Mr. Justice White concluded that "the death penalty is exacted with great infrequency even for the most atrocious crimes and ... there is no meaningful basis for distinguishing the few cases in which it is imposed from the many cases in which it is not." Indeed, the death sentences examined by the Court in *Furman* were

> cruel and unusual in the same way that being struck by lightning is cruel and unusual. For, of all the people convicted of [capital crimes], many just as reprehensible as these, the petitioners [in *Furman* were] among a capriciously selected random handful upon whom the sentence of death has in fact been imposed.... [T]he Eighth and Fourteenth Amendments cannot tolerate the infliction of a sentence of death under legal systems that permit this unique penalty to be so wantonly and so freakishly imposed.

Furman mandates that where discretion is afforded a sentencing body on a matter so grave as the determination of whether a human life should be taken or spared, that discretion must be suitably directed and limited so as to minimize the risk of wholly arbitrary and capricious action.

It is certainly not a novel proposition that discretion in the area of sentencing be exercised in an informed manner. We have long recognized that "[f]or the determination of sentences, justice generally requires ... that there be taken into account the circumstances of the offense together with the character and propensities of the offender." Otherwise, "the system cannot function in a consistent and a rational manner."

The cited studies assumed that the trial judge would be the sentencing authority. If an experienced trial judge, who daily faces the difficult task of imposing sentences, has a vital need for accurate information about a defendant and the crime he committed in order to be able to impose a rational sentence in the typical criminal case, then accurate sentencing information is an indispensable prerequisite to a reasoned determination of whether a defendant shall live or die by a jury of people who may never before have made a sentencing decision.

Jury sentencing has been considered desirable in capital cases in order "to maintain a link between contemporary community values and the penal system—a link without which the determination of punishment could hardly reflect 'the evolving standards of decency that mark the progress of a maturing society.'" But it creates special problems. Much of the information that is relevant to the sentencing decision may have no relevance to the question of guilt, or may even be extremely prejudicial to a fair determination of that question. This problem, however, is scarcely insurmountable. Those who have studied the question suggest that a bifurcated procedure—one in which the question of sentence is not considered until the determination of guilt has been made—is the best answer.... When a human life is at stake and when the jury must have information prejudicial to the question of guilt but relevant to the question of penalty in order to impose a rational sentence, a bifurcated system is more likely to ensure elimination of the constitutional deficiencies identified in *Furman*.

But the provision of relevant information under fair procedural rules is not alone sufficient to guarantee that the information will be properly used in the imposition of punishment, especially if sentencing is performed by a jury. Since the members of a jury will have had little, if any, previous experience in sentencing, they are unlikely to be skilled in dealing with the information they are given. To the extent that this problem is inherent in jury sentencing, it may not be totally correctible. It seems clear, however, that the problem will be alleviated if the jury is given guidance regarding the factors about the crime and the defendant that the State, representing organized society, deems particularly relevant to the sentencing decision.

... [T]he concerns expressed in *Furman* that the penalty of death not be imposed in an arbitrary or capricious manner can be met by a carefully drafted statute that ensures that the sentencing authority is given adequate information and guidance. As a general proposition these concerns are best met by a system that provides for a bifurcated proceeding at which the sentencing authority is apprised of the information relevant to the imposition of sentence and provided with standards to guide its use of the information.

We do not intend to suggest that only the above-described procedures would be permissible under *Furman* or that any sentencing system constructed along these general lines would inevitably satisfy the concerns of *Furman*, for each distinct system must be examined on an individual basis. Rather, we have embarked upon this general exposition to make clear that it is possible to construct capital-sentencing systems capable of meeting *Furman*'s constitutional concerns.

B

We now turn to consideration of the constitutionality of Georgia's capital-sentencing procedures. In the wake of *Furman*, Georgia amended its capital punishment statute, but chose not to narrow the scope of its murder provisions. Thus, now as before *Furman*, in Georgia "(a) person commits murder when he unlawfully and with malice aforethought, either express or implied, causes the death of another human being." Ga. Code Ann., §26-1101(a) (1972). All persons convicted of murder "shall be punished by death or by imprisonment for life." §26-1101(c) (1972).

Georgia did act, however, to narrow the class of murderers subject to capital punishment by specifying 10 statutory aggravating circumstances, one of which must be found by the jury to exist beyond a reasonable doubt before a death sentence can ever be imposed. In addition, the jury is authorized to consider any other appropriate aggravating or mitigating circumstances. The jury is not required to find any mitigating circumstance in order to make a recommendation of mercy that is binding on the trial court, but it must find a statutory aggravating circumstance before recommending a sentence of death.

These procedures require the jury to consider the circumstances of the crime and the criminal before it recommends sentence. No longer can a Georgia jury do as *Furman's* jury did: reach a finding of the defendant's guilt and then, without guidance or direction, decide whether he should live or die. Instead, the jury's attention is directed to the specific circumstances of the crime: Was it committed in the course of another capital felony? Was it committed for money? Was it committed upon a peace officer or judicial officer? Was it committed in a particularly heinous way or in a manner that endangered the lives of many persons? In addition, the jury's attention is focused on the characteristics of the person who committed the crime: Does he have a record of prior convictions for capital offenses? Are there any special facts about this defendant that mitigate against imposing capital punishment (*e.g.*, his youth, the extent of his cooperation with the police, his emotional state at the time of the crime). As a result, while some jury discretion still exists, "the discretion to be exercised is controlled by clear and objective standards so as to produce non-discriminatory application."

As an important additional safeguard against arbitrariness and caprice, the Georgia statutory scheme provides for automatic appeal of all death sentences to the State's Supreme Court. That court is required by statute to review each sentence of death and determine whether it was imposed under the influence of passion or prejudice, whether the evidence supports the jury's finding of a statutory aggravating circumstance, and whether the sentence is disproportionate compared to those sentences imposed in similar cases.

In short, Georgia's new sentencing procedures require as a prerequisite to the imposition of the death penalty, specific jury findings as to the circumstances of the crime or the character of the defendant. Moreover, to guard further against a situation comparable to that presented in *Furman*, the Supreme Court of Georgia compares each death sentence with the sentences imposed on similarly situated defendants to ensure that the sentence of death in a particular case is not disproportionate. On their face these procedures seem to satisfy the concerns of *Furman*. No longer should there be "no meaningful basis for distinguishing the few cases in which [the death penalty] is imposed from the many cases in which it is not." 408 U.S. at 313 (White, J., concurring).

V

The basic concern of *Furman* centered on those defendants who were being condemned to death capriciously and arbitrarily. Under the procedures before the Court in that case, sentencing authorities were not directed to give attention to the nature or circumstances of the crime committed or to the character or record of the defendant. Left unguided, juries imposed the death sentence in a way that could only be called freakish. The new Georgia sentencing procedures, by contrast, focus the jury's attention on the particularized nature of the crime and the particularized characteristics of the individual defendant. While the jury is permitted to consider any aggravating or mitigating circumstances, it must find and identify at least one statutory aggravating factor before it may impose a penalty of death. In this way the jury's discretion is channeled. No longer can a jury wantonly and freakishly impose the death sentence; it is always circumscribed by the legislative guidelines. In addition, the review function of the Supreme Court of Georgia affords additional assurance that the concerns that prompted our decision in *Furman* are not present to any significant degree in the Georgia procedure applied here.

For the reasons expressed in this opinion, we hold that the statutory system under which Gregg was sentenced to death does not violate the Constitution. Accordingly, the judgment of the Georgia Supreme Court is affirmed.

Statement of THE CHIEF JUSTICE and Mr. Justice REHNQUIST: We concur in the judgment and join the opinion of Mr. Justice White agreeing with its analysis that Georgia's system of capital punishment comports with the Court's holding in *Furman*.

[Justice Brennan and Justice Marshall dissented in *Gregg* and two companion cases, *Jurek v. Texas* and *Proffitt v. Florida*. Their dissents, published at 428 U.S. 227 (1976), are excerpted below.]

Mr. Justice BRENNAN, dissenting.

... This Court inescapably has the duty, as the ultimate arbiter of the meaning of our Constitution, to say whether, when individuals condemned to death stand before our Bar, "moral concepts" require us to hold that the law has progressed to the point where we should declare that the punishment of death, like punishments on the rack, the screw, and the wheel, is no longer morally tolerable in our civilized society. My opinion in *Furman* concluded that our civilization and the law had progressed to this point and that therefore the punishment of death, for whatever crime and under all circumstances, is "cruel and unusual" in violation of the Eighth and Fourteenth Amendments of the Constitution. I shall not again canvass the reasons that led to that conclusion. I emphasize only that foremost among the "moral concepts" recognized in our cases and inherent in the Clause is the primary moral principle that the State, even as it punishes, must treat its citizens in a manner consistent with their intrinsic worth as human beings—a punishment must not be so severe as to be degrading to human dignity. A judicial determination whether the punishment of death comports with human dignity is therefore not only permitted but compelled by the Clause....

The fatal constitutional infirmity in the punishment of death is that it treats "members of the human race as nonhumans, as objects to be toyed with and discarded. [It is] thus inconsistent with the fundamental premise of the Clause that even the vilest criminal remains a human being possessed of common human dignity." As such it is a penalty that "subjects the individual to a fate forbidden by the principle of civilized treatment guaranteed by the [Clause]." I therefore would hold, on that ground alone, that death is today a cruel and unusual punishment prohibited by the Clause. "Justice of this kind is obviously no less shocking than the crime itself, and the new 'official' murder, far from offering redress for the offense committed against society, adds instead a second defilement to the first." A. Camus, Reflections on the Guillotine 5–6 (Fridtjof-Karla Pub. 1960).

I dissent from the judgments in *Gregg v. Georgia, Proffitt v. Florida*, and *Jurek v. Texas*, insofar as each upholds the death sentences challenged in those cases. I would set aside the death sentences imposed in those cases as violative of the Eighth and Fourteenth Amendments.

Mr. Justice MARSHALL, dissenting.

... In *Furman* I concluded that the death penalty is constitutionally invalid for two reasons. First, the death penalty is excessive. And second, the American people, fully informed as to the purposes of the death penalty and its liabilities, would in my view reject it as morally unacceptable.

Since the decision in *Furman*, the legislatures of 35 States have enacted new statutes authorizing the imposition of the death sentence for certain crimes, and Congress has enacted a law providing the death penalty for air piracy resulting in death. I would be less than candid if I did not acknowledge that these developments have a significant bearing on a realistic assessment of the moral acceptability of the death penalty to the American people. But if the constitutionality of the death penalty turns, as I have urged, on the opinion of an informed citizenry, then even the enactment of new death statutes cannot be viewed as conclusive. In *Furman*, I observed that the American people are largely unaware of the information critical to a judgment on the morality of the death penalty, and concluded that if they were better informed they would consider it shocking, unjust, and unacceptable. A recent study, conducted after the enactment of the post-*Furman* statutes, has confirmed that the American people know little about the death penalty, and that the opinions of an informed public would differ significantly from those of a public unaware of the consequences and effects of the death penalty. Sarat & Vidmar, "Public Opinion, the Death Penalty, and the Eighth Amendment," 1976 Wis. L. Rev. 171.

Even assuming, however, that the post-*Furman* enactment of statutes authorizing the death penalty renders the prediction of the views of an informed citizenry an uncertain basis for a constitutional decision, the enactment of those statutes has no bearing whatsoever on the conclusion that the death penalty is unconstitutional because it is excessive. An excessive penalty is invalid under the Cruel and Unusual Punishments Clause "even though popular sentiment may favor" it. The inquiry here, then, is simply whether the death penalty is necessary to accomplish the legitimate legislative purposes in punishment, or whether a less severe penalty — life imprisonment — would do as well.

The two purposes that sustain the death penalty as nonexcessive in the Court's view are general deterrence and retribution. In *Furman*, I canvassed the relevant data on the deterrent effect of capital punishment. The state of knowledge at that point, after literally centuries of debate, was summarized as follows by a United Nations Committee: "It is generally agreed between the retentionists and abolitionists, whatever their opinions about the validity of comparative studies of deterrence, that the data which now exist show no correlation between the existence of capital punishment and lower rates of capital crime." The available evidence, I concluded in *Furman*, was convincing that "capital punishment is not necessary as a deterrent to crime in our society." ...

The other principal purpose said to be served by the death penalty is retribution. The notion that retribution can serve as a moral justification for the sanction of death finds credence in the opinion of my Brothers Stewart, Powell, and Stevens, and that of my Brother White in *Roberts v. Louisiana*, (*infra* this chapter). It is this notion that I find to be the most disturbing aspect of today's unfortunate decisions....

The [plurality's] contentions — that society's expression of moral outrage through the imposition of the death penalty pre-empts the citizenry from taking the law into its own hands and reinforces moral values — are not retributive in the purest sense. They are essentially utilitarian in that they portray the death penalty as valuable because of its beneficial results. These justifications for the death penalty are inadequate because the penalty is, quite clearly I think, not necessary to the accomplishment of those results.

There remains for consideration, however, what might be termed the purely retributive justification for the death penalty that the death penalty is appropriate, not because of its beneficial effect on society, but because the taking of the murderer's life is itself morally good. Some of the language of the opinion of my Brothers Stewart, Powell, and Stevens in [*Gregg*] appears positively to embrace this notion of retribution for its own sake as a justification for capital punishment. They state: "[T]he decision that capital punishment may be the appropriate sanction in extreme cases is an expression of the community's belief that certain crimes are themselves so grievous an affront to humanity that the only adequate response may be the penalty of death."

They then quote with approval from Lord Justice Denning's remarks before the British Royal Commission on Capital Punishment: "The truth is that some crimes are so outrageous that society insists on adequate punishment, because the wrong-doer deserves it, irrespective of whether it is a deterrent or not."

Of course, it may be that these statements are intended as no more than observations as to the popular demands that it is thought must be responded to in order to prevent anarchy. But the implication of the statements appears to me to be quite different—namely, that society's judgment that the murderer "deserves" death must be respected not simply because the preservation of order requires it, but because it is appropriate that society make the judgment and carry it out. It is this latter notion, in particular, that I consider to be fundamentally at odds with the Eighth Amendment. The mere fact that the community demands the murderer's life in return for the evil he has done cannot sustain the death penalty, for as Justices Stewart, Powell, and Stevens remind us, "the Eighth Amendment demands more than that a challenged punishment be acceptable to contemporary society." To be sustained under the Eighth Amendment, the death penalty must "compor[t] with the basic concept of human dignity at the core of the Amendment," the objective in imposing it must be "[consistent] with our respect for the dignity of [other] men." Under these standards, the taking of life "because the wrongdoer deserves it" surely must fall, for such a punishment has as its very basis the total denial of the wrong-doer's dignity and worth.

The death penalty, unnecessary to promote the goal of deterrence or to further any legitimate notion of retribution, is an excessive penalty forbidden by the Eighth and Fourteenth Amendments. I respectfully dissent from the Court's judgment upholding the sentences of death imposed upon the petitioners in these cases.

Note and Question

The *Gregg* plurality stated that the constitutional infirmities identified in *Furman* (the arbitrary and capricious imposition of the death penalty) are "best met by a system that provides for a bifurcated proceeding." Does this mean that bifurcated trials are constitutionally required in capital cases?

D. Summary of the 1976 Supreme Court Cases Applying the Eighth and Fourteenth Amendments to Post-*Furman* Death Penalty Statutes

On the same day the Court issued its landmark decision in *Gregg v. Georgia*, the Court decided four companion cases addressing the constitutionality of post-*Furman* death penalty statutes in Florida, Texas, North Carolina and Louisiana: *Proffitt v. Florida*, 428 U.S. 242 (1976); *Jurek v. Texas*, 428 U.S. 262 (1976); *Woodson v. North Carolina*, 428 U.S. 280 (1976); and *(Stanislaus) Roberts v. Louisiana*, 428 U.S. 325 (1976). In *Gregg* and the four companion cases, a three-member plurality consisting of Justices Stewart, Powell and Stevens joined in an opinion and announced the judgment of the Court.

In *Gregg*, the three-member plurality, joined by Chief Justice Burger and Justices White, Blackmun and Rehnquist, embraced *Furman's* holding that the death penalty "could not be imposed under sentencing procedures that created a substantial risk that it would be inflicted in an arbitrary and capricious manner," but concluded that the Eighth Amendment erected no *per se* barrier to the punishment of death. Moreover, these seven justices agreed that the Georgia death penalty statute remedied the constitutional defects which the *Furman* Court found fatal to capital sentencing procedures. Justice Stewart, joined by Justices Powell and Stevens, concluded that:

> the concerns expressed in *Furman* that the penalty of death not be imposed in an arbitrary or capricious manner can be met by a carefully drafted statute that ensures that the sentencing authority is given adequate information and guidance. As a general proposition, these concerns are best met by a system [like Georgia's] that provides for a bifurcated proceeding at which the sentencing authority is apprised of the information relevant to the imposition of sentence and provided with standards to guide its use of the information.

Justices Brennan and Marshall dissented in *Gregg*, *Proffitt* and *Jurek*. Their dissents built upon differing rationales, but both Brennan and Marshall embraced the argument that, regardless of the nature of the offense or the procedures followed in imposing sentence, the punishment of death invariably constitutes cruel and unusual punishment in violation of the Eighth and Fourteenth Amendments.

In *Proffitt* and *Jurek*, the same seven member majority of *Gregg* found that the death penalty statutes of Florida and Texas provided procedural safeguards similar to the Georgia death penalty statute and thus were constitutional.

Proffitt v. Florida, 428 U.S. 242 (1976)

Writing for the three-member plurality in *Proffitt*, Justice Powell described the mechanics of the Florida death penalty statute:

> Under the new statute, if a defendant is found guilty of a capital offense, a separate evidentiary hearing is held before the trial judge and jury to determine his sentence. Evidence may be presented on any matter the judge deems relevant to sentencing and must include matters relating to certain legislatively specified aggravating and mitigating circumstances. Both the prosecution and the defense may present argument on whether the death penalty shall be imposed.
>
> At the conclusion of the hearing the jury is directed to consider "[w]hether sufficient mitigating circumstances exist ... which outweigh the aggravating circumstances found to exist; and ... [b]ased on these considerations, whether the defendant should be sentenced to life [imprisonment] or death." The jury's verdict is determined by majority vote. It is only advisory; the actual sentence is determined by the trial judge. The Florida Supreme Court has stated, however, that "[i]n order to sustain a sentence of death following a jury recom-

mendation of life, the facts suggesting a sentence of death should be so clear and convincing that virtually no reasonable person could differ."

The trial judge is also directed to weigh the [eight] statutory aggravating and [seven] mitigating circumstances when he determines the sentence to be imposed on a defendant. The statute requires that if the trial court imposes a sentence of death, "it shall set forth in writing its findings upon which the sentence of death is based to the facts: (a) [t]hat sufficient [statutory] aggravating circumstances exist ... and (b) [t]hat there are insufficient [statutory] mitigating circumstances ... to outweigh the aggravating circumstances."

According to the plurality, the key difference between the statutory schemes in Florida and Georgia was that in Florida the trial judge imposed the death penalty; in Georgia the jury assessed punishment. Finding this distinction to be constitutionally insignificant, the plurality opinion focused on similarities between the two statutory schemes. In this regard, the Florida statute was similar to Georgia's statute in that the Florida statute "require[d] the trial judge to focus his determination of death on the circumstances of the crime and character of the individual defendant."

Both Georgia and Florida provided for automatic review by the highest state court of all cases in which death is imposed. Unlike the Georgia scheme, however, the Florida statute did not proscribe a specific form for appellate review. Nonetheless, the plurality concluded that the Florida procedure "has in effect adopted the type of proportionality review mandated by the Georgia statute."

The plurality rejected attacks on the Florida death penalty statute based on the grounds that aggravating and mitigating circumstances were vague, overbroad and imprecise. Justice Powell wrote, "[w]hile the various factors to be considered by the sentencing authorities do not have numerical weights assigned to them, the requirements of *Furman* are satisfied when the sentencing authority's discretion is guided and channeled by requiring examination of specific factors that argue in favor of or against imposition of the death penalty, thus eliminating total arbitrariness and capriciousness in its imposition."

Jurek v. Texas, 428 U.S. 262 (1976)

In *Jurek*, the Court upheld the death penalty statutory scheme in Texas. After *Furman*, the Texas legislature revised its death penalty statute and identified five offenses punishable by death: "[1] murder of a peace officer or fireman; [2] murder committed in the course of kidnapping, burglary, robbery, forcible rape or arson; [3] murder committed for remuneration; [4] murder committed while escaping or attempting to escape from a penal institution; and [5] murder committed by a prison inmate when the victim is a prison employee." During the guilt and innocence stage of the capital trial, the jury is required to determine whether the state proved beyond a reasonable doubt that the defendant committed one of the enumerated capital offenses.

If the jury finds the defendant guilty of a capital offense, the Texas statute, like those upheld in *Gregg* and *Proffitt*, provides for a separate sentencing proceeding during which both the prosecution and defense are permitted to introduce relevant evidence and present arguments for or against the punishment of death. Unlike Florida and Georgia, however, the Texas death penalty statute did not adopt a list of aggravating and mitigating factors and circumstances for the jury to consider during sentencing. Rather, Texas procedure required the jury to answer three questions to determine whether a defendant would be allowed to live in prison or be put to death:

(1) whether the conduct of the defendant that caused the death of the deceased was committed deliberately and with the reasonable expectation that the death of the deceased or another would result;

(2) whether there is a probability that the defendant would commit criminal acts of violence that would constitute a continuing threat to society; and

(3) if raised by the evidence, whether the conduct of the defendant in killing the deceased was unreasonable in response to the provocation, if any, by the deceased.

Although the Texas statute did not set out a list of aggravating circumstances, Justices Stewart, Powell and Stevens concluded that "each of the five classes of murders made capital by the Texas statute is encompassed in Georgia and Florida by one or more of their statutory aggravating factors." Writing for the plurality, Justice Stevens reasoned that, "in essence, the Texas statute requires that the jury find the existence of a statutory aggravating circumstance before the death penalty may be imposed." According to Justice Stevens' opinion, notwithstanding the absence of a defined group of statutory aggravators, the system in Texas, like those in Georgia and Florida, "requires the sentencing authority to focus on the particularized nature of the crime."

In upholding the constitutionality of the Texas statute, the plurality cautioned that consideration of only aggravating circumstances would fall short of the individualized sentencing required by the Eighth and Fourteenth Amendments. Such a statutory scheme, the plurality reasoned, would amount to a mandatory death sentence. "A jury must be allowed to consider on the basis of all relevant evidence not only why a death sentence should be imposed, but also why it should not be imposed." Because the three questions posed to the jurors sufficiently focused on mitigating circumstances, the system in Texas was constitutional.

Not all legislative attempts to cure the constitutional defects identified in *Furman* were as successful as those in Georgia, Florida and Texas. In *Woodson v. North Carolina* and (*Stanislaus*) *Roberts v. Louisiana*, a different coalition of justices combined to invalidate the post-*Furman* death penalty statutes of North Carolina and Louisiana. This time the three-member plurality of Justices Stewart, Powell and Stevens was joined by Justices Brennan and Marshall in striking down mandatory death penalty schemes in North Carolina and Louisiana. In both cases, the justices who had cast concurring votes in *Gregg*, *Proffitt* and *Jurek* (C.J. Burger, White, Blackmun and Rehnquist) assumed the role of dissenters.

Woodson v. North Carolina, 428 U.S. 280 (1976)

In response to *Furman*, the North Carolina legislature enacted a "new" death penalty statute in 1974. This statute was virtually identical to North Carolina's pre-*Furman* statute except that it made the death penalty mandatory for everyone convicted of first-degree murder or felony murder. According to Justice Stewart's plurality opinion, mandatory death sentences had long been viewed with disfavor because such mandatory sentencing practices were perceived as "unduly harsh and unworkably rigid."

[O]ne of the most significant developments in our society's treatment of capital punishment has been the rejection of the common-law practice of inexorably imposing a death sentence upon every person convicted of a specified offense. North Carolina's mandatory death penalty departs markedly from contemporary standards respecting the imposition of the punishment of death and thus cannot be applied consistently with the Eighth and Fourteenth Amendments' requirement that the State's power to punish "be exercised within the limits of civilized standards."

Justice Stewart identified two other reasons to strike down the North Carolina statute. First, the mandatory sentencing procedure did not address "*Furman*'s rejection of unbridled jury discretion in the imposition of capital sentences." "North Carolina's mandatory death penalty statute provides no standards to guide the jury in its inevitable exercise of the power to determine which first-degree murderers shall live and which shall die." Moreover, studies showed that jurors faced with mandatory death sentences were reluctant to return guilty verdicts because of the "enormity of the sentence automatically imposed."

The second reason Justice Stewart gave for invalidating the North Carolina statute is that the mandatory sentencing procedure did not allow for "particularized consideration of relevant aspects of the character and record of each convicted defendant before the imposition upon him of a sentence of death." "[W]e believe that in capital cases the fundamental respect for humanity underlying the Eighth Amendment ... requires consideration of the character and record of the individual offender and the circumstances of the particular offense as a constitutionally indispensable part of the process of inflicting the penalty of death." Thus, *Woodson* imposed a requirement of "individualized sentencing" in capital cases.

The guiding principle is the recognition that "death is different." According to *Woodson*,

> [T]he penalty of death is qualitatively different from a sentence of imprisonment, however long. Death, in its finality, differs more from life imprisonment than a 100-year prison term differs from one of only a year or two. Because of that qualitative difference, there is a corresponding difference in the need for reliability in the determination that death is the appropriate punishment in a specific case.

(Stanislaus) Roberts v. Louisiana, 428 U.S. 325 (1976)

Louisiana, like North Carolina, responded to *Furman* by replacing discretionary jury sentencing in capital cases with mandatory death sentences. Consequently, the Louisiana statute met a fate similar to North Carolina's statute. After *Furman*, Louisiana adopted a different and somewhat narrower definition of first-degree murder than North Carolina. Although North Carolina had decreed that all persons guilty of either "willful, deliberate and premeditated homicide" or felony-murder would automatically receive a death sentence, Louisiana took a more conservative approach. The Louisiana statute also imposed an automatic death sentence on all first-degree murderers, but defined first-degree murder to include only five categories of homicide: (1) killing in connection with certain felonies; (2) killing a fireman or police officer engaged in the performance of his duties; (3) killing for remuneration; (4) killing with the intent to inflict harm on more than one person; and (5) killing by a person with a prior murder conviction or under a current life sentence. Under the Louisiana scheme, when the state charged an individual with the offense of first-degree murder the jury was provided with, and instructed on, four potential verdicts: guilty of first-degree murder, guilty of second-degree murder, guilty of manslaughter, and not guilty. Second-degree murder was punished by life in prison. If a jury found the defendant guilty of first-degree murder, death was mandatory and appeals for mercy by the jury had no effect.

Writing for the three-member plurality, Justice Stevens concluded that limiting the range of offenses for which the death penalty could be imposed did not adequately respond to the harshness and inflexibility of a mandatory death sentence. According to Justice Stevens, even narrowly-tailored mandatory death penalty statutes had historically been rejected in favor of discretionary death penalty statutes. This historical trend revealed "our society's rejection of the belief that 'every offense in a like legal category calls for an identical punishment without regard to the past life and habits of the particular offender.'" "The Eighth Amendment, which draws much of its meaning from 'the evolving standards of decency that mark the progress of a maturing society,' simply cannot tolerate the reintroduction of a practice so thoroughly discarded." Moreover, the system of offering four verdicts to the jury "not only lacks standards to guide the jury in selecting among first-degree murderers, but it plainly invites the jurors to disregard their oaths and choose a verdict for a lesser offense whenever they feel the death penalty is inappropriate. There is an element of capriciousness in making the jurors' power to avoid the death penalty dependent on their willingness to accept this invitation to disregard the trial judge's instructions."

Justice White, along with Chief Justice Burger and Justices Blackmun and Rehnquist, dissented in *Woodson* and *Roberts*. Justice White rejected the plurality's view that historically mandatory death sentences were so disfavored that they should be deemed unconstitutional under the Eighth Amendment. Further, Justice White concluded that the mandatory provisions in the death penalty statute were designed to remove the unfettered jury discretion which rendered the death penalty in *Furman* unconstitutional. In *Roberts*, Justice White wrote: "As I see it, we are now in no position to rule that the State's present law, having eliminated the overt discretionary power of juries, suffers from the same constitutional infirmities which led this Court to invalidate the Georgia death penalty statute in *Furman v. Georgia.*"

Justice White criticized the distinctions drawn by the plurality between the mandatory death penalty statute of Louisiana and the statutory scheme of Texas:

> Furthermore, Justices Stewart, Powell, and Stevens uphold the capital punishment statute of Texas, under which capital punishment is required if the defendant is found guilty of the crime charged and the jury answers two additional questions in the affirmative. Once that occurs, no discretion is left to the jury; death is mandatory. Although Louisiana juries are not required to answer these precise questions, the Texas law is not constitutionally distinguishable from the Louisiana system under which the jury, to convict, must find the elements of the crime, including the essential intent to kill or inflict great bodily harm, which, according to the instructions given in this case, must be felonious, "that is, it must be wrong or without just cause or excuse."

In his *Woodson* dissent, Justice Rehnquist also viewed Texas' statutory scheme as requiring a mandatory death penalty and attacked the plurality's decision to uphold the Texas scheme while striking down North Carolina's statute.

> The Texas system much more closely approximates the mandatory North Carolina system which is struck down today. The jury is required to answer three statutory questions. If the questions are unanimously answered in the affirmative, the death penalty *must* be imposed. It is extremely difficult to see

how this system can be any less subject to the infirmities caused by juror nullification which the plurality concludes are fatal to North Carolina's statute. Justices Stewart, Powell, and Stevens apparently think they can sidestep this inconsistency because of their belief that one of the three questions will permit
consideration of mitigating factors justifying the imposition of a life sentence.
It is, however, as those Justices recognize ... far from clear that the statute is to
be read in such a fashion. In any event, while the imposition of such unlimited
consideration of mitigating factors conforms to the plurality's novel constitutional doctrine that "[a] jury must be allowed to consider on the basis of all
relevant evidence not only why a death sentence should be imposed, but also
why it should not be imposed," the resulting system seems as likely as any to
produce the unbridled discretion which was condemned by the separate opinions in *Furman*.

The plurality's insistence on individualized consideration of the sentencing ... does not depend upon any traditional application of the prohibition
against cruel and unusual punishment contained in the Eighth Amendment.
The punishment here is concededly not cruel and unusual, and that determination has traditionally ended judicial inquiry in our cases construing the
Cruel and Unusual Punishments Clause.... What the plurality opinion has actually done is to import into the Due Process Clause of the Fourteenth Amendment what it conceives to be desirable procedural guarantees where the punishment of death, concededly not cruel and unusual for the crime of which the
defendant was convicted, is to be imposed. This is squarely contrary to *Mc-
Gautha*, and unsupported by any other decision of this Court.

Notes and Questions

1. In *Roberts*, Justices Stewart, Stevens and Powell concluded that limiting the scope
of offenses subject to the death penalty did not cure the perceived harshness of
mandatory death sentences. How did Louisiana's more narrowly-tailored list of crimes
punishable by death differ from Georgia's and Florida's lists of aggravating circumstances, or Texas' list of offenses subject to the death penalty? How can you distinguish
the Louisiana statute from the Texas statute? Do you agree with Justices White's and
Rehnquist's assessments of the Texas statutory scheme as "not constitutionally distinguishable" from Louisiana's mandatory system and "no less subject to the infirmities
caused by juror nullification" which the plurality deemed fatal to the North Carolina
system?

2. In *Woodson* and *Roberts*, the Court rejected the mandatory death penalty schemes
of North Carolina and Louisiana in part because of the prospect of jury nullification.
Simply stated, jurors were being deterred from rendering verdicts of guilty of first-degree murder because of the enormity of the sentence automatically imposed. Would jurors operating under the sentencing schemes in Texas, Georgia and Florida be more
obedient to the trial court's instructions? What is there to prevent a juror in Texas from
deciding to answer "no" to one of the three questions—even though the evidence warranted an affirmative answer—in order to avoid inflicting death on a defendant? Similarly, could a trial judge in Florida refuse to find one of the eight aggravating factors in
order to avoid imposing death? Because of the irreversible nature of the death penalty
and the moral problems raised by killing another human being—for whatever
reason—can any death penalty scheme be free of this problem? Does requiring the con-

sideration of mitigating factors alleviate this potential infirmity in the punishment of death? How? Do the three questions in the Texas death penalty scheme resolve this problem?

3. Consider the following language, frequently quoted, from *Woodson*: "[T]he penalty of death is qualitatively different from a sentence of imprisonment, however long. Death, in its finality, differs more from life imprisonment than a 100-year prison term differs from one of only a year or two. Because of that qualitative difference, there is a corresponding difference in the need for reliability in the determination that death is the appropriate punishment in a specific case." Death penalty opponents interpret this language as requiring super due process in capital cases. Professor Adam Thurschwell has observed that the promise of *Woodson* has been observed largely in the breach. According to Thurschwell, the Supreme Court's admonishments for heightened reliability and increased accuracy in capital cases "have for the most part remained mere rhetoric, as the special protections theoretically afforded to capital defendants under the Eighth Amendment have turned out to be almost valueless in practice. The tendency among academics and defense lawyers has been to bewail this phenomenon as judicial hypocrisy. Whatever the merits of that view as a matter of individual judicial psychology or politics, it has deeper roots in an underlying conceptual weakness in the Court's attempt to use the Eighth Amendment as the primary vehicle for guaranteeing the heightened reliability of capital procedures." Thurschwell, "Federal Courts, the Death Penalty, and the Due Process Clause: The Original Understanding of the 'Heightened Reliability' of Capital Trials," 14 Fed. Sent. R. 14 (2001).

4. A majority of the Court concluded that the death penalty was not a *per se* violation of the Eighth Amendment in part because thirty-five states had recently enacted death penalty statutes which the states wished to enforce. Thus, "evolving standards of decency," as discerned from the conduct of various state legislatures, would appear to permit imposition of the death penalty. However, all Western nations except the United States have either abolished or refused to impose the penalty of death. If "evolving standards of decency" are measured on a global level, is the death penalty cruel and unusual? Should the death penalty be surveyed internationally to determine whether the penalty comports with the Eighth Amendment?

5. In 1987, the United States Supreme Court revisited the mandatory death penalty in *Sumner v. Shuman*, 483 U.S. 66. While serving a life sentence without possibility of parole for first degree murder, Shuman was convicted of the capital murder of a fellow inmate. Under the Nevada statute then in effect, Shuman received a mandatory death sentence. Relying on *Roberts* and *Woodson*, the Court held that the sentencing scheme was unconstitutional, in part, because it did not allow the defendant to present evidence in mitigation.

6. Which aspects of *Furman* remain intact after the 1976 decisions? According to one scholar, three aspects of *Furman* survive the 1976 cases:

(1) The limits of the Eighth Amendment's proscription are not static and not to be determined solely by reference to the intent of the founding fathers. Rather, the search is for an elastic concept governed by "evolving standards of decency."

(2) Discerning the content of the Eighth Amendment requires looking at the *process* by which a penalty is inflicted, rather than the inherent nature of the penalty itself.

(3) Death differs in kind, not just degree, from all other forms of criminal punishment.

Geimer, "Death At Any Cost: A Critique of the Supreme Court's Recent Retreat From Its Death Penalty Standards," 12 Fla. St. U.L. Rev. 737 (1985).

Analytically, it may be useful to divide the history of capital punishment in the United States into three periods. Prior to 1794, death was a mandatory punishment upon conviction of certain offenses including most homicides and virtually all murder. In 1794, Pennsylvania became the first state to distinguish among various degrees of murder. Although first degree murder was still automatically punished by death, jurors were given another option: second degree murder. Second degree murder did not carry a mandatory death sentence.

The second period of the death penalty in America began in the middle of the nineteenth century and endured until the *Furman* decision in 1972. During this period, defendants convicted of first degree murder were eligible to be sentenced to death. However, the decision of death or life was left to the unfettered discretion of the same judge or jury that had resolved the guilt issue against the defendant.

Finally, ever since *Gregg* was decided in 1976, capital punishment systems have been characterized by "guided discretion." Most states bifurcate capital trials; that is, guilt and innocence are decided during the first phase of the trial. Then, if the defendant is found guilty, a second penalty phase is convened to determine the appropriate punishment. The factfinder is still empowered to make the ultimate life or death decision. However, the punishment decision is reached only after aggravating and mitigating factors are weighed. For additional discussion of the various historical periods of capital punishment in America, see Kaplan, Weisberg and Binder, *Criminal Law: Cases and Materials* 429–435 (Aspen Pub. 2004). See also Tushnet, *The Death Penalty* 19–94 (Facts on File, Inc. 1994).

7. *Gregg* and the companion cases suggest a capital sentencing scheme where the discretion of imposing death is narrowed and channeled. This may be achieved by using specific aggravating factors, while simultaneously affording the jury wide discretion to consider any mitigating evidence offered by the defendant as the basis for a sentence other than death. The Court has adopted an expansive view of what constitutes mitigating evidence. See *Lockett v. Ohio, infra* chapter 8.

8. After reviewing post-*Gregg* death sentences for nearly eighteen years, Justice Harry Blackmun concluded, "[e]xperience has taught us that the constitutional goal of eliminating arbitrariness and discrimination from the administration of death can never be achieved without compromising an equally essential component of fundamental fairness—individualized sentencing." *Callins v. Collins*, 510 U.S. 1141 (1994) (Blackmun, J., dissenting from denial of certiorari).

Justice Blackmun's opinion follows:

Callins v. Collins
510 U.S. 1141 (1994)

Justice BLACKMUN, dissenting from denial of certiorari.

On February 23, 1994, at approximately 1:00 a.m., Bruce Edwin Callins will be executed by the State of Texas. Intravenous tubes attached to his arms will carry the instrument of death, a toxic fluid designed specifically for the purpose of killing human beings. The witnesses, standing a few feet away, will behold Callins, no longer a defendant, an appellant, or a petitioner, but a man, strapped to a gurney, and seconds away from extinction.

Within days, or perhaps hours, the memory of Callins will begin to fade. The wheels of justice will churn again, and somewhere, another jury or another judge will have the unenviable task of determining whether some human being is to live or die. We hope, of course, that the defendant whose life is at risk will be represented by competent counsel—someone who is inspired by the awareness that a less-than-vigorous defense truly could have fatal consequences for the defendant. We hope that the attorney will investigate all aspects of the case, follow all evidentiary and procedural rules, and appear before a judge who is still committed to the protection of defendants' rights—even now, as the prospect of meaningful judicial oversight has diminished. In the same vein, we hope that the prosecution, in urging the penalty of death, will have exercised its discretion wisely, free from bias, prejudice, or political motive, and will be humbled, rather than emboldened, by the awesome authority conferred by the State.

But even if we can feel confident that these actors will fulfill their roles to the best of their human ability, our collective conscience will remain uneasy. Twenty years have passed since this Court declared that the death penalty must be imposed fairly, and with reasonable consistency, or not at all, see *Furman v. Georgia*, 408 U.S. 238 (1972), and, despite the effort of the States and courts to devise legal formulas and procedural rules to meet this daunting challenge, the death penalty remains fraught with arbitrariness, discrimination, caprice, and mistake. This is not to say that the problems with the death penalty today are identical to those that were present 20 years ago. Rather, the problems that were pursued down one hole with procedural rules and verbal formulas have come to the surface somewhere else, just as virulent and pernicious as they were in their original form. Experience has taught us that the constitutional goal of eliminating arbitrariness and discrimination from the administration of death can never be achieved without compromising an equally essential component of fundamental fairness—individualized sentencing. See *Lockett v. Ohio*, 438 U.S. 586 (1978).

It is tempting, when faced with conflicting constitutional commands, to sacrifice one for the other or to assume that an acceptable balance between them already has been struck. In the context of the death penalty, however, such jurisprudential maneuvers are wholly inappropriate. The death penalty must be imposed "fairly, and with reasonable consistency, or not at all." *Eddings v. Oklahoma*, 455 U.S. 104, 112 (1982).

To be fair, a capital sentencing scheme must treat each person convicted of a capital offense with that "degree of respect due the uniqueness of the individual." *Lockett v. Ohio*, 438 U.S. at 605 (plurality opinion). That means affording the sentencer the power and discretion to grant mercy in a particular case, and providing avenues for the consideration of any and all relevant mitigating evidence that would justify a sentence less than death. Reasonable consistency, on the other hand, requires that the death penalty be inflicted evenhandedly, in accordance with reason and objective standards, rather than by whim, caprice, or prejudice. Finally, because human error is inevitable, and because our criminal justice system is less than perfect, searching appellate review of death sentences and their underlying convictions is a prerequisite to a constitutional death penalty scheme.

On their face, these goals of individual fairness, reasonable consistency, and absence of error appear to be attainable: Courts are in the very business of erecting procedural devices from which fair, equitable, and reliable outcomes are presumed to flow. Yet, in the death penalty area, this Court, in my view, has engaged in a futile effort to balance these constitutional demands, and now is retreating not only from the *Furman* promise of consistency and rationality, but from the requirement of individualized sentencing as well. Having virtually conceded that both fairness and rationality cannot be achieved in the administration of the death penalty, see *McCleskey v. Kemp*, 481 U.S. 279, 313, n. 37 (1987), the Court has chosen to deregulate the entire enterprise, replacing, it would seem, substantive constitutional requirements with mere aesthetics, and abdicating its statutorily and constitutionally imposed duty to provide meaningful judicial oversight to the administration of death by the States.

From this day forward, I no longer shall tinker with the machinery of death. For more than 20 years I have endeavored — indeed, I have struggled — along with a majority of this Court, to develop procedural and substantive rules that would lend more than the mere appearance of fairness to the death penalty endeavor. Rather than continue to coddle the Court's delusion that the desired level of fairness has been achieved and the need for regulation eviscerated, I feel morally and intellectually obligated simply to concede that the death penalty experiment has failed. It is virtually self-evident to me now that no combination of procedural rules or substantive regulations ever can save the death penalty from its inherent constitutional deficiencies. The basic question — does the system accurately and consistently determine which defendants "deserve" to die? — cannot be answered in the affirmative. It is not simply that this Court has allowed vague aggravating circumstances to be employed, see, e.g., *Arave v. Creech*, 507 U.S. 463 (1993), relevant mitigating evidence to be disregarded, see, e.g., *Johnson v. Texas*, 509 U.S. 350 (1993), and vital judicial review to be blocked, see, e.g., *Coleman v. Thompson*, 501 U.S. 722 (1991). The problem is that the inevitability of factual, legal, and moral error gives us a system that we know must wrongly kill some defendants, a system that fails to deliver the fair, consistent, and reliable sentences of death required by the Constitution.

I

In 1971, in an opinion which has proved partly prophetic, the second Justice Harlan, writing for the Court, observed:

> "Those who have come to grips with the hard task of actually attempting to draft means of channeling capital sentencing discretion have confirmed the lesson taught by the history recounted above. To identify before the fact those characteristics of criminal homicides and their perpetrators which call for the death penalty, and to express these characteristics in language which can be fairly understood and applied by the sentencing authority, appear to be tasks which are beyond present human ability.... For a court to attempt to catalog the appropriate factors in this elusive area could inhibit rather than expand the scope of consideration, for no list of circumstances would ever be really complete."

McGautha v. California, 402 U.S. 183, 204, 208 (1971).

In *McGautha*, the petitioner argued that a statute which left the penalty of death entirely in the jury's discretion, without any standards to govern its imposition, violated the Fourteenth Amendment. Although the Court did not deny that serious risks were associated with a sentencer's unbounded discretion, the Court found no remedy in the Constitution for the inevitable failings of human judgment.

A year later, the Court reversed its course completely in *Furman v. Georgia*, 408 U.S. 238 (1972) (per curiam, with each of the nine Justices writing separately). The concurring Justices argued that the glaring inequities in the administration of death, the standardless discretion wielded by judges and juries, and the pervasive racial and economic discrimination, rendered the death penalty, at least as administered, "cruel and unusual" within the meaning of the Eighth Amendment. Justice White explained that, out of the hundreds of people convicted of murder every year, only a handful were sent to their deaths, and that there was "no meaningful basis for distinguishing the few cases in which [the death penalty] is imposed from the many cases in which it is not." If any discernible basis could be identified for the selection of those few who were chosen to die, it was "the constitutionally impermissible basis of race." *Id.* at 310 (Stewart, J., concurring).

I dissented in *Furman*. Despite my intellectual, moral, and personal objections to the death penalty, I refrained from joining the majority because I found objectionable the Court's abrupt change of position in the single year that had passed since *McGautha*. While I agreed that the Eighth Amendment's prohibition against cruel and unusual punishments "may acquire meaning as public opinion becomes enlightened by a humane justice," 408 U.S. at 409, quoting *Weems v. United States*, 217 U.S. 349, 378 (1910), I objected to the "suddenness of the Court's perception of progress in the human attitude since decisions of only a short while ago." 408 U.S. at 410. Four years after *Furman* was decided, I concurred in the judgment in *Gregg v. Georgia*, 428 U.S. 153 (1976), and its companion cases which upheld death sentences rendered under statutes passed after *Furman* was decided. See *Proffitt v. Florida*, 428 U.S. 242, 261 (1976), and *Jurek v. Texas*, 428 U.S. 262, 279 (1976). Cf. *Woodson v. North Carolina*, 428 U.S. 280, 307 (1976), and *Roberts v. Louisiana*, 428 U.S. 325, 363 (1976).

A

There is little doubt now that *Furman*'s essential holding was correct. Although most of the public seems to desire, and the Constitution appears to permit, the penalty of death, it surely is beyond dispute that if the death penalty cannot be administered consistently and rationally, it may not be administered at all. *Eddings v. Oklahoma*, 455 U.S. at 112. I never have quarreled with this principle; in my mind, the real meaning of *Furman*'s diverse concurring opinions did not emerge until some years after *Furman* was decided. See *Gregg v. Georgia*, 428 U.S. at 189 (opinion of Stewart, Powell, and Stevens, JJ.) ("*Furman* mandates that where discretion is afforded a sentencing body on a matter so grave as the determination of whether a human life should be taken or spared, that discretion must be suitably directed and limited so as to minimize the risk of wholly arbitrary and capricious action"). Since *Gregg*, I faithfully have adhered to the *Furman* holding and have come to believe that it is indispensable to the Court's Eighth Amendment jurisprudence.

Delivering on the *Furman* promise, however, has proved to be another matter. *Furman* aspired to eliminate the vestiges of racism and the effects of poverty in capital sentencing; it deplored the "wanton" and "random" infliction of death by a government with constitutionally limited power. *Furman* demanded that the sentencer's discretion be directed and limited by procedural rules and objective standards in order to minimize the risk of arbitrary and capricious sentences of death.

In the years following *Furman*, serious efforts were made to comply with its mandate. State legislatures and appellate courts struggled to provide judges and juries with sensible and objective guidelines for determining who should live and who should die. Some States attempted to define who is "deserving" of the death penalty through the use of carefully chosen adjectives, reserving the death penalty for those who commit crimes that are "especially heinous, atrocious, or cruel," see Fla. Stat. §921.141(5)(h)

(Supp. 1976), or "wantonly vile, horrible or inhuman," see Ga. Code Ann. §27-2534.1(b)(7) (1978). Other States enacted mandatory death penalty statutes, reading *Furman* as an invitation to eliminate sentencer discretion altogether. See, e.g., N.C. Gen. Stat. §14-17 (Cum. Supp. 1975). But see *Woodson v. North Carolina*, 428 U.S. 280 (1976) (invalidating mandatory death penalty statutes). Still other States specified aggravating and mitigating factors that were to be considered by the sentencer and weighed against one another in a calculated and rational manner. See, e.g., Ga. Code. Ann. §17-10-30(c) (1982); cf. Tex. Code Crim. Proc. Ann., Art. §37.071(c)–(e) (Vernon 1981 and Supp. 1989) (identifying "special issues" to be considered by the sentencer when determining the appropriate sentence).

Unfortunately, all this experimentation and ingenuity yielded little of what *Furman* demanded. It soon became apparent that discretion could not be eliminated from capital sentencing without threatening the fundamental fairness due a defendant when life is at stake. Just as contemporary society was no longer tolerant of the random or discriminatory infliction of the penalty of death, evolving standards of decency required due consideration of the uniqueness of each individual defendant when imposing society's ultimate penalty.

This development in the American conscience would have presented no constitutional dilemma if fairness to the individual could be achieved without sacrificing the consistency and rationality promised in *Furman*. But over the past two decades, efforts to balance these competing constitutional commands have been to no avail. Experience has shown that the consistency and rationality promised in *Furman* are inversely related to the fairness owed the individual when considering a sentence of death. A step toward consistency is a step away from fairness.

B

There is a heightened need for fairness in the administration of death. This unique level of fairness is born of the appreciation that death truly is different from all other punishments a society inflicts upon its citizens. "Death, in its finality, differs more from life imprisonment than a 100-year prison term differs from one of only a year or two." *Woodson*, 428 U.S. at 305 (opinion of Stewart, Powell, and Stevens, JJ.). Because of the qualitative difference of the death penalty, "there is a corresponding difference in the need for reliability in the determination that death is the appropriate punishment in a specific case." In *Woodson*, a decision striking down mandatory death penalty statutes as unconstitutional, a plurality of the Court explained: "A process that accords no significance to relevant facets of the character and record of the individual offender or the circumstances of the particular offense excludes from consideration in fixing the ultimate punishment of death the possibility of compassionate or mitigating factors stemming from the diverse frailties of humankind." *Id*. at 304.

While the risk of mistake in the determination of the appropriate penalty may be tolerated in other areas of the criminal law, "in capital cases the fundamental respect for humanity underlying the Eighth Amendment ... requires consideration of the character and record of the individual offender and the circumstances of the particular offense as a constitutionally indispensable part of the process of inflicting the penalty of death." *Id*. Thus, although individualized sentencing in capital cases was not considered essential at the time the Constitution was adopted, *Woodson* recognized that American standards of decency could no longer tolerate a capital sentencing process that failed to afford a defendant individualized consideration in the determination whether he or she should live or die.

The Court elaborated on the principle of individualized sentencing in *Lockett v. Ohio*, 438 U.S. 586 (1978). In that case, a plurality acknowledged that strict restraints on sentencer discretion are necessary to achieve the consistency and rationality promised in *Furman*, but held that, in the end, the sentencer must retain unbridled discretion to afford mercy. Any process or procedure that prevents the sentencer from considering "as a mitigating factor, any aspect of a defendant's character or record and any circumstances of the offense that the defendant proffers as a basis for a sentence less than death," creates the constitutionally intolerable risk that "the death penalty will be imposed in spite of factors which may call for a less severe penalty." The Court's duty under the Constitution therefore is to "develop a system of capital punishment at once consistent and principled but also humane and sensible to the uniqueness of the individual." *Eddings v. Oklahoma*, 455 U.S. at 110.

C

I believe the *Woodson-Lockett* line of cases to be fundamentally sound and rooted in American standards of decency that have evolved over time. The notion of prohibiting a sentencer from exercising its discretion "to dispense mercy on the basis of factors too intangible to write into a statute," *Gregg*, 428 U.S. at 222 (White, J., concurring), is offensive to our sense of fundamental fairness and respect for the uniqueness of the individual. In *California v. Brown*, 479 U.S. 538 (1987), I said in dissent:

> "The sentencer's ability to respond with mercy towards a defendant has always struck me as a particularly valuable aspect of the capital sentencing procedure.... We adhere so strongly to our belief that a sentencer should have the opportunity to spare a capital defendant's life on account of compassion for the individual because, recognizing that the capital sentencing decision must be made in the context of 'contemporary values,' *Gregg v. Georgia*, 428 U.S. at 181 (opinion of Stewart, Powell, and Stevens, JJ.), we see in the sentencer's expression of mercy a distinctive feature of our society that we deeply value."

Id. at 562–563.

Yet, as several Members of the Court have recognized, there is real "tension" between the need for fairness to the individual and the consistency promised in *Furman*. See *Franklin v. Lynaugh*, 487 U.S. 164, 182 (1988) (plurality opinion); *California v. Brown*, 479 U.S. at 544 (O'Connor, J., concurring); *McCleskey v. Kemp*, 481 U.S. at 363 (Blackmun, J., dissenting); *Graham v. Collins*, 506 U.S. 461 (1993) (Thomas, J., concurring). On the one hand, discretion in capital sentencing must be "controlled by clear and objective standards so as to produce non-discriminatory [and reasoned] application." On the other hand, the Constitution also requires that the sentencer be able to consider "any relevant mitigating evidence regarding the defendant's character or background, and the circumstances of the particular offense." *California v. Brown*, 479 U.S. 538, 544 (1987) (O'Connor, J., concurring). The power to consider mitigating evidence that would warrant a sentence less than death is meaningless unless the sentencer has the discretion and authority to dispense mercy based on that evidence. Thus, the Constitution, by requiring a heightened degree of fairness to the individual, and also a greater degree of equality and rationality in the administration of death, demands sentencer discretion that is at once generously expanded and severely restricted.

This dilemma was laid bare in *Penry v. Lynaugh*, 492 U.S. 302 (1989). The defendant in *Penry* challenged the Texas death penalty statute, arguing that it failed to allow the sentencing jury to give full mitigating effect to his evidence of mental retardation and history of child abuse. The Texas statute required the jury, during the penalty phase, to answer three "special issues"; if the jury unanimously answered "yes" to each issue, the trial court was obligated to sentence the defendant to death. Only one of the three issues—whether the defendant posed a "continuing threat to society"—was related to the evidence *Penry* offered in mitigation. But Penry's evidence of mental retardation and child abuse was a two-edged sword as it related to that special issue: "it diminished his blameworthiness for his crime even as it indicated that there [was] a probability that he [would] be dangerous in the future." The Court therefore reversed Penry's death sentence, explaining that a reasonable juror could have believed that the statute prohibited a sentence less than death based upon his mitigating evidence. After *Penry*, the paradox underlying the Court's post-Furman jurisprudence was undeniable. Texas had complied with *Furman* by severely limiting the sentencer's discretion, but those very limitations rendered Penry's death sentence unconstitutional.

D

The theory underlying *Penry* and *Lockett* is that an appropriate balance can be struck between the *Furman* promise of consistency and the *Lockett* requirement of individualized sentencing if the death penalty is conceptualized as consisting of two distinct stages. In the first stage of capital sentencing, the demands of *Furman* are met by "narrowing" the class of death-eligible offenders according to objective, fact-bound characteristics of the defendant or the circumstances of the offense. Once the pool of death-eligible defendants has been reduced, the sentencer retains the discretion to consider whatever relevant mitigating evidence the defendant chooses to offer.

Over time, I have come to conclude that even this approach is unacceptable: It simply reduces, rather than eliminates, the number of people subject to arbitrary sentencing. It is the decision to sentence a defendant to death—not merely the decision to make a defendant eligible for death—that may not be arbitrary. While one might hope that providing the sentencer with as much relevant mitigating evidence as possible will lead to more rational and consistent sentences, experience has taught otherwise. It seems that the decision whether a human being should live or die is so inherently subjective—rife with all of life's understandings, experiences, prejudices, and passions—that it inevitably defies the rationality and consistency required by the Constitution.

E

The arbitrariness inherent in the sentencer's discretion to afford mercy is exacerbated by the problem of race. Even under the most sophisticated death penalty statutes, race continues to play a major role in determining who shall live and who shall die. Perhaps it should not be surprising that the biases and prejudices that infect society generally would influence the determination of who is sentenced to death, even within the narrower pool of death-eligible defendants selected according to objective standards. No matter how narrowly the pool of death-eligible defendants is drawn according to objective standards, *Furman*'s promise still will go unfulfilled so long as the sentencer is free to exercise unbridled discretion within the smaller group and thereby to discriminate. "'The power to be lenient [also] is the power to discriminate.'" *McCleskey v. Kemp*, 481 U.S. at 312, quoting K. Davis, Discretionary Justice 170 (1973).

A renowned example of racism infecting a capital-sentencing scheme is documented in *McCleskey v. Kemp*, 481 U.S. 279 (1987) (*infra* chapter 4). Warren McCleskey, an African-American, argued that the Georgia capital-sentencing scheme was administered in a racially discriminatory manner, in violation of the Eighth and Fourteenth Amendments. In support of his claim, he proffered a highly reliable statistical study (the Baldus study) which indicated that, "after taking into account some 230 nonracial factors that might legitimately influence a sentencer, the jury *more likely than not* would have spared McCleskey's life had his victim been black." 481 U.S. at 325 (emphasis in original) (Brennan, J., dissenting). The Baldus study further demonstrated that blacks who kill whites are sentenced to death "at nearly *22 times* the rate of blacks who kill blacks, and more than 7 times the rate of whites who kill blacks." *Id.* at 327 (emphasis in original).

Despite this staggering evidence of racial prejudice infecting Georgia's capital-sentencing scheme, the majority turned its back on McCleskey's claims, apparently troubled by the fact that Georgia had instituted more procedural and substantive safeguards than most other States since *Furman,* but was still unable to stamp out the virus of racism. Faced with the apparent failure of traditional legal devices to cure the evils identified in *Furman,* the majority wondered aloud whether the consistency and rationality demanded by the dissent could ever be achieved without sacrificing the discretion which is essential to fair treatment of individual defendants:

> "It is difficult to imagine guidelines that would produce the predictability sought by the dissent without sacrificing the discretion essential to a humane and fair system of criminal justice.... The dissent repeatedly emphasizes the need for 'a uniquely high degree of rationality in imposing the death penalty'.... Again, no suggestion is made as to how greater 'rationality' could be achieved under any type of statute that authorizes capital punishment.... Given these safeguards already inherent in the imposition and review of capital sentences, the dissent's call for greater rationality is no less than a claim that a capital punishment system cannot be administered in accord with the Constitution."

Id. at 314–315, n. 37.

I joined most of Justice Brennan's significant dissent which expounded McCleskey's Eighth Amendment claim, and I wrote separately, to explain that *McCleskey* also had a solid equal protection argument under the Fourteenth Amendment. I still adhere to the views set forth in both dissents, and, as far as I know, there has been no serious effort to impeach the Baldus study. Nor, for that matter, have proponents of capital punishment provided any reason to believe that the findings of that study are unique to Georgia.

The fact that we may not be capable of devising procedural or substantive rules to prevent the more subtle and often unconscious forms of racism from creeping into the system does not justify the wholesale abandonment of the *Furman* promise. To the contrary, where a morally irrelevant—indeed, a repugnant—consideration plays a major role in the determination of who shall live and who shall die, it suggests that the continued enforcement of the death penalty in light of its clear and admitted defects is deserving of a "sober second thought." Justice Brennan explained:

> "Those whom we would banish from society or from the human community itself often speak in too faint a voice to be heard above society's demand for punishment. It is the particular role of courts to hear these voices, for the Constitution declares that the majoritarian chorus may not alone dictate the conditions of social life. The Court thus fulfills, rather than disrupts, the scheme of separation of powers by closely scrutinizing the imposition of the death penalty, for no decision of a society is more deserving of the 'sober second thought.' Stone, The Common Law in the United States, 50 Harv. L. Rev. 4, 25 (1936)."

F

In the years since *McCleskey*, I have come to wonder whether there was truth in the majority's suggestion that discrimination and arbitrariness could not be purged from the administration of capital punishment without sacrificing the equally essential component of fairness — individualized sentencing. Viewed in this way, the consistency promised in *Furman* and the fairness to the individual demanded in *Lockett* are not only inversely related, but irreconcilable in the context of capital punishment. Any statute or procedure that could effectively eliminate arbitrariness from the administration of death would also restrict the sentencer's discretion to such an extent that the sentencer would be unable to give full consideration to the unique characteristics of each defendant and the circumstances of the offense. By the same token, any statute or procedure that would provide the sentencer with sufficient discretion to consider fully and act upon the unique circumstances of each defendant would "throw open the back door to arbitrary and irrational sentencing." *Graham v. Collins*, 113 S. Ct. at 912 (Thomas, J., concurring). All efforts to strike an appropriate balance between these conflicting constitutional commands are futile because there is a heightened need for both in the administration of death.

But even if the constitutional requirements of consistency and fairness are theoretically reconcilable in the context of capital punishment, it is clear that this Court is not prepared to meet the challenge. In apparent frustration over its inability to strike an appropriate balance between the *Furman* promise of consistency and the *Lockett* requirement of individualized sentencing, the Court has retreated from the field, allowing relevant mitigating evidence to be discarded, vague aggravating circumstances to be employed, and providing no indication that the problem of race in the administration of death will ever be addressed. In fact some members of the Court openly have acknowledged a willingness simply to pick one of the competing constitutional commands and sacrifice the other. These developments are troubling, as they ensure that death will continue to be meted out in this country arbitrarily and discriminatorily, and without that "degree of respect due the uniqueness of the individual." *Lockett*, 438 U.S. at 605. In my view, the proper course when faced with irreconcilable constitutional commands is not to ignore one or the other, nor to pretend that the dilemma does not exist, but to admit the futility of the effort to harmonize them. This means accepting the fact that the death penalty cannot be administered in accord with our Constitution.

II

My belief that this Court would not enforce the death penalty (even if it could) in accordance with the Constitution is buttressed by the Court's "obvious eagerness to do away with any restriction on the States' power to execute whomever and however they please." *Herrera*, 113 S. Ct. 853, 854 (Blackmun, J., dissenting). I have explained at length on numerous occasions that my willingness to enforce the capital punishment statutes enacted by the States and the Federal Government, "notwithstanding my own deep moral reservations ... has always rested on an understanding that certain procedural safeguards, chief among them the federal judiciary's power to reach and correct claims of constitutional error on federal habeas review, would ensure that death sentences are fairly imposed." *Sawyer v. Whitley*, 112 S. Ct. 2514, 2528 (1992) (Blackmun, J., concurring in the judgment). See also *Herrera v. Collins*, 113 S. Ct. at 880–881 (Blackmun, J., dissenting). In recent years, I have grown increasingly skeptical that "the death penalty really can be imposed fairly and in accordance with the requirements of the

Eighth Amendment," given the now limited ability of the federal courts to remedy constitutional errors. *Sawyer*, 112 S. Ct. at 2525 (Blackmun, J., concurring in the judgment).

Federal courts are required by statute to entertain petitions from state prisoners who allege that they are held "in violation of the Constitution or the treaties of the United States." 28 U.S.C. §2254(a). Serious review of these claims helps to ensure that government does not secure the penalty of death by depriving a defendant of his or her constitutional rights. At the time I voted with the majority to uphold the constitutionality of the death penalty in *Gregg v. Georgia*, 428 U.S. 153, 227 (1976), federal courts possessed much broader authority than they do today to address claims of constitutional error on habeas review. In 1976, there were few procedural barriers to the federal judiciary's review of a State's capital sentencing scheme, or the fairness and reliability of a State's decision to impose death in a particular case. Since then, however, the Court has "erected unprecedented and unwarranted barriers" to the federal judiciary's review of the constitutional claims of capital defendants. *Sawyer*, 112 S. Ct. at 2525 (Blackmun, J., concurring in the judgment).

The Court's refusal last term to afford Leonel Torres Herrera an evidentiary hearing, despite his colorable showing of actual innocence, demonstrates just how far afield the Court has strayed from its statutorily and constitutionally imposed obligations. In *Herrera*, only a bare majority of this Court could bring itself to state forthrightly that the execution of an actually innocent person violates the Eighth Amendment. This concession was made only in the course of erecting nearly insurmountable barriers to a defendant's ability to get a hearing on a claim of actual innocence. Certainly there will be individuals who are actually innocent who will be unable to make a better showing than what was made by *Herrera* without the benefit of an evidentiary hearing. The Court is unmoved by this dilemma, however; it prefers "finality" in death sentences to reliable determinations of a capital defendant's guilt. Because I no longer can state with any confidence that this Court is able to reconcile the Eighth Amendment's competing constitutional commands, or that the federal judiciary will provide meaningful oversight to the state courts as they exercise their authority to inflict the penalty of death, I believe that the death penalty, as currently administered, is unconstitutional.

III

Perhaps one day this Court will develop procedural rules or verbal formulas that actually will provide consistency, fairness, and reliability in a capital-sentencing scheme. I am not optimistic that such a day will come. I am more optimistic, though, that this Court eventually will conclude that the effort to eliminate arbitrariness while preserving fairness "in the infliction of [death] is so plainly doomed to failure that it—and the death penalty—must be abandoned altogether." *Godfrey v. Georgia*, 446 U.S. 420, 442 (1980) (Marshall, J., concurring in the judgment). I may not live to see that day, but I have faith that eventually it will arrive. The path the Court has chosen lessens us all. I dissent.

Note and Question on Justice Blackmun's Dissent in *Callins v. Collins, 510 U.S. 1141 (1994)*

In Justice Blackmun's dissent, three themes emerge with clarity: racism plays an unacceptable role in determining who will be condemned to die; the inevitability of error continues to ensure that innocent people will be executed; and federal courts no longer provide meaningful review of the constitutional claims pressed by death row inmates.

Regarding the Court's post-*Furman* jurisprudence, he explained, "the problems that were pursued down one hole with procedural rules and verbal formulas have come to the surface somewhere else, just as virulent and pernicious as they were in their original form." Is there a way to resolve the paradox which troubled Justice Blackmun?

Consider Justice Scalia's views on the inconsistencies inherent in the modern death penalty system.

Walton v. Arizona[1]
497 U.S. 639 (1990)

Justice SCALIA, concurring in part and concurring in the judgment.

Today a petitioner before this Court says that a state sentencing court (1) had unconstitutionally *broad* discretion to sentence him to death instead of imprisonment, *and* (2) had unconstitutionally *narrow* discretion to sentence him to imprisonment instead of death. An observer unacquainted with our death penalty jurisprudence (and in the habit of thinking logically) would probably say these positions cannot both be right. The ultimate choice in capital sentencing, he would point out, is a unitary one—the choice between death and imprisonment. One cannot have discretion whether to select the one yet lack discretion whether to select the other. Our imaginary observer would then be surprised to discover that, under this Court's Eighth Amendment jurisprudence of the past 15 years, petitioner would have a strong chance of winning on *both* of these antagonistic claims, simultaneously—as evidenced by the facts that four Members of this Court think he should win on both and that an en banc panel of a Federal Court of Appeals so held in an essentially identical case. But that just shows that our jurisprudence and logic have long since parted ways. I write separately to say that, and explain why, I will no longer seek to apply one of the two incompatible branches of that jurisprudence. I agree with the Court's analysis of petitioner's first claim, and concur in its opinion as to Parts I, II, and V. As to the second claim, I concur only in the judgment....

A

Since the 1976 cases, we have routinely read *Furman* as standing for the proposition that "channelling and limiting the sentencer's discretion in imposing the death penalty" is a "fundamental constitutional requirement," and have insisted that States furnish the sentencer with "clear and objective standards that provide specific and detailed guidance, and that make rationally reviewable the process for imposing a sentence of death." Only twice since 1976 have we actually invalidated a death sentence because of inadequate guidance to the sentencer, but we have repeatedly incanted the principle that "unbridled discretion" is unacceptable, that capital sentencing procedures must constrain and guide the sentencer's discretion to ensure "that the death penalty is not meted out arbitrarily and capriciously," that "the State must establish rational criteria that narrow the decisionmaker's judgment," that "death penalty statutes [must] be structured so as to prevent the penalty from being administered in an arbitrary and unpredictable fashion," that our cases require "procedural protections to ensure that the death penalty will be imposed in a consistent, rational manner," and that "[States] must administer [the

---

1. *Walton v. Arizona* was overturned in part by *Ring v. Arizona*, 536 U.S. 584 (2002), *infra* chapter 9.

death] penalty in a way that can rationally distinguish between those individuals for whom death is an appropriate sanction and those for whom it is not."

B

Shortly after introducing our doctrine *requiring* constraints on the sentencer's discretion to "impose" the death penalty, the Court began developing a doctrine *forbidding* constraints on the sentencer's discretion to "*decline* to impose" it. This second doctrine — counterdoctrine would be a better word — has completely exploded whatever coherence the notion of "guided discretion" once had....

In *Woodson* and *Lockett*, it emerged that uniform treatment of offenders guilty of the same capital crime was not only not *required* by the Eighth Amendment, but was all but *prohibited*. Announcing the proposition that "[c]entral to the application of the [Eighth] Amendment is a determination of contemporary standards regarding the infliction of punishment," *Woodson, supra*, 428 U.S., at 288, and pointing to the steady growth of discretionary sentencing systems over the previous 150 years (those very systems we had found unconstitutional in *Furman*), the pluralities in those cases determined that a defendant could not be sentenced to death unless the sentencer was convinced, by an unconstrained and unguided evaluation of offender and offense, that death was the appropriate punishment. In short, the practice which in *Furman* had been described as the discretion to sentence to death and pronounced constitutionally prohibited, was in *Woodson* and *Lockett* renamed the discretion not to sentence to death and pronounced constitutionally required.

As elaborated in the years since, the *Woodson-Lockett* principle has prevented States from imposing all but the most minimal constraints on the sentencer's discretion to decide that an offender eligible for the death penalty should nonetheless not receive it. We have, in the first place, repeatedly rebuffed States' efforts to channel that discretion by specifying objective factors on which its exercise should rest. It would misdescribe the sweep of this principle to say that "all mitigating evidence" must be considered by the sentencer. That would assume some objective criterion of what is mitigating, which is precisely what we have forbidden. Our cases proudly announce that the Constitution effectively prohibits the States from excluding from the sentencing decision *any* aspect of a defendant's character or record, or *any* circumstance surrounding the crime: that the defendant had a poor and deprived childhood, or that he had a rich and spoiled childhood; that he had a great love for the victim's race, or that he had a pathological hatred for the victim's race; that he has limited mental capacity, or that he has a brilliant mind which can make a great contribution to society; that he was kind to his mother, or that he despised his mother. *Whatever* evidence bearing on the crime or the criminal the defense wishes to introduce as rendering the defendant less deserving of the death penalty must be admitted into evidence and considered by the sentencer. Nor may States channel the sentencer's consideration of this evidence by defining the weight or significance it is to receive — for example, by making evidence of mental retardation relevant only insofar as it bears on the question whether the crime was committed deliberately. Rather, they must let the sentencer "give effect," to mitigating evidence in whatever manner it pleases. Nor, when a jury is assigned the sentencing task, may the State attempt to impose structural rationality on the sentencing decision by requiring that mitigating circumstances be found unanimously, each juror must be allowed to determine and "give effect" to his perception of what evidence favors leniency, regardless of whether those perceptions command the assent of (or are even comprehensible to) other jurors.

To acknowledge that "there perhaps is an inherent tension" between this line of cases and the line stemming from *Furman*, is rather like saying that there was perhaps an inherent tension between the Allies and the Axis Powers in World War II. And to refer to the two lines as pursuing "twin objectives," is rather like referring to the twin objectives of good and evil. They cannot be reconciled. Pursuant to *Furman*, and in order "to achieve a more rational and equitable administration of the death penalty," we require that States "channel the sentencer's discretion by 'clear and objective standards' that provide 'specific and detailed guidance.'" In the next breath, however, we say that "the State *cannot* channel the sentencer's discretion to consider any relevant [mitigating] information offered by the defendant," and that the sentencer must enjoy unconstrained discretion to decide whether any sympathetic factors bearing on the defendant or the crime indicate that he does not "deserve to be sentenced to death." The latter requirement quite obviously destroys whatever rationality and predictability the former requirement was designed to achieve.

The Court has attempted to explain the contradiction by saying that the two requirements serve different functions: The first serves to "narrow" according to rational criteria the class of offenders eligible for the death penalty, while the second guarantees that each offender who is death eligible is not actually sentenced to death without "an individualized assessment of the appropriateness of the death penalty." But it is not "individualized assessment" that is the issue here. No one asserts that the Constitution permits condemnation *en masse*. The issue is whether, in the process of the individualized sentencing determination, the society may specify which factors are relevant, and which are not—whether it may insist upon a rational scheme in which all sentencers making the individualized determinations apply the same standard. That is *precisely* the issue that was involved in *Furman*, no more and no less. Having held, in *Furman*, that the aggravating factors to be sought in the individualized determination must be specified in advance, we are able to refer to the defendants who will qualify under those factors as a "class of death eligibles"—from among whom those actually to receive death will be selected on the basis of unspecified mitigating factors. But if we had held in *Lockett* that the *mitigating* factors to be sought in the individualized determination must be specified in advance, we would equally have been able to refer to the defendants who will qualify under those factors as a "class of mercy eligibles"—from among whom those actually to receive mercy will be selected on the basis of unspecified aggravating factors. In other words, classification *versus* individuation does not *explain* the opposite treatment of aggravating and mitigating factors; it is merely one way of *describing the result* of that opposite treatment. What is involved here is merely setting standards for individualized determinations, and the question remains why the Constitution demands that the aggravating standards and mitigating standards be accorded opposite treatment. It is impossible to understand why. Since the individualized determination is a unitary one (does this defendant deserve death for this crime?) once one says each sentencer must be able to answer "no" for whatever reason it deems morally sufficient (and indeed, for whatever reason any one of 12 jurors deems morally sufficient), it becomes impossible to claim that the Constitution requires consistency and rationality among sentencing determinations to be preserved by strictly limiting the reasons for which each sentencer can say "yes." In fact, randomness and "freakishness" are even more evident in a system that requires aggravating factors to be found in great detail, since it permits sentencers to accord different treatment, for whatever mitigating reasons they wish, not only to two different murderers, but to two murderers whose crimes have been found to be of similar gravity. It is difficult enough to justify the *Furman* requirement so long as the States are *permitted* to allow random mitigation; but to impose it while simultaneously *requiring* random mitigation is absurd. I agree with Justice White's observation that the *Lockett* rule represents a sheer "about-face" from *Furman*, an outright negation of the principle of guided discretion that brought us down the path of regulating capital sentencing procedure in the first place....

Despite the fact that I think *Woodson* and *Lockett* find no proper basis in the Constitution, they have some claim to my adherence because of the doctrine of *stare decisis*. I do not reject that claim lightly, but I must reject it here. My initial and my fundamental problem, as I have described it in detail above, is not that *Woodson* and *Lockett* are wrong, but that *Woodson* and *Lockett* are rationally irreconcilable with *Furman*. It is that which led me into the inquiry whether either they or *Furman* was wrong. I would not know how to apply them—or, more precisely, how to apply both them and *Furman*—if I wanted to. I cannot continue to say, in case after case, what degree of "narrowing" is sufficient to achieve the constitutional objective enunciated in *Furman* when I know that that objective is in any case impossible of achievement because of *Woodson-Lockett*. And I cannot continue to say, in case after case, what sort of restraints upon sentencer discretion are unconstitutional under *Woodson-Lockett* when I know that the Constitution positively *favors* constraints under *Furman*. *Stare decisis* cannot command the impossible. Since I cannot possibly be guided by what seem to me incompatible principles, I must reject the one that is plainly in error.

The objectives of the doctrine of *stare decisis* are not furthered by adhering to *Woodson-Lockett* in any event. The doctrine exists for the purpose of introducing certainty and stability into the law and protecting the expectations of individuals and institutions that have acted in reliance on existing rules. As I have described, the *Woodson-Lockett* principle has frustrated this very purpose from the outset—contradicting the basic thrust of much of our death penalty jurisprudence, laying traps for unwary States, and generating a fundamental uncertainty in the law that shows no signs of ending or even diminishing.

I cannot adhere to a principle so lacking in support in constitutional text and so plainly unworthy of respect under *stare decisis*. Accordingly, I will not, in this case or in the future, vote to uphold an Eighth Amendment claim that the sentencer's discretion has been unlawfully restricted....

Aggravating and Mitigating Factors: The Paradox of Today's Arbitrary and Mandatory Capital Punishment Scheme

Jeffrey L. Kirchmeier, 6 Wm. & Mary Bill of Rights J. 345 (Spring 1998)

V. Resolving the Paradox

There is no perfect procedure for deciding in which cases governmental authority should be used to impose death.[507]

After rejecting capital sentencing statutes that gave sentencers complete discretion and after rejecting mandatory capital sentencing statutes, the Court has developed an Eighth Amendment jurisprudence that has embraced the evils of both of those systems. Over twenty years after *Furman*,[508] death penalty statutes continue to be broadened to increase the likelihood that defendants will be sentenced to death, resulting in a death

---

507. *Lockett v. Ohio*, 438 U.S. 586, 605 (1978) (Burger, C.J., plurality opinion).
508. *Furman v. Georgia*, 408 U.S. 238 (1972).

penalty that contains many similarities to harsh mandatory death penalty schemes. At the same time, the Court has permitted a system of sentencing factors that tolerates a substantial amount of arbitrary discretion, including the systemic factors discussed above, as well as prosecutorial discretion and racial bias.

Although it may seem paradoxical to claim that a system is both mandatory and arbitrary, that is the system we currently have. While obviously it is not completely one or the other, the system has the constitutional faults of both. We are left to wonder whether we would have only half of the constitutional problems we now face if the Court were to embrace one or the other completely.

None of the Justices or commentators suggest a return to the *McGautha* days when juries had almost complete and unfettered discretion in determining who received a death sentence. As Professor McCord suggested, attorneys probably do not want to return to such a system either.[511] In many ways, however, we now have that system. Perhaps the present system is worse than the old system in the sense that the present system has the false appearance of being a fair and nonarbitrary system. Although Professor McCord argued that the present system works, Professors Steiker and Steiker have argued that "the Supreme Court's detailed attention to death penalty law has generated negligible improvements over the pre-*Furman* era, but has helped people to accept without second thoughts—much less 'sober' ones—our profoundly failed system of capital punishment."[512] One may ask who is correct. Do we have a better system or only a system that allows the public to pretend that the system works?

The paradox is that McCord and the Steikers each are correct. Some narrowing has occurred, but it has not occurred in a significant or rational way. The system is better than the *McGautha* era because the present capital sentencing statutes eliminate some first-degree murders from the capital sentencing pool. The system is not better than the *McGautha* era because it is arbitrary in selecting who is eliminated from the pool and because it eliminates only a few defendants before reopening the system to unlimited arbitrariness.

The two best alternatives to the constitutional paradox of today's arbitrary mandatory death sentencing scheme are the solutions that individual Supreme Court Justices have suggested. In short, "capital punishment [must] be imposed fairly, and with reasonable consistency, or not at all."[513] One option is to impose it "fairly" by following the suggestion of Justices Scalia and Thomas by completely embracing a mandatory death penalty. Such a system would need to go beyond Justice Scalia's upholding of arbitrary factors, like victim impact evidence, by requiring a mandatory death sentence for all first-degree murderers. To permit the consideration of vague aggravating factors would open the door to the arbitrariness discussed in this Article, so under the proposed system every first-degree murderer or a clearly defined group would need to receive a death sentence. Although such a system would increase the harshness of today's death penalty, its arbitrariness would be eliminated.

---

511. So, while death penalty opponents rue the Court's failure to regulate death more severely, I doubt that there is one experienced capital defense lawyer in this country who would rather return to the pre-*Furman* era. Perhaps not even many prosecutors would want to return to the days before *Furman*, when such an unguided power of life and death rested in their hands.

512. *See also Callins v. Collins*, 510 U.S. 1141 (1994) (Blackmun, J., dissenting) ("I have struggled—along with a majority of this Court, to develop procedural and substantive rules that would lend more than the mere appearance of fairness to the death penalty endeavor.").

513. *Eddings v. Oklahoma*, 455 U.S. 104, 112 (1982).

The other option is to follow Justices Blackmun and Powell, who both originally voted to uphold today's death penalty scheme, and subsequently concluded that the death penalty should be imposed "not at all." Holding the death penalty unconstitutional would acknowledge that all attempts to impose the ultimate punishment in a fair manner have failed and that the only constitutional alternative is to abandon the punishment altogether.

Instead of embracing one of these two options, the Court has left us with a compromise and only the appearance of a fair process. In short, the Court's constitutional interpretation is one that has neither the stomach for the harshness of a mandatory death penalty nor the willingness to counter public opinion.

The question is which of the two choices is the better option—a mandatory death penalty or no death penalty. Perhaps part of the answer lies in examining the underlying reasoning for the positions taken by Justices Scalia and Blackmun, who both recognize the same problems but come to radically different conclusions.

Justice Scalia believes in the moral philosophies supporting capital punishment. For example, in one dissent Scalia argued that potential jurors who state during voir dire that they always will vote for the death penalty should be permitted to sit as jurors, while jurors who always will vote against the death penalty should be struck for cause.[515] In that opinion, Justice Scalia quoted Immanuel Kant in what may be his own view regarding retribution and the death penalty:

> Even if a Civil Society resolved to dissolve itself with the consent of all its members ... the last Murderer lying in the prison ought to be executed before the resolution was carried out. This ought to be done in order that every one may realize the desert of his deeds....

In contrast, before Justice Blackmun came to the conclusion that the death penalty is unconstitutional, he noted his moral distaste for capital punishment. Indeed, in his *Furman* dissent, even though he voted to uphold the death penalty, he stated: "I yield to no one in the depth of my distaste, antipathy, and, indeed, abhorrence, for the death penalty, with all its aspects of physical distress and fear and of moral judgment exercised by finite minds."[517] He added that for him, "it violates childhood's training and life's experiences, and is not compatible with the philosophical convictions I have been able to develop."[518]

Perhaps the decision of whether to eliminate today's death penalty scheme altogether or to replace it with a mandatory death penalty scheme depends upon the principles and philosophies underlying the constitutionality of the death penalty *per se* and whether such principles justify the harshness of mandatory death sentences. In other words, if the death penalty is absolutely necessary to American society, we must accept a mandatory death penalty. If, however, it is not so necessary that it justifies such harshness, it must be abandoned. Other factors that must be evaluated include aspects that undermine the constitutionality of the Court's capital punishment system. Such factors include claims of racial bias, lack of federal review, no constitutional right to state post-conviction review, inadequate funding for capital defense, and poor representation by capital defense counsel.

However, even without considering other factors affecting the constitutionality of the death penalty *per se*, the logical correct path is evident merely from the evolution of

---

515. *See Morgan v. Illinois*, 504 U.S. 719, 739 (1992) (Scalia, J., dissenting).
517. *Furman v. Georgia*, 408 U.S. 238, 405 (1972) (Blackmun, J., dissenting).
518. *Id.* at 405–06 (Blackmun, J., dissenting).

the present system. This view is illustrated by the conversion of Justice Powell, who wrote several opinions upholding the death penalty, including the Court's opinion in *McCleskey v. Kemp*.[519] Justice Powell did not believe that executions are never justified; however, his experience on the Court in attempting to regulate the punishment "taught him that the death penalty cannot be decently administered."[520]

Similarly, other judges have also concluded that the death penalty system does not work in practice and should be abolished. In a recent opinion, Judge Heaney of the United States Court of Appeals for the Eighth Circuit announced in his "view that this nation's administration of capital punishment is simply irrational, arbitrary, and unfair."[522] Chief Justice Gerald Kogan of the Florida Supreme Court, who is not morally opposed to the death penalty, recently began speaking out against capital punishment because the cumbersome system does not work. Although Thomas Zlaket, the Chief Justice of the Arizona Supreme Court, has stated that he will apply the death penalty as required, he has concluded that the system has failed. In 1995, Justice Robert Utter resigned from the Washington Supreme Court because of his opposition to capital punishment and because he could not be part of a death penalty system that "is fatally flawed."

Examining only the process used in implementing the death penalty, one notes that the United States has tried mandatory sentencing, unguided sentencing discretion, and guided sentencing discretion. The last two approaches clearly have been failures. Furthermore, mandatory death sentences have not worked historically. Additionally, as discussed above, scholars have failed to create a workable alternative to the present system, which is both mandatory and arbitrary in nature.

Because all attempts to impose the death penalty with a fair consistency have failed, the only alternative, as the Court has stated, is to apply it "not at all." The Court has never tried true abolition of the death penalty. After twenty years, it is time to take a new direction away from the failed experiment. Perhaps Justice Powell recognized the final paradox of today's death penalty: By attempting to save the constitutionality of the death penalty by imposing guidelines and permitting discretion at the same time, the Court has doomed the process and the punishment to being the ultimate failure in the United States criminal justice system.

VI. Conclusion

The modern era of the Court's evaluation of the constitutionality of the death penalty began with a simple principle: While treating all defendants equally, sentencers should fully and fairly consider each defendant and the crime committed before deciding whether to execute or to imprison. The Court's twenty-year struggle to attain this goal through regulating sentencing criteria has taught us that the goal is impossible to attain and has left us with an arbitrary mandatory death penalty system. As human beings, defendants are too complex for legislatures to design clear and specific guidelines for determining whether the accused should be destroyed. Thus, we are left only with the choice of executing all first-degree murderers or executing none.

---

519. In *McCleskey*, the Court upheld the constitutionality of the death penalty despite the defendant's statistics indicating a general racial bias in the use of the punishment. See *McCleskey v. Kemp*, 481 U.S. 279, 308 (1987). After retiring, Justice Powell stated that he regretted his vote in *McCleskey*.
    520. John C. Jeffries, Jr., Justice Lewis Powell, Jr.: A Biography 451 (1994).
    522. *Singleton v. Norris*, 108 F.3d 872, 876 (8th Cir. 1997) (Heaney, J., concurring). Judge Heaney noted, "I am confident that no death penalty system can ever be administered in a rational and consistent manner."

The capital punishment system used in the United States consumes a large amount of resources for little progress in trying to achieve a fair use of the ultimate punishment. Presently, there are well over 3,000 people on death rows around the country and, although the number of executions is increasing, the number of those living on death row continues to climb. The numbers are disturbing, but so is the process by which we have selected these individuals among thousands of others convicted of murder. The factors distinguishing those sentenced to death from those not sentenced to death are not well defined, resulting in a situation where among a large group of convicted first-degree murderers it is impossible to distinguish between those with life sentences and those with death sentences. "[T]he inevitability of factual, legal, and moral error gives us a system that we know must wrongly kill some defendants, a system that fails to deliver the fair, consistent, and reliable sentences of death required by the Constitution."[531]

The science of determining who should be executed is inexact. Maybe the present arbitrary mandatory process by which defendants are selected for the death penalty is the best compromise the Court can reach, and perhaps it is the only way to walk the line between a harsh mandatory system and an arbitrary unguided discretion system. "Such, it will be said, is human justice.... But that sad evaluation is bearable only in connection with ordinary penalties. It is scandalous in the face of verdicts of death."[532]

After a failed twenty-year experiment, the Court should reexamine the constitutionality of the death penalty and the overall process by which defendants are selected for the gas chamber, electric chair, rope, firing squad, or gurney. If the Court were to reexamine the system, its only logical conclusion would be that the paradox of the arbitrary mandatory death penalty system can be eliminated only be eliminating the death penalty.

Felony Murder and the Eighth Amendment Jurisprudence of Death
Richard Rosen, 31 B.C. L. Rev. 1103 (1990)

II. The Eighth Amendment and Capital Punishment—Rationalizing Death

It is no easy task to recount briefly the United States Supreme Court's venture into creating a new substantive and procedural jurisprudence of death. Perhaps the simplest way to understand it is to go back to the source—the 1972 decision in *Furman v. Georgia*, in which a majority of Justices held that the existing systems of capital punishment were constitutionally deficient. The Supreme Court's activity in death penalty cases since *Furman* can be viewed as an attempt to create an American system of capital punishment that would provide a more rational basis for choosing those to be executed than the systems the Justices examined in *Furman*. The Justices in *Furman* were neither concerned with the individual cases before them nor with the particular idiosyncracies of the state procedures that produced the specific death penalties. Instead, their concerns were more global, and their opinions reflected a condemnation of the nationwide system for imposing the death penalty.

---

531. *Callins v. Collins*, 510 U.S. 1141 (1994) (Blackmun, J., dissenting from the denial of the petition for writ of certiorari).

532. Albert Camus, Reflections on the Guillotine, in Resistance, Rebellion and Death 131, 165 (Justin O'Brien trans., 1960).

The pre-*Furman* state capital sentencing statutes in the various states were markedly similar. In murder cases, the defendant was made eligible for capital punishment by the substantive law of homicide. Most commonly, this eligibility meant that the jury had found the defendant guilty of first degree murder either because he or she killed with premeditation and deliberation, by operation of the felony murder rule, or, in rare cases, by use of a specified means, such as torture or poison. Then, the sentencer, usually as part of the same proceeding, was given unfettered discretion to impose the death penalty.

The Justices in the majority in *Furman* focused on the random, arbitrary, capricious, and discriminatory application of the death penalty under these statutes. To Justice Douglas, the state systems of capital punishment produced death penalties in a manner "pregnant with discrimination" against minorities and the poor. Justice White opined that he was unable to see any "meaningful basis for distinguishing the few cases in which [the death penalty] is imposed from the many cases in which it is not." To Justice Stewart, the death penalty was so "wantonly and freakishly imposed" that receiving it was like being "struck by lightning."

The states reacted to *Furman* by passing statutes designed to meet the objections of Justices Stewart, White, and Douglas. Four years after deciding *Furman*, the Court upheld the death penalty for deliberate murder, optimistically predicting that capital punishment systems providing some guidance to the sentencer would effectively end, or at least minimize, the evils identified in *Furman*. Having made this prediction, the Court, in a series of cases over the past fourteen years, has sought to guide the states in developing capital punishment systems that reduce, if not eliminate, discrimination, arbitrariness, and capriciousness in the selection of those to be executed.

At one time, it appeared that the Court was trying to achieve rationality in the process of selecting those to be spared as well as those to be executed — *Furman* seemed to demand as much. The Court, however, has essentially abandoned the former effort, holding that the eighth amendment is little concerned with consistency in sparing a life. The focus instead has been on the process of selecting those to be killed, with the overarching goal of ensuring that those defendants chosen for execution be in some way worse, or "materially more depraved," than those other first degree murderers not executed.

The Court has relied primarily on procedural protections to realize its eighth amendment goals. A state first must narrow the class of homicide defendants who are eligible for the death penalty to ensure that even if some "materially more depraved" murderers manage to avoid the death penalty, those chosen for this dubious honor will at least be among the worst offenders.

This narrowing, however, is insufficient by itself to satisfy the eighth amendment. The Court has prohibited a mandatory death penalty for even the narrowest class of murder defendants. Instead, after restricting the class of death-eligible defendants, a state must utilize additional procedures that assure "reliability in the determination that death is the appropriate punishment" in a given capital case.

To meet this reliability requirement, a state must permit the sentencer to make "an *individualized* determination on the basis of the character of the individual and the circumstances of the crime." The defendant is entitled to present and have the sentencer fully consider all relevant evidence in mitigation of sentence. The state also is allowed, but not required, to present a wide range of evidence in aggravation as long as it is relevant to the sentencing decision and promotes the reliability of that determination.

In theory, both the restriction of discretion attendant upon the narrowing requirement and the increase in discretion caused by the full and unfettered consideration of mitigation serve the underlying goal of winnowing out those who do not convincingly deserve the death penalty. Some defendants avoid the sanction of death because the characteristics of their crimes or backgrounds do not provide enough aggravation to distinguish them from all of the other murderers. Others avoid the death penalty because the unique characteristics of their crimes or backgrounds raise mitigating factors that separate them from the truly worst of the worst.

In addition to relying on procedural dictates, the Court has used sparingly the concept of disproportionality under the eighth amendment to rule out the death penalty for entire classes of offenders. Such classes include those who cause great harm but do not participate at all in the taking of human life; those who kill but are below a minimum age; those who become insane after trial; and those who, as felony murder accomplices, lack a minimum level of culpability regarding a killing. Under these holdings a defendant can be ineligible for execution, no matter how aggravated the case, if a single factor, i.e., a requisite degree of harm or culpability, is absent.

The extended effort by the Court to rationalize the imposition of death has been criticized, even from within the Court. Justice Harlan, writing in *McGautha v. California* the year before *Furman*, warned that any attempt to rationalize the imposition of capital punishment was a task "beyond human ability," and that the federal courts, therefore, should allow the states the freedom to choose how to impose this ultimate penalty. Justices Marshall and Brennan have concluded that capital punishment never can be imposed in a manner consistent with the demands of the eighth amendment. Other Justices have expressed doubts about the constitutionality of the capital punishment systems now being used by the states but have been unwilling to conclude that the venture is hopeless.

By shifting majorities, the Court has steered a path between the extremes. Keeping the goal of minimizing arbitrariness, caprice, and discrimination in front of them, the Justices have scrutinized various state procedures, approving some and disallowing others. Although rarely achieving unanimity on the result in any particular case, the Court seemingly has reached agreement on the questions to be asked in each case—questions relating to the evils identified in *Furman*, and the consequent need to limit the death penalty to the truly deserving.

Chapter 4

Race, Gender, and Sexual Orientation

A. Prosecutorial Discretion

Federal prosecutorial power derives from Article II, Section 3 of the United States Constitution which provides that the executive branch "shall take Care that the Laws be faithfully executed." Most state constitutions contain similar provisions.

Prosecutors enjoy broad discretion in making critical decisions. As U.S. Attorney General Robert H. Jackson noted in 1940, "The prosecutor has more control over life, liberty, and reputation than any other person in America." Douglas, *Ethical Issues in Prosecution* 9 (1988). As far as capital cases are concerned, "[i]t's local prosecutors, not judges or governors, who most often decide which criminals live or die for their crimes." Rosenberg, *Deadliest D.A.*, The New York Times Magazine, July 16, 1995, at 21.

"Tempered by his status as a minister of justice, the prosecutor exerts a profound influence on the adjudication of a criminal case, nowhere more pronounced than in the context of plea bargaining. Closely tied to political authority, plea bargaining historically served as a power resource and a prerogative of the prosecutor." Alfieri, "Prosecuting Violence/Reconstructing Community," 52 Stan. L. Rev. 809, 843 (2000). Of equal importance to modern prosecutors is the charging decision: "the determination whether a particular person should formally be accused of crime and, if so, on precisely what charge or charges." Whitebread & Slobogin, *Criminal Procedure* 508 (3d ed.) (Foundation Press, Inc. 1993). These decisions are unlikely to be disturbed. As the Supreme Court stated in *Bordenkircher v. Hayes*, 434 U.S. 357 (1978),

> so long as the prosecutor has probable cause to believe that the accused committed an offense defined by statute, the decision whether or not to prosecute, and what charge to file or bring before a grand jury, generally rests entirely in his discretion.

Simply stated, "the relevant standards, ethical rules, and cases provide that a prosecutor ought not proceed with a case without solid evidence of guilt, ought never use false testimony or evidence, and should promptly provide all information and material to the defense which tends to exculpate the offender or mitigate the penalty. The rules are well known to prosecutors. Tragically, they are occasionally violated in capital cases in which a conviction can cost an innocent person, or one in truth guilty of a lesser charge, his or her very life." McCann, "Opposing Capital Punishment: A Prosecutor's Perspective," 79 Marq. L. Rev. 649, 661–62 (1996).

Prosecutorial discretion is not wholly unfettered. In certain situations, the Constitution itself may impose constraints on a prosecutor's power. For example, discriminatory prosecutions are prohibited by the Equal Protection Clause, *Yick Wo v. Hopkins*, 118 U.S. 356 (1886), and vindictive prosecutions may violate the Due Process Clause. *Blackledge v. Perry*, 417 U.S. 21 (1974).

In *Capital Punishment: The Inevitability of Caprice and Mistake* (2d ed.) (W.W. Norton & Co. 1981), Charles Black argues that each step in the criminal justice system presents an opportunity for the exercise of broad discretion. Per Black, arrest, conviction, sentencing, appeal, and the exercise of clemency are equally subject to the application of inexact standards of decisionmaking. The inevitable result is a high degree of arbitrariness in the determination of who is ultimately executed. Black concludes that the possibility of mistake in the infliction of the death penalty and the presence of standardless arbitrariness in its imposition are ineradicable features of death penalty administration.

The American Bar Association has cautioned that prosecutors, in discharging both their investigative and charging functions, "should not invidiously discriminate against or in favor of any person on the basis of race, religion, sex, sexual preference, or ethnicity," whether the person appears as the defendant or the victim. Standards for Criminal Justice Standard 3-3.1(b) (comment).

A prosecutor's unconscious racism or the belief that African-Americans are more violent may persuade the prosecutor to seek the death penalty, for example, in an interracial case, but not in a similar non-interracial case. Further, a judge with a racial bias may not recognize or may fail to address racial discrimination throughout a criminal proceeding, ranging from jury selection, the decision whether to seek the death penalty, or the presentation of evidence during the trial or sentencing phases. Bright, "Discrimination, Death and Denial: The Tolerance of Racial Discrimination in Infliction of the Death Penalty," 35 Santa Clara L. Rev. 433, 437 (1995).

Richard Burr, formerly of the NAACP Legal Defense and Educational Fund, Inc., argues that racial bias often plays a role in the exercise of prosecutorial discretion.

> The first issue is that racial bias has very frequently influenced the prosecutor's judgment to seek death and the ability to obtain it. Racial bias works in a couple of ways; it creates an inflated concern for the value of white people's lives who are victims of murder and a corresponding lack of concern for the lives of black people who are the victims of murder. The white victim murder is invariably the more politically popular murder to prosecute in any jurisdiction in this country.

> Additionally, racial bias impacts the sentencing process by influencing the prosecutor's evaluation of a crime, apart from the race of the victim. There are still many racist assumptions that work against black defendants. Unfounded presumptions about violent behavior and tendencies which can lead to a skewed view of whether someone is guilty or whether they have been so closely related to a horrendous murder that death is the appropriate punishment. If one takes a cross-section of death row cases, race issues will have permeated at least three-fourths of that cross-section in some way or another. This will be true whether the defendant is white or black, but particularly if the defendant is black.

Burr, "Representing the Client on Death Row: The Politics of Advocacy," 59 UMKC L. Rev. 1 (1990). Similarly, a study of 1,017 homicide cases in Florida concluded that race "functions as an implicit aggravating factor in homicide cases." Radelet & Pierce, "Race and Prosecutorial Discretion in Homicide Cases," 19 L. & Soc'y Rev. 587, 615 (1985).

In his dissent in *McCleskey v. Kemp*, 481 U.S. 279 (1987) (*infra* this chapter), Justice Brennan warned: "It is tempting to pretend that minorities on death row share a fate in no way connected to our own, that our treatment of them sounds no echoes beyond the chambers in which they die. Such an illusion is ultimately corrosive, for the reverberations of injustice are not so easily confined."

Note on Prosecutorial Discretion in Maryland

A state-sponsored study released January 7, 2003 concluded that blacks who kill whites are significantly more likely to face the death penalty in Maryland than are blacks who kill blacks or white killers generally. By itself, the study found, the race of the defendant was largely irrelevant.

The study examined data from 6,000 homicides over two decades and found "enormous" differences in how often prosecutors in different Maryland jurisdictions seek the death penalty. According to Raymond Pasternoster, the study's principal investigator, one disparity was particularly noteworthy. "Baltimore County and Baltimore City are contiguous. But defendants in Baltimore County are 26 times more likely to get the death penalty. In social science, you don't find many things that huge." Baltimore City has a significantly larger percentage of blacks than Baltimore County.

The study found that two counties with the highest death sentencing rates—Baltimore and Hartford—were also the two counties with the highest rates of capital homicides involving white victims and black killers. Eight of Maryland's 13 death row inmates are black. All 13 death row inmates were sentenced to death for killing whites. Of the 1,311 death penalty-eligible cases in Maryland from 1978 to 1999, more than half involved black victims. But of the 76 death penalty sentences imposed during the same period, 80 percent involved white victims. Liptak, *Death Penalty Found More Likely When Victim is White*, New York Times A12, Jan. 8, 2003.

B. The Effects of Race

Decisions of Death[*]
David Bruck (Updated April 1, 2006)

Before John Spenkelink—a white murderer of a white victim—was executed by the state of Florida in May 1979, his lawyers tried to present to the state and federal courts a study which showed that the "new" Florida death penalty laws, much like the ones which they had replaced, were being applied far more frequently against persons who killed whites than against those who killed blacks. The appeals courts responded that the Supreme Court had settled all of these arguments in 1976 when it upheld the new

---

[*] Original version published in The New Republic, Dec. 12, 1983. [Ed.]

sentencing statutes: the laws were fair because the Supreme Court had said they were fair; mere evidence to the contrary was irrelevant.

After Spenkelink was electrocuted, the evidence continued to mount. In 1980 two Northeastern University criminologists, William Bowers and Glenn Pierce, published a study of homicide sentencing in Georgia, Florida, and Texas, the three states whose new death penalty statutes were the first to be approved by the Supreme Court after *Furman*. Bowers and Pierce tested the Supreme Court's prediction that these new statutes would achieve consistent and even-handed sentencing by comparing the lists of which convicted murderers had been condemned and which spared with the facts of their crimes as reported by the police. What they found was that in cases where white victims had been killed, black defendants in all three states were from four to six times more likely to be sentenced to death than were white defendants. Both whites and blacks, moreover, faced a much greater danger of being executed where the murder victims were white than where the victims were black. A black defendant in Florida was thirty-seven times more likely to be sentenced to death if his victim was white than if his victim was black; in Georgia, black-on-white killings were punished by death thirty-three times more often than were black-on-black killings; and in Texas, the ratio climbed to an astounding 84 to 1. Even when Bowers and Pierce examined only those cases which the police had reported as "felony-circumstance" murders (i.e., cases involving kidnapping or rape, and thus excluding mere domestic and barroom homicides), they found that both the race of the defendant and the race of the victim appeared to produce enormous disparities in death sentences in each state.

A more detailed analysis of charging decisions in several Florida counties even suggested that prosecutors tended to "upgrade" murders of white victims by alleging that they were more legally aggravated than had been apparent to the police who had written up the initial report, while "downgrading" murders of black victims in a corresponding manner, apparently to avoid the expensive and time-consuming process of trying such murders of blacks as capital cases. Their overall findings, Bowers and Pierce concluded

> are consistent with a single underlying racist tenet: that white lives are worth more than black lives. From this tenet it follows that death as punishment is more appropriate for the killers of whites than for the killers of blacks and more appropriate for black than for white killers.

Such stark evidence of discrimination by race of offender and by race of victim, they wrote, is "a direct challenge to the constitutionality of the post-*Furman* capital statutes ... [and] may represent a two-edged sword of racism in capital punishment which is beyond statutory control."

This new data was presented to the federal courts by attorneys for a Georgia death row inmate named John Eldon Smith in 1981. The court of appeals replied that the studies were too crude to have any legal significance, since they did not look at all the dozens of circumstances of each case, other than race, that might have accounted for the unequal sentencing patterns that Bowers and Pierce had detected.

The matter might have ended there, since the court's criticism implied that only a gargantuan (and extremely expensive) research project encompassing the most minute details of many hundreds of homicide cases would be worthy of its consideration. But as it happened, such a study was already under way, supported by a foundation grant and directed by University of Iowa law professor David Baldus. Using a staff of law students and relying primarily on official Georgia state records, Baldus gathered and coded more than 230 factual circumstances surrounding each of more than a thousand homicides, including 253 death penalty sentencing proceedings conducted under Georgia's current death penalty law. Baldus's results, presented in an Atlanta federal court hearing [during the summer of 1983], confirmed that among defendants convicted of murdering whites, blacks are substantially more likely to go to death row than are whites.

Although blacks account for some 60 percent of Georgia homicide victims, Baldus found that killers of black victims are punished by death less than one-tenth as often as are killers of white victims. With the scientific precision of an epidemiologist seeking to pinpoint the cause of a new disease, Baldus analyzed and reanalyzed his mountain of data on Georgia homicides, controlling for the hundreds of factual variables in each case, in search of any explanation other than race which might account for the stark inequalities in the operation of Georgia's capital sentencing system. He could find none. And when the state of Georgia's turn came to defend its capital sentencing record at the Atlanta federal court hearing, it soon emerged that the statisticians hired by the state to help it refute Baldus's research had no better success in *their* search for an alternative explanation. (In a telephone interview after the Atlanta hearing, the attorney general of Georgia, Michael Bowers, assured me that "the bottom line is that Georgia does not discriminate on the basis of race," but referred all specific questions to his assistant, who declined to answer on the grounds that the court proceeding was pending.)

The findings of research efforts like Baldus's document what anyone who has worked in the death-sentencing system will have sensed all along: the Supreme Court notwithstanding, there is no set of courtroom procedures set out in lawbooks which can change the prosecution practices of local district attorneys. Nor will even the most elaborate jury instructions ever ensure that an all-white jury will weigh a black life as heavily as a white life.

At bottom, the determination of whether or not a particular defendant should die for his crime is simply not a rational decision. Requiring that the jury first determine whether his murder was "outrageously or wantonly vile, horrible, or inhuman," as Georgia juries are invited to do, provides little assurance that death will be imposed fairly and consistently. Indeed, Baldus's research revealed that Georgia juries are more likely to find that a given murder was "outrageously or wantonly vile, horrible, or inhuman" when the victim was white, and likelier still when the murderer is black—hardly a vindication of the Supreme Court's confidence in *Gregg v. Georgia* that such guidelines would serve to eliminate racial discrimnation in sentencing.

At present, forty-five percent of the inhabitants of death row across the country are white, as were 580 of the 1004 inmates executed [between] the Supreme Court's *Gregg* decision and April 1, 2006. Ten percent of the condemned are Hispanic, and forty-two percent are black.** Since roughly half the people arrested and charged with intentional homicide each year in the United States are white, it could appear at first glance that the proportions of blacks and whites now on Death Row are about those that would be expected from a fair system of capital sentencing. But what studies like Baldus's now re-

---

** Statistics are current as of April 1, 2006. NAACP Legal Defense and Educational Fund, Inc. [Ed.]

veal is how such seemingly equitable racial distribution can actually be the product of racial discrimination, rather than proof that discrimination has been overcome.

The explanation for this seeming paradox is that the judicial system discriminates on the basis of the race of the *victim* as well as the race of the defendant. Each year, according to the F.B.I.'s crime report, about the same numbers of blacks as whites are arrested for murder throughout the United States, and the totals of black and white murder victims are also roughly equal. But like many other aspects of American life, our murders are segregated: white murderers almost always kill whites, and the large majority of black killers kill blacks. While blacks who kill whites tend to be singled out for harsher treatment—and more death sentences—than other murderers, there are relatively few of them, and so the absolute effect on the numbers of blacks sent to death row is limited. On the other hand, the far more numerous black murderers whose victims were also black are treated relatively leniently in the courts, and are only rarely sent to death row. Because these dual systems of discrimination operate simultaneously, they have the overall effect of keeping the numbers of blacks on death row roughly proportionate to the numbers of blacks convicted of murder—even while individual defendants are being condemned, and others spared, on the basis of race. In short, like the man who, with one foot in ice and the other in boiling water, describes his situation as "comfortable on average," the death sentencing system has created an illusion of fairness.

In theory, law being based on precedent, the Supreme Court might be expected to apply the principles of the *Furman* decision as it did in 1972 and strike down death penalty laws which have produced results as seemingly racist as these. But that's not going to happen. *Furman* was a product of its time: in 1972 public support for the death penalty had been dropping fairly steadily over several decades, and capital punishment appeared to be going the way of the stocks, the whipping post, and White and Colored drinking fountains. The resurgence of support for capital punishment in the country over the [past three] decade[s] has changed that, at least for now....

Note on Death Penalty for Rape

A decade before the Supreme Court struck down the punishment of death as disproportionate to the crime of raping an adult woman in *Coker v. Georgia*, 433 U.S. 584 (1977) (*supra* chapter 2), the NAACP Legal Defense Fund (LDF) orchestrated a nationwide due process based attack on death sentences imposed on black defendants convicted of raping white women. To support its claim that unfettered jury discretion gave free rein to arbitrariness, irrationality and racial bias, LDF hired University of Pennsylvania sociologist Marvin Wolfgang to conduct a statistical analysis of racial patterns in death sentences for rape. Professor Wolfgang's rape sentencing study examined 119 convicted rapists executed in twelve southern states between 1945 and 1965. Wolfgang found that 110 of the 119 men executed were black. After attempting to control for factors other than racial bias that might account for this apparent gross disparity, Wolfgang concluded that "in less than one time in a thousand could these [racial] associations have occurred by the operation of chance." (The results of Wolfgang's study were consistent with data from 1930–1970 indicating that 89% of the 455 inmates executed for rape were black. Williamson, *The Crucible of Race* 116–17, 183–84 (1984).) LDF used Wolfgang's study in William Maxwell's case. *Maxwell v. Bishop*, 257 F. Supp. 710 (D. Ark. 1966). Maxwell, a young black man, was sentenced to death in Arkansas for raping a 35-year-old white woman after breaking into her home. In rejecting Wolfgang's study, U.S. District Judge J. Smith Henly wrote, "Statistics are elusive at best, and it is a truism that almost anything can be proved by them."

Law and Statistics in Conflict:
Reflections on *McCleskey v. Kemp*

David C. Baldus, George Woodworth, and Charles A. Pulaski, Jr. (1991)

Two Studies of Georgia's Capital Charging and Sentencing System

The Design of the Studies

During the period 1979 to 1982, we conducted two separate, albeit related, studies of the application of Georgia's capital charging and sentencing system: the Procedural Reform Study (PRS) and the Charging and Sentencing Study (CSS). Under Georgia law, a defendant convicted of murder may receive a death sentence if the evidence persuades the sentencing jury that any 1 or more of 10 statutory aggravating circumstances are present in the case. Statistically, the statutory aggravating circumstances that most frequently lead to death sentences are (a) the presence of a serious contemporaneous felony such as rape, kidnapping, or armed robbery, or (b) the occurrence of "wanton or vile" circumstances, such as torture or sexual abuse.

Figure 13.1 depicts the operation of Georgia's system. It involves a multistage process consisting of five key decision points: (a) indictment for capital murder; (b) a prosecutorial decision to accept a guilty plea to a reduced charge or to a murder plea in exchange for a waiver of the death penalty; (c) among those cases that advance to trial on murder charges, a jury decision of guilty, not guilty, or guilty of a lesser included offense, such as voluntary manslaughter; (d) among those cases resulting in a capital murder conviction, the prosecutorial decision to advance the case to a penalty trial; and (e) among those cases that reach a penalty trial, a jury decision to impose a life or death sentence.

Although evidence from the PRS and CSS figured in the *McCleskey* [*v. Kemp*] case (*infra* this chapter), the most important evidence in the case was from the CSS, the larger of the two studies. The universe of this study consisted of 2,484 Georgia homicide cases, processed between 1973 and 1979, which had resulted in convictions for murder or voluntary manslaughter. According to our analysis, 65% of these cases, or 1,620, included facts that made the defendant death eligible under Georgia law. Of these cases, 128 resulted in a death sentence.

From this universe, we drew a stratified sample of approximately 1,050 cases, which included all cases that advanced to a penalty trial, and a sample of the remaining cases. For each case, during the summer of 1981, we collected data on over 200 variables from public records in Georgia, a task that engaged six people full-time for 3 months.

The purpose of the CSS was to determine the extent to which racially discriminatory factors influenced the succession of decisions that could lead to the imposition of a death sentence under Georgia's capital-sentencing system. In particular, we focused on the extent to which either the race of the defendant or the race of the victim, or both, appeared to influence decisions in the system.

The Results

Georgia's capital charging and sentencing system is characterized by the broad exercise of discretion. Figure 13.2 shows the extreme selectivity of the process as cases move through the system, principally because of prosecutorial choices. Of the death-eligible cases in the study, 97% resulted in a murder indictment (see Figure 13.2, bar 2). How-

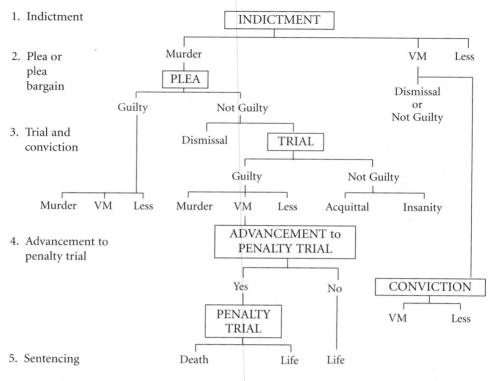

Figure 13.1. Georgia's capital charging and sentencing system. Decision stages in the capital charging and sentencing system are shown in boldface. Outcomes of decisions are in ordinary type. Stages following a voluntary manslaughter (VM) indictment are abbreviated. The Procedural Reform Study covered stages 4 and 5 only. The Charging and Sentencing Study covered stages 1 through 5, but included only those cases that resulted in a conviction for murder or voluntary manslaughter. A few murder plea cases were advanced to penalty trials before a judge.

ever, a comparison between bars 2 and 4 in Figure 13.2 indicates that a very significant proportion of the cases are resolved by negotiated guilty pleas, either to voluntary manslaughter or to murder. Bar 5 indicates that only 40% of the death-eligible cases result in a murder trial conviction, and a comparison between bars 5 and 6 indicates that prosecutors choose to pursue a penalty trial in fewer than 40% of the litigated cases that result in murder convictions. Finally, penalty trial juries impose death sentences in about 50% of the cases they hear, which means that only 8% of the original population of death-eligible offenders received a death sentence.

… [D]efendants in our study whose victims were white faced a significantly higher risk of receiving a death sentence than those with black victims. The disparity is 10 percentage points (0.11 minus 0.013%) or a ratio of 8.3:1.

Obviously, race was not the only factor that influenced Georgia's capital-sentencing system. There were many legitimate case characteristics that influenced prosecutorial and jury decisions. Accordingly, it was necessary to calculate "adjusted" racial disparities after controlling for the presence of these legitimate background factors in the cases. The confidence we have that the racial disparities that emerged from these analyses are real is principally based on the persistence of those effects across a wide variety of multivariate statistical methods that controlled for various combinations of legitimate case characteristics.

McCleskey v. Kemp
481 U.S. 279 (1987)

Justice POWELL delivered the opinion of the Court.

This case presents the question whether a complex statistical study that indicates a risk that racial considerations enter into capital sentencing determinations proves that petitioner McCleskey's capital sentence is unconstitutional under the Eighth or Fourteenth Amendment.

I

McCleskey, a black man, was convicted of two counts of armed robbery and one count of murder in the Superior Court of Fulton County, Georgia, on October 12, 1978. McCleskey's convictions arose out of the robbery of a furniture store and the killing of a white police officer during the course of the robbery. [The jury which convicted McCleskey recommended a death sentence for the murder.]

[After his conviction and death sentence were affirmed on direct appeal and in state post-conviction,] McCleskey ... filed a petition for a writ of habeas corpus in the federal District Court for the Northern District of Georgia. His petition raised 18 claims, one of which was that the Georgia capital sentencing process is administered in a racially discriminatory manner in violation of the Eighth and Fourteenth Amendments to the United States Constitution. In support of his claim, McCleskey proffered a statistical study performed by Professors David C. Baldus, George Woodworth, and Charles Pulaski, (the Baldus study) that purports to show a disparity in the imposition of the death sentence in Georgia based on the race of the murder victim and, to a lesser extent, the race of the defendant. The Baldus study is actually two sophisticated statistical studies that examine over 2,000 murder cases that occurred in Georgia during the 1970s. The raw numbers collected by Professor Baldus indicate that defendants charged with killing white persons received the death penalty in 11% of the cases, but defendants charged with killing blacks received the death penalty in only 1% of the cases. The raw numbers also indicate a reverse racial disparity according to the race of the defendant: 4% of the black defendants received the death penalty, as opposed to 7% of the white defendants.

Baldus also divided the cases according to the combination of the race of the defendant and the race of the victim. He found that the death penalty was assessed in 22% of the cases involving black defendants and white victims; 8% of the cases involving white defendants and white victims; 1% of the cases involving black defendants and black victims; and 3% of the cases involving white defendants and black victims. Similarly, Baldus found that prosecutors sought the death penalty in 70% of the cases involving black defendants and white victims; 32% of the cases involving white defendants and white victims; 15% of the cases involving black defendants and black victims; and 19% of the cases involving white defendants and black victims.

Baldus subjected his data to an extensive analysis, taking account of 230 variables that could have explained the disparities on nonracial grounds. One of his models concludes that, even after taking account of 39 nonracial variables, defendants charged with killing white victims were 4.3 times as likely to receive a death sentence as defendants charged with killing blacks. According to this model, black defendants were 1.1 times as likely to receive a death sentence as other defendants. Thus, the Baldus study indicates that black defendants, such as McCleskey, who kill white victims have the greatest likelihood of receiving the death penalty.

[Both the federal district court and the Court of Appeals for the Eleventh Circuit rejected McCleskey's claims that the racial considerations that enter into capital sentencing determinations violate the Eighth and Fourteenth Amendments.]

We granted certiorari and now affirm.

II

McCleskey's first claim is that the Georgia capital punishment statute violates the Equal Protection Clause of the Fourteenth Amendment.[7] He argues that race has infected the administration of Georgia's statute in two ways: persons who murder whites are more likely to be sentenced to death than persons who murder blacks, and black murderers are more likely to be sentenced to death than white murderers. As a black defendant who killed a white victim, McCleskey claims that the Baldus study demonstrates that he was discriminated against because of his race and because of the race of his victim. In its broadest form, McCleskey's claim of discrimination extends to every actor in the Georgia capital sentencing process, from the prosecutor who sought the death penalty and the jury that imposed the sentence, to the State itself that enacted the capital punishment statute and allows it to remain in effect despite its allegedly discriminatory application. We agree with the Court of Appeals, and every other court that has considered such a challenge, that this claim must fail.

A

Our analysis begins with the basic principle that a defendant who alleges an equal protection violation has the burden of proving "the existence of purposeful discrimination." A corollary to this principle is that a criminal defendant must prove that the purposeful discrimination "had a discriminatory effect" on him. Thus, to prevail under the Equal Protection Clause, McCleskey must prove that the decisionmakers in his case acted with discriminatory purpose. He offers no evidence specific to his own case that would support an inference that racial considerations played a part in his sentence. Instead, he relies solely on the Baldus study. McCleskey argues that the Baldus study compels an inference that his sentence rests on purposeful discrimination. McCleskey's claim that these statistics are sufficient proof of discrimination, without regard to the facts of a particular case, would extend to all capital cases in Georgia, at least where the victim was white and the defendant is black.

... McCleskey's statistical proffer must be viewed in the context of his challenge. McCleskey challenges decisions at the heart of the State's criminal justice system. "[O]ne of

---

7. Although the District Court rejected the findings of the Baldus study as flawed, the Court of Appeals assumed that the study is valid and reached the constitutional issues. Accordingly, those issues are before us. As did the Court of Appeals, we assume the study is valid statistically without reviewing the factual findings of the District Court. Our assumption that the Baldus study is statistically valid does not include the assumption that the study shows that racial considerations actually enter into any sentencing decisions in Georgia. Even a sophisticated multiple regression analysis such as the Baldus study can only demonstrate a risk that the factor of race entered into some capital sentencing decisions and a necessarily lesser risk that race entered into any particular sentencing decision.

society's most basic tasks is that of protecting the lives of its citizens and one of the most basic ways in which it achieves the task is through criminal laws against murder." Implementation of these laws necessarily requires discretionary judgments. Because discretion is essential to the criminal justice process, we would demand exceptionally clear proof before we would infer that the discretion has been abused. The unique nature of the decisions at issue in this case also counsel against adopting such an inference from the disparities indicated by the Baldus study. Accordingly, we hold that the Baldus study is clearly insufficient to support an inference that any of the decisionmakers in McCleskey's case acted with discriminatory purpose.

B

McCleskey also suggests that the Baldus study proves that the State as a whole has acted with a discriminatory purpose. He appears to argue that the State has violated the Equal Protection Clause by adopting the capital punishment statute and allowing it to remain in force despite its allegedly discriminatory application. But "'[d]iscriminatory purpose'... implies more than intent as volition or intent as awareness of consequences. It implies that the decisionmaker, in this case a state legislature, selected or reaffirmed a particular course of action at least in part 'because of,' not merely 'in spite of,' its adverse effects upon an identifiable group." For this claim to prevail, McCleskey would have to prove that the Georgia Legislature enacted or maintained the death penalty statute because of an anticipated racially discriminatory effect. In *Gregg v. Georgia*, 428 U.S. 153 (1976), this Court found that the Georgia capital sentencing system could operate in a fair and neutral manner. There was no evidence then, and there is none now, that the Georgia Legislature enacted the capital punishment statute to further a racially discriminatory purpose.[20]

Nor has McCleskey demonstrated that the legislature maintains the capital punishment statute because of the racially disproportionate impact suggested by the Baldus study. As legislatures necessarily have wide discretion in the choice of criminal laws and penalties, and as there were legitimate reasons for the Georgia Legislature to adopt and maintain capital punishment, we will not infer a discriminatory purpose on the part of the State of Georgia. Accordingly, we reject McCleskey's equal protection claims.

III

McCleskey also argues that the Baldus study demonstrates that the Georgia capital sentencing system violates the Eighth Amendment....

D

[After discussing the Court's Eighth Amendment death penalty jurisprudence, the Court stated:] In sum our decisions since *Furman v. Georgia*, 408 U.S. 238 (1972), have identified a constitutionally permissible range of discretion in imposing the death penalty. First, there is a required threshold below which the death penalty cannot be imposed. In this context, the State must establish rational criteria that narrow the deci-

---

20. McCleskey relies on "historical evidence" to support his claim of purposeful discrimination by the State. This evidence focuses on Georgia laws in force during and just after the Civil War. Of course, the "historical background of the decision is one evidentiary source" for proof of intentional discrimination. But unless historical evidence is reasonably contemporaneous with the challenged decision, it has little probative value. Although the history of racial discrimination in this country is undeniable, we cannot accept official actions taken long ago as evidence of current intent.

sionmaker's judgment as to whether the circumstances of a particular defendant's case meet the threshold. Moreover, a societal consensus that the death penalty is disproportionate to a particular offense prevents a State from imposing the death penalty for that offense. Second, States cannot limit the sentencer's consideration of any relevant circumstance that could cause it to decline to impose the penalty. In this respect, the State cannot channel the sentencer's discretion, but must allow it to consider any relevant information offered by the defendant.

IV

A

In light of our precedents under the Eighth Amendment, McCleskey cannot argue successfully that his sentence is "disproportionate to the crime in the traditional sense." He does not deny that he committed a murder in the course of a planned robbery, a crime for which this Court has determined that the death penalty constitutionally may be imposed. His disproportionality claim "is of a different sort." McCleskey argues that the sentence in his case is disproportionate to the sentences in other murder cases.

On the one hand, he cannot base a constitutional claim on an argument that his case differs from other cases in which defendants *did* receive the death penalty. On automatic appeal, the Georgia Supreme Court found that McCleskey's death sentence was not disproportionate to other death sentences imposed in the State. The court supported this conclusion with an appendix containing citations to 13 cases involving generally similar murders. Moreover, where the statutory procedures adequately channel the sentencer's discretion, such proportionality review is not constitutionally required.

On the other hand, absent a showing that the Georgia capital punishment system operates in an arbitrary and capricious manner, McCleskey cannot prove a constitutional violation by demonstrating that other defendants who may be similarly situated did not receive the death penalty. In *Gregg*, the Court confronted the argument that "the opportunities for discretionary action that are inherent in the processing of any murder case under Georgia law," specifically the opportunities for discretionary leniency, rendered the capital sentences imposed arbitrary and capricious. We rejected this contention:

> The existence of these discretionary stages is not determinative of the issues before us. At each of these stages an actor in the criminal justice system makes a decision which may remove a defendant from consideration as a candidate for the death penalty. *Furman*, in contrast, dealt with the decision to impose the death sentence on a specific individual who had been convicted of a capital offense. Nothing in any of our cases suggests that the decision to afford an individual defendant mercy violates the Constitution. *Furman* held only that, in order to minimize the risk that the death penalty would be imposed on a capriciously selected group of offenders, the decision to impose it had to be guided by standards so that the sentencing authority would focus on the particularized circumstances of the crime and the defendant.[28]

---

28. The Constitution is not offended by inconsistency in results based on the objective circumstances of the crime. Numerous legitimate factors may influence the outcome of a trial and a defendant's ultimate sentence, even though they may be irrelevant to his actual guilt. If sufficient evidence to link a suspect to a crime cannot be found, he will not be charged. The capability of the responsible law enforcement agency can vary widely. Also, the strength of the available evidence remains a variable throughout the criminal justice process and may influence a prosecutor's decision to offer a plea bargain or to go to trial. Witness availability, credibility, and memory also influence the results

Because McCleskey's sentence was imposed under Georgia sentencing procedures that focus discretion "on the particularized nature of the crime and the particularized characteristics of the individual defendant," we lawfully may presume that McCleskey's death sentence was not "wantonly and freakishly" imposed, and thus that the sentence is not disproportionate within any recognized meaning under the Eighth Amendment.

B

Although our decision in *Gregg* as to the facial validity of the Georgia capital punishment statute appears to foreclose McCleskey's disproportionality argument, he further contends that the Georgia capital punishment system is arbitrary and capricious in *application*, and therefore his sentence is excessive, because racial considerations may influence capital sentencing decisions in Georgia. We now address this claim.

To evaluate McCleskey's challenge, we must examine exactly what the Baldus study may show. Even Professor Baldus does not contend that his statistics prove that race enters into any capital sentencing decisions or that race was a factor in McCleskey's particular case.[29] Statistics at most may show only a likelihood that a particular factor entered into some decisions. There is, of course, some risk of racial prejudice influencing a jury's decision in a criminal case. There are similar risks that other kinds of prejudice will influence other criminal trials. The question "is at what point that risk becomes constitutionally unacceptable." McCleskey asks us to accept the likelihood allegedly shown by the Baldus study as the constitutional measure of an unacceptable risk of racial prejudice influencing capital sentencing decisions. This we decline to do.

Because of the risk that the factor of race may enter the criminal justice process, we have engaged in "unceasing efforts" to eradicate racial prejudice from our criminal justice system. Our efforts have been guided by our recognition that "the inestimable privilege of trial by jury ... is a vital principle, underlying the whole administration of criminal justice." Thus, it is the jury that is a criminal defendant's fundamental "protection of life and liberty against race or color prejudice." Specifically, a capital sentencing jury representative of a criminal defendant's community assures a "'diffused impartiality,'" in the jury's task of "express[ing] the conscience of the community on the ultimate question of life or death."

Individual jurors bring to their deliberations "qualities of human nature and varieties of human experience, the range of which is unknown and perhaps unknowable." The capital sentencing decision requires the individual jurors to focus their collective judgment on the unique characteristics of a particular criminal defendant. It is not surprising that such collective judgments often are difficult to explain. But the inherent lack of predictability of jury decisions does not justify their condemnation. On the contrary, it is the jury's function to make the difficult and uniquely human judgments that defy codification and that "buil[d] discretion, equity, and flexibility into a legal system."

---

of prosecutions. Finally, sentencing in state courts is generally discretionary, so a defendant's ultimate sentence necessarily will vary according to the judgment of the sentencing authority. The foregoing factors necessarily exist in varying degrees throughout our criminal justice system.

29. According to Professor Baldus:

"McCleskey's case falls in [a] grey area where ... you would find the greatest likelihood that some inappropriate consideration may have come to bear on the decision.

"In an analysis of this type, obviously one cannot say that we can say to a moral certainty what it was that influenced the decision. We can't do that."

McCleskey's argument that the Constitution condemns the discretion allowed decisionmakers in the Georgia capital sentencing system is antithetical to the fundamental role of discretion in our criminal justice system. Discretion in the criminal justice system offers substantial benefits to the criminal defendant. Not only can a jury decline to impose the death sentence, it can decline to convict, or choose to convict of a lesser offense. Whereas decisions against a defendant's interest may be reversed by the trial judge or on appeal, these discretionary exercises of leniency are final and unreviewable. Similarly, the capacity of prosecutorial discretion to provide individualized justice is "firmly entrenched in American law." As we have noted, a prosecutor can decline to charge, offer a plea bargain, or decline to seek a death sentence in any particular case. Of course, "the power to be lenient [also] is the power to discriminate," but a capital-punishment system that did not allow for discretionary acts of leniency "would be totally alien to our notions of criminal justice."

C

At most, the Baldus study indicates a discrepancy that appears to correlate with race. Apparent disparities in sentencing are an inevitable part of our criminal justice system. The discrepancy indicated by the Baldus study is "a far cry from the major systemic defects identified in *Furman*." As this Court has recognized, any mode for determining guilt or punishment "has its weaknesses and the potential for misuse." Specifically, "there can be no perfect procedure for deciding in which cases governmental authority should be used to impose death." Despite these imperfections, our consistent rule has been that constitutional guarantees are met when "the mode [for determining guilt or punishment] itself has been surrounded with safeguards to make it as fair as possible." Where the discretion that is fundamental to our criminal process is involved, we decline to assume that what is unexplained is invidious. In light of the safeguards designed to minimize racial bias in the process, the fundamental value of jury trial in our criminal justice system, and the benefits that discretion provides to criminal defendants, we hold that the Baldus study does not demonstrate a constitutionally significant risk of racial bias affecting the Georgia capital-sentencing process.

V

Two additional concerns inform our decision in this case. First, McCleskey's claim, taken to its logical conclusion, throws into serious question the principles that underlie our entire criminal justice system. The Eighth Amendment is not limited in application to capital punishment, but applies to all penalties. Thus, if we accepted McCleskey's claim that racial bias has impermissibly tainted the capital sentencing decision, we could soon be faced with similar claims as to other types of penalty. Moreover, the claim that his sentence rests on the irrelevant factor of race easily could be extended to apply to claims based on unexplained discrepancies that correlate to membership in other minority groups, and even to gender. Similarly, since McCleskey's claim relates to the race of his victim, other claims could apply with equally logical force to statistical disparities that correlate with the race or sex of other actors in the criminal justice system, such as defense attorneys or judges. Also, there is no logical reason that such a claim need be limited to racial or sexual bias. If arbitrary and capricious punishment is the touchstone under the Eighth Amendment, such a claim could — at least in theory — be based upon any arbitrary variable, such as the defendant's facial characteristics, or the physical attractiveness of the defendant or the victim, that some statistical study indicates may be influential in jury decisionmaking. As these examples illustrate, there is no limiting principle to the type of challenge brought by McCleskey. The Constitution does not require that a State eliminate any demonstrable disparity that correlates with a potentially irrelevant factor in order to operate a criminal justice system that includes capital punishment. As we have stated specifically in the context of capital punishment, the Constitution does not "plac[e] totally unrealistic conditions on its use."

Second, McCleskey's arguments are best presented to the legislative bodies. It is not the responsibility—or indeed even the right—of this Court to determine the appropriate punishment for particular crimes. It is the legislatures, the elected representatives of the people, that are "constituted to respond to the will and consequently the moral values of the people." Legislatures also are better qualified to weigh and "evaluate the results of statistical studies in terms of their own local conditions and with a flexibility of approach that is not available to the courts." Capital punishment is now the law in more than two-thirds of our States. It is the ultimate duty of courts to determine on a case-by-case basis whether these laws are applied consistently with the Constitution. Despite McCleskey's wide ranging arguments that basically challenge the validity of capital punishment in our multi-racial society, the only question before us is whether in his case the law of Georgia was properly applied. We agree with the District Court and the Court of Appeals for the Eleventh Circuit that this was carefully and correctly done in this case.

VI

Accordingly, we affirm the judgment of the Court of Appeals for the Eleventh Circuit.

Justice BRENNAN, with whom Justice Marshall joins, and with whom Justice Blackmun and Justice Stevens join in all but Part I, dissenting.

II

At some point in this case, Warren McCleskey doubtless asked his lawyer whether a jury was likely to sentence him to die. A candid reply to this question would have been disturbing. First, counsel would have to tell McCleskey that few of the details of the crime or of McCleskey's past criminal conduct were more important than the fact that his victim was white. Furthermore, counsel would feel bound to tell McCleskey that defendants charged with killing white victims in Georgia are 4.3 times as likely to be sentenced to death as defendants charged with killing blacks. In addition, frankness would compel the disclosure that it was more likely than not that the race of McCleskey's victim would determine whether he received a death sentence: 6 of every 11 defendants convicted of killing a white person would not have received the death penalty if their victims had been black, while, among defendants with aggravating and mitigating factors comparable to McCleskey, 20 of every 34 would not have been sentenced to die if their victims had been black. Finally, the assessment would not be complete without the information that cases involving black defendants and white victims are more likely to result in a death sentence than cases featuring any other racial combination of defendant and victim. The story could be told in a variety of ways, but McCleskey could not fail to grasp its essential narrative line: there was a significant chance that race would play a prominent role in determining if he lived or died.

The Court today holds that Warren McCleskey's sentence was constitutionally imposed. It finds no fault in a system in which lawyers must tell their clients that race casts a large shadow on the capital sentencing process. The Court arrives at this conclusion by stating that the Baldus Study cannot "*prove* that race enters into any capital sentencing decisions or that race was a factor in McCleskey's particular case." Since, according to Professor Baldus, we cannot say "to a moral certainty" that race influenced a decision, we can identify only "a likelihood that a particular factor entered into some decisions," and "a discrepancy that appears to correlate with race." This "likelihood" and "discrepancy," holds the Court, is insufficient to establish a constitutional violation. The Court reaches this conclusion by placing four factors on the scales opposite McCleskey's evidence: the desire to encourage sentencing discretion, the existence of "statutory safeguards" in the Georgia scheme, the fear of encouraging widespread challenges to other sentencing decisions, and the limits of the judicial role. The Court's evaluation of the significance of petitioner's evidence is fundamentally at odds with our consistent concern for rationality in capital sentencing, and the considerations that the majority invokes to discount that evidence cannot justify ignoring its force.

III

A

It is important to emphasize at the outset that the Court's observation that McCleskey cannot prove the influence of race on any particular sentencing decision is irrelevant in evaluating his Eighth Amendment claim. Since *Furman*, the Court has been concerned with the *risk* of the imposition of an arbitrary sentence, rather than the proven fact of one. *Furman* held that the death penalty "may not be imposed under sentencing procedures that create a substantial risk that the punishment will be inflicted in an arbitrary and capricious manner." As Justice O'Connor observed in *Caldwell v. Mississippi*, 472 U.S. 320, 343 (1985) (*infra* chapter 9), a death sentence must be struck down when the circumstances under which it has been imposed "creat[e] an unacceptable *risk* that 'the death penalty [may have been] meted out arbitrarily or capriciously' or through 'whim or mistake.'" This emphasis on risk acknowledges the difficulty of divining the jury's motivation in an individual case. In addition, it reflects the fact that concern for arbitrariness focuses on the rationality of the system as a whole, and that a system that features a significant probability that sentencing decisions are influenced by impermissible considerations cannot be regarded as rational. As we said in *Gregg*, "the petitioner looks to the sentencing system as a whole (as the Court did in *Furman* and we do today)": a constitutional violation is established if a plaintiff demonstrates a "*pattern* of arbitrary and capricious sentencing."

Defendants challenging their death sentences thus never have had to prove that impermissible considerations have actually infected sentencing decisions. We have required instead that they establish that the system under which they were sentenced posed a significant risk of such an occurrence. McCleskey's claim does differ, however, in one respect from these earlier cases: it is the first to base a challenge not on speculation about how a system *might* operate, but on empirical documentation of how it *does* operate.

The Court assumes the statistical validity of the Baldus study, and acknowledges that McCleskey has demonstrated a risk that racial prejudice plays a role in capital sentencing in Georgia. Nonetheless, it finds the probability of prejudice insufficient to create constitutional concern. Close analysis of the Baldus study, however, in light of both statistical principles and human experience, reveals that the risk that race influenced McCleskey's sentence is intolerable by any imaginable standard.

C

The Baldus study indicates that, after taking into account some 230 nonracial factors that might legitimately influence a sentencer, the jury *more likely than not* would have spared McCleskey's life had his victim been black. The study distinguishes between those cases in which (1) the jury exercises virtually no discretion because the strength or weakness of aggravating factors usually suggests that only one outcome is appropriate; and (2) cases reflecting an "intermediate" level of aggravation, in which the jury has considerable discretion in choosing a sentence. McCleskey's case falls into the intermediate range. In such cases, death is imposed in 34% of white-victim crimes and 14% of black-victim crimes, a difference of 139% in the rate of imposition of the death penalty. In other words, just under 59%—almost 6 in 10—defendants comparable to McCleskey would not have received the death penalty if their victims had been black.

Furthermore, even examination of the sentencing system as a whole, factoring in those cases in which the jury exercises little discretion, indicates the influence of race on capital sentencing. For the Georgia system as a whole, race accounts for a six percentage point difference in the rate at which capital punishment is imposed. Since death is imposed in 11% of all white-victim cases, the rate in comparably aggravated black-victim cases is 5%. The rate of capital sentencing in a white-victim case is thus 120% greater than the rate in a black-victim case. Put another way, over half—55%—of defendants in white-victim crimes in Georgia would not have been sentenced to die if their victims had been black. Of the more than 200 variables potentially relevant to a sentencing decision, race of the victim is a powerful explanation for variation in death sentence rates—as powerful as nonracial aggravating factors such as a prior murder conviction or acting as the principal planner of the homicide.

These adjusted figures are only the most conservative indication of the risk that race will influence the death sentences of defendants in Georgia. Data unadjusted for the mitigating or aggravating effect of other factors show an even more pronounced disparity by race. The capital sentencing rate for all white-victim cases was almost *11 times* greater than the rate for black-victim cases. Furthermore, blacks who kill whites are sentenced to death at nearly *22 times* the rate of blacks who kill blacks, and more than *7 times* the rate of whites who kill blacks. In addition, prosecutors seek the death penalty for 70% of black defendants with white victims, but for only 15% of black defendants with black victims, and only 19% of white defendants with black victims. Since our decision upholding the Georgia capital-sentencing system in *Gregg*, the State has executed 7 persons. All of the 7 were convicted of killing whites, and 6 of the 7 executed were black. Such execution figures are especially striking in light of the fact that, during the period encompassed by the Baldus study, only 9.2% of Georgia homicides involved black defendants and white victims, while 60.7% involved black victims.

The statistical evidence in this case thus relentlessly documents the risk that McCleskey's sentence was influenced by racial considerations. This evidence shows that there is a better than even chance in Georgia that race will influence the decision to impose the death penalty: a majority of defendants in white-victim crimes would not have been sentenced to die if their victims had been black. In determining whether this risk is acceptable, our judgment must be shaped by the awareness that "[t]he risk of racial prejudice infecting a capital sentencing proceeding is especially serious in light of the complete finality of the death sentence," and that "[i]t is of vital importance to the defendant and to the community that any decision to impose the death sentence be, and appear to be, based on reason rather than caprice or emotion." In determining the guilt of a defendant, a state must prove its case beyond a reasonable doubt. That is, we refuse to convict if the chance of error is simply less likely than not. Surely, we should not be willing to take a person's life if the chance that his death sentence was irrationally imposed is *more* likely than not. In light of the gravity of the interest at stake, petitioner's statistics on their face are a powerful demonstration of the type of risk that our Eighth Amendment jurisprudence has consistently condemned.

D

… For many years, Georgia operated openly and formally precisely the type of dual system the evidence shows is still effectively in place. The criminal law expressly differentiated between crimes committed by and against blacks and whites, distinctions whose lineage traced back to the time of slavery. During the colonial period, black slaves who killed whites in Georgia, regardless of whether in self-defense or in defense of another, were automatically executed.

By the time of the Civil War, a dual system of crime and punishment was well established in Georgia. The state criminal code contained separate sections for "Slaves and Free Persons of Color," and for all other persons. The code provided, for instance, for an automatic death sentence for murder committed by blacks, but declared that anyone else convicted of murder might receive life imprisonment if the conviction were founded solely on circumstantial testimony or simply if the jury so recommended. The code established that the rape of a free white female by a black "shall be" punishable by death. However, rape by anyone else of a free white female was punishable by a prison term not less than 2 nor more than 20 years. The rape of *blacks* was punishable "by fine and imprisonment, at the discretion of the court." A black convicted of assaulting a free white person with intent to murder could be put to death at the discretion of the court, but the same offense committed against a black, slave or free, was classified as a "minor" offense whose punishment lay in the discretion of the court, as long as such punishment did not "extend to life, limb, or health." Assault with intent to murder by a white person was punishable by a prison term of from 2 to 10 years. While sufficient provocation could reduce a charge of murder to manslaughter, the code provided that "[o]bedience and submission being the duty of a slave, much greater provocation is necessary to reduce a homicide of a white person by him to voluntary manslaughter, than is prescribed for white persons."

… History and its continuing legacy thus buttress the probative force of McCleskey's statistics. Formal dual criminal laws may no longer be in effect, and intentional discrimination may no longer be prominent. Nonetheless, as we acknowledged in *Turner v. Murray*, 476 U.S 28 (1986), "subtle, less consciously held racial attitudes" continue to be of concern, and the Georgia system gives such attitudes considerable room to operate. The conclusions drawn from McCleskey's statistical evidence are therefore consistent with the lessons of social experience.…

IV

It has now been over 13 years since Georgia adopted the provisions upheld in *Gregg*. Professor Baldus and his colleagues have compiled data on almost 2,500 homicides committed during the period 1973–1979. They have taken into account the influence of 230 nonracial variables, using a multitude of data from the State itself, and have produced striking evidence that the odds of being sentenced to death are significantly greater than average if a defendant is black or his or her victim is white. The challenge to the Georgia system is not speculative or theoretical; it is empirical. As a result, the Court cannot rely on the statutory safeguards in discounting McCleskey's evidence, for it is the very effectiveness of those safeguards that such evidence calls into question. While we may hope that a model of procedural fairness will curb the influence of race on sentencing, "we cannot simply assume that the model works as intended; we must critique its performance in terms of its results."

The Court next states that its unwillingness to regard the petitioner's evidence as sufficient is based in part on the fear that recognition of McCleskey's claim would open the door to widespread challenges to all aspects of criminal sentencing. Taken on its face, such a statement seems to suggest a fear of too much justice. Yet surely the majority would acknowledge that if striking evidence indicated that other minority groups, or women, or even persons with blond hair, were disproportionately sentenced to death, such a state of affairs would be repugnant to deeply rooted conceptions of fairness. The prospect that there may be more widespread abuse than McCleskey documents may be dismaying, but it does not justify complete abdication of our judicial role. The Constitution was framed fundamentally as a bulwark against governmental power, and preventing the arbitrary administration of punishment is a basic ideal of any society that purports to be governed by the rule of law....

The Court also maintains that accepting McCleskey's claim would pose a threat to all sentencing because of the prospect that a correlation might be demonstrated between sentencing outcomes and other personal characteristics. Again, such a view is indifferent to the considerations that enter into a determination of whether punishment is "cruel and unusual." Race is a consideration whose influence is expressly constitutionally proscribed. We have expressed a moral commitment, as embodied in our fundamental law, that this specific characteristic should not be the basis for allotting burdens and benefits. Three constitutional amendments, and numerous statutes, have been prompted specifically by the desire to address the effects of racism. "Over the years, this Court has consistently repudiated '[d]istinctions between citizens solely because of their ancestry' as being 'odious to a free people whose institutions are founded upon the doctrine of equality.'" Furthermore, we have explicitly acknowledged the illegitimacy of race as a consideration in capital sentencing, *Zant v. Stephens*, 462 U.S. 862, 885 (1983). That a decision to impose the death penalty could be influenced by race is thus a particularly repugnant prospect, and evidence that race may play even a modest role in levying a death sentence should be enough to characterize that sentence as "cruel and unusual."

The Court's projection of apocalyptic consequences for criminal sentencing is thus greatly exaggerated. The Court can indulge in such speculation only by ignoring its own jurisprudence demanding the highest scrutiny on issues of death and race. As a result, it fails to do justice to a claim in which both those elements are intertwined—an occasion calling for the most sensitive inquiry a court can conduct. Despite its acceptance of the validity of Warren McCleskey's evidence, the Court is willing to let his death sentence stand because it fears that we cannot successfully define a different standard for lesser punishments. This fear is baseless.

Finally, the Court justifies its rejection of McCleskey's claim by cautioning against usurpation of the legislatures' role in devising and monitoring criminal punishment. The Court is, of course, correct to emphasize the gravity of constitutional intervention and the importance that it be sparingly employed. The fact that "[c]apital punishment is now the law in more than two-thirds of our States," however, does not diminish the fact that capital punishment is the most awesome act that a State can perform. The judiciary's role in this society counts for little if the use of governmental power to extinguish life does not elicit close scrutiny. It is true that society has a legitimate interest in punishment. Yet, as Alexander Bickel wrote:

> It is a premise we deduce not merely from the fact of a written constitution but from the history of the race, and ultimately as a moral judgment of the good society, that government should serve not only what we conceive from time to time to be our immediate material needs but also certain enduring values. This in part is what is meant by government under law.

A. Bickel, The Least Dangerous Branch 24 (1962).

For these reasons, "[t]he methods we employ in the enforcement of our criminal law have aptly been called the measures by which the quality of our civilization may be judged." Those whom we would banish from society or from the human community itself often speak in too faint a voice to be heard above society's demand for punishment. It is the particular role of courts to hear these voices, for the Constitution declares that the majoritarian chorus may not alone dictate the conditions of social life. The Court thus fulfills, rather than disrupts, the scheme of separation of powers by closely scrutinizing the imposition of the death penalty, for no decision of a society is more deserving of the "sober second thought."

V

At the time our Constitution was framed 200 years ago this year, blacks "had for more than a century before been regarded as beings of an inferior order, and altogether unfit to associate with the white race, either in social or political relations; and so far inferior, that they had no rights which the white man was bound to respect." *Dred Scott v. Sandford*, 60 U.S. (19 How.) 393 (1857). Only 130 years ago, this Court relied on these observations to deny American citizenship to blacks. A mere three generations ago, this Court sanctioned racial segregation, stating that "[i]f one race be inferior to the other socially, the Constitution of the United States cannot put them upon the same plane."

In more recent times, we have sought to free ourselves from the burden of this history. Yet it has been scarcely a generation since this Court's first decision striking down racial segregation, and barely two decades since the legislative prohibition of racial discrimination in major domains of national life. These have been honorable steps, but we cannot pretend that in three decades we have completely escaped the grip of an historical legacy spanning centuries. Warren McCleskey's evidence confronts us with the subtle and persistent influence of the past. His message is a disturbing one to a society that has formally repudiated racism, and a frustrating one to a Nation accustomed to regarding its destiny as the product of its own will. Nonetheless, we ignore him at our peril, for we remain imprisoned by the past as long as we deny its influence in the present.

It is tempting to pretend that minorities on death row share a fate in no way connected to our own, that our treatment of them sounds no echoes beyond the chambers in which they die. Such an illusion is ultimately corrosive, for the reverberations of injustice are not so easily confined. "The destinies of the two races in this country are indissolubly linked together," and the way in which we choose those who will die reveals the depth of moral commitment among the living. The Court's decision today will not change what attorneys in Georgia tell other Warren McCleskeys about their chances of execution. Nothing will soften the harsh message they must convey, nor alter the prospect that race undoubtedly will continue to be a topic of discussion. McCleskey's evidence will not have obtained judicial acceptance, but that will not affect what is said on death row. However many criticisms of today's decision may be rendered, these painful conversations will serve as the most eloquent dissents of all.

Law and Statistics in Conflict:
Reflections on *McCleskey v. Kemp*

David C. Baldus, George Woodworth, and Charles A. Pulaski, Jr. (1991)

The most important single piece of evidence presented on McCleskey's behalf was the results of a 39-variable logistic multiple-regression model. We chose the variables selected for this core model either because we regarded them as conceptually important[4] or because we found them to be statistically important in explaining which defendants in the study ultimately received a death sentence.[5] The influence of the various case characteristics employed in this model also reflected the combined effects of all prosecutorial and jury decisions from the point of indictment to the jury's penalty trial decision. Table 13.2 [on the next page] presents the logistic regression coefficients and odds multipliers for the two racial variables and the 39 legitimate case characteristics from this model. The table lists the variables in the order of their statistical impact, with the mitigating case characteristics (1 thru 10) presented first, followed by the aggravating case characteristics. Items 10 and 30 in this table indicate the results for the race-of-defendant and race-of-victim variables.

For purposes of interpretation, the most important statistics in Table 13.2 are the "death-odds multipliers" in column B. Those numbers indicate the extent to which the odds of the average defendant are enhanced or reduced by the presence of each case characteristic in his case, after adjustment for the other variables in the analysis. For example, the 2.8 odds multiplier for variable 24, "victim was a stranger," means that after adjustment for the other factors in the analysis, a defendant's odds of receiving a death sentence were enhanced by a factor of 2.8 if his victim was a stranger. Thus, if after adjustment for all the other variables in the model, a defendant's odds of receiving a death sentence were even (1:1), those odds would rise to 2.8:1 (2.8 x 1:1) if the victim also was a stranger (Gross & Mauro, 1989, pp. 248–252).

The rank ordering of the legitimate case characteristics in Table 13.2 indicates that the system appears to operate in a reasonably coherent fashion. With respect to racial factors, the odds-multiplier for the race-of-defendant variable at item 10 indicates that, on the average, the offender's race is not an influential factor; that is, it is only .94 and is not statistically significant beyond the .05 level. In contrast, the odds-multiplier for the race-of-victim variable at item 30 is 4.3 and significant at the .003 level. This indicates that, on the average, after adjustment for the other factors in the model, a defendant's odds of receiving a death sentence are increased by a factor of 4.3 when the victim is white. Therefore, if a defendant's odds of receiving a death sentence were even (1:1) on the basis of all of the other case characteristics in the model, they would increase to 4.3 to 1 (4.3 x 1) if the victim were white. The relative size of the odds-multiplier for the race-of-victim variable in Table 13.2 suggests that, on the average, the presence of a white victim in a case has about the same effect on the defendant's chances of a death sentence as such legitimate aggravating factors as the presence of multiple stab wounds, an armed robbery, a child victim, or a prior record for murder, armed robbery, rape, kidnapping, or kidnapping with bodily injury....

---

4. By *conceptually important*, we mean factors that are widely recognized by criminologists, courts, prosecutors, and legislators as significant determinants of death-sentencing outcomes, e.g., serious prior record, multiple victims.

5. By *statistically important*, we mean variables that were, in fact, strongly correlated with the likelihood of a death sentence.

Figure 13.2. Proportion of death-eligible cases remaining at successive stages in Georgia's capital charging and sentencing process: 1973 to 1979. In 45 cases it is unknown whether there was a penalty trial. Penalty trials were held in 10 cases in which the defendant pled guilty to capital murder.

Variable label and name	Death-odds multiplier	Adjusted logistic regression coefficient (with level of statistical significance)
1. Defendant was not the triggerman (NOKILL)	.06	−2.75 (.0001)
2. Defendant admitted guilt and no defense asserted (DEFADMIT)	.28	−1.27 (.12)
3. Defendant had a history of drug or alcohol abuse (DRGHIS)	.36	−1.01 (.007)
4. Defendant was under 17 years of age (SYMOUTH)	.41	−.88 (.23)
5. Jealousy motive (JEALOUS)	.47	−.74 (.53)
6. Family, lover, liquor, or barroom quarrel (BLVICMOD)	.54	−.61 (.15)
7. Defendant was retired, student, juvenile, housewife (MITDFFN)	.54	−.61 (.64)
8. Hate motive (HATE)	.71	−.34 (.69)
9. Pecuniary motive for self/other (LDFB4)	.80	−.22 (.70)
10. *Defendant was black* (BLACKD)	.94	−.06 (.88)
11. Number of prior defendant felony prison terms (PRISONX)	1.1	.08 (.67)
12. Defendant caused death risk in public place to ≥ 2 people (LDFB3)	1.1	.14 (.74)
13. One or more coperpetrators involved (COPERP)	1.3	.24 (.56)
14. Defendant was a female (FEMDEF)	1.3	.28 (.70)
15. One or more convictions for a violent personal crime, burglary, or arson (VPCARBR)	1.35	.30 (.53)
16. Nonproperty-related contemporaneous crime (NONPROPC)	1.4	.35 (.64)
17. Killing to avoid, stop arrest of self, other (LDFB10)	1.5	.41 (.32)
18. Victim was a police or corrections officer on duty (LDFB8)	1.7	.52 (.58)
19. Defendant primary mover in planning homicide or contemporaneous offense (DLEADER)	1.7	.55 (.33)
20. Rape/armed robbery/kidnapping plus silence witness, execution, or victim pleaded for life (LDFB7D)	1.8	.60 (.16)
21. Coperpetrator received a lesser sentence (CPLESSEN)	2.2	.78 (.09)
22. Multiple shots (MULSH)	2.2	.79 (.04)
23. Victim was drowned (DROWN)	2.6	.96 (.24)
24. Victim was a stranger (STRANGER)	2.8	1.03 (.01)
25. Victim was bedridden/handicapped (VBED)	2.8	1.04 (.33)
26. Kidnapping involved (KIDNAP)	2.9	1.06 (.17)
27. Victim weak or frail (VWEAK)	3.1	1.13 (.19)
28. Defendant had a prior record for murder, armed robbery, rape, or kidnapping with bodily injured (LDFB1)	4.1	1.40 (.009)
29. Armed robbery involved (ARMROB)	4.2	1.43 (.02)
30. *One or more white victims* (WHVICRC)	4.3	1.45 (.003)
31. Multiple stabbing (MULTSTAB)	4.7	1.54 (.002)
32. Victim was 12 or younger (VICCHILD)	4.8	1.56 (.03)
33. Number of defendant prior murder convictions (MURPRIOR)	5.2	1.66 (.27)
34. Murder for hire (LDFB6)	5.9	1.77 (.08)
35. Defendant was a prisoner or escapee (LDFB9)	7.7	2.04 (.002)
36. Defendant killed two or more people (TWOVIC)	7.9	2.07 (.005)
37. Mental torture involved (MENTORT)	9.7	2.27 (.009)
38. Rape involved (RAPE)	12.8	2.55 (.001)
39. Defendant's motive was to collect insurance (INSMOT)	20.1	3.01 (.01)
40. Victim was tortured physically (TORTURE)	27.4	3.31 (.003)
41. Motive was to avenge role by judicial officer, DA, lawyer (AVENGE)	28.9	3.36 (.25)
Constant		−6.15 (.0001)

The *McCleskey* Decision

The Equal Protection Claim

McCleskey's attorneys offered the empirical results of our studies to support two legal claims. The first was that the persistent race-of-victim disparities, which our studies identified after adjusting for all plausible legitimate aggravating and mitigating circumstances, provided a sufficient basis for invalidating McCleskey's death sentence under the equal-protection clause of the Fourteenth Amendment. The second legal claim arose under the cruel and unusual punishments clause of the Eighth Amendment.

To make the necessary showing of purposeful discrimination under the equal-protection clause, McCleskey's lawyers relied on both the jury-selection model of proof and the employment discrimination model of proof that the Supreme Court had endorsed in earlier equal-protection cases. By analogy to the jury model, they first argued that our evidence of classwide purposeful discrimination in the imposition of the death penalty warranted relief, whether or not it demonstrated the existence of any race-of-victim discrimination in his particular case. Second, McCleskey's lawyers argued by analogy to the employment discrimination model of proof, that our unrebutted demonstration of classwide purposeful race-of-victim discrimination should, at a minimum, shift to the state the burden of demonstrating that McCleskey's death sentence was not the product of race-of-victim discrimination.

Of the three federal courts that considered McCleskey's equal-protection claims, the Supreme Court gave this claim the most extended treatment. Writing for the majority, Justice Powell held that no equal-protection violation had occurred warranting relief because McCleskey's attorneys did not prove "that the decision-makers in *his* case acted with discriminatory purpose." This failure of proof, said Justice Powell, stemmed from the absence of "evidence specific to his own case that would support an inference that racial considerations played a part in his sentence." Justice Powell further implied that "absent far stronger proof," statistical evidence of classwide purposeful discrimination was not even relevant to equal-protection claims of racial discrimination in death sentencing cases. The Court further held that any suggestion of discrimination in McCleskey's case created by this statistical evidence was fully rebutted by the presence of two statutory aggravating circumstances in his case; that is, it involved an armed robbery, and the victim was a police officer. Each circumstance provided a sufficient basis for the imposition of a death sentence, Justice Powell reasoned, even though the evidence indicated that the race of victim affected the sentencing outcomes in large groups of cases that involved the presence of one or more of these very statutory aggravating circumstances.

One effect of Justice Powell's Fourteenth Amendment holding in *McCleskey* is that equal protection claims of purposeful race discrimination in death-sentence cases will be subjected to a far heavier burden of proof than is applied in jury discrimination and employment discrimination cases. By limiting equal-protection claims in capital punishment cases to the most restrictive model of proof, the Court in *McCleskey* created a nearly insuperable barrier to the use of statistical methods in such cases. To secure relief, it now appears that capital defendants must demonstrate the existence of purposeful discrimination based on direct admissions by prosecutors or juries, or by circumstantial evidence of discriminatory intent in their individual cases—all without reference to evidence of classwide discrimination against their racial group....

Of course, that the Supreme Court might impose a burden of proof in death-sentencing cases that is different from those used in other situations cases would come as no surprise. What is surprising is that the Court imposed a more severe burden of proof in death-sentence cases than in jury and employment discrimination cases. As Justice Blackmun pointed out in his dissenting opinion, because death cases involve society's ultimate sanction, one would have expected the Court to impose a *lighter* rather than a heavier burden of proof.

The justification offered by Justice Powell to support the Court's holding also came as a surprise. First, he suggested that the imposition of an essentially unattainable burden of proof was necessary to maintain the legitimate discretion of prosecutors and jurors in the death-sentencing context. Indeed, he even asserted that permitting the type of statistical proof of systemwide racial disparities in death sentencing that McCleskey's attorneys offered would jeopardize the very heart of the state's criminal justice system. But he did not expand this argument much further.

Second, Justice Powell rejected the strictly statistical model of proof on the grounds that it would invalidate a significant number of death sentences without regard to whether they were individually the result of purposeful discrimination. This would be a reasonable basis for rejecting the purely statistical model because, as noted earlier, many death sentences are imposed in highly aggravated cases for which the race of victim or defendant clearly has no effect on the outcome. This rationale does not, however, justify a rejection of the hybrid model, which contemplates a case-by-case inquiry into the specifics of each case as a basis for awarding relief.

Justice Powell's third and principal argument was based on methodological grounds, which apply to both the purely statistical and the hybrid models of proof. In essence, he argued that the strength of the inference of purposeful discrimination in an individual case that flowed from evidence of purposeful classwide discrimination was different in the death-sentencing context than it was in jury and employment cases: "But the nature of the capital sentencing decision, and the relationship of the statistics to that decision, are fundamentally different from the corresponding elements in the [jury] venire-selection or Title VII cases."

Justice Powell offered three reasons for this judgment. First, he stated that more distinct and autonomous decision-making entities are involved in a death-sentencing system, and they operate without any "coordination." Second, because more characteristics of each case may influence death-sentencing decision, there is "no common standard" by which a court can "evaluate all defendants who have or have not received the death penalty." For these two reasons, Justice Powell concluded that "the application of an inference drawn from the general statistics to a specific decision in a trial and sentencing simply is not comparable to the application of an inference drawn from general statistics to a specific venire-selection or Title VII case." Our full response to these arguments is presented elsewhere (Baldus et al., 1990, pp. 370–394). Suffice it to say that we do not believe that the distinctions drawn by Justice Powell between the characteristics of decisionmaking in the death-sentencing context as compared to the employment or jury-selection contexts are a sufficient basis for rejecting entirely the probative force of McCleskey's statistical evidence.

The Eighth Amendment Arbitrariness Claim

McCleskey's second constitutional objection to his sentence was based on an Eighth Amendment arbitrariness theory. In this connection, he made two alternative arguments. The first was the race of the victim or the race of the defendant would constitute an arbitrary basis for a sentencing decision and that the strong evidence of purposeful racial discrimination in the system was sufficient to demonstrate a constitutionally impermissible risk of arbitrariness in McCleskey's case. In the alternative, McCleskey's lawyers argued that, at a minimum, the risk of purposeful discrimination in his case should shift to the state the burden of showing that race was not a determinative factor in either McCleskey's conviction or sentence. On either of these grounds they argued, McCleskey's death sentence should be invalidated.

McCleskey did not request the Court to invalidate the entire Georgia death-sentencing system. It was clear, however, that if the court decided to grant relief under the first arbitrariness argument, the implications of that decision would be far-reaching. Such a decision would have required the vacation of every death sentence imposed in Georgia in a white-victim case; and, although the issue is far more problematic, the federal courts might also have extended such relief to similarly situated black-victim cases as well. By contrast, the potential circumstances of relief granted pursuant to the second arbitrariness argument were less catastrophic from the state's perspective. To be sure, it would have required case-by-case evaluations. But it very likely would have resulted in vacated death sentences only in low or moderately aggravated cases for which there were discernible race effects. By contrast, in highly aggravated cases for which racial factors have no influence, there would be no basis for a court to conclude that race was a but-for cause of the defendant's death sentence.

… Justice Powell rejected McCleskey's Eighth Amendment claim as well. He reached this decision by holding that, although relevant, the statistical evidence that McCleskey offered failed to establish a "constitutionally significant risk" that racial bias affected Georgia's death-sentencing process.

Our detailed response to Justice Powell's methodological justification for his arbitrariness holding is presented elsewhere (Baldus et al., 1990, pp. 370–394). In summary, we believe, first, that Justice Powell misconceived the capacity of multivariate statistical analyses of the type we employed in *McCleskey* to prove both the fact that a pattern and practice of purposeful racial discrimination exists as well as the likelihood or "risk" that such practices *may* exist. Second, we regard his summary rejection of McCleskey's risk argument as unpersuasive because it fails to identify why the very considerable risk of racial discrimination suggested by our data was insufficient to establish a constitutional violation.

Notes and Questions

1. In Justice Brennan's *McCleskey* dissent he warned,

> [I]t has been scarcely a generation since this Court's first decision striking down racial segregation, and barely two decades since the legislative prohibition of racial discrimination in major domains of national life. These have been honorable steps, but we cannot pretend that in three decades we have completely escaped the grip of a historical legacy spanning centuries.... [W]e remain imprisoned by the past as long as we deny its influence on the present.

A. Leon Higginbotham Jr., the former Chief Judge of the United States Court of Appeals for the Third Circuit, put it this way:

> The impact of our heritage of slave laws will continue to make itself felt into the future. For there is a nexus between the brutal centuries of colonial slavery and the racial polarization and anxieties of today. The poisonous legacy of legalized oppression based upon the matter of color can never be adequately purged from our society if we act as if slave laws had never existed.

The Tallahassee Democrat newspaper picked up on the theme of residual effects of slavery in an editorial written shortly after *McCleskey* was handed down.

> It is the same reasoning that enabled the Court in the late 1800's to approve the "separate-but-equal" doctrine for the nation's schools.... In *McCleskey* the Court essentially says Blacks must accept a separate-and-unequal system of justice in capital cases.

Do you agree? Do you think Justice Powell's majority opinion in *McCleskey* fails to adequately consider the residual effects slavery has on modern racial attitudes? Or is slavery as an historical event too remote to form a basis for constitutional decisionmaking? How would you explain data collected by Watt Espy which indicates that from the 1910s to the 1950s between 60–70% of the people executed for murder in the South were black? Schnieder & Smykla, "A Summary Analysis of Execution in the United States, 1608–1987," in *The Death Penalty in America*, Current Research 1, 12 tbl.1.5 (Robert M. Bohm ed. 1991).

2. After *McCleskey*, is there any remedy available for a capital defendant whose conviction or sentence has been infected with undue racial bias? Of course, all criminal cases suffer from a risk that racial prejudice will influence the jury's decision. The question is, "at what point that risk becomes constitutionally unacceptable." *McCleskey*, 481 U.S. at 308–309.

In *Dobbs v. Zant*, 963 F.2d 1403, 1407–1408 (11th Cir. 1991), the court rejected an equal protection claim based in part on the fact that the trial judge referred to the defendant Dobbs as "colored" and Dobbs' trial attorney admitted believing that blacks in general are morally and intellectually inferior to whites. How did Dobbs' racial bias claim fail to satisfy *McCleskey*?

Similarly in *Griffin v. Dugger*, 874 F.2d 1397 (11th Cir. 1989), the court rejected a *McCleskey* claim. Griffin argued unsuccessfully that (1) the prosecutor improperly addressed the race of the victims in his case and in other death penalty cases, and (2) statistical studies demonstrated a correlation between the imposition of the death sentence and the victim's race. Taken together, Griffin claimed, these two forms of evidence demonstrated the unconstitutionality of his death sentence. Why do you suppose Griffin's equal protection argument failed? See *id.* at 1399–1402.

According to Professor David Baldus, "Only one American legislative body has adopted a law that would give murder defendants the right to advance claims of racial discrimination in the same manner available to racial minorities in the employment, housing, and public accommodations context. In 1998, Kentucky passed legislation that permits a capital defendant to challenge a prosecutorial decision to seek a death sentence on the ground that it was 'sought on the basis of race.' 1998 Ky. Acts 252." Baldus, et al., "Racial Discrimination and the Death Penalty in the Post-*Furman* Era," 83 Cornell L. Rev. 1638, 1644 & n.2 (1998). How do you explain that it is easier for plaintiffs to establish discrimination in housing, employment and public accommodations than it is for capital murder defendants to prove racial bias connected to their prosecution?

3. Death penalty supporters respond to arguments of racial bias in capital cases by arguing, principally, that society's interest in retribution, justice, and the concern for the victims of the crime and their families trump equal protection concerns. Further, they argue that racial discrimination in no way diminishes either the culpability of the defendants who are sentenced to death or society's justification for executing them. Finally, death penalty proponents claim that racial discrimination is inevitable and perva-

sive in all our social institutions. Eradicating racism in capital cases would require abolishing the death penalty, which many death penalty supporters find morally unacceptable. Do you believe that the costs of eliminating the death penalty clearly outweigh any harms caused by racial discrimination? See Baldus, et al., "Racial Discrimination and the Death Penalty in the Post-*Furman* Era," 83 Cornell L. Rev. 1638, 1652 (1998).

4. Consider the 1998 Texas murder of James Byrd, Jr., a black, disabled, 49-year-old former vacuum cleaner salesman and father of three. Shawn Berry and Bill King, two 23-year-old avowed white supremacists, along with their roommate, 31-year-old Russell Brewer, kidnapped and assaulted Byrd, sprayed black paint on his face, pulled his pants and underwear down, then chained him by his ankles to a pickup truck. The trio then dragged Byrd, alive and conscious, for three miles on a paved road until a concrete culvert beside the road decapitated him. The three white men dumped Byrd's "shredded torso, minus his head, an arm and shoulder" at the end of a country road situated "directly between a black cemetery and church." Alfieri, "Prosecuting Violence/Reconstructing Community," 52 Stan. L. Rev. 809, 819–20 (2000). All three defendants were charged with capital murder. In 1999, separate, predominantly white juries found King and Brewer guilty and sentenced them to death. An all-white jury found Berry guilty, but sentenced him to life in prison.

5. Race discrimination also pervaded the administration of the death penalty in the case of Walter McMillian, a black man framed and sentenced to die for the murder of a white woman. McMillian was convicted based on false testimony generated by law enforcement officials. McMillian's race, his history of dating a white woman, and the victim's race made him particularly vulnerable to a wrongful conviction and death sentence. See *McMillian v. State*, 616 So.2d 933 (Ala. Crim. App. 1993) (overturning McMillian's conviction).

6. In 1980, the nude body of blonde, blue-eyed cheerleader Cheryl Fergeson was found in the high school auditorium in Conroe, Texas. One week later, 28-year-old janitor Clarence Lee Brandley, the only black man at the scene of the crime, was charged with raping and strangling her. The day of the murder, a police officer, addressing Brandley and his white co-worker Icky Peace, predicted, "One of you two is going to hang for this." Turning to Brandley, the police officer continued: "Since you're the nigger, you're elected."

Brandley's first trial, before an all-white jury, resulted in a mistrial. Brandley's second trial, before another all-white jury, resulted in his conviction and death sentence. Brandley spent nine years on death row before the Texas Court of Criminal Appeals overturned his conviction in 1989. Prosecutors decided to drop charges against Brandley after the state courts which reversed his conviction characterized Brandley's trial as "lack[ing] the rudiments of fairness" and the police investigation which led to his arrest as "a blind focus aimed at convicting Brandley rather than finding the killer." McKay, *Brandley's Charges Dropped After Ruling*, Hous. Chron., Oct. 2, 1990, at A1. An account of the small town racism which led to Brandley's wrongful conviction and death sentence can be found in Davies, *White Lies: Rape, Murder and Justice Texas Style* (Pantheon Books, 1991).

7. *McCleskey* was not the first decision in which the Court wrestled with the issue of racism in capital cases. In his *Furman* concurrence (*supra* chapter 3), Justice Douglas touched upon the issue of discrimination and its relevance to the Eighth Amendment.

It would seem incontestable that the death penalty inflicted on one defendant is "unusual" if it discriminates against him by reason of his race, religion, wealth, social position, or class, or if it is imposed under a procedure that gives room for the play of such prejudices.

> [T]he discretion of judges and juries in imposing the death penalty enables the penalty to be selectively applied, feeding prejudices against the accused if he is poor and despised, and lacking political clout, or if he is a member of a suspect and unpopular minority, and saving those who, by social position, may be in a more protected position.

408 U.S. 238, 242 (1972) (Douglas, J., concurring).

Justice Thurgood Marshall's *Furman* opinion was characteristically more blunt:

> Regarding discrimination, it has been said that "[i]t is usually the poor, the illiterate, the underprivileged, the member of the minority group—the man who, because he is without means, and is defended by a court-appointed attorney—who becomes society's sacrificial lamb...." Indeed, a look at the bare statistics regarding executions is enough to betray much of the discrimination. A total of 3,859 persons have been executed since 1930, of whom 1,751 were white and 2,066 were Negro. Of the executions, 3,334 were for murder; 1,664 of the executed murderers were white and 1,630 were Negro; 455 persons, including 48 whites and 405 Negroes, were executed for rape. It is immediately apparent that Negroes were executed far more often than whites in proportion to their percentage of the population. Studies indicate that while the higher rate of execution among Negroes is partially due to a higher rate of crime, there is evidence of racial discrimination.... In *McGautha v. California*, 402 U.S. at 207, this Court held "that committing to the untrammelled discretion of the jury the power to pronounce life or death in capital cases is [not] offensive to anything in the Constitution." This was an open invitation to discrimination.

408 U.S. 238, 364–65 (Marshall, J. concurring).

In dissent, Justice Powell responded to Justice Marshall.

> [D]iscriminatory application of the death penalty in the past, admittedly indefensible, is no justification for holding today that capital punishment is invalid in all cases in which sentences are handed out to members of the class discriminated against....
>
> The possibility of racial bias in the trial and sentencing process has diminished in recent years. The segregation of our society in decades past, which contributed substantially to the severity of punishment for interracial crimes, is now no longer prevalent in this country. Likewise, the day is past when juries do not represent the minority group elements of the community. The assurance of fair trials for all citizens is greater today than at any previous time in our history. Because standards of criminal justice have "evolved" in a manner favorable to the accused, discriminatory imposition of capital punishment is far less likely today than in the past.

408 U.S. 238, 450 (Powell, J. dissenting).

8. Executions resumed almost immediately following the 1976 *Gregg* decision. Gary Gilmore, a white man convicted of murdering a white victim, waived all appeals and died before Utah's firing squad on January 17, 1977. The next inmate executed was John Spenkelink, a white man convicted of murdering another white man. Spenkelink died in Florida's electric chair on May 25, 1979. However, not until late 1991—fourteen years after executions resumed—was a white inmate executed for the murder of a black

victim. After an unsuccessful suicide attempt, Donald (Pee Wee) Gaskins, a white death row inmate in South Carolina, was electrocuted on September 6, 1991 for the murder of a black fellow inmate.

Prior to Gaskins, the last white person put to death in this country for killing a black person died in Kansas in 1944. At the time of Gaskins' execution, South Carolina had not executed a white person convicted of killing a black person since 1880.

9. Charles Brooks became the first black death row inmate executed after *Gregg.* Brooks was convicted of murdering a white man and died in Texas' lethal injection chamber on December 7, 1982. Brooks' execution also made history as the first legal execution by lethal injection in the United States.

10. Professor Baldus' study suggests a prosecutorial bias which favors defendants who kill black victims. As Justice Brennan's dissent noted, the Baldus study demonstrated that "6 of every 11 defendants convicted of killing a white person would not have received the death penalty if their victims had been black, while, among defendants with aggravating and mitigating factors comparable to McCleskey, 20 of every 34 would not have been sentenced to die if their victims had been black." According to Fred Tinsley, a veteran defense attorney in Dallas, Texas, "At one point, with a black-on-black murder, you could get it dismissed if the defendant would pay funeral expenses." What conclusions, if any, can be drawn from these statistics?

In 2001, Professor Jack Boger released a study of death penalty cases in North Carolina from the 1990s which concluded that the odds of getting a death sentence increased three and a half times if the victim was white rather than black or Hispanic. Professor Boger's study examined all 3,990 homicide cases in North Carolina from 1993 to 1997. Of the potentially capital cases brought during this period, 11.6% of nonwhite defendants charged with murdering white defendants were sentenced to death. In contrast, 6.1% of white defendants charged with murdering white victims and 5% of white defendants charged with murdering nonwhite victims were sentenced to death. Finally, 4.7% of nonwhite defendants charged with murdering nonwhite victims received the death penalty. According to Professor Boger, the study indicates not that prosecutors sought the death penalty more often for black defendants, but that prosecutors were more willing to plea bargain for sentences less than death if the victim was black. Butterfield, *Victims' Race Affects Decisions on Killers' Sentence, Study Finds*, The New York Times, Apr. 20, 2001, at A10.

In 2005, a study tallied the races of California homicide victims during the 1990s and found that defendants who murdered whites were almost 4 times more likely to be sentenced to death than those who killed Hispanics, and 3 times more likely to be sentenced to death than those who killed blacks. Of 263 death sentences handed down during that period, 142 were handed down for killing whites, 44 for killing blacks, 52 for killing Hispanics, and 25 for killing victims of other races. Eighty per cent of executions in California were for those convicted of killing whites, while only 27.6% of murder victims are white. Pierce & Radelet, "The Impact of Legally Inappropriate Factors on Death Sentencing for California Homicides, 1990–99," 46 Santa Clara L. Rev. 1 (2005).

11. According to a U.S. Justice Department study, of the 682 potential federal death penalty cases U.S. attorneys forwarded to Justice for review between 1995 and July 2000, 20 percent of the defendants were white and 80 percent were non-white. U.S. attorneys recommended the death penalty be sought for 183 defendants, 26 percent of them white and 74 percent non-white. Between 1988 and March of 2003, the federal government authorized seeking the death penalty against 211 defendants. Of the 211 approved

prosecutions, 158 (75%) were against minority defendants. Of these defendants, 53 were white, 39 Hispanic, 12 Asian/Indian/Pacific Islander, 2 Arab and 105 African American. Of the 38 inmates on federal death row as of May 24, 2005, 24 (63%) are members of a minority group. "Federal Death Row Prisoners," located at www.death-penaltyinfo.org. The federal death penalty is examined in chapter 18, *infra*.

12. Does the predominantly white control of the American criminal justice system contribute to the risk of racial discrimination in capital cases? According to Professor Baldus,

> In many places in the United States, prosecutors, judges, and penalty-trial jurors are predominantly white even though the defendants whose cases they hear are not. The conventional wisdom is that white jurors are less likely to sympathize with black defendants or to identify with black victims. Convincing evidence also suggests that many participants in the system, both black and nonblack, consider young black males more deserving of severe punishment because they are violence prone, morally inferior, and a threat to the community. The danger for black defendants in the system is particularly acute when the attorneys who represent them entertain racial stereotypes that diminish the quality and vigor of their representation.

> The risk of both race-of-defendant and race-of-victim discrimination is also enhanced when the jury selection processes result in the serious underrepresentation of blacks on criminal trial juries. This underrepresentation is a widespread problem. First, blacks are often underrepresented on both the voter and automobile registrations lists from which most jury venires are drawn. Second, low income citizens are less likely to appear for jury service, and courts are more likely to excuse them for hardship. Third, and most important, prosecutors have the wide-ranging discretion to strike prospective jurors through the exercise of "peremptory" challenges. The result is that many black defendants receive sentences from juries with only a few or no blacks. This problem is particularly acute when the attorneys assigned to represent them are inexperienced or indifferent, making it easier for prosecutors to strike blacks because their strikes are not effectively challenged.... Finally, explicit prosecutorial references to the jury of the race of the defendant or the victim (e.g., "Can you imagine her state of mind ... staring into the muzzle of a gun held by this black man?") as well as racial slurs and other appeals to racial prejudice, such as the use of animal metaphors in describing the defendant (e.g., "this animal" who "shouldn't be out of his cell unless he has a leash on him") exacerbate the risk of racial discrimination. Slurs of this type have come from prosecutors, judges, and defense counsel.

Baldus, et al., "Racial Discrimination and the Death Penalty in the Post-*Furman* Era," 83 Cornell L. Rev. 1638, 1724–25 (1998).

13. For further discussion of racial bias and jury selection, see *infra* chapter 6.

14. For the most recent statistics on the number of prisoners on death row nationwide and the race of these inmates and their victims, see Coyne & Entzeroth, Supplement to Capital Punishment and the Judicial Process.

Note on Justice Lewis Powell's Transformation

Justice Lewis Powell dissented in *Furman*, joined the majority in *Gregg*, and frequently voted to uphold capital convictions and death sentences. Nonetheless, soon after he retired from the Court in 1987, Justice Lewis Powell began to express growing doubts about the death penalty. In an analysis of capital punishment published in 1989, Powell surveyed the problems of "excessively repetitious litigation" in capital cases. "If capital punishment cannot be enforced even where innocence is not an issue and the fairness of the trial is not seriously questioned," Powell wrote, "perhaps Congress and the state legislatures should take a serious look at whether the retention of a punishment that is being enforced only haphazardly is in the public interest." Powell, "Commentary: Capital Punishment," 102 Harv. L. Rev. 1035–46 (1989).

The following year, during an interview, he echoed this sentiment: "[I]f I were in the state legislature, I would vote against capital punishment. There are approximately 2,500 people who have been convicted of murder and sentenced to death..., and there have been only about 125 to 130 executions. Capital punishment, though constitutional, is not being enforced. I think it reflects discredit on the law to have a major component of the law that is simply not enforced." DeBenedictis, *The Reasonable Man*, ABA Journal, Oct. 1990, p. 69.

One year later, in 1991, during a conversation with his biographer, Professor John C. Jeffries, Jr., Justice Powell "took the final step." Jeffries asked Justice Powell whether he would change his vote in any case:

> Yes. *McCleskey v. Kemp*.
>
> Do you mean you would now accept the argument from the statistics?
>
> No. I would vote the other way in any capital case.
>
> In *any* capital case?
>
> Yes.
>
> Even in *Furman v. Georgia*?
>
> Yes. I have come to think that capital punishment should be abolished.

Professor Jeffries has explained that, for Justice Powell,

> "the death penalty should be barred, not because it was intrinsically wrong but because it could not be fairly and expeditiously enforced. The endless waiting, merry-go-round litigation, last-minute stays, and midnight executions offended Powell's sense of dignity and his conception of the majesty of the law. The spectacle of nonenforcement bred cynicism about the law's announced purposes and contempt for the courts that could not or would not carry them out. Better to have done with the whole ugly mess than to continue an indecent, embarrassing, and wasteful charade."

Jeffries, *Justice Lewis F. Powell, Jr.*, 451–52 (Charles Scribner's Sons 1994).

As author of the 5–4 majority opinion in *McCleskey v. Kemp*, Justice Powell ensured that Warren McCleskey would be put to death. In 1991, the year Justice Powell renounced his vote in *McCleskey* and announced his belief that the death penalty should be abolished, Warren McCleskey died in Georgia's electric chair for a murder he committed 13 years earlier.

Note on Racial Discrimination During Jury Selection

Consider the invidious role race played in the capital conviction of Patricia Jackson, *Jackson v. Thigpen*, 752 F. Supp. 1551 (N.D. Ala. 1990). Trial counsel failed to properly prepare for the sentencing stage because he erroneously believed that Jackson's "'worse case scenario' [was] ... a manslaughter conviction—a view no doubt based upon the fact that both defendant and victim were black and that the case involved a 'shothouse killing.'" Counsel was wrong and Jackson was sentenced to death.

In addition, the jury selection process suffered from racially-motivated practices intended to prevent African-American jurors from serving on Jackson's jury in violation of the then-existing constitutional standard of *Swain v. Alabama*, 380 U.S. 202 (1965). According to the district court in *Jackson*:

> Petitioner's venire consisted of eighty-six persons—seventy whites and sixteen blacks. Six whites and four blacks were excused for cause, leaving a reduced venire of twelve blacks and sixty-four whites. The prosecutor used his twenty-two peremptory challenges to remove all of the twelve blacks and ten of the whites.

> Gerald Hudson, the lead prosecuting attorney, testified that he struck all blacks from petitioner's venire because, in his judgment, black jurors are less willing to give the State a fair trial and are less likely to convict. Hudson also testified that black jurors tend to be more forgiving and more willing to give a defendant a second or third chance than are white jurors.

> Credible anecdotal evidence shows that Hudson's opinion of black jurors was universally shared by other assistant district attorneys in Tuscaloosa County. Where a prosecutor was personally acquainted with a black venireperson, that venireperson might not be stricken by the prosecutor. Otherwise, the standard operating procedure of the Tuscaloosa County District Attorney's Office at the time of petitioner's trial was to use the peremptory challenges to strike as many blacks as possible from the venires in cases involving serious crimes.

> The statistical evidence confirms that the prosecutor's use of the peremptory challenges at petitioner's trial and prior thereto excluded black citizens from participation in the administration of the criminal justice system. The report of Dr. Chester I. Palmer, Jr., an expert called by respondent, indicates that ... [t]here can be no reasonable doubt that, both in all cases 1981–85 and in Hudson's case, there was a pattern that blacks were more likely to be subjected to peremptory strikes by the prosecution than were whites on the same venires. On the average, in 1981–85 the prosecution used 2.42 more peremptory strikes on blacks than expected by random selection; in Hudson's cases, the comparable figure is 2.58....

> Thus, these analyses indicate that the prosecution was more likely to exercise its peremptory challenges against blacks than against whites on the same venires. As indicated above, it is not possible to determine from the data the extent that effect might have been caused by differences other than race between the pools of blacks and whites on the venires.

> According to Dr. Palmer, the probability is *de minimis* that the disparate use of peremptory challenges against blacks is attributable to chance—less than three out of ten million. Reviewing the same evidence, petitioner's expert, Dr. Robert Sigler, a professor of Criminal Justice, agreed. Dr. Sigler concluded that blacks were systematically excluded from jury service in serious criminal cases by prosecutors who felt that blacks would not convict. The experts were in agreement that 28% fewer blacks served on criminal juries in Tuscaloosa County than would have been expected to serve by random selection; that blacks were underrepresented on 70% of the criminal juries in Tuscaloosa

County; and that the Tuscaloosa County District Attorney's Office struck 28% more blacks than would have been expected by random selection. This situation existed at the time of petitioner's trial and it continued for the next four years.

The Tuscaloosa County prosecutors also manipulated the trial docket in their effort to preserve the racial purity of criminal juries. Inasmuch as they actually set the criminal trial dockets until 1982, they implemented a scheme in which juries with fewer black venirepersons would be called for the serious cases.

The use of peremptory challenges by the Tuscaloosa County District Attorney's Office effectively resulted in the systematic exclusion of blacks from trial juries in serious criminal cases prior to 1982. In cases involving black defendants and white alleged victims, the exclusion of blacks also occurred in cases where both the defendant and the alleged victim were black and resulted in the all-white jury that tried petitioner.

[Defendant's trial counsel] testified that in his many years of practicing criminal law in Tuscaloosa County, he has never filed a motion attacking the racial composition of juries. He testified, to the astonishment of this court, that in his first few years of practice, the names of black venirepersons were removed by the circuit clerk prior to empanelment. While he served as an assistant district attorney in Tuscaloosa County, he was aware of a "tendency" on the part of young assistant district attorneys to strike black venirepersons. In fact, some of these assistants admitted to him that they always struck the available blacks from the jury venires. He was aware, of course, that the young assistant district attorney in this very case used the state's peremptory challenges to strike all the blacks from the jury that tried his client.

What is the appropriate remedy in this case?

Note on Allegations of Racial Discrimination in *Miller-El v. Dretke, 545 U.S. 231 (2005)*

Thomas Joe Miller was convicted and sentenced to death by a Texas jury. In finding Miller-El was entitled to relief based on his claim that the prosecutor used his peremptory challenges to improperly strike African-American jurors from the jury panel, the Supreme Court summarized some of the evidence of racial discrimination that infected the jury selection process in Miller-El's case. Miller-El's case is also discussed in chapter 6, Selecting the Capital Jury, and in chapter 13, Introduction to Federal Habeas Corpus Review. The following is an excerpt from Justice Souter's majority opinion in *Miller-El v. Dretke, 545 U.S. 231 (2005)*.

Miller-El v. Dretke
545 U.S. 231 (2005)

Justice SOUTER delivered the opinion of the Court.

III

A

The numbers describing the prosecution's use of peremptories are remarkable. Out of 20 black members of the 108-person venire panel for Miller-El's trial, only 1 served.

Although 9 were excused for cause or by agreement, 10 were peremptorily struck by the prosecution. "The prosecutors used their peremptory strikes to exclude 91% of the eligible African-American venire members.... Happenstance is unlikely to produce this disparity."....

B

The case for discrimination goes beyond these comparisons [between black and non-black potential jurors] to include broader patterns of practice during the jury selection. The prosecution's shuffling of the venire panel, its enquiry into views on the death penalty, its questioning about minimum acceptable sentences: all indicate decisions probably based on race. Finally, the appearance of discrimination is confirmed by widely known evidence of the general policy of the Dallas County District Attorney's Office to exclude black venire members from juries at the time Miller-El's jury was selected.

The first clue to the prosecutors' intentions, distinct from the peremptory challenges themselves, is their resort during voir dire to a procedure known in Texas as the jury shuffle. In the State's criminal practice, either side may literally reshuffle the cards bearing panel members' names, thus rearranging the order in which members of a venire panel are seated and reached for questioning. Once the order is established, the panel members seated at the back are likely to escape voir dire altogether, for those not questioned by the end of the week are dismissed. As we previously explained,

> "the prosecution's decision to seek a jury shuffle when a predominant number of African-Americans were seated in the front of the panel, along with its decision to delay a formal objection to the defense's shuffle until after the new racial composition was revealed, raise a suspicion that the State sought to exclude African-Americans from the jury. Our concerns are amplified by the fact that the state court also had before it, and apparently ignored, testimony demonstrating that the Dallas County District Attorney's Office had, by its own admission, used this process to manipulate the racial composition of the jury in the past."

In this case, the prosecution and then the defense shuffled the cards at the beginning of the first week of voir dire; the record does not reflect the changes in order. At the beginning of the second week, when a number of black members were seated at the front of the panel, the prosecution shuffled. At the beginning of the third week, the first four panel members were black. The prosecution shuffled, and these black panel members ended up at the back. Then the defense shuffled, and the black panel members again appeared at the front. The prosecution requested another shuffle, but the trial court refused. Finally, the defense shuffled at the beginning of the fourth and fifth weeks of voir dire; the record does not reflect the panel's racial composition before or after those shuffles.

The State notes in its brief that there might be racially neutral reasons for shuffling the jury, and we suppose there might be. But no racially neutral reason has ever been offered in this case, and nothing stops the suspicion of discriminatory intent from rising to an inference.

The next body of evidence that the State was trying to avoid black jurors is the contrasting voir dire questions posed respectively to black and nonblack panel members, on two different subjects. First, there were the prosecutors' statements preceding questions about a potential juror's thoughts on capital punishment. Some of these prefatory statements were cast in general terms, but some followed the so-called graphic script, describing the method of execution in rhetorical and clinical detail. It is intended, Miller-El contends, to prompt some expression of hesitation to consider the death penalty and thus to elicit plausibly neutral grounds for a peremptory strike of a potential juror subjected to it, if not a strike for cause. If the graphic script is given to a higher proportion of blacks than whites, this is evidence that prosecutors more often wanted blacks off the jury, absent some neutral and extenuating explanation....

The State concedes that this disparate questioning did occur but argues that use of the graphic script turned not on a panelist's race but on expressed ambivalence about the death penalty in the preliminary questionnaire. Prosecutors were trying, the argument goes, to weed out noncommittal or uncertain jurors, not black jurors. And while some white venire members expressed opposition to the death penalty on their questionnaires, they were not read the graphic script because their feelings were already clear. The State says that giving the graphic script to these panel members would only have antagonized them.

This argument, however, first advanced in dissent when the case was last here, *Miller-El v. Cockrell,* (opinion of Thomas, J.), and later adopted by the State and the Court of Appeals, simply does not fit the facts. Looking at the answers on the questionnaires, and at voir dire testimony expressly discussing answers on the questionnaires, we find that black venire members were more likely than nonblacks to receive the graphic script regardless of their expressions of certainty or ambivalence about the death penalty, and the State's chosen explanation for the graphic script fails in the cases of four out of the eight black panel members who received it....

The State's attempt at a race-neutral rationalization thus simply fails to explain what the prosecutors did. But if we posit instead that the prosecutors' first object was to use the graphic script to make a case for excluding black panel members opposed to or ambivalent about the death penalty, there is a much tighter fit of fact and explanation. Of the 10 nonblacks whose questionnaires expressed ambivalence or opposition, only 30% received the graphic treatment. But of the seven blacks who expressed ambivalence or opposition, 86% heard the graphic script. As between the State's ambivalence explanation and Miller-El's racial one, race is much the better, and the reasonable inference is that race was the major consideration when the prosecution chose to follow the graphic script.

The same is true for another kind of disparate questioning, which might fairly be called trickery. The prosecutors asked members of the panel how low a sentence they would consider imposing for murder. Most potential jurors were first told that Texas law provided for a minimum term of five years, but some members of the panel were not, and if a panel member then insisted on a minimum above five years, the prosecutor would suppress his normal preference for tough jurors and claim cause to strike. Two Terms ago, we described how this disparate questioning was correlated with race:

> "Ninety-four percent of whites were informed of the statutory minimum sentence, compared [with] only twelve and a half percent of African-Americans. No explanation is proffered for the statistical disparity....

The State concedes that the manipulative minimum punishment questioning was used to create cause to strike, but now it offers the extenuation that prosecutors omitted the 5-year information not on the basis of race, but on stated opposition to the death penalty, or ambivalence about it, on the questionnaires and in the voir dire testimony.

On the State's identification of black panel members opposed or ambivalent, all were asked the trick question. But the State's rationale flatly fails to explain why most white panel members who expressed similar opposition or ambivalence were not subjected to it. It is entirely true, as the State argues, that prosecutors struck a number of nonblack members of the panel (as well as black members) for cause or by agreement before they reached the point in the standard voir dire sequence to question about minimum punishment. But this is no answer; 8 of the 11 nonblack individuals who voiced opposition or ambivalence were asked about the acceptable minimum only after being told what state law required. Hence, only 27% of nonblacks questioned on the subject who expressed these views were subjected to the trick question, as against 100% of black members. Once again, the implication of race in the prosecutors' choice of questioning cannot be explained away.

There is a final body of evidence that confirms this conclusion. We know that for decades leading up to the time this case was tried prosecutors in the Dallas County office had followed a specific policy of systematically excluding blacks from juries, as we explained the last time the case was here.

> "Although most of the witnesses [presented at the *Swain* hearing in 1986] denied the existence of a systematic policy to exclude African-Americans, others disagreed. A Dallas County district judge testified that, when he had served in the District Attorney's Office from the late-1950's to early-1960's, his superior warned him that he would be fired if he permitted any African-Americans to serve on a jury. Similarly, another Dallas County district judge and former assistant district attorney from 1976 to 1978 testified that he believed the office had a systematic policy of excluding African-Americans from juries.

> "Of more importance, the defense presented evidence that the District Attorney's Office had adopted a formal policy to exclude minorities from jury service.... .A manual entitled 'Jury Selection in a Criminal Case' [sometimes known as the Sparling Manual] was distributed to prosecutors. It contained an article authored by a former prosecutor (and later a judge) under the direction of his superiors in the District Attorney's Office, outlining the reasoning for excluding minorities from jury service. Although the manual was written in 1968, it remained in circulation until 1976, if not later, and was available at least to one of the prosecutors in Miller-El's trial."

Prosecutors here "marked the race of each prospective juror on their juror cards."

The Court of Appeals concluded that Miller-El failed to show by clear and convincing evidence that the state court's finding of no discrimination was wrong, whether his evidence was viewed collectively or separately. We find this conclusion as unsupportable as the "dismissive and strained interpretation" of his evidence that we disapproved when we decided Miller-El was entitled to a certificate of appealability..It is true, of course, that at some points the significance of Miller-El's evidence is open to judgment calls, but when this evidence on the issues raised is viewed cumulatively its direction is too powerful to conclude anything but discrimination....

* * *

Justice Thomas wrote a lengthy dissent in *Miller-El* explaining in detail that he did not believe that Miller-El had presented clear and convincing evidence of racial discrimination. Chief Justice Rehnquist and Justice Scalia joined Justice Thomas' dissent.

C. The Effects of Gender

Are women disproportionately underrepresented on death row? In his concurring opinion in *Furman*, Justice Thurgood Marshall raised the prospect of gender discrimination in capital cases.

> There is also overwhelming evidence that the death penalty is employed against men and not women. Only 32 women have been executed since 1930, while 3,827 men have met a similar fate. It is difficult to understand why women have received such favored treatment since the purposes allegedly served by capital punishment seemingly are equally applicable to both sexes.

Furman v. Georgia, 408 U.S. 238, 365 (1972).

Nonetheless, in rejecting Warren McCleskey's claim that impermissible racism should invalidate Georgia's capital sentencing system, the Court strongly hinted that— even in the face of convincing evidence of gender discrimination—male death row inmates would be unsuccessful in challenging their sentences on the ground that men are disproportionately selected for death. Recall Justice Powell's majority opinion:

> Thus, if we accepted McCleskey's claim that racial bias has impermissibly tainted the capital sentencing decision, we could soon be faced with similar claims as to other types of penalty. Moreover, the claim that his sentence rests on the irrelevant factor of race easily could be extended to apply to claims based on unexplained discrepancies that correlate to membership in other minority groups, *and even to gender.*

McCleskey v. Kemp, 481 U.S. 279, 315–317 (1987) (emphasis added). Thus, as an additional reason for denying McCleskey relief, the Court explained that a contrary result would open the door to similar complaints about lesser penalties, and "throw[ ] into serious question the principles that underlie our entire criminal justice system."

Death Penalty for Female Offenders
Victor L. Streib, 58 U. Cin. L. Rev. 845 (1990)

Two categories of questions result from reviewing the imposition of the death penalty on females. First, why have so comparatively few females received this sentence, at least as compared to males sentenced to death and actually executed during the same time periods? Second, focussing upon those few females who were selected, what about them or their crimes might have led to this extremely rare consequence?

Gender-bias probably has two major sources—the express provisions of the law and the implicit attitudes, either conscious or subconscious, of key actors involved in the criminal justice process. Exploring the former, all current death penalty statutes list specific aggravating and mitigating factors that tend to increase or decrease the seriousness of the crime and the culpability of the offender. Also the statutes provide express guidance for the sentencing decision. None expressly mention the gender of the defendant as a factor to be considered, but they do include considerations which may tend to apply with different weight to male and female offenders.

… One such factor is the offender's previous criminal behavior, ranging from murder to attempted homicide to any threatened personal violence. Some states include this factor under both aggravating and mitigating circumstances. Obviously, this factor is intended to single out those present murderers who have engaged in the same or seemingly related behavior in the past and to rely in part upon their past behavior to increase the probability of more severe punishment (here, execution instead of imprisonment) for their present murder.

Consistent with the fact that women commit fewer crimes than men, female defendants tend to have less significant prior criminal records than do male defendants. Not only do they commit fewer crimes in general than men, but their crimes also tend to be less violent than those of men. This difference continues despite some recent increase in crimes by women generally. Also, women arrested for murder are more likely to be first offenders than women who are arrested for other crimes. Therefore, female defendants in capital sentencing proceedings are much less likely than their male counterparts to need to counter a damaging past criminal record and, in some instances, may be able to point to an absence of such a record as a mitigating circumstance in their favor.

A related aggravating factor is one which would increase the punishment for the present murder based in part upon a prediction of future violent crimes.... All other things being equal, research indicates that most observers do not see female offenders generally as being as dangerous to society as they see male offenders. Consistent with this is the perception among sentencing judges that women are better candidates for rehabilitation than are men. This tendency to predict a more benign future for female offenders, coupled with less retributive grounds from past offenses, would tend to benefit female defendants in capital sentencing.

Premeditation is commonly a requirement for capital murder or is at least a factor on the list of aggravating and mitigating factors. Having originally been the element that distinguished first degree murder from all other forms of criminal homicide, a premeditated killing seems somehow worse than one committed on impulse or in reaction to provocation. Research indicates that few homicides committed by women are premeditated. Homicides by women tend to involve sudden, unplanned acts in the context of a family squabble or drunken conflict. In fact, this typical lack of premeditation means that homicides by women will be less serious crimes, resulting in lighter sentences in general and often precluding the possibility of the death penalty being imposed. This factor may well carry over to capital cases as well, resulting in less chance that the aggravating factor of premeditation will be applied against female offenders.

Another aggravating factor of major significance is whether the homicide was part of a felony-murder. These crimes involve intentional killings integral to perpetration of a felony such as robbery or rape.... It is clear that females are only very rarely involved in felony murders. Thus, this aggravating factor tends to work only against male offenders, at least in the typical felony-murder case.

One common mitigating factor is that the capital crime was committed while the defendant was under extreme mental or emotional disturbance. Research findings indicate a common public perception that female murderers are more likely to be emotionally disturbed than are male murderers under identical circumstances. Though many would challenge the accuracy of this perception, the perception is widespread and presumably is present among sentencing judges and juries. If the female defendant can muster any reasonable evidence of such mental or emotional disturbance, the judge and jury may be more likely to weigh this mitigating factor in her favor.

Acting under the substantial domination of another person is another common mitigating factor in the capital sentencing process. Females often are perceived as more likely than males to be in this category. For cases in which a woman and a man are arrested together for the same crime, it is most common for a man to have been the principal actor and the woman to have been the lesser involved accessory. Many involved in the criminal justice system generally believe that a female offender is frequently involved in the crime because of her commitment to a husband or a lover. If these perceptions are held by sentencing judges and juries in capital cases, the result could be a gender-bias mitigating against sentencing females to death. As with the other factors, this mitigating factor is proved partly by producing objective evidence and partly by playing upon the presumptions and perceptions the judge and jury bring with them to the case.

The sentencing judge and jury must consider any relevant mitigating factor the defendant introduces. This encourages defense attorneys to bring in a variety of sympathetic evidence on the character and background of the defendant, perhaps hitting a particularly soft spot if the defendant is a woman or girl rather than a man or boy. Even when all of the specific aggravating and mitigating factors are the same for male and female defendants, females still tend to receive significantly lighter sentences in criminal cases generally. Judges admit that they tend to be more lenient toward female offenders in general. Also, juries generally tend to be more lenient toward female offenders, particularly in serious crimes, for a variety of ingrained, cultural reasons besides those analyzed above. This tendency is consistent with the extraordinarily low number of death sentences and executions of adult female offenders in our history.

Why Were These Females Condemned to Death?

If female offenders have been the recipients of gender-bias away from imposing death sentences and executions, why were 398 females executed [in this country during the past three centuries] and why were seventy females recently sentenced to death? Definitive answers to these questions are beyond the current capabilities of this research but some informed speculation may be helpful.

The executed females tended to be very poor, uneducated, and of the lowest social class in the community. Their victims tended to be white and of particularly protected classes, either children or socially prominent adults. Comparatively few executed females committed their crimes with a co-offender, so they could not claim they were under the domination of another. Most of the executed females manifested an attitude of violence, either from past behavior or present acts, that countered any presumption of nonviolence. Finally, and perhaps most fatally for them, they committed shockingly "unladylike" behavior, allowing the sentencing judges and juries to put aside any image of them as "the gentler sex" and to treat them as "crazed monsters" deserving of nothing more than extermination.

The seventy females sentenced to death in the recent era also tend to fit the pattern developed above. They tend to be poor, undereducated, and of the lowest social class in the community. Predictably, their victims tend to be white and of particularly protected classes.

While some of the recently sentenced females committed their crimes with accomplices, the females typically were proven to be the dominant actor in the group, which went against any presumption in their favor. Their crimes tended to be horribly violent felony-murders. Indeed, their crimes and behavior could be characterized as more like those of male killers than female killers, perhaps removing them from the normally protective constructs for female offenders.

Some Questions About Gender and the Death Penalty

Elizabeth Rapaport, 20 Golden Gate U.L. Rev. 501 (1990)

Although gender discrimination in the application of capital punishment is an unlikely candidate for litigation, the widespread impression, or suspicion, that women receive favorable treatment with respect to society's most severe penalty reverberates. It echoes the widely accepted chivalry thesis, that women receive preferential treatment in the criminal justice system. The death penalty, as society's most awesome sanction, symbolizes the power of society to exact justice for the violation of rights it chooses to protect. The impression that women are spared death, despite our gathering commitment to sexual equality, is indicative of the conviction, deep in the culture, that women will continue to lack full moral, political and legal stature, and that they gain certain protections in exchange for accepting these limitations. Ripples of corrosive sexism flow from the perception that female murderers are shielded from the society's most extreme punitive response. Interestingly, the information presently available does not support the proposition that female murderers have a substantial advantage over similarly situated male murderers in avoiding the death penalty. The limited information available suggests that women may be reaping both the rigors of equality and the detriments of the widespread suspicion of privilege.

Available evidence does not support the proposition that the American prosecutors, juries and courts refuse, out of chivalry, to death sentence women in circumstances where a capital sentence would be the fate of male offenders, certainly not to the egregious extent that Justice Marshall's complaint suggests: The fundamental reason why so few women murders are death sentenced is that women rarely commit the kinds of murders that are subject to capital punishment. Women commit one of every eight murders, but are far more likely to commit certain types of murders than others. Most offenders on death row, as many as eighty percent, have been convicted of felony murder, i.e., murder in the course of committing another felony. Women commit very few felony murders. Six percent of suspected perpetrators of felony murder are female. Women do hold their own, however, in the commission of intra-family homicide. They kill spouses and children almost as often as men do. Intra-family homicides rarely give rise to capital sentences, regardless of the sex of the defendant, unless the murder was committed for gain. These homicides are typically read as less blameworthy than those that merit the death penalty, lacking either or both of the qualities of coldbloodedness or predatoriness. Indeed, only the most aggravated murders can sustain a death sentence under modern era capital punishment law.

Those who have interpreted the extreme gender lopsidedness of the death row population to reflect chivalry towards women murders have failed to take into consideration the greater seriousness or heinousness ascribed by our criminal law to felony murder, and to predatory murders generally, as compared with typical family and other intimacy murders which are committed in the heat of anger. Consider robbery murder, by far the largest subclass of felony murders. Over the twelve year period, 1976–87, men were twenty-five times more likely to be robbery murder suspects than were women. Male murder defendants are more likely than female murder defendants to be capitally tried and sentenced in part for the legitimate, legally relevant reason that they are more likely to have prior histories of and convictions for violent crimes. More than ninety-five percent of those convicted of violent crimes are male. There are other indications, although by no means conclusive proofs, that women are not grossly advantaged in selection for death. Two sets of researchers who have studied post-*Furman* death sentencing report that gender had no significant effect on the fate of persons convicted of murder. These studies were conducted to investigate the impact of race on capital sentencing; because the number of women whose cases had the potential for aggravated first degree murder processing is small, it would be imprudent to overgeneralize from these results. Further research is necessary to determine whether prejudice in favor of women murderers plays any role in accounting for the rareness of women on death row.

... There is a consensus in criminological research that women benefit from leniency in some pre-sentencing phases of case processing and in sentencing for many relatively minor crimes. Researchers are divided as to whether women who commit serious or violent crime are more lightly sentenced than comparable male offenders. While some believe that leniency carries through into sentencing for serious crime, other researchers believe women convicted of serious or violent crime lose the advantage of being female and are treated no differently or even more harshly than men. Wherever and to the extent that criminologists see an advantage to female gender, they proffer the same explanatory hypothesis, the chivalry or paternalism hypothesis: women are treated as less responsible for their actions, hence less culpable, and perhaps also as posing less continuing danger to society. Researchers who find that women receive sentences as severe as comparable males hypothesize that when a woman is perceived as guilty of a severe or "male" offense she loses the advantage of her gender and is more harshly punished because of her violation of gender stereotypical expectations. There is some tendency to conflate two distinct hypotheses, either one of which is confusingly termed the "evil woman" hypothesis. The first hypothesis, which would more appropriately be called the "gender equality" theory, is that women, who perhaps contrary to gender norm expectations, commit high severity offenses, are treated no differently than men. The second, the true "evil woman" theory, is that women who commit high severity offenses are treated more harshly than similarly situated men: they are punished for violating sex role expectations in addition to being punished for their crimes.

[Professor Rapaport notes that most modern death penalty statutes are aimed at: (1) predatory murder, usually for pecuniary gain; (2) murder threatening law enforcement or governmental authority; and (3) murder involving exceptional cruelty or murder committed by an individual with a violent past. Domestic violence, on the other hand, is not singled out for special attention under death penalty statutes. According to Rapaport, women are much more likely to murder an intimate, *i.e.*, a family member or friend. Therefore, women are less likely to fall under the capital murder statutes.]

... It is striking from this perspective that while the capital statutes offer their special protection to representatives of the state and to the interaction of non-intimates, the third of the three spheres into which society can be divided, family life, is notably absent from the statutes' universe of concerns. Women's traditional interest in the sanctity of the home, its peace and safety, is not supported by the prestige that would be symbolically conveyed by the attachment of the capital sanction to the most egregious family homicides. Of course, if a family murder has a pecuniary motive, the alchemy of money transmutes it into a killing as heinous as one committed on a stranger. And capital statutes do reflect the opprobrium with which rape and other sexual offense killings, whose victims are far more likely to be women or children than adult men, are regarded. These provisions, although they might also apply to crimes against family victims, reflect the extreme disapprobation which our society reserves for crimes inflicted on other men's women and children.

Capital punishment, then, is used primarily to reinforce and solemnize the code of conduct governing relations among persons who do not warm themselves at the same hearth; the sanction is largely reserved for predatory murder, the kind of crime men (and women) fear that male strangers will inflict upon themselves and their families.

Our law of homicide reveals a moral outlook in which greater opprobrium normally attaches to the killing of strangers than to the killing of intimates. This hierarchy of opprobrium is chivalrous to women as perpetrators, since such a high percentage of the homicides women commit are domestic; but it is not chivalrous to women as victims, since the blameworthiness of domestic homicide is discounted relative to stranger killing.

Notes and Questions

1. If the American system of capital punishment suffers from gender discrimination, doesn't this benefit female offenders? Women comprise fewer than two percent of the 18,000–20,000 persons executed from colonial times to the present. Streib, *American Executions of Female Offenders: A Preliminary Inventory* (3d ed. 1982). Since 1972, approximately two percent of all persons sentenced to death have been women. Likewise, since executions resumed in 1977 more than 1000 men—and 11 women—have been executed.

Professor Elizabeth Rapaport suggests two theories which may account for the gender disparity among American death row inmates.

> *Does* the sparseness of women on death row result from a chivalrous disinclination to mete out death to women under circumstances in which men would be consigned to this fate? Or does the apparent underrepresentation of women have an explanation other than gender discrimination in our favor? Two hypotheses, singly or in combination, would account for the gender profile of America's death row: (1) women offenders are benefiting from gender discrimination in their favor; (2) women are represented on death row in numbers commensurate with the infrequency of female commission of those crimes our society labels sufficiently reprehensible to merit capital punishment.
>
> ... [A]lthough there is ample scope for further study before fully satisfactory conclusions can be reached, the explanation for much, if not all, of the apparent disparity between the proportion of murderers who are women and the proportion of women on death row is not chivalrous regard for the female sex. It is to be found in the differences between the kinds of murders men and women commit and the kinds of personal history they present to prosecutors and sentencers: Female murderers are dramatically less likely than male murderers to have committed predatory murder and to appear in the dock as habitual and exceptionally violent felons. The sparseness of women on death row reflects our society's judgments about the nature of the most reprehensible and hence most severely sanctioned crimes rather than our protectiveness of women.

See generally Rapaport, "The Death Penalty and Gender Discrimination," 25 L. & Soc'y Rev. 367 (1991).

2. The earliest documented execution of a female in the United States occurred in 1632, when Virginia put to death Jane Champion for murder. Since 1632, 409 women have been executed in this country. Of course, murder is not the only crime for which women have been executed. On June 1, 1660, Mary Dyer was executed in Massachusetts

for refusing to obey an order banning all Quakers from the Massachusetts Bay Colony. Perhaps the most famous execution of a woman was that of Ethel Rosenberg, convicted of espionage along with her husband Julius and put to death in New York's electric chair on June 19, 1953. Espionage, according to Judge Frank Kaufman who sentenced the Rosenbergs to death, was "worse than murder." Judge Kaufman held the Rosenbergs responsible both for the Americans who died during the Korean War and for putting countless other Americans at risk. Notwithstanding a worldwide clemency campaign, President Eisenhower allowed the execution to proceed. Ethel and Julius, parents of two small children, were executed within minutes of each other.

As of April 1, 2006, eleven women had been executed under the modern, post-*Furman* death penalty statutes. According to Professor Streib, 230 of the women executed over the past three-and-a-half centuries were black; 108 women were white; nine women were of American Indian or Hispanic descent; and the race of fifty-one women could not be established with a sufficient degree of certainty. At least 189 of the 398 women who were executed were known to be slaves. Sixty-one percent of these women killed their slave master, their mistress or some member of the slave master's family. However, other common capital offenses for female slaves included arson, attempted murder and conduct unbecoming a slave. Streib, "Death Penalty for Female Offenders," 58 U. Cin. L. Rev. 845 (1990).

Most of the women executed during the seventeenth century were white and many had been convicted of witchcraft. In the eighteenth and nineteenth centuries, executions of women increased dramatically; the majority of these women were black. In the eighteenth century, seventy percent of the women executed were black and in the nineteenth century eighty-three percent of the women executed were black. The highest concentration of female executions occurred in the decades preceding and during the Civil War.

In the twentieth century, the execution rate for female offenders fell markedly. In addition, almost two-thirds of the women executed in the twentieth century were white and approximately one third of the women were black.

Can you draw any conclusions from the differing treatment of white and black female death row inmates over the past three-and-a-half centuries? Why would female slaves comprise almost fifty percent of the women executed in American history?

One young, black slave executed in antebellum Missouri was a woman named Celia. Celia was fourteen years old when she was purchased by John Newsome, a widower from Calloway County, Missouri. During the next five years, Newsome repeatedly raped and sexually abused Celia. Eventually, Celia became romantically involved with another slave named George. At George's insistence, Celia attempted to end her sexual relationship with Newsome. When Newsome refused to end his sexual relations with Celia, Celia struck him with a club and killed him. Celia disposed of Newsome's body by burning it in the fireplace of her cabin.

At Celia's trial for the murder of Newsome, defense counsel argued that Celia had acted in self-defense and was justified in using force to repel Newsome's sexual advances. However, rape of a slave woman was not considered a crime in Missouri, and the trial judge refused to instruct the jury on Celia's defense. The jury found Celia guilty and, on October 13, 1855, the trial judge sentenced Celia to death. On December 21, 1855, the nineteen-year-old Celia was executed by hanging. See McLaurin, *Celia, A Slave* (Univ. Georgia Press 1991).

3. Twenty-seven women were executed in the seventeenth century for witchcraft. Streib, "Death Penalty for Female Offenders," 58 U. Cin. L. Rev. 845, 858 (1990).

Most of these executions occurred in Massachusetts. The infamous Salem witch trials have been the subject of much historical, psychological and literary study. For an interesting exploration of the subject see Starkey, *The Devil in Massachusetts* (Anchor Books 1969).

4. Should pregnant women be immune from capital punishment? One solution to the dilemma might be to await the birth of the child and then carry out the sentence. See Ariz. Crim. Code §§13-4025, 13-4026. Historically, executions of pregnant women have been suspended until they delivered the child. Misson, in his *Travels Over England* (written 1698, translated from the French by Ozell, 1719) p. 330, writes:

> The Women or Wenches that are condemn'd to Death, never fail to plead they are with Child (if they are old enough) in order to stop Execution till they are delivered. Upon this they are order'd to be visited by Matrons; if the Matrons do not find them Quick, they are sure to swing next Execution Day; but very often they declare that they are with Child, and often too the poor Criminals are so indeed; for tho' they came never so good Virgins into Prison, they are a Sett of Wags there that take Care of the Matters. No Doubt they are diligent to inform them the very Moment they come in, that if they are not with Child already, they must go to work immediately to be so; that in case they have the Misfortune to be condemn'd, they may get Time, and so perhaps save their Lives. Who would not hearken to such wholesome Advice?

Not all pregnant convicts have been so charitably treated. Blackstone asserted that granting a reprieve to a pregnant mother was "dictated by the law of nature." 4 W. Blackstone, Commentaries 395. Thus, he condemned the cruel execution on the Isle of Gurnsey accomplished by "burning a woman big with child; and when, through the violence of the flames, the infant sprang forth at the stake, and was preserved by the bystanders, after some deliberation of the priests who assisted at the sacrifice, they cast it again into the fire as a young heretic."

Should the pregnant condition of a capital defendant be considered a mitigating factor during sentencing? Why or why not? Under Chinese law, pregnant offenders may not be sentenced to death. *When The State Kills* 121 (Amnesty International 1989).

5. As noted above, as of April 1, 2006, eleven women have been executed in the United States since executions resumed in 1977. In 1984, North Carolina executed the first woman since *Gregg*. Velma Barfield, a nurse, was put to death for murdering Stewart Taylor, a patient under her care, by arsenic poisoning. Barfield also confessed to killing several other patients. Barfield was the first woman put to death in the United States since California executed Elizabeth Duncan, 22 years earlier. For an interesting and personal account of Barfield's execution, see Ingle, "Final Hours: The Execution of Velma Barfield," 23 Loy. L.A. L. Rev. 221 (1989).

6. What effect, if any, should evidence of the battered woman syndrome have in the capital sentencing decision of a woman who kills a husband or lover? For a discussion of the battered woman syndrome in capital sentencing decisions see Streib, "Death Penalty for Battered Women," 20 Fla. St. L. Rev. 163 (1992). Professor Streib argues that battered woman syndrome evidence should be considered a statutory mitigating circumstance during capital sentencing hearings. Streib further suggests that women who kill their batterers should be altogether exempt from the death penalty.

7. In 1991, Ellen Sweets reported that death sentencing for women had doubled since the early 1980s to about ten per year. In 1978, there were four women on death row. By 1988 there were fifteen; by 1990 there were thirty-three. *Women Facing Death Penalty in*

Increasing Numbers, The Dallas Morning News, May 9, 1991, p. 39A. As of January 1, 2006, there were 55 women awaiting execution in the United States.

8. In the following law review article, Professor Rapaport argues that the underrepresentation of women on death row results from the discounting of the seriousness of the sorts of murders women typically commit.

Equality of the Damned: The Execution of Women on the Cusp of the 21st Century

Elizabeth Rapaport, 26 Ohio N.U. L. Rev. 581 (2000)

In the period beginning with the reaffirmation of capital punishment in the United States in 1976, until the present day, more than 600 men but only four women have been executed. The execution of Karla Faye Tucker in 1998, the second of the four women to be executed, occurred in the midst of relentless publicity. The Tucker execution revived interest in gender equity in the administration of capital punishment. Although one woman, Velma Barfield, had been executed fourteen years earlier in a comparable media storm, the Tucker execution took place after weeks of speculation as to whether Governor Bush of Texas, and indeed any contemporary American governor, would allow a woman to be executed. Would George W. Bush, who styles himself a "compassionate conservative," allow a pretty white woman of childbearing age to be executed? Governor Bush, at the time that this decision was thrust upon him, was readying himself to run for re-election as governor of Texas in less than a year and was also a prominent contender for the Republican presidential nomination in the 2000 election. Governor Bush's decision should have surprised no one. The Tucker execution was nonetheless a signal event in the recent history of capital punishment; it should prepare us for the normalization of the execution of women. The execution of Karla Faye Tucker also "put a face on the death penalty," and in doing so, may contribute to the return of abolitionism to mainstream politics.

Few murderers are ever in jeopardy of a capital sentence. In 1996, for example 2.5% of persons convicted of murder or manslaughter received capital sentences. Among this capital elite, women are rare, comprising between 1% and 2% of death row, typically, since the death penalty was reinstated. To many, the meaning of such statistics is manifest: since women commit approximately one in eight homicides in the United States, the death row numbers prove that women are protected by cultural or even more fundamental inhibitions from paying the ultimate price for taking life. For opponents of capital punishment gender bias is one more powerful reason, if one more were needed, to condemn the injustice of capital punishment.

The statistics just reviewed tell a misleading story. Although women commit one in eight homicides, they commit a very much smaller percentage of offenses that are eligible for capital treatment. Demonstrably, the single most important explanatory factor accounting for the representation women on death row is the low rate of the commission of death penalty echelon offenses by women. The death penalty is reserved for offenses and offenders our society regards as the most reprehensible. Two-thirds of women who kill, kill family members and lovers. These crimes almost never result in death sentences, regardless of the sex of the killer, unless they are done for predatory motives or result in multiple deaths. More than 75% of those on death row killed in the course of committing a violent felony such as rape or robbery. These offenses, in which women's rates of participation are very low, are most severely condemned by our society. Women commit 4%, or slightly less, of killings by strangers, of robbery-murders, and of rape-murders.

They commit 7.2% of killings with multiple victims. In addition to the nature of the homicides they commit, women are protected from capital punishment by the criminal histories they present to prosecutors selecting those who will stand trial for their lives. It is the extremely low rate of participation in death penalty echelon crimes that most powerfully explains the low percentage of women on death row.

We have far less information about the impact of gender upon the fates of men and women after they are admitted to death row. A full account of the post-admission role of gender would include understanding how gender figures into selection for execution, in particular, for judicial relief from capital sentence and for executive clemency ...

Approximately one third of all death sentences imposed 1973–98, had been reversed by court action by the end of 1998. However, fewer capitally sentenced women remain on death row than do men. Of the 128 women capital sentenced since 1973, four, or 3.7%, have been executed, and seventy-six, or 59% have left death row due to judicial reversal of sentence or executive commutation of sentence.

There are several possible explanations of women's greater statistical likelihood of avoiding death after a capital sentence. One explanation is inhibition against the execution of women on the bench, among governors and clemency boards, and among other persons in the criminal justice system who individually and collectively influence the pace at which cases proceed, as well as their outcomes. It is also possible that gender is correlated with other factors that account for some or all outcomes. For example, some women's capital cases (by no means all) have involved gender-patterned mitigation factors insufficiently examined at trial. The contemporary death penalty was launched just as the law of homicide began its as yet incomplete effort to come to grips with domestic oppression as a factor affecting or mitigating culpability ...

I would like to offer two possible explanations, other than the decision-maker's inhibition against executing a woman, that may account for some of the longevity of the, as yet, small number of women sentenced to die in the contemporary death penalty era. The first is the sheer unusualness of being a woman on death row. To be unusual makes for closer attention, perhaps greater care in reviewing a case, whether judicially or in an executive clemency determination. Both the intrinsic interest of the unusual and the expectation that others are paying more attention—the public, the press, opponents, other jurists—would lead to closer scrutiny of a woman's case. At the end of 1998, there were forty-eight women on death row, conspicuous for their gender among a total of 3,452 prisoners on death row. Even the states having the largest number of women under capital sentence since *Furman* have had only a handful of women on their death rows at a time. California, with the largest death row in the country, 512, presently also has the largest number of women on death row, ten. California is followed by Texas, which has the second largest death row, 451, housing eight women. Only two other states currently have as many as four female death row inmates, while almost one third of the death penalty states have no female death row inmates. It is not unreasonable to conjecture that, in an area of law where cases are complex to try and error vitiating trial and sentencing results have been found by reviewing courts in approximately a third of all cases, cases closely sifted will more likely be found to contain reversible error or circumstances warranting clemency.

A second possible explanation of the removal of more women from death row than men—especially by executive clemency but also by action of elected judges and even life tenure judges—is the impact on a governor or judge of his belief that the public would regard the execution of a woman as inhumane. George W. Bush, who has overseen more than 120 executions during his tenure as governor of Texas, reports the concern felt in his administration that the execution of a woman would make him and the State of Texas appear inhumane and "bloodthirsty." If this kind of diffidence is a factor, the phenomenon at hand is not inhibition against executing a woman, but rather politically motivated caution or concern about losing popularity or support ...

The near-term future of execution of women in the United States is likely to resemble the recent past. The executions of Judi Buenoano in 1998, and Betty Lou Beets in 2000, were accompanied by only faint echoes of the excitement that swirled around the Barfield and Tucker executions. Unless renewal of the abolitionist sentiment forestalls the dramatic increase in the pace of executions of the last few years, we are likely to see further executions of women occur with as little strain as was felt in Buenoano's or Beets' departures. Indeed, with the Beets and Buenoano executions, we have seen a reassertion of the gender stereotyping that has historically dehumanized despised female murderers. Both these women were styled "Black Widows," a label that imposes psychic distance and deploys sexualized fear and hostility. A fifth woman was executed in Arkansas on May 2, 2000, with similarly modest publicity and no press speculation about whether the Governor would allow the execution of a woman. Whether there will be any lasting repercussions of Karla Faye Tucker's witness for the damned remains to be seen. If so, it will be as part of a renewed movement for abolition for the thousands on death row of both sexes.

Notes and Question

1. According to one scholar, women account for about one in eight (13 percent) murder arrests, one in 72 (1.4 percent) death sentences, and one in 140 (0.7 percent) actual executions. Of the more than 8,000 persons executed in the United States since 1900, only 44 (0.5 percent) have been women. If it's true that men are eight times as likely as women to be arrested for murder; 72 times as likely to be sentenced to death; and 140 times as likely to be executed, couldn't a male death row inmate raise a *McCleskey*-based equal protection challenge to his sentence? Of course, under *McCleskey*, a male alleging sex discrimination in capital sentencing would have to prove (1) a pattern of discrimination against men, perhaps in the charging decisions of prosecutors or the verdicts of juries; and (2) that gender bias infected his particular case. Streib, *Sentencing Women to Death*, Vol. 16 The Champion at p. 25–26 (Spring 2001).

2. When Professor Rapaport's article was written, only four women had been put to death in the modern era of American capital punishment. Her article notes that gender stereotyping contributes to the dehumanization of "despised female murderers." By labeling Betty Lou Beets and Judi Buenoano "Black Widows," prosecutors (and the media) created psychic distance and engendered "sexualized fear and hostility."

Dehumanization is a key goal of prosecutors seeking the death penalty. In discharging their awesome responsibilities, capital jurors are far more likely to sentence to death someone who has been demonized and made to appear, through presentation of evidence and prosecutorial argument, less than human. On the other hand, defense lawyers must remind jurors at every possible opportunity that the person whose life (or death) is in their hands is no less a human being than they are.

Consider the crimes committed by Tucker, Buenoano and Beets. Karla Faye Tucker may well provide the most shocking example of the "evil woman" hypothesis—that women who commit high severity offenses violate sex role expectations and therefore are treated more harshly than similarly situated men. Tucker, a Texas death row inmate executed in 1998, confessed to assisting her boyfriend in a particularly gruesome double murder. Tucker confided to a friend that she derived sexual pleasure from her murderous assault with a pickax. Prior to Tucker's lethal injection, Texas had not put a woman to death since hanging Chipita Rodriguez in 1863. See generally Rapaport, "Gender and the Death Penalty," 20 Golden Gate Univ. L. Rev. 501, 535 (1990).

Less than two months after Tucker was executed, Florida executed Judi Buenoano for poisoning her husband. Prior to Buenoano's 1998 execution, Florida's last execution of a female prisoner was the 1848 execution of Celia Bryan.

In 2000, Texas put to death Betty Lou Beets for killing her abusive husband. Two months later, Arkansas executed Christina Riggs, a licensed practical nurse, who became the first woman put to death in that state since 1868. Riggs smothered to death her two children, ages 2 and 5, then tried to kill herself by overdosing on drugs. Riggs confessed while hospitalized and eventually waived her appeals, becoming the first female volunteer. Oklahoma executed three women in 2001: Wanda Jean Allen, who shot her lesbian lover outside a police station; Marilyn Plantz, who hired her boyfriend and another man to kill her husband; and Lois Nadean Smith, who shot her son's former girlfriend. In 2002, Alabama electrocuted cop killer Lynda Block and Florida lethally injected serial killer Aileen Wuornos. Finally, in 2005, Texas executed Francis Newton, convicted of shooting her husband and two children to death. Thus, of the first eleven women put to death since executions resumed in 1977, six executees killed intimates in domestic violence cases.

3. A sampling of high-profile capital convictions and death sentences confirms the tendency of female killers to murder within their domestic circles. A California jury sentenced Caroline Young to death in 1995 for killing her two grandchildren, ages four and six. In October 1998, a California jury sentenced Dora Buenrostro to death for the stabbing murders of her three children, ages four to nine. The following year, Californian Susan Eubanks was condemned for shooting to death her three sons, ages four to seven. In March 2000, an Arizona jury sentenced Doris Carlson to death for the contract killing of her invalid mother-in-law as she lay helpless in a nursing home. In October 2000, arson-murderess Sandi Nieves joined California's death row for killing her four daughters.

4. Although female serial killers appear to be extremely rare, Florida death row prisoner Aileen Wournos had six death sentences before she was executed. Wournos' victims were middle-aged white men who picked her up for prostitution. Charlize Theron portrays Wournos in the 2003 Academy Award winning film, "Monster."

5. In March 2000, Kentucky jurors returned a death sentence in an extraordinarily unusual capital case, given the nearly unprecedented combination of gender and race. Virginia Caudill, a white woman, was condemned for the robbery and murder of a 73-year-old black woman.

6. Professor Streib's web-based report on the death penalty for female offenders, "Death Penalty for Female Offenders, January 1973 Through December 31, 2005," can be accessed from www.deathpenaltyinfo.org.

D. Is Sexual Orientation Relevant in Capital Cases?

Note and Questions on Homosexuality as a Hidden Aggravator

According to the Old Testament, death was considered the appropriate punishment for the "offense" of homosexuality. (See *supra* chapter 1.) Conversely, the right to be free from discrimination on the basis of sexual orientation is recognized in contemporary international treaties, including the International Covenant on Civil and Political Rights.

Is a capital defendant's sexual orientation at all relevant to sentencing in capital cases? Should evidence of a capital defendant's homosexuality be excluded under a probative-prejudice analysis?

The following article examines the pernicious use of allegations of homosexuality in death penalty cases.

Queer on Death Row; In Murder Cases, Being Gay Can Seal a Defendant's Fate

Richard Goldstein, Village Voice (Feb. 2001)

You may never have heard of Calvin Burdine, but his case should be familiar. Burdine is the Texas death-row inmate whose lawyer allegedly fell asleep during his trial. (The lawyer claimed he was merely concentrating.) The story surfaced during last year's presidential campaign as a stunning reminder of why Texas is known as the execution capital of the free world. The fact that Burdine's trial took only 13 hours did not seem unusual. But a federal court found the evidence of his attorney's naps disturbing enough to grant Burdine a stay of execution so his case could be reviewed. It is still pending. Yet, another aspect of Burdine's appeal has gone unaddressed. His gayness was used by the state in ways that may have marked him for death. Jurors—several of whom admitted animus toward gays—heard the prosecutor say during closing arguments that "sending a homosexual to the penitentiary certainly isn't a very bad punishment for a homosexual." Burdine's lawyer did not object, but then, he had no problem calling the codefendant in the case a "tush hog." He didn't object when the prosecutor described Burdine's "homosexual life" as "voluntary." Making that point was an effective way to counter any sympathy that might arise from testimony that Burdine had been raped as a child by his father, a truck driver who took him along on runs. Burdine's victim, too, had been a dark father figure. He took Burdine in only on the condition that he turn over his salary. Burdine testified that when his earnings didn't cover his rent, the benefactor insisted he hustle. When he refused, Burdine contends, he was beaten by the victim's friends.

The result was murder in the commission of a robbery—a capital crime in many states, but one that doesn't necessarily lead to death row. Indeed, only 1.2 percent of murder cases end in death sentences. Executing someone requires a separate proceeding in which aggravating factors are weighed against mitigating ones. When the defendant is gay, sexuality can become one of those aggravating factors—with fatal consequences.

In Burdine's case, the jurors were urged to order his execution by a prosecutor who told them that sending this man to prison would be like setting a kid loose in a candy store. Calvin Burdine is not the only queer on death row. In the past few years, five capital cases involving gay or lesbian defendants have raised charges that homophobia played a role in sentencing. But no one knows how many queers await execution in America. Though extensive data exist on the race, age, and gender of such inmates, there are few statistics about their sexuality. No one knows how often gayness is raised by prosecutors as a snide implication, an unfounded assertion, or a fact that may or may not be relevant to the case. But it comes up with such frequency and in such predictable ways that the allegations of antigay bias cannot be dismissed.

There are high barriers against injecting race into a trial, and rape-shield laws that prohibit introducing a victim's prior sexual history. But no such restrictions exist when it comes to homosexuality. "The courts are not there yet, especially in capital cases," says Richard Dieter, executive director of the Death Penalty Information Center. As Burdine's trial illustrates, the rules against statements that might inflame a jury are not necessarily enforced when the defendant is gay. Ambitious prosecutors are often free to play to stereotypical beliefs about homosexuals. And they have reason to single out gay defendants when deciding which cases might convince a jury to opt for execution. After all, a death sentence is never mandatory. No matter how heinous the crime, a jury can choose to spare the murderer's life. "It's all about emotion," says Dieter. "There's no legal formula for who gets the death penalty. And anyone who seems outside the bounds of what's acceptable is more likely to end up being executed." Race, class, and reduced mental capacity all play a major role in capital punishment. The queer defendants in the following cases also fit into one or more of those categories. Their sexuality was hardly the only factor in their fate. But in each case, it was used in ways that played to the most negative assumptions about gay people. And in the God-fearing counties where these trials took place, their gayness may have sealed their fate. Sometimes, the mere mention of homosexuality is enough to spell death.

That's what activists say happened to Stanley Lingar, who was executed in Missouri last month for the murder of a young man he and a friend had picked up. According to the friend, who pled guilty to second degree murder (and served six years), they forced their victim to undress and demanded that he masturbate. When he failed to perform, Lingar shot him, beat him, and ran him over twice. The friend was the only witness to the crime, but the jury bought his testimony, and in the penalty phase, they sentenced Lingar to die.

This second verdict followed a startling piece of evidence that the prosecutor had abruptly introduced. It was something even the defense was unaware of. Lingar and his friend had been lovers. But what did that have to do with the case? The prosecutor maintained it would help explain Lingar's motive—though he never made that point to the jury. No matter. The prosecutor had convinced the judge that Lingar's sexuality spoke to his character—and in Missouri a "depraved mind" is an aggravating factor. Lingar's appeal was partly successful. The court ruled that discussing his homosexuality would have been unconstitutional if it had influenced the jury. But the court also concluded that it had not. Missouri's attorney general called the charge of bias "absurd."

In fact, 12 percent of jurors say they could not be fair to a gay defendant, according to a survey by the National Law Journal. This suggests that homophobia will likely be present on any jury, not to mention one in rural Missouri. Yet because the prosecution chose to keep Lingar's sexuality a secret until the last minute, the defense had no way to deal with it, or even to poll the jury about homophobia. Situations like this are why activists urge defense lawyers to be proactive when their clients are gay.

Yet in places like Missouri, attorneys will often pretend the issue isn't there—until it's too late. Wanda Jean Allen's sexuality was never far from the surface of her case. She had killed her female lover in front of a police station; there was no disputing that. The issue was motive, and the defense demonstrated that Allen and her lover had a tumultuous, violent relationship requiring frequent interventions by the police. At her arrest, Allen bore scratches on her face, allegedly from being assaulted by her lover with a rake. This was a crime of passion, the defense argued, and in such cases the death penalty is rarely invoked.

But Allen had several strikes against her. For one thing, she was black and poor. (Her lawyer was paid only $800.) For another, she had killed before, albeit in a case so ambiguous that she was allowed to plead guilty to manslaughter and received the minimum sentence of four years. A prior homicide can be grounds for death. But according to the Death Penalty Information Center, only 8.4 percent of inmates awaiting execution have previous murder convictions.

What made Allen's crime so shocking that she became the first woman put to death in the state of Oklahoma? Possibly it was the prosecution's assertion that Allen "wore the pants in the family." Spurred on by testimony from the victim's mother, the state claimed that Allen was the man in the relationship, noting that she even liked to spell her middle name G-E-N-E, in the masculine way. The implication that Allen dominated her lover overwhelmed the evidence that both women had abused each other. And it raised the specter of the killer dyke that often haunts female defendants in murder cases. In the documentary Perverted Justice, CUNY law professor Ruthann Robson estimates that 40 percent of women accused of murder must contend with "some implication of lesbianism."

In capital cases, the prosecution aims to convince the jury that the defendant is inhuman. It's harder to do that when a woman is in the dock. "Before we can dehumanize her, we have to defeminize her," says Victor Streib, who has studied lesbians on death row. It's easier to kill a masculine woman, especially if she is what Streib calls "a tough customer." Ana Cardona was hardly that. She was frail and feminine, according to her defense. Cardona claimed it was her domineering female lover who had killed her child. But the strategy backfired: Her lover got 40 years while Cardona got sentenced to death. After all, she was the child's mother—or "lesbian mother," as the prosecution called her. She was also accused of being sadistic enough to have beaten and starved the child. But the image of the killer dyke gave her culpability added weight. As Streib notes: "The death penalty is fairly rare for mothers who kill their children." Susan Smith's life was spared, though she had watched her children drown in the car she rolled into a lake. But Smith was not a "lesbian mother."

Gay defendants, too, must deal with the image of the predatory queer, especially when the accomplice is a younger man. Even Calvin Burdine's dozing lawyer knew enough to base his defense on allegations that the victim was a "middle aged, king homosexual" who had victimized young boys.

Gregory Scott Dickens was 26 when he was charged with killing a couple outside Yuma, Arizona. He had been traveling with a 16-year-old who, according to Dickens's current attorney, was the most important person in his life. The youth admitted to firing the gun, but he testified that Dickens had given him the weapon and put him up to the crime. When the defense moved to present evidence that this teen fit the profile of a violent and impulsive liar, Judge Tom Cole intervened. If the defense took that route, said the judge, he might allow the prosecutor to raise an issue that had been kept from the jury: Dickens and his young friend were lovers. Then the nature of Dickens's two previous convictions—for fondling minors—might also come out. "The state could say that in this homosexual relationship, the older partner had control over the kid," says Dickens's current attorney. So the defense backed down.

This time it wasn't the prosecutor's tactics but the judge's behavior that figured in the appeal. Court papers filed on Dickens's behalf claim that Judge Cole had reacted with rage to his own son's homosexuality. He had written a letter expressing the hope that his son would "die in prison like all the rest of your faggot friends." Cole denies writing the letter, but he would not comment on the allegation that he believes his son was turned gay by unscrupulous friends. "It's insignificant," Cole says. But the defense contends that such an attitude could have induced Cole to allow homosexuality into the trial—especially when the accused might appear to be a sexual predator. In Arizona, the judge decides when a killer should be sentenced to death, and though Dickens was acquitted of premeditated murder, Cole found other grounds to condemn him. Dickens had committed a multiple murder that resulted in pecuniary gain. But so had his young friend, whose life was spared.

Assume that all these defendants are guilty. Grant that their sexuality may have some relevance to the case. The question, then, is not whether the subject should have come up but how it was used. Homosexuality was seen as a marker of perversion or pathology, the sign of a murderous bent. In these cases, the pretense of tolerance is ripped away, and one can see monsters from the homophobic id. But one can also recognize the biases that underlie ordinary life.

"Anyone can end up in court," notes Ruth E. Harlow, legal director of the Lambda Legal Defense and Education Fund. "And any time a gay man or lesbian goes into court, they have to be afraid that sexual orientation may play a role in their case." It might come up in family court, when the judge assumes a gay parent would expose a child to sexual activity. It could influence a prosecutor's decision about who gets to plea bargain and who must stand trial. It could even determine who is charged with a crime in the first place. "We tend to think of gay people as crime victims, not prisoners," says Bill Dobbs of Queer Watch. "But in fact, the criminal justice system touches us in many ways."

In New York, court clerks are required for monitoring purposes to list the sexual orientation of each defendant in a capital case. But the law does not address the way homosexuality can be used at trial. "I don't think there is any particular protection," says Pauline Toole, spokesperson for New York's Capital Defender Office. But at least homosexuality is not a crime in this state. In the South and West, where sodomy laws are common, the presumption of innocence for gay people is compromised to begin with. And when they are charged with murder, their sexuality is "like a powder keg," says Dobbs. "It can easily cause a jury to light the match."

Calvin Burdine knows how homophobia was used against him: from the jurors' pretrial comments to the prosecutor's closing remarks. "I did hear it," Burdine told the Voice from his cell on death row. "But it just kind of went over my head. I was scared to death."

Notes on Gay-Lesbian Bias in Capital Cases

1. The use of homophobia in death penalty prosecutions was the subject of an October 2002 panel discussion during the NCADP's annual conference in Chicago. Panelists concluded that American prosecutors are more likely to argue for death sentences

against gay and lesbian murder defendants because U.S. courts allow them to appeal to jurors' stereotypes and biases against homosexuals. According to Joey Mogul, an attorney with the People's Law Center, "It's easier for a prosecutor to get a death penalty if they can dehumanize people. They know merely raising the fact that we"re gay, lesbian or gender variant can do that."

Some examples cited by the panelists:

- During Bernina Mata's sentencing for a 1998 murder, prosecutors described her as a "hardcore lesbian." Mata's lawyer claimed that her trial was infested with anti-lesbian bias. They were insinuating that she deserved a death sentence mainly because she was an out gay person."

- Stanley Lingar was executed in Missouri in 2000 after prosecutors argued his relationship with another man was evidence of bad character and a factor the jury should consider in deciding on his sentence.

- In Texas, Calvin Burdine was sentenced to death after the prosecutor told the jury that sentencing Burdine to life would be wrong because "sending a homosexual to the penitentiary certainly isn't punishment for a homosexual."

- In Oklahoma, Wanda Jean Allen was executed for killing her female partner in a fight. During trial, prosecutors depicted Allen in various ways as the "man" in the relationship.

- Ana Cardona's lesbianism figured prominently when Florida sentenced her to die for killing her youngest child. At the same time, Susan Smith, Marilyn Lemak and Andrea Yates—three heterosexual women in prominent murder cases involving their children—were spared death sentences.

Barlow, *Life and Death; Death Penalty Opponents Cite Anti-Gay Bias in Sentences*, Chicago Free Press, Oct. 30, 2002.

2. Consider the remarks of the prosecutor during the capital sentencing of Jay Wesley Neill. In 1984, at age 19, Neill and his homosexual partner, 21-year-old Robert Johnson, decided to rob a bank in Geronimo, Oklahoma. During the robbery, three bank employees were stabbed to death and four customers (one of whom died) were shot. Three days later, both men were arrested in San Francisco.

In urging the jury to sentence Neill to death, the prosecutor said: "I want you to think briefly about the man you're sitting in judgment on and determining what the appropriate punishment should be.... I'd like to go through some things that to me depict the true person, what kind of person, he is. He is a homosexual. The person you're sitting in judgment on—disregard Jay Neill. You're deciding life or death on a person that's a vowed [sic] homosexual.... But these are areas you consider whenever you determine the type of person you're sitting in judgment on.... The individual's homosexual."

The Tenth Circuit Court of Appeals upheld Neill's death sentence, 2 to 1. Dissenting Judge Carlos Lucero argued that "the prosecutor's blatant homophobic hatemongering at sentencing has no place in the courtrooms of a civilized society." Per Judge Lucero, the comments were "susceptible of only one possible interpretation: among other factors, Neill should be put to death because he is gay.... I cannot sanction—because I have no confidence in—a proceeding tainted by a prosecutor's request that jurors impose a death sentence based, even in part, on who the defendant is rather than what he has done." Jay Wesley Neill was executed by lethal injection on December 12, 2002.

3. James T. Fisher, a male prostitute sentenced to death for stabbing to death a male customer in Oklahoma City, fared better before a different Tenth Circuit panel. In March 2002, the federal court of appeals overturned Fisher's conviction, ruling that E. Melvin Porter, Fisher's trial attorney, was "grossly inept" and harbored prejudice against homosexuals. The appeals court found that Porter had "sabotaged his client's defense by acting more as a prosecutor than a defense attorney." Deficient aspects of Porter's performance included failing to properly cross-examine prosecution witnesses, failing to explore contradictory statements by the prosecution's chief witness, and failing to seek out exculpatory evidence from police and prosecutors. Porter presented no opening statement, and waived his client's right to present evidence during the trial. During the sentencing stage — where the jury was asked to decide whether Fisher should live or die — Porter declined to make a closing statement, telling the judge and jury, "We waive."

Porter admitted that his antipathy towards homosexuals affected his representation. At a post-conviction hearing, the lawyer acknowledged, "At that time, I thought homosexuals were among the worst people in the world, and I did not like that aspect of the case." Chibbaro, *Court Throws Out "Gay" Death Row Conviction*, The Washington Blade, March 22, 2002.

Chapter 5

Constitutional Limitations on Death Eligibility

Even when a defendant's conduct fits within the statutory definition of capital murder, there may be good reason to rule out the death penalty as a criminal sanction. A death sentence necessarily reflects a moral judgment. And, consistent with principles of morality, certain categories of offenders or offenses may deserve to be exempted from the ultimate punishment.

A. Mens Rea

In criminal law, relative culpability is assessed by reference to the defendant's mens rea, or state of mind, and the harm caused by the defendant. At one level, all criminal homicides share a common harm: the death of a human being. Consequently, degrees of punishment for criminal homicide frequently vary according to the killer's state of mind. "Deeply ingrained in our legal tradition is the idea that the more purposeful the criminal conduct, the more serious is the offense, and, therefore, the more severely it ought to be punished." *Tison v. Arizona*, 481 U.S. 137, 156 (1987) (*infra* this chapter). Intentional killings, then, are generally punished more harshly than unintentional ones. Similarly, intentional killings committed in the heat of passion or in response to provocation may be considered less serious than intentional killings committed after premeditation and calm deliberation.

The following law review article examines the tension between two antithetical criminal law doctrines: "the felony murder rule of ancient, though disputed, lineage and the modern jurisprudence of capital punishment under the Eighth Amendment."

Felony Murder and the Eighth Amendment Jurisprudence of Death
Richard A. Rosen, 31 B.C. L. Rev. 1103 (1990)

A tension has developed between these two doctrines because they are, fundamentally, polar opposites. On the one hand, the felony murder rule, in its starkest form, provides that any participant in a specified felony that results in a death shall be punished as a murderer, no matter how accidental or unforeseeable the death, nor how attenuated the defendant's connection to the death. As such, the rule long has been criticized as a singular exception to the normal principles of criminal law, which require

251

that liability for a particular offense be predicated on the individual defendant's *mens rea* and degree of participation in the specific offense charged.

On the other hand, the Supreme Court's modern jurisprudence of death is based on a heightened refinement, not an exception, to these principles. This refinement requires an even more searching inquiry into all of the relevant aspects of the crime and the defendant than usually is found in criminal law to ensure the reliability and correctness of the decision to impose death.

[Professor Rosen describes how the felony-murder rule dramatically increases the pool of death-eligible offenders.]

In contrast to the winnowing out of the least culpable offenders through the application of the malice and premeditation/deliberation standards of non-felony murder homicide law, the felony murder rule thrusts an entire undifferentiated mass of defendants into the category of the supposedly worst murderers eligible for the death penalty. Some of these defendants indeed may be among the most culpable offenders—for example, the cold-blooded executioner of a store clerk during a robbery—but many are not. The rule makes no distinctions.

The felony murder rule disregards the normal rules of criminal culpability and provides homicide liability equally for both the deliberate rapist/killer and the robber whose victim dies of a heart attack, as well as for the robber's accomplice who is absent from the scene of the crime. In its traditional form, still used in some jurisdictions, the felony murder rule can make the defendant guilty of murder when an officer or victim mistakenly kills a third person or an accomplice during the felony or even when the defendant is involved in a traffic accident while fleeing the felony, resulting in death. A defendant who undertakes a felony only after extracting promises from his co-felon that no one will be hurt likewise is subject to the full force of the rule when the co-felon breaks the promise. In these situations, the felony murder rule has the potential to equate any participant in the felony with the cold-blooded deliberate killer, no matter how unforeseeable the death or how attenuated that defendant's participation in the felony or the events leading to death.

Therefore, notwithstanding all of the procedural requirements imposed upon the states, the possibility always exists that, with the felony murder rule as a basis for a capital sentence, some minimally culpable felony murder defendants, like accidental killers or attenuated accomplices to the felony, will be sentenced to die, even while many cold-blooded premeditated killers will be allowed to live. This possibility hardly reflects the proportionality—the reservation of the death penalty for the worst murderers—that underlies the Court's entire eighth amendment venture.

[The following cases illustrate the Supreme Court's attempts to minimize the tension caused by applying the felony-murder rule in capital cases.]

Enmund v. Florida

458 U.S. 782 (1982)

Justice WHITE delivered the opinion of the Court.

The facts of this case, taken principally from the opinion of the Florida Supreme Court, are as follows. On April 1, 1975, at approximately 7:45 a.m., Thomas and Eunice Kersey, aged 86 and 74, were robbed and fatally shot at their farmhouse in central Florida. The evidence showed that Sampson and Jeanette Armstrong had gone to the back door of the Kersey house and asked for water for an overheated car. When Mr. Kersey came out of the house, Sampson Armstrong grabbed him, pointed a gun at him, and told Jeanette Armstrong to take his money. Mr. Kersey cried for help, and his wife came out of the house with a gun and shot Jeanette Armstrong, wounding her. Sampson Armstrong, and perhaps Jeanette Armstrong, then shot and killed both of the Kerseys, dragged them into the kitchen, and took their money and fled.

Two witnesses testified that they drove past the Kersey house between 7:30 and 7:40 a.m. and saw a large cream- or yellow-colored car parked beside the road about 200 yards from the house and that a man was sitting in the car. Another witness testified that at approximately 6:45 a.m. he saw Ida Jean Shaw, petitioner's common-law wife and Jeanette Armstrong's mother, driving a yellow Buick with a vinyl top which belonged to her and petitioner Earl Enmund. Enmund was a passenger in the car along with an unidentified woman. At about 8 a.m. the same witness saw the car return at a high rate of speed. Enmund was driving, Ida Jean Shaw was in the front seat, and one of the other two people in the car was lying down across the back seat. [Based on this evidence, Enmund was convicted of capital murder and sentenced to death.]

... [T]he record supported no more than the inference that Enmund was the person in the car by the side of the road at the time of the killings, waiting to help the robbers escape. This was enough under Florida law to make Enmund a constructive aider and abettor and hence a principal in first-degree murder upon whom the death penalty could be imposed. It was thus irrelevant ... [under Florida law that Enmund] did not himself kill and was not present at the killings; also beside the point was whether he intended that the Kerseys be killed or anticipated that lethal force would or might be used if necessary to effectuate the robbery or a safe escape. We have concluded that imposition of the death penalty in these circumstances is inconsistent with the Eighth and Fourteenth Amendments.

The Cruel and Unusual Punishments Clause of the Eighth Amendment is directed, in part, "'against all punishments which by their excessive length or severity are greatly disproportioned to the offenses charged.'" [In determining whether a punishment is excessive, the Court, in the past, has] looked to the historical development of the punishment at issue, legislative judgments, international opinion, and the sentencing decisions juries have made before bringing its own judgment to bear on the matter. We proceed to analyze the punishment at issue in this case in a similar manner.

... [After a review of modern death penalty statutes, the Court found that] only a small minority of jurisdictions—eight—allow the death penalty to be imposed solely because the defendant somehow participated in a robbery in the course of which a murder was committed. Even if the nine States are included where such a defendant could be executed for an unintended felony murder if sufficient aggravating circumstances are present to outweigh mitigating circumstances—which often include the defendant's minimal participation in the murder—only about a third of American jurisdictions would ever permit a defendant who somehow participated in a robbery where a murder occurred to be sentenced to die. Moreover, of the eight States which have enacted new death penalty statutes since 1978, none authorize capital punishment in such circumstances. While the current legislative judgment with respect to imposition of the death penalty where a defendant did not take life, attempt to take it, or intend to take life is neither "wholly unanimous among state legislatures," nor as compelling as the legislative judgments considered in *Coker* [*v. Georgia*, 433 U.S. 584 (1977), in which the Court found that imposing the death penalty for rape was disproportionate and violated the Eighth Amendment], it nevertheless weighs on the side of rejecting capital punishment for the crime at issue.

Society's rejection of the death penalty for accomplice liability in felony murders is also indicated by the sentencing decisions that juries have made. As we have previously observed, "'[t]he jury ... is a significant and reliable objective index of contemporary values because it is so directly involved.'" The evidence is overwhelming that American juries have repudiated imposition of the death penalty for crimes such as petitioner's....

Although the judgments of legislatures, juries, and prosecutors weigh heavily in the balance, it is for us ultimately to judge whether the Eighth Amendment permits imposition of the death penalty on one such as Enmund who aids and abets a felony in the course of which a murder is committed by others but who does not himself kill, attempt to kill, or intend that a killing take place or that lethal force will be employed. We have concluded, along with most legislatures and juries, that it does not.

We have no doubt that robbery is a serious crime deserving serious punishment. It is not, however, a crime "so grievous an affront to humanity that the only adequate response may be the penalty of death." "[I]t does not compare with murder, which does involve the unjustified taking of human life. Although it may be accompanied by another crime, [robbery] by definition does not include the death of or even the serious injury to another person. The murderer kills; the [robber], if no more than that, does not. Life is over for the victim of the murderer; for the [robbery] victim, life ... is not over and normally is not beyond repair." As was said of the crime of rape in *Coker* [*supra*, chapter 1], we have the abiding conviction that the death penalty, which is "unique in its severity and irrevocability," is an excessive penalty for the robber who, as such, does not take human life.

Here the robbers did commit murder; but they were subjected to the death penalty only because they killed as well as robbed. The question before us is not the disproportionality of death as a penalty for murder, but rather the validity of capital punishment for Enmund's own conduct. The focus must be on his culpability, not on that of those who committed the robbery and shot the victims, for we insist on "individualized consideration as a constitutional requirement in imposing the death sentence," which means that we must focus on "relevant facets of the character and record of the individual offender." Enmund himself did not kill or attempt to kill; and, as construed by the Florida Supreme Court, the record before us does not warrant a finding that Enmund had any intention of participating in or facilitating a murder. Yet under Florida law death was an authorized penalty because Enmund aided and abetted a robbery in the course of which murder was committed. It is fundamental that "causing harm intentionally must be punished more severely than causing the same harm unintentionally." Enmund did not kill or intend to kill and thus his culpability is plainly different from that of the robbers who killed; yet the State treated them alike and attributed to Enmund the culpability of those who killed the Kerseys. This was impermissible under the Eighth Amendment.

In *Gregg v. Georgia*, 428 U.S. 153 (1976), the opinion announcing the judgment observed that "[t]he death penalty is said to serve two principal social purposes: retribution and deterrence of capital crimes by prospective offenders." Unless the death penalty when applied to those in Enmund's position measurably contributes to one or both of these goals, it "is nothing more than the purposeless and needless imposition of pain and suffering," and hence an unconstitutional punishment. We are quite unconvinced, however, that the threat that the death penalty will be imposed for murder will measurably deter one who does not kill and has no intention or purpose that life will be taken. Instead, it seems likely that "capital punishment can serve as a deterrent only when murder is the result of premeditation and deliberation," for if a person does not intend that life be taken or contemplate that lethal force will be employed by others, the possibility that the death penalty will be imposed for vicarious felony murder will not "enter into the cold calculus that precedes the decision to act."

It would be very different if the likelihood of a killing in the course of a robbery were so substantial that one should share the blame for the killing if he somehow participated in the felony. But competent observers have concluded that there is no basis in experience for the notion that death so frequently occurs in the course of a felony for which killing is not an essential ingredient that the death penalty should be considered as a justifiable deterrent to the felony itself. This conclusion was based on three comparisons of robbery statistics, each of which showed that only about one-half of one percent of robberies resulted in homicide. The most recent national crime statistics strongly support this conclusion. In addition to the evidence that killings only rarely occur during robberies is the fact, already noted, that however often death occurs in the course of a felony such as robbery, the death penalty is rarely imposed on one only vicariously guilty of the murder, a fact which further attenuates its possible utility as an effective deterrence.

As for retribution as a justification for executing Enmund, we think this very much depends on the degree of Enmund's culpability—what Enmund's intentions, expectations, and actions were. American criminal law has long considered a defendant's intention—and therefore his moral guilt—to be critical to "the degree of [his] criminal culpability," and the Court has found criminal penalties to be unconstitutionally excessive in the absence of intentional wrongdoing. In *Robinson v. California*, 370 U.S. 660, 667 (1962), a statute making narcotics addiction a crime, even though such addiction "is apparently an illness which may be contracted innocently or involuntarily," was struck down under the Eighth Amendment. Similarly, in *Weems v. United States*, 217 U.S. 349 (1910), the Court invalidated a statute making it a crime for a public official to make a false entry in a public record but not requiring the offender to "injur[e] any one by his act or inten[d] to injure any one." The Court employed a similar approach in *Godfrey v. Georgia*, 446 U.S. 420 (1980), reversing a death sentence based on the existence of an aggravating circumstance because the defendant's crime did not reflect "a consciousness materially more 'depraved' than that of any person guilty of murder."

For purposes of imposing the death penalty, Enmund's criminal culpability must be limited to his participation in the robbery, and his punishment must be tailored to his personal responsibility and moral guilt. Putting Enmund to death to avenge two killings that he did not commit and had no intention of committing or causing does not measurably contribute to the retributive end of ensuring that the criminal gets his just deserts. This is the judgment of most of the legislatures that have recently addressed the matter, and we have no reason to disagree with that judgment for purposes of construing and applying the Eighth Amendment.

Because the Florida Supreme Court affirmed the death penalty in this case in the absence of proof that Enmund killed or attempted to kill, and regardless of whether Enmund intended or contemplated that life would be taken, we reverse the judgment upholding the death penalty and remand for further proceedings not inconsistent with this opinion.

Note

1. Four years after *Enmund*, the Court in *Cabana v. Bullock*, 474 U.S. 376 (1986), faced the question "in whose hands the decision that a defendant possesses the requisite degree of culpability properly lies." Because the language of the capital murder statute defined capital murder to include a killing in the course of a robbery "'done with or

without any design to effect death'" and because of confusing or defective jury instructions, Mr. Bullock was sentenced to death by a jury that "may well have sentenced Bullock to death despite concluding that he had neither killed nor intended to kill; or it may have reached its decision without ever coming to any conclusion whatever on those questions." In considering how to deal with this problem, the Supreme Court stated:

> But the conclusion that the jury may not have found that the defendant killed, attempted to kill, or intended that a killing take place or that lethal force be employed does not end the inquiry into whether *Enmund v. Florida* bars the death sentence; rather, it is only the first step. In focusing only on instructions—and in requiring a new sentencing hearing before a jury before the death penalty might be reimposed—the Fifth Circuit apparently proceeded upon the premise that *Enmund* can be satisfied only at a sentencing hearing and by a jury's decision (presumably based upon proof beyond reasonable doubt) that the defendant possessed the requisite culpability. Examination of the nature of our ruling in *Enmund* reveals that this premise is erroneous.
>
> A defendant charged with a serious crime has the right to have a jury determine his guilt or innocence, and a jury's verdict cannot stand if the instructions provided the jury do not require it to find each element of the crime under the proper standard of proof. Findings made by a judge cannot cure deficiencies in the jury's finding as to the guilt or innocence of a defendant resulting from the court's failure to instruct it to find an element of the crime. But our ruling in *Enmund* does not concern the guilt or innocence of the defendant—it establishes no new elements of the crime of murder that must be found by the jury. Rather, as the Fifth Circuit itself has recognized, *Enmund* "does not affect the state's definition of any substantive offense, even a capital offense." *Enmund* holds only that the principles of proportionality embodied in the Eighth Amendment bar imposition of the death penalty upon a class of persons who may nonetheless be guilty of the crime of capital murder as defined by state law: that is, the class of murderers who did not themselves kill, attempt to kill, or intend to kill....
>
> Indeed, *Enmund* does not impose any particular form of procedure upon the States. The Eighth Amendment is satisfied so long as the death penalty is not imposed upon a person ineligible under *Enmund* for such punishment. If a person sentenced to death in fact killed, attempted to kill, or intended to kill, the Eighth Amendment itself is not violated by his or her execution regardless of who makes the determination of the requisite culpability; by the same token, if a person sentenced to death lacks the requisite culpability, the Eighth Amendment violation can be adequately remedied by any court that has the power to find the facts and vacate the sentence. At what precise point in its criminal process a State chooses to make the *Enmund* determination is of little concern from the standpoint of the Constitution. The State has considerable freedom to structure its capital sentencing system as it sees fit, for "[a]s the Court has several times made clear, we are unwilling to say that there is any one right way for a State to set up its capital sentencing scheme." ...
>
> The proceeding that the state courts must provide Bullock need not take the form of a new sentencing hearing before a jury. As indicated above, the Eighth Amendment does not require that a jury make the findings required by *Enmund*. Moreover, the sentence currently in force may stand provided only that the requisite findings are made in an adequate proceeding before some appro-

priate tribunal—be it an appellate court appropriate tribunal—be it an appellate court, a trial judge, or a jury. A new hearing devoted to the identification and weighing of aggravating and mitigating factors is thus, as far as we are concerned, unnecessary.

In his dissent in *Cabana*, Justice Blackmun, with whom Justice Brennan and Justice Marshall joined, stated:

> ... The central message of *Enmund* is that the death penalty cannot constitutionally be imposed without an intensely individual appraisal of the "personal responsibility and moral guilt" of the defendant.

> The focus must be on *his* culpability, ... for we insist on "individualized consideration as a constitutional requirement in imposing the death sentence," *Lockett v. Ohio*, 438 U.S. 586, 605 (1978), which means that we must focus on "relevant facets of the character and record of the individual offender." *Woodson v. North Carolina*, 428 U.S. 280, 304 (1976).

> Put simply, *Enmund* establishes a constitutionally required factual predicate for the valid imposition of the death penalty. Like the statutory aggravating circumstances..., the *Enmund* findings "circumscribe the class of persons eligible for the death penalty." Just as, absent the finding of a statutory aggravating circumstance, "'[a] case may not pass ... into that area in which the death penalty is authorized'" under Georgia law, so too, absent a finding of one of the *Enmund* factors, a case may not pass into that area in which the death penalty is authorized by the Eighth Amendment....

> The question of how to cure this constitutional violation remains. The Court holds that an adequate remedy for the absence of *Enmund* findings can be supplied by "any court that has the power to find the facts and vacate the sentence." I believe that, in this case, only a new sentencing proceeding before a jury can guarantee the reliability which the Constitution demands.

2. As Bryan Stevenson discusses in his article, "The Ultimate Authority on the Ultimate Punishment: The Requisite Role of the Jury in Capital Sentencing," 54 Ala. L. Rev. 1091, 1130–37 (2003), *Ring v. Arizona* (*infra* chapter 9) raises doubts about whether *Cabana* is consistent with the Court's more recent rulings on the constitutional requirements of jury sentencing determinations.

Tison v. Arizona
481 U.S. 137 (1987)

Justice O'CONNOR delivered the opinion of the Court.

The question presented is whether the petitioners' participation in the events leading up to and following the murder of four members of a family makes the sentences of death imposed by the Arizona courts constitutionally permissible although neither petitioner specifically intended to kill the victims and neither inflicted the fatal gunshot wounds. We hold that the Arizona Supreme Court applied an erroneous standard in making the findings required by *Enmund v. Florida*, 458 U.S. 782 (1982), and, therefore, vacate the judgments below and remand the case for further proceedings not inconsistent with this opinion.

I

Gary Tison was sentenced to life imprisonment as the result of a prison escape during the course of which he had killed a guard. After he had been in prison a number of years, Gary Tison's wife, their three sons Donald, Ricky, and Raymond, Gary's brother Joseph, and other relatives made plans to help Gary Tison escape again. The Tison family assembled a large arsenal of weapons for this purpose. Plans for escape were discussed with Gary Tison, who insisted that his cellmate, Randy Greenawalt, also a convicted murderer, be included in the prison break....

On July 30, 1978, the three Tison brothers entered the Arizona State Prison at Florence carrying a large ice chest filled with guns. The Tisons armed Greenawalt and their father, and the group, brandishing their weapons, locked the prison guards and visitors present in a storage closet. The five men fled the prison grounds in the Tisons' Ford Galaxy automobile. No shots were fired at the prison.

After leaving the prison, the men abandoned the Ford automobile and proceeded on to an isolated house in a white Lincoln automobile that the brothers had parked at a hospital near the prison. At the house, the Lincoln automobile had a flat tire; the only spare tire was pressed into service. After two nights at the house, the group drove towards Flagstaff. As the group traveled on back roads and secondary highways through the desert, another tire blew out. The group decided to flag down a passing motorist and steal a car. Raymond stood out in front of the Lincoln; the other four armed themselves and lay in wait by the side of the road. One car passed by without stopping, but a second car, a Mazda occupied by John Lyons, his wife Donnelda, his 2-year-old son Christopher and his 15-year-old niece, Theresa Tyson, pulled over to render aid.

As Raymond showed John Lyons the flat tire on the Lincoln, the other Tisons and Greenawalt emerged. The Lyons family was forced into the backseat of the Lincoln. Raymond and Donald drove the Lincoln down a dirt road off the highway and then down a gas line service road farther into the desert; Gary Tison, Ricky Tison and Randy Greenawalt followed in the Lyons' Mazda. The two cars were parked trunk to trunk and the Lyons family was ordered to stand in front of the Lincoln's headlights. The Tisons transferred their belongings from the Lincoln into the Mazda. They discovered guns and money in the Mazda which they kept and they put the rest of the Lyons' possessions in the Lincoln.

Gary Tison then told Raymond to drive the Lincoln still farther into the desert. Raymond did so, and, while the others guarded the Lyons and Theresa Tyson, Gary fired his shotgun into the radiator, presumably to completely disable the vehicle. The Lyons and Theresa Tyson were then escorted to the Lincoln and again ordered to stand in its headlights. Ricky Tison reported that John Lyons begged, in comments "more or less directed at everybody," "Jesus, don't kill me." Gary Tison said he was "thinking about it." John Lyons asked the Tisons and Greenawalt to "[g]ive us some water ... just leave us out here, and you all go home." Gary Tison then told his sons to go back to the Mazda and get some water. Raymond later explained that his father "was like in conflict with himself ... [w]hat it was, I think it was the baby being there and all this, and he wasn't sure about what to do."

... [I]t appears that both [petitioners, Raymond and Ricky Tison,] went back towards the Mazda, along with Donald, while Randy Greenawalt and Gary Tison stayed at the Lincoln guarding the victims. Raymond recalled being at the Mazda filling the water jug "when we started hearing the shots." Ricky said that the brothers gave the water jug to Gary Tison who then, with Randy Greenawalt went behind the Lincoln, where they spoke briefly, then raised the shotguns and started firing. In any event, petitioners agree they saw Greenawalt and their father brutally murder their four captives with repeated blasts from their shotguns. Neither made an effort to help the victims, though both later stated they were surprised by the shooting. The Tisons got into the Mazda and drove away, continuing their flight. Physical evidence suggested that Theresa Tyson managed to crawl away from the bloodbath, severely injured. She died in the desert after the Tisons left.

Several days later the Tisons and Greenawalt were apprehended after a shootout at a police roadblock. Donald Tison was killed. Gary Tison escaped into the desert where he subsequently died of exposure. Raymond and Ricky Tison and Randy Greenawalt were captured and tried jointly for the crimes associated with the prison break itself and the shootout at the roadblock; each was convicted and sentenced.

The State then individually tried each of the petitioners for capital murder of the four victims as well as for the associated crimes of armed robbery, kidnaping, and car theft. The capital murder charges were based on Arizona felony-murder law providing that a killing occurring during the perpetration of robbery or kidnaping is capital murder, and that each participant in the kidnaping or robbery is legally responsible for the acts of his accomplices. Each of the petitioners was convicted of the four murders under these accomplice liability and felony-murder statutes.

[In accordance with Arizona law, a judge sentenced the petitioners to death. The Arizona Supreme Court affirmed the convictions and sentences finding that the petitioners played an active role in the events leading up to the death of the four victims and there was sufficient evidence to evince an intent to kill and justify the sentence of death.] ...

II

... [Petitioners contend that their death sentences should be set aside because of *Enmund v. Florida*, 458 U.S. 782 (1982).] *Enmund* explicitly dealt with two distinct subsets of all felony murders in assessing whether Enmund's sentence was disproportional under the Eighth Amendment. At one pole was Enmund himself: the minor actor in an armed robbery, not on the scene, who neither intended to kill nor was found to have had any culpable mental state. Only a small minority of States even authorized the death penalty in such circumstances and even within those jurisdictions the death penalty was almost never exacted for such a crime. The Court held that capital punishment was disproportional in these cases. *Enmund* also clearly dealt with the other polar case: the felony murderer who actually killed, attempted to kill, or intended to kill. The Court clearly held that the equally small minority of jurisdictions that limited the death penalty to these circumstances could continue to exact it in accordance with local law when the circumstances warranted. The Tison brothers' cases fall into neither of these neat categories.

... The issue raised by this case is whether the Eighth Amendment prohibits the death penalty in the intermediate case of the defendant whose participation is major and whose mental state is one of reckless indifference to the value of human life. *Enmund* does not specifically address this point. We now take up the task of determining whether the Eighth Amendment proportionality requirement bars the death penalty under these circumstances.

[The Court concluded that a number of states authorize the death penalty where, although the "defendant's mental state fell short of intent to kill, the defendant was a major actor in a felony in which he knew death was highly likely to occur."] Against this backdrop, we now consider the proportionality of the death penalty in these mid-range felony-murder cases for which the majority of American jurisdictions clearly authorize capital punishment and for which American courts have not been nearly so reluctant to impose death as they are in the case of felony-murder *simpliciter*.

A critical facet of the individualized determination of culpability required in capital cases is the mental state with which the defendant commits the crime. Deeply ingrained in our legal tradition is the idea that the more purposeful is the criminal conduct, the more serious is the offense, and, therefore, the more severely it ought to be punished. The ancient concept of malice aforethought was an early attempt to focus on mental state in order to distinguish those who deserved death from those who through "Benefit of ... Clergy" would be spared. Over time, malice aforethought came to be inferred from the mere act of killing in a variety of circumstances; in reaction, Pennsylvania became the first American jurisdiction to distinguish between degrees of murder, reserving capital punishment to "wilful, deliberate and premeditated" killings and felony murders. More recently, in *Lockett v. Ohio*, 438 U.S. 586 (1978), the plurality opinion made clear that the defendant's mental state was critical to weighing a defendant's culpability under a system of guided discretion, vacating a death sentence imposed under an Ohio statute that did not permit the sentencing authority to take into account "[t]he absence of direct proof that the defendant intended to cause the death of the victim." In *Enmund v. Florida*, the Court recognized again the importance of mental state, explicitly permitting the death penalty in at least those cases where the felony murderer intended to kill and forbidding it in the case of a minor actor not shown to have had any culpable mental state.

A narrow focus on the question of whether or not a given defendant "intended to kill," however, is a highly unsatisfactory means of definitively distinguishing the most culpable and dangerous of murderers. Many who intend to, and do, kill are not criminally liable at all — those who act in self-defense or with other justification or excuse. Other intentional homicides, though criminal, are often felt undeserving of the death penalty — those that are the result of provocation. On the other hand, some nonintentional murderers may be among the most dangerous and inhumane of all — the person who tortures another not caring whether the victim lives or dies, or the robber who shoots someone in the course of the robbery, utterly indifferent to the fact that the desire to rob may have the unintended consequence of killing the victim as well as taking the victim's property. This reckless indifference to the value of human life may be every bit as shocking to the moral sense as an "intent to kill." Indeed it is for this very reason that the common law and modern criminal codes alike have classified behavior such as occurred in this case along with intentional murders. *Enmund* held that when "intent to kill" results in its logical though not inevitable consequence — the taking of human life — the Eighth Amendment permits the State to exact the death penalty after a careful weighing of the aggravating and mitigating circumstances. Similarly, we hold that the reckless disregard for human life implicit in knowingly engaging in criminal activities known to carry a grave risk of death represents a highly culpable mental state, a mental state that may be taken into account in making a capital sentencing judgment when that conduct causes its natural, though also not inevitable, lethal result.

The petitioners' own personal involvement in the crimes was not minor, but rather, as specifically found by the trial court, "substantial." Far from merely sitting in a car away from the actual scene of the murders acting as the getaway driver to a robbery, each petitioner was actively involved in every element of the kidnaping-robbery and was physically present during the entire sequence of criminal activity culminating in the murder of the Lyons family and the subsequent flight. The Tisons' high level of participation in these crimes further implicates them in the resulting deaths. Accordingly, they fall well within the overlapping second intermediate position which focuses on the defendant's degree of participation in the felony.

Only a small minority of those jurisdictions imposing capital punishment for felony murder have rejected the possibility of a capital sentence absent an intent to kill and we do not find this minority position constitutionally required. We will not attempt to precisely delineate the particular types of conduct and states of mind warranting imposition of the death penalty here. Rather, we simply hold that major participation in the felony committed, combined with reckless indifference to human life, is sufficient to satisfy the *Enmund* culpability requirement. The Arizona courts have clearly found that the former exists; we now vacate the judgments below and remand for determination of the latter in further proceedings not inconsistent with this opinion.

Justice BRENNAN, with whom Justice Marshall joins, and with whom Justice Blackmun and Justice Stevens join as to Parts I through IV-A, dissenting.

The murders that Gary Tison and Randy Greenawalt committed revolt and grieve all who learn of them. When the deaths of the Lyons family and Theresa Tyson were first reported, many in Arizona erupted "in a towering yell" for retribution and justice. Yet Gary Tison, the central figure in this tragedy, the man who had his family arrange his and Greenawalt's escape from prison, and the man who chose, with Greenawalt, to murder this family while his sons stood by, died of exposure in the desert before society could arrest him and bring him to trial. The question this case presents is what punishment Arizona may constitutionally exact from two of Gary Tison's sons for their role in these events. Because our precedents and our Constitution compel a different answer than the one the Court reaches today, I dissent....

II

[The Court's application of its new rule governing felony-murder is not justified in this case.] The evidence in the record overlooked today regarding petitioners' mental states with respect to the shootings is not trivial. For example, while the Court has found that petitioners made no effort prior to the shooting to assist the victims, the uncontradicted statements of both petitioners are that just prior to the shootings they were attempting to find a jug of water to give to the family. While the Court states that petitioners were on the scene during the shooting and that they watched it occur, Raymond stated that he and Ricky were still engaged in repacking the Mazda after finding the water jug when the shootings occurred. Ricky stated that they had returned with the water, but were still some distance ("farther than this room") from the Lincoln when the shootings started, and that the brothers then turned away from the scene and went back to the Mazda. Neither stated that they anticipated that the shootings would occur, or that they could have done anything to prevent them or to help the victims afterward. Both, however, expressed feelings of surprise, helplessness, and regret. This statement of Raymond's is illustrative:

> Well, I just think you should know when we first came into this we had an agreement with my dad that nobody would get hurt because we [the brothers] wanted no one hurt. And when this [killing of the kidnap victims] came about we were not expecting it. And it took us by surprise as much as it took the family [the victims] by surprise because we were not expecting this to happen. And

I feel bad about it happening. I wish we could [have done] something to stop it, but by the time it happened it was too late to stop it. And it's just something we are going to live with the rest of our lives. It will always be there....

IV

In 1922, "five negroes who were convicted of murder in the first degree and sentenced to death by the Court of the State of Arkansas" appealed to this Court from an order of the District Court dismissing their writ of habeas corpus. *Moore v. Dempsey*, 261 U.S. 86 (1923). The crux of their appeal was that they "were hurried to conviction under the pressure of a mob without any regard for their rights and without according to them due process of law." In reversing the order, Justice Holmes stated the following for the Court:

> It certainly is true that mere mistakes of law in the course of a trial are not to be corrected [by habeas corpus]. But if the case is that the whole proceeding is a mask — that counsel, jury, and judge were swept to the fatal end by an irresistible wave of public passion, and that the State Courts failed to correct the wrong, neither perfection in the machinery for correction nor the possibility that the trial court and counsel saw no other way of avoiding an immediate outbreak of the mob can prevent this Court from securing to the petitioners their constitutional rights.

A

... What makes this a difficult case is the challenge of giving substantive content to the concept of criminal culpability. Our Constitution demands that the sentencing decision itself, and not merely the procedures that produce it, respond to the reasonable goals of punishment. But the decision to execute these petitioners, like the state courts' decisions in *Moore*, appears responsive less to reason than to other, more visceral, demands. The urge to employ the felony-murder doctrine against accomplices is undoubtedly strong when the killings stir public passion and the actual murderer is beyond human grasp. And an intuition that sons and daughters must sometimes be punished for the sins of the father may be deeply rooted in our consciousness.[7] Yet pun-

---

7. These expressions are consistent with other evidence about the sons' mental states that this Court, like the lower courts, has neglected. Neither son had a prior felony record. Both lived at home with their mother and visited their father, whom they believed to be "a model prisoner," each week. They did not plan the breakout or escape; rather their father, after thinking about it himself for a year, mentioned the idea to Raymond for the first time one week before the breakout, and discussed with his sons the possibility of having them participate only the day before the breakout. The sons conditioned their participation on their father's promise that no one would get hurt; during the breakout, their father kept his word. The trial court found that the murders their father later committed were senseless and unnecessary to the felony of stealing a car in which the sons participated; and just prior to the shootings the sons were retrieving a water jug for the family. Given these circumstances, the sons' own testimony that they were surprised by the killings, and did not expect them to occur, appears more plausible than the Court's speculation that they "subjectively appreciated that their activities were likely to result in the taking of innocent life." The report of the psychologist, who examined both sons, also suggests that they may not have appreciated the consequences of their participation:

> "These most unfortunate youngsters were born into an extremely pathological family and were exposed to one of the premier sociopaths of recent Arizona history. In my opinion this very fact had a severe influence upon the personality structure of these youngsters....
> "I do believe their father, Gary Tison, exerted a strong, consistent, destructive but subtle pressure upon these youngsters and I believe that these young men got committed to

ishment that conforms more closely to such retributive instincts than to the Eighth Amendment is tragically anachronistic in a society governed by our Constitution.

B

This case thus illustrates the enduring truth of Justice Harlan's observation that the tasks of identifying "those characteristics of criminal homicides and their perpetrators which call for the death penalty, and [of] express[ing] these characteristics in language which can be fairly understood and applied by the sentencing authority appear to be ... beyond present human ability." *McGautha v. California*, 402 U.S. 183, 204 (1971).The persistence of doctrines (such as felony murder) that allow excessive discretion in apportioning criminal culpability, and of decisions (such as today's) that do not even attempt "precisely [to] delineate the particular types of conduct and states of mind warranting imposition of the death penalty," demonstrate that this Court has still not articulated rules that will ensure that capital sentencing decisions conform to the substantive principles of the Eighth Amendment. Arbitrariness continues so to infect both the procedure and substance of capital sentencing that any decision to impose the death penalty remains cruel and unusual. For this reason, as well as for the reasons expressed in *Gregg*, I adhere to my view that the death penalty is in all circumstances cruel and unusual punishment prohibited by the Eighth and Fourteenth Amendments, and dissent.

Notes

1. The United States' refusal to abandon the felony-murder rule as the basis for a capital sentence distinguishes it from other developed countries. In addition to being one of a few countries in the western hemisphere that retains capital punishment, the United States "remains virtually the only western country still recognizing a rule which makes it possible 'that the most serious sanctions known to law might be imposed for accidental homicide.'" Roth & Sunby, "The Felony-Murder Rule: A Doctrine at Constitutional Crossroads," 70 Cornell L. Rev. 446, 447–448 (1985).

2. For an argument against making felony murder the basis for a capital offense, see Acker & Lanier, "The Dimensions of Capital Murder," 29 Crim. L. Bull. 379, 390–397 (1993). Acker and Lanier report that in twenty-three death penalty states, offenders can be convicted of capital murder *even though they have no intent to kill or to inflict serious bodily injury*. Fourteen death penalty jurisdictions preclude capital punishment for unintentional felony murder by requiring that a killing be committed intentionally or knowingly to qualify as capital murder. In eighteen death penalty states, felony murder *simpliciter* (which requires no specific mens rea and applies to killings committed during certain dangerous felonies) is a capital offense. Nine states permit the death penalty even though the offender kills neither intentionally nor during the course of an enumerated felony. This type of culpability involves offenders who, although harboring no intent to kill, nonetheless consciously engage in high risk behavior which manifests a

---

an act which was essentially 'over their heads.' Once committed, it was too late and there does not appear to be any true defense based on brainwashing, mental deficiency, mental illness or irresistible urge. There was a family obsession, the boys were 'trained' to think of their father as an innocent person being victimized in the state prison but both boys have made perfectly clear that they were functioning of their own volition. At a deeper psychological level it may have been less of their own volition than as a result of Mr. Tison's 'conditioning' and rather amoral attitudes within the family home."

"don't give a damn" attitude about the consequences which predictably could include the loss of human life.

3. Consider and evaluate Professor David McCord's proposals to reduce the rate of wrongly imposed death sentences in felony murder cases.

State Death Sentences for Felony Murder Accomplices Under the *Enmund* and *Tison* Standards

David McCord, 32 Ariz. St. L.J. 843, 892–96 (2000)

VI. Conclusions and Proposals

Despite the ambiguities of the *Enmund/Tison* doctrine, the state appellate courts have developed a relatively consistent body of doctrine. Just because it is relatively consistent, though, does not mean that it is the best that can be done. My research has revealed three cases where death sentences were improper because there was no ironclad evidence that the defendants were even at the murder scene, at least eleven cases of wrongly imposed death sentences in less-than-positive-knowledge cases, with the potential that an indeterminable number of at-least-positive-knowledge cases were wrongly held death eligible due to incorrectly found facts. Implementation of the following proposals by state legislatures could significantly reduce many of the bases on which such mistakes were made.

1. Require at least prior positive knowledge for death eligibility. Defendants who intentionally kill, attempt to kill, intend that a cohort kill, or know well in advance that a cohort will kill all stand on the same base moral level. If we are going to have capital punishment, then four mental states can undebatably be treated as equally justifying death eligibility. A culpable mental state comprised of recklessness—even if it is extreme—has not traditionally been treated as conferring equal culpability. It is still true that much of the populace does not consider recklessness to be of equal heinousness. Why not err on the side of caution and set the minimum degree of culpability necessary for death eligibility at the level of at least prior positive knowledge that a cohort will kill? Montana reached this conclusion under its state constitution. I urge other states to follow suit.

2. Even in at-least-prior-positive-knowledge cases, require safeguards against casting the death eligibility net too widely. I have already mentioned my three proposals in this regard: (1) require clear corroboration of a turncoat cohort's testimony before a defendant is death eligible; (2) require the same for the testimony of a jailhouse informant; and (3) require that the sentencer be absolutely certain that the defendant had at least prior positive knowledge before imposing a death sentence.

3. On the other hand, do not follow the New Jersey approach, which casts the net of death eligibility too narrowly. New Jersey has a statute that permits death eligibility only for the actual killer, or for someone who hired a contract killer. This is an incorrect approach to the problem. As noted above, there is no moral distinction to be drawn between the actual killer and one who attempted to kill, intended to kill, or knew in advance that the killing was going to occur. Thus, a statute like New Jersey's injects arbitrariness into the system. To take the most obvious example, imagine that Cohort #1, the mastermind and ringleader in a robbery, orders Cohort #2 to kill the robbery victim. Cohort #2 does so. Cohort #1 is death ineligible; Cohort #2 is death eligible. Yet surely Cohort #1 is no more or less deathworthy than Cohort #2 (all other things being equal). This approach is too simplistic to reach just results.

4. If death eligibility premised on less-than-prior-positive-knowledge is to be retained, make clear that the defendant's presence at the murder scene is an absolute prerequisite, and that the sentencer must be absolutely convinced of it before imposing a death sentence. As explained earlier, it is unjust to infer that the defendant shared in the killing actions of his cohort unless the defendant was present and failed to exercise a restraining influence. Further, absolute certainty of the defendant's presence—not just a belief beyond a reasonable doubt—is necessary to minimize the possibility of unjust death sentences.

5. If death eligibility premised on less-than-prior-positive-knowledge is to be retained, it should never be found in cases of simple robbery gone quickly awry. As likewise argued earlier, there is no basis for imputing extreme indifference to human life in a simple robbery gone quickly and fatally awry. The planned duration of the crime is short, the potential punishment for the robbery is not so severe as to engender a large probability that a cohort will kill to eliminate a witness, the defendant usually has no reason to believe the cohort to have lethal propensity, and the defendant has no opportunity to restrain in the spur of the moment.

6. Appellate courts should apply reasoned—but not knee-jerk-intra-case proportionality review. Occasionally, appellate courts take a peek at the sentences the defendant's cohorts received, and adjust the defendant's sentence to something less than death on the basis of an unnamed doctrine that could be described as intra-case proportionality review. There is a knee-jerk way to use this doctrine that may be harmful, and a reasoned way to use it that is beneficial. The knee-jerk use of intra-case proportionality review is that if any of the cohorts received a sentence less than death, none of them are eligible to receive a death sentence. While this reduces the number of death sentences, this reduction comes at too great a cost of injecting patent arbitrariness into the system. Imagine two virtually identical robbery/murder cases, each with two cohorts. In the first case, the prosecutor strikes a deal with Cohort #1 in which he receives a life sentence in exchange for testifying against Cohort #2, who receives the death penalty. In the second case, the prosecutor successfully seeks death sentences against both cohorts. If a court were to engage in intra-case proportionality review, it would reduce the sentence of Cohort #2 in the first case, while upholding both death sentences in the second case. These differences in treatment would not be due to the merits of the cases, but rather to the vagaries of the prosecution's tactics. Under this knee-jerk approach, even the most culpable of the cohorts would be death ineligible. On the other hand, a reasoned use of intra-case proportionality review is for an appellate court to check to see if any cohorts who were as or more culpable than the defendant received sentences less than death; if so, defendant's sentence should also be less than death. Such a downward adjustment is particularly warranted where the cohort's lesser sentence is due to a plea bargain. While even this reasoned use of intra-case proportionality review injects some systemic arbitrariness, the benefits of undoing the arbitrariness within the group of co-felons outweighs the systemic concerns.

7. The burden of persuasion for major participation with reckless indifference should be absolute certainty. This goes along with the absolute certainty standard already proposed regarding the at-least-positive-knowledge cases, and the defendant's presence at the scene for purposes as a necessary component of major participation. These reforms would make death sentencing for felony murder accomplices more just and predictable. They would not, however, completely eliminate wrongful death sentences for felony murder accomplices.

B. Age of the Offender

Should eligibility for the death penalty depend upon the age of the offender? While there may be an agreement in principle that some offenders are too young to be "deserving of death," is there or should there be a constitutional age limit on the death penalty?

Death Penalty for Children: The American Experience with Capital Punishment for Crimes Committed While under Age Eighteen

Victor L. Streib, 36 Okla. L. Rev. 613 (1983)

Historical Background of Capital Punishment for Children

The United States inherited the bulk of its criminal law, including the tradition of capital punishment, primarily from England but also from other European countries. A fundamental premise of this criminal jurisprudence was then and is now that persons under age seven were conclusively presumed to be incapable of entertaining criminal intent and thus could not have criminal liability imposed upon them. For persons from age seven to age fourteen, the presumption of inability to entertain criminal intent was rebuttable, and if rebutted, such a person could be convicted of a crime and be sentenced to death. No such presumption applied to persons age fourteen or over. This view of children's liability in the criminal justice system was accepted by the United States Supreme Court in *In re Gault*, 387 U.S. 1 (1967): "At common law, children under seven were considered incapable of possessing criminal intent. Beyond that age, they were subjected to arrest, trial, and in theory to punishment like adult offenders." ...

Impact of the Juvenile Justice System, 1899 to 1930

During this period in the United States, the juvenile justice system began to emerge. The United States Supreme Court provided the conventional explanation:

> The early reformers were appalled by adult procedures and penalties, and by the fact that children could be given long prison sentences and mixed in jails with hardened criminals.... The apparent rigidities, technicalities, and harshness which they observed in both substantive and procedural criminal law were therefore to be discarded. The idea of crime and punishment was to be abandoned. The child was to be "treated" and "rehabilitated" and the procedures, from apprehension through institutionalization, were to be "clinical" rather than punitive.

Mid-nineteenth-century reformers focused primarily upon modifying the harshness of the correctional phase of the criminal justice system. The best-known reforms were the houses of refuge established in various cities by reformers anxious to separate youthful offenders from adult criminals. The success of these reforms was limited by the continuing criminal court jurisdiction over those youthful offenders. This led reformers to believe that a separate legal system for juveniles was needed.

... The appearance of the juvenile justice system can be seen as a codification of the previous unofficial and implicit policy of giving special treatment to young offenders. For the purpose of this article, the premise is accepted that a juvenile justice system should not punish the juvenile offender but must treat and rehabilitate him. Adoption of this premise requires rejection of the death penalty for juvenile offenders. During the early era of juvenile justice (1900–1930), however, seventy-seven persons were executed for crimes committed while under age eighteen. None were sentenced to death directly by juvenile courts but were condemned by adult criminal courts.

Prosecution of Children in Criminal Court

In most jurisdictions today, delinquent acts are defined as acts in violation of state or federal law, local ordinance, or an order of the juvenile court. Generally, this definition encompasses acts that would be crimes if committed by an adult. This broad category includes murder and other capital crimes unless they are specifically excluded from the jurisdiction of the juvenile court. The essentially criminal nature of these delinquent acts means that the cases could fall within the jurisdiction of criminal court, as has been recognized by the Supreme Court in *Gault*, 387 U.S. 1, 15–16 (1967):

> [T]he fact of the matter is that there is little or no assurance ... that a juvenile apprehended and interrogated by the police or even by the Juvenile Court itself will remain outside of the reach of adult courts as a consequence of the offense for which he has been taken into custody. In Arizona, as in other States, provision is made for Juvenile Courts to relinquish or waive jurisdiction to the ordinary criminal courts.

In 1975 the Supreme Court noted in passing that "an overwhelming majority of jurisdictions permits transfer in certain instances."

... A person under the age limit for juvenile court jurisdiction will nevertheless be tried in criminal court if the offense charged has been expressly excluded from the jurisdiction of juvenile court. Typically, only the most serious crimes such as murder, rape, and robbery are excluded. Some states expressly exclude capital offenses from juvenile court jurisdiction, leaving only criminal court jurisdiction over such offenses.

Finally, some states give the prosecuting attorney discretion to decide in which court the case should be filed. If the prosecutor files a juvenile petition, the case proceeds in juvenile court; if a criminal information is filed or a grand jury indictment is obtained, the case proceeds in criminal court.

Each of these three alternatives lodges the choice of court in a different primary decision-maker. The traditional court waiver alternative leaves the decision up to the judiciary—specifically the juvenile court judge. In the second alternative, the legislature has made the original and preemptive decision to place certain cases exclusively in criminal court. The prosecutor is the decision-maker as to the choice of court in the third alternative. Whichever means is followed, an offender under the juvenile court age limit is subjected to the full authority of the criminal court, typically including the power to impose capital punishment for certain crimes.

Criminological Purposes Served by Executing Children

Capital punishment for children has been common enough during the past 340 years to warrant attention. Even though the youthfulness of offenders has probably always been considered, and now must be specifically taken into account as a mitigating factor, the choice must still be made between execution and a long term, usually life, in prison. What factors unique to such cases should be considered?

A number of policies and presumptions underlie the continuing debate over the appropriateness of capital punishment for crimes by adults. Perhaps the most complete list has been provided by Justice Thurgood Marshall, concurring in *Furman v. Georgia*: "There are six purposes conceivably served by capital punishment: retribution, deterrence, prevention of repetitive criminal acts, encouragement of guilty pleas and confessions, eugenics, and economy." Each should be considered in the context of crimes committed by persons under age eighteen.

The goal of societal retribution or legal vengeance achieved through execution of a child seems difficult to justify. However, capital punishment can be characterized as an understandable expression of societal outrage at particular crimes. In this sense, Justice Stewart referred favorably to a retributive purpose in *Gregg v. Georgia* and in *Furman v. Georgia*. Chief Justice Burger has also approved this justification. In contrast, Justice Marshall has argued persuasively that the Eighth Amendment precludes retribution for its own sake.

Even if the execution of an adult solely for revenge is constitutionally permissible, this justification of capital punishment is less appealing when the object of righteous vengeance is a child. The spectacle of our society seeking legal vengeance through execution of a child raises fundamental questions about the nature of children's moral responsibility for their actions and about society's moral responsibility to protect and nurture children.

Probably the most complex issue is whether capital punishment is more effective than life imprisonment as a deterrent to crime. This key issue has been the subject of extensive research, but no consistent conclusions have been drawn by members of the Supreme Court. When applied to children, the key issues are adolescents' perception of death and whether that perception acts as a more significant deterrent to criminal acts than life imprisonment.

Even less is known about death as a deterrent for adolescents than is known about death as a deterrent for adults. Many social scientists would agree that adolescents live for today with little thought of the future consequences of their actions. The defiant attitudes and risk-taking behaviors of some adolescents are probably related to their "developmental stage of defiance about danger and death." Some adolescents may play games of chance with death from a feeling of omnipotence. They typically have not learned to accept the finality of death. Adolescents tend to view death as a remote possibility; old people die, not teenagers. Consider, for example, teenagers' propensity to flirt with death through reckless driving, ingestion of dangerous drugs, and other similar "death-defying" behavior.

The meager research on this issue suggests the conclusion that threatening a child with death probably does not have the same impact as threatening an adult with death. Even if some percentage of adults are deterred by the death penalty, the deterrent effect tends to lose much of its power when imposed upon an adolescent.

No one can deny that execution of a child will prevent repetitive criminal acts by that particular child. The death penalty does, however, seem an unnecessarily harsh solution to the problem of recidivism. Not only are murderers "extremely unlikely to commit other crimes either in prison or upon their release," but irreversibly abandoning all hope of the reform of a child is squarely in opposition to the fundamental premises of juvenile justice and comparable socio-legal systems. While the specific deterrence argument may be somewhat persuasive in the case of the 45-year-old habitual criminal, it is singularly inappropriate and defeatist when applied to the 16-year-old child.

Using capital punishment as leverage to encourage guilty pleas and confessions seems not only a questionable justification for this ultimate sanction but also unnecessary in a child's case. The threat of life imprisonment for an adolescent who has fifty to sixty years yet to live is so overwhelming that it should provide whatever leverage the government might need.

The potential fifty to sixty years of life in prison also gives rise to an economic argument—that it is simply an enormous and unjustifiable financial burden on society to support life imprisonment instead of executing youthful offenders. Given the extraordinarily high cost of capital trials and appeals, as well as the cost of maintaining death row and of performing executions, it would seem reasonable to conclude that "there can be no doubt that it costs more to execute a man than to keep him in prison for life."

Finally, the issue of using capital punishment for eugenic purposes or to improve the human race seems unworthy of serious consideration. In any event, the less severe alternatives of sterilization and/or life imprisonment would seem to be required by the Constitution.

This brief consideration of the purposes served by capital punishment for children is inconclusive at best, as is such a consideration *vis-à-vis* adults. Most of the justifications for capital punishment of adults lose whatever persuasiveness they have when applied to the case of an offender under age eighteen.

Note on Thompson v. Oklahoma, 487 U.S. 815 (1988), and Stanford v. Kentucky, 492 U.S. 361 (1989)

In *Thompson v. Oklahoma*, 487 U.S. 815 (1988), the Supreme Court addressed the question "whether the execution of [a death] sentence would violate the constitutional prohibition against the infliction of 'cruel and unusual punishments' because petitioner was only 15 years old at the time of his offense." In *Thompson*, four justices—Justices Stevens, Brennan, Marshall and Blackmun—concluded that the Eighth Amendment precluded Oklahoma from imposing the death penalty on an individual who was under the age of sixteen at the time he committed capital murder. Chief Justice Rehnquist, and Justices White and Scalia dissented. Justice O'Connor's swing vote tipped the scales in favor Thompson. In reaching her decision that the death penalty could not constitutionally be imposed on a fifteen-year-old, Justice O'Connor stated:

> … The case before us today raises some of the same concerns that have led us to erect barriers to the imposition of capital punishment in other contexts. Oklahoma has enacted a statute that authorizes capital punishment for murder, without setting any minimum age at which the commission of murder may lead to the imposition of that penalty. The State has also, but quite separately, provided that 15-year-old murder defendants may be treated as adults in some circumstances. Because it proceeded in this manner, there is a considerable risk that the Oklahoma Legislature either did not realize that its actions would have the effect of rendering 15-year-old defendants death eligible or did not give the question the serious consideration that would have been reflected in the explicit choice of some minimum age for death eligibility. Were it clear that no national consensus forbids the imposition of capital punishment for crimes committed before the age of 16, the implicit nature of the Oklahoma Legislature's decision would not be constitutionally problematic. In the peculiar circumstances we face today, however, the Oklahoma statutes have presented this Court with a result that is of very dubious constitutionality, and they have done so without the earmarks of careful consideration that we have required

for other kinds of decisions leading to the death penalty. In this unique situation, I am prepared to conclude that petitioner and others who were below the age of 16 at the time of their offense may not be executed under the authority of a capital punishment statute that specifies no minimum age at which the commission of a capital crime can lead to the offender's execution.

The following year, in *Stanford v. Kentucky* and *Wilkins v. Missouri*, the Court considered "whether the imposition of capital punishment on an individual for a crime committed at 16 or 17 years of age constitutes cruel and unusual punishment under the Eighth Amendment." In an opinion authored by Justice Scalia, in which Chief Justice Rehnquist, and Justices White and Kennedy joined, a plurality held that the Eighth Amendment did not preclude the imposition of the death penalty on persons who were 16 or 17 at the time of the commission of their capital crimes. The plurality stated: "We discern neither a historical nor a modern societal consensus forbidding the imposition of capital punishment on any person who murders at 16 or 17 years of age. Accordingly, we conclude that such punishment does not offend the Eighth Amendment's prohibition against cruel and unusual punishment." Justices Brennan, Marshall, Blackmun, and Stevens dissented concluding that the death penalty could not constitutionally be imposed on anyone who was under the age of 18 at the time of the commission of their crime. Once again, Justice O'Connor provided the swing vote; however, Justice O'Connor voted to uphold the imposition of the death penalty on 16 and 17 year olds. In distinguishing *Thompson*, Justice O'Connor stated:

> In *Thompson* I noted that "[t]he most salient statistic that bears on this case is that every single American legislature that has expressly set a minimum age for capital punishment has set that age at 16 or above." It is this difference between *Thompson* and these cases, more than any other, that convinces me there is no national consensus forbidding the imposition of capital punishment for crimes committed at the age of 16 and older. As the Court indicates, "a majority of the States that permit capital punishment authorize it for crimes committed at age 16 or above...." Three States, including Kentucky, [Indiana and Nevada], have specifically set the minimum age for capital punishment at 16, and a fourth, Florida, clearly contemplates the imposition of capital punishment on 16-year-olds in its juvenile transfer statute. Under these circumstances, unlike the "peculiar circumstances" at work in *Thompson*, I do not think it necessary to require a state legislature to specify that the commission of a capital crime can lead to the execution of a 16- or 17-year-old offender. Because it is sufficiently clear that today no national consensus forbids the imposition of capital punishment in these circumstances, "the implicit nature of the [Missouri] Legislature's decision [is] not ... constitutionally problematic." This is true, *a fortiori*, in the case of Kentucky, which has specified 16 as the minimum age for the imposition of the death penalty. The day may come when there is such general legislative rejection of the execution of 16- or 17-year-old capital murderers that a clear national consensus can be said to have developed. Because I do not believe that day has yet arrived, I concur in Parts ... of the Court's opinion, and I concur in its judgment....

Roper v. Simmons
543 U.S. 551 (2005)

KENNEDY, J., delivered the opinion of the Court, in which Stevens, Souter, Ginsburg, and Breyer, JJ., joined. Stevens, J., filed a concurring opinion, in which Ginsburg,

J., joined. O'Connor, J., filed a dissenting opinion. Scalia, J., filed a dissenting opinion, in which Rehnquist, C.J., and Thomas, J., joined.

This case requires us to address, for the second time in a decade and a half, whether it is permissible under the Eighth and Fourteenth Amendments to the Constitution of the United States to execute a juvenile offender who was older than 15 but younger than 18 when he committed a capital crime. In *Stanford v. Kentucky*, 492 U.S. 361 (1989), a divided Court rejected the proposition that the Constitution bars capital punishment for juvenile offenders in this age group. We reconsider the question.

I

At the age of 17, when he was still a junior in high school, Christopher Simmons, the respondent here, committed murder. About nine months later, after he had turned 18, he was tried and sentenced to death. There is little doubt that Simmons was the instigator of the crime. Before its commission Simmons said he wanted to murder someone. In chilling, callous terms he talked about his plan, discussing it for the most part with two friends, Charles Benjamin and John Tessmer, then aged 15 and 16 respectively. Simmons proposed to commit burglary and murder by breaking and entering, tying up a victim, and throwing the victim off a bridge. Simmons assured his friends they could "get away with it" because they were minors. . . .

The jury recommended the death penalty after finding the State had proved each of the three aggravating factors submitted to it. Accepting the jury's recommendation, the trial judge imposed the death penalty. . . .

After [direct appeal and habeas] proceedings in Simmons' case had run their course, this Court held that the Eighth and Fourteenth Amendments prohibit the execution of a mentally retarded person. *Atkins v. Virginia*, 536 U.S. 304 (2002) (see *infra* chapter 5). Simmons filed a new petition for state postconviction relief, arguing that the reasoning of *Atkins* established that the Constitution prohibits the execution of a juvenile who was under 18 when the crime was committed.

The Missouri Supreme Court agreed. It held that since *Stanford*,

> "a national consensus has developed against the execution of juvenile offenders, as demonstrated by the fact that eighteen states now bar such executions for juveniles, that twelve other states bar executions altogether, that no state has lowered its age of execution below 18 since Stanford, that five states have legislatively or by case law raised or established the minimum age at 18, and that the imposition of the juvenile death penalty has become truly unusual over the last decade."

On this reasoning it set aside Simmons' death sentence and resentenced him to "life imprisonment without eligibility for probation, parole, or release except by act of the Governor."

We granted certiorari and now affirm.

II

The Eighth Amendment provides: "Excessive bail shall not be required, nor excessive fines imposed, nor cruel and unusual punishments inflicted." The provision is applicable to the States through the Fourteenth Amendment. As the Court explained in *Atkins*, the Eighth Amendment guarantees individuals the right not to be subjected to excessive sanctions. The right flows from the basic " 'precept of justice that punishment for crime should be graduated and proportioned to [the] offense.'" By protecting even those convicted of heinous crimes, the Eighth Amendment reaffirms the duty of the government to respect the dignity of all persons.

The prohibition against "cruel and unusual punishments," like other expansive language in the Constitution, must be interpreted according to its text, by considering history, tradition, and precedent, and with due regard for its purpose and function in the constitutional design. To implement this framework we have established the propriety and affirmed the necessity of referring to "the evolving standards of decency that mark the progress of a maturing society" to determine which punishments are so disproportionate as to be cruel and unusual. *Trop v. Dulles*, 356 U.S. 86, 100–101 (1958) (plurality opinion).

In *Thompson v. Oklahoma*, 487 U.S. 815 (1988), a plurality of the Court determined that our standards of decency do not permit the execution of any offender under the age of 16 at the time of the crime. The plurality opinion explained that no death penalty State that had given express consideration to a minimum age for the death penalty had set the age lower than 16. The plurality also observed that "[t]he conclusion that it would offend civilized standards of decency to execute a person who was less than 16 years old at the time of his or her offense is consistent with the views that have been expressed by respected professional organizations, by other nations that share our Anglo-American heritage, and by the leading members of the Western European community." The opinion further noted that juries imposed the death penalty on offenders under 16 with exceeding rarity; the last execution of an offender for a crime committed under the age of 16 had been carried out in 1948, 40 years prior.

Bringing its independent judgment to bear on the permissibility of the death penalty for a 15-year-old offender, the *Thompson* plurality stressed that "[t]he reasons why juveniles are not trusted with the privileges and responsibilities of an adult also explain why their irresponsible conduct is not as morally reprehensible as that of an adult." According to the plurality, the lesser culpability of offenders under 16 made the death penalty inappropriate as a form of retribution, while the low likelihood that offenders under 16 engaged in "the kind of cost-benefit analysis that attaches any weight to the possibility of execution" made the death penalty ineffective as a means of deterrence. With Justice O'Connor concurring in the judgment on narrower grounds, the Court set aside the death sentence that had been imposed on the 15-year-old offender.

The next year, in *Stanford v. Kentucky*, 492 U.S. 361 (1989), the Court, over a dissenting opinion joined by four Justices, referred to contemporary standards of decency in this country and concluded the Eighth and Fourteenth Amendments did not proscribe the execution of juvenile offenders over 15 but under 18. The Court noted that 22 of the 37 death penalty States permitted the death penalty for 16-year-old offenders, and, among these 37 States, 25 permitted it for 17-year-old offenders. These numbers, in the Court's view, indicated there was no national consensus "sufficient to label a particular punishment cruel and unusual." A plurality of the Court also "emphatically reject[ed]" the suggestion that the Court should bring its own judgment to bear on the acceptability of the juvenile death penalty....

... [W]e now reconsider the issue decided in *Stanford*. The beginning point is a review of objective indicia of consensus, as expressed in particular by the enactments of legislatures that have addressed the question. This data gives us essential instruction. We then must determine, in the exercise of our own independent judgment, whether the death penalty is a disproportionate punishment for juveniles.

III

A

The evidence of national consensus against the death penalty for juveniles is similar, and in some respects parallel, to the evidence *Atkins* held sufficient to demonstrate a national consensus against the death penalty for the mentally retarded. When *Atkins* was decided, 30 States prohibited the death penalty for the mentally retarded. This number comprised 12 that had abandoned the death penalty altogether, and 18 that maintained it but excluded the mentally retarded from its reach. By a similar calculation in this case, 30 States prohibit the juvenile death penalty, comprising 12 that have rejected the death penalty altogether and 18 that maintain it but, by express provision or judicial interpretation, exclude juveniles from its reach. *Atkins* emphasized that even in the 20 States without formal prohibition, the practice of executing the mentally retarded was infrequent. Since *Penry*, only five States had executed offenders known to have an IQ under 70. In the present case, too, even in the 20 States without a formal prohibition on executing juveniles, the practice is infrequent. Since *Stanford*, six States have executed prisoners for crimes committed as juveniles. In the past 10 years, only three have done so: Oklahoma, Texas, and Virginia.... In December 2003 the Governor of Kentucky decided to spare the life of Kevin Stanford, and commuted his sentence to one of life imprisonment without parole, with the declaration that "'[w]e ought not to be executing people who, legally, were children.'" By this act the Governor ensured Kentucky would not add itself to the list of States that have executed juveniles within the last 10 years even by the execution of the very defendant whose death sentence the Court had upheld in *Stanford v. Kentucky*.

There is, to be sure, at least one difference between the evidence of consensus in *Atkins* and in this case. Impressive in *Atkins* was the rate of abolition of the death penalty for the mentally retarded. Sixteen States that permitted the execution of the mentally retarded at the time of *Penry* had prohibited the practice by the time we heard *Atkins*. By contrast, the rate of change in reducing the incidence of the juvenile death penalty, or in taking specific steps to abolish it, has been slower. Five States that allowed the juvenile death penalty at the time of *Stanford* have abandoned it in the intervening 15 years—four through legislative enactments and one through judicial decision.

Though less dramatic than the change from *Penry* to *Atkins* ("telling," to borrow the word *Atkins* used to describe this difference), we still consider the change from *Stanford* to this case to be significant. As noted in *Atkins*, with respect to the States that had abandoned the death penalty for the mentally retarded since *Penry*, "[i]t is not so much the number of these States that is significant, but the consistency of the direction of change." In particular we found it significant that, in the wake of *Penry*, no State that had already prohibited the execution of the mentally retarded had passed legislation to reinstate the penalty. The number of States that have abandoned capital punishment for juvenile offenders since *Stanford* is smaller than the number of States that abandoned capital punishment for the mentally retarded after *Penry*; yet we think the same consistency of direction of change has been demonstrated. Since *Stanford*, no State that previously prohibited capital punishment for juveniles has reinstated it. This fact, coupled with the trend toward abolition of the juvenile death penalty, carries special force in light of the general popularity of anticrime legislation, and in light of the particular trend in recent years toward cracking down on juvenile crime in other respects. . . . Any difference between this case and *Atkins* with respect to the pace of abolition is thus counterbalanced by the consistent direction of the change. . . .

As in *Atkins*, the objective indicia of consensus in this case—the rejection of the juvenile death penalty in the majority of States; the infrequency of its use even where it remains on the books; and the consistency in the trend toward abolition of the practice—provide sufficient evidence that today our society views juveniles, in the words *Atkins* used respecting the mentally retarded, as "categorically less culpable than the average criminal."

B

A majority of States have rejected the imposition of the death penalty on juvenile offenders under 18, and we now hold this is required by the Eighth Amendment.

Because the death penalty is the most severe punishment, the Eighth Amendment applies to it with special force. Capital punishment must be limited to those offenders who commit "a narrow category of the most serious crimes" and whose extreme culpability makes them "the most deserving of execution." This principle is implemented throughout the capital sentencing process. States must give narrow and precise definition to the aggravating factors that can result in a capital sentence. In any capital case a defendant has wide latitude to raise as a mitigating factor "any aspect of [his or her] character or record and any of the circumstances of the offense that the defendant proffers as a basis for a sentence less than death." . . . There are a number of crimes that beyond question are severe in absolute terms, yet the death penalty may not be imposed for their commission. The death penalty may not be imposed on certain classes of offenders, such as juveniles under 16, the insane, and the mentally retarded, no matter how heinous the crime. These rules vindicate the underlying principle that the death penalty is reserved for a narrow category of crimes and offenders.

Three general differences between juveniles under 18 and adults demonstrate that juvenile offenders cannot with reliability be classified among the worst offenders. First, as any parent knows and as the scientific and sociological studies respondent and his *amici* cite tend to confirm, "[a] lack of maturity and an underdeveloped sense of responsibility are found in youth more often than in adults and are more understandable among the young. These qualities often result in impetuous and ill-considered actions and decisions." It has been noted that "adolescents are overrepresented statistically in virtually every category of reckless behavior." In recognition of the comparative immaturity and irresponsibility of juveniles, almost every State prohibits those under 18 years of age from voting, serving on juries, or marrying without parental consent.

The second area of difference is that juveniles are more vulnerable or susceptible to negative influences and outside pressures, including peer pressure. This is explained in part by the prevailing circumstance that juveniles have less control, or less experience with control, over their own environment.

The third broad difference is that the character of a juvenile is not as well formed as that of an adult. The personality traits of juveniles are more transitory, less fixed. See generally E. Erikson, Identity: Youth and Crisis (1968).

These differences render suspect any conclusion that a juvenile falls among the worst offenders. The susceptibility of juveniles to immature and irresponsible behavior means "their irresponsible conduct is not as morally reprehensible as that of an adult." Their own vulnerability and comparative lack of control over their immediate surroundings mean juveniles have a greater claim than adults to be forgiven for failing to escape negative influences in their whole environment. The reality that juveniles still struggle to define their identity means it is less supportable to conclude that even a heinous crime committed by a juvenile is evidence of irretrievably depraved character. From a moral standpoint it would be misguided to equate the failings of a minor with those of an adult, for a greater possibility exists that a minor's character deficiencies will be reformed. Indeed, "[t]he relevance of youth as a mitigating factor derives from the fact that the signature qualities of youth are transient; as individuals mature, the impetuousness and recklessness that may dominate in younger years can subside." ...

Once the diminished culpability of juveniles is recognized, it is evident that the penological justifications for the death penalty apply to them with lesser force than to adults. We have held there are two distinct social purposes served by the death penalty: "'retribution and deterrence of capital crimes by prospective offenders.'" ... Whether viewed as an attempt to express the community's moral outrage or as an attempt to right the balance for the wrong to the victim, the case for retribution is not as strong with a minor as with an adult. Retribution is not proportional if the law's most severe penalty is imposed on one whose culpability or blameworthiness is diminished, to a substantial degree, by reason of youth and immaturity.

As for deterrence, it is unclear whether the death penalty has a significant or even measurable deterrent effect on juveniles, as counsel for the petitioner acknowledged at oral argument. In general we leave to legislatures the assessment of the efficacy of various criminal penalty schemes.... Here, however, the absence of evidence of deterrent effect is of special concern because the same characteristics that render juveniles less culpable than adults suggest as well that juveniles will be less susceptible to deterrence. In particular, as the plurality observed in *Thompson*, "[t]he likelihood that the teenage offender has made the kind of cost-benefit analysis that attaches any weight to the possibility of execution is so remote as to be virtually nonexistent." To the extent the juvenile death penalty might have residual deterrent effect, it is worth noting that the punishment of life imprisonment without the possibility of parole is itself a severe sanction, in particular for a young person....

Drawing the line at 18 years of age is subject, of course, to the objections always raised against categorical rules. The qualities that distinguish juveniles from adults do not disappear when an individual turns 18. By the same token, some under 18 have already attained a level of maturity some adults will never reach. For the reasons we have discussed, however, a line must be drawn. The plurality opinion in *Thompson* drew the line at 16. In the intervening years the *Thompson* plurality's conclusion that offenders under 16 may not be executed has not been challenged. The logic of *Thompson* extends to those who are under 18. The age of 18 is the point where society draws the line for many purposes between childhood and adulthood. It is, we conclude, the age at which the line for death eligibility ought to rest.

These considerations mean *Stanford v. Kentucky* should be deemed no longer controlling on this issue. To the extent *Stanford* was based on review of the objective indicia of consensus that obtained in 1989, it suffices to note that those indicia have changed. It should be observed, furthermore, that the *Stanford* Court should have considered those States that had abandoned the death penalty altogether as part of the consensus against the juvenile death penalty, a State's decision to bar the death penalty altogether of necessity demonstrates a judgment that the death penalty is inappropriate for all offenders, including juveniles. Last, to the extent *Stanford* was based on a rejection of the idea that this Court is required to bring its independent judgment to bear on the proportionality of the death penalty for a particular class of crimes or offenders, it suffices to note that this rejection was inconsistent with prior Eighth Amendment decisions....

IV

Our determination that the death penalty is disproportionate punishment for offenders under 18 finds confirmation in the stark reality that the United States is the only country in the world that continues to give official sanction to the juvenile death penalty. This reality does not become controlling, for the task of interpreting the Eighth Amendment remains our responsibility. Yet at least from the time of the Court's decision in *Trop*, the Court has referred to the laws of other countries and to international authorities as instructive for its interpretation of the Eighth Amendment's prohibition of "cruel and unusual punishments." ...

As respondent and a number of *amici* emphasize, Article 37 of the United Nations Convention on the Rights of the Child, which every country in the world has ratified save for the United States and Somalia, contains an express prohibition on capital punishment for crimes committed by juveniles under 18.... No ratifying country has entered a reservation to the provision prohibiting the execution of juvenile offenders. Parallel prohibitions are contained in other significant international covenants....

Respondent and his *amici* have submitted, and petitioner does not contest, that only seven countries other than the United States have executed juvenile offenders since 1990: Iran, Pakistan, Saudi Arabia, Yemen, Nigeria, the Democratic Republic of Congo, and China. Since then each of these countries has either abolished capital punishment for juveniles or made public disavowal of the practice. In sum, it is fair to say that the United States now stands alone in a world that has turned its face against the juvenile death penalty.

Though the international covenants prohibiting the juvenile death penalty are of more recent date, it is instructive to note that the United Kingdom abolished the juvenile death penalty before these covenants came into being. The United Kingdom's experience bears particular relevance here in light of the historic ties between our countries and in light of the Eighth Amendment's own origins. The Amendment was modeled on a parallel provision in the English Declaration of Rights of 1689, which provided: "[E]xcessive Bail ought not to be required nor excessive Fines imposed; nor cruel and unusual Punishments inflicted." ... As of now, the United Kingdom has abolished the death penalty in its entirety; but, decades before it took this step, it recognized the disproportionate nature of the juvenile death penalty; and it abolished that penalty as a separate matter....

The Eighth and Fourteenth Amendments forbid imposition of the death penalty on offenders who were under the age of 18 when their crimes were committed. The judgment of the Missouri Supreme Court setting aside the sentence of death imposed upon Christopher Simmons is affirmed.

Justice SCALIA, with whom The Chief Justice and Justice Thomas join, dissenting....

II

Of course, the real force driving today's decision is not the actions of four state legislatures, but the Court's own judgment that murderers younger than 18 can never be as morally culpable as older counterparts. The Court claims that this usurpation of the role of moral arbiter is simply a "retur[n] to the rul[e] established in decisions predating *Stanford*." That supposed rule—which is reflected solely in dicta and never once in a holding that purports to supplant the consensus of the American people with the Justices' views—was repudiated in *Stanford* for the very good reason that it has no foundation in law or logic. If the Eighth Amendment set forth an ordinary rule of law, it would indeed be the role of this Court to say what the law is. But the Court having pronounced that the Eighth Amendment is an ever-changing reflection of "the evolving standards of decency" of our society, it makes no sense for the Justices then to prescribe those standards rather than discern them from the practices of our people. On the evolving-standards hypothesis, the only legitimate function of this Court is to identify a moral consensus of the American people. By what conceivable warrant can nine lawyers presume to be the authoritative conscience of the Nation?

The reason for insistence on legislative primacy is obvious and fundamental: "[I]n a democratic society legislatures, not courts, are constituted to respond to the will and consequently the moral values of the people." For a similar reason we have, in our determination of society's moral standards, consulted the practices of sentencing juries: Juries "maintain a link between contemporary community values and the penal system" that this Court cannot claim for itself....

III

Though the views of our own citizens are essentially irrelevant to the Court's decision today, the views of other countries and the so-called international community take center stage.

The Court begins by noting that "Article 37 of the United Nations Convention on the Rights of the Child, which every country in the world has ratified save for the United States and Somalia, contains an express prohibition on capital punishment for crimes committed by juveniles under 18." The Court also discusses the International Covenant on Civil and Political Rights (ICCPR), December 19, 1966....

More fundamentally, however, the basic premise of the Court's argument—that American law should conform to the laws of the rest of the world—ought to be rejected out of hand. In fact the Court itself does not believe it. In many significant respects the laws of most other countries differ from our law—including not only such explicit provisions of our Constitution as the right to jury trial and grand jury indictment, but even many interpretations of the Constitution prescribed by this Court itself. The Court-pronounced exclusionary rule, for example, is distinctively American. When we adopted that rule in *Mapp v. Ohio*, 367 U.S. 643, 655 (1961), it was "unique to American Jurisprudence." Since then a categorical exclusionary rule has been "universally rejected" by other countries, including those with rules prohibiting illegal searches and police misconduct, despite the fact that none of these countries "appears to have any alternative form of discipline for police that is effective in preventing search violations." England, for example, rarely excludes evidence found during an illegal search or seizure and has only recently begun excluding evidence from illegally obtained confessions. Canada rarely excludes evidence and will only do so if admission will "bring the administration of justice into disrepute." The European Court of Human Rights has held that introduction of illegally seized evidence does not violate the "fair trial" requirement in Article 6, 1, of the European Convention on Human Rights....

And let us not forget the Court's abortion jurisprudence, which makes us one of only six countries that allow abortion on demand until the point of viability.... Though the

Government and *amici* in cases following *Roe v. Wade*, 410 U.S. 113 (1973), urged the Court to follow the international community's lead, these arguments fell on deaf ears....

The Court's special reliance on the laws of the United Kingdom is perhaps the most indefensible part of its opinion. It is of course true that we share a common history with the United Kingdom, and that we often consult English sources when asked to discern the meaning of a constitutional text written against the backdrop of 18th-century English law and legal thought. If we applied that approach today, our task would be an easy one. As we explained in *Harmelin v. Michigan*, 501 U.S. 957 (1991), the "Cruell and Unusuall Punishments" provision of the English Declaration of Rights was originally meant to describe those punishments "'out of [the Judges'] Power'"—that is, those punishments that were not authorized by common law or statute, but that were nonetheless administered by the Crown or the Crown's judges. Under that reasoning, the death penalty for under-18 offenders would easily survive this challenge. The Court has, however—I think wrongly—long rejected a purely originalist approach to our Eighth Amendment, and that is certainly not the approach the Court takes today. Instead, the Court undertakes the majestic task of determining (and thereby prescribing) our Nation's current standards of decency. It is beyond comprehension why we should look, for that purpose, to a country that has developed, in the centuries since the Revolutionary War—and with increasing speed since the United Kingdom's recent submission to the jurisprudence of European courts dominated by continental jurists—a legal, political, and social culture quite different from our own. If we took the Court's directive seriously, we would also consider relaxing our double jeopardy prohibition, since the British Law Commission recently published a report that would significantly extend the rights of the prosecution to appeal cases where an acquittal was the result of a judge's ruling that was legally incorrect.... We would also curtail our right to jury trial in criminal cases since, despite the jury system's deep roots in our shared common law, England now permits all but the most serious offenders to be tried by magistrates without a jury....

The Court should either profess its willingness to reconsider all these matters in light of the views of foreigners, or else it should cease putting forth foreigners' views as part of the reasoned basis of its decisions. To invoke alien law when it agrees with one's own thinking, and ignore it otherwise, is not reasoned decisionmaking, but sophistry.

The Court responds that "[i]t does not lessen our fidelity to the Constitution or our pride in its origins to acknowledge that the express affirmation of certain fundamental rights by other nations and peoples simply underscores the centrality of those same rights within our own heritage of freedom." To begin with, I do not believe that approval by "other nations and peoples" should buttress our commitment to American principles any more than (what should logically follow) disapproval by "other nations and peoples" should weaken that commitment. More importantly, however, the Court's statement flatly misdescribes what is going on here. Foreign sources are cited today, not to underscore our "fidelity" to the Constitution, our "pride in its origins," and "our own [American] heritage." To the contrary, they are cited to set aside the centuries-old American practice—a practice still engaged in by a large majority of the relevant States—of letting a jury of 12 citizens decide whether, in the particular case, youth should be the basis for withholding the death penalty. What these foreign sources "affirm," rather than repudiate, is the Justices' own notion of how the world ought to be, and their diktat that it shall be so henceforth in America. The Court's parting attempt to downplay the significance of its extensive discussion of foreign law is unconvincing. "Acknowledgment" of foreign approval has no place in the legal opinion of this Court unless it is part of the basis for the Court's judgment—which is surely what it parades as today.

Notes and Question

1. In this country, discussions about age as a barrier to capital punishment have focused exclusively on the defendant's youth. Should a defendant's elderly status make him ineligible for the death penalty? A few countries exempt the elderly. For example, in Guatemala and Sudan, no one over 70 years of age may be executed. In Mongolia, no man over 60 (or woman of any age) may be executed. Hood, *The Death Penalty: A World-Wide Perspective* 62 (Oxford Clarendon Press 1990).

2. In January of 2006, Governor Arnold Schwartzenegger refused to grant clemency to 76-year-old Clarence Ray Allen, sending California's oldest death row inmate to the lethal injection chamber.

3. With respect to juveniles who are excluded from the death penalty, the determination of whether a defendant falls within the exclusion is fairly straightforward: Was the defendant under the age of eighteen at the time of the commission of the crime? In the next two sections, which examine the imposition of the death penalty on the mentally ill and the mentally retarded, consider how much more complicated, difficult, and malleable the test for determining mental illness or mental retardation for purposes of exclusion from the death penalty can be.

Note on Age and Death Eligibility, Extradition and Mitigation

One effect of *Roper v. Simmons* is to bring the United States into comformity with prevailing standards of international law, which uniformly favor age 18. For example, Article 6(5) of the *International Covenant on Civil and Political Rights*, Can. T.S. 1976 No. 47, prohibits the execution of individuals who were under the age of 18 at the time of the commission of the offense. Article 37(a) of the *Convention on the Rights of the Child*, Can. T.S. 1992 No. 3, states a similar proposition. Section 47 of the Canadian *Extradition Act*, S.C. 1999, c. 18, permits Canada's Minister in certain circumstances to refuse to surrender persons who were under 18 at the time of the offense. According to the Canadian Supreme Court in *United States v. Burns*, 2001 SCC 7 (2001), "Canada's ratification of these international instruments, and the language of the new *Extradition Act*, support the conclusion that some degree of leniency for youth is an accepted value in the administration of justice." The *Burns* decision, involving two 18-year-old murder defendants, is reproduced *infra* chapter 19.

C. Insanity

Ford v. Wainwright
477 U.S. 399 (1986)

Justice MARSHALL announced the judgment of the Court and delivered the opinion of the Court and delivered the opinon of the Court with respect to Parts I and II and an opinion with respect to Parts III, IV and V in which Justice Brennan, Justice Blackmun and Justice Stevens join.

For centuries no jurisdiction has countenanced the execution of the insane, yet this Court has never decided whether the Constitution forbids the practice. Today we keep faith with our common-law heritage in holding that it does.

I

Alvin Bernard Ford was convicted of murder in 1974 and sentenced to death. There is no suggestion that he was incompetent at the time of his offense, at trial, or at sentencing. In early 1982, however, Ford began to manifest gradual changes in behavior. They began as an occasional peculiar idea or confused perception, but became more serious over time. After reading in the newspaper that the Ku Klux Klan had held a rally in nearby Jacksonville, Florida, Ford developed an obsession focused upon the Klan. His letters to various people reveal endless brooding about his "Klan work," and an increasingly pervasive delusion that he had become the target of a complex conspiracy, involving the Klan and assorted others, designed to force him to commit suicide. He believed that the prison guards, part of the conspiracy, had been killing people and putting the bodies in the concrete enclosures used for beds. Later, he began to believe that his women relatives were being tortured and sexually abused somewhere in the prison. This notion developed into a delusion that the people who were tormenting him at the prison had taken members of Ford's family hostage. The hostage delusion took firm hold and expanded, until Ford was reporting that 135 of his friends and family were being held hostage in the prison, and that only he could help them. By "day 287" of the "hostage crisis," the list of hostages had expanded to include "senators, Senator Kennedy, and many other leaders." In a letter to the Attorney General of Florida, written in 1983, Ford appeared to assume authority for ending the "crisis," claiming to have fired a number of prison officials. He began to refer to himself as "Pope John Paul, III," and reported having appointed nine new justices to the Florida Supreme Court.

Counsel for Ford asked a psychiatrist who had examined Ford earlier, Dr. Jamal Amin, to continue seeing him and to recommend appropriate treatment. On the basis of roughly 14 months of evaluation, taped conversations between Ford and his attorneys, letters written by Ford, interviews with Ford's acquaintances, and various medical records, Dr. Amin concluded in 1983 that Ford suffered from "a severe, uncontrollable, mental disease which closely resembles 'Paranoid Schizophrenia With Suicide Potential'"—a "major mental disorder ... severe enough to substantially affect Mr. Ford's present ability to assist in the defense of his life."

Ford subsequently refused to see Dr. Amin again, believing him to have joined the conspiracy against him, and Ford's counsel sought assistance from Dr. Harold Kaufman, who interviewed Ford in November 1983. Ford told Dr. Kaufman that "I know there is some sort of death penalty, but I'm free to go whenever I want because it would be illegal and the executioner would be executed." When asked if he would be executed, Ford replied: "I can't be executed because of the landmark case. I won. *Ford v. State* will prevent executions all over." These statements appeared amidst long streams of seemingly unrelated thoughts in rapid succession. Dr. Kaufman concluded that Ford had no understanding of why he was being executed, made no connection between the homicide of which he had been convicted and the death penalty, and indeed sincerely believed that he would not be executed because he owned the prisons and could control the Governor through mind waves. Kaufman found that there was "no reasonable possibility that Mr. Ford was dissembling, malingering or otherwise putting on a performance...." The following month, in an interview with his attorneys, Ford regressed further into nearly complete incomprehensibility, speaking only in a code characterized by intermittent use of the word "one," making statements such as "Hands one, face one. Mafia one. God one, father one, Pope one. Pope one. Leader one."

Counsel for Ford invoked the procedures of Florida law governing the determination of competency of a condemned inmate. Following the procedures set forth in the statute, the Governor of Florida appointed a panel of three psychiatrists to evaluate whether ... Ford had "the mental capacity to understand the nature of the death penalty and the reasons why it was imposed upon him." At a single meeting, the three psychiatrists together interviewed Ford for approximately 30 minutes. Each doctor then filed a separate two- or three-page report with the Governor, to whom the statute delegates the final decision. One doctor concluded that Ford suffered from "psychosis with paranoia" but had "enough cognitive functioning to understand the nature and the effects of the death penalty, and why it is to be imposed on him." Another found that, although Ford was "psychotic," he did "know fully what can happen to him." The third concluded that Ford had a "severe adaptational disorder," but did "comprehend his total situation including being sentenced to death, and all of the implications of that penalty." He believed that Ford's disorder, "although severe, seem[ed] contrived and recently learned." Thus, the interview produced three different diagnoses, but accord on the question of sanity as defined by state law.

The Governor's decision was announced on April 30, 1984, when, without explanation or statement, he signed a death warrant for Ford's execution.... [Ford then sought an evidentiary hearing in federal district court to determine his sanity in light of the conflicting evidence and reports on this issue. The district court denied Ford's request and the federal court of appeals upheld that denial.] This Court granted Ford's petition for certiorari in order to resolve the important issue whether the Eighth Amendment prohibits the execution of the insane and, if so, whether the District Court should have held a hearing on petitioner's claim....

II

A

We begin, then, with the common law. The bar against executing a prisoner who has lost his sanity bears impressive historical credentials; the practice consistently has been branded "savage and inhuman." 4 W. Blackstone, Commentaries (hereinafter Blackstone). Blackstone explained:

> [I]diots and lunatics are not chargeable for their own acts, if committed when under these incapacities: no, not even for treason itself. Also, if a man in his sound memory commits a capital offense, and before arraignment for it, he becomes mad, he ought not to be arraigned for it: because he is not able to plead to it with that advice and caution that he ought. And if, after he has pleaded, the prisoner becomes mad, he shall not be tried: for how can he make his defence? If, after he be tried and found guilty, he loses his senses before judgment, judgment shall not be pronounced; and if, after judgment, he becomes of nonsane memory, execution shall be stayed: for peradventure, says the humanity of the English law, had the prisoner been of sound memory, he might have alleged something in stay of judgment or execution.

... One explanation [for the common-law bar against executing the insane] is that the execution of an insane person simply offends humanity; another, that it provides no example to others and thus contributes nothing to whatever deterrence value is intended to be served by capital punishment. Other commentators postulate religious underpinnings: that it is uncharitable to dispatch an offender "into another world, when he is not of a capacity to fit himself for it." It is also said that execution serves no purpose in these cases because madness is its own punishment: *furiosus solo furore punitur.*

More recent commentators opine that the community's quest for "retribution"—the need to offset a criminal act by a punishment of equivalent "moral quality"—is not served by execution of an insane person, which has a "lesser value" than that of the crime for which he is to be punished. Unanimity of rationale, therefore, we do not find. "But whatever the reason of the law is, it is plain the law is so." We know of virtually no authority condoning the execution of the insane at English common law.[1]

Further indications suggest that this solid proscription was carried to America, where it was early observed that "the judge is bound" to stay the execution upon insanity of the prisoner.

B

This ancestral legacy has not outlived its time. Today, no State in the Union permits the execution of the insane. It is clear that the ancient and humane limitation upon the State's ability to execute its sentences has as firm a hold upon the jurisprudence of today as it had centuries ago in England. The various reasons put forth in support of the common-law restriction have no less logical, moral, and practical force than they did when first voiced. For today, no less than before, we may seriously question the retributive value of executing a person who has no comprehension of why he has been singled out and stripped of his fundamental right to life. Similarly, the natural abhorrence civilized societies feel at killing one who has no capacity to come to grips with his own conscience or deity is still vivid today. And the intuition that such an execution simply offends humanity is evidently shared across this Nation. Faced with such widespread evidence of a restriction upon sovereign power, this Court is compelled to conclude that the Eighth Amendment prohibits a State from carrying out a sentence of death upon a prisoner who is insane. Whether its aim be to protect the condemned from fear and pain without comfort of understanding, or to protect the dignity of society itself from the barbarity of exacting mindless vengeance, the restriction finds enforcement in the Eighth Amendment....

V

A

[Based on the foregoing discussion, the Court concluded that Ford's allegations of insanity, if proven, would bar his execution. After finding that Florida failed to provide Ford an adequate hearing on the question of sanity, the Court held that the federal district court was required to grant a hearing *de novo* to determine the issue. In reaching this conclusion, the Court condemned the Florida practice of allowing the determination of sanity to be made through a non-adversarial procedure wholly within the executive branch of government. Although the Court refused to articulate the precise procedure states should used in determining sanity, the Court found instructive analogies in proceedings to determine competency to stand trial and involuntary commitment proceedings. The Court further advised:]

... [T]he lodestar of any effort to devise a procedure must be the overriding dual imperative of providing redress for those with substantial claims and of encouraging accuracy in the factfinding determination. The stakes are high, and the "evidence" will al-

---

1. We emphasize that it is *American* conceptions of decency that are dispositive, rejecting the contention of petitioners and their various *amici* that the sentencing practices of other countries are relevant....

ways be imprecise. It is all the more important that the adversary presentation of relevant information be as unrestricted as possible. Also essential is that the manner of selecting and using the experts responsible for producing that "evidence" be conducive to the formation of neutral, sound, and professional judgments as to the prisoner's ability to comprehend the nature of the penalty. Fidelity to these principles is the solemn obligation of a civilized society.

... The judgment of the Court of Appeals is reversed, and the case is remanded for further proceedings consistent with this opinion.

Justice POWELL, concurring in part and concurring in the judgment.

I join Parts I and II of the Court's opinion. As Justice Marshall ably demonstrates, execution of the insane was barred at common law precisely because it was considered cruel and unusual. In *Solem v. Helm*, 463 U.S. 277 (1983), we explained that while the Framers "may have intended the Eighth Amendment to go beyond the scope of its English counterpart, their use of the language of the English Bill of Rights is convincing proof that they intended to provide at least the same protection." It follows that the practice of executing the insane is barred by our own Constitution.

That conclusion leaves two issues for our determination: (i) the meaning of insanity in this context, and (ii) the procedures States must follow in order to avoid the necessity of *de novo* review in federal courts under 28 U.S.C. §2254(d). The Court's opinion does not address the first of these issues, and as to the second, my views differ substantially from Justice Marshall's. I therefore write separately.

I

The Court holds today that the Eighth Amendment bars execution of a category of defendants defined by their mental state. The bounds of that category are necessarily governed by federal constitutional law. I therefore turn to the same sources that give rise to the substantive right to determine its precise definition: chiefly, our common-law heritage and the modern practices of the States, which are indicative of our "evolving standards of decency."

A

As the Court recognizes, the ancient prohibition on execution of the insane rested on differing theories. Those theories do not provide a common answer when it comes to defining the mental awareness required by the Eighth Amendment as a prerequisite to a defendant's execution. On the one hand, some authorities contended that the prohibition against executing the insane was justified as a way of preserving the defendant's ability to make arguments on his own behalf. See 1 M. Hale, Pleas of the Crown 35 (1736) ("if after judgment he become of *non sane memory*, his execution shall be spared; for were he of sound memory he might allege somewhat in stay of judgment or execution"); accord 4 W. Blackstone, Commentaries. Other authorities suggest, however, that the prohibition derives from more straightforward humanitarian concerns. Coke expressed the view that execution was intended to be an "example" to the living, but that the execution of "a mad man" was such "a miserable spectacle ... of extream inhumanity and cruelty" that it "can be no example to others." 3 E. Coke, Institutes 6 (—th ed. 1794). Hawles added that it is "against christian charity to send a great offender quick ... into another world, when he is not of a capacity to fit himself for it." Hawles, Remarks on the Trial of Mr. Charles Bateman, 11 How.St.Tr. 474, 477 (1685).

The first of these justifications has slight merit today. Modern practice provides far more extensive review of convictions and sentences than did the common law, including not only direct appeal but ordinarily both state and federal collateral review. Throughout this process, the defendant has access to counsel, by constitutional right at trial, and by employment or appointment at other stages of the process whenever the defendant raises substantial claims. Nor does the defendant merely have the right to counsel's assistance; he also has the right to the *effective* assistance of counsel at trial and on appeal. These guarantees are far broader than those enjoyed by criminal defendants at common law. It is thus unlikely indeed that a defendant today could go to his death with knowledge of undiscovered trial error that might set him free.

In addition, in cases tried at common law execution often followed fairly quickly after trial, so that incompetence at the time of execution was linked as a practical matter with incompetence at the trial itself. Our decisions already recognize, however, that a defendant must be competent to stand trial, and thus the notion that a defendant must be able to assist in his defense is largely provided for. See *Drope v. Missouri*, 420 U.S. 162, 95 S.Ct. 896, 43 L.Ed.2d 103 (1975).

B

The more general concern of the common law—that executions of the insane are simply cruel—retains its vitality. It is as true today as when Coke lived that most men and women value the opportunity to prepare, mentally and spiritually, for their death. Moreover, today as at common law, one of the death penalty's critical justifications, its retributive force, depends on the defendant's awareness of the penalty's existence and purpose. Thus, it remains true that executions of the insane both impose a uniquely cruel penalty and are inconsistent with one of the chief purposes of executions generally. For precisely these reasons, Florida requires the Governor to stay executions of those who "d[o] not have the mental capacity to understand the nature of the death penalty and why it was imposed" on them. Fla.Stat. §922.07 (1985 and Supp.1986). A number of States have more rigorous standards, but none disputes the need to require that those who are executed know the fact of their impending execution and the reason for it.

Such a standard appropriately defines the kind of mental deficiency that should trigger the Eighth Amendment prohibition. If the defendant perceives the connection between his crime and his punishment, the retributive goal of the criminal law is satisfied. And only if the defendant is aware that his death is approaching can he prepare himself for his passing. Accordingly, I would hold that the Eighth Amendment forbids the execution only of those who are unaware of the punishment they are about to suffer and why they are to suffer it.

Petitioner's claim of insanity plainly fits within this standard. According to petitioner's proffered psychiatric examination, petitioner does not know that he is to be executed, but rather believes that the death penalty has been invalidated. If this assessment is correct, petitioner cannot connect his execution to the crime for which he was convicted. Thus, the question is whether petitioner's evidence entitles him to a hearing in Federal District Court on his claim.

II

Petitioner concedes that the Governor of Florida has determined that he is not insane under the standard prescribed by Florida's statute, which is the same as the standard just described. Petitioner further concedes that there is expert evidence that supports the Governor's finding. Thus, if that finding is entitled to a presumption of correctness under 28 U.S.C. § 2254(d), there is no ground for holding a hearing on petitioner's federal habeas corpus petition.

I agree with Justice Marshall that the Governor's finding is not entitled to a presumption of correctness under § 2254(d). I reach this conclusion for two independent reasons. First, § 2254(d) requires deference to the factual findings of "a State court of competent jurisdiction." The term "State court" may have a certain amount of flexibility, but no amount of stretching can extend it to include the Governor. The essence of a "court" is independence from the prosecutorial arm of government and, as Justice Marshall correctly notes, the Governor is "[t]he commander of the State's corps of prosecutors." Unless the relevant language is to be read out of the statute, I see no basis for affording any deference to the Governor's determination.

Second, the presumption of correctness does not attach to the Governor's implicit finding of sanity because the State did not give petitioner's claim "a full and fair hearing," 28 U.S.C. § 2254(d)(2). This statutory phrase apparently was drawn from the Court's opinion in *Townsend v. Sain*, 372 U.S. 293, 313 (1963). There, the Court concluded that where the state court's "fact-finding procedure ... was not adequate for reaching reasonably correct results," or where the process "appear[ed] to be seriously inadequate for the ascertainment of the truth," no presumption of correctness would attach to the state court's findings when those findings were challenged on federal habeas corpus.

At least in the context of competency determinations prior to execution, this standard is no different from the protection afforded by procedural due process. It is clear that an insane defendant's Eighth Amendment interest in forestalling his execution unless or until he recovers his sanity cannot be deprived without a "fair hearing." Indeed, fundamental fairness is the hallmark of the procedural protections afforded by the Due Process Clause. Thus, the question in this case is whether Florida's procedures for determining petitioner's sanity comport with the requirements of due process.

Together with Justice Marshall and Justice O'Connor, I would hold that they do not. As Justice O'Connor states, "[i]f there is one 'fundamental requisite' of due process, it is that an individual is entitled to an 'opportunity to be heard.'" In this case, petitioner was deprived of that opportunity. The Florida statute does not require the Governor to consider materials submitted by the prisoner, and the present Governor has a "publicly announced policy of excluding" such materials from his consideration. Thus, the determination of petitioner's sanity appears to have been made solely on the basis of the examinations performed by state-appointed psychiatrists. Such a procedure invites arbitrariness and error by preventing the affected parties from offering contrary medical evidence or even from explaining the inadequacies of the State's examinations. It does not, therefore, comport with due process. It follows that the State's procedure was not "fair," and that the District Court on remand must consider the question of petitioner's competency to be executed.

III

While the procedures followed by Florida in this case do not comport with basic fairness, I would not require the kind of full-scale "sanity trial" that Justice Marshall appears to find necessary. Due process is a flexible concept, requiring only "such procedural protections as the particular situation demands." *Mathews v. Eldridge*, 424 U.S. 319, 334 (1976). In this instance, a number of considerations support the conclusion that the requirements of due process are not as elaborate as Justice Marshall suggests.

First, the Eighth Amendment claim at issue can arise only after the prisoner has been validly convicted of a capital crime and sentenced to death. Thus, in this case the State has a substantial and legitimate interest in taking petitioner's life as punishment for his crime. That interest is not called into question by petitioner's claim. Rather, the only question raised is not *whether*, but *when*, his execution may take place.[5] This question is important, but it is not comparable to the antecedent question whether petitioner should be executed at all. It follows that this Court's decisions imposing heightened procedural requirements on capital trials and sentencing proceedings do not apply in this context.

Second, petitioner does not make his claim of insanity against a neutral background. On the contrary, in order to have been convicted and sentenced, petitioner must have been judged competent to stand trial, or his competency must have been sufficiently clear as not to raise a serious question for the trial court. The State therefore may properly presume that petitioner remains sane at the time sentence is to be carried out, and may require a substantial threshold showing of insanity merely to trigger the hearing process.

Finally, the sanity issue in this type of case does not resemble the basic issues at trial or sentencing. Unlike issues of historical fact, the question of petitioner's sanity calls for a basically subjective judgment. And unlike the determination of whether the death penalty is appropriate in a particular case, the competency determination depends substantially on expert analysis in a discipline fraught with "subtleties and nuances." This combination of factors means that ordinary adversarial procedures—complete with live testimony, cross-examination, and oral argument by counsel—are not necessarily the best means of arriving at sound, consistent judgments as to a defendant's sanity.

We need not determine the precise limits that due process imposes in this area. In general, however, my view is that a constitutionally acceptable procedure may be far less formal than a trial. The State should provide an impartial officer or board that can receive evidence and argument from the prisoner's counsel, including expert psychiatric evidence that may differ from the State's own psychiatric examination. Beyond these basic requirements, the States should have substantial leeway to determine what process best balances the various interests at stake. As long as basic fairness is observed, I would find due process satisfied, and would apply the presumption of correctness of § 2254(d) on federal habeas corpus.

IV

Because petitioner has raised a viable claim under the Eighth Amendment, and because that claim was not adjudicated fairly within the meaning of due process or of § 2254(d), petitioner is entitled to have his claim adjudicated by the District Court on federal habeas corpus. I therefore join the Court's judgment.

Notes and Question

1. Common law rules prevent the criminal conviction of a person who was insane at the time she committed a capital offense. Moreover, persons properly convicted of capital offenses who subsequently become insane while awaiting execution may not be put to death.

Several rationales have been advanced in support of this aspect of the Eighth Amendment ban on cruel and unusual punishments:

---

5. It is of course true that some defendants may lose their mental faculties and never regain them, and thus avoid execution altogether. My point is only that if petitioner is cured of his disease, the State is free to execute him.

(a) executing an insane person offends humanity;

(b) executing insane persons does not further the penological goals of deterrence or retribution;

(c) insanity itself is adequate punishment;

(d) it is unfair to execute someone who cannot appreciate the moral significance of the relationship between her crime and her punishment;

(e) it is unfair to execute someone who cannot prepare for her death.

Do you find any of these reasons persuasive?

2. The *Ford* plurality vacated the death sentence for two reasons. First, Florida law, although ostensibly designed to insure that presently insane persons were not executed, failed to provide the condemned with sufficient procedural and evidentiary rights to prove present insanity. Second, under Florida law, the final determination of sanity for purposes of execution was left entirely within the executive branch. For an argument that the most effective way to develop adequate protections is to balance the interests of the condemned against those of the state, see Enzinna and Gill, "Capital Punishment and the Incompetent: Procedures for Determining Competency to be Executed After *Ford v. Wainwright*," 41 Fla. L. Rev. 115 (1989).

3. The problems involved in determining sanity in capital cases are highlighted by Charles Black in *Capital Punishment: The Inevitability of Caprice and Mistake* 52–55 (W. W. Norton & Co. 1974). According to Black:

[W]e have committed ourselves not to kill by law, or even to punish, anyone who satisfies certain criteria as to the connection of "insanity" with the commission of the act. Yet the astounding fact is that, having made this commitment, for what must be the most imperative moral reasons, we cannot state these criteria in any understandable form, in any form satisfying to the relevant specialists or comprehensible to either judge or jury, despite repeated and earnest trials. The upshot of the best writing on the subject is that we have so far failed in defining exculpatory "insanity," and that success is nowhere in sight. Yet we have to assume, unless the whole thing has been a solemn frolic, that we execute some people, and put others into medical custody, because we think that the ones we execute fall on one side of the line, and the others on the other side.

4. It has also been proposed by some scholars that individuals with certain severe or significant mental disabilities also be excluded from the penalty of death. *See* Slobogin, "Mental Disorder as an Exemption from the Death Penalty: The ABA-IRR Task Force Recommendations," 54 Cath. U. L. Rev. 1133 (2005).

Lowenfield v. Butler

485 U.S. 995 (1988)

On application for stay.

April 13, 1988. The application for stay of execution of the sentence of death presented to Justice White and by him referred to the Court is denied.

Justice BRENNAN, with whom Justice Marshall joins, dissenting.

Petitioner Leslie Lowenfield has been sentenced to death. The law of the State that is about to execute him entitles him to "rais[e] at any time" the issue of his "mental incapacity to proceed" with the execution. If there is a "reasonable ground to doubt" petitioner's sanity, the court "shall order a mental examination," and may permit "no further steps" in his punishment until he "is found to have the mental capacity to proceed." In any event, State law affords petitioner the right to pre-execution review by a sanity commission if he can "show by a preponderance of the evidence that he lacks the present capacity to undergo execution."

Petitioner moved for review by a sanity commission, presenting evidence that he is currently insane. The evidence consisted of a sworn affidavit by Dr. Marc L. Zimmerman, a duly licensed clinical psychologist who interviewed and tested petitioner for five hours on March 26, 1988, and concluded that "it is highly probable that Mr. Lowenfield is suffering from paranoid schizophrenia.... A study has found that 85% of persons who obtain the same profile as Mr. Lowenfield ... are diagnosed as paranoid schizophrenics." Dr. Zimmerman continued: "As a paranoid schizophrenic, Mr. Lowenfield's capacity to understand the death penalty would be impaired. Indeed, my clinical interview with Mr. Lowenfield indicated that *he is currently unable to understand the death penalty*." The State presented no evidence either to refute Dr. Zimmerman's conclusions or to question his credentials. In the face of that unrefuted evidence, the Louisiana trial court, and then the Louisiana Supreme Court, denied the motion without explanation.

Petitioner thereafter filed an application for habeas relief with the District Court. The District Court denied on the basis of an "extended conversation" with Dr. Zimmerman. From that conversation, which the District Court conducted without any notice to petitioner's counsel and apparently before petitioner's application was filed, the District Court concluded that, contrary to Dr. Zimmerman's affidavit, "petitioner has the capacity to understand the realities of the pending execution. Petitioner, though a paranoid schizophrenic, is apparently able to understand that the execution is going forward in accordance with law." A divided panel of the Court of Appeals affirmed in an opinion that reached this Chambers a mere fifteen minutes before the scheduled execution.

Every court that has considered petitioner's insanity claim has made a mockery of this Court's precedent and of the most fundamental principles of ordered justice. In *Ford v. Wainwright*, 477 U.S. 399, 410 (1986), we held "that the Eighth Amendment prohibits a State from carrying out a sentence of death upon a prisoner who is insane." In the course of the opinion, we characterized any such execution as "'savage and inhuman'"; "'a miserable spectacle, both against Law, and extreme inhumanity and cruelty,'" "'cruel and inhumane,'" and "abhorren[t]."

A majority of this Court did not agree on the precise procedures that the Constitution requires when the question is raised of a prisoner's sanity for execution. A majority did, however, hold that Due Process demands a hearing at least once the prisoner has made some "threshold showing" that he has become insane since his trial. Justice Powell, providing a fifth vote for that proposition, stated that "[t]he State may ... properly presume that petitioner remains sane at the time sentence is to be carried out, and may require a substantial threshold showing of insanity merely to trigger the hearing process."

The Louisiana legislature has set the requisite "threshold showing" at that level of evidence that would constitute a "reasonable ground to doubt" the prisoner's sanity. It is beyond me why Dr. Zimmerman's unrefuted affidavit did not meet that threshold. For that matter, I am at a loss to explain why the affidavit, which was the sole evidence before the courts, did not establish petitioner's insanity by a preponderance of the evidence, entitling petitioner not merely to a hearing but to the relief he seeks. Neither state court furnished any explanation. In fact, neither court so much as articulated the standard it was applying. For all we know, the state courts defaulted entirely on their obligation to consider petitioner's claim. The Louisiana courts, by declining to provide any explanation for their denial of relief, as a practical matter have required petitioner to meet not "a substantial threshold showing of insanity" but an insurmountable one. The effect extends far beyond this case, for the state courts have challenged all death-row inmates to a harrowing game of Russian roulette, in which each must take a wild guess at the "threshold" or suffer the consequences. Where, as here, there is no way to discern whether the state courts' "fact-finding procedure ... was not adequate for reaching reasonably correct results," their bare denial of relief is entitled to no presumption of correctness.

Even more outrageous was the injustice perpetrated by the federal courts to which petitioner resorted upon the state courts' default of their constitutional responsibilities. The District Court expressly adopted Dr. Zimmerman's conclusion that petitioner was a "paranoid schizophrenic." That conclusion should have compelled the District Court, at the very least, to "receive evidence and argument from [petitioner's] counsel" on whether petitioner is "aware that his death is approaching" and "perceives the connection between his crime and his punishment." Instead, the District Court excluded counsel entirely and conducted its own *ex parte* investigation in which it managed to extract from Dr. Zimmerman a concession ("Petitioner ... is apparently able to understand that the execution is going forward in accordance with law;") that contradicted his sworn affidavit dated three days earlier ("he is currently unable to understand the death penalty.") The District Court's consideration of petitioner's insanity claim fell far short of the *de novo* review that it was obliged to provide upon the state courts' default. Instead, its review was functionally equivalent to the "policy of excluding all advocacy on the part of the condemned," which we have held unconstitutional.

Worse, yet, petitioner alleges — and the State does not deny — that the District Court conducted its *ex parte* investigation before it even had jurisdiction over the case; as Judge Johnson, dissenting from the Court of Appeals' judgment, observed, "the district court failed to make any finding *on* the record." "Procedural shortcuts are always dangerous. Greater — surely not lesser — care should be taken to avoid the risk of error when its consequences are irreversible."

The Court of Appeals, for its part, compounded the District Court's abuse by ignoring it entirely and proceeding to address the sufficiency of Dr. Zimmerman's affidavit as an original matter, without a proper District Court predicate. Even that determination hopelessly conflated the principles articulated in *Ford*. From Justice Powell's observation that the "State ... *may* require a substantial threshold showing of insanity merely to trigger the hearing process," the Court of Appeals supposed that the State *must* do so, ("petitioner has not made a substantial threshold showing"), and overlooked the State's decision to require merely a showing of a "reasonable ground to doubt" in order to trigger further examination.

The abuses and mistakes in every court that has considered this case are no doubt attributable, at least in part, to the haste with which they proceeded:

* On the afternoon of April 11, petitioner filed in Louisiana state court a petition for post-conviction relief raising the claims that are now before us.
* Early the next afternoon, April 12, at 12:38 p.m. (Eastern Daylight Time), the state trial court denied relief.
* At 6:00 p.m. the Louisiana Supreme Court denied relief and petitioner applied to the District Court for a writ of habeas corpus.

* At 8:30 p.m. the District Court denied petitioner's application.
* At 12:10 a.m. that same night the Court of Appeals affirmed.
* At 12:45 a.m. (15 minutes before the scheduled execution) the Court of Appeals' opinions were circulated to this Court.
* At 1:05 a.m., with petitioner already strapped in the electric chair, this Court denied his application for a stay of execution.
* At 1:25 a.m. petitioner was pronounced dead. The New York Times, April 14, 1988, at A28, col. 1. Time ran out before we voted on the certiorari petition that accompanied petitioner's stay application.

The haste that attended disposition of this case is reprehensible. It is hardly surprising that a case scudding through the state courts in 24 hours should yield orders devoid of law or logic— the ones in this case simply read, "DENIED"—for which the description "terse" would be charitable. If the federal courts are intent on accelerating the pace at any cost, as they were in this case, their only choice is to take procedural short cuts and give short shrift to substance. And simply arithmetic suggests grave injustice when the Court of last resort takes 15 minutes to read and analyze 17 pages of opinions from the court below and cast a vote on life or death.

Due Process means little if it requires the courts to provide "an opportunity to be heard" without imposing on them a concomitant duty to listen—and, at least when a life is at stake, to listen very carefully. Presumably, it was in recognition of the injustice that four of us (one less than the requisite five) voted to stay petitioner's execution, so as to consider his insanity claim in an atmosphere that was not itself lunatic.

Regrettably, this case is not atypical. It is the natural product of a penal system conducive to inaccurate factfinding and shoddy analysis. And I doubt that any system could be devised to cure the evil, so long as States continue to impose punishments so severe as to be irrevocable. Even were I not convinced that the death penalty is in all circumstances cruel and unusual punishment prohibited by the Eighth Amendment, I would have no part of a penal system that permits a State's interest in meting out death on schedule to convert our constitutional duty to dispense justice into a license to dispense with it. I dissent.

Justice BLACKMUN and Justice STEVENS would grant the application for stay.

Medicating to Execute: Louisiana v. Perry, 610 So.2d 746 (La. 1992)

In *Washington v. Harper*, 494 U.S. 210 (1990), the Court held that treating a prisoner with antipsychotic drugs against his will did not violate substantive due process where (1) the prisoner was found to be dangerous to himself or others, and (2) treatment was in the prisoner's medical interest. Shortly thereafter, the Court in *Perry v. Louisiana*, 498 U.S. 38 (1990), remanded a case to a Louisiana trial court to determine whether, in light of *Washington v. Harper*, Louisiana could medicate an incompetent death row inmate with anti-psychotic drugs against his will in order to render the inmate sufficiently competent so that the state could execute him. The trial court found that the involuntary medication of an incompetent inmate was proper and ordered the state to medicate Perry so that his death sentence could be carried out. Perry appealed to the Louisiana Supreme Court. The Louisiana Supreme Court found that the state's "medicate-to-execute" scheme violated the state constitution and reversed the trial court's order. *Louisiana v. Perry*, 610 So.2d 746 (La. 1992).

The Louisiana Supreme Court distinguished *Washington v. Harper* from Perry's case on three grounds:

> First, forcing a prisoner to take antipsychotic drugs to facilitate his execution does not constitute medical treatment but is antithetical to the basic principles of the healing arts. Second, *Harper* held that due process requires the state to show that its prison regulation rationally seeks to further both the best medical interest of the prisoner and the state's own interest in prison safety before it may inject a prisoner with antipsychotic drugs against his will. The state in Perry's case has made neither showing but seeks forcible medication of a prisoner by court order as an instrument of his execution. Third, *Harper* not only fails to support the state's position; it strongly implies that forced administration of antipsychotic drugs may not be used by the state for the purpose of punishment.

The court examined the constitutionality of the state's proposed medication of Perry under the Louisiana Constitution. Specifically, the court focused on Article I, §5 of the 1974 Louisiana Constitution, which guarantees that every individual shall be secure in his "person" against "unreasonable searches, seizures, or invasions of privacy," and Article I, §20, which protects individuals from excessive punishment and cruel and unusual punishment.

The court observed that Article I, §5 of the Louisiana Constitution extends more protection to criminal defendants than does the Fourth Amendment of the United States Constitution. Moreover, the Louisiana state constitution "incorporates the principles of the United States Supreme Court privacy decisions in explicit statement, and includes the recognition of a patient's right to decide whether to obtain or reject medical treatment and what shall or shall not be done with his body." The court concluded "that the medicate-to-execute scheme infringes on Perry's [state] constitutionally protected interest in deciding whether to obtain or reject treatment and what shall be done medically with his mind and body." The court also found that "the state's plan to medicate and execute Perry would violate his bodily integrity, chemically alter his mind and will, and usurp his fundamental right to make decisions regarding his health or medical treatment. Each of these interests is protected from unwarranted governmental intrusion by Article I, §5's right of privacy or personhood."

Although the court recognized that the right to privacy or personhood is not absolute, it required the state to identify a narrowly confined, compelling state interest to override Perry's interests. Further, the purported state interest was subject to strict judicial scrutiny. The state argued that, under *Washington v. Harper*, it had a compelling interest in advancing Perry's medical interest and promoting prison safety. Ultimately the court concluded that the state's proposed action did not promote either of these interests. Similarly, the court rejected the state's claim that it had a compelling interest in medicating Perry to further the social goals of the death penalty, i.e., deterrence and retribution.

In analyzing this second alleged state interest — that the "medicate-to-execute" scheme furthered the social goals of the death penalty — the court turned to Article I, §20 of the Louisiana Constitution. Although Article I, §20 was derived from the Eighth Amendment to the federal Constitution, the state constitutional provision "adds … that no law shall subject any person to, 'euthanasia', 'torture', or 'excessive punishment', broadening the prior prohibition against 'excessive fines … cruel and unusual punishment.'" To withstand scrutiny under Article I, §20, the punishment inflicted "must not be (1) degrading to the dignity to human beings; (2) arbitrarily inflicted; (3) unacceptable to contemporary society; or (4) excessive, i.e., disproportionate to the crimes or failing to serve a penal purpose more effectively than a less severe punishment." The court concluded that the proposed medication of Perry: (1) did not comport with the standards of human dignity; (2) was arbitrary in its conception and practice; (3) offended "civilized standards of decency;" and (4) "makes no measurable contribution to the acceptable goals of capital punishment [i.e., retribution and deterrence] and hence is nothing more than purposeless and needless imposition of pain and suffering." Thus, the Louisiana court concluded that medicating Perry constituted cruel, excessive and unusual punishment. Accordingly, the court reversed the trial court's order to administer antipsychotic drugs to Perry against his will and ordered a stay of Perry's execution.

Within one year of *Louisiana v. Perry*, 610 So.2d 746 (La. 1992), medicated defendants were eligible to be tried in twenty-six of the then thirty-six death penalty states. See Crosby, "*State v. Perry*: Louisiana's Cure-to-Kill Scheme," 77 Minn. L. Rev. 1193, 1203 n.48 (1993) (list of states and citations).

Note and Questions on Riggins v. Nevada, 504 U.S. 127 (1992)

What result if a capital murder defendant claiming insanity is forcibly medicated during trial? In *Riggins v. Nevada*, 504 U.S. 127 (1992), the Supreme Court held that the trial court erred in denying Riggins' motion to terminate the administration of Mellaril, an antipsychotic drug. Although the state argued that the drug was necessary to render Riggins competent to stand trial, the Court disagreed. Indeed, the Court found a strong possibility that the drug impaired Riggins' defense. The side effects of Mellaril, according to the Court, may have impacted Riggins' outward appearance, the content of his testimony, his ability to follow the proceedings, and the substance of his communication with counsel.

Although the Court recognized that a pretrial detainee has a due process right to avoid involuntary administration of antipsychotic drugs, that right is not absolute. Thus, due process would be satisfied if the state had shown that the treatment was medically appropriate and, considering less intrusive alternatives, essential for Riggins' own safety or the safety of others.

Lawyers for Russell Weston, a 44-year-old paranoid schizophrenic charged with the 1998 murder of two U.S. Capitol police officers, embraced a radical defense strategy. They reportedly refused to permit doctors to treat Weston for his severe and worsening mental illness. Weston's lawyers feared that if he improved enough to be considered competent to stand trial, he would be sentenced to death for the shootings. Weston first refused medical treatment, and then his lawyers blocked efforts to force it on him. In pleadings filed in the case, Weston's attorneys said that they would permit him to be medicated if prosecutors would agree to not seek the death penalty. Professor James E. Coleman phrased the issue thus: "Is it better to control the mental illness and then face the death penalty, or is it better to remain mentally ill and not face the death penalty?" Eisley, *Lawyers Letting Client's Mental Illness Flourish*, www.newsobserver.com (Feb. 14, 2001). What should a lawyer do under these circumstances? Is their first duty to restore their client's mental health so that justice can proceed? Or is their first duty instead to use any means available to save his life.

Standards for evaluating competency are considered immediately below.

Evaluating Competency: Godinez v. Moran, 509 U.S. 389 (1993)

Evaluating a defendant's mental competency is essential for determining (1) capacity for forming the mens rea required to commit a crime; (2) competency to stand trial; (3)

competency to waive certain constitutional rights (primarily under the Fourth, Fifth, Sixth, and Eighth Amendments); and (4) competency to be executed. Until recently, debate centered around whether the competency standard for pleading guilty or waiving the right to counsel is higher than the competency standard for standing trial. In *Godinez v. Moran*, 509 U.S. 389 (1993), the Court held that it is not.

During a nine-day period, Richard Allan Moran shot and killed three persons, and then attempted suicide. After confessing to his crimes, Moran was examined by psychiatrists who found him competent to stand trial. Two-and-a-half months after these evaluations, Moran told the court he wanted to fire his attorney and plead guilty to prevent the presentation of mitigating evidence at his sentencing.

After warning Moran about the dangers of proceeding without counsel, the trial court found that he "understood the charges against him" and was "able to assist in his defense"; that he was "knowingly and intelligently" waiving his right to counsel; and that his guilty pleas were "freely and voluntarily" given. Moran received three death sentences.

During state postconviction proceedings, Moran claimed that he was not mentally competent to represent himself. The trial court held an evidentiary hearing before denying relief. Ultimately, the United States Court of Appeals for the Ninth Circuit granted federal habeas relief. That court concluded that due process required the trial court to hold a hearing to evaluate and determine Moran's competency before it accepted his decisions to waive counsel and plead guilty. It also found that the state postconviction hearing did not cure the error because the trial court's ruling was based on the wrong legal standard of competency.

According to the Ninth Circuit, waiver of constitutional rights

> "requires a higher level of mental functioning than that required to stand trial. [Although a defendant is competent to stand trial if he has] a rational and factual understanding of the proceedings and is capable of assisting his counsel, [a defendant is competent to waive counsel or plead guilty only if he has] the capacity for reasoned choice among the alternatives available to him."

The Ninth Circuit concluded that, when examined in light of the correct legal standard, the record did not support a finding that Moran was "mentally capable of the reasoned choice required for a valid waiver of constitutional rights."

Reversing the judgment of the Ninth Circuit, the Supreme Court held that the Due Process Clause does not require that the standard for competency to plead guilty and waive the right to counsel be higher than, or different from, the standard for competency to stand trial. Although states remain free to adopt more elaborate competency standards, due process is satisfied by applying to all three situations the two part standard first articulated in *Dusky v. United States*, 362 U.S. 402 (1960): (1) whether the defendant has "sufficient present ability to consult with his lawyer with a reasonable degree of rational understanding," and (2) whether the defendant has a "rational as well as factual understanding of the proceedings against him." This, however, does not end the inquiry with respect to waiver of certain constitutional rights. According to Justice Thomas' majority opinion in *Godinez v. Moran*,

> A finding that a defendant is competent to stand trial, however, is not all that is necessary before he may be permitted to plead guilty or waive his right to counsel. In addition to determining that a defendant who seeks to plead guilty or waive counsel is competent, a trial court must satisfy itself that the waiver of his constitutional rights is knowing and voluntary. In this sense there *is* a

"heightened" standard for pleading guilty and for waiving the right to counsel, but it is not a heightened standard of *competence.*

509 U.S. at 400–01.

In dissent, Justice Blackmun painted a more complete picture of the facts. Moran was deeply depressed and remorseful after his arrest; he was under significant dosages of four anti-depressant and anti-seizure medications; and he had abandoned his will to mount a defense. The record shows that the trial court never inquired into what medication Moran was taking at the time of the waivers, and at one point "prodded" Moran to give an affirmative answer to one of the necessary questions during the plea colloquy.

Note on *Sell v. United States,* 539 U.S. 166 (2003)

Eleven years after *Riggins,* the Court granted certiorari to consider whether the Constitution permits the government to forcibly administer antipsychotic drugs to a mentally ill defendant in order to render that defendant competent to stand trial for serious, but nonviolent crimes. In *Sell v. United States,* the Court held that the Constitution allows the government to administer those drugs, even against the defendant's will, but only in limited circumstances. Justice Breyer's opinion for the Court draws upon *Riggins* and *Washington v. Harper* and sets forth "requisite circumstances" which must exist before the government can wield this power. Although the question presented in *Sell* was limited to defendants charged with "serious, but nonviolent" crimes, it remains to be seen whether *Sell* will be applied to capital cases. Justice Breyer's opinion is excerpted below.

Sell v. United States
539 U.S. 166 (2003)

Justice BREYER delivered the opinion of the Court.

The question presented is whether the Constitution permits the Government to administer antipsychotic drugs involuntarily to a mentally ill criminal defendant—in order to render that defendant competent to stand trial for serious, but nonviolent, crimes. We conclude that the Constitution allows the Government to administer those drugs, even against the defendant's will, in limited circumstances, *i.e.,* upon satisfaction of conditions that we shall describe. Because the Court of Appeals did not find that the requisite circumstances existed in this case, we vacate its judgment.

I

A.

Petitioner Charles Sell, once a practicing dentist, has a long and unfortunate history of mental illness. In September 1982, after telling doctors that the gold he used for fillings had been contaminated by communists, Sell was hospitalized, treated with antipsychotic medication, and subsequently discharged. In June 1984, Sell called the police to say that a leopard was outside his office boarding a bus, and he then asked the police to shoot him. Sell was again hospitalized and subsequently released. On various occasions, he complained that public officials, for example, a State Governor and a police chief, were trying to kill him. In April 1997, he told law enforcement personnel that he "spoke to God last night," and that "God told me every [Federal Bureau of Investigation] person I kill, a soul will be saved."

In May 1997, the Government charged Sell with submitting fictitious insurance claims for payment. See 18 U.S.C. § 1035(a)(2). A Federal Magistrate Judge (Magistrate), after ordering a psychiatric examination, found Sell "currently competent," but noted that Sell might experience "a psychotic episode" in the future. The judge released Sell on bail. A grand jury later produced a superseding indictment charging Sell and his wife with 56 counts of mail fraud, 6 counts of Medicaid fraud, and 1 count of money laundering.

In early 1998, the Government claimed that Sell had sought to intimidate a witness. The Magistrate held a bail revocation hearing. Sell's behavior at his initial appearance was, in the judge's words, "totally out of control," involving "screaming and shouting," the use of "personal insults" and "racial epithets," and spitting "in the judge's face." A psychiatrist reported that Sell could not sleep because he expected the FBI to "come busting through the door," and concluded that Sell's condition had worsened. After considering that report and other testimony, the Magistrate revoked Sell's bail.

In April 1998, the grand jury issued a new indictment charging Sell with attempting to murder the FBI agent who had arrested him and a former employee who planned to testify against him in the fraud case. The attempted murder and fraud cases were joined for trial.

In early 1999, Sell asked the Magistrate to reconsider his competence to stand trial. The Magistrate sent Sell to the United States Medical Center for Federal Prisoners at Springfield, Missouri, for examination. Subsequently the Magistrate found that Sell was "mentally incompetent to stand trial." He ordered Sell to "be hospitalized for treatment" at the Medical Center for up to four months, "to determine whether there was a substantial probability that [Sell] would attain the capacity to allow his trial to proceed."

Two months later, Medical Center staff recommended that Sell take antipsychotic medication. Sell refused to do so. The staff sought permission to administer the medication against Sell's will. That effort is the subject of the present proceedings.

B.

... [T]he District Court reviewed the record and, in April 2001, issued an opinion. The court addressed the Magistrate's finding "that defendant presents a danger to himself or others sufficient" to warrant involuntary administration of antipsychotic drugs. After noting that Sell subsequently had "been returned to an open ward," the District Court held the Magistrate's "dangerousness" finding "clearly erroneous." The court limited its determination to Sell's "dangerousness *at this time* to himself and to those around him *in his institutional context.*"

Nonetheless, the District Court *affirmed* the Magistrate's order permitting Sell's involuntary medication. The court wrote that "anti-psychotic drugs are medically appropriate," that "they represent the only viable hope of rendering defendant competent to stand trial," and that "administration of such drugs appears necessary to serve the government's compelling interest in obtaining an adjudication of defendant's guilt or innocence of numerous and serious charges" (including fraud and attempted murder). The court added that it was "premature" to consider whether "the effects of medication might prejudice [Sell's] defense at trial." The Government and Sell both appealed.

... [A] divided panel of the Court of Appeals affirmed the District Court's judgment. The majority affirmed the District Court's determination that Sell was not dangerous. The majority noted that, according to the District Court, Sell's behavior at the Medical Center "amounted at most to an 'inappropriate familiarity and even infatuation' with a nurse." The Court of Appeals agreed, "[u]pon review," that "the evidence does not support a finding that Sell posed a danger to himself or others at the Medical Center."

The Court of Appeals also affirmed the District Court's order requiring medication in order to render Sell competent to stand trial. Focusing solely on the serious fraud charges, the panel majority concluded that the "government has an essential interest in bringing a defendant to trial." It added that the District Court "correctly concluded that there were no less intrusive means." After reviewing the conflicting views of the experts, the panel majority found antipsychotic drug treatment "medically appropriate" for Sell. It added that the "medical evidence presented indicated a reasonable probability that Sell will fairly be able to participate in his trial." One member of the panel dissented primarily on the ground that the fraud and money laundering charges were "not serious enough to warrant the forced medication of the defendant."

We granted certiorari to determine whether the Eighth Circuit "erred in rejecting" Sell's argument that "allowing the government to administer antipsychotic medication against his will solely to render him competent to stand trial for non-violent offenses" violated the Constitution — in effect by improperly depriving Sell of an important "liberty" that the Constitution guarantees, Amdt. 5....

III

We turn now to the basic question presented: Does forced administration of antipsychotic drugs to render Sell competent to stand trial unconstitutionally deprive him of his "liberty" to reject medical treatment? U.S. Const., Amdt. 5 (Federal Government may not "depriv[e] any person of liberty ... without due process of law"). Two prior precedents, [*Washington v.*] *Harper*, [494 U.S. 210 (1985),] and *Riggins* [*v. Nevada*, 504 U.S. 127 (1992),] set forth the framework for determining the legal answer.

In *Harper*, this Court recognized that an individual has a "significant" constitutionally protected "liberty interest" in "avoiding the unwanted administration of antipsychotic drugs." 494 U.S. at 221. The Court considered a state law authorizing forced administration of those drugs "to inmates who are ... gravely disabled or represent a significant danger to themselves or others." The State had established "by a medical finding" that Harper, a mentally ill prison inmate, had "a mental disorder ... which is likely to cause harm if not treated." The treatment decision had been made "by a psychiatrist," it had been approved by "a reviewing psychiatrist," and it "ordered" medication only because that was "in the prisoner's medical interests, given the legitimate needs of his institutional confinement."

The Court found that the State's interest in administering medication was "legitima[te]" and "importan[t];" and it held that "the Due Process Clause permits the State to treat a prison inmate who has a serious mental illness with antipsychotic drugs against his will, if the inmate is dangerous to himself or others and the treatment is in the inmate's medical interest." The Court concluded that, in the circumstances, the state law authorizing involuntary treatment amounted to a constitutionally permissible "accommodation between an inmate's liberty interest in avoiding the forced administration of antipsychotic drugs and the State's interests in providing appropriate medical treatment to reduce the danger that an inmate suffering from a serious mental disorder represents to himself or others."

In *Riggins*, the Court repeated that an individual has a constitutionally protected liberty "interest in avoiding involuntary administration of antipsychotic drugs" — an interest that only an "essential" or "overriding" state interest might overcome. The Court suggested that, in principle, forced medication in order to render a defendant competent to stand trial for murder was constitutionally permissible. The Court, citing *Harper,* noted that the State "would have satisfied due process if the prosecution had demonstrated ... that treatment with antipsychotic medication was medically appropriate and, considering less intrusive alternatives, essential for the sake of Riggins' *own safety or the safety of others.*" And it said that the State [s]imilarly ... might have been able to justify medically appropriate, involuntary treatment with the drug by establishing that it could not obtain an adjudication of Riggins' guilt or innocence" of the murder charge "by using less intrusive means." Because the trial court had permitted forced medication of Riggins without taking account of his "liberty interest," with a consequent possibility of trial prejudice, the Court reversed Riggins' conviction and remanded for further proceedings. Justice Kennedy, concurring in the judgment, emphasized that antipsychotic drugs might have side effects that would interfere with the defendant's ability to receive a fair trial.

These two cases, *Harper* and *Riggins,* indicate that the Constitution permits the Government involuntarily to administer antipsychotic drugs to a mentally ill defendant facing serious criminal charges in order to render that defendant competent to stand trial, but only if the treatment is medically appropriate, is substantially unlikely to have side effects that may undermine the fairness of the trial, and, taking account of less intrusive alternatives, is necessary significantly to further important governmental trial-related interests.

This standard will permit involuntary administration of drugs solely for trial competence purposes in certain instances. But those instances may be rare. That is because the standard says or fairly implies the following:

First, a court must find that *important* governmental interests are at stake. The Government's interest in bringing to trial an individual accused of a serious crime is important. That is so whether the offense is a serious crime against the person or a serious crime against property. In both instances the Government seeks to protect through application of the criminal law the basic human need for security.

Courts, however, must consider the facts of the individual case in evaluating the Government's interest in prosecution. Special circumstances may lessen the importance of that interest. The defendant's failure to take drugs voluntarily, for example, may mean lengthy confinement in an institution for the mentally ill—and that would diminish the risks that ordinarily attach to freeing without punishment one who has committed a serious crime. We do not mean to suggest that civil commitment is a substitute for a criminal trial. The Government has a substantial interest in timely prosecution. And it may be difficult or impossible to try a defendant who regains competence after years of commitment during which memories may fade and evidence may be lost. The potential for future confinement affects, but does not totally undermine, the strength of the need for prosecution. The same is true of the possibility that the defendant has already been confined for a significant amount of time (for which he would receive credit toward any sentence ultimately imposed, see 18 U.S.C. §3585(b)). Moreover, the Government has a concomitant, constitutionally essential interest in assuring that the defendant's trial is a fair one.

Second, the court must conclude that involuntary medication will *significantly further* those concomitant state interests. It must find that administration of the drugs is substantially likely to render the defendant competent to stand trial. At the same time, it must find that administration of the drugs is substantially unlikely to have side effects that will interfere significantly with the defendant's ability to assist counsel in conducting a trial defense, thereby rendering the trial unfair.

Third, the court must conclude that involuntary medication is *necessary* to further those interests. The court must find that any alternative, less intrusive treatments are unlikely to achieve substantially the same results. And the court must consider less intrusive means for administering the drugs, *e.g.,* a court order to the defendant backed by the contempt power, before considering more intrusive methods.

Fourth, as we have said, the court must conclude that administration of the drugs is *medically appropriate, i.e.,* in the patient's best medical interest in light of his medical condition. The specific kinds of drugs at issue may matter here as elsewhere. Different kinds of antipsychotic drugs may produce different side effects and enjoy different levels of success.

We emphasize that the court applying these standards is seeking to determine whether involuntary administration of drugs is necessary significantly to further a particular governmental interest, namely, the interest in rendering the defendant *competent to stand trial.* A court need not consider whether to allow forced medication for that kind of purpose, if forced medication is warranted for a *different* purpose, such as the purposes set out in *Harper* related to the individual's dangerousness, or purposes related to the individual's own interests where refusal to take drugs puts his health gravely at risk. There are often strong reasons for a court to determine whether forced administration of drugs can be justified on these alternative grounds *before* turning to the trial competence question.

For one thing, the inquiry into whether medication is permissible, say, to render an individual nondangerous is usually more "objective and manageable" than the inquiry into whether medication is permissible to render a defendant competent. The medical experts may find it easier to provide an informed opinion about whether, given the risk of side effects, particular drugs are medically appropriate and necessary to control a patient's potentially dangerous behavior (or to avoid serious harm to the patient himself) than to try to balance harms and benefits related to the more quintessentially legal questions of trial fairness and competence.

For another thing, courts typically address involuntary medical treatment as a civil matter, and justify it on these alternative, *Harper*-type grounds. Every State provides avenues through which, for example, a doctor or institution can seek appointment of a guardian with the power to make a decision authorizing medication when in the best interests of a patient who lacks the mental competence to make such a decision. And courts, in civil proceedings, may authorize involuntary medication where the patient's failure to accept treatment threatens injury to the patient or others. See, *e.g.,* 28 CFR §549.43 (2002); cf. 18 U.S.C. §4246.

If a court authorizes medication on these alternative grounds, the need to consider authorization on trial competence grounds will likely disappear. Even if a court decides medication cannot be authorized on the alternative grounds, the findings underlying such a decision will help to inform expert opinion and judicial decisionmaking in respect to a request to administer drugs for trial competence purposes. At the least, they will facilitate direct medical and legal focus upon such questions as: Why is it medically appropriate forcibly to administer antipsychotic drugs to an individual who (1) is *not* dangerous *and* (2) *is* competent to make up his own mind about treatment? Can bringing such an individual to trial *alone* justify in whole (or at least in significant part) administration of a drug that may have adverse side effects, including side effects that may to some extent impair a defense at trial? We consequently believe that a court, asked to approve forced administration of drugs for purposes of rendering a defendant competent to stand trial, should ordinarily determine whether the Government seeks, or has first sought, permission for forced administration of drugs on these other *Harper*-type grounds; and, if not, why not.

When a court must nonetheless reach the trial competence question, the factors discussed above, should help it make the ultimate constitutionally required judgment. Has the Government, in light of the efficacy, the side effects, the possible alternatives, and the medical appropriateness of a particular course of antipsychotic drug treatment, shown a need for that treatment sufficiently important to overcome the individual's protected interest in refusing it?

IV

The Medical Center and the Magistrate in this case, applying standards roughly comparable to those set forth here and in *Harper*, approved forced medication substantially, if not primarily, upon grounds of Sell's dangerousness to others. But the District Court and the Eighth Circuit took a different approach. The District Court found "clearly erroneous" the Magistrate's conclusion regarding dangerousness, and the Court of Appeals agreed. Both courts approved forced medication solely in order to render Sell competent to stand trial.

We shall assume that the Court of Appeals' conclusion about Sell's dangerousness was correct. But we make that assumption *only* because the Government did not contest, and the parties have not argued, that particular matter. If anything, the record before us, described in Part I, suggests the contrary.

The Court of Appeals apparently agreed with the District Court that "Sell's inappropriate behavior ... amounted at most to an 'inappropriate familiarity and even infatuation' with a nurse." That being so, it also agreed that "the evidence does not support a finding that Sell posed a danger to himself or others at the Medical Center." The Court of Appeals, however, did not discuss the potential differences (described by a psychiatrist testifying before the Magistrate) between ordinary "over-familiarity" and the same conduct engaged in persistently by a patient with Sell's behavioral history and mental illness. Nor did it explain why those differences should be minimized in light of the fact that the testifying psychiatrists concluded that Sell was dangerous, while Sell's own expert denied, not Sell's dangerousness, but the efficacy of the drugs proposed for treatment.

The District Court's opinion, while more thorough, places weight upon the Medical Center's decision, taken after the Magistrate's hearing, to return Sell to the general prison population. It does not explain whether that return reflected an improvement in Sell's condition or whether the Medical Center saw it as permanent rather than temporary.

Regardless, as we have said, we must assume that Sell was not dangerous. And on that hypothetical assumption, we find that the Court of Appeals was wrong to approve forced medication solely to render Sell competent to stand trial. For one thing, the Magistrate's opinion makes clear that he did *not* find forced medication legally justified on trial competence grounds alone. Rather, the Magistrate concluded that Sell *was* dangerous, and he wrote that forced medication was "the only way to render the defendant *not dangerous and* competent to stand trial."

Moreover, the record of the hearing before the Magistrate shows that the experts themselves focused mainly upon the dangerousness issue. Consequently the experts did not pose important questions—questions, for example, about trial-related side effects and risks—the answers to which could have helped determine whether forced medication was warranted on trial competence grounds alone. Rather, the Medical Center's experts conceded that their proposed medications had "significant" side effects and that "there has to be a cost benefit analysis." And in making their "cost-benefit" judgments, they primarily took into account Sell's dangerousness, not the need to bring him to trial.

The failure to focus upon trial competence could well have mattered. Whether a particular drug will tend to sedate a defendant, interfere with communication with counsel, prevent rapid reaction to trial developments, or diminish the ability to express emotions are matters important in determining the permissibility of medication to restore competence, but not necessarily relevant when dangerousness is primarily at issue. We cannot tell whether the side effects of antipsychotic medication were likely to undermine the fairness of a trial in Sell's case.

Finally, the lower courts did not consider that Sell has already been confined at the Medical Center for a long period of time, and that his refusal to take antipsychotic drugs might result in further lengthy confinement. Those factors, the first because a defendant ordinarily receives credit toward a sentence for time served, 18 U.S.C. § 3585(b), and the second because it reduces the likelihood of the defendant's committing future crimes, moderate—though they do not eliminate—the importance of the governmental interest in prosecution.

V

For these reasons, we believe that the present orders authorizing forced administration of antipsychotic drugs cannot stand. The Government may pursue its request for forced medication on the grounds discussed in this opinion, including grounds related to the danger Sell poses to himself or others. Since Sell's medical condition may have changed over time, the Government should do so on the basis of current circumstances.

The judgment of the Eighth Circuit is vacated, and the case is remanded for further proceedings consistent with this opinion.

Questions on Sell v. United States

In a dissent joined by Justices O'Connor and Thomas, Justice Scalia objected that the Sell's trial should have gone forward, with Dr. Sell's challenge to his involuntary medication put off until an appeal after conviction. Permitting pretrial appeals of this sort, Justice Scalia complained, provides an "obvious opportunity for gamesmanship" and invites "the disruption of criminal proceedings" by defendants challenging a variety of pretrial orders. For example, he said, "an order refusing to allow the defendant to wear a T-shirt that says 'Black Power' in front of the jury could be attacked as an immediate violation of First Amendment rights." Assuming, as Justice Scalia seems predisposed to do, that a defendant in Sell's position is convicted, he of course could raise a challenge to his trial on the ground that he was forcibly medicated and that the side effects interfered with his ability to assist in his own defense. If he succeeds on this ground, and retrial is required, haven't scarce judicial resources been needlessly squandered? On the other hand, if the defendant is acquitted after a trial during which he was forcibly medicated, what avenue of redress would remain open to the defendant?

Singleton v. Norris

319 F.3d 1018 (8th Cir. 2003)

WOLLMAN, Chief Judge.

Charles Laverne Singleton appeals the district court's order denying his petition for writ of habeas corpus. The district court rejected Singleton's contention that the administration of mandatory antipsychotic medication to a prisoner, initially constitutional under *Washington v. Harper*, 494 U.S. 210 (1990), becomes unconstitutional once an execution date is set because at that time it ceases to be in the prisoner's medical interest. After a divided panel of this court reversed, *Singleton v. Norris*, 267 F.3d 859 (8th

Cir. 2001), we granted the State's petition for rehearing en banc and vacated the panel opinion. We now affirm the district court's order.

I

In 1979, the State of Arkansas convicted Singleton of capital felony murder and aggravated robbery. He received a sentence of death for the murder and a sentence of life imprisonment for the robbery.... Singleton's conviction and sentence for capital felony murder were affirmed, but his conviction for the underlying felony of aggravated robbery was set aside.

After Singleton was denied post-conviction relief in state court, his execution was scheduled for June 4, 1982. Singleton then petitioned the district court for a stay of execution and writ of habeas corpus, raising claims including ineffective assistance of counsel, use of invalid aggravating factors, and that he was incompetent and thus ineligible for execution under *Ford v. Wainwright*, 477 U.S. 399 (1986). *Singleton v. Lockhart*, 653 F.Supp.1114, 1116 (E.D. Ark.1986). The district court sustained the conviction but reversed the sentence of death, holding that the pecuniary gain aggravating factor was invalid since it duplicated a factor in the underlying robbery-murder charge. On appeal, a panel of this court affirmed the order upholding the conviction, but reversed the order vacating the death sentence. *Singleton v. Lockhart*, 871 F.2d 1395, 1396 (8th Cir. 1989). Because the district court did not reach the *Ford* claim, it was not at issue on appeal.

In December 1992, Singleton filed an action in state court claiming that he was incompetent and could not be executed. He requested that his treatment with antipsychotic drugs be terminated and that a competency examination be held after the effect of the drugs had subsided. In addition, he asked for a declaratory judgment that he was not competent to be executed. The trial court denied his motion, and the Arkansas Supreme Court affirmed. *Singleton v. Endell*, 316 Ark. 133, 870 S.W.2d 742 (1994). In his second federal habeas petition, filed in 1993 but held in abeyance until the state proceedings concluded, Singleton raised the *Ford* claim, along with claims of double counting and actual innocence. The district court held two hearings and dismissed his petition. On appeal, Singleton conceded that he was competent because of the antipsychotic medication he was taking voluntarily. We affirmed the dismissal of his petition, noting that a future *Ford* claim based upon changed circumstances was not foreclosed by the decision. *Singleton v. Norris*, 108 F.3d 872, 874 (8th Cir.1997).

In 1997, the State placed Singleton on an involuntary medication regime after a medication review panel unanimously agreed that he posed a danger to himself and others. After the medication took effect, Singleton's psychotic symptoms abated. In January 2000, the State scheduled his execution for March 1, 2000. In February 2000, Singleton filed a petition for habeas corpus pursuant to 28 U.S.C. §2241, arguing that the State could not constitutionally restore his *Ford* competency through use of forced medication and then execute him. The district court denied the petition, finding "no evidence in this record that the actions and decisions of the medical personnel involved were in any degree motivated by the desire, purpose or intent to make Mr. Singleton competent so that he could be executed." Singleton appealed, and we granted a stay of execution.

We ordered a limited remand in March 2000 to answer two remaining questions of fact. First, whether Singleton was *Ford*-competent prior to the implementation of the *Harper* mandatory medication order in 1997. Second, whether Singleton would regress into psychosis and become *Ford*-incompetent if he stopped taking the medication. In answer to the first question, the district court found that Singleton was not *Ford*-competent at the time the involuntary medication regime began in 1997. The answer to the second question was less clear. The district court found that Singleton would regress into psychosis without medication, but could not say with certainty when psychotic symptoms would resume and whether he would become *Ford*-incompetent. Although the district court did not make a specific finding as to Singleton's present competence, Singleton does not argue that under medication he is unaware of his punishment and why he is to be punished.

II

B.

We turn now to consider the ... issues of whether the State may forcibly administer antipsychotic medication to a prisoner whose date of execution has been set and whether the State may execute a prisoner who has been involuntarily medicated under a *Washington v. Harper* procedure. Singleton argues that the involuntary medication regime, legal under *Harper* during a stay of execution, becomes illegal once an execution date is set because it is no longer in his best medical interest. This issue is one of first impression for this court and is a question of law we review *de novo*.

We are guided in our inquiry by *Ford v. Wainwright* and *Washington v. Harper*. In *Ford*, the Supreme Court addressed for the first time the limits imposed by the Eighth Amendment on a State's power to execute an insane prisoner. Reviewing the common law at the time the Bill of Rights was enacted, the Court found a clear rule against executing the insane despite divergent rationales for such a rule, including the inhumanity and the lack of deterrent and retributive value of such an act. In a concurring opinion, Justice Powell set out the governing standard for determining whether a prisoner is competent to be executed: "[T]he Eighth Amendment forbids the execution only of those who are unaware of the punishment they are about to suffer and why they are to suffer it."

In *Harper*, the Court addressed the question of what limit the Fourteenth Amendment Due Process Clause places on the power of a State to treat a mentally ill prisoner with antipsychotic drugs against his will. Harper, a state prisoner and diagnosed schizophrenic, refused to continue taking antipsychotic medication. After receiving medication against his will, Harper challenged as insufficient the procedural protections prisoners were afforded before being forcibly medicated. Noting that "procedural protections must be examined in terms of the substantive rights at stake," the Court analyzed the underlying substantive issue of what factual predicate is required before a State may forcibly administer antipsychotic drugs to a prisoner. The Court held that a State may forcibly administer antipsychotic drugs to "a prison inmate who has a serious mental illness ... if the inmate is dangerous to himself or others and the treatment is in the inmate's medical interest."

The limit of a State's authority to medicate a prisoner involuntarily has been developed further in the context of maintaining or restoring a defendant's competence to stand trial. In *Riggins v. Nevada*, the Court decided whether a defendant who was forcibly medicated with antipsychotic drugs to ensure his competence had been denied his right to a fair trial. Citing *Harper*, the Court found that the "substantial interference with [the prisoner's] liberty" was particularly severe due to the side effects often associated with those drugs. Declining to adopt a standard of strict scrutiny, the Court stated that due process required a showing of medical appropriateness and, considering less intrusive alternatives, a showing that treatment is "essential for the sake of [the defendant's] own safety or the safety of others." Riggins was medicated without "*any* determination of the need for [the medication] or *any* findings about reasonable alternatives." The Court held that this was inadequate, considering the "substantial probability of trial prejudice" in the form of the drug's effect on Riggins's appearance, testimony, and communication with counsel.

We recently considered a due process challenge to forced administration of medication where the state's sole purpose was to restore a defendant's competency for trial. *United States v. Sell*, 282 F.3d 560 (8th Cir.), cert. granted, 537 U.S. 999 (2002). In *Sell*, we held that the government had an "essential interest" in bringing Sell to trial that outweighed his liberty interest in refusing education. To justify forcibly medicating an individual to restore competency for trial, the government must (1) "present an essential state interest that outweighs the individual's interest in remaining free from medication," (2) "prove that there is no less intrusive way of fulfilling its essential interest," and (3) "prove by clear and convincing evidence that the medication is medically appropriate." "Medication is medically appropriate if: (1) it is likely to render the patient competent; (2) the likelihood and gravity of side effects do not overwhelm its benefits; and, (3) it is in the best medical interests of the patient." Where the charges against the defendant are serious, the government's essential interest in bringing a defendant to trial outweighs his significant liberty interest in avoiding unwanted medication.

We acknowledge, of course, *Sell*'s reservation of the question presented by Singleton's appeal ("[A]n entirely different case is presented when the government wishes to medicate a prisoner in order to render him competent for execution.") and its admonishment that "our holding must be read narrowly." Notwithstanding *Sell*'s cautionary comments, we believe that the standards set forth above are applicable to the district court's rulings in Singleton's case.

That the government has an essential interest in carrying out a lawfully imposed sentence cannot be doubted. *Moran v. Burbine*, 475 U.S. 412, 426 (1986) (recognizing "society's compelling interest in finding, convicting, and punishing those who violate the law"). We need not decide under what circumstances carrying out a particular sentence is not "essential." Society's interest in punishing offenders is at its greatest in the narrow class of capital murder cases in which aggravating factors justify imposition of the death penalty. This societal interest must be weighed against Singleton's interest in being free of unwanted antipsychotic medication. The record before us indicates that Singleton prefers to take the medication rather than be in an unmedicated and psychotic state. In addition, Singleton has suffered no substantial side effects. On these facts, the State's interest in carrying out its lawfully imposed sentence is the superior one.

Singleton has suggested no less intrusive means of ensuring his competence short of antipsychotic medication. The Eighth Amendment forbids the execution of an incompetent person, thus the State may achieve its essential interest in carrying out Singleton's sentence of execution only if Singleton is competent. In our order of limited remand, we did not ask the district court to make a finding as to Singleton's present competence. Other than his "artificial competence" theory, Singleton has never argued, and in fact has agreed repeatedly, that he is competent while he is medicated. In its report, the district court concluded that without medication Singleton would revert to a delusional psychotic state, but it is uncertain whether he would also become *Ford*-incompetent. On this record, treatment with antipsychotic drugs is necessary to alleviate Singleton's psychosis, and there is no less intrusive medical treatment by which the government can ensure Singleton's competence.

Finally, we reach the core of the dispute: whether the antipsychotic medication is medically appropriate for Singleton's treatment. We review the district court's findings of fact under the clearly erroneous standard. The first two determinations in the *Sell* analysis of medical appropriateness are not in serious dispute: first, whether the medication is likely to restore competence, and second whether the expected side effects overwhelm the benefits. The district court found that Singleton was *Ford*-incompetent at the time the mandatory medication was started in 1997. Singleton's symptoms have been kept almost completely under control since the initiation of the mandatory medication regime in 1997, and he has repeatedly conceded his competence while medicated. In its denial of Singleton's petition for habeas corpus, the district court found the record devoid of any significant negative side effects from the antipsychotic medication. These findings are not clearly erroneous, and they establish both that the medication is effective and that the expected side effects do not overwhelm the benefits of the medicine.

Central to Singleton's argument is his contention that medication "obviously is not in the prisoner's ultimate best medical interest" where one effect of the medication is rendering the patient competent for execution. Singleton does not dispute that the antipsychotic medication is in his medical interest during the pendency of a stay of execution. He has stated he takes it voluntarily because he does not like the symptoms he experiences without it. He also does not dispute the lack of serious side effects. The factor that Singleton contends takes him outside the scope of *Harper* is not the existence of serious harmful side effects or an insufficient medical need, but the very psychosis-reducing effect of the medicine. By focusing on his "ultimate best medical interest," Singleton presents the court with a choice between involuntary medication followed by execution and no medication followed by psychosis and imprisonment. Faced with these two unpleasant alternatives, he offers a third solution: a stay of execution until involuntary medication is no longer needed to maintain his competence.

By focusing on his long-term medical interest, Singleton implicitly concedes that the medication is in his short-term medical interest. Several doctors, both during the *Harper* determination and at other times, have found the medication to be effective in controlling Singleton's psychotic symptoms. Singleton's argument regarding his long-term medical interest boils down to an assertion that execution is not in his medical interest. Eligibility for execution is the only unwanted consequence of the medication. The due process interests in life and liberty that Singleton asserts have been foreclosed by the lawfully imposed sentence of execution and the *Harper* procedure. In the circumstances presented in this case, the best medical interests of the prisoner must be determined without regard to whether there is a pending date of execution. Thus we hold that the mandatory medication regime, valid under the pendency of a stay of execution, does not become unconstitutional under *Harper* when an execution date is set.

Closely related to his due process argument, Singleton also claims that the Eighth Amendment forbids the execution of a prisoner who is "artificially competent." Singleton relies principally on a case construing an analogous provision in the Louisiana Constitution. *State v. Perry*, 610 So.2d 746 (La.1992). The *Perry* court, noting that the Louisiana provision is an expansion on the protections of the Eighth Amendment, concluded that the execution of an insane inmate who had been forcibly medicated into competence would violate the state constitution. State courts of last resort may interpret their state constitutions as they see fit. We note, however, that the *Perry* court accepted the view of "best medical interests" that we have rejected. The court also found Perry's medication was ordered solely for purposes of punishment and not for legitimate reasons of prison security or medical need. We decline to undertake a difficult and unnecessary inquiry into the State's motives in circumstance where it has a duty to provide medical care. *DeShaney v. Winnebago County Dep't of Soc. Servs.*, 489 U.S. 189, 199–200 (1989); *Estelle v. Gamble*, 429 U.S. 97, 103 (1976) ("These elementary principles establish the government's obligation to provide medical care for those whom it is punishing by incarceration."). The findings below support a conclusion that the state was under an obligation to administer antipsychotic medication, thus any additional motive or effect is irrelevant. *Ford* prohibits only the execution of a prisoner who is unaware of the punishment he is about to receive and why he is to receive it. A State does not violate the Eighth Amendment as interpreted by *Ford* when it executes a prisoner who became incompetent during his long stay on death row but who subsequently regained competency through appropriate medical care.

We affirm the order of the district court denying Singleton's petition for writ of habeas corpus and vacate the stay of execution....

HEANEY, Circuit Judge, dissenting, in which BRIGHT, McMILLIAN, and BYE, Circuit Judges, join.

Charles Singleton suffers from mental illness that makes him psychotic. At times he has been forced to take powerful psychotropic drugs; at other times he takes the medication voluntarily. The drugs often mask his underlying psychosis. The majority believes this makes him fit for execution. I believe that to execute a man who is severely deranged without treatment, and arguably incompetent when treated, is the pinnacle of what Justice Marshall called "the barbarity of exacting mindless vengeance." *Ford v. Wainwright*, 477 U.S. 399, 410 (1986). My reasoning is guided by the decisions of the Supreme Court, and supported by the rulings of state courts which have considered the issue, the overwhelming majority of scholarly commentary, and the ethical standards of the medical profession. I dissent.

I

Charles Singleton has been on death row since 1979 as a result of his conviction for the capital felony murder of Mary Lou York. He has been on psychotropic medication during much of his stay in prison. This medication was prescribed initially to alleviate anxiety and depression. Beginning in 1987, however, Singleton's mental health began to deteriorate. He started to believe that his cell was possessed by demons and had "demon blood" in it. He reported that his brother would come to his locked prison cell and take him out of it for walks. He was under the impression that a prison doctor had planted some type of device in his right ear and that his thoughts were being stolen from him when he read the Bible. During this time, he sustained a considerable loss of weight.

Singleton was diagnosed as likely schizophrenic and placed on antipsychotic medication. He initially took it on his own, but when he refused, he was forcibly medicated. For the next several years, Singleton continued to be treated for his psychosis. His medication was administered voluntarily at times, and at times it was administered forcibly. Whenever he was off his medication, his symptoms would resurface, and he would again experience hallucinations. In 1991, Singleton's treating doctor took him off his medication in order to determine when symptoms of his illness would reappear. Within a few months, he was observed stripping off his clothes and speaking in a strange language. He became paranoid and delusional, and believed that he had already been executed.

Singleton was again put on an involuntary medication plan. From November of 1991 until March of 1995, he remained on this treatment plan. Despite being treated at the time, symptoms of Singleton's mental illness flared up again in the summer of 1993. During this period, Singleton was under the impression that he was the victim of a voodoo curse, and endured disturbing hallucinations in which his food turned to worms and cigarettes became bones. His medication was altered, and he became more stable.

Beginning in March of 1995, Singleton was put on a voluntary treatment regime. He regularly accepted his medication until September of 1996, when a prison psychiatrist agreed to take him off the medication. Within a few months, Singleton was withdrawn and again lost a substantial amount of weight. His speech had become unintelligible. He was prescribed another antipsychotic medication, but did not take it regularly. By July of 1997, Singleton's symptoms were much worse. Observations over the next few weeks have been summarized as follows:

On July 21, 1997, Mr. Singleton was described as very hostile, belligerent, and probably psychotic. The following day, he informed the staff he was "on a mission from God," and he had to kill [treating physician] Dr. Oglesby and the President. On August 7, 1997, Mr. Singleton was described as bizarre, delusional, and he expressed the belief that he had been "freed by the Eighth Circuit and the U.S. Supreme Court." On August 7, 1997, Mr. Singleton was described as exhibiting bad hygiene. He informed the staff he was "God and the Supreme Court" and that he had been set free. On August 13, Mr. Singleton was observed in his cell by mental health staff. He was described as nude and "zombie-like." He displayed a vacant stare and was almost nonresponsive. He had torn up his mattress and flushed it. The following day, Dr. Oglesby recommended Mr. Singleton be seen by a Medication Review Panel, because he believed Mr. Singleton was psychotic and gravely disabled. On August 15, Mr. Singleton flooded his cell. He was seen on August 18 by the Medication Review Panel. He informed them he believed the courts had overturned his sentence and there was a conspiracy to execute him anyway.

Based on Singleton's behavior, the panel again decided to forcibly medicate him. This medication alleviated Singleton's symptoms for a time, but by February of 1999 he was again withdrawn and exhibited a strange speech pattern. His medication was increased. In April of 1999, he reported that he was "hearing voices talking about doing something to him." Again, the prison responded by increasing his medication.

In March of 2000, a panel of this Court ordered a limited remand to determine issues surrounding Singleton's competency to be executed. As a result, the district court ordered an evaluation to be performed on Singleton at the Federal Medical Center in Springfield. Singleton was held for observation from June 29, 2000 through August 14, 2000. During that time, he was interviewed a number of times by Dr. Mrad, a psychologist in the Forensic Evaluation Unit. Dr. Mrad had seen Singleton in 1995 for a similar evaluation, giving him some point of reference as to Singleton's mental state.

During this evaluation period, Singleton's comments to Dr. Mrad led Dr. Mrad to question whether Singleton might be psychotic even while on his medication. Singleton admitted to having continued hallucinations, and "occasionally referred to himself as God or God-like and on a few occasions referred to himself as the Holy Spirit." Regarding Singleton's understanding of his punishment, Mrad stated:

I asked him if he was God, how could he be executed, and he slapped his arm and said I've got this. My understanding referring to a body. He could be—he could be executed and that it would—and I think he knew that the reason for the execution would be conviction for the murder of Mary Lou York and by that I believed he had a factual understanding. He could recite— basically recite basic facts that he would be—what the sentence was and why he would be given that sentence. The other part of it, the rational understanding I think was—has more to do with does he actually understand what this means, not only can he say it but does he actually understand what this means and what it means as applied to him, and it was not at all clear to me that he did. His thinking was so disorganized. He made these frequent comments about being the Holy Ghost or Holy Spirit. He talked about a—some beliefs about a parallel world, about being—an execution just being stopping breathing and then you start up again somewhere else and that—there was some statement made about correctional officers. Execution correctional officers stop you from breathing and then the judge can do something to start it up again.

Singleton explained that he had attempted to kill himself in 1997 and had cut his jugular vein, but that he was unable to die because the wound spontaneously stopped bleeding. There is no evidence in the record of any such suicide attempt. Singleton went on to tell Dr. Mrad that he was penning a book at the request of God, that he and St. John were on a mission to fight homosexuals, and that Sylvester Stallone and Arnold Schwartzenegger were somewhere between this universe and another one and were trying to save him.

When asked about Singleton's current mental status, Mrad stated he would technically classify Singleton as "psychotic because he was describing that he was still experiencing hallucinations, and clearly when I had interviewed him his mental status was noticeably different than it had been, for instance, five years earlier. His thinking was much more disorganized. He was very difficult to follow." In summary, Dr. Mrad determined that Singleton was not competent under the *Ford* standard when he was off his medication in 1997, and that he would clearly be psychotic if his medication was discontinued. He further opined that Singleton's current concept of death was not a rational one, and that "he may not be currently competent from what I was seeing."

There is some question of the cause of Singleton's psychosis during his observation period in the summer of 2000. Singleton did not take his medication in April of 2000, and Dr. Mrad thought that may have contributed to Singleton's behavior. However, Mrad also stated that disorders such as Singleton's often get worse with time. ("Generally, the disorder is chronic and usually lifelong and, if anything, a more common pattern would be to become more severe over time and that frequently as a patient has additional decompensations they often—once they're medicated, once their mental status is restored, they may not come back to the prior level of functioning they had before the last decompensation....")

On December 11, 2001, this Court received a letter directly from Singleton. In it, he declared that he did not believe Mary Lou York was dead, and that she "is somewhere on this earth waiting for me—her groom." He further stated that "[s]omebody sent me, the robot, to Mrs. York, I know the police is in it, you could be in it. So, if her service was/is in vain, its because that's the way you want it."

II

A.

In *Ford v. Wainwright*, 477 U.S. 399 (1986), the Supreme Court was faced with the question of whether the Eighth Amendment prohibition on cruel and unusual punishment proscribed the execution of insane prisoners. Ford was a death row inmate who suffered from serious mental illness. As a result of his disease, Ford began to refer to himself as a religious leader, believed he had appointed new justices to the Florida Supreme Court, and began to speak in a strange alphanumeric code. Importantly, Ford was also under the impression that he was no longer subject to the death penalty, and could leave the prison whenever he wanted to do so.

Justice Marshall outlined the historical contours of the prohibition on executing the insane. Finding support as far back as Sir Edward Coke's seventeenth century treatise on the subject, the Court determined that while legislatures, courts, and commentators provided diverse rationales for the prohibition, they all agreed on one thing: execution of the insane does not comport with the ideals of a civilized society. Consistent with this historical principle, the Court held that "the restriction [on executing the insane] finds enforcement in the Eighth Amendment." Justice Powell, in his concurrence, suggested that if the insane inmate becomes "cured of his disease, the State is [then] free to execute him."

The issue left unresolved by *Ford* is the very one in this case: whether the Eighth Amendment permits the execution of an insane inmate who is receiving treatment. At the outset, I believe that our analysis should consider what precisely "treatment" means in this context. Singleton has been forced to take antipsychotic medication, the stated goal of which is to stabilize his mental condition. However, receiving treatment is not synonymous with being cured. Antipsychotic drugs "merely calm and mask the psychotic symptoms which usually return to debilitate the patient when the medication is discontinued." *State v. Perry*, 610 So.2d 746, 759 (La.1992); Keith Alan Byers, *Incompetency, Execution, and the Use of Antipsychotic Drugs*, 47 Ark. L.Rev. 361, 377 (1994) (noting consensus in medical community that antipsychotic drugs provide only temporary relief); see also Rhonda K. Jenkins, Comment, *Fit to Die: Drug-Induced Competency for the Purpose of Execution*, 20 S. Ill. U. L.J. 149, 169 (Fall, 1995) ("A subset of psychotropic medications, psychoactive drugs diminish the symptoms of mental illness, but they do not cure the underlying mental illness."); Nancy S. Horton, Comment, *Restoration of Competency for Execution: Furious Solo Furore Punitur*, 44 Sw. L.J. 1191, 1204 (Winter, 1990) ("Despite their beneficial effects, antipsychotic drugs merely mask the debilitating symptoms of major mental disorders; the drugs do not cure the mental disorder.")

Thus, when antipsychotic medication results in an improved mental state, the patient is merely displaying what has been termed "artificial" or "synthetic" sanity. One of the pitfalls of equating true sanity with its medically-coerced cousin is that drug-induced sanity is temporary and unpredictable: "the effect of psychoactive drugs on a particular recipient is uncertain; the drugs may affect the same individual differently each time they are administered."

Singleton's case is exemplary of the unpredictable result antipsychotic drug treatment has on mentally ill prisoners. A review of the record establishes that since the outset of the Singleton's symptoms, the treatment plan for his mental disease has been consistently fluid. Singleton's medication has often been changed, either in dose or in type, in response to observations of his mental stability. Even when evaluated by Dr. Mrad pursuant to our court order, Singleton's behavior left Dr. Mrad with the impression that Singleton had decompensated and was currently psychotic, in spite of his treatment plan. Particularly because Singleton's treatment plan has never kept him consistently free of symptoms, "it would be very difficult to ensure that the prisoner was truly free of the effects of his psychosis and able to meet the [*Ford*] standard of competency at the exact moment of his execution."

Based on the medical history in this case, I am left with no alternative but to conclude that drug-induced sanity is not the same as true sanity. Singleton is not "cured;" his insanity is merely muted, at times, by the powerful drugs he is forced to take. Underneath this mask of stability, he remains insane.[6] *Ford* 's prohibition on executing the insane should apply with no less force to Singleton than to untreated prisoners. [7]

B.

It is beyond dispute that the forcible injection of psychotropic medication into a person's body represents a substantial interference with that person's liberty. *Riggins v. Nevada*; *Washington v. Harper*. The Court recognized that while such drugs often benefit the recipient, "it is also true that the drugs can have serious, even fatal, side effects." For this reason, forcing a prisoner to take antipsychotic drugs is "impermissible absent a finding of overriding justification and a determination of medical appropriateness." Specifically, the Due Process clause of the Fourteenth Amendment requires the State to show that the mind-altering medication is (1) necessary because the inmate is dangerous to himself or others, and (2) in the inmate's best medical interest.

The question for our court is whether *Harper* is satisfied where the consequence of forcibly medicating the inmate will be his execution. The majority believes that its analysis should focus on the State's intent in medicating the inmate, and concludes that it is constitutional for the State to forcibly medicate Singleton into a state of competency because the State's motive in medicating Singleton is to improve his well-being.

Even if I were to accept that the State's intent should control the analysis, the majority's reasoning remains unsound. It is beyond dispute that the State may not execute Singleton when he is unmedicated and displays the typical symptoms of his psychosis. *Ford*. It is also true, as the majority states, "[t]hat the government has an essential interest in carrying out a lawfully imposed sentence cannot be doubted." The State's vigor in pursuing this goal may well lead it to obscure the true reasons for forcibly medicating an inmate into competence.[8] *See* Bryan Lester Dupler, *The Uncommon Law: Insanity, Executions, and Oklahoma Criminal Procedure*, 55 Okla. L.Rev. 1, 54 (Spring 2002) ("As a matter of candor and common sense, the long-term health (or 'medical interest') of the insane capital prisoner is not the concern of the State that seeks to forcibly medicate him.").... [9]

The problem with pinning the constitutionality of a prisoner's execution to the State's intent in forcibly medicating him is that it will often be difficult to determine whether the State is medicating a prisoner to protect him from harming himself or others, or whether the State is medicating the inmate to render him competent for execu-

---

6. Singleton, in fact, exhibits some of the very same manifestations of psychosis that Ford himself did, including a belief that his sentence has been overturned and that he cannot be executed.

7. There is also some question as to whether forcing Singleton to take medication that will lead to his execution is violative of the Eighth Amendment's prohibition against excessive punishment. *Cf. Atkins v. Virginia*, 536 U.S. 304 (2002) ("The Eighth Amendment succinctly prohibits 'excessive' sanctions.") Two state supreme courts, under their state constitutions, found such punishment to be excessive and thus unconstitutional. *See generally, Singleton v. State*, 437 S.E.3d 53 (S.C.1993); *State v. Perry*, 610 So.2d 746 (La.1992). The Supreme Court has recognized the potentially debilitating side effects of psychotropic medication. *Washington v. Harper*, 494 U.S. 210, 229–30 (1990). It has been recognized that forcibly medicated condemned inmates have to endure greater suffering than the typical condemned inmates, *Perry*, 610 So.2d at 766– 68, and it is not beyond reason to suggest that the "evolving standards of decency that mark the progress of a maturing society" do not permit such a distinction, *Trop v. Dulles*, 356 U.S. 86, 101 (1958) (plurality opinion).

8. The State conceded in its brief and at the initial oral argument in this matter that it may not medicate Singleton for the express purpose of rendering him competent for execution.

9. Unlike the majority, I am not convinced that forced medical treatment is in Singleton's best medical interest when it may ultimately result in his execution.

tion. Moreover, such an inquiry rests on the faulty assumption that the State maintains one exclusive motive for its actions. Here, even the majority recognizes two competing State interests: the safety of the prison guards and inmates (including Singleton), and its interest in exacting punishment. In light of the record, it is simply illusory for our court to conclude that it can discern the State's single, directed motivation for forcibly medicating Singleton.

Once an execution date was set, I believe that the justification for medicating Singleton under *Harper* evaporated. An inquiry into the State's motivation is unhelpful, for it presupposes a single, directed motivation, which is not the case here. In fact, the evidence suggests two competing interests: the welfare of the prison, and the execution of the prisoner's sentence. At the very least, the setting of an execution date calls into question the State's true motivation for administering the medication in the first instance. The circumstances of Singleton's case changed once the execution date was set, and changed in such a way that *Harper* no longer supports the prison forcing him to take medication.

C.

Lastly, I am compelled to note that the majority holding will inevitably result in forcing the medical community to practice in a manner contrary to its ethical standards. Physicians are duty bound to act in the best interest of their patients. See *Perry*, 610 So.2d at 752 ("Under [the Hippocratic Oath], the physician pledges to do no harm and to act only in the best medical interests of his patients.") Consequently, the ethical standards of both the American Medical Association and the American Psychiatric Association prohibit members from assisting in the execution of a condemned prisoner. Needless to say, this leaves those doctors who are treating psychotic, condemned prisoners in an untenable position: treating the prisoner may provide short-term relief but ultimately result in his execution, whereas leaving him untreated will condemn him to a world such as Singleton's, filled with disturbing delusions and hallucinations.

The ethical dilemma outlined above is not simply a policy matter; courts have long recognized the integrity of the medical profession as an appropriate consideration in its decision-making process. In *Washington v. Glucksberg*, 521 U.S. 702 (1997), the Supreme Court considered the whether a statute outlawing physician-assisted suicide was constitutional. It noted that the American Medical Association and other physician groups had condemned the practice. The Court explicitly recognized the significance of this factor, giving credence to the State's "interest in protecting the integrity and ethics of the medical profession."

I see no reason for the majority's divergence from the Supreme Court in this matter. Here, as in *Glucksberg*, the medical community has spoken with a singular voice, opposing its members' assistance in executions. Instead of giving due consideration to this serious issue, the majority eschews it altogether, without so much as an acknowledgment of the dilemma it has created. I adhere to the Supreme Court's position that the integrity of the medical profession is an interest that the court should consider and protect.

III

Charles Singleton is an insane death row inmate. He is forced to submit to a treatment regime that includes powerful, mind-altering drugs. As a result of his treatment, he sometimes appears lucid and rational; other times he does not. The fact is, however, that he remains insane. I believe that we must continue to abide by the Supreme Court's prohibition on executing the insane, particularly in this case, where the State is motivated to medicate a person into competence in order to carry out its punishment. I am gravely concerned that the majority has created a serious ethical dilemma for the medical community as a result of its opinion. I would hold that the State may continue to medicate Singleton, voluntarily or involuntarily, if it is necessary to protect him or others and is in his best medical interest, but it may not execute him. I continue to believe that the appropriate remedy is for the district court to enter a permanent stay of execution. Accordingly, I have no alternative but to dissent.

Note and Questions on Singleton v. Norris

At the time of the Eighth Circuit's en banc ruling in *Singleton v. Norris*, the Eighth Circuit's decision in *Sell v. United States* was awaiting review in the Supreme Court. The *Singleton* majority acknowledged that Singleton's appeal—which raised the issue of whether the government can medicate a prisoner to render him competent for execution—presented "an entirely different case" than Sell's appeal—which raised a due process challenge to the forced administration of drugs where the state's sole purpose was to restore a defendant's competency for trial. Nonetheless, the Eighth Circuit appeared to apply its *Sell* standards to Singleton's case.

How does the Supreme Court's resolution of *Sell v. United States, supra*, differ from the Eighth Circuit's holding in *Sell*? The Supreme Court limited its holding in *Sell* to defendants charged with "serious, but nonviolent" crimes. Does the Supreme Court's refusal to apply its *Sell* standards to the issue presented by Singleton mean that the Eighth Circuit erred in doing so? Does the Supreme Court's denial of certiorari in *Singleton v. Norris* indicate that the Eighth Circuit did not err?

Note on Cooper v. Oklahoma, 517 U.S. 348 (1996)

The Supreme Court has held that a criminal trial of an incompetent person violates due process. The Court also has established that the standard by which competency is to be determined is (1) whether the defendant "has the present ability to consult with his attorney with reasonable degree of rational understanding," and (2) whether the defendant has a "rational as well as factual understanding of the proceedings against." *Dusky v. United States*, 362 U.S. 402 (1960). Within these parameters, states have crafted various ways to determine whether, under the *Dusky* standard, a defendant is competent to stand trial. In four states, including Oklahoma, the State placed the burden on the defendant to prove by clear and convincing evidence that he is not competent to stand trial. In *Cooper v. Oklahoma*, 517 U.S. 348 (1996), a unanimous Court struck down such a procedural rule on the grounds that it violated due process.

Byron Keith Cooper was charged with the brutal murder of an 86-year-old man. Cooper's competence to stand trial "was the focus of significant attention both before and during his trial." Several pre-trial hearings were held to determine Cooper's competence to stand trial. Although he eventually was found competent to stand trial, on the first day of trial Cooper's bizarre behavior prompted the trial court to conduct a further competency hearing. At the conclusion of that hearing, the trial court stated,

"Well, I think I've used the expression ... in the past that normal is like us. Anybody that's not like us is not normal, so I don't think normal is a proper definition that we are to use with incompetence. My shirtsleeve opinion of Mr. Cooper is that he is not normal. Now, to say he's not competent is something else.

"But you know, all things considered, I suppose it's possible for a client to be in such a predicament that he can't help his defense and still not be incompetent. I suppose that's a possibility, too.

"I think it's going to take smarter people than me to make a decision here. I'm going to say that I don't believe he has carried the burden by clear and convincing evidence of his incompetency and I'm going to say we're going to go to trial."

At trial, the jury found Cooper guilty of murder and sentenced him to death. The Oklahoma Court of Criminal Appeals affirmed his conviction and sentence, and Cooper sought relief in the United States Supreme Court.

Although the Court had held previously "that a State may presume that the defendant is competent and require him to shoulder the burden of proving his incompetence by a preponderance of the evidence," the Court found that placing the onerous burden of requiring the defendant to prove his incompetence by "clear and convincing evidence" was at odds with the common law traditions of this country. The Court found this deviance from tradition and modern procedural practice violated the fundamental principles of due process. In addition, the Court appeared particularly offended that a defendant, like Cooper, who displayed extreme and bizarre behavior and who was more likely than not incompetent, would still be forced to stand trial because he had not proved his incompetence under the heavier clear and convincing evidence burden. Accordingly, the Supreme Court remanded Cooper's case to state court.

Note on Incompetence: Rickey Ray Rector

Rickey Ray Rector shot and killed a police officer, then shot himself through the forehead. The bullet tore completely through the front of Rector's skull and lodged under the skin above his right ear. Rector underwent emergency brain surgery, during which three inches of frontal brain tissue were removed from his head. Although Rector survived, the damage to his brain was so severe that the surgery amounted to "a classic prefrontal lobotomy." A journalist characterized Rector's post-operative mental condition as follows:

> The clinical effect of such a substantial destruction of frontal brain tissue is that Rector, as it was presented in testimony over the ensuing months, would suffer from "gross memory loss," and particularly that when dealing with "content and meaning" he was "severely impaired," and would have a near-total inability to conceptualize beyond a response to immediate sensations or provocations; in fact, he "seemed unable to grasp either the concept of past or future." A state psychologist also noted that he had "difficulty maintaining concentration and attention to a task." In addition, although Rector did "demonstrate ... some abilities to handle his day-to-day life in terms of actions which are repetitive," he also demonstrated what is known as a flat affect, meaning that "when it comes down to the issues of emotion ... Rickey has absolutely no involvement in any of the dire circumstances of his life." In fact, the Little Rock clinical neuropsychologist found him to be "lacking a will or an understanding of a way to fight his present dilemma."

Following a pretrial competency hearing, which produced expert testimony a higher court would later characterize as "hopelessly in conflict," Rector was deemed fit to be tried. He stood trial and was convicted and sentenced to die.

In the four days just prior to Rector's execution, his every move and utterance were as-siduously recorded in a "death watch log" kept by prison guards. Rector spent much of his time howling, barking like a dog, stamping his feet, snapping his finger, and laughing. Occasionally Rector would scream, "Cold Duck, Cold Duck," the nickname of an old friend. From his death watch cell, Rector learned that Arkansas Governor Bill Clinton—who was running for president—refused clemency. Just hours before his execution, Rec-tor sat with his attorney and watched news broadcasts detailing both Rector's imminent execution and sexual harassment charges leveled at Governor Clinton by Gennifer Flow-ers. Rector mumbled to his attorney, "I'm gonna vote for him. Gonna vote for Clinton."

Rector confided to a death watch guard that "if you eat grass lethal injection won't kill you." Rector devoured all of his last meal except for dessert, a large portion of pecan pie. As was his habit, Rector put his dessert aside to be eaten later—after the execution. He died by lethal injection on January 24, 1992. Marshall Frady, *Death in Arkansas*, The New Yorker, Feb. 23, 1993 at 105, 111.

Differences Between Insanity and Mental Retardation

Insanity has been described as a social and legal phenomenon, rather than a medical one. Insane persons are "unfit to enjoy liberty of action because of the unreliability of [their] behavior with concomitant danger to [themselves] and others." *Black's Law Dic-tionary* 714 (5th ed.). In a legal sense, insanity is a mental illness which negates an indi-vidual's legal responsibility or capacity.

According to Professor James W. Ellis, "the cardinal difference [between mental ill-ness and mental retardation] is that mental retardation is not an illness." Ellis & Luckas-son, "Mentally Retarded Criminal Defendants," 53 Geo. Wash. L. Rev. 414, 423 (1985). "Mentally ill people encounter disturbances in their thought processes and emotions; mentally retarded people have limited abilities to learn." Mental retardation is a perma-nent development condition characterized by slowness or limitation in intellectual, functional, or emotional development and is usually characterized by low IQ scores. See Entzeroth, "Putting The Mentally Retarded Criminal Defendant to Death: Charting the Development of a National Consensus to Exempt the Mentally Retarded from the Death Penalty," 52 Ala. L. Rev. 911 (2001).

In *Penry v. Lynaugh*, immediately below, the Court addressed the double-edged na-ture of evidence of retardation. On one hand, retardation has a mitigating quality: ju-rors may believe retardation reduces both capability and culpability. On the other hand, retardation also has an aggravating quality: one whose intellectual and emotional devel-opment is impaired might be perceived as posing a greater risk of "commit[ting] crimi-nal acts of violence that would constitute a continuing threat to society." Texas Code Crim. Proc. Art. 37.071, §2(b)(2), *infra* chapter 7.

D. Mental Retardation

In 1989, a year after the Supreme Court considered the issue of juvenile executions in *Thompson v. Oklahoma*, and the same year it decided *Stanford v. Kentucky*, 492 U.S. 361 (1989), the Supreme Court considered whether a mentally retarded inmate could be put to death consistent with the U.S. Constitution. The Supreme Court defined the issue presented in *Penry v. Lynaugh*, 492 U.S. 302 (1989): "[W]hether ... the Eighth Amendment categorically prohibits Penry's execution because he is mentally retarded." The Court's opinion, authored by Justice O'Connor, resolved the issue as follows:

IV

... [Penry claims] that it would be cruel and unusual punishment, prohibited by the Eighth Amendment, to execute a mentally retarded person like himself with the reasoning capacity of a 7-year-old. He argues that because of their mental disabilities, mentally retarded people do not possess the level of moral culpability to justify imposing the death sentence. He also argues that there is an emerging national consensus against executing the mentally retarded. The State responds that there is insufficient evidence of a national consensus against executing the retarded, and that existing procedural safeguards adequately protect the interests of mentally retarded persons such as Penry.

B

The Eighth Amendment categorically prohibits the infliction of cruel and unusual punishments. At a minimum, the Eighth Amendment prohibits punishment considered cruel and unusual at the time the Bill of Rights was adopted. The prohibitions of the Eighth Amendment are not limited, however, to those practices condemned by the common law in 1789. The prohibition against cruel and unusual punishments also recognizes the "evolving standards of decency that mark the progress of a maturing society." *Trop v. Dulles*, 356 U.S. 86, 101 (1958) (plurality opinion); *Ford v. Wainwright*. In discerning those "evolving standards," we have looked to objective evidence of how our society views a particular punishment today. The clearest and most reliable objective evidence of contemporary values is the legislation enacted by the country's legislatures. We have also looked to data concerning the actions of sentencing juries.

It was well-settled at common law that "idiots," together with "lunatics," were not subject to punishment for criminal acts committed under those incapacities.... Idiocy was understood as "a defect of understanding from the moment of birth," in contrast to lunacy, which was "a partial derangement of the intellectual faculties, the senses returning at uncertain intervals." ... The common law prohibition against punishing "idiots" and "lunatics" for criminal acts was the precursor of the insanity defense, which today generally includes "mental defect" as well as "mental disease" as part of the legal definition of insanity.

In its emphasis on a permanent, congenital mental deficiency, the old common law notion of "idiocy" bears some similarity to the modern definition of mental retardation. The common law prohibition against punishing "idiots" generally applied, however, to persons of such severe disability that they lacked the reasoning capacity to form criminal intent or to understand the difference between good and evil. In the 19th and early 20th centuries, the term "idiot" was used to describe the most retarded of persons, corresponding to what is called "profound" and "severe" retardation today.

The common law prohibition against punishing "idiots" for their crimes suggests that it may indeed be "cruel and unusual" punishment to execute persons who are profoundly or severely retarded and wholly lacking the capacity to appreciate the wrongfulness of their actions. Because of the protections afforded by the insanity defense today, such a person is not likely to be convicted or face the prospect of punishment. Moreover, under *Ford v. Wainwright*, 477 U.S. 399 (1986), someone who is "unaware of the punishment they are about to suffer and why they are to suffer it" cannot be executed.

Such a case is not before us today. Penry was found competent to stand trial. In other words, he was found to have the ability to consult with his lawyer with a reasonable degree of rational understanding, and was found to have a rational as well as factual understanding of the proceedings against him. In addition, the jury rejected his insanity defense, which reflected their conclusion that Penry knew that his conduct was wrong and was capable of conforming his conduct to the requirements of the law.

Penry argues, however, that there is objective evidence today of an emerging national consensus against execution of the mentally retarded, reflecting the "evolving standards of decency that mark the progress of a maturing society." The federal Anti-Drug Abuse Act of 1988 prohibits execution of a person who is mentally retarded. Only one State, [Georgia], however, currently bans execution of retarded persons who have been found guilty of a capital offense.

In contrast, in *Ford v. Wainwright*, which held that the Eighth Amendment prohibits execution of the insane, considerably more evidence of a national consensus was available. No State permitted the execution of the insane, and 26 States had statutes explicitly requiring suspension of the execution of a capital defendant who became insane. Other States had adopted the common law prohibition against executing the insane. Moreover, in examining the objective evidence of contemporary standards of decency in *Thompson v. Oklahoma*, the plurality noted that 18 States expressly established a minimum age in their death penalty statutes, and all of them required that the defendant have attained at least the age of 16 at the time of the offense. In our view, the single state statute prohibiting execution of the mentally retarded, even when added to the 14 States that have rejected capital punishment completely, does not provide sufficient evidence at present of a national consensus....

C

Penry argues that execution of a mentally retarded person like himself with a reasoning capacity of approximately a 7-year-old would be cruel and unusual because it is disproportionate to his degree of personal culpability. Just as the plurality in *Thompson* reasoned that a juvenile is less culpable than an adult for the same crime, Penry argues that mentally retarded people do not have the judgment, perspective, and self-control of a person of normal intelligence. In essence, Penry argues that because of his diminished ability to control his impulses, to think in long-range terms, and to learn from his mistakes, he "is not capable of acting with the degree of culpability that can justify the ultimate penalty...."

On the record before the Court today ... I cannot conclude that all mentally retarded people of Penry's ability—by virtue of their mental retardation alone, and apart from any individualized consideration of their personal responsibility—inevitably lack the cognitive, volitional, and moral capacity to act with the degree of culpability associated with the death penalty....

In sum, mental retardation is a factor that may well lessen a defendant's culpability for a capital offense. But we cannot conclude today that the Eighth Amendment precludes the execution of any mentally retarded person of Penry's ability convicted of a capital offense simply by virtue of his or her mental retardation alone. So long as sentencers can consider and give effect to mitigating evidence of mental retardation in imposing sentence, an individualized determination whether "death is the appropriate punishment" can be made in each particular case. While a national consensus against execution of the mentally retarded may someday emerge reflecting the "evolving standards of decency that mark the progress of a maturing society," there is insufficient evidence of such a consensus today.

Notes

1. Johnny Paul Penry's mental problems started at birth. A difficult breach delivery left Penry with organic brain damage. His condition was aggravated during early childhood by his mother's brutal beatings. She struck Penry on the head, broke his arm several times, burned him with cigarette butts, and forced him to eat his own feces and drink urine. Penry's neighbors recalled hearing "terrible, terrible screams" coming from the Penry house every afternoon. Penry dropped out of the first grade and when he reached adulthood his mental age was still comparable to the average second-grader's. His aunt spent a year just trying to teach him to sign his name. As an adolescent, Penry was unable to recite the alphabet and could not count.

At age 21, Penry was convicted of rape and eventually was paroled. A report from the Texas Rehabilitation Commission warned that he had "very poor coordination between body drives and intellectual control. He also tends to be very defensive and may tend to protect himself from anticipation of hurt from others through aggressive acts."

During Penry's trial for the murder of Pamela Carpenter, "it became clear [that Penry] couldn't read or write.... He couldn't say how many nickels were in a dime or name the President of the United States." Beyond Reason: The Death Penalty and Offenders with Mental Retardation (DPIC) (March 2001).

Although the Court rejected Penry's argument that the execution of a mentally retarded criminal defendant violated the Eighth Amendment, the Court nonetheless reversed Penry's death sentence on the grounds that the jury was not able to adequately consider his mental retardation as a factor mitigating against the imposition of the death penalty. Penry returned to state court for a new sentencing hearing, and was again sentenced to death. Penry's November 16, 2000 execution date was stayed by the Supreme Court which granted certiorari to consider his challenge to the jury instructions in his second sentencing hearing. On June 5, 2001, the Court overturned Penry's second death sentence, because jury instructions again did not allow jurors to take his retardation sufficiently into account.

2. Legislative responses to *Penry* were dramatic. In 1989, only Maryland, Georgia and the federal government excluded the mentally retarded from the penalty of death. By 2002, eighteen death penalty states and the federal government protected the mentally retarded from the death penalty. *See* Entzeroth, "Constitutional Prohibition on the Execution of the Mentally Retarded Criminal Defendant," 38 Tul. L. Rev. 299 (2002); Entzeroth, "Putting the Mentally Retarded Criminal Defendant to Death: Charting the Development of a National Consensus to Exempt the Mentally Retarded from the Death Penalty," 52 Ala. L. Rev. 911 (2001).

3. Some state courts also expressed concern with the execution of mentally retarded criminal defendants. For example, in his dissent in *Lambert v. State*, 984 P.2d 221 (Okla. Crim. App. 1999), Presiding Judge Chapel described the mentally abilities of a capital defendant and the constitutionality under the Oklahoma Constitution of executing this man:

> A majority of the Court today approves the execution of a mentally retarded man who has the mental age of an eight-year-old boy. The Court blithely rejects the claim that the execution of the mentally retarded violates our state and federal constitutions. In deciding to allow the killing of mentally retarded citizens, the majority swallows all sense of decency, disregards the will of the people of Oklahoma and ignores the principles and values of Article II, section 9 of the Oklahoma Constitution.[10] Because our State constitution will not tolerate the execution of a mentally retarded man, I respectfully dissent to the imposition of the death penalty in this case. I concur in affirming Robert Wayne Lambert's convictions, but I would modify the sentences to life without the possibility of parole and order the sentences to run consecutively.
>
> Although he is a grown man, Lambert cannot make change. He spells no better than a seven-year-old and reads at a third grade level. When Lambert was seventeen years old, the Oklahoma Juvenile Services Division tested him. The State's testing revealed that Lambert has an IQ of 68 and that he is mentally retarded. Prior to this testing, Lambert struggled through special education classes. Lambert barely managed to get through kindergarten. Finally he dropped out of school when he was in the seventh grade. Lambert was never able to function successfully in a school setting, and after he dropped out of school, his mental retardation limited his ability to work or survive in the outside world. Lambert's entire life has been shaped by his mental retardation. Although he is now thirty years old, he has the mental age of an eight-year-old. His thinking and reasoning are equivalent to that of a child in the second or third grade. His moral culpability is, of necessity, on the same level.
>
> At issue is not whether Robert Wayne Lambert should be punished for his actions; he should. The question is how we as a society should punish the mentally retarded. The answer to this question speaks volumes about us as civilized, decent people. The majority's answer is shameful.
>
> Oklahoma does not execute children or the insane because to do so would violate our common, evolving sense of decency. It is incompatible with this sense of decency and it is morally indefensible then to kill someone who thinks, reasons and operates at the level of a third grader. Executing such a man is comparable to executing an eight-year-old boy.
>
> The Diagnostic and Statistical Manual of Mental Disorders (1994) (DSM-IV) defines a mentally retarded individual as one whose disability manifests itself before age eighteen and who has "significantly subaverage intellectual function," i.e., an IQ below seventy, accompanied with "significant limitations in adaptive functioning." Unlike mental illness, mental retardation is a permanent developmental condition marked by low intellectual capacity. This low intelligence affects and limits the mentally retarded person's ability to think, plan and function. It cannot be ameliorated by drugs or psychotherapy, although

---

10. Article II, section 9 of the Oklahoma Constitution prohibits cruel or unusual punishment.

the mentally retarded individual may be taught skills and strategies to better function in society. In contrast to mental illness, the likelihood of "faking" mental retardation is minimal....

Since *Penry* the national landscape has changed dramatically. Ten more states have banned the execution of the mentally retarded. Now, twelve death penalty states, the federal government and thirteen non-death penalty jurisdictions ban the execution of the mentally retarded. New Hampshire has not imposed the death penalty on anyone since 1976. Missouri currently has legislation pending to bar the execution of mentally retarded persons.

Other states, while not explicitly banning the execution of mentally retarded persons, prohibit the execution of persons with limited mental abilities. For example, Connecticut provides, "The court shall not impose the sentence of death on the defendant if ... at the time of the offense ... his mental capacity was significantly impaired or his ability to conform his conduct to the requirements of law was significantly impaired but not so impaired in either case as to constitute a defense to prosecution." California also provides "evidence of diminished capacity or of a mental disorder may be considered by the court ... at the time of sentencing or other disposition or commitment." Courts have overturned or modified death sentences in part because of a defendant's mental retardation.

As evidenced by state and federal legislation as well as public opinion polls, the American people disfavor executing the mentally retarded. A majority of Oklahomans oppose the imposition of the death penalty on mentally retarded defendants. The American Bar Association and the American Association of Mental Retardation recommend banning the execution of mentally retarded persons. Thus, while the death penalty continues to be an accepted form of punishment, the execution of the mentally retarded is out of step with the values of society.

The growing ban on the execution of the mentally retarded has much in common with the ban on the execution of two other traditionally protected groups: children and the insane. The rationale for barring the execution of children was set out in *Thompson v. Oklahoma*. Of great importance to the *Thompson* Court was the fact that under Oklahoma law children were treated differently from adults. The Court was also swayed by the eighteen states that specifically required that persons be at least sixteen years old to be eligible for the death penalty and by the American Bar Association's recommendation that children be exempt from the death penalty. In barring the execution of the insane, the United States Supreme Court had a visceral reaction against the execution of such persons finding that the execution of the insane offended humanity and constituted a barbaric act of "exacting mindless vengeance." ...

The Oklahoma Constitution bars "cruel or unusual punishments." It is our duty to interpret and enforce the Oklahoma Constitution. Given Oklahoma's traditional protection of the mentally retarded, the growing national ban on the execution of the mentally retarded, and the lack of penological goals advanced by the execution of these individuals, I believe the execution of the mentally retarded is a cruel or unusual punishment prohibited under Oklahoma law. I therefore respectfully dissent to the execution of a mentally retarded man who has the mental age of an eight-year-old boy.

3. This issue also arose before the California Supreme Court. In *People v. Smithey*, 978 P.2d 1171 (Cal. 1999) (Mosk, J., concurring) Justice Mosk concluded in a concur-

ring opinion that *Penry* is no longer valid under the Eighth Amendment in light of the legislative changes that have taken place since 1989. Justice Mosk stated:

> I would hold that the cruel and unusual punishments clause [of the United States Constitution] now prohibits execution of a sentence of death against mentally retarded persons. I am able to discern that, since *Penry*, "evolving standards of decency" have indeed evolved sufficiently in this area. Indeed, I cannot do otherwise. For I find that the requisite "national consensus" has, in fact, emerged.

In a footnote, Justice Mosk also stated that Article I, §17 of the California Constitution precluded the imposition of the death penalty on the mentally retarded. Like the Oklahoma Constitution, the California Constitution prohibits the imposition of cruel *or* unusual punishment and provides greater protection to defendants in California than does the Eighth Amendment.

4. The Diagnostic and Statistical Manual of Mental Disorders (1994) (DSM-IV) defines the mentally retarded individual as someone who has "significantly subaverage intellectual function" with "significant limitations in adaptive functioning in at least two of the following skill areas: communication, self-care, home living, social/interpersonal skills, use of community resources, self-direction, functional academic skills, work, leisure, health and safety," and whose adaptive and intellectual deficits are manifested by the time the individual is eighteen years old.

5. The mean score for intelligence is an IQ of 100. The DSM-IV rates the following IQ scores as indicative of mental retardation:

IQ 50–55 to approximately 70	mild mental retardation
IQ 35–40 to 50–55	moderate mental retardation
IQ 20–25 to 35–40	severe mental retardation
IQ below 20–25	profound mental retardation

6. The American Association of Mental Retardation (AAMR) sets forth similar, although not identical, standards for determining mental retardation. In 1992, the AAMR adopted a revised definition of "mentally retarded person." The 1992 definition provides:

> Mental retardation refers to substantial limitations in present functioning. It is characterized by significantly subaverage intellectual functioning, existing concurrently with related limitations in two or more of the following applicable adaptive skill areas: communication, self-care, home living, social skills, community use, self-direction, health and safety, functional academics, leisure, and work. Mental retardation manifests before age 18.

Prior to 1992, "mentally retarded persons" were described as having "significantly subaverage general intellectual functioning existing concurrently with deficits in adaptive behavior and manifested during the development period." American Association on Mental Deficiency (now Retardation), Classification in Mental Retardation 1 (H. Grossman ed. 1983).

Atkins v. Virginia

536 U.S. 304 (2002)

JUSTICE STEVENS delivered the opinion of the Court, in which O'Connor, Kennedy, Souter, Ginsburg, and Breyer, JJ., joined. Rehnquist, C.J., filed a dissenting opinion, in which Scalia and Thomas, JJ., joined. Scalia, J., filed a dissenting opinion, in which Rehnquist, C.J., and Thomas, J, joined.

Those mentally retarded persons who meet the law's requirements for criminal responsibility should be tried and punished when they commit crimes. Because of their disabilities in areas of reasoning, judgment, and control of their impulses, however, they do not act with the level of moral culpability that characterizes the most serious adult criminal conduct. Moreover, their impairments can jeopardize the reliability and fairness of capital proceedings against mentally retarded defendants. Presumably for these reasons, in the 13 years since we decided *Penry* v. *Lynaugh*, 492 U.S. 302 (1989), the American public, legislators, scholars, and judges have deliberated over the question whether the death penalty should ever be imposed on a mentally retarded criminal. The consensus reflected in those deliberations informs our answer to the question presented by this case: whether such executions are "cruel and unusual punishments" prohibited by the Eighth Amendment to the Federal Constitution.

I

Petitioner, Daryl Renard Atkins, was convicted of abduction, armed robbery, and capital murder, and sentenced to death....

In the penalty phase, the defense relied on one witness, Dr. Evan Nelson, a forensic psychologist who had evaluated Atkins before trial and concluded that he was "mildly mentally retarded."[3] His conclusion was based on interviews with people who knew Atkins, a review of school and court records, and the administration of a standard intelligence test which indicated that Atkins had a full scale IQ of 59.

The jury sentenced Atkins to death, but the Virginia Supreme Court ordered a second sentencing hearing because the trial court had used a misleading verdict form. At the resentencing, Dr. Nelson again testified. The State presented an expert rebuttal witness, Dr. Stanton Samenow, who expressed the opinion that Atkins was not mentally retarded, but rather was of "average intelligence, at least," and diagnosable as having antisocial personality disorder. The jury again sentenced Atkins to death.

The Supreme Court of Virginia affirmed the imposition of the death penalty....

Justice Hassell and Justice Koontz dissented. They rejected Dr. Samenow's opinion that Atkins possesses average intelligence as "incredulous as a matter of law," and concluded that "the imposition of the sentence of death upon a criminal defendant who has the mental age of a child between the ages of 9 and 12 is excessive." In their opinion, "it is indefensible to conclude that individuals who are mentally retarded are not to

---

3. The American Association on Mental Retardation (AAMR) defines mental retardation as follows: "*Mental retardation* refers to substantial limitations in present functioning. It is characterized by significantly subaverage intellectual functioning, existing concurrently with related limitations in two or more of the following applicable adaptive skill areas: communication, self-care, home living, social skills, community use, self-direction, health and safety, functional academics, leisure, and work. Mental retardation manifests before age 18." Mental Retardation: Definition, Classification, and Systems of Supports 5 (9th ed.1992).

The American Psychiatric Association's definition is similar: "The essential feature of Mental Retardation is significantly subaverage general intellectual functioning (Criterion A) that is accompanied by significant limitations in adaptive functioning in at least two of the following skill areas: communication, self-care, home living, social/interpersonal skills, use of community resources, self-direction, functional academic skills, work, leisure, health, and safety (Criterion B). The onset must occur before age 18 years (Criterion C). Mental Retardation has many different etiologies and may be seen as a final common pathway of various pathological processes that affect the functioning of the central nervous system." Diagnostic and Statistical Manual of Mental Disorders 41 (4th ed.2000). "Mild" mental retardation is typically used to describe people with an IQ level of 50–55 to approximately 70. *Id.*, at 42–43.

some degree less culpable for their criminal acts. By definition, such individuals have substantial limitations not shared by the general population. A moral and civilized society diminishes itself if its system of justice does not afford recognition and consideration of those limitations in a meaningful way."

Because of the gravity of the concerns expressed by the dissenters, and in light of the dramatic shift in the state legislative landscape that has occurred in the past 13 years, we granted certiorari to revisit the issue that we first addressed in the *Penry* case.

II

The Eighth Amendment succinctly prohibits "[e]xcessive" sanctions. It provides: "Excessive bail shall not be required, nor excessive fines imposed, nor cruel and unusual punishments inflicted." In *Weems v. United States,* 217 U.S. 349 (1910), we held that a punishment of 12 years jailed in irons at hard and painful labor for the crime of falsifying records was excessive. We explained "that it is a precept of justice that punishment for crime should be graduated and proportioned to [the] offense." We have repeatedly applied this proportionality precept in later cases interpreting the Eighth Amendment. Thus, even though "imprisonment for ninety days is not, in the abstract, a punishment which is either cruel or unusual," it may not be imposed as a penalty for "the 'status' of narcotic addiction," *Robinson v. California,* 370 U.S. 660, 666–667 (1962), because such a sanction would be excessive. As Justice Stewart explained in *Robinson:* "Even one day in prison would be a cruel and unusual punishment for the 'crime' of having a common cold."

A claim that punishment is excessive is judged not by the standards that prevailed in 1685 when Lord Jeffreys presided over the "Bloody Assizes" or when the Bill of Rights was adopted, but rather by those that currently prevail. As Chief Justice Warren explained in his opinion in *Trop v. Dulles,* 356 U.S. 86 (1958): "The basic concept underlying the Eighth Amendment is nothing less than the dignity of man.... The Amendment must draw its meaning from the evolving standards of decency that mark the progress of a maturing society."

Proportionality review under those evolving standards should be informed by " 'objective factors to the maximum possible extent.' " We have pinpointed that the "clearest and most reliable objective evidence of contemporary values is the legislation enacted by the country's legislatures." *Penry,* 492 U.S., at 331. Relying in part on such legislative evidence, we have held that death is an impermissibly excessive punishment for the rape of an adult woman, *Coker v. Georgia,* 433 U.S. 584 (1977), or for a defendant who neither took life, attempted to take life, nor intended to take life, *Enmund v. Florida,* 458 U.S. 782 (1982)....

We also acknowledged in *Coker* that the objective evidence, though of great importance, did not "wholly determine" the controversy, "for the Constitution contemplates that in the end our own judgment will be brought to bear on the question of the acceptability of the death penalty under the Eighth Amendment." ...

Thus, in cases involving a consensus, our own judgment is "brought to bear," by asking whether there is reason to disagree with the judgment reached by the citizenry and its legislators.

Guided by our approach in these cases, we shall first review the judgment of legislatures that have addressed the suitability of imposing the death penalty on the mentally retarded and then consider reasons for agreeing or disagreeing with their judgment.

III

The parties have not called our attention to any state legislative consideration of the suitability of imposing the death penalty on mentally retarded offenders prior to 1986. In that year, the public reaction to the execution of a mentally retarded murderer in Georgia apparently led to the enactment of the first state statute prohibiting such executions. In 1988, when Congress enacted legislation reinstating the federal death penalty, it expressly provided that a "sentence of death shall not be carried out upon a person who is mentally retarded." In 1989, Maryland enacted a similar prohibition. It was in that year that we decided *Penry*, and concluded that those two state enactments, "even when added to the 14 States that have rejected capital punishment completely, do not provide sufficient evidence at present of a national consensus."

Much has changed since then. Responding to the national attention received by the Bowden execution and our decision in *Penry*, state legislatures across the country began to address the issue. In 1990, Kentucky and Tennessee enacted statutes similar to those in Georgia and Maryland, as did New Mexico in 1991, and Arkansas, Colorado, Washington, Indiana, and Kansas in 1993 and 1994. In 1995, when New York reinstated its death penalty, it emulated the Federal Government by expressly exempting the mentally retarded. Nebraska followed suit in 1998. There appear to have been no similar enactments during the next two years, but in 2000 and 2001 six more States—South Dakota, Arizona, Connecticut, Florida, Missouri, and North Carolina—joined the procession. The Texas Legislature unanimously adopted a similar bill, and bills have passed at least one house in other States, including Virginia and Nevada.

It is not so much the number of these States that is significant, but the consistency of the direction of change. Given the well-known fact that anticrime legislation is far more popular than legislation providing protections for persons guilty of violent crime, the large number of States prohibiting the execution of mentally retarded persons (and the complete absence of States passing legislation reinstating the power to conduct such executions) provides powerful evidence that today our society views mentally retarded offenders as categorically less culpable than the average criminal. The evidence carries even greater force when it is noted that the legislatures that have addressed the issue have voted overwhelmingly in favor of the prohibition. Moreover, even in those States that allow the execution of mentally retarded offenders, the practice is uncommon. Some States, for example New Hampshire and New Jersey, continue to authorize executions, but none have been carried out in decades. Thus there is little need to pursue legislation barring the execution of the mentally retarded in those States. And it appears that even among those States that regularly execute offenders and that have no prohibition with regard to the mentally retarded, only five have executed offenders possessing a known IQ less than 70 since we decided *Penry*. The practice, therefore, has become truly unusual, and it is fair to say that a national consensus has developed against it.[21]

---

21. Additional evidence makes it clear that this legislative judgment reflects a much broader social and professional consensus. For example, several organizations with germane expertise have adopted official positions opposing the imposition of the death penalty upon a mentally retarded offender. See Brief for American Psychological Association et al. as *Amici Curiae*; Brief for AAMR et al. as *Amici Curiae*. In addition, representatives of widely diverse religious communities in the United States, reflecting Christian, Jewish, Muslim, and Buddhist traditions, have filed an *amicus curiae* brief explaining that even though their views about the death penalty differ, they all "share a conviction that the execution of persons with mental retardation cannot be morally justified." Brief for United States Catholic Conference et al. as *Amici Curiae* 2. Moreover, within the world commu-

To the extent there is serious disagreement about the execution of mentally retarded offenders, it is in determining which offenders are in fact retarded. . . .

IV

This consensus unquestionably reflects widespread judgment about the relative culpability of mentally retarded offenders, and the relationship between mental retardation and the penological purposes served by the death penalty. Additionally, it suggests that some characteristics of mental retardation undermine the strength of the procedural protections that our capital jurisprudence steadfastly guards.

As discussed above, clinical definitions of mental retardation require not only subaverage intellectual functioning, but also significant limitations in adaptive skills such as communication, self-care, and self-direction that became manifest before age 18. Mentally retarded persons frequently know the difference between right and wrong and are competent to stand trial. Because of their impairments, however, by definition they have diminished capacities to understand and process information, to communicate, to abstract from mistakes and learn from experience, to engage in logical reasoning, to control impulses, and to understand the reactions of others. There is no evidence that they are more likely to engage in criminal conduct than others, but there is abundant evidence that they often act on impulse rather than pursuant to a premeditated plan, and that in group settings they are followers rather than leaders. Their deficiencies do not warrant an exemption from criminal sanctions, but they do diminish their personal culpability.

In light of these deficiencies, our death penalty jurisprudence provides two reasons consistent with the legislative consensus that the mentally retarded should be categorically excluded from execution. First, there is a serious question as to whether either justification that we have recognized as a basis for the death penalty applies to mentally retarded offenders. *Gregg v. Georgia*, 428 U.S. 153, 183 (1976), identified "retribution and deterrence of capital crimes by prospective offenders" as the social purposes served by the death penalty. Unless the imposition of the death penalty on a mentally retarded person "measurably contributes to one or both of these goals, it 'is nothing more than the purposeless and needless imposition of pain and suffering,' and hence an unconstitutional punishment."

With respect to retribution—the interest in seeing that the offender gets his "just deserts"—the severity of the appropriate punishment necessarily depends on the culpability of the offender. Since *Gregg*, our jurisprudence has consistently confined the imposition of the death penalty to a narrow category of the most serious crimes. If the culpability of the average murderer is insufficient to justify the most extreme sanction available to the State, the lesser culpability of the mentally retarded offender surely does not merit that form of retribution. Thus, pursuant to our narrowing jurisprudence,

---

nity, the imposition of the death penalty for crimes committed by mentally retarded offenders is overwhelmingly disapproved. Brief for European Union as *Amicus Curiae* 4. Finally, polling data shows a widespread consensus among Americans, even those who support the death penalty, that executing the mentally retarded is wrong. Bonner & Rimer, Executing the Mentally Retarded Even as Laws Begin to Shift, New York Times, Aug. 7, 2000, p. A1; App. B to Brief for AAMR, et al. as *Amici Curiae* (appending approximately 20 state and national polls on the issue). Although these factors are by no means dispositive, their consistency with the legislative evidence lends further support to our conclusion that there is a consensus among those who have addressed the issue. See Thompson v. Oklahoma, 487 U.S. 815, 830, 831, n. 31 (1988) (considering the views of "respected professional organizations, by other nations that share our Anglo-American heritage, and by the leading members of the Western European community").

which seeks to ensure that only the most deserving of execution are put to death, an exclusion for the mentally retarded is appropriate.

With respect to deterrence—the interest in preventing capital crimes by prospective offenders—"it seems likely that 'capital punishment can serve as a deterrent only when murder is the result of premeditation and deliberation.'" Exempting the mentally retarded from that punishment will not affect the "cold calculus that precedes the decision" of other potential murderers.... Nor will exempting the mentally retarded from execution lessen the deterrent effect of the death penalty with respect to offenders who are not mentally retarded. Such individuals are unprotected by the exemption and will continue to face the threat of execution. Thus, executing the mentally retarded will not measurably further the goal of deterrence.

The reduced capacity of mentally retarded offenders provides a second justification for a categorical rule making such offenders ineligible for the death penalty. The risk "that the death penalty will be imposed in spite of factors which may call for a less severe penalty," is enhanced, not only by the possibility of false confessions, but also by the lesser ability of mentally retarded defendants to make a persuasive showing of mitigation in the face of prosecutorial evidence of one or more aggravating factors....

Our independent evaluation of the issue reveals no reason to disagree with the judgment of "the legislatures that have recently addressed the matter" and concluded that death is not a suitable punishment for a mentally retarded criminal. We are not persuaded that the execution of mentally retarded criminals will measurably advance the deterrent or the retributive purpose of the death penalty. Construing and applying the Eighth Amendment in the light of our "evolving standards of decency," we therefore conclude that such punishment is excessive and that the Constitution "places a substantive restriction on the State's power to take the life" of a mentally retarded offender.

The judgment of the Virginia Supreme Court is reversed and the case is remanded for further proceedings not inconsistent with this opinion.

CHIEF JUSTICE REHNQUIST, with whom Justice Scalia and Justice Thomas join, dissenting.

The question presented by this case is whether a national consensus deprives Virginia of the constitutional power to impose the death penalty on capital murder defendants like petitioner, *i.e.*, those defendants who indisputably are competent to stand trial, aware of the punishment they are about to suffer and why, and whose mental retardation has been found an insufficiently compelling reason to lessen their individual responsibility for the crime. The Court pronounces the punishment cruel and unusual primarily because 18 States recently have passed laws limiting the death eligibility of certain defendants based on mental retardation alone, despite the fact that the laws of 19 other States besides Virginia continue to leave the question of proper punishment to the individuated consideration of sentencing judges or juries familiar with the particular offender and his or her crime.

I agree with Justice Scalia, (dissenting opinion), that the Court's assessment of the current legislative judgment regarding the execution of defendants like petitioner more resembles a *post hoc* rationalization for the majority's subjectively preferred result rather than any objective effort to ascertain the content of an evolving standard of decency. I write separately, however, to call attention to the defects in the Court's decision to place weight on foreign laws, the views of professional and religious organizations, and opinion polls in reaching its conclusion. The Court's suggestion that these sources are relevant to the constitutional question finds little support in our precedents and, in my view, is antithetical to considerations of federalism, which instruct that any "permanent prohibition upon all units of democratic government must [be apparent] in the operative acts (laws and the application of laws) that the people have approved." ...

There are strong reasons for limiting our inquiry into what constitutes an evolving standard of decency under the Eighth Amendment to the laws passed by legislatures and the practices of sentencing juries in America. Here, the Court goes beyond these well-established objective indicators of contemporary values. It finds "further support to [its] conclusion" that a national consensus has developed against imposing the death penalty on all mentally retarded defendants in international opinion, the views of professional and religious organizations, and opinion polls not demonstrated to be reliable. Believing this view to be seriously mistaken, I dissent.

JUSTICE SCALIA, with whom the Chief Justice and Justice Thomas join, dissenting.

Today's decision is the pinnacle of our Eighth Amendment death-is-different jurisprudence. Not only does it, like all of that jurisprudence, find no support in the text or history of the Eighth Amendment; it does not even have support in current social attitudes regarding the conditions that render an otherwise just death penalty inappropriate. Seldom has an opinion of this Court rested so obviously upon nothing but the personal views of its Members....

Notes and Questions

1. After *Atkins*, Johnny Paul Penry, whom the Supreme Court described as mentally retarded in *Penry v. Lynaugh*, 492 U.S. 302 (1989), underwent a re-sentencing hearing to determine whether he should be sentenced to life or death. The jury considered mental retardation as part of the entire capital sentencing proceeding. "The trial court ... told the jury that mental retardation is a mitigating factor as a matter of law, and it defined mental retardation. The jury was instructed that, if it believed that the appellant is mentally retarded, it should answer the fourth special issue yes [indicating that Penry should be sentenced to life]. If the jury found that the appellant was not mentally retarded, the jury was instructed to "follow the Court's instructions previously given herein concerning the appropriate answer to Special Issue No. 4 and consider whether any other mitigating circumstance or circumstances exist...." *Penry v. Texas*, 178 S.W.3d 782 (Tex. Crim. App. 2005). The jury sentenced Penry to death. The death sentenced was reversed and remanded to the trial court for a new punishment proceeding due to errors in the jury instructions. 2. For a discussion of mental retardation and the role lawyers play in identifying and properly asserting this claim see Rebecca Klaren and Irene Rosenberg, "Splitting Hairs in Ineffective Assistance of Counsel Cases: An Essay on How Ineffective Assistance of Counsel Doctrine Undermines the Prohibition against Executing the Mentally Retarded," 31 Am. J. Crim. L. 339 (2004).

3. While *Atkins* forbids the execution of a mentally retarded criminal defendant, it did not dictate to states how to make this determination. Two years after *Atkins*, Daryl Atkins had yet to benefit from the Court's decision. "That is because the Supreme Court did not decide whether Mr. Atkins falls withing the accepted definitions of retardation. Nor did it give judges and legislatures much guidance on how the ban should be applied in other cases." In hundreds of cases throughout the U.S.—including challenges brought by death row prisoners and new capital prosecutions—courts struggled with questions left open by the *Atkins* ruling: Who qualifies as mentally retarded? What standards should be used? Should a judge or jury decide whether a capital defendant is retarded? When should that

determination be made? Before the capital trial? During the sentencing phase? Liptak, *New Challenge for Courts: How to Define Retardation*, The New York Times, March 14, 2004, at 12. Consider the following state statutes and how they address these issues.

Selected Statutes

Arkansas:

Arkansas Code Annotated § 5-4-618

(a)(1) As used in this section, "mental retardation" means:

(A) Significantly subaverage general intellectual functioning accompanied by significant deficits or impairments in adaptive functioning manifest in the developmental period, but no later than age eighteen (18); and

(B) Deficits in adaptive behavior.

(2) There is a rebuttable presumption of mental retardation when a defendant has an intelligence quotient of sixty-five (65) or below.(b) No defendant with mental retardation at the time of committing capital murder shall be sentenced to death.(c) The defendant has the burden of proving mental retardation at the time of committing the offense by a preponderance of the evidence.

(d)(1) A defendant on trial for capital murder shall raise the special sentencing provision of mental retardation by motion prior to trial.

(2) Prior to trial, the court shall determine if the defendant is mentally retarded.

(A) If the court determines that the defendant is not mentally retarded, the defendant may raise the question of mental retardation to the jury for determination de novo during the sentencing phase of the trial.

(i) At the time the jury retires to decide mitigating and aggravating circumstances, the jury shall be given a special verdict form on mental retardation.

(ii) If the jury unanimously determines that the defendant was mentally retarded at the time of the commission of capital murder, then the defendant will automatically be sentenced to life imprisonment without possibility of parole.

(B) If the court determines that the defendant is mentally retarded, then the jury shall not be "death qualified", but the jury shall sentence the defendant to life imprisonment without possibility of parole upon conviction.

(e) However, this section shall not be deemed to require unanimity for consideration of any mitigating circumstance, nor shall this section be deemed to supersede any suggested mitigating circumstance regarding mental defect or disease currently found in § 5-4-605.

Arizona:

Arizona §13-703.02. **Mental evaluations of capital defendants; hearing; appeal; prospective application; definitions**

A. In any case in which the state files a notice of intent to seek the death penalty, a person who is found to have mental retardation pursuant to this section shall not be sentenced to death but shall be sentenced to life or natural life.

B. If the state files a notice of intent to seek the death penalty, the court shall appoint a prescreening psychological expert in order to determine the defendant's intelligence quotient using current community, nationally and culturally accepted intelligence testing procedures. The prescreening psychological expert shall submit a written report of the intelligence quotient determination to the court within ten days of the testing of the defendant.

C. If the prescreening psychological expert determines that the defendant's intelligence quotient is higher than seventy-five, the notice of intent to seek the death penalty shall not be dismissed on the ground that the defendant has mental retardation. If the prescreening psychological expert determines that the defendant's intelligence quotient is higher than seventy-five, the report shall be sealed by the court and be available only to the defendant. The report shall be released on the motion of any party if the defendant introduces the report in the present case or is convicted of an offense in the present case and the sentence is final. A prescreening determination that the defendant's intelligence quotient is higher than seventy-five does not prevent the defendant from introducing evidence of the defendant's mental retardation or diminished mental capacity as a mitigating factor at the penalty phase of the sentencing proceeding.

D. If the prescreening psychological expert determines that the defendant's intelligence quotient is seventy-five or less, the trial court shall appoint one or more additional psychological experts to independently determine whether the defendant has mental retardation. If the prescreening psychological expert determines that the defendant's intelligence quotient is seventy-five or less, the trial court, within ten days of receiving the written report, shall order the state and the defendant to each nominate three psychological experts, or jointly nominate a single psychological expert. The trial court shall appoint one psychological expert nominated by the state and one psychological expert nominated by the defendant, or a single psychological expert jointly nominated by the state and the defendant, none of whom made the prescreening determination of the defendant's intelligence quotient. The trial court, in its discretion, may appoint an additional psychological expert who was neither nominated by the state nor the defendant, and who did not make the prescreening determination of the defendant's intelligence quotient. Within forty-five days after the trial court orders the state and the defendant to nominate psychological experts, or on the appointment of such experts, whichever is later, the state and the defendant shall provide to the psychological experts and the court any available records that may be relevant to the defendant's mental retardation status. The court may extend the deadline for providing records on good cause shown by the state or defendant.

E. Not less than twenty days after receipt of the records provided pursuant to subsection D of this section, or twenty days after the expiration of the deadline for providing the records, whichever is later, each psychological expert shall examine the defendant using current community, nationally and culturally accepted physical, developmental, psychological and intelligence testing procedures, for the purpose of determining whether the defendant has mental retardation. Within fifteen days of examining the defendant, each psychological expert shall submit a written report to the trial court that includes the expert's opinion as to whether the defendant has mental retardation.

F. If the scores on all the tests for intelligence quotient administered to the defendant are above seventy, the notice of intent to seek the death penalty shall not be dismissed on the ground that the defendant has mental retardation. This does not preclude the defendant from introducing evidence of the defendant's mental retardation or diminished mental capacity as a mitigating factor at the penalty phase of the sentencing proceeding.

G. No less than thirty days after the psychological experts' reports are submitted to the court and before trial, the trial court shall hold a hearing to determine if the defendant has mental retardation. At the hearing, the defendant has the burden of proving mental retardation by clear and convincing evidence. A determination by the trial court that the defendant's intelligence quotient is sixty-five or lower establishes a rebuttable presumption that the defendant has mental retardation. Nothing in this subsection shall preclude a defendant with an intelligence quotient of seventy or below from proving mental retardation by clear and convincing evidence.

H. If the trial court finds that the defendant has mental retardation, the trial court shall dismiss the intent to seek the death penalty, shall not impose a sentence of death on the defendant if the defendant is convicted of first degree murder and shall dismiss one of the attorneys appointed under rule 6.2, Arizona rules of criminal procedure unless the court finds that there is good cause to retain both attorneys. If the trial court finds that the defendant does not have mental retardation, the court's finding does not prevent the defendant from introducing evidence of the defendant's mental retardation or diminished mental capacity as a mitigating factor at the penalty phase of the sentencing proceeding.

I. Within ten days after the trial court makes a finding on mental retardation, the state or the defendant may file a petition for special action with the Arizona court of appeals pursuant to the rules of procedure for special actions. The filing of the petition for special action is governed by the rules of procedure for special actions, except that the court of appeals shall exercise jurisdiction and decide the merits of the claims raised.

J. This section applies to all capital sentencing proceedings.

K. For the purposes of this section, unless the context otherwise requires:

1. "Adaptive behavior" means the effectiveness or degree to which the defendant meets the standards of personal independence and social responsibility expected of the defendant's age and cultural group.

2. "Mental retardation" means a condition based on a mental deficit that involves significantly subaverage general intellectual functioning, existing concurrently with significant impairment in adaptive behavior, where the onset of the foregoing conditions occurred before the defendant reached the age of eighteen.

3. "Prescreening psychological expert" or "psychological expert" means a psychologist licensed pursuant to title 32, chapter 19.1 with at least two years' experience in the testing, evaluation and diagnosis of mental retardation.

4. "Significantly subaverage general intellectual functioning" means a full scale intelligence quotient of seventy or lower. The court in determining the intelligence quotient shall take into account the margin of error for the test administered.

Florida:

Fla. R. Crim. P. Rule 3.203

(a) **Scope.** This rule applies in all first-degree murder cases in which the state attorney has not waived the death penalty on the record and the defendant's mental retardation becomes an issue.

(b) **Definition of Mental Retardation.** As used in this rule, the term "mental retardation" means significantly subaverage general intellectual functioning existing concurrently with deficits in adaptive behavior and manifested during the period from conception to age 18. The term "significantly subaverage general intellectual functioning," for the purpose of this rule, means performance that is two or more standard deviations from the mean score on a standardized intelligence test authorized by the Department of Children and Family Services in rule 65B-4.032 of the Florida Administrative Code. The term "adaptive behavior," for the purpose of this rule, means the effectiveness or degree with which an individual meets the standards of personal independence and social responsibility expected of his or her age, cultural group, and community.

(c) Motion for Determination of Mental Retardation as a Bar to Execution: Contents; Procedures.

(1) A defendant who intends to raise mental retardation as a bar to execution shall file a written motion to establish mental retardation as a bar to execution with the court.

(2) The motion shall state that the defendant is mentally retarded and, if the defendant has been tested, evaluated, or examined by one or more experts, the names and addresses of the experts. Copies of reports containing the opinions of any experts named in the motion shall be attached to the motion. The court shall appoint an expert chosen by the state attorney if the state attorney so requests. The expert shall promptly test, evaluate, or examine the defendant and shall submit a written report of any findings to the parties and the court.

(3) If the defendant has not been tested, evaluated, or examined by one or more experts, the motion shall state that fact and the court shall appoint two experts who shall promptly test, evaluate, or examine the defendant and shall submit a written report of any findings to the parties and the court.

(4) Attorneys for the state and defendant may be present at the examinations conducted by court-appointed experts.

(5) If the defendant refuses to be examined or fully cooperate with the court appointed experts or the state's expert, the court may, in the court's discretion:

(A) order the defense to allow the court-appointed experts to review all mental health reports, tests, and evaluations by the defendant's expert;

(B) prohibit the defense experts from testifying concerning any tests, evaluations, or examinations of the defendant regarding the defendant's mental retardation; or

(C) order such relief as the court determines to be appropriate....

(e) Hearing on Motion to Determine Mental Retardation. The circuit court shall conduct an evidentiary hearing on the motion for a determination of mental retardation. At the hearing, the court shall consider the findings of the experts and all other evidence on the issue of whether the defendant is mentally retarded. The court shall enter a written order prohibiting the imposition of the death penalty and setting forth the court's specific findings in support of the court's determination if the court finds that the defendant is mentally retarded as defined in subdivision (b) of this rule. The court shall stay the proceedings for 30 days from the date of rendition of the order prohibiting the death penalty or, if a motion for rehearing is filed, for 30 days following the rendition of the order denying rehearing, to allow the state the opportunity to appeal the order. If the court determines that the defendant has not established mental retardation, the court shall enter a written order setting forth the court's specific findings in support of the court's determination....

(g) Finding of Mental Retardation; Order to Proceed. If, after the evidence presented, the court is of the opinion that the defendant is mentally retarded, the court shall order the case to proceed without the death penalty as an issue

E. Double Jeopardy Aspects of Capital Punishment

The Fifth Amendment to the United States Constitution provides that no person shall "be subject for the same offence to be twice put in jeopardy of life or limb." According to *Green v. United States*, 355 U.S. 184 (1957),

> The underlying idea, one that is deeply ingrained in at least the Anglo-American system of jurisprudence, is that the State with all its resources and power should not be allowed to make repeated attempts to convict an individual for an alleged offense, thereby subjecting him to embarrassment, expense and ordeal and compelling him to live in a continuing state of anxiety and insecurity, as well as enhancing the possibility that even though innocent he may be found guilty.

Three separate guarantees are embodied in the Double Jeopardy Clause: (1) no reprosecution for the same offense after an acquittal; (2) no reprosecution for the same offense after a conviction; and (3) no multiple punishments for the same offense. Although the multitudinous double jeopardy rules are convoluted, see 34 Geo. L. J. Crim. Proc. 411–453 (2005), and beyond the scope of this note, special rules do apply to capital cases. For example, if a defendant sentenced to life imprisonment (or life without parole) has her conviction reversed on appeal, double jeopardy prevents a death sentence following retrial. *Bullington v. Missouri*, 451 U.S. 430 (1981). In those circumstances, the first trial is said to have acquitted the capital defendant of the death penalty. *Id.* at 446. *Cf. Schiro v. Farley*, 510 U.S. 222 (1994).

This double jeopardy bar to the imposition of a death sentence apparently applies only in the case of an implied acquittal. Double jeopardy does not prevent the reimposition of a death sentence when the original death sentence was imposed in error. Thus, if a sentencer relied on a single invalid aggravating circumstance in sentencing the defendant to death, the defendant may be resentenced to death on the basis of another aggravating circumstance. *Poland v. Arizona*, 476 U.S. 147, 156–157 (1986). Unlike *Bullington*, the first trial did not result in an acquittal of the death penalty. Similarly, a judge's failure to consider nonstatutory mitigating circumstances may require that the defendant's death sentence be set aside, but it does not prevent the state from seeking death in another sentencing hearing in which all relevant mitigating circumstances are admitted into evidence. *Hitchcock v. Dugger*, 481 U.S. 393 (1987).

On occasion, sentencing errors inure to the benefit of capital defendants as a result of double jeopardy. Consequently, where a sentencing judge misconstrued the meaning of a statutory aggravating circumstance, and as a result found it inapplicable and sentenced the defendant to life, the defendant may not thereafter be sentenced to death. *Arizona v. Rumsey*, 467 U.S. 203, 212 (1984).

The expansion of the federal death penalty through the passage of the Anti-Drug Abuse Act of 1988, 21 U.S.C. §848 et seq., and the Federal Death Penalty Act of 1994, 18 U.S.C. §3591 et seq., suggests an increasingly important role for the dual sovereignty doctrine in capital cases. Certain murders may simultaneously violate federal and state law. Under the dual sovereignty doctrine, "an act denounced by both national and state sovereignties is an offense against the peace and dignity of both and may be punished by each." *United States v. Lanza*, 260 U.S. 377 (1922). Prosecutions by separate sovereigns are considered prosecutions for different offenses. Thus, the federal government is free to prosecute a defendant after a state prosecution for the same conduct, regardless of the outcome of the state prosecution. *Abbate v. United States*, 359 U.S. 187 (1959). Likewise, if the federal government prosecutes first, the state may prosecute for the same conduct, regardless of the result of the federal prosecution. *Bartkus v. Illinois*, 359 U.S. 121 (1959). For example, in 1997 Terry Nichols was convicted in federal court and sentenced to life without parole for his involvement in the 1995 Oklahoma City bombing mass murder. In 2003, Oklahoma state prosecutors tried Nichols in state court, seeking the death penalty for 161 counts of murder. Although Nichols was again convicted, the jury refused to sentence him to death. Moreover, under the dual sovereignty doctrine, successive prosecutions by different states for the same conduct are permitted. *Heath v. Alabama*, 474 U.S. 82 (1985). Thus, in *Heath*, the United States Supreme Court upheld the Alabama death sentence of a defendant who had earlier pleaded guilty to the same murder in Georgia in exchange for a life sentence.

The double jeopardy guarantees provided by the United States Constitution as interpreted by the United States Supreme Court should be viewed as a minimum of protections below which no State is free to go. Indeed, several state constitutions have been interpreted by state courts to provide greater protection for criminal defendants than is required by the federal Constitution. See, e.g., *Hunnicutt v. Oklahoma*, 755 P.2d 105 (Okla. Crim. App. 1988).

Note on Schiro v. Farley, 510 U.S. 222 (1994)

In *Schiro v. Farley*, 510 U.S. 222 (1994), the Supreme Court revisited the application of the Double Jeopardy Clause to capital sentencing proceedings. Schiro had been charged with separate counts of murdering a single victim. Count I charged that Schiro "knowingly" killed his victim. Count II charged that Schiro killed his victim while committing the crime of rape. The jury returned a verdict of guilty on Count II and left the remaining verdict sheets blank. The trial judge rejected the jury's unanimous recommendation that Schiro be spared and sentenced him to death. The sole aggravating circumstance found by the trial judge was that Schiro had intentionally killed his victim while attempting to commit rape. In the Supreme Court, Schiro argued that he was implicitly acquitted at the guilt phase of the same offense that the trial court used as the sole aggravating circumstance: intentionally killing his victim. Schiro also argued that the collateral estoppel component of the Fifth Amendment barred his death sentence. He claimed that at the guilt phase his mental state when he killed his victim was resolved against the state when the jury implicitly acquitted him of Count I, which required the state to prove that he killed intentionally.

The Court rejected both double jeopardy arguments and distinguished *Bullington v. Missouri*, 451 U.S. 430 (1981). First, Schiro's sentencing proceeding did not amount to a successive prosecution for intentional murder in violation of the Double Jeopardy Clause. The Court reasoned that because a second sentencing proceeding following retrial ordinarily is constitutional, an initial sentencing proceeding following trial on the issue of guilt does not violate the clause. Moreover, prior convictions may be constitutionally used to enhance sentences for subsequent convictions. Second, collateral estoppel did not require vacation of Schiro's death sentence. According to the majority, Schiro failed to establish the required factual predicate, namely that an issue of ultimate fact had once been determined in his favor. Examination of the entire record showed that the trial court's instructions on the issue of intent to kill were ambiguous. Also, uncertainty existed as to whether the jury believed it could return more than one verdict. Consequently, the verdict actually entered could have been grounded on an issue other than intent to kill.

Justices Blackmun and Stevens dissented. Justice Stevens' dissent, joined by Justice Blackmun, found nothing "even arguably ambiguous about the jury's verdict." Each of the verdict forms contained a space to be checked to record agreement with a proposed verdict. The only way to record disagreement was to leave the space blank. In Justice Stevens' view, the trial judge sentenced Schiro to death because he was guilty of intentional murder, even though the jury had found otherwise.

In a separate dissent, Justice Blackmun argued that *Bullington* provided a compelling ground for vacation of Schiro's death sentence. Justice Blackmun observed, "In *Bullington*, this Court held that once a capital defendant is acquitted of the death sentence, the Double Jeopardy Clause bars his again being placed in jeopardy of death at a subsequent sentencing proceeding." In Justice Blackmun's view, "the essential holding of *Bullington* ... was that capital sentencing proceedings uniquely can constitute a 'jeopardy' under the Double Jeopardy Clause." Even if the issue of Schiro's intent to kill was not "actually and necessarily decided" for collateral estoppel purposes, the jury's failure to convict Schiro of intentional murder impliedly acquitted him under the Double Jeopardy Clause, in Justice Blackmun's view. Justice Blackmun observed: "Over a unanimous jury recommendation of life and after a State Supreme Court remand, the trial judge condemned Schiro to death in reliance *nunc pro tunc* on the very conduct for which Schiro had been acquitted. This sentence cannot be tolerated under the Double Jeopardy Clause."

Note on Sattazahn v. Pennsylvania, 537 U.S. 101 (2003)

Under Pennsylvania law, the verdict in the penalty phase of a capital case must be death if the jury unanimously finds at least one aggravating circumstance and no mitigating circumstance and no mitigating circumstance or one or more aggravating circumstances outweighing any mitigating circumstances. In all other instances, the penalty must be life imprisonment. If the court determines that the jury will not unanimously agree on the sentence, the court may discharge the jury, but it must then sentence the defendant to life. 42 Pa. Cons. Stat. Section 9711(c).

David Allen Sattazahn's penalty-phase jury reported to the trial judge that it was hopelessly deadlocked 9-to-3 for life imprisonment. The court discharged the jury and sentenced Sattazahn to life. On appeal, the Pennsylvania Superior Court reversed Sattazahn's first-degree murder conviction, and remanded for a new trial. At the retrial, Sattazahn was again convicted, but this time the jury imposed a death sentence.

On appeal, Sattazahn challenged his death sentence on double jeopardy and due process grounds. The Supreme Court, in a 5–4 decision, rejected both arguments. Writing for the majority, Justice Scalia held that when a defendant is convicted of murder and sentenced to life imprisonment succeeds in having the conviction set aside on appeal, jeopardy has not terminated. Consequently, a life sentence imposed in connection with the initial conviction raises no double-jeopardy bar to a death sentence following retrial.

Justice Scalia conceded that the line of cases commencing with *Bullington v. Missouri*, 451 U.S. 430 (1981), have applied the Double Jeopardy Clause to capital sentencing proceedings that "have the hallmarks of the trial on guilt or innocence." Nonetheless, according to Justice Scalia, the relevant inquiry in that context is not whether the defendant received a life sentence the first time around, but whether a first life sentence was an "acquittal" based on findings sufficient to establish legal entitlement to the life sentence, for example, findings that the government failed to prove one or more aggravating circumstances beyond a reasonable doubt. *Arizona v. Rumsey*, 467 U.S. 203, 211 (1984).

In Sattazahn's case, double jeopardy protections were not triggered when the jury deadlocked at his first sentencing proceeding. The deadlocked jury made no findings with respect to the alleged aggravating circumstance. That result or non-result can not fairly be called an acquittal, based on findings sufficient to establish legal entitlement to a life sentence. Neither was the entry of a life sentence by the judge required by Pennsylvania law in Sattazahn's case an acquittal. Under Pennsylvania's scheme, a judge has no discretion to fashion a sentence once he finds that the jury is deadlocked. Similarly, he makes no findings and resolves no factual matters. Finally, the Pennsylvania Supreme Court, in rejecting Sattazahn's double jeopardy claim, also made no finding that the Pennsylvania legislature intended the statutorily required entry of a life sentence to create an "entitlement" even without an acquittal.

As to Sattazahn's due process claim, Justice Scalia noted that nothing in the 14th Amendment indicates that any life or liberty interest is immutable. Here, Sattazahn was "deprived" of any such interest only by operation of the "process" he invoked to invalidate the underlying first-degree murder conviction. The Court, per Scalia, declined to hold that the Due Process Clause provides greater double jeopardy protection than does the Double Jeopardy Clause.

Chapter 6

Selecting the Capital Jury

A. Overview

The role of the capital jury is critical. Not only does the capital jury determine the guilt or innocence of the accused, but also, in most states, it decides whether the accused lives or dies. Consequently, selecting a jury is one of the most important steps in a capital trial.

During a process known as *voir dire* (literally from the French meaning to see, to say, but more frequently translated to mean to speak the truth), the trial court, the prosecutor and defense counsel question jurors about a wide variety of issues to determine whether they are capable of impartially judging the case. If either the prosecutor or defense counsel believes a potential juror is partial, then that side may challenge the juror "for cause." If the judge agrees that the juror is partial, then that juror will be removed from the jury panel. For example, a juror may be struck for cause if she knows a member of the victim's family and, due to that relationship, is unable to impartially hear the case. Alternatively, a juror's religious beliefs may prevent her from sitting in judgment of others and, in such cases, the trial court will often grant a challenge for cause. Each side has an unlimited number of challenges for cause, although the trial court may conclude that the juror can serve impartially and refuse to grant the challenge.

In addition to challenges for cause, each side possesses a certain, limited number of peremptory challenges. Traditionally, peremptory challenges allow counsel to strike from the jury any juror who, for whatever reason, counsel feels will not be impartial. Peremptory challenges often are based on intuition. Nevertheless, experts are being employed with increasing frequency to assist counsel in weeding out jurors who may be less favorable to their side of the case.

Through this jury selection process a panel is assembled. Most often the panel consists of twelve individuals plus alternates. The fate of the accused — indeed, his very life — rests in the hands of the jury. As Justice Marshall stated in *Caldwell v. Mississippi*, 472 U.S. 320 (1985), the Court "has always premised its capital punishment decisions on the assumption that a capital sentencing jury recognizes the gravity of its task and proceeds with the appropriate awareness of its 'truly awesome responsibility.'" Who can and cannot become a member of such an important panel is plainly of paramount importance to the prosecutor and the defendant.

B. Death Qualification

In capital cases, one of the key issues which the trial court, the prosecutor, and defense counsel will explore with a potential juror is the juror's views on the death penalty.

The ability of the prosecutor and defense counsel to strike a juror, either for cause or by peremptory challenge, based on that juror's views on the death penalty has been vigorously debated and litigated.

Witherspoon v. Illinois
391 U.S. 510 (1968)

Mr. Justice STEWART delivered the opinion of the Court.

The petitioner was brought to trial in 1960 in Cook County, Illinois, upon a charge of murder. The jury found him guilty and fixed his penalty at death. At the time of his trial an Illinois statute provided:

> In trials for murder it shall be a cause for challenge of any juror who shall, on being examined, state that he has conscientious scruples against capital punishment, or that he is opposed to the same.

Through this provision the State of Illinois armed the prosecution with unlimited challenges for cause in order to exclude those jurors who, in the words of the State's highest court, "might hesitate to return a verdict inflicting (death)." At the petitioner's trial, the prosecution eliminated nearly half the venire of prospective jurors by challenging, under the authority of this statute, any venireman who expressed qualms about capital punishment. From those who remained were chosen the jurors who ultimately found the petitioner guilty and sentenced him to death. The Supreme Court of Illinois denied post-conviction relief, and we granted certiorari to decide whether the Constitution permits a State to execute a man pursuant to the verdict of a jury so composed.

I

The issue before us is a narrow one. It does not involve the right of the prosecution to challenge for cause those prospective jurors who state that their reservations about capital punishment would prevent them from making an impartial decision as to the defendant's guilt. Nor does it involve the State's assertion of a right to exclude from the jury in a capital case those who say that they could never vote to impose the death penalty or that they would refuse even to consider its imposition in the case before them. For the State of Illinois did not stop there, but authorized the prosecution to exclude as well all who said that they were opposed to capital punishment and all who indicated that they had conscientious scruples against inflicting it.

In the present case the tone was set when the trial judge said early in the *voir dire*, "Let's get these conscientious objectors out of the way, without wasting any time on them." In rapid succession, 47 veniremen were successfully challenged for cause on the basis of their attitudes toward the death penalty. Only five of the 47 explicitly stated that under no circumstances would they vote to impose capital punishment. Six said that they did not "believe in the death penalty" and were excused without any attempt to determine whether they could nonetheless return a verdict of death.[7] Thirty-nine veniremen, including four of the six who indicated that they did not believe in capital punishment, acknowledged having "conscientious or religious scruples against the infliction of

---

7. It is entirely possible, of course, that even a juror who believes that capital punishment should never be inflicted and who is irrevocably committed to its abolition could nonetheless subordinate his personal views to what he perceived to be his duty to abide by his oath as a juror and to obey the law of the State.

the death penalty" or against its infliction "in a proper case" and were excluded without any effort to find out whether their scruples would invariably compel them to vote against capital punishment.

Only one venireman who admitted to "a religious or conscientious scruple against the infliction of the death penalty in a proper case" was examined at any length. She was asked: "You don't believe in the death penalty?" She replied: "No. It's just I wouldn't want to be responsible." The judge admonished her not to forget her "duty as a citizen" and again asked her whether she had "a religious or conscientious scruple" against capital punishment. This time, she replied in the negative. Moments later, however, she repeated that she would not "like to be responsible for ... deciding somebody should be put to death." Evidently satisfied that this elaboration of the prospective juror's views disqualified her under the Illinois statute, the judge told her to "step aside."[9] ...

[The petitioner argued that the jury selection procedure in Illinois tended to favor the prosecution in determining guilt or innocence. The Court rejected this argument and refused to establish a *per se* constitutional rule requiring reversal whenever a jury is selected in a manner like the one used in this case.]

II

It does not follow, however, that the petitioner is entitled to no relief. For in this case the jury was entrusted with two distinct responsibilities: first, to determine whether the petitioner was innocent or guilty; and second, if guilty, to determine whether his sentence should be imprisonment or death. It has not been shown that this jury was biased with respect to the petitioner's guilt. But it is self-evident that, in its role as arbiter of the punishment to be imposed, this jury fell woefully short of that impartiality to which the petitioner was entitled under the Sixth and Fourteenth Amendments.

The only justification the State has offered for the jury-selection technique it employed here is that individuals who express serious reservations about capital punishment cannot be relied upon to vote for it even when the laws of the State and the instructions of the trial judge would make death the proper penalty. But in Illinois, as in other States, the jury is given broad discretion to decide whether or not death is "the proper penalty" in a given case, and a juror's general views about capital punishment play an inevitable role in any such decision.

A man who opposes the death penalty, no less than one who favors it, can make the discretionary judgment entrusted to him by the State and can thus obey the oath he

---

9. As the *voir dire* examination of this venireman illustrates, it cannot be assumed that a juror who describes himself as having "conscientious or religious scruples" against the infliction of the death penalty or against its infliction "in a proper case" thereby affirmed that he could never vote in favor of it or that he would not consider doing so in the case before him. Obviously many jurors "could, notwithstanding their conscientious scruples [against capital punishment], return ... (a) verdict [of death] and ... make their scruples subservient to their duty as jurors." Yet such jurors have frequently been deemed unfit to serve in a capital case. The critical question, of course, is not how the phrases employed in this area have been construed by courts and commentators. What matters is how they might be understood—or misunderstood—by prospective jurors. Any "layman ... [might] say he has scruples if he is somewhat unhappy about death sentences.... [Thus] a general question as to the presence of ... reservations [or scruples] is far from the inquiry which separates those who would never vote for the ultimate penalty from those who would reserve it for the direst cases." Unless a venireman states unambiguously that he would automatically vote against the imposition of capital punishment no matter what the trial might reveal, it simply cannot be assumed that that is his position.

takes as a juror. But a jury from which all such men have been excluded cannot perform the task demanded of it. Guided by neither rule nor standard, "free to select or reject as it [sees] fit," a jury that must choose between life imprisonment and capital punishment can do little more—and must do nothing less—than express the conscience of the community on the ultimate question of life or death. Yet, in a nation less than half of whose people believe in the death penalty, a jury composed exclusively of such people cannot speak for the community. Culled of all who harbor doubts about the wisdom of capital punishment—of all who would be reluctant to pronounce the extreme penalty—such a jury can speak only for a distinct and dwindling minority.

If the State had excluded only those prospective jurors who stated in advance of trial that they would not even consider returning a verdict of death, it could argue that the resulting jury was simply "neutral" with respect to penalty. But when it swept from the jury all who expressed conscientious or religious scruples against capital punishment and all who opposed it in principle, the State crossed the line of neutrality. In its quest for a jury capable of imposing the death penalty, the State produced a jury uncommonly willing to condemn a man to die.

It is, of course, settled that a State may not entrust the determination of whether a man is innocent or guilty to a tribunal "organized to convict." It requires but a short step from that principle to hold, as we do today, that a State may not entrust the determination of whether a man should live or die to a tribunal organized to return a verdict of death. Specifically, we hold that a sentence of death cannot be carried out if the jury that imposed or recommended it was chosen by excluding veniremen for cause simply because they voiced general objections to the death penalty or expressed conscientious or religious scruples against its infliction.[21] No defendant can constitutionally be put to death at the hands of a tribunal so selected.

Whatever else might be said of capital punishment, it is at least clear that its imposition by a hanging jury cannot be squared with the Constitution. The State of Illinois has stacked the deck against the petitioner. To execute this death sentence would deprive him of his life without due process of law. Reversed.

---

21. Just as veniremen cannot be excluded for cause on the ground that they hold such views, so too they cannot be excluded for cause simply because they indicate that there are some kinds of cases in which they would refuse to recommend capital punishment. And a prospective juror cannot be expected to say in advance of trial whether he would in fact vote for the extreme penalty in the case before him. The most that can be demanded of a venireman in this regard is that he be willing to *consider* all of the penalties provided by state law, and that he not be irrevocably committed, before the trial has begun, to vote against the penalty of death regardless of the facts and circumstances that might emerge in the course of the proceedings. If the *voir dire* testimony in a given case indicates that veniremen were excluded on any broader basis than this, the death sentence cannot be carried out even if applicable statutory or case law in the relevant jurisdiction would appear to support only a narrower ground of exclusion.

We repeat, however, that nothing we say today bears upon the power of a State to execute a defendant sentenced to death by a jury from which the only veniremen who were in fact excluded for cause were those who made unmistakably clear (1) that they would *automatically* vote against the imposition of capital punishment without regard to any evidence that might be developed at the trial of the case before them, or (2) that their attitude toward the death penalty would prevent them from making an impartial decision as to the defendant's *guilt*. Nor does the decision in this case affect the validity of any sentence *other* than one of death. Nor, finally, does today's holding render invalid the *conviction*, as opposed to the *sentence*, in this or any other case.

Note: *Adams v. Texas*, 448 U.S. 38 (1980)

Twelve years after *Witherspoon*, the Supreme Court reversed the conviction of Randall Dale Adams because of a *Witherspoon* error in jury selection. *Adams v. Texas*, 448 U.S. 38 (1980). At the time of Mr. Adams' trial, Texas required jurors to take an oath as set forth in § 12.31(b) of the Texas Penal Code. Section 12.31(b) provided:

> Prospective jurors shall be informed that the sentence of life imprisonment or death is mandatory on conviction of a capital felony. A prospective juror shall be disqualified from serving as a juror unless he states under oath that the mandatory penalty of death or imprisonment for life will not affect his deliberations on any issue of fact.

In analyzing the application of § 12.31(b) to Mr. Adams' case, the Court found that three jurors were excluded because they "stated that they would be 'affected' by the possibility of the death penalty, but who apparently meant only that the potentially lethal consequences of their decision would invest their deliberations with greater seriousness and gravity or would involve them emotionally." Four other jurors were excluded "only because they were unable positively to state whether or not their deliberations would in any way be 'affected.... '"

The Court found that the exclusion of the jurors under Texas' system deprived Mr. Adams of an impartial jury. In reversing Mr. Adams' conviction the Court stated:

> We repeat that the state may bar from jury service those whose beliefs about capital punishment would lead them to ignore the law or violate their oaths. But in the present case Texas has applied §12.31(b) to exclude jurors whose only fault was to take their responsibilities with special seriousness or to acknowledge honestly that they might or might not be affected. It does not appear in the record before us that these individuals were so irrevocably opposed to capital punishment as to frustrate the State's legitimate efforts to administer its constitutionally valid death penalty. Accordingly, the Constitution disentitles the state to execute a sentence of death imposed by a jury from which such prospective jurors have been excluded.

After the reversal of Mr. Adams' conviction, the Governor of Texas commuted his sentence to life in prison. Mr. Adams subsequently became the subject of the film, "The Thin Blue Line" (Miramax 1988). The film revealed that Mr. Adams was innocent of the murder for which he was sentenced to death. In 1989, Mr. Adams was exonerated and released from prison. Mr. Adams came within seventy-two hours of being executed before the Court stayed his execution and granted the writ of certiorari in the case of *Adams v. Texas*. Adams documented the systematic injustice in his case in the book, *Adams v. Texas* (St. Martin's Press 1991).

Re-examining *Witherspoon v. Illinois: Wainwright v. Witt*

Many courts accepted *Witherspoon*'s footnote 21 as setting the standard for determining whether a juror could be excluded for cause because of his or her opposition to the death penalty. Footnote 21 stated that jurors may be excluded for cause if they make it unmistakably clear (1) that they would automatically vote against the imposition of capital punishment without regard to any evidence that might be developed at the trial, or (2) that their attitude toward the death penalty would prevent them from making an impartial decision as to the defendant's guilt.

In *Adams v. Texas* 448 U.S. 38 (1980), the Court stated that a juror could not be excluded for cause "based on his views about capital punishment unless those views would prevent or substantially impair the performances of his duties as a juror in accordance with his instructions and his oath." In *Wainwright v. Witt*, 496 U.S. 412 (1985), the Court re-examined *Witherspoon* in light of the language in *Adams*.

Wainwright v. Witt
469 U.S. 412 (1985)

Justice REHNQUIST delivered the opinion of the Court.

This case requires us to examine once again the procedures for selection of jurors in criminal trials involving the possible imposition of capital punishment, and to consider standards for federal courts reviewing those procedures upon petition for a writ of habeas corpus.

I

[Respondent Johnny Paul Witt was convicted and sentenced to death for the murder of an eleven-year-old boy. On a petition for a writ of habeas corpus, the Eleventh Circuit reversed Witt's conviction based on a *Witherspoon* error in jury selection.] The [Eleventh Circuit] found the following exchange during *voir dire*, between the prosecutor and veniremember Colby, to be insufficient to justify Colby's excusal for cause:

[Q. Prosecutor]: Now, let me ask you a question, ma'am. Do you have any religious beliefs or personal beliefs against the death penalty?

[A. Colby]: I am afraid personally but not—

[Q]:   Speak up, please.

[A]:   I am afraid of being a little personal, but definitely not religious.

[Q]:   Now, would that interfere with you sitting as a juror in this case?

[A]:   I am afraid it would.

[Q]:   You are afraid it would?

[A]:   Yes, Sir.

[Q]:   Would it interfere with judging the guilt or innocence of the Defendant in this case?

[A]:   I think so.

[Q]:   You think it would.

[A]:   I think it would.

[Q]:   Your honor, I would move for cause at this point.

THE COURT: All right. Step down.

Defense counsel did not object or attempt rehabilitation.

… The Court of Appeals construed our decisions to require that jurors expressing objections to the death penalty be given "great leeway" before their expressions justify dismissal for cause. "A prospective juror may even concede that his or her feelings about the death penalty would possibly color an objective determination of the facts of a case without admitting of the necessary partiality to justify excusal." The court concluded that the colloquy with venireman Colby reprinted above did not satisfy the *Witherspoon* standard. Colby's limited expressions of "feelings and thoughts" failed to "unequivocally state that she would automatically be unable to apply the death penalty...." In part, the court found the ambiguity in the record was caused by the lack of clarity of the prosecutor's questions. The prosecutor's question whether Colby's feelings about the death penalty would "interfere" with her sitting was ambiguous, because the fact of such "interference" failed to satisfy *Witherspoon*'s requirement that she be unable to apply the death sentence under any circumstances. The court found its holding consistent with Circuit precedent applying the *Witherspoon* standard....

II

... [M]ore recent opinions of this Court demonstrate no ritualistic adherence to a requirement that a prospective juror make it "unmistakably clear ... that [she] would *automatically* vote against the imposition of capital punishment...." In *Lockett v. Ohio*, 438 U.S. 586, 595–596 (1978), prospective capital jurors were asked:

> [D]o you feel that you could take an oath to well and truely [*sic*] try this case ... and follow the law, or is your conviction so strong that you cannot take an oath, knowing that a possibility exists in regard to capital punishment?

We held that the veniremen who answered that they could not "take the oath" were properly excluded. Although the *Lockett* opinion alluded to the second half of the [*Witherspoon*] footnote 21 standard, dealing with a juror's inability to decide impartially a defendant's guilt, the Court did not refer to the "automatically" language. Instead, it simply determined that each of the excluded veniremen had made it "'unmistakably clear' that they could not be trusted to 'abide by existing law' and 'to follow conscientiously the instructions' of the trial judge."

This Court again examined the *Witherspoon* standard in *Adams v. Texas*, 448 U.S. 38 (1980). *Adams* involved the Texas capital sentencing scheme, wherein jurors were asked to answer three specific questions put by the trial judge. The court was required to impose the death sentence if each question was answered affirmatively. A Texas statute provided that a prospective capital juror "'shall be disqualified ... unless he states under oath that the mandatory penalty of death or imprisonment for life will not affect his deliberations on any issue of fact.'" Before deciding whether certain jurors had been properly excluded pursuant to this statute, this Court attempted to discern the proper standard for making such a determination. The Court discussed its prior opinions, noting the *Witherspoon* Court's recognition, in footnote 21, that States retained a "legitimate interest in obtaining jurors who could follow their instructions and obey their oaths." The Court concluded:

> This line of cases establishes the general proposition that a juror may not be challenged for cause based on his views about capital punishment unless those views would prevent or substantially impair the performance of his duties as a juror in accordance with his instructions and his oath. The State may insist, however, that jurors will consider and decide the facts impartially and conscientiously apply the law as charged by the court.

The Court went on to hold that as applied in that case certain veniremen had been improperly excluded under the Texas statute, because their acknowledgment that the possible imposition of the death penalty would or might "affect" their deliberations was meant only to indicate that they would be more emotionally involved or would view their task "with greater seriousness and gravity." The Court reasoned that such an "effect" did not demonstrate that the prospective jurors were unwilling or unable to follow the law or obey their oaths.

The state of this case law leaves trial courts with the difficult task of distinguishing between prospective jurors whose opposition to capital punishment will not allow them to apply the law or view the facts impartially and jurors who, though opposed to capital punishment, will nevertheless conscientiously apply the law to the facts adduced at trial. Although this task may be difficult in any event, it is obviously made more difficult by the fact that the standard applied in *Adams* differs markedly from the language of footnote 21. The tests with respect to sentencing and guilt, originally in two prongs, have been merged; the requirement that a juror may be excluded only if he would never vote for the death penalty is now missing; gone too is the extremely high burden of proof. In general, the standard has been simplified.

There is good reason why the *Adams* test is preferable for determining juror exclusion. First, although given *Witherspoon*'s facts a court applying the general principles of *Adams* could have arrived at the "automatically" language of *Witherspoon*'s footnote 21, we do not believe that language can be squared with the duties of present-day capital sentencing juries. In *Witherspoon* the jury was vested with unlimited discretion in choice of sentence. Given this discretion, a juror willing to *consider* the death penalty arguably was able to "follow the law and abide by his oath" in choosing the "proper" sentence. Nothing more was required. Under this understanding the only veniremembers who could be deemed excludable were those who would never vote for the death sentence or who could not impartially judge guilt.

After our decisions in *Furman v. Georgia*, 408 U.S. 238 (1972), and *Gregg v. Georgia*, 428 U.S. 153 (1976), however, sentencing juries could no longer be invested with such discretion. As in the State of Texas, many capital sentencing juries are now asked specific questions, often factual, the answers to which will determine whether death is the appropriate penalty. In such circumstances it does not make sense to require simply that a juror not "automatically" vote against the death penalty; whether or not a venireman might vote for death under certain personal standards, the State still may properly challenge that venireman if he refuses to follow the statutory scheme and truthfully answer the questions put by the trial judge. To hold that *Witherspoon* requires anything more would be to hold, in the name of the Sixth Amendment right to an impartial jury, that a State must allow a venireman to sit despite the fact that he will be unable to view the case impartially.

Second, the statements in the *Witherspoon* footnotes are in any event dicta. The Court's holding focused only on circumstances under which prospective jurors could not be excluded; under *Witherspoon*'s facts it was unnecessary to decide when they could be. This Court has on other occasions similarly rejected language from a footnote as "not controlling."

Finally, the *Adams* standard is proper because it is in accord with traditional reasons for excluding jurors and with the circumstances under which such determinations are made. We begin by reiterating *Adams*' acknowledgment that "*Witherspoon* is not a ground for challenging any prospective juror. It is rather a limitation on the State's power to exclude...." Exclusion of jurors opposed to capital punishment began with a recognition that certain of those jurors might frustrate the State's legitimate interest in administering constitutional capital sentencing schemes by not following their oaths. *Witherspoon* simply held that the State's power to exclude did not extend beyond its interest in removing those particular jurors. But there is nothing talismanic about juror exclusion under *Witherspoon* merely because it involves capital sentencing juries. *Witherspoon* is not grounded in the Eighth Amendment's prohibition against cruel and unusual punishment, but in the Sixth Amendment. Here, as elsewhere, the quest is for jurors who will conscientiously apply the law and find the facts. That is what an "impartial" jury consists of, and we do not think, simply because a defendant is being tried for a capital crime, that he is entitled to a legal presumption or standard that allows jurors to be seated who quite likely will be biased in his favor.

As with any other trial situation where an adversary wishes to exclude a juror because of bias, then, it is the adversary seeking exclusion who must demonstrate, through questioning, that the potential juror lacks impartiality. It is then the trial judge's duty to determine whether the challenge is proper. This is, of course, the standard and procedure outlined in *Adams*, but it is equally true of any situation where a party seeks to exclude a biased juror.

We therefore take this opportunity to clarify our decision in *Witherspoon*, and to reaffirm the above-quoted standard from *Adams* as the proper standard for determining when a prospective juror may be excluded for cause because of his or her views on capital punishment. That standard is whether the juror's views would "prevent or substantially impair the performance of his duties as a juror in accordance with his instructions and his oath."[5] We note that, in addition to dispensing with *Witherspoon*'s reference to "automatic" decisionmaking, this standard likewise does not require that a juror's bias be proved with "unmistakable clarity." This is because determinations of juror bias cannot be reduced to question-and-answer sessions which obtain results in the manner of a catechism. What common sense should have realized experience has proved: many veniremen simply cannot be asked enough questions to reach the point where their bias has been made "unmistakably clear;" these veniremen may not know how they will react when faced with imposing the death sentence, or may be unable to articulate, or may wish to hide their true feelings. Despite this lack of clarity in the printed record, however, there will be situations where the trial judge is left with the definite impression that a prospective juror would be unable to faithfully and impartially apply the law.

[The Court concluded that the Eleventh Circuit erred in finding that the dismissal of Juror Colby violated the Constitution, and reversed the decision of the federal court of appeals.]

Notes and Question

1. Writing for the majority in *Witherspoon*, Justice Stewart observed, "It is, of course, settled that a State may not entrust the determination of whether a man is innocent or guilty to a tribunal 'organized to convict.'" Research has shown that death-qualified jurors are more concerned with crime control and less with due process than *Witherspoon*-excludables; more likely to assume that the defendant is guilty before hearing any evidence; and less remorseful over a wrongful conviction. Ellsworth, "To Tell What We Know or Wait for Godot?," 15 Law and Human Behavior 50–76 (1991); Fitzgerald & Ellsworth, "Due Process vs. Crime Control: Death Qualification and Jury Attitudes," 8 Law and Human Behavior 31–51 (1984).

---

5. ... We adhere to the essential balance struck by the *Witherspoon* decision rendered in 1968, if not to the version of it presented by today's dissent; we simply modify the test stated in *Witherspoon*'s footnote 21 to hold that the State may exclude from capital sentencing juries that "class" of veniremen whose views would prevent or substantially impair the performance of their duties in accordance with their instructions or their oaths.

One important study demonstrated that under simulated trial conditions, juries composed entirely of death-qualified jurors were significantly more likely to convict than juries in which two to four excludable jurors had been included. Cowan, Thompson & Ellsworth, "The Effects of Death Qualification on Jurors' Predisposition to Convict and on the Quality of Deliberation," 8 Law and Human Behavior 53–79 (1984).

The issue of whether *Witherspoon*-excludables in fact would *ever* vote to impose the death penalty has also been studied. When *Witherspoon*-excludables were presented with five especially grisly murders, only 40% refused to consider the death penalty in all five cases. The remaining 60% indicated that they would consider the death penalty in one or more of the cases. Robinson, "What Does 'Unwilling' to Impose the Death Penalty Mean Anyway? Another Look at Excludable Jurors," 17 Law and Human Behavior 471–477 (1993).

2. Justices Brennan and Marshall dissented in *Witt*. In his dissent Justice Brennan wrote, "Like the death-qualified juries that the prosecution can now mold to its will to enhance the chances of victory, this Court increasingly acts as the adjunct of the State and its prosecutors in facilitating efficient and expedient conviction and execution irrespective of the Constitution's fundamental guarantees." Do you think that the Court's decision in *Witt* will make it easier for the prosecution to empanel "death-qualified" juries, i.e., juries more likely to sentence the defendant to death and/or more likely to convict the defendant?

Morgan v. Illinois
504 U.S. 719 (1992)

Justice WHITE delivered the opinion of the Court.

We decide here whether, during *voir dire* for a capital offense, a state trial court may, consistent with the Due Process Clause of the Fourteenth Amendment, refuse inquiry into whether a potential juror would automatically impose the death penalty upon conviction of the defendant.

I

[During jury selection in petitioner Derrick Morgan's capital murder trial, the prosecutor requested that the trial judge question the jurors as to "whether any potential juror would in all instances refuse to impose the death penalty upon conviction of the offense." The trial court so questioned the jurors and seventeen potential jurors were struck because they expressed "substantial doubts" about their ability to follow Illinois' death penalty law.

Counsel for Morgan then requested that the judge "ask all prospective jurors the following question: 'If you found Derrick Morgan guilty, would you automatically vote to impose the death penalty no matter what the facts are?'" The trial court refused to ask potential jurors this "life qualifying" or "reverse-*Witherspoon*" question.

The jury found Morgan guilty and sentenced him to death. Morgan appealed the trial court's refusal to ask the reverse-*Witherspoon* question.]

On appeal, the Illinois Supreme Court affirmed petitioner's conviction and death sentence, rejecting petitioner's claim that, pursuant to *Ross v. Oklahoma*, 487 U.S. 81 (1988), *voir dire* must include the "life qualifying" or "reverse-*Witherspoon*" question upon request. The Illinois Supreme Court concluded that nothing requires a trial court to question potential jurors so as to identify and exclude any who would vote for the death penalty in every case after conviction for a capital offense. That Court also found no violation of *Ross*, concluding instead that petitioner's jury "was selected from a fair cross-section of the community, each juror swore to uphold the law regardless of his or her personal feelings, and no juror expressed any views that would call his or her impartiality into question."

We granted certiorari because of the considerable disagreement among state courts of last resort on the question at issue in this case. We now reverse the judgment of the Illinois Supreme Court....

II

B

[*Wainwright v.*] *Witt* held that "the proper standard for determining when a prospective juror may be excused for cause because of his or her views on capital punishment ... is whether the juror's views would 'prevent or substantially impair the performance of his duties as a juror in accordance with his instructions and his oath.'" Under this standard, it is clear from *Witt* and *Adams*, the progeny of *Witherspoon*, that a juror who in no case would vote for capital punishment, regardless of his or her instructions, is not an impartial juror and must be removed for cause.

Thereafter, in *Ross v. Oklahoma*, 487 U.S. 81 (1988), a state trial court refused to remove for cause a juror who declared he would vote to impose death automatically if the jury found the defendant guilty. That juror, however, was removed by the defendant's use of a peremptory challenge, and for that reason the death sentence could be affirmed. But in the course of reaching this result, we announced our considered view that because the Constitution guarantees a defendant on trial for his life the right to an impartial jury, the trial court's failure to remove the juror for cause was constitutional error under the standard enunciated in *Witt*. We emphasized that "[h]ad [this juror] sat on the jury that ultimately sentenced petitioner to death, and had petitioner properly preserved his right to challenge the trial court's failure to remove [the juror] for cause, the sentence would have to be overturned."

We reiterate this view today. A juror who will automatically vote for the death penalty in every case will fail in good faith to consider the evidence of aggravating and mitigating circumstances as the instructions require him to do. Indeed, because such a juror has already formed an opinion on the merits, the presence or absence of either aggravating or mitigating circumstances is entirely irrelevant to such a juror. Therefore, based on the requirement of impartiality embodied in the Due Process Clause of the Fourteenth Amendment, a capital defendant may challenge for cause any prospective juror who maintains such views. If even one such juror is empaneled and the death sentence is imposed, the State is disentitled to execute the sentence....

III

Justice Scalia, in dissent, insists that Illinois is entitled to try a death penalty case with 1 or even 12 jurors who upon inquiry announce that they would automatically vote to impose the death penalty if the defendant is found guilty of a capital offense, no matter what the so-called mitigating factors, whether statutory or nonstatutory, might be. But such jurors obviously deem mitigating evidence to be irrelevant to their decision to impose the death penalty: they not only refuse to give such evidence any weight but are also plainly saying that mitigating evidence is not worth their consideration and that they will not consider it. While Justice Scalia's jaundiced view of our decision today may best be explained by his rejection of the line of cases tracing from *Woodson v. North Carolina* and *Lockett v. Ohio*, and developing the nature and role of mitigating evidence in the trial of capital offenses, it is a view long rejected by this Court. More important to our purposes here, however, his view finds no support in either the statutory or decisional law of Illinois because that law is consistent with the requirements concerning mitigating evidence described in this Court's cases.

The Illinois death penalty statute provides that "[t]he court shall consider, or shall instruct the jury to consider, any aggravating and any mitigating factors which are relevant to the imposition of the death penalty," and lists certain mitigating factors that the legislature must have deemed relevant to such imposition. The statute explicitly directs the procedure controlling this jury deliberation:

> If there is a unanimous finding by the jury that one or more of the factors [enumerated in aggravation] exist, the jury shall consider aggravating and mitigating factors as instructed by the court and shall determine whether the sentence of death shall be imposed. If the jury determines unanimously that there are no mitigating factors sufficient to preclude the imposition of the death sentence, the court shall sentence the defendant to death.

In accord with this statutory procedure, the trial judge in this case instructed the jury:

> In deciding whether the Defendant should be sentenced to death, you should consider all the aggravating factors supported by the evidence and all the mitigating factors supported by the evidence....
>
> If you unanimously find, from your consideration of all the evidence, that there are no mitigating factors sufficient to preclude imposition of the death sentence, then you should sign the verdict requiring the Court [to] sentence the Defendant to death.

Any juror who states that he or she will automatically vote for the death penalty without regard to the mitigating evidence is announcing an intention not to follow the instructions to consider the mitigating evidence and to decide if it is sufficient to preclude imposition of the death penalty. Any contrary reading of this instruction, or more importantly, the controlling statute, renders the term "sufficient" meaningless. The statute plainly indicates that a lesser sentence is available in every case where mitigating evidence exists; thus any juror who would invariably impose the death penalty upon conviction cannot be said to have reached this decision based on all the evidence. While Justice Scalia chooses to argue that such a "merciless juror" is not a "lawless" one, he is in error, for such a juror will not give mitigating evidence the consideration that the statute contemplates. Indeed, the Illinois Supreme Court recognizes that jurors are not impartial if they would automatically vote for the death penalty, and that questioning in the manner petitioner requests is a direct and helpful means of protecting a defendant's right to an impartial jury. The State has not suggested otherwise in this Court.

Surely if in a particular Illinois case the judge, who imposes sentence should the defendant waive his right to jury sentencing under the statute, was to announce that, to him or her, mitigating evidence is beside the point and that he or she intends to impose the death penalty without regard to the nature or extent of mitigating evidence if the defendant is found guilty of a capital offense, that judge is refusing in advance to follow the statutory direction to consider that evidence and should disqualify himself or herself. Any juror to whom mitigating factors are likewise irrelevant should be disqualified for cause, for that juror has formed an opinion concerning the merits of the case without basis in the evidence developed at trial. Accordingly, the defendant in this case was entitled to have the inquiry made that he proposed to the trial judge.

IV

Because the "inadequacy of *voir dire*" leads us to doubt that petitioner was sentenced to death by a jury empaneled in compliance with the Fourteenth Amendment, his sentence cannot stand. Accordingly, the judgment of the Illinois Supreme Court affirming petitioner's death sentence is reversed, and the case is remanded for further proceedings not inconsistent with this opinion.

Justice SCALIA, with whom the Chief Justice and Justice Thomas join, dissenting.

II

... In the Court's view, a juror who will always impose the death penalty upon proof of the required aggravating factors "will fail in good faith to consider the evidence of aggravating and mitigating circumstances as the instructions require him to do." I would agree with that if it were true that the instructions required jurors to deem certain evidence to be "mitigating" and to weigh that evidence in deciding the penalty. On that hypothesis, the juror's firm attachment to the death penalty would demonstrate an absence of the constitutionally requisite impartiality, which requires that the decisionmaker be able "conscientiously [to] apply the law and find the facts." The hypothesis, however, is not true as applied to the facts of the present case. Remarkably, the Court rests its judgment upon a juror's inability to comply with instructions, *without bothering to describe the key instructions.* When one considers them, it is perfectly clear that they do not preclude a juror from taking the view that, for capital murder, a death sentence is always warranted.

The jury in this case was instructed that "[a]ggravating factors are reasons why the Defendant should be sentenced to death"; that "[m]itigating factors are reasons why the Defendant should not be sentenced to death"; that the jury must "consider all the aggravating factors supported by the evidence and all the mitigating factors supported by the evidence"; and that the jury should impose a death sentence if it found, "from [its] consideration of all the evidence, that there are no mitigating factors sufficient to preclude imposition of a death sentence." The instructions did not in any way further define what constitutes a "mitigating" or an "aggravating" factor, other than to point out that the jury's finding, at the death-eligibility stage, that petitioner committed a contract killing was necessarily an aggravator. As reflected in these instructions, Illinois law permitted each juror to define for himself whether a particular item of evidence was mitigating, in the sense that it provided a "reaso[n] why the Defendant should not be sentenced to death." Thus, it is simply not the case that Illinois law precluded a juror from taking the bright-line position that there are no valid reasons why a defendant who has committed a contract killing should not be sentenced to death. Such a juror does not "fail ... to consider the evidence," he simply fails to give it the effect the defendant desires.

Nor can the Court's exclusion of these death-inclined jurors be justified on the theory that—regardless of what Illinois law purports to permit—the Eighth Amendment prohibits a juror from always advocating a death sentence at the weighing stage. Our cases in this area hold, not that the sentencer must give effect to (or even that he must consider) the evidence offered by the defendant as mitigating, but rather that he must "not be *precluded* from considering" it. Similarly, where the judge is the final sentencer we have held, not that he *must* consider mitigating evidence, but only that he may not, on *legal* grounds, refuse to consider it. *Woodson* and *Lockett* meant to ensure that the sentencing jury would function as a "link between contemporary community values and the penal system," they did not mean to specify what the content of those values must be. The "conscience of the community" also includes those jurors who are not swayed by mitigating evidence.

The Court relies upon dicta contained in our opinion in *Ross v. Oklahoma*, 487 U.S. 81 (1988). In that case, the defendant challenged for cause a juror who stated during voir dire that he would automatically vote to impose a death sentence if the defendant were convicted. The trial court rejected the challenge, and Ross used a peremptory [challenge] to remove the juror. Although we noted that the state appellate court had assumed that such a juror would not be able to follow the law, we held that Ross was not deprived of an impartial jury because none of the jurors who actually sat on the petit jury was partial. In reaching that conclusion, however, we expressed the view that had the challenged juror actually served, "the sentence would have to be overturned." The Court attaches great weight to this dictum, which it describes as "announc[ing] our considered view." This is hyperbole. It is clear on the face of the opinion that the dictum was based entirely on the fact that the state court had assumed that such a juror was unwilling to follow the law at the penalty phase — a point we did not purport to examine independently. The *Ross* dictum thus merely reflects the quite modest proposition that a juror who will not follow the law is not impartial.

III

Because Illinois would not violate due process by seating a juror who will not be swayed by mitigating evidence at the weighing stage, the Constitution does not entitle petitioner to identify such jurors during voir dire

.... Sixteen years ago, this Court decreed — by a sheer act of will, with no pretense of foundation in constitutional text or American tradition — that the People (as in We, the People) cannot decree the death penalty, absolutely and categorically, for any criminal act, even (presumably) genocide; the jury must always be given the option of extending mercy. Today, obscured within the fog of confusion that is our annually improvised Eighth-Amendment, "death-is-different" jurisprudence, the Court strikes a further blow against the People in its campaign against the death penalty. Not only must mercy be allowed, but now only the merciful may be permitted to sit in judgment. Those who agree with the author of Exodus, or with Immanuel Kant,[6] must be banished from American juries — not because the People have so decreed, but because such jurors do not share the strong penological preferences of this Court. In my view, that not only is not required by the Constitution of the United States; it grossly offends it.

Using Mitigating Evidence in Jury Selection in Capital Trials

Marshall Dayan, The Champion, July 1993

Voir dire is not provided as a tool for selecting a jury more favorable to one side or the other. Rather, consistent with our adversary system of justice, the rationale for *voir*

---

6. See Exodus 21:12 ("He that smiteth a man, so that he die, shall be surely put to death"); I. Kant, The Philosophy of Law 198 [1796] (W. Hastie transl. 1887) ("[W]hoever has committed Murder, must die.... Even if a Civil Society resolved to dissolve itself with the consent of all its members[,] ... the last Murderer lying in the prison ought to be executed before the resolution was carried out. This ought to be done in order that every one may realize the desert of his deeds ...").

dire is to obtain a petit jury which is impartial, able fairly to apply the law, and objectively to consider the evidence before it; further, *voir dire* allows the parties to exercise intelligently their peremptory challenges. Even when employed as a tool for the protection of the constitutional right to an impartial jury, the specific conduct of *voir dire*, i.e., whether to allow a particular question or line of questions, is left to the direction of the trial court. One of the critical determinations on the question of impartiality is the demeanor of the prospective juror, and the U.S. Supreme Court has noted that this determination is best left to the trial court.

Nevertheless, the Supreme Court has concluded that the due process clause of the Fourteenth Amendment requires a capital sentencing jury to be impartial. It also entitles a capital defendant to challenge for cause and have removed on the ground of bias any prospective juror who will automatically vote for the death penalty irrespective of the facts or the trial court's instructions of law. This necessarily requires the trial court, on defendant's request, to inquire into the prospective jurors' views on capital punishment and whether those views preclude the jurors' ability to consider a punishment alternative to death for first-degree murder.

As a further safeguard, the Supreme Court has concluded that the due process clause requires the trial court to conduct *voir dire* on specific areas of prejudice when special circumstances in a particular trial raise a constitutionally significant likelihood that, absent such questioning, the jury impanelled would not be impartial....

In *Morgan v. Illinois*, 504 U.S. 719 (1992), the United States Supreme Court held that a state trial court may not, consistent with the due process clause of the Fourteenth Amendment, refuse inquiry into whether a potential juror would automatically impose the death penalty upon conviction of the defendant. In so holding, the Court dealt with four issues: (1) whether a jury provided to a capital defendant at the sentencing phase must be impartial; (2) whether such defendant is entitled to challenge for cause on the ground of bias a prospective juror who will automatically vote for the death penalty irrespective of the facts or the trial court's instructions of law; (3) whether on *voir dire* the court must, on defendant's request, inquire into the prospective juror's views on capital punishment; and, (4) whether *voir dire* which inquires only whether the jurors can follow the law suffices to meet constitutional requirements.

As to whether an impartial jury is required, the Court concluded that "due process alone has long demanded that, if a jury is to be provided the defendant, regardless of whether the Sixth Amendment requires it, the jury must stand impartial and indifferent to the extent commanded by the Sixth Amendment." As to the second question, the Court concluded that a capital defendant may challenge for cause any prospective juror who will automatically vote for the death penalty in every case, regardless of the facts in aggravation or mitigation. The Court also concluded that the trial court must, upon request, make inquiry into whether or not jurors hold biased views that prevent or substantially impair their abilities to fulfill their duties as jurors.

As the Court noted, "[w]ere *voir dire* not available to lay bare the foundation of petitioner's challenge for cause," the petitioner would be in no position "to exercise intelligently his complementary challenge for cause against those biased persons on the venire...."

Therefore, *Morgan* instructs that just as the state seeks to challenge jurors who could never vote to impose a death sentence, regardless of the facts and circumstances of a given case or the instructions of law from the trial court, so too the defense may and should challenge jurors who would automatically vote to impose a death sentence, regardless of the facts and circumstances of a given case or the instructions of law from the trial court....

The requirement that the sentencer "may not refuse to consider any relevant mitigating evidence offered by the defendant as a basis for a sentence less than death," and the prescription cited in *Morgan* that "it is the adversary seeking exclusion who must demonstrate, *through questioning*, that the potential juror lacks impartiality," combine to require the state, as a matter of federal constitutional law, to allow inquiry as to whether prospective venire members can fairly consider, as mitigating, classes of evidence which might be deemed controversial.

As an example, consider the statutory mitigating circumstance that "the capacity of the defendant to appreciate the criminality of his conduct or to conform his conduct to the requirements of law was impaired." This mitigating circumstance has been held to apply to voluntary intoxication that affects the defendant's ability to understand and control his actions.

Many people, however, believe that voluntary intoxication ought not to mitigate criminal activity; it ought to aggravate criminal activity. Many people might colloquially respond to the mitigating circumstance by asking, "You mean you want me to give him extra credit for getting drunk before he robbed and killed the victim?" Yet as jurors, those people would have an obligation to consider and give mitigating weight to that mitigating circumstance if they found the evidence of the intoxication and the extent of its effect on the defendant to be true. Similarly, there are people who simply do not believe that mental health status can be scientifically explored; to them, the term "mental health professional" is an oxymoron.

In short, there are people who believe that psychiatry and psychology are spurious, and their practitioners charlatans. When the juror is duty-bound to consider mitigating evidence as mitigating, but either cannot consider it as mitigating or can consider it only as aggravating, the defendant must be provided an opportunity, through questioning, to establish the juror's inability to follow the law because of bias about that class of evidence. It is the subjective nature of capital sentencing that, in part, compels this result.

While *Morgan* does not explicitly say that the Constitution compels a state court to allow such inquiry, its rationale, and other cases of the United States Supreme Court, strongly imply just such a constitutional imperative. In *Turner v. Murray*, 476 U.S. 28 (1986), the Court held that when an interracial offense is involved, a capital defendant is entitled to inquiry about prospective jurors' attitudes about race. In so holding, the Court noted that "the [sentencing] jury in a capital case is called upon to make a highly subjective, unique, individualized judgment regarding the punishment that a particular person deserves." The Court reasoned that "[b]ecause of the range of discretion entrusted to a jury in a capital sentencing hearing, there is a unique opportunity for racial prejudice to operate but remain undetected."

Given the finality of the death penalty, the risk of racial prejudice infecting the capital sentencing proceeding was held to be unacceptable when weighed against the ease with which that risk could be minimized. Therefore, a plurality held "that a capital defendant accused of an interracial crime is entitled to have prospective jurors informed of the race of the victim and questioned on the issue of racial bias." On the other hand, in *Mu'min v. Virginia*, 500 U.S. 415 (1991), the Court rejected a contention that in a capital case a state court is bound constitutionally to inquire about the contents of what venire members had read, seen or heard in pre-trial publicity, at least absent a showing that the pre-trial publicity engendered a "wave of public passion" such that the defendant could not otherwise obtain a fair trial.

The situation in *Mu'min*, however, is far different from that proposed here. The jurors themselves, having read, seen or heard about the case, are in a position to answer a question of whether they can put their pre-existing knowledge to the side and judge the case solely on the evidence they hear from the witness stand and the law as given them by the trial judge. By contrast, jurors who are not questioned about their ability to consider mitigating circumstances cannot honestly answer whether they can judge the case solely on the evidence they hear and the law as instructed by the trial court. As the Supreme Court noted in *Morgan*, a juror who says he or she can follow the law without knowledge of the legal obligation to consider, *as a mitigating circumstance*, the background, character and record of the offender, before deciding on the appropriate sentence, promises in good conscience but mistakenly.

C. Fair Cross-Section Requirement

A defendant is entitled to a jury drawn from a pool of persons representing a fair cross-section of the community, even though the particular jury selected to hear the defendant's case may not necessarily reflect the precise ethnic, racial, or gender composition of the community. A defendant's right to a jury drawn from a fair cross-section of the community may be violated if large, distinct classes of persons, such as women or members of a particular racial or ethnic group, are systemically excluded from the jury pool. *Taylor v. Louisiana*, 419 U.S. 522 (1975). In capital cases, the question arises whether automatically excluding persons who oppose the death penalty constitutes a violation of the defendant's right to a fair cross-section of the community by depriving the defendant of a class of potential jurors holding particular moral or religious beliefs about the death penalty.

Lockhart v. McCree
476 U.S. 162 (1986)

Justice REHNQUIST delivered the opinion of the Court.

In this case we address the question left open by our decision nearly 18 years ago in *Witherspoon*: Does the Constitution prohibit the removal for cause, prior to the guilt phase of a bifurcated capital trial, of prospective jurors whose opposition to the death penalty is so strong that it would prevent or substantially impair the performance of their duties as jurors at the sentencing phase of the trial? We hold that it does not....

On the morning of February 14, 1978, a combination gift shop and service station in Camden, Arkansas, was robbed, and Evelyn Boughton, the owner, was shot and killed. That afternoon, Ardia McCree was arrested in Hot Springs, Arkansas, after a police officer saw him driving a maroon and white Lincoln Continental matching an eyewitness' description of the getaway car used by Boughton's killer. The next evening, McCree admitted to police that he had been at Boughton's shop at the time of the murder. He claimed, however, that a tall black stranger wearing an overcoat first asked him for a ride, then took McCree's rifle out of the back of the car and used it to kill Boughton. McCree also claimed that, after the murder, the stranger rode with McCree to a nearby dirt road, got out of the car, and walked away with the rifle. McCree's story was contradicted by two eyewitnesses who saw McCree's car between the time of the murder and the time when McCree said the stranger got out and walked away, and who stated that they saw only one person in the car. The police found McCree's rifle and a bank bag from Boughton's shop alongside the dirt road. Based on ballistics tests, a Federal Bureau of Investigation officer testified that the bullet that killed Boughton had been fired from McCree's rifle.

McCree was charged with capital felony murder. In accordance with Arkansas law, the trial judge at *voir dire* removed for cause, over McCree's objections, those prospective jurors who stated that they could not under any circumstances vote for the imposition of the death penalty. Eight prospective jurors were excluded for this reason. The jury convicted McCree of capital felony murder, but rejected the State's request for the death penalty, instead setting McCree's punishment at life imprisonment without parole....

[McCree relied on a number of social science studies to support his claim that excluding jurors under *Witherspoon* (*Witherspoon*-excludables) produced conviction-prone juries. Although the Court criticized these studies, it stated,] we will assume for purposes of this opinion that the studies are both methodologically valid and adequate to establish that "death qualification" in fact produces juries somewhat more "conviction-prone" than "non-death-qualified" juries. We hold, nonetheless, that the Constitution does not prohibit the States from "death qualifying" juries in capital cases.

The Eighth Circuit ruled that "death qualification" [of juries by means of excluding jurors under *Witherspoon*] violated McCree's right under the Sixth Amendment, as applied to the States via incorporation through the Fourteenth Amendment, to a jury selected from a representative cross section of the community. But we do not believe that the fair-cross-section requirement can, or should, be applied as broadly as that court attempted to apply it. We have never invoked the fair-cross-section principle to invalidate the use of either for-cause or peremptory challenges to prospective jurors, or to require petit juries, as opposed to jury panels or venires, to reflect the composition of the community at large. The limited scope of the fair-cross-section requirement is a direct and inevitable consequence of the practical impossibility of providing each criminal defendant with a truly "representative" petit jury, a basic truth that the Court of Appeals itself acknowledged for many years prior to its decision in the instant case. We remain convinced that an extension of the fair-cross-section requirement to petit juries would be unworkable and unsound, and we decline McCree's invitation to adopt such an extension.

But even if we were willing to extend the fair-cross-section requirement to petit juries, we would still reject the Eighth Circuit's conclusion that "death qualification" violates that requirement. The essence of a "fair-cross-section" claim is the systematic exclusion of "a 'distinctive' group in the community." In our view, groups defined solely in terms of shared attitudes that would prevent or substantially impair members of the group from performing one of their duties as jurors, such as the "*Witherspoon*-excludables" at issue here, are not "distinctive groups" for fair-cross-section purposes.

We have never attempted to precisely define the term "distinctive group," and we do not undertake to do so today. But we think it obvious that the concept of "distinctiveness" must be linked to the purposes of the fair-cross-section requirement. In *Taylor v. Louisiana*, 419 U.S. 522 (1975), we identified those purposes as (1) "guard[ing] against the exercise of arbitrary power" and ensuring that the "commonsense judgment of the community" will act as "a hedge against the overzealous or mistaken prosecutor," (2) preserving "public confidence in the fairness of the criminal justice system," and (3) implementing our belief that "sharing in the administration of justice is a phase of civic responsibility."

Our prior jury-representativeness cases, whether based on the fair-cross-section component of the Sixth Amendment or the Equal Protection Clause of the Fourteenth Amendment, have involved such groups as blacks, women and Mexican-Americans. The wholesale exclusion of these large groups from jury service clearly contravened all three of the aforementioned purposes of the fair-cross-section requirement. Because these groups were excluded for reasons completely unrelated to the ability of members of the group to serve as jurors in a particular case, the exclusion raised at least the possibility that the composition of juries would be arbitrarily skewed in such a way as to deny criminal defendants the benefit of the common-sense judgment of the community. In addition, the exclusion from jury service of large groups of individuals not on the basis of their inability to serve as jurors, but on the basis of some immutable characteristic such as race, gender, or ethnic background, undeniably gave rise to an "appearance of unfairness." Finally, such exclusion improperly deprived members of these often historically disadvantaged groups of their right as citizens to serve on juries in criminal cases.

The group of "*Witherspoon*-excludables" involved in the case at bar differs significantly from the groups we have previously recognized as "distinctive." "Death qualification," unlike the wholesale exclusion of blacks, women, or Mexican-Americans from jury service, is carefully designed to serve the State's concededly legitimate interest in obtaining a single jury that can properly and impartially apply the law to the facts of the case at both the guilt and sentencing phases of a capital trial. There is very little danger, therefore, and McCree does not even argue, that "death qualification" was instituted as a means for the State to arbitrarily skew the composition of capital-case juries.

Furthermore, unlike blacks, women, and Mexican-Americans, "*Witherspoon*-excludables" are singled out for exclusion in capital cases on the basis of an attribute that is within the individual's control. It is important to remember that not all who oppose the death penalty are subject to removal for cause in capital cases; those who firmly believe that the death penalty is unjust may nevertheless serve as jurors in capital cases so long as they state clearly that they are willing to temporarily set aside their own beliefs in deference to the rule of law. Because the group of "*Witherspoon*-excludables" includes only those who cannot and will not conscientiously obey the law with respect to one of the issues in a capital case, "death qualification" hardly can be said to create an "appearance of unfairness."

Finally, the removal for cause of "*Witherspoon*-excludables" in capital cases does not prevent them from serving as jurors in other criminal cases, and thus leads to no substantial deprivation of their basic rights of citizenship. They are treated no differently than any juror who expresses the view that he would be unable to follow the law in a particular case.

In sum, "*Witherspoon*-excludables," or for that matter any other group defined solely in terms of shared attitudes that render members of the group unable to serve as jurors in a particular case, may be excluded from jury service without contravening any of the basic objectives of the fair-cross-section requirement. It is for this reason that we conclude that "*Witherspoon*-excludables" do not constitute a "distinctive group" for fair-cross-section purposes, and hold that "death qualification" does not violate the fair-cross-section requirement.

McCree argues that, even if we reject the Eighth Circuit's fair-cross-section holding, we should affirm the judgment below on the alternative ground, adopted by the District

Court, that "death qualification" violated his constitutional right to an impartial jury. McCree concedes that the individual jurors who served at his trial were impartial.... He does not claim that pretrial publicity, *ex parte* communications, or other undue influence, affected the jury's deliberations. In short, McCree does not claim that his conviction was tainted by any of the kinds of jury bias or partiality that we have previously recognized as violative of the Constitution. Instead, McCree argues that his jury lacked impartiality because the absence of "*Witherspoon*-excludables" "slanted" the jury in favor of conviction.

We do not agree. McCree's "impartiality" argument apparently is based on the theory that, because all individual jurors are to some extent predisposed towards one result or another, a constitutionally impartial jury can be constructed only by "balancing" the various predispositions of the individual jurors. Thus, according to McCree, when the State "tips the scales" by excluding prospective jurors with a particular viewpoint, an impermissibly partial jury results. We have consistently rejected this view of jury impartiality, including as recently as last Term when we squarely held that an impartial jury consists of nothing more than "*jurors* who will conscientiously apply the law and find the facts." *Wainwright v. Witt*, 469 U.S. 412, 423 (1985).

The view of jury impartiality urged upon us by McCree is both illogical and hopelessly impractical. McCree characterizes the jury that convicted him as "slanted" by the process of "death qualification." But McCree admits that exactly the same 12 individuals could have ended up on his jury through the "luck of the draw," without in any way violating the constitutional guarantee of impartiality. Even accepting McCree's position that we should focus on the jury rather than the individual jurors, it is hard for us to understand the logic of the argument that a given jury is unconstitutionally partial when it results from a state-ordained process, yet impartial when exactly the same jury results from mere chance. On a more practical level, if it were true that the Constitution required a certain mix of individual viewpoints on the jury, then trial judges would be required to undertake the Sisyphean task of "balancing" juries, making sure that each contains the proper number of Democrats and Republicans, young persons and old persons, white-collar executives and blue-collar laborers, and so on. Adopting McCree's concept of jury impartiality would also likely require the elimination of peremptory challenges, which are commonly used by both the State and the defendant to attempt to produce a jury favorable to the challenger....

In our view, it is simply not possible to define jury impartiality, for constitutional purposes, by reference to some hypothetical mix of individual viewpoints. Prospective jurors come from many different backgrounds, and have many different attitudes and predispositions. But the Constitution presupposes that a jury selected from a fair cross section of the community is impartial, regardless of the mix of individual viewpoints actually represented on the jury, so long as the jurors can conscientiously and properly carry out their sworn duty to apply the law to the facts of the particular case. We hold that McCree's jury satisfied both aspects of this constitutional standard. The judgment of the Court of Appeals is therefore reversed.

Justice MARSHALL, with whom Justice Brennan and Justice Stevens join, dissenting.

I

... In the wake of *Witherspoon*, a number of researchers set out to supplement the data that the Court had found inadequate in that case. The results of these studies were exhaustively analyzed by the District Court in this case, and can be only briefly summarized here. The data strongly suggest that death qualification excludes a significantly large subset—at least 11% to 17%—of potential jurors who could be impartial during the guilt phase of trial. Among the members of this excludable class are a disproportionate number of blacks and women.

The perspectives on the criminal justice system of jurors who survive death qualification are systematically different from those of the excluded jurors. Death-qualified jurors are, for example, more likely to believe that a defendant's failure to testify is indicative of his guilt, more hostile to the insanity defense, more mistrustful of defense attorneys, and less concerned about the danger of erroneous convictions. This proprosecution bias is reflected in the greater readiness of death-qualified jurors to convict or to convict on more serious charges. And, finally, the very process of death qualification—which focuses attention on the death penalty before the trial has even begun—has been found to predispose the jurors that survive it to believe that the defendant is guilty....

II

B

The true impact of death qualification on the fairness of a trial is likely even more devastating than the studies show. *Witherspoon* placed limits on the State's ability to strike scrupled jurors for cause, unless they state "unambiguously that [they] would automatically vote against the imposition of capital punishment no matter what the trial might reveal." It said nothing, however, about the prosecution's use of peremptory challenges to eliminate jurors who do not meet that standard and would otherwise survive death qualification. There is no question that peremptories have indeed been used to this end, thereby expanding the class of scrupled jurors excluded as a result of the death-qualifying *voir dire* challenged here. The only study of this practice has concluded: "For the five-year period studied a *prima facie* case has been demonstrated that prosecutors in Florida's Fourth Judicial Circuit systematically used their peremptory challenges to eliminate from capital juries venirepersons expressing opposition to the death penalty...."

IV

On occasion, this Court has declared what I believe should be obvious—that when a State seeks to convict a defendant of the most serious and severely punished offenses in its criminal code, any procedure that "diminish[es] the reliability of the guilt determination" must be struck down. But in spite of such declarations, I cannot help thinking that respondent here would have stood a far better chance of prevailing on his constitutional claims had he not been challenging a procedure peculiar to the administration of the death penalty. For in no other context would a majority of this Court refuse to find any constitutional violation in a state practice that systematically operates to render juries more likely to convict, and to convict on the more serious charges. I dissent.

Note: Two Juries?

Justice Marshall suggested that two juries should be employed in capital cases: one jury to determine guilt or innocence, and the other to determine punishment. Justice Marshall believed this approach would eliminate the problems of death-qualified juries during the guilt and innocence phase of the trial. The majority responded to Justice Marshall's proposal stating, "it seems obvious to us that in most, if not all, capital cases much of the evidence adduced at the guilt phase of the trial will also have a bearing on the penalty phase; if two different juries were to be required, such testimony would have to be presented twice, once to each jury. As the Arkansas Supreme Court has noted, '[s]uch repetitive trials could not be consistently fair to the State and perhaps not even to the accused.'" The majority maintained that an additional benefit of the unitary capital jury is that "the defendant might benefit at the sentencing phase of the trial from the jury's 'residual doubts' about the evidence presented at the guilt phase."

Justice Marshall argued that a two-jury system would not be unduly costly or time consuming. Further, Marshall noted, "it ill-behooves the majority to allude to a defendant's power to appeal to 'residual doubts' at his sentencing when this Court has consistently refused to grant certiorari in state cases holding that these doubts cannot be considered during capital sentencing proceedings. Any suggestion that capital defendants will benefit from a single jury thus is more than disingenuous. It is cruel." Ultimately, the Court did resolve whether "residual doubts" may be considered during capital sentencing. See *Franklin v. Lynaugh*, 487 U.S. 164 (1988), *infra* chapter 8.

D. Racial Bias and Jury Selection

Turner v. Murray
476 U.S. 28 (1986)

Justice WHITE announced the judgment of the Court and delivered the opinion of the Court with respect to Parts I and III, and an opinion with respect to Parts II and IV, in which Justice Blackmun, Justice Stevens, and Justice O'Connor join.

Petitioner is a black man sentenced to death for the murder of a white storekeeper. The question presented is whether the trial judge committed reversible error at *voir dire* by refusing petitioner's request to question prospective jurors on racial prejudice.

I

On July 12, 1978, petitioner Willie Lloyd Turner entered a jewelry store in Franklin, Virginia, armed with a sawed-off shotgun. He demanded that the proprietor, W. Jack Smith, Jr., put jewelry and money from the cash register into some jewelry bags. Smith complied with petitioner's demand, but triggered a silent alarm, alerting the Police Department. When Alan Bain, a police officer, arrived to inquire about the alarm, petitioner surprised him and forced him to surrender his revolver.

Having learned that Smith had triggered a silent alarm, petitioner became agitated. He fired toward the rear wall of the store and stated that if he saw or heard any more police officers, he was going to start killing those in the store. When a police siren sounded, petitioner walked to where Smith was stationed behind a counter and without warning shot him in the head with Bain's pistol, wounding Smith and causing him to slump incapacitated to the floor.

Officer Bain attempted to calm petitioner, promising to take him anywhere he wanted to go and asking him not to shoot again. Petitioner angrily replied that he was going to kill Smith for "snitching," and fired two pistol shots into Smith's chest, fatally wounding him. As petitioner turned away from shooting Smith, Bain was able to disarm him and place him under arrest.

A Southampton County, Virginia, grand jury indicted petitioner on charges of capital murder, use of a firearm in the commission of a murder, and possession of a sawed-off shotgun in the commission of a robbery. Petitioner requested and was granted a change of venue to Northampton County, Virginia, a rural county some 80 miles from the location of the murder.

Prior to the commencement of *voir dire*, petitioner's counsel submitted to the trial judge a list of proposed questions, including the following:

> "The defendant, Willie Lloyd Turner, is a member of the Negro race. The victim, W. Jack Smith, Jr., was a white Caucasian. Will these facts prejudice you against Willie Lloyd Turner or affect your ability to render a fair and impartial verdict based solely on the evidence?"

The judge declined to ask this question, stating that it "has been ruled on by the Supreme Court." The judge did ask the venire, who were questioned in groups of five in petitioner's presence, whether any person was aware of any reason why he could not render a fair and impartial verdict, to which all answered "no." At the time the question was asked, the prospective jurors had no way of knowing that the murder victim was white.

The jury that was empaneled, which consisted of eight whites and four blacks, convicted petitioner on all of the charges against him. After a separate sentencing hearing on the capital charge, the jury recommended that petitioner be sentenced to death, a recommendation the trial judge accepted.

Petitioner appealed his death sentence to the Virginia Supreme Court. Among other points, he argued that the trial judge deprived him of his constitutional right to a fair and impartial jury by refusing to question prospective jurors on racial prejudice. The Virginia Supreme Court rejected this argument. Relying on our decision in *Ristaino v. Ross*, 424 U.S. 589 (1976), the court stated that a trial judge's refusal to ask prospective jurors about their racial attitudes, while perhaps not the wisest decision as a matter of policy, is not constitutionally objectionable in the absence of factors akin to those in *Ham v. South Carolina*, 409 U.S. 524 (1973).[3] The court held that "[t]he mere fact that a defendant is black and that a victim is white does not constitutionally mandate ... an inquiry [into racial prejudice]."

... We granted certiorari to review the Fourth Circuit's decision that petitioner was not constitutionally entitled to have potential jurors questioned concerning racial prejudice. We reverse.

---

3. In *Ham*, a young black man known in his small South Carolina hometown as a civil rights activist was arrested and charged with possession of marijuana. We held that the trial judge committed reversible error in refusing to honor Ham's request to question prospective jurors on racial prejudice. In *Ristaino*, we specified the factors which mandated an inquiry into racial prejudice in *Ham*:

"Ham's defense was that he had been framed because of his civil rights activities. His prominence in the community as a civil rights activist, if not already known to veniremen, inevitably would have been revealed to the members of the jury in the course of his presentation of that defense. Racial issues therefore were inextricably bound up with the conduct of the trial. Further, Ham's reputation as a civil rights activist and the defense he interposed were likely to intensify any prejudice that individual members of the jury might harbor." 424 U.S. at 596–597.

II

The Fourth Circuit's opinion correctly states the analytical framework for evaluating petitioner's argument: "The broad inquiry in each case must be ... whether under all of the circumstances presented there was a constitutionally significant likelihood that, absent questioning about racial prejudice, the jurors would not be indifferent as [they stand] unsworn." The Fourth Circuit was correct, too, in holding that under *Ristaino* the mere fact that petitioner is black and his victim white does not constitute a "special circumstance" of constitutional proportions. What sets this case apart from *Ristaino*, however, is that in addition to petitioner's being accused of a crime against a white victim, the crime charged was a capital offense.

In a capital sentencing proceeding before a jury, the jury is called upon to make a "highly subjective, 'unique, individualized judgment regarding the punishment that a particular person deserves.'" *Caldwell v. Mississippi*, 472 U.S. 320, 340 n.7 (1985). The Virginia statute under which petitioner was sentenced is instructive of the kinds of judgments a capital sentencing jury must make. First, in order to consider the death penalty, a Virginia jury must find either that the defendant is likely to commit future violent crimes or that his crime was "outrageously or wantonly vile, horrible or inhuman in that it involved torture, depravity of mind or an aggravated battery to the victim." Second, the jury must consider any mitigating evidence offered by the defendant. Mitigating evidence may include, but is not limited to, facts tending to show that the defendant acted under the influence of extreme emotional or mental disturbance, or that at the time of the crime the defendant's capacity "to appreciate the criminality of his conduct or to conform his conduct to the requirements of law was significantly impaired." Finally, even if the jury has found an aggravating factor, and irrespective of whether mitigating evidence has been offered, the jury has discretion not to recommend the death sentence, in which case it may not be imposed.

Virginia's death-penalty statute gives the jury greater discretion than other systems which we have upheld against constitutional challenge. However, our cases establish that every capital sentencer must be free to weigh relevant mitigating evidence before deciding whether to impose the death penalty, and that in the end it is the jury that must make the difficult, individualized judgment as to whether the defendant deserves the sentence of death.

Because of the range of discretion entrusted to a jury in a capital sentencing hearing, there is a unique opportunity for racial prejudice to operate but remain undetected. On the facts of this case, a juror who believes that blacks are violence prone or morally inferior might well be influenced by that belief in deciding whether petitioner's crime involved the aggravating factors specified under Virginia law. Such a juror might also be less favorably inclined toward petitioner's evidence of mental disturbance as a mitigating circumstance. More subtle, less consciously held racial attitudes could also influence a juror's decision in this case. Fear of blacks, which could easily be stirred up by the violent facts of petitioner's crime, might incline a juror to favor the death penalty.

The risk of racial prejudice infecting a capital sentencing proceeding is especially serious in light of the complete finality of the death sentence. "The Court, as well as the separate opinions of a majority of the individual Justices, has recognized that the qualitative difference of death from all other punishments requires a correspondingly greater degree of scrutiny of the capital sentencing determination." *California v. Brown*, 463 U.S. 992, 998–999 (1983). We have struck down capital sentences when we found that the circumstances under which they were imposed "created an unacceptable risk that 'the death penalty [may have been] meted out arbitrarily or capriciously' or through 'whim ... or mistake.'" In the present case, we find the risk that racial prejudice may have infected petitioner's capital sentencing unacceptable in light of the ease with which that risk could have been minimized. By refusing to question prospective jurors on racial prejudice, the trial judge failed to adequately protect petitioner's constitutional right to an impartial jury.

III

We hold that a capital defendant accused of an interracial crime is entitled to have prospective jurors informed of the race of the victim and questioned on the issue of racial bias. The rule we propose is minimally intrusive; as in other cases involving "special circumstances," the trial judge retains discretion as to the form and number of questions on the subject, including the decision whether to question the venire individually or collectively. Also, a defendant cannot complain of a judge's failure to question the venire on racial prejudice unless the defendant has specifically requested such an inquiry.

IV

The inadequacy of *voir dire* in this case requires that petitioner's death sentence be vacated. It is not necessary, however, that he be retried on the issue of guilt. Our judgment in this case is that there was an unacceptable risk of racial prejudice infecting the capital sentencing proceeding. This judgment is based on a conjunction of three factors: the fact that the crime charged involved interracial violence, the broad discretion given the jury at the death-penalty hearing, and the special seriousness of the risk of improper sentencing in a capital case. At the guilt phase of petitioner's trial, the jury had no greater discretion than it would have had if the crime charged had been noncapital murder. Thus, with respect to the guilt phase of petitioner's trial, we find this case to be indistinguishable from *Ristaino*, to which we continue to adhere.[12]

The judgment of the Court of Appeals is reversed, and the case is remanded for further proceedings consistent with this opinion.

Justice MARSHALL, with whom Justice Brennan joins, concurring in the judgment in part and dissenting in part.

For the reasons stated in my opinion in *Ross v. Massachusetts*, 414 U.S. 1080 (1973) (dissenting from denial of certiorari), I believe that a criminal defendant is entitled to inquire on *voir dire* about the potential racial bias of jurors whenever the case involves a violent interracial crime. As the Court concedes, "it is plain that there is some risk of

---

12. Justice Brennan incorrectly reads into our opinion a suggestion that "the constitutional entitlement to an impartial jury attaches only at the sentencing phase." The real question is not whether there is a constitutional right to an impartial jury throughout a criminal trial, but what prophylactic rules the Constitution imposes on the States in furtherance of that right. What we held in *Ristaino*, and reaffirm today, is that absent "special circumstances" that create a particularly compelling need to inquire into racial prejudice, the Constitution leaves the conduct of *voir dire* to the sound discretion of state trial judges.

The implication of Justice Brennan's opinion is that every crime of interracial violence is a "special circumstance." Over Justice Brennan's dissent, however, *Ristaino* squarely rejected this approach. Moreover, we are unpersuaded by Justice Brennan's view that "the opportunity for racial bias to taint the jury process is ... equally a factor at the guilt [and sentencing] phase[s] of a bifurcated capital trial." As we see it, the risk of racial bias at sentencing hearings is of an entirely different order, because the decisions that sentencing jurors must make involve far more subjective judgments than when they are deciding guilt or innocence.

racial prejudice influencing a jury whenever there is a crime involving interracial violence." To my mind that risk plainly outweighs the slight cost of allowing the defendant
to choose whether to make an inquiry concerning such possible prejudice. This Court
did not identify in *Ristaino v. Ross*, nor does it identify today, any additional burdens
that would accompany such a rule. I therefore cannot agree with the Court's continuing
rejection of the simple prophylactic rule proposed in *Ristaino*.

Even if I agreed with the Court that a *per se* rule permitting inquiry into racial bias is
appropriate only in capital cases, I could not accept the Court's failure to remedy the
denial of such inquiry in this capital case by reversing petitioner's conviction. Henceforth any capital defendant accused of an interracial crime may inquire into racial prejudice on *voir dire*. When, as here, the same jury sits at the guilt phase and the penalty
phase, these defendants will be assured an impartial jury at both phases. Yet petitioner
is forced to accept a conviction by what may have been a biased jury. This is an incongruous and fundamentally unfair result. I therefore concur only in the Court's judgment vacating petitioner's sentence, and dissent from the Court's refusal to reverse the
conviction as well.

E. Race-Based Peremptory Challenges

In general, an attorney may exercise a peremptory challenge to strike a juror from
the jury panel for any legitimate reason. However, what happens when the prosecutor,
or defense counsel, uses a peremptory challenge to strike a juror from the jury panel because of the juror's race?

Batson v. Kentucky
476 U.S. 79 (1986)

Justice POWELL delivered the opinion of the Court.

This case requires us to reexamine that portion of *Swain v. Alabama*, 380 U.S. 202
(1965), concerning the evidentiary burden placed on a criminal defendant who claims
that he has been denied equal protection through the State's use of peremptory challenges to exclude members of his race from the petit jury.

I

Petitioner James Kirkland Batson, a black man, was indicted in Kentucky on charges
of second-degree burglary and receipt of stolen goods. On the first day of trial in Jefferson Circuit Court, the judge conducted *voir dire* examination of the venire, excused certain jurors for cause, and permitted the parties to exercise peremptory challenges. The
prosecutor used his peremptory challenges to strike all four black persons on the venire,
and a jury composed only of white persons was selected. Defense counsel moved to discharge the jury before it was sworn on the ground that the prosecutor's removal of the
black veniremen violated petitioner's rights under the Sixth and Fourteenth Amendments to a jury drawn from a cross section of the community, and under the Fourteenth Amendment to equal protection of the laws. Counsel requested a hearing on his
motion. Without expressly ruling on the request for a hearing, the trial judge observed
that the parties were entitled to use their peremptory challenges to "strike anybody they

want to." The judge then denied petitioner's motion, reasoning that the cross-section requirement applies only to selection of the venire and not to selection of the petit jury itself....

II

A

More than a century ago, the Court decided that the State denies a black defendant equal protection of the laws when it puts him on trial before a jury from which members of his race have been purposefully excluded. *Strauder v. West Virginia*, 100 U.S. 303 (1880). That decision laid the foundation for the Court's unceasing efforts to eradicate racial discrimination in the procedures used to select the venire from which individual jurors are drawn. In *Strauder*, the Court explained that the central concern of the recently ratified Fourteenth Amendment was to put an end to governmental discrimination on account of race. Exclusion of black citizens from service as jurors constitutes a primary example of the evil the Fourteenth Amendment was designed to cure.

In holding that racial discrimination in jury selection offends the Equal Protection Clause, the Court in *Strauder* recognized, however, that a defendant has no right to a "petit jury composed in whole or in part of persons of his own race." "The number of our races and nationalities stands in the way of evolution of such a conception" of the demand of equal protection. *Akins v. Texas*, 325 U.S. 398, 403 (1945). But the defendant does have the right to be tried by a jury whose members are selected pursuant to nondiscriminatory criteria. The Equal Protection Clause guarantees the defendant that the State will not exclude members of his race from the jury venire on account of race, or on the false assumption that members of his race as a group are not qualified to serve as jurors.

Purposeful racial discrimination in selection of the venire violates a defendant's right to equal protection because it denies him the protection that a trial by jury is intended to secure. "The very idea of a jury is a body ... composed of the peers or equals of the person whose rights it is selected or summoned to determine; that is, of his neighbors, fellows, associates, persons having the same legal status in society as that which he holds." The petit jury has occupied a central position in our system of justice by safeguarding a person accused of crime against the arbitrary exercise of power by prosecutor or judge. Those on the venire must be "indifferently chosen," to secure the defendant's right under the Fourteenth Amendment to "protection of life and liberty against race or color prejudice."

Racial discrimination in selection of jurors harms not only the accused whose life or liberty they are summoned to try. Competence to serve as a juror ultimately depends on an assessment of individual qualifications and ability impartially to consider evidence presented at a trial. A person's race simply "is unrelated to his fitness as a juror." As long ago as *Strauder*, therefore, the Court recognized that by denying a person participation in jury service on account of his race, the State unconstitutionally discriminated against the excluded juror.

The harm from discriminatory jury selection extends beyond that inflicted on the defendant and the excluded juror to touch the entire community. Selection procedures that purposefully exclude black persons from juries undermine public confidence in the fairness of our system of justice. Discrimination within the judicial system is most pernicious because it is "a stimulant to that race prejudice which is an impediment to securing to [black citizens] that equal justice which the law aims to secure to all others."

B

In *Strauder*, the Court invalidated a state statute that provided that only white men could serve as jurors. We can be confident that no State now has such a law. The Constitution requires, however, that we look beyond the face of the statute defining juror qualifications and also consider challenged selection practices to afford "protection against action of the State through its administrative officers in effecting the prohibited discrimination." Thus, the Court has found a denial of equal protection where the procedures implementing a neutral statute operated to exclude persons from the venire on racial grounds, and has made clear that the Constitution prohibits all forms of purposeful racial discrimination in selection of jurors. While decisions of this Court have been concerned largely with discrimination during selection of the venire, the principles announced there also forbid discrimination on account of race in selection of the petit jury. Since the Fourteenth Amendment protects an accused throughout the proceedings bringing him to justice, the State may not draw up its jury lists pursuant to neutral procedures but then resort to discrimination at "other stages in the selection process."

Accordingly, the component of the jury selection process at issue here, the State's privilege to strike individual jurors through peremptory challenges, is subject to the commands of the Equal Protection Clause.[12] Although a prosecutor ordinarily is entitled to exercise permitted peremptory challenges "for any reason at all, as long as that reason is related to his view concerning the outcome" of the case to be tried, the Equal Protection Clause forbids the prosecutor to challenge potential jurors solely on account of their race or on the assumption that black jurors as a group will be unable impartially to consider the State's case against a black defendant.

III

The principles announced in *Strauder* never have been questioned in any subsequent decision of this Court. Rather, the Court has been called upon repeatedly to review the application of those principles to particular facts. A recurring question in these cases, as in any case alleging a violation of the Equal Protection Clause, was whether the defendant had met his burden of proving purposeful discrimination on the part of the State. That question also was at the heart of the portion of *Swain v. Alabama* we reexamine today.

A

Swain required the Court to decide, among other issues, whether a black defendant was denied equal protection by the State's exercise of peremptory challenges to exclude

---

12. We express no views on whether the Constitution imposes any limit on the exercise of peremptory challenges by defense counsel. Nor do we express any views on the techniques used by lawyers who seek to obtain information about the community in which a case is to be tried, and about members of the venire from which the jury is likely to be drawn. Prior to *voir dire* examination, which serves as the basis for exercise of challenges, lawyers wish to know as much as possible about prospective jurors, including their age, education, employment, and economic status, so that they can ensure selection of jurors who at least have an open mind about the case. In some jurisdictions, where a pool of jurors serves for a substantial period of time, counsel also may seek to learn which members of the pool served on juries in other cases and the outcome of those cases. Counsel even may employ professional investigators to interview persons who have served on a particular petit jury.

We have had no occasion to consider particularly this practice. Of course, counsel's effort to obtain possibly relevant information about prospective jurors is to be distinguished from the practice at issue here.

members of his race from the petit jury. The record in *Swain* showed that the prosecutor had used the State's peremptory challenges to strike the six black persons included on the petit jury venire. While rejecting the defendant's claim for failure to prove purposeful discrimination, the Court nonetheless indicated that the Equal Protection Clause placed some limits on the State's exercise of peremptory challenges.

The Court sought to accommodate the prosecutor's historical privilege of peremptory challenge free of judicial control, and the constitutional prohibition on exclusion of persons from jury service on account of race. While the Constitution does not confer a right to peremptory challenges, those challenges traditionally have been viewed as one means of assuring the selection of a qualified and unbiased jury. To preserve the peremptory nature of the prosecutor's challenge, the Court in *Swain* declined to scrutinize his actions in a particular case by relying on a presumption that he properly exercised the State's challenges.

The Court went on to observe, however, that a State may not exercise its challenges in contravention of the Equal Protection Clause. It was impermissible for a prosecutor to use his challenges to exclude blacks from the jury "for reasons wholly unrelated to the outcome of the particular case on trial" or to deny to blacks "the same right and opportunity to participate in the administration of justice enjoyed by the white population." Accordingly, a black defendant could make out a *prima facie* case of purposeful discrimination on proof that the peremptory challenge system was "being perverted" in that manner. For example, an inference of purposeful discrimination would be raised on evidence that a prosecutor, "in case after case, whatever the circumstances, whatever the crime and whoever the defendant or the victim may be, is responsible for the removal of Negroes who have been selected as qualified jurors by the jury commissioners and who have survived challenges for cause, with the result that no Negroes ever serve on petit juries." Evidence offered by the defendant in *Swain* did not meet that standard. While the defendant showed that prosecutors in the jurisdiction had exercised their strikes to exclude blacks from the jury, he offered no proof of the circumstances under which prosecutors were responsible for striking black jurors beyond the facts of his own case.

A number of lower courts following the teaching of *Swain* reasoned that proof of repeated striking of blacks over a number of cases was necessary to establish a violation of the Equal Protection Clause. Since this interpretation of *Swain* has placed on defendants a crippling burden of proof, prosecutors' peremptory challenges are now largely immune from constitutional scrutiny. For reasons that follow, we reject this evidentiary formulation as inconsistent with standards that have been developed since *Swain* for assessing a *prima facie* case under the Equal Protection Clause.

B

Since the decision in *Swain*, we have explained that our cases concerning selection of the venire reflect the general equal protection principle that the "invidious quality" of governmental action claimed to be racially discriminatory "must ultimately be traced to a racially discriminatory purpose." As in any equal protection case, the "burden is, of course," on the defendant who alleges discriminatory selection of the venire "to prove the existence of purposeful discrimination." In deciding if the defendant has carried his burden of persuasion, a court must undertake "a sensitive inquiry into such circumstantial and direct evidence of intent as may be available." Circumstantial evidence of invidious intent may include proof of disproportionate impact. We have observed that under some circumstances proof of discriminatory impact "may for all practical purposes demonstrate unconstitutionality because in various circumstances the discrimination is very difficult to explain on nonracial grounds." For example, "total or seriously disproportionate exclusion of Negroes from jury venires" "is itself such an 'unequal application of the law … as to show intentional discrimination.'"

Moreover, since *Swain*, we have recognized that a black defendant alleging that members of his race have been impermissibly excluded from the venire may make out a *prima facie* case of purposeful discrimination by showing that the totality of the relevant facts gives rise to an inference of discriminatory purpose. Once the defendant makes the requisite showing, the burden shifts to the State to explain adequately the racial exclusion. The State cannot meet this burden on mere general assertions that its officials did not discriminate or that they properly performed their official duties. Rather, the State must demonstrate that "permissible racially neutral selection criteria and procedures have produced the monochromatic result."

The showing necessary to establish a *prima facie* case of purposeful discrimination in selection of the venire may be discerned in this Court's decisions. The defendant initially must show that he is a member of a racial group capable of being singled out for differential treatment. In combination with that evidence, a defendant may then make a *prima facie* case by proving that in the particular jurisdiction members of his race have not been summoned for jury service over an extended period of time. Proof of systematic exclusion from the venire raises an inference of purposeful discrimination because the "result bespeaks discrimination."

Since the ultimate issue is whether the State has discriminated in selecting the defendant's venire, however, the defendant may establish a *prima facie* case "in other ways than by evidence of long-continued unexplained absence" of members of his race "from many panels." In cases involving the venire, this Court has found a *prima facie* case on proof that members of the defendant's race were substantially underrepresented on the venire from which his jury was drawn, and that the venire was selected under a practice providing "the opportunity for discrimination." This combination of factors raises the necessary inference of purposeful discrimination because the Court has declined to attribute to chance the absence of black citizens on a particular jury array where the selection mechanism is subject to abuse. When circumstances suggest the need, the trial court must undertake a "factual inquiry" that "takes into account all possible explanatory factors" in the particular case.

Thus, since the decision in *Swain*, this Court has recognized that a defendant may make a *prima facie* showing of purposeful racial discrimination in selection of the venire by relying solely on the facts concerning its selection in his case. These decisions are in accordance with the proposition, articulated in *Arlington Heights v. Metropolitan Housing Department Corp.*, 429 U.S. 252 (1977), that "a consistent pattern of official racial discrimination" is not "a necessary predicate to a violation of the Equal Protection Clause. A single invidiously discriminatory governmental act" is not "immunized by the absence of such discrimination in the making of other comparable decisions." For evidentiary requirements to dictate that "several must suffer discrimination" before one could object would be inconsistent with the promise of equal protection to all.

C

The standards for assessing a *prima facie* case in the context of discriminatory selection of the venire have been fully articulated since *Swain*. These principles support our conclusion that a defendant may establish a *prima facie* case of purposeful discrimination in selection of the petit jury solely on evidence concerning the prosecutor's exercise of peremptory challenges at the defendant's trial. To establish such a case, the defendant first must show that he is a member of a cognizable racial group, and that the prosecutor has exercised peremptory challenges to remove from the venire members of the defendant's race. Second, the defendant is entitled to rely on the fact, as to which there can be no dispute, that peremptory challenges constitute a jury selection practice that permits "those to discriminate who are of a mind to discriminate." Finally, the defendant must show that these facts and any other relevant circumstances raise an inference that the prosecutor used that practice to exclude the veniremen from the petit jury on account of their race. This combination of factors in the empaneling of the petit jury, as in the selection of the venire, raises the necessary inference of purposeful discrimination.

In deciding whether the defendant has made the requisite showing, the trial court should consider all relevant circumstances. For example, a "pattern" of strikes against black jurors included in the particular venire might give rise to an inference of discrimination. Similarly, the prosecutor's questions and statements during *voir dire* examination and in exercising his challenges may support or refute an inference of discriminatory purpose. These examples are merely illustrative. We have confidence that trial judges, experienced in supervising *voir dire*, will be able to decide if the circumstances concerning the prosecutor's use of peremptory challenges creates a *prima facie* case of discrimination against black jurors.

Once the defendant makes a *prima facie* showing, the burden shifts to the State to come forward with a neutral explanation for challenging black jurors. Though this requirement imposes a limitation in some cases on the full peremptory character of the historic challenge, we emphasize that the prosecutor's explanation need not rise to the level justifying exercise of a challenge for cause. But the prosecutor may not rebut the defendant's *prima facie* case of discrimination by stating merely that he challenged jurors of the defendant's race on the assumption — or his intuitive judgment — that they would be partial to the defendant because of their shared race. Just as the Equal Protection Clause forbids the States to exclude black persons from the venire on the assumption that blacks as a group are unqualified to serve as jurors, so it forbids the States to strike black veniremen on the assumption that they will be biased in a particular case simply because the defendant is black. The core guarantee of equal protection, ensuring citizens that their State will not discriminate on account of race, would be meaningless were we to approve the exclusion of jurors on the basis of such assumptions, which arise solely from the jurors' race. Nor may the prosecutor rebut the defendant's case merely by denying that he had a discriminatory motive or "affirm[ing] [his] good faith in making individual selections." If these general assertions were accepted as rebutting a defendant's *prima facie* case, the Equal Protection Clause "would be but a vain and illusory requirement." The prosecutor therefore must articulate a neutral explanation related to the particular case to be tried. The trial court then will have the duty to determine if the defendant has established purposeful discrimination....

V

In this case, petitioner made a timely objection to the prosecutor's removal of all black persons on the venire. Because the trial court flatly rejected the objection without requiring the prosecutor to give an explanation for his action, we remand this case for further proceedings. If the trial court decides that the facts establish, *prima facie*, purposeful discrimination and the prosecutor does not come forward with a neutral explanation for his action, our precedents require that petitioner's conviction be reversed.[25]

---

25. To the extent that anything in *Swain v. Alabama* is contrary to the principles we articulate today, that decision is overruled.

Notes and Questions

1. Justice Rehnquist dissented in *Batson* and criticized the Court's willingness to intrude upon "the historic scope of peremptory challenges." In contrast, Justice Marshall, in his concurrence, opined, "The inherent potential of peremptory challenges to distort the jury process by permitting the exclusion of jurors on racial grounds should ideally lead the Court to ban them entirely from the criminal justice system."

2. Under *Batson*, once the defendant establishes a *prima facie* case showing race was a factor in a prosecutor's decision to exercise a peremptory challenge, the burden shifts to the prosecutor to come forward with a neutral, legitimate explanation to justify his striking of the juror. An explanation which is mere pretext and not legitimate will not be adequate to meet the prosecutor's burden of proof.

How would you evaluate the following actions by a prosecutor? In a capital murder trial, the prosecutor struck ten African-American jurors from the jury. The prosecutor justified striking the first two black men on the jury panel on the ground that the jurors were dressed inappropriately. One juror wore gray dress slacks, a white shirt and a knit tie. The prosecutor noted the juror was also wearing maroon socks and "pointy New York shoes." The other juror was not wearing a suit or tie. After striking these two jurors, the prosecutor allowed a white male, who was wearing an open collared shirt and a black leather jacket, to remain on the panel. The prosecutor then struck two black jurors who initially expressed reservations about imposing the death penalty. Both of these jurors later stated that they would follow the law and recommend the death sentence if warranted. The prosecutor also struck a thirty-year-old black woman from the panel on the ground that she was single and unemployed. An unemployed white female remained on the jury panel. The prosecutor excused three other black jurors on the grounds that they were single, but did not challenge five white jurors who were single. The prosecutor struck the ninth black juror because she was a woman and he preferred a predominantly male jury. The prosecutor did not challenge thirteen white women in the jury pool and eventually six of these women served on the defendant's jury. Finally, the prosecutor struck a tenth black juror because of her felony arrest record. Are all of these challenges sufficiently race-neutral and legitimate? Would you characterize any of the prosecutor's explanations as mere pretext? What factors would you consider in determining whether the prosecutor's challenges were legitimate or merely a sham? See *Roundtree v. State*, 546 So.2d 1042 (Fla. 1989). In analyzing the challenges described above, the Florida court in *Roundtree* found that the first nine challenges were not race-neutral and concluded that the prosecutor's explanations were mere pretext. The court reversed the defendant's conviction and sentence of death.

3. May a white defendant complain when the prosecutor excludes black or other minority jurors from the venire? In *Powers v. Ohio*, 499 U.S. 400 (1991), the Supreme Court concluded that a white defendant suffers a "cognizable injury" when the prosecutor excludes black jurors on account of race "because racial discrimination in the selection of jurors 'casts doubt on the integrity of the judicial process,' and places the fairness of a criminal proceeding in doubt." The Court also found that the exclusion of black jurors for racially motivated reasons harms the individual jurors and the jury system as a whole. The Court reasoned that "[t]o bar petitioner's claim because his race differs from that of the excluded jurors would be to condone the arbitrary exclusion of citizens from the duty, honor, and privilege of jury service." The Court thus held that a white defendant had standing to object to the prosecutor's peremptory challenges to black or other minority jurors. In so holding, the *Powers* Court stated:

The emphasis in *Batson* on racial identity between the defendant and the excused prospective juror is not inconsistent with our holding today that race is irrelevant to a defendant's standing to object to the discriminatory use of peremptory challenges. Racial identity between the defendant and the excused person might in some cases be the explanation for the prosecution's adoption of the forbidden stereotype, and if the alleged race bias takes this form, it may provide one of the easier cases to establish both a *prima facie* case and a conclusive showing that wrongful discrimination has occurred. But to say that the race of the defendant may be relevant to discerning bias in some cases does not mean that it will be a factor in others, for race prejudice stems from various causes and may manifest itself in different forms.

499 U.S. at 416.

4. Finding that there was "a conscious strategy to exclude" black jurors, a Pennsylvania judge overturned the capital conviction of William Basemore in 2001. At Basemore's trial, the prosecutor eliminated 19 potential jurors, all of whom were black. The same prosecutor, Jack McMahon, had been videotaped in the 1980s instructing a group of young prosecutors on how to exclude certain types of black jurors from jury service. Associated Press, Dec. 20, 2001.

Georgia v. McCollum
505 U.S. 42 (1992)

Justice BLACKMUN delivered the opinion of the Court.

For more than a century, this Court consistently and repeatedly has reaffirmed that racial discrimination by the State in jury selection offends the Equal Protection Clause. Last Term this Court held that racial discrimination in a civil litigant's exercise of peremptory challenges also violates the Equal Protection Clause. See *Edmonson v. Leesville Concrete Co.*, 500 U.S. 614 (1991). Today, we are asked to decide whether the Constitution prohibits a criminal defendant from engaging in purposeful racial discrimination in the exercise of peremptory challenges.

I

On August 10, 1990, a grand jury sitting in Dougherty County, Ga., returned a six-count indictment charging respondents with aggravated assault and simple battery. The indictment alleged that respondents beat and assaulted Jerry and Myra Collins. Respondents are white; the alleged victims are African-Americans. Shortly after the events, a leaflet was widely distributed in the local African-American community reporting the assault and urging community residents not to patronize respondents' business.

Before jury selection began, the prosecution moved to prohibit respondents from exercising peremptory challenges in a racially discriminatory manner. The State explained that it expected to show that the victims' race was a factor in the alleged assault. According to the State, counsel for respondents had indicated a clear intention to use peremptory strikes in a racially discriminatory manner, arguing that the circumstances of their case gave them the right to exclude African-American citizens from participating as jurors in the trial. Observing that 43 percent of the county's population is African-American, the State contended that, if a statistically representative panel is assembled for jury selection, 18 of the potential 42 jurors would be African-American. With 20 peremptory challenges, respondents therefore would be able to remove all the African-American potential jurors. Relying on *Batson v. Kentucky*, the Sixth Amendment, and the Georgia Constitution, the State sought an order providing that, if it succeeded in making out a *prima facie* case of racial discrimination by respondents, the latter would be required to articulate a racially neutral explanation for peremptory challenges.

The trial judge denied the State's motion, holding that "[n]either Georgia nor federal law prohibits criminal defendants from exercising peremptory strikes in a racially discriminatory manner." The issue was certified for immediate appeal.

The Supreme Court of Georgia, by a 4–3 vote, affirmed the trial court's ruling. The court acknowledged that in *Edmonson v. Leesville Concrete Co.*, this Court had found that the exercise of a peremptory challenge in a racially discriminatory manner "would constitute an impermissible injury" to the excluded juror. The court noted, however, that *Edmonson* involved private civil litigants, not criminal defendants. "Bearing in mind the long history of jury trials as an essential element of the protection of human rights," the court "decline[d] to diminish the free exercise of peremptory strikes by a criminal defendant." Three justices dissented, arguing that *Edmonson* and other decisions of this Court establish that racially based peremptory challenges by a criminal defendant violate the Constitution. A motion for reconsideration was denied.

We granted certiorari to resolve a question left open by our prior cases—whether the Constitution prohibits a criminal defendant from engaging in purposeful racial discrimination in the exercise of peremptory challenges.

II

… Last term this Court applied the *Batson v. Kentucky* framework in two other contexts. In *Powers v. Ohio*, it held that in the trial of a white criminal defendant, a prosecutor is prohibited from excluding African-American jurors on the basis of race. In *Edmonson v. Leesville Concrete Co.*, the Court decided that in a civil case, private litigants cannot exercise their peremptory strikes in a racially discriminatory manner.

In deciding whether the Constitution prohibits criminal defendants from exercising racially discriminatory peremptory challenges, we must answer four questions. First, whether a criminal defendant's exercise of peremptory challenges in a racially discriminatory manner inflicts the harms addressed by *Batson*. Second, whether the exercise of peremptory challenges by a criminal defendant constitutes state action. Third, whether prosecutors have standing to raise this constitutional challenge. And fourth, whether the constitutional rights of a criminal defendant nonetheless preclude the extension of our precedents to this case.

The majority in *Powers* recognized that "*Batson* was designed to serve multiple ends, only one of which was to protect individual defendants from discrimination in the selection of jurors." As in *Powers* and *Edmonson*, the extension of *Batson* in this context is designed to remedy the harm done to the "dignity of persons" and to the "integrity of the courts."

III

A

… One of the goals of our jury system is "to impress upon the criminal defendant and the community as a whole that a verdict of conviction or acquittal is given in accordance with the law by persons who are fair." Selection procedures that purposefully exclude African-Americans from juries undermine that public confidence—as well they should. "The overt wrong, often apparent to the entire jury panel, casts doubt over the obligation of the parties, the jury, and indeed the court to adhere to the law throughout the trial of the cause."

The need for public confidence is especially high in cases involving race-related crimes. In such cases, emotions in the affected community will inevitably be heated and volatile. Public confidence in the integrity of the criminal justice system is essential for preserving community peace in trials involving race-related crimes.

Be it at the hands of the State or the defense, if a court allows jurors to be excluded because of group bias, it is a willing participant in a scheme that could only undermine the very foundation of our system of justice—our citizens' confidence in it. Just as public confidence in criminal justice is undermined by a conviction in a trial where racial discrimination has occurred in jury selection, so is public confidence undermined where a defendant, assisted by racially discriminatory peremptory strikes, obtains an acquittal.

The fact that a defendant's use of discriminatory peremptory challenges harms the jurors and the community does not end our equal protection inquiry. Racial discrimination, although repugnant in all contexts, violates the Constitution only when it is attributable to state action. Thus, the second question that must be answered is whether a criminal defendant's exercise of a peremptory challenge constitutes state action for purposes of the Equal Protection Clause....

B

... The exercise of a peremptory challenge differs significantly from other actions taken in support of a defendant's defense. In exercising a peremptory challenge, a criminal defendant is wielding the power to choose a quintessential governmental body—indeed, the institution of government on which our judicial system depends. Thus, as we held in *Edmonson*, when "a government confers on a private body the power to choose the government's employees or officials, the private body will be bound by the constitutional mandate of race neutrality."

Lastly, the fact that a defendant exercises a peremptory challenge to further his interest in acquittal does not conflict with a finding of state action. Whenever a private actor's conduct is deemed "fairly attributable" to the government, it is likely that private motives will have animated the actor's decision. Indeed, in *Edmonson*, the Court recognized that the private party's exercise of peremptory challenges constituted state action, even though the motive underlying the exercise of the peremptory challenge may be to protect a private interest.

C

Having held that a defendant's discriminatory exercise of a peremptory challenge is a violation of equal protection, we move to the question whether the State has standing to challenge a defendant's discriminatory use of peremptory challenges. In *Powers*, this Court held that a white criminal defendant has standing to raise the equal protection rights of black jurors wrongfully excluded from jury service. While third-party standing is a limited exception, the *Powers* Court recognized that a litigant may raise a claim on behalf of a third party if the litigant can demonstrate that he has suffered a concrete injury, that he has a close relation to the third party, and that there exists some hindrance to the third party's ability to protect its own interests. In *Edmonson*, the Court applied the same analysis in deciding that civil litigants had standing to raise the equal protection rights of jurors excluded on the basis of their race.

... The State's relation to potential jurors in this case is closer than the relationships approved in *Powers* and *Edmonson*. As the representative of all its citizens, the State is the logical and proper party to assert the invasion of the constitutional rights of the excluded jurors in a criminal trial. Indeed, the Fourteenth Amendment forbids the State from denying persons within its jurisdiction the equal protection of the laws.

... [T]he *Powers* Court recognized that, although individuals excluded from jury service on the basis of race have a right to bring suit on their own behalf, the "barriers to a suit by an excluded juror are daunting." The barriers are no less formidable in this context. Accordingly, we hold that the State has standing to assert the excluded jurors' rights.

D

The final question is whether the interests served by *Batson* must give way to the rights of a criminal defendant. As a preliminary matter, it is important to recall that peremptory challenges are not constitutionally protected fundamental rights; rather, they are but one state-created means to the constitutional end of an impartial jury and a fair trial. This Court repeatedly has stated that the right to a peremptory challenge may be withheld altogether without impairing the constitutional guarantee of an impartial jury and a fair trial.

Yet in *Swain*, the Court reviewed the "very old credentials" of the peremptory challenge and noted the "long and widely held belief that the peremptory challenge is a necessary part of trial by jury." This Court likewise has recognized that "the role of litigants in determining the jury's composition provides one reason for wide acceptance of the jury system and of its verdicts."

We do not believe that this decision will undermine the contribution of the peremptory challenge to the administration of justice. Nonetheless, "if race stereotypes are the price for acceptance of a jury panel as fair," we reaffirm today that such a "price is too high to meet the standard of the Constitution." Defense counsel is limited to "legitimate, lawful conduct." It is an affront to justice to argue that a fair trial includes the right to discriminate against a group of citizens based upon their race.

Nor does a prohibition of the exercise of discriminatory peremptory challenges violate a defendant's Sixth Amendment right to the effective assistance of counsel. Counsel can ordinarily explain the reasons for peremptory challenges without revealing anything about trial strategy or any confidential client communications. In the rare case in which the explanation for a challenge would entail confidential communications or reveal trial strategy, an *in camera* discussion can be arranged. In any event, neither the Sixth Amendment right nor the attorney-client privilege gives a criminal defendant the right to carry out through counsel an unlawful course of conduct.

Lastly, a prohibition of the discriminatory exercise of peremptory challenges does not violate a defendant's Sixth Amendment right to a trial by an impartial jury. The goal of the Sixth Amendment is "jury impartiality with respect to both contestants."

We recognize, of course, that a defendant has the right to an impartial jury that can view him without racial animus, which so long has distorted our system of criminal justice. We have, accordingly, held that there should be a mechanism for removing those on the venire whom the defendant has specific reason to believe would be incapable of confronting and suppressing their racism.

But there is a distinction between exercising a peremptory challenge to discriminate invidiously against jurors on account of race and exercising a peremptory challenge to remove an individual juror who harbors racial prejudice. This Court firmly has rejected the view that assumptions of partiality based on race provide a legitimate basis for disqualifying a person as an impartial juror. As this Court stated just last Term in *Powers*, "[w]e may not accept as a defense to racial discrimination the very stereotype the law condemns." "In our heterogeneous society policy as well as constitutional considerations militate against the divisive assumption — as a *per se* rule — that justice in a court of law may turn upon the pigmentation of skin, the accident of birth, or the choice of religion." We therefore reaffirm today that the exercise of a peremptory challenge must not be based on either the race of the juror or the racial stereotypes held by the party.

IV

We hold that the Constitution prohibits a criminal defendant from engaging in purposeful discrimination on the ground of race in the exercise of peremptory challenges. Accordingly, if the State demonstrates a *prima facie* case of racial discrimination by the defendants, the defendants must articulate a racially neutral explanation for peremptory challenges. The judgment of the Supreme Court of Georgia is reversed and the case is remanded for further proceedings not inconsistent with this opinion. It is so ordered.

Justice O'CONNOR, dissenting.

II

What really seems to bother the Court is the prospect that leaving criminal defendants and their attorneys free to make racially motivated peremptory challenges will undermine the ideal of nondiscriminatory jury selection we espoused in *Batson*. The concept that the government alone must honor constitutional dictates, however, is a fundamental tenet of our legal order, not an obstacle to be circumvented. This is particularly so in the context of criminal trials, where we have held the prosecution to uniquely high standards of conduct.

Considered in purely pragmatic terms, moreover, the Court's holding may fail to advance nondiscriminatory criminal justice. It is by now clear that conscious and unconscious racism can affect the way white jurors perceive minority defendants and the facts presented at their trials, perhaps determining the verdict of guilt or innocence. Using peremptory challenges to secure minority representation on the jury may help to overcome such racial bias, for there is substantial reason to believe that the distorting influence of race is minimized on a racially mixed jury.

As *amicus* NAACP Legal Defense and Educational Fund explained in this case:

> The ability to use peremptory challenges to exclude majority race jurors may be crucial to empaneling a fair jury. In many cases an African-American, or other minority defendant, may be faced with a jury array in which his racial group is underrepresented to some degree, but not sufficiently to permit challenge under the Fourteenth Amendment. The only possible chance the defendant may have of having any minority jurors on the jury that actually tries him will be if he uses his peremptories to strike members of the majority race.

In a world where the outcome of a minority defendant's trial may turn on the misconceptions or biases of white jurors, there is cause to question the implications of this Court's good intentions.

That the Constitution does not give federal judges the reach to wipe all marks of racism from every courtroom in the land is frustrating, to be sure. But such limitations are the necessary and intended consequence of the Fourteenth Amendment's state action requirement. Because I cannot accept the Court's conclusion that government is responsible for decisions criminal defendants make while fighting state prosecution, I respectfully dissent.

Justice SCALIA, dissenting.

I agree with the Court that its judgment follows logically from *Edmonson v. Leesville Concrete Co., Inc.* [H]owever, I think that case was wrongly decided. Barely a year later, we witness its reduction to the terminally absurd: A criminal defendant, in the process of defending himself against the state, is held to be acting on behalf of the state.…

Today's decision gives the lie once again to the belief that an activist, "evolutionary" constitutional jurisprudence always evolves in the direction of greater individual rights. In the interest of promoting the supposedly greater good of race relations in the society as a whole (make no mistake that that is what underlies all this), we use the Constitution to destroy the ages-old right of criminal defendants to exercise peremptory challenges as they wish, to secure a jury that they consider fair. I dissent.

Note on Defendant's Burden of Proof When Raising Batson Objection: Johnson v. California, 545 U.S. 162 (2005)

In *Johnson v. California*, 545 U.S. 162, 125 S.Ct. 2410 (2005), the Supreme Court in an 8–1 decision clarified the first step of the *Batson* analysis in which the defendant must make a prima facie case of racial discrimination in the use of a peremptory challenge. The Court rejected California's rule that to make a *prima facie* case of discrimination, the defendant must persuade the trier of fact that it is more likely than not that the peremptory strike was based on a discriminatory purpose. Writing for the majority, Justice Stevens stated:

II

The question before us is whether *Batson* permits California to require at step one that "the objector must show that it is more likely than not the other party's peremptory challenges, if unexplained, were based on impermissible group bias." Although we recognize that States do have flexibility in formulating appropriate procedures to comply with *Batson*, we conclude that California's "more likely than not" standard is an inappropriate yardstick by which to measure the sufficiency of a prima facie case.…

Thus, in describing the burden-shifting framework, we assumed in Batson that the trial judge would have the benefit of all relevant circumstances, including the prosecutor's explanation, before deciding whether it was more likely than not that the challenge was improperly motivated. We did not intend the first step to be so onerous that a defendant would have to persuade the judge— on the basis of all the facts, some of which are impossible for the defendant to know with certainty—that the challenge was more likely than not the product of purposeful discrimination. Instead, a defendant satisfies the requirements of *Batson* 's first step by producing evidence sufficient to permit the trial judge to draw an inference that discrimination has occurred.

125 S.Ct. 2410, at 2417.

In dissent, Justice Thomas wrote:

Because *Batson's* burden-shifting approach is "a prophylactic framework" that polices racially discriminatory jury selection rather than "an independent constitutional command," States have "wide discretion, subject to the minimum requirements of the Fourteenth Amendment, to experiment with solutions to difficult problems of policy." California's procedure falls comfortably within its broad discretion to craft its own rules of criminal procedure, and I therefore respectfully dissent.

125 S.Ct. 2410, at 2419.

Note on Miller-El v. Dretke, 545 U.S. 231 (2005)

Chapter 4 lays out some of the arguments of racial discrimination in jury selection raised in *Miller-el v. Dretke*, and chapter 13 addresses the habeas corpus issues in *Miller-El*. Reprinted below is the *Batson* discussion in *Miller-El*. Pay particular attention to the Court's description of the prosecution's use of peremptory strikes against African-American veniremen.

Miller-El v. Dretke

545 U.S. 231 (2005)

Justice SOUTER delivered the opinion of the Court.

I

In the course of robbing a Holiday Inn in Dallas, Texas in late 1985, Miller-El and his accomplices bound and gagged two hotel employees, whom Miller-El then shot, killing one and severely injuring the other. During jury selection in Miller-El's trial for capital murder, prosecutors used peremptory strikes against 10 qualified black venire members. Miller-El objected that the strikes were based on race and could not be presumed legitimate, given a history of excluding black members from criminal juries by the Dallas County District Attorney's Office. The trial court received evidence of the practice alleged but found no "systematic exclusion of blacks as a matter of policy" by that office, and therefore no entitlement to relief under Swain v. Alabama, 380 U.S. 202 (1965), the case then defining and marking the limits of relief from racially biased jury selection. The court denied Miller-El's request to pick a new jury, and the trial ended with his death sentence for capital murder.

While an appeal was pending, this Court decided *Batson v. Kentucky*, 476 U.S. 79 (1986), which replaced *Swain's* threshold requirement to prove systemic discrimination under a Fourteenth Amendment jury claim, with the rule that discrimination by the prosecutor in selecting the defendant's jury sufficed to establish the constitutional violation. The Texas Court of Criminal Appeals then remanded the matter to the trial court to determine whether Miller-El could show that prosecutors in his case peremptorily struck prospective black jurors because of race.

The trial court found no such demonstration. After reviewing the voir dire record of the explanations given for some of the challenged strikes, and after hearing one of the prosecutors, Paul Macaluso, give his justification for those previously unexplained, the trial court accepted the stated race-neutral reasons for the strikes, which the judge called "completely credible [and] sufficient" as the grounds for a finding of "no purposeful discrimination." The Court of Criminal Appeals affirmed, stating it found "ample support" in the voir dire record for the race-neutral explanations offered by prosecutors for the peremptory strikes.

Miller-El then sought habeas relief under 28 U.S.C. § 2254, again pressing his *Batson* claim, among others not now before us. The District Court denied relief, and the Court of Appeals for the Fifth Circuit precluded appeal by denying a certificate of appealability. We granted certiorari to consider whether Miller-El was entitled to review on the *Batson* claim, and reversed the Court of Appeals. After examining the record of Miller-El's extensive evidence of purposeful discrimination by the Dallas County District Attorney's Office before and during his trial, we found an appeal was in order, since the merits of the *Batson* claim were, at the least, debatable by jurists of reason. *Miller-El v. Cockrell*, 537 U.S. 322 (2003). After granting a certificate of appealability, the Fifth Circuit rejected Miller-El's *Batson* claim on the merits. We again granted certiorari, and again we reverse....

III

A

The numbers describing the [Miller-El] prosecution's use of peremptories are remarkable. Out of 20 black members of the 108-person venire panel for Miller-El's trial, only 1 served. Although 9 were excused for cause or by agreement, 10 were peremptorily struck by the prosecution. "The prosecutors used their peremptory strikes to exclude 91% of the eligible African-American venire members.... Happenstance is unlikely to produce this disparity."

More powerful than these bare statistics, however, are side-by-side comparisons of some black venire panelists who were struck and white panelists allowed to serve. If a prosecutor's proffered reason for striking a black panelist applies just as well to an otherwise-similar nonblack who is permitted to serve, that is evidence tending to prove purposeful discrimination to be considered at *Batson*'s third step. While we did not develop a comparative juror analysis last time, we did note that the prosecution's reasons for exercising peremptory strikes against some black panel members appeared equally on point as to some white jurors who served. The details of two panel member comparisons bear this out.

The prosecution used its second peremptory strike to exclude Billy Jean Fields, a black man who expressed unwavering support for the death penalty. On the questionnaire filled out by all panel members before individual examination on the stand, Fields said that he believed in capital punishment, and during questioning he disclosed his belief that the State acts on God's behalf when it imposes the death penalty. "Therefore, if the State exacts death, then that's what it should be." He testified that he had no religious or philosophical reservations about the death penalty and that the death penalty deterred crime. He twice averred, without apparent hesitation, that he could sit on Miller-El's jury and make a decision to impose this penalty.

Although at one point in the questioning, Fields indicated that the possibility of rehabilitation might be relevant to the likelihood that a defendant would commit future acts of violence, he responded to ensuing questions by saying that although he believed anyone could be rehabilitated, this belief would not stand in the way of a decision to impose the death penalty:

> "[B]ased on what you [the prosecutor] said as far as the crime goes, there are only two things that could be rendered, death or life in prison. If for some reason the testimony didn't warrant death, then life imprisonment would give an individual an opportunity to rehabilitate. But, you know, you said that the ju-

rors didn't have the opportunity to make a personal decision in the matter with reference to what I thought or felt, but it was just based on the questions according to the way the law has been handed down."

Fields also noted on his questionnaire that his brother had a criminal history. During questioning, the prosecution went into this, too:

"Q Could you tell me a little bit about that?

"A He was arrested and convicted on [a] number of occasions for possession of a controlled substance.

"Q Was that here in Dallas?

"A Yes.

"Q Was he involved in any trials or anything like that?

"A I suppose of sorts. I don't really know too much about it.

"Q Was he ever convicted?

"A Yeah, he served time.

"Q Do you feel that that would in any way interfere with your service on this jury at all?

"A No."

Fields was struck peremptorily by the prosecution, with prosecutor James Nelson offering a race-neutral reason:

"[W]e ... have concern with reference to some of his statements as to the death penalty in that he said that he could only give death if he thought a person could not be rehabilitated and he later made the comment that any person could be rehabilitated if they find God or are introduced to God and the fact that we have a concern that his religious feelings may affect his jury service in this case."

Thus, Nelson simply mischaracterized Fields's testimony. He represented that Fields said he would not vote for death if rehabilitation was possible, whereas Fields unequivocally stated that he could impose the death penalty regardless of the possibility of rehabilitation. Perhaps Nelson misunderstood, but unless he had an ulterior reason for keeping Fields off the jury we think he would have proceeded differently. In light of Fields's outspoken support for the death penalty, we expect the prosecutor would have cleared up any misunderstanding by asking further questions before getting to the point of exercising a strike.

If, indeed, Fields's thoughts on rehabilitation did make the prosecutor uneasy, he should have worried about a number of white panel members he accepted with no evident reservations. Sandra Hearn said that she believed in the death penalty "if a criminal cannot be rehabilitated and continues to commit the same type of crime." Hearn went so far as to express doubt that at the penalty phase of a capital case she could conclude that a convicted murderer "would probably commit some criminal acts of violence in the future." "People change," she said, making it hard to assess the risk of someone's future dangerousness. "[T]he evidence would have to be awful strong." But the prosecution did not respond to Hearn the way it did to Fields, and without delving into her views about rehabilitation with any further question, it raised no objection to her serving on the jury. White panelist Mary Witt said she would take the possibility of rehabilitation into account in deciding at the penalty phase of the trial about a defendant's probability of future dangerousness, but the prosecutors asked her no further question about her views on reformation, and they accepted her as a juror. Latino venireman Fernando Gutierrez, who served on the jury, said that he would consider the death penalty for someone who could not be rehabilitated, but the prosecutors did not question him further about this view. In sum, nonblack jurors whose remarks on rehabilitation could well have signaled a limit on their willingness to impose a death sentence were not questioned further and drew no objection, but the prosecution expressed apprehension about a black juror's belief in the possibility of reformation even though he repeatedly stated his approval of the death penalty and testified that he could impose it according to state legal standards even when the alternative sentence of life imprisonment would give a defendant (like everyone else in the world) the opportunity to reform.

The unlikelihood that his position on rehabilitation had anything to do with the peremptory strike of Fields is underscored by the prosecution's response after Miller-El's lawyer pointed out that the prosecutor had misrepresented Fields's responses on the subject. A moment earlier the prosecutor had finished his misdescription of Fields's views on potential rehabilitation with the words, "Those are our reasons for exercising our ... strike at this time." When defense counsel called him on his misstatement, he neither defended what he said nor withdrew the strike. Instead, he suddenly came up with Fields's brother's prior conviction as another reason for the strike.

It would be difficult to credit the State's new explanation, which reeks of afterthought. While the Court of Appeals tried to bolster it with the observation that no seated juror was in Fields's position with respect to his brother, the court's readiness to accept the State's substitute reason ignores not only its pretextual timing but the other reasons rendering it implausible. Fields's testimony indicated he was not close to his brother, ("I don't really know too much about it"), and the prosecution asked nothing further about the influence his brother's history might have had on Fields, as it probably would have done if the family history had actually mattered. There is no good reason to doubt that the State's afterthought about Fields's brother was anything but makeweight.

... In sum, when we look for nonblack jurors similarly situated to Fields, we find strong similarities as well as some differences. But the differences seem far from significant, particularly when we read Fields's *voir dire* testimony in its entirety. Upon that reading, Fields should have been an ideal juror in the eyes of a prosecutor seeking a death sentence, and the prosecutors' explanations for the strike cannot reasonably be accepted.

The prosecution's proffered reasons for striking Joe Warren, another black venireman, are comparably unlikely. Warren gave this answer when he was asked what the death penalty accomplished:

"I don't know. It's really hard to say because I know sometimes you feel that it might help to deter crime and then you feel that the person is not really suffering. You're taking the suffering away from him. So it's like I said, sometimes you have mixed feelings about whether or not this is punishment or, you know, you're relieving personal punishment."

The prosecution said nothing about these remarks when it struck Warren from the panel, but prosecutor Paul Macaluso referred to this answer as the first of his reasons when he testified at the later *Batson* hearing:

"I thought [Warren's statements on *voir dire*] were inconsistent responses. At one point he says, you know, on a case-by-case basis and at another point he said, well, I think—I got the impression, at least, that he suggested that the death penalty was an easy way out, that they should be made to suffer more."

On the face of it, the explanation is reasonable from the State's point of view, but its plausibility is severely undercut by the prosecution's failure to object to other panel members who expressed views much like Warren's. Kevin Duke, who served on the jury, said, "sometimes death would be better to me than—being in prison would be like dying every day and, if you were in prison for life with no hope of parole, I['d] just as soon have it over with than be in prison for the rest of your life." Troy Woods, the one black panelist to serve as juror, said that capital punishment "is too easy. I think that's a quick relief.... I feel like [hard labor is] more of a punishment than putting them to sleep." Sandra Jenkins, whom the State accepted (but who was then struck by the defense) testified that she thought "a harsher treatment is life imprisonment with no parole." Leta Girard, accepted by the State (but also struck by the defense) gave her opinion that "living sometimes is a worse—is worse to me than dying would be." The fact that Macaluso's reason also applied to these other panel members, most of them white, none of them struck, is evidence of pretext.

The suggestion of pretext is not, moreover, mitigated much by Macaluso's explanation that Warren was struck when the State had 10 peremptory challenges left and could afford to be liberal in using them. If that were the explanation for striking Warren and later accepting panel members who thought death would be too easy, the prosecutors should have struck Sandra Jenkins, whom they examined and accepted before Warren. Indeed, the disparate treatment is the more remarkable for the fact that the prosecutors repeatedly questioned Warren on his capacity and willingness to impose a sentence of death and elicited statements of his ability to do so if the evidence supported that result and the answer to each special question was yes, whereas the record before us discloses no attempt to determine whether Jenkins would be able to vote for death in spite of her view that it was easy on the convict. Yet the prosecutors accepted the white panel member Jenkins and struck the black venireman Warren.

Macaluso's explanation that the prosecutors grew more sparing with peremptory challenges as the jury selection wore on does, however, weaken any suggestion that the State's acceptance of Woods, the one black juror, shows that race was not in play. Woods was the eighth juror, qualified in the fifth week of jury selection. When the State accepted him, 11 of its 15 peremptory strikes were gone, 7 of them used to strike black panel members. The juror questionnaires show that at least three members of the venire panel yet to be questioned on the stand were opposed to capital punishment, Janice Mackey; Paul Bailey; and Anna Keaton. With at least three remaining panel members highly undesirable to the State, the prosecutors had to exercise prudent restraint in using strikes. This late-stage decision to accept a black panel member willing to impose a death sentence does not, therefore, neutralize the early-stage decision to challenge a comparable venireman, Warren. In fact, if the prosecutors were going to accept any black juror to obscure the otherwise consistent pattern of opposition to seating one, the time to do so was getting late....

As for law, the rule in *Batson* provides an opportunity to the prosecutor to give the reason for striking the juror, and it requires the judge to assess the plausibility of that reason in light of all evidence with a bearing on it. It is true that peremptories are often the subjects of instinct, and it can sometimes be hard to say what the reason is. But when illegitimate grounds like race are in issue, a prosecutor simply has got to state his reasons as best he can and stand or fall on the plausibility of the reasons he gives. A *Batson* challenge does not call for a mere exercise in thinking up any rational basis. If the stated reason does not hold up, its pretextual significance does not fade because a trial judge, or an appeals court, can imagine a reason that might not have been shown up as false. The Court of Appeals's and the dissent's substitution of a reason for eliminating Warren does nothing to satisfy the prosecutors' burden of stating a racially neutral explanation for their own actions.

The whole of the voir dire testimony subject to consideration casts the prosecution's reasons for striking Warren in an implausible light. Comparing his strike with the treatment of panel members who expressed similar views supports a conclusion that race was significant in determining who was challenged and who was not.

B

... In the course of drawing a jury to try a black defendant, 10 of the 11 qualified black venire panel members were peremptorily struck. At least two of them, Fields and Warren, were ostensibly acceptable to prosecutors seeking a death verdict, and Fields was ideal. The prosecutors' chosen race-neutral reasons for the strikes do not hold up and are so far at odds with the evidence that pretext is the fair conclusion, indicating the very discrimination the explanations were meant to deny.

The strikes that drew these incredible explanations occurred in a selection process replete with evidence that the prosecutors were selecting and rejecting potential jurors because of race. At least two of the jury shuffles conducted by the State make no sense except as efforts to delay consideration of black jury panelists to the end of the week, when they might not even be reached. The State has in fact never offered any other explanation. Nor has the State denied that disparate lines of questioning were pursued: 53% of black panelists but only 3% of nonblacks were questioned with a graphic script meant to induce qualms about applying the death penalty (and thus explain a strike), and 100% of blacks but only 27% of nonblacks were subjected to a trick question about the minimum acceptable penalty for murder, meant to induce a disqualifying answer. The State's attempts to explain the prosecutors' questioning of particular witnesses on nonracial grounds fit the evidence less well than the racially discriminatory hypothesis.

If anything more is needed for an undeniable explanation of what was going on, history supplies it. The prosecutors took their cues from a 20-year old manual of tips on jury selection, as shown by their notes of the race of each potential juror. By the time a jury was chosen, the State had peremptorily challenged 12% of qualified nonblack panel members, but eliminated 91% of the black ones.

It blinks reality to deny that the State struck Fields and Warren, included in that 91%, because they were black. The strikes correlate with no fact as well as they correlate with race, and they occurred during a selection infected by shuffling and disparate questioning that race explains better than any race-neutral reason advanced by the State. The State's pretextual positions confirm Miller-El's claim, and the prosecutors' own notes proclaim that the Sparling Manual's emphasis on race was on their minds when they considered every potential juror.

The state court's conclusion that the prosecutors' strikes of Fields and Warren were not racially determined is shown up as wrong to a clear and convincing degree; the state court's conclusion was unreasonable as well as erroneous. The judgment of the Court of Appeals is reversed, and the case is remanded for entry of judgment for petitioner together with orders of appropriate relief.

JUSTICE BREYER, concurring.

III

I recognize that peremptory challenges have a long historical pedigree. They may help to reassure a party of the fairness of the jury. But long ago, Blackstone recognized the peremptory challenge as an "arbitrary and capricious species of [a] challenge." If used to express stereotypical judgments about race, gender, religion, or national origin, peremptory challenges betray the jury's democratic origins and undermine its representative function.... And, of course, the right to a jury free of discriminatory taint is constitutionally protected—the right to use peremptory challenges is not.

Justice Goldberg, dissenting in *Swain v. Alabama*, 380 U.S. 202 (1965), wrote, "Were it necessary to make an absolute choice between the right of a defendant to have a jury chosen in conformity with the requirements of the Fourteenth Amendment and the right to challenge peremptorily, the Constitution compels a choice of the former." This case suggests the need to confront that choice. In light of the considerations I have mentioned, I believe it necessary to reconsider *Batson's* test and the peremptory challenge system as a whole. With that qualification, I join the Court's opinion.

Note

Justice Thomas dissented along with Chief Justice Rehnquist and Justice Scalia. In his lengthy dissent, Justice Thomas concluded that the evidence did not provide clear and convincing evidence of racial discrimination in the jury selection process.

Gender-Based Peremptory Challenges: *J.E.B. v. Alabama ex rel. T.B., 511 U.S. 127 (1994)*

Following *Batson* and its progeny, litigants raised the issue of whether *Batson's* principles should be extended to gender-based peremptory challenges. In *J.E.B. v. Alabama ex rel. T.B.*, 511 U.S. 127 (1994), the United States Supreme Court answered this question in the affirmative.

J.E.B. arose out of a paternity suit brought by the State of Alabama, on behalf of the child's mother, against James E. Bowman. At issue in that case was whether Bowman was the biological father of Teresia Bible's two-year-old son and thus obligated to provide child support.

During jury selection, the state's attorneys used nine of their ten allotted peremptory challenges to remove male jurors from the jury panel. Bowman used all but one of his peremptory challenges to remove female jurors. An all-female jury was empaneled.

The jury concluded that Bowman was the child's biological father and ordered him to pay $415 per month in child support. Bowman appealed claiming that the state's use of its peremptory challenges to exclude jurors solely on the basis of gender violated the Equal Protection Clause. The United States Supreme Court granted certiorari and, by a 6–3 vote, held that state attorneys in Alabama violated the Constitution's guarantee of equal protection when they excluded prospective jurors based solely on gender. Writing for the majority, Justice Blackmun stated:

> When state actors exercise peremptory challenges in reliance on gender stereotypes, they ratify and reinforce prejudicial views of the relative abilities of men and women. Because these stereotypes have wreaked injustice in so many other spheres of our country's public life, active discrimination by litigants on the basis of gender during jury selection "invites cynicism respecting

the jury's neutrality and its obligation to adhere to the law." *Powers v. Ohio*, 499 U.S. at 412. The potential for cynicism is particularly acute in cases where gender-related issues are prominent, such as cases involving rape, sexual harassment, or paternity. Discriminatory use of peremptory challenges may create the impression that the judicial system has acquiesced in suppressing full participation by one gender or that the "deck has been stacked" in favor of one side.

Equal opportunity to participate in the fair administration of justice is fundamental to our democratic system. It not only furthers the goals of the jury system. It reaffirms the promise of equality under the law—that all citizens, regardless of race, ethnicity, or gender, have the chance to take part directly in our democracy.... When persons are excluded from participation in our democratic processes solely because of race or gender, this promise of equality dims, and the integrity of our judicial system is jeopardized.

In view of these concerns, the Equal Protection Clause prohibits discrimination in jury selection on the basis of gender, or on the assumption that an individual will be biased in a particular case for no reason other than the fact that the person happens to be a woman or happens to be a man. As with race, the "core guarantees of equal protection, ensuring citizens that their State will not discriminate..., would be meaningless were we to approve the exclusion of jurors on the basis of such assumptions, which arise solely from the jurors' [gender]." *Batson*, 476 U.S. at 97–98.

In a concurring opinion, Justice O'Connor urged that "today's holding ... be limited to the government's use of gender-based peremptory strikes." Justice O'Connor was troubled by the effect this decision would place on a private attorney's ability to effectively exercise peremptory challenges. She wrote:

... I adhere to my position that the Equal Protection Clause does not limit the exercise of peremptory challenges by private civil litigants and criminal defendants. This case itself presents no state action dilemma, for here the State of Alabama itself filed the paternity suit on behalf of petitioner. But what of the next case? Will we, in the name of fighting gender discrimination, hold the battered wife—on trial for wounding her abusive husband—is a state actor? Will we preclude her from using her peremptory challenges to ensure that the jury of her peers contains as many women members as possible? I assume we will, but I hope we will not.

In dissent, Justice Scalia, joined by Chief Justice Rehnquist and Justice Thomas, was characteristically caustic:

Today's opinion is an inspiring demonstration of how thoroughly up-to-date and right-thinking we Justices are in matters pertaining to the sexes (or as the Court would have it, the genders), and how sternly we disapprove of the male chauvinist attitudes of our predecessors....

In order, it seems to me, not to eliminate any real denial of equal protection, but simply to pay conspicuous obeisance to the equality of the sexes, the Court imperils a practice that has been considered an essential part of fair jury trial since the dawn of the common law. The Constitution of the United States neither requires nor permits this vandalizing of our people's traditions.

Note and Questions on Assumptions Underlying Peremptory Challenges

Professor David C. Baldus, chief architect of the Baldus study—which the Supreme Court acknowledged demonstrated a risk that racial prejudice plays a role in capital sentencing in Georgia (see *McCleskey v. Kemp*, 481 U.S. 279 (1987), *supra* chapter 4)—published an empirical study in 2001 which examined peremptory strike decisions made by prosecutors and defense counsel. Professor Baldus and his colleagues identified four types of peremptory challenges:

> Peremptory challenges fall into four different categories. First are those based on direct evidence of potential bias that is otherwise insufficient to support a challenge for cause. For example, a venire member's reservations about the death penalty may be insufficient to support a challenge for cause but sufficient to alarm the government and provide the basis for a peremptory challenge.
>
> The second category of peremptories is based on the appearance, attitude, and demeanor of the venire member during the *voir dire* process. This information may also suggest something about venire member attitudes and their likely reactions as jurors.
>
> The third category of peremptories is premised on perceptions about the extent to which a juror's race or gender is likely to bias his or her decisions because of an affinity for or antipathy against the defendant or victim. For example, it is commonly believed that in rape cases, women are better jurors for the state than are men. It is also widely believed that non-black and black jurors react quite differently to black defendants.
>
> The fourth category of peremptories is based on widely shared stereotypes that hypothesize either a general anti-defendant or anti-government bias, principally on the basis of demographics (race, gender, age, occupation, or education), intelligence, or prior contact with the criminal justice system. In general, prosecutors perceive minorities as a threat, especially blacks, younger people, women, college educated and bright people, people with disabilities, non-conformists, "free thinkers," liberals, teachers, and people from the helping professions, such as doctors, lawyers, and social workers. In the words of Texas prosecutor Jon Sparling, who prepared a training manual for prosecutors in the 1970's: "You are not looking for a fair juror, but rather a strong, biased and sometimes hypocritical individual who believes that Defendants are different from them in kind, rather than degree." Defense counsel prefer "jurors with apparent biases in the opposite direction;" accordingly, they look for the "young, the better educated, the non-white, the odd or whatever." The literature suggests that prosecutors and defense counsel share a common set of stereotypes of who are good and bad jurors for the State and the defense.

Baldus & Woodworth, "The Use of Peremptory Challenges in Capital Murder Trials: A Legal and Empirical Analysis," 3 U. Pa. J. Const. L. 3 (2001).

If you were a prosecutor, would you use your peremptory challenges to strike minorities, younger people, women, college educated and bright people, people with disabilities, non-conformists, "free thinkers," liberals, teachers, and people from the helping professions? If you were a capital defense attorney, what would your ideal juror-type be? See if the following article changes any of your preconceptions.

The Use of Peremptory Challenges in Capital Murder Trials: A Legal and Empirical Analysis

David Baldus and George Woodworth, et al., 3 U. Pa. J. Const. L. 3 (2001)

[Professor Baldus and his team of researchers examined the venires in 317 capital murder trials held in Philadelphia between 1981 and 1987.] Our findings on the use of peremptory strikes in Philadelphia capital cases support much of the argument in the literature and in judicial opinions about racial and gender disparities in the use of peremptories, the motivations driving their discriminatory use, the effectiveness of *Batson*, *McCollum*, and *J.E.B.* in limiting the influence of race and gender in their use, and the impact they are having on the participation of jurors and the outcomes of penalty trials. The following [is a] summary of our findings and conclusions....

A. Peremptory Strike Patterns

Our findings indicate that venire member race was a major determinant in the use of peremptories by both prosecutors and defense counsel, with the prosecution disproportionately striking black venire members and defense counsel disproportionately striking non-blacks. In addition, the racial make up of a venire member's neighborhood of residence was also an important factor, especially in prosecutorial strikes against non-black venire members who resided in a neighborhood with more than 1% black residents.

Gender was also a significant influence, but much less so than race, with prosecutors favoring men and defense counsel favoring women.

Overall, defense counsel's use of peremptories was a mirror image of the Commonwealth's strike pattern except that, on average, prosecutors exercised about three fewer peremptories per case. Venire member race and gender effects were evident in both unadjusted analyses and logistic multiple regression analyses that controlled for the venire member's age, occupation, education, answers to voir dire questions, and the race of the defendant and victim in the case.

The data clearly indicate that both prosecutors and defense counsel were influenced by their perceptions of how the race of the defendant and victim will interact with the venire member's race. In this regard, our findings validated the perception of the United States Supreme Court that the facts of the case are an important influence on how venire member race and gender influence the use of peremptories. Our data also indicate that both sides' peremptory strike strategies were heavily driven by racially based prosecutorial and defense counsel beliefs that have nothing to do with the possibility of juror identification with, or hostility toward, defendants and victims on the basis of their race or gender. Instead, the strike patterns document race—and gender-based stereotypes that reflect fundamental differences in perceptions of how male and female and black and non-black jurors view issues of criminal responsibility, culpability, and punishment (i.e., the stereotypes cogently captured in Jack McMahon's training tape and widely shared among defense counsel).

The pattern of race discrimination in these cases reflects the kind of motivation condemned by the United States Supreme Court in *Swain v. Alabama*, because it was often unrelated to the facts of the cases in which the venire members were struck.

Venire member age was another factor of great importance to both sides in their use of peremptories. Specifically, prosecutors had a strong preference for older jurors and a distinct aversion toward young jurors; the preferences of defense counsel were the opposite.

In terms of race, gender, and age, the prime targets and clearest choices for the Commonwealth strikes were young black women and men and middle-aged black women. The prime targets and clearest choices for defense counsel strikes were older non-black men, middle-aged non-black men, and older non-black women. The pervasive impact of race in the system was demonstrated by the fact that none of the Commonwealth's top six targets (defined in terms of race, gender, and age) was non-black and none of defense counsel's top six targets was black.

B. The Impact of United States Supreme Court Decisions on the Discriminatory Use of Peremptories

Our data indicate that in Philadelphia capital trials, the *Batson, McCollum,* and *J.E.B.* prohibitions against the use of race and gender as the basis for the use of peremptories have had, at best, only a marginal impact on the peremptory strike strategies of each side. One reason for the small impact of the Supreme Court's decisions is that, in spite of evidence of statistically significant race disparities in about half the cases, prosecutors and defense counsel appeared to raise race discrimination claims very infrequently. One possible explanation for this pattern is that each side tolerates the other side's discriminatory use of peremptories out of fear that if they raise a claim, the other side will reciprocate with a claim, with the outcome uncertain for both sides. Our data suggest that such claims are raised in fewer than 10% of cases.

Another possible explanation for the infrequent claims, in spite of evidence that the discrimination is widespread, is that counsel for both sides have little expectation that the courts will sustain a claim of discrimination even if it is based on solid evidence. Among the twenty-four capital cases in this study in which claims appear to have been made, appellate relief does not appear to have been granted in a single case.

This finding is something of a surprise, given the strong predictions of many members of the Supreme Court that the system would be inundated with claims of race and gender discrimination.

It also appears that both sides believe that their discriminatory use of peremptories is based on a rational assessment of human behavior, and is essential for the protection of their client's interests given the use of such strategies by the other side. The lack of judicial oversight further suggests that the courts implicitly concur with this assessment. Our findings strongly support Professor Ogletree's argument that in *Batson,* the United States Supreme Court completely misunderstood the conviction of both prosecutors and defense counsel that race and gender discrimination are rational, ethical, and necessary strategies to protect the interests of their clients.

C. The Impact of the Race and Gender Composition of Juries on Penalty Trial Outcomes

The literature provides some support for the validity of prosecutorial and defense counsel race-based perceptions concerning both guilt trial outcomes (non-black jurors are generally more conviction prone than black jurors) and penalty trial outcomes (non-black jurors are more prone to give a death sentence than are black jurors). Moreover, our Philadelphia findings indicate that predominantly black juries (ones with five or more blacks) were less likely to impose death sentences than were juries with four or fewer black jurors. That disparity was principally explained by a substantially higher death-sentencing rate in black defendant cases—eleven percentage points—when the jury was predominantly non-black than when it was predominantly black. The data also indicate that predominantly non-black juries sentenced black and non-black defendants to death at quite different rates—a sixteen percentage point black defendant disparity. For the predominantly black juries, black defendants were also sentenced at a higher rate than non-blacks, but the disparity was smaller—eight percentage points.

Our data did not reveal a similar relationship between the gender composition of juries and death-sentencing outcomes. The data indicate that predominantly female juries (with eight or more women) were associated with a slightly higher overall death-sentencing rate (four percentage points) that was not statistically significant. This disparity reflects a five point higher rate in black defendant cases and a seven point lower rate in non-black defendant cases. In fact, gender had much less effect on jury sentencing behavior than did race and age, the two factors that joined gender in defining each side's prime strike target groups. The slightly higher death-sentencing outcomes associated with the predominantly female juries is explained by the fact that these juries were also predominantly non-black.

D. The "Canceling Out" Hypothesis and the Comparative Effectiveness of the Commonwealth and Defense Counsel in Their Use of Peremptory Challenges

A major focus of this research has been on the "canceling out" hypothesis, which suggests that the use of peremptories is not an important problem because both sides discriminate and any harm caused by one side is immediately canceled or offset by the reciprocal strikes of the other side. At one level, our findings can be viewed as supporting this hypothesis, because the strike rates of both sides mirrored each other and the proportions of blacks and women on the juries we studied were almost identical to their proportions on the venires from which they were selected.

However, closer examination of the system indicates that the effects of the two sides' use of the peremptories in fact did not offset each other. The reason for this imbalance in impact is that the principal targets of the Commonwealth and defense counsel were not defined simply in terms of race and gender. For example, the McMahon tape draws sharp distinctions between older and younger black men, which are reflected in the Commonwealth's strike rates against these groups. Instead, each side's target populations were defined in terms of a combination of race, age, and gender, and these characteristics defined target groups of quite different sizes. Specifically, the prime targets of the Commonwealth typically were substantially smaller in number than were defense counsel's prime targets.

As a result of this disparity in the sizes of their respective target groups, the Commonwealth was more effective than defense counsel in depleting target group members from the pools of death eligible cases that each side considered. In addition, in terms of the combined impact of each side's peremptory strike strategies on jury representation, the Commonwealth enjoyed a distinct advantage over defense counsel in terms of the representation of the target groups each side favored and feared.

In terms of target selection, defense counsel appears to have been somewhat more successful. When its prime target groups were represented on juries at above their median rate, death-sentencing rates were distinctly higher, suggesting that they were accurately selected targets. Also, the Commonwealth's prime targets, middle-aged and older women, were associated with lower than average death-sentencing rates in black defendant cases with non-black victims. However, our data suggest that the prime target of the Commonwealth, young black women, posed no significant threat to it in terms of death-sentencing. It further appears that in cases involving non-black defendants, black jurors were quite willing to impose death sentences, suggesting that the Commonwealth may have overstruck black venire members when the defendant was non-black.

One distinct advantage enjoyed by the Commonwealth is that its prosecutors appear to have been more successful in striking life-prone black venire members than were defense counsel in striking death-prone non-black venire members. The data indicate that when both sides made a substantial strike effort — the prosecution against black venire members and defense counsel against non-black venire members — each had a substantial effect on the racial composition of the jury. However, the consequences of the enhanced strike effort of the two sides were different. A strong prosecutorial strike effort against black venire members resulted in a significantly elevated death-sentencing rate (ten percentage points higher) as well as significant race-of-defendant disparities in the rates at which black and non-black defendants received a death sentence (a 24-percentage point effect).

Although a strong defense counsel effort to strike non-black venire members did influence the number of blacks on the juries, this additional defense effort did not have as dramatic an effect in reducing the overall death-sentencing rate as did the prosecution's enhanced effort had in increasing the rate. However, the enhanced effort of defense counsel did substantially reduce the black defendant death-sentencing disparity — to only one percentage point, a sharp contrast to the sixteen point disparity observed when defense counsel's effort to strike non-black venire members was below the median.

The prosecution's greater effectiveness in influencing sentencing outcomes was likely explained in part by the fact that support for capital punishment was probably stronger among non-black than black jurors. In addition, on average, prosecutors appear to have had greater experience in trying capital cases and to have been more skillful at identifying and striking life-prone black venire members than defense counsel were at identifying and striking death-prone non-black venire members.

A final point on the canceling out issue is that the contrast between the percentages of blacks and women on Philadelphia's juries and their percentages on the venires from which they are selected overlooks the substantial numbers of venire members struck each year on the basis of their race and gender. Specifically, we estimate that during the 17-year period covered by this study, over 800 strikes against men and women, and over 2,000 strikes against blacks and non-blacks, were in excess of what we would have seen if peremptories had been applied even-handedly, i.e., without reliance on venire member race and gender. From the standpoint of the interest of venire members in even-handed treatment, these are not trivial effects.

E. Effects on the Defendant's Chances of Drawing a Jury of His Peers

Our data indicate that another consequence of Philadelphia's system of peremptory strikes is that black men, especially young black men, had a distinctly lower chance of being tried by their "peers" than did non-black defendants. Again, however, we note that criminal defendants have no explicit legal right to be tried by a jury of their "peers."

F. Conclusions

The law that has developed in America since *Batson v. Kentucky* in 1986 has had limited effectiveness in controlling race and gender discrimination in the use of peremptory challenges because of its inability to resolve a basic tension apparent in *Batson* itself. On one side, as a nation, we embrace the goal of eradicating race and gender discrimination in the administration of justice, a goal eloquently stated by the Supreme

Court's majority opinion. On the other side, trial lawyers perceive their reliance on race and gender stereotypes to be a long-standing, appropriate, and necessary means of promoting the legitimate interests of their clients, a position earnestly argued in the *Batson* dissent.

The regulatory system that has evolved in Philadelphia capital cases, the subject of this study, represents a symbolic compromise of those goals. In spite of compelling evidence of systemic disregard for *Batson*, *McCollum*, and *J.E.B.*, the system appears to be acquiesced in both by litigants (who raise few claims) and by courts (who rarely grant relief for violations). The consequence is that race and gender discrimination continue to flourish with corrective judicial action likely in only the most extreme circumstances. Moreover, because the issue has little visibility beyond the professionals who administer the system, it is not a matter of public concern or general political interest.

Our Philadelphia research has demonstrated, however, that in spite of the general acceptance of the current system, it carries serious costs. First, many venire members are routinely rejected for jury service because of their race and gender. Second, the system of peremptory strikes affects jury sentencing decisions in two important ways that arise from the Commonwealth's comparative advantage in its competition with defense counsel to influence the composition of the juries. This advantage flows in part from the simple fact that each side has an equal number of peremptory challenges, but the prime target groups of the prosecution are smaller in number than those of defense counsel. The advantage also appears to reflect greater experience and expertise in jury selection on the part of the Commonwealth's prosecutors during the period of this study.

One result of the Commonwealth's comparative advantage is that in many cases, we saw an under-representation of black jurors, who, on average, were more life sentence prone than their non-black counterparts. Another result is that, in general, Philadelphia prosecutors appeared to be more successful in identifying and striking life sentence prone jurors than were defense counsel in identifying and striking death sentence prone jurors. The upshot of the Commonwealth's comparative advantage in its use of peremptory strikes appears to be enhanced death-sentencing rates, particularly in cases involving black defendants.

The connection between the Commonwealth's comparative advantage in jury selection and race of defendant discrimination in jury sentencing decisions is of obvious moment for black defendants, who comprised 80% of the defendants in our sample.

When we consider alternatives, one obvious question is whether the current system is better or worse than the pre-*Batson* system, in which claims under *Swain v. Alabama* were even more difficult to establish than they are now under *Batson* and its progeny. We believe that in spite of its limitations, the current system is better because it appears at least to inhibit strategies designed to exclude nearly all blacks from the juries. It is worth noting in this regard that Philadelphia prosecutors used on average three fewer strikes than defense counsel in capital cases.

In deciding whether the current system is the "least worst" available, consider the prospect of total abolition suggested by Justice Marshall. Our data indicate that abolition would result in a system of random selection and therefore would end the systematic exclusion of venire members on the basis of race and gender as well as age and other arbitrary factors that are frequently offered to justify strikes that have been challenged. It would result, on average, in the proportional representation of all subgroups on the venires. It would also eliminate the adverse effects on jury decision making, which are a by-product of the current system. Finally, it would clear the courts of a time-consuming intractable issue that the judiciary seems unable or unwilling to resolve. We find the justification for the current system—each side's felt necessity to exclude what it considers to be "bad" jurors—wholly insufficient in the face of the substantial costs associated with the status quo.

However, as noted above, this is a low visibility issue and only a few criminal law practitioners appear willing to counter the strong and widespread belief on both sides that peremptories are critical to protect their clients' interests.

Judicial abolition, therefore, seems unlikely, as the United States Supreme Court and most state and federal courts appear content with the symbolic compromise they have created. The prospects of abolition by State legislatures seem equally unlikely. So also is the prospect of the United States Supreme Court's limiting the prohibitions of *Batson* and *J.E.B.* only to the prosecution.

However, our findings suggest that change short of complete abolition would be desirable. On the issue of enhanced enforcement of *Batson*, *McCollum*, and *J.E.B.*, our findings suggest that more systematic forms of data analysis of the type we have applied in this study may facilitate the detection of race and gender discrimination.

Also, our findings document that most of the adverse impact of the current system on jury decision making flows from the aggressive use of peremptories by prosecutors against blacks and defense counsel against non-blacks. Courts might usefully consider creating a strike rate limit against these groups, say 50%, that neither side could exceed.

Our hypothetical affirmative selection analysis indicates that if applied in Philadelphia, it would have resulted in significantly enhanced jury representation of each side's prime targets. In the interest of fairness, therefore, it is worth considering an alternative system that would give each side the option of picking the jury through a system of affirmative selection.

Our hypothetical restricted selection analysis, which would limit the Commonwealth's peremptories to five and defense counsel's strikes to ten, would have significantly reduced race and gender discrimination and limited its adverse impact on the jury decision making system. If peremptories are critical to protect each side against truly oddball jurors, then fewer than five strikes should be enough. Also, an imbalance in authorized strikes favoring the defendant would counteract somewhat the Commonwealth's comparative advantage in its competition to control the racial composition of the jury with peremptory strikes.

Our final judgment is that the empirical findings of this project document a significant source of injustice in the peremptory strike system currently used in Philadelphia capital trials. We do not believe such a system can be justified legally or morally. We hope, therefore, that the findings presented in this Article will help focus the debate on the problems associated with such systems and the possibilities for meaningful reform.

Note

Issues surrounding race, gender, and sexual orientation in capital cases are considered in greater depth in chapter 4, *supra*.

Chapter 7

The Role of Aggravating Circumstances

As discussed in earlier chapters, not everyone found guilty of murder will be condemned to die. Before imposing a death sentence, the sentencer—either the judge or jury—usually must find the existence of at least one "aggravating circumstance" which differentiates the capital defendant's crime from crimes which are not punishable by death. An aggravating circumstance increases the enormity of the crime, thus singling it out for special, harsher treatment. The burden of proving the existence of aggravating circumstances rests with the prosecutor. As the following statutes demonstrate, what constitutes an aggravating circumstance varies among jurisdictions.

A. Selected Death Penalty Statutes

Texas

Texas Code Crim. Proc. Art. 37.071. Procedure in capital case

Sec. 1. If a defendant is found guilty in a capital felony case in which the state does not seek the death penalty, the judge shall sentence the defendant to life imprisonment.

Sec. 2. (a) If a defendant is tried for a capital offense in which the state seeks the death penalty, on a finding that the defendant is guilty of a capital offense, the court shall conduct a separate sentencing proceeding to determine whether the defendant shall be sentenced to death or life imprisonment. The proceeding shall be conducted in the trial court and except as provided by Article 44.29(c) of this code, before the trial jury as soon as practicable. In the proceeding, evidence may be presented by the state and the defendant or the defendant's counsel as to any matter that the court deems relevant to sentence, including evidence of the defendant's background or character or the circumstances of the offense that mitigates against the imposition of the death penalty. This subsection shall not be construed to authorize the introduction of any evidence secured in violation of the Constitution of the United States or of the State of Texas. The state and the defendant or the defendant's counsel shall be permitted to present argument for or against sentence of death. The court, the attorney representing the state, the defendant, or the defendant's counsel may not inform a juror or a prospective juror of the effect of a failure of a jury to agree on issues submitted under Subsection (c) or (e) of this article.

(b) On conclusion of the presentation of the evidence, the court shall submit the following issues to the jury:

(1)　whether there is a probability that the defendant would commit criminal acts of violence that would constitute a continuing threat to society; and

(2)　in cases in which the jury charge at the guilt or innocence stage permitted the jury to find the defendant guilty as a party under Sections 7.01 and 7.02, Penal Code, whether the defendant actually caused the death of the deceased or did not actually cause the death of the deceased but intended to kill the deceased or another or anticipated that a human life would be taken.

(c) The state must prove each issue submitted under Subsection (b) of this article beyond a reasonable doubt, and the jury shall return a special verdict of "yes" or "no" on each issue submitted under Subsection (b) of this Article.

(d) The court shall charge the jury that:

(1)　in deliberating on the issues submitted under Subsection (b) of this article, it shall consider all evidence admitted at the guilt or innocence stage and the punishment stage, including evidence of the defendant's background or character or the circumstances of the offense that militates for or mitigates against the imposition of the death penalty;

(2)　it may not answer any issue submitted under Subsection (b) of this article "yes" unless it agrees unanimously and it may not answer any issue "no" unless 10 or more jurors agree; and

(3)　members of the jury need not agree on what particular evidence supports a negative answer to any issue submitted under Subsection (b) of this article.

(e)(1) The court shall instruct the jury that if the jury returns an affirmative finding to each issue submitted under Subsection (b) of this article, it shall answer the following issue:

Whether, taking into consideration all of the evidence, including the circumstances of the offense, the defendant's character and background, and the personal moral culpability of the defendant, there is a sufficient mitigating circumstance or circumstances to warrant that a sentence of life imprisonment rather than a death sentence be imposed.

(2)　The court, on the written request of the attorney representing the defendant, shall:

(A) instruct the jury that if the jury answers that a circumstance or circumstances warrant that a sentence of life imprisonment rather than a death sentence be imposed, the court will sentence the defendant to imprisonment in the institutional division of the Texas Department of Criminal Justice for life; and

(B) charge the jury in writing as follows:

"Under the law applicable in this case, if the defendant is sentenced to imprisonment in the institutional division of the Texas Department of Criminal Justice for life, the defendant will become eligible for release on parole, but not until the actual time served by the defendant equals 40 years, without consideration of any good conduct time. It cannot accurately be predicted how the parole laws might be applied to this defendant if the defendant is sentenced to a term of imprisonment for life because the application of those laws will depend on decisions made by prison and parole authorities, but eligibility for parole does not guarantee that parole will be granted."

(f) The court shall charge the jury that in answering the issue submitted under Subsection (e) of this article, the jury:

(1) shall answer the issue "yes" or "no";

(2) may not answer the issue "no" unless it agrees unanimously and may not answer the issue "yes" unless 10 or more jurors agree;

(3) need not agree on what particular evidence supports an affirmative finding on the issue; and

(4) shall consider mitigating evidence to be evidence that a juror might regard as reducing the defendant's moral blameworthiness.

(g) If the jury returns an affirmative finding on each issue submitted under Subsection (b) of this article and a negative finding on an issue submitted under Subsection (e) of this article, the court shall sentence the defendant to death. If the jury returns a negative finding on any issue submitted under Subsection (b) of this article or an affirmative finding on an issue submitted under Subsection (e) of this article or is unable to answer any issue submitted under Subsection (b) or (e) of this article, the court shall sentence the defendant to confinement in the institutional division of the Texas Department of Criminal Justice for life.

(h) The judgment of conviction and sentence of death shall be subject to automatic review by the Court of Criminal Appeals.

Oklahoma

21 Okla. Stat. §701.7. Murder in the first degree

A. A person commits murder in the first degree when that person unlawfully and with malice aforethought causes the death of another human being. Malice is that deliberate intention unlawfully to take away the life of a human being, which is manifested by external circumstances capable of proof.

B. A person also commits the crime of murder in the first degree, regardless of malice, when that person takes the life of a human being during, or if the death of a human being results from, the commission or attempted commission of murder of another person, shooting or discharge of a firearm or crossbow with intent to kill, intentional discharge of a firearm or other deadly weapon into any dwelling or building as provided in Section 1289.17A of this title, forcible rape, robbery with a dangerous weapon, kidnapping, escape from lawful custody, first degree burglary, first degree arson, unlawful distributing or dispensing of controlled dangerous substances, or trafficking in illegal drugs.

C. A person commits murder in the first degree when the death of a child results from the willful or malicious injuring, torturing, maiming or using of unreasonable force by said person or who shall willfully cause, procure or permit any of said acts to be done upon the child pursuant to Section 7115 of Title 10 of the Oklahoma Statutes. It is sufficient for the crime of murder in the first degree that the person either willfully tortured or used unreasonable force upon the child or maliciously injured or maimed the child.

D. A person commits murder in the first degree when that person unlawfully and with malice aforethought solicits another person or persons to cause the death of a human being in furtherance of unlawfully manufacturing, distributing or dispensing controlled dangerous substances, as defined in the Uniform Controlled Dangerous Substances Act, unlawfully possessing with intent to distribute or dispense controlled dangerous substances, or trafficking in illegal drugs.

21 Okla. Stat. §701.9. Punishment for murder

A. A person who is convicted of or pleads guilty or nolo contendere to murder in the first degree shall be punished by death, by imprisonment for life without parole or by imprisonment for life.

21 Okla. Stat. §701.10. Sentencing proceeding—Murder in the first degree

A. Upon conviction or adjudication of guilt of a defendant of murder in the first degree, the court shall conduct a separate sentencing proceeding to determine whether the defendant should be sentenced to death, life imprisonment without parole or life imprisonment. The proceeding shall be conducted by the trial judge before the same trial jury as soon as practicable without presentence investigation.

B. If the trial jury has been waived by the defendant and the state, or if the defendant pleaded guilty or nolo contendere, the sentencing proceeding shall be conducted before the court.

C. In the sentencing proceeding, evidence may be presented as to any mitigating circumstances or as to any of the aggravating circumstances enumerated in Section 701.7 et seq. of this title. Only such evidence in aggravation as the state has made known to the defendant prior to his trial shall be admissible. In addition, the state may introduce evidence about the victim and about the impact of the murder on the family of the victim.

D. This section shall not be construed to authorize the introduction of any evidence secured in violation of the Constitutions of the United States or of the State of Oklahoma. The state and the defendant or his counsel shall be permitted to present argument for or against sentence of death.

21 Okla. Stat. §701.11. Instructions—Jury findings of aggravating circumstance

In the sentencing proceeding, the statutory instructions as determined by the trial judge to be warranted by the evidence shall be given in the charge and in writing to the jury for its deliberation. The jury, if its verdict be a unanimous recommendation of death, shall designate in writing, signed by the foreman of the jury, the statutory aggravating circumstance or circumstances which it unanimously found beyond a reasonable doubt. In nonjury cases the judge shall make such designation. Unless at least one of the statutory aggravating circumstances enumerated in this act is so found or if it is found that any such aggravating circumstance is outweighed by the finding of one or more mitigating circumstances, the death penalty shall not be imposed. If the jury cannot, within a reasonable time, agree as to punishment, the judge shall dismiss the jury and impose a sentence of imprisonment for life without parole or imprisonment for life.

21 Okla. Stat. §701.12. Aggravating circumstances

Aggravating circumstances shall be:

1. The defendant was previously convicted of a felony involving the use or threat of violence to the person;
2. The defendant knowingly created a great risk of death to more than one person;
3. The person committed the murder for remuneration or the promise of remuneration or employed another to commit the murder for remuneration or the promise of remuneration;
4. The murder was especially heinous, atrocious, or cruel;
5. The murder was committed for the purpose of avoiding or preventing a lawful arrest or prosecution;

6.   The murder was committed by a person while serving a sentence of imprisonment on conviction of a felony;

7.   The existence of a probability that the defendant would commit criminal acts of violence that would constitute a continuing threat to society; or

8.   The victim of the murder was a peace officer as defined by Section 99 of Title 21 of the Oklahoma Statutes, or guard of an institution under the control of the Department of Corrections, and such person was killed while in performance of official duty.

Florida

Fla. Stat. §921.141. Sentence of death or life imprisonment for capital felonies; further proceedings to determine sentence

(1) **Separate proceedings on issue of penalty.**—Upon conviction or adjudication of guilt of a defendant of a capital felony, the court shall conduct a separate sentencing proceeding to determine whether the defendant should be sentenced to death or life imprisonment as authorized by §775.082. The proceeding shall be conducted by the trial judge before the trial jury as soon as practicable. If, through impossibility or inability, the trial jury is unable to reconvene for a hearing on the issue of penalty, having determined the guilt of the accused, the trial judge may summon a special juror or jurors as provided in chapter 913 to determine the issue of the imposition of the penalty. If the trial jury has been waived, or if the defendant pleaded guilty, the sentencing proceeding shall be conducted before a jury impaneled for that purpose, unless waived by the defendant. In the proceeding, evidence may be presented as to any matter that the court deems relevant to the nature of the crime and the character of the defendant and shall include matters relating to any of the aggravating or mitigating circumstances enumerated in subsections (5) and (6). Any such evidence which the court deems to have probative value may be received, regardless of its admissibility under the exclusionary rules of evidence, provided the defendant is accorded a fair opportunity to rebut any hearsay statements. However, this subsection shall not be construed to authorize the introduction of any evidence secured in violation of the Constitution of the United States or the Constitution of the State of Florida. The state and the defendant or the defendant's counsel shall be permitted to present argument for or against sentence of death.

(2) **Advisory sentence by the jury.**—After hearing all the evidence, the jury shall deliberate and render an advisory sentence to the court, based upon the following matters:

(a)   Whether sufficient aggravating circumstances exist as enumerated in subsection (5);

(b)   Whether sufficient mitigating circumstances exist which outweigh the aggravating circumstances found to exist; and

(c)   Based on these considerations, whether the defendant should be sentenced to life imprisonment or death.

(3) **Findings in support of sentence of death.**—Notwithstanding the recommendation of a majority of the jury, the court, after weighing the aggravating and mitigating circumstances, shall enter a sentence of life imprisonment or death, but if the court imposes a sentence of death, it shall set forth in writing its findings upon which the sentence of death is based as to the facts:

(a)   That sufficient aggravating circumstances exist as enumerated in subsection (5), and

(b) That there are insufficient mitigating circumstances to outweigh the aggravating circumstances.

In each case in which the court imposes the death sentence, the determination of the court shall be supported by specific written findings of fact based upon the circumstances in subsections (5) and (6) and upon the records of the trial and the sentencing proceedings. If the court does not make the findings requiring the death sentence within 30 days after the rendition of the judgment and sentence, the court shall impose sentence of life imprisonment in accordance with §775.082.

(5) **Aggravating circumstances.** — Aggravating circumstances shall be limited to the following:

(a) The capital felony was committed by a person previously convicted of a felony and under sentence of imprisonment or placed on community control or on felony probation.

(b) The defendant was previously convicted of another capital felony or of a felony involving the use or threat of violence to the person.

(c) The defendant knowingly created a great risk of death to many persons.

(d) The capital felony was committed while the defendant was engaged, or was an accomplice, in the commission of, or an attempt to commit, or flight after committing or attempting to commit, any robbery; sexual battery; aggravated child abuse; abuse of an elderly person or disabled adult resulting in great bodily harm, permanent disability or permanent disfigurement; arson; burglary; kidnapping; aircraft piracy; or unlawful throwing, placing, or discharging of a destructive device or bomb.

(e) The capital felony was committed for the purpose of avoiding or preventing a lawful arrest or effecting an escape from custody.

(f) The capital felony was committed for pecuniary gain.

(g) The capital felony was committed to disrupt or hinder the lawful exercise of any governmental function or the enforcement of laws.

(h) The capital felony was especially heinous, atrocious, or cruel.

(i) The capital felony was a homicide and was committed in a cold, calculated, and premeditated manner without any pretense of moral or legal justification.

(j) The victim of the capital felony was a law enforcement officer engaged in the performance of his or her official duties.

(k) The victim of the capital felony was an elected or appointed public official engaged in the performance of his or her official duties if the motive for the capital felony was related, in whole or in part, to the victim's official capacity.

(l) The victim of the capital felony was a person less than 12 years of age.

(m) The victim of the capital felony was particularly vulnerable due to advanced age or disability, or because the defendant stood in a position of familial or custodial authority over the victim.

(n) The capital felony was committed by a criminal street gang member, as defined in section 874.03.

(6) **Mitigating circumstances.** — Mitigating circumstances shall be the following:

(a) The defendant has no significant history of prior criminal activity.

(b) The capital felony was committed while the defendant was under the influence of extreme mental or emotional disturbance.

(c) The victim was a participant in the defendant's conduct or consented to the act.

(d) The defendant was an accomplice in the capital felony committed by another person and his or her participation was relatively minor.

(e) The defendant acted under extreme duress or under the substantial domination of another person.

(f) The capacity of the defendant to appreciate the criminality of his or her conduct or to conform his conduct to the requirements of law was substantially impaired.

(g) The age of the defendant at the time of the crime.

(h) The existence of any other factors in the defendant's background that would mitigate against imposition of the death penalty.

(7) **Victim impact evidence.**—Once the prosecution has provided evidence of the existence of one or more aggravating circumstances as described in subsection (5), the prosecution may introduce, and subsequently argue, victim impact evidence. Such evidence shall be designed to demonstrate the victim's uniqueness as an individual human being and the resultant loss to the community's members by the victim's death. Characterizations and opinions about the crime, the defendant, and the appropriate sentence shall not be permitted as a part of victim impact evidence.

(8) **Applicability.**—This section does not apply to a person convicted or adjudicated guilty of a capital drug trafficking felony under §893.135.

Georgia

Georgia Code Ann. §17-10-30. Procedure for imposition of death penalty generally.

(a) The death penalty may be imposed for the offenses of aircraft hijacking or treason in any case.

(b) In all cases of other offenses for which the death penalty may be authorized, the judge shall consider, or he shall include in his instructions to the jury for it to consider, any mitigating circumstances or aggravating circumstances otherwise authorized by law and any of the following statutory aggravating circumstances which may be supported by the evidence:

(1) the offense of murder, rape, armed robbery, or kidnapping was committed by a person with a prior record of conviction for a capital felony;

(2) The offense of murder, rape, armed robbery, or kidnapping was committed while the offender was engaged in the commission of another capital felony or aggravated battery, or the offense of murder was committed while the offender was engaged in the commission of burglary or arson in the first degree;

(3) The offender, by his act of murder, armed robbery, or kidnapping, knowingly created a great risk of death to more than one person in a public place by means of a weapon or device which would normally be hazardous to the lives of more than one person;

(4) The offender committed the offense of murder for himself or another, for the purpose of receiving money or any other thing of monetary value;

(5) The murder of a judicial officer, former judicial officer, district attorney or solicitor-general, or former district attorney or solicitor, solicitor-general was committed during or because of the exercise of his or her official duties;

(6)   The offender caused or directed another to commit murder or committed murder as an agent or employee of another person;

(7)   The offense of murder, rape, armed robbery, or kidnapping was outrageously or wantonly vile, horrible, or inhuman in that it involved torture, depravity of mind, or an aggravated battery to the victim;

(8)   The offense of murder was committed against any peace officer, corrections employee, or fireman while engaged in the performance of his official duties;

(9)   The offense of murder was committed by a person in, or who has escaped from, the lawful custody of a peace officer or place of lawful confinement; or

(10) The murder was committed for the purpose of avoiding, interfering with, or preventing a lawful arrest or custody in a place of lawful confinement, of himself or another.

(c) The statutory instructions as determined by the trial judge to be warranted by the evidence shall be given in charge and in writing to the jury for its deliberation. The jury, if its verdict is a recommendation of death, shall designate in writing, signed by the foreman of the jury, the aggravating circumstance or circumstances which it found beyond a reasonable doubt. In nonjury cases the judge shall make such designation. Except in cases of treason or aircraft hijacking, unless at least one of the statutory aggravating circumstances enumerated in subsection (b) of this Code section is so found, the death penalty shall not be imposed.

California

California Penal Code Ann. §190.2. Death Penalty or Life imprisonment without the possibility of parole; special circumstances

(a) The penalty for a defendant who is found guilty of murder in the first degree is death or imprisonment in the state prison for life without the possibility of parole if one or more of the following special circumstances has been found under Section 190.4 to be true:

(1) The murder was intentional and carried out for financial gain.

(2) The defendant was convicted previously of murder in the first or second degree. For the purpose of this paragraph, an offense committed in another jurisdiction, which if committed in California would be punishable as first or second degree murder, shall be deemed murder in the first or second degree.

(3) The defendant, in this proceeding, has been convicted of more than one offense of murder in the first or second degree.

(4) The murder was committed by means of a destructive device, bomb, or explosive planted, hidden, or concealed in any place, area, dwelling, building, or structure, and the defendant knew, or reasonably should have known, that his or her act or acts would create a great risk of death to one or more human beings.

(5) The murder was committed for the purpose of avoiding or preventing a lawful arrest, or perfecting or attempting to perfect, an escape from lawful custody.

(6) The murder was committed by means of a destructive device, bomb, or explosive that the defendant mailed or delivered, attempted to mail or deliver, or caused to be mailed or delivered, and the defendant knew, or reasonably should have known, that his or her act or acts would create a great risk of death to one or more human beings.

(7) The victim was a peace officer ... who, while engaged in the course of the performance of his or her duties, was intentionally killed, and the defendant knew, or reasonably should have known, that the victim was a peace officer engaged in the performance of his or her duties; or the victim was a peace officer, as defined in the above-enumerated sections, or a former peace officer under any of those sections, and was intentionally killed in retaliation for the performance of his or her official duties.

(8) The victim was a federal law enforcement officer or agent who, while engaged in the course of the performance of his or her duties, was intentionally killed, and the defendant knew, or reasonably should have known, that the victim was a federal law enforcement officer or agent engaged in the performance of his or her duties; or the victim was a federal law enforcement officer or agent, and was intentionally killed in retaliation for the performance of his or her official duties.

(9) The victim was a firefighter, as defined in Section 245.1, who, while engaged in the course of the performance of his or her duties, was intentionally killed, and the defendant knew, or reasonably should have known, that the victim was a firefighter engaged in the performance of his or her duties.

(10) The victim was a witness to a crime who was intentionally killed for the purpose of preventing his or her testimony in any criminal or juvenile proceeding, and the killing was not committed during the commission or attempted commission, of the crime to which he or she was a witness; or the victim was a witness to a crime and was intentionally killed in retaliation for his or her testimony in any criminal or juvenile proceeding. As used in this paragraph, "juvenile proceeding" means a proceeding brought pursuant to Section 602 or 707 of the Welfare and Institutions Code.

(11) The victim was a prosecutor or assistant prosecutor or a former prosecutor or assistant prosecutor of any local or state prosecutor's office in this or any other state, or of a federal prosecutor's office, and the murder was intentionally carried out in retaliation for, or to prevent the performance of, the victim's official duties.

(12) The victim was a judge or former judge of any court of record in the local, state, or federal system in this or any other state, and the murder was intentionally carried out in retaliation for, or to prevent the performance of, the victim's official duties.

(13) The victim was an elected or appointed official or former official of the federal government, or of any local or state government of this or any other state, and the killing was intentionally carried out in retaliation for, or to prevent the performance of, the victim's official duties.

(14) The murder was especially heinous, atrocious, or cruel, manifesting exceptional depravity. As used in this section, the phrase "especially heinous, atrocious, or cruel, manifesting exceptional depravity" means a conscienceless or pitiless crime that is unnecessarily torturous to the victim.

(15) The defendant intentionally killed the victim by means of lying in wait.

(16) The victim was intentionally killed because of his or her race, color, religion, nationality, or country of origin.

(17) The murder was committed while the defendant was engaged in, or was an accomplice in, the commission of, attempted commission of, or the immediate flight after committing, or attempting to commit, the following felonies:

  (A) Robbery in violation of Section 211 or 212.5.

(B) Kidnapping in violation of Section 207, 209, or 209.5.

(C) Rape in violation of Section 261.

(D) Sodomy in violation of Section 286.

(E) The performance of a lewd or lascivious act upon the person of a child under the age of 14 years in violation of Section 288.

(F) Oral copulation in violation of Section 288a.

(G) Burglary in the first or second degree in violation of Section 460.

(H) Arson in violation of subdivision (b) of Section 451.

(I) Train wrecking in violation of Section 219.

(J) Mayhem in violation of Section 203.

(K) Rape by instrument in violation of Section 289.

(L) Carjacking, as defined in Section 215.

(M) To prove the special circumstances of kidnapping in subparagraph (B), or arson in subparagraph (H), if there is specific intent to kill, it is only required that there be proof of the elements of those felonies. If so established, those two special circumstances are proven even if the felony of kidnapping or arson is committed primarily or solely for the purpose of facilitating the murder.

(18) The murder was intentional and involved the infliction of torture.

(19) The defendant intentionally killed the victim by the administration of poison.

(20) The victim was a juror in any court of record in the local, state, or federal system in this or any other state, and the murder was intentionally carried out in retaliation for, or to prevent the performance of, the victim's official duties.

(21) The murder was intentional and perpetrated by means of discharging a firearm from a motor vehicle, intentionally at another person or persons outside the vehicle with the intent to inflict death. For purposes of this paragraph, "motor vehicle" means any vehicle as defined in Section 415 of the Vehicle Code.

(22) The defendant intentionally killed the victim while the defendant was an active participant in a criminal street gang, as defined in subdivision (f) of Section 186.22, and the murder was carried out to further the activities of the criminal street gang.

(b) Unless an intent to kill is specifically required under subdivision (a) for a special circumstance enumerated therein, an actual killer, as to whom the special circumstance has been found to be true under Section 190.4, need not have had any intent to kill at the time of the commission of the offense which is the basis of the special circumstance in order to suffer death or confinement in the state prison for life without the possibility of parole.

(c) Every person, not the actual killer, who, with the intent to kill, aids, abets, counsels, commands, induces, solicits, requests, or assists any actor in the commission of murder in the first degree shall be punished by death or imprisonment in the state prison for life without the possibility of parole if one or more of the special circumstances enumerated in subdivision (a) has been found to be true under Section 190.4.

(d) Notwithstanding subdivision (c), every person, not the actual killer, who, with reckless indifference to human life and as a major participant, aids, abets, counsels, commands, induces, solicits, requests, or assists in the commission of a felony enumerated in paragraph (17) of subdivision (a) which results in the death of some person or persons, and who is found guilty of murder in the first degree therefor, shall be punished by death or imprisonment in the state prison for life without the possibility of parole if a special circumstance enumerated in paragraph (17) of subdivision (a) has been found to be true under Section 190.4.

California Penal Code Ann. §190.3. Determination of death penalty or life imprisonment; evidence of aggravating and mitigating circumstances; considerations

If the defendant has been found guilty of murder in the first degree, and a special circumstance has been charged and found to be true, or if the defendant may be subject to the death penalty after having been found guilty of violating subdivision (a) of Section 1672 of the Military and Veterans Code or Sections 37, 128, 219, or 4500 of this code, the trier of fact shall determine whether the penalty shall be death or confinement in state prison for a term of life without the possibility of parole. In the proceedings on the question of penalty, evidence may be presented by both the people and the defendant as to any matter relevant to aggravation, mitigation, and sentence including, but not limited to, the nature and circumstances of the present offense, any prior felony conviction or convictions whether or not such conviction or convictions involved a crime of violence, the presence or absence of other criminal activity by the defendant which involved the use or attempted use of force or violence or which involved the express or implied threat to use force or violence, and the defendant's character, background, history, mental condition and physical condition.

However, no evidence shall be admitted regarding other criminal activity by the defendant which did not involve the use or attempted use of force or violence or which did not involve the express or implied threat to use force or violence. As used in this section, criminal activity does not require a conviction.

However, in no event shall evidence of prior criminal activity be admitted for an offense for which the defendant was prosecuted and acquitted. The restriction on the use of this evidence is intended to apply only to proceedings pursuant to this section and is not intended to affect statutory or decisional law allowing such evidence to be used in any other proceedings.

Except for evidence in proof of the offense or special circumstances which subject a defendant to the death penalty, no evidence may be presented by the prosecution in aggravation unless notice of the evidence to be introduced has been given to the defendant within a reasonable period of time as determined by the court, prior to trial. Evidence may be introduced without such notice in rebuttal to evidence introduced by the defendant in mitigation.

The trier of fact shall be instructed that a sentence of confinement to state prison for a term of life without the possibility of parole may in future after sentence is imposed, be commuted or modified to a sentence that includes the possibility of parole by the Governor of the State of California.

In determining the penalty, the trier of fact shall take into account any of the following factors if relevant:

(a) The circumstances of the crime of which the defendant was convicted in the present proceeding and the existence of any special circumstances found to be true pursuant to Section 190.1.

(b) The presence or absence of criminal activity by the defendant which involved the use or attempted use of force or violence or the express or implied threat to use force or violence.

(c) The presence or absence of any prior felony conviction.

(d) Whether or not the offense was committed while the defendant was under the influence of extreme mental or emotional disturbance.

(e) Whether or not the victim was a participant in the defendant's homicidal conduct or consented to the homicidal act.

(f) Whether or not the offense was committed under circumstances which the defendant reasonably believed to be a moral justification or extenuation for his conduct.

(g) Whether or not defendant acted under extreme duress or under the substantial domination of another person.

(h) Whether or not at the time of the offense the capacity of the defendant to appreciate the criminality of his conduct or to conform his conduct to the requirements of law was impaired as a result of mental disease or defect, or the effects of intoxication.

(i) The age of the defendant at the time of the crime.

(j) Whether or not the defendant was an accomplice to the offense and his participation in the commission of the offense was relatively minor.

(k) Any other circumstance which extenuates the gravity of the crime even though it is not a legal excuse for the crime.

After having heard and received all of the evidence, and after having heard and considered the arguments of counsel, the trier of fact shall consider, take into account and be guided by the aggravating and mitigating circumstances referred to in this section, and shall impose a sentence of death if the trier of fact concludes that the aggravating circumstances outweigh the mitigating circumstances. If the trier of fact determines that the mitigating circumstances outweigh the aggravating circumstances the trier of fact shall impose a sentence of confinement in state prison for a term of life without the possibility of parole.

Note on Notice of Intent to Seek Death: Lankford v. Idaho, 500 U.S. 110 (1991)

In order to make a defendant eligible for a death sentence, the prosecution must prove the existence of at least one statutory aggravating circumstance. Would it be fair to sentence to death someone who is unaware that death might be imposed as a sanction? In *Lankford v. Idaho*, 500 U.S. 110 (1991), the Supreme Court held that a defendant is entitled to adequate notice that the death penalty might be imposed during sentencing. At Lankford's murder trial, the district attorney told both the judge and Lankford that the state would not recommend death. The death penalty was not discussed during sentencing and the prosecutor recommended a sentence of 10 to 20 years. The judge disregarded the recommendation and sentenced Lankford to death. The Supreme Court reversed Lankford's death sentence. According to the Court, Lankford's "lack of adequate notice that the judge was contemplating the imposition of the death sentence created an impermissible risk that the adversary process may have malfunctioned in this case."

B. Vagueness as a Constitutional Defect

Godfrey v. Georgia
446 U.S. 420 (1980)

Mr. Justice STEWART announced the judgment of the Court and delivered an opinion, in which Mr. Justice Blackmun, Mr. Justice Powell, and Mr. Justice Stevens joined.

Under Georgia law, a person convicted of murder may be sentenced to death if it is found beyond a reasonable doubt that the offense "was outrageously or wantonly vile, horrible or inhuman in that it involved torture, depravity of mind, or an aggravated battery to the victim." Ga. Code §27-2534.1 (b)(7) (1978). In *Gregg v. Georgia*, 428 U.S. 153 (1976), the Court held that this statutory aggravating circumstance [§(b)(7) of the Georgia death penalty statute] is not unconstitutional on its face. Responding to the argument that the language of the provision is "so broad that capital punishment could be imposed in any murder case," the joint opinion [in *Gregg*] said:

> It is, of course, arguable that any murder involves depravity of mind or an aggravated battery. But this language need not be construed in this way, and there is no reason to assume that the Supreme Court of Georgia will adopt such an open-ended construction.

Nearly four years have passed since the *Gregg* decision, and during that time many death sentences based in whole or in part on §(b)(7) have been affirmed by the Supreme Court of Georgia. The issue now before us is whether, in affirming the imposition of the sentences of death in the present case, the Georgia Supreme Court has adopted such a broad and vague construction of the §(b)(7) aggravating circumstance as to violate the Eighth and Fourteenth Amendments to the United States Constitution.[2]

I

On a day in early September in 1977, the petitioner and his wife of 28 years had a heated argument in their home. During the course of this altercation, the petitioner, who had consumed several cans of beer, threatened his wife with a knife and damaged some of her clothing. At this point, the petitioner's wife declared that she was going to leave him, and departed to stay with relatives. That afternoon she went to a Justice of the Peace and secured a warrant charging the petitioner with aggravated assault. A few days later, while still living away from home, she filed suit for divorce. Summons was served on the petitioner, and a court hearing was set on a date some two weeks later. Before the date of the hearing, the petitioner on several occasions asked his wife to return to their home. Each time his efforts were rebuffed. At some point during this period, his wife moved in with her mother. The petitioner believed that his mother-in-law was actively instigating his wife's determination not to consider a possible reconciliation.

In the early evening of September 20, according to the petitioner, his wife telephoned him at home. Once again they argued. She asserted that reconciliation was impossible and allegedly demanded all the proceeds from the planned sale of their house. The conversation was terminated after she said that she would call back later. This she did in an

---

2. The other statutory aggravating circumstances upon which a death sentence may be based after conviction of murder in Georgia are considerably more specific or objectively measurable than §(b)(7).

hour or so. The ensuing conversation was, according to the petitioner's account, even more heated than the first. His wife reiterated her stand that reconciliation was out of the question, said that she still wanted all proceeds from the sale of their house, and mentioned that her mother was supporting her position. Stating that she saw no further use in talking or arguing, she hung up.

At this juncture, the petitioner got out his shotgun and walked with it down the hill from his home to the trailer where his mother-in-law lived. Peering through a window, he observed his wife, his mother-in-law, and his 11-year-old daughter playing a card game. He pointed the shotgun at his wife through the window and pulled the trigger. The charge from the gun struck his wife in the forehead and killed her instantly. He proceeded into the trailer, striking and injuring his fleeing daughter with the barrel of the gun. He then fired the gun at his mother-in-law, striking her in the head and killing her instantly.

The petitioner then called the local sheriff's office, identified himself, said where he was, explained that he had just killed his wife and mother-in-law, and asked that the sheriff come and pick him up. Upon arriving at the trailer, the law enforcement officers found the petitioner seated on a chair in open view near the driveway. He told one of the officers that "they're dead, I killed them" and directed the officer to the place where he had put the murder weapon. Later the petitioner told a police officer: "I've done a hideous crime, ... but I have been thinking about it for eight years.... I'd do it again."

The petitioner was subsequently indicted on two counts of murder and one count of aggravated assault. He pleaded not guilty and relied primarily on a defense of temporary insanity at his trial. The jury returned verdicts of guilty on all three counts.

The sentencing phase of the trial was held before the same jury. No further evidence was tendered, but counsel for each side made arguments to the jury. Three times during the course of his argument, the prosecutor stated that the case involved no allegation of "torture" or of an "aggravated battery." When counsel had completed their arguments, the trial judge instructed the jury orally and in writing on the standards that must guide them in imposing sentence. Both orally and in writing, the judge quoted to the jury the statutory language of the §(b)(7) aggravating circumstance in its entirety.

The jury imposed sentences of death on both of the murder convictions. As to each, the jury specified that the aggravating circumstance they had found beyond a reasonable doubt was "that the offense of murder was outrageously or wantonly vile, horrible and inhuman."

In accord with Georgia law in capital cases, the trial judge prepared a report in the form of answers to a questionnaire for use on appellate review. One question on the form asked whether or not the victim had been "physically harmed or tortured." The trial judge's response was "No, as to both victims, excluding the actual murdering of the two victims."

The Georgia Supreme Court affirmed the judgments of the trial court in all respects. With regard to the imposition of the death sentence for each of the two murder convictions, the court rejected the petitioner's contention that §(b)(7) is unconstitutionally vague. The court noted that Georgia's death penalty legislation had been upheld in *Gregg* and cited its prior decisions upholding §(b)(7) in the face of similar vagueness challenges. As to the petitioner's argument that the jury's phraseology was, as a matter of law, an inadequate statement of §(b)(7), the court responded by simply observing that the language "was not objectionable." The court found no evidence that the sentence had been "imposed under the influence of passion, prejudice, or any other arbitrary factor," held that the sentence was neither excessive nor disproportionate to the penalty imposed in similar cases, and stated that the evidence supported the jury's finding of the §(b)(7) statutory aggravating circumstance. Two justices dissented.

II

In *Furman v. Georgia*, 408 U.S. 238 (1972), the Court held that the penalty of death may not be imposed under sentencing procedures that create a substantial risk that the punishment will be inflicted in an arbitrary and capricious manner. *Gregg* reaffirmed this holding:

> [W]here discretion is afforded a sentencing body on a matter so grave as the determination of whether a human life should be taken or spared, that discretion must be suitably directed and limited so as to minimize the risk of wholly arbitrary and capricious action.

A capital sentencing scheme must, in short, provide a "'meaningful basis for distinguishing the few cases in which [the death penalty] is imposed from the many cases in which it is not.'"

This means that if a State wishes to authorize capital punishment it has a constitutional responsibility to tailor and apply its law in a manner that avoids the arbitrary and capricious infliction of the death penalty. Part of a State's responsibility in this regard is to define the crimes for which death may be the sentence in a way that obviates "standardless [sentencing] discretion." It must channel the sentencer's discretion by "clear and objective standards" that provide "specific and detailed guidance," and that "make rationally reviewable the process for imposing a sentence of death." As was made clear in *Gregg*, a death penalty "system could have standards so vague that they would fail adequately to channel the sentencing decision patterns of juries with the result that a pattern of arbitrary and capricious sentencing like that found unconstitutional in *Furman* could occur."

In the case before us the Georgia Supreme Court has affirmed a sentence of death based upon no more than a finding that the offense was "outrageously or wantonly vile, horrible and inhuman." There is nothing in these few words, standing alone, that implies any inherent restraint on the arbitrary and capricious infliction of the death sentence. A person of ordinary sensibility could fairly characterize almost every murder as "outrageously or wantonly vile, horrible and inhuman." Such a view may, in fact, have been one to which the members of the jury in this case subscribed. If so, their preconceptions were not dispelled by the trial judge's sentencing instructions. These gave the jury no guidance concerning the meaning of any of §(b)(7)'s terms. In fact, the jury's interpretation of §(b)(7) can only be the subject of sheer speculation.

The standardless and unchanneled imposition of death sentences in the uncontrolled discretion of a basically uninstructed jury in this case was in no way cured by the affirmance of those sentences by the Georgia Supreme Court. Under state law that court may not affirm a judgment of death until it has independently assessed the evidence of record and determined that such evidence supports the trial judge's or jury's finding of an aggravating circumstance.

In past cases the State Supreme Court has apparently understood this obligation as carrying with it the responsibility to keep §(b)(7) within constitutional bounds....

... [B]y 1977 [the Georgia Supreme Court had] reached three separate but consistent conclusions respecting the §(b)(7) aggravating circumstance. The first was that the evidence that the offense was "outrageously or wantonly vile, horrible or inhuman" had to demonstrate "torture, depravity of mind, or an aggravated battery to the victim." The second was that the phrase, "depravity of mind," comprehended only the kind of mental state that led the murderer to torture or to commit an aggravated battery before killing his victim. The third ... was that the word, "torture," must be construed *in pari materia* with "aggravated battery" so as to require evidence of serious physical abuse of the victim before death. Indeed, the circumstances proved in a number of the §(b)(7) death sentence cases affirmed by the Georgia Supreme Court have met all three of these criteria.

The Georgia courts did not, however, so limit §(b)(7) in the present case. No claim was made, and nothing in the record before us suggests, that the petitioner committed an aggravated battery upon his wife or mother-in-law or, in fact, caused either of them to suffer any physical injury preceding their deaths. Moreover, in the trial court, the prosecutor repeatedly told the jury—and the trial judge wrote in his sentencing report—that the murders did not involve "torture." Nothing said on appeal by the Georgia Supreme Court indicates that it took a different view of the evidence. The circumstances of this case, therefore, do not satisfy the criteria laid out by the Georgia Supreme Court itself.... In holding that the evidence supported the jury's §(b)(7) finding, the State Supreme Court simply asserted that the verdict was "factually substantiated."

Thus, the validity of the petitioner's death sentences turns on whether, in light of the facts and circumstances of the murders that he was convicted of committing, the Georgia Supreme Court can be said to have applied a constitutional construction of the phrase "outrageously or wantonly vile, horrible or inhuman in that [they] involved ... depravity of mind...." We conclude that the answer must be no. The petitioner's crimes cannot be said to have reflected a consciousness materially more "depraved" than that of any person guilty of murder. His victims were killed instantaneously. They were members of his family who were causing him extreme emotional trauma. Shortly after the killings, he acknowledged his responsibility and the heinous nature of his crimes. These factors certainly did not remove the criminality from the petitioner's acts. But, as was said in *Gardner v. Florida*, 430 U.S. 349, 358 (1977), it "is of vital importance to the defendant and to the community that any decision to impose the death sentence be, and appear to be, based on reason rather than caprice or emotion."

That cannot be said here. There is no principled way to distinguish this case, in which the death penalty was imposed, from the many cases in which it was not. Accordingly, the judgment of the Georgia Supreme Court insofar as it leaves standing the petitioner's death sentences is reversed, and the case is remanded to that court for further proceedings.

Mr. Justice MARSHALL, with whom Mr. Justice Brennan joins, concurring in the judgment.

II

... The Georgia Supreme Court has given no real content to §(b)(7) in by far the majority of the cases in which it has had an opportunity to do so. In the four years since *Gregg*, the Georgia court has never reversed a jury's finding of a §(b)(7) aggravating circumstance. With considerable frequency the Georgia court has, as here, upheld the imposition of the death penalty on the basis of a simple conclusory statement that the evidence supported the jury's finding under §(b)(7). Instances of a narrowing construction are difficult to find, and those narrowing constructions that can be found have not been adhered to with any regularity. In no case has the Georgia court required a narrowing construction to be given to the jury—an indispensable method for avoiding the "standardless and unchanneled imposition of death sentences." Genuinely independent review has been exceedingly rare. In sum, I agree with the analysis of a recent commentator who, after a careful examination of the Georgia cases, concluded that the Georgia court has made no substantial effort to limit the scope of §(b)(7), but has instead defined the provision so broadly that practically every murder can fit within its reach.

The Georgia court's inability to administer its capital punishment statute in an even-handed fashion is not necessarily attributable to any bad faith on its part; it is, I believe, symptomatic of a deeper problem that is proving to be genuinely intractable. Just five years before *Gregg*, Mr. Justice Harlan [in *McGautha v. California, supra* chapter 3] stated for the Court that the tasks of identifying "before the fact those characteristics of criminal homicides and their perpetrators which call for the death penalty, and [of] express[ing] these characteristics in language which can be fairly understood and applied by the sentencing authority, appear to be ... beyond present human ability."

... I believe that the Court in *McGautha* was substantially correct in concluding that the task of selecting in some objective way those persons who should be condemned to die is one that remains beyond the capacities of the criminal justice system. For this reason, I remain hopeful that even if the Court is unwilling to accept the view that the death penalty is so barbaric that it is in all circumstances cruel and unusual punishment forbidden by the Eighth and Fourteenth Amendments, it may eventually conclude that the effort to eliminate arbitrariness in the infliction of that ultimate sanction is so plainly doomed to failure that it—and the death penalty—must be abandoned altogether.

Maynard v. Cartwright

486 U.S. 356 (1988)

Justice WHITE delivered the opinion for an unanimous Court.

On May 4, 1982, after eating their evening meal in their Muskogee County, Oklahoma, home, Hugh and Charma Riddle watched television in their living room. At some point, Mrs. Riddle left the living room and was proceeding towards the bathroom when she encountered respondent Cartwright standing in the hall holding a shotgun.

She struggled for the gun and was shot twice in the legs. The man, whom she recognized as a disgruntled ex-employee, then proceeded to the living room where he shot and killed Hugh Riddle. Mrs. Riddle dragged herself down the hall to a bedroom where she tried to use a telephone. Respondent, however, entered the bedroom, slit Mrs. Riddle's throat, stabbed her twice with a hunting knife the Riddles had given him for Christmas, and then left the house. Mrs. Riddle survived and called the police. Respondent was arrested two days later and charged with first-degree murder.

Respondent was tried and found guilty as charged. The State, relying on three statutory aggravating circumstances, sought the death penalty. The jury found two of them to have been established: first, the defendant "knowingly created a great risk of death to more than one person"; second, the murder was "especially heinous, atrocious, or cruel." Finding that the aggravating circumstances outweighed the mitigating evidence, the jury imposed the death penalty. The Oklahoma Court of Criminal Appeals and the federal district court affirmed respondent's conviction. A panel of the Court of Appeals for the Tenth Circuit [also] affirmed [respondent's conviction], but rehearing en banc was granted limited to the claim concerning the challenged aggravating circumstance.

The en banc court recognized that the jury had found two aggravating circumstances, one of them being unchallenged. But it noted that in cases where a death sentence rested in part on an invalid aggravating circumstance, the Oklahoma courts did not reweigh the aggravating and mitigating circumstances in an effort to save the death penalty; rather, the death sentence was vacated and a life-imprisonment sentence automatically imposed. Oklahoma had "no provision for curing on appeal a sentencer's consideration of an invalid aggravating circumstance." It was therefore necessary to consider the vagueness challenge to one of the aggravating circumstances. The court proceeded to do so and unanimously sustained the challenge. It stated that the words "heinous," "atrocious," and "cruel" did not on their face offer sufficient guidance to the jury to escape the strictures of our judgment in *Furman v. Georgia*, 408 U.S. 238 (1972). Nor, in the court's view, had the Oklahoma courts adopted a limiting construction that cured the infirmity and that was relied upon to affirm the death sentence in this case. It concluded that the Oklahoma Court of Criminal Appeals' construction of the aggravating circumstance was "unconstitutionally vague" under the Eighth Amendment. The death sentence, accordingly, was held to be invalid and its execution enjoined, but "without prejudice to further proceedings by the state for redetermination of the sentence on the conviction."

[The State] sought review here of the Tenth Circuit's holding that the aggravating circumstance was unconstitutionally vague. Because of the conflict between the Court of Appeals for the Tenth Circuit and the Court of Criminal Appeals of Oklahoma and because of the importance of this constitutional issue to the orderly and proper administration of state death-penalty statutes, we granted certiorari, limited to that issue. We affirm the judgment of the [Tenth Circuit] Court of Appeals.

The [Tenth Circuit] Court of Appeals, with some care, reviewed the evolution in the interpretation of the "especially heinous, atrocious, or cruel" aggravating circumstance by the Oklahoma Court of Criminal Appeals up to and including its decision in this case. Its reading of the cases was that while the Oklahoma court had considered the attitude of the killer, the manner of the killing, and the suffering of the victim to be relevant and sufficient to support the aggravating circumstance, that court had "refused to hold that any one of those factors must be present for a murder to satisfy this aggravating circumstance." Rather, the Oklahoma court simply had reviewed all of the circumstances of the murder and decided whether the facts made out the aggravating circumstance. We normally defer to courts of appeals in their interpretation of state law, and we see no reason not to accept the Court of Appeals' statements about state law in this case, especially since the State does not challenge this reading of the Oklahoma cases.

The State, however, takes issue with the Court of Appeals' conclusion that this approach, which was also employed in this case, to interpreting and applying the challenged aggravating circumstance is unconstitutional. It insists that in some cases there are factual circumstances that so plainly characterize the killing as "especially heinous, atrocious, or cruel" that affirmance of the death penalty is proper. As we understand the argument, it is that a statutory provision governing a criminal case is unconstitutionally vague only if there are no circumstances that could be said with reasonable certainty to fall within reach of the language at issue. Or to put it another way, that if there are circumstances that any reasonable person would recognize as covered by the statute, it is not unconstitutionally vague even if the language would fail to give adequate notice that it covered other circumstances as well.

The difficulty with the State's argument is that it presents a Due Process Clause approach to vagueness and fails to recognize the rationale of our cases construing and applying the Eighth Amendment. Objections to vagueness under the Due Process Clause rest on the lack of notice, and hence may be overcome in any specific case where reasonable persons would know that their conduct is at risk. Vagueness challenges to statutes not threatening First Amendment interests are examined in light of the facts of the case at hand; the statute is judged on an as-applied basis. Claims of vagueness directed at aggravating circumstances defined in capital punishment statutes are analyzed under the Eighth Amendment and characteristically assert that the challenged provision fails adequately to inform juries what they must find to impose the death penalty and as a result leaves them and appellate courts with the kind of open-ended discretion which was held invalid in *Furman*....

We think ... that *Godfrey v. Georgia*, 446 U.S. 420 (1980), controls this case. First, the language of the Oklahoma aggravating circumstance at issue — "especially heinous, atrocious, or cruel" — gave no more guidance than the "outrageously or wantonly vile, horrible or inhuman" language that the jury returned in its verdict in *Godfrey*. The State's contention that the addition of the word "especially" somehow guides the jury's discretion, even if the term "heinous" does not, is untenable. To say that something is "especially heinous" merely suggests that the individual jurors should determine that the murder is more than just "heinous," whatever that means, and an ordinary person could honestly believe that every unjustified, intentional taking of human life is "especially heinous." Likewise, in *Godfrey* the addition of "outrageously or wantonly" to the term "vile" did not limit the overbreadth of the aggravating factor.

Second, the conclusion of the Oklahoma court that the events recited by it "adequately supported the jury's finding" was indistinguishable from the action of the Georgia court in *Godfrey*, which failed to cure the unfettered discretion of the jury and to satisfy the commands of the Eighth Amendment. The Oklahoma court relied on the facts that Cartwright had a motive of getting even with the victims, that he lay in wait for them, that the murder victim heard the blast that wounded his wife, that he again brutally attacked the surviving wife, that he attempted to conceal his deeds, and that he attempted to steal the victims' belongings. Its conclusion that on these facts the jury's verdict that the murder was especially heinous, atrocious, or cruel was supportable did not cure the constitutional infirmity of the aggravating circumstance.

The State complains, however, that the [Tenth Circuit] Court of Appeals ruled that to be valid the "especially heinous, atrocious, or cruel" aggravating circumstance must be construed to require torture or serious physical abuse and that this was error. We do not, however, agree that the Court of Appeals imposed this requirement. It noted cases in which such a requirement sufficed to validate an otherwise vague aggravating circumstance, but it expressly refrained from directing the State to adopt any specific curative construction of the aggravating circumstance at issue here. We also do not hold that some kind of torture or serious physical abuse is the only limiting construction of the heinous, atrocious, or cruel aggravating circumstance that would be constitutionally acceptable....

It is true that since the decision of the [Tenth Circuit] Court of Appeals, the Oklahoma Court of Criminal Appeals has restricted the "heinous, atrocious, or cruel" aggravating circumstance to those murders in which torture or serious physical abuse is present. At the same time, that court decided that it would not necessarily set aside a death penalty where on appeal one of several aggravating circumstances has been found invalid or unsupported by the evidence.

What significance these decisions of the Court of Criminal Appeals have for the present case is a matter for the state courts to decide in the first instance. Like that of the [Tenth Circuit] Court of Appeals, our judgment is without prejudice to further proceedings in the state courts for redetermination of the appropriate sentence.

The judgment of the Court of Appeals is affirmed.

Arave v. Creech

507 U.S. 463 (1993)

Justice O'CONNOR delivered the opinion of the Court in which Rehnquist, C.J., and White, Scalia, Kennedy, Souter and Thomas, JJ., joined.

In 1981 Thomas Eugene Creech beat and kicked to death a fellow inmate at the Idaho State Penitentiary. He pleaded guilty to first-degree murder and was sentenced to death. The sentence was based in part on the statutory aggravating circumstance that "by the murder, or circumstances surrounding its commission, the defendant exhibited utter disregard for human life." Idaho Code §19-2515(g)(6) (1987). The sole question we must decide is whether the "utter disregard" circumstance, as interpreted by the Idaho Supreme Court, adequately channels sentencing discretion as required by the Eighth and Fourteenth Amendments.

I

The facts underlying this case could not be more chilling. Thomas Creech has admitted to killing or participating in the killing of at least 26 people. The bodies of 11 of his victims—who were shot, stabbed, beaten, or strangled to death—have been recovered in seven States. Creech has said repeatedly that, unless he is completely isolated from humanity, he likely will continue killing. And he has identified by name three people outside prison walls he intends to kill if given the opportunity.

Creech's most recent victim was David Dale Jensen, a fellow inmate in the maximum security unit of the Idaho State Penitentiary. When he killed Jensen, Creech was already serving life sentences for other first-degree murders. Jensen, about seven years Creech's junior, was a nonviolent car thief. He was also physically handicapped. Part of Jensen's brain had been removed prior to his incarceration, and he had a plastic plate in his skull.

The circumstances surrounding Jensen's death remain unclear, primarily because Creech has given conflicting accounts of them. In one version, Creech killed Jensen in self-defense. In another—the version that Creech gave at his sentencing hearing—other inmates offered to pay Creech or help him escape if he killed Jensen. Creech, through an intermediary, provided Jensen with makeshift weapons and then arranged for Jensen to attack him, in order to create an excuse for the killing....

Creech pleaded guilty to first-degree murder. After the [sentencing] hearing, the judge issued written findings in the format prescribed by Rule 33.1 of the Idaho Criminal Rules. Under the heading "Facts and Argument Found in Mitigation," he listed that Creech "did not instigate the fight with the victim, but the victim, without provocation, attacked him. [Creech] was initially justified in protecting himself." Under the heading "Facts and Argument Found in Aggravation," the judge stated:

> The victim, once the attack commenced, was under the complete domination and control of the defendant. The murder itself was extremely gruesome evidencing an excessive violent rage. With the victim's attack as an excuse, the ... murder then took on many aspects of an assassination. These violent ac-

tions ... went well beyond self-defense.... The murder, once commenced, appears to have been an intentional, calculated act.

The judge then found beyond a reasonable doubt five statutory aggravating circumstances, including that Creech, "by the murder, or circumstances surrounding its commission, ... exhibited utter disregard for human life." He observed in this context that "after the victim was helpless [Creech] killed him." Next, the judge concluded that the mitigating circumstances did not outweigh the aggravating circumstances. Reiterating that Creech "intentionally destroyed another human being at a time when he was completely helpless," the judge sentenced Creech to death.

... [The Idaho Supreme Court affirmed Creech's conviction. The Ninth Circuit Court of Appeals reversed the conviction finding that the "utter disregard" aggravating circumstances was facially invalid.] We granted certiorari, limited to the narrow question whether the "utter disregard" circumstance, as interpreted by the Idaho Supreme Court in *State v. Osborn,* 102 Idaho 405, 631 P.2d 187 (1981), is unconstitutionally vague.

II

This case is governed by the standards we articulated in *Walton v. Arizona,* 497 U.S. 639 (1990), and *Lewis v. Jeffers,* 497 U.S. 764 (1990). In *Jeffers* we reaffirmed the fundamental principle that, to satisfy the Eighth and Fourteenth Amendments, a capital sentencing scheme must "'suitably direct and limit'" the sentencer's discretion "'so as to minimize the risk of wholly arbitrary and capricious action.'" The State must "'channel the sentencer's discretion by clear and objective standards that provide specific and detailed guidance, and that make rationally reviewable the process for imposing a sentence of death.'"

In *Walton* we set forth the inquiry that a federal court must undertake when asked to decide whether a particular aggravating circumstance meets these standards:

> The federal court ... must first determine whether the statutory language defining the circumstance is itself too vague to provide any guidance to the sentencer. If so, then the federal court must attempt to determine whether the state courts have further defined the vague terms and if they have done so, whether those definitions are constitutionally sufficient, *i.e.,* whether they provide *some* guidance to the sentencer.

Where, as in Idaho, the sentencer is a judge rather than a jury, the federal court must presume that the judge knew and applied any existing narrowing construction.

Unlike the [Ninth Circuit] Court of Appeals, we do not believe it is necessary to decide whether the statutory phrase "utter disregard for human life" itself passes constitutional muster. The Idaho Supreme Court [in *State v. Osborn,* 102 Idaho 405, 631 P.2d 187 (1981)], has adopted a limiting construction [that the phrase "utter disregard" requires a showing of the highest, callous disregard for human life, i.e., the cold-blooded, pitiless slayer], and we believe that construction meets constitutional requirements.

Contrary to the dissent's assertions, the phrase "cold-blooded, pitiless slayer" is not without content. Webster's Dictionary defines "pitiless" to mean devoid of, or unmoved by, mercy or compassion. The lead entry for "cold-blooded" gives coordinate definitions. One, "marked by absence of warm feelings: without consideration, compunction, or clemency," mirrors the definition of "pitiless." The other defines "cold-blooded" to mean "matter of fact, emotionless." It is true that "cold-blooded" is sometimes also used to describe "premeditation," a mental state that may coincide with, but is distinct from, a lack of feeling or compassion. But premeditation is clearly not the sense in which the Idaho Supreme Court used the word "cold-blooded" in *Osborn.* Other terms in the limiting construction — "callous" and "pitiless" — indicate that the court used the word "cold-blooded" in its first sense. "Premeditation," moreover, is specifically addressed elsewhere in the Idaho homicide statutes; had the *Osborn* court meant premeditation, it likely would have used the statutory language....

Determining whether a capital defendant killed without feeling or sympathy is undoubtedly more difficult than, for example, determining whether he "was previously convicted of another murder." But that does not mean that a State cannot, consistent with the Federal Constitution, authorize sentencing judges to make the inquiry and to take their findings into account when deciding whether capital punishment is warranted. This is the import of *Walton*. In that case we considered Arizona's "especially heinous, cruel, or depraved" circumstance. The Arizona Supreme Court had held that a crime is committed in a "depraved" manner when the perpetrator " 'relishes the murder, evidencing debasement or perversion,' or 'shows an indifference to the suffering of the victim and evidences a sense of pleasure' in the killing." We concluded that this construction adequately guided sentencing discretion, even though "the proper degree of definition of an aggravating factor of this nature is not susceptible of mathematical precision."

The language at issue here is no less "clear and objective" than the language sustained in *Walton*. Whether a defendant "relishes" or derives "pleasure" from his crime arguably may be easier to determine than whether he acts without feeling or sympathy, since enjoyment is an affirmative mental state, whereas the cold-bloodedness inquiry in a sense requires the sentencer to find a negative. But we do not think so subtle a distinction has constitutional significance. The *Osborn* limiting construction, like the one upheld in *Walton*, defines a state of mind that is ascertainable from surrounding facts. Accordingly, we decline to invalidate the "utter disregard" circumstance on the ground that the Idaho Supreme Court's limiting construction is insufficiently "objective."

Of course, it is not enough for an aggravating circumstance, as construed by the state courts, to be determinate. Our precedents make clear that a State's capital sentencing scheme also must "genuinely narrow the class of defendants eligible for the death penalty." When the purpose of a statutory aggravating circumstance is to enable the sentencer to distinguish those who deserve capital punishment from those who do not, the circumstance must provide a principled basis for doing so. If the sentencer fairly could conclude that an aggravating circumstance applies to every defendant eligible for the death penalty, the circumstance is constitutionally infirm.

Although the question is close, we believe the *Osborn* construction satisfies this narrowing requirement. The class of murderers eligible for capital punishment under Idaho law is defined broadly to include all first-degree murderers. And the category of first-degree murderers is also broad. It includes premeditated murders and those carried out by means of poison, lying in wait, or certain kinds of torture. In addition, murders that otherwise would be classified as second degree — including homicides committed without "considerable provocation" or under circumstances demonstrating "an abandoned and malignant heart" — become first degree if they are accompanied by one of a number of enumerated circumstances. For example, murders are classified as first degree when the victim is a fellow prison inmate, or a law enforcement or judicial officer performing official duties; when the defendant is already serving a sentence for murder; and when the murder occurs during a prison escape, or the commission or attempted commission of arson, rape, robbery, burglary, kidnapping, or mayhem. In other words, a sizable class of even those murderers who kill with some provocation or without specific intent may receive the death penalty under Idaho law.

We acknowledge that, even within these broad categories, the word "pitiless," standing alone, might not narrow the class of defendants eligible for the death penalty. A sentencing judge might conclude that every first-degree murderer is "pitiless," because it is difficult to imagine how a person with any mercy or compassion could kill another human being without justification. Given the statutory scheme, however, we believe that a sentencing judge reasonably could find that not all Idaho capital defendants are "cold-blooded." That is because some within the broad class of first-degree murderers do exhibit feeling. Some, for example, kill with anger, jealousy, revenge, or a variety of other emotions. In *Walton* we held that Arizona could treat capital defendants who take pleasure in killing as more deserving of the death penalty than those who do not. Idaho similarly has identified the subclass of defendants who kill without feeling or sympathy as more deserving of death. By doing so, it has narrowed in a meaningful way the category of defendants upon whom capital punishment may be imposed....

III

... The Court of Appeals granted Creech relief on two other claims: that the trial judge improperly refused to allow him to present new mitigating evidence when he was resentenced in open court, and that the judge applied two aggravating circumstances without making a finding required under state law. On the basis of the first claim, Creech is entitled to resentencing in state trial court. Accordingly, we hold today only that the "utter disregard" circumstance, as defined in *Osborn*, on its face meets constitutional requirements.

Justice BLACKMUN, with whom Justice Stevens joins, dissenting.

Confronted with an insupportable limiting construction of an unconstitutionally vague statute, the majority in turn concocts its own limiting construction of the state court's formulation. Like "nonsense upon stilts," however, the majority's reconstruction only highlights the deficient character of the nebulous formulation that it seeks to advance. Because the metaphor "cold-blooded" by which Idaho defines its "utter disregard" circumstance is both vague and unenlightening, and because the majority's recasting of that metaphor is not dictated by common usage, legal usage, or the usage of the Idaho courts, the statute fails to provide meaningful guidance to the sentencer as required by the Constitution. Accordingly, I dissent....

II

... Under *Osborn*, an offense demonstrates "utter disregard for human life" when the "acts or circumstances surrounding the crime ... exhibit the highest, the utmost, callous disregard for human life, i.e., the cold-blooded, pitiless slayer." Jettisoning all but the term, "cold-blooded," the majority contends that this cumbersome construction clearly singles out the killing committed "without feeling or sympathy." As an initial matter, I fail to see how "without feeling or sympathy" is meaningfully different from "devoid of ... mercy or compassion"—the definition of "pitiless" that the majority concedes to be constitutionally inadequate.

... In its eagerness to boil the phrase down to a serviceable core, the majority virtually ignores the very definition it cites. Instead, the majority comes up with a hybrid all its own—"without feeling or sympathy"—and then goes one step further, asserting that because the term "cold-blooded" so obviously means "without feeling," it cannot refer as ordinarily understood to murderers who "kill with anger, jealousy, revenge, or a variety of other emotions." That is incorrect. In everyday parlance, the term "cold-blooded" routinely is used to describe killings that fall outside the major-ity's definition. In the first nine weeks of this year alone, [newspaper articles have used] the label "cold-blooded" to [describe] a murder by an ex-spouse angry over vis-itation rights, a killing by a jealous lover, a revenge killing, an ex-spouse "full of ha-tred," the close-range assassination of an enemy official by a foe in a bitter ethnic con-flict, a murder prompted by humiliation and hatred, killings by fanatical cult members, a murderer who enjoyed killing, and, perhaps most appropriately, all mur-ders. All these killings occurred with "feelings" of one kind or another. All were de-scribed as cold-blooded. The majority's assertion that the Idaho construction narrows the class of capital defendants because it rules out those who "kill with anger, jealousy, revenge, or a variety of other emotions" clearly is erroneous, because in ordinary usage the nebulous description "cold-blooded" simply is not limited to defendants who kill without emotion.

In legal usage, the metaphor "cold blood" does have a specific meaning. "Cold blood" is used "to designate a willful, deliberate, and premeditated homicide." As such, the term is used to differentiate between first- and second-degree murders. For ex-ample, in *United States v. Frady*, 456 U.S. 152 (1982), Justice O'Connor, writing for the Court, described the District of Columbia's homicide statute: "'In homespun termi-nology, intentional murder is in the first degree if committed in cold blood, and is murder in the second degree if committed on impulse or in the sudden heat of pas-sion.'" Murder in cold blood is, in this sense, the opposite of murder in "hot blood." Arguably, then, the *Osborn* formulation covers every intentional or first-degree mur-der. An aggravating circumstance so construed would clearly be unconstitutional under *Godfrey*.

… The futility of the Idaho courts' attempt to bring some rationality to the "utter disre-gard" circumstance is glaringly evident in the sole post-*Osborn* case that endeavors to ex-plain the construction in any depth. In *State v. Fain*, 116 Idaho 82, 774 P.2d 252 (1989), the court declared that the "utter disregard" factor refers to "the defendant's lack of con-scientious scruples against killing another human being." Thus, the latest statement from the Idaho Supreme Court on the issue says nothing about emotionless crimes, but, in-stead, sweepingly includes every murder committed that is without "conscientious scru-ples against killing." I can imagine no crime that would not fall within that construc-tion.…

III

Let me be clear about what the majority would have to show in order to save the Idaho statute: that, on its face, the *Osborn* construction—"the highest, the utmost, callous dis-regard for human life, i.e., the cold-blooded, pitiless slayer"—refers clearly and exclu-sively to crimes that occur "without feeling or sympathy," that is, to those that occur without "anger, jealousy, revenge, or a variety of other emotions." No such showing has been made.

There is, of course, something distasteful and absurd in the very project of parsing this lexicon of death. But as long as we are in the death business, we shall be in the pars-ing business as well. Today's majority stretches the bounds of permissible construction past the breaking point. "'Vague terms do not suddenly become clear when they are de-fined by reference to other vague terms,'" nor do sweeping categories become narrow by mere restatement. The *Osborn* formulation is worthless, and neither common usage, nor legal terminology, nor the Idaho cases support the majority's attempt to salvage it. The statute is simply unconstitutional and Idaho should be busy repairing it.

I would affirm the judgment of the Court of Appeals.

Notes

1. The California death penalty scheme provides that before a jury may consider imposing the death penalty the jury must find a defendant guilty of first-degree murder and find the existence of one or more special circumstances which are set out in the California Penal Code. Once a jury makes these findings, the case proceeds to the sentencing phase during which the jury determines whether death or some lesser penalty should be imposed. During the sentencing phase the jury considers the relevant sentencing factors set forth in §190.3 of the California Penal Code. (The California statute is reproduced on pages 399–400 of the casebook.)

In *Tuilaepa v. California*, 512 U.S. 967 (1994), two capital defendants, Paul Palalaua Tuilaepa and William Arnold Proctor, challenged the constitutionality of three factors set out in §190.3:

(a) The circumstances of the crime of which the defendant was convicted in the present proceeding and the existence of any special circumstances found to be true pursuant to Section 190.1.

(b) The presence or absence of criminal activity by the defendant which involved the use or attempted use of force or violence or the express or implied threat to use force or violence.

* * *

(i) The age of the offender.

Justice Kennedy's opinion for the five-member majority is excerpted below.

Because "the proper degree of definition" of eligibility and selection factors often "is not susceptible of mathematical precision," our vagueness review is quite deferential. *Walton v. Arizona*, 497 U.S. 639, 655 (1990); see *Gregg*, 428 U.S. at 193–194 (factors "are by necessity somewhat general"). Relying on the basic principle that a factor is not unconstitutional if it has some "common-sense core of meaning ... that criminal juries should be capable of understanding," *Jurek v. Texas*, 428 U.S. 262, 279 (1976) (White, J., concurring in judgment), we have found only a few factors vague, and those in fact are quite similar to one another. See *Maynard*, at 363–364 (question whether murder was "especially heinous, atrocious, or cruel"); *Godfrey*, at 427–429 (question whether murder was "outrageously or wantonly vile, horrible or inhuman"); cf. *Arave*, 507 U.S. 463 (1993) ("We are not faced with pejorative adjectives ... that describe a crime as a whole"). In providing for individualized sentencing, it must be recognized that the States may adopt capital sentencing processes that rely upon the jury, in its sound judgment, to exercise wide discretion. That is evident from the numerous factors we have upheld against vagueness challenges.

In our decisions holding a death sentence unconstitutional because of a vague sentencing factor, the State had presented a specific proposition that the sentencer had to find true or false (*e.g.*, whether the crime was especially heinous, atrocious, or cruel). We have held, under certain sentencing schemes, that a vague propositional factor used in the sentencing decision creates an unacceptable risk of randomness, the mark of the arbitrary and capricious sentencing process prohibited by *Furman v. Georgia*, 408 U.S. 238 (1972). Those concerns are mitigated when a factor does not require a yes or a no answer to a specific question, but instead only points the sentencer to a subject matter. See Cal. Penal Code §190.3 (a), (k) (West 1988). Both types of factors (and the distinction between the two is not always clear) have their utility. For purposes of vagueness analysis, however, in examining the propositional content of a factor, our concern is that the factor have some "common-sense core of meaning ... that criminal juries should be capable of understanding." *Jurek*, at 279 (White, J., concurring in judgment).

Petitioners' challenge to factor (a) is at some odds with settled principles, for our capital jurisprudence has established that the sentencer should consider the circumstances of the crime in deciding whether to impose the death penalty. See, e.g., *Woodson*, 428 U.S. at 304 ("consideration of ... the circumstances of the particular offense [is] a constitutionally indispensable part of the process of inflicting the penalty of death"). We would be hard pressed to invalidate a jury instruction that implements what we have said the law requires. In any event, this California factor instructs the jury to consider a relevant subject matter and does so in understandable terms. The circumstances of the crime are a traditional subject for consideration by the sentencer, and an instruction to consider the circumstances is neither vague nor otherwise improper under our Eighth Amendment jurisprudence.

Tuilaepa also challenges factor (b), which requires the sentencer to consider the defendant's prior criminal activity. The objection fails for many of the same reasons. Factor (b) is phrased in conventional and understandable terms and rests in large part on a determination whether certain events occurred, thus asking the jury to consider matters of historical fact. Under other sentencing schemes, in Texas for example, jurors may be asked to make a predictive judgment, such as "whether there is a probability that the defendant would commit criminal acts of violence that would constitute a continuing threat to society." Both a backward-looking and a forward-looking inquiry are a permissible part of the sentencing process, however, and the States have considerable latitude in determining how to guide the sentencer's decision in this respect. Here, factor (b) is not vague.

Tuilaepa's third challenge is to factor (i), which requires the sentencer to consider "the age of the defendant at the time of the crime." This again is an unusual challenge in light of our precedents. See *Eddings v. Oklahoma*, 455 U.S. 104, 115–117 (1982) (age may be relevant factor in sentencing decision). The factual inquiry is of the most rudimentary sort, and there is no suggestion that the term "age" is vague. Petitioner contends, however, that the age factor is equivocal and that in the typical case the prosecution argues in favor of the death penalty based on the defendant's age, no matter how old or young he was at the time of the crime. It is neither surprising nor remarkable that the relevance of the defendant's age can pose a dilemma for the sentencer. But difficulty in application is not equivalent to vagueness. Both the prosecution and the defense may present valid arguments as to the significance of the defendant's age in a particular case. Competing arguments by adversary parties bring perspective to a problem, and thus serve to promote a more reasoned decision, providing guidance as to a factor jurors most likely would discuss in any event. We find no constitutional deficiency in factor (I).

2. For a discussion of the constitutionality of judge sentencing in capital cases, see *Ring v. Arizona*, 536 U.S. 584 (2002), *infra* chapter 9.

C. Unauthorized Aggravating Circumstances

Unauthorized aggravating circumstances are those introduced by the prosecution during the capital sentencing phase which are not permitted. What happens when the sentencing authority condemns a defendant to die, relying in part on an aggravating circumstance not enumerated in the sentencing statute? The answer depends upon whether the relevant death penalty statute permits the introduction of nonstatutory aggravators during the sentencing phase. The Florida statute, at issue below in *Barclay v. Florida*, requires the sentencer to find at least one valid statutory aggravating circumstance before the death penalty may even be considered, and permits the trial court to admit any evidence that may be relevant to the proper sentence. However, Florida law requires the sentencer to balance statutory aggravating circumstances against all mitigating circumstances and does not permit non-statutory aggravating circumstances to enter into this weighing process.

Barclay v. Florida
463 U.S. 939 (1983)

Justice REHNQUIST announced the judgment of the Court and delivered an opinion in which the Chief Justice, Justice White, and Justice O'Connor joined.

The central question in this case is whether Florida may constitutionally impose the death penalty on petitioner Elwood Barclay when one of the "aggravating circumstances" relied upon by the trial judge to support the sentence was not among those established by the Florida death penalty statute.

[The sentencing judge found that five young black men — petitioner Barclay, Dougan, Crittendon, Evans, and Hearn — belonged to the Black Liberation Army, whose avowed purpose was "to kill white persons and to start a revolution and a racial war." On June 17, 1974, the five men set out in a car to find a victim. They picked up a hitchhiker, a white man named Stephen Orlando. The men drove Orlando to an isolated trash dump, ordered him out of the car, stabbed him with a knife, and then Dougan fatally shot Orlando twice in the head. The men left a note with Orlando's body declaring that the revolution had begun. Subsequently, Barclay and Dougan made tape recordings describing Orlando's death and sent those recordings to Orlando's mother.]

Barclay and Dougan were convicted by a jury of first-degree murder.[1] As required by the Florida death penalty statute, a separate sentencing hearing was held before the same jury. The jury rendered advisory sentences ... recommending that Dougan be sentenced to death and, by a 7 to 5 vote, that Barclay be sentenced to life imprisonment. The trial judge, after receiving a presentence report, decided to sentence both men to death. He

---

1. Evans and Crittendon, who did not actually kill Orlando, were convicted of second-degree murder and sentenced to 199 years in prison. Hearns pleaded guilty to second-degree murder and testified for the prosecution.

made written findings of fact concerning aggravating and mitigating circumstances as required by [Florida law]. The trial judge found that several of the aggravating circumstances set out in the [Florida death penalty] statute were present. He found that Barclay had knowingly created a great risk of death to many persons, had committed the murder while engaged in a kidnapping, had endeavored to disrupt governmental functions and law enforcement, and had been especially heinous, atrocious and cruel.

The trial judge did not find any mitigating circumstances. He noted in particular that Barclay had an extensive criminal record, and therefore did not qualify for the mitigating circumstance of having no significant history of prior criminal activity. He found that Barclay's record constituted an aggravating, rather than a mitigating circumstance. The trial judge also noted that the aggravating circumstance [that "the capital felony was committed by a convict under sentence of imprisonment"] was not present, but restated Barclay's criminal record and again found it to be an aggravating circumstance. He made a similar finding as to the aggravating circumstance [that "the defendant was previously convicted of another capital felony or of a felony involving the use or threat of violence to the person"]. Barclay had been convicted of breaking and entering with intent to commit the felony of grand larceny, but the trial judge did not know whether it involved the use or threat of violence. He pointed out that crimes such as this often involve the use or threat of violence, and stated that "there are more aggravating than mitigating circumstances."

The trial judge concluded that "[t]here are sufficient and great aggravating circumstances which exist to justify the sentence of death as to both defendants." He therefore rejected part of the jury's recommendation, and sentenced Barclay as well as Dougan to death.

... [Although the Florida Supreme Court initially affirmed Barclay's conviction and sentence,] the [c]ourt later vacated its judgment, *sua sponte*, in light of our decision in *Gardner v. Florida*, 430 U.S. 349 (1977), and remanded to the trial court to give Barclay a full opportunity to rebut the information in the presentence report that was prepared for the trial judge. The trial court held a resentencing hearing, and reaffirmed the death sentence on the basis of findings that are essentially identical to its original findings. On appeal, the Florida Supreme Court again affirmed, holding that Barclay had not been denied any rights under *Gardner*. Rehearing was denied by an equally divided court.

I

Barclay has raised numerous objections to the trial judge's findings....

C

Barclay also contends that his sentence must be vacated because the trial judge, in explaining his sentencing decision, discussed the racial motive for the murder and compared it with his own experiences in the army in World War II, when he saw Nazi concentration camps and their victims.[6] Barclay claims that the trial judge improperly

---

6. COMMENTS OF JUDGE

"My twenty-eight years of legal experience have been almost exclusively in the field of Criminal Law. I have been a defense attorney in criminal cases, an Advisor to the Public Defender's Office, a prosecutor for eight and one-half years and a Criminal Court and Circuit Judge — Felony Division — for almost ten years. During these twenty-eight years I have defended, prosecuted and held trial in almost every type of serious crime.

"Because of this extensive experience, I believe I have come to know and understand when, or when not, a crime is heinous, atrocious and cruel and deserving of the maximum possible sentence.

"My experience with the sordid, tragic and violent side of life has not been confined to the

added a non-statutory aggravating circumstance of racial hatred and should not have considered his own experiences.

We reject this argument. The United States Constitution does not prohibit a trial judge from taking into account the elements of racial hatred in this murder. The judge in this case found Barclay's desire to start a race war relevant to several statutory aggravating factors. The judge's discussion is neither irrational nor arbitrary. In particular, the comparison between this case and the Nazi concentration camps does not offend the United States Constitution. Such a comparison is not an inappropriate way of weighing the "especially heinous, atrocious and cruel" statutory aggravating circumstance in an attempt to determine whether it warrants imposition of the death penalty.

Any sentencing decision calls for the exercise of judgment. It is neither possible nor desirable for a person to whom the State entrusts an important judgment to decide in a vacuum, as if he had no experiences. The thrust of our decisions on capital punishment has been that "'discretion must be suitably directed and limited so as to minimize the risk of wholly arbitrary and capricious action.'" This very day we said in another capital case:

> In returning a conviction, the jury must satisfy itself that the necessary elements of the particular crime have been proved beyond a reasonable doubt. In fixing a penalty, however, there is no similar "central issue" from which the jury's attention may be diverted. Once the jury finds that the defendant falls within the legislatively defined category of persons eligible for the death penalty, as did respondent's jury in determining the truth of the alleged special circumstance, the jury then is free to consider a myriad of factors to determine whether death is the appropriate punishment. *California v. Ramos.*

We have never suggested that the United States Constitution requires that the sentencing process should be transformed into a rigid and mechanical parsing of statutory aggravating factors. But to attempt to separate the sentencer's decision from his experiences would inevitably do precisely that. It is entirely fitting for the moral, factual, and legal judgment of judges and juries to play a meaningful role in sentencing. We expect that sentencers will exercise their discretion in their own way and to the best of their ability. As long as that discretion is guided in a constitutionally adequate way, and as

---

Courtroom. I, like so many American Combat Infantry Soldiers, walked the battlefields of Europe and saw the thousands of dead American and German soldiers and I witnessed the concentration camps where innocent civilians and children were murdered in a war of racial and religious extermination.

"To attempt to initiate such a race war in this country is too horrible to contemplate for both our black and white citizens. Such an attempt must be dealt with by just and swift legal process and when justified by a Jury verdict of guilty—then to terminate and remove permanently from society those who would choose to initiate this diabolical course.

"Had the defendant been exposed to the carnage of the battlefields and the horrors of the concentration camps instead of movies, television programs and revolutionary tracts glorifying violence and racial strife—then perhaps his thoughts and actions would have taken a less violent course.

"Having set forth my personal experiences above, it is understandable that I am not easily shocked or moved by tragedy—but this present murder and call for racial war is especially shocking and meets every definition of heinous, atrocious and cruel. The perpetrator thereby forfeits further right to life—for certainly his life is no more sacred than that of the innocent eighteen year old victim, Stephen Anthony Orlando."

long as the decision is not so wholly arbitrary as to offend the Constitution, the Eighth Amendment cannot and should not demand more.

II

In this case, the state courts have considered an aggravating factor that is not a proper aggravating circumstance under state law. Barclay argues that a system that permits this sort of consideration does not meet the standards established by this Court under the Eighth and Fourteenth Amendments for the imposition of the death penalty....

B

The trial judge's consideration of Barclay's criminal record as an aggravating circumstance was improper as a matter of state law: that record did not fall within the definition of any statutory aggravating circumstance, and Florida law prohibits consideration of nonstatutory aggravating circumstances. In this case, like in *Zant v. Stephens*, 462 U.S. 862 (1983), nothing in the United States Constitution prohibited the trial court from considering Barclay's criminal record. The trial judge did not consider any constitutionally protected behavior to be an aggravating circumstance. And, again like in *Zant*, nothing in the Eighth Amendment or in Florida law prohibits the admission of the evidence of Barclay's criminal record. On the contrary, this evidence was properly introduced to prove that the mitigating circumstance of absence of a criminal record did not exist. This statutory aggravating circumstance "plausibly described aspects of the defendant's background that were properly before the [trial judge] and whose accuracy was unchallenged."

C

[After concluding that the trial court erred in considering Barclay's criminal record as an aggravating circumstance, the Supreme Court agreed with the Florida Supreme Court that the error was harmless and affirmed Barclay's sentence of death. For discussions of the harmless error doctrine and the appellate reweighing of aggravating and mitigating circumstances, see *infra* chapter 8 (appellate reweighing), chapter 10 (harmless error on direct appeal), and chapter 13 (harmless error in federal habeas corpus).]

The judgment of the Supreme Court of Florida is affirmed.

Justice MARSHALL, with whom Justice Brennan joins, dissenting.

Based on a sentencing order rife with errors, the trial judge condemned petitioner Elwood Barclay to death. The Florida Supreme Court then conducted a perfunctory review and affirmed the sentence. Today the plurality approves this miscarriage of justice. In doing so it is utterly faithless to the safeguards established by the Court's prior decisions. I dissent....

II

A

... The trial judge found that none of the statutory mitigating circumstances applied to Barclay.[2] Instead, the judge concluded that the absence of one of the mitigating cir-

---

2. The trial judge did not mention the subject of nonstatutory mitigating circumstances. During closing argument at the sentencing trial, petitioner's counsel had contended that such circumstances were present. For example, counsel noted that petitioner was the father of five children and was gainfully employed, and he argued that petitioner was a follower and not a leader among the murderers. He also pointed to the disparity in treatment among the various participants in the crime,

cumstances itself constituted an aggravating circumstance. Florida law identifies as a mitigating circumstance the fact that a defendant "has no significant history of prior criminal activity." The statute does not make the presence of a significant history of prior criminal activity an aggravating circumstance. Nonetheless, after finding that petitioner had a criminal record, the trial judge stated that the prior record constituted an aggravating circumstance. This determination was clearly lawless. The Florida Supreme Court has expressly held that a "substantial history of prior criminal activity is not an aggravating circumstance under the statute."

The trial judge then turned to the eight aggravating circumstances that the Florida Legislature had actually established. Even though the State had relied on only one of these circumstances during the sentencing hearing, the trial judge managed to find that six were relevant.

The first aggravating circumstance applies if a capital felony has been "committed by a person under sentence of imprisonment." The judge stated that Barclay was not under imprisonment at the time of the capital offense—a fact which should have been dispositive under the plain language of the statute. Nonetheless, the judge then pointed to Barclay's prior arrests and the fact that he had previously been on probation for a felony, and he again stated that petitioner's record constituted an aggravating circumstance. Reliance on the arrests was certainly improper under Florida law, because any charge which has "not resulted in a conviction at the time of the [capital] trial" is "a nonstatutory aggravating factor." Reliance on the fact that petitioner had formerly been on probation was also error, since the sentence of imprisonment must exist at the time of the capital felony. The second aggravating circumstance found by the trial judge was that petitioner had been "previously convicted of another capital felony or of a felony involving the use or threat of violence to the person." The court based this finding on petitioner's presentence report, which showed an earlier conviction for breaking and entering with intent to commit grand larceny. Although there was absolutely no evidence that this prior felony involved the use or threat of violence, the judge asserted that "such crime can and often does involve violence or threat of violence." The judge's reliance on this aggravating circumstance was contrary to Florida law. This statutory factor applies only where "the judgment of conviction discloses that it involved violence," and the Florida Supreme Court has explicitly held that the crime of breaking and entering with intent to commit a felony does not constitute a crime of violence within the meaning of this provision. Moreover, the trial judge's reliance on information contained in the presentence report to establish this aggravating circumstance itself constituted an error under state law.

The trial court next found that petitioner had "knowingly created a great risk of death to many persons." This statutory circumstance was directed at conduct creating a serious danger to a large group of people, such as exploding a bomb in a public place or hijacking an airplane. Thus, something in the nature of the homicidal act itself or in the conduct immediately surrounding the act must create a great risk to many people.... The trial judge incorrectly relied on conduct occurring both before and after the capital felony. Invocation of this aggravating circumstance was therefore clearly unauthorized by state law.

The trial court's remaining findings are also problematic. For example, the judge found as a fourth aggravating circumstance that the murder was committed during a

---

three of whom faced punishment for only second-degree murder. The jury's finding that sufficient mitigating circumstances existed which outweighed any aggravating circumstances indicates that the jury found some mitigating circumstances.

kidnapping. However, the only witness who testified about the circumstances prior to the murder noted that the victim, a hitchhiker, willingly entered the car and rode with the defendants voluntarily. At the close of the trial on the issue of guilt, the trial judge himself had deemed the evidence insufficient to establish a kidnapping for purposes of giving a jury instruction as to felony-murder.

The trial judge's explanation of his sentence is all the more remarkable in light of two salient requirements of the Florida death penalty scheme. First, each of the statutory aggravating circumstances "must be proved beyond a reasonable doubt before being considered by judge or jury." Second, when the jury has recommended a life sentence, the judge may not impose a death sentence unless "'the facts suggesting a sentence of death [are] so clear and convincing that no reasonable person could differ.'" In light of these standards, the judge's sentencing order in this case was totally inadequate.

B

Nor can the sentencing judge's abysmal performance be deemed inadvertent or aberrant. To begin with, after the Florida Supreme Court had vacated the original sentence and remanded the case for reconsideration in light of *Gardner v. Florida*, petitioner's counsel brought to the attention of the trial judge several flagrant legal errors in the original sentencing order. For example, counsel noted that defendant's prior criminal record was not a proper aggravating circumstance, citing a controlling decision of the Florida Supreme Court. Even the plurality acknowledges that the trial judge erred in this finding. Nonetheless, the trial judge drafted a new sentencing order which simply repeated his prior, erroneous analysis.

The trial judge's actions in other capital cases are also instructive. Judge Olliff has sentenced three other defendants to death besides petitioner and his co-defendant. In each of these cases, as in petitioner's case, Judge Olliff ignored a jury's advisory sentence of life imprisonment.[10] In each of the cases, as in petitioner's case, the judge failed to find a single mitigating circumstance. The judge has repeatedly found that the felony was committed by a person under a sentence of imprisonment, that the defendant had previously been convicted of a violent felony, and that the defendant created a great risk of death to many persons, even though virtually all of these findings had no foundation in Florida law. And each time, Judge Olliff has recounted his experiences during World War II and recited boiler-plate language to the effect that he was not easily shocked but that the offense involved shocked him....

IV

This case illustrates the capital sentencing process gone awry. Relying on factors not mentioned in Florida law and statutory factors distorted beyond recognition, Judge Olliff overrode the jury's recommendation of life and sentenced petitioner to death. The Florida Supreme Court failed to conduct any meaningful review and instead showered the trial judge with praise for his performance. "Justice of this kind is obviously no less shocking than the crime itself, and the new 'official' murder, far from offering redress for the offense committed against society, adds instead a second defilement to the first."

---

10. There is only one reported decision in which Judge Olliff did not give a convicted capital felon a death sentence. In that case, however, the Judge attempted to sentence the defendant to a term of 199 years and to reserve review of any release of the defendant for 66 years, even though such a sentence was not authorized by law. The Florida appellate court vacated the sentence and remanded for resentencing.

A. Camus, Reflections on the Guillotine 5–6 (Fridtjof-Karla Pub., R. Howard, trans. 1960). I therefore dissent.

Question

Did the trial court in *Barclay* err by admitting Barclay's criminal record into evidence? Isn't past criminal conduct always relevant to sentence? If the trial court did not err by permitting the introduction of Barclay's criminal record into evidence, did it err in the consideration it gave to that evidence? How?

Note on Trifurcation

Three states—Florida, Indiana and Alabama—have adopted trifurcated procedures for identifying the persons convicted of a capital felony who shall be sentenced to death. Trifurcation consists of (1) a determination of guilt or innocence by the jury; (2) an advisory sentence by the jury; and (3) an actual sentence imposed by the trial judge, who can override the jury's recommended sentence. Given the Court's holding in *Ring v. Arizona*, 536 U.S. 584 (2002) (*infra* chapter 9), the constitutionality of these sentencing procedures are thrown into serious doubt.

Notes on Use of Racism as Aggravating Evidence

1. In *Dawson v. Delaware*, 503 U.S.159 (1992), the Supreme Court ruled that the state's evidence that the defendant was a member of the Aryan Brotherhood white racist prison gang, introduced during the penalty phase of a capital trial, was not relevant to any aggravating circumstance. Nor was the evidence relevant to rebut mitigating character evidence introduced by the defendant. The Court concluded that the evidence violated the First and Fourteenth Amendments because it did no more than show the defendant's abstract beliefs. The Court suggested that its decision might have been different if the evidence showed that the gang was associated with drugs or violence, or if the defendant's racist beliefs had been in some way connected with the murder of the victim. Compare *Barclay v. Florida*, 463 U.S. 939, 949 (1983) (racial motivation for murder held relevant to determination of statutory aggravating circumstances).

2. Consider the prosecution's use of evidence of racial animus in the 1999 capital murder trials of three white men, convicted of killing James Byrd, Jr., a disabled black man and father of three. The evidence showed that the three defendants kidnapped Byrd, sprayed his face with black paint, pulled his pants and underwear down, chained him by his ankles to a pickup truck, and dragged him for 3 miles before dumping his decapitated and mutilated body between a black church and a black cemetery. After *Barclay* and *Dawson*, should the prosecutor be permitted to present the following evidence and arguments?

—letters replete with racist language, offered to prove the men had a motive to kill a black man;

—while in prison, two of the men charged with killing Byrd joined the Confederate Knights of America, a Ku Klux Klan splinter group;

—two of the defendants murdered Byrd as a racially-motivated publicity event staged to launch their own fledgling hate group, the Texas Rebel Soldiers, a branch of the Confederate Knights of America;

— two defendants were adorned with white supremacist tattoos which depicted Nazi SS symbols, satanic stars, and the lynching of a black man.

Are the following arguments by prosecutors permissible?

— at the trial of the third defendant, which followed convictions and death sentences of the other two, the prosecutor remarked, "Up until [the two earlier trials], no Klansman had ever been convicted of harming a black man. Now they see that a white man can be given a death sentence for killing a black man."

— "By giving [the defendant] a life sentence, you're giving him at least 40 years to catch a black guard, a black nurse, a black doctor, a Jewish guard, a Jewish nurse, a Jewish doctor or anybody else. You're giving him a chance to catch anybody ... who doesn't believe in his satanic racist views."

Alfieri, "Prosecuting Violence, Reconstructing Community," 52 Stan. L. Rev. 809 (2000) (*passim*).

Note

The Indiana Supreme Court reversed a capital defendant's death sentence because the trial court judge relied too heavily on a non-statutory aggravating circumstance in imposing the death sentence. While awaiting sentencing for capital murder, the defendant acquired a jailhouse tattoo of a knife dripping blood. The judge concluded that the tattoo demonstrated a lack of remorse on the part of the defendant. In sentencing the defendant to death, the judge further stated that the tattoo relieved his uncertainty and concern about what he perceived as a close case in sentencing the defendant. The state supreme court concluded that the non-statutory aggravating circumstance was a "determinative factor" in sentencing. Reliance on this factor and the emphasis which the trial court placed on the tattoo was error and the case was remanded for resentencing. *Bellmore v. Indiana*, 602 N.E.2d 111 (Ind. 1992).

D. Nonstatutory Aggravating Circumstances

Aggravating and Mitigating Factors: The Paradox of Today's Arbitrary and Mandatory Capital Punishment Scheme
Jeffrey L. Kirchmeier, 6 Wm. & Mary Bill of Rights J. 345 (1998)

C. Nonstatutory Aggravating Factors

The federal government[202] and some states[203] allow the sentencing authority to consider nonstatutory aggravating factors, that is, aggravating factors approved by the individual court in a specific case but not listed in the jurisdiction's death penalty statute. Although at least one statutory aggravating factor also must be present before a defendant may be sentenced to death, the consideration of nonstatutory aggravating factors

---

202. See 18 U.S.C. 3592(c) (1994).

203. Some states, however, are "weighing" states, and sentencers in those states may not consider nonstatutory aggravating factors....

increases the potential for arbitrariness in capital cases by allowing an unlimited number of considerations to be presented to the sentencing authority.

In *Barclay v. Florida,* the Court held that

> [a]lthough a death sentence may not rest solely on a nonstatutory aggravating factor, ... the Constitution does not prohibit consideration at the sentencing phase of information not directly related to either statutory aggravating or statutory mitigating factors, as long as that information is relevant to the character of the defendant or the circumstances of the crime.

In *Barclay,* the Florida judge considered the defendant's criminal record a nonstatutory aggravating factor. The Supreme Court concluded that while the consideration of that factor may have violated state law, it did not violate the defendant's Eighth and Fourteenth Amendment rights.

In *Zant v. Stephens,* in addressing the use of an invalid aggravating factor, the Court noted that the use of nonstatutory aggravating factors is permissible to provide for individualized sentencing. The Court explained that statutory aggravating factors "play a constitutionally necessary function" in determining the class of persons eligible for the death penalty, "[b]ut the Constitution does not require the jury to ignore other possible aggravating factors in the process of selecting, from among that class, those defendants who will actually be sentenced to death."

Since *Barclay* and *Zant,* courts have permitted sentencers to consider a wide range of nonstatutory factors. For example, a number of courts permit the sentencing body to weigh the "nature and circumstances of the crime." The sentencer may consider an unlimited range of events under such a nonstatutory aggravating circumstance. For example, in *State v. Clark,* the sentencing judge wrote several pages about the particular circumstances and details surrounding the deaths of the victims in upholding this nonstatutory aggravating circumstance. In *State v. Manley,* the Delaware Superior Court permitted the use of several nonstatutory aggravating circumstances, including the fact that one of the defendant's motives for committing the robbery that led to the murder was to pay a debt that he owed to a Philadelphia gang. In *Mathenia v. Delo,* the Eighth Circuit Court of Appeals upheld the jury's consideration of several nonstatutory aggravating factors, including the fact that the defendant was a twenty-five-year-old male and the two victims were females over seventy years old. In *United States v. McCullah,*[219] a federal capital case, the United States Court of Appeals for the Tenth Circuit upheld the use of the nonstatutory aggravating circumstance of "use of a deadly weapon." The court reasoned that because not all murders are committed with a deadly weapon, "this factor genuinely narrows the class of defendants eligible for the death penalty and aids in individualized sentencing."

Courts also have upheld the use of "lack of remorse" as a nonstatutory aggravating circumstance. As one court has explained, however, "[l]ack of remorse is a subjective state of mind, difficult to gage [sic] objectively since behavior and words don't necessarily correlate with internal feelings." Further, "[i]n a criminal context, [lack of remorse] is particularly ambiguous since guilty persons have a constitutional right to be silent, to rest on a presumption of innocence and to require the government to prove their guilt beyond a reasonable doubt." For example, the aggravating factor may be misapplied if a truly remorseful defendant did not testify at trial, but, to protect himself when placed in a threatening jail environment, boasted to another inmate, who did testify.

---

219. 76 F.3d 1087 (10th Cir. 1996).

Perhaps the broadest of the nonstatutory aggravating factors relating to the offense is the factor of whether the defendant "committed the offenses charged in the indictment," which was upheld in *McCullah*. In that case, the court recognized that the factor allowed the jury to consider the circumstances surrounding the crime, including the fact that the "murder was committed in furtherance of an illegal drug operation." The court in *McCullah* noted that the Supreme Court in *Lowenfield v. Phelps* held that it was "permissible to count an element of the underlying offense as an aggravating factor where the 'narrowing' function is performed at the guilt phase." Thus, the court in *McCullah* reasoned, "an aggravating factor that does not add anything above and beyond the offense is constitutionally permissible provided that the statute itself narrows the class of death-eligible defendants."

In addition to the various circumstances surrounding the offense, courts have permitted the consideration of other nonstatutory aggravating circumstances. Several courts have permitted the consideration of the defendant's prior record—including juvenile convictions and crimes for which the defendant was never convicted—as a nonstatutory aggravating circumstance. For example, in *Wright v. State*,[231] the Delaware Supreme Court held that the defendant's occupation as a drug dealer for several years was admissible as a nonstatutory aggravating factor, along with two other such factors.

In addition to looking at prior acts, some courts have permitted the consideration of the defendant as a future threat to society as a nonstatutory aggravating factor....

The number of categories of potential nonstatutory aggravating factors is unlimited. In *State v. Gattis*,[235] the Delaware Superior Court sentenced the defendant to death after considering several nonstatutory aggravating circumstances, including the defendant's lack of respect toward authority as shown by his military record and his behavior while on probation for pleading guilty to assault charges. In *McCullah*, the court upheld the consideration of several nonstatutory aggravating circumstances, including the fact that repeated attempts to rehabilitate the defendant were unsuccessful. In *United States v. Bradley*,[239] one of the nonstatutory aggravating factors presented was that the government was "unaware of any evidence which would constitute 'mitigating factors.'"

Courts have considered numerous nonstatutory aggravating circumstances. These factors generally have some relevance in sentencing, and courts that permit consideration of nonstatutory aggravating circumstances require findings of at least one statutory aggravating circumstance.[241] Also, unlike the *McGautha* days, the use of unlimited nonstatutory aggravating and nonstatutory mitigating circumstances—because they are defined by the trial court—results in the sentencing body having a list of specific factors to consider.

The problem, however, is that open-ended consideration of relevant nonstatutory aggravating factors adds a substantial amount of arbitrariness to the equation. First, unlike statutory aggravating factors, nonstatutory factors are not determined by the

---

231. 633 A.2d 329 (Del. 1993).
235. No. IN90-05-1017, 1992 Del. Super. LEXIS 474 (Del. Super. Ct. Oct. 29, 1992).
239. 880 F. Supp. 271 (M.D. Penn. 1994).
241. *See Barclay v. Florida*, 463 U.S. 939, 966–67 (1983) (holding that the Constitution did not prohibit consideration of nonstatutory aggravating factors although a death sentence could not "rest solely on a nonstatutory aggravating factor"); *Zant v. Stephens*, 462 U.S. 862 (1983) (suggesting that statutory aggravating factors define the class of persons eligible for the death penalty and that a jury may consider nonstatutory aggravating factors to determine which defendants within that class will be sentenced to death).

elected legislatures, so nonstatutory factors are not applied in the cases of all capital defendants in the state. Instead, much depends on the creativity of the prosecutor to raise and style the nonstatutory aggravating circumstances. Depending on the prosecutor and the court, a prior juvenile record of a twenty-two-year-old defendant may be raised as a nonstatutory aggravating circumstance of prior record, failed attempts to rehabilitate, and/or future dangerousness. Second, the addition of more factors to an already large pool of statutory aggravating circumstances has given juries and sentencing judges broad discretion in imposing the death penalty, in contrast with the focused and channeled discretion foreseen in *Gregg* and *Godfrey*.[242]

One of the justifications for allowing a prosecutor to present nonstatutory aggravating factors is that if the Constitution requires that a defendant's presentation of mitigating factors not be limited, then aggravating factors should not be so limited. It is important to note, however, that while the Constitution requires that a defendant be able to present all mitigating factors, the Court has not held that the Constitution requires that the prosecutor be able to present all possible aggravating factors. The Court's holding in *Barclay* was only that states may permit the prosecutor to present nonstatutory aggravating factors. The Court thus has reasoned that nonstatutory aggravating factors, which are permitted, are not as constitutionally significant as nonstatutory mitigating factors, which are required.

Although there is no constitutional basis for requiring nonstatutory aggravating factors, there is a constitutional basis for prohibiting the use of nonstatutory aggravating factors: *Furman* and *Gregg*, which held that the Constitution abhors arbitrariness in capital sentencing. Justice Scalia has stated that the requirement that sentencing bodies be permitted to consider all nonstatutory mitigating factors "quite obviously destroys whatever rationality and predictability" *Furman* attempted to achieve.[247] That problem is exacerbated by also permitting consideration of nonstatutory aggravating factors. By allowing an unlimited number of potential nonstatutory aggravating factors, courts are approaching the days of unfettered jury discretion.

E. The Narrowing Function of Aggravating Circumstances

Lowenfield v. Phelps
484 U.S. 231 (1988)

Chief Justice REHNQUIST delivered the opinion of the Court, in which White, Blackmun, O'Connor, and Scalia, JJ., joined, and in Part III of which, except for the last sentence thereof, Stevens, J., joined.

---

242. Indeed, in several of the cases in which courts have permitted consideration of nonstatutory aggravating circumstances, the courts have allowed a large number of such factors to be considered. *See, e.g., Nguyen*, 928 F. Supp. at 1538 (five nonstatutory aggravating factors); *Bradley*, 880 F. Supp. at 271 (finding two out of seven proposed nonstatutory aggravating factors duplicative of statutory aggravating factors); *United States v. Perry*, No. 92-474, 1994 U.S. Dist. LEXIS 20462, at *15 (D.D.C. Jan. 11, 1994) (in a federal death penalty case, the Government argued 11 nonstatutory aggravating factors); *State v. Manley*, No. 9511007022, 1997 Del. Super. LEXIS 5, at *22 (Del. Super. Ct. Jan. 10, 1997) (eight nonstatutory aggravating circumstances).

247. *Walton v. Arizona*, 497 U.S. 639, 664–65 (1990) (Scalia, J., concurring).

III

... Petitioner advances as a second ground for vacating his sentence of death that the sole aggravating circumstance found by the jury at the sentencing phase was identical to an element of the capital crime of which he was convicted. Petitioner urges that this overlap left the jury at the sentencing phase free merely to repeat one of its findings in the guilt phase, and thus not to narrow further in the sentencing phase the class of death-eligible murderers. Upon consideration of the Louisiana capital punishment scheme in the light of the decisions of this Court we reject this argument.

Louisiana has established five grades of homicide: first-degree murder, second-degree murder, manslaughter, negligent homicide, and vehicular homicide. Second-degree murder includes intentional murder and felony murder, and provides for punishment of life imprisonment without the possibility of parole. Louisiana defines first-degree murder to include a narrower class of homicides:

First degree murder is the killing of a human being:

(1) When the offender has specific intent to kill or to inflict great bodily harm and is engaged in the perpetration or attempted perpetration of aggravated kidnapping, aggravated escape, aggravated arson, aggravated rape, aggravated burglary, armed robbery, or simple robbery;

(2) When the offender has a specific intent to kill or to inflict great bodily harm upon a fireman or peace officer engaged in the performance of his lawful duties;

(3) When the offender has a specific intent to kill or to inflict great bodily harm upon more than one person;

(4) When the offender has specific intent to kill or inflict great bodily harm and has offered, has been offered, has given, or has received anything of value for the killing; or

(5) When the offender has the specific intent to kill or to inflict great bodily harm upon a victim under the age of twelve years.

An individual found guilty of first-degree murder is sentenced by the same jury in a separate proceeding to either death or life imprisonment without benefit of parole, probation, or suspension of sentence. "A sentence of death shall not be imposed unless the jury finds beyond a reasonable doubt that at least one statutory aggravating circumstance exists and, after consideration of any mitigating circumstances, recommends that the sentence of death be imposed." Louisiana has established 10 statutory aggravating circumstances.[6] If the jury returns a sentence of death, the sentence is automatically reviewable for excessiveness by the Supreme Court of Louisiana.

---

6. The following shall be considered aggravating circumstances:

(a) the offender was engaged in the perpetration or attempted perpetration of aggravated rape, aggravated kidnapping, aggravated burglary, aggravated arson, aggravated escape, armed robbery, or simple robbery;

(b) the victim was a fireman or peace officer engaged in his lawful duties;

(c) the offender was previously convicted of an unrelated murder, aggravated rape, or aggravated kidnapping or has a significant prior history of criminal activity;

(d) the offender knowingly created a risk of death or great bodily harm to more than one person;

(e) the offender offered or has been offered or has given or received anything of value for the commission of the offense;

(f) the offender at the time of the commission of the offense was imprisoned after sentence for the commission of an unrelated forcible felony;

(g) the offense was committed in an especially heinous, atrocious, or cruel manner; or

Petitioner was found guilty of three counts of first-degree murder under §14:30.A.(3): "[T]he offender has a specific intent to kill or to inflict great bodily harm upon more than one person." The sole aggravating circumstance both found by the jury and upheld by the Louisiana Supreme Court was that "the offender knowingly created a risk of death or great bodily harm to more than one person." In these circumstances, these two provisions are interpreted in a "parallel fashion" under Louisiana law. Petitioner's argument that the parallel nature of these provisions requires that his sentences be set aside rests on a mistaken premise as to the necessary role of aggravating circumstances.

To pass constitutional muster, a capital sentencing scheme must "genuinely narrow the class of persons eligible for the death penalty and must reasonably justify the imposition of a more severe sentence on the defendant compared to others found guilty of murder." Under the capital sentencing laws of most States, the jury is required during the sentencing phase to find at least one aggravating circumstance before it may impose death. By doing so, the jury narrows the class of persons eligible for the death penalty according to an objective legislative definition.

In *Zant v. Stephens*, 462 U.S. 862 (1983), we upheld a sentence of death imposed pursuant to the Georgia capital sentencing statute, under which "the finding of an aggravating circumstance does not play any role in guiding the sentencing body in the exercise of its discretion, apart from its function of narrowing the class of persons convicted of murder who are eligible for the death penalty." We found no constitutional deficiency in that scheme because the aggravating circumstances did all that the Constitution requires.

The use of "aggravating circumstances" is not an end in itself, but a means of genuinely narrowing the class of death-eligible persons and thereby channeling the jury's discretion. We see no reason why this narrowing function may not be performed by jury findings at either the sentencing phase of the trial or the guilt phase. Our opinion in *Jurek v. Texas*, 428 U.S. 262 (1976), establishes this point. The *Jurek* Court upheld the Texas death penalty statute, which, like the Louisiana statute, narrowly defined the categories of murders for which a death sentence could be imposed. If the jury found the defendant guilty of such a murder, it was required to impose death so long as it found beyond a reasonable doubt that the defendant's acts were deliberate, the defendant would probably constitute a continuing threat to society, and, if raised by the evidence, the defendant's acts were an unreasonable response to the victim's provocation. We concluded that the latter three elements allowed the jury to consider the mitigating aspects of the crime and the unique characteristics of the perpetrator, and therefore sufficiently provided for jury discretion. But the opinion announcing the judgment noted the difference between the Texas scheme, on the one hand, and the Georgia and Florida schemes discussed in the cases of *Gregg* and *Proffitt*:

> While Texas has not adopted a list of statutory aggravating circumstances the existence of which can justify the imposition of the death penalty as have Georgia and Florida, its action in narrowing the categories of murders for which a death sentence may ever be imposed serves much the same purpose.... In fact,

---

(h) the victim was a witness in a prosecution against the defendant, gave material assistance to the state in any investigation or prosecution of the defendant, or was an eyewitness to a crime alleged to have been committed by the defendant or possessed other material evidence against the defendant;

(i) the victim was a correctional officer or any other employee of the Louisiana Department of Corrections who, in the normal course of his employment was required to come in close contact with persons incarcerated in a state prison facility, and the victim was engaged in his lawful duties at the time of the offense. La. Code Crim. Proc. Ann., Art. 905.4 (West 1984).

each of the five classes of murders made capital by the Texas statute is encompassed in Georgia and Florida by one or more of their statutory aggravating circumstances. . . . Thus, in essence, the Texas statute requires that the jury find the existence of a statutory aggravating circumstance before the death penalty may be imposed. So far as consideration of aggravating circumstances is concerned, therefore, the principal difference between Texas and the other two States is that the death penalty is an available sentencing option — even potentially — for a smaller class of murders in Texas.*

It seems clear to us from this discussion that the narrowing function required for a regime of capital punishment may be provided in either of these two ways: The legislature may itself narrow the definition of capital offenses, as Texas and Louisiana have done, so that the jury finding of guilt responds to this concern, or the legislature may more broadly define capital offenses and provide for narrowing by jury findings of aggravating circumstances at the penalty phase.

Here, the "narrowing function" was performed by the jury at the guilt phase when it found defendant guilty of three counts of murder under the provision that "the offender has a specific intent to kill or to inflict great bodily harm upon more than one person." The fact that the sentencing jury is also required to find the existence of an aggravating circumstance in addition is no part of the constitutionally required narrowing process, and so the fact that the aggravating circumstance duplicated one of the elements of the crime does not make this sentence constitutionally infirm. There is no question but that the Louisiana scheme narrows the class of death-eligible murderers and then at the sentencing phase allows for the consideration of mitigating circumstances and the exercise of discretion. The Constitution requires no more. The judgment of the Court of Appeals for the Fifth Circuit is accordingly affirmed.

Justice MARSHALL, with whom Justice Brennan joins, and Justice Stevens joins as to Part I, dissenting.

II

. . . Since our decision in *Furman* we have required that there be a "meaningful basis for distinguishing the few cases in which [the death sentence] is imposed from the many cases in which it is not." We have held consistently that statutory aggravating circumstances considered during the sentencing process provide one of the means by which the jury's discretion is guided in making such constitutionally mandated distinctions.

The Court today suggests that our emphasis on aggravating circumstances has been mere happenstance and holds that the critical narrowing function may be performed prior to and distinct from the sentencing process. This holding misunderstands the significance of the narrowing requirement. The Court treats the narrowing function as a merely technical requirement that the number of those eligible for the death penalty be made smaller than the number of those convicted of murder. But narrowing the class of death eligible offenders is not "an end in itself" any more than aggravating circumstances are. Rather, as our cases have emphasized consistently, the narrowing requirement is meant to channel the discretion of the sentencer. It forces the capital sentencing jury to approach its task in a structured, step-by-step way, first determining whether a defendant is eligible for the death penalty and then determining whether all of the circumstances

---

* [If this is true, why does Texas have one of the largest death row populations in the country? Ed.]

justify its imposition. The only conceivable reason for making narrowing a constitutional requirement is its function in structuring sentencing deliberations. By permitting the removal of the narrowing function from the sentencing process altogether, the Court reduces it to a mechanical formality entirely unrelated to the choice between life and death.

The Court's relegation of the narrowing function to the guilt phase of a capital trial implicates the concerns we expressed in another context in *Caldwell v. Mississippi*, 472 U.S. 320 (1985). In *Caldwell*, we vacated petitioner's sentence of death when the prosecutor had argued to the jury that the appellate court would review the imposition of the death sentence for correctness, concluding that "it is constitutionally impermissible to rest a death sentence on a determination made by a sentencer who has been led to believe that the responsibility for determining the appropriateness of the defendant's death rests elsewhere." Here, the sentencing jurors were led to believe that petitioner's eligibility for the death sentence was already established by their findings during the guilt phase — findings arrived at without any contemplation of their implication for petitioner's sentence. Indeed, the court specifically instructed the jury at the start of its guilt phase deliberations: "You are not to discuss, in any way, the possibility of any penalties whatsoever." Then, during the penalty hearing, the prosecutor twice reminded the jury that it had already found during the guilt phase one of the aggravating circumstances that the State urged was applicable to petitioner's sentence. The prosecutor's argument might well have convinced the jury that it had no choice about and hence no responsibility for the defendant's eligibility for the death penalty. This situation cannot be squared with our promise to ensure that "a capital sentencing jury recognizes the gravity of its task and proceeds with the appropriate awareness of its 'truly awesome responsibility.'"

In sum, the application of the Louisiana sentencing scheme in cases like this one, where there is a complete overlap between aggravating circumstances found at the sentencing phase and elements of the offense previously found at the guilt phase, violates constitutional principles in ways that will inevitably tilt the sentencing scales toward the imposition of the death penalty. The State will have an easier time convincing a jury beyond a reasonable doubt to find a necessary element of a capital offense at the guilt phase of a trial if the jury is unaware that such a finding will make the defendant eligible for the death penalty at the sentencing phase. Then the State will have an even easier time arguing for the imposition of the death penalty, because it can remind the jury at the sentencing phase, as it did in this case, that the necessary aggravating circumstances already have been established beyond a reasonable doubt. The State thus enters the sentencing hearing with the jury already across the threshold of death eligibility, without any awareness on the jury's part that it had crossed that line. By permitting such proceedings in a capital case, the Court ignores our early pronouncement that "a State may not entrust the determination of whether a man should live or die to a tribunal organized to return a verdict of death."

F. Victim Impact Evidence

Inflicting *Payne* on Oklahoma: The Use of Victim Impact Evidence During the Sentencing Phase of Capital Cases

Randall Coyne, 45 Okla. L. Rev. 589 (1992)

In *Booth v. Maryland*, 482 U.S. 496 (1987), John Booth and an accomplice entered the home of Irvin and Rose Bronstein, an elderly couple, for the purpose of stealing money to buy heroin. Two days later, the Bronsteins' son discovered his parents' bodies bound, gagged, and perforated with stab wounds from a kitchen knife. Booth was convicted of two counts of first-degree murder, two counts of robbery, and conspiracy to commit robbery. Prior to the sentencing phase, the Maryland Division of Parole and Probation (DPP) prepared a presentence report which described Booth's background, education and employment history, and criminal record. As required by Maryland statute, the report also contained a victim impact statement (VIS) which described the effect of the crime on the victims and the victims' family.[16] In Booth's case, the VIS was based on interviews with the victims' son, daughter, son-in-law, and granddaughter.

Much of the VIS emphasized the victims' outstanding personal qualities and stressed how deeply the victims would be missed. For example, the victims' son reported that his father was a lifelong hard worker, his mother was young at heart, and both parents had many devout friends.

In addition, the VIS described the emotional and personal problems the family members encountered as a result of the crimes. The victims' son reported that he suffered from depression and lack of sleep and "is fearful for the first time in his life." Similarly, the victims' daughter reported that she suffered from a lack of sleep and had become withdrawn and distrustful. The daughter also stated that she could no longer watch violent movies or look at kitchen knives without being reminded of the murders. The victims' granddaughter reported that the deaths had ruined her sister's wedding a few days later and that the granddaughter had received counseling for several months, only to quit when she concluded "no one could help her."

Finally, the VIS set forth the family members' opinions and characterizations of the crimes and of Booth. In this regard, the son opined that his parents had been "butchered like animals," while the daughter concluded that she could never forgive the murderer and that "such a person could [n]ever be rehabilitated." Moreover, the state official who conducted the family interviews concluded the VIS by expressing doubt that the family "will ever be able to fully recover from this tragedy and not be haunted by the memory of the brutal manner in which their loved ones were murdered and taken from them."

Booth's trial attorney moved to suppress the VIS on the ground that this information was both irrelevant and unduly inflammatory and that therefore its use in a capital case violated the Eighth Amendment to the United States Constitution. After the trial court

---

16. A Maryland statute in effect at the time of the *Booth* decision set forth the information to be included in the VIS:
   (i)   Identify the victim of the offense;
   (ii) Itemize any economic loss suffered by the victim as a result of the offense;
   (iii) Identify any physical injury suffered by the victim as a result of the offense along with its seriousness and permanence;
   (iv) Describe any change in the victim's personal welfare or familial relationships as a result of the offense;
   (v)   Identify any request for psychological services initiated by the victim or the victim's family as a result of the offense; and
   (vi) Contain any other information related to the impact of the offense upon the victim or the victim's family that the trial court requires.
Md. Ann. Code art. 41, §4-609(c)(3) (1986).

denied the motion, defense counsel requested that the prosecutor simply read the VIS to the jury rather than call the family members to testify before the jury.[27] The prosecutor agreed to this arrangement. After considering the presentence report and the victim impact evidence therein, the jury sentenced Booth to death on one count of murder and to life imprisonment on the second count.

On direct appeal, Booth argued that the VIS injected an arbitrary factor into the sentencing decision. The Maryland Court of Appeals affirmed Booth's conviction and sentence, holding that the jury's decision to impose the death sentence was not influenced by passion, prejudice, or other arbitrary factors. According to the court of appeals, the VIS in Booth's case was a "relatively straightforward and factual description of the effects of these murders on members of the Bronstein family." Moreover, the VIS served an important interest because it informed the sentencer of the full measure of harm caused by Booth's crime.

The United States Supreme Court granted certiorari to decide "whether the Eighth Amendment prohibits a capital sentencing jury from considering victim impact evidence." Five members of the Court concluded that the introduction of a VIS at the sentencing phase of a capital murder trial violated the Eighth Amendment and vacated Booth's death sentence. Four justices dissented.

Essential to Booth's victory in the Supreme Court was the well-established principle that a jury's discretion to impose the death sentence must be "suitably directed and limited so as to minimize the risk of wholly arbitrary and capricious action." Sharp disagreement among the majority and dissenting justices centered on whether victim impact evidence "suitably directed" a jury's discretion (as the dissenters believed) or enhanced the risk of "arbitrary and capricious" action (as the majority believed).

Writing for the majority, Justice Powell emphasized that "a jury must make an '*individualized* determination' whether the defendant in question should be executed, based on the 'character of the individual and the circumstances of the crime.'" According to the Court, a state statute requiring consideration of other factors (including information contained in a VIS) must be scrutinized closely to ensure that the evidence has some "bearing on the defendant's 'personal responsibility and moral guilt'" so that a death sentence will not be based on considerations that are "constitutionally impermissible or totally irrelevant to the sentencing process." Indeed, the VIS focuses on the character and reputation of the *victim* and the effect of the crime on his or her *family*. Thus, VIS information diverts the jury's attention away from the defendant's background and record, and the circumstances of the crime. As a result, a sentencing decision based in part on VIS information may turn on irrelevant factors such as the degree to which the victim's family is willing and able to articulate its grief, or the relative worth of the victim's character. In support of its conclusion that victim impact evidence should be excluded from the sentencing phase of capital cases, the majority scrutinized the VIS submitted in Booth's capital murder trial. For purposes of analysis, the Court identified two types of information which the VIS in Booth's case provided to the jury:

---

27. Defense counsel was obviously aware that the use of live witnesses would dramatically increase the inflammatory effect of the VIS. There are other potential reasons supporting a prosecutor's use of a written VIS rather than live testimony, including: (1) family members may wish to be spared the anxiety of taking the stand and being subjected to cross-examination; and (2) because reading a written VIS is likely to consume less time than live testimony, the court may view this procedure as conserving scarce judicial resources.

(1) descriptions of the personal characteristics of the victims and the emotional impact of the crimes on the family; and (2) family members' opinions and characterizations of the crimes and the defendant.

Within two years of the *Booth* decision, the Court reaffirmed its principles in *South Carolina v. Gathers*, 490 U.S. 805 (1989). Demetrius Gathers was convicted of the brutal murder of Richard Haynes, a former mental patient who referred to himself as "Reverend Minister." During closing arguments at the sentencing phase of Gathers' capital murder trial, the prosecutor read to the jury at length from a religious tract that Haynes was carrying when he was killed[100] and commented on personal qualities he inferred from Haynes' possession of the religious tract and a voter registration card.[101] The jury sentenced Gathers to death. Because the prosecutor's remarks "conveyed the suggestion that [Gathers] deserved a death sentence because the victim was a religious man and a registered voter," the South Carolina Supreme Court, relying on *Booth*, reversed Gathers' death sentence and remanded for a new sentencing proceeding.

In another 5–4 decision, the United States Supreme Court affirmed. Although the state did not rely on a VIS, the majority found that the prosecutor's comments regarding the victim's personal characteristics could result in a death sentence because of fac-

---

100. At the time he was killed, Richard Haynes was carrying a card on which was inscribed "The Game Guy's Prayer." The prayer, which the prosecutor recited in its entirety to the jury, reads:

"Dear God, help me to be a sport in this little game of life. I don't ask for any easy place in this lineup. Play me anywhere you need me. I only ask you for the stuff to give you one hundred percent of what I have got. If all the hard drives seem to come my way, I thank you for the compliment. Help me to remember that you won't ever let anything come my way that you and I can't handle. And help me to take the bad break as part of the game. Help me to understand that the game is full of knots and knocks and trouble, and make me thankful for them. Help me to be brave so that the harder they come the better I like it. And, oh God, help me to always play on the square. No matter what the other players do, help me to come clean. Help me to study the book so that I'll know the rules, to study and think a lot about the greatest player that ever lived and other players that are portrayed in the book. If they ever found out the best part of the game was helping other guys who are out of luck, help me to find it out, too. Help me to be regular, and also an inspiration with the other players. Finally, oh God, if fate seems to uppercut me with both hands, and I am laid on the shelf in sickness or old age or something, help me to take that as part of the game, too. Help me not to whimper or squeal that the game was a frameup or that I had a raw deal. When in the falling dusk I get the final bell, I ask for no lying, complimentary tombstones. I'd only like to know that you feel that I have been a good guy, a good game guy, a saint in the game of life."

101. The prosecutor's closing argument is excerpted below:

"We know from the proof that Reverend Minister Haynes was a religious person. He had his religious items out there. This defendant strewn [sic] them across the bike path, thinking nothing of that.... He had this [sic] religious items, his beads. He had a plastic angel. Of course, he is with the angels now, but this defendant Demetrius Gathers could care little about the fact that he is a religious person. Cared little of the pain and agony he inflicted upon a person who is trying to enjoy one of our public parks." ...

"You will find some other exhibits in this case that tell you more about a just verdict. Again, this is not easy. No one takes any pleasure from it, but the proof cries out from the grave in this case. Among the personal effects that this defendant could care little about when he went through it is something that we all treasure. Speaks a lot about Reverend Minister Haynes. Very simple yet very profound. Voting. A voter's registration card. Reverend Haynes believed in this community. He took part. And he believed that in Charleston County, in the United States of America, that in this country you could go to a public park and sit on a public bench and not be attacked by the likes of Demetrius Gathers.

tors about which Gathers was unaware and that were irrelevant to the decision to kill.[105] Writing for the majority, Justice Brennan stressed that "the content of the various papers the victim happened to be carrying when he was attacked was purely fortuitous, and cannot provide any information relevant to [Gathers'] moral culpability."

Notwithstanding two 5–4 decisions squarely holding that victim impact evidence violated the Eighth Amendment, changes in Court personnel underscored the precarious position of *Booth* and *Gathers* as enduring precedent. Significantly, the author of the majority opinion in *Booth*, Justice Powell, resigned at the end of the 1987 term and was replaced by Justice Kennedy, who became one of the four dissenters in *Gathers*. Replacing Powell (a moderate) with Kennedy (a conservative) should have tipped the 5–4 balance decisively in favor of the *Booth* dissenters. However, Justice White, himself a *Booth* dissenter, mysteriously joined the majority in *Gathers*, and grumbled in a separate concurrence: "Unless *Booth* is to be overruled, the judgment below must be affirmed." Justice Scalia, writing a separate dissent, picked up on White's invitation and called for *Booth* to be overruled.[108] Similarly, Justice O'Connor's dissent revealed that she, Chief Justice Rehnquist and Justice Kennedy stood "ready to overrule" *Booth*. In their view, "*Booth* should not be read ... to preclude prosecutorial comment which gives the sentencer a 'glimpse of the life' a defendant 'chose to extinguish.'" Moreover, "nothing in the Eighth Amendment precludes the prosecutor from conveying to the jury a sense of the unique human being whose life the defendant has taken."

Although Justice White's bizarre vote in *Gathers* preserved the rule of *Booth*, ultimately it merely delayed the inevitable. Within two years, Justice Brennan (a liberal) retired, Justice Souter (a conservative) replaced him, and Justice White retreated from his apparent reverence for *stare decisis*.

Payne v. Tennessee
501 U.S. 808 (1991)

Chief Justice REHNQUIST delivered the opinion of the court, in which White, O'Connor, Scalia, Kennedy, and Souter, JJ., joined.

In this case we reconsider our holdings in *Booth v. Maryland* and *South Carolina v. Gathers*, that the Eighth Amendment bars the admission of victim impact evidence during the penalty phase of a capital trial.

---

105. Recall that *Booth* described three categories of victim impact evidence: (1) the victims' personal characteristics; (2) statements concerning the emotional impact of the crime on the victims' family; and (3) family members' opinions about the crime and the defendant. Only the first category of victim impact evidence was implicated in *Gathers*. And, unlike *Booth* where the victims' family members characterized the victims' personal qualities, *Gathers* involved a prosecutor's characterization of a victim's personal qualities. 490 U.S. at 810–811.

108. Justice Scalia anticipated the criticism which would flow from the Court's reversal of a recent decision:

"It has been argued that we should not overrule so recent a decision, lest our action 'appear to be ... occasioned by nothing more than a change in the Court's personnel,' and the rules we announce no more than 'the opinions of a small group of men who temporarily occupy high office.' I doubt that overruling *Booth* will so shake the citizenry's faith in the Court. Overrulings of precedent rarely occur without a change in the Court's personnel. The only distinctive feature here is that the overruling would follow not long after the recent decision. But that is hardly unprecedented." 490 U.S. at 824.

The petitioner, Pervis Tyrone Payne, was convicted by a jury on two counts of first-degree murder and one count of assault with intent to commit murder in the first degree. [The evidence showed that Payne, who had been injecting cocaine and drinking beer much of the day, entered an apartment occupied by 28-year-old Charisse Christopher, her 2-year-old daughter Lacie, and her 3-year-old son Nicholas. When Charisse resisted his sexual advances, Payne stabbed to death Charisse and Lacie. Nicholas, who had been stabbed several times by a butcher knife which completely penetrated through his body from front to back, miraculously survived.] [Payne] was sentenced to death for each of the murders, and to 30 years in prison for the assault.

[During the sentencing phase of the trial, the] State presented the testimony of Charisse's mother, Mary Zvolanek. When asked how Nicholas had been affected by the murders of his mother and sister, she responded:

> He cries for his mom. He doesn't seem to understand why she doesn't come home. And he cries for his sister Lacie. He comes to me many times during the week and asks me, Grandmama, do you miss my Lacie. And I tell him yes. He says, I'm worried about my Lacie.

In arguing for the death penalty during closing argument, the prosecutor commented on the continuing effects of Nicholas' experience, stating:

> But we do know that Nicholas was alive. And Nicholas was in the same room. Nicholas was still conscious. His eyes were open. He responded to the paramedics. He was able to follow their directions. He was able to hold his intestines in as he was carried to the ambulance. So he knew what happened to his mother and baby sister.

> There is nothing you can do to ease the pain of any of the families involved in this case. There is nothing you can do to ease the pain of Bernice or Carl Payne, and that's a tragedy. There is nothing you can do basically to ease the pain of Mr. and Mrs. Zvolanek, and that's a tragedy. They will have to live with it the rest of their lives. There is obviously nothing you can do for Charisse and Lacie Jo. But there is something that you can do for Nicholas.

> Somewhere down the road Nicholas is going to grow up, hopefully. He's going to want to know what happened. And he is going to know what happened to his baby sister and his mother. He is going to want to know what type of justice was done. He is going to want to know what happened. With your verdict, you will provide the answer.

… We granted certiorari to reconsider our holdings in *Booth* and *Gathers* that the Eighth Amendment prohibits a capital sentencing jury from considering "victim impact" evidence relating to the personal characteristics of the victim and the emotional impact of the crimes on the victim's family.…

Booth and *Gathers* were based on two premises: that evidence relating to a particular victim or to the harm that a capital defendant causes a victim's family do[es] not in general reflect on the defendant's "blameworthiness," and that only evidence relating to "blameworthiness" is relevant to the capital sentencing decision. However, the assessment of harm caused by the defendant as a result of the crime charged has understandably been an important concern of the criminal law, both in determining the elements of the offense and in determining the appropriate punishment. Thus, two equally blameworthy criminal defendants may be guilty of different offenses solely because their acts cause differing amounts of harm. "If a bank robber aims his gun at a guard, pulls the trigger, and kills his target, he may be put to death. If the gun unexpectedly misfires, he may not. His moral guilt in both cases is identical, but his responsibility in the former is greater." The same is true with respect to two defendants, each of whom participates in a robbery, and each of whom acts with reckless disregard for human life; if the robbery in which the first defendant participated results in the death of a victim, he may be subjected to the death penalty, but if the robbery in which the second defendant participates does not result in the death of a victim, the death penalty may not be imposed.

..."We have held that a State cannot preclude the sentencer from considering 'any relevant mitigating evidence' that the defendant proffers in support of a sentence less than death." Thus we have, as the Court observed in *Booth*, required that the capital defendant be treated as a "'uniquely individual human bein[g]'" (quoting *Woodson v. North Carolina*, 428 U.S. at 304). But it was never held or even suggested in any of our cases preceding *Booth* that the defendant, entitled as he was to individualized consideration, was to receive that consideration wholly apart from the crime which he had committed. The language quoted from *Woodson* in the *Booth* opinion was not intended to describe a class of evidence that could not be received, but a class of evidence which must be received.... This misreading of precedent in *Booth* has, we think, unfairly weighted the scales in a capital trial; while virtually no limits are placed on the relevant mitigating evidence a capital defendant may introduce concerning his own circumstances, the State is barred from either offering "a glimpse of the life" which a defendant "chose to extinguish," or demonstrating the loss to the victim's family and to society which have resulted from the defendant's homicide.

Booth reasoned that victim impact evidence must be excluded because it would be difficult, if not impossible, for the defendant to rebut such evidence without shifting the focus of the sentencing hearing away from the defendant, thus creating a "'mini-trial' on the victim's character." In many cases the evidence relating to the victim is already before the jury at least in part because of its relevance at the guilt phase of the trial. But even as to additional evidence admitted at the sentencing phase, the mere fact that for tactical reasons it might not be prudent for the defense to rebut victim impact evidence makes the case no different than others in which a party is faced with this sort of a dilemma. As we explained in rejecting the contention that expert testimony on future dangerousness should be excluded from capital trials, "the rules of evidence generally extant at the federal and state levels anticipate that relevant, unprivileged evidence should be admitted and its weight left to the factfinder, who would have the benefit of cross examination and contrary evidence by the opposing party." *Barefoot v. Estelle*, 463 U.S. 880 (1983) (*infra* chapter 10).

Payne echoes the concern voiced in *Booth*'s case that the admission of victim impact evidence permits a jury to find that defendants whose victims were assets to their community are more deserving of punishment than those whose victims are perceived to be less worthy. As a general matter, however, victim impact evidence is not offered to encourage comparative judgments of this kind—for instance, that the killer of a hardworking, devoted parent deserves the death penalty, but that the murderer of a reprobate does not. It is designed to show instead each victim's "uniqueness as an individual human being," whatever the jury might think the loss to the community resulting from his death might be. The facts of *Gathers* are an excellent illustration of this: the evidence showed that the victim was an out of work, mentally handicapped individual, perhaps not, in the eyes of most, a significant contributor to society, but nonetheless a murdered human being.

Under our constitutional system, the primary responsibility for defining crimes against state law, fixing punishments for the commission of these crimes, and establishing procedures for criminal trials rests with the States. The state laws respecting crimes, punishments, and criminal procedure are of course subject to the overriding provisions of the United States Constitution. Where the State imposes the death penalty for a particular crime, we have held that the Eighth Amendment imposes special limitations upon that process....

... We are now of the view that a State may properly conclude that for the jury to assess meaningfully the defendant's moral culpability and blameworthiness, it should have before it at the sentencing phase evidence of the specific harm caused by the defendant. "[T]he State has a legitimate interest in counteracting the mitigating evidence which the defendant is entitled to put in, by reminding the sentencer that just as the murderer should be considered as an individual, so too the victim is an individual whose death represents a unique loss to society and in particular to his family." By turning the victim into a "faceless stranger at the penalty phase of a capital trial," *Booth* deprives the State of the full moral force of its evidence and may prevent the jury from having before it all the information necessary to determine the proper punishment for a first-degree murder.

The present case is an example of the potential for such unfairness. The capital sentencing jury heard testimony from Payne's girlfriend that they met at church, that he was affectionate, caring, kind to her children, that he was not an abuser of drugs or alcohol, and that it was inconsistent with his character to have committed the murders. Payne's parents testified that he was a good son, and a clinical psychologist testified that Payne was an extremely polite prisoner and suffered from a low IQ. None of this testimony was related to the circumstances of Payne's brutal crimes. In contrast, the only evidence of the impact of Payne's offenses during the sentencing phase was Nicholas' grandmother's description—in response to a single question—that the child misses his mother and baby sister. Payne argues that the Eighth Amendment commands that the jury's death sentence must be set aside because the jury heard this testimony. But the testimony illustrated quite poignantly some of the harm that Payne's killing had caused; there is nothing unfair about allowing the jury to bear in mind that harm at the same time as it considers the mitigating evidence introduced by the defendant. The Supreme Court of Tennessee in this case obviously felt the unfairness of the rule pronounced by *Booth* when it said "[i]t is an affront to the civilized members of the human race to say that at sentencing in a capital case, a parade of witnesses may praise the background, character and good deeds of Defendant (as was done in this case), without limitation as to relevancy, but nothing may be said that bears upon the character of, or the harm imposed, upon the victims."

In *Gathers*, as indicated above, we extended the holding of *Booth* barring victim impact evidence to the prosecutor's argument to the jury. Human nature being what it is, capable lawyers trying cases to juries try to convey to the jurors that the people involved in the underlying events are, or were, living human beings, with something to be gained or lost from the jury's verdict. Under the aegis of the Eighth Amendment, we have given the broadest latitude to the defendant to introduce relevant mitigating evidence reflecting on his individual personality, and the defendant's attorney may argue that evidence to the jury. Petitioner's attorney in this case did just that. For the reasons discussed above, we now reject the view—expressed in *Gathers*—that a State may not permit the prosecutor to similarly argue to the jury the human cost of the crime of which the defendant stands convicted. We reaffirm the view expressed by Justice Cardozo in *Snyder v. Massachusetts*, 291 U.S. 97 (1934): "justice, though due to the accused, is due to the accuser also. The concept of fairness must not be strained till it is narrowed to a filament. We are to keep the balance true."

We thus hold that if the State chooses to permit the admission of victim impact evidence and prosecutorial argument on that subject, the Eighth Amendment erects no *per se* bar. A State may legitimately conclude that evidence about the victim and about the impact of the murder on the victim's family is relevant to the jury's decision as to whether or not the death penalty should be imposed. There is no reason to treat such evidence differently than other relevant evidence is treated.

Payne and his *amicus* argue that despite these numerous infirmities in the rule created by *Booth* and *Gathers*, we should adhere to the doctrine of *stare decisis* and stop short of overruling those cases. *Stare decisis* is the preferred course because it promotes the evenhanded, predictable, and consistent development of legal principles, fosters reliance on judicial decisions, and contributes to the actual and perceived integrity of the judicial process. Adhering to precedent "is usually the wise policy, because in most matters it is more important that the applicable rule of law be settled than it be settled right." Nevertheless, when governing decisions are unworkable or are badly reasoned, "this Court has never felt constrained to follow precedent." *Stare decisis* is not an inexorable command; rather, it "is a principle of policy and not a mechanical formula of adherence to the latest decision." This is particularly true in constitutional cases, because in such cases "correction through legislative action is practically impossible." Considerations in favor of *stare decisis* are at their acme in cases involving property and contract rights, where reliance interests are involved; the opposite is true in cases such as the present one involving procedural and evidentiary rules.

Applying these general principles, the Court has during the past 20 Terms overruled in whole or in part 33 of its previous constitutional decisions. *Booth* and *Gathers* were decided by the narrowest of margins, over spirited dissents challenging the basic underpinnings of those decisions. They have been questioned by members of the Court in later decisions, and have defied consistent application by the lower courts. Reconsidering these decisions now, we conclude for the reasons heretofore stated, that they were wrongly decided and should be, and now are, overruled.[2] We accordingly affirm the judgment of the Supreme Court of Tennessee.

Justice MARSHALL, with whom Justice Blackmun joins, dissenting.

Power, not reason, is the new currency of this Court's decisionmaking. Four Terms ago, a five-Justice majority of this Court held that "victim impact" evidence of the type at issue in this case could not constitutionally be introduced during the penalty phase of a capital trial. By another 5–4 vote, a majority of this Court rebuffed an attack upon this ruling just two Terms ago. *South Carolina v. Gathers*. Nevertheless, having expressly invited respondent to renew the attack, today's majority overrules *Booth* and *Gathers* and credits the dissenting views expressed in those cases. Neither the law nor the facts supporting *Booth* and *Gathers* underwent any change in the last four years. Only the personnel of this Court did.

---

2. Our holding today is limited to the holdings of *Booth v. Maryland* and *South Carolina v. Gathers* that evidence and argument relating to the victim and the impact of the victim's death on the victim's family are inadmissible at a capital sentencing hearing. *Booth* also held that the admission of a victim's family members' characterizations and opinions about the crime, the defendant, and the appropriate sentence violates the Eighth Amendment. No evidence of the latter sort was presented at the trial in this case.

In dispatching *Booth* and *Gathers* to their graves, today's majority ominously suggests that an even more extensive upheaval of this Court's precedents may be in store. Renouncing this Court's historical commitment to a conception of "the judiciary as a source of impersonal and reasoned judgments," the majority declares itself free to discard any principle of constitutional liberty which was recognized or reaffirmed over the dissenting votes of four Justices and with which five or more Justices now disagree. The implications of this radical new exception to the doctrine of *stare decisis* are staggering. The majority today sends a clear signal that scores of established constitutional liberties are now ripe for reconsideration, thereby inviting the very type of open defiance of our precedents that the majority rewards in this case. Because I believe that this Court owes more to its constitutional precedents in general and to *Booth* and *Gathers* in particular, I dissent.

I

... There is nothing new in the majority's discussion of the supposed deficiencies in *Booth* and *Gathers*. Every one of the arguments made by the majority can be found in the dissenting opinions filed in those two cases, and, ... each argument was convincingly answered by Justice Powell and Justice Brennan.

But contrary to the impression that one might receive from reading the majority's lengthy rehearsing of the issues addressed in *Booth* and *Gathers*, the outcome of this case does not turn simply on who — the *Booth* and *Gathers* majorities or the *Booth* and *Gathers* dissenters — had the better of the argument. Justice Powell and Justice Brennan's position carried the day in those cases and became the law of the land. The real question, then, is whether today's majority has come forward with the type of extraordinary showing that this Court has historically demanded before overruling one of its precedents. In my view, the majority clearly has not made any such showing. Indeed, the striking feature of the majority's opinion is its radical assertion that it need not even try.

II

... [T]he majority candidly explains why this particular contingency, which until now has been almost universally understood not to be sufficient to warrant overruling a precedent, is sufficient to justify overruling *Booth* and *Gathers*. "Considerations in favor of *stare decisis* are at their acme," the majority explains, "in cases involving property and contract rights, where reliance interests are involved[;] the opposite is true in cases such as the present one involving procedural and evidentiary rules." In addition, the majority points out, "*Booth* and *Gathers* were decided by the narrowest of margins, over spirited dissents" and thereafter were "questioned by members of the Court." Taken together, these considerations make it legitimate, in the majority's view, to elevate the position of the *Booth* and *Gathers* dissenters into the law of the land.

This truncation of the Court's duty to stand by its own precedents is astonishing. By limiting full protection of the doctrine of *stare decisis* to "cases involving property and contract rights," the majority sends a clear signal that essentially all decisions implementing the personal liberties protected by the Bill of Rights and the Fourteenth Amendment are open to reexamination. Taking into account the majority's additional criterion for overruling — that a case either was decided or reaffirmed by a 5–4 margin "over spirited dissen[t]," — the continued vitality of literally scores of decisions must be understood to depend on nothing more than the proclivities of the individuals who now comprise a majority of this Court.

In my view, this impoverished conception of *stare decisis* cannot possibly be reconciled with the values that inform the proper judicial function. Contrary to what the majority suggests, *stare decisis* is important not merely because individuals rely on precedent to structure their commercial activity but because fidelity to precedent is part and parcel of a conception of "the judiciary as a source of impersonal and reasoned judgments." Indeed, this function of *stare decisis* is in many respects even more critical in adjudication involving constitutional liberties than in adjudication involving commercial entitlements. Because enforcement of the Bill of Rights and the Fourteenth Amendment frequently requires this Court to rein in the forces of democratic politics, this Court can legitimately lay claim to compliance with its directives only if the public understands the Court to be implementing "principles ... founded in the law rather than in the proclivities of individuals." Thus, as Justice Stevens has explained, the "stron[g] presumption of validity" to which "recently decided cases" are entitled "is an essential thread in the mantle of protection that the law affords the individual.... It is the unpopular or beleaguered individual—not the man in power—who has the greatest stake in the integrity of the law."

Carried to its logical conclusion, the majority's debilitated conception of *stare decisis* would destroy the Court's very capacity to resolve authoritatively the abiding conflicts between those with power and those without. If this Court shows so little respect for its own precedents, it can hardly expect them to be treated more respectfully by the state actors whom these decisions are supposed to bind. By signaling its willingness to give fresh consideration to any constitutional liberty recognized by a 5–4 vote "over spirited dissen[t]," the majority invites state actors to renew the very policies deemed unconstitutional in the hope that this Court may now reverse course, even if it has only recently reaffirmed the constitutional liberty in question.

Indeed, the majority's disposition of this case nicely illustrates the rewards of such a strategy of defiance. The Tennessee Supreme Court did nothing in this case to disguise its contempt for this Court's decisions in *Booth* and *Gathers*. Summing up its reaction to those cases, it concluded:

> It is an affront to the civilized members of the human race to say that at sentencing in a capital case, a parade of witnesses may praise the background, character and good deeds of Defendant (as was done in this case), without limitation as to relevancy, but nothing may be said that bears upon the character of, or harm imposed, upon the victims.

Offering no explanation for how this case could possibly be distinguished from *Booth* and *Gathers*—for obviously, there is none to offer—the court perfunctorily declared that the victim-impact evidence and the prosecutor's argument based on this evidence "did not violate either [of those decisions]." It cannot be clearer that the court simply declined to be bound by this Court's precedents.

Far from condemning this blatant disregard for the rule of law, the majority applauds it. In the Tennessee Supreme Court's denigration of *Booth* and *Gathers* as "an affront to the civilized members of the human race," the majority finds only confirmation of "the unfairness of the rule pronounced by" the majorities in those cases. It is hard to imagine a more complete abdication of this Court's historic commitment to defending the supremacy of its own pronouncements on issues of constitutional liberty. In light of the cost that such abdication exacts on the authoritativeness of all of this Court's pronouncements, it is also hard to imagine a more short-sighted strategy for effecting change in our constitutional order.

III

Today's decision charts an unmistakable course. If the majority's radical reconstruction of the rules for overturning this Court's decisions is to be taken at face value—and the majority offers us no reason why it should not—then the overruling of *Booth* and *Gathers* is but a preview of an even broader and more far-reaching assault upon this Court's precedents. Cast aside today are those condemned to face society's ultimate penalty. Tomorrow's victims may be minorities, women, or the indigent. Inevitably, this campaign to resurrect yesterday's "spirited dissents" will squander the authority and the legitimacy of this Court as a protector of the powerless. I dissent.*

Shooting the Wounded: First Degree Murder and Second Class Victims

Randall Coyne, 28 Okla. City U. L. Rev. 93, 99–102 (2003)

In August, 2002, Murder Victims' Families for Reconciliation (MVFR)[19] published an important report which cogently demonstrated that notwithstanding the victims' rights revolution, all members of the victim community are not treated equally. *Dignity Denied: The Experience of Murder Victims' Family Members Who Oppose the Death Penalty*,[20] chronicles the indifference, discrimination, and in some instances, abuse that the criminal justice system metes out to the family members of murder victims whose opposition to capital punishment makes them at best useless—and at worst dangerous—to prosecutors committed to persuading jurors that killers should be sentenced to death.

Part of the blame, of course, rests with the portion of *Booth v. Maryland*—prohibiting the victim impact evidence that characterizes the defendant or conveys opinions as to appropriate sentence—which survives *Payne*.[21] This prohibition made sense in the context of a total ban on victim impact evidence during capital sentencing proceedings. Standing alone, however, the ban on victim testimony or evidence as to an appropriate sentence has the perverse effect of silencing only one segment of the victim community: those family members of murder victims who oppose the imposition of a death sentence.

It is true, in a formal sense, that murder victims' family members who support the imposition of a death sentence are prevented by *Payne* from bluntly sharing this preference with jurors while testifying. Consistent with *Payne*, family members of victims may not be asked, nor may they offer, their opinions as to the sentence they believe the defendant deserves. And yet even when this rule is scrupulously observed, and no such testimony is sought or offered, the very appearance of murder victims' family members

---

* Within two short hours of reading this dissent from the bench, Justice Marshall announced his retirement. See Coyne, "Taking the Death Penalty Personally: Justice Thurgood Marshall," 47 Okla. L. Rev. 35 (1994).

19. MVFR, a remarkable coalition of persons opposed to the death penalty who have lost family members through murder or legal execution, was founded in 1976. According to MVFR's mission statement:

> MVFR is a national organization of family members of victims of both homicide and state killings who oppose the death penalty in all cases. Our mission is to abolish the death penalty. We advocate for programs and policies that reduce the rate of homicide and promote crime prevention and alternatives to violence. We support programs that address the needs of victims of violence, enabling them to heal and to rebuild their lives.

More information on MVFR can be obtained through their website. *See* Murder Victims' Families for Reconciliation, *at* http://www.mvfr.org

20. Robert Renny Cushing & Susannah Sheffer, Dignity Denied: The Experience of Murder Victims' Family Members Who Oppose the Death Penalty, (Murder Victims' Families for Reconciliation 2002) [hereinafter, Dignity Denied].

21. 482 U.S. 496 (1987).

as prosecution witnesses during capital sentencing hearings in which the prosecution is seeking death leaves precious little room to doubt just what their opinion might be. If they did not want the defendant killed in retribution for the loss of their murdered family member, they would have stayed home perhaps, or at least refused to testify.

Thus, *Payne* permits prosecutors to perpetuate the cruel charade that pro-death murder victim family members who testify as prosecution witnesses are not lending their voices in support of the prosecution's goal of seeking the defendant's death.

Dignity Denied emphasizes the importance of all victims being "informed of, present, and *heard* at critical stages of the criminal justice process" and condemns the practices of victim's advocacy offices, controlled by prosecutors, that "silence[], marginalize[], and abandon[] … family members who oppose the death penalty." Robert Renny Cushing, MVFR's executive director whose father was murdered, recounts being told by one Victim Witness Coordinator that Cushing's opposition to the death penalty prevented victims from healing. This presumption—that universal support for a death sentence is necessary to promote victim healing—ignores the reality that for some families, executing a murderer only adds to their pain and superimposes an additional trauma which, far from helping restore some sense of peace and security, actually revictimizes these victims.

Worse, failing to recognize the needs and heed the voices of anti-death penalty victims exiles a significant number of victims from the community of support services which the federal government and most states have mandated for all victims, regardless of their views on capital punishment. The baleful result, according to Cushing, goes beyond the politically expedient but nonetheless callous deprivation of support services to anti-death penalty victims. The more pernicious effect, perhaps, is to cast doubt on the legitimacy of suffering endured by these victims. As Cushing, borrowing from Sojourner Truth, cogently frames the issue, "'ain't *I* a victim?' Even though I oppose the death penalty and would not find resolution in another killing, am I not a victim as well, with a loss as piercing as the losses of victims who do support the death penalty?"

There does not appear to be even "a single protocol in the office of any prosecutor in the United States that alerts victim assistants to the possibility that some family members of murder victims may oppose the death penalty" and that admonishes these same assistants that these family members are entitled to the same assistance as those who support" capital punishment. Similarly, there appear to be no "laws or policies prohibiting discrimination against victims who oppose the death penalty, or mandating that services intended for survivors of homicide victims be provided equally to those who support the death penalty and those who oppose it." Thus, the pattern and practice of widespread silencing and discrimination against anti-death penalty victims should surprise no one.

According to *Dignity Denied*, victims' family members who oppose the death penalty seek "from prosecutors, judges, police officers, policymakers, and the victim services community" two things: (1) awareness of their perspective; and (2) "recognition that victims who oppose the death penalty are as deserving of respect and dignity as those who support it."[22]

---

22. It perhaps goes without saying that family members who oppose the death penalty are every bit as deserving of the support services rendered by victims' assistance programs to those who support the death penalty.

Selected Victim Impact Evidence Statutes

Georgia

Georgia Code §17-10-1.2. Oral victim impact statement; presentation of evidence; cross-examination and rebuttal by defendant; effect of noncompliance; no creation of cause of action or right of appeal.

(a) (1) In all cases in which the death penalty may be imposed, subsequent to an adjudication of guilt and in conjunction with the procedures in Code Section 17-10-30, the court may allow evidence from the family of the victim, or such other witness having personal knowledge of the victim's personal characteristics and the emotional impact of the crime on the victim, the victim's family, or the community. Such evidence shall be given in the presence of the defendant and of the jury and shall be subject to cross-examination. The admissibility of such evidence shall be in the sole discretion of the judge and in any event shall be permitted only in such a manner and to such a degree as not to inflame or unduly prejudice the jury.

(2) In all cases other than those in which the death penalty may be imposed, prior to fixing of the sentence as provided for in Code Section 17-10-1 or the imposing of life imprisonment as mandated by law, and before rendering the appropriate sentence, including any order of restitution, the court, within its discretion, may allow evidence from the victim, the family of the victim, or such other witness having personal knowledge of the impact of the crime on the victim, the family of the victim, or community. Such evidence shall be given in the presence of the defendant and shall be subject to cross-examination.

(b) In presenting such evidence, the victim, the family of the victim, or such other witness having personal knowledge of the impact of the crime on the victim, the victim's family, or the community shall, if applicable:

(1) Describe the nature of the offense;

(2) Itemize any economic loss suffered by the victim or the family of the victim, if restitution is sought;

(3) Identify any physical injury suffered by the victim as a result of the offense along with its seriousness and permanence;

(4) Describe any change in the victim's personal welfare or familial relationships as a result of the offense;

(5) Identify any request for psychological services initiated by the victim or the victim's family as a result of the offense; and

(6) Include any other information related to the impact of the offense upon the victim, the victim's family, or the community that the court inquires of.

(c) The court shall allow the defendant the opportunity to cross-examine and rebut the evidence presented of the victim's personal characteristics and the emotional impact of the crime on the victim, the victim's family, or the community, and such cross-examination and rebuttal evidence shall be subject to the same discretion set forth in paragraph (1) of subsection (a) of this Code section.

(d) No sentence shall be invalidated because of failure to comply with the provisions of this Code section. This Code section shall not be construed to create any cause of action or any right of appeal on behalf of any person.

Pennsylvania

42 Pa. C.S.A. §9711. Sentencing Procedure for Murder in the First Degree

(a) Procedure in jury trials. —

(1) After a verdict of murder of the first degree is recorded and before the jury is discharged, the court shall conduct a separate sentencing hearing in which the jury shall determine whether the defendant shall be sentenced to death or life imprisonment.

(2) In the sentencing hearing, evidence concerning the victim and the impact that the death of the victim has had on the family of the victim is admissible. Additionally, evidence may be presented as to any other matter that the court deems relevant and admissible on the question of the sentence to be imposed. Evidence shall include matters relating to any of the aggravating or mitigating circumstances specified in subsections (d) and (e), and information concerning the victim and the impact that the death of the victim has had on the family of the victim. Evidence of aggravating circumstances shall be limited to those circumstances specified in subsection (d).

(3) After the presentation of evidence, the court shall permit counsel to present argument for or against the sentence of death. The court shall then instruct the jury in accordance with subsection (c).

(4) Failure of the jury to unanimously agree upon a sentence shall not impeach or in any way affect the guilty verdict previously recorded.

(b) Procedure in nonjury trials and guilty pleas. — If the defendant has waived a jury trial or pleaded guilty, the sentencing proceeding shall be conducted before a jury impaneled for that purpose unless waived by the defendant with the consent of the Commonwealth, in which case the trial judge shall hear the evidence and determine the penalty in the same manner as would a jury as provided in subsection (a).

(c) Instructions to jury. —

(1) Before the jury retires to consider the sentencing verdict, the court shall instruct the jury on the following matters:

(i) the aggravating circumstances specified in subsection (d) as to which there is some evidence.

(ii) the mitigating circumstances specified in subsection (e) as to which there is some evidence.

(iii) aggravating circumstances must be proved by the Commonwealth beyond a reasonable doubt; mitigating circumstances must be proved by the defendant by a preponderance of the evidence.

(iv) the verdict must be a sentence of death if the jury unanimously finds at least one aggravating circumstance specified in subsection (d) and no mitigating circumstance or if the jury unanimously finds one or more aggravating circumstances which outweigh any mitigating circumstances. The verdict must be a sentence of life imprisonment in all other cases.

(v) the court may, in its discretion, discharge the jury if it is of the opinion that further deliberation will not result in a unanimous agreement as to the sentence, in which case the court shall sentence the defendant to life imprisonment.

(2) The court shall instruct the jury that if it finds at least one aggravating circumstance and at least one mitigating circumstance, it shall consider, in weighing the aggravating and mitigating circumstances, any evidence presented about the victim and about the impact of the murder on the victim's family. The court shall also instruct the jury on any other matter that may be just and proper under the circumstances ...

Oklahoma

22 Okla. Stat. §984. Definitions

As used in this act:

1. "Victim impact statement" means information about the financial, emotional, psychological, and physical effects of a violent crime on each victim and members of their immediate family, or person designated by the vicim or by family members of the victim and includes information about the victim, circumstances surrounding the crime, the manner in which the crime was perpetrated, and the victim's opinion of a recommended sentence;

2. "Member of the immediate family" means the spouse, a child by birth or adoption, a stepchild, a parent, or a sibling of each victim; and

3. "Violent crime" means any crime listed in paragraph 5 of Section 571 of Title 57 of the Oklahoma Statutes or any attempt, conspiracy or solicitation to commit any such crime or the crime of negligent homicide pursuant to Section 11-903 of Title 47 of the Oklahoma Statutes or the crime of causing great bodily injury while driving under the influence of intoxicating substance, pursuant to Section 11-904 of Title 47 of the Oklahoma Statutes.

22 Okla. Stat. §984.1. Presentation and use of victim impact statement at sentencing and parole proceedings

A. Each victim, or members of the immediate family of each victim or person designated by the victim or by family members of the victim, may present a written victim impact statement or appear personally at the sentence proceeding and present the statement orally. Provided, however, if a victim or any member of the immediate family or person designated by the victim or by family members of a victim wishes to appear personally, such person shall have the absolute right to do so.

B. If a presentence investigation report is prepared, the person preparing the report shall consult with each victim or members of the immediate family or a designee of members of the immediate family if the victim is deceased, incapacitated or incompetent, and include any victim impact statements in the presentence investigation report. If the individual to be consulted cannot be located or declines to cooperate, a notation to that effect shall be included.

C. The judge shall make available to the parties copies of any victim impact statements.

D. In any case which is plea bargained, victim impact statements shall be presented at the time of sentencing or attached to the district attorney narrative report. In determining the appropriate sentence, the court shall consider among other factors any victim impact statements if submitted to the jury, or the judge in the event a jury was waived.

E. The Department of Corrections and the Pardon and Parole Board, in deciding whether to release an individual on parole, shall consider any victim impact statements submitted to the jury, or the judge in the event a jury was waived.

22 Okla. Stat. §984.2. Disclosure of certain information regarding victim may be prohibited

The court, upon the request of a victim or the district attorney, may order that the victim's address, telephone number, place of employment, or other personal information shall not be disclosed in any law enforcement record or any court document, other than the transcript of a court proceeding, if it is determined by the court to be necessary to protect the victim or immediate family of the victim from harassment or physical harm and if the court determines that the information is immaterial to the defense.

Notes and Questions

1. Victim impact evidence raises troubling ethical issues for prosecutors and defense attorneys alike. For example, how actively should prosecutors seek the aid of grieving friends and family members in attempting to secure a death sentence? Is the grief of victims a legitimate factor to consider when deciding whether to seek the death penalty? Does the Sixth Amendment's guarantee of effective assistance of counsel require defense attorneys to search for evidence that the deceased somehow deserved to die? For a discussion of these issues, see Coyne, "Inflicting *Payne* on Oklahoma," 45 Okla. L. Rev. 589 (1992). For a contrary view, see Douglass, "Oklahoma's Victim Impact Legislation: A New Voice for Victims and Their Families: A Response to Professor Coyne," 46 Okla. L. Rev. 283 (1993).

2. Evaluate the following proposed defense strategies for diffusing victim impact evidence.

   (a) Establish contact with victims' family members to determine whether they are going to insist that capital charges be filed.

   (b) During voir dire, ask potential jurors whether they feel that the jury's job is to render a verdict satisfactory to the deceased's family.

   (c) Thoroughly investigate the background and character of the *deceased*, paying particular attention to bad character evidence. Threaten to air this dirty laundry if the prosecution insists upon using victim impact evidence.

   (d) Investigate the victim's background for the purpose of contrasting the victim's background (assuming it was filled with love and encouragement) and the defendant's background (assuming it was characterized by abject neglect or abuse).

   (e) File a *Brady* motion specifically requesting bad-character-of-the-victim evidence, arguing that it is relevant to rebut any VIS and may affect punishment.

   (f) Tactfully inform VIS witnesses of the defense attorney's duty to vigorously cross-examine all witnesses.

   (g) Through gentle cross-examination, ask whether family members are receiving help coping with the tragedy, being especially careful to express the defendant's remorse through the tone and substance of the questions.

   (h) Seek to introduce expert testimony to the effect that killing the defendant will not help the survivors.

   (i) Endeavor to portray family members of the defendant as other victims, destined to suffer greatly if a death sentence is returned.

   (j) Ask the surviving spouse if the deceased was a compassionate, forgiving person.

   (k) Discover how the victim's family treated the victim. If evidence of child abuse or neglect is uncovered, argue that it should be admissible for impeachment.

45 Okla. L. Rev. at 612–615.

3. In light of the emotional tug-of-war created by *Payne*, should the defense be permitted to offer evidence of the effect of the defendant's execution on his family and

friends in order to restore a semblance of procedural even-handedness historically required in capital cases? Would such evidence be considered relevant mitigating evidence? For several arguments in favor of admitting execution impact evidence during capital sentencing proceedings, see Logan, "When Balance and Fairness Collide: An Argument for Execution Impact Evidence in Capital Trials," 33 U. Mich. J.L. Ref. 1 (2000).

Note on Congressional Interference in an On-Going Capital Trial on Behalf of Victims in United States v. McVeigh and Nichols

The following decision illustrates the enormous momentum the victims' rights movement enjoyed in the wake of the April 19, 1995 Oklahoma City bombing. Distressed that Chief Judge Matsch's ruling under Rule 615 would prevent victims who intended to testify in support of death sentences from attending trial proceedings (which could taint their testimony), victims appealed to Congress. Congress embraced the victims' arguments and passed a federal law (the Victims' Rights Clarification Act of 1997) specifically designed to overrule Chief Judge Matsch's order in Timothy McVeigh's on-going capital trial. Chief Judge Matsch's response to the statute follows.

United States v. McVeigh and Nichols
958 F. Supp. 512 (D.Colo. 1997)

MATSCH, Chief Judge.

On October 20, 1995, the government filed notices of intention to seek the death penalty as to each of the defendants upon conviction of any of the charges against them, thereby invoking the provisions of the Federal Death Penalty Act, 18 U.S.C. §§3591–3596. Among the aggravating factors identified in those notices is the following:

> 4. Victim impact evidence concerning the effect of the defendant's offense(s) on the victims and the victims' families, as evidenced by oral testimony and victim impact statements that identify the victims of the offense(s) and the extent and scope of injury and loss suffered by the victims and the victims' families.

Congress expressly authorized including this factor in such a notice pursuant to §3593(a) but did not particularize the scope of the information that may be presented to the jury at a sentencing hearing. As observed in this court's earlier Memorandum Opinion and Order on Motions Addressed to Death Penalty Notice, entered September 25, 1996, 944 F. Supp. 1478 (D. Colo.1996), this is the most problematical of the aggravating factors and may present the greatest difficulty in determining the admissibility of information at a penalty hearing. In 1987, the Supreme Court declared in *Booth v. Maryland*, 482 U.S. 496 (1987), that the use of a victim impact statement based on interviews with the family survivors of a murdered elderly couple violated the Eighth Amendment. Two years later, the Court held in *South Carolina v. Gathers*, 490 U.S. 805 (1989), that a prosecutor's closing argument was grounds for reversing a death sentence in a murder case because of extensive reference to inferences regarding the victim because a prayer card and a voter's registration card were found near his body.

In 1991, the Supreme Court overruled those prior decisions insofar as they imposed a *per se* rule of inadmissibility of victim impact evidence. The Court held in *Payne v. Tennessee*, 501 U.S. 808 (1991), that there was no Eighth Amendment violation in a penalty hearing which included testimony from a grandmother about the effects on her young grandson of the murders of his mother and sister and the prosecutor's comments on those effects in his closing argument. In the Court's opinion and in concurring opinions, the justices recognized the potential for inflammatory effects of such evidence and cautioned that it could render the proceeding fundamentally unfair in violation of the Due Process Clause. In reversing the *per se* exclusion in the prior cases, the Court expressly recognized the requirement that trial courts exercise their discretion to avoid the influence of passion or prejudice.

Because §3593(a) refers to "the effect of the offense on the victim and the victim's family," this court concluded that persons scheduled to testify about such effects at a penalty hearing should be excluded from pretrial proceedings and the trial to avoid any influence from that experience on their testimony. Accordingly, such potential penalty witnesses were excluded from the courtroom under Fed. R. Evid. 615 in an oral ruling on the first day of a suppression hearing on June 26, 1996. On July 29, 1996, the government filed a motion to reconsider that ruling, arguing that §3593(c) explicitly provides that "information" at capital sentencing hearings is not limited by the rules governing admission of evidence at criminal trials "except that information may be excluded if its probative value is outweighed by the danger of creating unfair prejudice, confusing the issues, or misleading the jury."

At a hearing on October 4, 1996, the court denied the motion for reconsideration and adhered to the exclusion order to avoid any prejudicial impact from possible emotionally traumatizing effects of what penalty phase witnesses may see and hear at the trial. Thus, the court elected to continue to apply Rule 615 as a prophylactic measure.

On March 19, 1997, the President signed Public Law 105-6, bearing the short title "Victim Rights Clarification Act of 1997." That statute, now in effect, enacted a new provision, codified as 18 U.S.C. §3510, which includes the following:

> (b) Capital Cases. — Notwithstanding any statute, rule, or other provision of law, a United States district court shall not order any victim of an offense excluded from the trial of a defendant accused of that offense because such victim may, during the sentencing hearing, testify as to the effect of the offense on the victim and the victim's family or as to any other factor for which notice is required under section 3593(a).

It also amended 18 U.S.C. §3593(c) to read, in pertinent part, as follows:

> Information is admissible regardless of its admissibility under the rules governing admission of evidence at criminal trials except that information may be excluded if its probative value is outweighed by the danger of creating unfair prejudice, confusing the issues, or misleading the jury. *For the purposes of the preceding sentence, the fact that a victim, as defined in section 3510, attended or observed the trial shall not be construed to pose a danger of creating unfair prejudice, confusing the issues, or misleading the jury.*

(Amended language in italics.)

This legislation began as H.R. 924. The House Committee on the Judiciary published its report on March 17, 1997, together with dissenting views. The members of Congress who were signatory to those dissenting views expressed concern about the constitutionality of the legislation as applied to this case, and the floor debate on March 18, 1997, published in the Congressional Record for March 18, 1997, includes statements of concern about constitutionality from two of those dissenters.

The trial of Timothy McVeigh is scheduled to begin on March 31, 1997. A debate now on the constitutionality of this new legislation would result in a delay of that trial.

In this court's view, any motions raising constitutional questions about this legislation would be premature and would present issues that are not now ripe for decision. It is clear that the new legislation has no application to fact witnesses testifying at the trial of the charges against Mr. McVeigh. If Timothy McVeigh is acquitted of these charges there will be no sentencing hearing and, therefore, no justiciable issue will arise.

If there is a conviction, the court can protect against any prejudicial effect from victim impact witnesses' attendance at the trial, including the closed circuit telecast of the trial proceedings, by permitting voir dire of victim witnesses outside the presence of the jury before they testify. All interests, including the public interest in proceeding with Mr. McVeigh's trial, can be accommodated by construing Public Law 105-6 as simply reversing the presumption of a prejudicial effect on victim impact testimony of observation of the trial proceedings. Thus, the distinction between the effects of the crime of conviction and any effects from the adjudicative process will still be preserved if this court now reverses the exclusionary order, permits observation of the trial proceedings by potential penalty phase victim impact witnesses and reserves ruling on the admissibility of the testimony of particular witnesses who observed any part of the trial proceedings. Accordingly, it is ordered that the order excluding witnesses under Rule 615 of the Federal Rules of Evidence is amended to permit observation of the trial proceedings in the courtroom and through means of the closed circuit telecast by persons whose potential participation is limited to providing written victim impact statements or testimony at a capital sentencing hearing.

Notes and Questions

1. What questions would you ask to determine whether the testimony of victim impact witnesses who attended trial was influenced by the emotionally traumatizing effects of what these victim witnesses saw and heard at trial?

2. In 2004, MVFR board member Bud Welch — whose daughter Julie was one of 168 persons killed in the 1995 Oklahoma City bombing (and who nonetheless opposed the execution of her killers) testified on behalf of Terry Nichols at his state trial sentencing hearing. Although Nichols was found guilty of more than 160 capital offenses, four jurors voted against a death sentence. Consequently, Nichols received 161 consecutive life sentences. "Victims Testify Against Death Sentence for OK City Bombing Defendant Terry Nichols," The Voice, Fall/Winter 2004.

3. How far should victims' rights be extended? The execution chamber at the federal prison in Terre Haute, Indiana has seats for ten victim witnesses. The June 11, 2001 execution of Timothy McVeigh — convicted of the 1995 bombing of the Oklahoma City federal building which killed 168 people and injured hundreds more — was broadcast on a closed-circuit feed to victims interested in witnessing McVeigh's death. More than 250 victims expressed an interest in attending the broadcast. Attorney General Ashcroft said that the FBI and other agencies will make sure that the broadcast is not recorded or pirated. He described the broadcast as "state-of-the-art videoconferencing" and said that it may help victims "close this chapter on their lives." One victim, whose wife died in the bombing, said, "It just pleases me to no end." Does this seem like a reasonable accommodation of victims' interests? Should it matter that McVeigh did not oppose the broadcast and suggested that his execution be televised nationally?

4. Zacarias Moussaoui, the sole individual tried in connection with the September 11, 2001 terrorist attacks on the United States, belittled the victim impact witnesses

who testified in support of the government's plea that he be executed. During his sentencing hearing, he testified that he had "no regret, no remorse," and said, "I find it disgusting that people come here to share their grief." Nonetheless, Moussaoui was sentenced to life without the possibility of parole. Meek, *Moussaoui Takes Stand, Mocks Victims' Families*, N.Y Daily News, April 14, 2006.

Chapter 8

The Role of Mitigating Circumstances

A. General Principles of Mitigation

Once the prosecution presents evidence of aggravating circumstances to justify sentencing a defendant to death, the defense has the opportunity to introduce evidence to persuade the jury to impose a lesser sentence. Mitigating evidence does not justify or excuse the offense in question, but it is evidence which, "in fairness and mercy, may be considered as extenuating or reducing the degree of moral culpability." *Black's Law Dictionary* 903 (5th ed.) (West Pub. Co. 1979).

1. All Aspects of Defendant's Character, Record and Circumstances of the Offense

Lockett v. Ohio

438 U.S. 586 (1978)

Mr. Chief Justice BURGER delivered the opinion of the Court with respect to the constitutionality of petitioner's conviction (Parts I and II) together with an opinion (Part III) in which Mr. Justice Stewart, Mr. Justice Powell, and Mr. Justice Stevens joined, on the constitutionality of the statute under which petitioner was sentenced to death, and announced the judgment of the court.

We granted certiorari in this case to consider, among other questions, whether Ohio violated the Eighth and Fourteenth Amendments by sentencing Sandra Lockett to death pursuant to a statute that narrowly limits the sentencer's discretion to consider the circumstances of the crime and the record and character of the offender as mitigating factors.

I

Lockett was charged with aggravated murder with the aggravating specifications (1) that the murder was "committed for the purpose of escaping detection, apprehension, trial, or punishment" for aggravated robbery, and (2) that the murder was "committed while ... committing, attempting to commit, or fleeing immediately after committing or attempting to commit ... aggravated robbery." That offense was punishable by death in Ohio. She was also charged with aggravated robbery. The State's case against her depended largely upon the testimony of a co-participant, one Al Parker, who gave the following account of her participation in the robbery and murder.... [Parker testified that he, Lockett and two others planned to rob a pawnshop. No one intended to kill the

451

owner of the pawnshop. However, during the course of the robbery, Parker shot and killed the owner. Lockett was not in the pawnshop during the robbery and murder; she was waiting in the car for the others. Based on this evidence, the jury found Lockett guilty of aggravated murder with aggravating specifications.]

Once a verdict of aggravated murder with specifications had been returned, the Ohio death penalty statute required the trial judge to impose a death sentence unless, after "considering the nature and circumstances of the offense" and Lockett's "history, character, and condition," he found by a preponderance of the evidence that (1) the victim had induced or facilitated the offense, (2) it was unlikely that Lockett would have committed the offense but for the fact that she "was under duress, coercion, or strong provocation," or (3) the offense was "primarily the product of [Lockett's] psychosis or mental deficiency."

In accord with the Ohio statute, the trial judge requested a presentence report as well as psychiatric and psychological reports. The reports contained detailed information about Lockett's intelligence, character, and background. The psychiatric and psychological reports described her as a 21-year-old with low-average or average intelligence, and not suffering from a mental deficiency. One of the psychologists reported that "her prognosis for rehabilitation" if returned to society was favorable. The presentence report showed that Lockett had committed no major offenses although she had a record of several minor ones as a juvenile and two minor offenses as an adult. It also showed that she had once used heroin but was receiving treatment at a drug abuse clinic and seemed to be "on the road to success" as far as her drug problem was concerned. It concluded that Lockett suffered no psychosis and was not mentally deficient.

After considering the reports and hearing argument on the penalty issue, the trial judge concluded that the offense had not been primarily the product of psychosis or mental deficiency. Without specifically addressing the other two statutory mitigating factors, the judge said that he had "no alternative, whether [he] like[d] the law or not" but to impose the death penalty. He then sentenced Lockett to death....

[On appeal, Lockett argued her death sentence was invalid because the Ohio statute under which she was sentenced did not permit the sentencing judge to consider, as mitigating factors, Lockett's character, prior record, age, lack of specific intent to cause death, and her relatively minor role in the crime.]

III

A

... In the last decade, many of the States have been obliged to revise their death penalty statutes in response to the various opinions supporting the judgments in *Furman v. Georgia*, 408 U.S. 238 (1972), and *Gregg v. Georgia*, 428 U.S. 227 (1976), and its companion cases. The signals from this Court have not, however, always been easy to decipher. The States now deserve the clearest guidance that the Court can provide; we have an obligation to reconcile previously differing views in order to provide that guidance.

B

With that obligation in mind we turn to Lockett's attack on the Ohio statute. Essentially she contends that the Eighth and Fourteenth Amendments require that the sentencer be given a full opportunity to consider mitigating circumstances in capital cases and that the Ohio statute does not comply with that requirement. She relies, in large part, on the plurality opinions in *Woodson v. North Carolina*, 428 U.S. 280 (1976), and *Roberts (Stanislaus) v. Louisiana*, 428 U.S. 325 (1976), and the joint opinion in *Jurek v. Texas*, 428 U.S. 262 (1976), but she goes beyond them.

We begin by recognizing that the concept of individualized sentencing in criminal cases generally, although not constitutionally required, has long been accepted in this country. Consistent with that concept, sentencing judges traditionally have taken a wide range of factors into account. That States have authority to make aiders and abettors equally responsible, as a matter of law, with principals, or to enact felony-murder statutes is beyond constitutional challenge. But the definition of crimes generally has not been thought automatically to dictate what should be the proper penalty. And where sentencing discretion is granted, it generally has been agreed that the sentencing judge's "possession of the fullest information possible concerning the defendant's life and characteristics" is "[h]ighly relevant—if not essential—[to the] selection of an appropriate sentence...."

The opinions of this Court going back many years in dealing with sentencing in capital cases have noted the strength of the basis for individualized sentencing. For example, Mr. Justice Black, writing for the Court in *Williams v. New York*, 337 U.S. 241 (1949)—a capital case—observed that the "whole country has traveled far from the period in which the death sentence was an automatic and commonplace result of convictions—even for offenses today deemed trivial." Ten years later, in *Williams v. Oklahoma*, 358 U.S. 576 (1959), another capital case, the Court echoed Mr. Justice Black, stating that "[i]n discharging his duty of imposing a proper sentence, the sentencing judge is authorized, if not required, to consider all of the mitigating and aggravating circumstances involved in the crime." Most would agree that "the 19th century movement away from mandatory death sentences marked an enlightened introduction of flexibility into the sentencing process."

Although legislatures remain free to decide how much discretion in sentencing should be reposed in the judge or jury in noncapital cases, the plurality opinion in *Woodson*, after reviewing the historical repudiation of mandatory sentencing in capital cases, concluded that "in capital cases the fundamental respect for humanity underlying the Eighth Amendment ... requires consideration of the character and record of the individual offender and the circumstances of the particular offense as a constitutionally indispensable part of the process of inflicting the penalty of death." That declaration rested "on the predicate that the penalty of death is qualitatively different" from any other sentence. We are satisfied that this qualitative difference between death and other penalties calls for a greater degree of reliability when the death sentence is imposed. The mandatory death penalty statute in *Woodson* was held invalid because it permitted no consideration of "relevant facets of the character and record of the individual offender or the circumstances of the particular offense." The plurality did not attempt to indicate, however, which facets of an offender or his offense it deemed "relevant" in capital sentencing or what degree of consideration of "relevant facets" it would require.

We are now faced with those questions and we conclude that the Eighth and Fourteenth Amendments require that the sentencer, in all but the rarest kind of capital case, not be precluded from considering, as a mitigating factor, any aspect of a defendant's character or record and any of the circumstances of the offense that the defendant proffers as a basis for a sentence less than death. We recognize that, in noncapital cases, the established practice of individualized sentences rests not on constitutional commands, but on public policy enacted into statutes. The considerations that account for the wide acceptance of individualization of sentences in noncapital cases surely cannot be thought less important in capital cases. Given that the imposition of death by public authority is so profoundly different from all other penalties, we cannot avoid the conclusion that an individualized decision is essential in capital cases. The need for treating each defendant in a capital case with that degree of respect due the uniqueness of the individual is far more important than in noncapital cases. A variety of flexible techniques—probation, parole, work furloughs, to name a few—and various postconviction remedies may be available to modify an initial sentence of confinement in noncapital cases. The nonavailability of corrective or modifying mechanisms with respect to an executed capital sentence underscores the need for individualized consideration as a constitutional requirement in imposing the death sentence.

There is no perfect procedure for deciding in which cases governmental authority should be used to impose death. But a statute that prevents the sentencer in all capital cases from giving independent mitigating weight to aspects of the defendant's character and record and to circumstances of the offense proffered in mitigation creates the risk that the death penalty will be imposed in spite of factors which may call for a less severe penalty. When the choice is between life and death, that risk is unacceptable and incompatible with the commands of the Eighth and Fourteenth Amendments.

C

The Ohio death penalty statute does not permit the type of individualized consideration of mitigating factors we now hold to be required by the Eighth and Fourteenth Amendments in capital cases. Its constitutional infirmities can best be understood by comparing it with the statutes upheld in *Gregg, Proffitt,* and *Jurek.*

In upholding the Georgia statute in *Gregg,* Justices Stewart, Powell, and Stevens noted that the statute permitted the jury "to consider any aggravating or mitigating circumstances," and that the Georgia Supreme Court had approved "open and far-ranging argument" in presentence hearings. Although the Florida statute approved in *Proffitt* contained a list of mitigating factors, six Members of this Court assumed, in approving the statute, that the range of mitigating factors listed in the statute was not exclusive. *Jurek* involved a Texas statute which made no explicit reference to mitigating factors. Rather, the jury was required to answer three questions in the sentencing process, the second of which was "whether there is a probability that the defendant would commit criminal acts of violence that would constitute a continuing threat to society." The statute survived the petitioner's Eighth and Fourteenth Amendment attack because three Justices concluded that the Texas Court of Criminal Appeals had broadly interpreted the second question—despite its facial narrowness—so as to permit the sentencer to consider "whatever mitigating circumstances" the defendant might be able to show. None of the statutes we sustained in *Gregg* and the companion cases clearly operated at that time to prevent the sentencer from considering any aspect of the defendant's character and record or any circumstances of his offense as an independently mitigating factor.

In this regard the statute now before us is significantly different. Once a defendant is found guilty of aggravated murder with at least one of seven specified aggravating circumstances, the death penalty must be imposed unless, considering "the nature and circumstances of the offense and the history, character, and condition of the offender," the sentencing judge determines that at least one of the following mitigating circumstances is established by a preponderance of the evidence:

"(1) The victim of the offense induced or facilitated it.

"(2) It is unlikely that the offense would have been committed, but for the fact that the offender was under duress, coercion, or strong provocation.

"(3) The offense was primarily the product of the offender's psychosis or mental deficiency, though such condition is insufficient to establish the defense of insanity."

The Ohio Supreme Court has concluded that there is no constitutional distinction between the statute approved in *Proffitt* and Ohio's statute because the mitigating circumstances in Ohio's statute are "liberally construed in favor of the accused," and because the sentencing judge or judges may consider factors such as the age and criminal record of the defendant in determining whether any of the mitigating circumstances is established. But even under the Ohio court's construction of the statute, only the three factors specified in the statute can be considered in mitigation of the defendant's sentence. We see therefore, that once it is determined that the victim did not induce or facilitate the offense, that the defendant did not act under duress or coercion, and that the offense was not primarily the product of the defendant's mental deficiency, the Ohio statute mandates the sentence of death. The absence of direct proof that the defendant intended to cause the death of the victim is relevant for mitigating purposes only if it is determined that it sheds some light on one of the three statutory mitigating factors. Similarly, consideration of a defendant's comparatively minor role in the offense, or age, would generally not be permitted, as such, to affect the sentencing decision.

The limited range of mitigating circumstances which may be considered by the sentencer under the Ohio statute is incompatible with the Eighth and Fourteenth Amendments. To meet constitutional requirements, a death penalty statute must not preclude consideration of relevant mitigating factors. Accordingly, the judgment under review is reversed to the extent that it sustains the imposition of the death penalty, and the case is remanded for further proceedings.

Note and Question

Lockett requires that a capital sentencer must consider in mitigation all aspects of the defendant's character and record and the circumstances of the offense proffered as the basis for a sentence less than death. On remand, the trial court must consider, among other things, Lockett's "comparatively minor role in the offense." What result if the prosecution's evidence shows that Lockett suggested robbing two other stores and offered to furnish a gun; guided her accomplices to the pawnshop; remained in the car because she knew the pawnshop owner; hid the murder weapon in her purse; and hid two of her accomplices in her parents' attic?

Note on Evidence Possessing Aggravating and Mitigating Qualities

Some evidence proffered during sentencing may tend both to aggravate and mitigate the offense. In particular, evidence of mental illness often is double-edged. The mitigating nature of mental illness, disease and defect seems self-evident. The mentally ill person did not choose to be disordered. Her disability may significantly limit her ability to perceive reality and to make rational and appropriate choices. Nonetheless, mentally ill persons are particularly vulnerable to assertions of future dangerousness or continuing threat aggravators. As Justice O'Connor observed in *Penry v. Lynaugh,* (*supra* chapter 4 and *infra* chapter 15), "Penry's mental retardation and history of abuse is thus a two-edged sword: it may diminish his blameworthiness for his crime even as it indicates that there is a probability that he will be dangerous in the future."

Consider the mitigating and aggravating aspects of anti-social personality disorder (ASPD). According to the American Psychiatric Association's Diagnostic and Statistical Manual of Mental Disorders (DSM-IV), persons who suffer from ASPD must be at least 18 years of age, have evidenced a conduct disorder before the age of 15, and exhibit a pervasive pattern of disregard for and violation of the rights of others occurring since age 15, as indicated by 3 (or more) of the following:

(1) failure to conform to social norms with respect to lawful behaviors as indicated by repeatedly performing acts that are grounds for arrest;

(2) deceitfulness, as indicated by repeated lying, use of aliases, or conning others for personal profit or pleasure;

(3) impulsivity or failure to plan ahead;

(4) irritability and aggressiveness, as indicated by repeated physical fights or assaults;

(5) reckless disregard for safety of self or others;

(6) consistent irresponsibility, as indicated by repeated failure to sustain consistent work behavior or honor financial obligations;

(7) lack of remorse, as indicated by being indifferent to or rationalizing having hurt, mistreated, or stolen from another....

DSM-IV at 649–50. See Sevilla, "Anti-Social Personality Disorder: Justification for the Death Penalty?," 10 J. Contemp. Legal Issues 247 (1999) (arguing that it is immoral to use as an aggravating factor leading to a penalty of death a condition over which a defendant lacks choice and control and asserting that ASPD and other involuntary mental illnesses should be limited to mitigating use only).

Green v. Georgia
442 U.S. 95 (1979)

PER CURIAM.

Petitioner and Carzell Moore were indicted together for the rape and murder of Teresa Carol Allen. Moore was tried separately, was convicted of both crimes, and has been sentenced to death. Petitioner subsequently was convicted of murder, and also received a capital sentence. The Supreme Court of Georgia upheld the conviction and sentence, and petitioner has sought review of so much of the judgment as affirmed the capital sentence. We grant the motion for leave to proceed *in forma pauperis* and the petition for certiorari and vacate the sentence. The evidence at trial tended to show that petitioner and Moore abducted Allen from the store where she was working alone and, acting either in concert or separately, raped and murdered her. After the jury determined that petitioner was guilty of murder, a second trial was held to decide whether capital punishment would be imposed. At this second proceeding, petitioner sought to prove he was not present when Allen was killed and had not participated in her death. He attempted to introduce the testimony of Thomas Pasby, who had testified for the State at Moore's trial. According to Pasby, Moore had confided to him that he had killed Allen, shooting her twice after ordering petitioner to run an errand. The trial court refused to allow introduction of this evidence, ruling that Pasby's testimony constituted hearsay that was inadmissible under Ga.Code §§38-301 (1978). The State then argued to the jury that in the absence of direct evidence as to the circumstances of the crime, it could infer that petitioner participated directly in Allen's murder from the fact that more than one bullet was fired into her body.[2]

Regardless of whether the proffered testimony comes within Georgia's hearsay rule, under the facts of this case its exclusion constituted a violation of the Due Process Clause of the Fourteenth Amendment. The excluded testimony was highly relevant to a critical issue in the punishment phase of the trial, see *Lockett v. Ohio*, 438 U.S. 586, 604–605, (1978) (plurality opinion); *id.*, at 613–616, (opinion of Blackmun, J.), and substantial reasons existed to assume its reliability. Moore made his statement spontaneously to a close friend. The evidence corroborating the confession was ample, and indeed sufficient to procure a conviction of Moore and a capital sentence. The statement was against interest, and there was no reason to believe that Moore had any ulterior motive in making it. Perhaps most important, the State considered the testimony sufficiently reliable to use it against Moore, and to base a sentence of death upon it. In these unique circumstances, "the hearsay rule may not be applied mechanistically to defeat the ends of justice." *Chambers v. Mississippi*, 410 U.S. 284, 302, (1973). Because the exclusion of Pasby's testimony denied petitioner a fair trial on the issue of punishment, the sentence is vacated and the case is remanded for further proceedings not inconsistent with this opinion.

Mr. Justice REHNQUIST, dissenting.

The Court today takes another step toward embalming the law of evidence in the Due Process Clause of the Fourteenth Amendment to the United States Constitution. I think it impossible to find any justification in the Constitution for today's ruling, and take comfort only from the fact that since this is a capital case, it is perhaps an example of the maxim that "hard cases make bad law." The Georgia trial court refused to allow in evidence certain testimony at petitioner's sentencing trial on the ground that it constituted inadmissible hearsay under Ga. Code §§38-301 (1978). This Court does not, and could not, dispute the propriety of that ruling. Instead, it marshals a number of ad hoc reasons why Georgia should adopt a code of evidence that would allow this particular testimony to be admitted, and concludes that "[i]n these unique circumstances, 'the hearsay rule may not be applied mechanistically to defeat the ends of justice.'"

Nothing in the United States Constitution gives this Court any authority to supersede a State's code of evidence because its application in a particular situation would defeat what this Court conceives to be "the ends of justice." The Court does not disagree that the testimony at issue is hearsay or that it fails to come within any of the exceptions to the hearsay rule provided by Georgia's rules of evidence. The Court obviously is troubled by the fact that the same testimony was admissible at the separate trial of petitioner's codefendant at the behest of the State. But this fact by no means demonstrates that the Georgia courts have not evenhandedly applied their code of evidence, with its various hearsay exceptions, so as to deny petitioner a fair trial. No practicing lawyer can

---

2. The District Attorney stated to the jury:

"We couldn't possibly bring any evidence other than the circumstantial evidence and the direct evidence that we had pointing to who did it, and I think it's especially significant for you to remember what Dr. Dawson said in this case. When the first shot, in his medical opinion, he stated that Miss Allen had positive blood pressure when both shots were fired but I don't know whether Carzell Moore fired the first shot and handed the gun to Roosevelt Green and he fired the second shot or whether it was vice versa or whether Roosevelt Green had the gun and fired the shot or Carzell Moore had the gun and fired the first shot or the second, but I think it can be reasonably stated that you Ladies and Gentlemen can believe that each one of them fired the shots so that they would be as equally involved and one did not exceed the other's part in the commission of this crime." Pet. for Cert. 10.

have failed to note that Georgia's evidentiary rules, like those of every other State and of the United States, are such that certain items of evidence may be introduced by one party, but not by another. This is a fact of trial life, embodied throughout the hearsay rule and its exceptions. This being the case, the United States Constitution must be strained to or beyond the breaking point to conclude that all capital defendants who are unable to introduce all of the evidence which they seek to admit are denied a fair trial. I therefore dissent from the vacation of petitioner's sentence.

2. Standard of Proof Governing Mitigating Circumstances

Although *Walton v. Arizona*, 497 U.S. 1050 (1990), was overruled in part by *Ring v. Arizona*, 536 U.S. 584 (2002) (*infra* chapter 9), Justice White's opinion, excerpted below, contains a useful—and still valid—discussion of the mitigating circumstances.

Walton v. Arizona
497 U.S. 1050 (1990)

Justice WHITE announced the judgment of the Court and delivered the opinion of the Court with respect to Parts I, II, and V, and an opinion with respect to Parts III and IV, in which the Chief Justice, Justice O'Connor, and Justice Kennedy joined.

At issue in this case is the validity of the death sentence imposed by an Arizona trial court after a jury found petitioner Jeffrey Walton guilty of committing first-degree murder.

The Arizona statutes provide that a person commits first-degree murder if "[i]ntending or knowing that his conduct will cause death, such person causes the death of another with premeditation" or if in the course of committing certain specified offenses and without any mental state other than what is required for the commission of such offenses, he causes the death of any person. Ariz. Rev. Stat. Ann. §13-1105 (1989). After a person has been found guilty of first-degree murder, the sentence for such crime is determined in accordance with the provisions of §13-703(B). It is there directed that a "separate sentencing hearing shall be conducted before the court alone" to determine whether the sentence shall be death or life imprisonment. In the course of such hearing, the judge is instructed to determine the existence or nonexistence of any of the aggravating or mitigating circumstances defined in subsections (F) and (G) of §13-703. Subsection (F) defines 10 aggravating circumstances that may be considered. One of them is whether the offense was committed with the expectation of receiving anything of pecuniary value. Another is whether the defendant committed the offense in an especially heinous, cruel, or depraved manner. Subsection (G) defines mitigating circumstances as any factors "which are relevant in determining whether to impose a sentence less than death, including any aspect of the defendant's character, propensities or record and any of the circumstances of the offense, including but not limited to" five specified factors. The burden of establishing the existence of any of the aggravating circumstances is on the prosecution, while the burden of establishing mitigating circumstances is on the defendant. The court is directed to return a special verdict setting forth its findings as to aggravating and mitigating circumstances and then "shall impose a sentence of death if the court finds one or more of the aggravating circumstances enumerated in subsection (F) of this section and that there are no mitigating circumstances sufficiently substantial to call for leniency."

I

Petitioner Walton and his two codefendants, Robert Hoover and Sharold Ramsey, went to a bar in Tucson, Arizona, on the night of March 2, 1986, intending to find and rob someone at random, steal his car, tie him up, and leave him in the desert while they fled the State in the car. In the bar's parking lot, the trio encountered Thomas Powell, a young, off-duty Marine. The three robbed Powell at gunpoint and forced him into his car which they then drove out into the desert. While driving out of Tucson, the three asked Powell questions about where he lived and whether he had any more money. When the car stopped, Ramsey told a frightened Powell that he would not be hurt. Walton and Hoover then forced Powell out of the car and had him lie face down on the ground near the car while they debated what to do with him. Eventually, Walton instructed Hoover and Ramsey to sit in the car and turn the radio up loud. Walton then took a .22 caliber derringer and marched Powell off into the desert. After walking a short distance, Walton forced Powell to lie down on the ground, placed his foot on Powell's neck, and shot Powell once in the head. Walton later told Hoover and Ramsey that he had shot Powell and that he had "never seen a man pee in his pants before." Powell's body was found approximately a week later, after Walton was arrested and led police to the murder site. A medical examiner determined that Powell had been blinded and rendered unconscious by the shot but was not immediately killed. Instead, Powell regained consciousness, apparently floundered about in the desert, and ultimately died from dehydration, starvation, and pneumonia approximately a day before his body was found.

A jury convicted Walton of first-degree murder after being given instructions on both premeditated and felony murder. The trial judge then conducted the separate sentencing hearing required by §13-703(B). The State argued that two aggravating circumstances were present: (1) The murder was committed "in an especially heinous, cruel or depraved manner," the murder was committed for pecuniary gain. In mitigation Walton presented testimony from a psychiatrist who opined that Walton had a long history of substance abuse which impaired his judgment, and that Walton may have been abused sexually as a child. Walton's counsel also argued Walton's age, 20 at the time of sentencing, as a mitigating circumstance. At the conclusion of the hearing, the trial court found "beyond any doubt" that Walton was the one who shot Powell. The court also found that the two aggravating circumstances pressed by the State were present. The court stated that it had considered Walton's age and his capacity to appreciate the wrongfulness of his conduct, as well as all of the mitigating factors urged by defendant's counsel. The court then concluded that there were "no mitigating circumstances sufficiently substantial to call for leniency." The court sentenced Walton to death.

The Arizona Supreme Court affirmed Walton's conviction and sentence. Relying on its prior decisions, the court rejected various specific challenges to the constitutionality of the Arizona death penalty statute, some of which are pressed here, and then proceeded to conduct its independent review of Walton's sentence in order to "ensure that aggravating factors were proven beyond a reasonable doubt and all appropriate mitigation was considered." The court began by examining the "especially heinous, cruel or depraved" aggravating circumstance found by the trial judge. The court pointed out that it previously had determined that a murder is committed in an especially cruel manner when "the perpetrator inflicts mental anguish or physical abuse before the victim's death," (citations omitted), and that "[m]ental anguish includes a victim's uncertainty as to his ultimate fate." In this case, the court concluded that there was ample evidence that Powell suffered mental anguish prior to his death. The Arizona Supreme Court also found the evidence sufficient to conclude that the crime was committed in an especially depraved manner, pointing out that it had defined a depraved murder as one where "the perpetrator relishes the murder, evidencing debasement or perversion." Additionally, the court found that the pecuniary gain circumstance was present. After examining Walton's mitigating evidence regarding his substance abuse and his youth, the court concluded that there were "no mitigating circumstances sufficient to call for leniency." Finally, the court conducted its proportionality review and determined that Walton's death sentence was "proportional to sentences imposed in similar cases."

Because the United States Court of Appeals for the Ninth Circuit has held the Arizona death penalty statute to be unconstitutional for the reasons submitted by Walton in this case, *Adamson v. Ricketts*, we granted certiorari, to resolve the conflict and to settle issues that are of importance generally in the administration of the death penalty. We now affirm the judgment of the Arizona Supreme Court....

III

[We find] ... unpersuasive ... Walton's contention that the Arizona statute violates the Eighth and Fourteenth Amendments because it imposes on defendants the burden of establishing, by a preponderance of the evidence, the existence of mitigating circumstances sufficiently substantial to call for leniency. It is true that the Court has refused to countenance state-imposed restrictions on what mitigating circumstances may be considered in deciding whether to impose the death penalty. See, *e.g., Lockett v. Ohio*, 438 U.S. 586, 604 (1978) (plurality opinion). But Walton is not complaining that the Arizona statute or practice excludes from consideration any particular type of mitigating evidence; and it does not follow from *Lockett* and its progeny that a State is precluded from specifying how mitigating circumstances are to be proved. Indeed, in *Lockett* itself, we expressly reserved opinion on whether "it violates the Constitution to require defendants to bear the risk of nonpersuasion as to the existence of mitigating circumstances in capital cases."

In *Martin v. Ohio*, 480 U.S. 228 (1987), we upheld the Ohio practice of imposing on a capital defendant the burden of proving by a preponderance of the evidence that she was acting in self-defense when she allegedly committed the murder. In *Leland v. Oregon*, 343 U.S. 790 (1952), the Court upheld, in a capital case, a requirement that the defense of insanity be proved beyond a reasonable doubt by the defendant, see also *Rivera v. Delaware*, 429 U.S. 877 (1976), and in *Patterson v. New York*, 432 U.S. 197 (1977), we rejected the argument that a State violated due process by imposing a preponderance of the evidence standard on a defendant to prove the affirmative defense of extreme emotional disturbance.

The basic principle of these cases controls the result in this case. So long as a State's method of allocating the burdens of proof does not lessen the State's burden to prove every element of the offense charged, or in this case to prove the existence of aggravating circumstances, a defendant's constitutional rights are not violated by placing on him the burden of proving mitigating circumstances sufficiently substantial to call for leniency. *Mullaney v. Wilbur*, 421 U.S. 684 (1975), is not to the contrary. *Mullaney* struck down on due process grounds a state statute that required a convicted murder defendant to negate an element of the offense of murder in order to be entitled to a sentence for voluntary manslaughter. No such burden is placed on defendants by Arizona's capital sentencing scheme. We therefore decline to adopt as a constitutional imperative a rule that would require the court to consider the mitigating circumstances claimed by a defendant unless the State negated them by a preponderance of the evidence.

Neither does *Mills v. Maryland*, 486 U.S. 367 (1988), lend support to Walton's position. There this Court reversed a death sentence because it concluded that the jury instructions given at the sentencing phase likely led the jury to believe that any particular mitigating circumstance could not be considered unless the jurors unanimously agreed that such circumstance was present. The Court's focus was on whether reasonable jurors would have read the instructions to require unanimity and, if so, the possible consequences of such an understanding. Here, of course, the judge alone is the sentencer, and *Mills* is therefore beside the point.

Furthermore, *Mills* did not suggest that it would be forbidden to require each individual juror, before weighing a claimed mitigating circumstance in the balance, to be convinced in his or her own mind that the mitigating circumstance has been proved by a preponderance of the evidence. To the contrary, the jury in that case was instructed that it had to find that any mitigating circumstances had been proved by a preponderance of the evidence. Neither the petitioner in *Mills* nor the Court in its opinion hinted that there was any constitutional objection to that aspect of the instructions.

We therefore reject Walton's argument that Arizona's allocation of the burdens of proof in a capital sentencing proceeding violates the Constitution.

IV

Walton insists that because §13-703(E) provides that the court "shall" impose the death penalty if one or more aggravating circumstances are found and mitigating circumstances are held insufficient to call for leniency, the statute creates an unconstitutional presumption that death is the proper sentence. Our recent decisions in *Blystone v. Pennsylvania*, 494 U.S. 299 (1990), and *Boyde v. California*, 494 U.S. 370 (1990), foreclose this submission. *Blystone* rejected a challenge to a jury instruction based on a Pennsylvania statute requiring the imposition of the death penalty if aggravating circumstances were found to exist but no mitigating circumstances were present. We pointed out that "[t]he requirement of individualized sentencing in capital cases is satisfied by allowing the jury to consider all relevant mitigating evidence," and concluded that because the Pennsylvania statute did not preclude the sentencer from considering any type of mitigating evidence, it was consonant with that principle. In addition, the Court concluded that the statute was not "impermissibly 'mandatory' as that term was understood" in *Woodson v. North Carolina*, 428 U.S. 280 (1976), and *Roberts v. Louisiana*, 428 U.S. 325 (1976), because it did not automatically impose death upon conviction for certain types of murder. The same is true of the Arizona statute.

Similarly, *Boyde v. California* upheld a pattern jury instruction which stated that "[i]f you conclude that the aggravating circumstances outweigh the mitigating circumstances, you shall impose a sentence of death." The Court specifically noted that "there is no constitutional requirement of unfettered sentencing discretion in the jury, and States are free to structure and shape consideration of mitigating evidence 'in an effort to achieve a more rational and equitable administration of the death penalty.'" Walton's arguments in this case are no more persuasive than those made in *Blystone and Boyde....*

The judgment of the Arizona Supreme Court is affirmed.

Note

Justice Scalia's dissenting opinion in *Walton,* in which he identifies the inconsistencies inherent in the modern system of capital punishment, is reproduced in chapter 3, *supra.*

3. Age as a Mitigating Factor

As chapter 5 demonstrates, an offender's youth at the time she commits a capital offense may render her ineligible for the death penalty. However, even when a defendant is old enough to be fully punished under the law, youth may play a critical role during sentencing.

Eddings v. Oklahoma
455 U.S. 104 (1982)

Justice POWELL delivered the opinion of the Court.

Petitioner Monty Lee Eddings was convicted of first-degree murder and sentenced to death. Because this sentence was imposed without "the type of individualized consideration of mitigating factors ... required by the Eighth and Fourteenth Amendments in capital cases," we reverse.

I

On April 4, 1977, Eddings, a 16-year-old youth, and several younger companions ran away from their Missouri homes. They traveled in a car owned by Eddings' brother, and drove without destination or purpose in a southwesterly direction eventually reaching the Oklahoma Turnpike. Eddings had in the car a shotgun and several rifles he had taken from his father. After he momentarily lost control of the car, he was signalled to pull over by Officer Crabtree of the Oklahoma Highway Patrol. Eddings did so, and when the officer approached the car, Eddings stuck a loaded shotgun out of the window and fired, killing the officer.

Because Eddings was a juvenile, the State moved to have him certified to stand trial as an adult. Finding that there was prosecutive merit to the complaint and that Eddings was not amenable to rehabilitation within the juvenile system, the trial court granted the motion. The ruling was affirmed on appeal. Eddings was then charged with murder in the first degree, and the District Court of Creek County found him guilty upon his plea of *nolo contendere.*

The Oklahoma death penalty statute provides in pertinent part: "Upon conviction ... of guilt of a defendant of murder in the first degree, the court shall conduct a separate sentencing proceeding to determine whether the defendant should be sentenced to death or life imprisonment.... In the sentencing proceeding, evidence may be presented as to any mitigating circumstances or as to any of the aggravating circumstances enumerated in this act." Section 701.12 [of Okla. Stat., Tit. 21] lists seven separate aggravating circumstances; the statute nowhere defines what is meant by "any mitigating circumstances."

At the sentencing hearing, the State alleged three of the aggravating circumstances enumerated in the statute: that the murder was especially heinous, atrocious, or cruel, that the crime was committed for the purpose of avoiding or preventing a lawful arrest, and that there was a probability that the defendant would commit criminal acts of violence that would constitute a continuing threat to society.

In mitigation, Eddings presented substantial evidence at the hearing of his troubled youth. The testimony of his supervising Juvenile Officer indicated that Eddings had been raised without proper guidance. His parents were divorced when he was 5 years old, and until he was 14 Eddings lived with his mother without rules or supervision. There is the suggestion that Eddings' mother was an alcoholic and possibly a prostitute. By the time Eddings was 14 he no longer could be controlled, and his mother sent him to live with his father. But neither could the father control the boy. Attempts to reason and talk gave way to physical punishment. The Juvenile Officer testified that Eddings was frightened and bitter, that his father overreacted and used excessive physical punishment: "Mr. Eddings found the only thing that he thought was effectful with the boy was actual punishment, or physical violence — hitting with a strap or something like this."[3]

Testimony from other witnesses indicated that Eddings was emotionally disturbed in general and at the time of the crime, and that his mental and emotional development were at a level several years below his age. A state psychologist stated that Eddings had a sociopathic or antisocial personality and that approximately 30% of youths suffering from such a disorder grew out of it as they aged. A sociologist specializing in juvenile offenders testified that Eddings was treatable. A psychiatrist testified that Eddings could be rehabilitated by intensive therapy over a 15- to 20-year period. He testified further that Eddings "did pull the trigger, he did kill someone, but I don't even think he knew that he was doing it." The psychiatrist suggested that, if treated, Eddings would no longer pose a serious threat to society.

At the conclusion of all the evidence, the trial judge weighed the evidence of aggravating and mitigating circumstances. He found that the State had proved each of the three alleged aggravating circumstances beyond a reasonable doubt. Turning to the evidence of mitigating circumstances, the judge found that Eddings' youth was a mitigating factor of great weight: "I have given very serious consideration to the youth of the Defendant when this particular crime was committed. Should I fail to do this, I think I would not be carrying out my duty." But he would not consider in mitigation the circumstances of Eddings' unhappy upbringing and emotional disturbance: "[T]he Court cannot be persuaded entirely by the ... fact that the youth was sixteen years old when this heinous crime was committed. *Nor can the Court in following the law, in my opinion, consider the fact of this young man's violent background.*" Finding that the only mitigating circumstance was Eddings' youth and finding further that this circumstance could not outweigh the aggravating circumstances present, the judge sentenced Eddings to death. [The Oklahoma Court of Criminal Appeals affirmed Eddings' conviction.] ...

III

We now apply the rule [established] in *Lockett v. Ohio*, 438 U.S. 586 (1978), to the circumstances of this case. The trial judge stated that "in following the law," he could not "consider the fact of this young man's violent background." There is no dispute that by "violent background" the trial judge was referring to the mitigating evidence of Eddings' family history. From this statement it is clear that the trial judge did not evaluate

---

3. There was evidence that immediately after the shooting Eddings said: "I would rather have shot an Officer than go back to where I live."

the evidence in mitigation and find it wanting as a matter of fact; rather he found that as a matter of law he was unable even to consider the evidence.

The Court of Criminal Appeals took the same approach. It found that the evidence in mitigation was not relevant because it did not tend to provide a legal excuse from criminal responsibility. Thus the court conceded that Eddings had a "personality disorder," but cast this evidence aside on the basis that "he knew the difference between right and wrong ... and that is the test of criminal responsibility." Similarly, the evidence of Eddings' family history was "useful in explaining" his behavior, but it did not "excuse" the behavior. From these statements it appears that the Court of Criminal Appeals also considered only that evidence to be mitigating which would tend to support a legal excuse from criminal liability.

We find that the limitations placed by these courts upon the mitigating evidence they would consider violated the rule in *Lockett*. Just as the State may not by statute preclude the sentencer from considering any mitigating factor, neither may the sentencer refuse to consider, as a matter of law, any relevant mitigating evidence. In this instance, it was as if the trial judge had instructed a jury to disregard the mitigating evidence Eddings proffered on his behalf. The sentencer, and the Court of Criminal Appeals on review, may determine the weight to be given relevant mitigating evidence. But they may not give it no weight by excluding such evidence from their consideration.[10]

Nor do we doubt that the evidence Eddings offered was relevant mitigating evidence. Eddings was a youth of 16 years at the time of the murder. Evidence of a difficult family history and of emotional disturbance is typically introduced by defendants in mitigation. In some cases, such evidence properly may be given little weight. But when the defendant was 16 years old at the time of the offense there can be no doubt that evidence of a turbulent family history, of beatings by a harsh father, and of severe emotional disturbance is particularly relevant.

The trial judge recognized that youth must be considered a relevant mitigating factor. But youth is more than a chronological fact. It is a time and condition of life when a person may be most susceptible to influence and to psychological damage. Our history is replete with laws and judicial recognition that minors, especially in their earlier years, generally are less mature and responsible than adults. Particularly "during the formative years of childhood and adolescence, minors often lack the experience, perspective, and judgment" expected of adults.

Even the normal 16-year-old customarily lacks the maturity of an adult. In this case, Eddings was not a normal 16-year-old; he had been deprived of the care, concern, and paternal attention that children deserve. On the contrary, it is not disputed that he was a juvenile with serious emotional problems, and had been raised in a neglectful, sometimes even violent, family background. In addition, there was testimony that Eddings' mental and emotional development were at a level several years below his chronological age. All of this does not suggest an absence of responsibility for the crime of murder, deliberately committed in this case. Rather, it is to say that just as the chronological age of a minor is itself a relevant mitigating factor of great weight, so must the background and mental and emotional development of a youthful defendant be duly considered in sentencing....

---

10. We note that the Oklahoma death penalty statute permits the defendant to present evidence "as to any mitigating circumstances." *Lockett* requires the sentencer to listen.

On remand, the state courts must consider all relevant mitigating evidence and weigh it against the evidence of the aggravating circumstances. We do not weigh the evidence for them. Accordingly, the judgment is reversed to the extent that it sustains the imposition of the death penalty, and the case is remanded for further proceedings not inconsistent with this opinion.

Johnson v. Texas

509 U.S. 350 (1993)

Justice KENNEDY delivered the opinion of the Court.

[During the penalty phase of petitioner Dorsie Johnson's capital murder trial, the defense presented as its only witness Johnson's father. Johnson's father testified that his son's criminal activities were the result of his drug use and youth. On certiorari from direct appeal, Johnson argued that the future dangerousness inquiry under the then-existing Texas law[1] did not provide sufficient room for consideration of the mitigating circumstance of youth.]

II

B

... [W]e considered the Texas statute in *Penry v. Lynaugh*, 492 U.S. 302 (1989), the pivotal case from petitioner's point of view, for there we set aside a capital sentence because the Texas special issues did not allow for sufficient consideration of the defendant's mitigating evidence. In *Penry* (*supra* chapter 5), the condemned prisoner had presented mitigating evidence of his mental retardation and childhood abuse. We agreed that the jury instructions were too limited for the appropriate consideration of this mitigating evidence in light of Penry's particular circumstances. We noted that "[t]he jury was never instructed that it could consider the evidence offered by Penry as mitigating evidence and that it could give mitigating effect to that evidence in imposing sentence." Absent any definition for the term "deliberately," we could not "be sure that the jury was able to give effect to the mitigating evidence ... in answering the first special issue," so we turned to the second special issue, future dangerousness. The evidence in the case suggested that Penry's mental retardation rendered him unable to learn from his mistakes. As a consequence, we decided the mitigating evidence was relevant to the second special issue "only as an aggravating factor because it suggests a 'yes' answer to the question of future dangerousness." The Court concluded that the trial court had

---

1. The Texas Legislature amended the statute in 1991. See Art. 37.071(2) (Vernon Supp. 1992–1993). At the time of Johnson's trial, Texas law provided that the trial court instruct the jury to answer two special issues:

(1) Was the conduct of Johnson, that caused the death of the deceased, committed deliberately with the reasonable expectation that the death of the deceased or another would result?

(2) Is there a probability that Johnson would commit criminal acts of violence that would constitute a continuing threat to society?

The trial judge also instructed the jury, "In determining each of these Issues, you may take into consideration all the evidence submitted to you in the trial of this case, whether aggravating or mitigating in nature, that is, all the evidence in the first part of the trial when you were called upon to determine the guilt or innocence of the Defendant and all the evidence, if any, in the second part of the trial wherein you are called upon to determine the answers to the Special Issues."

erred in not instructing the jury that it could "consider and give effect to the mitigating evidence of Penry's mental retardation and abused background by declining to impose the death penalty." ...

III

... There is no dispute that a defendant's youth is a relevant mitigating circumstance that must be within the effective reach of a capital sentencing jury if a death sentence is to meet the requirements of *Lockett* and *Eddings*. Our cases recognize that "youth is more than a chronological fact. It is a time and condition of life when a person may be most susceptible to influence and psychological damage." A lack of maturity and an underdeveloped sense of responsibility are found in youth more often than in adults and are more understandable among the young. These qualities often result in impetuous and ill-considered actions and decisions. A sentencer in a capital case must be allowed to consider the mitigating qualities of youth in the course of its deliberations over the appropriate sentence.

The question presented here is whether the Texas special issues allowed adequate consideration of petitioner's youth. An argument that youth can never be given proper mitigating force under the Texas scheme is inconsistent with our holdings in *Jurek v. Texas*, *Graham v. Collins*, 506 U.S. 461 (1993), and *Penry* itself. The standard against which we assess whether jury instructions satisfy the rule of *Lockett* and *Eddings* was set forth in *Boyde v. California*, 494 U.S. 370 (1990). There we held that a reviewing court must determine "whether there is a reasonable likelihood that the jury has applied the challenged instruction in a way that prevents the consideration of constitutionally relevant evidence." Although the reasonable likelihood standard does not require that the defendant prove that it was more likely than not that the jury was prevented from giving effect to the evidence, the standard requires more than a mere possibility of such a bar. In evaluating the instructions, we do not engage in a technical parsing of this language of the instructions, but instead approach the instructions in the same way that the jury would—with a "common-sense understanding of the instructions in the light of all that has taken place at the trial."

We decide that there is no reasonable likelihood that the jury would have found itself foreclosed from considering the relevant aspects of petitioner's youth. Pursuant to the second special issue, the jury was instructed to decide whether there was "a probability that [petitioner] would commit criminal acts of violence that would constitute a continuing threat to society." The jury also was told that, in answering the special issues, it could consider all the mitigating evidence that had been presented during the guilt and punishment phases of petitioner's trial. Even on a cold record, one cannot be unmoved by the testimony of petitioner's father urging that his son's actions were due in large part to his youth. It strains credulity to suppose that the jury would have viewed the evidence of petitioner's youth as outside its effective reach in answering the second special issue. The relevance of youth as a mitigating factor derives from the fact that the signature qualities of youth are transient; as individuals mature, the impetuousness and recklessness that may dominate in younger years can subside. We believe that there is ample room in the assessment of future dangerousness for a juror to take account of the difficulties of youth as a mitigating force in the sentencing determination. As we recognized in *Graham*, the fact that a juror might view the evidence of youth as aggravating, as opposed to mitigating, does not mean that the rule of *Lockett* is violated. As long as the mitigating evidence is within "the effective reach of the sentencer," the requirements of the Eighth Amendment are satisfied.

That the jury had a meaningful basis to consider the relevant mitigating qualities of petitioner's youth is what distinguishes this case from *Penry*. In *Penry*, there was expert medical testimony that the defendant was mentally retarded and that his condition prevented him from learning from experience. Although the evidence of the mental illness fell short of providing Penry a defense to prosecution for his crimes, the Court held that the second special issue did not allow the jury to give mitigating effect to this evidence. Penry's condition left him unable to learn from his mistakes, and the Court reasoned that the only logical manner in which the evidence of his mental retardation could be considered within the future dangerousness inquiry was as an aggravating factor. *Penry* remains the law and must be given a fair reading. The evidence of petitioner's youth, however, falls outside *Penry's* ambit. Unlike Penry's mental retardation, which rendered him unable to learn from his mistakes, the ill effects of youth that a defendant may experience are subject to change and, as a result, are readily comprehended as a mitigating factor in consideration of the second special issue.

Petitioner does not contest that the evidence of youth could be given some effect under the second special issue. Instead, petitioner argues that the forward-looking perspective of the future dangerousness inquiry did not allow the jury to take account of how petitioner's youth bore upon his personal culpability for the murder he committed. According to petitioner, "[a] prediction of future behavior is not the same thing as an assessment of moral culpability for a crime already committed." Contrary to petitioner's suggestion, however, this forward-looking inquiry is not independent of an assessment of personal culpability. It is both logical and fair for the jury to make its determination of a defendant's future dangerousness by asking the extent to which youth influenced the defendant's conduct. If any jurors believed that the transient qualities of petitioner's youth made him less culpable for the murder, there is no reasonable likelihood that those jurors would have deemed themselves foreclosed from considering that in evaluating petitioner's future dangerousness. It is true that Texas has structured consideration of the relevant qualities of petitioner's youth, but in so doing, the State still "allow[s] the jury to give effect to [this] mitigating evidence in making the sentencing decision." Although Texas might have provided other vehicles for consideration of petitioner's youth, no additional instruction beyond that given as to future dangerousness was required in order for the jury to be able to consider the mitigating qualities of youth presented to it.

In a related argument, petitioner, quoting a portion of our decision in *Penry*, claims that the jurors were not able to make a "reasoned moral response" to the evidence of petitioner's youth because the second special issue called for a narrow factual inquiry into future dangerousness. We, however, have previously interpreted the Texas special issues system as requiring jurors to "exercise a range of judgment and discretion." This view accords with a "commonsense understanding" of how the jurors were likely to view their instructions and to implement the charge that they were entitled to consider all mitigating evidence from both the trial and sentencing phases. The crucial term employed in the second special issue—"continuing threat to society"—affords the jury room for independent judgment in reaching its decision. Indeed, we cannot forget that "a Texas capital jury deliberating over the Special Issues is aware of the consequences of its answers, and is likely to weigh mitigating evidence as it formulates these answers in a manner similar to that employed by capital juries in 'pure balancing' States." In *Blystone v. Pennsylvania*, 494 U.S. 299 (1990), four Members of the Court in dissent used the Texas statute as an example of a capital sentencing system that permitted the exercise of judgment. That opinion stated:

> [The two special issues] require the jury to do more than find facts supporting a legislatively defined aggravating circumstance. Instead, by focusing on the deliberateness of the defendant's actions and his future dangerousness, the questions compel the jury to make a moral judgment about the severity of the

crime and the defendant's culpability. The Texas statute directs the imposition of the death penalty only after the jury has decided that the defendant's actions were sufficiently egregious to warrant death.

The Texas Court of Criminal Appeals' view of the future dangerousness inquiry supports our conclusion that consideration of the second special issue is a comprehensive inquiry that is more than a question of historical fact. In reviewing death sentences imposed under the former Texas system, that court has consistently looked to a nonexclusive list of eight factors, which includes the defendant's age, in deciding whether there was sufficient evidence to support a yes answer to the second special issue.

There might have been a juror who, on the basis solely of sympathy or mercy, would have opted against the death penalty had there been a vehicle to do so under the Texas special issues scheme. But we have not construed the *Lockett* line of cases to mean that a jury must be able to dispense mercy on the basis of a sympathetic response to the defendant. Indeed, we have said that "[i]t would be very difficult to reconcile a rule allowing the fate of a defendant to turn on the vagaries of particular jurors' emotional sensitivities with our longstanding recognition that, above all, capital sentencing must be reliable, accurate, and nonarbitrary."

For us to find a constitutional defect in petitioner's death sentence, we would have to alter in significant fashion this Court's capital sentencing jurisprudence. The first casualty of a holding in petitioner's favor would be *Jurek*. The inevitable consequence of petitioner's argument is that the Texas special issues system in almost every case would have to be supplemented by a further instruction. As we said in *Graham*,

> [H]olding that a defendant is entitled to special instructions whenever he can offer mitigating evidence that has some arguable relevance beyond the special issues ... would be to require in all cases that a fourth "special issue" be put to the jury: "Does any mitigating evidence before you, whether or not relevant to the above [three] questions, lead you to believe that the death penalty should not be imposed?"

In addition to overruling *Jurek*, accepting petitioner's arguments would entail an alteration of the rule of *Lockett* and *Eddings*. Instead of requiring that a jury be able to consider in some manner all of a defendant's relevant mitigating evidence, the rule would require that a jury be able to give effect to mitigating evidence in every conceivable manner in which the evidence might be relevant.

The fundamental flaw in petitioner's position is its failure to recognize that "[t]here is a simple and logical difference between rules that govern what factors the jury must be permitted to consider in making its sentencing decision and rules that govern how the State may guide the jury in considering and weighing those factors in reaching a decision." To rule in petitioner's favor, we would have to require that a jury be instructed in a manner that leaves it free to depart from the special issues in every case. This would, of course, remove all power on the part of the States to structure the consideration of mitigating evidence—a result we have been consistent in rejecting. The reconciliation of competing principles is the function of law. Our capital sentencing jurisprudence seeks to reconcile two competing, and valid, principles in *Furman*, which are to allow mitigating evidence to be considered and to guide the discretion of the sentencer. Our holding in *Jurek* reflected the understanding that the Texas sentencing scheme "accommodates both of these concerns." The special issues structure in this regard satisfies the Eighth Amendment and our precedents that interpret its force. There was no constitutional infirmity in its application here. The judgment of the Texas Court of Criminal Appeals is affirmed.

Justice SCALIA, concurring.

In my view the *Lockett-Eddings* principle that the sentencer must be allowed to consider "all relevant mitigating evidence" is quite incompatible with the *Furman* principle that the sentencer's discretion must be channeled. That will continue to be true unless and until the sort of "channeling" of mitigating discretion that Texas has engaged in here is not merely permitted (as the Court today holds), but positively required—a further elaboration of our intricate Eighth Amendment jurisprudence that I neither look forward to nor would support.

Today's decision, however, is simply a clarification (and I think a plainly correct one) of this Court's opinions in *Franklin v. Lynaugh*, 487 U.S. 164 (1988) (plurality opinion), and *Boyde v. California*, 494 U.S. 370 (1990), which I joined. In fact, the essence of today's holding (to the effect that discretion may constitutionally be channeled) was set forth in my dissent in *Penry v. Lynaugh*, 492 U.S. 302, 350 (1989). Accordingly, I join the opinion of the Court.

Notes and Questions

1. *Eddings* and *Johnson* focus on youth as a mitigating circumstance. Should old age at the time of the crime be viewed as a mitigating circumstance? Of course for very old defendants even a modest term of years could amount to a life sentence. Might a jury wishing to punish an elderly defendant impose death because it believes that a lesser sentence (life or life without parole) will only amount to a small term of years?

2. The federal Anti-Drug Abuse Act of 1988 provides as a mitigating circumstance that "[t]he defendant was youthful, although not under the age of 18." 21 U.S.C. §848(m). Those under 18 at the time the crime was committed may not be sentenced to death under that statute. 21 U.S.C. §848 (1). See chapter 18 for more information about the federal death penalty.

3. In *Johnson*, the Court refers to two other cases arising out of Texas: *Penry v. Lynaugh*, 492 U.S. 302 (1989), and *Graham v. Collins*, 506 U.S. 461 (1993). In *Penry*, the Court held that the Texas death penalty statutory scheme did not allow the jury to give proper effect to the mitigating evidence of the defendant's mental retardation and abused childhood. See *supra* chapter 5. In *Graham*, the Court was asked to determine whether, under the Texas death penalty scheme, the jury was able to give effect to the mitigating circumstances presented by Graham which included youth, family background, and positive character traits. The Court, however, did not reach this issue because it found that Graham was barred from raising this claim under the procedural rules governing federal habeas corpus review. See *infra* chapter 15.

4. Adjustment to Prison as a Mitigating Factor

Skipper v. South Carolina
476 U.S. 1 (1986)

Justice WHITE delivered the opinion of the Court.

Petitioner Ronald Skipper was convicted in a South Carolina trial court of capital murder and rape. The State sought the death penalty, and a separate sentencing hearing was held before the trial jury under S.C. Code §16-3-20 (1985), which provides for a bifurcated trial and jury sentencing in capital cases. Following introduction by the State of evidence in aggravation of the offense (principally evidence of petitioner's history of sexually assaultive behavior), petitioner presented as mitigating evidence his own testimony and that of his former wife, his mother, his sister, and his grandmother. This testimony, for the most part, concerned the difficult circumstances of his upbringing. Petitioner and his former wife, however, both testified briefly that petitioner had conducted himself well during the 7 1/2 months he spent in jail between his arrest and trial. Petitioner also testified that during a prior period of incarceration he had earned the equivalent of a high school diploma and that, if sentenced to life imprisonment rather than to death, he would behave himself in prison and would attempt to work so that he could contribute money to the support of his family.

Petitioner also sought to introduce testimony of two jailers and one "regular visitor" to the jail to the effect that petitioner had "made a good adjustment" during his time spent in jail. The trial court, however, ruled that ... such evidence would be irrelevant and hence inadmissible. The decision in *Koon I*, 278 S.C. 528, 298 S.E.2d 769 (1982), the judge stated, stood for the rule that "whether [petitioner] can adjust or not adjust" was "not an issue in this case."

After hearing closing arguments—during the course of which the prosecutor contended that petitioner would pose disciplinary problems if sentenced to prison and would likely rape other prisoners—the jury sentenced petitioner to death. On appeal, petitioner contended that the trial court had committed constitutional error in excluding the testimony of the jailers and the visitor: the testimony of these witnesses, petitioner argued, would have constituted relevant mitigating evidence, and exclusion of such evidence was improper under this Court's decisions in *Lockett* and *Eddings*. The Supreme Court of South Carolina rejected petitioner's contention, stating: "The trial judge properly refused to admit evidence of [petitioner's] future adaptability to prison life. However, evidence of his past adaptability was admitted through testimony of his former wife, his mother and his own testimony. This contention is without merit."

We granted certiorari to consider petitioner's claim that the South Carolina Supreme Court's decision is inconsistent with this Court's decisions in *Lockett* and *Eddings*, and we now reverse.

There is no disputing that this Court's decision in *Eddings* requires that in capital cases "'the sentencer.... not be precluded from considering, as a mitigating factor, any aspect of a defendant's character or record and any of the circumstances of the offense that the defendant proffers as a basis for a sentence less than death.'" Equally clear is the corollary rule that the sentencer may not refuse to consider or be precluded from considering "any relevant mitigating evidence." These rules are now well established, and the State does not question them.

Accordingly, the only question before us is whether the exclusion from the sentencing hearing of the testimony petitioner proffered regarding his good behavior during the over seven months he spent in jail awaiting trial deprived petitioner of his right to place before the sentencer relevant evidence in mitigation of punishment. It can hardly be disputed that it did. The State does not contest that the witnesses petitioner attempted to place on the stand would have testified that petitioner had been a well-behaved and well-adjusted prisoner, nor does the State dispute that the jury could have drawn favorable inferences from this testimony regarding petitioner's character and his probable future conduct if sentenced to life in prison. Although it is true that any such inferences would not relate specifically to petitioner's culpability for the crime he committed, there is no question but that such inferences would be "mitigating" in the sense that they might serve "as a basis for a sentence less than death." Consideration of a defendant's past conduct as indicative of his probable future behavior is an inevitable and not undesirable element of criminal sentencing: "any sentencing authority must predict a convicted person's probable future conduct when it engages in the process of determining what punishment to impose." The Court has therefore held that evidence that a defendant would in the future pose a danger to the community if he were not executed may be treated as establishing an "aggravating factor" for purposes of capital sentencing. Likewise, evidence that the defendant would not pose a danger if spared (but incarcerated) must be considered potentially mitigating.[1] Under *Eddings*, such evidence may not be excluded from the sentencer's consideration....

The exclusion by the state trial court of relevant mitigating evidence impeded the sentencing jury's ability to carry out its task of considering all relevant facets of the character and record of the individual offender. The resulting death sentence cannot stand, although the State is of course not precluded from again seeking to impose the death sentence, provided that it does so through a new sentencing hearing at which petitioner is permitted to present any and all relevant mitigating evidence that is available. The judgment of the Supreme Court of South Carolina is therefore reversed insofar as it affirms the death sentence, and the case is remanded for further proceedings not inconsistent with this opinion.

Note

Justice Powell issued a concurring opinion which was joined by Chief Justice Burger and Justice Rehnquist. These three justices concluded that the Eighth Amendment, as construed in *Lockett* and *Eddings*, did not require the admission of evidence that Skipper had behaved well while in prison. Justice Powell wrote:

> The Eighth Amendment requires that the sentencing authority consider "relevant mitigating evidence" concerning the defendant's "character or record" and "the circumstances of the offense." But the States, and not this Court, retain "the traditional authority" to determine what particular evidence within the broad categories described in *Lockett* and *Eddings* is relevant in the first instance. As long as those determinations are reasonable — as long as they do not foreclose consideration of factors that may tend to reduce the defendant's culpability for his crime — this Court should respect them.

Despite this conclusion regarding the scope of the Eighth Amendment, Justice Powell reasoned that Skipper's sentence should be reversed and remanded for resentencing on due process grounds. During sentencing, the prosecutor argued to the jury that Skipper would present disciplinary problems in prison and would likely rape other prisoners. Skipper was not allowed to present evidence to rebut the prosecutor's argument. Justice Powell found that Skipper, therefore, was denied due process because he was not per-

---

1. The relevance of evidence of probable future conduct in prison as a factor in aggravation or mitigation of an offense is underscored in this particular case by the prosecutor's closing argument, which urged the jury to return a sentence of death in part because petitioner could not be trusted to behave if he were simply returned to prison. Where the prosecution specifically relies on a prediction of future dangerousness in asking for the death penalty, it is not only the rule of *Lockett* and *Eddings* that requires that the defendant be afforded an opportunity to introduce evidence on this point; it is also the elemental due process requirement that a defendant not be sentenced to death "on the basis of information which he had no opportunity to deny or explain." *Gardner v. Florida*, 430 U.S. 349, 362 (1977).

mitted to deny or explain evidence on which his sentence of death may have rested. For further discussion of due process during sentencing, see *Gardner v. Florida*, 430 U.S. 349 (1977), *infra* chapter 9.

Evans v. Muncy

498 U.S. 927 (1990)

Justice MARSHALL, dissenting from denial of stay of execution.

This Court's approval of the death penalty has turned on the premise that given sufficient procedural safeguards the death penalty may be administered fairly and reliably. Wilbert Evans' plea to be spared from execution demonstrates the fallacy of this assumption. Notwithstanding the panoply of procedural protections afforded Evans by this Court's capital jurisprudence, Evans today faces an imminent execution that even the State of Virginia appears to concede is indefensible in light of the undisputed facts proffered by Evans. Because an execution under these circumstances highlights the inherently cruel and unusual character of capital punishment, I dissent.

I

Evans was convicted of capital murder and sentenced to death. At the sentencing phase, the jury's verdict was predicated on a *single* aggravating circumstance: that if allowed to live Evans would pose a serious threat of future danger to society. Without this finding, Evans could not have been sentenced to death.

While Evans was on death row at the Mecklenberg Correctional Facility, an event occurred that casts grave doubt on the jury's prediction of Evans' future dangerousness. On May 31, 1984, six death row inmates at Mecklenberg attempted to engineer an escape. Armed with makeshift knives, these inmates took hostage twelve prison guards and two female nurses. The guards were stripped of their clothes and weapons, bound and blindfolded. The nurses also were stripped of their clothes, and one was bound to an inmate's bed.

According to uncontested affidavits presented by guards taken hostage during the uprising, Evans took decisive steps to calm the riot, saving the lives of several hostages, and preventing the rape of one of the nurses.[2] For instance, Officer Ricardo Holmes, who was bound by the escaping inmates and forced into a closet with other hostages, states that he heard Evans imploring to the escaping inmates, " 'Don't hurt anybody and everything will be alright.' " Officer Holmes continues:

> "It was very clear to me that [Evans] was trying to keep [the escaping inmates] calm and prevent them from getting out of control.... Based on what I saw and heard, it is my firm belief that if any of the escaping inmates had tried to harm us, Evans would have come to our aid. It is my belief that had it not been for Evans, I might not be here today."

Other guards taken hostage during the uprising verify Officer Holmes' judgment that Evans protected them and the other hostages from danger. According to Officer Prince Thomas, Evans interceded to prevent the rape of Nurse Ethyl Barksdale by one of the escaping inmates. Officer Harold Crutchfield affirms that Evans' appeals to the escapees not to harm anyone may have meant the difference between life and death for the

---

2. The affiant prison officials all attest that Evans played no role in instigating the riot.

hostages. "It is … my firm belief that if Evans had not been present during the escape, things may have blown up and people may have been harmed." According to Officer Crutchfield, after the escapees had left the area in which they were holding the guards hostage, Evans tried to force open the closet door and free the guards—albeit unsuccessfully. Officers Holmes, Thomas, and Crutchfield, and five other prison officials all attest that Evans' conduct during the May 31, 1984, uprising was consistent with his exemplary behavior during his close to ten years on death row.

Evans filed a writ of habeas corpus and application for a stay of his execution before the United State District Court for the Eastern District of Virginia. He urged that the jury's prediction of his future dangerousness be re-examined in light of his conduct during the Mecklenberg uprising. Evans proffered that these events would prove that the jury's prediction was unsound and thereby invalidate the sole aggravating circumstance on which the jury based its death sentence. For this reason, Evans argued that his death sentence must be vacated. The District Court stayed the execution and ordered a hearing. The Court of Appeals reversed and vacated the stay.

II

Remarkably, the State of Virginia's opposition to Evans' application to stay the execution barely contests either Evans' depiction of the relevant events, or Evans' conclusion that these events reveal the clear error of the jury's prediction of Evans' future dangerousness.[3] In other words, the State concedes that the sole basis for Evans' death sentence—future dangerousness—in fact *does not exist*.

The only ground asserted by the State for permitting Evans' execution to go forward is its interest in procedural finality. According to the State, permitting a death row inmate to challenge a finding of future dangerousness by reference to facts occurring after the sentence will unleash an endless stream of litigation. Each instance of an inmate's post-sentencing nonviolent conduct, the State argues, will form the basis of a new attack upon a jury's finding of future dangerousness, and with each new claim will come appeals and collateral attacks. By denying Evans' application for a stay, this Court implicitly endorses the State's conclusion that it is entitled to look the other way when late-arriving evidence upsets its determination that a particular defendant can lawfully be executed.

In my view, the Court's decision to let Wilbert Evans be put to death is a compelling statement of the failure of this Court's capital jurisprudence. This Court's ap-

---

3. Equally remarkable is the sheer gall of the manner in which the State makes its feeble challenge. For six years, Evans' counsel has tried to pry loose from the State copies of its investigative reports of the uprising. Counsel steadfastly has contended that these reports would support Evans' account of the relevant events and thereby strengthen Evans' claims for both legal relief and executive clemency. The State has refused to release its iron grip on these materials and to this moment has not made them available to him. According to Evans' counsel, late last evening he was contacted by counsel for Willie Lloyd Turner, another Virginia death row inmate involved in the Mecklenberg uprising. Notwithstanding its refusal to cooperate with Evans' request for the investigative reports, the State, without protest, provided these reports to Turner's counsel. Upon learning of Evans' impending execution, Turner's counsel immediately delivered these materials to Evans' counsel, and Evans has now been able to make them available to us.

Now that Evans finally has possession of information the State has so deliberately denied him for six years, the State cites two isolated excerpts from a lengthy set of materials in a mean and deceitful attempt to belittle Evans' claims. A more honest and thorough review of these materials, which include numerous interviews with the hostages and reports of the State's investigators, reveals that these materials in no way diminish Evans' account of the relevant events.

proach since *Gregg v. Georgia* has blithely assumed that strict procedures will satisfy the dictates of the Eighth Amendment's ban on cruel and unusual punishment. As Wilbert Evans' claim makes crystal clear, even the most exacting procedures are fallible. Just as the jury occasionally "gets it wrong" about whether a defendant charged with murder is innocent or guilty, so, too, can the jury "get it wrong" about whether a defendant convicted of murder is deserving of death, notwithstanding the exacting procedures imposed by the Eighth Amendment. The only difference between Wilbert Evans' case and that of many other capital defendants is that the defect in Evans' sentence has been made unmistakably clear for us even before his execution is to be carried out.

The State's interest in "finality" is no answer to this flaw in the capital-sentencing system. It may indeed be the case that a state cannot realistically accommodate post-sentencing evidence casting doubt on a jury's finding of future dangerousness; but it hardly follows from this that it is *Wilbert Evans* who should bear the burden of this procedural limitation. In other words, if it is impossible to construct a system capable of accommodating *all* evidence relevant to a man's entitlement to be spared death — no matter when that evidence is disclosed — then it is the *system*, not the life of the man sentenced to death, that should be dispatched.

The indifferent shrug of the shoulders with which the Court answers the failure of its procedures in this case reveals the utter bankruptcy of its notion that a system of capital punishment can co-exist with the Eighth Amendment. A death sentence that is *dead wrong* is no less so simply because its deficiency is not uncovered until the eleventh hour. A system of capital punishment that would permit Wilbert Evans' execution notwithstanding as-to-now unrefuted evidence showing that death is an improper sentence is a system that cannot stand.

I would stay Wilbert Evans' execution.

Note on Partial Paralysis, Future Dangerousness and Charles Stamper

Interesting future dangerousness questions were raised in the case of Charles Sylvester Stamper, a Virginia death row inmate. Stamper, who killed three people during a 1978 restaurant robbery, was the first person in a wheelchair to be executed since the Supreme Court reinstated capital punishment in 1976. In September 1988, Stamper was partially paralyzed after he was thrown to the floor in a fight with another death row inmate. Stamper suffered a severe spinal injury and was unable to walk without the aid of leg braces and a walker. He was bedridden for nearly a year after his injury and went through extensive therapy to learn to walk again. Stamper's post-conviction attorney argued that Stamper was no longer dangerous and should be spared.

According to James S. Gilmore, the commonwealth's attorney of Henrico County where Stamper was tried, "He's not being executed for being disabled. He's being executed for killing three people and damaging the lives of all the victims." Gilmore said, "[Y]ou have to hold the line [on executions]. It's the absolute reaffirmation of civilized behavior, of civilized standards in our society. Otherwise anything goes." Other prosecutors agreed. According to Paul B. Ebert, commonwealth's attorney for Prince William County, "A physical malady, to my way of thinking, favors the death penalty."

Ultimately, Virginia Governor Douglas Wilder refused to grant clemency. After reviewing information supplied by Stamper's attorneys, observations of nearly 20 nurses and corrections officers who were responsible for his care and custody, and an examination by a neurologist hired by the state, Virginia's deputy secretary of public safety, T.L. Twitty, noted that Stamper still had sufficient grip in his left hand to be able to use a gun or knife. Thus, according to the state, Stamper remained dangerous.

Hugo Bedau, a Tufts University philosophy professor, commented on Stamper's execution. According to Bedau, Stamper was worthy of consideration for clemency because "his capacity to endanger others was either zero or very slight." In addition, Bedau argued that Virginia owed Stamper a serious moral obligation since Stamper was injured while in custody. Bedau said, "Before we took the politically correct view toward the physically impaired, it used to be correct to pity people who were in this condition. It seems to me that we're a little less than human if we don't even consider that argument."

Stamper was executed in Virginia's electric chair on January 19, 1993. Stamper's last request—that he be allowed to walk to his execution with the aid of leg braces and a walker—was denied. He attempted to walk anyway. Three guards surrounded him, one at each side and one following directly behind. Stamper's legs went into spasms and he had to be dragged, and eventually carried, into the execution chamber. Miller, *The Execution of a Disabled Killer Rekindles the Debate on Capital Punishment*, The Washington Post, Feb. 2, 1993.

5. Consideration of Non-Statutory Mitigating Factors

Hitchcock v. Dugger
481 U.S. 393 (1987)

Justice SCALIA delivered the opinion of the Court.

We have held that in capital cases, "'the sentencer'" may not refuse to consider or "'be precluded from considering'" any relevant mitigating evidence. Certiorari was granted in the present case to consider petitioner's contention that he was sentenced to death under a Florida statute that operated in a manner inconsistent with this requirement.

I

On July 31, 1976, 13-year-old Cynthia Driggers was strangled to death. At the time of the murder, both Cynthia and petitioner resided with Richard Hitchcock, who was Cynthia's stepfather and petitioner's brother. Petitioner initially confessed to the murder, stating that he had killed Cynthia after she threatened to tell her parents that she and petitioner had engaged in consensual sexual intercourse. At his trial for first-degree murder, however, petitioner recanted and testified that it was his brother Richard who murdered Cynthia, after finding out about the intercourse. The State contended that petitioner had sexually assaulted Cynthia and then murdered her to avoid discovery....

II

Petitioner claims that the advisory jury and the sentencing judge were precluded by law from considering some of the evidence of mitigating circumstances before them. The Florida death-penalty statute in effect at the time (which has since been amended in various respects) provided for separate postconviction proceedings to determine whether those convicted of capital felonies should be sentenced to death or to life imprisonment. Those proceedings were typically held before the trial jury, which heard evidence "as to any matter that the court deem[ed] relevant to sentence." Fla. Stat. §921.14(1) (1975). After hearing that evidence, the jury was to render an advisory verdict by determining "(a) [w]hether sufficient aggravating circumstances exist as enumerated in [Fla. Stat. §921.141(5)];[2] (b) [w]hether sufficient mitigating circumstances exist as enumerated in [Fla. Stat. §921.141(6)],[3] which outweigh the aggravating circumstances found to exist; and (c) [b]ased on these considerations, whether the defendant should be sentenced to life [imprisonment] or death." Fla. Stat. §921.141(2). The trial court then was to weigh the aggravating and mitigating circumstances itself and enter a sentence of life imprisonment or death. If it imposed a sentence of death, it was required to set forth in writing its findings "(a) [t]hat sufficient aggravating circumstances exist as enumerated in [Fla. Stat. §921.141(5)], and (b) [t]hat there are insufficient mitigating circumstances, as enumerated in [Fla. Stat. §921.141(6)], to outweigh the aggravating circumstances." ...

In the sentencing phase of this case, petitioner's counsel introduced before the advisory jury evidence that as a child petitioner had the habit of inhaling gasoline fumes from automobile gas tanks; that he had once passed out after doing so; that thereafter his mind tended to wander; that petitioner had been one of seven children in a poor family that earned its living by picking cotton; that his father had died of cancer; and that petitioner had been a fond and affectionate uncle to the children of one of his brothers. In argument to the advisory jury, petitioner's counsel referred to various considerations, some of which were the subject of factual dispute, making a sentence of death inappropriate: petitioner's youth (he was 20 at the time of the murder), his innocence of significant prior criminal activity or violent behavior, the difficult circumstances of his upbringing, his potential for rehabilitation, and his voluntary surrender to authorities. Although petitioner's counsel stressed the first two considerations, which related to mitigating circumstances specifically enumerated in the statute, he told the jury that in reaching its sentencing decision it was to "look at the overall picture ... consider everything together ... consider the whole picture, the whole ball of wax." In contrast, the prosecutor told the jury that it was "to consider the mitigating circumstances and consider those by number," and then went down the statutory list item by item, arguing that only one (petitioner's youth) was applicable. Before proceeding to their deliberations, the members of the jury were told by the trial judge that he would instruct them "on the factors in aggravation and mitigation that you may consider under our law." He then instructed them that "[t]he mitigating circumstances which you may consider shall be the following ..." (listing the statutory mitigating circumstances).

---

2. Section 921.141(5) provided that the aggravating circumstances "shall be limited to the following": that the crime was committed while the defendant was under sentence of imprisonment; that the defendant had previously been convicted of a felony involving the use or threat of violence; that the defendant knowingly created a great risk of death to many persons; that the crime was committed while the defendant was involved in the commission of specified other felonies; that the crime was committed for the purpose of avoiding arrest or escaping from custody; that the crime was committed for pecuniary gain; that the crime was intended to disrupt the government or the enforcement of the laws; and that the crime was especially heinous, atrocious, or cruel.

3. Section 921.141(6) provided that the mitigating circumstances "shall be the following": that the defendant had no significant history of prior criminal activity; that the crime was committed while the defendant was under the influence of extreme mental or emotional disturbance; that the victim participated in or consented to the crime; that defendant was merely an accomplice whose participation in the crime was relatively minor; that the defendant acted under duress or domination; that the capacity of the defendant to appreciate the criminality of his conduct or to conform that conduct to the requirements of law was substantially impaired; and the age of the defendant at the time of the crime.

After receiving the advisory jury's recommendation (by majority vote) of death, and despite the argument of petitioner's counsel that the court should take into account the testimony concerning petitioner's family background and his capacity for rehabilitation, the sentencing judge found that "there [were] insufficient mitigating circumstances *as enumerated in Florida Statute §921.141(6)* to outweigh the aggravating circumstances." He described the process by which he reached his sentencing judgment as follows: "In determining whether the defendant should be sentenced to death or life imprisonment, this Court is mandated to apply the facts to *certain enumerated* 'aggravating' and 'mitigating' circumstances." The only mitigating circumstance he found was petitioner's youth.

We think it could not be clearer that the advisory jury was instructed not to consider, and the sentencing judge refused to consider, evidence of nonstatutory mitigating circumstances, and that the proceedings therefore did not comport with the requirements of *Skipper v. South Carolina*. Respondent has made no attempt to argue that this error was harmless, or that it had no effect on the jury or the sentencing judge. In the absence of such a showing our cases hold that the exclusion of mitigating evidence of the sort at issue here renders the death sentence invalid. As in [*Skipper* and *Eddings*], however, the State is not precluded from seeking to impose a death sentence upon petitioner, "provided that it does so through a new sentencing hearing at which petitioner is permitted to present any and all relevant mitigating evidence that is available."

We reverse the judgment and remand the case to the Court of Appeals. That court is instructed to remand to the District Court with instructions to enter an order granting the application for a writ of habeas corpus, unless the State within a reasonable period of time either resentences petitioner in a proceeding that comports with the requirements of *Lockett* or vacates the death sentence and imposes a lesser sentence consistent with law. It is so ordered.

Note on Hitchcock v. Dugger, 481 U.S. 393 (1987)

According to author David von Drehle, *Hitchcock* teaches a much greater lesson:

> [C]ourts can change their minds very quickly. That was the message of the second death penalty ruling published on that April day in 1986, *Hitchcock v. Dugger*. Technically, the U.S. Supreme Court had never ruled on whether Florida's death penalty law limited a defendant's right to present evidence in favor of a life sentence. But the Court had been asked repeatedly to take the question under consideration, and repeatedly the Court had refused. And sixteen people had gone to Old Sparky. That suggests the majority had made up their minds. Now they changed them: The justices ruled unanimously—all of them, the conservatives, the moderates, the liberals—that the law had been "authoritatively interpreted by the Florida Supreme Court" to mean that mitigating evidence was limited.
>
> Craig Barnard [Hitchcock's attorney] was right. The Florida Supreme Court had denied this for some eight years—sixteen executions—but Barnard had kept at it, kept hammering, despite scoldings and even ridicule from judges and prosecutors. The public had complained bitterly about lawyers like him, with their delaying tactics and technicalities. Politicians had proposed all sorts of bills to limit his access, and the access of his colleagues, to the appellate courts.

Now the U.S. Supreme Court said unanimously that Barnard had been right all along. Justice Scalia, the new conservative tiger, wrote the opinion. "We think it could not be clearer," he intoned, in his confident, definitive way, that the judge and the jury believed they could consider only a few favorable factors. It could not be clearer.

The Court's opinion in *Hitchcock* was brief, scarcely hinting at the years of litigation that had gone into Barnard's victory. In the end, the subtle shift Barnard had made in his argument was the fig leaf the justices grasped to cover their sudden change of heart. "The sentencing judge assumed ... a prohibition [on favorable evidence] and instructed the jury accordingly," Scalia wrote. Therefore, "we need not reach the question whether that was in fact the requirement of Florida law." But Scalia did note that other judges in other cases had reached the same mistaken conclusion about the law. And he mentioned with obvious approval that Florida's legislature had changed the wording of its death penalty statute to make it clear that all favorable evidence should be considered.

The opinion was written to make it seem that a very small point had been decided, but Craig Barnard could see that a new generation of appeals had been opened for the men who had been on Florida's death row the longest. What was true for James Hitchcock was at least arguably true for all of them—dozens of them, and they were the men closest to Old Sparky. And *Hitchcock* had an even larger meaning for Barnard. After the ruling, he proudly told his troops: When people ask why we keep appealing, why we raise these issues over and over, why we never give up fighting ... tell them to look at *Hitchcock*.

von Drehle, *Among the Lowest of the Dead: The Culture of Death Row* 300–301 (Times Books 1995).

Note and Question

What if a capital defendant asks the judge to instruct the jury on a particular mitigating circumstance but proffers no evidence to support it? In *Delo v. Lashley*, 507 U.S. 1057 (1993), Frederick Lashley, a 17-year-old, was convicted of stabbing to death his handicapped foster mother. At a pre-sentencing conference defense counsel sought an instruction on the mitigating circumstance that "[T]he defendant ha[d] no significant history of prior criminal activity." The trial court ruled that it would not give the instruction absent supporting evidence and indicated that if such evidence was introduced, he would likely allow the state to introduce Lashley's juvenile record. Defense counsel presented no supporting evidence.

The Supreme Court denied relief. Although *Lockett* requires that the jury be allowed to consider the defendant's background, character and circumstances of the crime which "the defendant proffers as a basis for a sentence less than death," defendant proferred no evidence on the mitigating circumstance at issue. "Today we make explicit the clear implication of our precedents: Nothing in the Constitution obligates state courts to give mitigating circumstance instructions when no evidence is offered to support them." In dissent Justice Stevens (joined by Justice Blackmun) argued that the instruction should have been given. In their view, "[t]he presumption of innocence, when uncontradicted, is an adequate substitute for affirmative evidence."

6. Juror Unanimity Not Required

Mills v. Maryland
486 U.S. 367 (1988)

Justice BLACKMUN delivered the opinion of the Court.

I

... Petitioner Ralph Mills was tried by a state-court jury and convicted of the first-degree murder of his cellmate in the Maryland Correctional Institution in Hagerstown. The jury found that petitioner repeatedly had stabbed his victim with a "shank" or homemade knife. In the sentencing phase of the trial, the same jury found that the State had established the one statutory aggravating circumstance it propounded, namely, that petitioner "committed the murder at a time when he was confined in a correctional institution." Defense counsel sought to persuade the jury of the presence of certain mitigating circumstances, in particular, petitioner's relative youth, his mental infirmity, his lack of future dangerousness, and the State's failure to make any meaningful attempt to rehabilitate petitioner while he was incarcerated. On the verdict form provided by the trial court pursuant to the then-existing, but since rescinded, Maryland Rule of Procedure 772A, the jury marked "no" beside each referenced mitigating circumstance and returned a sentence of death.

Petitioner challenged his conviction and sentence on various grounds, including an argument that the Maryland capital-punishment statute, as applied to him, was unconstitutionally mandatory. Petitioner construed the statute, as explained to the jury by the court's instructions and as implemented by the verdict form, to require the imposition of the death sentence if the jury unanimously found an aggravating circumstance, but could not agree unanimously as to the existence of any particular mitigating circumstance. According to petitioner's view, even if some or all of the jurors were to believe some mitigating circumstance or circumstances were present, unless they could unanimously agree on the existence of the same mitigating factor, the sentence necessarily would be death....

II

Petitioner's argument is straightforward, and well illustrated by a hypothetical situation he contends is possible under the Maryland capital sentencing scheme:

> If eleven jurors agree that there are six mitigating circumstances, the result is that no mitigating circumstance is found. Consequently, there is nothing to weigh against any aggravating circumstance found and the judgment is death even though eleven jurors think the death penalty wholly inappropriate.

The dissent below postulated a situation just as intuitively disturbing: All 12 jurors might agree that some mitigating circumstances were present, and even that those mitigating circumstances were significant enough to outweigh any aggravating circumstance found to exist. But unless all 12 could agree that the same mitigating circumstance was present, they would never be permitted to engage in the weighing process or any deliberation on the appropriateness of the death penalty.

Although jury discretion must be guided appropriately by objective standards, it would certainly be the height of arbitrariness to allow or require the imposition of the death penalty under the circumstances so postulated by petitioner or the dissent. It is beyond dispute that in a capital case "'the sentencer [may] not be precluded from considering, as a mitigating factor, any aspect of a defendant's character or record and any of the circumstances of the offense that the defendant proffers as a basis for a sentence less than death.'" The corollary that "the sentencer may not refuse to consider or be precluded from considering 'any relevant mitigating evidence'" is equally "well established."

Under Maryland's sentencing scheme, if the sentencer finds that any mitigating circumstance or circumstances have been proved to exist, it then proceeds to decide whether those mitigating circumstances outweigh the aggravating circumstances and sentences the defendant accordingly. But if petitioner is correct, a jury that does not unanimously agree on the existence of any mitigating circumstance may not give mitigating evidence any effect whatsoever, and must impose the sentence of death. Under our decisions, it is not relevant whether the barrier to the sentencer's consideration of all mitigating evidence is interposed by statute, by the sentencing court, or by an evidentiary ruling. The same must be true with respect to a single juror's holdout vote against finding the presence of a mitigating circumstance. Whatever the cause, if petitioner's interpretation of the sentencing process is correct, the conclusion would necessarily be the same: "Because the [sentencer's] failure to consider all of the mitigating evidence risks erroneous imposition of the death sentence, in plain violation of *Lockett*, it is our duty to remand this case for resentencing."

III

B

… [W]e cannot conclude, with any degree of certainty, that the jury did not adopt petitioner's interpretation of the jury instructions and verdict form. At the conclusion of the sentencing phase, the judge distributed copies of the form to the jurors. (This form is reproduced in its entirety, with the answers given, in the Appendix to this opinion.) After reading aloud the instruction part of the form's Section I and stressing the unanimity requirement, the judge explained: "[Y]ou must consider whether the aggravating circumstance number two has been proven beyond a reasonable doubt. If you unanimously conclude that it has been so proven, you should answer that question yes. If you are not so satisfied, then of course you must answer no." We find it difficult to read into that statement a requirement that the "no" answer, like the "yes" answer, must be unanimous. Indeed, the verdict form establishes at least a rough equivalence between the lack of unanimity to write "yes," and writing "no": the jury learns from the form that its failure to write "yes" beside any aggravating circumstance leads to the imposition of a life sentence, the same result that obtains if the jury answers "no" for every aggravating circumstance.

The judge then moved on to Section II of the form, which addresses the jury's determination of which, if any, mitigating circumstances exist. The language at the beginning of that section is identical to that at the beginning of Section I, except that the standard of proof is by a preponderance of the evidence rather than beyond a reasonable doubt, see Appendix to this opinion, and we presume that, unless instructed to the contrary, the jury would read similar language throughout the form consistently. The jury was instructed to mark each answer "yes" or "no." Although it was clear that the jury could not mark "yes" in any box without unanimity, nothing the judge said dispelled the probable inference that "no" is the opposite of "yes," and therefore the appropriate answer to reflect an inability to answer a question in the affirmative. Nothing in the verdict form or the judge's instructions even arguably is construable as suggesting the jury could leave an answer blank and proceed to the next stage in its deliberations.

The only place on the form where the jury had an opportunity to write anything more than "yes" or "no" was with respect to mitigating circumstance number eight, see Appendix to this opinion, which permits the jury to recognize as mitigating anything, in addition to the enumerated mitigating factors, that petitioner offered as a basis for a sentence less than death. The judge explained to the jury that if it found any such "other" mitigating circumstances, it must list them in the space provided, and "[i]f you find no other mitigating circumstance then you make no entry upon those lines under number eight." No instruction was given indicating what the jury should do if some but not all of the jurors were willing to recognize something about petitioner, his background, or the circumstances of the crime, as a mitigating factor.

Ordinarily, a Maryland jury reaches the balancing stage of the deliberation process any time it unanimously finds at least one mitigating circumstance, or, under the interpretation adopted by the Court of Appeals in this case, any time the jury does not unanimously reject all mitigating circumstances. Had the jurors that sentenced petitioner reached Section III,[13] they would have found that even if they had read the verdict form as the Court of Appeals suggests they could have, and marked "yes" or "no" only on the basis of unanimity as to either, they were not free at this point to consider *all* relevant evidence in mitigation as they balanced aggravating and mitigating circumstances. Section III instructed the jury to weigh only those mitigating circumstances marked "yes" in Section II. Any mitigating circumstance not so marked, even if not unanimously rejected, could not be considered by any juror. A jury following the instructions set out in the verdict form could be "precluded from considering, as a mitigating factor, [an] aspect of a defendant's character or record [or a] circumstanc[e] of the offense that the defendant proffer[ed] as a basis for a sentence less than death," if even a single juror adhered to the view that such a factor should not be so considered.

C

There is, of course, no extrinsic evidence of what the jury in this case actually thought. We have before us only the verdict form and the judge's instructions. Our reading of those parts of the record leads us to conclude that there is at least a substantial risk that the jury was misinformed....

One additional bit of evidence about the natural interpretation of the form has become available since this case was decided below on June 25, 1987. On an emergency basis, the Court of Appeals promulgated a new Findings and Sentencing Determination form. The new form expressly incorporates the unanimity requirement as to both accepting and rejecting aggravating circumstances. More significantly, however, the section concerning mitigating circumstances is completely rewritten and changed. Now, under each statutory mitigating circumstance, the jury is asked to choose from among three options:

> "(Mark only one)
> ____(a) We unanimously find by a preponderance of the evidence that the above circumstance exists.

---

13. The jury in this case apparently never reached the balancing stage of the process. When the jury returned to the courtroom to report its verdict, even the judge was confused by their failure to complete Section III, in accordance with the form's instructions. The prosecutor suggested, during a colloquy with the court, that the jurors were "hung up on that language."

___(b) We unanimously find by a preponderance of the evidence that the above circumstance does not exist.

___(c) After a reasonable period of deliberation, one or more of us, but fewer than all 12, find by a preponderance of the evidence that the above circumstance exists."

As before, the new verdict form also provides the jury the opportunity to articulate "additional mitigating circumstances." The new form, however, unlike the one used in petitioner's case, explicitly directs the jury to articulate any such "additional" circumstances that the jurors unanimously agree exist, *and* any found by "[o]ne or more..., but fewer than all 12" of the jurors.

With respect to the consideration of mitigating evidence during the weighing and balancing process, the new verdict form instructs jurors as follows: "(If the jury unanimously determines in Section III that no mitigating circumstances exist, do not complete Section IV. Proceed to Section V and enter 'Death.' If the jury *or any juror* determines that one or more mitigating circumstances exist, complete Section IV.)"

Section IV now reflects the requirement that jurors not be prevented from considering all evidence in mitigation: "*Each individual juror shall weigh* the aggravating circumstances found unanimously to exist against any mitigating circumstances found unanimously to exist, *as well as against any mitigating circumstances found by that individual juror to exist.*"

Although we are hesitant to infer too much about the prior verdict form from the Court of Appeals' well-meant efforts to remove ambiguity from the State's capital sentencing scheme, we cannot avoid noticing these significant changes effected in instructions to the jury. We can and do infer from these changes at least *some* concern on the part of that court that juries could misunderstand the previous instructions as to unanimity and the consideration of mitigating evidence by individual jurors. We also note, for what it may be worth, that in two cases tried since a Maryland jury has been given the option of reporting non-unanimous votes, the jury has done so.

No one on this Court was a member of the jury that sentenced Ralph Mills, or of any similarly instructed jury in Maryland. We cannot say with any degree of confidence which interpretation Mills' jury adopted. But common sense and what little extrinsic evidence we possess suggest that juries do not leave blanks and do not report themselves as deadlocked over mitigating circumstances after reasonable deliberation, unless they are expressly instructed to do so.

The decision to exercise the power of the State to execute a defendant is unlike any other decision citizens and public officials are called upon to make. Evolving standards of societal decency have imposed a correspondingly high requirement of reliability on the determination that death is the appropriate penalty in a particular case. The possibility that petitioner's jury conducted its task improperly certainly is great enough to require resentencing.

IV

We conclude that there is a substantial probability that reasonable jurors, upon receiving the judge's instructions in this case, and in attempting to complete the verdict form as instructed, well may have thought they were precluded from considering any mitigating evidence unless all 12 jurors agreed on the existence of a particular such circumstance. Under our cases, the sentencer must be permitted to consider all mitigating evidence. The possibility that a single juror could block such consideration, and consequently require the jury to impose the death penalty, is one we dare not risk.

We therefore vacate the judgment of the Court of Appeals insofar as it sustained the imposition of the death penalty. The case is remanded to that court for further proceedings not inconsistent with this opinion.

APPENDIX TO OPINION OF THE COURT FINDINGS AND SENTENCE DETERMINATION FORM EMPLOYED AT PETITIONER'S TRIAL

"Section I

"Based upon the evidence we unanimously find that each of the following aggravating circumstances which is marked 'yes' has been proven BEYOND A REASONABLE DOUBT and each aggravating circumstance which is marked 'no' has not been proven BEYOND A REASONABLE DOUBT:

"1. The victim was a law enforcement officer who was murdered while in the performance of his duties.

yes   X no

"2. The defendant committed the murder at a time when he was confined in a correctional institution.

X yes   no

"3. The defendant committed the murder in furtherance of an escape from or an attempt to escape from or evade the lawful custody, arrest or detention of or by an officer or guard of a correctional institution or by a law enforcement officer.

yes   X no

"4. The victim was a hostage taken or attempted to be taken in the course of a kidnapping or abduction or an attempt to kidnap or abduct.

yes   X no

"5. The victim was a child abducted in violation of Code, Article 27, §2.

yes   X no

"6. The defendant committed the murder pursuant to an agreement to contract for remuneration or the promise of remuneration to commit the murder.

yes   X no

"7. The defendant engaged or employed another person to commit the murder and the murder was committed pursuant to an agreement or contract for remuneration or the promise of remuneration.

yes   X no

"8. At the time of the murder, the defendant was under the sentence of death or imprisonment for life.

yes   X no

"9. The defendant committed more than one offense of murder in the first degree arising out of the same incident.

yes   X no

"10. The defendant committed the murder while committing or attempting to commit robbery, arson or rape or sexual offense in the first degree.

     yes   X no

"(If one or more of the above are marked 'yes', complete Section II. If all of the above are marked 'no', do not complete Sections II and III.)

"Section II

"Based upon the evidence we unanimously find that each of the following mitigating circumstances which is marked 'yes' has been proven to exist by A PREPONDERANCE OF THE EVIDENCE and each mitigating circumstance marked 'no' has not been proven by A PREPONDERANCE OF THE EVIDENCE:

"1. The defendant previously (i) has not been found guilty of a crime of violence; and (ii) has not entered a plea of guilty or nolo contendere to a charge of a crime of violence; and (iii) has not been granted probation on stay or entry of judgment pursuant to a charge or a crime of violence. As used in this paragraph, 'crime of violence' means abduction, arson, escape, kidnapping, manslaughter, except involuntary manslaughter, mayhem, murder, robbery, or rape or sexual offense in the first or second degree, or an attempt to commit any of these offenses, or the use of a handgun in the commission of a felony or another crime of violence.

     yes   X no

"2. The victim was a participant in the defendant's conduct or consented to the act which caused the victim's death.

     yes   X no

"3. The defendant acted under substantial duress, domination or provocation of another person, but not so substantial as to constitute a complete defense to the prosecution.

     yes   X no

"4. The murder was committed while the capacity of the defendant to appreciate the criminality of his conduct or to conform his conduct to the requirements of law was substantially impaired as a result of mental incapacity, mental disorder or emotional disturbance.

     yes   X no

"5. The youthful age of the defendant at the time of the crime.

     yes   X no

"6. The act of the defendant was not the sole proximate cause of the victim's death.

     yes   X no

"7. It is unlikely that the defendant will engage in further criminal activity that would constitute a continuing threat to society.

     yes   X no

"8. Other mitigating circumstances exist, as set forth below: None.

"(If one or more of the above in Section II have been marked 'yes', complete Section III. If all of the above in Section II are marked 'no', you do not complete Section III.)

"Section III

"Based on the evidence we unanimously find that it has been proven by A PREPON-DERANCE OF THE EVIDENCE that the mitigating circumstances marked 'yes' in Section II outweigh the aggravating circumstances marked 'yes' in Section I.

     yes   no

"Determination of Sentence

"Enter the determination of sentence either 'Life Imprisonment' or 'Death' according to the following instructions:

"1. If all of the answers in Section I are marked 'no' enter 'Life Imprisonment.'

"2. If Section III was completed and was marked 'yes' enter 'Life Imprisonment.'

"3. If Section II was completed and all of the answers were marked 'no' then enter 'Death.'

"4. If Section III was completed and was marked 'no' enter 'Death.'

"We unanimously determine the sentence to be Death."

7. Special Issues and Residual Doubt

Franklin v. Lynaugh
487 U.S. 164 (1988)

Justice WHITE announced the judgment of the Court, and delivered an opinion, in which the Chief Justice, Justice Scalia, and Justice Kennedy joined.

I

... [The jury found petitioner Donald Gene Franklin guilty of the capital murder of Mary Margaret Moran.] At the penalty phase of petitioner's trial, the State called four police officers who testified that petitioner had a bad reputation as a law-abiding citizen. The State also proved that petitioner Donald Gene Franklin had a prior conviction for rape, and called a witness who testified that petitioner had raped her the year before this crime was committed. The sole mitigating evidence petitioner presented was the stipulation that petitioner's disciplinary record while incarcerated from 1971–1974 and 1976–1980 was without incident. At the conclusion of this penalty hearing, the trial court, pursuant to [Texas law], submitted two "Special Issues" to the jury,[3] instructing the jury that if they determined the answer to both these questions to be "Yes," petitioner would be sentenced to death.

Earlier, petitioner had submitted five "special requested" jury instructions to direct the jury's consideration of the Special Issues. In essence, the requested instructions

---

3. The two Special Issues, as presented to the jury in this case, were: "Do you find from the evidence beyond a reasonable doubt that the conduct of the Defendant, Donald Gene Franklin, that caused the death of Mary Margaret Moran, was committed deliberately and with the reasonable expectation that the death of the deceased or another would result? Do you find from the evidence beyond a reasonable doubt that there is a probability that the Defendant, Donald Gene Franklin, would commit criminal acts of violence that would constitute a continuing threat to society?"

would have told the jury that any evidence considered by them to mitigate against the death penalty should be taken into account in answering the Special Issues, and could alone be enough to return a negative answer to either one or both of the questions submitted to them—even if the jury otherwise believed that "Yes" answers to the Special Issues were warranted. [The trial court refused to give the instructions. The jury answered "Yes" to both special issues and petitioner was sentenced to death.]

... We granted certiorari to determine if the trial court's refusal to give the requested instructions violated petitioner's Eighth Amendment right to present mitigating evidence at his capital sentencing trial, and now affirm the judgment below....

II

... Petitioner ... complains that the instructions [given] and Special Issues did not provide sufficient opportunity for the jury, in the process of answering the two Special Issues, to consider whatever "residual doubt" it may have had about petitioner's guilt. The instructions also allegedly did not allow the jury to give adequate weight to the mitigating evidence of petitioner's good behavior while in prison. In addition, petitioner contends that the Eighth Amendment was violated because the jury was not afforded an opportunity to "giv[e] independent mitigating weight" to the circumstances the defense presented; *i.e.*, not permitted to weigh petitioner's mitigating evidence and circumstances apart from its deliberation over the Texas Special Issues, and return a verdict requiring a life sentence....

A

(1)

[Petitioner first claims that the trial court should have instructed the jury to consider any "residual doubts" that it may have about his guilt.] At the outset, we note that this Court has never held that a capital defendant has a constitutional right to an instruction telling the jury to revisit the question of his identity as the murderer as a basis for mitigation....

Our edict that, in a capital case, "the sentencer ... [may] not be precluded from considering, as a mitigating factor, any aspect of a defendant's character or record and any of the circumstances of the offense," in no way mandates reconsideration by capital juries, in the sentencing phase, of their "residual doubts" over a defendant's guilt. Such lingering doubts are not over any aspect of petitioner's "character," "record," or a "circumstance of the offense." This Court's prior decisions, as we understand them, fail to recognize a constitutional right to have such doubts considered as a mitigating factor.

Most importantly, even if we were inclined to discern such a right in the Eighth Amendment, we would not find any violation of it *in this case*. For even if such a right existed, nothing done by the trial court impaired petitioner's exercise of this "right." The trial court placed no limitation whatsoever on petitioner's opportunity to press the "residual doubts" question with the sentencing jury. Moreover, in our view, the trial court's rejection of petitioner's proffered jury instructions was without impact on the jury's consideration of the "residual doubts" issue. We reject petitioner's complaint that the possibility of residual doubt was not "self-evidently relevant to either of the special issue questions," and that "[u]nless told that *residual* doubt ... could be considered in relation to [the special issue] question[s], the jurors could logically have concluded that such doubt was irrelevant." Among other problems with this argument is the simple fact that petitioner's requested instructions on mitigating evidence themselves offered *no* specific direction to the jury concerning the potential consideration of "residual doubt." The proposed instructions did not suggest that lingering doubts about the petitioner's guilt were to be a subject of deliberations in the sentencing phase. Consequently, it is difficult to see how the rejection of these instructions denied petitioner the benefit of any "residual doubts" about his guilt....

B

The second mitigating circumstance which petitioner claims that the jury did not adequately consider is his good disciplinary record during his period of incarceration, both before and after the murder of Ms. Moran. As noted above, petitioner's prison disciplinary record was presented to the jury in this case — in fact, it was the sole bit of evidence in mitigation petitioner presented during the penalty phase of his trial. This case is therefore unlike *Skipper v. South Carolina*, 476 U.S. 1, 3 (1986), where evidence of the defendant's conduct while incarcerated was wholly excluded from the jury's consideration in its sentencing deliberations. To the contrary, petitioner here was permitted to press, with some emphasis, his good behavior in prison when he urged the jury, at the close of the sentencing hearing, to return a "No" answer to the second Special Issue concerning future dangerousness. Petitioner acknowledged as much before this Court.

Petitioner objects, however, that — absent his requested jury instructions — there was no opportunity for the jury to give "independent" mitigating weight to his prison record. He argues that this mitigating evidence had significance independent of its relevance to the Special Issues — as a reflection on his "character." Petitioner contends that his prison disciplinary record reflected so positively on his "character" that the instructions in this case should have provided the jury with a "mechanism through which to impose a life sentence" even if the jury otherwise believed that both Special Issues should have been answered "Yes." For several reasons, we do not find these arguments convincing.

First, petitioner was accorded a full opportunity to have his sentencing jury consider and give effect to any mitigating impulse that petitioner's prison record might have suggested to the jury as they proceeded with their task. In resolving the second Texas Special Issue the jury was surely free to weigh and evaluate petitioner's disciplinary record as it bore on his "character" — that is, his "character" as measured by his likely future behavior. We have never defined what the term "character" means when we have held that a defendant's "character" is a relevant consideration in capital sentencing. But nothing in our cases supports petitioner's contention that relevant aspects of his "character," as far as they were illuminated by the presentation of evidence concerning petitioner's disciplinary record, encompassed anything more than those matters fully considered by the jury when it was asked to answer the second Special Issue.

Indeed, our discussion in *Skipper* of the relevancy of such disciplinary record evidence in capital sentencing decisions dealt exclusively with the question of how such evidence reflects on a defendant's likely future behavior. Nothing in *Skipper* suggests that such evidence has any further relevancy with respect to a defendant's "character" or with respect to the punishment decision. Moreover, *Skipper*'s discussion of the proper use of a defendant's prison disciplinary record in a jury's sentencing decision focused precisely on the way in which such evidence is encompassed by the Texas future-dangerousness question, and on the Court's previous decision in *Jurek*. Furthermore, we note that nothing in petitioner's presentation or discussion of his prison record at the sentencing hearing urged the jury to consider petitioner's record as probative of anything more than that the answer to the question posed by Special Issue Two should be "No." Even in this Court, in seeking to define how his prison record sheds light on his "character," petitioner has cast his argument in terms of future dangerousness.

We find unavailing petitioner's [contention] ... that the sentencing jury may not be precluded from considering "any relevant, mitigating evidence." This statement leaves unanswered the question: relevant to what? While *Lockett v. Ohio* answers this question at least in part—making it clear that a State cannot take out of the realm of relevant sentencing considerations the questions of the defendant's "character," "record," or the "circumstances of the offense"—*Lockett* does not hold that the State has no role in structuring or giving shape to the jury's consideration of these mitigating factors. Given the awesome power that a sentencing jury must exercise in a capital case, it may be advisable for a State to provide the jury with some framework for discharging these responsibilities. And we have never held that a specific method for balancing mitigating and aggravating factors in a capital sentencing proceeding is constitutionally required.

We are thus quite sure that the jury's consideration of petitioner's prison record was not improperly limited. The jury was completely free to give that evidence appropriate weight in arriving at its answers to the Special Issues. And as for the claim that the jury should have been instructed that, even if its answer to the Special Issues was "Yes," it was still entitled to cast an "independent" vote against the death penalty, we note that this submission is foreclosed by *Jurek v. Texas*, which held that Texas could constitutionally impose the death penalty if a jury returned "Yes" answers to the two Special Issues. *Jurek* has not been overruled; and we are not inclined to take any such action now.

III

Our specific rejection of petitioner's claims is well supported by the general principles governing the role of mitigating evidence in capital sentencing which have been developed since our decisions in *Gregg v. Georgia* and *Jurek v. Texas*.

It is true that since *Jurek* was decided, this Court has gone far in establishing a constitutional entitlement of capital defendants to appeal for leniency in the exercise of juries' sentencing discretion. But even in so doing, this Court has never held that jury discretion must be unlimited or unguided; we have never suggested that jury consideration of mitigating evidence must be undirected or unfocused; we have never concluded that States cannot channel jury discretion in capital sentencing in an effort to achieve a more rational and equitable administration of the death penalty.

Much in our cases suggests just the opposite. This Court has previously held that the States "must channel the [capital] sentencer's discretion by 'clear and objective standards' that provide 'specific and detailed guidance' and that 'make rationally reviewable the process for imposing a sentence of death.'" Our cases before and since have similarly suggested that "sentencers may not be given unbridled discretion in determining the fates of those charged with capital offenses" and that the "Constitution ... requires that death penalty statutes be structured so as to prevent the penalty from being administered in an arbitrary and unpredictable fashion."

IV

... Because we do not believe that the jury instructions or the Texas Special Issues precluded jury consideration of any relevant mitigating circumstances in this case, or otherwise unconstitutionally limited the jury's discretion here, we reject petitioner's

Eighth Amendment challenge to his death sentence. Consequently, the Fifth Circuit's judgment in this case is affirmed.

Notes and Questions

1. The plurality in *Franklin v. Lynaugh* recognized the tension between cases holding that the jury's discretion must be directed so as to avoid arbitrary and capricious sentencing and cases holding that the jury be allowed to consider any relevant mitigating evidence. The plurality reconciled this tension as follows:

> Arguably these two lines of cases—*Eddings* and *Lockett* on the one hand, and *Gregg* and *Proffitt* on the other—are somewhat in "tension" with each other. Yet the Texas capital sentencing system has been upheld by this Court, and its method for providing for the consideration of mitigating evidence has been cited repeatedly with favor, precisely because of the way in which the Texas scheme accommodates both of these concerns. Doubtlessly this is why this Court originally approved Texas' use of Special Issues to guide jury discretion in the sentencing phase, notwithstanding the fact—expressly averted to in the plurality opinion for the Court—that mitigating evidence is employed in the Texas scheme only to inform the jury's consideration of the answers to the Special Issue questions.[12] No doubt this is also why the Texas scheme has continued to pass constitutional muster, even when the Court laid down its broad rule in *Lockett* concerning the consideration of mitigating evidence. Simply put, we have previously recognized that the Texas Special Issues adequately "allo[w] the jury to consider the mitigating aspects of the crime and the unique characteristics of the perpetrator, and therefore sufficiently provid[e] for jury discretion." We adhere to this prior conclusion.

The dissent, however, noted, "our holding in *Jurek* did not turn on an understanding that the Special Issues performed a narrowing function; rather our concern there, as it is here, was whether the Special issues interfered with the jury's full consideration of mitigating evidence." The dissent criticized the majority for limiting the scope of mitigating evidence the jury may consider.

> The plurality errs in suggesting that under our precedents Texas may "structur[e]" or "giv[e] shape" to the jury's consideration of character as a mitigating factor by defining character to include only that evidence that reflects on future dangerousness. The notion that a State may permissibly provide such a "framework" for the sentencer's discharge of its "awesome power" is inconsistent with our holdings in *Lockett* and *Hitchcock* that a State may not limit the sentencer's consideration to certain enumerated mitigating factors. There is no constitutionally meaningful distinction between allowing the jury to hear all the evidence the defendant would like to introduce and then telling the jury to consider that evidence only to the extent that it is probative of one of the enumerated mitigating circumstances, which we held unconstitutional in both

---

12. We also repeat our previous acknowledgment, that—as a practical matter—a Texas capital jury deliberating over the Special Issues is aware of the consequences of its answers, and is likely to weigh mitigating evidence as it formulates these answers in a manner similar to that employed by capital juries in "pure balancing" States. Thus, the difference between the two systems may be even less than it appears at first examination.

Lockett and *Hitchcock*, and allowing the jury to hear whatever evidence the defendant would like to introduce and then telling the jury to consider that evidence only to the extent that it is probative of future dangerousness, which the plurality here finds constitutional.

Petitioner does not contend that the jury required special instructions in order to give complete consideration to any mitigating evidence that was relevant to whether he acted deliberately or to whether he constituted a future threat to society. His argument is limited to the rather simple truism that absent some instruction, given the structure of the Texas scheme, it is probable that the jury misapprehended the significance it could attach to mitigating evidence that was descriptive of petitioner's character rather than predictive of his future behavior. The instructions he sought would only have informed the jury that it could answer either or both of the Special Issues "no" if it found that the mitigating evidence justified a sentence less than death—whether or not that evidence was relevant to deliberateness or future dangerousness—authority the jury assuredly had under the Constitution and under the Texas sentencing scheme as we have previously construed it. . . .

Which do you find more persuasive on the need for special instructions on mitigating evidence, the plurality or the dissenting view?

2. In *Penry v. Lynaugh*, 492 U.S. 302 (1989), another death penalty case arising out of Texas, the jury rejected Penry's insanity defense and found him guilty of capital murder. The following day, at the close of the penalty hearing, the jury decided the sentence to be imposed on Penry by answering three "special issues":

(1) whether the conduct of the defendant that caused the death of the deceased was committed deliberately and with the reasonable expectation that the death of the deceased or another would result;

(2) whether there is a probability that the defendant would commit criminal acts of violence that would constitute a continuing threat to society; and

(3) if raised by the evidence, whether the conduct of the defendant in killing the deceased was unreasonable in response to the provocation, if any, by the deceased.

The jury answered "yes" to all three special issues, and Penry was sentenced to death.

The Court granted certiorari to resolve whether Penry was sentenced to death in violation of the Eighth Amendment because the jury was not adequately instructed to take into consideration all of his mitigating evidence and because the terms in the Texas special issues were not defined in such a way that the jury could consider and give effect to his mitigating evidence in answering them.

Although Penry offered mitigating evidence of his mental retardation and abused childhood as the basis for a sentence of life imprisonment rather than death, the jury that sentenced him was only able to express its views on the appropriate sentence by answering three questions: Did Penry act deliberately when he murdered Pamela Carpenter? Is there a probability that he will be dangerous in the future? Did he act unreasonably in response to provocation? The jury was never instructed that it could consider the evidence offered by Penry as mitigating evidence and that it could give mitigating effect to that evidence in imposing sentence.

Like the petitioner in *Franklin v. Lynaugh*, Penry contended that in the absence of his requested jury instructions, the Texas death penalty statute was applied in an unconstitutional manner by precluding the jury from acting upon the particular mitigating evidence he introduced. The Court agreed.

> In this case, in the absence of instructions informing the jury that it could consider and give effect to the mitigating evidence of Penry's mental retardation and abused background by declining to impose the death penalty, we conclude that the jury was not provided with a vehicle for expressing its "reasoned moral response" to that evidence in rendering its sentencing decision. Our reasoning in *Lockett* and *Eddings* thus compels a remand for resentencing so that we do not "risk that the death penalty will be imposed in spite of factors which may call for a less severe penalty."

3. How broad should the scope of mitigating evidence be? For example, should a capital defendant be allowed to introduce evidence that heavy metal or rap music influenced him to commit murder? What about a history of drug or alcohol abuse? What about evidence that a defendant was mentally impaired due to long exposure to violent pornography so that the defendant was unable to determine the wrongfulness of his actions during a violent rape and homicide? If the family of the victim opposes the death penalty, should they be allowed to ask the jury to impose a sentence less than death?

4. In *Oregon v. Guzek*, 126 S.Ct. 1226 (2006), the United States Supreme Court reversed the Oregon high court which had held that the Eighth and Fourteenth Amendments gave Guzek a federal constitutional right to introduce live alibi testimony from his mother at his upcoming resentencing hearing. The Oregon Supreme Court had interpreted the federal admissibility requirement in *Lockett v. Ohio* and *Green v. Georgia* (*supra* this chapter) to include evidence such as the proffered alibi testimony. According to the U.S. Supreme Court, the Constitution does not prohibit states from limiting the innocence-related evidence that a capital defendant can introduce at a sentencing proceeding to the evidence introduced during the guilt phase. First, there is a relevance problem. Sentencing traditionally concerns *how*, not *whether*, a defendant committed the crime. Second, allowing the introduction of new alibi evidence at sentencing would amount to permitting a collateral attack on a previously determined matter (guilt) during a proceeding in which that matter is not at issue.

Individualized Sentencing and "Mere Sympathy"

Although capital defendants are free to introduce evidence that might justify a sentence less than death, *Furman* prevents the sentencer from exercising "unfettered discretion." As long as the sentencer is able to consider mitigating circumstances, a defendant's right to individualized sentencing is protected. Thus, in *Blystone v. Pennsylvania*, 494 U.S. 299 (1990), the Court upheld a statute which required a death sentence when the sentencer found no mitigating evidence and at least one statutory aggravating circumstance. Likewise, in *Boyde v. California*, 494 U.S. 370 (1990), the Court upheld a statute which required a death sentence when aggravating circumstances were found to outweigh mitigating circumstances.

What role then is sympathy to play in capital sentencing? Mitigating evidence is of course intended to evoke a merciful response from the sentencer. Nonetheless, jury instructions which admonish jurors not to be swayed by "mere sentiment, conjecture, sympathy, passion, prejudice, public opinion or public feeling" in deciding the appropriate sentence are constitutional. In *California v. Brown*, 479 U.S. 538, 542 (1987), the Court concluded that a reasonable juror would interpret the anti-sympathy instruction to mean that he should "ignore emotional responses that are not rooted in the aggravating and mitigating evidence." Although *Brown* may be read to suggest that emotional responses which *are* rooted in mitigating evidence are permissible, *Saffle v. Parks*, 494 U.S. 484, 493–494 (1990), suggests the contrary.

8. The Requirement That Jurors Give Effect to Mitigating Evidence

In *Smith v. Texas*, 543 U.S. 37 (2004) (per curiam), the Court reiterated its holding in *Penry v. Johnson*, (*Penry II*), 532 U.S. 782 (2001)—that a jury must be given a vehicle to give effect to mitigating evidence—and rejected a supplemental "nullification instruction" as providing sufficient guidance in assessing mitigation evidence in the sentencing phase of a Texas capital murder trial. This nullification instruction "directed the jury to give effect to mitigation evidence, but allowed the jury to do so only by negating what would otherwise be affirmative responses to two special issues relating to deliberateness and future dangerousness." The Supreme Court stated in *Smith v. Texas*:

III

The Texas Court of Criminal Appeals held that even if petitioner did proffer relevant mitigation evidence, the supplemental "nullification instruction" provided to the jury adequately allowed the jury to give effect to that evidence. The court found it significant that the supplemental instruction in this case "told the jury that it 'shall' consider all mitigating evidence, even evidence unrelated to the special issues, [and] it also told the jury how to answer the special issues to give effect to that mitigation evidence." The court also concluded that the nullification instruction made it clear to the jury that a "No" answer was required if it "believed that the death penalty was not warranted because of the mitigating circumstances."

In *Penry II*, we held that "the key under Penry I is that the jury be able to 'consider and give effect to [a defendant's mitigation] evidence in imposing sentence.'" We explained at length why the supplemental instruction employed by the Texas courts did not provide the jury with an adequate vehicle for expressing a "reasoned moral response" to all of the evidence relevant to the defendant's culpability. Although there are some distinctions between the *Penry II* supplemental instruction and the instruction petitioner's jury received, those distinctions are constitutionally insignificant.

Penry II identified a broad and intractable problem—a problem that the state court ignored here—inherent in any requirement that the jury nullify special issues contained within a verdict form.

> "We generally presume that jurors follow their instructions. Here, however, it would have been both logically and ethically impossible for a juror to follow both sets of instructions. Because Penry's mitigating evidence did not fit within the scope of the special issues, answering those issues in the manner prescribed on the verdict form necessarily meant ignoring the command of the supplemental instruction. And answering the special issues in the mode prescribed by the supplemental instruction necessarily meant ignoring the verdict form instructions. Indeed, jurors who wanted to answer one of the special is-

sues falsely to give effect to the mitigating evidence would have had to violate their oath to render a "'true verdict.'"

"The mechanism created by the supplemental instruction thus inserted 'an element of capriciousness' into the sentencing decision, 'making the jurors' power to avoid the death penalty dependent on their willingness' to elevate the supplemental instruction over the verdict form instructions. There is, at the very least, 'a reasonable likelihood that the jury ... applied the challenged instruction in a way that prevent[ed] the consideration' of Penry's mental retardation and childhood abuse. The supplemental instruction therefore provided an inadequate vehicle for the jury to make a reasoned moral response to Penry's mitigating evidence."

It is certainly true that the mandatory aspect of the nullification instruction made petitioner's instruction distinct from Penry's. Indeed, the "shall" command in the nullification instruction resolved the ambiguity inherent in the *Penry II* instruction, which we held was either a nullification instruction or an instruction that "'shackled and confined'" Penry's mitigating evidence within the scope of the impermissibly narrow special issues. That being said, the clearer instruction given to petitioner's jury did not resolve the ethical problem described *supra*, at this page. To the contrary, the mandatory language in the charge could possibly have intensified the dilemma faced by ethical jurors. Just as in *Penry II*, petitioner's jury was required by law to answer a verdict form that made no mention whatsoever of mitigation evidence. And just as in *Penry II*, the burden of proof on the State was tied by law to findings of deliberateness and future dangerousness that had little, if anything, to do with the mitigation evidence petitioner presented. Even if we were to assume that the jurors could easily and effectively have comprehended an orally delivered instruction directing them to disregard, in certain limited circumstances, a mandatory written instruction given at a later occasion, that would not change the fact that the "jury was essentially instructed to return a false answer to a special issue in order to avoid a death sentence."

There is no principled distinction, for Eighth Amendment purposes, between the instruction given to petitioner's jury and the instruction in *Penry II*. Petitioner's evidence was relevant mitigation evidence for the jury under *Tennard* [*v. Dretke*, 124 S.Ct. 2562 (2004), *infra* chapter 13] and *Penry I*. We therefore hold that the nullification instruction was constitutionally inadequate under *Penry II*. The judgment of the Texas Court of Criminal Appeals is reversed, and the case is remanded for further proceedings not inconsistent with this opinion.

B. Balancing Aggravating and Mitigating Circumstances

Introduction

The jury or trial court which imposes sentence on the capital defendant must make an individualized determination as to whether the defendant should be sentenced to death. This constitutional requirement mandates that the defendant be allowed to present, and the sentencer be required to listen to, mitigating evidence presented on the defendant's behalf. However, the precise method by which the jury or the trial judge is to evaluate all the aggravating and mitigating circumstances varies among states. For example, in Georgia, the jury must find the existence of one aggravating circumstance before imposing a sentence of death. However, in Georgia "aggravating circumstances as such have no specific function in the jury's decision whether a defendant who has been found to be eligible for the death penalty should receive it under all the circumstances of the case. Instead, under the Georgia scheme, '[i]n making the decision as to the penalty, the factfinder takes into consideration all circumstances before it from both the guilt-innocence and the sentence phases of the trial. These circumstances relate both to the offense and the defendant.'" *Stringer v. Black*, 503 U.S. 222 (1992), quoting *Zant v. Stephens*, 462 U.S. 862, 872 (1983). Thus, in Georgia, the aggravating circumstance serves to narrow the class of persons who may be subject to the death penalty, but beyond establishing this initial hurdle, the aggravating circumstance itself does not play a specific, defined role during sentencing.

In contrast, other states specifically require the factfinder to engage in a "weighing" process in which the trier of fact weighs the aggravating and mitigating circumstances to determine whether the defendant should be sentenced to life imprisonment or death. The factfinder must find the existence of one or more aggravating circumstances as a prerequisite to a death sentence. If the factfinder fails to find the existence of at least one aggravating circumstance, then a sentence less than death must be imposed. On the other hand, if the factfinder finds one or more aggravating circumstances, then the factfinder must weigh the aggravating circumstance(s) against the mitigating circumstance(s) to determine the appropriate sentence. The United States Constitution does not proscribe a specific method or standard for weighing the aggravating and mitigating circumstances. *Zant v. Stephens*, 462 U.S. 862 (1983).

Pennsylvania's sentencing scheme differs from those in most other weighing jurisdictions. In cases in which the jury finds at least one statutory aggravating circumstance, the jury then determines whether a mitigating circumstance is also present. If the jury finds a mitigating circumstance (which requires the affirmative vote of only a single juror), the jury then weighs the aggravating circumstances against the mitigating circumstances. However, if the jury fails to find at least one mitigating circumstance, the court instructs the jury that it must return a sentence of death—whether or not it considers a death sentence appropriate or just. Despite allegations that this limitation on the jury's discretion results in unlawful "mandatory" death sentencing, the Supreme Court has upheld this procedure. *Blystone v. Pennsylvania*, 494 U.S. 299, 305 (1990).

1. Appellate Review of the Death Sentence in Non-Weighing States

The question arises in both weighing and non-weighing states: What happens if, on appeal, one of the aggravating circumstances the factfinder relied upon to impose the death sentence is invalidated due to lack of evidence or a deficiency in the statutory aggravating circumstance itself? See e.g., *Maynard v. Cartwright*, 486 U.S. 356 (1988). In both weighing and non-weighing states, if the sole aggravating circumstance relied upon by the factfinder is invalidated the defendant's death sentence cannot stand. However, may the appellate court in a non-weighing state affirm the sentence of death if there is at least one valid aggravating circumstance supporting its imposition, or must the court remand the case for resentencing?

Zant v. Stephens
462 U.S. 862 (1983)

Justice STEVENS delivered the opinion of the Court.

The question presented is whether respondent's death penalty must be vacated because one of the three statutory aggravating circumstances found by the jury was subsequently held to be invalid by the Supreme Court of Georgia, although the other two aggravating circumstances were specifically upheld. The answer depends on the function of the jury's finding of an aggravating circumstance under Georgia's capital sentencing statute, and on the reasons that the aggravating circumstance at issue in this particular case was found to be invalid....

At the sentencing phase of the trial the State relied on the evidence adduced at the guilt phase and also established that respondent's prior criminal record included convictions on two counts of armed robbery, five counts of burglary, and one count of murder. Respondent testified that he was "sorry" and knew he deserved to be punished, that his accomplice actually shot Asbell, and that they had both been "pretty high" on drugs. The State requested the jury to impose the death penalty and argued that the evidence established the aggravating circumstances identified in subparagraphs (b)(1), (b)(7), and (b)(9) of the Georgia capital sentencing statute.[1]

[In accordance with the trial judge's instructions, the jury found two aggravating circumstances: (1) that the murder was committed by a person with a prior record of conviction for a capital felony, or committed by a person with a substantial history of serious assaultive criminal convictions; and (2) that the murder was committed by a person who had escaped from the custody of a police officer or place of confinement. The jury made no finding as to whether the murder was committed in an outrageously or wantonly vile, horrible or inhuman manner.] It should be noted that the jury's finding ... encompassed both alternatives identified in the judge's instructions and in subsection (b)(1) of the statute—that respondent had a prior conviction of a capital felony and that he had a substantial history of serious assaultive convictions. These two alternatives and the finding that the murder was committed by an escapee are described by the parties as the three aggravating circumstances found by the jury, but they may also be viewed as two statutory aggravating circumstances, one of which rested on two grounds.

---

1. Georgia Code §27-2534.1(b) (1978) provided, in part: "In all cases of other offenses for which the death penalty may be authorized, the judge shall consider, or he shall include in his instructions to the jury for it to consider, any mitigating circumstances or aggravating circumstances otherwise authorized by law and any of the following statutory aggravating circumstances which may be supported by the evidence:

"(1) The offense of murder, rape, armed robbery, or kidnapping was committed by a person with a prior record of conviction for a capital felony, or the offense of murder was committed by a person who has a substantial history of serious assaultive criminal convictions....

"(7) The offense of murder, rape, armed robbery, or kidnapping was outrageously or wantonly vile, horrible or inhuman in that it involved torture, depravity of mind, or an aggravated battery to the victim....

"(9) The offense of murder was committed by a person in, or who has escaped from, the lawful custody of a peace officer or place of lawful confinement."

... While [respondent's] appeal was pending, however, the Georgia Supreme Court held in *Arnold v. State*, 236 Ga. 534, 224 S.E.2d 386 (1976), that the aggravating circumstance described in the second clause of (b)(1)—"a substantial history of serious assaultive criminal convictions"—was unconstitutionally vague. Because such a finding had been made by the jury in this case, the Georgia Supreme Court, on its own motion, considered whether it impaired respondent's death sentence. It concluded that the two other aggravating circumstances adequately supported the sentence....

... [The Fifth Circuit Court of Appeals] held, however, that the death penalty was invalid because one of the aggravating circumstances found by the jury was later held unconstitutional.

The Court of Appeals ... read *Stromberg v. California*, 283 U.S. 359 (1931), as requiring that a jury verdict based on multiple grounds must be set aside if the reviewing court cannot ascertain whether the jury relied on an unconstitutional ground....

We granted [the State's] petition for certiorari. The briefs on the merits revealed that different state appellate courts have reached varying conclusions concerning the significance of the invalidation of one of multiple aggravating circumstances considered by a jury in a capital case.

... [W]e must confront three separate issues in order to decide this case. First, does the limited purpose served by the finding of a statutory aggravating circumstance in Georgia allow the jury a measure of discretion that is forbidden by *Furman* and subsequent cases? Second, has the rule of *Stromberg* been violated? Third, in this case, even though respondent's prior criminal record was properly admitted, does the possibility that the reference to the invalid statutory aggravating circumstance in the judge's instruction affected the jury's deliberations require that the death sentence be set aside? We discuss these issues in turn.

I

In Georgia, unlike some other States, the jury is not instructed to give any special weight to any aggravating circumstance, to consider multiple aggravating circumstances any more significant than a single such circumstance, or to balance aggravating against mitigating circumstances pursuant to any special standard. Thus, in Georgia, the finding of an aggravating circumstance does not play any role in guiding the sentencing body in the exercise of its discretion, apart from its function of narrowing the class of persons convicted of murder who are eligible for the death penalty. For this reason, respondent argues that Georgia's statutory scheme is invalid under the holding in *Furman*....

The Georgia scheme provides for categorical narrowing at the definition stage, and for individualized determination and appellate review at the selection stage. We therefore remain convinced, as we were in 1976 [when the Court decided *Gregg v. Georgia*], that the structure of the statute is constitutional. Moreover, the narrowing function has been properly achieved in this case by the two valid aggravating circumstances upheld by the Georgia Supreme Court—that respondent had escaped from lawful confinement, and that he had a prior record of conviction for a capital felony. These two findings adequately differentiate this case in an objective, evenhanded, and substantively rational way from the many Georgia murder cases in which the death penalty may not be imposed. Moreover, the Georgia Supreme Court in this case reviewed the death sentence to determine whether it was arbitrary, excessive, or disproportionate. Thus the absence of legislative or court-imposed standards to govern the jury in weighing the significance of either or both of those aggravating circumstances does not render the Georgia capital sentencing statute invalid as applied in this case.

II

Respondent contends that under the rule of *Stromberg v. California* and subsequent cases, the invalidity of one of the statutory aggravating circumstances underlying the jury's sentencing verdict requires that its entire death sentence be set aside. In order to evaluate this contention, it is necessary to identify two related but different rules that have their source in the *Stromberg* case....

One rule derived from the *Stromberg* case requires that a general verdict must be set aside if the jury was instructed that it could rely on any of two or more independent grounds, and one of those grounds is insufficient, because the verdict may have rested exclusively on the insufficient ground. The cases in which this rule has been applied all involved general verdicts based on a record that left the reviewing court uncertain as to the actual ground on which the jury's decision rested. This rule does not require that respondent's death sentence be vacated, because the jury did not merely return a general verdict stating that it had found at least one aggravating circumstance. The jury expressly found aggravating circumstances that were valid and legally sufficient to support the death penalty.

The second rule derived from the *Stromberg* case is illustrated by *Thomas v. Collins*, 323 U.S. 516 (1945), and *Street v. New York*, 394 U.S. 576 (1969). In those cases we made clear that the reasoning of *Stromberg* encompasses a situation in which the general verdict on a single-count indictment or information rested on both a constitutional and an unconstitutional ground....

The rationale of *Thomas* and *Street* applies to cases in which there is no uncertainty about the multiple grounds on which a general verdict rests. If, under the instructions to the jury, one way of committing the offense charged is to perform an act protected by the Constitution, the rule of these cases requires that a general verdict of guilt be set aside even if the defendant's unprotected conduct, considered separately, would support the verdict. It is a difficult theoretical question whether the rule of *Thomas* and *Street* applies to the Georgia death penalty scheme. The jury's imposition of the death sentence after finding more than one aggravating circumstance is not precisely the same as the jury's verdict of guilty on a single-count indictment after finding that the defendant has engaged in more than one type of conduct encompassed by the same criminal charge, because a wider range of considerations enters into the former determination. On the other hand, it is also not precisely the same as the imposition of a single sentence of imprisonment after guilty verdicts on each of several separate counts in a multiple-count indictment, because the qualitatively different sentence of death is imposed only after a channeled sentencing procedure. We need not answer this question here. The second rule derived from *Stromberg*, embodied in *Thomas* and *Street*, applies only in cases in which the State has based its prosecution, at least in part, on a charge that constitutionally protected activity is unlawful. No such charge was made in respondent's sentencing proceeding.

In *Stromberg*, *Thomas*, and *Street*, the trial courts' judgments rested, in part, on the fact that the defendant had been found guilty of expressive activity protected by the First Amendment. In contrast, in this case there is no suggestion that any of the aggravating circumstances involved any conduct protected by the First Amendment or by any other provision of the Constitution. Accordingly, even if the *Stromberg* rules may sometimes apply in the sentencing context, a death sentence supported by at least one valid aggravating circumstance need not be set aside under the second *Stromberg* rule simply because another aggravating circumstance is "invalid" in the sense that it is insufficient by itself to support the death penalty. In this case, the jury's finding that respondent was a person who has a "substantial history of serious assaultive criminal convictions" did not provide a sufficient basis for imposing the death sentence. But it raised none of the concerns underlying the holdings in *Stromberg, Thomas,* and *Street,* for it did not treat constitutionally protected conduct as an aggravating circumstance.

III

Two themes have been reiterated in our opinions discussing the procedures required by the Constitution in capital sentencing determinations. On the one hand, as the general comments in the *Gregg* plurality opinion indicated, there can be "no perfect procedure for deciding in which cases governmental authority should be used to impose death." On the other hand, because there is a qualitative difference between death and any other permissible form of punishment, "there is a corresponding difference in the need for reliability in the determination that death is the appropriate punishment in a specific case." "It is of vital importance to the defendant and to the community that any decision to impose the death sentence be, and appear to be, based on reason rather than caprice or emotion." Thus, although not every imperfection in the deliberative process is sufficient, even in a capital case, to set aside a state court judgment, the severity of the sentence mandates careful scrutiny in the review of any colorable claim of error.

Respondent contends that the death sentence was impaired because the judge instructed the jury with regard to an invalid statutory aggravating circumstance, a "substantial history of serious assaultive criminal convictions," for these instructions may have affected the jury's deliberations. In analyzing this contention it is essential to keep in mind the sense in which that aggravating circumstance is "invalid." It is not invalid because it authorizes a jury to draw adverse inferences from conduct that is constitutionally protected. Georgia has not, for example, sought to characterize the display of a red flag, the expression of unpopular political views, or the request for trial by jury, as an aggravating circumstance. Nor has Georgia attached the "aggravating" label to factors that are constitutionally impermissible or totally irrelevant to the sentencing process, such as for example the race, religion, or political affiliation of the defendant, or to conduct that actually should militate in favor of a lesser penalty, such as perhaps the defendant's mental illness. If the aggravating circumstance at issue in this case had been invalid for reasons such as these, due process of law would require that the jury's decision to impose death be set aside.

But the invalid aggravating circumstance found by the jury in this case was struck down in *Arnold* because the Georgia Supreme Court concluded that it fails to provide an adequate basis for distinguishing a murder case in which the death penalty may be imposed from those cases in which such a penalty may not be imposed. The underlying evidence is nevertheless fully admissible at the sentencing phase. As we noted in *Gregg,* the Georgia statute provides that, at the sentencing hearing, the judge or jury

> shall hear additional evidence in extenuation, mitigation, and aggravation of punishment, *including the record of any prior criminal convictions and pleas of guilty or pleas of nolo contendere of the defendant,* or the absence of any prior conviction and pleas: Provided, however, that only such evidence in aggrava-

tion as the State has made known to the defendant prior to his trial shall be admissible.

... [T]he [Fifth Circuit] Court of Appeals ... expressed the concern that the trial court's instructions "may have unduly directed the jury's attention to his prior conviction." But, assuming that the instruction did induce the jury to place greater emphasis upon the respondent's prior criminal record than it would otherwise have done, the question remains whether that emphasis violated any constitutional right. In answering this question, it is appropriate to compare the instruction that was actually given with an instruction on the same subject that would have been unobjectionable. Nothing in the United States Constitution prohibits a trial judge from instructing a jury that it would be appropriate to take account of a defendant's prior criminal record in making its sentencing determination, even though the defendant's prior history of noncapital convictions could not by itself provide sufficient justification for imposing the death sentence. There would have been no constitutional infirmity in an instruction stating, in substance: "If you find beyond a reasonable doubt that the defendant is a person who has previously been convicted of a capital felony, or that he has escaped from lawful confinement, you will be authorized to impose the death sentence, and in deciding whether or not that sentence is appropriate you may consider the remainder of his prior criminal record." ...

Our decision [to uphold respondent's sentence of death] in this case depends in part on the existence of an important procedural safeguard, the mandatory appellate review of each death sentence by the Georgia Supreme Court to avoid arbitrariness and to assure proportionality. We accept that court's view that the subsequent invalidation of one of several statutory aggravating circumstances does not automatically require reversal of the death penalty, having been assured that a death sentence will be set aside if the invalidation of an aggravating circumstance makes the penalty arbitrary or capricious. The Georgia Supreme Court, in its response to our certified question, expressly stated, "A different result might be reached in a case where evidence was submitted in support of a statutory aggravating circumstance which was not otherwise admissible, and thereafter the circumstance failed." As we noted in *Gregg*, we have also been assured that a death sentence will be vacated if it is excessive or substantially disproportionate to the penalties that have been imposed under similar circumstances.

Finally, we note that in deciding this case we do not express any opinion concerning the possible significance of a holding that a particular aggravating circumstance is "invalid" under a statutory scheme in which the judge or jury is specifically instructed to weigh statutory aggravating and mitigating circumstances in exercising its discretion whether to impose the death penalty. As we have discussed, the Constitution does not require a State to adopt specific standards for instructing the jury in its consideration of aggravating and mitigating circumstances, and Georgia has not adopted such a system. Under Georgia's sentencing scheme, and under the trial judge's instructions in this case, no suggestion is made that the presence of more than one aggravating circumstance should be given special weight. Whether or not the jury had concluded that respondent's prior record of criminal convictions merited the label "substantial" or the label "assaultive," the jury was plainly entitled to consider that record, together with all of the other evidence before it, in making its sentencing determination.

The judgment of the Court of Appeals is reversed.

Justice MARSHALL, with whom Justice Brennan joins, dissenting.

II

B

... More than a decade ago this Court struck down an Ohio statute that permitted a death sentence only if the jury found that the victim of the murder was a police officer, but gave the jury unbridled discretion once that aggravating factor was found. *Duling v. Ohio*, 408 U.S. 936 (1972). There is no difference of any consequence between the Ohio scheme held impermissible in *Duling* and the "threshold" scheme that the Court endorses today. If, as *Duling* establishes, the Constitution prohibits a State from defining a crime (such as murder of a police officer) and then leaving the decision whether to impose the death sentence to the unchecked discretion of the jury, it must also prohibit a State from defining a lesser crime (such as murder) and then permitting the jury to make a standardless sentencing decision once it has found a single aggravating factor (such as that the victim was a police officer). In both cases the ultimate decision whether the defendant will be killed is left to the discretion of the sentencer, unguided by any legislative standards. Whether a particular preliminary finding was made at the guilt phase of the trial or at the sentencing phase is irrelevant; a requirement that the finding be made at the sentencing phase in no way channels the sentencer's discretion once that finding has been made.[5] If the Constitution forbids one form of standardless discretion, it must forbid the other as well....

III

B

... There is simply no way for this Court to know whether the jury would have sentenced respondent to death if the unconstitutional statutory aggravating circumstance had not been included in the judge's charge. If it is important for the State to authorize and for the prosecution to request the submission of a particular statutory aggravating circumstance to the jury, "we must assume that in some cases [that circumstance] will be decisive in the [jury's] choice between a life sentence and a death sentence."

As Justice Stewart pointed out in a similar case, "under Georgia's capital punishment scheme, only the trial judge or jury can know and determine what to do when upon appellate review it has been concluded that a particular aggravating circumstance should not have been considered in sentencing the defendant to death." *Drake v. Zant*, 449 U.S. 999, 1001 (1980) (dissenting from denial of certiorari). Although the Court labors mightily in an effort to demonstrate that submission of the unconstitutional statutory aggravating circumstance did not affect the jury's verdict, there is no escape from the

---

5. This Court has repeatedly recognized that a capital sentencing statute does not satisfy the Constitution simply because it requires a bifurcated trial and permits presentation at the penalty phase of evidence concerning the circumstances of the crime, the defendant's background and history, and other factors in aggravation and mitigation of punishment. Although the creation of a separate sentencing proceeding permits the exclusion from the guilt phase of information that is relevant only to sentencing and that might prejudice the determination of guilt, merely bifurcating the trial obviously does nothing to guide the discretion of the sentencer.

Nor is mandatory appellate review a substitute for legislatively defined criteria to guide the jury in imposing sentence. Although appellate review may serve to reduce arbitrariness and caprice "[w]here the sentencing authority is required to specify the factors it relied upon in reaching its decision," appellate review cannot serve this function where statutory aggravating circumstances play only a threshold role and an appellate court therefore has no means of ascertaining the factors underlying the jury's ultimate sentencing decision.

conclusion—reached by Justice Powell only last Term—that respondent was sentenced to death "under instructions that could have misled the jury." Where a man's life is at stake, this inconvenient fact should not be simply swept under the rug....

2. Reweighing on Appeal

In weighing states, aggravating circumstances play a specific role in determining the defendant's sentence: the aggravating circumstances must be specifically weighed and balanced against the mitigating circumstances. The effect this role has on appellate review of the capital defendant's death sentence is discussed in the cases below.

Clemons v. Mississippi
494 U.S. 738 (1990)

Justice WHITE delivered the opinion of the Court.

The Mississippi Supreme Court upheld the death sentence imposed on Chandler Clemons even though the jury instruction regarding one of the aggravating factors pressed by the State, that the murder was "especially heinous, atrocious, or cruel," was constitutionally invalid in light of our decision in *Maynard v. Cartwright*, 486 U.S. 356 (1988). Although we hold that the Federal Constitution does not prevent a state appellate court from upholding a death sentence that is based in part on an invalid or improperly defined aggravating circumstance either by reweighing of the aggravating and mitigating evidence or by harmless error review, we vacate the judgment below and remand, because it is unclear whether the Mississippi Supreme Court correctly employed either of these methods....

II

We deal first with petitioner's submission that it is constitutionally impermissible for an appellate court to uphold a death sentence imposed by a jury that has relied in part on an invalid aggravating circumstance. In *Zant v. Stephens*, 462 U.S. 862 (1983), we determined that in a State like Georgia, where aggravating circumstances serve only to make a defendant eligible for the death penalty and not to determine the punishment, the invalidation of one aggravating circumstance does not necessarily require an appellate court to vacate a death sentence and remand to a jury. We withheld opinion, however, "concerning the possible significance of a holding that a particular aggravating circumstance is 'invalid' under a statutory scheme in which the judge or jury is specifically instructed to weigh statutory aggravating and mitigating circumstances in exercising its discretion whether to impose the death penalty."

In Mississippi, unlike the Georgia scheme considered in *Zant*, the finding of aggravating factors is part of the jury's sentencing determination, and the jury is required to weigh any mitigating factors against the aggravating circumstances. Although these differences complicate the questions raised, we do not believe that they dictate reversal in this case.

A

Nothing in the Sixth Amendment as construed by our prior decisions indicates that a defendant's right to a jury trial would be infringed where an appellate court invalidates one of two or more aggravating circumstances found by the jury but affirms the death sentence after itself finding that the one or more valid remaining aggravating factors outweigh the mitigating evidence. Any argument that the Constitution requires that a jury impose the sentence of death or make the findings prerequisite to imposition of such a sentence has been soundly rejected by prior decisions of this Court.... [N]either the Sixth Amendment, the Eighth Amendment, nor any other constitutional provision provides a defendant with the right to have a jury determine the appropriateness of a capital sentence; neither is there a Double Jeopardy prohibition on a judge's override of a jury's recommended sentence. Likewise, the Sixth Amendment does not require that a jury specify the aggravating factors that permit the imposition of capital punishment, nor does it require jury sentencing, even where the sentence turns on specific findings of fact....

C

Clemons also submits that appellate courts are unable to fully consider and give effect to the mitigating evidence presented by defendants at the sentencing phase in a capital case and that it therefore violates the Eighth Amendment for an appellate court to undertake to reweigh aggravating and mitigating circumstances in an attempt to salvage the death sentence imposed by a jury. He insists, therefore, that he is entitled to a new sentencing hearing before a jury and that the decision below must be reversed. We are unpersuaded, however, that our cases require this result. Indeed, they point in the opposite direction.

The primary concern in the Eighth Amendment context has been that the sentencing decision be based on the facts and circumstances of the defendant, his background, and his crime. In scrutinizing death penalty procedures under the Eighth Amendment, the Court has emphasized the "twin objectives" of "measured consistent application and fairness to the accused." Nothing inherent in the process of appellate reweighing is inconsistent with the pursuit of the foregoing objectives. We see no reason to believe that careful appellate weighing of aggravating against mitigating circumstances in cases such as this would not produce "measured consistent application" of the death penalty or in any way be unfair to the defendant. It is a routine task of appellate courts to decide whether the evidence supports a jury verdict and in capital cases in "weighing" States, to consider whether the evidence is such that the sentencer could have arrived at the death sentence that was imposed. And, as the opinion below indicates, a similar process of weighing aggravating and mitigating evidence is involved in an appellate court's proportionality review. Furthermore, this Court has repeatedly emphasized that meaningful appellate review of death sentences promotes reliability and consistency. It is also important to note that state supreme courts in States authorizing the death penalty may well review many death sentences and that typical jurors, in contrast, will serve on only one such case during their lifetimes. Therefore, we conclude that state appellate courts can and do give each defendant an individualized and reliable sentencing determination based on the defendant's circumstances, his background, and the crime....

We accordingly see nothing in appellate weighing or reweighing of the aggravating and mitigating circumstances that is at odds with contemporary standards of fairness or that is inherently unreliable and likely to result in arbitrary imposition of the death sentence. Nor are we impressed with the claim that without written jury findings concerning mitigating circumstances, appellate courts cannot perform their proper role.... An appellate court ... is able adequately to evaluate any evidence relating to mitigating factors without the assistance of written jury findings.

III

Clemons argues that even if appellate reweighing is permissible, the Mississippi Supreme Court did not actually reweigh the evidence in this case and instead simply held that when an aggravating circumstance relied on by the jury has been invalidated, the sentence may be affirmed as long as there remains at least one valid and undisturbed aggravating circumstance, an approach that requires no weighing whatsoever. The State on the other hand insists that a proper reweighing of aggravating circumstances was undertaken.

We find the opinion below unclear with respect to whether the Mississippi Supreme Court did perform a weighing function either by disregarding entirely the "especially heinous" factor and weighing only the remaining aggravating circumstance against the mitigating evidence or by including in the balance the "especially heinous" factor as narrowed by its prior decisions and embraced in this case. At one point the court recites the proper limiting construction of the "especially heinous" aggravating factor, and at times the court's opinion seems to indicate that the court was reweighing the mitigating circumstances and both aggravating factors by applying the proper definition to the "especially heinous" factor. For example, at one point the court refers to the "brutal and torturous facts" surrounding Shorter's murder and elsewhere states that "the punishment of death is not too great when the aggravating and mitigating circumstances are weighed against each other." At other times, however, the opinion indicates the court may have been employing the other approach and disregarding the "especially heinous" factor entirely. "[T]his Court (Mississippi) has held and established unequivocally through the years that when one aggravating circumstance is found to be invalid or unsupported by the evidence, a remaining valid aggravating circumstance will nonetheless support the death penalty verdict."

In addition, although the latter statement does not necessarily indicate that no reweighing was undertaken, the court's statement can be read as a rule authorizing or requiring affirmance of a death sentence so long as there remains at least one valid aggravating circumstance. If that is what the Mississippi Supreme Court meant, then it was not conducting appellate reweighing as we understand the concept. An automatic rule of affirmance in a weighing State would be invalid under *Lockett v. Ohio*, 438 U.S. 586 (1978), and *Eddings v. Oklahoma*, 455 U.S. 104 (1982), for it would not give defendants the individualized treatment that would result from actual reweighing of the mix of mitigating factors and aggravating circumstances. Additionally, because the Mississippi Supreme Court's opinion is virtually silent with respect to the particulars of the allegedly mitigating evidence presented by Clemons to the jury, we cannot be sure that the court fully heeded our cases emphasizing the importance of the sentencer's consideration of a defendant's mitigating evidence. We must, therefore, vacate the judgment below, and remand for further proceedings, insofar as the judgment purported to rely on the State Supreme Court's reweighing of aggravating and mitigating circumstances.

IV

Even if under Mississippi law, the weighing of aggravating and mitigating circumstances were not an appellate, but a jury function, it was open to the Mississippi Supreme Court to find that the error which occurred during the sentencing proceeding was harmless. As the plurality in *Barclay v. Florida*, 463 U.S. 939 (1983), opined, the Florida Supreme Court could apply harmless error analysis when reviewing a death sentence imposed by a trial judge who relied on an aggravating circumstance not available for his consideration under Florida law:

> Cases such as [those cited by the petitioner] indicate that the Florida Supreme Court does not apply its harmless-error analysis in an automatic or mechanical fashion, but rather upholds death sentences on the basis of this analysis only when it actually finds that the error is harmless. There is no reason why the Florida Supreme Court cannot examine the balance struck by the trial judge and decide that the elimination of improperly considered aggravating circumstances could not possibly affect the balance.... What is important ... is an *individualized* determination on the basis of the character of the individual and the circumstances of the crime.

Clemons argues, however, that the Mississippi Supreme Court incorrectly applied the harmless error rule, that the court acted arbitrarily in applying it to his case when it refused to do so in a similar case, and that the State failed to prove beyond a reasonable doubt that any error was harmless.

With regard to harmless error, the Mississippi Supreme Court made only the following statement: "We likewise are of the opinion beyond a reasonable doubt that the jury's verdict would have been the same with or without the 'especially heinous, atrocious or cruel' aggravating circumstance." Although the court applied the proper [harmless error] "beyond a reasonable doubt" standard, its cryptic holding suggests that it was beyond reasonable doubt that the sentence would have been the same even if there had been no "especially heinous" instruction at all and only the aggravating circumstance that the murder was committed in the course of a robbery for pecuniary gain was to be balanced against the mitigating circumstances. We agree that it would be permissible to approach the harmless error question in this fashion, but if this is the course the court took, its ultimate conclusion is very difficult to accept. As Clemons points out, the State repeatedly emphasized and argued the "especially heinous" factor during the sentencing hearing. The State placed little emphasis on the "robbery for pecuniary gain" factor. Under these circumstances, it would require a detailed explanation based on the record for us possibly to agree that the error in giving the invalid "especially heinous" instruction was harmless.

It is perhaps possible, however, that the Mississippi Supreme Court intended to ask whether beyond reasonable doubt the result would have been the same had the especially heinous aggravating circumstance been properly defined in the jury instructions; and perhaps on this basis it could have determined that the failure to instruct properly was harmless error. Because we cannot be sure which course was followed in Clemons's case, however, we vacate the judgment insofar as it rested on harmless error and remand for further proceedings.

V

Nothing in this opinion is intended to convey the impression that state appellate courts are required to or necessarily should engage in reweighing or harmless error analysis when errors have occurred in a capital sentencing proceeding. Our holding is only that such procedures are constitutionally permissible. In some situations, a state appellate court may conclude that peculiarities in a case make appellate reweighing or harmless error analysis extremely speculative or impossible. We have previously noted that appellate courts may face certain difficulties in determining sentencing questions in the first instance. See *Caldwell v. Mississippi*, 472 U.S. 320, 330–331 (1985). Nevertheless, that decision is for state appellate courts, including the Mississippi Supreme Court in this case, to make....

VI

For the foregoing reasons the judgment of the Mississippi Supreme Court is vacated, and the case is remanded for further proceedings not inconsistent with this opinion.

Justice BLACKMUN, with whom Justice Brennan, Justice Marshall, and Justice Stevens join, concurring in part and dissenting in part.

II

... I dissent from the majority's gratuitous suggestion that on remand the Mississippi Supreme Court itself may reweigh aggravating and mitigating circumstances and thereby salvage petitioner's death sentence. That portion of the Court's discussion is a pure and simple advisory opinion, something I thought this Court avoided and was disinclined to issue. The majority recognizes, as it must, that the Mississippi Supreme Court has given no clear indication that it intends to reweigh or that under state law it has the power to do so. The Court's determination that reweighing is constitutional has no bearing upon our conclusion, which is to vacate the Mississippi judgment and remand the case for further proceedings in the state courts. Rather than awaiting, and then reviewing, the decisions of other tribunals, the Court today assumes that its role is to offer helpful suggestions to state courts seeking to expedite the capital sentencing process. Of course the Court's discussion of reweighing may have an effect on the form that the state proceedings will take. But the impropriety of an advisory opinion is not eliminated by the possibility that the state court will act upon the advice.

In my view, the majority's discussion of the reweighing issue is sadly flawed. If a jury's verdict rests in part upon a constitutionally impermissible aggravating factor, and the State's appellate court upholds the death sentence based upon its own reweighing of legitimate aggravating and mitigating circumstances, the appellate court, in any real sense, has not approved or affirmed the verdict of the jury. Rather, the reviewing court in that situation has assumed for itself the role of sentencer. The logical implication of the majority's approach is that no trial-level sentencing procedure need be conducted at all. Instead, the record of a capital trial (including a sentencing hearing conducted before a court reporter) might as well be shipped to the appellate court, which then would determine the appropriate sentence in the first instance....

... [But] trial and appellate tribunals respectively perform distinct functions. In explaining the requirement that courts of appeals must defer to district court findings of fact unless these findings are clearly erroneous, [this Court] has noted that "only the trial judge can be aware of the variations in demeanor and tone of voice that bear so heavily on the listener's understanding of and belief in what is said." The Federal Rules, of course, are not of constitutional stature; the States are not required to mimic the federal system in their allocation of responsibilities between trial and appellate courts. But, given the heightened concern for reliability when a sentence of death is imposed, I find inexplicable the majority's willingness in a capital case to countenance the resolution of disputed factual issues by means of a procedure that this Court has deemed insufficiently reliable even for the adjudication of a civil lawsuit....

In part, therefore, the impropriety of appellate sentencing rests on the appellate court's diminished ability to act as a factfinder. But I think there is more to it than that. An appellate court is ill-suited to undertake the task of capital sentencing, not simply because of its general deficiencies as a factfinder, or because the costs of erroneous factfinding are so high, but also because the capital sentencing decision by its very nature is peculiarly likely to turn on considerations that cannot adequately be conveyed through the medium of a written record. In *Caldwell v. Mississippi*, 472 U.S. 320 (1985), this Court emphasized that

> an appellate court, unlike a capital sentencing jury, is wholly ill-suited to evaluate the appropriateness of death in the first instance. Whatever intangibles a jury might consider in its sentencing determination, few can be gleaned from an appellate record. This inability to confront and examine the individuality of the defendant would be particularly devastating to any argument for consideration of what this Court has termed "[those] compassionate or mitigating factors stemming from the diverse frailties of humankind." When we held that a defendant has a constitutional right to the consideration of such factors, we clearly envisioned that that consideration would occur among sentencers who were present to hear the evidence and arguments and see the witnesses.[21]

The petitioner in this case, for example, argued that his remorse for the crime constituted a mitigating factor. It would verge on the surrealistic to suggest that Chandler Clemons' right to present that contention would be adequately protected by an appellate court's consideration of the written transcript of his testimony. More than any other decision known to our law, the decision whether to impose the death penalty involves an assessment of the defendant himself, not simply a determination as to the facts surrounding a particular event. And an adequate assessment of the defendant—a procedure which recognizes the "need for treating each defendant in a capital case with that degree of respect due the uniqueness of the individual,"—surely requires a sentencer who confronts him in the flesh. I therefore conclude that a capital defendant's right to present mitigating evidence cannot be fully realized if that evidence can be submitted only through the medium of a paper record. I also believe that, if a sentence of death is to be imposed, it should be pronounced by a decisionmaker who will look upon the face of the defendant as he renders judgment. The bloodless alternative approved by the majority conveniently may streamline the process of capital sentencing, but at a cost that seems to me to be intolerable....

Notes and Question

1. The petitioner in *Clemons* also argued that the state of Mississippi had created a liberty interest by having a jury make particular findings in capital sentencing proceedings. Petitioner asserted that to allow an appellate court to reweigh his sentence of death would deprive him of his state law liberty interest in violation of the Due Process Clause. The majority rejected this argument, finding that Mississippi courts' interpretation of state law did not support this particular liberty interest.

2. In reweighing the valid aggravating and mitigating circumstances, the appellate court is confined to the "cold record" and does not have the benefit of listening to and observing live witnesses. Justice Blackmun believed that this is a significant problem in reweighing. Do you agree?

3. "Where the death sentence has been infected by a vague or otherwise invalid aggravating factor, the state appellate court or some other state sentencer must actually

---

21. The majority opinion today includes a single, perfunctory reference to *Caldwell v. Mississippi*, citing it for the bland proposition that "appellate courts may face certain difficulties in determining sentencing questions in the first instance." The majority does not attempt to reconcile its decision with *Caldwell's* analysis of the institutional limitations of appellate courts.

perform a new sentencing calculus, if the sentence is to stand." *Richmond v. Lewis*, 506 U.S. 40 (1992). In *Richmond v. Lewis*, the Court reversed the petitioner's sentence of death because the "death sentence was tainted by Eighth Amendment error when the sentencing judge gave weight to an unconstitutionally vague aggravating factor. The Supreme Court of Arizona did not cure this error, because two justices who concurred in affirming the sentence did not actually perform the reweighing calculus." To let the sentences stand where the appellate court failed to properly reweigh would violate the Eighth Amendment.

Parker v. Dugger
498 U.S. 308 (1991)

Justice O'CONNOR delivered the opinion of the Court.

III

... On direct review of Robert Lacy Parker's [death] sentence, the Florida Supreme Court struck two of the aggravating circumstances on which the trial judge had relied. The Supreme Court nonetheless upheld the death sentence because "[t]he trial court found no mitigating circumstances to balance against the aggravating factors." The Florida Supreme Court erred in its characterization of the trial judge's findings, and consequently erred in its review of Parker's sentence.

As noted, Florida is a weighing state; the death penalty may be imposed only where specified aggravating circumstances outweigh all mitigating circumstances. In a weighing state, when a reviewing court strikes one or more of the aggravating factors on which the sentencer relies, the reviewing court may, consistent with the Constitution, reweigh the remaining evidence or conduct a harmless error analysis. *Clemons v. Mississippi*, 494 U.S. 738 (1990). It is unclear what the Florida Supreme Court did here. It certainly did not conduct an independent reweighing of the evidence. In affirming Parker's sentence, the court explicitly relied on what it took to be the trial judge's finding of no mitigating circumstances. Had it conducted an independent review of the evidence, the court would have had no need for such reliance. More to the point, the Florida Supreme Court has made it clear on several occasions that it does not reweigh the evidence of aggravating and mitigating circumstances. See, *e.g.*, *Hudson v. State*, 538 So.2d 829, 831 (*per curiam*), ("It is not within this Court's province to reweigh or reevaluate the evidence presented as to aggravating or mitigating circumstances"); *Brown v. Wainwright*, 392 So.2d 1327, 1331–1332 (1981) (*per curiam*).

The Florida Supreme Court may have conducted a harmless error analysis. At the time it heard Parker's appeal, this was its general practice in cases in which it had struck aggravating circumstances and the trial judge had found no mitigating circumstances. Perhaps the Florida Supreme Court conducted a harmless error analysis here: Believing that the trial judge properly had found four aggravating circumstances, and no mitigating circumstances to weigh against them, the Florida Supreme Court may have determined that elimination of two additional aggravating circumstances would have made no difference to the sentence.

But, as we have explained, the trial judge must have found mitigating circumstances. The Florida Supreme Court's practice in such cases—where the court strikes one or more aggravating circumstances relied on by the trial judge and mitigating circumstances are present—is to remand for a new sentencing hearing. Following *Clemons*, a reviewing court is not compelled to remand. It may instead reweigh the evidence or conduct a harmless error analysis based on what the sentencer actually found. What the Florida Supreme Court could not do, but what it did, was to ignore the evidence of mitigating circumstances in the record and misread the trial judge's findings regarding mitigating circumstances, and affirm the sentence based on a mischaracterization of the trial judge's findings.

In *Wainwright v. Goode*, 464 U.S. 78, 83–85 (1983), the Court held that a federal court on habeas review must give deference to a state appellate court's resolution of an ambiguity in a state trial court statement. We did not decide in *Goode* whether the issue resolved by the state appellate court was properly characterized as one of law or of fact. In this case, we conclude that a determination of what the trial judge found is an issue of historical fact. It depends on an examination of the transcript of the trial and sentencing hearing, and the sentencing order. This is not a legal issue; no determination of the legality of Parker's sentence under Florida law necessarily follows from a resolution of the question of what the trial judge found.

Because it is a factual issue, the deference we owe is that designated by 28 U.S.C. §2254. In ruling on a petition for a writ of habeas corpus, a federal court is not to overturn a factual conclusion of a state court, including a state appellate court, unless the conclusion is not "fairly supported by the record." §2254(d)(8). For the reasons stated, we find that the Florida Supreme Court's conclusion that the trial judge found no mitigating circumstances is not fairly supported by the record in this case.

IV

"If a State has determined that death should be an available penalty for certain crimes, then it must administer that penalty in a way that can rationally distinguish between those individuals for whom death is an appropriate sanction and those for whom it is not." *Spaziano v. Florida*, 468 U.S. 447, 460 (1984). The Constitution prohibits the arbitrary or irrational imposition of the death penalty. We have emphasized repeatedly the crucial role of meaningful appellate review in ensuring that the death penalty is not imposed arbitrarily or irrationally. We have held specifically that the Florida Supreme Court's system of independent review of death sentences minimizes the risk of constitutional error, and have noted the "crucial protection" afforded by such review in jury override cases. The Florida Supreme Court did not conduct an independent review here. In fact, there is a sense in which the court did not review Parker's sentence at all.

It cannot be gainsaid that meaningful appellate review requires that the appellate court consider the defendant's actual record. "What is important ... is an *individualized* determination on the basis of the character of the individual and the circumstances of the crime." *Zant v. Stephens*, 462 U.S. 862, 879 (1983). The Florida Supreme Court affirmed Parker's death sentence neither based on a review of the individual record in this case nor in reliance on the trial judge's findings based on that record, but in reliance on some other nonexistent findings.

The jury found sufficient mitigating circumstances to outweigh the aggravating circumstances, and recommended that Parker be sentenced to life imprisonment for the Sheppard murder. The trial judge found nonstatutory mitigating circumstances related to the Sheppard murder. The judge also declined to override the jury's recommendation as to the Padgett murder, even though he found five statutory aggravating circumstances and no statutory mitigating circumstances related to that crime. The Florida Supreme Court then struck two of the aggravating circumstances on which the trial judge had relied. On these facts, the Florida Supreme Court's affirmance of Parker's death sentence based on four aggravating circumstances and the trial judge's "finding" of no mitigating circumstances was arbitrary.

This is not simply an error in assessing the mitigating evidence. Had the Florida Supreme Court conducted its own examination of the trial and sentencing hearing records and concluded that there were no mitigating circumstances, a different question would be presented. Similarly, if the trial judge had found no mitigating circumstances and the Florida Supreme Court had relied on that finding, our review would be very different. But the Florida Supreme Court did not come to its own independent factual conclusion, and it did not rely on what the trial judge actually found; it relied on "findings" of the trial judge that bear no necessary relation to this case. After striking two aggravating circumstances, the Florida Supreme Court affirmed Parker's death sentence without considering the mitigating circumstances. This affirmance was invalid because it deprived Parker of the individualized treatment to which he is entitled under the Constitution.

V

We reverse the judgment of the Court of Appeals and remand with instructions to return the case to the District Court to enter an order directing the State of Florida to initiate appropriate proceedings in state court so that Parker's death sentence may be reconsidered in light of the entire record of his trial and sentencing hearing and the trial judge's findings. The District Court shall give the State a reasonable period of time to initiate such proceedings. We express no opinion as to whether the Florida courts must order a new sentencing hearing....

3. Assessing the Effect of Invalid Aggravators

In a 5–4 decision upholding a California death sentence, the Supreme Court effected a major change in the Court's death penalty jurisprudence by abandoning the distinction between "weighing" and "non-weighing" states when determining whether a jury's consideration of an improper aggravating circumstance invalidates a death sentence. According to the new, simplified approach, when a capital sentencing jury has imposed a death sentence based in part on an aggravating factor that is later declared invalid, the sentence may nevertheless be constitutional if some other, valid sentencing factor allowed the sentencing judge or jury to give aggravating weight to the same facts and circumstances.

Brown v. Sanders
126 S.Ct. 884 (2006)

Justice SCALIA delivered the opinion of the Court.

We consider the circumstances in which an invalidated sentencing factor will render a death sentence unconstitutional by reason of its adding an improper element to the aggravation scale in the jury's weighing process.

I

Respondent Ronald Sanders and a companion invaded the home of Dale Boender, where they bound and blindfolded him and his girlfriend, Janice Allen. Both of the victims were then struck on the head with a heavy, blunt object; Allen died from the blow. Sanders was convicted of first-degree murder, of attempt to murder Boender, and of robbery, burglary, and attempted robbery.

Sanders' jury found four "special circumstances" under California law, each of which independently rendered him eligible for the death penalty. See Cal.Penal Code Ann. § 190.2 (West Supp.1995). The trial then moved to a penalty phase, at which the jury was instructed to consider a list of sentencing factors relating to Sanders' background and the nature of the crime, one of which was "[t]he circumstances of the crime of which the defendant was convicted in the present proceeding and the existence of any special circumstances found to be true." The jury sentenced Sanders to death.

On direct appeal, the California Supreme Court declared invalid two of the four special circumstances found by the jury. It nonetheless affirmed Sanders' death sentence, relying on our decision in *Zant v. Stephens,* 462 U.S. 862 (1983), which, it said, "upheld a death penalty judgment despite invalidation of one of several aggravating factors." It affirmed the conviction and sentence in all other respects. We denied certiorari.

Sanders then filed a petition for a writ of habeas corpus pursuant to 28 U.S.C. § 2254 in the United States District Court for the Eastern District of California, arguing, as relevant here, that the jury's consideration of invalid special circumstances rendered his death sentence unconstitutional. After Sanders exhausted various state remedies, the District Court denied relief.

The Court of Appeals for the Ninth Circuit reversed. *Sanders v. Woodford,* 373 F.3d 1054 (2004). It concluded that "the California court erroneously believed that it could apply the rule of *Zant v. Stephens,* 462 U.S. 862 (1983)—which is applicable only to non-weighing states—and uphold the verdict despite the invalidation of two special circumstances because it was upholding other special circumstances." Finding California to be a weighing State, and applying the rules we have announced for such States, the Ninth Circuit concluded that California courts could uphold Sanders' death sentence only by finding the jury's use of the invalid special circumstances to have been harmless beyond a reasonable doubt or by independently reweighing the sentencing factors under § 190.3. Since, it continued, the state courts had done neither, Sanders had been unconstitutionally deprived of an "individualized death sentence." We granted certiorari.

II

Since *Furman v. Georgia,* 408 U.S. 238 (1972) *(per curiam),* we have required States to limit the class of murderers to which the death penalty may be applied. This narrowing requirement is usually met when the trier of fact finds at least one statutorily defined eligibility factor at either the guilt or penalty phase. See *Tuilaepa v. California,* 512 U.S. 967, 971–972 (1994).[2] Once the narrowing requirement has been satisfied, the sentencer is called upon to determine whether a defendant thus found eligible for the death penalty should in fact receive it. Most States channel this function by specifying the ag-

---

2. Our cases have frequently employed the terms "aggravating circumstance" or "aggravating factor" to refer to those statutory factors which determine death eligibility in satisfaction of *Furman's* narrowing requirement. See, *e.g., Tuilaepa v. California,* 512 U.S., at 972. This terminology becomes confusing when, as in this case, a State employs the term "aggravating circumstance" to refer to factors that play a different role, determining which defendants *eligible* for the death penalty will actually *receive* that penalty. To avoid confusion, this opinion will use the term "eligibility factor" to describe a factor that performs the constitutional narrowing function.

gravating factors (sometimes identical to the eligibility factors) that are to be weighed against mitigating considerations. The issue in the line of cases we confront here is what happens when the sentencer imposes the death penalty after at least one valid eligibility factor has been found, but under a scheme in which an eligibility factor or a specified aggravating factor is later held to be invalid.

To answer that question, our jurisprudence has distinguished between so-called weighing and non-weighing States. The terminology is somewhat misleading, since we have held that in *all* capital cases the sentencer must be allowed to weigh the facts and circumstances that arguably justify a death sentence against the defendant's mitigating evidence. See, *e.g., Eddings v. Oklahoma,* 455 U.S. 104, 110 (1982). The terminology was adopted, moreover, relatively early in the development of our death-penalty jurisprudence, when we were perhaps unaware of the great variety of forms that state capital-sentencing legislation would ultimately take. We identified as "weighing State[s]" those in which the only aggravating factors permitted to be considered by the sentencer were the specified eligibility factors. Since the eligibility factors by definition identified distinct and particular aggravating features, if one of them was invalid the jury could not consider the facts and circumstances relevant to that factor as aggravating in some other capacity—for example, as relevant to an omnibus "circumstances of the crime" sentencing factor such as the one in the present case. In a weighing State, therefore, the sentencer's consideration of an invalid eligibility factor necessarily skewed its balancing of aggravators with mitigators, *Stringer,* 503 U.S., at 232, and required reversal of the sentence (unless a state appellate court determined the error was harmless or reweighed the mitigating evidence against the valid aggravating factors).

By contrast, in a non-weighing State—a State that permitted the sentencer to consider aggravating factors different from, or in addition to, the eligibility factors—this automatic skewing would not necessarily occur. It would never occur if the aggravating factors were entirely different from the eligibility factors. Nor would it occur if the aggravating factors *added* to the eligibility factors a category (such as an omnibus "circumstances of the crime" factor, which is quite common) that would allow the very facts and circumstances relevant to the invalidated eligibility factor to be weighed in aggravation under a different rubric. We therefore set forth different rules governing the consequences of an invalidated eligibility factor in a non-weighing State. The sentencer's consideration of an invalid eligibility factor amounts to constitutional error in a non-weighing State in two situations. First, due process requires a defendant's death sentence to be set aside if the reason for the invalidity of the eligibility factor is that it "authorizes a jury to draw adverse inferences from conduct that is constitutionally protected," or that it "attache[s] the 'aggravating' label to factors that are constitutionally impermissible or totally irrelevant to the sentencing process, ... or to conduct that actually should militate in favor of a lesser penalty." *Zant,* 462 U.S., at 885. Second, the death sentence must be set aside if the jury's consideration of the invalidated eligibility factor allowed it to hear evidence that would not otherwise have been before it. See *Tuggle v. Netherland,* 516 U.S. 10, 13–14 (1995) (*per curiam*).

This weighing/non-weighing scheme is accurate as far as it goes, but it now seems to us needlessly complex and incapable of providing for the full range of possible variations. For example, the same problem that gave rise to our weighing-State jurisprudence would arise if it were a sentencing factor, and *not* an eligibility factor, that was later found to be invalid. The weighing process would just as clearly have been prima facie "skewed," and skewed for the same basic reason: The sentencer might have given weight to a statutorily or constitutionally invalid aggravator. And the prima facie skewing could in appropriate cases be shown to be illusory for the same reason that separates weighing States from non-weighing States: One of the *other* aggravating factors, usually an omnibus factor but conceivably another one, made it entirely proper for the jury to consider as aggravating the facts and circumstances underlying the invalidated factor.

We think it will clarify the analysis, and simplify the sentence-invalidating factors we have hitherto applied to non-weighing States, if we are henceforth guided by the following rule: An invalidated sentencing factor (whether an eligibility factor or not) will render the sentence unconstitutional by reason of its adding an improper element to the aggravation scale in the weighing process[6] *unless* one of the other sentencing factors enables the sentencer to give aggravating weight to the same facts and circumstances.

This test is not, as Justice Breyer describes it, "an inquiry based solely on the admissibility of the underlying evidence." If the presence of the invalid sentencing factor allowed the sentencer to consider evidence that would not otherwise have been before it, due process would mandate reversal without regard to the rule we apply here. The issue we confront is the skewing that could result from the jury's considering *as aggravation* properly admitted evidence that should not have weighed in favor of the death penalty. See, *e.g., Stringer,* 503 U.S., at 232 ("[W]hen the sentencing body is told to weigh an invalid factor in its decision, a reviewing court may not assume it would have made no difference if the thumb had been removed from death's side of the scale."). As we have explained, such skewing will occur, and give rise to constitutional error, only where the jury could not have given aggravating weight to the same facts and circumstances under the rubric of some other, valid sentencing factor.

III

In California, a defendant convicted of first-degree murder is eligible for the death penalty if the jury finds one of the "special circumstances" listed in Cal.Penal Code Ann. § 190.2 (West Supp.2005) to be true. These are the eligibility factors designed to satisfy *Furman.* If the jury finds the existence of one of the special circumstances, it is instructed to "take into account" a *separate* list of sentencing factors describing aspects of the defendant and the crime. These sentencing factors include, as we have said, "[t]he circumstances of the crime of which the defendant was convicted in the present proceeding."

The Court of Appeals held that California is a weighing State because " 'the sentencer [is] restricted to a "weighing" of aggravation against mitigation' and 'the sentencer [is] prevented from considering evidence in aggravation other than discrete, statutorily-defined factors.' " The last statement is inaccurate. The "circumstances of the crime" factor can hardly be called "discrete." It has the effect of rendering all the specified factors nonexclusive, thus causing California to be (in our prior terminology) a non-weighing State. Contrary to Sanders' contention, and Justice Stevens' views in dissent, the mere fact that the sentencing factors included "the existence of any special circumstances [eligibility factors] found to be true," did not make California a weighing State. That fact was redundant for purposes of our weighing jurisprudence because it in no way narrowed the universe of aggravating facts the jury was entitled to consider in determining

---

6. There may be other distortions caused by the invalidated factor beyond the mere addition of an improper aggravating element. For example, what the jury was instructed to consider as an aggravating factor might have "actually ... militate[d] in favor of a lesser penalty," Zant, at 885.

a sentence. But leaving aside the weighing/non-weighing dichotomy and proceeding to the more direct analysis set forth earlier in this opinion: All of the aggravating facts and circumstances that the invalidated factor permitted the jury to consider were also open to their proper consideration under one of the other factors. The erroneous factor could not have "skewed" the sentence, and no constitutional violation occurred.

More specifically, Sanders' jury found four special circumstances to be true: that "[t]he murder was committed while the defendant was engaged in ... Robbery," § 190.2(a)(17)(A) (West Supp.2005); that it was "committed while the defendant was engaged in ... Burglary in the first or second degree," § 190.2(a)(17)(G); that "[t]he victim [Allen] was a witness to a crime who was intentionally killed for the purpose of preventing ... her testimony in any criminal ... proceeding," § 190.2(a)(10); and that "[t]he murder was especially heinous, atrocious, or cruel," § 190.2(a)(14). The California Supreme Court set aside the burglary-murder special circumstance under state merger law because the instructions permitted the jury to find a burglary (and thus the burglary-murder special circumstance) based on Sanders' intent to commit assault, which is already an element of homicide. The court invalidated the "heinous, atrocious, or cruel" special circumstance because it had previously found that to be unconstitutionally vague.

As the California Supreme Court noted, however, "the jury properly considered two special circumstances [eligibility factors] (robbery-murder and witness-killing)." These are sufficient to satisfy *Furman's* narrowing requirement, and alone rendered Sanders eligible for the death penalty. Moreover, the jury's consideration of the invalid eligibility factors in the weighing process did not produce constitutional error because all of the facts and circumstances admissible to establish the "heinous, atrocious, or cruel" and burglary-murder eligibility factors were also properly adduced as aggravating facts bearing upon the "circumstances of the crime" sentencing factor. They were properly considered whether or not they bore upon the invalidated eligibility factors.

Sanders argues that the weighing process was skewed by the fact that the jury was asked to consider, as one of the sentencing factors, "the existence of any special circumstances [eligibility factors] found to be true." In Sanders' view, that placed special emphasis upon those facts and circumstances relevant to the invalid eligibility factor. Virtually the same thing happened in *Zant*. There the Georgia jury was permitted to "'conside[r] all evidence in extenuation, mitigation and aggravation of punishment,'" but also instructed specifically that it could consider "'any of [the] statutory aggravating circumstances which you find are supported by the evidence,'" This instruction gave the facts underlying the eligibility factors special prominence. Yet, even though one of the three factors (that the defendant had "substantial history of serious assaultive convictions,"was later invalidated, we upheld the sentence. We acknowledged that the erroneous instruction "might have caused the jury to give somewhat greater weight to respondent's prior criminal record than it otherwise would have given;" indeed, we *assumed* such an effect. But the effect was "merely a consequence of the statutory label 'aggravating circumstanc[e].'" We agreed with the Georgia Supreme Court that any such impact was "'inconsequential,'" and held that it "cannot fairly be regarded as a constitutional defect in the sentencing process." The same is true here....

Because the jury's consideration of the invalid "special circumstances" gave rise to no constitutional violation, the Court of Appeals erred in ordering habeas relief. The judgment of the Court of Appeals is reversed, and the case is remanded for further proceedings consistent with this opinion.

Chapter 9

The Sentencing Phase of Capital Cases

A. Introduction

Capital sentencing laws vary from state to state. After a capital defendant is found guilty, a separate proceeding is typically conducted to determine which penalty—life, life without parole, or death—is appropriate. Regardless of whether the defendant pled guilty, was tried by a judge, or was tried by a jury during the guilt phase, most states permit the defendant to choose whether the judge or jury will determine the penalty. If the defendant elects to have a jury determine the penalty, the same jury which found the defendant guilty will usually decide his punishment.

The sentencing phase greatly resembles a trial. The prosecutor and defense counsel are permitted to make opening statements, call witnesses and introduce exhibits into evidence. Closing arguments are presented and the jury, if any, is instructed as to the law. During penalty deliberations, the factfinder usually weighs aggravating circumstances against mitigating circumstances. Generally, if aggravating circumstances outweigh mitigating circumstances, death is imposed.

The extent to which the Eighth Amendment regulates capital sentencing proceedings has been vigorously debated. One view, espoused by Justice Scalia in *Walton v. Arizona*, 497 U.S. 639 (1990) (Scalia, J. concurring) (*supra* chapter 3), and derived primarily from the opinions of Justices Stewart and White in *Furman v. Georgia*, 408 U.S. 238 (1972), is that the Eighth Amendment merely protects against arbitrariness in capital sentencing. Under this view, the Eighth Amendment is satisfied as long as the sentencer's discretion to choose between life and death is narrowed by sentencing guidelines.

Others have argued that the Eighth Amendment imposes substantive limitations on a sentencer's ability to decree death. For example, Professor Scott Howe has proposed that states create systems to implement a desert-oriented system of capital punishment. Howe, "Resolving the Conflict in the Capital Sentencing Cases: A Desert-Oriented Theory of Regulation," 26 Ga. L. Rev. 323 (1992). Professor Howe's proposal recognizes that a majority of the Court has declared that the defendant's "culpability" is the appropriate focus of the capital sentencing hearing. Thus, an individual's blameworthiness or personal responsibility for the capital crime must be evaluated. In addition, however, Professor Howe has argued that the Eighth Amendment requires an assessment of an offender's "general deserts" or "moral merit." The sentencer should evaluate the offender's deserts based on all of his life works.

To assess culpability, Professor Howe suggests posing to the sentencer the following question:

Considering the defendant's moral responsibility for the murder itself, is the appropriate sentence one of life imprisonment or death?

Assessing general deserts would be accomplished by answering a second question:

If the answer to the first question is that the death penalty is warranted, evaluate the defendant's overall deserts based on all of his actions in life considered in light of all of the evidence you have heard about him. Under this broader standard, does the defendant deserve to be sentenced to life imprisonment or to death?

If either an offender's culpability (for the capital offense) or his general deserts (based on his entire life) indicates that he does not deserve death, Professor Howe argues that a life sentence should be imposed.

Notes and Questions

1. What standard should the factfinder apply when weighing aggravating circumstances against mitigating circumstances? Is death appropriate if the factfinder is convinced by a preponderance of the evidence that aggravators outweigh mitigators? Or should clear and convincing evidence that aggravators outweigh mitigators be required? In part because the capital sentencing proceeding so closely resembles a trial and the stakes are extraordinarily high, Professor Linda E. Carter has proposed that capital sentencing determinations be subjected to a "beyond a reasonable doubt" standard.

According to Professor Carter, most statutes fail to provide a specific standard of proof. As a result, by default many states have adopted a preponderance of the evidence standard. In at least eleven states (Alabama, California, Florida, Idaho, Illinois, Indiana, Maryland, Mississippi, Missouri, New Mexico and Oklahoma), courts have explicitly rejected a beyond a reasonable doubt standard in the penalty phase. At least seven states (Arkansas, Colorado, New Jersey, Ohio, Texas, Utah and Washington) have imposed the beyond a reasonable doubt standard in their capital sentencing proceedings.

Professor Carter suggests that we should "require that, if death is to be imposed, the sentencer be certain of that decision. Moreover, the certainty of a decision of death should be no less than the highest degree in our legal system, beyond a reasonable doubt." This is so because

[t]he same solemnity that attaches to the decision of guilt or innocence should apply to a decision whether a defendant lives or dies. The Court has repeatedly expressed its view that the death penalty decision is different and requires the utmost reliability. As the Court stated in a case reaffirming the principle that all mitigating evidence must be considered, regardless whether the jurors were unanimous in finding a particular mitigating circumstance:

"The decision to exercise the power of the State to execute a defendant is unlike any other decision citizens and public officials are called upon to make. Evolving standards of societal decency have imposed a correspondingly high requirement of reliability on the determination that death is the appropriate penalty in a particular case." *Mills v. Maryland*, 486 U.S. 367, 383–384 (1988).

The nature of the decision itself, life or death, thus speaks forcefully for using the heightened standard of beyond a reasonable doubt. Carter, "A Beyond a Reasonable Doubt Standard in Death Penalty Proceedings: A Neglected Element of Fairness," 52 Ohio St. L.J. 195, 208, 211–12 (1991).

2. William S. Geimer and Jonathan Amsterdam studied ten Florida death penalty cases to identify reasons affecting jurors' decisions to recommend execution or a life sentence. The authors concluded that the statutory list of aggravating and mitigating circumstances did not have any appreciable effect on trial level decision making. Indeed, their admittedly small sampling of capital cases indicated that "the operative list of sentencing factors only occasionally resemble[d] the statutory list, and the factors that actually influence[d] jurors are only occasionally dealt with in appellate review of death sentences." The operative factors identified by the authors include demeanor of defendant; performance of defense attorney; manner of the killing; prior record of defendant; race; multiple victims; pecuniary gain; defendant under sentence of imprisonment; fear of early release; and future dangerousness. In addition, more than half the jurors interviewed indicated either that they would vote for death in all first degree murder cases or that they understood there to be a presumption in favor of death during sentencing—that is, death was to be imposed unless the defendant provided some reason to vote for life. Geimer & Amsterdam, "Why Jurors Vote Life or Death: Operative Factors in Ten Florida Death Penalty Cases," 15 Am. J. Crim. L. 1, 3–4, 40–41 (1988).

B. Presentence Investigation Reports

Gardner v. Florida

430 U.S. 349 (1977)

Mr. Justice STEVENS announced the judgment of the Court and delivered an opinion, in which Mr. Justice Stewart and Mr. Justice Powell joined.

I

[A Florida jury found Daniel Gardner, the petitioner, guilty of first-degree murder. The jury recommended that Gardner be sentenced to life imprisonment after it expressly found that the mitigating circumstances outweighed the aggravating circumstances. When the trial judge reviewed the jury's findings, he also reviewed a presentence investigation report prepared by the Florida Parole and Probation Commission after the jury had made its recommendation. The presentence report contained a confidential portion that was not disclosed to defense counsel.

After reviewing the jury's findings and the presentence report, the trial court rejected the jury's recommendation that Gardner be sentenced to life imprisonment and imposed a sentence of death.] ... The trial judge did not comment on the contents of the confidential portion [of the presentence report]. His findings do not indicate that there was anything of special importance in the undisclosed portion, or that there was any reason other than customary practice for not disclosing the entire report to the parties.

On appeal to the Florida Supreme Court, petitioner argued that the sentencing court had erred in considering the presentence investigation report, including the confidential portion, in making the decision to impose the death penalty. The *per curiam* opinion of the Supreme Court did not specifically discuss this contention, but merely recited the trial judge's finding, stated that the record had been carefully reviewed, and concluded that the conviction and sentence should be affirmed. The record on appeal, however, did not include the confidential portion of the presentence report.

... Petitioner's execution was stayed pending determination of the constitutionality of the Florida capital-sentencing procedure. Following the decision in *Proffitt v. Florida*, 428 U.S. 242, holding that the Florida procedure, on its face, avoids the constitutional deficiencies identified in *Furman v. Georgia*, the Court granted certiorari in this case, to consider the constitutionality of the trial judge's use of a confidential presentence report in this capital case....

III

First, five Members of the Court have now expressly recognized that death is a different kind of punishment from any other which may be imposed in this country. From the point of view of the defendant, it is different in both its severity and its finality. From the point of view of society, the action of the sovereign in taking the life of one of its citizens also differs dramatically from any other legitimate state action. It is of vital importance to the defendant and to the community that any decision to impose the death sentence be, and appear to be, based on reason rather than caprice or emotion.

Second, it is now clear that the sentencing process, as well as the trial itself, must satisfy the requirements of the Due Process Clause. Even though the defendant has no substantive right to a particular sentence within the range authorized by statute, the sentencing is a critical stage of the criminal proceeding at which he is entitled to the effective assistance of counsel. The defendant has a legitimate interest in the character of the procedure which leads to the imposition of sentence even if he may have no right to object to a particular result of the sentencing process.[9]

In the light of these developments we consider the justifications offered by the State for a capital-sentencing procedure which permits a trial judge to impose the death sentence on the basis of confidential information which is not disclosed to the defendant or his counsel.

The State first argues that an assurance of confidentiality to potential sources of information is essential to enable investigators to obtain relevant but sensitive disclosures from persons unwilling to comment publicly about a defendant's background or character. The availability of such information, it is argued, provides the person who prepares the report with greater detail on which to base a sentencing recommendation and, in turn, provides the judge with a better basis for his sentencing decision. But consideration must be given to the quality, as well as the quantity, of the information on which the sentencing judge may rely. Assurances of secrecy are conducive to the transmission of confidences which may bear no closer relation to fact than the average rumor or item of gossip, and may imply a pledge not to attempt independent verification of the information received. The risk that some of the information accepted in confidence may be erroneous, or may be misinterpreted, by the investigator or by the sentencing judge, is manifest.

If, as the State argues, it is important to use such information in the sentencing process, we must assume that in some cases it will be decisive in the judge's choice be-

---

9. The fact that due process applies does not, of course, implicate the entire panoply of criminal trial procedural rights. "Once it is determined that due process applies, the question remains what process is due. It has been said so often by this Court and others as not to require citation of authority that due process is flexible and calls for such procedural protections as the particular situation demands.... Its flexibility is in its scope once it has been determined that some process is due; it is a recognition that not all situations calling for procedural safeguards call for the same kind of procedure." *Morrissey v. Brewer*, 408 U.S. 471, 481.

tween a life sentence and a death sentence. If it tends to tip the scales in favor of life, presumably the information would be favorable and there would be no reason why it should not be disclosed. On the other hand, if it is the basis for a death sentence, the interest in reliability plainly outweighs the State's interest in preserving the availability of comparable information in their cases.

The State also suggests that full disclosure of the presentence report will unnecessarily delay the proceeding. We think the likelihood of significant delay is overstated because we must presume that reports prepared by professional probation officers, as the Florida procedure requires, are generally reliable. In those cases in which the accuracy of a report is contested, the trial judge can avoid delay by disregarding the disputed material. Or if the disputed matter is of critical importance, the time invested in ascertaining the truth would surely be well spent if it makes the difference between life and death.

The State further urges that full disclosure of presentence reports, which often include psychiatric and psychological evaluations, will occasionally disrupt the process of rehabilitation. The argument, if valid, would hardly justify withholding the report from defense counsel. Moreover, whatever force that argument may have in noncapital cases, it has absolutely no merit in a case in which the judge has decided to sentence the defendant to death. Indeed, the extinction of all possibility of rehabilitation is one of the aspects of the death sentence that makes it different in kind from any other sentence a State may legitimately impose.

Finally, Florida argues that trial judges can be trusted to exercise their discretion in a responsible manner, even though they may base their decisions on secret information. However acceptable that argument might have been before *Furman v. Georgia*, it is now clearly foreclosed. Moreover, the argument rests on the erroneous premise that the participation of counsel is superfluous to the process of evaluating the relevance and significance of aggravating and mitigating facts. Our belief that debate between adversaries is often essential to the truth-seeking function of trials requires us also to recognize the importance of giving counsel an opportunity to comment on facts which may influence the sentencing decision in capital cases.

Even if it were permissible to withhold a portion of the report from a defendant, and even from defense counsel, pursuant to an express finding of good cause for nondisclosure, it would nevertheless be necessary to make the full report a part of the record to be reviewed on appeal. Since the State must administer its capital-sentencing procedures with an even hand, it is important that the record on appeal disclose to the reviewing court the considerations which motivated the death sentence in every case in which it is imposed. Without full disclosure of the basis for the death sentence, the Florida capital-sentencing procedure would be subject to the defects which resulted in the holding of unconstitutionality in *Furman v. Georgia*. In this particular case, the only explanation for the lack of disclosure is the failure of defense counsel to request access to the full report. That failure cannot justify the submission of a less complete record to the reviewing court than the record on which the trial judge based his decision to sentence petitioner to death.

Nor do we regard this omission by counsel as an effective waiver of the constitutional error in the record. There are five reasons for this conclusion. First, the State does not urge that the objection has been waived. Second, the Florida Supreme Court has held that it has a duty to consider "the total record" when it reviews a death sentence. Third, since two members of that court expressly considered this point on the appeal in this case, we presume that the entire court passed on the question. Fourth, there is no basis for presuming that the defendant himself made a knowing and intelligent waiver, or that counsel could possibly have made a tactical decision not to examine the full report. Fifth, since the judge found, in disagreement with the jury, that the evidence did not establish any mitigating circumstance, and since the presentence report was the only item considered by the judge but not by the jury, the full review of the factual basis for the judge's rejection of the advisory verdict is plainly required. For if the jury, rather than the judge, correctly assessed the petitioner's veracity, the death sentence rests on an erroneous factual predicate.

We conclude that petitioner was denied due process of law when the death sentence was imposed, at least in part, on the basis of information which he had no opportunity to deny or explain.

IV

There remains only the question of what disposition is now proper. Petitioner's conviction, of course, is not tainted by the error in the sentencing procedure. The State argues that we should merely remand the case to the Florida Supreme Court with directions to have the entire presentence report made a part of the record to enable that court to complete its reviewing function. That procedure, however, could not fully correct the error. For it is possible that full disclosure, followed by explanation or argument by defense counsel, would have caused the trial judge to accept the jury's advisory verdict. Accordingly, the death sentence is vacated, and the case is remanded to the Florida Supreme Court with directions to order further proceedings at the trial court level not inconsistent with this opinion.

Mr. Justice MARSHALL, dissenting.

Last Term, this Court carefully scrutinized the Florida procedures for imposing the death penalty and concluded that there were sufficient safeguards to insure that the death sentence would not be "wantonly" and "freakishly" imposed. This case, however, belies that hope. While I continue to believe that the death penalty is unconstitutional in all circumstances, and therefore would remand this case for resentencing to a term of life, nevertheless, now that Florida may legally take a life, we must insist that it be in accordance with the standards enunciated by this Court. In this case I am appalled at the extent to which Florida has deviated from the procedures upon which this Court expressly relied. It is not simply that the trial judge, in overriding the jury's recommendation of life imprisonment, relied on undisclosed portions of the presentence report. Nor is it merely that the Florida Supreme Court affirmed the sentence without discussing the omission and without concern that it did not even have the entire report before it. Obviously that alone is enough to deny due process and require that the death sentence be vacated as the Court now holds. But the blatant disregard exhibited by the courts below for the standards devised to regulate imposition of the death penalty calls into question the very basis for this Court's approval of that system in *Proffitt v. Florida*.

… In the present case … the Florida Supreme Court engaged in precisely the "cursory or rubber-stamp review" that the joint opinion in *Proffit* trusted would not occur. The jury, after considering the evidence, recommended a life sentence…. The judge, however, ignored the jury's findings. His statutorily required written findings consisted of:

> [T]he undersigned concludes and determines that aggravating circumstances exist, to-wit: The capital felony was especially heinous, atrocious or cruel; and that such aggravating circumstances outweighs [sic] the mitigating circumstance, to-wit: none; and based upon the records of such trial and sentencing

proceedings makes the following findings of facts, to-wit: 1. That the victim died as a result of especially heinous, atrocious and cruel acts committed by the defendant, the nature and extent of which are reflected by the testimony of Dr. William H. Shutze, District Medical Examiner of the Fifth Judicial Circuit of the State of Florida, as follows: [followed by a list of 11 injuries to the deceased].

The Florida Supreme Court affirmed with two justices dissenting. The *per curiam* consisted of a statement of the facts of the murder, a verbatim copy of the trial judge's "findings," a conclusion that no new trial was warranted, and the following "analysis":

Upon considering all the mitigating and aggravating circumstances and careful review of the entire record in the cause, the trial court imposed the death penalty for the commission of the afore-described atrocious and heinous crime. Accordingly, the judgment and sentence of the Circuit Court are hereby affirmed....

From this quotation, which includes the entire legal analysis of the opinion, it is apparent that the State Supreme Court undertook none of the analysis it had previously proclaimed to be its duty. The opinion does not say that the Supreme Court evaluated the propriety of the death sentence. It merely says the trial judge did so. Despite its professed obligation to do so, the Supreme Court thus failed "to determine independently" whether death was the appropriate penalty. The Supreme Court also appears to have done nothing "to guarantee" consistency with other death sentences. Its opinion makes no comparison with the facts in other similar cases. Nor did it consider whether the trial judge was correct in overriding the jury's recommendation. There was no attempt to ascertain whether the evidence sustaining death was "so clear and convincing that virtually no reasonable person could differ." Indeed, it is impossible for me to believe that that standard can be met in this case....

Clearly, this is not a case where the evidence suggesting death is "so clear and convincing that virtually no reasonable person could differ." Had the Florida Supreme Court examined the evidence in the manner this Court trusted it would, I have no doubt that the jury recommendation of life imprisonment would have been reinstated....

In *Proffitt*, a majority of this Court was led to believe that Florida had established capital-sentencing procedures that would "assure that the death penalty will not be imposed in an arbitrary or capricious manner." This case belies that promise and suggests the need to reconsider that assessment.

C. Use of Criminal Convictions as Aggravating Evidence

Johnson v. Mississippi
486 U.S. 578 (1988)

Justice STEVENS delivered the opinion of the Court.

In 1982, petitioner Samuel Bice Johnson was convicted of murder and sentenced to death. The sentence was predicated, in part, on the fact that petitioner had been convicted of a felony in New York in 1963. After the Mississippi Supreme Court affirmed petitioner's death sentence, the New York Court of Appeals reversed the 1963 conviction. Petitioner thereafter unsuccessfully sought post-conviction relief from the Mississippi Supreme Court. The question presented to us is whether the state court was correct in concluding that the reversal of the New York conviction did not affect the validity of a death sentence based on that conviction.

I

On December 31, 1981, petitioner and three companions were stopped for speeding by a Mississippi highway patrolman. While the officer was searching the car, petitioner stabbed him and, in the ensuing struggle, one of his companions obtained the officer's gun and used it to kill him. Petitioner was apprehended, tried and convicted of murder, and sentenced to death. At the conclusion of the sentencing hearing, the jury found three aggravating circumstances,[1] any one of which, as a matter of Mississippi law, would have been sufficient to support a capital sentence. After weighing mitigating circumstances and aggravating circumstances "one against the other," the jury found "that the aggravating circumstances do outweigh the mitigating circumstances and that the Defendant should suffer the penalty of death." The Mississippi Supreme Court affirmed the conviction and sentence and we denied certiorari.

The sole evidence supporting the aggravating circumstance that petitioner had been "previously convicted of a felony involving the use or threat of violence to the person of another" consisted of an authenticated copy of petitioner's commitment to Elmira Reception Center in 1963 following his conviction in Monroe County, New York, for the crime of second-degree assault with intent to commit first-degree rape. The prosecutor repeatedly referred to that evidence in the sentencing hearing, stating in so many words: "I say that because of having been convicted of second degree assault with intent to commit first degree rape and capital murder that Samuel Johnson should die."

Prior to the assault trial in New York in 1963, the police obtained an incriminating statement from petitioner. Despite petitioner's objection that the confession had been coerced, it was admitted into evidence without a prior hearing on the issue of voluntariness. Moreover, after petitioner was convicted, he was never informed of his right to appeal. He made three efforts to do so without the assistance of counsel, each of which was rejected as untimely. After his Mississippi conviction, however, his attorneys successfully prosecuted a post-conviction proceeding in New York in which they persuaded the Monroe County Court that petitioner had been unconstitutionally deprived of his right to appeal. The County Court then entered a new sentencing order from which petitioner was able to take a direct appeal. In that proceeding, the New York Court of Appeals reversed his conviction.

Petitioner filed a motion in the Mississippi Supreme Court seeking post-conviction relief from his death sentence on the ground that the New York conviction was invalid and could not be used as an aggravating circumstance. That motion was filed before the New York proceeding was concluded, but it was supplemented by prompt notification of the favorable action taken by the New York Court of Appeals. Nevertheless, over the

---

1. The jury found the following aggravating circumstances:
   "(1) That the defendant, Samuel Johnson, was previously convicted of a felony involving the use or threat of violence to the person of another.
   "(2) That the defendant, Samuel Johnson, committed the capital murder for the purpose of avoiding arrest or effecting an escape from custody.
   "(3) The capital murder was especially heinous, atrocious and cruel."

dissent of three justices, the Mississippi Supreme Court denied the motion. The majority supported its conclusion with four apparently interdependent arguments. First, it stated that the petitioner had waived his right to challenge the validity of the New York conviction because he had not raised the point on direct appeal. Second, it expressed concern that Mississippi's capital sentencing procedures would become capricious and standardless if the post-sentencing decision of another State could have the effect of invalidating a Mississippi death sentence. Third, it questioned whether the New York proceedings were "truly adversarial." Finally, it concluded that the New York conviction provided adequate support for the death penalty even if it was invalid, stating:

> The fact remains that Johnson was convicted in 1963 by a New York court of a serious felony involving violence to a female for which he was imprisoned in that state. No New York court extended Johnson relief from his conviction before Johnson paid his debt to the state. If his crime was serious enough for him to be convicted and final enough for him to serve time in a penal institution, it had sufficient finality to be considered as an aggravating circumstance by a jury of this state. No death penalty verdict based upon this conviction need be vitiated by the subsequent relief granted more than twenty years later by the New York Court of Appeals.

In reaching this conclusion, the court expressly disavowed any reliance on the fact that two of the aggravating circumstances found by the jury did not turn on the evidence of petitioner's prior conviction.[5]

We granted certiorari to consider whether the Federal Constitution requires a reexamination of petitioner's death sentence. We conclude that it does.

II

The fundamental respect for humanity underlying the Eighth Amendment's prohibition against cruel and unusual punishment gives rise to a special " 'need for reliability in the determination that death is the appropriate punishment' " in any capital case. Although we have acknowledged that "there can be 'no perfect procedure for deciding in which cases governmental authority should be used to impose death,' " we have also made it clear that such decisions cannot be predicated on mere "caprice" or on "factors that are constitutionally impermissible or totally irrelevant to the sentencing process." The question in this case is whether allowing petitioner's death sentence to stand although based in part on a vacated conviction violates this principle.

In its opinion the Mississippi Supreme Court drew no distinction between petitioner's 1963 conviction for assault and the underlying conduct that gave rise to that conviction. In Mississippi's sentencing hearing following petitioner's conviction for murder, however, the prosecutor did not introduce any evidence concerning the alleged

---

5. Three justices dissented. Relying on the logic of *Phillips v. State*, 421 So.2d 476 (Miss. 1982), and the fact that there was "no way of ascertaining with confidence whether the prior conviction was a significant factor in the jury's determination that [petitioner] should suffer the penalty of death," the dissenters concluded that when an " 'aggravating' prior conviction is vacated," "the defendant [is] entitled to relief from his enhanced sentence." They criticized the majority for giving the decision of the New York Court of Appeals "less than full faith and credit," refusing themselves to "indulge in the cynical assumption that the New York Court did less than its duty when it ordered [petitioner's] 1963 conviction vacated." The dissenters rejected the majority's invocation of a procedural bar, asserting that under Mississippi law petitioner had acted properly in first seeking relief in the New York courts and that he had no basis for a claim in the Mississippi courts until he obtained that relief.

assault itself; the only evidence relating to the assault consisted of a document establishing that petitioner had been convicted of that offense in 1963. Since that conviction has been reversed, unless and until petitioner should be retried, he must be presumed innocent of that charge. Indeed, even without such a presumption, the reversal of the conviction deprives the prosecutor's sole piece of documentary evidence of any relevance to Mississippi's sentencing decision.

Contrary to the opinion expressed by the Mississippi Supreme Court, the fact that petitioner served time in prison pursuant to an invalid conviction does not make the conviction itself relevant to the sentencing decision. The possible relevance of the conduct which gave rise to the assault charge is of no significance here because the jury was not presented with any evidence describing that conduct—the document submitted to the jury proved only the facts of conviction and confinement, nothing more. That petitioner was imprisoned is not proof that he was guilty of the offense; indeed, it would be perverse to treat the imposition of punishment pursuant to an invalid conviction as an aggravating circumstance.

It is apparent that the New York conviction provided no legitimate support for the death sentence imposed on petitioner. It is equally apparent that the use of that conviction in the sentencing hearing was prejudicial. The prosecutor repeatedly urged the jury to give it weight in connection with its assigned task of balancing aggravating and mitigating circumstances "one against the other." Even without that express argument, there would be a possibility that the jury's belief that petitioner had been convicted of a prior felony would be "decisive" in the "choice between a life sentence and a death sentence."

We do not share the Mississippi Supreme Court's concern that its procedures would become capricious if it were to vacate a death sentence predicated on a prior felony conviction when such a conviction is set aside. A similar problem has frequently arisen in Mississippi, as well as other States, in cases involving sentences imposed on habitual criminals. Thus, in *Phillips v. State*, 421 So.2d 476 (Miss. 1982), the court held that the reversal of a Kentucky conviction that had provided the basis for an enhanced sentence pursuant to Mississippi's habitual criminal statute justified post-conviction relief. A rule that regularly gives a defendant the benefit of such post-conviction relief is not even arguably arbitrary or capricious. To the contrary, especially in the context of capital sentencing, it reduces the risk that such a sentence will be imposed arbitrarily.

In this Court the Mississippi Attorney General advances an argument for affirmance that was not relied upon by the State Supreme Court. He argues that the decision of the Mississippi Supreme Court should be affirmed because when that court conducted its proportionality review of the death sentence on petitioner's initial appeal, it did not mention petitioner's prior conviction in upholding the sentence. Whether it is true, as the Attorney General argues, that even absent evidence of petitioner's prior conviction a death sentence would be consistent with Mississippi's practice in other cases, however, is not determinative of this case. First, the Mississippi Supreme Court expressly refused to rely on harmless-error analysis in upholding petitioner's sentence; on the facts of this case, that refusal was plainly justified. Second, and more importantly, the error here extended beyond the mere invalidation of an aggravating circumstance supported by evidence that was otherwise admissible. Here the jury was allowed to consider evidence that has been revealed to be materially inaccurate.

Accordingly, the judgment is reversed, and the case is remanded to the Mississippi Supreme Court for further proceedings not inconsistent with this opinion.

Note

In his *Johnson v. Mississippi* concurrence, Justice White noted: "I join the Court's opinion, agreeing that the death sentence cannot stand, given the introduction of inadmissible and prejudicial evidence at the hearing before the jury. That evidence, however, was irrelevant to the other two aggravating circumstances found to be present, and I note that the case is remanded for further proceedings not inconsistent with the Court's opinion. It is left to the Mississippi Supreme Court to decide whether a new sentencing hearing must be held or whether that court should itself decide the appropriate sentence without reference to the inadmissible evidence, thus undertaking to reweigh the two untainted aggravating circumstances against the mitigating circumstances." The Mississippi Supreme Court ordered that Samuel Johnson receive a new sentencing hearing. Notwithstanding "the two untainted aggravating circumstances," Johnson was resentenced to life.

Unadjudicated Offenses and the Need For Heightened Reliability in Capital Sentencing Determinations

Should the state be allowed to introduce during the sentencing phase of a capital trial evidence that the defendant committed extraneous, unadjudicated criminal offenses in addition to the crime for which he was just tried and convicted? Is, as many claim, the reliability of the sentencing decision enhanced by its introduction? Or does unfair prejudice inevitably result when untried charges are hurled at someone freshly found guilty of capital murder?

Recall that the guiding principle in capital sentencing procedures is "death is different." According to the Court in *Woodson v. North Carolina*, 428 U.S. 280, 305 (1976),

> [T]he penalty of death is qualitatively different from a sentence of imprisonment, however long. Death, in its finality, differs more from life imprisonment than a 100-year prison term differs from one of only a year or two. Because of that qualitative difference, there is a corresponding difference in the need for reliability in the determination that death is the appropriate punishment in a specific case.

As a result, the Court has held that individualized sentencing is constitutionally mandated. *Lockett v. Ohio*, 438 U.S. 586 (1978). Sentences in capital cases are personally tailored through the guided balancing of aggravating and mitigating circumstances. Reliability is arguably enhanced by laying before the jury all relevant evidence about the individual defendant bearing on the aggravating and mitigating factors. Compare *Lockett v. Ohio*, 438 U.S. 586 (1978) with *Barefoot v. Estelle*, 463 U.S. 880 (1983). However, as *Gardner v. Florida*, 430 U.S. 349 (1977), demonstrates, more than mere relevance is required to satisfy the constitutional requirements for admissibility of sentencing phase evidence. Due process demands that the introduction and consideration of relevant information comply with procedural fairness.

Of twenty-four states which have resolved the issue, sixteen[1] admit evidence of unadjudicated offenses during the capital sentencing phase. Of these, six states[2] admit the ev-

---

1. Arkansas, California, Delaware, Georgia, Illinois, Louisiana, Missouri, Nebraska, Nevada, North Carolina, Oklahoma, Oregon, South Carolina, Texas, Utah and Virginia.
2. Missouri, North Carolina, Oklahoma, Oregon, Texas and Virginia.

idence with virtually no limitation. For example, Virginia courts have held that unadjudicated offense evidence is "highly relevant" to the issue of future dangerousness and have rejected arguments that the evidence is "not reliable" and is instead "highly inflammatory or inherently prejudicial."[3]

The other ten states[4] which admit unadjudicated offense evidence require either a heightened standard of reliability or a limiting instruction regarding the proper use of the evidence. For example, several states hold that unadjudicated criminal conduct must be proved beyond a reasonable doubt. Others have adopted a "clear and convincing evidence" standard.

Eight states[5] flatly prohibit the introduction of unadjudicated criminal offense evidence during the capital penalty phase. Various rationales are offered in support of excluding this evidence, including freedom from unfair prejudice, reliability, and procedural fairness.

Note and Questions

1. The constitutional issues raised by unadjudicated criminal offense evidence are thoroughly examined in Smith, "Unreliable and Prejudicial: The Use of Extraneous Unadjudicated Offenses in the Penalty Phase of Capital Trials," 93 Colum. L. Rev. 1249 (1993).

2. What effect does the introduction of unadjudicated criminal offense evidence have on the presumption of innocence?

3. Is a capital sentencing proceeding an adequate substitute for a full blown sentencing trial?

4. Does a conviction for capital murder inevitably increase the likelihood that the defendant committed other unrelated crimes?

D. The "Truly Awesome Responsibility" of Capital Jurors

Caldwell v. Mississippi

472 U.S. 320 (1985)

Justice MARSHALL delivered the opinion of the Court, except as to Part IV-A.

This case presents the issue whether a capital sentence is valid when the sentencing jury is led to believe that responsibility for determining the appropriateness of a death sentence rests not with the jury but with the appellate court which later reviews the case. In this case, a prosecutor urged the jury not to view itself as determining whether

---

3. Compare *Williams v. Commonwealth*, 360 S.E.2d 371, 370 (Va. 1987) with *Beaver v. Commonwealth*, 352 S.E.2d 342, 346–347 (Va. 1987) and *Gray v. Commonwealth*, 356 S.E.2d 157, 175–176 (Va. 1987).

4. Arkansas, California, Delaware, Georgia, Illinois, Louisiana, Nebraska, Nevada, South Carolina and Utah.

5. Alabama, Florida, Indiana, Maryland, Ohio, Pennsylvania, Tennessee and Washington.

the defendant would die, because a death sentence would be reviewed for correctness by the State Supreme Court. We granted certiorari to consider petitioner's contention that the prosecutor's argument rendered the capital sentencing proceeding inconsistent with the Eighth Amendment's heightened "need for reliability in the determination that death is the appropriate punishment in a specific case." Agreeing with the contention, we vacate the sentence.

I

Petitioner shot and killed the owner of a small grocery store in the course of robbing it. In a bifurcated proceeding conducted pursuant to Mississippi's capital punishment statute, petitioner was convicted of capital murder and sentenced to death.

In their case for mitigation, petitioner's lawyers put on evidence of petitioner's youth, family background, and poverty, as well as general character evidence. In their closing arguments they referred to this evidence and then asked the jury to show mercy. The arguments were in large part pleas that the jury confront both the gravity and the responsibility of calling for another's death, even in the context of a capital sentencing proceeding.

> [E]very life is precious and as long as there's life in the soul of a person, there is hope. There is hope, but life is one thing and death is final. So I implore you to think deeply about this matter. It is his life or death—the decision you're going to have to make, and I implore you to exercise your prerogative to spare the life of Bobby Caldwell.... I'm sure [the prosecutor is] going to say to you that Bobby Caldwell is not a merciful person, but I say unto you he is a human being. That he has a life that rests in your hands. You can give him life or you can give him death. It's going to be your decision. I don't know what else I can say to you but we live in a society where we are taught that an eye for an eye is not the solution.... You are the judges and you will have to decide his fate. It is an awesome responsibility, I know—an awesome responsibility.

In response, the prosecutor sought to minimize the jury's sense of the importance of its role. Indeed, the prosecutor forcefully argued that the defense had done something wholly illegitimate in trying to force the jury to feel a sense of responsibility for its decision. The prosecutor's argument, defense counsel's objection, and the trial court's ruling were as follows:

> "ASSISTANT DISTRICT ATTORNEY: Ladies and gentlemen, I intend to be brief. I'm in complete disagreement with the approach the defense has taken. I don't think it's fair. I think it's unfair. I think the lawyers know better. Now, they would have you believe that you're going to kill this man and they know—they know that your decision is not the final decision. My God, how unfair can you be? Your job is reviewable. They know it. Yet they...

> "COUNSEL FOR DEFENDANT: Your Honor, I'm going to object to this statement. It's out of order.

> "ASSISTANT DISTRICT ATTORNEY: Your Honor, throughout their argument, they said this panel was going to kill this man. I think that's terribly unfair.

> "THE COURT: Alright, go on and make the full expression so the Jury will not be confused. I think it proper that the jury realizes that it is reviewable automatically as the death penalty commands. I think that information is now needed by the Jury so they will not be confused.

"ASSISTANT DISTRICT ATTORNEY: Throughout their remarks, they attempted to give you the opposite, sparing the truth. They said 'Thou shalt not kill.' If that applies to him, it applies to you, insinuating that your decision is the final decision and that they're gonna take Bobby Caldwell out in the front of this Courthouse in moments and string him up and that is terribly, terribly unfair. For they know, as I know, and as Judge Baker has told you, that the decision you render is automatically reviewable by the Supreme Court. Automatically, and I think it's unfair and I don't mind telling them so."

On review, the Mississippi Supreme Court unanimously affirmed the conviction but divided 4–4 on the validity of the death sentence, thereby affirming the sentence by an equally divided court....

III

A

On reaching the merits, we conclude that it is constitutionally impermissible to rest a death sentence on a determination made by a sentencer who has been led to believe that the responsibility for determining the appropriateness of the defendant's death rests elsewhere. This Court has repeatedly said that under the Eighth Amendment "the qualitative difference of death from all other punishments requires a correspondingly greater degree of scrutiny of the capital sentencing determination." *California v. Ramos*, 463 U.S. 992, 998–999 (1983). Accordingly, many of the limits that this Court has placed on the imposition of capital punishment are rooted in a concern that the sentencing process should facilitate the responsible and reliable exercise of sentencing discretion.

In evaluating the various procedures developed by States to determine the appropriateness of death, this Court's Eighth Amendment jurisprudence has taken as a given that capital sentencers would view their task as the serious one of determining whether a specific human being should die at the hands of the State. Thus, as long ago as the pre-*Furman* case of *McGautha v. California*, Justice Harlan, writing for the Court, upheld a capital sentencing scheme in spite of its reliance on jury discretion. The sentencing scheme's premise, he assumed, was "that jurors confronted with the truly awesome responsibility of decreeing death for a fellow human will act with due regard for the consequences of their decision...." Belief in the truth of the assumption that sentencers treat their power to determine the appropriateness of death as an "awesome responsibility" has allowed this Court to view sentencer discretion as consistent with—and indeed as indispensable to—the Eighth Amendment's "need for reliability in the determination that death is the appropriate punishment in a specific case."

B

In the capital sentencing context there are specific reasons to fear substantial unreliability as well as bias in favor of death sentences when there are state-induced suggestions that the sentencing jury may shift its sense of responsibility to an appellate court.

(1)

Bias against the defendant clearly stems from the institutional limits on what an appellate court can do—limits that jurors often might not understand. The "delegation" of sentencing responsibility that the prosecutor here encouraged would thus not simply postpone the defendant's right to a fair determination of the appropriateness of his death; rather it would deprive him of that right, for an appellate court, unlike a capital sentencing jury, is wholly ill-suited to evaluate the appropriateness of death in the first instance. Whatever intangibles a jury might consider in its sentencing determination, few can be gleaned from an appellate record. This inability to confront and examine the individuality of the defendant would be particularly devastating to any argument for consideration of what this Court has termed "[those] compassionate or mitigating factors stemming from the diverse frailties of humankind." When we held that a defendant has a constitutional right to the consideration of such factors, we clearly envisioned that that consideration would occur among sentencers who were present to hear the evidence and arguments and see the witnesses. As the dissenters below noted:

> The [mercy] plea is made directly to the jury as only they may impose the death sentence. Under our standards of appellate review mercy is irrelevant. There is no appellate mercy. Therefore, the fact that review is mandated is irrelevant to the thought processes required to find that an accused should be denied mercy and sentenced to die.

Given these limits, most appellate courts review sentencing determinations with a presumption of correctness. This is the case in Mississippi, where, as the dissenters below pointed out: "Even a novice attorney knows that appellate courts do not impose a death penalty, they merely review the jury's decision and that review is with a presumption of correctness."

(2)

Writing on this kind of prosecutorial argument in a prior case, Justice Stevens noted another reason why it presents an intolerable danger of bias toward a death sentence: Even when a sentencing jury is unconvinced that death is the appropriate punishment, it might nevertheless wish to "send a message" of extreme disapproval for the defendant's acts. This desire might make the jury very receptive to the prosecutor's assurance that it can more freely "err because the error may be corrected on appeal." A defendant might thus be executed, although no sentencer had ever made a determination that death was the appropriate sentence.

(3)

Bias could similarly stem from the fact that some jurors may correctly assume that a sentence of life in prison could not be increased to a death sentence on appeal. The chance that this will be the assumption of at least some jurors is increased by the fact that, in an argument like the one in this case, appellate review is only raised as an issue with respect to the reviewability of a death sentence. If the jury understands that only a death sentence will be reviewed, it will also understand that any decision to "delegate" responsibility for sentencing can only be effectuated by returning that sentence. But for a sentencer to impose a death sentence out of a desire to avoid responsibility for its decision presents the specter of the imposition of death based on a factor wholly irrelevant to legitimate sentencing concerns. The death sentence that would emerge from such a sentencing proceeding would simply not represent a decision that the State had demonstrated the appropriateness of the defendant's death. This would thus also create the danger of a defendant's being executed in the absence of any determination that death was the appropriate punishment.

(4)

In evaluating the prejudicial effect of the prosecutor's argument, we must also recognize that the argument offers jurors a view of their role which might frequently be highly attractive. A capital sentencing jury is made up of individuals placed in a very unfamiliar situation and called on to make a very difficult and uncomfortable choice. They are confronted with evidence and argument on the issue of whether another should die, and they are asked to decide that issue on behalf of the community. Moreover, they are given only partial guidance as to how their judgment should be exercised, leaving them with substantial discretion. Given such a situation, the uncorrected suggestion that the responsibility for any ultimate determination of death will rest with others presents an intolerable danger that the jury will in fact choose to minimize the importance of its role. Indeed, one can easily imagine that in a case in which the jury is divided on the proper sentence, the presence of appellate review could effectively be used as an argument for why those jurors who are reluctant to invoke the death sentence should nevertheless give in.

This problem is especially serious when the jury is told that the alternative decision-makers are the justices of the state supreme court. It is certainly plausible to believe that many jurors will be tempted to view these respected legal authorities as having more of a "right" to make such an important decision than has the jury. Given that the sentence will be subject to appellate review only if the jury returns a sentence of death, the chance that an invitation to rely on that review will generate a bias toward returning a death sentence is simply too great.

C

It is, therefore, not surprising that legal authorities almost uniformly have strongly condemned the sort of argument offered by the prosecutor here. For example, this has been the view of almost all of the State Supreme Courts that have dealt with this question since *Furman*. Indeed, even before *Furman* the sort of argument offered by the prosecutor here was viewed as clearly improper by most state courts, whether in capital or noncapital cases. The American Bar Association, in its standards for prosecutorial conduct, agrees with this judgment. And even the Mississippi Supreme Court, since deciding *Caldwell*, has adopted the position that arguments very similar to that used here are sufficiently improper to merit vacating a death sentence....

V

This Court has always premised its capital punishment decisions on the assumption that a capital sentencing jury recognizes the gravity of its task and proceeds with the appropriate awareness of its "truly awesome responsibility." In this case, the State sought to minimize the jury's sense of responsibility for determining the appropriateness of death. Because we cannot say that this effort had no effect on the sentencing decision, that decision does not meet the standard of reliability that the Eighth Amendment requires. The sentence of death must therefore be vacated. Accordingly, the judgment is reversed to the extent that it sustains the imposition of the death penalty, and the case is remanded for further proceedings.

Notes and Questions

1. In an empirical study which included post-sentencing interviews with 153 capital jurors, researchers concluded that capital jurors felt little responsibility for death sentences and less for executions. "On the whole, jurors simply do not believe that defendants sentenced to death will in fact ever be executed.... A clear majority say that 'very few' death-sentenced defendants will ever be executed, and about 70 percent ... believe

that 'less than half' or 'very few' will be executed." Eisenberg et al., "Jury Responsibility in Capital Sentencing: An Empirical Study," 44 Buff. L. Rev. 339, 352–54, 362–64 (1996).

2. In *Wheat v. Thigpen*, 793 F.2d 621 (5th Cir. 1986), the Fifth Circuit found that a prosecutor's attempts to minimize the jury's sense of responsibility in violation of *Caldwell v. Mississippi*, 472 U.S. 320 (1985), could not be excused on the grounds that defense counsel "invited" the error. During closing argument defense counsel argued as follows:

> I approached you yesterday and told you how heavy a burden that I felt. If I felt a heavy burden yesterday, I feel like I have the weight of the world on my shoulders today.

> You know, I can't imagine what it would be like, truthfully, to be in your position. I guess, maybe, you can imagine what it would be like to be in my position, knowing that what you say may actually have a great determination whether a man lives or dies. I can't imagine what it would be like to sit on a jury like you are, and have to make a decision as to whether a man is killed or not. I truthfully can't. I don't know if it's hard, never having been in the position, and I just can't imagine it.

> You know, what you decide here today when you go out of here, when you come back, the decision if he should be killed, somewhere, it may take—truthfully the way appeals go, it may take two or three years. But someday, just as sure as we're here now, they'll take that man over there, and they'll walk him into a little gray-looking chamber—I've seen it before—a little eight-sided thing, about, maybe, a little bit bigger than that witness box, and there's a metal chair that's got leather straps to it, and they'll strap him in there. And it's got glass where people can look through it. And they have a man who stands over behind there where people can't see him, and he pulls the little lever; and these little tablets drop in there, and it makes a gas, cyanide gas. And it comes into there, and they have things, I think, strapped to the body to check the heartbeat, and so forth. They stay in there until they're dead, and then they bring them out. Someday, I want you to understand that; someday—I'm not doing this to be morbid with you. I'm doing it to make sure that you really understand the gravity of the thing.

* * *

> Now, I said all of that to say this: you can be wrong about it. People can be wrong. It's just that simple. No matter what, no matter what a thing looks like, you can be wrong about it. There is no question that you can be wrong about it.

> Now, you have said by your verdict that you believe that he killed him, and that you have no reasonable doubt of it. But consider, what if? Consider that possibility. What if I'm wrong? What if it really wasn't him. If you come back with a sentence of death, it can never be reversed. Once he's dead, he's gone. He'll never be brought back if you're wrong. But what if you're wrong? What if there is a man, really, out there. That man who I argued about yesterday. What if he really exists? Consider that possibility. If you haven't—if you let the thought come into your mind, consider it. What if he exists? You can never bring that man back if you kill him.

The state responded to this argument by explaining the state and federal appellate processes. The prosecutor also stated, "[J]ust remember this, if your verdict is that of the death penalty, that's not final." The prosecutor further informed the jury that, if they made a mistake, one of the reviewing courts would send the case back for retrial. The prosecutor advised the jury:

And another thing Mr. Stegall said, Kenneth Wheat still gets another chance even if you find that he should suffer the penalty of death. This will not happen tomorrow. It will not happen next. It will not happen next year. Why? Because, in the first place, there will be so many different panels reviewing your decision as to see if you made the right decision. First, His Own Honor here, will review your decision at a later time to see if you've made any error; or if the lawyers made any errors. If the Judge finds that I have committed some type of error in this case, this Judge right here has the authority to grant another trial. If he thinks that your verdict is not in accordance with the law, he has a right to grant a new trial, and let twelve more people decide. And if he finds that he's in accordance — in accord with your verdict, then we have nine supreme court justices at our state level who will look at ever[y] word that has been spoken, that this lady has taken down, will be all transcribed into a book form. Ever[y] piece of evidence that you see will go yonder to the Supreme Court, and nine men and with all of their wisdom, and knowledge, and compassion, and mercy, and understanding, and legal experience will look at all of this and determine whether Kenneth William Wheat got a fair trial at the hands of you twelve people in Harrison County, Mississippi. Then if they decide, they have a right to send it back to another jury to look at if they think we committed error in this case. If they find that no error was committed, then he has a right to go all the way to the United States Supreme Court. And this doesn't cost him one dime. Our system provides him this relief at no cost to him. And he goes all the way to the Supreme Court in Washington, where nine more men will have all of the same evidence to look at and determine whether this Judge here, or those nine judges in Jackson made a mistake. And if they find that he did, then they will send it back for a new trial. Or they can go the Federal Court route after that, and then have Federal Judges to look at and see if all the evidence was presented fairly and impartially.

So, you see, Ladies and Gentlemen, it's not like he will be killed tomorrow. Mississippi hasn't had anyone executed in a long time.

* * *

Again, I say to you, and then I'll leave it to you, just remember this, if your verdict is that of the death penalty, that's not final. There's so many more people who will look at this case after you have made your decision in this case. Others will look at it, and look at your work, and see if you've made the right decision. And I can assure you, Ladies and Gentlemen, that if one finds that you have not, that they will send him back, and tell us to try it over, because someone made a mistake.

BY MR. STEGALL: May It Please The Court, I'm gonna object to that again. He's telling this jury to go ahead and do something even if it's wrong, because if it's wrong, they're gonna send it back. That's not right. I'm gonna object.

BY THE COURT: I think the argument was allowed — it was opened up on your argument. I'll overrule it.

The federal court of appeals concluded that the prosecutor's argument was unexcused, constitutional error, and that the defendant was entitled to a new sentencing proceeding. Do you think the prosecutor was legitimately responding to an issue raised by defense counsel? Should a prosecutor be permitted to respond in some form to this type of defense argument? If so, how?

Note and Question on Romano v. Oklahoma, 512 U.S. 1 (1994)

In *Romano v. Oklahoma*, 512 U.S. 1 (1994), the Supreme Court addressed the question: "Does admission of evidence that a capital defendant already has been sentenced to death in another case impermissibly undermine the sentencing jury's sense of responsibility for determining the appropriateness of the defendant's death, in violation of the Eighth and Fourteenth Amendments?" The Court answered this question in the negative.

At issue was Romano's conviction and death sentence for the 1985 murder of Roger Sarfaty. Prior to his trial in Sarfaty's case, Romano was convicted and sentenced to death for the murder of Lloyd Thompson. During the sentencing phase of the Sarfaty trial, the state introduced a copy of Romano's judgment and sentence from the Thompson trial which revealed that a different jury had previously convicted and sentenced Romano to death for another murder. The Thompson judgment and sentence also revealed to the jury that Romano was appealing his conviction and sentence in that case. After the introduction of this evidence as well as other evidence supporting the imposition of the death sentence, the Sarfaty jury sentenced Romano to death. Subsequently, Romano's conviction and sentence in the Thompson case was reversed and remanded for a new trial.

Romano argued that the admission of evidence regarding his prior death sentence violated the Eighth and Fourteenth Amendments by undermining the Sarfaty jury's sense of responsibility for determining the appropriateness of the death penalty. In particular, Romano contended that the admission of the prior judgment and sentence violated the jury's sentencing responsibilities as set out in *Caldwell v. Mississippi*, 472 U.S. 320 (1985). A majority of the Court disagreed. Chief Justice Rehnquist, writing for the five-member majority, stated:

> It is helpful to begin by placing petitioner's challenge within the larger context of our Eighth Amendment death penalty jurisprudence. We have held that the Eighth Amendment's concern that the death penalty be both appropriate, and not randomly imposed, requires the States to perform two somewhat contradictory tasks in order to impose the death penalty.

> First, States must properly establish a threshold below which the penalty cannot be imposed. *McCleskey v. Kemp*, 481 U.S. 279, 305 (1987). To ensure that this threshold is met, the "State must establish rational criteria that narrow the decisionmaker's judgment as to whether the circumstances of a particular defendant's case meet the threshold." Petitioner does not allege that Oklahoma's sentencing scheme fails to adequately perform the requisite narrowing.

> Second, States must ensure that "capital sentencing decisions rest on [an] individualized inquiry," under which the "character and record of the individual offender and the circumstances of the particular offense" are considered. *McCleskey, supra*, at 302 (internal quotation marks omitted); see also *Clemons v. Mississippi*, 494 U.S. 738, 748 (1990). To this end, "States cannot limit the

sentencer's consideration of any relevant circumstance that could cause it to decline to impose the penalty. In this respect, the State cannot channel the sentencer's discretion, but must allow it to consider any relevant information offered by the defendant." *McCleskey*, at 306.

Within these constitutional limits, "the States enjoy their traditional latitude to prescribe the method by which those who commit murder shall be punished." *Blystone v. Pennsylvania*, 494 U.S. 299, 309 (1990). This latitude extends to evidentiary rules at sentencing proceedings....

We have also held, in *Caldwell v. Mississippi*, that the jury must not be misled regarding the role it plays in the sentencing decision. The prosecutor in *Caldwell*, in remarks which "were quite focused, unambiguous, and strong," misled the jury to believe that the responsibility for sentencing the defendant lay elsewhere. The trial judge "not only failed to correct the prosecutor's remarks, but in fact openly agreed with them."

The plurality concluded that the prosecutor's remarks, along with the trial judge's affirmation, impermissibly "minimized the jury's sense of responsibility for determining the appropriateness of death." Such a diminution, the plurality felt, precluded the jury from properly performing its responsibility to make an individualized determination of the appropriateness of the death penalty. Justice O'Connor, in her opinion concurring in part and concurring in the judgment, identified more narrowly the infirmity in the prosecutor's remarks: "In my view, the prosecutor's remarks were impermissible because they were inaccurate and misleading in a manner that diminished the jury's sense of responsibility."

As Justice O'Connor supplied the fifth vote in *Caldwell*, and concurred on grounds narrower than those put forth by the plurality, her position is controlling. Accordingly, we have since read *Caldwell* as "relevant only to certain types of comment—those that mislead the jury as to its role in the sentencing process in a way that allows the jury to feel less responsible than it should for the sentencing decision." *Darden v. Wainwright*, 477 U.S. 168, 184, n. 15 (1986). Thus, "to establish a *Caldwell* violation, a defendant necessarily must show that the remarks to the jury improperly described the role assigned to the jury by local law."

Petitioner argues that *Caldwell* controls this case. He contends that the evidence of his prior death sentence impermissibly undermined the sentencing jury's sense of responsibility, in violation of the principle established in *Caldwell*. We disagree. The infirmity identified in *Caldwell* is simply absent in this case: Here, the jury was not affirmatively misled regarding its role in the sentencing process. The evidence at issue was neither false at the time it was admitted, nor did it even pertain to the jury's role in the sentencing process. The trial court's instructions, moreover, emphasized the importance of the jury's role. As the Court of Criminal Appeals observed:

> "The jury was instructed that it had the responsibility for determining whether the death penalty should be imposed.... It was never conveyed or intimated in any way, by the court or the attorneys, that the jury could shift its responsibility in sentencing or that its role in any way had been minimized."

Romano II, 847 P.2d, at 390.

We do not believe that the admission of evidence regarding petitioner's prior death sentence affirmatively misled the jury regarding its role in the sentencing process so as to diminish its sense of responsibility. The admission of this evidence, therefore, did not contravene the principle established in *Caldwell*.

That this case is different from *Caldwell* only resolves part of petitioner's challenge. In addition to raising a "*Caldwell*" claim, petitioner presents a more general contention: He argues that because the evidence of his prior death sentence was inaccurate and irrelevant, the jury's consideration of it rendered his sentencing proceeding so unreliable that the proceeding violated the Eighth Amendment. The Oklahoma Court agreed that the "evidence of the imposition of the death penalty by another jury is not relevant in determining the appropriateness of the other death sentence for the instant offense." *Romano II*, at 391. That the evidence may have been irrelevant as a matter of state law, however, does not render its admission federal constitutional error....

Romano held that a juror may be told that the defendant is already under sentence of death in another case, even though this information is irrelevant and creates a danger that the jury will treat the imposition of an additional death sentence as less serious than imposing a first death sentence. Doesn't *Romano* unwisely neutralize *Caldwell*'s effort to assure that juries feel a sense of responsibility for imposing the death penalty?

Romano also argued that the jury was misled about his prior conviction and sentence because the Thompson conviction was reversed on appeal and remanded for a new trial and that therefore the evidence supporting one of the aggravating factors — previously convicted of a prior violent felony — had been rendered invalid. A majority of the Court found that this argument did not entitle Romano to relief. Chief Justice Rehnquist opined:

Petitioner also cites *Johnson v. Mississippi*, 486 U.S. 578 (1988), but it, too, is inapposite. There we reversed the imposition of Johnson's death sentence because the only evidence supporting an aggravating factor turned out to be invalid, and because the Mississippi Supreme Court refused to reweigh the remaining, untainted aggravating circumstances against the mitigating circumstances. Similarly, in this case the only evidence supporting the "prior violent felony" aggravating circumstance was the judgment from petitioner's conviction for the Thompson murder. That evidence, like the evidence in *Johnson*, was rendered invalid by the reversal of petitioner's conviction on appeal.

Here, however, the Oklahoma Court of Criminal Appeals struck the "prior violent felony" aggravator, reweighed the three untainted aggravating circumstances against the mitigating circumstances, and still concluded that the death penalty was warranted. The Court of Criminal Appeals' approach is perfectly consistent with our precedents, including *Johnson*, where we remanded without limiting the Mississippi Supreme Court's authority to reweigh the remaining aggravating circumstances against the mitigating circumstances. Contrary to petitioner's assertion, *Johnson* does not stand for the proposition that the mere admission of irrelevant and prejudicial evidence requires the overturning of a death sentence.

Notes and Questions on Juror Confusion

1. In May 1999, Justice Sandra Day O'Connor delivered a speech in which she suggested that jurors routinely rendered verdicts without enough information to do their

jobs. "Too often, jurors are allowed to do nothing but listen impassively to the testimony, without any idea what the legal issues are in the case, not allowed to take notes or participate in any way, and finally to be read a virtually incomprehensible set of instructions and sent into the jury room to reach a verdict in a case they may not understand much better than they did before the trial began." Consider *Buchanan v. Angelone*, 522 U.S. 269 (1998), in which the Court reviewed the following pattern jury instruction used in Virginia:

> If you find from the evidence that the Commonwealth has proved beyond a reasonable doubt either of the two [aggravating factors], and as to that [aggravating factor] you are unanimous, then you may fix the punishment of the defendant at death or if you believe from all the evidence that the death penalty is not justified, then you shall fix the punishment of the defendant at life imprisonment or imprisonment for life and a fine of a specific amount, but not more than $100,000.

Petitioner Buchanan claimed that this instruction offended case law which requires that a capital sentencing jury be allowed to consider and give effect to mitigating evidence. Previously, in *Boyde v. California*, 494 U.S. 370 (1990), the Supreme Court held that the proper standard for determining whether an instruction was constitutionally flawed was whether there was a reasonable likelihood that the jury applied the instruction in such a way as to prevent consideration of constitutionally relevant evidence. Applying the test of *Boyde*, the Supreme Court concluded that there was no reasonable likelihood that the jury would apply the pattern instruction so as to prevent consideration of constitutionally relevant evidence.

2. The same Virginia pattern instruction came before the Supreme Court in *Weeks v. Angelone*, 528 U.S. 225 (2000). Weeks unsuccessfully sought habeas relief after being sentenced to death for killing a law enforcement officer. The Court held that when jurors who are deliberating the fate of a convicted capital defendant send out a question that touches on the proper consideration of mitigating circumstances, the trial court can satisfy the demands of the Constitution by referring the jurors to the relevant language in a constitutionally sufficient instruction that the jury has already heard.

Weeks' jury was instructed that at least one aggravating factor had to be found beyond a reasonable doubt before the death penalty could be imposed. That instruction was followed by the language of the pattern instruction previously upheld in *Buchanan* (see note 1). The instruction ended with a paragraph saying that if the prosecution failed to prove either alleged aggravator, the jury was to choose between the life and life-with-fine options. The trial judge also told the jury that "[y]ou must consider a mitigating circumstance if you find there is evidence to support it."

During deliberations, the jury sent out a written question asking whether, if it believed that Weeks was guilty of at least one aggravating factor, its duty was "to *issue* the death penalty" or to "*decide* (even though he is guilty of one of the [aggravators]) whether or not to issue the death penalty, or one of the life sentences?"

Weeks' lawyer asked the trial court to tell the jurors that even if they found one or both aggravators, they could still impose one of the life sentences. The court refused. Instead, the judge told counsel that it could not improve on its previous instruction and referred the jury to the passage quoted in note 1, above. After two more hours of deliberations, the jury sentenced Weeks to death.

According to the Supreme Court, faced with the jury's question about the consequences of finding an aggravating factor, the trial court was constitutionally justified in merely directing the jury's attention to "the precise paragraph of the constitutionally adequate instruction that answer[ed] its inquiry." Moreover, the Court applied the usual presumption that a jury understands a judge's answer to its question. That presumption, per the Court, was strengthened in Weeks' case by several facts:

— the verdict, which each juror affirmed in open court, included a finding that the jurors had "considered the evidence in mitigation of the offense;"

— the jury deliberated four and one half hours before asking the question and deliberated more than two hours after receiving the judge's answer, suggesting that the jury had found an aggravator by the time the question was asked and spent the remainder of the deliberations weighing the mitigating evidence against the aggravator;

— the question was the second posed by the jury, suggesting that if the jury found the trial judge's response unsatisfactory it would have sent out another question;

— Weeks' lawyer told the jury in closing argument that it could impose a life sentence, even if the jury found both aggravators.

Given these factors, the Court concluded that although there was a "slight possibility" that the jury thought it could not consider mitigating evidence once it found an aggravating factor, the "reasonable likelihood" standard of *Boyde* had not been met.

The dissenters, led by Justice Stevens (who was joined by Justices Ginsburg and Breyer, and in part by Justice Souter) contended that there was a "virtual certainty" that the jury was mistaken about its options. The majority dismissed this view as "extravagant hyperbole."

3. When capital jurors ask the trial judge to clarify a sentencing instruction, chances are good that they didn't understand the instruction. The trial judge in *Weeks* did nothing more than refer the jurors to a specific portion of the very instruction they found confusing in the first place. Was this an adequate response? A Supreme Court majority found that, when all was said and done, there was only a "slight possibility" that jury members were confused. The dissenting justices concluded that juror confusion was a "virtual certainty."

Researchers designed an experiment to test the majority's conclusion that there was only a "slight possibility" of confusion in the minds of jurors regarding whether they were required to sentence Weeks to death. (Most of Weeks' jurors wept openly when the death sentence was announced.) The results of the experiment, which replicated the facts of *Weeks* as much as possible, led to this conclusion:

The jurors who sentenced Lonnie Weeks to death did not understand the law. They asked the trial judge for help. Based on our mock study, the answer he gave probably did precious little good. Consequently, when the jurors voted to condemn Weeks, some of them probably didn't understand the law and continued to think that they had to vote for death. Yet no capital juror is ever required to vote for death. The Supreme Court upheld Weeks' death sentence nonetheless. But the Court's judgment is ultimately based on nothing more than instinct and conjecture. Sadly, the evidence presented ... leads to one conclusion: The Court got this one wrong, both on the facts and on the law.

Garvey, et al., "Correcting Deadly Confusion: Responding to Jury Inquiries in Capital Cases," 85 Cornell L. Rev. 627 (2000).

Garvey's findings are supported by another researcher who concluded:

[A]t least three jurors in the *Weeks* case were so profoundly confused about the judge's instructions that they wrongly believed that the law might require them to impose a death sentence. Two of them made that clear by questions they sent to the judge during deliberations, and the third later told me that they believed "we weren't there to discuss the penalty. We were there just to find out whether he was guilty or innocent, and we all understood that it was the death penalty if he was guilty."

Berlow, *A Jury of Your Peers? Only If You're Clueless*, The Washington Post, Aug. 11, 2002.

E. Closing Arguments and Fundamental Fairness

Darden v. Wainwright
477 U.S. 168 (1986)

Justice POWELL delivered the opinion of the Court.

This case presents [the question] ... whether the prosecution's closing argument during the guilt phase of a bifurcated trial rendered the trial fundamentally unfair and deprived the sentencing determination of the reliability required by the Eighth Amendment....

II

Because of the nature of petitioner's claims, the facts of this case will be stated in more detail than is normally necessary in this Court. On September 8, 1973, at about 5:30 p.m., a black adult male entered Carl's Furniture Store near Lakeland, Florida. The only other person in the store was the proprietor, Mrs. Turman, who lived with her husband in a house behind the store. Mr. Turman, who worked nights at a juvenile home, had awakened at about 5:00 p.m., had a cup of coffee at the store with his wife, and returned home to let their dogs out for a run. Mrs. Turman showed the man around the store. He stated that he was interested in purchasing about $600 worth of furniture for a rental unit, and asked to see several different items. He left the store briefly, stating that his wife would be back to look at some of the items.

The same man returned just a few minutes later asking to see some stoves, and inquiring about the price. When Mrs. Turman turned toward the adding machine, he grabbed her and pressed a gun to her back, saying "Do as I say and you won't get hurt." He took her to the rear of the store and told her to open the cash register. He took the money, then ordered her to the part of the store where some box springs and mattresses were stacked against the wall. At that time Mr. Turman appeared at the back door. Mrs. Turman screamed while the man reached across her right shoulder and shot Mr. Turman between the eyes. Mr. Turman fell backwards, with one foot partially in the building. Ordering Mrs. Turman not to move, the man tried to pull Mr. Turman into the building and close the door, but could not do so because one of Mr. Turman's feet was caught in the door. The man left Mr. Turman face-up in the rain, and told Mrs. Turman to get down on the floor approximately five feet from where her husband lay dying. While she begged to go to her husband, he told her to remove her false teeth. He unzipped his pants, unbuckled his belt, and demanded that Mrs. Turman perform oral sex on him. She began to cry "Lord, have mercy." He told her to get up and go towards the front of the store.

Meanwhile, a neighbor family, the Arnolds, became aware that something had happened to Mr. Turman. The mother sent her 16-year-old son Phillip, a part-time employee at the furniture store, to help. When Phillip reached the back door he saw Mr. Turman lying partially in the building. When Phillip opened the door to take Turman's body inside, Mrs. Turman shouted "Phillip, no, go back." Phillip did not know what she meant and asked the man to help get Turman inside. He replied, "Sure, buddy, I will help you." As Phillip looked up, the man was pointing a gun in his face. He pulled the trigger and the gun misfired; he pulled the trigger again and shot Phillip in the mouth. Phillip started to run away, and was shot in the neck. While he was still running, he was shot a third time in the side. Despite these wounds, Phillip managed to stumble to the home of a neighbor, Mrs. Edith Hill. She had her husband call an ambulance while she tried to stop Phillip's bleeding. While she was helping Phillip, she saw a late model green Chevrolet leave the store and head towards Tampa on state highway 92. Phillip survived the incident; Mr. Turman, who never regained consciousness, died later that night.

Minutes after the murder petitioner was driving towards Tampa on highway 92, just a few miles away from the furniture store. He was out on furlough from a Florida prison, and was driving a car borrowed from his girlfriend in Tampa. He was driving fast on a wet road. Petitioner testified that as he came up on a line of cars in his lane, he was unable to slow down. He attempted to pass, but was forced off the road to avoid a head-on collision with an oncoming car. Petitioner crashed into a telephone pole. The driver of the oncoming car, John Stone, stopped his car and went to petitioner to see if he could help. Stone testified that as he approached the car, petitioner was zipping up his pants and buckling his belt. Police at the crash site later identified petitioner's car as a 1969 Chevrolet Impala of greenish golden brown color. Petitioner paid a bystander to give him a ride to Tampa. Petitioner later returned with a wrecker, only to find that the car had been towed away by the police.

By the time the police arrived at the scene of the accident, petitioner had left. The fact that the car matched the description of the car leaving the scene of the murder, and that the accident had occurred within three and one-half miles of the furniture store and within minutes of the murder, led police to suspect that the car was driven by the murderer. They searched the area. An officer found a pistol — a revolver — about forty feet from the crash site. The arrangement of shells within the chambers exactly matched the pattern that should have been found in the murder weapon: one shot, one misfire, followed by three shots, with a live shell remaining in the next chamber to be fired. A specialist for the FBI examined the pistol and testified that it was a Smith & Wesson .38 special revolver. It had been manufactured as a standard .38; it later was sent to England to be rebored, making it a much rarer type of gun than the standard .38. An examination of the bullet that killed Mr. Turman revealed that it came from a .38 Smith & Wesson special.

On the day following the murder petitioner was arrested at his girlfriend's house in Tampa. A few days later Mrs. Turman identified him at a preliminary hearing as her husband's murderer. Phillip Arnold selected petitioner's picture out of a spread of six photographs as the man who had shot him.[1] ...

---

1. There are some minor discrepancies in the eyewitness identification. Mrs. Turman first described her assailant immediately after the murder while her husband was being taken to the emergency room. She told the investigating officer that the attacker was a heavyset man. When asked if he was "neat in his appearance, clean-looking, clean-shaven," she responded "[a]s far as I can re-

IV

Petitioner ... contends that the prosecution's closing argument at the guilt-innocence stage of the trial rendered his conviction fundamentally unfair and deprived the sentencing determination of the reliability that the Eighth Amendment requires.

It is helpful as an initial matter to place these remarks in context. Closing argument came at the end of several days of trial. Because of a state procedural rule petitioner's counsel had the opportunity to present the initial summation as well as a rebuttal to the prosecutors' closing arguments. The prosecutors' comments must be evaluated in light of the defense argument that preceded it, which blamed the Polk County Sheriff's Office for a lack of evidence,[5] alluded to the death penalty,[6] characterized the perpetrator of the crimes as an "animal,"[7] and contained counsel's personal opinion of the strength of the state's evidence.[8]

The prosecutors then made their closing argument. That argument deserves the condemnation it has received from every court to review it, although no court has held that the argument rendered the trial unfair. Several [of the prosecutor's] comments attempted to place some of the blame for the crime on the Division of Corrections, because Darden was on weekend furlough from a prison sentence when the crime occurred.[9] Some [of the prosecutor's] comments implied that the death penalty would be

member, yes, sir." She also stated to the officer that she thought that the attacker was about her height, 5'6" tall, and that he was wearing a pullover shirt with a stripe around the neck. The first time she saw petitioner after the attack was when she identified him at the preliminary hearing. She had not read any newspaper accounts of the crime, nor had she seen any picture of petitioner. When she was asked if petitioner was the man who had committed the crimes, she said yes. She also repeatedly identified him at trial.

Phillip Arnold first identified petitioner in a photo line-up while in the hospital. He could not speak at the time, and in response to the written question whether petitioner had a mustache, Phillip wrote back "I don't think so."

Phillip also testified at trial that the attacker was a heavyset man wearing a dull, light color knit shirt with a ring around the neck. He testified that the man was almost his height, about 6'2" tall.

A motorist who stopped at the scene of the accident testified that petitioner was wearing a white or off-grey button-down shirt and that he had a slight mustache. In fact, the witness stated that he "didn't know it was that [the mustache] or the raindrops on him or not. I couldn't really tell that much to it, it was real thin, that's all." Petitioner is about 5'10" tall, and at the time of trial testified that he weighed about 175 pounds.

5. "The Judge is going to tell you to consider the evidence or the lack of evidence. We have a lack of evidence, almost criminally negligent on the part of the Polk County Sheriff's Office in this case. You could go on and on about it."

6. "They took a coincidence and magnified that into a capital case. And they are asking you to kill a man on coincidence."

7. "The first witness you saw was Mrs. Turman, who was a pathetic figure; who worked and struggled all of her life to build what little she had, the little furniture store; and a woman who would be robbed, sexually assaulted, and then had her husband slaughtered before her eyes, by what would have to be a vicious animal." "And this murderer ran after him, aimed again, and this poor kid with half his brains blown away.... It's the work of an animal, there's no doubt about it."

8. "So they come up here and ask Citrus County people to kill the man. You will be instructed on lesser included offenses.... The question is, do they have enough evidence to kill that man, enough evidence? And I honestly do not think they do."

9. "As far as I am concerned, there should be another Defendant in this courtroom, one more, and that is the division of corrections, the prisons.... Can we expect him to stay in a prison when they go there? Can we expect them to stay locked up once they go there? Do we know that they're going to be out on the public with guns, drinking?" "Yes, there is another Defendant, but I regret that I know of no charges to place upon him, except the public condemnation of them, condemn them."

the only guarantee against a future similar act.[10] Others incorporated the defense's use of the word "animal."[11] Prosecutor McDaniel made several offensive comments reflecting an emotional reaction to the case.[12] These comments undoubtedly were improper. But as both the District Court and the original panel of the Court of Appeals (whose opinion on this issue still stands) recognized, it "is not enough that the prosecutors' remarks were undesirable or even universally condemned." The relevant question is whether the prosecutors' comments "so infected the trial with unfairness as to make the resulting conviction a denial of due process." Moreover, the appropriate standard of review for such a claim on writ of habeas corpus is "the narrow one of due process, and not the broad exercise of supervisory power."

Under this standard of review, we agree with the reasoning of every court to consider these comments that they did not deprive petitioner of a fair trial. The prosecutors' argument did not manipulate or misstate the evidence, nor did it implicate other specific rights of the accused such as the right to counsel or the right to remain silent. Much of the objectionable content was invited by or was responsive to the opening summation of the defense. As we explained in *United States v. Young*, 470 U.S. 1 (1985), the idea of "invited response" is used not to excuse improper comments, but to determine their effect on the trial as a whole. The trial court instructed the jurors several times that their decision was to be made on the basis of the evidence alone, and that the arguments of counsel were not evidence. The weight of the evidence against petitioner was heavy; the "overwhelming eyewitness and circumstantial evidence to support a finding of guilt on all charges" reduced the likelihood that the jury's decision was influenced by argument. Finally, defense counsel made the tactical decision not to present any witness other than petitioner. This decision not only permitted them to give their summation prior to the prosecution's closing argument, but also gave them the opportunity to make a final rebuttal argument. Defense counsel were able to use the opportunity for rebuttal very effectively, turning much of the prosecutors' closing argument against them by placing many of the prosecutors' comments and actions in a light that was more likely to engender strong disapproval than result in inflamed passions against petitioner.[14] For these

---

10. "I will ask you to advise the Court to give him death. That's the only way I know that he is not going to get out on the public. It's the only way I know. It's the only way I can be sure of it. It's the only way anybody can be sure of it now, because the people that turned him loose—."

11. "As far as I am concerned, and as Mr. Maloney said as he identified this man as an animal, this animal was on the public for one reason."

12. "He shouldn't be out of his cell unless he has a leash on him and a prison guard at the other end of that leash." "I wish [Mr. Turman] had had a shotgun in his hand when he walked in the back door and blown his [Darden's] face off. I wish I could see him sitting here with no face, blown away by a shotgun." "I wish someone had walked in the back door and blown his head off at that point." "He fired in the boy's back, number five saving one. Didn't get a chance to use it. I wish he had used it on himself." "I wish he had been killed in the accident, but he wasn't. Again, we are unlucky that time." "Don't forget what he has done according to those witnesses, to make every attempt to change his appearance from September the 8th, 1973. The hair, the goatee, even the moustache and the weight. The only thing he hasn't done that I know of is cut his throat." After this, the last in a series of such comments, defense counsel objected for the first time.

14. "Mr. McDaniel made an impassioned plea ... how many times did he repeat [it]? I wish you had been shot, I wish they had blown his face away. My God, I get the impression he would like to be the man that stands there and pulls the switch on him." One of Darden's counsel testified at the habeas corpus hearing that he made the tactical decision not to object to the improper comments. Based on his long experience with prosecutor McDaniel, he knew McDaniel would "get much more vehement in his remarks if you allowed him to go on." By not immediately objecting, he hoped to encourage the prosecution to commit reversible error.

reasons, we agree with the District Court below that "Darden's trial was not perfect—few are—but neither was it fundamentally unfair." ...

VI

The judgment of the Court of Appeals is affirmed, and the case is remanded for proceedings consistent with this opinion.

Justice BLACKMUN, with whom Justice Brennan, Justice Marshall, and Justice Stevens join, dissenting.

Although the Constitution guarantees a criminal defendant only "a fair trial [and] not a perfect one," this Court has stressed repeatedly in the decade since *Gregg v. Georgia* that the Eighth Amendment requires a heightened degree of reliability in any case where a State seeks to take the defendant's life. Today's opinion, however, reveals a Court willing to tolerate not only imperfection but a level of fairness and reliability so low it should make conscientious prosecutors cringe.

I

A

The Court's discussion of Darden's claim of prosecutorial misconduct is noteworthy for its omissions. Despite the fact that earlier this Term the Court relied heavily on standards governing the professional responsibility of defense counsel in ruling that an attorney's actions did not deprive his client of any constitutional right, today it entirely ignores standards governing the professional responsibility of prosecutors in reaching the conclusion that the summations of Darden's prosecutors did not deprive him of a fair trial.

The prosecutors' remarks in this case reflect behavior as to which "virtually all the sources speak with one voice," that is, a voice of strong condemnation. The following brief comparison of established standards of prosecutorial conduct with the prosecutors' behavior in this case merely illustrates, but hardly exhausts, the scope of the misconduct involved:

1. "A lawyer shall not ... state a personal opinion as to ... the credibility of a witness ... or the guilt or innocence of an accused." Model Rules of Professional Conduct, Rule 3.4(e); see also Code of Professional Responsibility, DR 7-106(C)(4); ABA Standards for Criminal Justice: The Prosecution Function, Standard 3-5.8(b). Yet one prosecutor, White, stated: "I am convinced, as convinced as I know I am standing before you today, that Willie Jasper Darden is a murderer, that he murdered Mr. Turman, that he robbed Mrs. Turman and that he shot to kill Phillip Arnold. I will be convinced of that the rest of my life." And the other prosecutor, McDaniel, stated, with respect to Darden's testimony: "Well, let me tell you something: If I am ever over in that chair over there, facing life or death, life imprisonment or death, I guarantee you I will lie until my teeth fall out."

2. "The prosecutor should refrain from argument which would divert the jury from its duty to decide the case on the evidence, by injecting issues broader than the guilt or innocence of the accused under the controlling law, or by making predictions of the consequences of the jury's verdict." ABA Standards for Criminal Justice: The Prosecution Function, Standard 3-5.8(d); cf. Model Rules of Professional Conduct, Rule 3.4(e); Code of Professional Responsibility, DR 7-106(C)(7); ABA Standards for Criminal Justice: The Prosecution Function, Standard 3-6.1(c). Yet McDaniel's argument was filled

with references to Darden's status as a prisoner on furlough who "shouldn't be out of his cell unless he has a leash on him." Again and again, he sought to put on trial an absent "defendant," the State Department of Corrections that had furloughed Darden. He also implied that defense counsel would use improper tricks to deflect the jury from the real issue. Darden's status as a furloughed prisoner, the release policies of the Department of Corrections, and his counsel's anticipated tactics obviously had no legal relevance to the question the jury was being asked to decide: whether he had committed the robbery and murder at the Turmans' furniture store. Indeed, the State argued before this Court that McDaniel's remarks were harmless precisely because he "failed to discuss the issues, the weight of the evidence, or the credibility of the witnesses."

3. "The prosecutor should not use arguments calculated to inflame the passions or prejudices of the jury." ABA Standards for Criminal Justice: The Prosecution Function, Standard 3-5.8(c). Yet McDaniel repeatedly expressed a wish "that I could see [Darden] sitting here with no face, blown away by a shotgun." Indeed, I do not think McDaniel's summation, taken as a whole, can accurately be described as anything but a relentless and single-minded attempt to inflame the jury.

C

… The Court presents what is, for me, an entirely unpersuasive one-page laundry list of reasons for ignoring this blatant misconduct. First, the Court says that the summations "did not manipulate or misstate the evidence [or] … implicate other specific rights of the accused such as the right to counsel or the right to remain silent." With all respect, that observation is quite beside the point. The "solemn purpose of endeavoring to ascertain the truth … is the *sine qua non* of a fair trial," and the summations cut to the very heart of the Due Process Clause by diverting the jury's attention "from the ultimate question of guilt or innocence that should be the central concern in a criminal proceeding."

Second, the Court says that "[m]uch of the objectionable content was invited by or was responsive to the opening summation of the defense." The Court identifies four portions of the defense summation that it thinks somehow "invited" McDaniel's sustained barrage. The State, however, did not object to any of these statements, and, to my mind, none of them is so objectionable that it would have justified a tactical decision to interrupt the defense summation and perhaps irritate the jury.

The Court begins by stating that defense counsel "blamed" the sheriff's office for a lack of evidence. The Court does not identify which, if any, of McDaniel's remarks represented a response to this statement. I cannot believe that the Court is suggesting, for example, that defense counsel's one mention of the "almost crimina[l] negligen[ce] on the part of the Polk County Sheriff's Office" justified McDaniel's express and repeated wish that he could try the Department of Corrections for murder.

Next, the Court notes that defense counsel "alluded" to the death penalty. While this allusion might have justified McDaniel's statement that "you are merely to determine his innocence or guilt, nothing else," it could hardly justify, for example, McDaniel's expressions of his personal wish that Darden be "blown away by a shotgun."

Moreover, the Court says, defense counsel twice referred to the perpetrator as an "animal." It is entirely unclear to me why this characterization called for any response from the prosecutor at all. Taken in context, defense counsel's statements did nothing more than tell the jury that, although everyone agreed that a heinous crime had been committed, the issue on which it should focus was whether Darden had committed it.

Finally, the Court finds that Darden brought upon himself McDaniel's tirade because defense counsel gave his "personal opinion of the strength of the State's evidence." Again, the Court gives no explanation of how the statement it quotes—a single, mild expression of defense counsel's overall assessment of the evidence—justified the "response" that followed, which consisted, to the extent it represented a comment on the evidence at all, of accusations of perjury and personal disparagements of opposing counsel. In sum, McDaniel went so far beyond "respond[ing] substantially in order to 'right the scale'" that the reasoning in *United States v. Young*, 470 U.S. 1 (1985), provides no basis at all for the Court's holding today.

The third reason the Court gives for discounting the effects of the improper summations is the supposed curative effect of the trial judge's instructions: the judge had instructed the jury that it was to decide the case on the evidence and that the arguments of counsel were not evidence. But the trial court overruled Darden's objection to McDaniel's repeated expressions of his wish that Darden had been killed, thus perhaps leaving the jury with the impression that McDaniel's comments were somehow relevant to the question before them. The trial judge's instruction that the attorneys were "trained in the law," and thus that their "analysis of the issues" could be "extremely helpful," might also have suggested to the jury that the substance of McDaniel's tirade was pertinent to their deliberations.

Fourth, the Court suggests that because Darden enjoyed the tactical advantage of having the last summation, he was able to "tur[n] much of the prosecutors' closing argument against them." But the issue before the jury was whether Darden was guilty, not whether McDaniel's summation was proper. And the question before this Court is not whether we agree with defense counsel's criticism of the summation but whether the jury was affected by it. Since Darden was ultimately convicted, it is hard to see what basis the Court has for its naked assertion that "[d]efense counsel were able to use the opportunity for rebuttal very effectively."

Fifth, the Court finds, in essence, that any error was harmless: "The weight of the evidence against petitioner was heavy; the 'overwhelming eyewitness and circumstantial evidence to support a finding of guilt on all charges,' reduced the likelihood that the jury's decision was influenced by argument." The Court rejects the "no effect" test set out in *Caldwell v. Mississippi*, but it does not identify the standard it does use to decide the harmlessness of the error....

Regardless of which test is used, I simply do not believe the evidence in this case was so overwhelming that this Court can conclude, on the basis of the written record before it, that the jury's verdict was not the product of the prosecutors' misconduct. The three most damaging pieces of evidence—the identifications of Darden by Phillip Arnold and Helen Turman and the ballistics evidence—are all sufficiently problematic that they leave me unconvinced that a jury not exposed to McDaniel's egregious summation would necessarily have convicted Darden.

Arnold first identified Darden in a photo array shown to him in the hospital. The trial court suppressed that out-of-court identification following a long argument concerning the reliability and constitutionality of the procedures by which it was obtained.

Mrs. Turman's initial identification was made under even more suggestive circumstances. She testified at trial that she was taken to a preliminary hearing at which Darden appeared in order "[t]o identify him." Instead of being asked to view Darden in a lineup, Mrs. Turman was brought into the courtroom, where Darden apparently was the only black man present. Over defense counsel's objection, after the prosecutor asked her whether "this man sitting here" was "the man that shot your husband," she identified Darden.

The use of showups has long been condemned by this Court, precisely because they can result in unreliable identifications. See, e.g., *Stovall v. Denno*, 388 U.S. 293, 302 (1967). Similarly, the Court has condemned the use of photo arrays in which the suspect's photograph "is in some way emphasized." *Simmons v. United States*, 390 U.S. 377, 383 (1968). While the question whether the various in- and out-of-court identifications ought to have been suppressed is not now before the Court, my confidence in their reliability is nonetheless undermined by the suggestiveness of the procedures by which they were obtained, particularly in light of Mrs. Turman's earlier difficulties in describing the criminal.

Finally, the ballistics evidence is hardly overwhelming. The purported murder weapon was tied conclusively neither to the crime nor to Darden. Special Agent Cunningham of the FBI's Firearms Identification Unit testified that the bullets recovered at the scene of the crime "could have been fired" from the gun, but he was unwilling to say that they in fact had come from that weapon. He also testified, contrary to the Court's assertion, that rebored Smith & Wessons were fairly common. Deputy Sheriff Weatherford testified that the gun was discovered in a roadside ditch adjacent to where Darden had wrecked his car on the evening of the crime. But the gun was discovered the next day and the ditch was also next to a bar's parking lot.

Darden testified at trial on his own behalf and denied any involvement in the robbery and murder. His account of his actions on the day of the crime was contradicted only by Mrs. Turman's and Arnold's identifications. Indeed, a number of the State's witnesses corroborated parts of Darden's account. The trial judge who had seen and heard Darden testify found that he "emotionally and with what appeared on its face to be sincerity, proclaimed his innocence." In setting sentence, he viewed the fact that Darden "repeatedly professed his complete innocence of the charges" as a mitigating factor.

Thus, at bottom, this case rests on the jury's determination of the credibility of three witnesses—Helen Turman and Phillip Arnold, on the one side, and Willie Darden, on the other. I cannot conclude that McDaniel's sustained assault on Darden's very humanity did not affect the jury's ability to judge the credibility question on the real evidence before it. Because I believe that he did not have a trial that was fair, I would reverse Darden's conviction; I would not allow him to go to his death until he has been convicted at a fair trial....

III

Twice during the past year—in *United States v. Young* and again today—this Court has been faced with clearly improper prosecutorial misconduct during summations. Each time, the Court has condemned the behavior but affirmed the conviction....

I believe this Court must do more than wring its hands when a State ... permits prosecutors to pervert the adversary process. I therefore dissent.

Notes and Questions on Prosecutorial Misconduct

1. In *Darden*, the Court characterized the issue as whether the prosecutor's improper comments were so unfair as to make the conviction a denial of due process. Does this standard offer anything by way of specific guidance or is it merely circular?

2. The practice of affirming convictions while simultaneously denouncing government counsel for misconduct was condemned by Judge Jerome N. Frank in *United States v. Antonelli Fireworks Co.*, 155 F.2d 631, 661 (2d Cir. 1946) (dissenting). According to Judge Frank, such "helpless piety" compounds the error of condoning misconduct by sending a message to prosecutors that the rules against misconduct are "pretend-rules" which are "purely ceremonial." In Judge Frank's words:

> Government counsel, employing such tactics, are the kind who, eager to win victories, will gladly pay the small price of a ritualistic verbal spanking. The practice of this court—recalling the bitter tear shed by the Walrus as he ate the oysters—breeds a deplorably cynical attitude towards the judiciary.

Can you think of any ways, short of reversal, to deter prosecutorial misconduct?

3. According to the Supreme Court, the prosecutor's duty in a criminal case is to seek justice. In *Berger v. United States*, 295 U.S. 78, 89 (1935), the Court ordered a new trial because the prosecutor had misstated facts, put words in witnesses' mouths, spoke as if he had personal knowledge about the case, bullied witnesses, and conducted himself in a "thoroughly indecorous and improper manner." The Court explained:

> [the prosecutor] is the representative not of an ordinary party to a controversy, but of a sovereignty whose obligation to govern impartially is as compelling as its obligation to govern at all; and whose interest, therefore, in a criminal prosecution, is not that it shall win a case, but that justice shall be done.

Id. at 88. Although prosecutors are expected to "prosecute with earnestness and vigor," they must not use "improper methods calculated to produce a wrongful conviction." *Id.*

4. Recall that in *Darden*, improper comments formed the basis for the prosecutorial misconduct allegation. Prosecutors have been admonished to avoid making unfair or improper remarks about the defendant, *United States v. Francis*, 170 F.3d 546, 549 (6th Cir. 1999) (prosecutor's calling defendant a "con man" and a "liar" was reversible error in the absence of curative instructions and overwhelming evidence of guilt); defense counsel, *United States v. Friedman*, 909 F.2d 705, 709–10 (2d Cir. 1990) (prosecutor's statements that defense counsel would "make any argument he can to get that guy off" and that "while some people prosecute drug dealers, there are others who try to get them off, perhaps even for high fees" was reversible error because curative instructions were insufficient and evidence of defendant's guilt was not overwhelming); or defense witnesses, *United States v. Mitchell*, 1 F.3d 235, 240 (4th Cir. 1993) (prosecutor's argument that defendant's brother's testimony should be disbelieved because defendant's brother's own jury had disbelieved him was reversible error because comments were repeated and evidence was not overwhelming). Comment on the defendant's failure to testify is also improper. *Griffin v. California*, 380 U.S. 609, 615 (1965). Personal opinions about the defendant's guilt or credibility are likewise forbidden. *United States v. Smith*, 982 F.2d 681, 682–85 (1st Cir. 1993) (prosecution's repeated characterization of defendant's testimony as "a lie," "one tall tale," and "a complete fabrication," and improper statements that defendant was guilty was not reversible error because the government's evidence was uncontested and defendant failed as a matter of law to establish affirmative defense).

As the Court made clear, improper comments alone do not warrant reversal. "[T]he relevant question is whether the prosecutors' comments so infected the trial with unfairness as to make the resulting conviction a denial of due process." *Darden*, 477 U.S. at 181.

Other types of actions which commonly form the basis for prosecutorial misconduct charges include knowingly presenting false testimony, *Napue v. Illinois*, 360 U.S. 264,

269 (1959), and failing to disclose evidence favorable to the defendant upon request, *Brady v. Maryland*, 373 U.S. 83 (1963). In addition, misstating the law or the facts is obviously prohibited. Can you think of any other actions which might constitute prosecutorial misconduct? Consider the Court's recent opinion dealing with prosecutorial misconduct:

In *Banks v. Dretke*, 540 U.S. 668 (2004), the Supreme Court found that Texas prosecutors deliberately withheld information that would have undermined and/or discredited the testimony of two state witnesses who testified against Delma Banks in Banks' capital murder trial. In describing the state's actions, the Supreme Court stated:

> Petitioner Delma Banks, Jr., was convicted of capital murder and sentenced to death. Prior to trial, the State advised Banks's attorney there would be no need to litigate discovery issues, representing: "[W]e will, without the necessity of motions[,] provide you with all discovery to which you are entitled." Despite that undertaking, the State withheld evidence that would have allowed Banks to discredit two essential prosecution witnesses. The State did not disclose that one of those witnesses was a paid police informant, nor did it disclose a pretrial transcript revealing that the other witness' trial testimony had been intensively coached by prosecutors and law enforcement officers.
>
> Furthermore, the prosecution raised no red flag when the informant testified, untruthfully, that he never gave the police any statement and, indeed, had not talked to any police officer about the case until a few days before the trial. Instead of correcting the informant's false statements, the prosecutor told the jury that the witness "ha[d] been open and honest with you in every way," and that his testimony was of the "utmost significance." Similarly, the prosecution allowed the other key witness to convey, untruthfully, that his testimony was entirely unrehearsed. Through direct appeal and state collateral review proceedings, the State continued to hold secret the key witnesses' links to the police and allowed their false statements to stand uncorrected.
>
> Ultimately, through discovery and an evidentiary hearing authorized in a federal habeas corpus proceeding, the long-suppressed evidence came to light. The District Court granted Banks relief from the death penalty, but the Court of Appeals reversed. In the latter court's judgment, Banks had documented his claims of prosecutorial misconduct too late and in the wrong forum; therefore he did not qualify for federal-court relief. We reverse that judgment. When police or prosecutors conceal significant exculpatory or impeaching material in the State's possession, it is ordinarily incumbent on the State to set the record straight.

5. Capital cases, which by definition involve the most serious crimes and the most draconian penalties, are especially susceptible to episodes of prosecutorial misconduct. Given the "Eighth Amendment's heightened need for reliability," *Caldwell v. Mississippi*, 472 U.S. 320, 340 (1985), should courts reduce the burden on capital defendants seeking to establish due process violations as a result of prosecutorial misconduct?

6. If you believe that courts should not reduce the burden of establishing prosecutorial misconduct which rises to the level of a due process violation, can the political processes be relied upon to sanction prosecutors who abjure their obligations to act fairly? An investigative reporter describing the capital trial tactics of Oklahoma City District Attorney Robert Macy suggests that the answer is "no." According to the reporter, Macy, the former head of the National Association of District Attorneys,

has lied. He has bullied. Even when a man's life is at stake, Macy has spurned the rules of a fair trial, concealing evidence, misrepresenting evidence, or launching into abusive, improper arguments that had nothing to do with the evidence, according to appellate rulings condemning his tactics. In the court of law, Macy meets with constant and sometimes severe criticism. But in the court of public opinion he consistently wins re-election—usually with more than 70 percent of the vote.

Armstrong, *"Cowboy Bob" Ropes Win—But at Considerable Cost*, Chicago Tribune, Jan. 10, 1999.

Others have observed that prosecutors rarely get punished for concealing the truth in order to secure undeserved convictions, even if their conduct is outrageous. One study found nearly 400 cases in which prosecutors obtained homicide convictions by committing extreme acts of deception. "They hid evidence which could have set defendants free. They allowed witnesses to lie. All in defiance of law.... The premium is on winning, not justice." What becomes of prosecutors whose misbehavior perverts the criminal justice system?

A dramatic example is provided by the 381 homicide defendants who received new trials [in the U.S. between 1965 and 1999] because prosecutors hid evidence or allowed witnesses to lie. The appellate courts denounced the prosecutors' actions with words like "unforgivable," "intolerable," "beyond reprehension," and "illegal, improper and dishonest." At least a dozen of the prosecutors were investigated by state agencies charged with policing lawyers for misconduct.

But here is what has happened to the prosecutors in those hundreds of cases: One was fired, but appealed and was reinstated with back pay. Another received an in-house suspension of 30 days. A third prosecutor's law license was suspended for 59 days, but because of other misconduct in the case.

Not one received any kind of public sanction from a state lawyer disciplinary agency or was convicted of any crime for hiding evidence or presenting false evidence.... Two were indicted, but the charges were dismissed before trial.

Instead, the prosecutor's career advances. In Georgia, George "Buddy" Darden became a congressman after a court concluded that he withheld evidence in a case where seven men, later exonerated, were convicted of murder and one was sentenced to death. In New Mexico, Virginia Ferrara failed to disclose evidence of another suspect in a murder case. By the time the conviction was reversed she had become chief disciplinary counsel for the New Mexico agency that polices lawyers for misconduct.

Armstrong & Possley, *The Verdict: Dishonor*, Chicago Tribune, Jan. 10, 1999, at N1. The study of the aftermath of hundreds of judicial reversals of homicide convictions due to prosecutorial misconduct concluded that "winning a [homicide] conviction can accelerate a prosecutor's career, but getting rebuked on appeal will rarely stall it, contributing to a culture that fosters misconduct. And the deterrents that confront prosecutors are fearsome only in theory." Armstrong & Possley, *Break Rules, Be Promoted*, Chicago Tribune, Jan. 14, 1999, at N1.

7. There seems to be a symbiotic relationship between egregious prosecutorial misconduct in court and trial judges who permit capital trials to take place in an atmosphere of "near anarchy." For example, the Illinois Supreme Court, while unanimously overturning the conviction of a police killer despite overwhelming evidence of guilt,

criticized Cook County Circuit Judge Daniel Kelly "for failing to halt the prosecutors' egregious misconduct and for allowing prosecutors to place in the courtroom a headless mannequin wearing the victim's police uniform, which had blood and brain matter on it." Armstrong & Mills, *Death Row Conviction on Cop Death Overturned*, Chicago Tribune, Jan. 28, 2000. Another Illinois trial judge mocked defense lawyers for seeking DNA tests for their client. When the Illinois Supreme Court ordered that the testing be done, it demonstrated the defendant's innocence. Armstrong & Mills, *Death Row Justice Derailed*, Chicago Tribune, Nov. 14, 1999, at N1.

Evidence suggests that political pressure on judges may contribute to high death sentencing rates which, in turn, may contribute to high error rates. That leads, of course, to low rates of execution. Liebman et al, "Capital Attrition: Error Rates in Capital Cases, 1973–1995," 78 Tex. L. Rev. 1839 (2000). The full version of Professor Liebman's report, "A Broken System: Error Rates in Capital Cases, 1973–1995," is available electronically at <http://www.law.columbia.edu/instructionalservices/liebman/>.

The effect of political pressure on judges in capital cases is examined by Bright & Keenan, "Judges and the Politics of Death: Deciding Between the Bill of Rights and the Next Election in Capital Cases," 75 B.U. L. Rev. 759, 776–80 (1995) (showing that judges in nearly all capital punishment states are elected).

8. At worst, crime victims pay with their lives for police and prosecutorial misconduct in capital cases. For every innocent defendant convicted, a guilty murderer remains free. For example, 13 years after the "Ford Heights Four" were falsely convicted (two capitally) of two rape-murders, and four years before they were exonerated, one of the actual killers, who was still at large, suffocated a third woman to death in a vacant apartment near the scene of the earlier crimes. During the trial of the Ford Heights Four, prosecutors (1) presented false and misleading scientific evidence; (2) used a variety of undisclosed benefits to induce three witnesses to finger the defendants, then permitted the witnesses to lie about the inducements on the stand at trial; and (3) capitalized on a weak case presented by defense attorneys who were often ill-prepared or incompetent. Three attorneys who represented members of the Ford Heights Four have had their licenses revoked or suspended for other matters. Armstrong & Possley, *Reversal of Fortune*, Chicago Tribune, Jan. 13, 1999, at N1.

9. Catching prosecutors who have engaged in unlawful deception at murder trials can be extremely difficult. In the past, evidence of prosecutorial misconduct has surfaced, for example, "only after a judge directed the U.S. marshal to seize the prosecutors' documents, or because newspapers sued under the Freedom of Information Act, or because of anonymous tips, conversations accidentally overheard or papers spied in a prosecutor's hand." Several exonerations resulted after the actual killer took the almost unbelievably self-destructive step of confessing to a crime the police and the courts had claimed to have solved by convicting and condemning someone else. Armstrong & Possley, *The Verdict: Dishonor*, Chicago Tribune, Jan. 10, 1999, at N1.

10. By a 5–4 vote, the United States Supreme Court in *Kyles v. Whitley*, 514 U.S. 419 (1995), reversed petitioner Kyles' conviction and sentence of death because the state had withheld exculpatory evidence in violation of *United States v. Bagley*, 473 U.S. 667 (1985), and *Brady v. Maryland*, 373 U.S. 83 (1963). *Brady* provides that due process is violated when the state withholds evidence favorable to the accused where that evidence is material to either guilt or punishment. Under *Bagley*, evidence is material "if there is a reasonable probability that, had the evidence been disclosed to the defense, the result of the proceeding would have been different." 473 U.S. at 682. Writing for the majority in

Kyles, Justice Souter focused on the materiality aspect of the *Brady-Bagley* line of cases, and concluded that under *Brady* and *Bagley* (1) "materiality does not require a demonstration by a preponderance that disclosure of suppressed evidence would have resulted ultimately in the defendant's acquittal"; (2) the "defendant need not demonstrate that after discounting the inculpatory evidence in light of the undisclosed evidence, there would not have been enough left to convict"; (3) "once a reviewing court applying *Bagley* had found constitutional error there is no need for further harmless-error review"; and (4) the question of materiality is viewed "in terms of the suppressed evidence collectively, not item-by-item."

In *Kyles*, the police and prosecutor failed to turn over certain exculpatory evidence, including contemporaneous statements made by some of the eyewitnesses, records of communications between an informant and the police, and an internal police memorandum. Although acknowledging that the state withheld such evidence, the state courts and the lower federal courts all denied Kyles relief. After undertaking a very close and thorough review of the record, the Supreme Court found that the cumulative effect of this suppressed evidence deprived Kyles of due process and ordered that his conviction and sentence be reversed.

In his dissent, Justice Scalia criticized the majority's fact-intensive review of Kyles' conviction and noted:

> The greatest puzzle of today's decision is what caused *this* capital case to be singled out for favored treatment. Perhaps it has been randomly selected as a symbol, to reassure America that the United States Supreme Court is reviewing capital convictions to make sure no factual error has been made. If so, it is a false symbol, for we assuredly do not do that.... The reality is that responsibility for factual accuracy, in capital cases as in other cases, rests elsewhere — with trial judges and juries, state appellate courts, and the lower federal courts; we do nothing but encourage foolish reliance to pretend otherwise.

11. In *Strickler v. Greene*, 527 U.S. 263, 289–96 (1999), the Court found that a capital prosecutor's suppression of exculpatory evidence was not unconstitutional because the withheld evidence was not "material" in the sense that it probably affected the outcome.

12. Issues of fundamental fairness are raised when the newly-convicted defendant is placed in handcuffs, leg irons or other visible restraints during his sentencing proceeding. In *Deck v. Missouri*, 544 U.S. 622 (2005), the Court held "that the Constitution forbids the use of visible shackles during the penalty phase, as it forbids their use during the guilt phase, unless that use is "justified by an essential state interest — such as the interest in courtroom security — specific to the defendant on trial." In reaching this conclusion, the Court stated:

> We must conclude that courts cannot routinely place defendants in shackles or other physical restraints visible to the jury during the penalty phase of a capital proceeding. The constitutional requirement, however, is not absolute. It permits a judge, in the exercise of his or her discretion, to take account of special circumstances, including security concerns, that may call for shackling. In so doing, it accommodates the important need to protect the courtroom and its occupants. But any such determination must be case specific; that is to say, it should reflect particular concerns, say special security needs or escape risks, related to the defendant on trial.

Moreover, the *Deck* Court concluded that shackling is "inherently prejudicial." The Court opined:

> That statement [that shackling is inherently prejudicial] is rooted in our belief that the practice will often have negative effects, but—like "the consequences of compelling a defendant to wear prison clothing" or of forcing him to stand trial while medicated—those effects "cannot be shown from a trial transcript." *Riggins*, at 137. Thus, where a court, without adequate justification, orders the defendant to wear shackles that will be seen by the jury, the defendant need not demonstrate actual prejudice to make out a due process violation. The State must prove "beyond a reasonable doubt that the [shackling] error complained of did not contribute to the verdict obtained." *Chapman v. California*, 386 U.S. 18, 24 (1967).

Allocution

In closing arguments, defense counsel frequently emphasize their clients' humanity and present them as persons expressing remorse and deserving of a penalty less than death. However, many believe that the most effective spokesman on behalf of the defendant's life is likely to be the defendant himself. Balske, "New Strategies for the Defense of Capital Cases," 13 Akron L. Rev. 331, 356–357 (1979). Nonetheless, capital defendants with significant criminal records are almost always discouraged from testifying during sentencing because the prosecution will undoubtedly impeach their testimony with evidence of their criminal histories.

Allocution is "[t]he traditional formal inquiry under the common law, which exists by force of statute in American jurisdictions with some variations, to be directed by the court to one convicted of a felony before sentence: whether the one convicted has anything to say why the sentence should not be pronounced against him." *Ballentine's Law Dictionary* 62 (3d ed.) (1969). Federal Rule of Criminal Procedure 32(a) provides a right of allocution in federal criminal cases.

"In the capital sentencing context, allocution can be employed powerfully as an opportunity for the convicted person to speak to the jury without threat or fear of cross-examination just before the jury receives its instructions and begins its sentencing deliberations." Dayan, "Allocution in Capital Sentencing," The Champion 39, Nov. 1992.

The Supreme Court has acknowledged the importance of the right to allocution. "The most persuasive counsel may not be able to speak for a defendant as the defendant might, with halting eloquence, speak for himself." *Green v. United States*, 365 U.S. 301, 304 (1962). At least four federal circuit courts of appeal have held that the right to allocution is constitutionally protected. *Ashe v. North Carolina*, 586 F.2d 334 (4th Cir. 1978); *United States v. Moree*, 928 F.2d 654 (5th Cir. 1991); *Boardman v. Estelle*, 957 F.2d 1523 (9th Cir. 1992); *United States v. Jackson*, 923 F.2d 1494 (11th Cir. 1991). Consider the Ninth Circuit's *Boardman* opinion.

> [T]he personal nature of the Sixth Amendment's guarantee of the right to make a defense, the unique ability of a defendant to plead on his own behalf, and the Supreme Court's acknowledgment of the continuing vitality of the practice of permitting a defendant to allocute before sentencing, [compel us to] hold that allocution is a right guaranteed by the due process clause of the Constitution.

Before being formally sentenced to death for his role in the Oklahoma City bombing, convicted terrorist Timothy McVeigh exercised his right to address Judge Richard Matsch. McVeigh quoted Justice Louis Brandeis' dissent in *Olmstead v. United States*, 277 U.S. 438 (1928): McVeigh said, "If the Court please, I wish to use the words of Justice Brandeis dissenting in *Olmstead* to speak for me. He wrote, 'Our government is the potent, the omnipresent teacher. For good or for ill, it teaches the whole people by its example.'[1] That's all I have." McVeigh's cryptic remark was variously interpreted to mean (1) that the bombing of the Murrah Federal Building in Oklahoma City—which claimed 168 lives and injured hundreds—followed an example the government set in 1995 by causing the deaths of the inhabitants of the Davidian compound at Waco, Texas; and (2) whenever the government executes someone for the crime of murder it endorses killing.

F. Lesser Included Offense Instructions

Beck v. Alabama
447 U.S. 625 (1980)

Mr. Justice STEVENS delivered the opinion of the Court.

We granted certiorari to decide the following question: "May a sentence of death constitutionally be imposed after a jury verdict of guilt of a capital offense, when the jury was not permitted to consider a verdict of guilt of a lesser included non-capital offense, and when the evidence would have supported such a verdict?" We now hold that the death penalty may not be imposed under these circumstances.

Petitioner was tried for the capital offense of "[r]obbery or attempts thereof when the victim is intentionally killed by the defendant." Under the Alabama death penalty statute the requisite intent to kill may not be supplied by the felony-murder doctrine. Felony murder is thus a lesser included offense of the capital crime of robbery-intentional killing. However, under the statute the judge is specifically prohibited from giving the jury the option of convicting the defendant of a lesser included offense. Instead, the jury is given the choice of either convicting the defendant of the capital crime, in which case it is required to impose the death penalty, or acquitting him, thus allowing him to escape all penalties for his alleged participation in the crime. If the defendant is convicted and the death penalty imposed, the trial judge must then hold a hearing with respect to aggravating and mitigating circumstances; after hearing the evidence, the judge may refuse to impose the death penalty, sentencing the defendant to life imprisonment without possibility of parole.

---

1. The full quotation from *Olmstead* reads: "Decency, security, and liberty alike demand that government officials shall be subjected to the same rules of conduct that are commands to the citizen. In a government of laws, existence of the government will be imperiled if it fails to observe the law scrupulously. Our government is the potent, the omnipresent teacher. For good or for ill, it teaches the whole people by its example. Crime is contagious. If the government becomes a lawbreaker, it breeds contempt for law; it invites every man to become a law unto himself; it invites anarchy. To declare that in the administration of the criminal law the end justifies the means—to declare that the government may commit crimes in order to secure the conviction of a private criminal—would bring terrible retribution. Against that pernicious doctrine this court should resolutely set its face." 277 U.S. 438, 484 (1925) (Brandeis, J., dissenting).

In this case petitioner's own testimony established his participation in the robbery of an 80-year-old man named Roy Malone. Petitioner consistently denied, however, that he killed the man or that he intended his death. Under petitioner's version of the events, he and an accomplice entered their victim's home in the afternoon, and, after petitioner had seized the man intending to bind him with a rope, his accomplice unexpectedly struck and killed him. As the State has conceded, absent the statutory prohibition on such instructions, this testimony would have entitled petitioner to a lesser included offense instruction on felony murder as a matter of state law.

Because of the statutory prohibition, the court did not instruct the jury as to the lesser included offense of felony murder. Instead, the jury was told that if petitioner was acquitted of the capital crime of intentional killing in the course of a robbery, he "must be discharged" and "he can never be tried for anything that he ever did to Roy Malone." The jury subsequently convicted petitioner and imposed the death penalty; after holding a hearing with respect to aggravating and mitigating factors, the trial court refused to overturn that penalty.

In the courts below petitioner attacked the prohibition on lesser included offense instructions in capital cases, arguing that the Alabama statute was constitutionally indistinguishable from the mandatory death penalty statutes struck down in *Woodson v. North Carolina*, 428 U.S. 280, and *Roberts v. Louisiana*, 428 U.S. 325. The Alabama Court of Criminal Appeals rejected this argument on the ground that the jury's only function under the Alabama statute is to determine guilt or innocence and that the death sentence it is required to impose after a finding of guilt is merely advisory. In a brief opinion denying review, the Alabama Supreme Court also rejected petitioner's arguments, citing *Jacobs v. State*, 361 So.2d 640 (Ala. 1978), in which it had upheld the constitutionality of the Alabama death penalty statute against a similar challenge.

In this Court petitioner contends that the prohibition on giving lesser included offense instructions in capital cases violates both the Eighth Amendment ... and the Due Process Clause of the Fourteenth Amendment by substantially increasing the risk of error in the factfinding process. Petitioner argues that, in a case in which the evidence clearly establishes the defendant's guilt of a serious noncapital crime such as felony murder, forcing the jury to choose between conviction on the capital offense and acquittal creates a danger that it will resolve any doubts in favor of conviction. In response, Alabama argues that the preclusion of lesser included offense instructions does not impair the reliability of the factfinding process or prejudice the defendant in any way. Rather, it argues that the apparently mandatory death penalty will make the jury more prone to acquit in a doubtful case and that the jury's ability to force a mistrial by refusing to return a verdict acts as a viable third option in a case in which the jury has doubts but is nevertheless unwilling to acquit. The State also contends that prohibiting lesser included offense instructions is a reasonable way of assuring that the death penalty is not imposed arbitrarily and capriciously as a result of compromise verdicts. Finally, it argues that any error in the imposition of the death penalty by the jury can be cured by the judge after a hearing on aggravating and mitigating circumstances.

I

At common law the jury was permitted to find the defendant guilty of any lesser offense necessarily included in the offense charged. This rule originally developed as an aid to the prosecution in cases in which the proof failed to establish some element of the crime charged. But it has long been recognized that it can also be beneficial to the defendant because it affords the jury a less drastic alternative than the choice between conviction of the offense charged and acquittal. As Mr. Justice Brennan explained in his opinion for the Court in *Keeble v. United States*, 412 U.S. 205, 208, providing the jury with the "third option" of convicting on a lesser included offense ensures that the jury will accord the defendant the full benefit of the reasonable-doubt standard....

Alabama's failure to afford capital defendants the protection provided by lesser included offense instructions is unique in American criminal law. In the federal courts, it has long been "beyond dispute that the defendant is entitled to an instruction on a lesser included offense if the evidence would permit a jury rationally to find him guilty of the lesser offense and acquit him of the greater." Similarly, the state courts that have addressed the issue have unanimously held that a defendant is entitled to a lesser included offense instruction where the evidence warrants it. Indeed, for all noncapital crimes Alabama itself gives the defendant a right to such instructions under appropriate circumstances.

While we have never held that a defendant is entitled to a lesser included offense instruction as a matter of due process, the nearly universal acceptance of the rule in both state and federal courts establishes the value to the defendant of this procedural safeguard. That safeguard would seem to be especially important in a case such as this. For when the evidence unquestionably establishes that the defendant is guilty of a serious, violent offense — but leaves some doubt with respect to an element that would justify conviction of a capital offense — the failure to give the jury the "third option" of convicting on a lesser included offense would seem inevitably to enhance the risk of an unwarranted conviction.

Such a risk cannot be tolerated in a case in which the defendant's life is at stake. As we have often stated, there is a significant constitutional difference between the death penalty and lesser punishments:

> [D]eath is a different kind of punishment from any other which may be imposed in this country.... From the point of view of the defendant, it is different in both its severity and its finality. From the point of view of society, the action of the sovereign in taking the life of one of its citizens also differs dramatically from any other legitimate state action. It is of vital importance to the defendant and to the community that any decision to impose the death sentence be, and appear to be, based on reason rather than caprice or emotion. *Gardner v. Florida*, 430 U.S. 349, 357–358 (opinion of Stevens, J.)

To insure that the death penalty is indeed imposed on the basis of "reason rather than caprice or emotion," we have invalidated procedural rules that tended to diminish the reliability of the sentencing determination. The same reasoning must apply to rules that diminish the reliability of the guilt determination. Thus, if the unavailability of a lesser included offense instruction enhances the risk of an unwarranted conviction, Alabama is constitutionally prohibited from withdrawing that option from the jury in a capital case.

II

Alabama argues, however, that petitioner's factual premise is wrong and that, in the context of an apparently mandatory death penalty statute, the preclusion of lesser included offense instructions heightens, rather than diminishes, the reliability of the guilt determination. The State argues that, because the jury is led to believe that a death sentence will automatically follow a finding of guilt,[2] it will be more likely to acquit than to

---

2. The jury is not told that the judge is the final sentencing authority. Rather, the jury is instructed that it must impose the death sentence if it finds the defendant guilty and is led to believe, by implication, that its sentence will be final.

convict whenever it has anything approaching a reasonable doubt. In support of this theory the State relies on the historical data described in *Woodson v. North Carolina*, 428 U.S. at 293 (opinion of Stewart, Powell, and Stevens, JJ.), which indicated that American juries have traditionally been so reluctant to impose the death penalty that they have "with some regularity, disregarded their oaths and refused to convict defendants where a death sentence was the automatic consequence of a guilty verdict."

The State's argument is based on a misreading of our cases striking down mandatory death penalties. In *Furman v. Georgia*, the Court held unconstitutional a Georgia statute that vested the jury with complete and unguided discretion to impose the death penalty or not as it saw fit, on the ground that such a procedure led to the "wanton" and "freakish" imposition of the penalty. In response to *Furman* several States enacted statutes that purported to withdraw any and all discretion from the jury with respect to the punishment decision by making the death penalty automatic on a finding of guilt. But, as the prevailing opinion noted in *Woodson v. North Carolina*, in so doing the States "simply papered over the problem of unguided and unchecked jury discretion." For, as historical evidence indicated, juries faced with a mandatory death penalty statute often created their own sentencing discretion by distorting the fact-finding process, acquitting even a clearly guilty defendant if they felt he did not deserve to die for his crime. Because the jury was given no guidance whatsoever for determining when it should exercise this *de facto* sentencing power, the mandatory death statutes raised the same possibility that the death penalty would be imposed in an arbitrary and capricious manner as the statute held invalid in *Furman*.

The Alabama statute, which was enacted after *Furman* but before *Woodson*, has many of the same flaws that made the North Carolina statute unconstitutional. Thus, the Alabama statute makes the guilt determination depend, at least in part, on the jury's feelings as to whether or not the defendant deserves the death penalty, without giving the jury any standards to guide its decision on this issue.

In *Jacobs v. State*, 361 So.2d 640 (Ala. 1978), Chief Justice Torbert attempted to distinguish the Alabama death statute from the North Carolina and Louisiana statutes on the ground that the unavailability of lesser included offense instructions substantially reduces the risk of jury nullification. Thus, because of their reluctance to acquit a defendant who is obviously guilty of some serious crime, juries will be unlikely to disregard their oaths and acquit a defendant who is guilty of a capital crime simply because of their abhorrence of the death penalty. However, because the death penalty is mandatory, the State argues that the jury will be especially careful to accord the defendant the full benefit of the reasonable-doubt standard. In the State's view the end result is a perfect balance between competing emotional pressures that ensures the defendant a reliable procedure, while at the same time reducing the possibility of arbitrary and capricious guilt determinations.

The State's theory, however, is supported by nothing more than speculation. The 96% conviction rate achieved by prosecutors under the Alabama statute hardly supports the notion that the statute creates such a perfect equipoise.[18] Moreover, it seems unlikely

---

18. Forty-eight out of the first 50 defendants tried under the Alabama statute were convicted. In this case the State has argued that the reason for the high conviction rate is that prosecutors rarely indict for capital offenses except in the clearest of cases because of the risk that a failure of proof on an essential element of the crime might lead to an acquittal. Assuming that this is the reason for the high conviction rate, the statistics still do not support the hypothesis that juries will be more likely to acquit than convict in a doubtful case.

that many jurors would react in the theoretically perfect way the State suggests. As Justice Shores stated in dissent in *Jacobs v. State*:

> The Supreme Court of the United States did remark in *Furman*, and again in *Woodson*, that this nation abhorred the mandatory death sentence.... I suggest that, although there is no historical data to support it, most, if not all, jurors at this point in our history perhaps equally abhor setting free a defendant where the evidence establishes his guilt of a serious crime. We have no way of knowing what influence either of these factors have on a jury's deliberation, and which of these unappealing alternatives a jury opts for in a particular case is a matter of purest conjecture. We cannot know that one outweighs the other. Jurors are not expected to come into the jury box and leave behind all that their human experience has taught them. The increasing crime rate in this country is a source of concern to all Americans. To expect a jury to ignore this reality and to find a defendant innocent and thereby set him free when the evidence establishes beyond doubt that he is guilty of some violent crime requires of our juries clinical detachment from the reality of human experience....

In the final analysis the difficulty with the Alabama statute is that it interjects irrelevant considerations into the factfinding process, diverting the jury's attention from the central issue of whether the State has satisfied its burden of proving beyond a reasonable doubt that the defendant is guilty of a capital crime. Thus, on the one hand, the unavailability of the third option of convicting on a lesser included offense may encourage the jury to convict for an impermissible reason—its belief that the defendant is guilty of some serious crime and should be punished. On the other hand, the apparently mandatory nature of the death penalty may encourage it to acquit for an equally impermissible reason—that, whatever his crime, the defendant does not deserve death. In any particular case these two extraneous factors may favor the defendant or the prosecution or they may cancel each other out. But in every case they introduce a level of uncertainty and unreliability into the factfinding process that cannot be tolerated in a capital case.

III

The State also argues that, whatever the effect of precluding lesser included offense instructions might otherwise be, there is no possibility of harm under the Alabama statute because of two additional safeguards. First, although the jury may not convict the defendant of a lesser included offense, the State argues that it may refuse to return any verdict at all in a doubtful case, thus creating a mistrial. After a mistrial, the State may reindict on the capital offense or on lesser included offenses. In this case the jury was instructed that a mistrial would be declared if it was unable to agree on a verdict or if it was unable to agree on fixing the death penalty; it was also told that, in the event of a mistrial, the defendant could be tried again.

We are not persuaded by the State's argument that the mistrial "option" is an adequate substitute for proper instructions on lesser included offenses. It is extremely doubtful that juries will understand the full implications of a mistrial or will have any confidence that their choice of the mistrial option will ultimately lead to the right result. Thus, they could have no assurance that a second trial would end in the conviction of the defendant on a lesser included offense. Moreover, invoking the mistrial option in a case in which the jury agrees that the defendant is guilty of some offense, though not the offense charged, would require the jurors to violate their oaths to acquit in a proper case — contrary to the State's assertions that juries should not be expected to make such lawless choices. Finally, the fact that lesser included offense instructions have traditionally been given in noncapital cases despite the availability of the mistrial "option" indicates that such instructions provide a necessary additional measure of protection for the defendant.

The State's second argument is that, even if a defendant is erroneously convicted, the fact that the judge has the ultimate sentencing power will ensure that he is not improperly sentenced to death. Again, we are not persuaded that sentencing by the judge compensates for the risk that the jury may return an improper verdict because of the unavailability of a "third option."

If a fully instructed jury would find the defendant guilty only of a lesser, noncapital offense, the judge would not have the opportunity to impose the death sentence. Moreover, it is manifest that the jury's verdict must have a tendency to motivate the judge to impose the same sentence that the jury did. Indeed, according to statistics submitted by the State's Attorney General, it is fair to infer that the jury verdict will ordinarily be followed by the judge even though he must hold a separate hearing in aggravation and mitigation before he imposes sentence. Under these circumstances, we are unwilling to presume that a post-trial hearing will always correct whatever mistakes have occurred in the performance of the jury's factfinding function.

Accordingly, the judgment of the Alabama Supreme Court is reversed.

Notes and Question

1. In *Schad v. Arizona*, 501 U.S. 624 (1991), the Court held that a defendant is not entitled to an instruction on *every* lesser included offense supported by the evidence, as long as the jury has been provided with a "third option" to acquittal or capital conviction.

2. Is the defendant entitled to a lesser included offense instruction if the statute of limitations has expired on the lesser offense? In *Spaziano v. Florida*, 468 U.S. 447, 455–456 (1984), the Court held that the defendant is *not* entitled to such an instruction unless she chooses to waive her statute of limitations defense.

G. Life Without Parole Instructions

Simmons v. South Carolina

512 U.S. 154 (1994)

Justice BLACKMUN announced the judgment of the Court and delivered an opinion in which Justice Stevens, Justice Souter, and Justice Ginsburg join.

This case presents the question whether the Due Process Clause of the Fourteenth Amendment was violated by the refusal of a state trial court to instruct the jury in the penalty phase of a capital trial that under state law the defendant was ineligible for parole. We hold that where the defendant's future dangerousness is at issue, and state law prohibits the defendant's release on parole, due process requires that the sentencing jury be informed that the defendant is parole ineligible.

I

A

In July 1990, petitioner beat to death an elderly woman, Josie Lamb, in her home in Columbia, South Carolina. The week before petitioner's capital murder trial was scheduled to begin, he pleaded guilty to first degree burglary and two counts of criminal sexual conduct in connection with two prior assaults on elderly women. Petitioner's guilty pleas resulted in convictions for violent offenses, and those convictions rendered petitioner ineligible for parole if convicted for any subsequent violent-crime offense. S.C. Code Ann. 24-21-640 (Supp. 1993).

Prior to jury selection, the prosecution advised the trial judge that the State "obviously [was] going to ask you to exclude any mention of parole throughout this trial." Over defense counsel's objection, the trial court granted the prosecution's motion for an order barring the defense from asking any question during voir dire regarding parole. Under the court's order, defense counsel was forbidden even to mention the subject of parole, and expressly was prohibited from questioning prospective jurors as to whether they understood the meaning of a "life" sentence under South Carolina law.[1] After a 3-day trial, petitioner was convicted of the murder of Ms. Lamb.

During the penalty phase, the defense brought forward mitigating evidence tending to show that petitioner's violent behavior reflected serious mental disorders that stemmed from years of neglect and extreme sexual and physical abuse petitioner endured as an adolescent. While there was some disagreement among witnesses regarding the extent to which petitioner's mental condition properly could be deemed a "disorder," witnesses for both the defense and the prosecution agreed that petitioner posed a continuing danger to elderly women.

In its closing argument the prosecution argued that petitioner's future dangerousness was a factor for the jury to consider when fixing the appropriate punishment. The question for the jury, said the prosecution, was "what to do with [petitioner] now that he is in our midst." The prosecution further urged that a verdict for death would be "a response of society to someone who is a threat. Your verdict will be an act of self-defense."

Petitioner sought to rebut the prosecution's generalized argument of future dangerousness by presenting evidence that, due to his unique psychological problems, his dangerousness was limited to elderly women, and that there was no reason to expect further acts of violence once he was isolated in a prison setting. In support of his argument, petitioner introduced testimony from a female medical assistant and from two supervising officers at the Richland County jail where petitioner had been held prior to trial. All three testified that petitioner had adapted well to prison life during his pretrial confinement and had not behaved in a violent manner toward any of the other inmates or staff. Petitioner also offered expert opinion testimony from Richard L. Boyle, a clinical social worker and former correctional employee, who had viewed and observed petitioner's institutional adjustment. Mr. Boyle expressed the view that, based on petitioner's background and his current functioning, petitioner would successfully adapt to prison if he was sentenced to life imprisonment.

---

1. The venire was informed, however, of the meaning of the term "death" under South Carolina law. The trial judge specifically advised the prospective jurors that "by the death penalty, we mean death by electrocution." The sentencing jury was also so informed.

Concerned that the jury might not understand that "life imprisonment" did not carry with it the possibility of parole in petitioner's case, defense counsel asked the trial judge to clarify this point by defining the term "life imprisonment" for the jury in accordance with S.C. Code §24-21-640 (Supp. 1993).[2] To buttress his request, petitioner proffered, outside the presence of the jury, evidence conclusively establishing his parole ineligibility. On petitioner's behalf, attorneys for the South Carolina Department of Corrections and the Department of Probation, Parole and Pardons testified that any offender in petitioner's position was in fact ineligible for parole under South Carolina law. The prosecution did not challenge or question petitioner's parole ineligibility. Instead, it sought to elicit admissions from the witnesses that, notwithstanding petitioner's parole ineligibility, petitioner might receive holiday furloughs or other forms of early release. Even this effort was unsuccessful, however, as the cross-examination revealed that Department of Corrections regulations prohibit petitioner's release under early release programs such as work-release or supervised furloughs, and that no convicted murderer serving life without parole ever had been furloughed or otherwise released for any reason.

Petitioner then offered into evidence, without objection, the results of a statewide public-opinion survey conducted by the University of South Carolina's Institute for Public Affairs. The survey had been conducted a few days before petitioner's trial, and showed that only 7.1 percent of all jury-eligible adults who were questioned firmly believed that an inmate sentenced to life imprisonment in South Carolina actually would be required to spend the rest of his life in prison. Almost half of those surveyed believed that a convicted murderer might be paroled within 20 years; nearly three-quarters thought that release certainly would occur in less than 30 years. More than 75 percent of those surveyed indicated that if they were called upon to make a capital-sentencing decision as jurors, the amount of time the convicted murderer actually would have to spend in prison would be an "extremely important" or a "very important" factor in choosing between life and death.

Petitioner argued that, in view of the public's apparent misunderstanding about the meaning of "life imprisonment" in South Carolina, there was a reasonable likelihood that the jurors would vote for death simply because they believed, mistakenly, that petitioner eventually would be released on parole.

The prosecution opposed the proposed instruction, urging the court "not to allow ... any argument by state or defense about parole and not charge the jury on anything concerning parole." Citing the South Carolina Supreme Court's opinion in *State v. Torrence*, 305 S.C. 45, 406 S.E.2d 315 (1991), the trial court refused petitioner's requested instruction. Petitioner then asked alternatively for the following instruction:

> "I charge you that these sentences mean what they say. That is, if you recommend that the defendant Jonathan Simmons be sentenced to death, he actually will be sentenced to death and executed. If, on the other hand, you recommend that he be sentenced to life imprisonment, he actually will be sentenced to imprisonment in the state penitentiary for the balance of his natural life.

---

2. Section 24-21-640 states: "The board must not grant parole nor is parole authorized to any prisoner serving a sentence for a second or subsequent conviction, following a separate sentencing from a prior conviction, for violent crimes as defined in §16-1-60." Petitioner's earlier convictions for burglary in the first degree and criminal sexual assault in the first degree are violent offenses under §16-1-60.

"In your deliberations, you are not to speculate that these sentences mean anything other than what I have just told you, for what I have told you is exactly what will happen to the defendant, depending on what your sentencing decision is."

The trial judge also refused to give this instruction, but indicated that he might give a similar instruction if the jury inquired about parole eligibility.

After deliberating on petitioner's sentence for 90 minutes, the jury sent a note to the judge asking a single question: "Does the imposition of a life sentence carry with it the possibility of parole?" Over petitioner's objection, the trial judge gave the following instruction:

"You are instructed not to consider parole or parole eligibility in reaching your verdict. Do not consider parole or parole eligibility. That is not a proper issue for your consideration. The terms life imprisonment and death sentence are to be understood in their plan [sic] and ordinary meaning."

Twenty-five minutes after receiving this response from the court, the jury returned to the courtroom with a sentence of death.

On appeal to the South Carolina Supreme Court, petitioner argued that the trial judge's refusal to provide the jury accurate information regarding his parole ineligibility violated the Eighth Amendment and the Due Process Clause of the Fourteenth Amendment.[3] The South Carolina Supreme Court declined to reach the merits of petitioner's challenges. With one Justice dissenting, it concluded that, regardless of whether a trial court's refusal to inform a sentencing jury about a defendant's parole ineligibility might be error under some circumstances, the instruction given to petitioner's jury "satisfied in substance [petitioner's] request for a charge on parole ineligibility," and thus there was no reason to consider whether denial of such an instruction would be constitutional error in this case. We granted certiorari.

II

The Due Process Clause does not allow the execution of a person "on the basis of information which he had no opportunity to deny or explain." *Gardner v. Florida*, 430 U.S. at 362. In this case, the jury reasonably may have believed that petitioner could be released on parole if he were not executed. To the extent this misunderstanding pervaded the jury's deliberations, it had the effect of creating a false choice between sentencing petitioner to death and sentencing him to a limited period of incarceration. This grievous misperception was encouraged by the trial court's refusal to provide the jury with accurate information regarding petitioner's parole ineligibility, and by the State's repeated suggestion that petitioner would pose a future danger to society if he

---

3. Specifically, petitioner argued that under the Eighth Amendment his parole ineligibility was "'mitigating' in the sense that [it] might serve 'as a basis for a sentence less than death,'" *Skipper v. South Carolina*, 476 U.S. 1, 4–5 (1986), quoting *Lockett v. Ohio*, 438 U.S. 586, 604 (1978) (plurality opinion), and that therefore he was entitled to inform the jury of his parole ineligibility. He also asserted that by withholding from the jury the fact that it had a life-without-parole sentencing alternative, the trial court impermissibly diminished the reliability of the jury's determination that death was the appropriate punishment. *Cf. Beck v. Alabama*, 447 U.S. 625 (1980). Finally, relying on the authority of *Gardner v. Florida*, 430 U.S. 349 (1977), petitioner argued that his due process right to rebut the State's argument that petitioner posed a future danger to society had been violated by the trial court's refusal to permit him to show that a noncapital sentence adequately could protect the public from any future acts of violence by him.

were not executed. Three times petitioner asked to inform the jury that in fact he was ineligible for parole under state law; three times his request was denied. The State thus succeeded in securing a death sentence on the ground, at least in part, of petitioner's future dangerousness, while at the same time concealing from the sentencing jury the true meaning of its noncapital sentencing alternative, namely, that life imprisonment meant life without parole. We think it is clear that the State denied petitioner due process.[4]

A

This Court has approved the jury's consideration of future dangerousness during the penalty phase of a capital trial, recognizing that a defendant's future dangerousness bears on all sentencing determinations made in our criminal justice system. See *Jurek v. Texas*, 428 U.S. 262, 275 (1976) (plurality opinion) (noting that "any sentencing authority must predict a convicted person's probable future conduct when it engages in the process of determining what punishment to impose"); *California v. Ramos*, 463 U.S. 992, 1003, n. 17 (1983) (explaining that it is proper for a sentencing jury in a capital case to consider "the defendant's potential for reform and whether his probable future behavior counsels against the desirability of his release into society").

Although South Carolina statutes do not mandate consideration of the defendant's future dangerousness in capital sentencing, the State's evidence in aggravation is not limited to evidence relating to statutory aggravating circumstances. See *Barclay v. Florida*, 463 U.S. 939, 948–951 (1983) (plurality opinion); *California v. Ramos*, 463 U.S. at 1008 ("Once the jury finds that the defendant falls within the legislatively defined category of persons eligible for the death penalty ... the jury then is free to consider a myriad of factors to determine whether death is the appropriate punishment"). Thus, prosecutors in South Carolina, like those in other States that impose the death penalty, frequently emphasize a defendant's future dangerousness in their evidence and argument at the sentencing phase; they urge the jury to sentence the defendant to death so that he will not be a danger to the public if released from prison. Eisenberg & Wells, Deadly Confusion: Juror Instructions in Capital Cases, 79 Cornell L. Rev. 1, 4 (1993).

Arguments relating to a defendant's future dangerousness ordinarily would be inappropriate at the guilt phase of a trial, as the jury is not free to convict a defendant simply because he poses a future danger; nor is a defendant's future dangerousness likely relevant to the question whether each element of an alleged offense has been proved beyond a reasonable doubt. But where the jury has sentencing responsibilities in a capital trial, many issues that are irrelevant to the guilt-innocence determination step into the foreground and require consideration at the sentencing phase. The defendant's character, prior criminal history, mental capacity, background, and age are just a few of the many factors, in addition to future dangerousness, that a jury may consider in fixing appropriate punishment. See *Lockett v. Ohio*, 438 U.S. 586 (1978); *Eddings v. Oklahoma*, 455 U.S. 104, 110 (1982); *Barclay v. Florida*, 463 U.S. at 948–951.

In assessing future dangerousness, the actual duration of the defendant's prison sentence is indisputably relevant. Holding all other factors constant, it is entirely reasonable for a sentencing jury to view a defendant who is eligible for parole as a greater threat to society than a defendant who is not. Indeed, there may be no greater assurance of a defendant's future nondangerousness to the public than the fact that he never will

---

4. We express no opinion on the question whether the result we reach today is also compelled by the Eighth Amendment.

be released on parole. The trial court's refusal to apprise the jury of information so crucial to its sentencing determination, particularly when the prosecution alluded to the defendant's future dangerousness in its argument to the jury, cannot be reconciled with our well-established precedents interpreting the Due Process Clause.

B

In *Skipper v. South Carolina*, 476 U.S. 1 (1986), this Court held that a defendant was denied due process by the refusal of the state trial court to admit evidence of the defendant's good behavior in prison in the penalty phase of his capital trial. Although the majority opinion stressed that the defendant's good behavior in prison was "relevant evidence in mitigation of punishment," and thus admissible under the Eighth Amendment, the *Skipper* opinion expressly noted that the Court's conclusion also was compelled by the Due Process Clause. The Court explained that where the prosecution relies on a prediction of future dangerousness in requesting the death penalty, elemental due process principles operate to require admission of the defendant's relevant evidence in rebuttal.

The Court reached a similar conclusion in *Gardner v. Florida*, 430 U.S. 349 (1977). In that case, a defendant was sentenced to death on the basis of a presentence report which was not made available to him and which he therefore could not rebut. A plurality of the Court explained that sending a man to his death "on the basis of information which he had no opportunity to deny or explain" violated fundamental notions of due process. The principle announced in *Gardner* was reaffirmed in *Skipper*, and it compels our decision today.

Like the defendants in *Skipper* and *Gardner*, petitioner was prevented from rebutting information that the sentencing authority considered, and upon which it may have relied, in imposing the sentence of death. The State raised the specter of petitioner's future dangerousness generally, but then thwarted all efforts by petitioner to demonstrate that, contrary to the prosecutor's intimations, he never would be released on parole and thus, in his view, would not pose a future danger to society.[5] The logic and effectiveness of petitioner's argument naturally depended on the fact that he was legally ineligible for parole and thus would remain in prison if afforded a life sentence. Petitioner's efforts to focus the jury's attention on the question whether, in prison, he would be a future danger were futile, as he repeatedly was denied any opportunity to inform the jury that he never would be released on parole. The jury was left to speculate about petitioner's parole eligibility when evaluating petitioner's future dangerousness, and was denied a straight answer about petitioner's parole eligibility even when it was requested.

C

The State and its *amici* contend that petitioner was not entitled to an instruction informing the jury that petitioner is ineligible for parole because such information is inherently misleading. Essentially, they argue that because future exigencies such as leg-

---

5. Of course, the fact that a defendant is parole ineligible does not prevent the State from arguing that the defendant poses a future danger. The State is free to argue that the defendant will pose a danger to others in prison and that executing him is the only means of eliminating the threat to the safety of other inmates or prison staff. But the State may not mislead the jury by concealing accurate information about the defendant's parole ineligibility. The Due Process Clause will not tolerate placing a capital defendant in a straitjacket by barring him from rebutting the prosecution's arguments of future dangerousness with the fact that he is ineligible for parole under state law.

islative reform, commutation, clemency, and escape might allow petitioner to be released into society, petitioner was not entitled to inform the jury that he is parole ineligible. Insofar as this argument is targeted at the specific wording of the instruction petitioner requested, the argument is misplaced. Petitioner's requested instruction ("If ... you recommend that [the defendant] be sentenced to life imprisonment, he actually will be sentenced to imprisonment in the state penitentiary for the balance of his natural life"), was proposed only after the trial court ruled that South Carolina law prohibited a plain-language instruction that petitioner was ineligible for parole under state law. To the extent that the State opposes even a simple parole-ineligibility instruction because of hypothetical future developments, the argument has little force. Respondent admits that an instruction informing the jury that petitioner is ineligible for parole is legally accurate. Certainly, such an instruction is more accurate than no instruction at all, which leaves the jury to speculate whether "life imprisonment" means life without parole or something else.

The State's asserted accuracy concerns are further undermined by the fact that a large majority of States which provide for life imprisonment without parole as an alternative to capital punishment inform the sentencing authority of the defendant's parole ineligibility.[7] The few States that do not provide capital-sentencing juries with any information regarding parole ineligibility seem to rely, as South Carolina does here, on the proposition that *California v. Ramos*, 463 U.S. 992 (1983), held that such determinations are purely matters of state law.

… It is true that *Ramos* stands for the broad proposition that we generally will defer to a State's determination as to what a jury should and should not be told about sentencing. In a State in which parole is available, how the jury's knowledge of parole availability will affect the decision whether or not to impose the death penalty is speculative, and we shall not lightly second-guess a decision whether or not to inform a jury of information regarding parole. States reasonably may conclude that truthful information regarding the availability of commutation, pardon, and the like, should be kept from the jury in order to provide "greater protection in [the States'] criminal justice system than the Federal Constitution requires." Concomitantly, nothing in the Constitution prohibits the prosecution from arguing any truthful information relating to parole or other forms of early release.

But if the State rests its case for imposing the death penalty at least in part on the premise that the defendant will be dangerous in the future, the fact that the alternative sentence to death is life without parole will necessarily undercut the State's argument regarding the threat the defendant poses to society. Because truthful information of parole ineligibility allows the defendant to "deny or explain" the showing of future dangerousness, due process plainly requires that he be allowed to bring it to the jury's attention by way of argument by defense counsel or an instruction from the court.

III

There remains to be considered whether the South Carolina Supreme Court was correct in concluding that the trial court "satisfie[d] in substance [petitioner's] request for a charge on parole ineligibility" when it responded to the jury's query by stating that life

---

7. At present, there are 26 States that both employ juries in capital sentencing and provide for life imprisonment without parole as an alternative to capital punishment. In 17 of these, the jury expressly is informed of the defendant's ineligibility for parole. Nine States simply identify the jury's sentencing alternatives as death and life without parole....

imprisonment was to be understood in its "plain and ordinary meaning." In the court's view, petitioner basically received the parole-ineligibility instruction he requested. We disagree.

It can hardly be questioned that most juries lack accurate information about the precise meaning of "life imprisonment" as defined by the States. For much of our country's history, parole was a mainstay of state and federal sentencing regimes, and every term (whether a term of life or a term of years) in practice was understood to be shorter than the stated term. Increasingly, legislatures have enacted mandatory sentencing laws with severe penalty provisions, yet the precise contours of these penal laws vary from State to State. Justice Chandler of the South Carolina Supreme Court observed that it is impossible to ignore "the reality, known to the 'reasonable juror,' that, historically, life-term defendants have been eligible for parole." [8]

An instruction directing juries that life imprisonment should be understood in its "plain and ordinary" meaning does nothing to dispel the misunderstanding reasonable jurors may have about the way in which any particular State defines "life imprisonment."[9] See *Boyde v. California*, 494 U.S. 370, 380 (1990) (where there is a "reasonable likelihood that the jury has applied the challenged instruction in a way that prevents the consideration of constitutionally relevant evidence," the defendant is denied due process).

It is true, as the State points out, that the trial court admonished the jury that "you are instructed not to consider parole" and that parole "is not a proper issue for your consideration." Far from ensuring that the jury was not misled, however, this instruction actually suggested that parole was available but that the jury, for some unstated reason, should be blind to this fact. Undoubtedly, the instruction was confusing and frustrating to the jury, given the arguments by both the prosecution and the defense relating to petitioner's future dangerousness, and the obvious relevance of petitioner's parole ineligibility to the jury's formidable sentencing task. While juries ordinarily are presumed to follow the court's instructions, we have recognized that in some circumstances "the risk that the jury will not, or cannot, follow instructions is so great, and the consequences of failure so vital to the defendant, that the practical and human limitations of the jury system cannot be ignored." *Bruton v. United States*, 391 U.S. 123, 135 (1968). See also *Beck v. Alabama*, 447 U.S. 625, 642 (1980); *Barclay v. Florida*, 463 U.S. at 950 ("Any sentencing decision calls for the exercise of judgment. It is neither possible nor desirable for a person to whom the State entrusts an important judgment to decide in a vacuum, as if he had no experiences").

But even if the trial court's instruction successfully prevented the jury from considering parole, petitioner's due process rights still were not honored. Because petitioner's future dangerousness was at issue, he was entitled to inform the jury of his parole ineligibility. An instruction directing the jury not to consider the defendant's likely conduct

---

8. Public opinion and juror surveys support the commonsense understanding that there is a reasonable likelihood of juror confusion about the meaning of the term "life imprisonment." See Paduano & Smith, Deadly Errors: Juror Misperceptions Concerning Parole in the Imposition of the Death Penalty, 18 Colum. Human Rights L. Rev. 211, 222–225 (1987); Note, The Meaning of "Life" for Virginia Jurors and Its Effect on Reliability in Capital Sentencing, 75 Va. L. Rev. 1605, 1624 (1989); Eisenberg & Wells, Deadly Confusion: Juror Instructions in Capital Cases, 79 Cornell L. Rev. 1 (1993); Bowers, Capital Punishment & Contemporary Values: People's Misgivings and the Court's Misperceptions, 27 Law & Society 157, 169–170 (1993).

9. It almost goes without saying that if the jury in this case understood that the "plain meaning" of "life imprisonment" was life without parole in South Carolina, there would have been no reason for the jury to inquire about petitioner's parole eligibility.

in prison would not have satisfied due process in *Skipper,* and, for the same reasons, the instruction issued by the trial court in this case does not satisfy due process.

IV

The State may not create a false dilemma by advancing generalized arguments regarding the defendant's future dangerousness while, at the same time, preventing the jury from learning that the defendant never will be released on parole. The judgment of the South Carolina Supreme Court accordingly is reversed and the case is remanded for further proceedings not inconsistent with this opinion.

Justice SCALIA, with whom Justice Thomas joins, dissenting.

... The rule the majority adopts in order to overturn this sentence ... goes well beyond what would be necessary to counteract prosecutorial misconduct (a disposition with which I might agree). It is a rule at least as sweeping as this: that the Due Process Clause overrides state law limiting the admissibility of information concerning parole *whenever* the prosecution argues future dangerousness. Justice Blackmun appears to go even further, requiring the admission of parole-ineligibility even when the prosecutor does *not* argue future dangerousness. I do not understand the basis for this broad prescription. As a general matter, the Court leaves it to the States to strike what *they* consider the appropriate balance among the many factors — probative value, prejudice, reliability, potential for confusion, among others — that determine whether evidence ought to be admissible. Even in the capital punishment context, the Court has noted that "the wisdom of the decision to permit juror consideration of [post-sentencing contingencies] is best left to the States." *California v. Ramos,* 463 U.S. 992, 1014 (1983). "The States, and not this Court, retain 'the traditional authority' to determine what particular evidence ... is relevant." *Skipper v. South Carolina,* 476 U.S. 1, 11 (1986) (Powell, J., concurring). One reason for leaving it that way is that a sensible code of evidence cannot be invented piecemeal. Each item cannot be considered in isolation, but must be given its place within the whole. Preventing the *defense* from introducing evidence regarding parolability is only half of the rule that prevents the *prosecution* from introducing it as well. If the rule is changed for defendants, many will think that evenhandedness demands a change for prosecutors as well. State's attorneys ought to be able to say that if, ladies and gentlemen of the jury, you do not impose capital punishment upon this defendant (or if you impose anything less than life without parole) he may be walking the streets again in eight years! Many would not favor the admission of such an argument — but would prefer it to a State scheme in which defendants can call attention to the unavailability of parole, but prosecutors cannot note its availability. This Court should not force state legislators into such a difficult choice unless the isolated state evidentiary rule that the Court has before it is not merely less than ideal, but beyond a high threshold of unconstitutionality.

The low threshold the Court constructs today is difficult to reconcile with our almost simultaneous decision in *Romano v. Oklahoma,* 512 U.S. 1 (1994). There, the Court holds that the proper inquiry when evidence is admitted in contravention of a state law is "whether the admission of evidence ... so infected the sentencing proceedings with unfairness as to render the jury's imposition of the death penalty a denial of due process." I do not see why the unconstitutionality criterion for *excluding* evidence *in accordance with state law* should be any less demanding than the unconstitutionality criterion *Romano* recites for *admitting* evidence *in violation of* state law: "fundamental unfairness." And "fundamentally unfair" the South Carolina rule is assuredly not. The notion that the South Carolina jury imposed the death penalty "just in case" Simmons might be released on parole seems to me quite far-fetched. And the notion that the decision taken on such grounds would have been altered by information on the *current state of the law* concerning parole (which could of course be amended) is even more far-fetched. And the scenario achieves the ultimate in far-fetchedness when there is added the fact that, according to uncontroverted testimony of prison officials in this case, even *current* South Carolina law (as opposed to discretionary prison regulations) does not prohibit furloughs and work-release programs for life-without-parole inmates.

When the prosecution has not specifically suggested parolability, I see no more reason why the United States Constitution should compel the admission of evidence showing that, under the State's current law, the defendant would be nonparolable, than that it should compel the admission of evidence showing that parolable life-sentence murderers are in fact almost never paroled, or are paroled only after age 70; or evidence to the effect that escapes of life-without-parole inmates are rare; or evidence showing that, though under current law the defendant will be parolable in 20 years, the recidivism rate for elderly prisoners released after long incarceration is negligible. All of this evidence may be thought relevant to whether the death penalty should be imposed, and a petition raising the last of these claims has already arrived.

As I said at the outset, the regime imposed by today's judgment is undoubtedly reasonable as a matter of policy, but I see nothing to indicate that the Constitution requires it to be followed coast-to-coast. I fear we have read today the first page of a whole new chapter in the "death-is-different" jurisprudence which this Court is in the apparently continuous process of composing. It adds to our insistence that State courts admit "all relevant mitigating evidence," *see, e.g., Eddings v. Oklahoma*, 455 U.S. 104 (1982); *Lockett v. Ohio*, 438 U.S. 586 (1978), a requirement that they adhere to distinctive rules, more demanding than what the Due Process Clause normally requires, for admitting evidence of other sorts—Federal Rules of Death Penalty Evidence, so to speak, which this Court will presumably craft (at great expense to the swiftness and predictability of justice) year-by-year. The heavily outnumbered opponents of capital punishment have successfully opened yet another front in their guerilla war to make this unquestionably constitutional sentence a practical impossibility.

Notes and Question

1. One week after announcing *Simmons*, a 7–2 majority of the Court ruled that a federal jury does not have to be instructed that a verdict of not guilty by reason of insanity will result in involuntary commitment. *Shannon v. United States*, 512 U.S. 573 (1994). According to Justice Thomas' majority opinion, neither the Insanity Defense Reform Act of 1984 nor federal practice requires such an instruction.

2. In *Ramdass v. Angelone*, 530 U.S. 156 (2000), the Supreme Court rejected a habeas petititioner's claim that the state courts took an overly technical approach to defining his parole ineligibility and, therefore, his entitlement to a *Simmons* instruction.

Ramdass was convicted in Virginia state court of murdering a convenience store clerk during an armed robbery. During Ramdass' sentencing phase, the state argued future dangerousness as an aggravating factor. To establish future dangerousness, the state introduced evidence of other crimes committed by Ramdass. At the time of his penalty phase, Ramdass had been found guilty in another case of a separate armed robbery but the judge in that case had not yet entered a judgment of guilt. Ramdass' lawyer did not argue that Ramdass was parole ineligible at that time. The jury recommended death, and the trial judge imposed a death sentence.

While the case was pending on direct review, the Supreme Court handed down *Simmons*. The Virginia Supreme Court examined Ramdass' sentence in light of *Simmons* but held that Ramdass had not conclusively established that he was ineligible for parole under Virginia's three-strikes law. According to the state, the entry of judgment in the unrelated armed robbery case is what rendered that conviction a "strike" for purposes of parole eligibility.

During federal habeas review, Ramdass argued that due process requires a more "functional" and less technical approach to determining whether a defendant is entitled to an instruction on parole ineligibility. The U.S. Court of Appeals for the Fourth Circuit disagreed, and held that the question of whether a defendant is ineligible for parole is a question of state law.

Justice Kennedy, joined in a plurality opinion by Chief Justice Rehnquist, and Justices Scalia and Thomas, approved the Court of Appeals' decision to deny relief. Justice O'Connor added the fifth vote for affirmance in an opinion concurring in the judgment.

Under 28 U.S.C. §2254(d)(1), as amended by the 1996 Antiterrorism and Effective Death Penalty Act, Ramdass could not obtain habeas relief unless he demonstrated that the state court's decision was contrary to or an unreasonable application of a clearly established U.S. Supreme Court precedent. Applying this test, the plurality rejected Ramdass' contentions that his case was functionally indistinguishable from *Simmons*. Justice Kennedy wrote: "We have not extended *Simmons* to cases where parole ineligibility has not been established as a matter of state law at the time of the jury's future dangerousness deliberations in a capital case."

Ramdass argued that the record in *Simmons* revealed that Simmons technically would not have been ineligible for parole under South Carolina law until the parole board met and formally determined his status. The plurality was unpersuaded, stressing that at the time of Ramdass' capital sentencing, Ramdass' record was such that he was still eligible for parole.

Moreover, a state court's failure to glean information from the briefs and record of a controlling U.S. Supreme Court decision does not necessarily render the state court's ruling contrary to or an unreasonable application of that precedent for purposes of the habeas statute. A federal habeas court can hold a state court responsible only for a "faithful application of the principles set out in the controlling opinion of the Court," according to the plurality.

Ramdass also argued that in *Simmons*, as in his case, future events could have affected whether the defendant was ever to reenter society. For example, the defendant in *Simmons* could have escaped or been pardoned, or the state laws regarding parole eligibility could change. In the plurality's view, however, Ramdass' case represented the opposite of *Simmons* in that Ramdass was eligible for parole at the time of his sentencing hearing and it was he, rather than the state, who was raising future hypothetical events.

"*Simmons* applies only to instances where, as a legal matter, there is no possibility of parole if the jury decides that the appropriate sentence is life in prison." Ramdass' proposed "functional" approach would require courts to evaluate the probability of future events and potentially take a sentencing jury too far away from the core issues before it. The plurality found no arbitrariness in the fact that Virginia kept the petitioner from using crimes not reduced to judgment to trigger *Simmons* while it imposed no such limitation on the state's use of evidence of those crimes at sentencing to aid in obtaining a death sentence.

The plurality also noted that the entry of judgment of conviction in Ramdass' other case was not a foregone conclusion and represented more than a ministerial act. At the time of the penalty phase proceedings, the time for filing post-trial motions in the other case had not expired and Ramdass had not indicated that he was not going to file such motions.

Finally, the plurality noted that states are free to adopt rules that go beyond the Constitution's minimum standards regarding jury instructions on parole ineligibility. In fact, Virginia did so in cases post-dating this one.

3. In *Simmons*, the Court for the first time ruled that prosecutors could not simultaneously seek the death penalty based on future dangerousness and yet withhold from the jury the fact that the alternative to a death sentence is life without parole. The Court narrowly construed *Simmons* when in *Ramdass* it concluded that state judges may decline to give a life without parole instruction as an alternative to the death penalty if they find that, despite a statute mandating the LWOP alternative, a defendant given that sentence might still become eligible for parole at some point.

4. The Court also has refused to extend the *Simmons* ruling to impose a requirement that capital jurors be informed of lengthy minimum sentences that apply in states that do not provide for life without parole. See *Brown v. Texas*, 522 U.S. 940, 940–43 (1997) (Stevens, J., respecting the denial of certiorari). Is the Court's refusal to extend *Simmons* unfair given that the Court in *California v. Ramos*, 463 U.S. 992, 1001–03 (1983), upheld the constitutionality of a California law requiring that capital sentencing jurors be told of the governor's power to commute death sentences?

5. An 11-state statistical study of capital sentencing jurors found that "very few jurors believe that LWOP is the punishment usually served by those not given death," even in states where LWOP is the mandatory alternative to a death sentence. "[J]urors grossly underestimate how long capital murderers not sentenced to death usually stay in prison" and "people generally believe murderers not given a death sentence will be back on the streets in relatively few years; most said ten or less." Moreover, "mistaken estimates of early release [of capital defendants] appear to be decisive in the decision-making of jurors who have not made up their minds before deliberations begin or by the time of the jury's first vote on punishment." Bowers & Steiner, "Death by Default: An Empirical Demonstration of False and Forced Choices in Capital Sentencing," 77 Tex. L. Rev. 605 (1999).

6. When life without parole is offered as an option, support for the death penalty drops dramatically. In an ABC News poll, 64% of Americans said they support the death penalty for people convicted of murder. That percentage dropped to 48% when life without parole is an option. ABCNEWS.com, Split Decision on Death Penalty (Oct. 13, 2000).

Four years before *Simmons*, the Mississippi Supreme Court held that life without parole instructions were required in at least some capital cases.

Turner v. Mississippi

573 So.2d 657 (Miss. 1990) (En Banc)*

Part One: Guilt Phase

ROY NOBLE LEE, Chief Justice, for the Court:

Kevin Lewis Turner was indicted in the Circuit Court of Pike County, Mississippi, for the capital robbery/murder of Elizabeth Blakely, and, as an habitual criminal. Venue

---

* Note that different judges authored Part I and Part III of the majority opinion. [Ed.]

was changed to Hinds County where the trial began on May 26, 1987. Turner was found guilty of capital murder on May 28, 1987, and in a bifurcated trial, the jury imposed the death penalty upon Turner the next day. Thereafter, the trial judge conducted a hearing on the habitual criminal charge and Turner was adjudged to be an habitual offender. Turner has appealed to this Court and assigns twenty-two (22) errors in the trial below.

I. Factual Background

The facts of this case are undisputed. On December 2, 1985, appellant Kevin Turner and Eric Jones went to the "Forget Me Not" grocery in Summit, Mississippi, for the purpose of burglarizing it. When they arrived at the store, they found the front door to be unlocked. They opened the door and entered the store. Elizabeth Blakely, the owner and only occupant, came from the back to wait on them. Jones asked for change to use the cigarette machine and Ms. Blakely went to the rear of the store to make the change. Upon her return to the front, Kevin Turner pulled a .38 revolver, pointed it at her and said that it was a stickup. Immediately, Turner shot the victim and moments thereafter shot her two more times. Two of the wounds were fatal, one being to the brain and another through the heart. The third was a flesh wound. After shooting Ms. Blakely, Turner and Jones searched and ransacked the building looking for valuables. Approximately $190.00 in cash was found and taken by Turner. They took the victim's car keys, house keys and purse, and went next door to her home which they searched for things of value. After leaving the premises in disarray, they returned to the store, wrapped the victim's body in a blanket and put it in the trunk of her car.

Turner and Jones then went to the house where Jones lived, changed clothes, and told Jones' mother that they were going to New Orleans. Turner went back to the store, got the victim's car, and picked up Jones around the corner. They drove around for a while and then decided to drive to Memphis and dump the victim's body. When they arrived in Memphis, they decided to drive on to Chicago.

Appellant Turner lived in his mother's house in Chicago and had gone to the Summit, Mississippi, community for a visit. When Turner and Jones arrived in Chicago, they went to the home of appellant's mother and stayed there. During their stay, they committed crimes, including robberies, in Chicago. In the meantime, family members, being concerned about the disappearance of Ms. Blakely, began to make inquiries and notified law enforcement officials. They entered the victim's home and store, where they discovered the evidence of foul play. The investigation indicated Turner and Jones were suspects, the Chicago Police Department was contacted, and the license plate number of Ms. Blakely's car was given the Chicago police along with the address of appellant's mother. The Chicago police went to the Turner home, where they found Kevin Turner and Eric Jones and arrested them. They opened the trunk of the victim's car and found her body. This occurred on December 8, 1985, seven (7) days after the robbery/murder....

Part Three: Reversible Error

PRATHER, Justice, for the Court:

XXI. The Preclusion of Evidence of Appellant's Habitual-Offender Status and the Lower Court's Refusal to Instruct the Jury That Appellant Would Never be Eligible For Parole Was Reversible Error

This Court's principal concern in capital-murder cases has been with the substance which is presented a jury as a basis for imposing a life or death sentence. In this section of the case *sub judice*, the concern is with the procedure by which a sentence is imposed.

The concern stems from Turner's petition through which he asks the Court to reconsider its majority opinion regarding "assigned error No. 10." No. 10 asks whether the trial judge erred when he refused to give the following instruction: "Kevin Turner has been indicted as an habitual offender. If given a life sentence, Kevin Turner shall never be eligible for parole because he will be an habitual offender."

The majority concluded that the trial judge did not err. For the following reasons, this Court *now* holds that the jury should have been informed of Turner's ineligibility for parole.[6] This conclusion is based, for the most part, upon constitutional principles of due process and fundamental fairness. These principles have been intrinsic themes in numerous decisions of the United States Supreme Court.

For example, in one case, the Supreme Court deemed as "wise" Georgia's choice "not to impose unnecessary restrictions on the evidence that can be offered at [sentencing] hearing[s] and to approve *open and far-ranging argument*." *Gregg v. Georgia*, 428 U.S. 153, 203 (1976). The Court added: "We think it desirable for the jury to have *as much information before it as possible* when it makes the sentencing decision." Almost immediately after *Gregg* was decided, the Supreme Court emphasized that it is "*essential* that the jury have before it *all* possible relevant information about the individual defendant whose fate it must determine." *Jurek v. Texas*, 428 U.S. 262, 276 (1976). In another case, the Court reiterated that under the Eighth Amendment, the "qualitative difference of death from all other punishments requires a correspondingly greater degree of scrutiny of the capital sentencing determination." *California v. Ramos*, 463 U.S. 992, 998–999 (1983). And more recently, the Court held that the federal Constitution "limits" states' "ability" to "narrow" a jury's consideration of any relevant evidence that could "cause it to decline to impose the death sentence." *McCleskey v. Kemp*, 481 U.S. 279, 304 (1987).

Notably, nearly thirty years ago, a prophetic proposal by the American Law Institute provided: (1) that besides aggravating and mitigating factors, the sentencing jury "shall take into account ... any other factors that it deems relevant," and (2) that the jury shall be informed "of the nature of the sentence of imprisonment that may be imposed, *including its implication with respect to possible release upon parole, if the jury verdict is against the sentence of death*." See ALI Model Penal Code §210.6 (Prop. Off. Draft 1962) (emphasis added), quoted in *Ramos*, 463 U.S. at 1009 n. 23.

In capital-murder cases like the one *sub judice*, the jury generally is instructed that its options are to impose sentences of life or death. Juries are often not informed that "life" means, or could mean, "life without parole." This is the consequence of trial judges exercising their power of discretion and deciding to conduct the sentencing phase prior to the phase during which the defendant's habitual-offender status is determined. When the sentencing phase is conducted first, the State argues that information regarding the defendant's eligibility for parole should be withheld from the jury because it is "totally speculative at the time of sentencing." This Court concurs with the State's argument to the extent that evidence which is "totally speculative" should be withheld from a jury deliberating the fate of a convicted defendant. Thus, this opinion should not be construed as modifying or re-writing substantive case law.

---

6. Mississippi's habitual-offender statute actually provides that the offender's sentence "shall not be reduced or suspended nor shall such person be eligible for parole or probation." Miss. Code Ann. §99-19-83 (1990 Supp.).

Substantive matters aside, no rationale has been offered to explain why procedurally the sentencing phase should be conducted first or why the judge should be empowered with discretion to decide the order in which post-conviction phases will be conducted. See Miss. Unif. Crim. R. Cir. Ct. Prac. 6.04 (as amended 1982) (delineating post-conviction procedure: "If the defendant is convicted ... on the principal charge, a hearing ... without the jury will then be conducted on the previous convictions."); Miss. Code. Ann. §99-19-101 (1990) (delineating the procedure for the sentencing phase of a capital-murder trial).

This Court simply cannot accept as logical or justifiable the procedure by which many, if not most or all, capital-murder trials have thus far been conducted. The procedure as it stands leaves a defendant's eligibility for parole uncertain and "narrows" a jury's consideration of clearly relevant information that could "cause it to decline to impose the death sentence." *McCleskey*, 481 U.S. at 304. Such uncertainty (or "total speculativeness") would be eliminated[7] *without* undue inconvenience[8] *if* the hearing on the status phase was conducted *prior* to the sentencing phase of the trial. Such simple yet compelling logic is not difficult to comprehend.

Accordingly, this Court directs that in future cases the status phase *must be* conducted prior to the sentencing phase. At the sentencing phase, the jury *shall be* entitled to know by instruction whether the defendant is eligible for parole. See *Ex parte Rutledge*, 482 So.2d 1262, 1264 (Ala. 1984) (jurors informed: (1) that they may consider death or life without parole, and (2) "that life without parole mean[s] life without parole"); *State v. Willie*, 410 So.2d 1019, 1033 (La. 1982) (jury instructed that "[t]he sentence will be life imprisonment without parole, probation or suspension of sentence"). Providing juries with such *non*-speculative information would be compliant with the dictates of logic and constitutional principles of due process and fundamental fairness. In other words, the procedure would meet the "essential" requirement that juries have before them "*all* possible relevant information about the individual defendant whose fate it must determine." *Jurek*, 428 U.S. at 276.

In sum, Turner's guilt of capital murder and status as an habitual offender is affirmed, but his death sentence is vacated. The case is remanded for re-sentencing with instructions consistent with this opinion.

ROY NOBLE LEE, Chief Justice, dissenting as to part III:

I do not agree that the lower court erred in its refusal to grant an instruction that appellant was an habitual offender and would never be eligible for parole. Therefore, I dissent from the actions of the majority, on the petition for rehearing, to so hold and grant the petition. The issue presented to this Court on direct appeal, and rejected, arises by refusal in the lower court of the following instruction: "Kevin Turner has been indicted as an habitual offender. If given a life sentence, Kevin Turner shall never be eligible for parole because he will be an habitual offender."

---

7. The State argues that many cases, which involve an habitual offender sentenced to life without possibility of parole, inhere an element of speculativeness since the offender could successfully challenge a prior felony. *See, e.g., Johnson v. Mississippi*, 486 U.S. 578 (1988). In addition, the governor could grant a reprieve or pardon. See Miss. Const. art. 5, §123. The chance that any of these events could occur, however, are infinitesimal.

8. During oral argument before this Court, the prosecuting district attorney conceded that establishment of Turner's habitual-offender status prior to the sentencing phase would not have resulted in undue inconvenience. Indeed, this Court's review of transcripts of the numerous cases involving an habitual offender has revealed that the status phase consumes an average of thirty minutes.

This Court has consistently held that the State may not introduce evidence or comment upon the fact that a person convicted of capital murder and sentenced to life in prison will be eligible for parole in ten (10) years. The same shoe must be worn by the appellant. The same law must apply to the defendant/appellant as to the State/prosecution. Both are entitled to a fair trial under the same rules and procedures. This Court has consistently rejected such a jury instruction and arguments on the question....

In the case *sub judice*, appellant was indicted as an habitual offender, as stated, but the hearing on the habitual offender part of the indictment would be considered and addressed by the court after the bifurcated trial involving the guilt phase and sentence phase....

The record reflects that counsel for appellant stated to the jury panel on *voir dire* that appellant would never be paroled, if given life imprisonment. In closing argument, both counsel for appellant argued specifically and at length, without objection from the State, that, if given life imprisonment, appellant would spend the rest of his life at the Mississippi State Penitentiary....

The lower court, in being more than fair to the appellant, went beyond the law and granted the following instructions at the request of the appellant:

> Regardless of the balance of aggravating and mitigating circumstances, you may afford Kevin Turner mercy in this proceeding.

> The Court instructs the Jury that you need not find any mitigating circumstances in order to return a sentence of life imprisonment.

> The Court instructs you that mitigating circumstances are those which do not constitute a justification or excuse for the offense in question but which, in fairness and mercy, may be considered as extenuating or reducing the degree of moral culpability of blame.

The lower court followed the law stated long ago, and recently, in granting and refusing instructions in the present case. Now in one swoop the majority is overruling established cases, destroying procedure and policy and nullifying the jury's verdict in this serious, but well tried and fully instructed, death penalty case. The law forbid!

After this reversal, an astute district attorney should never charge an habitual offender, as such, in the trial of a capital murder case, which the jury may decide deserves the death penalty. On the contrary, if a verdict less than death is returned, other procedures will be available. I dissent from the majority opinion vacating the death penalty and remanding for a new sentencing hearing.

Shafer v. South Carolina
532 U.S. 36 (2001)

Justice GINSBURG delivered the opinion of the Court.

This case concerns the right of a defendant in a capital case to inform the jury that, under the governing state law, he would not be eligible for parole in the event that the jury sentences him to life imprisonment. In *Simmons v. South Carolina*, 512 U.S. 154 (1994), this Court held that where a capital defendant's future dangerousness is at issue, and the only sentencing alternative to death available to the jury is life imprisonment without possibility of parole, due process entitles the defendant "to inform the jury of [his] parole ineligibility, either by a jury instruction or in arguments by counsel." *Ramdass v. Angelone*, 530 U.S. 156, 165 (2000) (plurality opinion) (describing *Simmons*' premise and plurality opinion). The case we now confront involves a death sentence returned by a jury instructed both that "life imprisonment means until death of the offender," and that "[p]arole eligibility or ineligibility is not for your consideration." It presents the question whether the South Carolina Supreme Court misread our precedent when it declared *Simmons* inapplicable to South Carolina's current sentencing scheme. We hold that South Carolina's Supreme Court incorrectly limited *Simmons* and therefore reverse that court's judgment.

I

In April 1997, in the course of an attempted robbery in Union County, South Carolina, then-18-year-old Wesley Aaron Shafer, Jr., shot and killed a convenience store cashier. A grand jury indicted Shafer on charges of murder, attempted armed robbery, and criminal conspiracy. Prior to trial, the prosecutor notified Shafer that the State would seek the death penalty for the murder. In that pursuit, the prosecutor further informed Shafer, the State would present evidence of Shafer's "prior bad acts," as well as his "propensity for [future] violence and unlawful conduct."

Under South Carolina law, juries in capital cases consider guilt and sentencing in separate proceedings. S.C.Code Ann. §§16-3-20(A), (B) (2000 Cum. Supp.). In the initial (guilt phase) proceeding, the jury found Shafer guilty on all three charges. Governing the sentencing proceeding, South Carolina law instructs: "[T]he jury ... shall hear additional evidence in extenuation, mitigation, or aggravation of the punishment.... The State, the defendant, and his counsel are permitted to present arguments for or against the sentence to be imposed."

Under amendments effective January 1, 1996, South Carolina capital jurors face two questions at sentencing. They decide first whether the State has proved beyond a reasonable doubt the existence of any statutory aggravating circumstance. If the jury fails to agree unanimously on the presence of a statutory aggravator, "it shall not make a sentencing recommendation." "[T]he trial judge," in that event, "shall sentence the defendant to either life imprisonment or a mandatory minimum term of imprisonment for thirty years." If, on the other hand, the jury unanimously finds a statutory aggravator, it then recommends one of two potential sentences — death or life imprisonment without the possibility of parole. No sentencing option other than death or life without parole is available to the jury.

During the sentencing proceeding in Shafer's case, the State introduced evidence of his criminal record, past aggressive conduct, probation violations, and misbehavior in prison. The State urged the statutory aggravating circumstance that Shafer had committed the murder in the course of an attempted robbery while armed with a deadly weapon. The defense presented evidence of Shafer's abusive childhood and mental problems.

Near the completion of the parties' sentencing presentations, the trial judge conducted an in camera hearing on jury instructions. Shafer's counsel maintained that due process, and our decision in *Simmons v. South Carolina*, 512 U.S. 154 (1994), required the judge to instruct that under South Carolina law a life sentence carries no possibility of parole. The prosecutor, in opposition, urged that Shafer was not entitled to a *Simmons* instruction because "the State has not argued at any point ... that he would be a danger to anybody in the future, nor will we argue [that] in our closing argument...." Shafer's counsel replied: "The State cannot introduce evidence of future dangerousness, and then say we are not going to argue it and [thereby avoid] a charge on the law....

They have introduced [evidence of a] post arrest assault, [and] post arrest violations of the rules of the jail.... If you put a jailer on to say that [Shafer] is charged with assault ... on [the jailer], that is future dangerousness." Ruling that "the matter of parole ineligibility will not be charged," the trial judge stated: "I find that future dangerousness [was] not argued[;] if it's argued [in the prosecutor's closing], it may become different."

Unsuccessful in his effort to gain a court instruction on parole ineligibility, Shafer's counsel sought permission to impart the information to the jury himself. He sought leave to read in his closing argument lines from the controlling statute, §16-3-20(A), stating plainly that a life sentence in South Carolina carries no possibility of parole. In accord with the State's motion "to prevent the defense from arguing in their closing argument anything to the effect that [Shafer] will never get out of prison," the judge denied the defense permission to read the statute's text to the jury.

After the prosecution's closing argument, and out of the presence of the jury, Shafer's counsel renewed his plea for "a life without parole charge." He referred to his earlier submissions and urged, in addition, that the State had placed future dangerousness at issue during closing argument by repeating the words of an alarmed witness at the crime scene: "[T]hey [Shafer and his two accomplices] might come back, they might come back." The trial judge denied the request. The judge "admit[ted he] had some concern [as to whether the State's] argument ... had crossed the line," but in the end he found "that it comes close, but did not."

Instructing the jury, the judge explained:

"If you do not unanimously find the existence of the aggravating circumstance as set forth on the form [murder during the commission of an attempted armed robbery], you do not need to go any further.

"If you find unanimously the existence of a statutory aggravating circumstance ... you will go further and continue your deliberations.

"Once you have unanimously found and signed as to the presence of an aggravated circumstance, you then further deliberate, and determine whether or not Wesley Aaron Shafer should be sentence[d] to life imprisonment or death."

The judge twice told the jury, quoting words from §16-3-20(A), that "life imprisonment means until the death of the defendant." In line with his prior rulings, the judge did not instruct that a life sentence, if recommended by the jury, would be without parole. In the concluding portion of his charge, he told the jury that "the sentence you send to me by way of a recommendation will in fact be the sentence that the court imposes on the defendant." After the judge instructed the jury, the defense once more renewed its "objection to the statutory language [on parole ineligibility] not being charged," and the judge again overruled the objection.

Three hours and twenty-five minutes into its sentencing deliberations, the jury sent a note to the trial judge containing two questions:

"1) Is there any remote chance for someone convicted of murder to become elig-[i]ble for parole?

"2) Under what conditions would someone convicted for murder be elig[i]ble."

Shafer's counsel urged the court to read to the jury the following portion of §16-3-20(A):

"If the State seeks the death penalty and a statutory aggravating circumstance is found beyond a reasonable doubt ... and a recommendation of death is not made, the trial judge must impose a sentence of life imprisonment. For purposes of this section, *'life imprisonment' means until death of the offender.* **No person sentenced to life imprisonment pursuant to this section is eligible for parole, community supervision, or any early release program, nor is the person eligible to receive any work credits, education credits, good conduct credits, or any other credits that would reduce the mandatory life imprisonment required by this section."**

He argued that the court's charge, which partially quoted from §16-3-20 (above in italics), but omitted the provision's concluding sentence (above in boldface), had left the jurors confused about Shafer's parole eligibility. The State adhered to its position that "the jury should not be informed as to any parole eligibility." South Carolina law, the prosecutor insisted, required the judge to "instruct the jury that it shall not consider parole eligibility in reaching its decision, and that the term life imprisonment and a death sentence should be understood in their ordinary and plain meaning."

The trial judge decided "not ... to charge the jury about parole ineligibility," and informed counsel that he would instruct:

> "Your consideration is restricted to what sentence to recommend. I will, as trial judge, impose the sentence you recommend. Section 16-3-20 of the South Carolina Code of Laws provides that for the purpose of this section life imprisonment means until the death of the offender. Parole eligibility is not for your consideration."

Shafer's counsel asked the judge "to take off the language of parole eligibility." The statement that "parole eligibility is not to be considered by [the jury]," counsel argued, "impl[ies] that it is available." (Shafer's counsel reiterated: "[I]f you tell them they can't consider parole eligibility ... that certainly implies that he may be eligible.").

Following counsels' arguments, and nearly an hour after the jury tendered its questions, the trial judge instructed:

> "Section 16-3-20 of our Code of Laws as applies to this case in the process we're in, states that, quote, for the purposes of this section life imprisonment means until the death of the offender, end quote. Parole eligibility or ineligibility is not for your consideration."

The jury returned some 80 minutes later. It unanimously found beyond a reasonable doubt the aggravating factor of murder while attempting armed robbery, and recommended the death penalty. The jury was polled, and each member indicated his or her assent to the aggravated circumstance finding and to the death penalty recommendation. Defense counsel asked that the jury be polled on "the specific question as to whether parole eligibility, their belief therein, gave rise to the verdict," and "whether juror number 233 who works for probation and parole, expressed personal knowledge in the jury's deliberation outside of the evidence and the given law." The judge denied both requests and imposed the death sentence.

Shafer appealed his death sentence to the South Carolina Supreme Court. Noting our decision in *Simmons*, the South Carolina Supreme Court acknowledged that "[w]hen the State places the defendant's future dangerousness at issue and the only available alternative sentence to the death penalty is life imprisonment without parole, due process entitles the defendant to inform the jury he is parole ineligible." Without considering whether the prosecutor's evidentiary submissions or closing argument in fact placed Shafer's future dangerousness at issue, the court held *Simmons* generally inapplicable to

South Carolina's "new sentencing scheme." Under that scheme, life without the possibility of parole and death are not the only authorized sentences, the court said, for there is a third potential sentence, "a mandatory minimum thirty year sentence."[3]

Shafer had urged that a *Simmons* instruction was warranted under the new sentencing scheme, for when the jury serves as sentencer, i.e., when it finds a statutory aggravating circumstance, sentencing discretion is limited to death or life without the possibility of parole. The South Carolina Supreme Court read *Simmons* differently. In its view, "*Simmons* requires the trial judge instruct the jury the defendant is parole ineligible only if no other sentence than death, other than life without the possibility of parole, is legally available to the defendant." "At the time [Shafer's] jury began its deliberations," the court observed, "three alternative sentences were available"; "[s]ince one of these alternatives to death was not life without the possibility of parole," the court concluded, "*Simmons* was inapplicable."

Chief Justice Finney dissented. "[T]he overriding principle to be drawn from [*Simmons*]," he stated, "is that due process is violated when a jury's speculative misunderstanding about a capital defendant's parole eligibility is allowed to go uncorrected." Due process mandates reversal here, he concluded, because "the jury's inquiry prompted a misleading response which suggested parole was a possibility." Moreover, Chief Justice Finney added, when "a capital jury inquires about parole," even if the question "is simply one of policy, as the majority suggests [it is], then why not adopt a policy which gives the jurors the simpl[e] truth: no parole."

We granted certiorari, to determine whether the South Carolina Supreme Court properly held *Simmons* inapplicable to the State's current sentencing regime. We conclude that South Carolina's Supreme Court misinterpreted *Simmons*, and we therefore reverse that court's judgment.

II

South Carolina has consistently refused to inform the jury of a capital defendant's parole eligibility status.[4] We first confronted this practice in *Simmons*. The South Car-

---

3. South Carolina's "new" sentencing scheme changed the punishments available for a capital murder conviction that did not result in a death sentence. The capital sentencing law in effect at the time we decided *Simmons* read: "A person who is convicted of or pleads guilty to murder must be punished by death or by imprisonment for life and is not eligible for parole until the service of twenty years; provided, however, that when the State seeks the death penalty and an aggravating circumstance is specifically found beyond a reasonable doubt..., and a recommendation of death is not made, the court must impose a sentence of life imprisonment without eligibility for parole until the service of thirty years." S.C. Code Ann. §16-3-20(A) (Supp.1993). What made Simmons parole ineligible was the provision stating: "The board must not grant parole nor is parole authorized to any prisoner serving a sentence for a second or subsequent conviction, following a separate sentencing for a prior conviction, for violent crimes...." §24-21-640. This latter provision has not been amended; however, it did not apply to Shafer. Here, we consider whether South Carolina's wholesale elimination of parole for capital defendants sentenced to life in prison, see S.C. Code Ann. §16-3-20 (2000 Cum. Supp.), requires a *Simmons* instruction in all South Carolina capital cases in which future dangerousness is "at issue."

4. At the time we decided *Simmons v. South Carolina*, 512 U.S. 154 (1994), South Carolina was one of only three States—Pennsylvania and Virginia were the others—that "ha[d] a life-without-parole sentencing alternative to capital punishment for some or all convicted murderers but refuse[d] to inform sentencing juries of th[at] fact." Since *Simmons*, Virginia has abandoned this practice. *Yarbrough v. Commonwealth*, 258 Va. 347, 374 (1999) ("[W]e hold that in the penalty-determination phase of a trial where the defendant has been convicted of capital murder, in response to a proffer of a proper instruction from the defendant prior to submitting the issue of penalty-de-

olina sentencing scheme then in effect, S.C. Code Ann. §§16-3-20(A) and 24-21-610 (Supp. 1993), did not categorically preclude parole for capital defendants sentenced to life imprisonment. Simmons, however, was parole ineligible under that scheme because of prior convictions for crimes of violence. Simmons' jury, in a note to the judge during the penalty phase deliberations, asked: "Does the imposition of a life sentence carry with it the possibility of parole?" Over defense counsel's objection, the trial judge in *Simmons* instructed: "Do not consider parole or parole eligibility [in reaching your verdict]. That is not a proper issue for your consideration." After receiving this response from the court, Simmons' jury returned a sentence of death, which Simmons unsuccessfully sought to overturn on appeal to the South Carolina Supreme Court.

Mindful of the "longstanding practice of parole availability," we recognized that Simmons' jury, charged to chose between death and life imprisonment, may have been misled. Given no clear definition of "life imprisonment" and told not to consider parole eligibility, that jury "reasonably may have believed that [Simmons] could be released on parole if he were not executed." It did not comport with due process, we held, for the State to "secur[e] a death sentence on the ground, at least in part, of [defendant's] future dangerousness, while at the same time concealing from the sentencing jury the true meaning of its [only] noncapital sentencing alternative, namely, that life imprisonment meant life without parole."

As earlier stated, the South Carolina Supreme Court held in *Simmons* "inapplicable under the [State's] new sentencing scheme." *Simmons* is not triggered the South Carolina court said, unless life without parole is "the only legally available sentence alternative to death." Currently, the court observed, when a capital case jury begins its sentencing deliberations, three alternative sentences are available: "1) death, 2) life without the possibility of parole, or 3) a mandatory minimum thirty year sentence." "Since one of these alternatives to death [is] not life without the possibility of parole," the court concluded, *Simmons* no longer constrains capital sentencing in South Carolina.

This reasoning might be persuasive if the jury's sentencing discretion encompassed the three choices the South Carolina court identified. But, that is not how the State's new scheme works. Under the law now governing, in any case in which the jury does not unanimously find a statutory aggravator, death is not a permissible sentence and *Simmons* has no relevance. In such a case, the judge alone becomes the sentencer. S.C. Code Ann. §16-3-20(C) (2000 Cum. Supp.). Only if the jury finds an aggravating circumstance does it decide on the sentence. And when it makes that decision, as was the case in *Simmons*, only two sentences are legally available under South Carolina law: death or life without the possibility of parole.

The South Carolina Supreme Court was no doubt correct to this extent: At the time the trial judge instructed the jury in Shafer's case, it was indeed possible that Shafer would receive a sentence other than death or life without the possibility of parole. That is so because South Carolina, in line with other States, gives capital juries, at the penalty phase, discrete and sequential functions. Initially, capital juries serve as factfinders in determining whether an alleged aggravating circumstance exists. Once that factual threshold is passed, the jurors exercise discretion in determining the punishment that ought to be imposed. The trial judge in Shafer's case recognized the critical difference in the two functions. He charged that "[a] statutory aggravating circumstance is a fact, an

termination to the jury or where the defendant asks for such an instruction following an inquiry from the jury during deliberations, the trial court shall instruct the jury that the words 'imprisonment for life' mean 'imprisonment for life without possibility of parole.'").

incident, a detail or an occurrence," the existence of which must be found beyond a reasonable doubt. Turning to the sentencing choice, he referred to considerations of "fairness and mercy," and the defendant's "moral culpability." He also instructed that the jury was free to decide "whether ... for any reason or no reason at all Mr. Shafer should be sentenced to life imprisonment rather than to death."

In sum, when the jury determines the existence of a statutory aggravator, a tightly circumscribed factual inquiry, none of *Simmons'* due process concerns arise. There are no "misunderstanding[s]" to avoid, no "false choice[s]" to guard against. See *Simmons*, 512 U.S., at 161 (plurality opinion). The jury, as aggravating circumstance factfinder, exercises no sentencing discretion itself. If no aggravator is found, the judge takes over and has sole authority to impose the mandatory minimum so heavily relied upon by the South Carolina Supreme Court. It is only when the jury endeavors the moral judgment whether to impose the death penalty that parole eligibility may become critical. Correspondingly, it is only at that stage that *Simmons* comes into play, a stage at which South Carolina law provides no third choice, no 30-year mandatory minimum, just death or life without parole. See *Ramdass*, 530 U.S., at 169 (*Simmons* applies where "as a legal matter, there is no possibility of parole if the jury decides the appropriate sentence is life in prison.").[5] We therefore hold that whenever future dangerousness is at issue in a capital sentencing proceeding under South Carolina's new scheme, due process requires that the jury be informed that a life sentence carries no possibility of parole.

III

South Carolina offers two other grounds in support of the trial judge's refusal to give Shafer's requested parole ineligibility instruction. First, the State argues that the jury was properly informed of the law on parole ineligibility by the trial court's instructions and by defense counsel's own argument. Second, the State contends that no parole ineligibility instruction was required under *Simmons* because the State never argued Shafer would pose a future danger to society. We now turn to those arguments.

A

"Even if this Court finds *Simmons* was triggered," the State urges, "the defense's closing argument and the judge's charge fulfilled the requirements of *Simmons*." To support that contention, the State sets out defense counsel's closing pleas that, if Shafer's life is spared, he will "die in prison" after "spend[ing] his natural life there." Next, the State recites passages from the trial judge's instructions reiterating that "life imprisonment means until the death of the defendant."

The South Carolina Supreme Court, we note, never suggested that counsel's arguments or the trial judge's instructions satisfied *Simmons*. That court simply held *Simmons* inapplicable under the State's new sentencing scheme. We do not find the State's position persuasive. Displacement of "the longstanding practice of parole availability" remains a relatively recent development, and "common sense tells us that many jurors might not know whether a life sentence carries with it the possibility of parole." South

---

5. Tellingly, the State acknowledged at oral argument that if future dangerousness was a factor, and the jury first reported finding an aggravator before going on to its sentencing recommendation, a *Simmons* charge would at that point be required. We see no significant difference between that situation and the one presented here. Nor does Justice Thomas' dissent in this case plausibly urge any such distinction. If the jurors should be told life means no parole in the hypothesized bifurcated sentencing proceeding, they should be equally well informed in the actual uninterrupted proceeding.

Carolina's situation is illustrative. Until two years before Shafer's trial, as we earlier noted, the State's law did not categorically preclude parole for capital defendants sentenced to life imprisonment. Most plainly contradicting the State's contention, Shafer's jury left no doubt about its failure to gain from defense counsel's closing argument or the judge's instructions any clear understanding of what a life sentence means. The jurors sought further instruction, asking: "Is there any remote chance for someone convicted of murder to become elig[i]ble for parole?" The jury's comprehension was hardly aided by the court's final instruction: "Parole eligibility or ineligibility is not for your consideration." That instruction did nothing to ensure that the jury was not misled and may well have been taken to mean "that parole was available but that the jury, for some unstated reason, should be blind to this fact."

In sum, a life sentence for Shafer would permit no "parole, community supervision, ... early release program, ... or any other credits that would reduce the mandatory imprisonment," S.C. Code Ann. §16-3-20(A) (2000 Cum. Supp.); this reality was not conveyed to Shafer's jury by the court's instructions or by the arguments defense counsel was allowed to make.

B

Ultimately, the State maintains that "[t]he prosecution did not argue future dangerousness," so the predicate for a *Simmons* charge is not present here. That issue is not ripe for our resolution.

In the trial court, the prosecutor and defense counsel differed on what it takes to place future dangerousness "at issue." The prosecutor suggested that the State must formally argue future dangerousness. Defense counsel urged that once the prosecutor introduces evidence showing future dangerousness, the State cannot avoid a *Simmons* charge by saying the point was not argued or calling the evidence by another name.

As earlier recounted, the trial judge determined that future dangerousness was not at issue, but acknowledged, at one point, that the prosecutor had come close to crossing the line. The South Carolina Supreme Court, in order to rule broadly that *Simmons* no longer governs capital sentencing in the State, apparently assumed, *arguendo*, that future dangerousness had been shown at Shafer's sentencing proceeding. Because the South Carolina Supreme Court did not home in on the question whether the prosecutor's evidentiary submissions or closing argument in fact placed Shafer's future dangerousness at issue, we leave that question open for the state court's attention and disposition.

For the reasons stated, the judgment of the South Carolina Supreme Court is reversed, and the case is remanded for further proceedings not inconsistent with this opinion.

Justice SCALIA, dissenting.

While I concede that today's judgment is a logical extension of *Simmons v. South Carolina*, 512 U.S. 154 (1994), I am more attached to the logic of the Constitution, whose Due Process Clause was understood as an embodiment of common-law tradition, rather than as authority for federal courts to promulgate wise national rules of criminal procedure.

As I pointed out in *Simmons*, that common-law tradition does not contain special jury-instruction requirements for capital cases. Today's decision is the second page of the "whole new chapter" of our improvised "'death-is-different' jurisprudence" that

Simmons began. The third page (or the fourth or fifth) will be the (logical-enough) extension of this novel requirement to cases in which the jury did not inquire into the possibility of parole. Providing such information may well be a good idea (though it will sometimes harm rather than help the defendant's case) — and many States have indeed required it. The Constitution, however, does not. I would limit *Simmons* to its facts.

Justice THOMAS, dissenting.

For better or, as I believe, worse, the majority's decision in this case is the logical next step after *Simmons v. South Carolina*, 512 U.S. 154 (1994). Now, whenever future dangerousness is placed at issue and the jury's potential sentencing choice is between life without parole and death, the trial court must instruct the jury on the impossibility of release even if there is an alternative sentence available to the court under which the defendant could be released. However, even accepting that sentencing courts in South Carolina must now permit the jury to learn about the impossibility of parole when life imprisonment is a sentencing possibility, I believe that the court's instructions and the arguments made by counsel in Shafer's case were sufficient to inform the jury of what "life imprisonment" meant for Shafer. I therefore respectfully dissent.

In *Simmons*, a majority of this Court was concerned that the jury in Simmons' trial reasonably could have believed that, if he were sentenced to life, he would be eligible for parole. Therefore, Simmons' defense to future dangerousness — that because he sexually assaulted only elderly women, he would pose no danger to fellow inmates, would not have been effective. To correct the jury's possible misunderstanding of the availability of parole, Simmons requested several jury instructions, including one that would explain that, if he were sentenced to life imprisonment, "he actually w[ould] be sentenced to imprisonment in the state penitentiary for the balance of his natural life." The trial court rejected this instruction and instead ambiguously informed the jury that the term life imprisonment is to be understood according to its "plain and ordinary meaning," which did "nothing to dispel the misunderstanding reasonable jurors may have about the way in which any particular State defines 'life imprisonment.'"

In this case, by contrast, the judge repeatedly explained that "life imprisonment means until the death of the defendant." The judge defined "life imprisonment" as "incarceration of the defendant until his death," and informed the jury that, if it chose the punishment of life imprisonment, the verdict form would read "We, the jury ... unanimously recommend that the defendant, Wesley Aaron Shafer, be imprisoned in the state penitentiary for the balance of his natural life." Emphasizing this very point, Shafer's counsel argued to the jury that Shafer would never leave prison if he received a life sentence. ("The question is will the State execute him or will he just die in prison"); ("putting a 19 year old in prison until he is dead" and "you can put him some place until he is dead"); ("When they say give [him] life, he's not going home ... I'm just asking for the smallest amount of mercy it takes to make a man, a child spend the rest of his life in prison").

Given these explanations of what life imprisonment means, which left no room for speculation by the jury, I can only infer that the jury's questions regarding parole referred not to Shafer's parole eligibility in the event the jury sentenced Shafer to life, but rather to his parole eligibility in the event it did not sentence him at all. In fact, both of the jury's questions referred only to parole eligibility of someone "convicted of murder," ("[I]s there any remote chance that someone convicted of murder could become eligible for parole."); ("[U]nder what conditions would someone convicted for murder be eligible [for parole]"), rather than parole eligibility of someone sentenced to life imprisonment. Under South Carolina law, if the jury does not find an aggravating circumstance, someone convicted of murder could be sentenced to a term of 30 years' imprisonment or greater. See S.C. Code Ann. §16-3-20(C) (2000 Cum. Supp.). If the jury thought Shafer's release from prison was a possibility in the event the judge sentenced him, they would have been correct. To be sure, under South Carolina's sentencing scheme, the jury did not need to know what sentencing options were available to the judge in the event the jury did not find an aggravating circumstance. But that is precisely why the trial court's answers were appropriate. It explained what "life" meant for purposes of the jury's sentencing option, and then added that "[p]arole eligibility or ineligibility is not for your consideration."

The majority appears to believe that it could develop jury instructions that are more precise than those offered to Shafer's jury. It may well be right. But it is not this Court's role to micromanage state sentencing proceedings or to develop model jury instructions. I would decline to interfere further with matters that the Constitution leaves to the States.

Note: Is Future Dangerousness Always "At Issue" in Every Capital Case?

Based on data collected from interviews with South Carolina capital jurors, Professors Blume, Garvey, and Johnson have shown that future dangerousness is on the minds of most capital jurors, and is thus "at issue" in virtually all capital trials, regardless of the prosecution's conduct. That is, whether the state alleges "future dangerousness" or "continuing threat" as an aggravating factor, most capital jurors are mindful of the possibility that the defendant, if not sentenced to death and executed, could one day gain release and kill again. Accordingly, the authors argue that the "at issue" requirement of *Simmons* serves no real purpose and should be eliminated.

> Under existing doctrine, due process entitles a capital defendant to inform the jurors who will decide his fate that, if not sentenced to death, he will never be eligible for parole—but only if his future dangerousness is "at issue." Yet the fact of the matter is that future dangerousness is on the minds of most capital jurors and thus "at issue" in virtually all capital trials, even if the prosecution says nothing about it. Ironically, a capital defendant is therefore better off, all else being equal, if the prosecutor argues that he will pose a danger to society—in which case the defendant would be entitled to a *Simmons* instruction—than if the prosecutor remains silent. Indeed, the prosecutor in *Shafer* was well aware of this irony; otherwise, he would not have gone to such lengths to avoid a *Simmons* instruction.

Blume, Garvey & Johnson, "Future Dangerousness in Capital Cases: Always 'At Issue,'" 86 Cornell L. Rev. 397 (2001).

Note: California v. Ramos, 463 U.S. 992 (1983)

In *California v. Ramos*, the Court considered the constitutionality of the "*Briggs* Instruction" statute. The statute required a California jury to be informed that, if it returned a sentence of life imprisonment without the possibility of parole, the sentence could in the future be commuted by the governor to a sentence that includes the possibility of parole. Ramos argued that the "*Briggs* Instruction" was misleading, and therefore unconstitutional, because "it inject[ed] an unacceptable level of unreliability into the capital sentencing determination," and because it "deflect[ed] the jury from its constitutionally mandated task of basing the penalty decision on the character of the defendant and the nature of the offense."

Relying heavily on the accuracy of the proposed instruction, the Court held that it did not offend the federal Constitution. Subsequently, the California Supreme Court declared the statute unconstitutional because it offended the state constitution's due process guarantee of fundamental fairness. *People v. Ramos*, 689 P.2d 430, 439–440 (1984). For an argument that the Supreme Court's *Ramos* decision is at odds with the Court's declaration that the Constitution requires reliability in capital sentencing, see Paduano and Smith, "Deathly Errors: Juror Misperceptions Concerning Parole in the Imposition of the Death Penalty," 18 Colum. Hum. Rts. L. Rev. 211, 232–238 (1987) (excerpted below).

Deathly Errors: Juror Misperceptions Concerning Parole in the Imposition of the Death Penalty

Anthony Paduano & Clive A. Stafford Smith
18 Colum. Hum. Rts. L. Rev. 211 (1987)

Nothing, it seems, is worth what is used to be, and the criminal justice system's administration of capital punishment has not escaped unscathed. There was a time when a sentence of death meant swift execution and the only alternative, a sentence of life imprisonment, was imposed without hope of subsequent parole. Nowadays, however, in the evaluation of whether a capital defendant should live or die, the options are not as clearly defined for jurors as they once were. As a consequence, jurors in capital cases labor under the fundamental misperception that their verdict of either life or death will not count for much in the grand scheme of death penalty jurisprudence.

[T]he typical juror at the sentencing phase of a capital trial perceives the imposition of a sentence of "life imprisonment" to mean there is a good chance that the capital defendant will in fact be released from prison on parole. In some states the typical capital juror believes that the capital murderer sentenced to life may go free in just seven years. The option of life to a typical juror means disproportionately little punishment for the convicted capital murderer. A juror, then, laboring under the misperception that a sentence of "life" is a ticket to "get out of jail free" on parole, feels constrained to vote for a penalty of death. This misperception is compounded by the widely-held view that the federal courts are an all-but-impenetrable barrier to carrying out any death sentence. The frequent and widely-disseminated stories of never-ending appeals and last-minute stays of executions orchestrated by allegedly overly-zealous lawyers have made the imposition of a death sentence less real, and less likely, to a typical juror. The juror may well not believe—at the time he or she votes for sentence—that a death sentence is likely to ever be carried out. Indeed, that juror may well believe that a death sentence may result merely in a longer prison term while the protracted appellate process follows its course.

"Is There Life Without Parole?": A Capital Defendant's Right to a Meaningful Alternative Sentence

J. Mark Lane, 26 Loy. L.A. L. Rev. 327 (1993)

[T]here are substantial objective indicators that, although contemporary American society does not reject the death penalty outright, the majority nevertheless believes that there should be, in every capital case, an alternative sentence that would effectively incapacitate the defendant short of death. Such an alternative would differ from the traditional "life" sentence, in that it would expressly eliminate the possibility of the defendant's ultimate release on parole. Views favoring such an alternative have found expression in public opinion polls, which indicate a significant drop in support for the death penalty when a no-parole or limited-parole alternative is offered, and in legislative enactments, by which an increasing number of states have eliminated or limited parole eligibility for capital defendants sentenced to life imprisonment. Perhaps most importantly, such a view has manifested itself in the reactions of juries to existing sentencing schemes which provide only the alternatives of death or a traditional "life" sentence with possibility of parole. [J]uries have had strongly negative reactions to such a scheme, and have frequently sentenced defendants to death because they felt that, given only these options, they faced no meaningful alternative.

This situation has serious constitutional implications. First, a death sentence returned under such a sentencing scheme cannot be relied upon to reflect a properly guided and reasoned decision that death is the most appropriate punishment. Second, where a jury is primarily concerned with the defendant's incapacitation from committing further crimes, but is forced to return a death verdict because of the State's failure to offer any other means of doing so, such a sentence constitutes excessive punishment in violation of the Eighth Amendment, for the simple reason that incapacitation is not a constitutionally sufficient basis upon which to execute a criminal defendant. Finally, where there is such clear evidence that contemporary values require the availability of a life without parole alternative in any capital case, the failure to provide such an alternative, and to inform the sentencer of its availability, infringes upon the "evolving standards of decency" protected by the Eighth Amendment.

In contrast to the harm caused by failure to offer a life without parole alternative, the remedy is simple, straightforward and virtually costless. As demonstrated by states that have already done so, it would be a simple matter to provide, in every case where the death penalty is sought, an alternative sentence which would ensure that the defendant will be incarcerated for life, either completely or substantially without the possibility of parole. Moreover, in order to make that alternative sentence fully meaningful to the sentencing process, the sentencer must be made to understand its availability and its exact meaning. Where jury sentencing is used, therefore, the jury should be fully and accurately instructed as to the exact meaning of all its sentencing options, and should be reassured (accurately) that, if sentenced to life imprisonment, the defendant will never be released into society again. Such provisions would in no way limit the ability of the State to seek the death penalty when such a sentence is deemed appropriate, and would not affect the ability of the sentencer to impose it when, upon reasoned reflection, such a result is thought proper. As the Supreme Court stated in invalidating the mandatory scheme at issue in *Sumner v. Shuman* (*supra* chapter 2) in favor of a guided discretion statute, "[t]hose who deserve to die according to the judgment of the sentencing authority will be condemned to death under such a statute." On the other hand, once an appropriate alternative is made available, it will become less likely that those who, in the judgment of the sentencing authority, do *not* deserve to die, will nonetheless be condemned to death.

H. Special Problems of Volunteers

Gilmore v. Utah
429 U.S. 1012 (1976)

Order

On October 7, 1976, Gary Mark Gilmore was convicted of murder and sentenced to death by a judgment entered after a jury trial in a Utah court. On December 3, 1976, this Court granted an application for a stay of execution of the judgment and sentence, pending the filing here by the State of Utah of a response to the application together with transcripts of various specified hearings in the Utah courts and Board of Pardons, and until "further action of the Court on the application for stay."

The State of Utah has now filed its response and has substantially complied with the Court's request for transcripts of the specified hearings. After carefully examining the materials submitted by the State of Utah, the Court is convinced that Gary Mark Gilmore made a knowing and intelligent waiver of any and all federal rights he might have asserted after the Utah trial court's sentence was imposed, and, specifically, that the State's determinations of his competence knowingly and intelligently to waive any and all such rights were firmly grounded.

Accordingly, the stay of execution granted on December 3, 1976, is hereby terminated.

Mr. Chief Justice BURGER, with whom Mr. Justice Powell joins, concurring.

On December 2, 1976, Bessie Gilmore, claiming to act as "next friend" on behalf of her son, Gary Mark Gilmore, filed with this Court an application for stay of execution of the death sentence then scheduled for December 6, 1976.[1] Since only a limited record was then before the Court, we granted a temporary stay of execution on December 3, 1976 in order to secure a response from the State of Utah. That response was received on December 7, 1976. On December 8, 1976, a response was filed by Gary Mark Gilmore, by and through his attorneys of record, Ronald R. Stanger and Robert L. Moody, challenging the standing of Bessie Gilmore to initiate any proceedings in his behalf.

When the application for a stay was initially filed on December 2, a serious question was presented as to whether Bessie Gilmore had standing to seek the requested relief or any relief from this Court. Assuming the Court would otherwise have jurisdiction with respect to a "next friend" application, that jurisdiction would arise only if it were demonstrated that Gary Mark Gilmore is unable to seek relief in his own behalf. See

---

1. This case may be unique in the annals of the Court. Not only does Gary Mark Gilmore request no relief himself; on the contrary he has expressly and repeatedly stated since his conviction in the Utah courts that he had received a fair trial and had been well treated by the Utah authorities. Nor does he claim to be innocent of the crime for which he was convicted. Indeed, his only complaint against Utah or its judicial process, including that raised in the state habeas corpus petition … has been with respect to the delay on the part of the State in carrying out the sentence.

Rosenberg v. United States, 346 U.S. 273, 291 (1953) (separate opinion of Mr. Justice Jackson for six Members of the Court). However, in view of Gary Mark Gilmore's response on December 8, 1976, it is now clear that the "next friend" concept is wholly inapplicable to this case. Since Gary Mark Gilmore has now filed a response and appeared in his own behalf, through his retained attorneys, any basis for the standing of Bessie Gilmore to seek relief in his behalf is necessarily eliminated. The only possible exception to this conclusion would be if the record suggested, despite the representations of Gary Mark Gilmore's attorneys, that he was incompetent to waive his right of appeal under state law and was at the present time incompetent to assert rights or to challenge Bessie Gilmore's standing to assert rights in his behalf as "next friend."

After examining with care the pertinent portions of the transcripts and reports of state proceedings, and the response of Gary Mark Gilmore filed on December 8, I am in complete agreement with the conclusion expressed in the Court's order that Gary Mark Gilmore knowingly and intelligently, with full knowledge of his right to seek an appeal in the Utah Supreme Court, has waived that right.[4] I further agree that the State's determinations of his competence to waive his rights knowingly and intelligently were firmly grounded.[5]

---

4. At a hearing on November 1, 1976, on a motion for a new trial, Gilmore's attorneys informed the trial court that they had been told by Gilmore not to file an appeal and not to seek a stay of execution of sentence on his behalf. They also informed the trial court that they had advised Gilmore of his right to appeal that they believed there were substantial grounds for appeal, that the constitutionality of the Utah death penalty statute had not yet been reviewed by either the Utah Supreme Court or the United States Supreme Court, and that in their view there was a chance that the statute would eventually be held unconstitutional. The trial court itself advised Gilmore that he had a right to appeal, that the constitutional issue had not yet been resolved, and that both counsel for the State and Gilmore's own counsel would attempt to expedite an appeal to avoid unnecessary delay. Gilmore stated that he did not "care to languish in prison for another day," that the decision was his own, and that he had not made the decision as a result of the influence of drugs or alcohol or as a result of the way he was treated in prison. On November 4, the state trial court concluded that Gilmore fully understood his right to appeal and the consequences of a decision not to appeal.

On November 10, the Utah Supreme Court held a hearing on the Utah Attorney General's motion to vacate a stay of execution of sentence entered two days earlier by that Court. Gilmore was present, and, in response to questions from several Justices, stated that he thought he had received a fair trial and a proper sentence, that he opposed any appeal in the case, and that he wished to withdraw an appeal previously filed without his consent by appointed trial counsel.

Finally, at a hearing before the trial court on December 1, Gilmore again informed the court that he opposed all appeals that had been filed.

5. In the pretrial period, from August 5 to October 6, 1976, the trial court appointed psychiatrists to examine Gilmore on two occasions, to determine his competency to stand trial and his sanity at the time of the offense. Three of the five psychiatrists who examined Gilmore in that period found no evidence of mental illness or insanity. The record before us does not include the findings of the other two psychiatrists, which were presented to the trial court when it concluded that Gilmore was sane for the purpose of standing trial.

After trial, at the November 1 hearing, the state trial court ordered *sua sponte* that the Utah State Prison Psychiatrist, or other available psychiatric personnel of the prison, examine Gilmore to determine his ability to decide not to appeal. In the order, the court noted that Gilmore had instructed his attorneys not to appeal after they had informed him that there was substantial legal merit to such an appeal. On November 3 the Prison Psychiatrist submitted a report, based on a one-hour psychiatric interview and a review of Gilmore's medical records, concluding that Gilmore's decision to waive appeal was the "product of an organized thought process" and that Gilmore had not "become 'insane' or mentally ill." On the same day, two prison psychologists submitted a second report, based on psychological tests and an individual interview, concluding that "(Gilmore) presently has the mental capacity and the emotional stability to make the necessary decision concerning his sentence and to understand the consequences."

When the record establishing a knowing and intelligent waiver of Gary Mark Gilmore's right to seek appellate review is combined with the December 8 written response submitted to this Court,[6] it is plain that the Court is without jurisdiction to entertain the "next friend" application filed by Bessie Gilmore. This Court has jurisdiction pursuant to Art. III of the Constitution only over "cases and controversies," and we can issue stays only in aid of our jurisdiction. 28 U.S.C. §§1651, 2101(f). There is no dispute, presently before us, between Gary Mark Gilmore and the State of Utah, and the application of Bessie Gilmore manifestly fails to meet the statutory requirements to invoke this Court's power to review the action of the Supreme Court of Utah. No authority to the contrary has been brought to our attention, and nothing suggested in dissent bears on the threshold question of jurisdiction.

In his dissenting opinion, Mr. Justice White suggests that Gary Mark Gilmore is "unable" as a matter of law to waive the right to state appellate review. Whatever may be said as to the merits of this suggestion, the question simply is not before us. Gilmore, duly found to be competent by the Utah courts, has had available meaningful access to this Court and has declined expressly to assert any claim here other than his explicit repudiation of Bessie Gilmore's effort to speak for him as next friend. It follows, therefore, that the Court is without jurisdiction to consider the question posed by the dissent.

Mr. Justice WHITE, joined by Mr. Justice Brennan and Mr. Justice Marshall, dissenting.

As Justice Wilkins said in dissent below, there are substantial questions under *Furman v. Georgia*, 408 U.S. 238 (1972), about the constitutionality of the Utah death penalty statute. Because of Gary Gilmore's purported waiver of his right to challenge the statute, none of these questions was resolved in the Utah courts. I believe, however, that the consent of a convicted defendant in a criminal case does not privilege a State to impose a punishment otherwise forbidden by the Eighth Amendment.[2] Until the state courts have resolved the obvious serious doubts about the validity of the state statute, the imposition of the death penalty in this case should be stayed.

Given the inability of Gary Gilmore to waive resolution in the state courts of the serious questions concerning the constitutional legality of his death sentence, there is no jurisdictional barrier to addressing the question upon the petition of the defendant's mother. See *Rosenberg v. United States*, 346 U.S. 273, 291 (1953) (separate opinion of Justice Jackson). Without examining the constitutionality of the Utah death statute, on November 10, 1976, the Utah Supreme Court vacated its stay of Gilmore's sentence and dismissed the appeal which his then attorneys had filed on his behalf.

Pending the filing of a timely petition for certiorari, I would continue the stay previously issued by this Court; and upon said filing it would appear that the judgment of the Supreme Court of Utah should be vacated and the case remanded to the state courts for reconsideration in the light of the death penalty decisions announced by this Court

---

Gilmore apparently attempted to take his own life on November 16. The Prison Psychiatrist subsequently reported to the Board of Pardons that Gilmore's mental state on November 24 was "exactly as described" in the Psychiatrist's report to the court on November 3.

6. On December 8, 1976, Gilmore, by counsel, advised this Court of the filing of a petition in a Utah state court seeking habeas corpus relief. Although that petition is not in the papers before us, it is understood that the ground relied upon is not the deprivation of any constitutional right but that there is a 60-day limitation under Utah law upon the carrying out of the sentence of death, an issue which has not been presented to the Utah Supreme Court as of this date.

2. Nor in the absence of a state court decision sustaining the death penalty statute would a purported waiver of the Eighth Amendment necessarily be a defense to a wrongful-death action, see Utah Code Ann. §78-11-7, based on an execution imposed under an unconstitutional statute.

last Term. Cf. *Collins v. Arkansas*, 429 U.S. 808 (1976); *Neal v. Arkansas*, 429 U.S. 808 (1976).

Mr. Justice MARSHALL, dissenting.

I fully agree with my Brother White that a criminal defendant has no power to agree to be executed under an unconstitutional statute. I believe that the Eighth Amendment not only protects the right of individuals not to be victims of cruel and unusual punishment, but that it also expresses a fundamental interest of society in ensuring that state authority is not used to administer barbaric punishments. Irrespective of this, however, I cannot agree with the view expressed by the Chief Justice that Gilmore has competently, knowingly, and intelligently decided to let himself be killed. Less than five months have passed since the commission of the crime; just over two months have elapsed since sentence was imposed. That is hardly sufficient time for mature consideration of the question, nor does Gilmore's erratic behavior from his suicide attempt to his state habeas petition evidence such deliberation. No adversary hearing has been held to examine the experts,[1] all employed by the State of Utah, who have pronounced Gilmore sane.[2] The decision of the Utah Supreme Court finding a valid waiver can be given little weight. In the transcripts that the court prepared for us, it omitted a portion of its proceedings as having "no pertinency" to the issue of Gilmore's "having voluntarily and intelligently waived his right to appeal." That "irrelevant" portion involved a discussion by Gilmore's trial counsel of his opinion of Gilmore's competence and the constitutionality of the Utah statute. It is appalling that any court could consider these questions irrelevant to that determination. It is equally shocking that the Utah court, in a matter of such importance, failed even to have a court reporter present to transcribe the proceeding, instead relying on recordings made by dictating machines which have produced a partly unintelligible record. These inexplicable actions by a court charged with life or death responsibility underscore the failure of the State to determine adequately the validity of Gilmore's purported waiver and the propriety of imposing capital punishment.

Constitutional Rights Discarded as Many Pursue Grasso's Wish to Die

Randall Coyne, Oklahoma Gazette, May 6, 1993

Condemned murderer Thomas Grasso wants desperately to die. And his attorney, Tulsa County Public Defender Johnie O'Neal, is doing everything in his power to see that his client's death wish is granted. If Grasso and O'Neal are successful, serious damage will be done to Oklahoma's criminal justice system. Grasso's trenchant pursuit of self-destruction charts a course littered with the debris of discarded constitutional rights.

Grasso pled guilty to the 1990 strangling of an 87-year-old Tulsa woman and waived his constitutional right to a trial by jury. To determine whether Grasso was mentally competent to plead guilty, Grasso's attorneys had him examined by a psychologist. Subsequently, Grasso's lawyers joined the prosecution in arguing that Grasso was competent. Ultimately the trial judge accepted Grasso's guilty plea.

---

1. If Gilmore's own lawyers refused to question his competence, the court could certainly ask other counsel acting as *amicus curiae* to present that side of the issue.

2. As the Chief Justice notes, the opinion of the Prison Psychiatrist, the only doctor who has considered Gilmore's competency since the waiver decision was publicly announced, was based on a review of Gilmore's medical records and a one-hour interview.

Under Oklahoma law, cases punishable by death require a separate sentencing proceeding to determine the appropriate punishment. The judge or jury must balance aggravating evidence (presented by the prosecution as a basis for a death sentence) against mitigating evidence (presented by the defense as a basis for a sentence less than death). Only by balancing both types of evidence may the sentencer decide which of three possible punishments — life, life without parole, or death by poison injection — fits the crime.

The district attorney prosecuting the case performed his duty and presented abundant aggravating evidence. Grasso's extensive criminal record, which includes convictions for armed robbery, burglary, aggravated battery and drug possession, was offered as justification for killing him. However, due to the deliberate decisions of Grasso and his attorneys the adversary system miscarried once again. To facilitate Grasso's wish to die, his lawyers agreed that they would not present any mitigating evidence. Not surprisingly, after a shockingly one-sided presentation of evidence, the trial judge sentenced Grasso to death.

Remarkably, the Oklahoma Court of Criminal Appeals permitted Grasso to waive his rights to appeal his conviction and death sentence. And in a move which effectively silenced all voices raised in opposition to Grasso and O'Neal's manipulation of Oklahoma's criminal justice system, the Court refused to grant the Oklahoma Appellate Indigent Defender System permission to file an *amicus* brief.

Eventually, Grasso's death march stumbled upon a right which is not waivable under Oklahoma statutes: mandatory sentence review. On Tuesday, April 20, 1993, the Oklahoma Court of Criminal Appeals hosted oration (oral argument by definition requires dispute) in *State v. Grasso* for the narrow purpose of performing sentence review. This time Assistant Attorney General Diane Blalock added her voice to the unanimous chorus demanding Grasso's speedy execution.

To further complicate matters, Grasso was convicted of second degree murder in New York before his Oklahoma trial. New York — which has no death penalty — allowed Grasso to be brought to Oklahoma temporarily to stand trial and now wants him back. Grasso, of course, prefers to remain here and face execution.

Scholars believe that serial killer Ted Bundy selected Florida because it offered the best hope of execution. And psychiatrists who extensively examined Gary Gilmore wondered whether he would have killed if Utah had no death penalty. Ultimately, the *Grasso* decision may determine whether Oklahoma will become a mecca for murderers who kill in order to invoke the state's capital punishment system as a means of committing suicide.

Let me suggest several additional reasons why the Court should be reluctant to embrace the monotonous chorus of arguments proffered in unison by the defendant, the defense lawyer and the attorney general. First, the quintessential attribute of the American criminal justice system is that its adversarial nature helps to ensure reliable results. The quintessential attribute of Grasso's case has been the complete absence of adversariness. Second, defendants are not entitled to select their punishment. That responsibility rests with the sentencer. And when the sentencer is deliberately deprived of relevant mitigating evidence, the sentencer's decision becomes arbitrary. Third, the state has a compelling interest in preventing the manipulation of its criminal justice system by a murderer bent on suicide. Finally, the integrity of Oklahoma's death penalty system depends on scrupulous adversarial proceedings which ensure that those who are sentenced to death actually deserve to die.

Grasso v. Oklahoma

857 P.2d 802 (Okla. Crim. App. 1993)

Judge CHAPEL, specially concurring:

Under the unique facts of this case, I conclude Thomas Grasso's conviction and sentence of death should be affirmed. However, I am concerned about the issues raised by this case and the impact that this case will have on future cases. Although Grasso's desire to be executed may seem unusual, this case is not unique. Over ten percent of the executions in the United States since 1976 have been carried out on individuals who, at some point, elected to die. Because this case raises difficult and troubling issues, I specially concur to explain my concerns and address the problems raised when a defendant, who having been convicted of First Degree Murder, seeks the imposition of the death penalty.

The first area of concern is the issue of a defendant's competency to waive his appeals and seek the imposition of the death penalty. By waiving his discretionary appeal, a defendant will expedite and may render certain the imposition of death. Such a waiver begs the question of the defendant's competence and the permanence of his decision....

Given the basic human desire to live in spite of tremendous adversity and difficulties, a defendant's decision to be executed is fraught with questions and concerns. Commentators have noted that it is not unusual for a defendant facing the death penalty to at some point express the desire to die only to recant that desire later. When ultimately facing death most people agree with the observations of Claudio in Shakespeare's *Measure for Measure*:

> The weariest and most loathed worldly life
> That age, ache, penury, and imprisonment
> Can lay on nature is a paradise
> To what we fear of death.

W. Shakespeare, *Measure for Measure*, act III, scene i, li. 129–133.

Further, the State of Oklahoma has a keen interest in assuring that its system of justice is not being manipulated or abused by a defendant. The State must not become an unwitting partner in a defendant's suicide by placing the personal desires of the defendant above the societal interests in assuring that the death penalty is imposed in a rational, non-arbitrary fashion.

The State's interest in assuring the rational and appropriate application of the death sentence and Grasso's interest in asserting his personal desire to waive his appeal must be balanced. Although the consequences and risks that attend waiving an appeal in a capital case are high, a defendant should not be precluded from waiving his discretionary appeals. In other contexts, a competent defendant's ability to waive his rights is well recognized. For example, under appropriate circumstances, a defendant may waive his right to counsel, he may waive his right to silence, and he may waive trial by pleading guilty to an offense.

I agree with the majority that a capital defendant may waive his statutory right to a direct appeal, although he may not waive his right to the mandatory sentence review. I also agree with the majority that the standard for determining whether a capital defendant is competent to waive his direct appeal is whether (1) the defendant has the capacity to understand the choice between life and death, and (2) the defendant has the capacity to knowingly and intelligently waive any and all rights to appeal his sentence. My concern is with the application of this standard to Grasso and future criminal defendants seeking to waive their capital appeals....

Reviewing the factors and evidence other courts have relied upon to determine the competency of a capital defendant to waive his appeals provides a useful guide to this Court. A competency evaluation should address the defendant's ability to truly comprehend his own death. The examiner should determine whether the defendant understands all of his options and that his perception of those options is rational, coherent, and based on reality. The defendant's mental health history and I.Q. should be closely scrutinized. Any suicidal or paranoid tendencies, which may distort the defendant's ability to make a rational decision, should be addressed and carefully examined. It seems the competency examination, as best as is possible, should also address the possibility that the defendant may change his mind. Thus, it seems that once a defendant decides to waive his appeals, a separate and independent evaluation of the defendant should be conducted to address the unique issues surrounding competency to waive capital discretionary appeals as set out in the competency standard we adopted today.

In reviewing the record in this case and the observations that this Court has made of Grasso, I agree with the majority that Grasso is competent to waive his discretionary appeal....

Nonetheless, many individuals facing the death penalty may very well be burdened by mental and emotional problems that would render them incompetent to waive their appeals. For example, the record in this case would hardly be adequate for an individual who was borderline mentally retarded and sought to waive an appeal of his death sentence. Nor would the record before us today be adequate for someone with a history of mental illness or who had been diagnosed with a mental illness such as paranoid schizophrenia. The cursory record prepared in this case may very well be rejected in the next case in which a person facing the sentence of death seeks to waive his appeal so that he can die. I conclude that a separate competency evaluation conducted by an appropriate mental health professional should be conducted to specifically determine competency to waive one's appeals.

Further, in my view, a waiver of a discretionary capital appeal must be viewed with great caution. This Court is obligated to ensure that the death penalty be carried out only in a rational manner which comports with the Oklahoma and federal constitutions. Simply because a defendant chooses to waive his sentence of death does not mean this Court is obligated to carry out the defendant's wishes.

In addition, I am greatly concerned about the possibility that a defendant could manipulate the judicial system and on the eve of the execution change his mind and seek review in federal court claiming incompetence, ineffective assistance of counsel, and a whole myriad of other issues.[3] By carefully assuring on the record that the defendant is competent and that he is knowingly, voluntarily and intelligently waiving his appeal, this potential problem will be minimized.

---

3. A further concern is the syndrome that the commentators call the "murder-suicide" phenomenon which "refers to the clinically recognized syndrome in which an individual intentionally commits murder in a state with a death penalty hoping that, once caught, the State will execute and thereby accomplish [the suicide that] he himself cannot bring about by his own hand." The classic case is James French who was executed by Oklahoma in 1966 for the murder of his prison cell mate. According to some commentators, French was unable to carry out his own suicide. French's motive in murdering his cell mate was to force the State to execute him.

As to the mandatory sentence review, I also agree that the evidence presented below supports the imposition of the sentence of death.[4] However, I feel that allowing *amicus curiae* to participate would have aided the Court in its review of Grasso's sentence. Nonetheless, based on the record before this Court, I agree that the imposition of the sentence of death was proper in this case.[5] ...

Notes and Questions

1. For a discussion on the moral and ethical dilemma facing defense counsel who represent clients who "volunteer" to be executed see, Dieter, "Ethical Choices for Attorneys Whose Clients Elect Execution," 3 Geo. J. Legal Ethics 799 (1990); W.S. Welsh, "Defendants Who Elect Execution," 48 U. Pitt. L. Rev. 853, 855–861 (1987); Carter, "Maintaining Systemic Integrity in Capital Cases: The Use of Court-Appointed Counsel to Present Mitigating Evidence When the Defendant Advocates Death," 55 Tenn. L. Rev. 95 (1987).

Consider the following questions posed by Professor Linda E. Carter. "Three interrelated ethical concerns arise when the defendant wants to forego mitigating evidence. First, to what extent are decisions regarding tactics and the presentation of evidence the defendant's? Second, as a 'zealous advocate,' what is the attorney's obligation to the defendant? Third, is the obligation to represent one's client zealously tempered to any extent by virtue of the lawyer's status as an 'officer of the court.'?" 55 Tenn. L. Rev. at 130.

2. According to Professor Carter, "[t]he heart of the problem when a defendant in a capital case refuses to present mitigating evidence is ensuring the non-arbitrary imposition of death." Carter, "Maintaining Systemic Integrity in Capital Cases: The Use of Court-Appointed Counsel to Present Mitigating Evidence When the Defendant Advocates Death," 55 Tenn. L. Rev. 95, 151 (1987). Professor Carter suggests that society's interest in ensuring the reliability of the decision of death outweighs the interest of a defendant who advocates death. Rather than require the court, the prosecutor or the defense counsel to present mitigating evidence over the defendant's objections, Carter proposes that courts appoint counsel whose specific role is to present mitigating evidence. Do you agree with Professor Carter that "the presentation of mitigating evidence, not merely the opportunity to present it, is constitutionally required"?

3. Some states require mandatory review of the imposition of the death sentence. In such states, defendants who wish to be executed may waive discretionary appeals but not the mandatory review of their sentence. See *Grasso v. State*, 857 P.2d 802 (Okla. Crim. App. 1993); *State v. Brewer*, 826 P.2d 783 (Ariz. 1992); *State v. Dodd*, 838 P.2d 86 (Wash. 1992).

---

4. It is possible that a defendant's effort to have the death sentence imposed upon him could, in and of itself, constitute an arbitrary factor rendering the death sentence invalid. Although I do not find that Grasso's actions inserted an improper and arbitrary element into the sentencing process in this case, there may be cases in the future where this would be a problem.

5. During the sentencing phase below, Grasso instructed his attorneys not to put on any mitigating evidence. One commentator has argued, and at least one court has found, that absence of mitigating evidence distorts the sentencing process and prevents the imposition of a rational, non-arbitrary sentence. In spite of the serious concerns raised by waiving mitigating evidence, I believe that the right can be waived. However, I believe that the waiver should be clear and on the record and that the trial court must make a determination that the defendant is competent to waive the presentation of mitigating evidence.

4. A defendant's waiver of his right to appeal must be knowing, voluntary, and intelligent to be effective. What evidence is necessary to show a knowing, voluntary, and intelligent waiver? Should a competency hearing be held after sentencing but before execution to determine the defendant's competence? Should a psychiatrist examine the defendant to assure his mental competence? If so, is the prison psychiatrist adequate, or should an outside psychiatrist be appointed? What should the scope and nature of that examination be? Should the court independently review the defendant's waiver to ensure that it is knowing, voluntary, and intelligent? If so, what should be the scope of that review?

5. Assuming a defendant is found to be competent and waives all appeals, what remedy, if any, should be granted if twelve hours before his execution the defendant changes his mind?

6. Should the state permit death row inmates to commit suicide? Socrates, the ancient Greek philosopher, was sentenced to death after being found guilty of "corruption of the young" and "neglect of the gods whom the city worships and the practice of religious novelties." Athenian custom permitted the condemned to "drink the hemlock" within 24 hours of the death sentence and avoid a more gruesome fate. Volume 27, *The New Encyclopaedia Britannica* 436 (15th ed.). More recently, in 1991 Donald "Pee Wee" Gaskins swallowed a razor blade, coughed it up and slit his wrists, shortly before his scheduled electrocution in South Carolina. Twenty stitches and several hours later, Gaskins became the first white person actually executed for killing a black person in this country since 1944.

Notes and Questions on Jury Overrides: Spaziano v. Florida, 468 U.S. 447 (1984)

1. The majority of capital punishment jurisdictions vest the life-or-death decision exclusively in the jury. In many states, a death sentence may be imposed only if the jury unanimously agrees that death is the appropriate punishment. Nonetheless, at one point four states — Alabama, Delaware, Florida and Indiana — permitted the trial judge to overrule the jury and impose a death sentence, even if all jurors voted for a life sentence.

The constitutionality of Florida's jury override provision was before the Court in *Spaziano v. Florida*, 468 U.S. 447 (1984). After Joseph Spaziano was found guilty of first degree murder, a majority of jurors recommended life imprisonment. Under Florida law, a capital jury's recommendation of appropriate sentence is merely advisory. Thus, after independently weighing the aggravating and mitigating circumstances, the trial judge has the power to override the jury's recommendation. If the judge overrides the jury and imposes death, specific written findings are required. In Spaziano's case, the trial judge conducted its own weighing and determined that the proper sentence was death.

Writing for the majority, Justice Blackmun rejected Spaziano's argument that juries, not judges, are better equipped to make reliable capital-sentencing decisions and therefore a jury's recommendation of life should be inviolate. According to Justice Blackmun's opinion, although the fundamental issue in a capital sentencing proceeding is the determination of the appropriate punishment, nothing in the Constitution guarantees a right to a jury determination of that issue. Moreover, the fact that a majority of jurisdictions with capital sentencing statutes give the life-or-death decision to the jury does not establish that contemporary standards of fairness and decency are offended by the jury override. What constitutional provisions are implicated by Spaziano's argument?

2. As early as 1977, the United States Supreme Court permitted the execution of an inmate, notwithstanding a Florida jury's 10–2 recommendation of a life sentence. See *Dobbert v. Florida*, 432 U.S. 282, 304 n.1 (1977) (Stevens, J., dissenting).

3. The petitioner in *Harris v. Alabama*, 513 U.S. 504 (1995), challenged the constitutionality of Alabama's jury override statute. In capital cases in Alabama, the jury rendered an advisory verdict of either death or life without parole, but the ultimate sentencing power rested with the trial judge. While the trial court could consider the advisory jury verdict in imposing sentence, Alabama law did not specify the weight to be attached to that special verdict. In declaring Alabama's sentencing scheme constitutional, the Court held that "the Eighth Amendment does not require the state to define the weight the sentencing judge must accord an advisory verdict." In dissent, Justice Stevens stated, "Not surprisingly, given the political pressures they face, judges are far more likely than juries to impose the death penalty." 513 U.S. at 521. Justice Stevens observed, "Alabama judges have vetoed only five jury recommendations of death, but they have condemned 47 defendants whom juries would have spared." Statistics from the two other judge over-ride states—Florida and Indiana—showed similar patterns. 513 U.S. at 521 & n.8.

Note on Dispensing with Capital Sentencing Juries

At the time the Court decided *Spaziano*, the Sixth Amendment "never ha[d] been thought to guarantee a right to jury determination" of the "appropriate punishment to be imposed on an individual." 468 U.S. 447, 459 (1989). Consequently, Colorado's decision in 1995 to dispense altogether with juries in capital sentencing proceedings, and to vest the sentencing decision in a three-judge panel appeared to raise no federal constitutional problems. §16-11-103, Colo. Rev. Stat. Nonetheless, the Colorado sentencing scheme drew criticism. The local newspaper predicted a death sentence in one murder case in Colorado Springs: "There's a strong chance that the judges in the Colorado Springs case will vote for death ... because of the public outrage which erupted last year when [the co-defendant] was allowed to live." A local defense lawyer noted, "A non-death verdict is a ticket to public outrage in this county. Any judge who votes for life is going to be unemployed when they come up for retention." The Colorado Gazette, Mar. 27, 2000, at M1.

Nevada's system—which relied upon three-judge panels to decide between life and death sentences in cases in which juries can not reach agreement, and which permitted judges to opt out of service on such panels—also drew heavy criticism. According to one skeptic, "In a state where voters directly elect them, judges disinclined to support the death penalty have every incentive to beg off rather than risk creating a campaign issue for a future opponent." Las Vegas Rev.-J., July 10, 2000, at B6.

I. Requirement of Jury Determination of Any Fact Which Increases Punishment

When considering the Supreme Court's opinion in *Ring v. Arizona*, ask whether the Court called into question the continuing constitutionality of jury override systems and judge sentencing.

Ring v. Arizona

536 U.S. 584 (2002)

Justice GINSBURG delivered the opinion of the Court.

This case concerns the Sixth Amendment right to a jury trial in capital prosecutions. In Arizona, following a jury adjudication of a defendant's guilt of first-degree murder, the trial judge, sitting alone, determines the presence or absence of the aggravating factors required by Arizona law for imposition of the death penalty.

In *Walton v. Arizona*, 497 U.S. 639 (1990), this Court held that Arizona's sentencing scheme was compatible with the Sixth Amendment because the additional facts found by the judge qualified as sentencing considerations, not as "element[s] of the offense of capital murder." Ten years later, however, we decided *Apprendi v. New Jersey*, 530 U.S. 466 (2000), which held that the Sixth Amendment does not permit a defendant to be "expose[d] ... to a penalty exceeding the maximum he would receive if punished according to the facts reflected in the jury verdict alone." This prescription governs, *Apprendi* determined, even if the State characterizes the additional findings made by the judge as "sentencing factor[s]."

Apprendi's reasoning is irreconcilable with *Walton*'s holding in this regard, and today we overrule *Walton* in relevant part. Capital defendants, no less than non-capital defendants, we conclude, are entitled to a jury determination of any fact on which the legislature conditions an increase in their maximum punishment.

I

... [Timothy] Ring [was convicted] of felony murder occurring in the course of armed robbery. [Along with James Greeham and William Ferguson, Ring robbed an armored van and killed the driver, John Magoch.].

Under Arizona law, Ring could not be sentenced to death, the statutory maximum penalty for first-degree murder, unless further findings were made. The State's first-degree murder statute prescribes that the offense "is punishable by death or life imprisonment as provided by § 13-703." Ariz.Rev.Stat. Ann. § 13-1105(C) (West 2001). The cross-referenced section, § 13-703, directs the judge who presided at trial to "conduct a separate sentencing hearing to determine the existence or nonexistence of [certain enumerated] circumstances ... for the purpose of determining the sentence to be imposed." § 13-703(C) (West Supp. 2001). The statute further instructs: "The hearing shall be conducted before the court alone. The court alone shall make all factual determinations required by this section or the constitution of the United States or this state."

At the conclusion of the sentencing hearing, the judge is to determine the presence or absence of the enumerated "aggravating circumstances" and any "mitigating circumstances." The State's law authorizes the judge to sentence the defendant to death only if there is at least one aggravating circumstance and "there are no mitigating circumstances sufficiently substantial to call for leniency."

The judge then turned to the determination of aggravating and mitigating circumstances. He found two aggravating factors. First, the judge determined that Ring committed the offense in expectation of receiving something of "pecuniary value," "[t]aking the cash from the armored car was the motive and reason for Mr. Magoch's murder and not just the result." Second, the judge found that the offense was committed "in an especially heinous, cruel or depraved manner." In support of this finding, he cited Ring's comment, as reported by Greenham at the sentencing hearing, expressing pride in his marksmanship. The judge found one nonstatutory mitigating factor: Ring's "minimal" criminal record. In his judgment, that mitigating circumstance did not "call for leniency"; he therefore sentenced Ring to death.

On appeal, Ring argued that Arizona's capital sentencing scheme violates the Sixth and Fourteenth Amendments to the U.S. Constitution because it entrusts to a judge the finding of a fact raising the defendant's maximum penalty. The State, in response, noted that this Court had upheld Arizona's system in *Walton v. Arizona*, 497 U.S. 639 (1990), and had stated in *Apprendi* that *Walton* remained good law.

After reciting this Court's divergent constructions of Arizona law in *Apprendi*, the Arizona Supreme Court described how capital sentencing in fact works in the State. The Arizona high court concluded that "the present case is precisely as described in Justice O'Connor's dissent [in *Apprendi*] — Defendant's death sentence required the judge's factual findings." Although it agreed with the *Apprendi* dissent's reading of Arizona law, the Arizona court understood that it was bound by the Supremacy Clause to apply *Walton*, which this Court had not overruled. It therefore rejected Ring's constitutional attack on the State's capital murder judicial sentencing system.

The court agreed with Ring that the evidence was insufficient to support the aggravating circumstance of depravity, but it upheld the trial court's finding on the aggravating factor of pecuniary gain. The Arizona Supreme Court then reweighed that remaining factor against the sole mitigating circumstance (Ring's lack of a serious criminal record), and affirmed the death sentence.

We granted Ring's petition for a writ of certiorari, to allay uncertainty in the lower courts caused by the manifest tension between *Walton* and the reasoning of *Apprendi*. We now reverse the judgment of the Arizona Supreme Court.

II

Based solely on the jury's verdict finding Ring guilty of first-degree felony murder, the maximum punishment he could have received was life imprisonment. This was so because, in Arizona, a "death sentence may not legally be imposed ... unless at least one aggravating factor is found to exist beyond a reasonable doubt." The question presented is whether that aggravating factor may be found by the judge, as Arizona law specifies, or whether the Sixth Amendment's jury trial guarantee, made applicable to the States by the Fourteenth Amendment, requires that the aggravating factor determination be entrusted to the jury.[4]

---

4. Ring's claim is tightly delineated: He contends only that the Sixth Amendment required jury findings on the aggravating circumstances asserted against him. No aggravating circumstance related to past convictions in his case; Ring therefore does not challenge *Almendarez-Torres v. United States*, 523 U.S. 224 (1998), which held that the fact of prior conviction may be found by the judge even if it increases the statutory maximum sentence. He makes no Sixth Amendment claim with respect to mitigating circumstances. See *Apprendi v. New Jersey*, 530 U.S. 466 (2000) (noting "the distinction the Court has often recognized between facts in aggravation of punishment and facts in mitigation"). Nor does he argue that the Sixth Amendment required the jury to make the ultimate determination whether to impose the death penalty. See *Proffitt v. Florida*, 428 U.S. 242 (1976) (plurality opinion) ("[I]t has never [been] suggested that jury sentencing is constitutionally required."). He does not question the Arizona Supreme Court's authority to reweigh the aggravating and mitigating circumstances after that court struck one aggravator. See *Clemons v. Mississippi*, 494 U.S. 738, 100 S.Ct. 1441 (1990). Finally, Ring does not contend that his indictment was constitutionally de-

As earlier indicated, this is not the first time we have considered the constitutionality of Arizona's capital sentencing system. In *Walton v. Arizona*, 497 U.S. 639 (1990), we upheld Arizona's scheme against a charge that it violated the Sixth Amendment. The Court had previously denied a Sixth Amendment challenge to Florida's capital sentencing system, in which the jury recommends a sentence but makes no explicit findings on aggravating circumstances; we so ruled, *Walton* noted, on the ground that "the Sixth Amendment does not require that the specific findings authorizing the imposition of the sentence of death be made by the jury." *Walton* found unavailing the attempts by the defendant-petitioner in that case to distinguish Florida's capital sentencing system from Arizona's. In neither State, according to *Walton*, were the aggravating factors "elements of the offense"; in both States, they ranked as "sentencing considerations" guiding the choice between life and death.

Walton drew support from *Cabana v. Bullock*, 474 U.S. 376 (1986), in which the Court held there was no constitutional bar to an appellate court's finding that a defendant killed, attempted to kill, or intended to kill, as *Enmund v. Florida*, 458 U.S. 782 (1982), required for imposition of the death penalty in felony-murder cases. The *Enmund* finding could be made by a court, *Walton* maintained, because it entailed no "'element of the crime of capital murder'"; it "only place[d] 'a substantive limitation on sentencing.'" "If the Constitution does not require that the *Enmund* finding be proved as an element of the offense of capital murder, and does not require a jury to make that finding," *Walton* stated, "we cannot conclude that a State is required to denominate aggravating circumstances 'elements' of the offense or permit only a jury to determine the existence of such circumstances."

In dissent in *Walton*, Justice Stevens urged that the Sixth Amendment requires "a jury determination of facts that must be established before the death penalty may be imposed." Aggravators "operate as statutory 'elements' of capital murder under Arizona law," he reasoned, "because in their absence, [the death] sentence is unavailable." "If th[e] question had been posed in 1791, when the Sixth Amendment became law," Justice Stevens said, "the answer would have been clear," for "[b]y that time, "the English jury's role in determining critical facts in homicide cases was entrenched. As fact-finder, the jury had the power to determine not only whether the defendant was guilty of homicide but also the degree of the offense. Moreover, the jury's role in finding facts that would determine a homicide defendant's eligibility for capital punishment was particularly well established. Throughout its history, the jury determined which homicide defendants would be subject to capital punishment by making factual determinations, many of which related to difficult assessments of the defendant's state of mind. By the time the Bill of Rights was adopted, the jury's right to make these determinations was unquestioned." Id., at 710–711 (quoting White, Fact-Finding and the Death Penalty: The Scope of a Capital Defendant's Right to Jury Trial, 65 Notre Dame L.Rev. 1, 10–11 (1989)).

[In] 2000, the Court decided *Apprendi v. New Jersey*, 530 U.S. 466 (2000). The defendant-petitioner in that case was convicted of, inter alia, second-degree possession of a firearm, an offense carrying a maximum penalty of ten years under New Jersey law. On the prosecutor's motion, the sentencing judge found by a preponderance of the evidence that Apprendi's crime had been motivated by racial animus. That finding triggered application of New Jersey's "hate crime enhancement," which doubled Apprendi's

---

fective. See *Apprendi*, (Fourteenth Amendment "has not ... been construed to include the Fifth Amendment right to 'presentment or indictment of a Grand Jury'").

maximum authorized sentence. The judge sentenced Apprendi to 12 years in prison, 2 years over the maximum that would have applied but for the enhancement.

We held that Apprendi's sentence violated his right to "a jury determination that [he] is guilty of every element of the crime with which he is charged, beyond a reasonable doubt." That right attached not only to Apprendi's weapons offense but also to the "hate crime" aggravating circumstance. New Jersey, the Court observed, "threatened Apprendi with certain pains if he unlawfully possessed a weapon and with additional pains if he selected his victims with a purpose to intimidate them because of their race." "Merely using the label 'sentence enhancement' to describe the [second act] surely does not provide a principled basis for treating [the two acts] differently."

The dispositive question, we said, "is one not of form, but of effect." If a State makes an increase in a defendant's authorized punishment contingent on the finding of a fact, that fact—no matter how the State labels it—must be found by a jury beyond a reasonable doubt. A defendant may not be "expose[d] … to a penalty exceeding the maximum he would receive if punished according to the facts reflected in the jury verdict alone."

Walton could be reconciled with *Apprendi*, the Court finally asserted. The key distinction, according to the *Apprendi* Court, was that a conviction of first-degree murder in Arizona carried a maximum sentence of death. "[O]nce a jury has found the defendant guilty of all the elements of an offense which carries as its maximum penalty the sentence of death, it may be left to the judge to decide whether that maximum penalty, rather than a lesser one, ought to be imposed."

In an effort to reconcile its capital sentencing system with the Sixth Amendment as interpreted by *Apprendi*, Arizona first restates the *Apprendi* majority's portrayal of Arizona's system: Ring was convicted of first-degree murder, for which Arizona law specifies "death or life imprisonment" as the only sentencing options; Ring was therefore sentenced within the range of punishment authorized by the jury verdict. This argument overlooks *Apprendi*'s instruction that "the relevant inquiry is one not of form, but of effect." In effect, "the required finding [of an aggravated circumstance] expose[d] [Ring] to a greater punishment than that authorized by the jury's guilty verdict." The Arizona first-degree murder statute "authorizes a maximum penalty of death only in a formal sense," for it explicitly cross-references the statutory provision requiring the finding of an aggravating circumstance before imposition of the death penalty.

Arizona also supports the distinction relied upon in Walton between elements of an offense and sentencing factors. As to elevation of the maximum punishment, however, *Apprendi* renders the argument untenable; *Apprendi* repeatedly instructs in that context that the characterization of a fact or circumstance as an "element" or a "sentencing factor" is not determinative of the question "who decides," judge or jury.

Even if facts increasing punishment beyond the maximum authorized by a guilty verdict standing alone ordinarily must be found by a jury, Arizona further urges, aggravating circumstances necessary to trigger a death sentence may nonetheless be reserved for judicial determination. As Arizona's counsel maintained at oral argument, there is no doubt that "[d]eath is different." States have constructed elaborate sentencing procedures in death cases, Arizona emphasizes, because of constraints we have said the Eighth Amendment places on capital sentencing.

Arizona suggests that judicial authority over the finding of aggravating factors "may … be a better way to guarantee against the arbitrary imposition of the death penalty." The Sixth Amendment jury trial right, however, does not turn on the relative rationality, fairness, or efficiency of potential factfinders. Entrusting to a judge the finding of facts necessary to support a death sentence might be "an admirably fair and efficient scheme of criminal justice designed for a society that is prepared to leave criminal justice to the State.... The founders of the American Republic were not prepared to leave it to the State, which is why the jury-trial guarantee was one of the least controversial provisions of the Bill of Rights. It has never been efficient; but it has always been free." *Apprendi*, 530 U.S., at 498 (Scalia, J., concurring).

In any event, the superiority of judicial factfinding in capital cases is far from evident. Unlike Arizona, the great majority of States responded to this Court's Eighth Amendment decisions requiring the presence of aggravating circumstances in capital cases by entrusting those determinations to the jury.[6]

Although "'the doctrine of stare decisis is of fundamental importance to the rule of law[,]'... [o]ur precedents are not sacrosanct." "[W]e have overruled prior decisions where the necessity and propriety of doing so has been established." We are satisfied that this is such a case.

For the reasons stated, we hold that *Walton* and *Apprendi* are irreconcilable; our Sixth Amendment jurisprudence cannot be home to both. Accordingly, we overrule *Walton* to the extent that it allows a sentencing judge, sitting without a jury, to find an aggravating circumstance necessary for imposition of the death penalty. Because Arizona's enumerated aggravating factors operate as "the functional equivalent of an element of a greater offense," the Sixth Amendment requires that they be found by a jury....

"The guarantees of jury trial in the Federal and State Constitutions reflect a profound judgment about the way in which law should be enforced and justice administered.... If the defendant preferred the common-sense judgment of a jury to the more tutored but perhaps less sympathetic reaction of the single judge, he was to have it." *Duncan v. Louisiana*, 391 U.S. 145, 155–156 (1968).

The right to trial by jury guaranteed by the Sixth Amendment would be senselessly diminished if it encompassed the factfinding necessary to increase a defendant's sentence by two years, but not the factfinding necessary to put him to death. We hold that the Sixth Amendment applies to both. The judgment of the Arizona Supreme Court is therefore reversed, and the case is remanded for further proceedings not inconsistent with this opinion.

Justice SCALIA, with whom Justice Thomas joins, concurring.

The question whether *Walton v. Arizona*, 497 U.S. 639 (1990), survives our decision in *Apprendi v. New Jersey*, 530 U.S. 466 (2000), confronts me with a difficult choice. What compelled Arizona (and many other States) to specify particular "aggravating factors" that must be found before the death penalty can be imposed, was the line of this Court's cases beginning with *Furman v. Georgia*, 408 U.S. 238 (1972) (per curiam). In my view, that line of decisions had no proper foundation in the Constitution. I am therefore reluctant to magnify the burdens that our *Furman* jurisprudence imposes on the States. Better for the Court to have invented an evidentiary requirement that a judge can find by a preponderance of the evidence, than to invent one that a unanimous jury must find beyond a reasonable doubt.

---

6. Of the 38 States with capital punishment, 29 generally commit sentencing decisions to juries. Other than Arizona, only four States commit both capital sentencing fact-finding and the ultimate sentencing decision entirely to judges. Four States have hybrid systems, in which the jury renders an advisory verdict but the judge makes the ultimate sentencing determinations.

On the other hand, as I wrote in my dissent in *Almendarez-Torres v. United States*, 523 U.S. 224, 248 (1998), and as I reaffirmed by joining the opinion for the Court in *Apprendi*, I believe that the fundamental meaning of the jury-trial guarantee of the Sixth Amendment is that all facts essential to imposition of the level of punishment that the defendant receives—whether the statute calls them elements of the offense, sentencing factors, or Mary Jane—must be found by the jury beyond a reasonable doubt.

The quandary is apparent: Should I continue to apply the last-stated principle when I know that the only reason the fact is essential is that this Court has mistakenly said that the Constitution requires state law to impose such "aggravating factors"? In *Walton*, to tell the truth, the Sixth Amendment claim was not put with the clarity it obtained in *Almendarez-Torres* and *Apprendi*. There what the appellant argued had to be found by the jury was not all facts essential to imposition of the death penalty, but rather "every finding of fact underlying the sentencing decision," including not only the aggravating factors without which the penalty could not be imposed, but also the mitigating factors that might induce a sentencer to give a lesser punishment. But even if the point had been put with greater clarity in *Walton*, I think I still would have approved the Arizona scheme—I would have favored the States' freedom to develop their own capital sentencing procedures (already erroneously abridged by *Furman*) over the logic of the *Apprendi* principle.

Since *Walton*, I have acquired new wisdom that consists of two realizations—or, to put it more critically, have discarded old ignorance that consisted of the failure to realize two things: First, that it is impossible to identify with certainty those aggravating factors whose adoption has been wrongfully coerced by *Furman*, as opposed to those that the State would have adopted in any event. Some States, for example, already had aggravating-factor requirements for capital murder ... when *Furman* was decided. When such a State has added aggravating factors, are the new ones the *Apprendi*-exempt product of *Furman*, and the old ones not? And even as to those States that did not previously have aggravating-factor requirements, who is to say that their adoption of a new one today—or, for that matter, even their retention of old ones adopted immediately post-*Furman*—is still the product of that case, and not of a changed social belief that murder simpliciter does not deserve death?

Second, and more important, my observing over the past 12 years the accelerating propensity of both state and federal legislatures to adopt "sentencing factors" determined by judges that increase punishment beyond what is authorized by the jury's verdict, and my witnessing the belief of a near majority of my colleagues that this novel practice is perfectly OK, cause me to believe that our people's traditional belief in the right of trial by jury is in perilous decline. That decline is bound to be confirmed, and indeed accelerated, by the repeated spectacle of a man's going to his death because a judge found that an aggravating factor existed. We cannot preserve our veneration for the protection of the jury in criminal cases if we render ourselves callous to the need for that protection by regularly imposing the death penalty without it.

Accordingly, whether or not the States have been erroneously coerced into the adoption of "aggravating factors," wherever those factors exist they must be subject to the usual requirements of the common law, and to the requirement enshrined in our Constitution, in criminal cases: they must be found by the jury beyond a reasonable doubt....

Justice BREYER, concurring in the judgment.

I

Given my views in *Apprendi v. New Jersey*, 530 U.S. 466, 555 (2000) (dissenting opinion), and *Harris v. United States*, 122 S.Ct. 2406 (Breyer, J., concurring in part and concurring in judgment), I cannot join the Court's opinion. I concur in the judgment, however, because I believe that jury sentencing in capital cases is mandated by the Eighth Amendment.

II

This Court has held that the Eighth Amendment requires States to apply special procedural safeguards when they seek the death penalty. Otherwise, the constitutional prohibition against "cruel and unusual punishments" would forbid its use. Justice Stevens has written that those safeguards include a requirement that a jury impose any sentence of death. *Harris v. Alabama*, 513 U.S. 504, 515–526 (1995) (dissenting opinion); *Spaziano v. Florida*, 468 U.S. 447, 467–490 (1984) (Stevens, J., joined by Brennan and Marshall, JJ., concurring in part and dissenting in part). Although I joined the majority in *Harris v. Alabama*, I have come to agree with the dissenting view, and with the related views of others upon which it in part relies. I therefore conclude that the Eighth Amendment requires that a jury, not a judge, make the decision to sentence a defendant to death.

I am convinced by the reasons that Justice Stevens has given. These include (1) his belief that retribution provides the main justification for capital punishment, and (2) his assessment of the jury's comparative advantage in determining, in a particular case, whether capital punishment will serve that end.

As to the first, I note the continued difficulty of justifying capital punishment in terms of its ability to deter crime, to incapacitate offenders, or to rehabilitate criminals. Studies of deterrence are, at most, inconclusive. See, e.g., Sorenson, Wrinkle, Brewer, & Marquart, Capital Punishment and Deterrence: Examining the Effect of Executions on Murder in Texas, 45 Crime & Delinquency 481 (1999) (no evidence of a deterrent effect); Bonner & Fessenden, Absence of Executions: A Special Report, States With No Death Penalty Share Lower Homicide Rates, N.Y. Times, Sept. 22, 2000, p. A1 (during last 20 years, homicide rate in death penalty States has been 48% to 101% higher than in non-death-penalty States); see also Radelet & Akers, Deterrence and the Death Penalty: The Views of the Experts, 87 J.Crim. L. & C. 1, 8 (1996) (over 80% of criminologists believe existing research fails to support deterrence justification).

As to incapacitation, few offenders sentenced to life without parole (as an alternative to death) commit further crimes. See, e.g., Sorensen & Pilgrim, An Actuarial Risk Assessment of Violence Posed by Capital Murder Defendants, 90 J.Crim. L. & C. 1251, 1256 (2000) (studies find average repeat murder rate of .002% among murderers whose death sentences were commuted); Marquart & Sorensen, A National Study of the *Furman*-Commuted Inmates: Assessing the Threat to Society from Capital Offenders, 23 Loyola (LA) L.Rev. 5, 26 (1989) (98% did not kill again either in prison or in free society). And rehabilitation, obviously, is beside the point.

In respect to retribution, jurors possess an important comparative advantage over judges. In principle, they are more attuned to "the community's moral sensibility," because they "reflect more accurately the composition and experiences of the community as a whole." Hence they are more likely to "express the conscience of the community on the ultimate question of life or death," and better able to determine in the particular case the need for retribution, namely, "an expression of the community's belief that certain crimes are themselves so grievous an affront to humanity that the only adequate response may be the penalty of death."

Justice O'CONNOR, with whom the Chief Justice joins, dissenting.

I understand why the Court holds that the reasoning of *Apprendi v. New Jersey*, 530 U.S. 466 (2000), is irreconcilable with *Walton v. Arizona*, 497 U.S. 639, 110 S.Ct. 3047, 111 L.Ed.2d 511 (1990). Yet in choosing which to overrule, I would choose *Apprendi*, not *Walton*.

I continue to believe, for the reasons I articulated in my dissent in *Apprendi*, that the decision in *Apprendi* was a serious mistake. As I argued in that dissent, *Apprendi*'s rule that any fact that increases the maximum penalty must be treated as an element of the crime is not required by the Constitution, by history, or by our prior cases. Indeed, the rule directly contradicts several of our prior cases. And it ignores the "significant history in this country of … discretionary sentencing by judges." The Court has failed, both in *Apprendi* and in the decision announced today, to "offer any meaningful justification for deviating from years of cases both suggesting and holding that application of the 'increase in the maximum penalty' rule is not required by the Constitution."

Not only was the decision in *Apprendi* unjustified in my view, but it has also had a severely destabilizing effect on our criminal justice system. I predicted in my dissent that the decision would "unleash a flood of petitions by convicted defendants seeking to invalidate their sentences in whole or in part on the authority of [*Apprendi*]." As of May 31, 2002, less than two years after *Apprendi* was announced, the United States Courts of Appeals had decided approximately 1,802 criminal appeals in which defendants challenged their sentences, and in some cases even their convictions, under *Apprendi*. These federal appeals are likely only the tip of the iceberg, as federal criminal prosecutions represent a tiny fraction of the total number of criminal prosecutions nationwide. The number of second or successive habeas corpus petitions filed in the federal courts also increased by 77% in 2001, a phenomenon the Administrative Office of the United States Courts attributes to prisoners bringing *Apprendi* claims. It is simply beyond dispute that *Apprendi* threw countless criminal sentences into doubt and thereby caused an enormous increase in the workload of an already overburdened judiciary.

The decision today is only going to add to these already serious effects. The Court effectively declares five States' capital sentencing schemes unconstitutional. There are 168 prisoners on death row in these States, each of whom is now likely to challenge his or her death sentence. I believe many of these challenges will ultimately be unsuccessful, either because the prisoners will be unable to satisfy the standards of harmless error or plain error review, or because, having completed their direct appeals, they will be barred from taking advantage of today's holding on federal collateral review. Nonetheless, the need to evaluate these claims will greatly burden the courts in these five States. In addition, I fear that the prisoners on death row in Alabama, Delaware, Florida, and Indiana, which the Court identifies as having hybrid sentencing schemes in which the jury renders an advisory verdict but the judge makes the ultimate sentencing determination, may also seize on today's decision to challenge their sentences. There are 529 prisoners on death row in these States.

By expanding on *Apprendi*, the Court today exacerbates the harm done in that case. Consistent with my dissent, I would overrule *Apprendi* rather than *Walton*.

Note on the Aftermath of Ring

In the aftermath of the *Ring* decision, four states that had used judge sentencing in capital cases enacted laws authorizing jury sentencing. As a result, only five states—Alabama, Delaware, Florida, Montana and Nebraska—still require some type of judge sentencing.

Note on Retroactivity of Ring

In *Schriro v. Summerlin*, 542 U.S. 348 (2004), the Supreme Court refused to apply *Ring* retroactively to death row inmates whose conviction and sentences were final at the time the Court decided *Ring*. As a result of *Schriro*, more than 100 death row inmates who were improperly sentenced to death by a judge, but whose convictions and sentences were final when the Court decided *Ring* in 2002, will not be entitled to new sentencing proceedings. A conviction and sentence are considered final after a defendant has completed his direct appeal.

Chapter 10

Use of Psychiatric Experts in Capital Cases

A. Introduction

The appropriate role of psychiatric experts in criminal trials has generated significant debate. Before trial, these experts may be called upon to examine a defendant to determine competency to stand trial and to waive certain constitutional rights. During trial, experts may be called upon to testify as to the defendant's capacity to possess the requisite mens rea and proclivity to commit violent acts in the future. Following trial, expert testimony may be useful in deciding whether the defendant is competent to waive further appeals. Finally, psychiatric assistance may be required to determine whether a death-sentenced inmate is competent to be executed.

B. Predicting Future Dangerousness

Jurors in several states, including Oklahoma, Texas, Oregon and Idaho, are asked to predict whether a defendant is likely to commit criminal acts of violence in the future. Oklahoma uses future dangerousness by defining as an aggravating circumstance (rendering the defendant death-eligible) "[t]he existence of a probability that the defendant would commit criminal acts of violence that would constitute a continuing threat to society." 21 Okla. Stat. §701.12 (7).

In Texas, which leads the nation in executions, and Oregon, future dangerousness predictions play a critical role in determining whether a convicted murderer is sentenced to death. Before imposing a death penalty in either of those two states, a jury must find—unanimously and beyond a reasonable doubt—that there is "a probability that the defendant would commit criminal acts of violence that would constitute a continuing threat to society."

Idaho's capital punishment statute takes a somewhat more restrictive view of future dangerousness. It lists as an aggravating circumstance a finding that the defendant has "a propensity to commit murder which will probably constitute a continuing threat to society." I.C. §19-2515(g)(8).

The issue of future dangerousness is particularly controversial because it requires the jury to make a life-or-death decision based upon a prediction of the future. Jurors are allowed to punish the defendant with the ultimate sanction of death, not only for the crime she has committed, but for crimes she *might* commit later. According to Univer-

603

sity of Houston law professor David Dow, who considers future dangerousness predictions to be "quackery," "[Y]ou're being sentenced to death not only for something that you haven't done, but for something that the evidence suggests you will never do." Hanson, *A Dangerous Assessment*, ABA Journal Oct. 2004, p. 26.

Although all prediction is difficult, some scholars argue that jury predictions of future dangerousness are particularly suspect. See Marquart, Ekland-Olson & Sorenson, "Gazing Into the Crystal Ball: Can Jurors Accurately Predict Dangerousness in Capital Cases?," 23 L. & Soc. Rev. 449 (1989). Significant disagreement centers around whether the accuracy of jury predictions of future dangerousness is enhanced by permitting juries to rely on expert opinions.

Barefoot v. Estelle
463 U.S. 880 (1983)

Justice WHITE delivered the opinion of the Court.

I

... On November 14, 1978, petitioner was convicted of the capital murder of a police officer in Bell County, Texas. A separate sentencing hearing before the same jury was then held to determine whether the death penalty should be imposed. Under Tex. Code Crim. Proc. Ann. §37.071, two special questions were to be submitted to the jury: whether the conduct causing death was "committed deliberately and with reasonable expectation that the death of the deceased or another would result"; and whether "there is a probability that the defendant would commit criminal acts of violence that would constitute a continuing threat to society." The State introduced into evidence petitioner's prior convictions and his reputation for lawlessness. The State also called two psychiatrists, John Holbrook and James Grigson, who, in response to hypothetical questions, testified that petitioner would probably commit further acts of violence and represent a continuing threat to society. The jury answered both of the questions put to them in the affirmative, a result which required the imposition of the death penalty....

III

Petitioner's ... submission is that his death sentence must be set aside because the Constitution of the United States barred the testimony of the two psychiatrists who testified against him at the punishment hearing. There are several aspects to this claim. First, it is urged that psychiatrists, individually and as a group, are incompetent to predict with an acceptable degree of reliability that a particular criminal will commit other crimes in the future and so represent a danger to the community. Second, it is said that in any event, psychiatrists should not be permitted to testify about future dangerousness in response to hypothetical questions and without having examined the defendant personally. Third, it is argued that in the particular circumstances of this case, the testimony of the psychiatrists was so unreliable that the sentence should be set aside. As indicated below, we reject each of these arguments.

A

The suggestion that no psychiatrist's testimony may be presented with respect to a defendant's future dangerousness is somewhat like asking us to disinvent the wheel. In the first place, it is contrary to our cases. If the likelihood of a defendant committing further crimes is a constitutionally acceptable criterion for imposing the death penalty, which it is, and if it is not impossible for even a lay person sensibly to arrive at that conclusion, it makes little sense, if any, to submit that psychiatrists, out of the entire universe of persons who might have an opinion on the issue, would know so little about the subject that they should not be permitted to testify....

In the second place, the rules of evidence generally extant at the federal and state levels anticipate that relevant, unprivileged evidence should be admitted and its weight left to the fact finder, who would have the benefit of cross examination and contrary evidence by the opposing party. Psychiatric testimony predicting dangerousness may be countered not only as erroneous in a particular case but as generally so unreliable that it should be ignored. If the jury may make up its mind about future dangerousness unaided by psychiatric testimony, jurors should not be barred from hearing the views of the State's psychiatrists along with opposing views of the defendant's doctors.

Third, petitioner's view mirrors the position expressed in the *amicus* brief of the American Psychiatric Association (APA).... [H]owever, the same view was presented and rejected in *Estelle v. Smith*, 451 U.S. 454 (1981). We are no more convinced now that the view of the APA should be converted into a constitutional rule barring an entire category of expert testimony. We are not persuaded that such testimony is almost entirely unreliable and that the factfinder and the adversary system will not be competent to uncover, recognize, and take due account of its shortcomings.

The [APA as] *amicus* does not suggest that there are not other views held by members of the Association or of the profession generally. Indeed, as this case and others indicate, there are those doctors who are quite willing to testify at the sentencing hearing, who think, and will say, that they know what they are talking about, and who expressly disagree with the Association's point of view. Furthermore, their qualifications as experts are regularly accepted by the courts. If they are so obviously wrong and should be discredited, there should be no insuperable problem in doing so by calling members of the Association who are of that view and who confidently assert that opinion in their *amicus* brief. Neither petitioner nor the Association suggests that psychiatrists are always wrong with respect to future dangerousness, only most of the time. Yet the submission is that this category of testimony should be excised entirely from all trials. We are unconvinced, however, at least as of now, that the adversary process cannot be trusted to sort out the reliable from the unreliable evidence and opinion about future dangerousness, particularly when the convicted felon has the opportunity to present his own side of the case.

We are unaware of and have been cited to no case, federal or state, that has adopted the categorical views of the Association. Certainly it was presented and rejected at every stage of the present proceeding. After listening to the two schools of thought testify not only generally but also about the petitioner and his criminal record, the District Court found:

> The majority of psychiatric experts agree that where there is a pattern of repetitive assault and violent conduct, the accuracy of psychiatric predictions of future dangerousness dramatically rises. The accuracy of this conclusion is reaffirmed by the expert medical testimony in the case at the evidentiary hearing.... It would appear that petitioner's complaint is not the diagnosis and prediction made by Drs. Holbrook and Grigson at the punishment phase of his trial, but that Dr. Grigson expressed extreme certainty in his diagnosis and prediction.... In any event, the differences among the experts were quantitative,

not qualitative. The differences in opinion go to the weight of the evidence and not the admissibility of such testimony.... Such disputes are within the province of the jury to resolve. Indeed, it is a fundamental premise of our entire system of criminal jurisprudence that the purpose of the jury is to sort out the true testimony from the false, the important matters from the unimportant matters, and, when called upon to do so, to give greater credence to one party's expert witnesses than another's. Such matters occur routinely in the American judicial system, both civil and criminal.

We agree with the District Court, as well as with the Court of Appeals' judges who dealt with the merits of the issue and agreed with the District Court in this respect.

B

Whatever the decision may be about the use of psychiatric testimony, in general, on the issue of future dangerousness, petitioner urges that such testimony must be based on personal examination of the defendant and may not be given in response to hypothetical questions. We disagree. Expert testimony, whether in the form of an opinion based on hypothetical questions or otherwise, is commonly admitted as evidence where it might help the factfinder do its assigned job....

Today, in the federal system, Federal Rules of Evidence 702–706 provide for the testimony of experts. The advisory committee notes touch on the particular objections to hypothetical questions, but none of these caveats lends any support to petitioner's constitutional arguments. Furthermore, the Texas Court of Criminal Appeals could find no fault with the mode of examining the two psychiatrists under Texas law:

> The trial court did not err by permitting the doctors to testify on the basis of the hypothetical question. The use of hypothetical questions is a well-established practice. That the experts had not examined appellant went to the weight of their testimony, not to its admissibility.

Like the Court of Criminal Appeals, the District Court, and the Court of Appeals, we reject petitioner's constitutional arguments against the use of hypothetical questions. Although cases such as this involve the death penalty, we perceive no constitutional barrier to applying the ordinary rules of evidence governing the use of expert testimony.

C

As we understand petitioner, he contends that even if the use of hypothetical questions in predicting future dangerousness is acceptable as a general rule, the use made of them in his case violated his right to due process of law. For example, petitioner insists that the doctors should not have been permitted to give an opinion on the ultimate issue before the jury, particularly when the hypothetical questions were phrased in terms of petitioner's own conduct; that the hypothetical questions referred to controverted facts; and that the answers to the questions were so positive as to be assertions of fact and not opinion. These claims of misuse of the hypothetical questions, as well as others, were rejected by the Texas courts, and neither the District Court nor the Court of Appeals found any constitutional infirmity in the application of the Texas Rules of Evidence in this particular case. We agree.

IV

In sum, we affirm the judgment of the District Court. There is no doubt that the psychiatric testimony increased the likelihood that petitioner would be sentenced to death, but this fact does not make that evidence inadmissible, any more than it would with respect to other relevant evidence against any defendant in a criminal case. At bottom, to agree with petitioner's basic position would seriously undermine and in effect overrule *Jurek v. Texas*. Petitioner conceded as much at oral argument. We are not inclined, however, to overturn the decision in that case.

Justice BLACKMUN, with whom Justice Brennan and Justice Marshall join [except as to the last paragraph], dissenting.

II

A

The American Psychiatric Association (APA), participating in this case as *amicus curiae*, informs us that "[t]he unreliability of psychiatric predictions of long-term future dangerousness is by now an established fact within the profession." The APA's best estimate is that two out of three predictions of long-term future violence made by psychiatrists are wrong. The Court does not dispute this proposition, and indeed it could not do so; the evidence is overwhelming. For example, the APA's Draft Report of the Task Force on the Role of Psychiatry in the Sentencing Process (Draft Report) states that "[c]onsiderable evidence has been accumulated by now to demonstrate that long-term prediction by psychiatrists of future violence is an extremely inaccurate process." John Monahan, recognized as "the leading thinker on this issue" even by the State's expert witness at Barefoot's federal habeas corpus hearing, concludes that "the 'best' clinical research currently in existence indicates that psychiatrists and psychologists are accurate in no more than one out of three predictions of violent behavior," even among populations of individuals who are mentally ill and have committed violence in the past. Another study has found it impossible to identify any subclass of offenders "whose members have a greater-than-even chance of engaging again in an assaultive act." Yet another commentator observes that "[i]n general, mental health professionals ... are more likely to be wrong than right when they predict legally relevant behavior. When predicting violence, dangerousness, and suicide, they are far more likely to be wrong than right." Neither the Court nor the State of Texas has cited a single reputable scientific source contradicting the unanimous conclusion of professionals in this field that psychiatric predictions of long-term future violence are wrong more often than they are right.

The APA also concludes, as do researchers that have studied the issue, that psychiatrists simply have no expertise in predicting long-term future dangerousness. A layman with access to relevant statistics can do at least as well and possibly better; psychiatric training is not relevant to the factors that validly can be employed to make such predictions, and psychiatrists consistently err on the side of overpredicting violence. Thus, while Doctors Grigson and Holbrook were presented by the State and by self-proclamation as experts at predicting future dangerousness, the scientific literature makes crystal clear that they had no expertise whatever. Despite their claims that they were able to predict Barefoot's future behavior "within reasonable psychiatric certainty," or to a "one hundred percent and absolute" certainty, there was in fact no more than a one in three chance that they were correct.

B

It is impossible to square admission of this purportedly scientific but actually baseless testimony with the Constitution's paramount concern for reliability in capital sentencing. Death is a permissible punishment in Texas only if the jury finds beyond a reasonable doubt that there is a probability the defendant will commit future acts of criminal violence. The admission of unreliable psychiatric predictions of future violence, offered with unabashed claims of "reasonable medical certainty" or "absolute" professional reliability, creates an intolerable danger that death sentences will be imposed erroneously....

IV

... Our constitutional duty is to ensure that the State proves future dangerousness, if at all, in a reliable manner, one that ensures that "any decision to impose the death sentence be, and appear to be, based on reason rather than caprice or emotion." Texas' choice of substantive factors does not justify loading the factfinding process against the defendant through the presentation of what is, at bottom, false testimony.

V

I would vacate petitioner's death sentence, and remand for further proceedings consistent with these views.

Notes and Questions

1. Doctor James Grigson, the forensic psychiatrist who examined Thomas Barefoot, has testified in numerous capital murder prosecutions throughout Texas, helping place more than 120 inmates on death row. Grigson's effectiveness, which earned him the sobriquet "Doctor Death," was called into question when Randall Dale Adams was released from prison after serving 12 years for a murder which most persons now believe he did not commit. Dr. Grigson examined Mr. Adams briefly prior to Adams' capital trial for the murder of a Dallas police officer. Struck by Adams' lack of remorse for the crime which Adams denied committing, Dr. Grigson testified that Adams was the type of person who could "work all day and creep at night." After Grigson testified that Adams most certainly would kill again, the jury sentenced Adams to death.

Adams was released from prison after New York filmmaker Errol Morris, who originally planned to make a movie about Dr. Grigson, stumbled onto the facts of Adams' case. Eventually Morris succeeded in getting Adams' chief accuser — on death row for another murder — to admit that he, not Adams, fired the fatal bullets at the police officer. Morris' film, *The Thin Blue Line*, may have been instrumental in helping securing Adams' release from a wrongful conviction, but it did not shake Grigson's belief in his powers of prediction. In 1990, while testifying in the capital murder trial of Gayland Bradford, Grigson reiterated his belief that Adams killed the Dallas police officer and his certainty that Adams "will kill again." See *Travels With Dr. Death*, by Ron Rosenbaum, Vanity Fair (May 1990).

2. In a brief submitted to the Supreme Court in *Barefoot v. Estelle*, the American Psychiatric Association launched a blistering attack on Dr. Grigson's methods:

Psychiatrists should not be permitted to offer a prediction concerning the long-term future dangerousness of a defendant in a capital case, at least ... where the psychiatrist purports to testify *as a medical expert* possessing predictive expertise.... The large body of research in this area indicates that, even under the best of conditions, *psychiatric predictions of long-term future dangerousness are wrong in at least two out of every three cases.* The forecast of future violent conduct ... is, at bottom, a lay determination ... made on the basis of essential actuarial data to which *psychiatrists can bring no special interpretive skills*.... The use of psychiatric testimony on this issue causes serious prejudice to the defendant. By dressing up the actuarial data with an "expert" opinion, the psychiatrist's testimony is likely to receive undue weight. [It] provides a false aura of certainty [which] impermissibly distorts the fact-finding process in capital cases.

(Emphasis added.)

3. Basing an expert opinion on a hypothetical carefully crafted by the prosecutor to reflect the particular characteristics of the defendant and his crime allows an expert to diagnose a defendant without having examined him. The colloquy between district attorney and expert witness might proceed as follows.

> D.A.   Doctor, based upon that hypothetical, those facts that I have explained to you, do you have an opinion within reasonable medical probability as to whether the defendant will commit criminal acts of violence that will constitute a continuing threat to society?
>
> Expert Yes, sir, I most certainly do have an opinion with regard to that.
>
> D.A.   What is your opinion, please, sir?
>
> Expert That absolutely there is no question, no doubt whatsoever, that the individual you described, that has been involved in repeated escalating behavior of violence, will commit acts of violence in the future and will represent a very serious threat to any society in which he finds himself.
>
> D.A.   Do you mean that he will be a threat in any society, even the prison society?
>
> Expert Absolutely, yes, sir. He will do the same thing there that he will do outside.

Dr. Grigson's practice of diagnosing a defendant as a severe sociopath on the basis of a prosecutor's hypothetical question, without examining the defendant—and then telling the jury that the diagnosis of sociopath is the scientific basis for guaranteeing future dangerousness—also drew criticism from the American Psychiatric Association:

> Such a diagnosis simply cannot be made on the basis of a hypothetical question.... The psychiatrist cannot exclude alternative diagnoses [such as] illnesses that plainly do not indicate a general propensity to commit criminal acts.... These deficiencies strip the psychiatric testimony of all value in the present context.

The Dallas Morning News reported that Dr. Grigson had been expelled from the American Psychiatric Association (APA) and the Texas Society of Psychiatric Physicians for alleged ethics violations. According to a statement released by the APA, Dr. Grigson violated the APA's ethics code by:

> arriving at a psychiatric diagnosis without first having examined the individuals in question, and for indicating, while testifying in court as an expert witness, that he could predict with 100 percent certainty that the individuals would engage in future violent acts.

Dr. Grigson said that his license would not be jeopardized by the charges. Laura Beil, *Groups Expel Psychiatrist Known for Murder Cases*, The Dallas Morning News (July 26, 1995).

4. A 2004 study of the Texas Defender Service examined 155 cases in which prosecutors used expert witnesses to predict a defendant's future dangerousness. The study concluded that the experts were wrong 95 percent of the time.

"Of the 155 inmates against whom state experts testified, eight—5 percent—had engaged in serious assaultive behavior, defined by the study as an injury requiring more than the administration of first aid. In addition 31 inmates—20 percent—had no disciplinary record. The remaining 116 inmates—75 percent—had committed disciplinary infractions involving conduct not amounting to seriously assaultive behavior, such as having food in their cells, refusing to shave or yelling obscenities in the hallway.

None of the inmates had killed again, the study showed. Only two had been prosecuted for crimes committed while in prison." Hansen, *A Dangerous Assessment: In Capital Cases Some Predictions of Violence Don't Come True, Study Shows*, ABA Journal Oct. 2004, p. 26.

5. After *Furman v. Georgia*, 408 U.S. 238 (1972) (*supra* chapter 3), emptied death rows throughout the country, the formerly condemned prisoners were sentenced to life terms that, in some states, meant between 10 and 30 years. Many feared the release of *Furman*-commuted inmates into the general population. Prison guards, prison administrators and psychiatrists believed that these 611 inmates posed a special security risk and predicted that they would commit serious acts of violence. A team of researchers examined the institutional disciplinary behavior of the commuted inmates from 1972 to 1987. Their data indicated that

> over a fifteen-year period, slightly less than one-third of the former death row inmates committed serious prison rule violations. Over one-half (84 or 51.9%) of those inmates committing serious rule violations were involved in only one rule violation, and another quarter (38 or 23.5%) were involved in only two rule violations. These data demonstrate, at least among these violators, that most serious infractions were one-time events or situations. In short, most of the *Furman* inmates were not violent menaces to the institutional order. As a group, they were not a disproportionate threat to guards and other inmates.

During this same 15-year period, the *Furman* commutees committed six homicides while in prison (four prisoners and two guards). Marquart & Sorenson, "A National Study of the *Furman*-Commuted Inmates: Assessing the Threat to Society From Capital Offenders," 23 Loy. L.A. L. Rev. 5, 19, 20, 21 (1989).

Perhaps of greater concern after *Furman* was the prospect of condemned murderers being released into society after earning parole. In 1989, Marquart and Sorenson reported that of the 558 *Furman*-commuted inmates they studied, 243 (44%) were released to society. "Of these, 191 (78.6%) have not been returned to prison: 147 are on their original parole, 19 discharged their sentences, 17 successfully completed their parole, 6 died in the community, and 2 were pardoned." Fifty-two (21%) of those paroled returned to prison for technical violations or new offenses. Although twenty-one percent recidivated and were reincarcerated, only twelve percent committed new felonies.

Marquart and Sorenson concluded that the *Furman*-commuted capital murderers who were paroled did not represent a disproportionate threat to society. Their data revealed that after five years on parole, only one murderer committed a second murder. All told, then, seven (1.3%) *Furman*-commuted prisoners were responsible for seven additional murders.

Executing all 558 inmates on death row in 1972 certainly would have prevented the seven killings. However, among the group of 558, Marquart and Sorenson identify four innocent prisoners. Does the question then become—as Marquart and Sorenson suggest—"whether saving the lives of seven victims was worth the execution of four innocent inmates"? If so, how would you answer it? Recall van den Haag's article excerpted in chapter 1. How would he react to these statistics?

More recent information about the *Furman* commutees surfaced in 2002. By then, 310—more than half of those who were on death rows in 1972—completed their sentences or earned parole. Three of these former death row inmates killed again, once they were out of prison. About 90 parolees returned to prison briefly for parole violations, but most were paroled again. Only 4 percent were convicted of aggravated felonies. Six were ultimately found to be innocent of the crimes for which they had been sentenced to death. Cheever, *A Chance Reprieve, and Another Chance at Life*, New York Times, June 29, 2002.

6. Expert testimony assessing the likelihood of future dangerousness was ruled constitutional by the U.S. Supreme Court in 1983, over the strong objections of the American Psychiatric Association. *Barefoot v. Estelle*. However, the Court has yet to reconsider its holding in *Barefoot* in light of its 1993 decision in *Daubert v. Merrell Dow Pharmaceuticals*, 509 U.S. 579. In *Daubert*, the high Court held that trial judges must act as "gatekeepers" and assess the reliability of scientific evidence before it is presented to a jury. Should expert predictions of future dangerousness survive application of the *Daubert* standards? Consider the opinion of Judge Emilio Garza of the U.S. Court of Appeals for the Fifth Circuit: "Overall, the theory that scientific reliability underlies predictions of future dangerousness has been uniformly rejected by the scientific community absent those individuals who routinely testify to, and profit from, predictions of dangerousness." *Flores v. Johnson*, 210 F.3d 456 (5th Cir. 2000) (Garza, J., concurring).

C. Fifth and Sixth Amendment Issues

Confessions frequently play a key role in capital prosecutions. For many jurors, evidence of incriminating statements allegedly made by the defendant can eradicate reasonable doubt. In some cases, a confession may be the best evidence of a person's guilt. And in many cases confessions relieve jurors of the fear that they might be convicting an innocent person.

Two separate constitutional provisions are implicated by the use of confessions. First, the Fifth Amendment guarantee that "[n]o person ... shall be compelled in any criminal case to be a witness against himself" creates a privilege against *compelled* self-incrimination. Simply put, statements secured by the police in a coercive manner may not be used against a defendant whose Fifth Amendment rights have attached.

Second, the Sixth Amendment guarantees that "[i]n all criminal prosecutions, the accused shall enjoy the right to ... the Assistance of Counsel for his defence." The Sixth Amendment may be violated when the government deliberately elicits statements from a suspect without either the presence of his counsel or a waiver of the right to have counsel present.

The testimony of psychiatric experts may assist in resolving issues presented by both the Fifth and Sixth Amendments. Under the Fifth Amendment a confession's admissibility will often turn on whether the incriminating remarks were made voluntarily as "the product of [the defendant's] free choice." *Miranda v. Arizona*, 384 U.S. 436 (1966). Expert testimony, therefore, may illuminate whether the defendant had the capacity to volunteer incriminating statements. Similarly, the Sixth Amendment analysis focuses on the defendant's capacity to waive his right to have counsel present during questioning.

As the next case demonstrates, issues of fundamental fairness are raised when a psychiatrist, appointed by the court to determine a defendant's competency to stand trial, testifies as to the substance of the defendant's disclosures made during the pretrial psychiatric exam.

Estelle v. Smith
451 U.S. 454 (1981)

Chief Justice BURGER delivered the opinion of the Court.

We granted certiorari to consider whether the prosecution's use of psychiatric testimony at the sentencing phase of respondent's capital murder trial to establish his future dangerousness violated his constitutional rights.

I

A

On December 28, 1973, respondent Ernest Benjamin Smith was indicted for murder arising from his participation in the armed robbery of a grocery store during which a clerk was fatally shot, not by Smith, but by his accomplice. In accordance with [Texas law] concerning the punishment for murder with malice aforethought, the State of Texas announced its intention to seek the death penalty. Thereafter, a judge of the 195th Judicial District Court of Dallas County, Texas, informally ordered the State's attorney to arrange a psychiatric examination of Smith by Dr. James P. Grigson to determine Smith's competency to stand trial.[1]

Dr. Grigson, who interviewed Smith in jail for approximately 90 minutes, concluded that he was competent to stand trial. In a letter to the trial judge, Dr. Grigson reported his findings: "[I]t is my opinion that Ernest Benjamin Smith, Jr., is aware of the difference between right and wrong and is able to aid an attorney in his defense." This letter was filed with the court's papers in the case. Smith was then tried by a jury and convicted of murder....

At the commencement of Smith's sentencing hearing, the State rested "[s]ubject to the right to reopen." Defense counsel called three lay witnesses: Smith's stepmother, his aunt, and the man who owned the gun Smith carried during the robbery. Smith's relatives testified as to his good reputation and character. The owner of the pistol testified as to Smith's knowledge that it would not fire because of a mechanical defect. The State then called Dr. Grigson as a witness....

After detailing his professional qualifications by way of foundation, Dr. Grigson testified before the jury on direct examination: (a) that Smith "is a very severe sociopath"; (b) that "he will continue his previous behavior"; (c) that his sociopathic condition will "only get worse"; (d) that he has no "regard for another human being's property or for their life, regardless of who it may be"; (e) that "[t]here is no treatment, no medicine ...

---

1. This psychiatric evaluation was ordered even though defense counsel had not put into issue Smith's competency to stand trial or his sanity at the time of the offense. The trial judge later explained: "In all cases where the State has sought the death penalty, I have ordered a mental evaluation of the defendant to determine his competency to stand trial. I have done this for my benefit because I do not intend to be a participant in a case where the defendant receives the death penalty and his mental competency remains in doubt." No question as to the appropriateness of the trial judge's order for the examination has been raised by Smith.

that in any way at all modifies or changes this behavior"; (f) that he "is going to go ahead and commit other similar or same criminal acts if given the opportunity to do so"; and (g) that he "has no remorse or sorrow for what he has done." Dr. Grigson, whose testimony was based on information derived from his 90-minute "mental status examination" of Smith (*i.e.*, the examination ordered to determine competency to stand trial), was the State's only witness at the sentencing hearing. [After hearing this evidence, the jury sentenced Smith to death.]

II

A

… [W]e turn first to whether the admission of Dr. Grigson's testimony at the penalty phase violated respondent's Fifth Amendment privilege against compelled self-incrimination because respondent was not advised before the pretrial psychiatric examination that he had a right to remain silent and that any statement he made could be used against him at a sentencing proceeding. Our initial inquiry must be whether the Fifth Amendment privilege is applicable in the circumstances of this case.

(1)

The State argues that respondent was not entitled to the protection of the Fifth Amendment because Dr. Grigson's testimony was used only to determine punishment after conviction, not to establish guilt. In the State's view, "incrimination is complete once guilt has been adjudicated," and, therefore, the Fifth Amendment privilege has no relevance to the penalty phase of a capital murder trial. We disagree.

The Fifth Amendment, made applicable to the states through the Fourteenth Amendment, commands that "[n]o person … shall be compelled in any criminal case to be a witness against himself." The essence of this basic constitutional principle is "the requirement that the State which proposes to convict and punish an individual produce the evidence against him by the independent labor of its officers, not by the simple, cruel expedient of forcing it from his own lips."

The Court has held that "the availability of the [Fifth Amendment] privilege does not turn upon the type of proceeding in which its protection is invoked, but upon the nature of the statement or admission and the exposure which it invites." In this case, the ultimate penalty of death was a potential consequence of what respondent told the examining psychiatrist. Just as the Fifth Amendment prevents a criminal defendant from being made "'the deluded instrument of his own conviction,'" it protects him as well from being made the "deluded instrument" of his own execution.

We can discern no basis to distinguish between the guilt and penalty phases of respondent's capital murder trial so far as the protection of the Fifth Amendment privilege is concerned. Given the gravity of the decision to be made at the penalty phase, the State is not relieved of the obligation to observe fundamental constitutional guarantees. Any effort by the State to compel respondent to testify against his will at the sentencing hearing clearly would contravene the Fifth Amendment. Yet the State's attempt to establish respondent's future dangerousness by relying on the unwarned statements he made to Dr. Grigson similarly infringes Fifth Amendment values.

(2)

The State also urges that the Fifth Amendment privilege is inapposite here because respondent's communications to Dr. Grigson were nontestimonial in nature. The State seeks support from our cases holding that the Fifth Amendment is not violated where the evidence given by a defendant is neither related to some communicative act nor used for the testimonial content of what was said.

However, Dr. Grigson's diagnosis, as detailed in his testimony, was not based simply on his observation of respondent. Rather, Dr. Grigson drew his conclusions largely from respondent's account of the crime during their interview, and he placed particular emphasis on what he considered to be respondent's lack of remorse. Dr. Grigson's prognosis as to future dangerousness rested on statements respondent made, and remarks he omitted, in reciting the details of the crime. The Fifth Amendment privilege, therefore, is directly involved here because the State used as evidence against respondent the substance of his disclosures during the pretrial psychiatric examination.

The fact that respondent's statements were uttered in the context of a psychiatric examination does not automatically remove them from the reach of the Fifth Amendment. The state trial judge, *sua sponte*, ordered a psychiatric evaluation of respondent for the limited, neutral purpose of determining his competency to stand trial, but the results of that inquiry were used by the State for a much broader objective that was plainly adverse to respondent. Consequently, the interview with Dr. Grigson cannot be characterized as a routine competency examination restricted to ensuring that respondent understood the charges against him and was capable of assisting in his defense. Indeed, if the application of Dr. Grigson's findings had been confined to serving that function, no Fifth Amendment issue would have arisen.

Nor was the interview analogous to a sanity examination occasioned by a defendant's plea of not guilty by reason of insanity at the time of his offense. When a defendant asserts the insanity defense and introduces supporting psychiatric testimony, his silence may deprive the State of the only effective means it has of controverting his proof on an issue that he interjected into the case. Accordingly, several Courts of Appeals have held that, under such circumstances, a defendant can be required to submit to a sanity examination conducted by the prosecution's psychiatrist.

Respondent, however, introduced no psychiatric evidence, nor had he indicated that he might do so. Instead, the State offered information obtained from the court-ordered competency examination as affirmative evidence to persuade the jury to return a sentence of death. Respondent's future dangerousness was a critical issue at the sentencing hearing, and one on which the State had the burden of proof beyond a reasonable doubt. To meet its burden, the State used respondent's own statements, unwittingly made without an awareness that he was assisting the State's efforts to obtain the death penalty. In these distinct circumstances, ... [Smith's] Fifth Amendment privilege was implicated....

(3)

In *Miranda v. Arizona*, 384 U.S. 436, 467 (1966), the Court acknowledged that "the Fifth Amendment privilege is available outside of criminal court proceedings and serves to protect persons in all settings in which their freedom of action is curtailed in any significant way from being compelled to incriminate themselves." *Miranda* held that "the prosecution may not use statements, whether exculpatory or inculpatory, stemming from custodial interrogation of the defendant unless it demonstrates the use of procedural safeguards effective to secure the privilege against self-incrimination." Thus, absent other fully effective procedures, a person in custody must receive certain warnings before any official interrogation, including that he has a "right to remain silent" and that "anything said can and will be used against the individual in court." The purpose of these admonitions is to combat what the Court saw as "inherently compelling pressures" at work on the person and to provide him with an awareness of the Fifth Amendment privilege and the consequences of forgoing it, which is the prerequisite for "an intelligent decision as to its exercise."

The considerations calling for the accused to be warned prior to custodial interrogation apply with no less force to the pretrial psychiatric examination at issue here. Respondent was in custody at the Dallas County Jail when the examination was ordered and when it was conducted. That respondent was questioned by a psychiatrist designated by the trial court to conduct a neutral competency examination, rather than by a police officer, government informant, or prosecuting attorney, is immaterial. When Dr. Grigson went beyond simply reporting to the court on the issue of competence and testified for the prosecution at the penalty phase on the crucial issue of respondent's future dangerousness, his role changed and became essentially like that of an agent of the State recounting unwarned statements made in a postarrest custodial setting. During the psychiatric evaluation, respondent assuredly was "faced with a phase of the adversary system" and was "not in the presence of [a] perso[n] acting solely in his interest." Yet he was given no indication that the compulsory examination would be used to gather evidence necessary to decide whether, if convicted, he should be sentenced to death. He was not informed that, accordingly, he had a constitutional right not to answer the questions put to him.

A criminal defendant, who neither initiates a psychiatric evaluation nor attempts to introduce any psychiatric evidence, may not be compelled to respond to a psychiatrist if his statements can be used against him at a capital sentencing proceeding. Because respondent did not voluntarily consent to the pretrial psychiatric examination after being informed of his right to remain silent and the possible use of his statements, the State could not rely on what he said to Dr. Grigson to establish his future dangerousness. If, upon being adequately warned, respondent had indicated that he would not answer Dr. Grigson's questions, the validly ordered competency examination nevertheless could have proceeded upon the condition that the results would be applied solely for that purpose. In such circumstances, the proper conduct and use of competency and sanity examinations are not frustrated, but the State must make its case on future dangerousness in some other way.

"Volunteered statements ... are not barred by the Fifth Amendment," but under *Miranda v. Arizona* we must conclude that, when faced while in custody with a court-ordered psychiatric inquiry, respondent's statements to Dr. Grigson were not "given freely and voluntarily without any compelling influences" and, as such, could be used as the State did at the penalty phase only if respondent had been apprised of his rights and had knowingly decided to waive them. These safeguards of the Fifth Amendment privilege were not afforded respondent and, thus, his death sentence cannot stand.

B

When respondent was examined by Dr. Grigson, he already had been indicted and an attorney had been appointed to represent him.... [Smith] had a Sixth Amendment right to the assistance of counsel before submitting to the pretrial psychiatric interview. The Court of Appeals concluded that he had a Sixth Amendment right to assistance of counsel before submitting to the pretrial psychiatric interview. We agree.

The Sixth Amendment, made applicable to the states through the Fourteenth Amendment, provides that "[i]n all criminal prosecutions, the accused shall enjoy the right … to have the assistance of counsel for his defence." The "vital" need for a lawyer's advice and aid during the pretrial phase was recognized by the Court nearly 50 years ago in *Powell v. Alabama*, 287 U.S. 45, 57, 71 (1932). Since then, we have held that the right to counsel granted by the Sixth Amendment means that a person is entitled to the help of a lawyer "at or after the time that adversary judicial proceedings have been initiated against him … whether by way of formal charge, preliminary hearing, indictment, information, or arraignment."

Here, respondent's Sixth Amendment right to counsel clearly had attached when Dr. Grigson examined him at the Dallas County Jail, and their interview proved to be a "critical stage" of the aggregate proceedings against respondent. Defense counsel, however, were not notified in advance that the psychiatric examination would encompass the issue of their client's future dangerousness, and respondent was denied the assistance of his attorneys in making the significant decision of whether to submit to the examination and to what end the psychiatrist's findings could be employed.

Because "[a] layman may not be aware of the precise scope, the nuances, and the boundaries of his Fifth Amendment privilege," the assertion of that right "often depends upon legal advise from someone who is trained and skilled in the subject matter." As the Court of Appeals observed, the decision to be made regarding the proposed psychiatric evaluation is "literally a life or death matter" and is "difficult … even for an attorney" because it requires "a knowledge of what other evidence is available, of the particular psychiatrist's biases and predilections, [and] of possible alternative strategies at the sentencing hearing." It follows logically from our precedents that a defendant should not be forced to resolve such an important issue without "the guiding hand of counsel."

Therefore, in addition to Fifth Amendment considerations, the death penalty was improperly imposed on respondent because the psychiatric examination on which Dr. Grigson testified at the penalty phase proceeded in violation of respondent's Sixth Amendment right to the assistance of counsel.

C

Our holding based on the Fifth and Sixth Amendments will not prevent the State in capital cases from proving the defendant's future dangerousness as required by statute. A defendant may request or consent to a psychiatric examination concerning future dangerousness in the hope of escaping the death penalty. In addition, a different situation arises where a defendant intends to introduce psychiatric evidence at the penalty phase.…

III

Respondent's Fifth and Sixth Amendment rights were abridged by the State's introduction of Dr. Grigson's testimony at the penalty phase, and, as the Court of Appeals concluded, his death sentence must be vacated. Because respondent's underlying conviction has not been challenged and remains undisturbed, the State is free to conduct further proceedings not inconsistent with this opinion. Accordingly, the judgment of the Court of Appeals is affirmed.

Notes and Question

1. The *Estelle v. Smith* Court concluded that Smith's Fifth Amendment privilege was violated "because the State used as evidence against [him] the substance of his disclosures during the pretrial psychiatric examination." This conclusion was necessarily

premised upon a finding that if the results of the psychiatric examination were to be used against him, the defendant had a Fifth Amendment privilege to decline to answer questions during the examination.

2. *Estelle v. Smith*'s Fifth Amendment holding is limited. The Court expressly refused to decide whether the Fifth Amendment would apply to governmental psychiatric examination of a defendant who pleads insanity. Should a defendant who raises an issue related to mental capacity or who presents expert psychiatric testimony at any stage of the proceedings be precluded from asserting Fifth Amendment objections to a government-ordered psychiatric examination or to particular questions asked during the examination?

D. Harmless Error

Although the Constitution guarantees each criminal defendant the right to a fair trial, no one is entitled to a perfect, error-free trial. Nonetheless, until the mid-1960s, most courts automatically reversed criminal convictions upon a finding that the trial was tainted by *constitutional* error. In 1967, the Supreme Court in *Chapman v. California*, 386 U.S. 18, 22 (1967), held that, unless prejudice resulted from the mistake, even constitutional errors do not require reversal. The purpose of the harmless error rule is to avoid "setting aside convictions for small errors or defects that have little, if any, likelihood of having changed the result of the trial."

The *Chapman* rule requires the beneficiary of the constitutional error — usually the government — to prove beyond a reasonable doubt "that the error complained of did not contribute to the verdict." Thus, if overwhelming error-free evidence supports the conviction, it will not be reversed.

Satterwhite v. Texas
486 U.S. 249 (1988)

Justice O'CONNOR delivered the opinion of the Court.

In *Estelle v. Smith*, 451 U.S. 454 (1981), we recognized that defendants formally charged with capital crimes have a Sixth Amendment right to consult with counsel before submitting to psychiatric examinations designed to determine their future dangerousness. The question in this case is whether it was harmless error to introduce psychiatric testimony obtained in violation of that safeguard in a capital sentencing proceeding.

I

... [Without notice to and without the knowledge of petitioner John T. Satterwhite's attorney, petitioner was examined by several doctors including the psychiatrist Dr. James P. Grigson]. Satterwhite was tried by jury and convicted of capital murder. In accordance with Texas law, a separate proceeding was conducted before the same jury to determine whether he should be sentenced to death or to life imprisonment. The State produced Dr. Grigson as a witness in support of its case for the death penalty. Over defense counsel's objection, Dr. Grigson testified that, in his opinion, Satterwhite presented a continuing threat to society through acts of criminal violence.

At the conclusion of the evidence, the court instructed the jury to decide whether the State had proved, beyond a reasonable doubt, (1) that "the conduct of the defendant that caused the death [was] committed deliberately and with the reasonable expectation that the death of [the victim] would result," and (2) that there is "a probability that the defendant would commit criminal acts of violence that would constitute a continuing threat to society." Texas law provides that if a jury returns affirmative findings on both special verdict questions, "the court shall sentence the defendant to death." The jury answered both questions affirmatively, and the trial court sentenced Satterwhite to death.

[On appeal, the Texas Court of Criminal Appeals found that the admission of Dr. Grigson's testimony violated petitioner's Sixth Amendment right to counsel as guaranteed in *Estelle v. Smith*, but concluded that admission of this evidence constituted harmless error. Accordingly the Texas court affirmed Satterwhite's death sentence. Satterwhite appealed his death sentence to the Supreme Court on the grounds that the admission of Dr. Grigson's testimony violated his Sixth Amendment right to assistance of counsel as recognized in *Estelle v. Smith*.] [L]ike the Texas Court of Criminal Appeals, we agree and conclude that the use of Dr. Grigson's testimony at the capital sentencing proceeding on the issue of future dangerousness violated the Sixth Amendment.

Our conclusion does not end the inquiry because not all constitutional violations amount to reversible error. We generally have held that if the prosecution can prove beyond a reasonable doubt that a constitutional error did not contribute to the verdict, the error is harmless and the verdict may stand. The harmless error rule " 'promotes public respect for the criminal process by focusing on the underlying fairness of the trial rather than on the virtually inevitable presence of immaterial error.' "

Some constitutional violations, however, by their very nature cast so much doubt on the fairness of the trial process that, as a matter of law, they can never be considered harmless. Sixth Amendment violations that pervade the entire proceeding fall within this category. Since the scope of a violation such as a deprivation of the right to conflict-free representation cannot be discerned from the record, any inquiry into its effect on the outcome of the case would be purely speculative....

Satterwhite urges us to adopt an automatic rule of reversal for violations of the Sixth Amendment right recognized in *Estelle v. Smith*. He relies heavily upon the statement in *Holloway v. Arkansas*, 435 U.S. 475 (1978), that "when a defendant is deprived of the presence and assistance of his attorney, either throughout the prosecution or during a critical stage in, at least, the prosecution of a capital offense, reversal is automatic." His reliance is misplaced, however, for *Holloway*, *Gideon v. Wainright*, 732 U.S. 335 (1963), *Hamilton v. Alabama*, 368 U.S. 52 (1961), and *White v. Maryland*, 373 U.S. 59 (1962), were all cases in which the deprivation of the right to counsel affected—and contaminated—the entire criminal proceeding. In this case, the effect of the Sixth Amendment violation is limited to the admission into evidence of Dr. Grigson's testimony. We have permitted harmless error analysis in both capital and noncapital cases where the evil caused by a Sixth Amendment violation is limited to the erroneous admission of particular evidence at trial. In *Milton v. Wainwright*, 407 U.S. 371 (1972), for example, the Court held the admission of a confession obtained in violation of *Massiah v. United States*, 377 U.S. 201 (1964), to be harmless beyond a reasonable doubt. And we have held that harmless error analysis applies to the admission of identification testimony obtained in violation of the right to counsel at a postindictment lineup. Just last year we indicated that harmless error analysis would apply in a noncapital case to constitutional error in the use of a psychological evaluation at trial.

It is important to avoid error in capital sentencing proceedings. Moreover, the evaluation of the consequences of an error in the sentencing phase of a capital case may be more difficult because of the discretion that is given to the sentencer. Nevertheless, we believe that a reviewing court can make an intelligent judgment about whether the erroneous admission of psychiatric testimony might have affected a capital sentencing jury. Accordingly, we hold that the *Chapman v. California*, 386 U.S. 18 (1967), harmless error rule applies to the admission of psychiatric testimony in violation of the Sixth Amendment right set out in *Estelle v. Smith*.

III

Applying the *Chapman* harmless error test, we cannot agree with the [Texas] Court of Criminal Appeals that the erroneous admission of Dr. Grigson's testimony was harmless beyond a reasonable doubt. A Texas court can sentence a defendant to death only if the prosecution convinces the jury, beyond a reasonable doubt, that "there is a probability that the defendant would commit criminal acts of violence that would constitute a continuing threat to society." The Court of Criminal Appeals thought that the admission of Dr. Grigson's expert testimony on this critical issue was harmless because "the properly admitted evidence was such that the minds of an average jury would have found the State's case [on future dangerousness] sufficient ... even if Dr. Grigson's testimony had not been admitted." The question, however, is not whether the legally admitted evidence was sufficient to support the death sentence, which we assume it was, but rather, whether the State has proved "beyond a reasonable doubt that the error complained of did not contribute to the verdict obtained."

The evidence introduced at sentencing showed that, in addition to his conviction in this case, Satterwhite had four prior convictions of crimes ranging from aggravated assault to armed robbery. Eight police officers testified that Satterwhite's reputation for being a peaceful and law-abiding citizen was bad, and Satterwhite's mother's former husband testified that Satterwhite once shot him during an argument. The State also introduced the testimony of Bexar County psychologist Betty Lou Schroeder. Dr. Schroeder testified that she found Satterwhite to be a "cunning individual" and a "user of people," with an inability to feel empathy or guilt. She testified that in her opinion, Satterwhite would be a continuing threat to society through acts of criminal violence.

Dr. Grigson was the State's final witness. His testimony stands out both because of his qualifications as a medical doctor specializing in psychiatry and because of the powerful content of his message. Dr. Grigson was the only licensed physician to take the stand. He informed the jury of his educational background and experience, which included teaching psychiatry at a Dallas medical school and practicing psychiatry for over 12 years. He stated unequivocally that, in his expert opinion, Satterwhite "will present a continuing threat to society by continuing acts of violence." He explained that Satterwhite has "a lack of conscience" and is "as severe a sociopath as you can be." To illustrate his point, he testified that on a scale of 1 to 10—where "ones" are mild sociopaths and "tens" are individuals with complete disregard for human life—Satterwhite is a "ten plus." Dr. Grigson concluded his testimony on direct examination with perhaps his most devastating opinion of all: he told the jury that Satterwhite was beyond the reach of psychiatric rehabilitation.

The District Attorney highlighted Dr. Grigson's credentials and conclusions in his closing argument:

> Doctor James Grigson, Dallas psychiatrist and medical doctor. And he tells you that on a range from 1 to 10 he's ten plus. Severe sociopath. Extremely dangerous. A continuing threat to our society. Can it be cured? Well, it's not a disease. It's not an illness. That's his personality. That's John T. Satterwhite.

The finding of future dangerousness was critical to the death sentence. Dr. Grigson was the only psychiatrist to testify on this issue, and the prosecution placed significant weight on his powerful and unequivocal testimony. Having reviewed the evidence in this case, we find it impossible to say beyond a reasonable doubt that Dr. Grigson's expert testimony on the issue of Satterwhite's future dangerousness did not influence the sentencing jury. Accordingly, we reverse the judgment of the Texas Court of Criminal Appeals insofar as it affirms the death sentence, and we remand the case for further proceedings not inconsistent with this opinion.

Justice MARSHALL, with whom Justice Brennan joins and with whom Justice Blackmun joins as to Part II, concurring in part and concurring in the judgment.

I

I agree with the Court that the psychiatric examination on which Dr. Grigson testified at the capital sentencing proceeding was in bald violation of *Estelle v. Smith* and that petitioner's death sentence should be vacated. I write separately because I believe the Court errs in applying harmless-error analysis to this Sixth Amendment violation. It is my view that the unique nature of a capital sentencing determination should cause this Court to be especially hesitant ever to sanction harmless-error review of constitutional errors that taint capital sentencing proceedings, and even if certain constitutional errors might properly be subject to such harmless-error analysis, a violation of *Estelle v. Smith* is not such an error.

Until today's ruling, this Court never had applied harmless-error analysis to constitutional violations that taint the sentencing phase of a capital trial. In deciding to apply harmless-error analysis to the Sixth Amendment violation in this case, I believe the Court fails to adequately consider the unique nature of a capital sentencing proceeding and a sentencer's decision whether a defendant should live or die. The Court's analysis is also flawed in that it fails to accord any noticeable weight to the qualitative difference of death from all other punishments.

Unlike the determination of guilt or innocence, which turns largely on an evaluation of objective facts, the question whether death is the appropriate sentence requires a profoundly moral evaluation of the defendant's character and crime. Moreover, although much of the Court's capital jurisprudence since *Furman* has been focused on guiding and channeling the decision whether death is the appropriate sentence in a specific case, the sentencer nonetheless is afforded substantial discretion. Even in the face of overwhelming aggravating evidence, the sentencer has discretion to act with leniency and refuse to impose the death sentence.

Because of the moral character of a capital sentencing determination and the substantial discretion placed in the hands of the sentencer, predicting the reaction of a sentencer to a proceeding untainted by constitutional error on the basis of a cold record is a dangerously speculative enterprise. As the Court recognized in *Caldwell v. Mississippi*, 472 U.S. 320, 330 (1985), "[w]hatever intangibles a jury might consider in its sentencing determination, few can be gleaned from an appellate record." In the same vein, an appellate court is ill-equipped to evaluate the effect of a constitutional error on a sentencing determination. Such sentencing judgments, even when guided and channeled, are inherently subjective, and the weight a sentencer gives an instruction or a significant piece of evidence that is later determined to violate a defendant's constitutional rights is nowhere apparent in the record. In *McCleskey v. Kemp*, the Court acknowledged that "[i]ndividual jurors bring to their deliberations 'qualities of human nature and varieties of human experience, the range of which is unknown and perhaps unknowable,'" and their collective judgment of the appropriate sentence is marked by an "inherent lack of predictability." The threat of an erroneous harmless-error determination thus looms much larger in the capital sentencing context than elsewhere.

That threat is of particular concern because of the unique nature of the death sentence. The awesome severity of a sentence of death makes it qualitatively different from all other sanctions. For this reason, the Court has emphasized the greater need for reliability in capital cases, and has required that "capital proceedings be policed at all stages by an especially vigilant concern for procedural fairness and for the accuracy of factfinding." Because of this heightened concern for reliability, "[t]ime and again the Court has condemned procedures in capital cases that might be completely acceptable in an ordinary case." Harmless-error analysis impinges directly on the reliability of the capital sentencing decision by allowing a court to substitute its judgment of what the sentencer would have done in the absence of constitutional error for an actual judgment of the sentencer untainted by constitutional error.

I therefore have serious doubts whether a constitutional error that infects the sentencing phase of a capital case ever may be considered harmless beyond a reasonable doubt. But even if I could agree that harmless-error analysis is appropriate for certain constitutional errors at the sentencing phase, such a situation is not presented when the error is a violation of the Sixth Amendment under *Estelle v. Smith*.

II

… [I]t is difficult, if not impossible, to accurately measure the degree of prejudice arising from the failure to notify defense counsel of an impending psychiatric examination and the subsequent admission at the sentencing phase of evidence acquired from the examination. As I discussed above, the decision whether a defendant should live or die is a discretionary, moral judgment involving a balancing of often intangible factors. Divining the effect of psychiatric testimony on a sentencer's determination whether death is an appropriate sentence is thus more in the province of soothsayers than appellate judges. In addition, contrary to the Court's claim, the prejudice arising from an *Estelle v. Smith* violation is not limited to the illegal admission of psychiatric testimony. If defense counsel is properly notified under *Smith* of the State's intention to perform a psychiatric examination, the course of subsequent proceedings may be altered significantly. For instance, defense counsel might extensively prepare his client for the examination, or perhaps advise his client to refuse to participate in the examination by the particular psychiatrist; defense counsel also might urge that a different psychiatrist perform the examination. I therefore believe that any attempt to predict the effect of such an *Estelle v. Smith* violation would require the appellate court to engage in unguided speculation. The confluence of these factors—the likelihood of prejudice and the difficulty in evaluating the degree of that prejudice—together with the heightened concern for reliability in capital cases, convinces me that a psychiatric examination conducted in violation of *Estelle v. Smith*, and the later admission at a capital sentencing proceeding of psychiatric testimony based on this examination, may never be considered harmless error.

Notes

1. **Per Se Reversible Error.** As *Satterwhite v. Texas* makes plain, the error of admitting, during the sentencing phase, psychiatric testimony obtained in violation of the Sixth Amendment, is subject to harmless error analysis. Certain types of error are so basic to a

fair trial that they are never subjected to harmless error analysis. According to the United States Supreme Court, these include wholesale denial of the right to counsel, the right to an impartial judge, the right to a public trial, the right to self-representation at trial, and the right to be free from racial discrimination in the selection of a grand jury. See *Arizona v. Fulminante*, 499 U.S. 279 (1991). In addition, the Court has refused to apply harmless error analysis in a case involving the improper removal of a potential juror for cause in a capital trial. See *Gray v. Mississippi*, 481 U.S. 648, 660–664 (1987). In *Sullivan v. Louisiana*, 508 U.S. 275 (1993), the United States Supreme Court refused to apply harmless error analysis to an improper jury instruction regarding reasonable doubt.

Federal circuit courts of appeal have refused to apply harmless error analysis to errors involving an egregious violation of the right to a fair trial, *United States v. Noushfar*, 78 F.3d 1442, 1445 (9th Cir. 1996) (harmless error analysis not applicable because jury took into deliberations taped conversations never played at trial, violating rules of evidence and undermining fundamental tenet that conviction must rest on evidence presented and tested in front of judge, jury and defendant); the right to choose counsel, *United States v. Romano*, 849 F.2d 812, 820 (3d Cir. 1988) (per se reversible error because court appointed counsel over defendant's objection after revoking right to pro se representation); improper amendments to the indictment, *United States v. Vebeliunas*, 76 F.3d 1283, 1290 (2d Cir. 1996) (per se reversible error because indictment constructively amended); failure to determine if the defendant understands the nature of the charges, *United States v. Suarez*, 155 F.3d 521, 525 (5th Cir. 1998) (if court fails to address whether defendant understands nature of charges before accepting guilty plea, defendant's substantial rights are affected and automatic reversal is required); failure to inform the defendant of his right to appeal his conviction, *United States v. Sanchez*, 88 F.3d 1243, 1247 (D.C. Cir. 1996) (per se reversible error because judge failed to inform defendant of his right to appeal sentence); impairment of the defendant's right to peremptory challenges, *United States v. Taylor*, 92 F.3d 1313, 1325 (2d Cir. 1996) (per se reversible error because defendant's right to peremptory challenges denied or impaired); denial of the right to a jury trial, *United States v. Duarte-Higareda*, 113 F.3d 1000, 1003 (9th Cir. 1997) (per se reversible error for failure to determine if defendant voluntarily, knowingly and intelligently waived jury trial).

2. **Errors Subject to the *Chapman* Rule.** The vast majority of errors are subject to harmless error analysis. These include errors in jury selection, *Ross v. Oklahoma*, 487 U.S. 81, 88 (1988); certain grand jury procedural violations, *United States v. Mechanik*, 475 U.S. 66, 72–73 (1986); confrontation clause violations, *Coy v. Iowa*, 487 U.S. 1012, 1022 (1988); admission of evidence in violation of a defendant's Fourth, Fifth, or Sixth Amendment rights, *Milton v. Wainwright*, 407 U.S. 371, 377–378 (1972) (harmless error in admitting evidence of confession obtained in violation of defendant's right to counsel, because evidence of guilt, including three confessions, was overwhelming); admission of coerced confessions, *Arizona v. Fulminante*, 499 U.S. 279, 310–11 (1991); the absence of the defendant from the return of a death verdict, *Rice v. Wood*, 77 F.3d 1138, 1145 (9th Cir. 1996) (en banc) (absence of defendant harmless because defendant had been twice convicted, there was a strong showing of aggravating factors, and few mitigating factors); and prosecutorial misconduct, *Bank of Nova Scotia v. United States*, 487 U.S. 250, 263–264 (1988). For an interesting discussion of the harmless error rule, see Chapel, "The Irony of Harmless Error," 51 Okla. L. Rev. 501 (1998).

3. **Harmless Error in Federal Post-Conviction.** The "harmless beyond a reasonable doubt standard" set forth in *Chapman v. California*, 386 U.S. 18 (1967), applies to courts on direct appeal but does not apply to federal habeas corpus review of constitu-

tional errors committed at trial. Instead, the Court in *Brecht v. Abrahamson*, 507 U.S. 619 (1993), held that federal courts on habeas may not grant relief unless the error "had substantial and injurious effect or influence in determining the jury's verdict." See discussion of *Brecht v. Abrahamson* in chapter 13.

E. The Right to a Court-Appointed Psychiatrist

Perhaps the most important opportunity for psychiatrists to assist during capital litigation is when a defendant's sanity is in issue. As a threshold matter, a court must determine a defendant's "present sanity," that is, his competency to stand trial. Later, if an insanity defense is raised, the defendant's mental condition at the time of the offense becomes critical. Both sanity determinations may benefit from the expert assistance of psychiatrists.

Ake v. Oklahoma
470 U.S. 68 (1985)

Justice MARSHALL delivered the opinion of the Court.

The issue in this case is whether the Constitution requires that an indigent defendant have access to the psychiatric examination and assistance necessary to prepare an effective defense based on his mental condition, when his sanity at the time of the offense is seriously in question.

I

Late in 1979, Glen Burton Ake was arrested and charged with murdering a couple and wounding their two children. He was arraigned in the District Court for Canadian County, Okla., in February 1980. His behavior at arraignment, and in other prearrangment incidents at the jail, was so bizarre that the trial judge, *sua sponte*, ordered him to be examined by a psychiatrist "for the purpose of advising with the Court as to his impressions of whether the Defendant may need an extended period of mental observation." The examining psychiatrist reported: "At times [Ake] appears to be frankly delusional.... He claims to be the 'sword of vengeance' of the Lord and that he will sit at the left hand of God in heaven." He diagnosed Ake as a probable paranoid schizophrenic and recommended a prolonged psychiatric evaluation to determine whether Ake was competent to stand trial.

In March, Ake was committed to a state hospital to be examined with respect to his "present sanity," *i.e.*, his competency to stand trial. On April 10, less than six months after the incidents for which Ake was indicted, the chief forensic psychiatrist at the state hospital informed the court that Ake was not competent to stand trial. The court then held a competency hearing, at which a psychiatrist testified:

> [Ake] is a psychotic ... his psychiatric diagnosis was that of paranoid schizophrenia — chronic, with exacerbation, that is with current upset, and that in addition ... he is dangerous.... [B]ecause of the severity of his mental illness and because of the intensities of his rage, his poor control, his delusions, he requires a maximum security facility within — I believe — the State Psychiatric Hospital system.

The court found Ake to be a "mentally ill person in need of care and treatment" and incompetent to stand trial, and ordered him committed to the state mental hospital.

Six weeks later, the chief forensic psychiatrist informed the court that Ake had become competent to stand trial. At the time, Ake was receiving 200 milligrams of Thorazine, an antipsychotic drug, three times daily, and the psychiatrist indicated that, if Ake continued to receive that dosage, his condition would remain stable. The State then resumed proceedings against Ake.

At a pretrial conference in June, Ake's attorney informed the court that his client would raise an insanity defense. To enable him to prepare and present such a defense adequately, the attorney stated, a psychiatrist would have to examine Ake with respect to his mental condition at the time of the offense. During Ake's 3-month stay at the state hospital, no inquiry had been made into his sanity at the time of the offense, and, as an indigent, Ake could not afford to pay for a psychiatrist. Counsel asked the court either to arrange to have a psychiatrist perform the examination, or to provide funds to allow the defense to arrange one. The trial judge rejected counsel's argument that the Federal Constitution requires that an indigent defendant receive the assistance of a psychiatrist when that assistance is necessary to the defense, and he denied the motion for a psychiatric evaluation at state expense....

Ake was tried for two counts of murder in the first degree, a crime punishable by death in Oklahoma, and for two counts of shooting with intent to kill. At the guilt phase of trial, his sole defense was insanity. Although defense counsel called to the stand and questioned each of the psychiatrists who had examined Ake at the state hospital, none testified about his mental state at the time of the offense because none had examined him on that point. The prosecution, in turn, asked each of these psychiatrists whether he had performed or seen the results of any examination diagnosing Ake's mental state at the time of the offense, and each doctor replied that he had not. *As a result, there was no expert testimony for either side on Ake's sanity at the time of the offense.* The jurors were then instructed that Ake could be found not guilty by reason of insanity if he did not have the ability to distinguish right from wrong at the time of the alleged offense. They were further told that Ake was to be presumed sane at the time of the crime unless he presented evidence sufficient to raise a reasonable doubt about his sanity at that time. If he raised such a doubt in their minds, the jurors were informed, the burden of proof shifted to the State to prove sanity beyond a reasonable doubt. The jury rejected Ake's insanity defense and returned a verdict of guilty on all counts.

At the sentencing proceeding, the State asked for the death penalty. No new evidence was presented. The prosecutor relied significantly on the testimony of the state psychiatrists who had examined Ake, and who had testified at the guilt phase that Ake was dangerous to society, to establish the likelihood of his future dangerous behavior. Ake had no expert witness to rebut this testimony or to introduce on his behalf evidence in mitigation of his punishment. The jury sentenced Ake to death on each of the two murder counts, and to 500 years' imprisonment on each of the two counts of shooting with intent to kill. [The Oklahoma Court of Criminal Appeals affirmed Ake's conviction and sentence.] ...

[This Court granted certiorari to address whether Ake should have been provided a court-appointed psychiatrist.] We hold that when a defendant has made a preliminary showing that his sanity at the time of the offense is likely to be a significant factor at trial, the Constitution requires that a State provide access to a psychiatrist's assistance on this issue if the defendant cannot otherwise afford one....

III

This Court has long recognized that when a State brings its judicial power to bear on an indigent defendant in a criminal proceeding, it must take steps to assure that the defendant has a fair opportunity to present his defense. This elementary principle, grounded in significant part on the Fourteenth Amendment's due process guarantee of fundamental fairness, derives from the belief that justice cannot be equal where, simply as a result of his poverty, a defendant is denied the opportunity to participate meaningfully in a judicial proceeding in which his liberty is at stake. In recognition of this right, this Court held almost 30 years ago that once a State offers to criminal defendants the opportunity to appeal their cases, it must provide a trial transcript to an indigent defendant if the transcript is necessary to a decision on the merits of the appeal. *Griffin v. Illinois*, 351 U.S. 12 (1956). Since then, this Court has held that an indigent defendant may not be required to pay a fee before filing a notice of appeal of his conviction, *Burns v. Ohio*, 360 U.S. 252 (1959), that an indigent defendant is entitled to the assistance of counsel at trial, *Gideon v. Wainwright*, 372 U.S. 335 (1963), and on his first direct appeal as of right, *Douglas v. California*, 372 U.S. 353 (1963), and that such assistance must be effective. Indeed, in *Little v. Streater*, 452 U.S. 1 (1981), we extended this principle of meaningful participation to a "quasi-criminal" proceeding and held that, in a paternity action, the State cannot deny the putative father blood grouping tests, if he cannot otherwise afford them.

Meaningful access to justice has been the consistent theme of these cases. We recognized long ago that mere access to the courthouse doors does not by itself assure a proper functioning of the adversary process, and that a criminal trial is fundamentally unfair if the State proceeds against an indigent defendant without making certain that he has access to the raw materials integral to the building of an effective defense. Thus, while the Court has not held that a State must purchase for the indigent defendant all the assistance that his wealthier counterpart might buy, it has often reaffirmed that fundamental fairness entitles indigent defendants to "an adequate opportunity to present their claims fairly within the adversary system." To implement this principle, we have focused on identifying the "basic tools of an adequate defense or appeal," and we have required that such tools be provided to those defendants who cannot afford to pay for them.

To say that these basic tools must be provided is, of course, merely to begin our inquiry. In this case we must decide whether, and under what conditions, the participation of a psychiatrist is important enough to preparation of a defense to require the State to provide an indigent defendant with access to competent psychiatric assistance in preparing the defense. Three factors are relevant to this determination. The first is the private interest that will be affected by the action of the State. The second is the governmental interest that will be affected if the safeguard is to be provided. The third is the probable value of the additional or substitute procedural safeguards that are sought, and the risk of an erroneous deprivation of the affected interest if those safeguards are not provided. *Mathews v. Eldridge*, 424 U.S. 319, 335 (1976). We turn, then, to apply this standard to the issue before us.

A

The private interest in the accuracy of a criminal proceeding that places an individual's life or liberty at risk is almost uniquely compelling. Indeed, the host of safeguards fashioned by this Court over the years to diminish the risk of erroneous conviction stands as a testament to that concern. The interest of the individual in the outcome of the State's effort to overcome the presumption of innocence is obvious and weighs heavily in our analysis.

We consider, next, the interest of the State. Oklahoma asserts that to provide Ake with psychiatric assistance on the record before us would result in a staggering burden to the State. We are unpersuaded by this assertion. Many States, as well as the Federal Government, currently make psychiatric assistance available to indigent defendants, and they have not found the financial burden so great as to preclude this assistance. This is especially so when the obligation of the State is limited to provision of one competent psychiatrist, as it is in many States, and as we limit the right we recognize today. At the same time, it is difficult to identify any interest of the State, other than that in its economy, that weighs against recognition of this right. The State's interest in prevailing at trial—unlike that of a private litigant—is necessarily tempered by its interest in the fair and accurate adjudication of criminal cases. Thus, also unlike a private litigant, a State may not legitimately assert an interest in maintenance of a strategic advantage over the defense, if the result of that advantage is to cast a pall on the accuracy of the verdict obtained. We therefore conclude that the governmental interest in denying Ake the assistance of a psychiatrist is not substantial, in light of the compelling interest of both the State and the individual in accurate dispositions.

Last, we inquire into the probable value of the psychiatric assistance sought, and the risk of error in the proceeding if such assistance is not offered. We begin by considering the pivotal role that psychiatry has come to play in criminal proceedings. More than 40 States, as well as the Federal Government, have decided either through legislation or judicial decision that indigent defendants are entitled, under certain circumstances, to the assistance of a psychiatrist's expertise. For example, in subsection (e) of the Criminal Justice Act, 18 U.S.C. §3006A, Congress has provided that indigent defendants shall receive the assistance of all experts "necessary for an adequate defense." Numerous state statutes guarantee reimbursement for expert services under a like standard. And in many States that have not assured access to psychiatrists through the legislative process, state courts have interpreted the State or Federal Constitution to require that psychiatric assistance be provided to indigent defendants when necessary for an adequate defense, or when insanity is at issue.

These statutes and court decisions reflect a reality that we recognize today, namely, that when the State has made the defendant's mental condition relevant to his criminal culpability and to the punishment he might suffer, the assistance of a psychiatrist may well be crucial to the defendant's ability to marshal his defense. In this role, psychiatrists gather facts, through professional examination, interviews, and elsewhere, that they will share with the judge or jury; they analyze the information gathered and from it draw plausible conclusions about the defendant's mental condition, and about the effects of any disorder on behavior; and they offer opinions about how the defendant's mental condition might have affected his behavior at the time in question. They know the probative questions to ask of the opposing party's psychiatrists and how to interpret their answers. Unlike lay witnesses, who can merely describe symptoms they believe might be relevant to the defendant's mental state, psychiatrists can identify the "elusive and often deceptive" symptoms of insanity, and tell the jury why their observations are relevant. Further, where permitted by evidentiary rules, psychiatrists can translate a medical diagnosis into language that will assist the trier of fact, and therefore offer evidence in a form that has meaning for the task at hand. Through this process of investigation, interpretation, and testimony, psychiatrists ideally assist lay jurors, who generally have no training in psychiatric matters, to make a sensible and educated determination about the mental condition of the defendant at the time of the offense.

Psychiatry is not, however, an exact science, and psychiatrists disagree widely and frequently on what constitutes mental illness, on the appropriate diagnosis to be attached to given behavior and symptoms, on cure and treatment, and on likelihood of future dangerousness. Perhaps because there often is no single, accurate psychiatric conclusion on legal insanity in a given case, juries remain the primary factfinders on this issue, and they must resolve differences in opinion within the psychiatric profession on the basis of the evidence offered by each party. When jurors make this determination about issues that inevitably are complex and foreign, the testimony of psychiatrists can be crucial and "a virtual necessity if an insanity plea is to have any chance of success." By organizing a defendant's mental history, examination results and behavior, and other information, interpreting it in light of their expertise, and then laying out their investigative and analytic process to the jury, the psychiatrists for each party enable the jury to make its most accurate determination of the truth on the issue before them. It is for this reason that States rely on psychiatrists as examiners, consultants, and witnesses, and that private individuals do as well, when they can afford to do so. In so saying, we neither approve nor disapprove the widespread reliance on psychiatrists but instead recognize the unfairness of a contrary holding in light of the evolving practice.

The foregoing leads inexorably to the conclusion that, without the assistance of a psychiatrist to conduct a professional examination on issues relevant to the defense, to help determine whether the insanity defense is viable, to present testimony, and to assist in preparing the cross-examination of a State's psychiatric witnesses, the risk of an inaccurate resolution of sanity issues is extremely high. With such assistance, the defendant is fairly able to present at least enough information to the jury, in a meaningful manner, as to permit it to make a sensible determination.

A defendant's mental condition is not necessarily at issue in every criminal proceeding, however, and it is unlikely that psychiatric assistance of the kind we have described would be of probable value in cases where it is not. The risk of error from denial of such assistance, as well as its probable value, is most predictably at its height when the defendant's mental condition is seriously in question. When the defendant is able to make an *ex parte* threshold showing to the trial court that his sanity is likely to be a significant factor in his defense, the need for the assistance of a psychiatrist is readily apparent. It is in such cases that a defense may be devastated by the absence of a psychiatric examination and testimony; with such assistance, the defendant might have a reasonable chance of success. In such a circumstance, where the potential accuracy of the jury's determination is so dramatically enhanced, and where the interests of the individual and the State in an accurate proceeding are substantial, the State's interest in its fisc must yield.

We therefore hold that when a defendant demonstrates to the trial judge that his sanity at the time of the offense is to be a significant factor at trial, the State must, at a minimum, assure the defendant access to a competent psychiatrist who will conduct an appropriate examination and assist in evaluation, preparation, and presentation of the defense. This is not to say, of course, that the indigent defendant has a constitutional right to choose a psychiatrist of his personal liking or to receive funds to hire his own. Our concern is that the indigent defendant have access to a competent psychiatrist for the purpose we have discussed, and as in the case of the provision of counsel we leave to the State the decision on how to implement this right.

B

Ake also was denied the means of presenting evidence to rebut the State's evidence of his future dangerousness. The foregoing discussion compels a similar conclusion in the context of a capital sentencing proceeding, when the State presents psychiatric evidence of the defendant's future dangerousness. We have repeatedly recognized the defendant's compelling interest in fair adjudication at the sentencing phase of a capital case. The State, too, has a profound interest in assuring that its ultimate sanction is not erroneously imposed, and we do not see why monetary considerations should be more persuasive in this context than at trial. The variable on which we must focus is, therefore, the probable value that the assistance of a psychiatrist will have in this area, and the risk attendant on its absence.

This Court has upheld the practice in many States of placing before the jury psychiatric testimony on the question of future dangerousness, at least where the defendant has had access to an expert of his own. In so holding, the Court relied, in part, on the assumption that the factfinder would have before it both the views of the prosecutor's psychiatrists and the "opposing views of the defendant's doctors" and would therefore be competent to "uncover, recognize, and take due account of ... shortcomings" in predictions on this point. Without a psychiatrist's assistance, the defendant cannot offer a well-informed expert's opposing view, and thereby loses a significant opportunity to raise in the jurors' minds questions about the State's proof of an aggravating factor. In such a circumstance, where the consequence of error is so great, the relevance of responsive psychiatric testimony so evident, and the burden on the State so slim, due process requires access to a psychiatric examination on relevant issues, to the testimony of the psychiatrist, and to assistance in preparation at the sentencing phase....

IV

We turn now to apply these standards to the facts of this case. On the record before us, it is clear that Ake's mental state at the time of the offense was a substantial factor in his defense, and that the trial court was on notice of that fact when the request for a court-appointed psychiatrist was made. For one, Ake's sole defense was that of insanity. Second, Ake's behavior at arraignment, just four months after the offense, was so bizarre as to prompt the trial judge, *sua sponte*, to have him examined for competency. Third, a state psychiatrist shortly thereafter found Ake to be incompetent to stand trial, and suggested that he be committed. Fourth, when he was found to be competent six weeks later, it was only on the condition that he be sedated with large doses of Thorazine three times a day, during trial. Fifth, the psychiatrists who examined Ake for competency described to the trial court the severity of Ake's mental illness less than six months after the offense in question, and suggested that this mental illness might have begun many years earlier. Finally, Oklahoma recognizes a defense of insanity, under which the initial burden of producing evidence falls on the defendant. Taken together, these factors make clear that the question of Ake's sanity was likely to be a significant factor in his defense.

In addition, Ake's future dangerousness was a significant factor at the sentencing phase. The state psychiatrist who treated Ake at the state mental hospital testified at the guilt phase that, because of his mental illness, Ake posed a threat of continuing criminal violence. This testimony raised the issue of Ake's future dangerousness, which is an aggravating factor under Oklahoma's capital sentencing scheme, and on which the prosecutor relied at sentencing. We therefore conclude that Ake also was entitled to the assistance of a psychiatrist on this issue and that the denial of that assistance deprived him of due process. Accordingly, we reverse and remand for a new trial.

Notes and Questions

1. Glen Burton Ake was ultimately retried and received a life sentence. Brooks Douglass, one of the children Ake shot and left for dead, recovered, attended law school, and was elected to the Oklahoma State Senate. Soon after *Payne v. Tennessee*, 501 U.S. 808 (1991), opened the door to the use of victim impact evidence in capital sentencing proceedings, Senator Douglass led a successful effort to amend Oklahoma's criminal code to permit victims to testify during the penalty phase of capital trials. Ake's accomplice, Stephen Hatch—who was sitting outside in the getaway car when Ake shot and killed Reverend and Mrs. Douglass and wounded their two children—was executed in 1996. Prior to Hatch's execution, Senator Douglass prevailed upon his colleagues in the Oklahoma state legislature to amend the law to allow victims to witness executions. Senator Douglass attended Hatch's execution. See generally Coyne, "Inflicting *Payne* on Oklahoma," 45 Okla. L. Rev. 589 (1992). For a discussion of victim impact evidence, see *supra* chapter 7.

2. According to *Ake*, a trial court must provide expert psychiatrist assistance to an indigent defendant where insanity is a significant factor during the trial. Failure to do so results in a violation of due process. Ake's sanity was at issue during both phases of his trial. During the guilt phase, Ake's mental state at the time of the offense was a substantial factor in his defense. During sentencing, Ake's future dangerousness was at issue. Note, however, that *Ake* does not necessarily limit the right to expert psychiatric assistance to the trial proceedings.

3. Is *Ake* limited to the right to psychiatric assistance? Or is *Ake* authority for obtaining any type of assistance necessary to present an adequate defense? Should *Ake* be read expansively to require the state to provide to indigents the assistance of private investigators? Forensic specialists? Polygraph examiners? Statistical experts?

4. An expert can assist a criminal defendant in two essential ways. First, she can gather facts, inspect tangible evidence, or conduct tests or examinations that may aid defense counsel in confronting the prosecution's case—including its expert witnesses—or in fashioning a theory of defense. Second, the expert can provide opinion testimony to rebut prosecution evidence or to establish an affirmative defense, such as insanity. Nonetheless, defense counsel requesting expert assistance under *Ake* are well advised to make a specific request. Counsel "must inform the court of the nature of the prosecution's case and how the requested expert would be useful. At the very least, he must inform the court about the nature of the crime and the evidence linking him to the crime." Moreover, "the defendant's showing must include a specific description of the expert or experts desired." *Moore v. Kemp*, 809 F.2d 702 (11th Cir. 1987) (upholding the denial of vague request for appointment of "criminologist or other expert witness"). According to *Moore*, the issue on appeal of a denial of expert assistance under *Ake* is, "having heard petitioner's explanation, should the trial judge have concluded that unless he granted his request petitioner would likely be denied an adequate opportunity fairly to confront the State's case and to present his defense?"

5. Assuming an indigent defendant is entitled to have the state provide psychiatric assistance, should the defendant be allowed to hire the psychiatrist of his choice? Under *Ake*, an indigent is entitled "to provision of one competent psychiatrist," but he is not entitled "to choose a psychiatrist of his personal liking or to receive funds to hire his own." 470 U.S. at 79, 83. Are you persuaded by the prosecutor's argument (reprinted in *Moore v. Kemp*, 809 F.2d at 716) that state crime laboratory employees would make proper defense witnesses?

Of course, the State has expert witnesses or people that are expert in these fields employed to do these investigations. They don't actually represent work for us or work for the defendant, they just analyze these items when they're sent to them at the State Crime Laboratory and whatever the results are, that's what they are. We say, or course, that he doesn't have any right to have someone else appointed and actually, when you really look to the substance of it, I don't know who the Court would appoint to do something like that and the only people that the State [has] to do those type things are the people at the Crime Laboratory.

6. *The Diagnostic and Statistical Manual of Mental Disorders*, or DSM, is the bible of American psychiatry. The DSM is the standard reference book that mental health professionals rely on to diagnose patients, researchers use to study mental illness, private and public insurers require to determine compensation for therapy, and courts turn to when ruling on insanity pleas and child custody decisions.

Chapter 11

Assistance of Counsel

A. Introduction

> In all criminal prosecutions, the accused shall enjoy the right ... to have
> the assistance of counsel for his defence. U.S. Const. amend. VI.

The Sixth Amendment, which provides a constitutional right to counsel at trial, says nothing of the quality of counsel required. This chapter examines standards governing the performance of counsel in capital cases. Drawing upon the "death is different" doctrine, the American Bar Association appears to hold defense counsel to a higher standard in capital as opposed to noncapital cases:

> Since the death penalty differs from other criminal penalties in its finality, defense counsel in a capital case should respond to this difference by making extraordinary efforts on behalf of the accused.

Standard 4-1.2(c) of the ABA Standards for Criminal Justice (3d ed. 1991).

Long before the Court recognized a Sixth Amendment right to court-appointed counsel for indigent defendants in capital cases, it held that the Fourteenth Amendment Due Process Clause embodied that guarantee.

Powell v. Alabama
287 U.S. 45 (1932)

Mr. Justice SUTHERLAND delivered the opinion of the Court.

These cases were argued together and submitted for decision as one case. The petitioners, hereinafter referred to as defendants, are negroes charged with the crime of rape, committed upon the persons of two white girls. The crime is said to have been committed on March 25, 1931. The indictment was returned in a state court of first instance on March 31, and the record recites that on the same day the defendants were arraigned and entered pleas of not guilty. There is a further recital to the effect that upon the arraignment they were represented by counsel. But no counsel had been employed, and aside from a statement made by the trial judge several days later during a colloquy immediately preceding the trial, the record does not disclose when, or under what circumstances, an appointment of counsel was made, or who was appointed. During the colloquy referred to, the trial judge, in response to a question, said that he had appointed all the members of the bar for the purpose of arraigning the defendants and then of course anticipated that the members of the bar would continue to help the defendants if no counsel appeared. Upon the argument here both sides accepted that as a correct statement of the facts concerning the matter.

There was a severance upon the request of the state, and the defendants were tried in three several groups, as indicated above. As each of the three cases was called for trial, each defendant was arraigned, and, having the indictment read to him, entered a plea of not guilty. Whether the original arraignment and pleas were regarded as ineffective is not shown. Each of the three trials was completed within a single day. Under the Alabama statute the punishment for rape is to be fixed by the jury, and in its discretion may be from ten years imprisonment to death. The juries found defendants guilty and imposed the death penalty upon all. The trial court overruled motions for new trials and sentenced defendants in accordance with the verdicts. The judgments were affirmed by the state supreme court. Chief Justice Anderson [of the Alabama Supreme Court] thought defendants had not been accorded a fair trial and strongly dissented.

In this court the judgments are assailed upon the grounds that defendants, and each of them, were denied due process of law and equal protection of the laws, in contravention of the Fourteenth Amendment, specifically as follows: (1) they were not given a fair, impartial and deliberate trial; (2) they were denied the right of counsel, with the accustomed incidents of consultation and opportunity of preparation for trial; and (3) they were tried before juries from which qualified members of their own race were systematically excluded. These questions were properly raised and saved in the courts below.

The only one of the assignments which we shall consider is the second, in respect of the denial of counsel; and it becomes unnecessary to discuss the facts of the case or the circumstances surrounding prosecution except in so far as they reflect light upon that question.

The record does not disclose [the defendants'] ages, except one of them was nineteen; but the record clearly indicates that most, if not all, of them were youthful, and they are constantly referred to as "the boys." They were ignorant and illiterate. All of them were residents of other states, where alone members of their families or friends resided.

However guilty defendants, upon due inquiry, might prove to have been, they were, until convicted, presumed to be innocent. It was duty of the court having their cases in charge to see that they were denied no necessary incident of a fair trial. With any error of the state court involving alleged contravention of the state statutes or Constitution we, of course, have nothing to do. The sole inquiry which we permitted to make is whether the federal Constitution was contravened; and as to that, we confine ourselves, as already suggested, to the inquiry whether the defendants were in substance denied the right of counsel and if so, whether such denial infringes the due process clause of the Fourteenth Amendment.

First. The record shows that immediately upon the return of indictment defendants were arraigned and pleaded not guilty. Apparently they were not asked whether they had, or were able to employ counsel, or wished to have counsel appointed; or whether they had friends or relatives who might assist in that regard if communicated with. That it would not have been an idle ceremony to have given defendants reasonable opportunity to communicate with their families and endeavor to obtain counsel is demonstrated by the fact that, very soon after conviction, able counsel appeared in their behalf. This was pointed out by Chief Justice Anderson in the course of his dissenting opinion. "They were nonresidents," he said, "and had little time or opportunity to get in touch with their families and friends who were scattered throughout two other states, and time has demonstrated that they could or would have been represented by able counsel had a better opportunity been given by a reasonable delay in the trial of the cases, judging from the number and activity of counsel that appeared immediately or shortly after their conviction."

It is hardly necessary to say that, the right to counsel being conceded, a defendant should be afforded a fair opportunity to secure counsel of his own choice. Not only was that not done here, but such designation of counsel as was attempted was either so indefinite or so close upon the trial as to amount to a denial of effective and substantial aid in that regard. This will be amply demonstrated by a brief review of the record.

April 6, six days after indictment, the trials began. When the first case was called, the court inquired whether the parties were ready for trial. The state's attorney replied that he was ready to proceed. No one answered for the defendants or appeared to represent or defend them. Mr. Roddy, a Tennessee lawyer not a member of the local bar, addressed the court, saying that he had not been employed, but that people who were interested had spoken to him about the case. He was asked by the court whether he intended to appear for the defendants, and answered that he would like to appear along with counsel that the court might appoint.

It thus will be seen that until the very morning of the trial no lawyer had been named or definitely designated to represent the defendants. Prior to that time, the trial judge had "appointed all the members of the bar" for the limited "purpose of arraigning the defendants." Whether they would represent the defendants thereafter if no counsel appeared in their behalf, was a matter of speculation only, or, as the judge indicated, of mere anticipation on the part of the court. Such a designation, even if made for all purposes, would, in our opinion, have fallen far short of meeting, in any proper sense, a requirement for the appointment of counsel. How many lawyers were members of the bar does not appear; but, in the very nature of things, whether many or few, they would not, thus collectively named, have been given that clear appreciation of responsibility or impressed with that individual sense of duty which should and naturally would accompany the appointment of a selected member of the bar, specifically named and assigned.

That this action of the trial judge in respect of appointment of counsel was little more than an expansive gesture, imposing no substantial or definite obligation upon any one, is borne out by the fact that prior to the calling of the case for trial on April 6, a leading member of the local bar accepted employment on the side of the prosecution and actively participated in the trial. It is true that he said that before doing so he had understood Mr. Roddy would be employed as counsel for the defendants. This the lawyer in question, of his own accord, frankly stated to the court; and no doubt he acted with the utmost good faith. Probably other members of the bar had a like understanding. In any event, the circumstance lends emphasis to the conclusion that during perhaps the most critical period of the proceedings against these defendants, that is to say, from the time of their arraignment until the beginning of their trial, when consultation, thoroughgoing investigation and preparation were vitally important, the defendants did not have the aid of counsel in any real sense, although they were as much entitled to such aid during that period as at the trial itself.

Nor do we think the situation was helped by what occurred on the morning of the trial. At that time, as appears from the [record], Mr. Roddy stated to the court that he did not appear as counsel, but that he would like to appear along with counsel that the court might appoint; that he had not been given an opportunity to prepare the case; that he was not familiar with the procedure in Alabama, but merely came down as a friend of the people who were interested; that he thought the boys would be better off if he should step entirely out of the case. Mr. Moody, a member of the local bar, expressed a willingness to help Mr. Roddy in anything he could do under the circumstances. To this the court responded, "All right, all the lawyers that will; of course I would not require a lawyer to appear if—." And Mr. Moody continued, "I am willing to do that for him as a member of the bar; I will go ahead and help do any thing I can do." With this dubious understanding, the trials immediately proceeded. The defendants, young, ignorant, illiterate, surrounded by hostile sentiment, haled back and forth under guard soldiers, charged with an atrocious crime regarded with especial horror in the community where they were to be tried, were thus put in peril of their lives within a few moments after counsel for the first time charged with any degree of responsibility began to represent them.

It is not enough to assume that counsel thus precipitated into this case thought there was no defense, and exercised their best judgment proceeding to trial without preparation. Neither they nor the court could say what a prompt and thoroughgoing investigation might disclose as to the facts. No attempt was made to investigate. No opportunity to do so was given. Defendants were immediately hurried to trial. Chief Justice Anderson, after disclaiming any intention to criticize harshly counsel who attempted to represent defendants at the trials, said: "The record indicates that the appearance was rather *pro forma* than zealous and active." Under the circumstances disclosed, we hold that defendants were not accorded the right of counsel in any substantial sense. To decide otherwise, would simply be to ignore actualities.

It is true that great and inexcusable delay in the enforcement of our criminal law is one of the grave evils of our time. Continuances are frequently granted for unnecessarily long periods of time, and delays incident to the disposition of motions for new trial and hearings upon appeal have come in many cases to be a distinct reproach to the administration of justice. The prompt disposition of criminal cases is to be commended and encouraged. But in reaching that result a defendant charged with a serious crime must not be stripped of his right to have sufficient time to advise with counsel and prepare his defense. To do that is not to proceed promptly in the calm spirit of regulated justice but to go forward with the haste of the mob.

Second. The Constitution of Alabama provides that in all criminal prosecutions the accused shall enjoy the right to have the assistance of counsel; and a state statute requires the court in a capital case, where the defendant is unable to employ counsel, to appoint counsel for him. The state supreme court held that these provisions had not been infringed, and with that holding we are powerless to interfere. The question, however, which it is our duty, and within our power, to decide, is whether the denial of the assistance of counsel contravenes the due process clause of the Fourteenth Amendment to the Federal Constitution.

It never has been doubted by this court, or any other so far as we know, that notice and hearing are preliminary steps essential to the passing of an enforceable judgment, and that they, together with a legally competent tribunal having jurisdiction of the case, constitute basic elements of the constitutional requirement of due process of law. The words of Webster, so often quoted, that by "the law of the land" is intended "a law which hears before it condemns," have been repeated in varying forms of expression in a multitude of decisions.

What, then, does a hearing include? Historically and in practice, in our own country at least, it has always included the right to the aid of counsel when desired and provided by the party asserting the right. The right to be heard would be, in many cases, of little avail if it did not comprehend the right to be heard by counsel. Even the intelligent and educated layman has small and sometimes no skill in the science of law. If charged with crime, he is incapable, generally, of determining for himself whether the indictment is good or bad. He is unfamiliar with the rules of evidence. Left without the aid of counsel he may be put on trial without a proper charge, and convicted upon incompetent evidence, or evidence irrelevant to the issue or otherwise inadmissible. He lacks both the skill and knowledge adequately to prepare his defense, even though he have a perfect one. He requires the guiding hand of counsel at every step in the proceedings against him. Without it, though he be not guilty, he faces the danger of conviction because he does not know how to establish his innocence. If that be true of men of intelligence, how much more true is it of the ignorant and illiterate, or those of feeble intellect. If in any case, civil or criminal, a state or federal court were arbitrarily to refuse to hear a party by counsel, employed by and appearing for him, it reasonably may not be doubted that such a refusal would be a denial of a hearing, and, therefore, of due process in the constitutional sense.

In the light of the facts outlined in the forepart of this opinion — the ignorance and illiteracy of the defendants, their youth, the circumstances of public hostility, the imprisonment and the close surveillance of the defendants by the military forces, the fact that their friends and families were all in other states and communication with them necessarily difficult, and above all that they stood in deadly peril of their lives — we think the failure of the trial court to give them reasonable time and opportunity to secure counsel was a clear denial of due process.

But passing that, and assuming their inability, even if opportunity had been given, to employ counsel, as the trial court evidently did assume, we are of opinion that, under the circumstances just stated, the necessity of counsel was so vital and imperative that the failure of the trial court to make an effective appointment of counsel was likewise a denial of due process within the meaning of the Fourteenth Amendment. Whether this would be so in other criminal prosecutions, or under other circumstances, we need not determine. All that it is necessary now to decide, as we do decide, is that in a capital case, where the defendant is unable to employ counsel, and is incapable adequately of making his own defense because of ignorance, feeble mindedness, illiteracy, or the like, it is the duty of the court, whether requested or not, to assign counsel for him as a necessary requisite of due process of law; and that duty is not discharged by an assignment at such a time or under such circumstances as to preclude the giving of effective aid in the preparation and trial of the case. To hold otherwise would be to ignore the fundamental postulate, already adverted to, "that there are certain immutable principles of justice which inhere in the very idea of free government which no member of the Union may disregard."

The judgments must be reversed and the causes remanded for further proceedings not inconsistent with this opinion.

Mr. Justice BUTLER, dissenting.

If there had been any lack of opportunity for preparation, trial counsel would have applied to the court for postponement. No such application was made. There was no suggestion, at the trial or in the motion for a new trial which they made, that Mr. Roddy or Mr. Moody was denied such opportunity or that they were not in fact fully prepared. The amended motion for new trial, by counsel who succeeded them, contains the first suggestion that defendants were denied counsel or opportunity to prepare for trial. But neither Mr. Roddy nor Mr. Moody has given any support to that claim. Their silence requires a finding that the claim is groundless, for if it had any merit they would be bound to support it. And no one has come to suggest any lack of zeal or good faith on their part.

B. The Constitutional Standard of Effective Assistance of Counsel

Strickland v. Washington
466 U.S. 668 (1984)

Justice O'CONNOR delivered the opinion of the Court.

This case requires us to consider the proper standards for judging a criminal defendant's contention that the Constitution requires a conviction or death sentence to be set aside because counsel's assistance at the trial or sentencing was ineffective.

I

A

During a ten-day period in September 1976, respondent David Washington planned and committed three groups of crimes, which included three brutal stabbing murders, torture, kidnapping, severe assaults, attempted murders, attempted extortion, and theft. After his two accomplices were arrested, respondent surrendered to police and voluntarily gave a lengthy statement confessing to the third of the criminal episodes. The State of Florida indicted respondent for kidnapping and murder and appointed an experienced criminal lawyer to represent him.

Counsel actively pursued pretrial motions and discovery. He cut his efforts short, however, and he experienced a sense of hopelessness about the case, when he learned that, against his specific advice, respondent had also confessed to the first two murders. By the date set for trial, respondent was subject to indictment for three counts of first degree murder and multiple counts of robbery, kidnapping for ransom, breaking and entering and assault, attempted murder, and conspiracy to commit robbery. Respondent waived his right to a jury trial, again acting against counsel's advice, and pleaded guilty to all charges, including the three capital murder charges.

In the plea colloquy, respondent told the trial judge that, although he had committed a string of burglaries, he had no significant prior criminal record and that at the time of his criminal spree he was under extreme stress caused by his inability to support his family. He also stated, however, that he accepted responsibility for the crimes. The trial judge told respondent that he had "a great deal of respect for people who are willing to step forward and admit their responsibility" but that he was making no statement at all about his likely sentencing decision.

Counsel advised respondent to invoke his right under Florida law to an advisory jury at his capital sentencing hearing. Respondent rejected the advice and waived the right. He chose instead to be sentenced by the trial judge without a jury recommendation.

In preparing for the sentencing hearing, counsel spoke with respondent about his background. He also spoke on the telephone with respondent's wife and mother, though he did not follow up on the one unsuccessful effort to meet with them. He did not otherwise seek out character witnesses for respondent. Nor did he request a psychiatric examination, since his conversations with his client gave no indication that respondent had psychological problems.

Counsel decided not to present and hence not to look further for evidence concerning respondent's character and emotional state. That decision reflected trial counsel's sense of hopelessness about overcoming the evidentiary effect of respondent's confessions to the gruesome crimes. It also reflected the judgment that it was advisable to rely on the plea colloquy for evidence about respondent's background and about his claim of emotional stress: the plea colloquy communicated sufficient information about these subjects, and by foregoing the opportunity to present new evidence on these subjects, counsel prevented the State from cross-examining respondent on his claim and from putting on psychiatric evidence of its own.

Counsel also excluded from the sentencing hearing other evidence he thought was potentially damaging. He successfully moved to exclude respondent's "rap sheet." Because he judged that a presentence report might prove more detrimental than helpful, as it would have included respondent's criminal history and thereby undermined the claim of no significant history of criminal activity, he did not request that one be prepared.

At the sentencing hearing, counsel's strategy was based primarily on the trial judge's remarks at the plea colloquy as well as on his reputation as a sentencing judge who thought it important for a convicted defendant to own up to his crime. Counsel argued that respondent's remorse and acceptance of responsibility justified sparing him from the death penalty. Counsel also argued that respondent had no history of criminal activity and that respondent committed the crimes under extreme mental or emotional disturbance, thus coming within the statutory list of mitigating circumstances. He further argued that respondent should be spared death because he had surrendered, confessed, and offered to testify against a co-defendant and because respondent was fundamentally a good person who had briefly gone badly wrong in extremely stressful circumstances. The State put on evidence and witnesses largely for the purpose of describing the details of the crimes. Counsel did not cross-examine the medical experts who testified about the manner of death of respondent's victims.

… [T]he trial judge found numerous aggravating circumstances and no (or a single comparatively insignificant) mitigating circumstance. With respect to each of the three convictions for capital murder, the trial judge concluded: "A careful consideration of all matters presented to the court impels the conclusion that there are insufficient mitigating circumstances … to outweigh the aggravating circumstances…." He therefore sentenced respondent to death on each of the three counts of murder and to prison terms for the other crimes.…

II

… [Respondent subsequently sought relief, claiming that he received ineffective assistance of counsel at his capital sentencing proceeding. Initially, the Court found that a] capital sentencing proceeding like the one involved in this case … is sufficiently like a trial in its adversarial format and in the existence of standards for decision, that counsel's role in the proceeding is comparable to counsel's role at trial—to ensure that the adversarial testing process works to produce a just result under the standards governing decision. For purposes of describing counsel's duties, therefore, Florida's capital sentencing proceeding need not be distinguished from an ordinary trial.

III

A convicted defendant's claim that counsel's assistance was so defective as to require reversal of a conviction or death sentence has two components. First, the defendant must show that counsel's performance was deficient. This requires showing that counsel made errors so serious that counsel was not functioning as the "counsel" guaranteed the defendant by the Sixth Amendment. Second, the defendant must show that the deficient performance prejudiced the defense. This requires showing that counsel's errors were so serious as to deprive the defendant of a fair trial, a trial whose result is reliable. Unless a defendant makes both showings, it cannot be said that the conviction or death sentence resulted from a breakdown in the adversary process that renders the result unreliable.

A

As all the Federal Courts of Appeals have now held, the proper standard for attorney performance is that of reasonably effective assistance. The Court indirectly recognized as much when it stated in *McMann v. Richardson*, 397 U.S., at 770, 771, that a guilty plea cannot be attacked as based on inadequate legal advice unless counsel was not "a reasonably competent attorney" and the advice was not "within the range of competence demanded of attorneys in criminal cases." When a convicted defendant complains of the ineffectiveness of counsel's assistance, the defendant must show that counsel's representation fell below an objective standard of reasonableness.

More specific guidelines are not appropriate. The Sixth Amendment refers simply to "counsel," not specifying particular requirements of effective assistance. It relies instead on the legal profession's maintenance of standards sufficient to justify the law's presumption that counsel will fulfill the role in the adversary process that the Amendment envisions. The proper measure of attorney performance remains simply reasonableness under prevailing professional norms.

Representation of a criminal defendant entails certain basic duties. Counsel's function is to assist the defendant, and hence counsel owes the client a duty of loyalty, a duty to avoid conflicts of interest. From counsel's function as assistant to the defendant derive the overarching duty to advocate the defendant's cause and the more particular duties to consult with the defendant on important decisions and to keep the defendant informed of important developments in the course of the prosecution. Counsel also has a duty to bring to bear such skill and knowledge as will render the trial a reliable adversarial testing process.

These basic duties neither exhaustively define the obligations of counsel nor form a checklist for judicial evaluation of attorney performance. In any case presenting an ineffectiveness claim, the performance inquiry must be whether counsel's assistance was reasonable considering all the circumstances. Prevailing norms of practice as reflected in American Bar Association standards and the like are guides to determining what is reasonable, but they are only guides. No particular set of detailed rules for counsel's conduct can satisfactorily take account of the variety of circumstances faced by defense counsel or the range of legitimate decisions regarding how best to represent a criminal defendant. Any such set of rules would interfere with the constitutionally protected independence of counsel and restrict the wide latitude counsel must have in making tactical decisions. Indeed, the existence of detailed guidelines for representation could distract counsel from the overriding mission of vigorous advocacy of the defendant's cause. Moreover, the purpose of the effective assistance guarantee of the Sixth Amendment is not to improve the quality of legal representation, although that is a goal of considerable importance to the legal system. The purpose is simply to ensure that criminal defendants receive a fair trial.

Judicial scrutiny of counsel's performance must be highly deferential. It is all too tempting for a defendant to second-guess counsel's assistance after conviction or adverse sentence, and it is all too easy for a court, examining counsel's defense after it has proved unsuccessful, to conclude that a particular act or omission of counsel was unreasonable. A fair assessment of attorney performance requires that every effort be made to eliminate the distorting effects of hindsight, to reconstruct the circumstances of counsel's challenged conduct, and to evaluate the conduct from counsel's perspective at the time. Because of the difficulties inherent in making the evaluation, a court must indulge a strong presumption that counsel's conduct falls within the wide range of reasonable professional assistance; that is, the defendant must overcome the presumption that, under the circumstances, the challenged action "might be considered sound trial strategy." There are countless ways to provide effective assistance in any given case. Even the best criminal defense attorneys would not defend a particular client in the same way. Thus, a court deciding an actual ineffectiveness claim must judge the reasonableness of counsel's challenged conduct on the facts of the particular case, viewed as of the time of counsel's conduct. A convicted defendant making a claim of ineffective assistance must identify the acts or omissions of counsel that are alleged not to have been the result of reasonable professional judgment. The court must then determine whether, in light of all the circumstances, the identified acts or omissions were outside the wide range of professionally competent assistance. In making that determination, the court should keep in mind that counsel's function, as elaborated in prevailing professional norms, is to make the adversarial testing process work in the particular case. At the same time, the court should recognize that counsel is strongly presumed to have rendered adequate assistance and made all significant decisions in the exercise of reasonable professional judgment.

These standards require no special amplification in order to define counsel's duty to investigate, the duty at issue in this case. As the Court of Appeals concluded, strategic choices made after thorough investigation of law and facts relevant to plausible options are virtually unchallengeable; and strategic choices made after less than complete investigation are reasonable precisely to the extent that reasonable professional judgments support the limitations on investigation. In other words, counsel has a duty to make reasonable investigations or to make a reasonable decision that makes particular investigations unnecessary. In any ineffectiveness case, a particular decision not to investigate must be directly assessed for reasonableness in all the circumstances, applying a heavy measure of deference to counsel's judgments.

The reasonableness of counsel's actions may be determined or substantially influenced by the defendant's own statements or actions. Counsel's actions are usually based, quite properly, on informed strategic choices made by the defendant and on information supplied by the defendant. In particular, what investigation decisions are reasonable depends critically on such information. For example, when the facts that support a certain potential line of defense are generally known to counsel because of what the defendant has said, the need for further investigation may be considerably diminished or eliminated altogether. And when a defendant has given counsel reason to believe that pursuing certain investigations would be fruitless or even harmful, counsel's failure to pursue those investigations may not later be challenged as unreasonable. In short, inquiry into counsel's conversations with the defendant may be critical to a proper assessment of counsel's investigation decisions, just as it may be critical to a proper assessment of counsel's other litigation decisions.

B

An error by counsel, even if professionally unreasonable, does not warrant setting aside the judgment of a criminal proceeding if the error had no effect on the judgment. The purpose of the Sixth Amendment guarantee of counsel is to ensure that a defendant has the assistance necessary to justify reliance on the outcome of the proceeding. Accordingly, any deficiencies in counsel's performance must be prejudicial to the defense in order to constitute ineffective assistance under the Constitution.

... [T]he appropriate test for prejudice ... [requires a defendant to] show that there is a reasonable probability that, but for counsel's unprofessional errors, the result of the proceeding would have been different. A reasonable probability is a probability sufficient to undermine confidence in the outcome....

The governing legal standard plays a critical role in defining the question to be asked in assessing the prejudice from counsel's errors. When a defendant challenges a conviction, the question is whether there is a reasonable probability that, absent the errors, the factfinder would have had a reasonable doubt respecting guilt. When a defendant challenges a death sentence such as the one at issue in this case, the question is whether there is a reasonable probability that, absent the errors, the sentencer — including an appellate court, to the extent it independently reweighs the evidence — would have concluded that the balance of aggravating and mitigating circumstances did not warrant death.

In making this determination, a court hearing an ineffectiveness claim must consider the totality of the evidence before the judge or jury. Some of the factual findings will have been unaffected by the errors, and factual findings that were affected will have been affected in different ways. Some errors will have had a pervasive effect on the inferences to be drawn from the evidence, altering the entire evidentiary picture, and some will have had an isolated, trivial effect. Moreover, a verdict or conclusion only weakly supported by the record is more likely to have been affected by errors than one with overwhelming record support. Taking the unaffected findings as a given, and taking due account of the effect of the errors on the remaining findings, a court making the prejudice inquiry must ask if the defendant has met the burden of showing that the decision reached would reasonably likely have been different absent the errors....

V

Having articulated general standards for judging ineffectiveness claims, we think it useful to apply those standards to the facts of this case in order to illustrate the meaning of the general principles....

Application of the governing principles is not difficult in this case. [The facts] make clear that the conduct of respondent's counsel at and before respondent's sentencing proceeding cannot be found unreasonable. They also make clear that, even assuming the challenged conduct of counsel was unreasonable, respondent suffered insufficient prejudice to warrant setting aside his death sentence.

With respect to the performance component, the record shows that respondent's counsel made a strategic choice to argue for the extreme emotional distress mitigating circumstance and to rely as fully as possible on respondent's acceptance of responsibility for his crimes. Although counsel understandably felt hopeless about respondent's prospects, nothing in the record indicates ... that counsel's sense of hopelessness distorted his professional judgment. Counsel's strategy choice was well within the range of professionally reasonable judgments, and the decision not to seek more character or psychological evidence than was already in hand was likewise reasonable.

The trial judge's views on the importance of owning up to one's crimes were well known to counsel. The aggravating circumstances were utterly overwhelming. Trial counsel could reasonably surmise from his conversations with respondent that character and psychological evidence would be of little help. Respondent had already been able to mention at the plea colloquy the substance of what there was to know about his financial and emotional troubles. Restricting testimony on respondent's character to what had come in at the plea colloquy ensured that contrary character and psychological evidence and respondent's criminal history, which counsel had successfully moved to exclude, would not come in. On these facts, there can be little question, even without application of the presumption of adequate performance, that trial counsel's defense, though unsuccessful, was the result of reasonable professional judgment.

With respect to the prejudice component, the lack of merit of respondent's claim is even more stark. The evidence that respondent says his trial counsel should have offered at the sentencing hearing would barely have altered the sentencing profile presented to the sentencing judge. As the state courts and District Court found, at most this evidence shows that numerous people who knew respondent thought he was generally a good person and that a psychiatrist and a psychologist believed he was under considerable emotional stress that did not rise to the level of extreme disturbance. Given the overwhelming aggravating factors, there is no reasonable probability that the omitted evidence would have changed the conclusion that the aggravating circumstances outweighed the mitigating circumstances and, hence, the sentence imposed. Indeed, admission of the evidence respondent now offers might even have been harmful to his case: his "rap sheet" would probably have been admitted into evidence, and the psychological reports would have directly contradicted respondent's claim that the mitigating circumstance of extreme emotional disturbance applied to his case....

Failure to make the required showing of either deficient performance or sufficient prejudice defeats the ineffectiveness claim. Here there is a double failure. More generally, respondent has made no showing that the justice of his sentence was rendered unreliable by a breakdown in the adversary process caused by deficiencies in counsel's assistance. Respondent's sentencing proceeding was not fundamentally unfair.

We conclude, therefore, that the District Court properly declined to issue a writ of habeas corpus. The judgment of the Court of Appeals is accordingly reversed.

Notes and Questions

1. As the Court held in *Strickland,* an error by counsel, even if professionally unreasonable, does not warrant setting aside a conviction or sentence unless the defendant also shows he was prejudiced by the error. In *United States v. Cronic,* 466 U.S. 648 (1984), the Court addressed whether counsel's performance may be so deficient that prejudice may be presumed. The Court stated, "[t]he presumption that counsel's assistance is essential requires us to conclude that a trial is unfair if the accused is denied counsel at a critical stage of the trial." In such cases, prejudice may be presumed. Further, the Court noted that in some cases where counsel is provided prejudice may be presumed if, "although counsel is available to assist the accused during trial, the likelihood that any lawyer, even a fully competent one, could provide effective assistance is so small that a presumption of prejudice is appropriate without inquiry into the actual

conduct of the trial." What circumstances do you think would give rise to a presumption of prejudice? What if counsel were appointed to represent a defendant charged with capital murder only days before trial? What if the defendant were only charged with petty larceny? What if an attorney who practices family law is appointed to represent a capital defendant in a highly complex murder trial? What if counsel suffers from alcoholism, drug addiction or senility during the course of the trial? What about Alzheimer's disease?

2. Prejudice may also be presumed where counsel is burdened by an actual conflict of interest. The *Strickland* Court stated, "[g]iven the obligation of counsel to avoid conflicts of interest and the ability of trial courts to make early inquiry in certain situations likely to give rise to conflicts, it is reasonable for the criminal justice system to maintain a fairly rigid rule of presumed prejudice for conflicts of interest.... Prejudice is presumed only if the defendant demonstrates that counsel 'actively represented conflicting interests' and 'that an actual conflict of interest adversely affected his lawyer's performance.'"

3. Justice Marshall dissented in *Strickland*, complaining that "the performance standard adopted by the Court is ... so malleable that, in practice, it will have no grip at all or will yield excessive variation in the manner in which the Sixth Amendment is interpreted and applied by different courts." Justice Marshall further commented:

> First, it is often very difficult to tell whether a defendant convicted after a trial on which he was ineffectively represented would have fared better if his lawyer had been competent. Seemingly impregnable cases can sometimes be dismantled by good defense counsel. On the basis of a cold record, it may be impossible for a reviewing court confidently to ascertain how the government's evidence and arguments would have stood up against rebuttal and cross-examination by a shrewd, well prepared lawyer....

> Second and more fundamentally, the assumption on which the Court's holding rests is that the only purpose of the constitutional guarantee of effective assistance of counsel is to reduce the chance that innocent persons will be convicted. In my view, the guarantee also functions to ensure that convictions are obtained only through fundamentally fair procedures.... Every defendant is entitled to a trial in which his interests are vigorously and conscientiously advocated by an able lawyer. A proceeding in which the defendant does not receive meaningful assistance in meeting the forces of the state does not, in my opinion, constitute due process.

How does the ABA Standard 4-1.2(c) quoted on the first page of this chapter compare to the *Strickland* standard?

4. Is the following interpretation of *Strickland* unnecessarily cynical?

> The Constitution, as interpreted by the courts, does not require that the accused, even in a capital case, be represented by able or effective counsel. It requires representation only by a lawyer who is not ineffective under the standard set by *Strickland v. Washington.* Proof that the lawyer was ineffective requires proof not only that the lawyer bungled but also that his errors likely affected the result. Ineffectiveness is not measured by the standards set by good lawyers but by the average — "reasonableness under prevailing professional norms" — and "judicial scrutiny of counsel's performance must be highly deferential." Consequently, accused persons who are represented by "not-legally-ineffective" lawyers may be condemned to die when the same accused, if represented by *effective* counsel, would receive at least the clemency of a life sentence.

Riles v. McCotter, 799 F.2d 947 (5th Cir. 1986) (Alvin B. Rubin, J., concurring).

5. In *Florida v. Nixon*, 543 U.S. 175, 193 (2004), the Court considered whether defense counsel's failure to obtain express consent from the defendant to a trial strategy in which guilt was conceded and that focused on the sentencing phase of the capital trial should be evaluated under the standards set forth in *United States v. Cronic*, 466 U.S. 648 (1984), or *Strickland v. Washington*, 466 U.S. 668 (1984). The Court concluded:

> To summarize, in a capital case, counsel must consider in conjunction both the guilt and penalty phases in determining how best to proceed. When counsel informs the defendant of the strategy counsel believes to be in the defendant's best interest and the defendant is unresponsive, counsel's strategic choice is not impeded by any blanket rule demanding the defendant's explicit consent. Instead, if counsel's strategy, given the evidence bearing on the defendant's guilt, satisfies the *Strickland* standard, that is the end of the matter; no tenable claim of ineffective assistance would remain.

Lockhart v. Fretwell
506 U.S. 364 (1993)

Chief Justice REHNQUIST delivered the opinion of the Court.

In this case we decide whether counsel's failure to make an objection in a state criminal sentencing proceeding—an objection that would have been supported by a decision which subsequently was overruled—constitutes "prejudice" within the meaning of our decision in *Strickland v. Washington*, 466 U.S. 668 (1984). Because the result of the sentencing proceeding in this case was rendered neither unreliable nor fundamentally unfair as a result of counsel's failure to make the objection, we answer the question in the negative. To hold otherwise would grant criminal defendants a windfall to which they are not entitled.

In August 1985, an Arkansas jury convicted respondent Bobby Ray Fretwell of capital felony murder. During the penalty phase, the State argued that the evidence presented during the guilt phase established two aggravating factors: (1) the murder was committed for pecuniary gain, and (2) the murder was committed to facilitate respondent's escape. [After the jury found that the evidence supported the first aggravating circumstance, but not the second, it] sentenced respondent to death.

On direct appeal, respondent argued, *inter alia*, that his sentence should be reversed in light of *Collins v. Lockhart*, 754 F.2d 258 (8th Cir. 1985). In that case the Court of Appeals for the Eighth Circuit held that a death sentence is unconstitutional if it is based on an aggravating factor that duplicates an element of the underlying felony, because such a factor does not genuinely narrow the class of persons eligible for the death penalty. Accordingly, respondent argued that his death sentence was unconstitutional because pecuniary gain is an element of the underlying felony in his capital felony murder conviction—murder in the course of a robbery. The Arkansas Supreme Court declined to consider whether to follow *Collins* because respondent failed to object to the use of the pecuniary gain aggravator during the sentencing proceeding. [The Arkansas court affirmed respondent's conviction and sentence.] ...

[Subsequently] respondent filed a petition seeking federal habeas corpus relief ... in the United States District Court for the Eastern District of Arkansas. Among other things, he argued that his trial counsel did not perform effectively because he failed to raise the *Collins* objection. The District Court held that counsel "had a duty to be aware of all law relevant to death penalty cases," and that failure to make the *Collins* objection amounted to prejudice under *Strickland*. The District Court granted habeas relief and conditionally vacated respondent's death sentence.

The Court of Appeals affirmed by a divided vote, even though it had two years earlier overruled its decision in *Collins* in light of our decision in *Lowenfield v. Phelps*, 484 U.S. 231 (1988) [*supra* chapter 7]. The majority believed that the Arkansas trial court was bound under the Supremacy Clause to obey the Eighth Circuit's interpretation of the Federal Constitution. Based on this belief, it reasoned that had counsel made the objection, the trial court would have sustained the objection and the jury would not have sentenced respondent to death. The court remanded, ordering the district court to sentence respondent to life imprisonment without the possibility of parole. It held that since respondent was entitled to the benefit of *Collins* at the time of his original sentencing proceeding, it would only "perpetuate the prejudice caused by the original sixth amendment violation" to resentence him under current law....

... In *Strickland*, we identified the two components to any ineffective assistance claim: (1) deficient performance and (2) prejudice.[1] Under our decisions, a criminal defendant alleging prejudice must show "that counsel's errors were so serious as to deprive the defendant of a fair trial, a trial whose result is reliable." Thus, an analysis focussing solely on mere outcome determination, without attention to whether the result of the proceeding was fundamentally unfair or unreliable, is defective. To set aside a conviction or sentence solely because the outcome would have been different but for counsel's error may grant the defendant a windfall to which the law does not entitle him.

Our decision in *Nix v. Whiteside*, 475 U.S. 157 (1986), makes this very point. The respondent in that case argued that he received ineffective assistance because his counsel refused to cooperate in presenting perjured testimony. Obviously, had the respondent presented false testimony to the jury, there might have been a reasonable probability that the jury would not have returned a verdict of guilty. Sheer outcome determination, however, was not sufficient to make out a claim under the Sixth Amendment. We held that "as a matter of law, counsel's conduct ... cannot establish the prejudice required for relief under the second strand of the *Strickland* inquiry." The touchstone of an ineffective assistance claim is the fairness of the adversary proceeding, and "in judging prejudice and the likelihood of a different outcome, '[a] defendant has no entitlement to the luck of a lawless decisionmaker.'"

The result of the sentencing proceeding in the present case was neither unfair nor unreliable. The Court of Appeals, which had decided *Collins* in 1985, overruled it in *Perry v. Lockhart*, 871 F.2d 1384 (8th Cir. 1989), four years later. Had the trial court chosen to follow *Collins*, counsel's error would have "deprived respondent of the chance to have the state court make an error in his favor."

Respondent argues that the use of hindsight is inappropriate in determining "prejudice" under *Strickland*, and that this element should be determined under the laws existing at the time of trial. For support, he relies upon language used in *Strickland* in discussing the first part of the necessary showing—deficient performance. We held that in order to determine whether counsel performed below the level expected from a reasonably competent attorney, it is necessary to "judge ... counsel's challenged conduct on the facts of the particular case, viewed as of the time of counsel's conduct."

---

1. Petitioner concedes that counsel's performance was deficient. He therefore focusses his argument exclusively on the prejudice component.

Ineffective assistance of counsel claims will be raised only in those cases where a defendant has been found guilty of the offense charged, and from the perspective of hindsight there is a natural tendency to speculate as to whether a different trial strategy might have been more successful. We adopted the rule of contemporary assessment of counsel's conduct because a more rigid requirement "could dampen the ardor and impair the independence of defense counsel, discourage the acceptance of assigned cases, and undermine the trust between attorney and client." But the "prejudice" component of the *Strickland* test does not implicate these concerns. It focusses on the question whether counsel's deficient performance renders the result of the trial unreliable or the proceeding fundamentally unfair. Unreliability or unfairness does not result if the ineffectiveness of counsel does not deprive the defendant of any substantive or procedural right to which the law entitles him. As we have noted, it was the premise of our grant in this case that *Perry* was correctly decided, *i.e.*, that respondent was not entitled to an objection based on "double counting." Respondent therefore suffered no prejudice from his counsel's deficient performance....

The judgment of the Court of Appeals is reversed.

Justice STEVENS, with whom Justice Blackmun joins, dissenting.

Concerned that respondent Fretwell would otherwise receive the "windfall" of life imprisonment, the Court today reaches the astonishing conclusion that deficient performance by counsel does not prejudice a defendant even when it results in the erroneous imposition of a death sentence. The Court's aversion to windfalls seems to disappear, however, when the State is the favored recipient. For the end result in this case is that the State, through the coincidence of inadequate representation and fortuitous timing, may carry out a death sentence that was invalid when imposed.

This extraordinary result rests entirely on the retrospective application of two changes in the law occurring after respondent's trial and sentencing. The first of these changes, on which the Court relies explicitly, affected the eligibility of defendants like Fretwell for the death penalty. The second change, never directly identified as such, is the Court's unprincipled transformation of the standards governing ineffective assistance claims, through the introduction of an element of hindsight that has no place in our Sixth Amendment jurisprudence.

I

... Hindsight has no place in a Sixth Amendment jurisprudence that focuses, quite rightly, on protecting the adversarial balance at trial. Respondent was denied "the assistance necessary to justify reliance on the outcome of the proceeding," because his counsel's performance was so far below professional standards that it satisfied *Strickland*'s first prong, and so severely lacking that the verdict "would reasonably likely have been different absent the errors" under the second prong. It is simply irrelevant that we can now say, with hindsight, that had counsel failed to make a [*Collins*] objection four years after the fact, his performance would have been neither deficient nor prejudicial. For as it happened, counsel's failure to object came at a time when it signified a breakdown in the adversarial process. A *post hoc* vision of what would have been the case years later has no bearing on the force of this showing.

Not surprisingly, the Court's reliance on hindsight finds no support in *Strickland* itself. *Strickland* makes clear that the merits of an ineffective assistance claim must be "viewed as of the time of counsel's conduct." As the Court notes, this point is stated explicitly with respect to *Strickland*'s first prong, the quality of counsel's performance.

What the Court ignores, however, is that the same point is implicit in *Strickland*'s entire discussion of the second prong. By defining prejudice in terms of the effect of counsel's errors on the outcome of the proceedings, based on the "totality of the evidence before the judge or jury," the *Strickland* Court establishes its point of reference firmly at the time of trial or sentencing.

To justify its revision of the *Strickland* standards for judging ineffective assistance claims, the Court relies in large part on *Nix v. Whiteside*. *Nix* cannot, however, perform the heavy duty the Court assigns it. A rather unusual case, *Nix* involved a claim that counsel was ineffective because he refused to present a defense based on perjured testimony. It should suffice to say here that reliance on perjured testimony and reliance on current Court of Appeals case law are not remotely comparable, and that to suggest otherwise is simply disingenuous. But if further distinction is needed, we need not search far to find it.

First, the Court's decision in *Nix* rests in part on the conclusion that counsel's refusal to cooperate in presentation of perjury falls "well within ... the range of reasonable professional conduct acceptable under *Strickland*." In other words, ineffective assistance claims predicated on failure to make wholly frivolous or unethical arguments will generally be dispensed with under *Strickland*'s first prong, without recourse to the second, and hence will not raise the questions at issue in this case.

To the extent that *Nix* does address *Strickland*'s second, or "prejudice," prong, it does so in a context quite different from that presented here. In *Strickland*, the Court cautioned that assessment of the likelihood of a different outcome should exclude the possibility of "a lawless decisionmaker," who fails to "reasonably, conscientiously, and impartially apply [ ] the standards that govern the decision." The *Nix* Court faced what is perhaps a paradigmatic example of the "lawlessness" to which *Strickland* referred, in the suggestion that perjured testimony might have undermined the decisionmaker's judgment, and concluded quite correctly that the defendant could not rely on any outcome-determinative effects of perjury to make his claim. I do not read the Court's decision today as suggesting that a state trial court need fear the label "lawless" if it follows the decision of a United States Court of Appeals on a matter of federal constitutional law. Accordingly, *Nix*'s discussion of perjury and lawlessness is simply inapposite to the issues presented here....

II

Respondent was convicted of committing murder in the course of a robbery. The Arkansas trial court then held a separate sentencing hearing, devoted exclusively to the question whether respondent was eligible for the death penalty, or would instead receive a life sentence without parole. The State relied on two aggravating circumstances to establish its right to execute respondent. The first—the alleged purpose of avoiding arrest—was found by the jury to be unsupported by the evidence. The second—that the felony was committed for purposes of pecuniary gain—was obviously supported by the evidence, as respondent had already been convicted of robbery in connection with the murder. Thus, the critical question on which respondent's death-eligibility turned was whether it was permissible, as a matter of law, to "double count" by relying on pecuniary gain as an aggravating circumstance and also on robbery as an element of the crime.

Counsel's duty at this stage of the proceedings was clear. In addition to general investigation and preparation for the penalty phase, counsel's primary obligation was to advise the trial judge about the correct answer to this crucial question of law. Had he handled this professional responsibility with anything approaching the "reasonableness" demanded by *Strickland*, he would have found an Eighth Circuit case directly on point, addressing the same Arkansas statute under which respondent was sentenced and holding such double counting unconstitutional. The failure to find that critically important case constitutes irrefutable evidence of counsel's inadequate performance. The fact that *Collins* was later overruled does not minimize in the slightest the force of that evidence.

Moreover, had counsel made a *Collins* objection to the pecuniary gain aggravating circumstance, we must assume that the trial court would have sustained it. As the District Court stated: "Although *Collins* has since been overruled, it was the law in the Eighth Circuit at the time of [respondent's] trial and this Court has no reason to believe that the trial court would have chosen to disregard it." Neither petitioner nor the Court relies on disagreement with this finding. Nor could they. As we explained in *Strickland*, it is not open to the State to argue that an idiosyncratic state trial judge might have refused to follow circuit precedent and overruled a *Collins* objection.

Applying *Strickland* to these facts, the District Court correctly held that counsel's failure to call the trial judge's attention to *Collins* constituted ineffective assistance and "seriously undermined the proper functioning of the adversarial process." Because it granted relief on this basis, the District Court found it unnecessary to reach additional ineffective assistance claims predicated on counsel's alleged failure to investigate or prepare for the penalty phase. By the time the case reached the Court of Appeals, deficient performance was conceded, and the Eighth Circuit had only to affirm the District Court conclusion that "a reasonable state trial court would have sustained an objection based on *Collins* had Fretwell's attorney made one."

... Under the *Strickland* standard that prevailed until today, respondent is entitled to relief on his ineffective assistance claim, having shown both deficient performance and a reasonable likelihood of a different outcome. The Court can avoid this result only by effecting a dramatic change in that standard, and then applying it retroactively to respondent's case. In my view, the Court's decision marks a startling and most unwise departure from our commitment to a system that ensures fairness and reliability by subjecting the prosecution's case to meaningful adversarial testing....

Terry Williams v. Taylor
529 U.S. 362 (2000)

Justice STEVENS announced the judgment of the Court and delivered the opinion of the Court with respect to Parts, I, III, and IV, and an opinion with respect to Parts II and V. Justice Souter, Justice Ginsburg, and Justice Breyer join Justice Stevens' opinion in its entirety. Justice O'CONNOR and Justice Kennedy joined Parts I, III, and IV of this opinion. Chief Justice Rehnquist, Justice Scalia and Justice Thomas dissent as to the Court's resolution of the petitioner's ineffective assistance of counsel claim.

[Parts I, III and IV of Justice Stevens' opinion concern the facts of this case and Terry Williams' ineffective assistance of trial counsel claim. These portions of the opinion are set forth below. Part II of Justice Stevens' opinion, and part II Justice O'Connor's concurring opinion, discuss the standard for reviewing such claims under the applicable federal habeas corpus statute. That portion of the decision is set forth more fully in chapter 13.]

The questions presented are whether Terry Williams' constitutional right to the effective assistance of counsel as defined in *Strickland v. Washington*, 466 U.S. 668 (1984), was violated, and whether the judgment of the Virginia Supreme Court refusing to set aside his death sentence "was contrary to, or involved an unreasonable application of, clearly established Federal law, as determined by the Supreme Court of the United States," within the meaning of 28 U.S.C. §2254(d)(1). We answer both questions affirmatively.

I

On November 3, 1985, Harris Stone was found dead in his residence on Henry Street in Danville, Virginia. Finding no indication of a struggle, local officials determined that the cause of death was blood alcohol poisoning, and the case was considered closed. Six months after Stone's death, Terry Williams, who was then incarcerated in the "I" unit of the city jail for an unrelated offense, wrote a letter to the police stating that he had killed "that man down on Henry Street" and also stating that he "did it" to that "lady down on West Green Street" and was "very sorry." The letter was unsigned, but it closed with a reference to "I cell." App. 41. The police readily identified Williams as its author, and, on April 25, 1986, they obtained several statements from him. In one Williams admitted that, after Stone refused to lend him "a couple of dollars," he had killed Stone with a mattock and took the money from his wallet. In September 1986, Williams was convicted of robbery and capital murder.

At Williams' sentencing hearing, the prosecution proved that Williams had been convicted of armed robbery in 1976 and burglary and grand larceny in 1982. The prosecution also introduced the written confessions that Williams had made in April. The prosecution described two auto thefts and two separate violent assaults on elderly victims perpetrated after the Stone murder. On December 4, 1985, Williams had started a fire outside one victim's residence before attacking and robbing him. On March 5, 1986, Williams had brutally assaulted an elderly woman on West Green Street—an incident he had mentioned in his letter to the police. That confession was particularly damaging because other evidence established that the woman was in a "vegetative state" and not expected to recover. Williams had also been convicted of arson for setting a fire in the jail while awaiting trial in this case. Two expert witnesses employed by the State testified that there was a "high probability" that Williams would pose a serious continuing threat to society.

The evidence offered by Williams' trial counsel at the sentencing hearing consisted of the testimony of Williams' mother, two neighbors, and a taped excerpt from a statement by a psychiatrist. One of the neighbors had not been previously interviewed by defense counsel, but was noticed by counsel in the audience during the proceedings and asked to testify on the spot. The three witnesses briefly described Williams as a "nice boy" and not a violent person. The recorded psychiatrist's testimony did little more than relate Williams' statement during an examination that in the course of one of his earlier robberies, he had removed the bullets from a gun so as not to injure anyone.

In his cross-examination of the prosecution witnesses, Williams' counsel repeatedly emphasized the fact that Williams had initiated the contact with the police that enabled them to solve the murder and to identify him as the perpetrator of the recent assaults, as well as the car thefts. In closing argument, Williams' counsel characterized Williams' confessional statements as "dumb," but asked the jury to give weight to the fact that he had "turned himself in, not on one crime but on four ... that the [police otherwise] would not have solved." The weight of defense counsel's closing, however, was devoted to explaining that it was difficult to find a reason why the jury should spare Williams' life.

The jury found a probability of future dangerousness and unanimously fixed Williams' punishment at death. The trial judge concluded that such punishment was "proper" and "just" and imposed the death sentence. The Virginia Supreme Court affirmed the conviction and sentence....

State Habeas Corpus Proceedings

In 1988 Williams filed for state collateral relief.... .[T]he Circuit Court (the same judge who had presided over Williams' trial and sentencing) held an evidentiary hearing on Williams' claim that trial counsel had been ineffective. Based on the evidence adduced after two days of hearings, Judge Ingram found that Williams' conviction was valid, but that his trial attorneys had been ineffective during sentencing. Among the evidence reviewed that had not been presented at trial were documents prepared in connection with Williams' commitment when he was 11 years old that dramatically described mistreatment, abuse, and neglect during his early childhood, as well as testimony that he was "borderline mentally retarded," had suffered repeated head injuries, and might have mental impairments organic in origin. The habeas hearing also revealed that the same experts who had testified on the State's behalf at trial believed that Williams, if kept in a "structured environment," would not pose a future danger to society.

Counsel's failure to discover and present this and other significant mitigating evidence was "below the range expected of reasonable, professional competent assistance of counsel." Counsels' performance thus "did not measure up to the standard required under the holding of *Strickland v. Washington,* and [if it had,] there is a reasonable probability that the result of the sentencing phase would have been different." Judge Ingram therefore recommended that Williams be granted a rehearing on the sentencing phase of his trial.

The Virginia Supreme Court did not accept that recommendation. Although it assumed, without deciding, that trial counsel had been ineffective, it disagreed with the trial judge's conclusion that Williams had suffered sufficient prejudice to warrant relief.... First, relying on our decision in *Lockhart v. Fretwell,* 506 U.S. 364 (1993), the [Virginia Supreme] [C]ourt held that it was wrong for the trial judge to rely " 'on mere outcome determination' " when assessing prejudice. Second, it construed the trial judge's opinion as having "adopted a *per se* approach" that would establish prejudice whenever any mitigating evidence was omitted.

The court then reviewed the prosecution evidence supporting the "future dangerousness" aggravating circumstance, reciting Williams' criminal history, including the several most recent offenses to which he had confessed. In comparison, it found that the excluded mitigating evidence—which it characterized as merely indicating "that numerous people, mostly relatives, thought that defendant was nonviolent and could cope very well in a structured environment,"—"barely would have altered the profile of this defendant that was presented to the jury." On this basis, the court concluded that there was no reasonable possibility that the omitted evidence would have affected the jury's sentencing recommendation, and that Williams had failed to demonstrate that his sentencing proceeding was fundamentally unfair.

Federal Habeas Corpus Proceedings

Having exhausted his state remedies, Williams sought a federal writ of habeas corpus pursuant to 28 U.S.C. §2254. After reviewing the state habeas hearing transcript and the state courts' findings of fact and conclusions of law, the federal trial judge agreed with the Virginia trial judge: The death sentence was constitutionally infirm....

The Federal Court of Appeals reversed. 163 F.3d 860 (C.A.4 1998).... It explained that the evidence that Williams presented a future danger to society was "simply overwhelming," it endorsed the Virginia Supreme Court's interpretation of *Lockhart,* and it characterized the state court's understanding of the facts in this case as "reasonable."

We granted certiorari, and now reverse....

III

In this case, Williams contends that he was denied his constitutionally guaranteed right to the effective assistance of counsel when his trial lawyers failed to investigate and to present substantial mitigating evidence to the sentencing jury.... We explained in *Strickland* that a violation of the right on which Williams relies has two components:

> First, the defendant must show that counsel's performance was deficient. This requires showing that counsel made errors so serious that counsel was not functioning as the 'counsel' guaranteed the defendant by the Sixth Amendment. Second, the defendant must show that the deficient performance prejudiced the defense. This requires showing that counsel's errors were so serious as to deprive the defendant of a fair trial, a trial whose result is reliable.

To establish ineffectiveness, a "defendant must show that counsel's representation fell below an objective standard of reasonableness." To establish prejudice he "must show that there is a reasonable probability that, but for counsel's unprofessional errors, the result of the proceeding would have been different. A reasonable probability is a probability sufficient to undermine confidence in the outcome." ...

IV

The Virginia Supreme Court erred in holding that our decision in *Lockhart v. Fretwell,* modified or in some way supplanted the rule set down in *Strickland.* It is true that while the *Strickland* test provides sufficient guidance for resolving virtually all ineffective-assistance-of-counsel claims, there are situations in which the overriding focus on fundamental fairness may affect the analysis. Thus, on the one hand, as *Strickland* itself explained, there are a few situations in which prejudice may be presumed. And, on the other hand, there are also situations in which it would be unjust to characterize the likelihood of a different outcome as legitimate "prejudice." Even if a defendant's false testimony might have persuaded the jury to acquit him, it is not fundamentally unfair to conclude that he was not prejudiced by counsel's interference with his intended perjury. *Nix v. Whiteside,* 475 U.S. 157, 175–176 (1986).

Similarly, in *Lockhart,* we concluded that, given the overriding interest in fundamental fairness, the likelihood of a different outcome attributable to an incorrect interpretation of the law should be regarded as a potential "windfall" to the defendant rather than the legitimate "prejudice" contemplated by our opinion in *Strickland.* The death sentence that Arkansas had imposed on Bobby Ray Fretwell was based on an aggravating circumstance (murder committed for pecuniary gain) that duplicated an element of the underlying felony (murder in the course of a robbery). Shortly before the trial, the United States Court of Appeals for the Eighth Circuit had held that such "double counting" was impermissible, see *Collins v. Lockhart,* 754 F.2d 258, 265 (1985), but Fretwell's lawyer (presumably because he was unaware of the *Collins* decision) failed to object to the use of the pecuniary gain aggravator. Before Fretwell's claim for federal habeas corpus relief reached this Court, the *Collins* case was overruled. Accordingly, even though the Arkansas trial judge probably would have sustained a timely objection to the double counting, it had become clear that the State had a right to rely on the disputed aggravating circumstance. Because the ineffectiveness of Fretwell's counsel had not deprived him of any substantive or procedural right to which the law entitled him, we held that his claim did not satisfy the "prejudice" component of the *Strickland* test.

Cases such as *Nix v. Whiteside,* and *Lockhart v. Fretwell,* do not justify a departure from a straightforward application of *Strickland* when the ineffectiveness of counsel *does* deprive the defendant of a substantive or procedural right to which the law entitles him. In the instant case, it is undisputed that Williams had a right — indeed, a constitutionally protected right — to provide the jury with the mitigating evidence that his trial counsel either failed to discover or failed to offer.

Nevertheless, the Virginia Supreme Court read our decision in *Lockhart* to require a separate inquiry into fundamental fairness even when Williams is able to show that his lawyer was ineffective and that his ineffectiveness probably affected the outcome of the proceeding.... Unlike the Virginia Supreme Court, the state trial judge omitted any reference to *Lockhart* and simply relied on our opinion in *Strickland* as stating the correct standard for judging ineffective-assistance claims.... The trial judge analyzed the ineffective-assistance claim under the correct standard; the Virginia Supreme Court did not.

We are likewise persuaded that the Virginia trial judge correctly applied both components of that standard to Williams' ineffectiveness claim. Although he concluded that counsel competently handled the guilt phase of the trial, he found that their representation during the sentencing phase fell short of professional standards — a judgment barely disputed by the State in its brief to this Court. The record establishes that counsel did not begin to prepare for that phase of the proceeding until a week before the trial. They failed to conduct an investigation that would have uncovered extensive records graphically describing Williams' nightmarish childhood, not because of any strategic calculation but because they incorrectly thought that state law barred access to such records. Had they done so, the jury would have learned that Williams' parents had been imprisoned for the criminal neglect of Williams and his siblings, that Williams had been severely and repeatedly beaten by his father, that he had been committed to the custody of the social services bureau for two years during his parents' incarceration (including one stint in an abusive foster home), and then, after his parents were released from prison, had been returned to his parents' custody.

Counsel failed to introduce available evidence that Williams was "borderline mentally retarded" and did not advance beyond sixth grade in school. They failed to seek prison records recording Williams' commendations for helping to crack a prison drug ring and for returning a guard's missing wallet, or the testimony of prison officials who described Williams as among the inmates "least likely to act in a violent, dangerous or provocative way." Counsel failed even to return the phone call of a certified public accountant who had offered to testify that he had visited Williams frequently when Williams was incarcerated as part of a prison ministry program, that Williams "seemed to thrive in a more regimented and structured environment," and that Williams was proud of the carpentry degree he earned while in prison.

Of course, not all of the additional evidence was favorable to Williams. The juvenile records revealed that he had been thrice committed to the juvenile system — for aiding and abetting larceny when he was 11 years old, for pulling a false fire alarm when he was 12, and for breaking and entering when he was 15. But ... the failure to introduce the comparatively voluminous amount of evidence that did speak in Williams' favor was not justified by a tactical decision to focus on Williams' voluntary confession. Whether or not those omissions were sufficiently prejudicial to have affected the outcome of sentencing, they clearly demonstrate that trial counsel did not fulfill their obligation to conduct a thorough investigation of the defendant's background.

We are also persuaded ... that counsel's unprofessional service prejudiced Williams within the meaning of *Strickland*. After hearing the additional evidence developed in the postconviction proceedings, the very judge who presided at Williams' trial and who once determined that the death penalty was "just" and "appropriate," concluded that there existed "a reasonable probability that the result of the sentencing phase would have been different" if the jury had heard that evidence. We do not agree ... that Judge Ingram's conclusion should be discounted because he apparently adopted "a *per se* approach to the prejudice element" that placed undue "emphasis on mere outcome determination." Judge Ingram did stress the importance of mitigation evidence in making his "outcome determination," but it is clear that his predictive judgment rested on his assessment of the totality of the omitted evidence rather than on the notion that a single item of omitted evidence, no matter how trivial, would require a new hearing....

V

In our judgment, the state trial judge was correct both in his recognition of the established legal standard for determining counsel's effectiveness, and in his conclusion that the entire postconviction record, viewed as a whole and cumulative of mitigation evidence presented originally, raised "a reasonable probability that the result of the sentencing proceeding would have been different" if competent counsel had presented and explained the significance of all the available evidence ...

Accordingly, the judgment of the Court of Appeals is reversed, and the case is remanded for further proceedings consistent with this opinion.

Note on Procedural Bar and Claims of Ineffective Assistance of Counsel

In *Massaro v. United States*, 538 U.S. 500 (2003), a non-capital case, the Supreme Court refused to limit federal appeals involving claims of ineffective assistance of counsel. Joseph Massaro, described by prosecutors as a soldier in the Luchese organized crime family, was sentenced to life for the 1990 killing of a mob partner in a dispute over gambling profits. Three days into Massaro's trial, prosecutors introduced new evidence—a bullet—which apparently caught Massaro's defense attorney by surprise. However, on direct appeal from his conviction, Massaro did not claim that his trial counsel was ineffective.

Massaro raised the ineffectiveness claim for the first time in his federal habeas petition. The Bush administration urged the Supreme Court to hold that Massaro had raised the issue too late, and to use Massaro's case to limit the appeal options of persons convicted of federal crimes.

Justice Kennedy, writing for a majority of the Court, rejected the government's argument and held that it is appropriate to raise an ineffective assistance of counsel claim in post-conviction proceedings. Failure to raise the claim on direct appeal does not constitute a default of the claim.

Macias v. Collins

979 F.2d 1067 (5th Cir. 1992)

Patrick E. HIGGINBOTHAM, Circuit Judge:

We review today the judgment of the United States District Court granting a writ of habeas corpus on the petition of Federico Martinez Macias convicted of capital murder in Texas and now on death row in that state. We affirm the judgment below for essentially the reasons stated by the magistrate-judge in her report and recommendation, and the order of the district court adopting it. We have read the record, read the briefs, and heard oral argument. We are left with the firm conviction that Macias was denied his constitutional right to adequate counsel in a capital case in which actual innocence was a close question. The state paid defense counsel $11.84 per hour. Unfortunately, the justice system got only what it paid for.

The judgment granting the petition for habeas corpus is affirmed. The judgment of conviction is vacated and Federico Martinez Macias shall be released from custody if the State of Texas has not commenced a new trial within 120 days of our mandate.

Notes and Questions

1. Mr. Macias' post-conviction attorneys claimed that Macias' court-appointed trial attorney, Gary Weiser, was ineffective, *inter alia*, for failing to call an alibi witness, failing to adequately investigate the case and failing to do any meaningful preparation for the sentencing phase. A federal magistrate agreed, stating, "the errors that occurred in this case are inherent in a system which paid attorneys such a meager amount." Report and Recommendation of Magistrate Judge Ruesch, April 26, 1991, p. 5. Weiser, who spent more than ten years as a district attorney, had prosecuted seven or eight capital murder cases, and was partner in a prominent El Paso law firm at the time of his appointment to represent Macias. At a federal habeas hearing, Weiser testified that the inadequacy of his fee did not affect his representation. Magistrate Ruesch found that Weiser had been ineffective, even though "Mr. Weiser is, and in 1984 was, one of the best attorneys in El Paso. Thus, the trite-but-true lesson is that 'it can happen to the best of us.'" Do you agree with Magistrate Ruesch that ineffectiveness "can happen to the best" criminal attorneys? Can prosecutors be ineffective? Is the *state* entitled to effective assistance of counsel?

2. As illustrated by the *Macias* case, defense counsel who are appointed to represent indigent capital defendants are often grossly underpaid. Do you believe that compensation plays a role in the representation of capital defendants?

3. After nine and one half years on death row, Mr. Macias was set free on June 23, 1993 because an El Paso grand jury refused to reindict him. *Man Freed in Machete Murder Case*, El Paso Times, June 24, 1993, p. 1. Randall Coyne, one of Macias' post-conviction attorneys, calculated that he had been paid $7.76 per hour for his representation of Macias. National Law Journal, April 26, 1993, p. 3.

4. Justice Thurgood Marshall certainly believed that poverty was a natural ally of capital punishment.

> It ... is evident that the burden of capital punishment falls upon the poor, the ignorant, and the underprivileged members of society. It is the poor and the members of minority groups who are least able to voice their complaints

against capital punishment. Their impotence leaves them victims of a sanction that the wealthier, better-represented, just-as-guilty person can escape.

Furman v. Georgia, 408 U.S. 238, 365–66 (1972) (Marshall, J. concurring).

Similarly, Lewis E. Lawes, former warden of Sing Sing who presided over numerous executions, wrote:

Not only does capital punishment fail in its justification, but no punishment could be invented with so many inherent defects. It is an unequal punishment in the way it is applied to the rich and the poor. The defendant of wealth and position never goes to the electric chair or to the gallows. Juries do not intentionally favor the rich, the law is theoretically impartial, but the defendant with ample means is able to have his case presented with every favorable aspect, while the poor defendant often has a lawyer assigned by the court. Sometimes such assignment is considered part of political patronage; usually the lawyer assigned has had no experience whatever in a capital case.

Life and Death in Sing Sing 155–160 (1928).

Justice Powell responded to these arguments in his *Furman* dissent:

Certainly the claim is justified that this criminal sanction falls more heavily on the relatively impoverished and underprivileged elements of society. The "have-nots" in every society always have been subject to greater pressure to commit crimes and to fewer constraints than their more affluent fellow citizens. This is, indeed, a tragic byproduct of social and economic deprivation, but it is not an argument of constitutional proportions under the Eighth or Fourteenth Amendment. The same discriminatory impact argument could be made with equal force and logic with respect to those sentenced to prison terms. The Due Process Clause admits of no distinction between the deprivation of "life" and the deprivation of "liberty." If discriminatory impact renders capital punishment cruel and unusual, it likewise renders invalid most of the prescribed penalties for crimes of violence. The root causes of the higher incidence of criminal penalties on "minorities and the poor" will not be cured by abolishing the system of penalties. Nor, indeed, could any society have a viable system of criminal justice if sanctions were abolished or ameliorated because most of those who commit crimes happen to be underprivileged. The basic problem results not from the penalties imposed for criminal conduct but from social and economic factors that have plagued humanity since the beginning of recorded history, frustrating all efforts to create in any country at any time the perfect society in which there are no "poor," no "minorities" and no "underprivileged." The causes underlying this problem are unrelated to the constitutional issue before the Court.

Who has the better argument, Justice Marshall or Justice Powell?

5. State courts have wrestled with collateral Sixth Amendment issues. For example, in *Amadeo v. State*, 384 S.E.2d 181 (Ga. 1989), the court held that an indigent defendant's preference for a particular attorney, where the defendant had developed a confidential relationship of trust and confidence with the attorney, was entitled to some weight. And, where the newly-appointed counsel argued in favor of representation by the prior lawyers, based on the legal and factual complexities of the case, the defendant's interests outweighed the state's interest in involving local lawyers.

6. Statutory limitations placed on attorney's fees also have generated vigorous litigation. In *White v. Board of County Commissioners*, 537 So.2d 1376 (Fla. 1989), counsel

successfully challenged a statutory scheme which provided for a maximum fee cap of $3,500 unless the case was extraordinary and unusual. Counsel spent 134 hours as a court-appointed attorney for a first degree murder suspect and earned $26.12 per hour. The Florida Supreme Court found the statute unconstitutional as applied and observed:

> When an attorney is called upon by the state to represent an indigent defendant in a criminal case, not only is the attorney expected to provide legal services as part of his or her professional ethical obligation, but the state, as part of its constitutional obligation, must reasonably compensate the attorney for those services.

Moreover, any conflicts between the treasury and the fundamental constitutional rights of a criminal defendant were to be "firmly and unhesitatingly resolve[d] ... in favor of the latter."

In a 1988 Mississippi capital case, the hourly fee of defense attorneys worked out to be $2.98 as a result of that state's statutory limit on reimbursable hours. Paduano and Smith, "The Unconscionability of Sub-Minimum Wages Paid Appointed Counsel in Capital Cases," 43 Rutgers L. Rev. 281, 310–14 (1991).

How would you expect an attorney's fee to affect the quality of her representation? Might she spend fewer hours knowing that she would not be compensated beyond a certain point? What effect, if any, would a maximum fee cap have on her willingness to plea bargain? What about states, like Oklahoma, which award indigent defense contracts for an entire county to the lowest and best bidder in an auction? See Uphoff, "The Right to Appointed Counsel: Why Defendants in Oklahoma Still Are Unrepresented," 64 Okla. B.J. 918 (1993). Should capital cases be exempt from such a procedure?

In Alabama, low maximum hourly rates for work performed by appointed capital trial counsel and trial courts' exercise of discretion to deny compensation for hours admittedly worked has resulted in Alabama trial lawyers "often" limiting themselves to 50 hours or less on capital cases, even though "adequate preparation ... should take 500 to 1,000 hours." Lawyers who put in the necessary hours are compensated at a rate of about $5 per hour. This harsh reality convinced one under-compensated capital defense attorney to vow: "I will go to jail before I handle another capital case." Rimer, *Questions of Death Row Justice for Poor People in Alabama*, The New York Times, Feb. 5, 2000, at A1.

The harsh realities capital defense attorneys have faced in Alabama for the last two decades are well known to attorney Bob French, appointed to handle the 1983 capital murder defense of indigent Judith Ann Neelley. French argued that Neelley was a battered wife, and that her husband had forced her to inject a 13-year-old girl with drain cleaner and then shoot her in the back. French reported that he worked thousands of hours preparing Neelley's defense, sinking nearly $340,000 into the case. However, the state paid French less than $1,000 for his work, approximately 50 cents an hour, to try to save Neelley's life. The case pushed French into bankruptcy. Not surprisingly, he said, "I don't want any more capital murder cases." French's case is an extreme example of the constraints Alabama's death penalty lawyers suffered under for years. At the time of Neelley's case, the state wouldn't pay a lawyer more than $2,000 plus overhead expenses for work on a capital case, despite the fact that the ABA decreed that a capital defense lawyer should work 500 hours or more on a case. In October, 2001, the legislature lifted this limit so that lawyers who represent indigent clients in capital cases now earn $40 an hour for out-of-court work and $60 an hour for in-court work. Nevertheless, a great number of inmates on Alabama's death row were convicted under the old limits. Birmingham Post-Herald Online, Dec. 14, 2001.

Similarly, Mississippi's flat, unwaivable $1,000 statutory cap, equivalent to a fee of about $5 per hour for many lawyers, has been described as "wholly unrealisitic," creating "disincentives to thorough trial investigation and preparation." Coyle, et al., *Fatal Defense: Trial and Error in the Nation's Death Belt*, Nat'l L.J. June 11, 1990, at 30.

In *Williamson v. Ward*, 110 F.3d 1508, 1512–21 (10th Cir. 1997), a federal habeas court overturned Ron Williamson's capital conviction because appointed counsel, who received no funding for expert or investigative services and was paid Oklahoma's statutory maximum of $3,200, failed to investigate a videotaped statement by another person confessing to the crime. Williamson's attorney also failed to uncover extensive evidence of Williamson's mental illness and likely incompetence to stand trial. When DNA testing later established that Williamson was innocent, he became the 78th person in the United States since 1970 to be cleared after being on death row.

For an argument that mandatory maximum fee caps amount to an unconstitutional taking of an attorney's property without reasonable compensation, see *Wilson v. State*, 574 So.2d 1338 (Miss. 1990).

7. The American Bar Association described state techniques for appointing lawyers in capital cases, ranging from patronage selections off a general list of all local attorneys — regardless of capital or criminal experience — to contract systems under which all cases go to the lowest bidder (with the flat fee bid covering experts and other expenses), including complex capital cases that unexpectedly appear on the county's docket. Other reimbursement schemes limit capital lawyers to, for example, $2,500 for the entire representation plus "$50 for each motion ... filed, up to five motions." The result is that the number of motions filed in almost every case is exactly five. Coyne & Entzeroth, "Report Regarding Implementation of the American Bar Association's Recommendations and Resolutions Concerning the Death Penalty and Calling for a Moratorium on Executions," 4 Geo. J. on Fighting Poverty, 3, 14, 16, 18 (1996).

8. As a practical matter, don't race and money affect the outcome and punishment in every criminal case? Given the lengthy appeals process and intense post-conviction scrutiny that death penalty cases receive, is it not more likely that the death penalty, when finally inflicted, is carried out in a more equitable manner than a sentence of twenty years imprisonment, or life imprisonment, or life imprisonment without the possibility of parole? Cost considerations are examined in greater detail in chapter 1.

C. Conflict of Interest

Burger v. Kemp
483 U.S. 776 (1987)

Justice STEVENS delivered the opinion of the Court.

A jury in the Superior Court of Wayne County, Georgia, found petitioner Christopher Burger guilty of murder and sentenced him to death on January 25, 1978. In this habeas corpus proceeding, he contends that he was denied his constitutional right to the effective assistance of counsel because his lawyer labored under a conflict of interest and failed to make an adequate investigation of the possibly mitigating circumstances of his offense. After a full evidentiary hearing, the District Court rejected the claim. We are persuaded, as was the Court of Appeals, that the judgment of the District Court must be affirmed.

I

... On [the] evening [of September 4, 1977], petitioner and ... Thomas Stevens, both privates [in the army], were drinking at a club on the post. They talked on the telephone with Private James Botsford, who had just arrived at the Savannah Airport, and agreed to pick him up and bring him back to the base. They stole a butcher knife and a sharpening tool from the mess hall and called a cab that was being driven by Roger Honeycutt, a soldier who worked part-time for a taxi company. On the way to the airport, petitioner held the knife and Stevens held the sharpening tool against Honeycutt. They forced him to stop the automobile, robbed him of $16, and placed him in the backseat. Petitioner took over the driving. Stevens then ordered Honeycutt to undress, threw each article of his clothing out of the car window after searching it, blindfolded him, and tied his hands behind his back. As petitioner drove, Stevens climbed into the backseat with Honeycutt, where he compelled Honeycutt to commit oral sodomy on him and anally sodomized him. After stopping the car a second time, petitioner and Stevens placed their victim, nude, blindfolded, and hands tied behind his back, in the trunk of the cab. They then proceeded to pick up Botsford at the airport. During the ride back to Fort Stewart, they told Botsford that they had stolen the cab and confirmed their story by conversing with Honeycutt in the trunk. In exchange for Botsford's promise not to notify the authorities, they promised that they would not harm Honeycutt after leaving Botsford at the base.

Ultimately, however, petitioner and Stevens drove to a pond in Wayne County where they had gone swimming in the past. They removed the cab's citizen-band radio and, while Stevens was hiding the radio in the bushes, petitioner opened the trunk and asked Honeycutt if he was all right. He answered affirmatively. Petitioner then closed the trunk, started the automobile, and put it in gear, getting out before it entered the water. Honeycutt drowned.

A week later Botsford contacted the authorities, and the military police arrested petitioner and Stevens. The two men made complete confessions. Petitioner also took the military police to the pond and identified the point where Honeycutt's body could be found. Petitioner's confession and Private Botsford's testimony were the primary evidence used at Burger's trial. That evidence was consistent with the defense thesis that Stevens, rather than petitioner, was primarily responsible for the plan to kidnap the cabdriver, the physical abuse of the victim, and the decision to kill him. Stevens was 20 years old at the time of the killing. Petitioner was 17; a psychologist testified that he had an IQ of 82 and functioned at the level of a 12-year-old child.

II

Alvin Leaphart was appointed to represent petitioner about a week after his arrest. Leaphart had been practicing law in Wayne County for about 14 years, had served as the county's attorney for most of that time, and had served on the Board of Governors of the State Bar Association. About 15 percent of his practice was in criminal law, and he had tried about a dozen capital cases. It is apparent that he was a well-respected lawyer, thoroughly familiar with practice and sentencing juries in the local community. He represented petitioner during the proceedings that resulted in his conviction and sentence, during an appeal to the Georgia Supreme Court which resulted in a vacation of the death penalty, during a second sentencing hearing, and also during a second appeal which resulted in affirmance of petitioner's capital sentence in 1980. Leaphart was paid approximately $9,000 for his services.

After exhausting his state collateral remedies, petitioner (then represented by a different attorney) filed a habeas corpus proceeding in the United States District Court for the Southern District of Georgia. He advanced several claims, including a charge that Leaphart's representation had been constitutionally inadequate. [On remand, the federal district court rejected petitioner's claim, and the Court of Appeals affirmed. Judge Johnson of the Court of Appeals dissented, finding that Leaphart had a conflict of interest because Leaphart's law partner represented the co-defendant Stevens at a later trial, and Leaphart assisted his law partner in that representation.]

III

There is certainly much substance to petitioner's argument that the appointment of two partners to represent coindictees in their respective trials creates a possible conflict of interest that could prejudice either or both clients. Moreover, the risk of prejudice is increased when the two lawyers cooperate with one another in the planning and conduct of trial strategy, as Leaphart and his partner did. Assuming without deciding that two law partners are considered as one attorney, it is settled that "[r]equiring or permitting a single attorney to represent codefendants, often referred to as joint representation, is not *per se* violative of constitutional guarantees of effective assistance of counsel." We have never held that the possibility of prejudice that "inheres in almost every instance of multiple representation" justifies the adoption of an inflexible rule that would presume prejudice in all such cases. Instead, we presume prejudice "only if the defendant demonstrates that counsel 'actively represented conflicting interests' and that 'an actual conflict of interest adversely affected his lawyer's performance.'"

... [T]he overlap of counsel, if any, did not so infect Leaphart's representation as to constitute an active representation of competing interests. Particularly in smaller communities where the supply of qualified lawyers willing to accept the demanding and unrewarding work of representing capital prisoners is extremely limited, the defendants may actually benefit from the joint efforts of two partners who supplement one another in their preparation. In many cases a "'common defense ... gives strength against a common attack.'" Moreover, we generally presume that the lawyer is fully conscious of the overarching duty of complete loyalty to his or her client. Trial courts appropriately and "necessarily rely in large measure upon the good faith and good judgment of defense counsel." In addition, petitioner and Stevens were tried in separate proceedings; as we noted in *Cuyler v. Sullivan*, 446 U.S. 335, 347 (1980), the provision of separate murder trials for the three coindictees "significantly reduced the potential for a divergence in their interests."

In an effort to identify an actual conflict of interest, petitioner points out that Leaphart prepared the briefs for both him and Stevens on their second appeal to the Georgia Supreme Court, and that Leaphart did not make a "lesser culpability" argument in his appellate brief on behalf of petitioner, even though he had relied on petitioner's lesser culpability as a trial defense. Given the fact that it was petitioner who actually killed Honeycutt immediately after opening the trunk to ask if he was all right, and the further fact that the Georgia Supreme Court expressed the opinion that petitioner's actions were "outrageously and wantonly vile and inhuman under any reasonable standard of human conduct," the decision to forgo this issue had a sound strategic basis. [T]he "process of winnowing out weaker claims on appeal and focusing on those more likely to prevail, far from being evidence of incompetence, is the hallmark of effective advocacy."

In addition, determining that there was an actual conflict of interest requires the attribution of Leaphart's motivation for not making the "lesser culpability" argument to the fact that his partner was Stevens' lawyer, or to the further fact that he assisted his partner in that representation.... [W]hen the lower courts have found that a lawyer has performed his or her solemn duties in such a case at or above the lower boundary of professional competence, both respect for the bar and deference to the shared conclusion of two reviewing courts prevent us from substituting speculation for their considered opinions. The district judge, who presumably is familiar with the legal talents and character of the lawyers who practice at the local bar and who saw and heard the witness testify, is in a far better position than we are to evaluate a charge of this kind, and the regional courts of appeals are in a far better position than we are to conduct appellate review of these heavily fact-based rulings.

We also conclude that the asserted actual conflict of interest, even if it had been established, did not harm his lawyer's advocacy. Petitioner argues that the joint representation adversely affected the quality of the counsel he received in two ways: Leaphart did not negotiate a plea agreement resulting in a life sentence, and he failed to take advantage of petitioner's lesser culpability when compared with his coindictee Stevens. We find that neither argument provides a basis for relief.

The notion that the prosecutor would have been receptive to a plea bargain is completely unsupported in the record. The evidence of both defendants' guilt, including their confessions, and eyewitness and tangible evidence, was overwhelming and uncontradicted; the prosecutor had no need for petitioner's eyewitness testimony to persuade the jury to convict Stevens and to sentence him to death.... [Further,] [a]s the District Court found, Leaphart "constantly attempted to plea bargain with the prosecutor," but was rebuffed. "The prosecutor's flat refusal to engage in plea bargaining is not surprising when viewed in light of the strength of the case against Burger."

The argument that his partner's representation of Stevens inhibited Leaphart from arguing petitioner's lesser culpability because such reliance would be prejudicial to Stevens is also unsupported by the record. Such an argument might have been more persuasive if the two defendants had been tried together. As the State conducted the prosecutions, however, each defendant's confession was used in his trial but neither was used against the coindictee. Because the trials were separate, Leaphart would have had no particular reason for concern about the possible impact of the tactics in petitioner's trial on the outcome of Stevens' trial. Moreover, in the initial habeas corpus proceeding, the District Court credited Leaphart's uncontradicted testimony that "he in no way tailored his strategy toward protecting Stevens." The District Court concluded that his "testimony is strongly supported by examination of the trial record, which shows considerable effort to gain mercy for petitioner by portraying Stevens as the chief architect of the crime."

In an effort to bolster his claim that an adverse effect resulted from Leaphart's actual conflict of interest, petitioner argues that because he was tried in a small community in which the facts of the crime were widely known, "it necessarily follows that the public, and very possibly members of the jury, knew that the cases were being tried on inherently inconsistent theories." But this observation does nothing to establish an actual, deleterious conflict of interest between Leaphart's work for his client and his partner's representation of Stevens. If two unaffiliated lawyers, complete strangers to one another, had represented Burger and Stevens respectively and had advanced the same defenses that were advanced, the community would have had the same awareness that the theories were inherently inconsistent. There was undoubtedly a conflict of interest between Burger and Stevens because of the nature of their defenses. But this inherent conflict between two participants in a single criminal undertaking cannot be transformed into a Sixth Amendment violation simply because the community might be aware that their respective attorneys were law partners....

V

Petitioner has not established that "in light of all the circumstances, the identified acts or omissions [of counsel] were outside the wide range of professionally competent assistance." He "has made no showing that the justice of his sentence was rendered unreliable by a breakdown in the adversary process caused by deficiencies in counsel's assistance."

Accordingly, the judgment of the Court of Appeals is affirmed.

Note and Question

On occasion in notorious cases, trial counsel will seek to augment their fees by negotiating book and movie rights. E. Ray Andrews, an attorney who represented Texas death row inmate Betty Lou Beets at trial, reportedly knew that the state's principal argument in favor of a death sentence—that Beets had killed her husband to recover insurance proceeds—was false, because Andrews knew that Beets was unaware of the policy until he told her of it a year after her husband's death. Andrews chose not to so inform the jury because doing so would have required him to stop representing Beets and testify. Not only would Andrews lose whatever pay he earned representing Beets, he would have been required to forfeit the literary and film rights to her story. Andrews later served three years in prison for extorting a bribe in another murder case. Berlow, *Lethal Injustice*, The American Prospect Mar. 27—Apr. 10, 2000, at 54. What conflict of interest problems arise when an attorney represents a client and is compensated, in part, by royalties expected to be earned through selling movie and book rights to her client's story?

Stephen Jones, lead counsel in the Oklahoma City bombing trial of Timothy McVeigh, was removed as counsel on McVeigh's direct appeal after McVeigh complained to the Tenth Circuit Court of Appeals that Jones had entered into a book contract with Doubleday Publishing without McVeigh's knowledge. The book contract reportedly required Doubleday to pay Jones $300,000 upon Jones' signing the contract and another $300,000 when Jones delivered a manuscript to the publisher.

According to McVeigh's affidavit, "Mr. Jones did this book deal without informing me and without my consent. I cannot believe that his account will not be based upon confidential communications. I consider this to be a betrayal."

Professor Drew Kershen, a legal ethics expert, provided an affidavit which concluded that Jones' actions posed "a genuine and serious risk" of a conflict of interest. Professor Kershen's affidavit cited the rule of professional responsibility which states that a lawyer who represents a client "shall not make or negotiate an agreement giving the lawyer literary or media rights to a portrayal or account" based on the case. According to Professor Kershen, Jones' book deal created three dangers: (1) that Jones would violate the attorney-client privilege; (2) that Jones would shape the appeal in a fashion designed to yield the best material for the book; and (3) that Jones would usurp McVeigh's right to set his own legal objectives. Loe, *Book Deal of Former McVeigh Attorney Criticized*, The Dallas Morning News, Dec. 19, 1997. Do you agree that Jones' actions present a "genuine and serious risk" of a conflict of interest? To learn how the federal court resolved these issues, see *United States v. McVeigh*, 118 F. Supp. 2d 1137 (D. Colo. 2000).

Mickens v. Taylor

535 U.S. 162 (2002)

Justice SCALIA delivered the opinion of the Court.

The question presented in this case is what a defendant must show in order to demonstrate a Sixth Amendment violation where the trial court fails to inquire into a potential conflict of interest about which it knew or reasonably should have known.

I

In 1993, a Virginia jury convicted petitioner Mickens of the premeditated murder of Timothy Hall during or following the commission of an attempted forcible sodomy. Finding the murder outrageously and wantonly vile, it sentenced petitioner to death. In June 1998, Mickens filed a petition for writ of habeas corpus, see 28 U.S.C. §2254, in the United States District Court for the Eastern District of Virginia, alleging, *inter alia,* that he was denied effective assistance of counsel because one of his court-appointed attorneys had a conflict of interest at trial. Federal habeas counsel had discovered that petitioner's lead trial attorney, Bryan Saunders, was representing Hall (the victim) on assault and concealed-weapons charges at the time of the murder. Saunders had been appointed to represent Hall, a juvenile, on March 20, 1992, and had met with him once for 15 to 30 minutes some time the following week. Hall's body was discovered on March 30, 1992, and four days later a juvenile court judge dismissed the charges against him, noting on the docket sheet that Hall was deceased. The one-page docket sheet also listed Saunders as Hall's counsel. On April 6, 1992, the same judge appointed Saunders to represent petitioner. Saunders did not disclose to the court, his co-counsel, or petitioner that he had previously represented Hall. Under Virginia law, juvenile case files are confidential and may not generally be disclosed without a court order, but petitioner learned about Saunders' prior representation when a clerk mistakenly produced Hall's file to federal habeas counsel.

The District Court held an evidentiary hearing and denied petitioner's habeas petition.... [On rehearing en banc,] the Court of Appeals assumed that the juvenile court judge had neglected a duty to inquire into a potential conflict, but rejected petitioner's argument that this failure either mandated automatic reversal of his conviction or relieved him of the burden of showing that a conflict of interest adversely affected his representation. Relying on *Cuyler v. Sullivan*, 446 U.S. 335 (1980), the court held that a defendant must show "both an actual conflict of interest and an adverse effect even if the trial court failed to inquire into a potential conflict about which it reasonably should have known." Concluding that petitioner had not demonstrated adverse effect, it affirmed the District Court's denial of habeas relief. We granted a stay of execution of petitioner's sentence and granted certiorari.

II

The Sixth Amendment provides that a criminal defendant shall have the right to "the assistance of counsel for his defense." This right has been accorded, we have said, "not for its own sake, but because of the effect it has on the ability of the accused to receive a fair trial." *United States v. Cronic*, 466 U.S. 648, 658 (1984). It follows from this that assistance which is ineffective in preserving fairness does not meet the constitutional mandate, see *Strickland v. Washington,* 466 U.S. 668, 685–686 (1984); and it also follows that defects in assistance that have no probable effect upon the trial's outcome do not establish a constitutional violation. As a general matter, a defendant alleging a Sixth Amendment violation must demonstrate "a reasonable probability that, but for counsel's unprofessional errors, the result of the proceeding would have been different."

There is an exception to this general rule. We have spared the defendant the need of showing probable effect upon the outcome, and have simply presumed such effect, where assistance of counsel has been denied entirely or during a critical stage of the proceeding. When that has occurred, the likelihood that the verdict is unreliable is so high that a case-by-case inquiry is unnecessary. But only in "circumstances of that magnitude" do we forgo individual inquiry into whether counsel's inadequate performance undermined the reliability of the verdict.

We have held in several cases that "circumstances of that magnitude" may also arise when the defendant's attorney actively represented conflicting interests. The nub of the question before us is whether the principle established by these cases provides an exception to the general rule of *Strickland* under the circumstances of the present case. To answer that question, we must examine those cases in some detail.

In *Holloway v. Arkansas,* 435 U.S. 475 (1978), defense counsel had objected that he could not adequately represent the divergent interests of three codefendants. Without inquiry, the trial court had denied counsel's motions for the appointment of separate counsel and had refused to allow counsel to cross-examine any of the defendants on behalf of the other two. The *Holloway* Court deferred to the judgment of counsel regarding the existence of a disabling conflict, recognizing that a defense attorney is in the best position to determine when a conflict exists, that he has an ethical obligation to advise the court of any problem, and that his declarations to the court are "virtually made under oath." *Holloway* presumed, moreover, that the conflict, "which [the defendant] and his counsel tried to avoid by timely objections to the joint representation," undermined the adversarial process. The presumption was justified because joint representation of conflicting interests is inherently suspect, and because counsel's conflicting obligations to multiple defendants "effectively sea[l] his lips on crucial matters" and make it difficult to measure the precise harm arising from counsel's errors. *Holloway* thus creates an automatic reversal rule only where defense counsel is forced to represent codefendants over his timely objection, unless the trial court has determined that there is no conflict.

In *Cuyler v. Sullivan,* 446 U.S. 335 (1980), the respondent was one of three defendants accused of murder who were tried separately, represented by the same counsel. Neither counsel nor anyone else objected to the multiple representation, and counsel's opening argument at Sullivan's trial suggested that the interests of the defendants were aligned. We declined to extend *Holloway*'s automatic reversal rule to this situation and held that, absent objection, a defendant must demonstrate that "a conflict of interest actually affected the adequacy of his representation." In addition to describing the defendant's burden of proof, *Sullivan* addressed separately a trial court's duty to inquire into the propriety of a multiple representation, construing *Holloway* to require inquiry only when "the trial court knows or reasonably should know that a particular conflict exists,"—which is not to be confused with when the trial court is aware of a vague, unspecified possibility of conflict, such as that which "inheres in almost every instance of multiple representation." In *Sullivan,* no "special circumstances" triggered the trial court's duty to inquire.

Finally, in *Wood v. Georgia,* 450 U.S. 261 (1981), three indigent defendants convicted of distributing obscene materials had their probation revoked for failure to make the requisite $500 monthly payments on their $5,000 fines. We granted certiorari to consider whether this violated the Equal Protection Clause, but during the course of our consideration certain disturbing circumstances came to our attention: At the probation-revocation hearing (as at all times since their arrest) the defendants had been represented by the lawyer for their employer (the owner of the business that purveyed the obscenity), and their employer paid the attorney's fees. The employer had promised his employees he would pay their fines, and had generally kept that promise but had not done so in these defendants' case. This record suggested that the employer's interest in establishing a favorable equal-protection precedent (reducing the fines he would have to pay for his indigent employees in the future) diverged from the defendants' interest in obtaining leniency or paying lesser fines to avoid imprisonment. Moreover, the possibility that counsel was actively representing the conflicting interests of employer and defendants "was sufficiently apparent at the time of the revocation hearing to impose upon the court a duty to inquire further." Because "[o]n the record before us, we [could not] be sure whether counsel was influenced in his basic strategic decisions by the interests of the employer who hired him," we remanded for the trial court "to determine whether the conflict of interest that this record strongly suggests actually existed."

Petitioner argues that the remand instruction in *Wood* established an "unambiguous rule" that where the trial judge neglects a duty to inquire into a potential conflict, the defendant, to obtain reversal of the judgment, need only show that his lawyer was subject to a conflict of interest, and need not show that the conflict adversely affected counsel's performance. He relies upon the language in the remand instruction directing the trial court to grant a new revocation hearing if it determines that "an actual conflict of interest existed," without requiring a further determination that the conflict adversely affected counsel's performance. As used in the remand instruction, however, we think "an actual conflict of interest" meant precisely a conflict that affected counsel's performance—as opposed to a mere theoretical division of loyalties. It was shorthand for the statement in *Sullivan* that "'a defendant who shows that a conflict of interest actually affected the adequacy of his representation need not demonstrate prejudice in order to obtain relief." This is the only interpretation consistent with the *Wood* Court's earlier description of why it could not decide the case without a remand: "On the record before us, we cannot be sure whether counsel was influenced in his basic strategic decisions by the interests of the employer who hired him. If this was the case, the due process rights of petitioners were not respected...." The notion that *Wood* created a new rule *sub silentio*—and in a case where certiorari had been granted on an entirely different question, and the parties had neither briefed nor argued the conflict-of-interest issue—is implausible.

Petitioner's proposed rule of automatic reversal when there existed a conflict that did not affect counsel's performance, but the trial judge failed to make the *Sullivan*-mandated inquiry, makes little policy sense. As discussed, the rule applied when the trial judge is not aware of the conflict (and thus not obligated to inquire) is that prejudice will be presumed only if the conflict has significantly affected counsel's performance—thereby rendering the verdict unreliable, even though *Strickland* prejudice cannot be shown. The trial court's awareness of a potential conflict neither renders it more likely that counsel's performance was significantly affected nor in any other way renders the verdict unreliable. Nor does the trial judge's failure to make the *Sullivan*-mandated inquiry often make it harder for reviewing courts to determine conflict and effect, particularly since those courts may rely on evidence and testimony whose importance only becomes established at the trial.

Nor, finally, is automatic reversal simply an appropriate means of enforcing *Sullivan's* mandate of inquiry. Despite Justice Souter's belief that there must be a threat of sanction (to-wit, the risk of conferring a windfall upon the defendant) in order to induce "resolutely obdurate" trial judges to follow the law, we do not presume that judges are as careless or as partial as those police officers who need the incentive of the exclusionary rule. And in any event, the *Sullivan* standard, which requires proof of effect upon representation but (once such effect is shown) presumes prejudice, already creates an "incentive" to inquire into a potential conflict. In those cases where the potential conflict is in fact an actual one, only inquiry will enable the judge to avoid all possibility of reversal by either seeking waiver or replacing a conflicted attorney. We doubt that the deterrence of "judicial dereliction" that would be achieved by an automatic reversal rule is significantly greater.

Since this was not a case in which (as in *Holloway*) counsel protested his inability simultaneously to represent multiple defendants; and since the trial court's failure to make the *Sullivan*-mandated inquiry does not reduce the petitioner's burden of proof; it was at least necessary, to void the conviction, for petitioner to establish that the conflict of interest adversely affected his counsel's performance. The Court of Appeals having found no such effect, the denial of habeas relief must be affirmed.

III

Lest today's holding be misconstrued, we note that the only question presented was the effect of a trial court's failure to inquire into a potential conflict upon the *Sullivan* rule that deficient performance of counsel must be shown. The case was presented and argued on the assumption that (absent some exception for failure to inquire) *Sullivan* would be applicable — requiring a showing of defective performance, but *not* requiring in addition (as *Strickland* does in other ineffectiveness-of-counsel cases), a showing of probable effect upon the outcome of trial. That assumption was not unreasonable in light of the holdings of Courts of Appeals, which have applied *Sullivan* "unblinkingly" to "'all kinds of alleged attorney ethical conflicts.'" They have invoked the *Sullivan* standard not only when (as here) there is a conflict rooted in counsel's obligations to former clients, but even when representation of the defendant somehow implicates counsel's personal or financial interests, including a book deal, a job with the prosecutor's office, the teaching of classes to Internal Revenue Service agents, a romantic "entanglement" with the prosecutor, or fear of antagonizing the trial judge.

It must be said, however, that the language of *Sullivan* itself does not clearly establish, or indeed even support, such expansive application.... [T]he Federal Rules of Criminal Procedure treat concurrent representation and prior representation differently, requiring a trial court to inquire into the likelihood of conflict whenever jointly charged defendants are represented by a single attorney (Rule 44(c)), but not when counsel previously represented another defendant in a substantially related matter, even where the trial court is aware of the prior representation.

This is not to suggest that one ethical duty is more or less important than another. The purpose of our *Holloway* and *Sullivan* exceptions from the ordinary requirements of *Strickland,* however, is not to enforce the Canons of Legal Ethics, but to apply needed prophylaxis in situations where *Strickland* itself is evidently inadequate to assure vindication of the defendant's Sixth Amendment right to counsel. In resolving this case on the grounds on which it was presented to us, we do not rule upon the need for the *Sullivan* prophylaxis in cases of successive representation. Whether *Sullivan* should be extended to such cases remains, as far as the jurisprudence of this Court is concerned, an open question....

For the reasons stated, the judgment of the Court of Appeals is affirmed.

Justice STEVENS, dissenting.

This case raises three uniquely important questions about a fundamental component of our criminal justice system — the constitutional right of a person accused of a capital offense to have the effective assistance of counsel for his defense. The first is whether a capital defendant's attorney has a duty to disclose that he was representing the defendant's alleged victim at the time of the murder. Second, is whether, assuming disclosure of the prior representation, the capital defendant has a right to refuse the appointment of the conflicted attorney. Third, is whether the trial judge, who knows or should know of such prior representation, has a duty to obtain the defendant's consent before appointing that lawyer to represent him.

Ultimately, the question presented by this case is whether, if these duties exist and if all of them are violated, there exist "circumstances that are so likely to prejudice the accused that the cost of litigating their effect in a particular case is unjustified." *United States v. Cronic*, 466 U.S. 648, 658 (1984).

I

The first critical stage in the defense of a capital case is the series of pretrial meetings between the accused and his counsel when they decide how the case should be defended. A lawyer cannot possibly determine how best to represent a new client unless that client is willing to provide the lawyer with a truthful account of the relevant facts. When an indigent defendant first meets his newly appointed counsel, he will often falsely maintain his complete innocence. Truthful disclosures of embarrassing or incriminating facts are contingent on the development of the client's confidence in the undivided loyalty of the lawyer. Quite obviously, knowledge that the lawyer represented the victim would be a substantial obstacle to the development of such confidence.

It is equally true that a lawyer's decision to conceal such an important fact from his new client would have comparable ramifications. The suppression of communication and truncated investigation that would unavoidably follow from such a decision would also make it difficult, if not altogether impossible, to establish the necessary level of trust that should characterize the "delicacy of relation" between attorney and client.

In this very case, it is likely that Mickens misled his counsel, Bryan Saunders, given the fact that Mickens gave false testimony at his trial denying any involvement in the crime despite the overwhelming evidence that he had killed Timothy Hall after a sexual encounter. In retrospect, it seems obvious that the death penalty might have been avoided by acknowledging Mickens' involvement, but emphasizing the evidence suggesting that their sexual encounter was consensual. Mickens' habeas counsel garnered evidence suggesting that Hall was a male prostitute; that the area where Hall was killed was known for prostitution; and that there was no evidence that Hall was forced to the secluded area where he was ultimately murdered. An unconflicted attorney could have put forward a defense tending to show that Mickens killed Hall only after the two engaged in consensual sex, but Saunders offered no such defense. This was a crucial omission — a finding of forcible sodomy was an absolute prerequisite to Mickens' eligibility for the death penalty. Of course, since that strategy would have led to conviction of a noncapital offense, counsel would have been unable to persuade the defendant to divulge the information necessary to support such a defense and then ultimately to endorse the strategy unless he had earned the complete confidence of his client.

Saunders' concealment of essential information about his prior representation of the victim was a severe lapse in his professional duty. The lawyer's duty to disclose his representation of a client related to the instant charge is not only intuitively obvious, it is as old as the profession.... Mickens' lawyer's violation of this fundamental obligation of disclosure is indefensible. The relevance of Saunders' prior representation of Hall to the new appointment was far too important to be concealed.

II

If the defendant is found guilty of a capital offense, the ensuing proceedings that determine whether he will be put to death are critical in every sense of the word. At those proceedings, testimony about the impact of the crime on the victim, including testimony about the character of the victim, may have a critical effect on the jury's decision. Because a lawyer's fiduciary relationship with his deceased client survives the client's death, Saunders necessarily labored under conflicting obligations that were irreconcilable. He had a duty to protect the reputation and confidences of his deceased client, and a duty to impeach the impact evidence presented by the prosecutor.[4]

Saunders' conflicting obligations to his deceased client, on the one hand, and to his living client, on the other, were unquestionably sufficient to give Mickens the right to insist on different representation.[5] For the "right to counsel guaranteed by the Constitution contemplates the services of an attorney devoted solely to the interests of his client."[6]

III

When an indigent defendant is unable to retain his own lawyer, the trial judge's appointment of counsel is itself a critical stage of a criminal trial. At that point in the proceeding, by definition, the defendant has no lawyer to protect his interests and must rely entirely on the judge. For that reason it is "the solemn duty of a ... judge before whom a defendant appears without counsel to make a thorough inquiry and to take all steps necessary to insure the fullest protection of this constitutional right at every stage of the proceedings."

This duty with respect to indigent defendants is far more imperative than the judge's duty to investigate the possibility of a conflict that arises when retained counsel represents either multiple or successive defendants.... [W]hen, as was true in this case, the judge is not merely reviewing the permissibility of the defendants' choice of counsel, but is responsible for making the choice herself, and when she knows or should know that a conflict does exist, the duty to make a thorough inquiry is manifest and unqualified. Indeed, under far less compelling circumstances, we squarely held that when a record discloses the "possibility of a conflict" between the interests of the defendants

---

4. For example, at the time of Hall's death, Saunders was representing Hall in juvenile court for charges arising out of an incident involving Hall's mother. She had sworn out a warrant for Hall's arrest charging him with assault and battery. Despite knowledge of this, Mickens' lawyer offered no rebuttal to the victim impact statement submitted by Hall's mother that "'all [she] lived for was that boy.'"

5. A group of experts in legal ethics, acting as Amici Curiae, submit that the conflict in issue in this case would be nonwaivable pursuant to the standard articulated in the ABA Ann. Unfortunately, because Mickens was not informed of the fact that his appointed attorney was the lawyer of the alleged victim, the questions whether Mickens would have waived this conflict and consented to the appointment, or whether governing standards of professional responsibility would have precluded him from doing so, remain unanswered.

6. Although the conflict in this case is plainly intolerable, I, of course, do not suggest that every conflict, or every violation of the code of ethics, is a violation of the Constitution.

and the interests of the party paying their counsel's fees, the Constitution imposes a duty of inquiry on the state court judge even when no objection was made.

IV

Mickens had a constitutional right to the services of an attorney devoted solely to his interests. That right was violated. The lawyer who did represent him had a duty to disclose his prior representation of the victim to Mickens and to the trial judge. That duty was violated. When Mickens had no counsel, the trial judge had a duty to "make a thorough inquiry and to take all steps necessary to insure the fullest protection of" his right to counsel. Despite knowledge of the lawyer's prior representation, she violated that duty.

We will never know whether Mickens would have received the death penalty if those violations had not occurred nor precisely what effect they had on Saunders' representation of Mickens. We do know that he did not receive the kind of representation that the Constitution guarantees. If Mickens had been represented by an attorney-impostor who never passed a bar examination, we might also be unable to determine whether the impostor's educational shortcomings "'actually affected the adequacy of his representation.'" We would, however, surely set aside his conviction if the person who had represented him was not a real lawyer....

Death is a different kind of punishment from any other that may be imposed in this country. "From the point of view of the defendant, it is different in both its severity and its finality. From the point of view of society, the action of the sovereign in taking the life of one of its citizens also differs dramatically from any other legitimate state action. It is of vital importance to the defendant and to the community that any decision to impose the death sentence be, and appear to be, based on reason rather than caprice or emotion." A rule that allows the State to foist a murder victim's lawyer onto his accused is not only capricious; it poisons the integrity of our adversary system of justice.

Justice BREYER, with whom Justice Ginsburg joins, dissenting.

The Commonwealth of Virginia seeks to put the petitioner, Walter Mickens, Jr., to death after having appointed to represent him as his counsel a lawyer who, at the time of the murder, was representing the very person Mickens was accused of killing. I believe that, in a case such as this one, a categorical approach is warranted and automatic reversal is required. To put the matter in language this Court has previously used: By appointing this lawyer to represent Mickens, the Commonwealth created a "structural defect affecting the framework within which the trial [and sentencing] proceeds, rather than simply an error in the trial process itself." *Arizona v. Fulminante*, 499 U.S. 279, 310 (1991).

The parties spend a great deal of time disputing how this Court's precedents of *Holloway v. Arkansas, Cuyler v. Sullivan,* and *Wood v. Georgia,* resolve the case.... Although I express no view at this time about how our precedents should treat *most* ineffective-assistance-of-counsel claims involving an alleged conflict of interest (or, for that matter, whether *Holloway, Sullivan,* and *Wood* provide a sensible or coherent framework for dealing with those cases at all), I am convinced that *this* case is not governed by those precedents, for the following reasons.

First, this is the kind of representational incompatibility that is egregious on its face. Mickens was represented by the murder victim's lawyer; that lawyer had represented the victim on a criminal matter; and that lawyer's representation of the victim had continued until one business day before the lawyer was appointed to represent the defendant.

Second, the conflict is exacerbated by the fact that it occurred in a capital murder case. In a capital case, the evidence submitted by both sides regarding the victim's character may easily tip the scale of the jury's choice between life or death. Yet even with extensive investigation in post-trial proceedings, it will often prove difficult, if not impossible, to determine whether the prior representation affected defense counsel's decisions regarding, for example: which avenues to take when investigating the victim's background; which witnesses to call; what type of impeachment to undertake; which arguments to make to the jury; what language to use to characterize the victim; and, as a general matter, what basic strategy to adopt at the sentencing stage. Given the subtle forms that prejudice might take, the consequent difficulty of proving actual prejudice, and the significant likelihood that it will nonetheless occur when the same lawyer represents both accused killer and victim, the cost of litigating the existence of actual prejudice in a particular case cannot be easily justified.

Third, the Commonwealth itself created the conflict in the first place. Indeed, it was the *same judge* who dismissed the case against the victim who then appointed the victim's lawyer to represent Mickens one business day later. In light of the judge's active role in bringing about the incompatible representation, I am not sure why the concept of a judge's "duty to inquire" is thought to be central to this case. No "inquiry" by the trial judge could have shed more light on the conflict than was obvious on the face of the matter, namely, that the lawyer who would represent Mickens today is the same lawyer who yesterday represented Mickens' alleged victim in a criminal case.

This kind of breakdown in the criminal justice system creates, at a minimum, the appearance that the proceeding will not "'reliably serve its function as a vehicle for determination of guilt or innocence,'" and the resulting "'criminal punishment'" will not "'be regarded as fundamentally fair.'" *Fulminante*. This appearance, together with the likelihood of prejudice in the typical case, are serious enough to warrant a categorical rule—a rule that does not require proof of prejudice in the individual case....

D. Failure to Investigate

Burger v. Kemp
483 U.S. 776 (1987)

Justice STEVENS delivered the opinion of the Court.

[Below, the Court addresses whether Burger's trial counsel's failure to present any mitigating evidence at the sentencing phase constituted ineffective assistance of counsel.]

IV

... The evidence that might have been presented [during sentencing] would have disclosed that petitioner had an exceptionally unhappy and unstable childhood. Most of this evidence was described by petitioner's mother, who testified at length at the habeas corpus hearing. At the age of 14 she married Burger's father, who was 16. She was divorced from petitioner's father when petitioner was nine years old. She remarried twice, and neither of petitioner's stepfathers wanted petitioner in the home; one of them beat his mother in petitioner's presence when he was 11 and the other apparently "got him involved with marijuana, and that was the whole point of his life, where the next bag was coming from, or the next bottle of beer. And, this was the kind of influence that he had." When his mother moved from Indiana to Florida, petitioner ran away from his father and hitchhiked to Tampa. After he became involved in an auto accident, she returned him to Indiana where he was placed in a juvenile detention home until he was released to his father's custody. Except for one incident of shoplifting, being absent from school without permission, and being held in juvenile detention — none of which was brought to the jury's attention — petitioner apparently had no criminal record before entering the Army.

Leaphart [petitioner's attorney] was aware of some, but not all, of this family history prior to petitioner's trial. He talked with petitioner's mother on several occasions, an attorney in Indiana who had befriended petitioner and his mother, and a psychologist whom Leaphart had employed to conduct an examination of petitioner in preparation for trial. He reviewed psychologists' reports that were obtained with the help of petitioner's mother. He also interviewed Stevens and other men at Fort Stewart. Based on these interviews, Leaphart made the reasonable decision that his client's interest would not be served by presenting this type of evidence.

His own meetings with petitioner, as well as the testimony of the psychologist at the hearing on the admissibility of petitioner's confession, convinced Leaphart that it would be unwise to put petitioner himself on the witness stand. The record indicates that petitioner never expressed any remorse about his crime, and the psychologist's testimony indicates that he might even have bragged about it on the witness stand. Leaphart formed the opinion that Burger enjoyed talking about the crimes; he was worried that the jury might regard Burger's attitude on the witness stand as indifferent or worse. Quite obviously ... an experienced trial lawyer could properly have decided not to put either petitioner or the psychologist who had thus evaluated him in a position where he would be subjected to cross-examination that might be literally fatal.

The other two witnesses that Leaphart considered using were petitioner's mother and the Indiana lawyer who had acted as petitioner's "big brother." Leaphart talked with the mother on several occasions and concluded that her testimony would not be helpful and might have been counterproductive. As the record stood, there was absolutely no evidence that petitioner had any prior criminal record of any kind. Her testimony indicates that petitioner had committed at least one petty offense. The District Judge who heard all of the testimony that she would have given on direct examination at the sentencing hearing was not convinced that it would have aided petitioner's case; it was surely not unreasonable for Leaphart to have concluded that cross-examination might well have revealed matters of historical fact that would have harmed his client's chances for a life sentence.

The Indiana lawyer was willing to travel to Georgia to testify on petitioner's behalf, but nothing in the record describes the content of the testimony he might have given. Although Leaphart was unable to recall the details of the background information that he received from the Indiana lawyer, he testified that the information was not helpful to petitioner, and the Indiana lawyer apparently agreed with that assessment. Consistently with that conclusion, petitioner's present counsel — even with the benefit of hindsight — has submitted no affidavit from that lawyer establishing that he would have offered substantial mitigating evidence if he had testified. Accordingly, while Leaphart's judgment may have been erroneous, the record surely does not permit us to reach that conclusion.

Finally, petitioner submitted several affidavits to the court to describe the evidence that Leaphart might have used if he had conducted a more thorough investigation.

These affidavits present information about petitioner's troubled family background that could have affected the jury adversely by introducing facts not disclosed by his clean adult criminal record. The affidavits indicate that the affiants, had they testified, might well have referred on direct examination or cross-examination to his encounters with law enforcement authorities. For example, a former neighbor, Phyllis Russell, stated that petitioner's father did not want to associate with him when he "got into trouble and was on juvenile probation." Petitioner's uncle, Earnest Holtsclaw, narrated that petitioner "got involved with drugs" while in Florida. Cathy Russell Ray, petitioner's friend in junior high school, stated that "Chris's father was supposed to go with him to juvenile court to get a release so that he could join the service [Army]."

Even apart from their references to damaging facts, the papers are by no means uniformly helpful to petitioner because they suggest violent tendencies that are at odds with the defense's strategy of portraying petitioner's actions on the night of the murder as the result of Stevens' strong influence upon his will....

The record at the habeas corpus hearing does suggest that Leaphart could well have made a more thorough investigation than he did. Nevertheless, in considering claims of ineffective assistance of counsel, "[w]e address not what is prudent or appropriate, but only what is constitutionally compelled." We have decided that "strategic choices made after less than complete investigation are reasonable precisely to the extent that reasonable professional judgments support the limitations on investigation." Applying this standard, we agree with the courts below that counsel's decision not to mount an all-out investigation into petitioner's background in search of mitigating circumstances was supported by reasonable professional judgment. It appears that he did interview all potential witnesses who had been called to his attention and that there was a reasonable basis for his strategic decision that an explanation of petitioner's history would not have minimized the risk of the death penalty. Having made this judgment, he reasonably determined that he need not undertake further investigation to locate witnesses who would make statements about Burger's past. We hold that the Court of Appeals complied with the directives of *Strickland*....

Justice BLACKMUN, with whom Justice Brennan and Justice Marshall join and, as to Part II, Justice Powell joins, dissenting.

II

[P]etitioner was deprived of the effective assistance of counsel in connection with his capital-sentencing proceeding. His counsel failed to investigate mitigating evidence and failed to present any evidence at the sentencing hearing despite the fact that petitioner was an adolescent with psychological problems and apparent diminished mental capabilities....

The limitation counsel placed on his investigation of the evidence of petitioner's mental capabilities and psychological makeup despite the indications that petitioner had problems in these respects was not supported by reasonable professional judgment.

Counsel stated that he based his decision not to move the court for a complete psychological examination of petitioner on his prior experience with the mental hospital where, he assumed, petitioner would be sent for the examination. He stated that "the results I've had with personnel at Central Hospital as far as the defense is concerned ... hasn't been good at all." He added that he thought that any further examinations would yield the same psychopathic diagnosis reached by the psychologist who had examined petitioner once briefly and primarily to administer an IQ test for purposes of the hearing on whether petitioner's confession was admissible.

Counsel's failure to request an examination because of what he considered to be a biased procedure constituted a breakdown in the adversarial process. If in fact the procedure for psychological examinations of an indigent criminal defendant in that jurisdiction was biased, the role of petitioner's counsel at least was to seek an alternative examination process or to challenge the biased procedure. Counsel's decision to forgo the psychological examination imperiled petitioner's ability to counter the prosecutor's argument that he deserved to be executed for his role in the murder and therefore undermined the reliability of the sentencing proceeding. Moreover, such a decision to proceed without the examination in a case in which an adolescent with indications of significant psychological problems and diminished mental capabilities faces the death penalty is contrary to professional norms of competent assistance. The usefulness of a thorough evaluation in a case where there are indications that the capital defendant has problems of that kind is obvious.

Counsel's decision not to investigate petitioner's family or childhood background also was not within the range of professionally reasonable judgment. Viewed as of the time he decided not to get in touch with any family member or to investigate any place where petitioner had lived, counsel provided inadequate assistance. He relied on petitioner to suggest possible witnesses or mitigating evidence. But his question to petitioner whether he could produce evidence of "anything good about him" hardly could be expected to yield information about petitioner's childhood and broken home. It is unlikely that in response to that question a defendant would volunteer the facts that his father threw him out of the house, that his mother did the same, that his stepfathers beat him and his mother, or that one stepfather involved him in drugs and alcohol at age 11.... Furthermore, counsel testified that he spoke with petitioner perhaps "half a dozen times," the longest being "[p]robably about an hour." These bare six hours provided counsel little time to discuss possible mitigating evidence for the sentencing proceeding because counsel surely also had to discuss in detail the circumstances surrounding petitioner's confession which he was challenging and all the other features of the guilt/innocence phase of the trial. Moreover, after petitioner's death sentence was vacated [on other grounds] on appeal and the case was remanded, counsel did not perform any further investigation whatsoever during the 9-month period before the second hearing. He simply proceeded in the same manner that had resulted in petitioner's being sentenced to death at the first hearing.

The only reason counsel spoke to petitioner's mother at all was because she sought him out after learning elsewhere that her son was charged with murder. Even after petitioner's mother initiated the contact, counsel's conduct was inexplicable. He testified that he never explained the penalty phase of the trial to petitioner's mother or what evidence then could be presented. The Court finds reasonable counsel's decision not to have petitioner's mother testify because he concluded that her testimony might be counterproductive in that it might reveal a petty offense petitioner had committed. That decision is a prime example, however, of a strategic choice made after less-than-adequate investigation, which therefore is not supported by informed professional judgment. Counsel could not reasonably determine whether presenting character witnesses would pose a risk of disclosing past criminal behavior by petitioner without first determining whether there was any such criminal behavior. Although there is a reference in the record to an incident of shoplifting a candy bar, another reference to an automobile accident, there is no indication that counsel ever determined whether petitioner in fact had a prior criminal record. The account provided by petitioner's mother of petitioner's hitchhiking to Florida to be with her after having been thrown out of his father's house and having to sell his shoes during the trip to get food may well have outweighed the relevance of any earlier petty theft.

I also find troubling the fact that defense counsel rejected the assistance of another lawyer (who had known petitioner) merely on the basis that the lawyer was black. The lawyer offered to come to Georgia at his own expense to provide what assistance he could. Counsel thought his assistance might have "an ill effect," however, on the trial of petitioner who is white. Counsel testified that he and the lawyer agreed that because of his race it was not wise to have the lawyer testify. I question whether this is a reasonable professional decision. The adversarial duty of petitioner's counsel was to pursue a means by which to present testimony from such a witness while doing his best to safe-guard the trial from racial prejudice. Counsel apparently made no effort to investigate possible racial bias of petitioner's jury. Like counsel's abandonment of the psychological investigation because of the suspected unfairness of the examination procedure, his sur-render to the perceived risk of racial discrimination without any effort to eliminate that risk is inconsistent with his adversarial role and his responsibility to further the reliabil-ity of the court proceeding.

Acceptance of the unpleasant likelihood of racial prejudice in such a trial, however, does not justify counsel's failure to accept assistance from the lawyer in any number of ways, such as investigating petitioner's childhood background in Indianapolis where the lawyer had known petitioner. Testimony by petitioner's mother at the federal habeas corpus hearing revealed that when the lawyer was in law school he had worked in a vol-unteer "big brother" organization for men who spent time with children who did not have a father-son relationship or a big brother. He was undoubtedly familiar with some of petitioner's friends and family members there. The affidavits submitted at the federal hearing indicate that many of those persons still reside in Indianapolis but were never approached by counsel. In sum, I reluctantly conclude that counsel fell short in his "duty to make reasonable investigations or to make a reasonable decision that makes particular investigations unnecessary." Application of the *Strickland* standard to this case convinces me that further investigation was compelled constitutionally because there was inadequate information on which a reasonable professional judgment to limit the investigation could have been made.

Having concluded that the conduct of petitioner's lawyer in failing to pursue an in-vestigation into petitioner's psychological problems or into his family and childhood background was professionally unreasonable, given the circumstances known to counsel at the time, I must also address the question whether this inadequate perfor-mance prejudiced petitioner. In my view, if more information about this adolescent's psychological problems, troubled childhood, and unfortunate family history had been available, "there is a reasonable probability that ... the sentencer — including an appellate court, to the extent it independently reweighs the evidence — would have concluded that the balance of aggravating and mitigating circumstances did not war-rant death."

... But for defense counsel's disinterest in developing any mitigating evidence to per-mit an informed decision, there is a reasonable possibility that the outcome of the sen-tencing hearing would have been different. Counsel's conduct "so undermined the proper functioning of the adversarial process" that the sentencing hearing cannot "be relied on as having produced a just result."

Wiggins v. Smith

539 U.S. 510 (2003)

Justice O'CONNOR delivered the opinion of the Court.

Petitioner, Kevin Wiggins, argues that his attorneys' failure to investigate his background and present mitigating evidence of his unfortunate life history at his capital sentencing proceedings violated his Sixth Amendment right to counsel. In this case, we consider whether the United States Court of Appeals for the Fourth Circuit erred in upholding the Maryland Court of Appeals' rejection of this claim.

I

A.

On September 17, 1988, police discovered 77-year-old Florence Lacs drowned in the bathtub of her ransacked apartment in Woodlawn, Maryland. The State indicted petitioner for the crime on October 20, 1988, and later filed a notice of intention to seek the death penalty. Two Baltimore County public defenders, Carl Schlaich and Michelle Nethercott, assumed responsibility for Wiggins' case. In July 1989, petitioner elected to be tried before a judge in Baltimore County Circuit Court. On August 4, after a 4-day trial, the court found petitioner guilty of first-degree murder, robbery, and two counts of theft.

After his conviction, Wiggins elected to be sentenced by a jury, and the trial court scheduled the proceedings to begin on October 11, 1989. On September 11, counsel filed a motion for bifurcation of sentencing in hopes of presenting Wiggins' case in two phases. Counsel intended first to prove that Wiggins did not act as a "principal in the first degree," i.e., that he did not kill the victim by his own hand. Counsel then intended, if necessary, to present a mitigation case. In the memorandum in support of their motion, counsel argued that bifurcation would enable them to present each case in its best light; separating the two cases would prevent the introduction of mitigating evidence from diluting their claim that Wiggins was not directly responsible for the murder.

On October 12, the court denied the bifurcation motion, and sentencing proceedings commenced immediately thereafter. In her opening statement, Nethercott told the jurors they would hear evidence suggesting that someone other than Wiggins actually killed Lacs. Counsel then explained that the judge would instruct them to weigh Wiggins' clean record as a factor against a death sentence. She concluded: "You're going to hear that Kevin Wiggins has had a difficult life. It has not been easy for him. But he's worked. He's tried to be a productive citizen, and he's reached the age of 27 with no convictions for prior crimes of violence and no convictions, period.... I think that's an important thing for you to consider." During the proceedings themselves, however, counsel introduced no evidence of Wiggins' life history.

Before closing arguments, Schlaich made a proffer to the court, outside the presence of the jury, to preserve bifurcation as an issue for appeal. He detailed the mitigation case counsel would have presented had the court granted their bifurcation motion. He explained that they would have introduced psychological reports and expert testimony demonstrating Wiggins' limited intellectual capacities and childlike emotional state on the one hand, and the absence of aggressive patterns in his behavior, his capacity for empathy, and his desire to function in the world on the other. At no point did Schlaich proffer any evidence of petitioner's life history or family background. On October 18, the court instructed the jury on the sentencing task before it, and later that afternoon, the jury returned with a sentence of death. A divided Maryland Court of Appeals affirmed.

B.

In 1993, Wiggins sought postconviction relief in Baltimore County Circuit Court. With new counsel, he challenged the adequacy of his representation at sentencing, arguing that his attorneys had rendered constitutionally defective assistance by failing to investigate and present mitigating evidence of his dysfunctional background. To support his claim, petitioner presented testimony by Hans Selvog, a licensed social worker certified as an expert by the court. Selvog testified concerning an elaborate social history report he had prepared containing evidence of the severe physical and sexual abuse petitioner suffered at the hands of his mother and while in the care of a series of foster parents. Relying on state social services, medical, and school records, as well as interviews with petitioner and numerous family members, Selvog chronicled petitioner's bleak life history.

According to Selvog's report, petitioner's mother, a chronic alcoholic, frequently left Wiggins and his siblings home alone for days, forcing them to beg for food and to eat paint chips and garbage. Mrs. Wiggins' abusive behavior included beating the children for breaking into the kitchen, which she often kept locked. She had sex with men while her children slept in the same bed and, on one occasion, forced petitioner's hand against a hot stove burner—an incident that led to petitioner's hospitalization.

At the age of six, the State placed Wiggins in foster care. Petitioner's first and second foster mothers abused him physically, and, as petitioner explained to Selvog, the father in his second foster home repeatedly molested and raped him. At age 16, petitioner ran away from his foster home and began living on the streets. He returned intermittently to additional foster homes, including one in which the foster mother's sons allegedly gang-raped him on more than one occasion. After leaving the foster care system, Wiggins entered a Job Corps program and was allegedly sexually abused by his supervisor.

During the postconviction proceedings, Schlaich testified that he did not remember retaining a forensic social worker to prepare a social history, even though the State made funds available for that purpose. He explained that he and Nethercott, well in advance of trial, decided to focus their efforts on "retry[ing] the factual case" and disputing Wiggins' direct responsibility for the murder. In April 1994, at the close of the proceedings, the judge observed from the bench that he could not remember a capital case in which counsel had not compiled a social history of the defendant, explaining, "[n]ot to do a social history, at least to see what you have got, to me is absolute error. I just—I would be flabbergasted if the Court of Appeals said anything else." In October 1997, however, the trial court denied Wiggins' petition for postconviction relief. The court concluded that "when the decision not to investigate ... is a matter of trial tactics, there is no ineffective assistance of counsel."

The Maryland Court of Appeals affirmed the denial of relief, concluding that trial counsel had made "a deliberate, tactical decision to concentrate their effort at convincing the jury" that appellant was not directly responsible for the murder. The court observed that counsel knew of Wiggins' unfortunate childhood. They had available to them both the presentence investigation (PSI) report prepared by the Division of Parole and Probation, as required by Maryland law, as well as "more detailed social service records that recorded incidences of physical and sexual abuse, an alcoholic mother, placements in foster care, and borderline retardation." The court acknowledged that this evidence was neither as detailed nor as graphic as the history elaborated in the Selvog report but emphasized that "counsel *did* investigate and *were* aware of appellant's background" (emphasis in original). Counsel knew that at least one uncontested mitigating factor—Wiggins' lack of prior convictions—would be before the jury should their attempt to disprove Wiggins' direct responsibility for the murder fail. As a result, the court concluded, Schlaich and Nethercott "made a reasoned choice to proceed with what they thought was their best defense."

C.

In September 2001, Wiggins filed a petition for writ of habeas corpus in Federal District Court. The trial court granted him relief, holding that the Maryland courts' rejection of his ineffective assistance claim "involved an unreasonable application of clearly established federal law." [The Fourth Circuit reversed, and the Supreme Court granted certiorari.]

II

A

... We established the legal principles that govern claims of ineffective assistance of counsel in *Strickland v. Washington,* 466 U.S. 668 (1984). An ineffective assistance claim has two components: A petitioner must show that counsel's performance was deficient, and that the deficiency prejudiced the defense. To establish deficient performance, a petitioner must demonstrate that counsel's representation "fell below an objective standard of reasonableness." We have declined to articulate specific guidelines for appropriate attorney conduct and instead have emphasized that "[t]he proper measure of attorney performance remains simply reasonableness under prevailing professional norms."

In this case, as in *Strickland,* petitioner's claim stems from counsel's decision to limit the scope of their investigation into potential mitigating evidence. Here, as in *Strickland,* counsel attempt to justify their limited investigation as reflecting a tactical judgment not to present mitigating evidence at sentencing and to pursue an alternate strategy instead....

In light of these standards, our principal concern in deciding whether Schlaich and Nethercott exercised "reasonable professional judgmen[t]" is not whether counsel should have presented a mitigation case. Rather, we focus on whether the investigation supporting counsel's decision not to introduce mitigating evidence of Wiggins' background was itself reasonable.

B.

1.

The record demonstrates that counsel's investigation drew from three sources. Counsel arranged for William Stejskal, a psychologist, to conduct a number of tests on petitioner. Stejskal concluded that petitioner had an IQ of 79, had difficulty coping with demanding situations, and exhibited features of a personality disorder. These reports revealed nothing, however, of petitioner's life history.

With respect to that history, counsel had available to them the written PSI, which included a one-page account of Wiggins' "personal history" noting his "misery as a youth," quoting his description of his own background as "'disgusting,'" and observing that he spent most of his life in foster care. Counsel also "tracked down" records kept by the Baltimore City Department of Social Services (DSS) documenting petitioner's various placements in the State's foster care system. In describing the scope of counsel's investigation into petitioner's life history, both the Fourth Circuit and the Maryland Court of Appeals referred only to these two sources of information.

Counsel's decision not to expand their investigation beyond the PSI and the DSS records fell short of the professional standards that prevailed in Maryland in 1989. As Schlaich acknowledged, standard practice in Maryland in capital cases at the time of Wiggins' trial included the preparation of a social history report. Despite the fact that the Public Defender's office made funds available for the retention of a forensic social worker, counsel chose not to commission such a report. Counsel's conduct similarly fell short of the standards for capital defense work articulated by the American Bar Association (ABA)—standards to which we long have referred as "guides to determining what is reasonable." *Strickland.* The ABA Guidelines provide that investigations into mitigating evidence "should comprise efforts to discover *all reasonably available* mitigating evidence and evidence to rebut any aggravating evidence that may be introduced by the prosecutor." ABA Guidelines for the Appointment and Performance of Counsel in Death Penalty Cases 11.4.1(C), p. 93 (1989) (emphasis added). Despite these well-defined norms, however, counsel abandoned their investigation of petitioner's background after having acquired only rudimentary knowledge of his history from a narrow set of sources.

The scope of their investigation was also unreasonable in light of what counsel actually discovered in the DSS records. The records revealed several facts: Petitioner's mother was a chronic alcoholic; Wiggins was shuttled from foster home to foster home and displayed some emotional difficulties while there; he had frequent, lengthy absences from school; and, on at least one occasion, his mother left him and his siblings alone for days without food. As the Federal District Court emphasized, any reasonably competent attorney would have realized that pursuing these leads was necessary to making an informed choice among possible defenses, particularly given the apparent absence of any aggravating factors in petitioner's background. Indeed, counsel uncovered no evidence in their investigation to suggest that a mitigation case, in its own right, would have been counterproductive, or that further investigation would have been fruitless; this case is therefore distinguishable from our precedents in which we have found limited investigations into mitigating evidence to be reasonable.... Had counsel investigated further, they may well have discovered the sexual abuse later revealed during state postconviction proceedings.

The record of the actual sentencing proceedings underscores the unreasonableness of counsel's conduct by suggesting that their failure to investigate thoroughly resulted from inattention, not reasoned strategic judgment. Counsel sought, until the day before sentencing, to have the proceedings bifurcated into a retrial of guilt and a mitigation stage. On the eve of sentencing, counsel represented to the court that they were prepared to come forward with mitigating evidence, and that they intended to present such evidence in the event the court granted their motion to bifurcate. In other words, prior to sentencing, counsel never actually abandoned the possibility that they would present a mitigation defense. Until the court denied their motion, then, they had every reason to develop the most powerful mitigation case possible.

What is more, during the sentencing proceeding itself, counsel did not focus exclusively on Wiggins' direct responsibility for the murder. After introducing that issue in her opening statement, Nethercott entreated the jury to consider not just what Wiggins "is found to have done," but also "who [he] is." Though she told the jury it would "hear that Kevin Wiggins has had a difficult life," counsel never followed up on that suggestion with details of Wiggins' history. At the same time, counsel called a criminologist to testify that inmates serving life sentences tend to adjust well and refrain from further violence in prison—testimony with no bearing on whether petitioner committed the murder by his own hand. Far from focusing exclusively on petitioner's direct responsibility, then, counsel put on a halfhearted mitigation case, taking precisely the type of "shotgun" approach the Maryland Court of Appeals concluded counsel sought to avoid. When viewed in this light, the "strategic decision" the state courts and respondents all invoke to justify counsel's limited pursuit of mitigating evidence resembles more a *post-hoc* rationalization of counsel's conduct than an accurate description of their deliberations prior to sentencing.

In rejecting petitioner's ineffective assistance claim, the Maryland Court of Appeals appears to have assumed that because counsel had *some* information with respect to petitioner's background—the information in the PSI and the DSS records—they were in a position to make a tactical choice not to present a mitigation defense. In assessing the reasonableness of an attorney's investigation, however, a court must consider not only the quantum of evidence already known to counsel, but also whether the known evidence would lead a reasonable attorney to investigate further. Even assuming Schlaich and Nethercott limited the scope of their investigation for strategic reasons, *Strickland* does not establish that a cursory investigation automatically justifies a tactical decision with respect to sentencing strategy. Rather, a reviewing court must consider the reasonableness of the investigation said to support that strategy....

3.

In finding that Schlaich and Nethercott's investigation did not meet *Strickland*'s performance standards, we emphasize that *Strickland* does not require counsel to investigate every conceivable line of mitigating evidence no matter how unlikely the effort would be to assist the defendant at sentencing. Nor does *Strickland* require defense counsel to present mitigating evidence at sentencing in every case. Both conclusions would interfere with the "constitutionally protected independence of counsel" at the heart of *Strickland*. We base our conclusion on the much more limited principle that "strategic choices made after less than complete investigation are reasonable" only to the extent that "reasonable professional judgments support the limitations on investigation." A decision not to investigate thus "must be directly assessed for reasonableness in all the circumstances."

Counsel's investigation into Wiggins' background did not reflect reasonable professional judgment. Their decision to end their investigation when they did was neither consistent with the professional standards that prevailed in 1989, nor reasonable in light of the evidence counsel uncovered in the social services records—evidence that would have led a reasonably competent attorney to investigate further. Counsel's pursuit of bifurcation until the eve of sentencing and their partial presentation of a mitigation case suggest that their incomplete investigation was the result of inattention, not reasoned strategic judgment. In deferring to counsel's decision not to pursue a mitigation case despite their unreasonable investigation, the Maryland Court of Appeals unreasonably applied *Strickland*....

III

In order for counsel's inadequate performance to constitute a Sixth Amendment violation, petitioner must show that counsel's failures prejudiced his defense. In *Strickland*, we made clear that, to establish prejudice, a "defendant must show that there is a reasonable probability that, but for counsel's unprofessional errors, the result of the proceeding would have been different. A reasonable probability is a probability sufficient to undermine confidence in the outcome." In assessing prejudice, we reweigh the evidence in aggravation against the totality of available mitigating evidence. In this case, our review is not circumscribed by a state court conclusion with respect to prejudice, as neither of the state courts below reached this prong of the *Strickland* analysis.

The mitigating evidence counsel failed to discover and present in this case is powerful. As Selvog reported based on his conversations with Wiggins and members of his family, Wiggins experienced severe privation and abuse in the first six years of his life while in the custody of his alcoholic, absentee mother. He suffered physical torment, sexual molestation, and repeated rape during his subsequent years in foster care. The time Wiggins spent homeless, along with his diminished mental capacities, further augment his mitigation case. Petitioner thus has the kind of troubled history we have declared relevant to assessing a defendant's moral culpability. *Penry v. Lynaugh*, 492 U.S. 302, 319 (1989) ("'[E]vidence about the defendant's background and character is relevant because of the belief, long held by this society, that defendants who commit criminal acts that are attributable to a disadvantaged background ... may be less culpable than defendants who have no such excuse'").

Given both the nature and the extent of the abuse petitioner suffered, we find there to be a reasonable probability that a competent attorney, aware of this history, would have introduced it at sentencing in an admissible form. While it may well have been strategically defensible upon a reasonably thorough investigation to focus on Wiggins' direct responsibility for the murder, the two sentencing strategies are not necessarily mutually exclusive. Moreover, given the strength of the available evidence, a reasonable attorney may well have chosen to prioritize the mitigation case over the direct responsibility challenge, particularly given that Wiggins' history contained little of the double edge we have found to justify limited investigations in other cases....

Wiggins' sentencing jury heard only one significant mitigating factor—that Wiggins had no prior convictions. Had the jury been able to place petitioner's excruciating life history on the mitigating side of the scale, there is a reasonable probability that at least one juror would have struck a different balance. Cf. *Borchardt v. Maryland*, 367 Md. 91, 139–140, 786 A.2d 631, 660 (2001) (noting that as long as a single juror concludes that mitigating evidence outweighs aggravating evidence, the death penalty cannot be imposed).

Moreover, in contrast to the petitioner in *Williams v. Taylor* [*supra*, this chapter], Wiggins does not have a record of violent conduct that could have been introduced by the State to offset this powerful mitigating narrative. As the Federal District Court found, the mitigating evidence in this case is stronger, and the State's evidence in support of the death penalty far weaker, than in *Williams*, where we found prejudice as the result of counsel's failure to investigate and present mitigating evidence. We thus conclude that the available mitigating evidence, taken as a whole, "might well have influenced the jury's appraisal" of Wiggins' moral culpability. Accordingly, the judgment of the United States Court of Appeals for the Fourth Circuit is reversed, and the case is remanded for further proceedings consistent with this opinion.

Note on *Rompilla v. Beard*, 545 U.S. 374 (2005)

Ronald Rompilla was convicted of murder and other crimes. During the penalty phase, the jury found the aggravating factors that the murder was committed during a felony, that it was committed by torture, and that Rompilla had a significant history of felony convictions indicating the use or threat of violence. In mitigation, five members of Rompilla's family beseeched the jury for mercy. He was sentenced to death, and the Pennsylvania Supreme Court affirmed.

Rompilla's new lawyers filed for state postconviction relief, claiming ineffective assistance by his trial counsel in failing to present significant mitigating evidence about Rompilla's childhood, mental capacity and health, and alcoholism. The state courts found that trial counsel had sufficiently investigated the mitigation possibilities.

Rompilla then raised inadequate representation in a federal habeas petition. The district court found that the state Supreme Court had unreasonably applied *Strickland v. Washington*, 466 U.S. 668, concluding that trial counsel had not investigated obvious signs that Rompilla had a troubled childhood and suffered from mental illness and alcoholism, unjustifiably relying instead on Rompilla's own description of an unexceptional background.

In reversing, the U.S Court of Appeals for the Third Circuit found nothing unreasonable in the state court's application of *Strickland*, given defense counsel's efforts to uncover mitigation evidence from Rompilla, certain family members, and three mental health experts. The court distinguished *Wiggins v. Smith*, 539 U.S. 510—in which counsel had failed to investigate adequately to the point of ignoring the leads their limited enquiry yielded—noting that, although trial counsel did not unearth useful information in Rompilla's school, medical, police, and prison records, their investigation had gone far enough to give them reason to think that further efforts would not be a wise use of their limited resources.

The Supreme Court reversed, holding that even when a capital defendant and his family members have suggested that no mitigating evidence is available, his lawyer is bound to make reasonable efforts to obtain and review material that counsel knows the prosecution will probably rely on as evidence of aggravation at the trial's sentencing phase.

According to Justice Souter's opinion for the Court, Rompilla's entitlement to federal habeas relief turned on showing that the state court's resolution of his ineffective-assistance claim under *Strickland* "resulted in a decision that was contrary to, or involved an unreasonable application of, clearly established Federal law, as determined by" this Court. 28 U.S.C. § 2254(d)(1). To prevail, Rompilla must demonstrate that the state court's result was not only incorrect but also objectively unreasonable. *Wiggins, supra,* at 520–521. The Court noted that, in judging the defense's investigation in preparing for a capital trial's sentencing phase, hindsight is discounted by pegging adequacy to "counsel's perspective at the time" investigative decisions were made and by giving deference to counsel's judgments. *Strickland, supra,* at 689, 691.

The Court concluded that Rompilla's trial lawyers were deficient in failing to examine the court file on Rompilla's prior rape and assault conviction. They knew that the Commonwealth intended to seek the death penalty by proving that Rompilla had a significant history of felony convictions indicating the use or threat of violence, that it would attempt to establish this history by proving the prior conviction, and that it would emphasize his violent character by introducing a transcript of the rape victim's trial testimony. Although the prior conviction file was a public record, readily available at the courthouse where Rompilla was to be tried, counsel looked at no part of it until warned by the prosecution a second time, and even then did not examine the entire file.

With every effort to view the facts as a defense lawyer would have at the time, the Court noted that it was difficult to see how counsel could have failed to realize that not examining the file would seriously compromise their opportunity to respond to an aggravation case. Their duty to make all reasonable efforts to learn what they could about the offense the prosecution was going to use certainly included obtaining the Commonwealth's own readily available file to learn what it knew about the crime, to discover any mitigating evidence it would downplay, and to anticipate the details it would emphasize.

The Court viewed the obligation to examine the file as particularly pressing in Rompilla's case because the violent prior offense was similar to the crime charged and because Rompilla's sentencing strategy stressed residual doubt. According to the Court, this obligation is not just common sense, but is also described in the American Bar Association Standards for Criminal Justice, which are " 'guides to determining what is reasonable,' " *Wiggins, supra,* at 524.

The state court's conclusion that defense counsel's efforts to find mitigating evidence by other means were enough to free them from further enquiry was wrong, to the point of being objectively unreasonable. In the Court's opinion, no reasonable lawyer would forgo examination of the file thinking he could do as well by asking the defendant or family relations what they recalled. Nor would a reasonable lawyer compare possible searches for school reports, juvenile records, and evidence of drinking habits to the opportunity to take a look at a file disclosing what the prosecutor knows and plans to read from in his case.

Because the state courts found counsel's representation adequate, they never reached the prejudice element of a *Strickland* claim, whether "there is a reasonable probability that, but for counsel's unprofessional errors, the result … would have been different," 466 U.S., at 694. The Court conducted a *de novo* examination of this element and found that counsel's lapse was prejudicial. Had they looked at the prior conviction file, they would have found a range of mitigation leads that no other source had opened up. The imprisonment records contained in that file pictured Rompilla's childhood and mental health very differently from anything they had seen or heard. The accumulated entries — e.g., that Rompilla had a series of incarcerations, often related to alcohol; and test results that would have pointed the defense's mental health experts to schizophrenia and other disorders — would have destroyed the benign conception of Rompilla's upbringing and mental capacity counsel had formed from talking to five family members and from the mental health experts' reports.

Further effort would presumably have unearthed much of the material postconviction counsel found. Alerted to the school, medical, and prison records that trial counsel never saw, postconviction counsel found red flags pointing up a need for further testing, which revealed organic brain damage and childhood problems probably related to fetal alcohol syndrome. These findings in turn would probably have prompted a look at easily available school and juvenile records, which showed additional problems, including evidence of a highly abusive home life. The evidence adds up to a mitigation case bearing no relation to the few naked pleas for mercy actually put before the jury. The undiscovered "mitigating evidence, taken as a whole, 'might well have influenced the jury's appraisal' of [Rompilla's] culpability," *Wiggins, supra,* at 538, and the likelihood of a different result had the evidence gone in is "sufficient to undermine confidence in the outcome" actually reached at sentencing, *Strickland, supra,* at 694.

E. Effective Assistance of Counsel in Capital Sentencing Proceedings

Darden v. Wainwright

477 U.S. 168 (1986)

Justice POWELL delivered the opinion of the Court.

[The facts of *Darden v. Wainwright* are set forth in chapter 9, *supra.*]

V

... Petitioner contends that he was denied effective assistance of counsel at the sentencing phase of trial.... Petitioner argues that his trial counsel did not delve sufficiently into his background, and as a result were unprepared to present mitigating evidence at the sentencing hearing.

As an initial matter, petitioner contends that trial counsel devoted only the time between the close of the guilt phase of trial and the start of the penalty phase—approximately one-half hour—to preparing the case in mitigation. That argument is without merit. Defense counsel engaged in extensive preparation prior to trial, in a manner that included preparation for sentencing. Mr. Jack Johnson, head of the Public Defender's office at the time, stated to the habeas court that "we had expended hundreds of hours on [Darden's] behalf trying to represent him." Mr. Goodwill, an experienced criminal trial lawyer, testified that he "spent more time on this case than I spent on ... any capital case I have been involved in, probably more time than any case I've ever been involved in." That included time investigating petitioner's alibi, and driving petitioner around the scene of events to establish each point of his story. Counsel obtained a psychiatric report on petitioner, with an eye toward using it in mitigation during sentencing. Counsel also learned in pre-trial preparation that Mrs. Turman [wife of the deceased] was opposed to the death penalty, and considered the possibility of putting her on the stand at the sentencing phase. The record clearly indicates that a great deal of time and effort went into the defense of this case; a significant portion of that time was devoted to preparation for sentencing.

Petitioner also claims that his trial counsel interpreted Fla. Stat. §921.141(6), a statutory list of mitigating factors, as an exclusive list. He contends that their failure to introduce any evidence in mitigation was the result of this interpretation of the statute, and that he was thereby deprived of effective assistance of counsel. We express no view about the reasonableness of that interpretation of Florida law, because in this case, the trial court specifically informed petitioner and his counsel just prior to the sentencing phase of trial that they could "go into any other factors that might really be pertinent to full consideration of your case and the analysis of you and your family situation, your causes, or anything else that might be pertinent to what is the appropriate sentence." At that point, even if counsel previously believed the list to be exclusive, they knew they were free to offer nonstatutory mitigating evidence, and chose not to do so.

As we recognized in *Strickland*, "[j]udicial scrutiny of counsel's performance must be highly deferential.... A fair assessment of attorney performance requires that every effort be made to eliminate the distorting effects of hindsight, to reconstruct the circumstances of counsel's challenged conduct, and to evaluate the conduct from counsel's perspective at the time." In particular, "a court must indulge a strong presumption that counsel's conduct falls within the wide range of reasonable professional assistance; that is, the defendant must overcome the presumption that, under the circumstances, the challenged action 'might be considered sound trial strategy.'" In this case, there are several reasons why counsel reasonably could have chosen to rely on a simple plea for mercy from petitioner himself. Any attempt to portray petitioner as a non-violent man would have opened the door for the State to rebut with evidence of petitioner's prior convictions. This evidence had not previously been admitted in evidence, and trial counsel reasonably could have viewed it as particularly damaging. The head of the Public Defender's Office testified at the habeas corpus hearing that petitioner "had been in and out of jails and prisons for most of his adult life...." Petitioner had, for example, previously been convicted of assault with intent to commit rape. In addition, if defense counsel had attempted to offer testimony that petitioner was incapable of committing the crimes at issue here, the state could have responded with a psychiatric report that indicated that petitioner "very well could have committed the crime; that he was, as I recall his [the psychiatrist's] term, sociopathic type personality; that he would act entirely on impulse with no premeditation from the standpoint of planning. But that when a situation arose, the decision would be made simultaneously to commit the act." For that reason, after consultation with petitioner, defense counsel rejected use of the psychiatric testimony. Similarly, if defense counsel had attempted to put on evidence that petitioner was a family man, they would have been faced with his admission at trial that, although still married, he was spending the weekend furlough with a girlfriend. In sum, petitioner has not "overcome the presumption that, under the circumstances, the challenged action 'might be considered sound trial strategy.'" Petitioner has failed to satisfy the first part of the *Strickland* test, that his trial counsel's performance fell below an objective standard of reasonableness. We agree with both the District Court and the Court of Appeals that petitioner was not deprived of the effective assistance of counsel.

The Trial For Life: Effective Assistance of Counsel in Death Penalty Cases

Gary Goodpaster, 58 N.Y.U. L. Rev. 299 (1983)

Bernardino Sierra was mean, big, and ugly, and he had done evil and inhuman things. In eight hours, he had committed twelve robberies, two maimings, and three killings. He had terrorized and tortured people. While one of his victims was lying on the ground with his face in a pile of broken glass, Sierra kicked him in the back of the head to drive glass into his eyes. Another victim also lay face down. Sierra raked his shotgun up the spine of this one, then fired into the wooden floor beside his head, exploding wood fragments into his head and cheek. The experts said it was the "most likely case for capital punishment perhaps in the history of Harris County."

The jury heard the state's case and found Sierra guilty of capital murder. Now the jury was hearing further evidence to decide whether to sentence him to death.

When he was a little boy, his stepfather would come home drunk at night and beat him with a wire whip, catching him while he was asleep. His stepfather would lock him out of the house at night sometimes, and he would crawl under it to make his miserable bed and try to sleep. Often he was hungry and had no food. He ate out of garbage cans. He brought the best food he found there home for his mother and little sister.

His mother told this to the jury. Then his son, a beautiful little boy, got on the stand and told the jury, "That's my father." And the lawyer asked him, "What's the jury going to decide?" "Whether he lives or whether he dies," said the little boy.

The jury spared Sierra's life....

Earl Lloyd Jackson, too, committed terrible crimes. He beat eighty-one-year-old Vernita Curtis about the face, neck and chest so severely that she died four days later. He raped ninety-year-old Gladys Ott with a wine bottle and then beat her to death. He told a friend and a relative that he did it for the money, that they were "two old bags [who] were a nuisance and got ... what they deserved. The jury found him guilty of capital murder, and now would hear evidence to decide whether Jackson should die for his crimes.

His ninety-year-old grandmother was at the trial every day. After his parents had abandoned him, she had raised him. He had been kind to her, and she loved him and believed in him. She knew his parents had cruelly neglected him as a child. Defense counsel did not put her on the stand although her testimony could have been favorable to the defendant.

There was evidence, too, that Jackson was not very intelligent, perhaps was on the borderline of mental retardation. Defense counsel did not introduce this evidence, indeed, did not introduce any evidence at all. Instead, he appealed to the jury through argument:

> [Y]ou have heard testimony, terrible testimony, gruesome testimony.... It is a terrible crime on both ladies.... [W]e are not talking about civilized acts. We are talking about uncivilized acts on two old ladies....
>
> ... No matter what you decide here in this particular jury, it isn't going to stop with Earl Jackson. It isn't going to stop with Earl Jackson because there is [sic] a lot of Earl Jacksons coming, more and more.... [W]hat is important here is that you recognize that in this society we have created certain monsters.... He exists, this Jackson and a lot of other Jacksons. What are we going to do with them? What are we going to do with these young blacks? Is this the answer right here, the way this trial went down ... ? When it comes out, we will kill them whenever we can. What are we going to do with these young blacks? One thing for sure. One thing for sure is you are not going to take them all out and you are not going to shoot them. If you think that you are crazy.
>
> Another thing for sure, you are not going to take them out and put them on a boat and ship them back to Africa, that is for sure.

The jury sentenced Jackson to die.

These two cases graphically illustrate a pervasive problem and major cause of unequal treatment of defendants in capital cases: competency of defense counsel at the penalty or sentencing phase of the capital trial. The defendants committed roughly comparable capital crimes. Both had life histories that helped explain their crimes; both had friends or relatives willing to testify in their favor. Each defendant had a case which, if properly presented, would have permitted the jury to see the defendant as a human being, to understand the crime, and to have some basis for mercy. In the more terrible Texas case, involving three killings, two maimings, and twelve robberies, the jury showed mercy. In *People v. Jackson*, 618 P.2d 149 (Cal. 1980), which involved two killings and burglaries, the jury sentenced the defendant to death.

The different results in these cases may be attributed to the presence or absence of a meaningful penalty trial. In *Jackson*, there was not a true penalty *trial*, whereas in *Sierra* there was. Although evidence of the defendant's life history, character, and mental condition was available in *Jackson*, defense counsel introduced none of it. He did not place before the jury any witness whose testimony might have indicated that the defendant was not completely evil, or who might have asked that his life be spared. Instead, when deciding Jackson's fate, the jury heard only evidence of the defendant's awful crimes, the same evidence used to convict the defendant at the guilt phase of the trial—that, and the incredible argument of the defense counsel. The jury in *Jackson* was given no reason even to consider mercy.

Sierra and *Jackson* demonstrate that lives depend upon the effectiveness of counsel in trying capital cases, particularly at the penalty phase of the trial. The existence of a penalty phase in capital trials makes such trials radically different from ordinary criminal trials. A full capital trial is in fact two separate but intimately related trials: a preliminary guilt trial focusing on issues pertaining to the commission of a capital offense, and a subsequent penalty trial about the convicted defendant's worthiness to live. The guilt trial establishes the elements of the capital crime. The penalty trial is a trial for life. It is a trial *for* life in the sense that the defendant's life is at stake, and it is a trial *about* life, because a central issue is the meaning and value of the defendant's life.

Notes and Questions

1. In the early morning hours of February 19, 1983, three young men entered a gambling club in the Chinatown section of Seattle, tied and robbed fourteen patrons and employees, and shot them. Thirteen victims died. One defendant was sentenced to life without parole after his attorney put on substantial mitigating evidence. A second defendant was captured in Canada and extradited on condition that the state would not seek the death penalty. He received seven consecutive life terms. The third defendant, Kwan Fai Mak, received a death sentence after his court-appointed attorneys failed to put on any mitigating evidence.

In federal habeas proceedings, Mak argued that he received ineffective assistance of counsel. Specifically, Mak alleged that trial counsel failed to present any mitigating evidence regarding Mak's background, family relationships or cultural dislocations that might have affected his behavior. A summary of the evidence Mak claimed should have been presented by trial counsel follows.

> Family members would have testified that [Mak] was the beloved youngest son of a traditional Chinese family; that he had been a good student and dutiful son in Hong Kong; that after coming to this country he did well in citizenship, and in some school subjects, for the first few years; that he worked and gave money to the family; that he helped his parents in other ways; that he was kind to other members of the extended family; and that he was a "favorite uncle" to young nieces and nephews.

> The expert testimony of Dr. Johnson would have discussed serious assimilation problems experienced by many Chinese who are moved during adolescence from Hong Kong to North America, and certain values in the Chinese culture of Hong Kong which could help to explain petitioner's involvement in criminal activities here. [The testimony] would also suggest that petitioner's apparent

lack of emotion at trial did not necessarily indicate disinterest or coldness, but was consistent with cultural expectations of Chinese males.

Applying *Strickland*, should Mak receive relief? Why or why not? See *Mak v. Blodgett*, 970 F.2d 614 (9th Cir. 1992). Does it make a difference under *Strickland* that Mak's court-appointed trial attorneys were three and four years out of law school, respectively? Does it matter that neither lawyer had experience in defending capital cases?

2. Consider the following newspaper account:

Courts Turn Their Backs on the Poor: Murder Defendants Often Assigned Inept Lawyers
Kathryn Kahler, The Plain Dealer (June 10, 1990)

Poor people accused of murder and facing the death penalty routinely are represented by inexperienced, incompetent and unskilled lawyers who fail to vigorously defend them. A review of more than 30 cases and thousands of pages of trial transcripts, and interviews with more than 100 judges, defense lawyers and prosecutors, revealed glaring deficiencies in the quality of legal representation by court-appointed counsel in death penalty cases. Even though these cases literally are matters of life and death, defense lawyers appeared in court drunk or on drugs and repeatedly failed to raise basic constitutional issues during the trial. Some lawyers use the term "legal lynching" to describe proceedings in which little or no pretrial preparation and investigation is done and virtually no defense is mounted.

Eddie Lee Ross experienced this firsthand. His two lawyers—one court-appointed and the other one a Ku Klux Klan official who later surrendered his law license—performed no independent investigation and never discussed their defense strategy before the trial began. As a result, the two lawyers put on antagonistic defenses that helped to land Ross on Georgia's death row.

In Kentucky, one-quarter of the lawyers who represented the 26 convicts on death row last year have been either disbarred or suspended. In Georgia, serious questions about the quality of lawyering were raised in a majority of the 14 cases of men executed there.

State and federal courts rarely reverse death sentences based on a defendant's claim that his trial lawyer was ineffective, even in cases where court documents show seemingly egregious errors.

Freddie Kirkpatrick sits on death row in Louisiana and could be executed for murder any day now. Two days into the trial, his court-appointed lawyer saw a photograph of the victim and realized that he had been a fishing buddy and lawyer for the victim's family for 25 years. The lawyer had not discovered this obvious conflict of interest before the trial because he had done no preparation.

During the trial, the defense lawyer told the jurors they would be "justified" if they voted the death penalty, which they did. Kirkpatrick's co-defendant, represented by a different lawyer, got a life sentence.

Defense lawyer Gould H. K. Blair was defending Judy Hancy, charged with murdering her abusive husband in Talladega, Ala., when he was ordered to spend the night in the city jail because he was drunk in court. Earlier, he had passed out in the library. The lawyer was released from jail the following morning to return to court, having been unable to prepare for the next day. Hancy was sentenced to death and sits on Alabama's death row.

Georgia lawyer O. L. Collins has represented several poor defendants facing the death penalty. When it became clear that he was unfamiliar with two U.S. Supreme Court decisions that establish the legal framework for death penalty litigation, Collins was asked by the court to name any criminal law decisions from any court that he could remember. He named two, one of which was the Dred Scott decision, which is not a criminal case. He could not name any death penalty decisions. Nevertheless, he was not held by a federal court panel to be an ineffective lawyer.

A Kenton County, Ky. judge placed a desperate plea on the courthouse bulletin board seeking a lawyer for Gregory Wilson, accused of murder. The only lawyer to answer the ad was William Hagedorn, who listed a number that was the telephone at the local bar. Wilson pleaded to have Hagedorn removed from the case after Hagedorn prepared no defense and put on no evidence in the penalty phase of the trial. But the judge refused. He told him his only alternative was to represent himself. Wilson stuck with Hagedorn, and today sits on death row. His co-defendant will be eligible for parole soon.

3. Professor James S. Liebman described the lawyers who represent capital defendants in most death penalty states as "abysmally ineffectual," "chronically under-remunerated; often young and inexperienced, patently unqualified and incompetent, unethical, or bar-disciplined; sometimes drug-impaired, drunken, comatose, psychotic, or senile; very often grossly negligent; and nearly always out-gunned." Liebman argues that this counsel situation is worse in capital than in noncapital cases in two important respects:

> First, capital trials are much harder to litigate well than noncapital trials. Built into them are a hugely complicated body of specialized law, a second, sentencing trial that almost always is more far-ranging, expert-dependent, and factually complex than the guilt phase, and a host of peculiar tactical and strategic decisions caused by the need to "unify" one's defense strategy at two individually daunting and jointly contradictory proceedings (the defendant didn't commit capital murder; even though the defendant committed capital murder, it wasn't (or he isn't) so bad that he deserves a death sentence).
>
> Second, although most criminal defense lawyers are overworked and (even more so than in noncapital cases) underpaid, what they do for a living in the main is settle cases for lower sentences than would be imposed after a trial. To use (Columbia Law Professor) Vivian Berger's metaphor, what they do most of the time is hardly brain surgery. But capital cases settle much less frequently, and when they do, the bargaining is far harder and more sophisticated than in other kinds of cases—hence the many depredations (in Professor Berger's full phrase) of "the chiropractor as brain surgeon." Indeed, because a case in which the death sentence was imposed is virtually certain to have gone to trial—not many lawyers are reckless enough to advise clients to plead guilty to capital murder without an agreement or understanding that doing so will avoid the death penalty—it is highly likely that any capitally-sentenced defendant who finds himself in that fix got there after a settlement-specializing chiropractor attempted to open up that capital defendant's cranium at trial.

Liebman, "The Overproduction of Death," 100 Colum. L. Rev. 2030, 2102–2108 (Dec. 2000).

4. Which of the following descriptions of lawyers actually assigned to represent capital defendants suggest a probability of unreasonable professional assistance? Would you consider any of the lawyers to be per se "abysmally ineffectual" (to borrow Professor Liebman's phrase)?

—lawyers with no criminal, much less capital, experience, who have been admitted to the bar for only a few months;

—a third year law student;

—a lawyer who announced he was ready for trial without having read the state's capital sentencing statute;

—a lawyer who thought that the governing statute was one which was actually overturned years before;

—co-counsel who disagreed with each other over the appropriate defense, and consequently presented inconsistent defenses;

—co-counsel, each of whom thought the other had agreed to conduct the investigation of the defendant's guilt-innocence issues so that neither did so;

—co-counsel, each of whom thought the other had agreed to conduct the investigation of the defendant's sentencing issues so that neither did so;

—alcohol or drug dependent lawyers;

—lawyers who recently had been suspended or otherwise disciplined;

—lawyers who admitted their client was guilty of the capital charge;

—lawyers who permit their client to plead guilty to capital murder without securing a deal to avoid the death penalty;

—a lawyer who consented to the removal from the jury of the one juror who was holding out for a life sentence;

—lawyers who failed to make objections to the obvious legal errors that later led to the reversal of the codefendants' convictions or sentences (because the codefendants' counsel did object);

—lawyers who inform the jury that they don't think much of their clients;

—lawyers who refer to their own clients as "boy," "nigger," "animal";

—lawyers who fail to interview any witnesses or the client;

—lawyers who did not view the state's evidence before trial;

—lawyers who did not seek expert examinations of obviously mentally impaired clients;

—lawyers who conducted no investigation of either sentencing or guilt phase issues.

Liebman, "The Overproduction of Death," 100 Colum. L. Rev. 2030 (2000).

5. What responsibility do judges bear for appointing lawyers of questionable ability (or proven incompetence) to represent capital defendants? Texas, the nation's undisputed leader in executions, has a "partisan patronage" system for selecting lawyers to represent indigent capital clients. Texas judges repeatedly appoint lawyers despite "documented incompetence," including several who frequently sleep through trial proceedings; and another attorney who was an active alcoholic and cocaine user at the time of trial and could not file the appeal because his law license had been suspended due to substance abuse. Duggan, *Attorneys' Ineptitude Doesn't Halt Executions*, Wash. Post, May 12, 2000, at A1.

One Illinois trial judge appointed a previously disbarred lawyer to represent a capital defendant, seated a juror whose husband, a former judge, had previously sentenced the capital defendant to prison, and had six of his nine capital sentences reversed on appeal. Armstrong & Mills, *Death Row Justice Derailed*, Chi. Trib., Nov. 14, 1999, at N1.

According to death penalty defense expert Stephen Bright:

> Judges have appointed to capital cases lawyers who have never tried a case before. A study of homicide cases in Philadelphia found that the quality of lawyers appointed to capital cases in Philadelphia is so bad that "even officials in charge of the system say they wouldn't want to be represented in Traffic Court by some of the people appointed to defend poor people accused of murder." The study found that many of the attorneys were appointed by judges based on political connections, not legal ability. "Philadelphia's poor defendants often find themselves being represented by ward leaders, ward committeemen, failed politicians, the sons of judges and party leaders, and contributors to the judge's election campaigns."
>
> An Alabama judge refused to relieve counsel even when they filed a motion to be relieved of the appointment because they had inadequate experience in defending criminal cases and considered themselves incompetent to defend a capital case.[7] Georgia trial judges have repeatedly refused to appoint or compensate the experienced attorneys who, doing pro bono representation in postconviction stages of review, had successfully won new trials for clients who had been sentenced to death.[8] In several of those cases, the Georgia Supreme Court ordered continued representation at the new trials by the lawyers who were familiar with the case and the client. Despite those precedents, a Georgia judge refused to appoint an expert capital litigator from the NAACP Legal Defense and Educational Fund to continue representation of an indigent defendant, even though the Legal Defense Fund lawyer had won a new trial for the client by showing in federal habeas corpus proceedings that he had received ineffective assistance from the lawyer appointed by the judge at the initial capital trial.[9] And the lower court judges who have been reversed for failing to allow continuity in representation are still appointing lawyers when new cases come through the system. Those new defendants have no one to assist them in securing competent representation.

Bright, "Counsel for the Poor: The Death Sentence Not for the Worst Crime but for the Worst Lawyer," 103 Yale L.J. 1835, 1856 (1994).

At what point does incompetent representation degrade the American system of justice to the point where defendants are better off being rich and guilty than poor and innocent? Consider the examples provided by Professor Stephen Bright in the following law review article.

Counsel for the Poor: The Death Sentence Not for the Worst Crime but for the Worst Lawyer

Stephen B. Bright, 103 Yale L.J. 1835, 1859–65 (1994)

John Young was sentenced to death…. Young was represented at his capital trial by an attorney who was dependent on amphetamines and other drugs which affected his

---

7. *Parker v. State*, 587 So. 2d 1071, 1100–03 (Ala. Crim. App. 1991).
8. *Davis v. State*, 404 S.E.2d 800 (Ga. 1991); *Birt v. Montgomery*, 387 S.E.2d 879 (Ga. 1990); *Amadeo v. State*, 384 S.E.2d 181 (Ga. 1989).
9. *Roberts v. State*, No. S93A1857, 1994 Ga. (Ga. Feb. 21, 1994).

ability to concentrate. At the same time, the lawyer was physically exhausted, suffering severe emotional strain, and distracted from his law practice because of marital problems, child custody arrangements, difficulties in a relationship with a lover, and the pressures of a family business. As a result, the lawyer made little preparation for Young's trial, where his performance was inept. Young was sentenced to death. A few weeks later, Young met his attorney at the prison yard in the county jail. The lawyer had been sent there after pleading guilty to state and federal drug charges. Georgia executed John Young on March 20, 1985.

James Messer was "represented" at trial by an attorney who, at the guilt phase, gave no opening statement, presented no defense case, conducted cursory cross-examination, made no objections, and then emphasized the horror of the crime in some brief closing remarks that could not be fairly described as a "closing argument."[148] Even though severe mental impairment was important to issues of mitigation at both the guilt and penalty phases, the lawyer was unable to present any evidence of it because he failed to make an adequate showing to the judge that he needed a mental health expert. He also failed to introduce Messer's steady employment record, military record, church attendance, and cooperation with police. In closing, the lawyer repeatedly hinted that death was the most appropriate punishment for his own client. This too was good enough for a capital case in Georgia. Messer was executed July 28, 1988.

In light of Messer's case, one cannot help but wonder what progress has been made since the Supreme Court held that there is a right to counsel in capital cases in *Powell v. Alabama*. The nine black youths tried in Scottsboro, Alabama, in 1931 for the rapes of two white girls were represented by a lawyer described as "an able member of the local bar of long and successful experience in the trial of criminal as well as civil cases" who conducted "rigorous and rigid cross-examination" of the state's witnesses.[151] That is more than James Messer received at his capital trial.

Another case in which the attorney did nothing was that of Billy Mitchell, executed by Georgia on September 1, 1987. Following a guilty plea, Mitchell was sentenced to death at a sentencing hearing at which defense counsel called no witnesses, presented no mitigating evidence, and made no inquiries into his client's academic, medical, or psychological history.[152] A great deal of information of this kind was available and, if presented, could well have reduced the sentence imposed on Mitchell. In postconviction proceedings, new counsel submitted 170 pages of affidavits summarizing the testimony of individuals who could have appeared on Mitchell's behalf. Among them were family members, a city council member, a former prosecutor, a professional football player, a bank vice president, and several teachers, coaches, and friends.

The same ineptitude is frequently tolerated on appeal. The brief on direct appeal to the Alabama Supreme Court in the case of Larry Gene Heath, executed by Alabama on March 20, 1992, consisted of only one page of argument and cited only one case, which it distinguished.[154] Counsel, who had filed a six-page brief on the same issue in the Al-

---

148. *Messer v. Kemp*, 474 U.S. 1008, 1090 (1986) (Marshall, J., dissenting from denial of certiorari).

151. *Powell v. Alabama*, 287 U.S. 45, 75 (1932) (Butler, J., dissenting) (quoting decision of Alabama Supreme Court).

152. *Mitchell v. Kemp*, 483 U.S. 1026, 1026–27 (1987) (Marshall, J., dissenting from denial of certiorari.).

154. [See Note and Question on Appellate Brief in *Heath v. Jones*, immediately following this law review article. Eds.]

abama Court of Criminal Appeals,[155] did not appear for oral argument in the case. Although the United States Court of Appeals later found counsel's performance deficient for failing to raise issues regarding denial of a change of venue, denial of sixty-seven challenges for cause of jurors who knew about the defendant's conviction in a neighboring state arising out of the same facts, and use of the defendant's assertion of his Fifth Amendment rights against him, it found no prejudice.[156]

While such incompetence as has been described here passes muster as "effective assistance of counsel" under the Supreme Court's view of the Sixth Amendment, counsel's performance often fails to satisfy the increasingly strict procedural doctrines developed by the Supreme Court since 1977. Failure of counsel to recognize and preserve an issue, due to ignorance, neglect, or failure to discover and rely upon proper grounds or facts, even in the heat of trial, will bar federal review of that issue.[157] A lawyer whose total knowledge of criminal law is *Miranda* and *Dred Scott* may be "not legally-ineffective" counsel under *Strickland*,[158] but such a lawyer will of course not recognize or preserve many constitutional issues. The result has been what Justice Thurgood Marshall described as an "increasingly pernicious visegrip" for the indigent accused: courts refuse to address constitutional violations because they were not preserved by counsel, but counsel's failure to recognize and raise those issues is not considered deficient legal assistance.[160]

Together, the lax standard of *Strickland* and the strict procedural default doctrines reward the provision of deficient representation. By assigning the indigent accused inadequate counsel, the state increases the likelihood of obtaining a conviction and death sentence at trial and reduces the scope of review. So long as counsel's performance passes muster under *Strickland*, those cases in which the accused received the poorest

---

155. *Heath v. Jones*, 941 F.2d 1126, 1131 (11th Cir. 1991).

156. However, Judge J.L. Edmondson, in concurring, disagreed even with the court's comment regarding counsel's performance. He stated, "I cannot agree that the quality of counsel's performance can be judged much by the length of brief or the number of issues raised. Effective lawyering involves the ability to discern strong arguments from weak ones and the courage to eliminate the unnecessary so that the necessary may be seen most clearly." The brief in *Heath*, however, and counsel's failure to appear for oral argument hardly constitute sterling examples of such ability or courage.

157. See *Smith v. Murray*, 477 U.S. 527, 533–36 (1986); *Engle v. Isaacs*, 456 U.S. 107, 130–34 (1982); *Wainwright v. Sykes*, 433 U.S. 72, 88–91 (1977); see also Richard J. Bonnie, Preserving Justice in Capital Cases While Streamlining the Process of Collateral Review, 23 U. Tol. L. Rev. 99, 109–13 (1991); Timothy J. Foley, The New Arbitrariness: Procedural Default of Federal Habeas Claims in Capital Cases, 23 Loy. L.A. L. Rev. 193 (1989).

158. The lawyer who testified that those were the only two "criminal" cases he knew has twice been found to satisfy the *Strickland* standard. *Birt v. Montgomery*, 725 F.2d 587, 596–601 (11th Cir. 1984) (en banc); *Williams v. State*, 368 S.E.2d 742, 747–50 (Ga. 1988).

160. Justice Robert Benham of the Georgia Supreme Court was "struck by the powerful irony" of the majority's refusal to consider an issue of "flagrantly improper" prosecutorial misconduct in one case because it was not preserved by counsel, but holding that counsel was not ineffective. *Todd v. State*, 410 S.E.2d 725, 735 n.1 (Ga. 1991) (Benham, J., dissenting). The majority disposed of the ineffective assistance claim in four sentences. The Mississippi Supreme Court refused to consider two issues on direct appeal because they were not properly preserved by trial counsel in *Hill v. State*, 432 So. 2d 427, 438–40 (Miss. 1983), over a dissent which argued, "We can think of no more arbitrary factor than having nimbleness of counsel on points of procedure determine whether Alvin Hill lives or dies." The same court later rejected in a single paragraph an assertion that counsel was ineffective. *In re Hill*, 460 So. 2d 792, 801 (Miss. 1984). The dissent argued: "Where two clear cut reversible errors were not available on direct appeal to a condemned defendant solely because his lawyer goofed, that would seem to make a prima facie case for ineffective assistance of counsel." Id. at 811 (Robertson, J., concurring in part and dissenting in part).

legal representation will receive the least scrutiny on appeal and in postconviction review because of failure of the lawyer to preserve issues.

In applying *Strickland,* courts indulge in presumptions and assumptions that have no relation to the reality of legal representation for the poor, particularly in capital cases. One scholar has aptly called the idea that bar membership automatically qualifies one to defend a capital case "lethal fiction." The reality is that most attorneys are not qualified to represent criminal defendants and certainly not those accused of capital crimes.

There is no basis for the presumption of competence in capital cases where the accused is represented by counsel who lacks the training, experience, skill, knowledge, inclination, time, and resources to provide adequate representation in a capital case. The presumption should be just the opposite—where one or more of these deficiencies exist, it is reasonable to expect that the lawyer is not capable of rendering effective representation. Indeed, the presumption of competence was adopted even though the Chief Justice of the Supreme Court, who joined in the majority in *Strickland,* had written and lectured about the lack of competence of trial attorneys.

Another premise underlying *Strickland* is that "[t]he government is not responsible for, and hence not able to prevent, attorney errors."[165] However, the notion of government innocence is simply not true in cases involving poor people accused of crimes. The poor person does not choose an attorney; one is assigned by a judge or some other government official. The government may well be responsible for attorney errors when it appoints a lawyer who lacks the experience and skill to handle the case, or when it denies the lawyer the time and resources necessary to do the job. In addition, as observed by Justice Blackmun:

> The county's control over the size of and funding for the public defender's office, as well as over the number of potential clients, effectively dictates the size of an individual attorney's caseload and influences substantially the amount of time the attorney is able to devote to each case. The public defender's discretion in handling individual cases—and therefore his ability to provide effective assistance to clients—is circumscribed to an extent not experienced by privately retained attorneys.

The assumption that deficient representation makes no difference,[167] which underlies a finding of lack of prejudice under *Strickland,* is also flawed. In cases where constitutional violations were not preserved and the defendant was executed while an identically situated defendant received relief for the same constitutional violation, it is apparent that the ineptitude of the lawyer did make a difference in the outcome of the case. In other more subtle but equally determinative ways, competent legal assistance can make a difference in the outcome which may not be detectable by reviewing courts.

A lawyer may muddle through a case with little or no preparation, but it is impossible to determine how the case might have been handled differently if he had investigated and prepared. Other difficulties may be even more difficult to detect. Rapport with the client and the family may lead to cooperation and the disclosure of compelling

---

165. *Strickland v. Washington,* 466 U.S. 688, 693 (1984).

167. "It is the belief—rarely articulated, but, I am afraid, widely held—that most criminal defendants are guilty anyway. From this assumption it is a short path to the conclusion that the quality of representation is of small account." David L. Bazelon, The Defective Assistance of Counsel, 42 U. Cin. L. Rev. 1, 26 (1973).

mitigating evidence that might not be found by a less skillful attorney. Good negotiating skills may bring about a plea offer to resolve the case with a sentence less than death, and a good relationship with the client may result in acceptance of an offer that might otherwise be rejected. Nor are reviewing courts able to determine after the fact the difference made by other skills that are often missing in the defense of criminal cases—such as conducting a good voir dire examination of jurors, effective examination and cross-examination of witnesses, and presenting well-reasoned and persuasive closing arguments.

The prejudice standard is particularly inappropriate for application to deficient representation at the penalty phase of a capital case. It is impossible for reviewing courts to assess the difference that investigation into mitigating circumstances and the effective presentation of mitigating evidence might make on a jury's sentencing decision.

The Supreme Court has consistently reaffirmed that in a capital case any aspect of the life and background of the accused offered by the defense must be considered as "mitigating circumstances" in determining punishment.[172] Those who have tried capital cases have found that the competent presentation of such evidence often results in sentences less than death. But the right to have any of the "diverse frailties of humankind"[174] taken into account is meaningless if the accused is not provided with counsel capable of finding and effectively presenting mitigating circumstances.

A court-appointed defense lawyer's only reference to his client during the penalty phase of a Georgia capital case was: "You have got a little ole nigger man over there that doesn't weigh over 135 pounds. He is poor and he is broke. He's got an appointed lawyer. He is ignorant. I will venture to say he has an IQ of not over 80."[175] The defendant was sentenced to death.

Had that lawyer done any investigation into the life and background of his client, he would have found that his client was not simply "ignorant." Instead, he was mentally retarded. For that reason, he had been rejected from military service. And he had been unable to function in school or at any job except the most repetitive and menial ones. His actual IQ was far from 80; it was 68. He could not do such basic things as make change or drive an automobile. After his death sentence was set aside because of failure to grant a change of venue,[176] an investigation was conducted, these facts were documented, and the defendant received a life sentence.

So long as juries and judges are deprived of critical information and the Bill of Rights is ignored in the most emotionally and politically charged cases due to deficient legal representation, the courts should not be authorized to impose the extreme and irrevo-

---

172. *Lockett v. Ohio*, 438 U.S. 586, 604 (1978) (holding that sentencer must consider "any aspect of a defendant's character or record that the defendant proffers as a basis for a sentence less than death"); *Penry v. Lynaugh*, 492 U.S. 302 (1989) (mental retardation must be considered in mitigation); *Hitchcock v. Dugger*, 481 U.S. 393 (1987) (jury instructions may not limit the jury's consideration of mitigating circumstances); *Skipper v. South Carolina*, 476 U.S. 1 (1986) (good behavior in prison must be considered as mitigating factor); *Eddings v. Oklahoma*, 455 U.S. 104 (1982) (troubled childhood must be considered as mitigating factor); *Bell v. Ohio*, 438 U.S. 637 (1978) (same holding as *Lockett*).

174. *Woodson v. North Carolina*, 428 U.S. 280, 304 (1976).

175. Transcript of Opening and Closing Arguments at 39, *State v. Dungee*, Record Excerpts at 102, (11th Cir.) (No. 85-8202), decided sub nom. *Isaacs v. Kemp*, 778 F.2d 1482 (11th Cir. 1985), cert. denied, 476 U.S. 1164 (1986).

176. The court did not address the issue of ineffective assistance of counsel, which had been rejected by the district court.

cable penalty of death. Otherwise, the death penalty will continue to be imposed, not upon those who commit the worst crimes, but upon those who have the misfortune to be assigned the worst lawyers.

Note and Question on Appellate Brief Filed in *Heath v. Jones*, 941 F.2d 1126 (11th Cir. 1991)

What follows is the complete brief submitted by defense counsel on appeal in *Heath v. Jones*, 941 F.2d 1126, 1131 (11th Cir. 1991). The only parts of the brief not reproduced below are the cover page and certificate of service:

THE RECORD AFFIRMATIVELY SHOWS THAT THE APPELLANT WAS CONVICTED OF THE SAME OFFENSE, WHICH IS PRECISELY THE SAME IN LAW AND FACT IN VIOLATION OF THE 5th AMENDMENT OF THE UNITED STATES CONSTITUTION.

In the opinion of the Court of Criminal Appeals rendered on July 5, 1983, the Court failed to address the issue as to whether or not the Appellant was tried and convicted of the same offense, which is precisely the same in law and fact as the offense of which he was convicted in the State of Georgia.

As the Court pointed out on Page 3 of it's [sic] opinion, there were no cited cases to any Federal case law involving jeopardy in multiple State prosecutions and because there are no Federal cases cited, the Court apparently ignored the law relative to multiple prosecutions for an offense, which are precisely the same in law and fact. Apparently the Court relied on the case of *Hare v State*, 387 So. 2 d [sic] 299, 300 (Ala. Crim. App. 1980) in reaching it's [sic] decision in this case. The *Hare* case can be distinguished simply by looking at the facts in the *Hare* case, wherein the Court in Tennessee was dealing with the offense of possession of drugs in the State of Alabama, which are not precisely the same in law and fact.

Appellant plead [sic] guilty to the offense of murder, which was a lesser included offense of the charge of murder caused and directed by the Appellant under the laws of the State of Georgia and received a life sentence. After the Appellant was sentenced in the State of Georgia to life imprisonment, he was returned to the State of Alabama and was prosecuted and convicted of the offense of murder during kidnapping, 1st degree in the State of Alabama for the murder of his wife, Rebecca Heath.

Apparently this case is one of first impression in the State of Alabama, and this Court has not ruled on a similar case involving the offense of murder where only one victim is involved.

Conclusion

Appellant contends that his constitutional rights guaranteed under the 5th Amendment of the United States Constitution and his rights guaranteed by Article I Section 9 of the Alabama Constitution prohibiting Double Jeopardy and Double Punishment have been violated. Further, Appellant contends that he relied upon his guaranteed Constitutional rights as set forth above in pleading guilty to a lesser included offense of murder of his wife, in the state of Georgia, and that the prosecution in the State of Alabama on the offense of murder during the course of kid napping [sic] of his wife, should be barred.

Therefore, after considering the facts, law and argument of Appellant, a Writ of Certiorari should be issued from this Court to the Court of Criminal Appeals correcting the errors complained of and reversing the judgment of the Court of Criminal Appeals and rendering such judgments as said Court have [sic] rendered in addition to such other relief as Petitioner may be entitled.

Respectfully submitted,

LARRY W. RONEY, ATTORNEY AT LAW, P.C.

Appellant's Brief and Argument in Support of Petition for Writ of Certiorari, at 1–2, *Heath v. Alabama*, 455 So.2d 905 (Ala. 1984).

Alabama requires that the brief and petition for certiorari be submitted at the same time. Ala. R. Crim. P. 32.2 (1990). Thus, the Alabama Supreme Court decided Heath's case on the basis of this brief alone. Assuming he was able to read and write, do you think Heath might have been better served if he wrote and filed his own brief?

Notes and Questions on Napping Lawyers

1. Joe Frank Cannon, a Houston attorney who earned a living through court appointments in capital cases (at least 10 of which resulted in death sentences) reportedly "boast[ed] of hurrying through [capital] trials 'like greased lightning'" to save the county money, and had a history of making elementary legal mistakes and a reputation for sleeping through capital trials. Barrett, *Lawyer's Fast Work on Death Cases Raises Serious Doubts About System*, Wall St. J., Sept. 7, 1994, at A1. Cannon's napping though substantial portions of Calvin Burdine's capital murder trial furnished the basis for Burdine's ineffective assistance of counsel claim. In 1999, federal district judge David Hittner ordered a new trial for Burdine, saying that a sleeping lawyer was equivalent to no lawyer at all. According to Judge Hittner, "Burdine's interests, including his life, were at stake. Hence, every witness should have compelled Cannon's fastidious and exacting attention." Judge Hittner's ruling was reversed 2–1 by a panel of the U.S. Court of Appeals for the Fifth Circuit which noted, "It is impossible to determine whether … counsel slept during presentation of crucial, exculpatory evidence, or during the introduction of unobjectionable, uncontested evidence." Burdine's habeas attorney, Robert McGlasson said, "This lawyer slept repeatedly during the state's presentation of its case. Of course it's substantial and of course it's crucial. How much time in a day-and-a-half trial is unimportant and not crucial?" Dissenting from the panel decision, U.S. Circuit Judge Fortunato Benavides wrote that Cannon should be presumed ineffective based on lower court findings that he slept during extended stretches of the trial. "It shocks the conscience that a defendant could be sentenced to death under the circumstances surrounding counsel's representation of Burdine," Benavides wrote.

2. Defense attorney John Benn reportedly "spent much" of George McFarland's capital-sentencing trial "in apparent deep sleep," "[h]is mouth falling open and his head loll[ing] back on his shoulders." Benn acknowledged that he was sleeping, and commented, "It's boring." The trial judge dismissed the problem, stating that "[t]he Constitution doesn't say the lawyer has to be awake." Makeig, *Asleep on the Job? Slay Trial Boring, Lawyer Says*, Hous. Chron., Aug. 14, 1992, at A35. The Texas Court of Criminal Appeals refused to order a new trial for McFarland. Judge Cathy Cochran wrote: "We conclude that, although one of his attorneys slept through portions of his trial, [McFarland] was not deprived of the assistance of counsel under the Sixth Amendment because his second attorney was present and an active advocate at all times." Cochran's opinion noted that Benn's napping worsened as the trial progressed and that the bailiff

would nudge Benn's chair to awaken him from time to time. At a hearing on McFarland's motion for a new trial, Benn testified: "I'm 72 years old. I customarily take a short nap in the afternoon." Hous. Chron., May 19, 2005.

For more examples of lawyers who slept through significant portions of capital trials, see Bright, "The American Bar Association's Recognition of the Sacrifice of Fairness for Results: Will We Pay the Price for Justice?," 4 Geo. J. on Fighting Poverty 183, 184–85 (1996).

3. Consider the following remark, made by Justice Ruth Bader Ginsburg, in a public address: "I have yet to see a death case, among the dozens coming to the Supreme Court on eve of execution petitions, in which the defendant was well represented at trial." "In Pursuit of the Public Good: Lawyers Who Care," Joseph L. Rauh Lecture, April 9, 2001.

Note and Questions on Impaired Lawyers

What should a federal court do in the following circumstances? Ronald Wayne Frye sought to avoid execution for the 1993 stabbing death and robbery of his 70-year-old landlord, Ralph Childress. After Frye exhausted his appeals in North Carolina state court, federal habeas counsel discovered new evidence and asked the Supreme Court to stay his execution. According to Frye's habeas lawyers, one of Frye's former defense attorneys admitted that he didn't pay attention to the trial and should have intervened to help the other defense attorney, who admitted a drinking habit. In an affidavit, Ted Cummings, Jr. said that he handled the guilt stage and that attorney Tom Portwood handled the sentencing phase. According to Frye's habeas petition, "One of Frye's counsel, Tom Portwood, has repeatedly admitted to an incredible decade-long drinking habit. He has testified that he did no work outside of the courtroom and that he did not search for one document or talk to one eyewitness. "Lead counsel, Ted Cummings, now admits in a sworn affidavit that he too was ineffective, in that he paid absolutely no attention to the sentencing phase and that if he had interacted with co-counsel he would, of course, have realized the depth of his co-counsel's addition and would have stepped in to do some work."

Of course, *Strickland* is not satisfied by showing only that counsel provided representation that fell below an objective standard of reasonableness. Any deficiencies in counsel's performance must be prejudicial; that is, the defendant must show a reasonable probability that, but for counsel's unprofessional errors, the result of the proceeding would have been different. According to Frye's petition, had his trial attorneys done their job, the jury would have heard mitigating evidence that could help explain Frye's behavior and his substance abuse. Frye and his brother were given away to strangers when Frye was 4, and their new father routinely hit them with a bullwhip.

Is it possible to provide drunk-but-effective representation during a capital sentencing proceeding? Consider Professor Jeffrey L. Kirchmeier's proposal for analyzing ineffective assistance claims where counsel slept during trial.

Drinks, Drugs and Drowsiness: The Constitutional Right to Effective Assistance of Counsel and the *Strickland* Prejudice Requirement

Jeffrey L. Kirchmeier, 75 Neb. L. Rev. 425 (1996)

The May 19, 2005 Houston Chronicle reported that the Texas Court of Criminal Appeals refused to order a new trial for McFarland. Judge Cathy Cochran wrote: "We conclude that, although one of his attorneys slept through portions of his trial, [McFarland] was not deprived of the assistance of counsel under the Sixth Amendment because his second attorney was present and an active advocate at all times." Cochran's opinion noted that Benn's napping worsened as the trial progressed and that the bailiff would nudge Benn's chair to awaken him from time to time. At a hearing on McFarland's motion for a new trial, Benn testified: "I'm 72 years old. I customarily take a short nap in the afternoon." The one area of attorney mental "impairment" where courts have applied a per se ineffective assistance rule is where a criminal defense attorney sleeps through a substantial portion of the trial. In *Javor v. United States*, 724 F.2d 831 (9th Cir. 1984), a pre-*Strickland* case, the Ninth Circuit Court of Appeals held that "when an attorney for a criminal defendant sleeps through a substantial portion of the trial, such conduct is inherently prejudicial and thus no separate showing of prejudice is necessary." In *Javor*, a federal magistrate found no prejudice but found that defense counsel slept or was not alert during a substantial portion of the trial for sale and possession of heroin. The court reasoned that requiring a show of prejudice would require "unguided speculation" and could not be applied even-handedly "because an attorney's absence prejudices a defendant more by what was not done than by what was done."

In *Tippins v. Walker*, 77 F.3d 682 (2d Cir. 1996), [a] post-*Strickland* case, the Second Circuit Court of Appeals followed the reasoning of *Javor* by applying a per se rule in certain situations where counsel slept during trial. However, the Second Circuit rejected the *Javor* test that required a finding of per se prejudice when counsel sleeps during a "substantial" portion of the trial. The court noted that the word "substantial" was unhelpful because the *Javor* court did not explain what was meant by "substantial," which could refer to the length of time counsel slept, the significance of the proceedings, or the proportion of the proceedings missed. The court stated that ordinarily the *Strickland* analysis would be sufficient for episodes of inattention or sleep, noting that:

> [p]rolonged inattention during stretches of a long trial (by sleep, preoccupation, or otherwise), particularly during periods concerned with other defendants, uncontested issues, or matters peripheral to a particular defendant, may be quantitatively substantial but without consequence. At such times, even alert and resourceful counsel cannot affect the proceedings to a client's advantage.

The court noted, however, that the *Strickland* standard allows a court to consider an improper decision by counsel as a strategy decision, but the underlying assumption in such a situation is that counsel is alert and able to exercise judgment. Specifically, the court stated:

> [A]s the majority reasoned in *Javor*, "prejudice is inherent" at some point, "because unconscious or sleeping counsel is equivalent to no counsel at all." Effectiveness of counsel depends in part on the ability to confer with the client during trial on a continuous basis, and the attorney must be "present and attentive" in order to make adequate cross-examination — "a matter of constitutional importance" by virtue of the Sixth Amendment. Moreover, if counsel sleeps, the ordinary analytical tools for identifying prejudice are unavailable. The errors and lost opportunities may not be visible in the record, and the reviewing court applying the traditional *Strickland* analysis may be forced to engage in "unguided speculation."

Thus, the *Tippins* court applied the following test: the defendant "suffered prejudice, by presumption or otherwise, if his counsel was repeatedly unconscious at trial for periods of time in which defendant's interests were at stake." The court then noted that the district court found that the defendant's attorney slept every day of the trial and during critical testimony. The court further noted that the record showed that the attorney was actually unconscious and his "sleeping was not a fitful inattention or a meditative focusing of the mind's powers."

Finally, the court concluded that the defendant's interests were at stake during the time of unconsciousness. Witnesses later testified that counsel was sleeping during specific key witnesses. Further, reprimands by the trial court did not cure the sleeping problem, although the reprimands illustrated the "dangerous character of the problem." Thus the court found the defendant was deprived of effective assistance of counsel in violation of his Sixth Amendment right to counsel.

[Professor Kirchmeier criticized the *Javor* "substantial portion" test as not providing enough guidance to courts and the *Tippins* requirement of "repeated and prolonged lapses" as too narrow to address situations where counsel only sleeps during the testimony of one key witness. He offered the following alternative proposal.]

Courts should apply a refined version of the *Javor* and *Tippins* tests, presuming prejudice: (1) if counsel sleeps through a relatively large portion of the overall trial proceedings; (2) if counsel sleeps during a large amount of time; or (3) if counsel sleeps through specific critical portions of the trial. Because every case differs factually, courts should have some discretion in determining what constitutes "sleeping," although an attorney with her eyes closed should not automatically be found to be sleeping. This test will presume prejudice where counsel sleeps 10 minutes of a one-hour trial, where counsel sleeps several different times over a 30-day trial, and where counsel sleeps only during crucial portions of the testimony of the state's key witness. In each of these situations, a defendant was effectively without counsel. Courts would find a Sixth Amendment violation in these cases if counsel were absent for the same amounts of time, and they should find such a violation if counsel is asleep. The *Javor* test probably would only presume prejudice in the first situation (where counsel slept during a "substantial portion" of the trial), while the *Tippins* test would likely only presume prejudice in the second situation (where there were "repeated and prolonged lapses"). Prejudice, however, should be presumed in both situations, as well as the situation where counsel sleeps during critical portions of the trial.

Notes and Questions

1. Will Professor Kirchmeier's proposed test result in a rash of victories for defendants raising ineffective assistance of counsel claims? Is his test too easy for defendants to meet? Should court reporters be instructed to record when attorneys appear to be napping during trial?

2. Professor Kirchmeier has described a "continuum of ineffective assistance of counsel cases, with one extreme being no counsel and the other extreme being competent counsel. If ... one were to rank the various right to counsel situations from the most egregious constitutional violations to the least egregious situations, the list would look like this:

(1) no counsel at all;

(2) no counsel at a 'critical stage' of the trial;

(3) surrounding circumstances prevent defense attorney from being able to act as counsel;

(4) 'counsel' does not meet the substantive requirements for Bar admission;

(5) counsel has a conflict of interest and an objection is made at trial;

(6) counsel sleeps during a portion of the trial;

(7) counsel is egregiously ineffective, such as where counsel refuses to participate in the trial, does not file an appeal, or concedes guilt;

(8) counsel has a conflict of interest and no objection is made at trial;

(9) counsel is drunk, using drugs, or otherwise substantially mentally impaired;

(10) counsel made errors at trial that may or may not have prejudiced the client; and

(11) counsel made no errors."

Kirchmeier, "Drink, Drugs and Drowsiness: The Constitutional Right to Effective Assistance of Counsel and the *Strickland* Prejudice Requirement," 75 Neb. L. Rev. 425, 463 (1996).

F. Direct Appeal

The Court has firmly held that "direct appeal is the primary avenue for relief of a conviction or sentence, and death penalty cases are no exception." *Barefoot v. Estelle*, 463 U.S. 880, 887 (1983). When the direct appeal process comes to an end—typically when an inmate raising a federal question petitions the United States Supreme Court for a writ of certiorari and the Court acts on the petition—a presumption of legality and finality attaches to the conviction and sentence. Consequently, "the role of federal habeas proceedings, while important in assuring that constitutional rights are observed, is secondary and limited."

1. No Constitutional Right to Appeal

Since 1894, the Supreme Court has uniformly held that a state is not constitutionally required to provide appellate review of criminal convictions. *McKane v. Durston*, 153 U.S. 684 (1894), left little room to argue that this general rule should be modified in capital cases under the Court's "death is different" jurisprudence. According to *McKane*,

> An appeal from a judgment of conviction is not a matter of absolute right, independent of [state] constitutional or statutory provisions allowing such appeal. A review by an appellate court of the final judgment in a criminal case, *however grave the offense of which the accused is convicted*, was not at common-law and is not now a necessary element of due process of law. It is wholly within the discretion of the State to allow or not to allow such a review.

Id. (emphasis added). See LaFave & Israel, *Criminal Procedure* 1136–1137 (2d ed.) (West Pub. Co. 1992). Thus, the right to appeal a criminal conviction, whether state or federal, exists purely as a matter of legislative grace. Nonetheless, all states, as well as the federal system, provide some mechanism for review of criminal convictions. Most states and the federal system supply a statutory right to appellate review. Several states simply provide the opportunity for appellate review at the discretion of the state's highest court.

2. Constitutional Protection of Statutory Right

Once the right to appeal is granted, however, constitutional protections attach. For example, states which choose to provide an appeal are prohibited from imposing "unnecessary impediments" to the exercise of that right. Whitebread & Slobogin, *Criminal Procedure* 691 (2d ed.) (Foundation Press 1986). Thus, the Court has held that due process was violated where a defendant who successfully appealed his conviction was subsequently reconvicted and received a greater punishment than originally imposed. *North Carolina v. Pearce*, 395 U.S. 711 (1969). To punish more severely, and overcome a "presumption of vindictiveness," the court must provide a reasonable explanation, on the record, for increasing the sentence. Similarly, due process may be violated where a prosecutor decides to increase the charge against a defendant who successfully appeals her conviction on a lesser charge. Again, the key is vindictive motivation and the concern is that prosecutors not be allowed to "up the ante" to discourage defendants from exercising their appeal rights. See Whitebread & Slobogin, *supra* at 691–92.

Equal protection guarantees also safeguard the right to appeal, once granted. Therefore, if a state decides to provide a right to appeal, it may not condition the exercise of that right in a way which discriminates against indigent defendants. For example, the Court in *Griffin v. Illinois*, 351 U.S. 12 (1956), held that due process and equal protection were violated when a state which conditioned appellate review on defendant's presentation of a trial record refused to provide an indigent defendant with a free trial transcript.

3. Right to Counsel on Direct Appeal

The Sixth Amendment by its terms does not confer a right to counsel on appeal. That amendment merely guarantees a person the assistance of counsel "for his *defence*" in "criminal *prosecutions*." Once convicted and sentenced, a defendant's prosecution is completed. Nonetheless, drawing upon the equal protection and due process guarantees of the Fourteenth Amendment, the Court has held that a state must provide counsel for an indigent's first appeal as of right. *Douglas v. California*, 372 U.S. 353 (1963). Therefore, even though a state is not required to provide a right to appeal, when it does so it undertakes the additional obligation of providing counsel to indigents.

Where a constitutional right to counsel on appeal exists, counsel must be effective. *Evitts v. Lucey*, 469 U.S. 387 (1985). Of course, effectiveness is judged under the standard of *Strickland v. Washington*, 466 U.S. 668 (1984). See *supra*, this chapter.

4. No Constitutional Right to Counsel on Certiorari or in State or Federal Post-Conviction

In *Ross v. Moffitt*, 417 U.S. 600 (1974), the Court refused to extend the principles of *Griffin* and *Douglas* to require appointed counsel to assist indigent defendants in their second, discretionary state appeals and in preparing petitions for certiorari to the United States Supreme Court. Similarly, the Court in *Pennsylvania v. Finley*, 481 U.S. 551 (1987), held that there is no right to appointed counsel in state post-conviction proceedings. The majority stated:

Postconviction relief is even further removed from the criminal trial than is discretionary direct review. It is not part of the criminal proceedings itself, and it is in fact considered to be civil in nature. It is a collateral attack that normally occurs only after the defendant has failed to secure relief through direct review of his conviction. States have no obligation to provide this avenue of relief, and when they do, the fundamental fairness mandated by the Due Process Clause does not require that the State supply a lawyer as well.

Murray v. Giarratano
492 U.S. 1 (1989)

Chief Justice REHNQUIST announced the judgment of the Court and delivered an opinion, in which Justice White, Justice O'Connor, and Justice Scalia join.

Virginia death row inmates brought a civil rights suit against various officials of the Commonwealth of Virginia. The prisoners claimed, based on several theories, that the Constitution required that they be provided with counsel at the Commonwealth's expense for the purpose of pursuing collateral proceedings related to their convictions and sentences. The courts below ruled that appointment of counsel upon request was necessary for the prisoners to enjoy their constitutional right to access to the courts in pursuit of state habeas corpus relief. We think this holding is inconsistent with our decision two Terms ago in *Pennsylvania v. Finley*, 481 U.S. 551 (1987), and rests on a misreading of our decision in *Bounds v. Smith*, 430 U.S. 817 (1977).

Joseph M. Giarratano is a Virginia prisoner under a sentence of death. He initiated this action under 42 U.S.C. §§1983, by *pro se* complaint in Federal District Court, against various state officials including Edward W. Murray who is the Director of the Virginia Department of Corrections. Some months later, the District Court certified a class comprising all current and future Virginia inmates awaiting execution who do not have and cannot afford counsel to pursue postconviction proceedings. The inmates asserted a number of constitutional theories for an entitlement to appointed counsel and the case was tried to the court....

In *Finley* we ruled that neither the Due Process Clause of the Fourteenth Amendment nor the equal protection guarantee of "meaningful access" required the State to appoint counsel for indigent prisoners seeking state postconviction relief. The Sixth and Fourteenth Amendments to the Constitution assure the right of an indigent defendant to counsel at the trial stage of a criminal proceeding, and an indigent defendant is similarly entitled as a matter of right to counsel for an initial appeal from the judgment and sentence of the trial court. But we held in *Ross v. Moffitt*, 417 U.S. 600 (1974), that the right to counsel at these earlier stages of a criminal procedure did not carry over to a discretionary appeal provided by North Carolina law from the intermediate appellate court to the Supreme Court of North Carolina. We contrasted the trial stage of a criminal proceeding, where the State by presenting witnesses and arguing to a jury attempts to strip from the defendant the presumption of innocence and convict him of a crime, with the appellate stage of such a proceeding, where the defendant needs an attorney "not as a shield to protect him against being 'haled into court' by the State and stripped of his presumption of innocence, but rather as a sword to upset the prior determination of guilt."

We held in *Finley* that the logic of *Ross v. Moffitt* required the conclusion that there was no federal constitutional right to counsel for indigent prisoners seeking state postconviction relief:

Postconviction relief is even further removed from the criminal trial than is discretionary direct review. It is not part of the criminal proceeding itself, and it is in fact considered to be civil in nature.... States have no obligation to provide this avenue of relief, and when they do, the fundamental fairness mandated by the Due Process Clause does not require that the state supply a lawyer as well.

Respondents ... argue that, under the Eighth Amendment, "evolving standards of decency" do not permit a death sentence to be carried out while a prisoner is unrepresented. In the same vein, they contend that due process requires appointed counsel in postconviction proceedings, because of the nature of the punishment and the need for accuracy.

We have recognized on more than one occasion that the Constitution places special constraints on the procedures used to convict an accused of a capital offense and sentence him to death. The finality of the death penalty requires "a greater degree of reliability" when it is imposed.

These holdings, however, have dealt with the trial stage of capital offense adjudication, where the court and jury hear testimony, receive evidence, and decide the questions of guilt and punishment. In *Pulley v. Harris*, 465 U.S. 37 (1984), we declined to hold that the Eighth Amendment required appellate courts to perform proportionality review of death sentences. And in *Satterwhite v. Texas*, 486 U.S. 249 (1988), we applied the traditional appellate standard of harmless error review set out in *Chapman v. California*, 386 U.S. 18 (1967), when reviewing a claim of constitutional error in a capital case.

We have similarly refused to hold that the fact that a death sentence has been imposed requires a different standard of review on federal habeas corpus. In *Smith v. Murray*, 477 U.S. 527, 538 (1986), a case involving federal habeas corpus, this Court unequivocally rejected "the suggestion that the principles [governing procedural default] of *Wainwright v. Sykes*, 433 U.S. 72 (1977), apply differently depending on the nature of the penalty a State imposes for the violation of its criminal laws" and similarly discarded the idea that "there is anything 'fundamentally unfair' about enforcing procedural default rules...." And, in *Barefoot v. Estelle*, 463 U.S. 880, 887 (1983), we observed that "direct appeal is the primary avenue for review of a conviction or sentence, and death penalty cases are no exception."

Finally, in *Ford v. Wainwright*, 477 U.S. 399 (1986), we held that the Eighth Amendment prohibited the State from executing a validly convicted and sentenced prisoner who was insane at the time of his scheduled execution. Five Justices of this Court, however, rejected the proposition that "the ascertainment of a prisoner's sanity as a predicate to lawful execution calls for no less stringent standards than those demanded in any other aspect of a capital proceeding." Justice Powell recognized that the prisoner's sanity at the time of execution was "not comparable to the antecedent question of whether the petitioner should be executed at all." "It follows that this Court's decisions imposing heightened procedural requirements on capital trials and sentencing proceedings do not apply in this context."

We think that these cases require the conclusion that the rule of *Pennsylvania v. Finley* should apply no differently in capital cases than in noncapital cases. State collateral proceedings are not constitutionally required as an adjunct to the state criminal proceedings and serve a different and more limited purpose than either the trial or appeal. The additional safeguards imposed by the Eighth Amendment at the trial stage of a capital case are, we think, sufficient to assure the reliability of the process by which the death penalty is imposed. We therefore decline to read either the Eighth Amendment or the Due Process Clause to require yet another distinction between the rights of capital case defendants and those in noncapital cases.... Reversed.

Justice KENNEDY, with whom Justice O'Connor joins, concurring in the judgment.

It cannot be denied that collateral relief proceedings are a central part of the review process for prisoners sentenced to death. As Justice Stevens observes, a substantial proportion of these prisoners succeed in having their death sentences vacated in habeas corpus proceedings. The complexity of our jurisprudence in this area, moreover, makes it unlikely that capital defendants will be able to file successful petitions for collateral relief without the assistance of persons learned in the law.

The requirement of meaningful access can be satisfied in various ways, however. This was made explicit in our decision in *Bounds v. Smith*, 430 U.S. 817 (1977). The intricacies and range of options are of sufficient complexity that state legislatures and prison administrators must be given "wide discretion" to select appropriate solutions. Indeed, judicial imposition of a categorical remedy such as that adopted by the court below might pretermit other responsible solutions being considered in Congress and state legislatures. Assessments of the difficulties presented by collateral litigation in capital cases are now being conducted by committees of the American Bar Association and the Judicial Conference of the United States, and Congress has stated its intention to give the matter serious consideration.

Unlike Congress, this Court lacks the capacity to undertake the searching and comprehensive review called for in this area, for we can decide only the case before us. While Virginia has not adopted procedures for securing representation that are as far reaching and effective as those available in other States, no prisoner on death row in Virginia has been unable to obtain counsel to represent him in postconviction proceedings, and Virginia's prison system is staffed with institutional lawyers to assist in preparing petitions for postconviction relief. I am not prepared to say that this scheme violates the Constitution. On the facts and record of this case, I concur in the judgment of the Court.

Justice STEVENS, with whom Justice Brennan, Justice Marshall, and Justice Blackmun join, dissenting.

Two Terms ago this Court reaffirmed that the Fourteenth Amendment to the Federal Constitution obligates a State "to assure the indigent defendant an adequate opportunity to present his claims fairly in the context of the State's appellate process." The narrow question presented is whether that obligation includes appointment of counsel for indigent death row inmates who wish to pursue state postconviction relief. Viewing the facts in light of our precedents, we should answer that question in the affirmative.

II

... [T]he appropriate question in this case is not whether there is an absolute "right to counsel" in collateral proceedings, but whether due process requires that these respondents be appointed counsel in order to pursue legal remedies. Three critical differences between *Finley* and this case demonstrate that even if it is permissible to leave an ordinary prisoner to his own resources in collateral proceedings, it is fundamentally unfair to require an indigent death row inmate to initiate collateral review without counsel's guiding hand. I shall address each of these differences in turn.

First. These respondents ... have been condemned to die. Legislatures conferred greater access to counsel on capital defendants than on persons facing lesser punishment even in colonial times. Our First Congress required assignment of up to two attorneys to a capital defendant at the same time it initiated capital punishment; nearly a century passed before Congress provided for appointment of counsel in other contexts. Similarly, Congress at first limited the federal right of appeal to capital cases. Just last year, it enacted a statute [the Anti-Drug Abuse Act of 1988] requiring provision of counsel for state and federal prisoners seeking federal postconviction relief—but only if they are under sentence of death....

The unique nature of the death penalty not only necessitates additional protections during pretrial, guilt, and sentencing phases, but also enhances the importance of the appellate process. Generally there is no constitutional right to appeal a conviction. "[M]eaningful appellate review" in capital cases, however, "serves as a check against the random or arbitrary imposition of the death penalty." It is therefore an integral component of a State's "constitutional responsibility to tailor and apply its law in a manner that avoids the arbitrary and capricious infliction of the death penalty."

Ideally, "direct appeal is the primary avenue for review of a conviction or sentence, and death penalty cases are no exception. When the process of direct review ... comes to an end, a presumption of finality and legality attaches to the conviction and sentence." *Barefoot v. Estelle*, 463 U.S. 880, 887 (1983). There is, however, significant evidence that in capital cases what is ordinarily considered direct review does not sufficiently safeguard against miscarriages of justice to warrant this presumption of finality. Federal habeas courts granted relief in only 0.25% to 7% of noncapital cases in recent years; in striking contrast, the success rate in capital cases ranged from 60% to 70%. Such a high incidence of uncorrected error demonstrates that the meaningful appellate review necessary in a capital case extends beyond the direct appellate process.

Second. In contrast to the collateral process discussed in *Finley*, Virginia law contemplates that some claims ordinarily heard on direct review will be relegated to postconviction proceedings. Claims that trial or appellate counsel provided constitutionally ineffective assistance, for instance, usually cannot be raised until this stage. Furthermore, some irregularities, such as prosecutorial misconduct, may not surface until after the direct review is complete. Occasionally, new evidence even may suggest that the defendant is innocent. Given the irreversibility of capital punishment, such information deserves searching, adversarial scrutiny even if it is discovered after the close of direct review....

Nor may a defendant circumvent the state postconviction process by filing a federal habeas petition. In *Rose v. Lundy*, 455 U.S. 509 (1982), this Court held that in order to comply with the exhaustion provision of 28 U.S.C. §2254(c), federal courts should dismiss petitions containing claims that have not been "fairly presented to the state courts," for both direct and postconviction review. Given the stringency with which this Court adheres to procedural default rules, it is of great importance to the prisoner that all his substantial claims be presented fully and professionally in his first state collateral proceeding.

Third. As the District Court's findings reflect, the plight of the death row inmate constrains his ability to wage collateral attacks far more than does the lot of the ordinary inmate considered in *Finley*. The District Court found that the death row inmate has an extremely limited period to prepare and present his postconviction petition and any necessary applications for stays of execution. Unlike the ordinary inmate, who presumably has ample time to use and reuse the prison library and to seek guidance from other prisoners experienced in preparing *pro se* petitions, a grim deadline imposes a finite limit on the condemned person's capacity for useful research.

Capital litigation, the District Court observed, is extremely complex. Without regard to the special characteristics of Virginia's statutory procedures, this Court's death penalty jurisprudence unquestionably is difficult even for a trained lawyer to master. A judgment that it is not unfair to require an ordinary inmate to rely on his own resources to prepare a petition for postconviction relief does not justify the same conclusion for the death row inmate who must acquire an understanding of this specialized area of the law and prepare an application for stay of execution as well as a petition for collateral relief. This is especially true, the District Court concluded, because the "evidence gives rise to a fair inference that an inmate preparing himself and his family for impending death is incapable of performing the mental functions necessary to adequately pursue his claims." ...

III

Of the 37 States authorizing capital punishment, at least 18 automatically provide their indigent death row inmates counsel to help them initiate state collateral proceedings. Thirteen of the 37 States have created governmentally funded resource centers to assist counsel in litigating capital cases. Virginia is among as few as five States that fall into neither group and have no system for appointing counsel for condemned prisoners before a postconviction petition is filed. In *Griffin v. Illinois*, 351 U.S. 12 (1956), the Court proscribed Illinois' discriminatory barrier to appellate review in part because many other States already had rejected such a barrier. Similarly, the trend in most States to expand legal assistance for their death row inmates further dilutes Virginia's weak justifications for refusing to do so, and "lends convincing support to the conclusion" of the courts below that these respondents have a fundamental right to the relief they seek....

Notes and Question

1. *Finley* was not a capital case but *Murray v. Giarratano*, 492 U.S. 1 (1989), was. There a plurality held that *Finley* should apply no differently in capital cases than noncapital cases. The *Giarratano* Court reiterated that there is no right to appointed counsel in state post-conviction proceedings, even those brought by capital defendants. See *supra* this chapter. Similarly, in *Coleman v. Thompson*, 501 U.S. 722 (1991), the Court rejected a claim that attorney error in failing to file a state habeas appeal on time constituted "cause" sufficient to excuse petitioner's procedural default. Earlier, the Court had held that attorney error can be "cause" only if it constitutes ineffective assistance of counsel violative of the Sixth Amendment. Because there is no constitutional right to an attorney in state post-conviction proceedings, there can be no claim of constitutionally ineffective assistance of counsel in those proceedings.

Thus far the Supreme Court has not directly addressed the issue of whether a death row inmate has a constitutional right to appointed counsel during federal habeas corpus proceedings. In all likelihood, the Court would draw upon *Moffitt*, *Finley* and *Giarratano* and hold that no such constitutional right exists. Lower federal courts have held that there is no constitutional right to counsel in federal habeas corpus proceedings. *Bonin v. Vasquez*, 999 F.2d 425 (9th Cir. 1993).

2. The Supreme Court has thus far not addressed whether due process requires appointed counsel where a discretionary appeal is the only appeal available to a defendant.

3. In some jurisdictions, state law provides that a claim of ineffective assistance of trial counsel cannot be raised on direct appeal but must be presented in a state post-conviction proceeding. Should there be an exception to *Finley* in such circumstances?

4. *Coleman v. Thompson*, 501 U.S. 722 (1991), raised the precise issue described in note 3. Coleman's attorney during state post-conviction raised an ineffectiveness claim, which was rejected. The issue before the Court involved the possible ineffective assistance of state post-conviction counsel for failure to properly pursue an appeal from the rejection of the ineffective-assistance-at-trial claim. The Court specifically left open the possibility of an exception to *Finley*. The Court noted that even if such an exception existed and the collateral challenge was treated as the equivalent of a direct appeal, any subsequent appeal from its rejection would certainly not fall within any such exception. For a fuller discussion of *Coleman v. Thompson*, see *infra* chapter 14.

5. Statutory Right to Counsel in Federal Habeas Corpus

McFarland v. Scott
512 U.S. 849 (1994)

Justice BLACKMUN delivered the opinion of the Court.

In establishing a federal death penalty for certain drug offenses under the Anti-Drug Abuse Act of 1988, 21 U.S.C. §848(e), Congress created a statutory right to qualified legal representation for capital defendants in federal habeas corpus proceedings. §848(q)(4)(B). This case presents the question whether a capital defendant must file a formal habeas corpus petition in order to invoke this statutory right and to establish a federal court's jurisdiction to enter a stay of execution.

I

Petitioner Frank Basil McFarland was convicted of capital murder on November 13, 1989, in the State of Texas and sentenced to death. The Texas Court of Criminal Appeals affirmed the conviction and sentence and on June 7, 1993, this Court denied certiorari. Two months later, on August 16, 1993, the Texas trial court scheduled McFarland's execution for September 23, 1993. On September 19, McFarland filed a *pro se* motion requesting that the trial court stay or withdraw his execution date to allow the Texas Resource Center an opportunity to recruit volunteer counsel for his state habeas corpus proceeding. Texas opposed a stay of execution, arguing that McFarland had not filed an application for writ of habeas corpus and that the court thus lacked jurisdiction to enter a stay. The trial court declined to appoint counsel, but modified McFarland's execution date to October 27, 1993.

On October 16, 1993, the Resource Center informed the trial court that it had been unable to recruit volunteer counsel and asked the court to appoint counsel for McFarland. Concluding that Texas law did not authorize the appointment of counsel for state habeas corpus proceedings, the trial court refused either to appoint counsel or to modify petitioner's execution date. McFarland then filed a *pro se* motion in the Texas Court of Criminal Appeals requesting a stay and a remand for appointment of counsel. The court denied the motion without comment.

Having failed to obtain either the appointment of counsel or a modification of his execution date in state court, McFarland, on October 22, 1993, commenced the present action in the United States District Court for the Northern District of Texas by filing a *pro se* motion stating that he "wished to challenge [his] conviction and sentence under [the federal habeas corpus statute,] 28 U.S.C. §2254." McFarland requested the appointment of counsel under 21 U.S.C. §848(q)(4)(B) and a stay of execution to give that counsel time to prepare and file a habeas corpus petition.[1]

The District Court denied McFarland's motion on October 25, 1993, concluding that because no "post conviction proceeding" had been initiated pursuant to 28 U.S.C. §2254 or §2255, petitioner was not entitled to appointment of counsel and the court lacked jurisdiction to enter a stay of execution. The court later denied a certificate of probable cause to appeal.

On October 26, the eve of McFarland's scheduled execution, the Court of Appeals for the Fifth Circuit denied his application for stay. The court noted that federal law expressly authorizes federal courts to stay state proceedings while a federal habeas corpus proceeding is pending, 28 U.S.C. §2251, but held that no such proceeding was pending, because a "motion for stay and for appointment of counsel [is not] the equivalent of an application for habeas relief." The court concluded that any other federal judicial interference in state court proceedings was barred by the Anti-Injunction Act, 28 U.S.C. §2283.

Shortly before the Court of Appeals ruled, a federal magistrate judge located an attorney willing to accept appointment in McFarland's case and suggested that if the attorney would file a skeletal document entitled "petition for writ of habeas corpus," the District Court might be willing to appoint him and grant McFarland a stay of execution. The attorney accordingly drafted and filed a *pro forma* habeas petition, together with a motion for stay of execution and appointment of counsel. As in the *Gosch* case, see n. 1, *supra*, despite the fact that Texas did not oppose a stay, the District Court found the petition to be insufficient and denied the motion for stay on the merits.

On October 27, 1993, this Court granted a stay of execution in McFarland's original suit pending consideration of his petition for certiorari. The Court later granted certiorari, to resolve an apparent conflict with *Brown v. Vasquez*, 952 F.2d 1164 (CA9 1991).

II

A

Section 848(q)(4)(B) of Title 21 provides:

---

1. Traditionally in Texas, capital defendants had invoked their federal right to appointed counsel by filing a perfunctory habeas corpus petition, often reciting a single claim. Texas customarily did not oppose a stay following the filing of such a *pro forma* petition, and federal district courts regularly granted a stay of execution under these circumstances and appointed counsel to file a legally sufficient habeas application.

In the month prior to McFarland's scheduled execution, however, a capital defendant facing imminent execution filed such a *pro forma* habeas petition in District Court. Texas did not oppose the filing, but the District Court denied the stay and dismissed the skeletal petition on the merits. *Gosch v. Collins*, No. SA-93-CA-731 (WD Tex., Sept. 15, 1993). The Court of Appeals for the Fifth Circuit affirmed, *Gosch v. Collins*, 8 F.3d 20, cert. pending, No. 93-6025. Gosch then filed a subsequent, substantive habeas petition, which the District Court dismissed as successive and abusive. *Gosch v. Collins*, No. SA-93-CA-736 (WD Tex. Oct. 12, 1993).

In a letter supporting McFarland's motion in the District Court, the Resource Center indicated that the *Gosch* case had left capital defendants reluctant to invoke their federal right to counsel by filing *pro forma* habeas petitions, given the substantial possibility that the petition might be dismissed on the merits, and that any habeas petition later filed would be dismissed summarily as an abuse of the writ.

> "In any post conviction proceeding under section 2254 or 2255 of title 28, seeking to vacate or set aside a death sentence, any defendant who is or becomes financially unable to obtain adequate representation or investigative, expert, or other reasonably necessary services shall be entitled to the appointment of one or more attorneys and the furnishing of such other services in accordance with paragraphs (5), (6), (7), (8), and (9)" (emphasis added).

On its face, this statute grants indigent capital defendants a mandatory right to qualified legal counsel[2] and related services "in any [federal] post conviction proceeding." The express language does not specify, however, how a capital defendant's right to counsel in such a proceeding shall be invoked.

Neither the federal habeas corpus statute, 28 U.S.C. §2241 et seq., nor the rules governing habeas corpus proceedings define a "post conviction proceeding" under §2254 or §2255 or expressly state how such a proceeding shall be commenced. Construing §848(q)(4)(B) in light of its related provisions, however, indicates that the right to appointed counsel adheres prior to the filing of a formal, legally sufficient habeas corpus petition. Section 848(q)(4)(B) expressly incorporates 21 U.S.C. §848(q)(9), which entitles capital defendants to a variety of expert and investigative services upon a showing of necessity:

> "Upon a finding in ex parte proceedings that investigative, expert or other services are reasonably necessary for the representation of the defendant, ... the court *shall authorize* the defendant's attorneys to obtain such services on behalf of the defendant and shall order the payment of fees and expenses therefore" (emphasis added).

The services of investigators and other experts may be critical in the preapplication phase of a habeas corpus proceeding, when possible claims and their factual bases are researched and identified. Section §848(q)(9) clearly anticipates that capital defense counsel will have been appointed under §848(q)(4)(B) before the need for such technical assistance arises, since the statute requires "the defendant's attorneys to obtain such services" from the court. In adopting §848(q)(4)(B), Congress thus established a right to preapplication legal assistance for capital defendants in federal habeas corpus proceedings.

This interpretation is the only one that gives meaning to the statute as a practical matter. Congress' provision of a right to counsel under §848(q)(4)(B) reflects a determination that quality legal representation is necessary in capital habeas corpus proceedings in light of "the seriousness of the possible penalty and ... the unique and complex nature of the litigation." §848(q)(7). An attorney's assistance prior to the filing of a capital defendant's habeas corpus petition is crucial, because "the complexity of our jurisprudence in this area ... makes it unlikely that capital defendants will be able to file successful petitions for collateral relief without the assistance of persons learned in the law."

Habeas corpus petitions must meet heightened pleading requirements and comply with this Court's doctrines of procedural default and waiver. Federal courts are authorized to dismiss summarily any habeas petition that appears legally insufficient on its

---

2. Counsel appointed to represent capital defendants in post conviction proceedings must meet more stringent experience criteria than attorneys appointed to represent noncapital defendants under the Criminal Justice Act of 1964, 18 U.S.C. §3006A. At least one attorney appointed to represent a capital defendant must have been authorized to practice before the relevant court for at least five years, and must have at least three years of experience in handling felony cases in that court. 21 U.S.C. §848(q)(6).

face, see 28 U.S.C. §2254 Rule 4, and to deny a stay of execution where a habeas petition fails to raise a substantial federal claim. Moreover, should a defendant's *pro se* petition be summarily dismissed, any petition subsequently filed by counsel could be subject to dismissal as an abuse of the writ. Requiring an indigent capital petitioner to proceed without counsel in order to obtain counsel thus would expose him to the substantial risk that his habeas claims never would be heard on the merits. Congress legislated against this legal backdrop in adopting §848(q)(4)(B), and we safely assume that it did not intend for the express requirement of counsel to be defeated in this manner.

The language and purposes of §848(q)(4)(B) and its related provisions establish that the right to appointed counsel includes a right to legal assistance in the preparation of a habeas corpus application. We therefore conclude that a "post conviction proceeding" within the meaning of §848(q)(4)(B) is commenced by the filing of a death row defendant's motion requesting the appointment of counsel for his federal habeas corpus proceeding.[3] McFarland filed such a motion and was entitled to the appointment of a lawyer.

B

Even if the District Court had granted McFarland's motion for appointment of counsel and had found an attorney to represent him, this appointment would have been meaningless unless McFarland's execution also was stayed. We therefore turn to the question whether the District Court had jurisdiction to grant petitioner's motion for stay.

Federal courts cannot enjoin state court proceedings unless the intervention is authorized expressly by federal statute or falls under one of two other exceptions to the Anti-Injunction Act. The federal habeas corpus statute grants any federal judge "before whom a habeas corpus proceeding is pending" power to stay a state court action "for any matter involved in the habeas corpus proceeding." 28 U.S.C. §2251 (emphasis added). McFarland argues that his request for counsel in a "post conviction proceeding" under §848(q)(4)(B) initiated a "habeas corpus proceeding" within the meaning of §2251, and that the District Court thus had jurisdiction to enter a stay. Texas contends, in turn, that even if a "post conviction proceeding" under §848(q)(4)(B) can be triggered by a death row defendant's request for appointment of counsel, no "habeas corpus proceeding" is "pending" under §2251, and thus no stay can be entered, until a legally sufficient habeas petition is filed.

… Section 2251 does not mandate the entry of a stay, but dedicates the exercise of stay jurisdiction to the sound discretion of a federal court. Under ordinary circumstances, a capital defendant presumably will have sufficient time to request the appointment of counsel and file a formal habeas petition prior to his scheduled execution. But the right to counsel necessarily includes a right for that counsel meaningfully to research and present a defendant's habeas claims. Where this opportunity is not afforded, "approving the execution of a defendant before his [petition] is decided on the merits

---

3. Justice Thomas argues in dissent that reading §848(q)(4)(B) to allow the initiation of a habeas corpus proceeding through the filing of a motion for appointment of counsel ignores the fact that such proceedings traditionally have been commenced by the filing of a habeas corpus petition and creates a divergent practice for capital defendants. As Justice O'Connor agrees, however, §848(q)(4)(B) bestows upon capital defendants a mandatory right to counsel, including a right to preapplication legal assistance, that is unknown to other criminal defendants. Because noncapital defendants have no equivalent right to the appointment of counsel in federal habeas corpus proceedings, it is not surprising that their habeas corpus proceedings typically will be initiated by the filing of a habeas corpus petition.

would clearly be improper." *Barefoot*, 463 U.S. at 889. On the other hand, if a dilatory capital defendant inexcusably ignores this opportunity and flouts the available processes, a federal court presumably would not abuse its discretion in denying a stay of execution.

II

A criminal trial is the "main event" at which a defendant's rights are to be determined, and the Great Writ is an extraordinary remedy that should not be employed to "relitigate state trials." At the same time, criminal defendants are entitled by federal law to challenge their conviction and sentence in habeas corpus proceedings. By providing indigent capital defendants with a mandatory right to qualified legal counsel in these proceedings, Congress has recognized that federal habeas corpus has a particularly important role to play in promoting fundamental fairness in the imposition of the death penalty.

We conclude that a capital defendant may invoke this right to a counseled federal habeas corpus proceeding by filing a motion requesting the appointment of habeas counsel, and that a district court has jurisdiction to enter a stay of execution where necessary to give effect to that statutory right. McFarland filed a motion for appointment of counsel and for stay of execution in this case, and the District Court had authority to grant the relief he sought.

The judgment of the Court of Appeals is reversed.

G. Fatal Consequences of Attorney Error

Below are two cases involving co-defendants, a husband and wife who were tried separately. Although counsel for the wife timely objected to a constitutional error in the jury composition, counsel for the husband did not.

Machetti v. Linahan

679 F.2d 236 (11th Cir. 1982)

HATCHETT, Circuit Judge:

Appellant, Rebecca Machetti, seeks federal habeas corpus relief ... from two consecutive death sentences....

Machetti was convicted on February 28, 1975, of two counts of murder in the brutal slaying of her ex-husband, Joseph Ronald Akins, and his wife, Juanita. Machetti planned the murders so that her three teenage daughters might receive the benefits of their father's insurance policies. At the sentencing hearing, Machetti's attorney introduced no new evidence but begged the jury to find mitigating factors without suggesting any such circumstances. The jury recommended death on both counts, and the court sentenced Machetti to two consecutive death sentences....

Machetti's counsel first raised the jury composition issue at the state habeas corpus hearing.[4] She contends that the operation of section 59-124 systematically excluded

---

4. Generally, a federal court will honor a valid state procedural rule that a defendant's failure to object to a grand or petit jury before or during trial constitutes waiver of that objection as a basis for habeas corpus relief. A Georgia decisional rule in force at the time of appellant's trial in February

women from the venire; and therefore, she was indicted by a grand jury and convicted by a traverse jury drawn from jury boxes in which women were unfairly underrepresented. Machetti thus contends that the Georgia jury selection procedure deprived her of her right to a fair trial by jury of a representative segment of the community....

We hold that Machetti's proof sufficiently established that the underrepresentation of women resulted from their systematic exclusion in Georgia's jury selection procedure. Her undisputed showing that this significant disparity occurred over a period of twenty months, from February, 1974, through September, 1975, unmistakably indicates that the cause of the imbalance was inherent in the jury selection procedure under Ga.Code Ann. §59-124. *Duren v. Missouri*, 439 U.S. 357 (1979), established that the existence of an opt-out system, as embodied by statute, in conjunction with the resulting disproportionate and consistent exclusion of women from the final jury pool was prima facie evidence of systematic exclusion of women. Moreover, appellee introduced no evidence to rebut Machetti's case. We therefore conclude that the Georgia jury-selection system in effect at the time of Machetti's trial deprived her of her sixth and fourteenth amendment right to an impartial jury trial.

... We therefore reverse and remand to the district court with directions to issue the writ of habeas corpus. Reversed and remanded with directions.

Smith v. Kemp

715 F.2d 1459 (11th Cir. 1983)

RONEY and JAMES C. HILL, Circuit Judges:

Joseph Ronald Akins and his wife of twenty days, Juanita Knight Akins, were killed in a secluded area of a new housing development in Bibb County, Georgia, on August 31, 1974, by shotgun blasts fired at close range. Petitioner, John Eldon Smith, also known as Tony Machetti, charged with firing the shotgun, was convicted of murder and sentenced to death.

Briefly, the evidence was that petitioner and his wife, Rebecca Akins Smith Machetti, together with John Maree, plotted to kill Akins, a former husband of Rebecca's and the father of her three children, in order to collect his life insurance proceeds. John Maree testified that he and petitioner lured Akins to the area of the crime on the pretense of installing a television antenna. When Akins appeared with his wife, petitioner shot them both.

Before this Court is the appeal from a denial of a second federal habeas corpus petition that asserted [among other grounds for relief that] ... the underrepresentation of women made the jury that convicted him unconstitutional under *Taylor v. Louisiana*, 419 U.S. 522 (1975)....

Smith made no challenge to the jury because of the underrepresentation of women at or before trial. The Georgia procedural rule requires that a defendant's challenge to jury composition be made at or before the time the jury is "put upon him." Smith also

---

and March, 1975, mandated that result. Where, however, the state habeas court entertains the federal constitutional claims on the merits, as in the instant case, the federal habeas court must also adjudicate the merits.

failed to raise the jury composition issue on direct appeal to the Georgia Supreme Court, in his initial state habeas corpus action, or in his initial federal habeas corpus petition. Smith's wife, however, while not raising the issue at trial did in her first habeas corpus proceeding challenge the underrepresentation of women on the jury under *Taylor v. Louisiana*, 419 U.S. 522 (1975). Although she failed to obtain state relief, she did succeed in her first federal habeas corpus appeal. This Court held the Georgia "opt-out" provision for women led to unconstitutional underrepresentation of women under *Duren v. Missouri*, 439 U.S. 357 (1979). Petitioner and his wife were tried within a few weeks of each other in the same county so that the Georgia provision applied to both juries. The questions before this Court are (1) whether Smith's failure to comply with this state procedural rule constitutes a waiver of his right to challenge the jury composition, and (2) if there was such a waiver, whether Smith is entitled under any theory to be relieved of its preclusive effect.

We hold that Smith has not established "cause and prejudice" for his failure to raise the allegation of illegal jury composition until his second, successive state habeas corpus petition. We affirm the district court's holding that it was prohibited from considering this claim on its merits....

It was not until after *Machetti* [*v. Linahan*] was decided that Smith sought to litigate the jury composition issue in his second state habeas corpus petition, first in the Superior Court of Butts County and then in the Georgia Supreme Court. The state habeas corpus court applied the state procedural waiver rule and did not consider the issue of alleged illegal jury composition on the merits. The Supreme Court of Georgia found that Smith had not shown grounds for raising this issue in his second habeas petition. The federal district court held that it was precluded from considering this claim because the state court applied the state procedural rule and did not consider the merits of the claim.

To show cause for his failure to object before the second state habeas corpus petition, Smith has presented affidavits that his trial lawyers were unaware of the *Taylor* decision at the time of his trial, and he argues that *Duren* and *Machetti* were intervening changes in the law which justify his failure to raise the issue until his second state habeas corpus petition. Smith's argument fails....

We thus hold that Smith has not shown that the federal court could consider the merits of this claim under the existing legal authorities. The stay of execution hereinbefore granted is vacated. The judgment of the district court is affirmed.

HATCHETT, concurring in part and dissenting in part.

Machetti, the mastermind in this murder, has had her conviction overturned, has had a new trial and has received a life sentence. This court overturned her first conviction because in the county where her trial was held, women were unconstitutionally underrepresented in the jury pool. *Machetti v. Linahan*, 679 F.2d 236 (11th Cir. 1982). Her lawyers timely raised this constitutional objection. They won; she lives.

John Eldon Smith was tried in the same county, by a jury drawn from the same unconstitutionally composed jury pool, but because his lawyers did not timely raise the unconstitutionality of the jury pool, he faces death by electrocution. His lawyers waived the jury issue. Judicial economy, as required by recent decisions of the United States Supreme Court, dictate that we not reach the underrepresentation of women issue, even under principles of "manifest injustice." The fairness promised in *Furman v. Georgia*, 408 U.S. 238 (1972), has long been forgotten.

Note

John Eldon Smith was executed in Georgia's electric chair on December 15, 1983.

Death by Lottery—Procedural Bar of Constitutional Claims in Capital Cases Due to Inadequate Representation of Indigent Defendants

Stephen B. Bright, 92 W. Va. L. Rev. 679 (1990)

II. Deciding Who Dies: A Principled Selection Process or The Luck of the Draw?

The judicial process for selecting "the few cases in which [the death penalty is imposed] from the many cases in which it is not" is supposed to be a principled one, in which those most deserving of death are identified based upon the circumstances of the crime and the background of the offender. The United States Supreme Court has repeatedly held that the eighth amendment prohibits the arbitrary or capricious imposition of the death penalty. In theory, at least, death is reserved for those who have committed the most heinous murders and are so far beyond redemption that they should be eliminated from the human community.

In practice, however, the system for imposing capital punishment is most often a game of chance in which the winners and the losers are distinguished not by their criminal and moral capability, but by the luck of the lawyers they draw. This is illustrated by the cases of Smith and Machetti, two codefendants sentenced to death at separate trials by unconstitutionally composed juries within a few weeks of each other in the same county in Georgia. Machetti's lawyers challenged the jury composition in state court; Smith's lawyers did not because they were unaware of a United States Supreme Court decision decided only five days before Smith's trial began. A new trial was ordered for Machetti by the Eleventh Circuit Court of Appeals, and, at that trial, a jury which fairly represented the community imposed a sentence of life imprisonment. The Eleventh Circuit refused to consider the identical issue in Smith's case because his lawyers did not preserve it. Smith was executed, becoming the first person to die under the Georgia statute previously held constitutional in *Gregg v. Georgia.*

If Machetti had been represented by Smith's lawyers and vice versa in state court, Machetti would have been executed and Smith would have obtained federal habeas corpus relief. This is not how a principled selection process should work. Yet *Smith* is hardly an isolated example. The second person executed in Georgia was a mentally retarded offender, who was denied relief despite a jury instruction which unconstitutionally shifted the burden of proof on intent because his attorney did not preserve the issue by raising an objection at trial. His more culpable codefendant was granted a new trial on the unconstitutional instruction. Again, a switch of the lawyers would have reversed the outcomes of the two cases.

Many other executions have been carried out after courts refused to examine constitutional questions because of counsel's failure to preserve them. Two executions occurred after decisions by the United States Supreme Court that meritorious constitutional claims were barred because trial or appellate lawyers failed to recognize or preserve the issues. Many others have been carried out after federal courts refused to address the merits of issues because of procedural bars invoked by the state under *Wainwright v. Sykes*, 433 U.S. 72 (1977).

Notes and Questions

1. For a discussion of the law of procedural default, see *Wainwright v. Sykes*, 433 U.S. 72 (1977) (*infra* chapter 14).

2. Consider Justice Thurgood Marshall's assessment of attorneys called upon to represent capital defendants.

> First, capital defendants frequently suffer the consequences of having trial counsel who are ill-equipped to handle capital cases. Death penalty litigation has become a specialized field of practice, and even the most well intentioned attorneys often are unable to recognize, preserve, and defend their client's rights. Often trial counsel simply are unfamiliar with the special rules that apply in capital cases. Counsel—whether appointed or retained—often are handling their first criminal cases, or their first murder cases, when confronted with the prospect of a death penalty. Though acting in good faith, they inevitably make very serious mistakes. For example, I have read cases in which counsel was unaware that certain death penalty issues were pending before the appellate courts and that the claims should be preserved, or that a separate sentencing phase would follow a conviction. The federal reports are filled with stories of counsel who presented no evidence in mitigation of their client's sentences because they did not know what to offer or how to offer it, or had not read the state's sentencing statute.

> … Trial counsel's lack of expertise takes a heavy toll. A capital defendant seeking post-conviction relief is today caught in an increasingly pernicious visegrip. Pressing against him from one side is the Supreme Court's continual restriction of what federal courts can remedy on post-conviction review. It has accomplished this by expanding the "presumption of correctness" afforded state court findings, and by imposing rigid doctrines of procedural default that often turn on technical pleading rules at the expense of fundamental fairness. The problem is even more acute for capital defendants. The Court purports to have created a host of rights that protect a capital defendant at the sentencing phase of a proceeding. But at the same time it has limited appellate and collateral review of those rights, and of the correctness of the sentencer's decision. These rules of limitation often deny capital defendants the kind of personalized inquiry to which they have an indisputable right. Thus, errors at sentencing are often irremediable.

Marshall, "Remarks on the Death Penalty Made at the Judicial Conference of the Second Circuit," 86 Colum. L. Rev. 1 (1986).

3. Is providing effective assistance of counsel to capital clients consistent with lying? Consider the following justifications for ethical violations by capital defense lawyers.

(1) My job is to save my client's life. That critical end justifies almost any means.
(2) The prosecution is much worse than the defense could ever be, so we're simply fighting fire with fire.
(3) Legal ethics don't apply to criminal lawyers, at least not in capital cases.

Streib, "Would You Lie to Save Your Client's Life?," 42 Brandeis L.J. 405 (2004).

Chapter 12

Stays of Execution and State Post-Conviction Relief Proceedings

A. Stays of Execution

1. Introduction

Securing a stay of execution while appealing a conviction and death sentence is a critical and time-sensitive endeavor. In a number of states, courts or executive officials are obligated to set execution dates for capital defendants upon certain triggering events. States often provide automatic stays of execution upon the filing of a direct appeal or, in certain circumstances, a state post-conviction application; however, the stay will often expire upon the conclusion of an appeal or post-conviction proceeding and a new execution date will then be set. See, *e.g.*, Ala. Code §12-22-150; Ark. Stat. §16-91-202; West Ann. Cal. Penal Code §1243; Fla. Stat. §922.06; Idaho Stat. §19-2719; Mo. Rule of Crim. Pro. 30.15; Okla. Stat. tit. 22, §1001.1; Tenn. Code §40-30-120.

Under 28 U.S.C. §2251, federal judges have the power to grant stays of execution for condemned prisoners whose habeas petitions are properly pending before the court. However, amendments to the statutes governing federal habeas proceedings require counsel to comply with certain procedural requirements and to file habeas petitions within a certain period of time. Accordingly, counsel for the defendant must act promptly and observe all applicable rules and procedures in order to secure a stay of execution so that her client may appeal, or continue appealing, his conviction. Liebman & Hertz, *Federal Habeas Corpus Practice and Procedure* §§13.1–13.6 (Lexis 5th ed. 2005). See chapter 13, *infra*, for a discussion of the procedures, including the relevant statute of limitations, applicable to capital defendants seeking federal habeas relief under the Anti-terrorism and Effective Death Penalty Act.

In *McFarland v. Scott*, 512 U.S. 849 (1994)(*supra* chapter 11), the Supreme Court held that a condemned inmate seeking federal habeas review of his conviction or sentence is entitled, under 21 U.S.C. §848(q)(4)(B), to the assistance of a properly trained attorney. This right to appointed counsel attaches prior to the filing of a formal, legally sufficient habeas corpus petition. McFarland argued that his request for counsel under §848 initiated a "habeas corpus proceeding" within the meaning of 28 U.S.C. §2251. According to that statute, "[a] justice or judge of the United States before whom a habeas corpus proceeding is pending, may ... stay any proceeding against the person detained in any State court." The Court agreed that McFarland's motion for appointment of counsel initiated a habeas proceeding under §2251. As Justice Blackmun's majority opinion wryly observed, McFarland's right to appointed counsel "would have been meaningless unless McFarland's execution also was stayed."

Justice Blackmun, however, cautioned against reading too much into the *McFarland* majority opinion:

> This conclusion [that a capital defendant's request for counsel under §848 initiates a habeas proceeding for purposes of §2251] by no means grants capital defendants a right to an automatic stay of execution. Section 2251 does not mandate the entry of a stay, but dedicates the exercise of stay jurisdiction to the sound discretion of a federal court. Under ordinary circumstances, a capital defendant presumably will have sufficient time to request the appointment of counsel and file a formal habeas petition prior to his scheduled execution. But the right to counsel necessarily includes a right for that counsel meaningfully to research and present a defendant's habeas claims. Where this opportunity is not afforded, "approving the execution of a defendant before his [petition] is decided on the merits clearly would be improper." *Barefoot v. Estelle*, 463 U.S. at 889. On the other hand, if a dilatory capital defendant inexcusably ignores this opportunity and flouts the available processes, a federal court presumably would not abuse its discretion in denying a stay of execution.

For further discussion of pre–petition stays and the application of the AEDPA in both opt-in and non-opt-in jurisdictions, see Liebman & Hertz, *Federal Habeas Corpus Practice and Procedure* §13.2(a)(b) (Lexis 5th ed. 2005).

Note on Supreme Court's Internal Rules Governing Stays

A minority of four justices is sufficient to grant certiorari and to force the entire Court to conduct a full review of a case. Only three justices are required to place a "hold" on any certiorari petition that they consider related to a case already pending before the Court. The purpose of the "hold rule" is to ensure that the parties to every case still pending on certiorari will receive the benefit of whatever changes in the law the Court might announce in an upcoming decision. When capital defendants appeal to the Court with an execution date already set, a certiorari grant or a hold vote is meaningless unless the Court also grants a stay of execution. In other words, a case the Court decided to hear (by granting certiorari) or decided to hold (because issues in a case pending before the Court might benefit the capital petitioner) would be rendered moot by the petitioner's execution. Absent a stay, which requires five votes, the petitioner would be killed before the Court took final action on his case. Lazarus, *Closed Chambers* 157–59 (Times Books 1998). Just such an event was described by Professor John C. Jeffries, Jr., in his biography of Justice Lewis Powell:

> The tug of war over stays of execution became public in the case of Ronald Straight. The state of Florida proposed to execute Straight for torture and murder. After exhausting his remedies in state court, Straight filed a federal habeas petition, which was denied by the Supreme Court of the United States. The day before his scheduled execution, Straight filed a second habeas petition raising similar claims. The case came to [Justice] Powell, who put it over for one day while his colleagues considered the matter and then voted to deny the stay. His refusal to provide the necessary fifth

vote to hold Straight's petition caused [Justice] Brennan to erupt in anger. "For the Court to deny a stay to a petitioner who is under sentence of death, and whose petition four Justices have determined to hold," was "new and gruesome." It was, said Brennan, "a wrong to which I may not be a silent witness."

Powell answered that Ronald Straight had been to the Supreme Court once before, that his claims had been fully and fairly considered, and that there was no reason to go into them again. The exchange revealed a growing bitterness about capital cases. Brennan continued to fight executions tooth and nail, while Powell grew increasingly impatient with the guerilla warfare tactics of delay.

Jeffries, *Justice Lewis F. Powell, Jr.* 446 (Charles Scribner's Sons 1994).

2. The Tension Between Full and Fair Adjudication and Expedited Review

Capital defendants seeking relief through federal habeas corpus often face imminent execution. When the federal courts grant stays of execution, however, the state may feel its interests and objectives are being frustrated. This is especially true when the federal courts take several years to rule on the merits of a case after having granted a stay of execution.

In Re Blodgett
502 U.S. 236 (1992)

PER CURIAM.

The Court has before it a petition from the State of Washington for a writ of mandamus to the Court of Appeals for the Ninth Circuit. The petition seeks an order directing the Court of Appeals to issue its decision on an appeal from the District Court's denial of a second federal habeas petition in a capital case. The appeal was argued and submitted to the Court of Appeals on June 27, 1989, and no decision has been forthcoming.

Charles Rodman Campbell was convicted of multiple murders in 1982 in the State of Washington and sentenced to death. After his conviction was affirmed on direct appeal and we denied certiorari, his first federal habeas petition was filed in July 1985 in the United States District Court for the Western District of Washington. Proceedings in that matter were completed when we denied certiorari in November 1988. No relief was granted.

In March 1989 Campbell filed a second federal habeas petition in the same District Court. The court acted with commendable dispatch, holding a hearing and issuing a written opinion denying a stay or other relief within days after the second petition was filed. On March 28, 1989, Campbell appealed to the Ninth Circuit. The Court of Appeals granted an indefinite stay of execution and set a briefing schedule. The case was argued and submitted in June 1989, but no decision was announced and the stay of execution remains in effect. The Washington Attorney General sent letters to the panel in

April and October of 1990 inquiring about the status of the case, but neither letter was answered.

In January 1990 Campbell filed a motion to withdraw certain issues from consideration by the Ninth Circuit panel, and he renewed this motion in April. The panel took no action. In July 1990 Campbell filed his third state action for collateral relief, a personal restraint petition, with the Washington Supreme Court. In September, Campbell again moved the Court of Appeals to withdraw three issues from consideration in the case that it was still holding under submission, leaving eight others to be decided. The panel did not respond until by order of February 21, 1992, it noted Campbell's motion to withdraw the issues, requested a report on the status of the state court proceedings, and vacated its own submission of the case. Both Washington and Campbell responded that all of the issues pending before the Ninth Circuit had been exhausted. The State requested that the case be resubmitted, but the panel did not do so.

The Washington Supreme Court denied Campbell's third personal restraint petition on its merits on March 21, 1991. On June 10, 1991, Campbell filed a document advising the Court of Appeals panel that he desired to discharge his attorneys and proceed *pro se* and that he would file a third federal habeas petition in the District Court. At that point more than two years had passed since the Ninth Circuit had heard oral argument in the case. Almost two months later, on August 7, 1991, the panel granted the motion to relieve counsel, directed Campbell to file his third federal habeas petition by August 30, and announced its intention to wait for the District Court's ruling before taking further action. The District Court has set a briefing schedule for the third petition.

On October 25, 1991, the Washington Attorney General filed the mandamus petition now before us and on November 22 the Court of Appeals and the members of the panel filed a response. Neither the response nor the record reveals any plausible explanation or reason for the panel's delay in resolving the case from June 1989 until July 1990. The response addresses the events after Campbell's third personal restraint petition was filed in the Washington Supreme Court. The response indicates that the panel vacated submission in February 1991 because, if the Washington Supreme Court had granted the state petition, the appeal before the Ninth Circuit would have become moot. It further stated that the panel desired to avoid piecemeal appeals by awaiting the decision of the District Court on the third federal habeas petition. The response noted that the Ninth Circuit has formed a Death Penalty Task Force with the objective of eliminating successive habeas petitions and that the consolidation of the last two petitions is consistent with that objective.

The delay of over a year before the third personal restraint was filed in Washington state court remains unexplained, and was in fact compounded by the events that followed. The orders by the Ninth Circuit to vacate submission of the case until completion of the state collateral proceeding and then to hold the case in abeyance pending filing and resolution of the third federal habeas proceeding in the District Court raise the very concerns regarding delay that were part of the rationale for this Court's decisions in *Rose v. Lundy*, 455 U.S. 509 (1982) and *McCleskey v. Zant*, 499 U.S. 467 (1991). Adherence to those decisions, and their prompt enforcement by the district courts and courts of appeals, will obviate in many cases what the Court of Appeals here seems to perceive to be the necessity for accommodating multiple filings.

As to the Death Penalty Task Force, reports of joint committees of the bench and bar should be of urgent concern to all persons with the responsibility for the administration of justice in the Ninth Circuit, but the ordinary course of legal proceedings and the constant duty of all judges to discharge their duties with diligence and precision cannot be suspended to await its recommendations.

None of the reasons offered in the response dispels our concern that the State of Washington has sustained severe prejudice by the two-and-a-half year stay of execution. The stay has prevented Washington from exercising its sovereign power to enforce the criminal law, an interest we found of great weight in *McCleskey* when discussing the importance of finality in the context of federal habeas corpus proceedings. Given the potential for prejudice to the State of Washington, the Ninth Circuit was under a duty to consider Campbell's claim for relief without delay. Our case law suggests that expedited review of this second habeas petition would have been proper. The delay in this case demonstrates the necessity for the rule that we now make explicit. In a capital case the grant of a stay of execution directed to a State by a federal court imposes on that court the concomitant duty to take all steps necessary to ensure a prompt resolution of the matter, consistent with its duty to give full and fair consideration to all of the issues presented in the case.

Despite our continuing concerns, we decline to issue mandamus to the Court of Appeals at this time....

As we do not now issue a writ of mandamus, the Court of Appeals should determine how best to expedite the appeal, given the present posture of the case. Denial of the writ is without prejudice to the right of the State to again seek mandamus relief or to request any other extraordinary relief by motion or petition if unnecessary delays or unwarranted stays occur in the panel's disposition of the matter. In view of the delay that has already occurred any further postponements or extensions of time will be subject to a most rigorous scrutiny in this Court if the State of Washington files a further and meritorious petition for relief.

The motion of respondent Charles R. Campbell for leave to proceed *in forma pauperis* is granted. The petition for writ of mandamus is denied.

Notes and Questions

1. Prior to 1996, 28 U.S.C. §2253 provided that an appeal may not be taken to the federal court of appeals from a final order in a habeas corpus proceeding where the detention complained of arises out of process issued by a state court "unless the justice or judge who rendered the order or a circuit justice or judge issues a certificate of probable cause." In *Barefoot v. Estelle*, 463 U.S. 880, 892–896 (1983), the Supreme Court issued the following procedural guidelines for handling applications for stays of execution on habeas appeals pursuant to a certificate of probable cause:

   (A) A certificate of probable cause requires more than a showing of the absence of frivolity of the appeal. The petitioner must make a substantial showing of the denial of a federal right, the severity of the penalty itself not sufficing to warrant automatic issuance of a certificate.

   (B) When a certificate of probable cause is issued, the petitioner must be afforded an opportunity to address the merits, and the court of appeals must decide the merits.

   (C) A court of appeals may adopt expedited procedures for resolving the merits of habeas corpus appeals, notwithstanding the issuance of a certificate of probable cause, but local rules should be promulgated stating the manner in which such cases will be handled and informing counsel that the merits of the appeal may be decided on the motion for a stay.

(D) Where there are second or successive federal habeas corpus petitions, it is proper for the district court to expedite consideration of the petition, even where it cannot be concluded that the petition should be dismissed under 28 U.S.C. §2254 Rule 9(b) because it fails to allege new or different grounds for relief.

(E) Stays of execution are not automatic pending the filing and consideration of a petition for certiorari from this Court to a court of appeals which has denied a writ of habeas corpus. Applications for stays must contain the information and materials necessary to make a careful assessment of the merits and so reliably to determine whether a plenary review and a stay are warranted. A stay of execution should first be sought from the court of appeals.

In 1996, 28 U.S.C. §2253 was amended to read, "Unless a circuit justice or judge issues a certificate of appealability, an appeal may not be taken to the court of appeals...." Section 2253 provides further that "[a] certificate of appealability may issue ... only if the applicant has made a substantial showing of the denial of a constitutional right." For capital litigants seeking federal habeas relief in non-opt-in states, that is, states that have not opted for the special procedures applicable under Chapter 154 of the habeas statutes, *Barefoot* remains the applicable standard for issuing stays of execution although the AEDPA has erected more substantial procedural hurdles particularly for second or successive habeas petitions. Liebman & Hertz, *Federal Habeas Corpus Practice and Procedure* §13.2(d)(e) (Lexis 5th 3d. 2005). For further discussion on federal habeas and §2253, see chapters 13 and 17, *infra*.

2. The *Barefoot* Court addressed the proper role of federal habeas proceedings:

Federal courts are not the forums in which to relitigate state trials. Even less is federal habeas a means by which a defendant is entitled to delay an execution indefinitely. The procedures adopted to facilitate the orderly consideration and disposition of habeas petitions are not legal entitlements that a defendant has a right to pursue irrespective of the contribution these procedures make toward uncovering constitutional error. "It is natural that counsel for the condemned in a capital case should lay hold of every ground which, in their judgment, might tend to the advantage of their client, but the administration of justice ought not to be interfered with on mere pretexts."

463 U.S. at 887–888 (citation omitted).

Because, unlike a term of years, a death sentence can not be carried out by the state while substantial legal issues remain outstanding, federal courts "must isolate the exceptional cases where constitutional error requires retrial or resentencing as certainly and swiftly as orderly procedures will permit. They need not, and should not, however, fail to give nonfrivolous claims of constitutional error the careful attention that they deserve." What limitations does the Court in *Barefoot* place on a defense attorney's representation of his condemned client?

3. Below is 22 Okla. Stat. tit. 22, §1001.1, in which Oklahoma sets out its procedures by which execution dates are set and stays of execution are granted in that state.

1001.1. Execution of judgment — Time — Stay of execution

A. The execution of the judgment in cases where sentence of death is imposed shall be ordered by the Court of Criminal Appeals to be carried out thirty (30) days after the defendant fails to meet any of the following time conditions:

1. If a defendant does not file a petition for writ of certiorari in the United States Supreme Court within ninety (90) days from the issuance of the mandate in the original state direct appeal unless a first application for post-conviction relief is pending;

2. If a defendant does not file an original application for post-conviction relief in the Court of Criminal Appeals within ninety (90) days from the filing of the appellee's brief on direct appeal or, if a reply brief is filed, ninety (90) days from the filing of that reply brief, or a petition in error to the Court of Criminal Appeals after remand within thirty (30) days from entry of judgment by the district court disposing of the application for post-conviction relief;

3. If a defendant does not file a writ of certiorari to the United States Supreme Court within ninety (90) days from a denial of state post-conviction relief by the Oklahoma Court of Criminal Appeals;

4. If a defendant does not file the first petition for a federal writ of habeas corpus within sixty (60) days from a denial of the certiorari petition or from a decision by the United States Supreme Court from post-conviction relief;

5. If a defendant does not file an appeal in the United States Court of Appeals for the Tenth Circuit from a denial of a federal writ of habeas corpus within seventy (70) days; or

6. If a defendant does not file a petition for writ of certiorari with the United States Supreme Court from a denial of the appeal of the federal writ of habeas corpus within ninety (90) days.

B. The filing of a petition for rehearing in any federal court shall not serve to stay the execution dates or the time restraints set forth in the above section unless the defendant makes the showing set forth in subsection C of this section. The provisions of subsection A do not apply to second or subsequent petitions or appeals filed in any court. The filing of a second or subsequent petition or appeal in any court does not prevent the setting of an execution date.

C. When an action challenging the conviction or sentence of death is pending before it, the Court of Criminal Appeals may stay an execution date, or issue any order which effectively stays an execution date only upon a showing by the defendant that there exists a significant possibility of reversal of the defendant's conviction, or vacation of the defendant's sentence, and that irreparable harm will result if no stay is issued.

D. Should a stay of execution be issued by any state or federal court, a new execution date shall be set by operation of law sixty (60) days after the dissolution of the stay of execution. The new execution date shall be set by the Court of Criminal Appeals without necessity of application by the state, but the Attorney General, on behalf of the state, shall bring to the attention of the Court of Criminal Appeals the fact of the dissolution of a stay of execution and suggest the appropriateness of the setting of a new execution date.

E. After an execution date has been set pursuant to the provisions of this section, should a stay of execution be issued by any state or federal court, a new execution date shall be set by operation of law thirty (30) days after the dissolution of the stay of execution. The new execution date shall be set by the Court of Criminal Appeals without necessity of application by the state, but the Attorney General, on behalf of the state, shall bring to the attention of the Court of Criminal Appeals the fact of the dissolution of a stay of execution and suggest the appropriateness of setting a new execution date.

F. After an execution date has been set pursuant to the provisions of this section, should a stay of execution be issued by any state or federal court and then vacated by such court, the sentence of death shall be carried out as ordered prior to the issuance of such vacated stay of execution. If the prior execution date has expired prior to the vacation of the stay of execution, a new execution date shall be set by operation of law thirty (30) days after the vacation of the stay of execution. The new execution date shall be set by the Court of Criminal Appeals without necessity of application by the state, but the Attorney General, on behalf of the state, shall bring to the attention of the Court of Criminal Appeals the fact of a vacation of the stay of execution and suggest the appropriateness of the setting of a new execution date.

G. After an execution date has been set pursuant to the provisions of this section, should the Governor of the State of Oklahoma issue a stay of execution pursuant to the powers articulated in Section 10 of Article VI of the Oklahoma Constitution, the Governor shall, simultaneous to the granting of the stay, set a new execution date. The sentence of death shall be carried out not more than thirty (30) days after the dissolution of the stay of execution; however, nothing shall prevent the Governor from ordering the new execution date to be on the first day immediately following dissolution of the stay.

Compare the Oklahoma statute with §§922.052, 922.06, and 924.14 of Florida statutes, which provide the following rules for issuing stays of execution in capital cases:

Section 922.052:

(1) When a person is sentenced to death, the clerk of the court shall prepare a certified copy of the record of the conviction and sentence, and the sheriff shall send the record to the Governor. The sentence shall not be executed until the Governor issues a warrant, attaches it to the copy of the record, and transmits it to the warden, directing the warden to execute the sentence at a time designated in the warrant.

(2) If, for any reason, the sentence is not executed during the week designated, the warrant shall remain in full force and effect and the sentence shall be carried out as provided in §922.06.

Section 922.06:

(1) The execution of a death sentence may be stayed only by the Governor or incident to an appeal.

(2)(a) If execution of the death sentence is stayed by the Governor, and the Governor subsequently lifts or dissolves the stay, the Governor shall immediately notify the Attorney General that the stay has been lifted or dissolved. Within 10 days after such notification, the Governor must set the new date for execution of the death sentence.

(b) If execution of the death sentence is stayed incident to an appeal, upon certification by the Attorney General that the stay has been lifted or dissolved, within 10 days after such certification, the Governor must set the new date for execution of the death sentence.

When the new date for execution of the death sentence is set by the Governor under this subsection, the Attorney General shall notify the inmate's counsel of record of the date and time of execution of the death sentence.

Section 924.14:

An appeal by a defendant from either the judgment or sentence shall stay execution of the sentence, subject to the provisions of §924.065.

What is your view of the Oklahoma and Florida statutes? Does one statute provide greater protection to a capital defendant than the other?

4. Collateral lawsuits might also give rise to stays of execution. For example, in Oklahoma a class action suit was filed in federal district court on behalf of all death row inmates challenging a policy which denied inmates reasonable access to counsel. The district court found the system for attorney visitation of death row inmates in Oklahoma to be constitutionally inadequate and ordered certain changes implemented. The court temporarily stayed all execution dates pending compliance with the court's order. The order provided that the stays would be vacated by written order once compliance with the proscribed injunctive relief was achieved. *Mann v. Reynolds*, 828 F. Supp 894 (W.D. Okla. 1993).

5. Collateral attacks on criminal convictions, launched both from state and federal court, undoubtedly cause years of delay between sentencing and final judicial resolution. Ad Hoc Comm. on Federal Habeas Corpus in Capital Cases, Judicial Conference of the United States, Comm. Report and Proposal 1 (1989). According to Judge Henry J. Friendly,

> [A]fter trial, conviction, sentence, appeal, affirmance, and denial of certiorari by the Supreme Court, in proceedings where the defendant had the assistance of counsel at every step, the criminal process, in Winston Churchill's phrase, has not reached the end, or even the beginning of the end, but only the end of the beginning.

Friendly, "Is Innocence Irrelevant? Collateral Attack on Criminal Judgments," 38 U. Chi. L. Rev. 142 (1970). Partly in response to concerns over such delays, in 1996, Congress enacted the Anti-terrorism and Effective Death Penalty Act. See chapters 13–17, *infra*.

6. On rare occasions, a stay of execution is granted belatedly. For example, Caryl Chessman received a telephonic stay after he was strapped into California's gas chamber and the pellets had dropped. Because there was no way to halt the execution, Chessman died. Gray & Stanley, *A Punishment in Search of a Crime* 153 (Avon Books 1989). Should there be any remedy to surviving relatives under these circumstances? If so, what? What if the stay would have only been for 30 minutes to enable a judge to consider a habeas petition?

7. In *Autry v. McKaskle*, 465 U.S. 1090 (1984), Justice Brennan along with Justice Marshall issued a dissent to a denial of certiorari and an application for stay of execution for a death sentence. Justice Brennan wrote:

> [T]he particular circumstances of this case only serve to reinforce my conviction that the imposition of the death penalty in our society inevitably amounts to an inexcusable affront to "the dignity of man." *Trop v. Dulles*, 356 U.S. 86, 100 (1958). Mr. Autry has already endured the profound psychological torment of lying strapped to a gurney for over an hour with an intravenous needle in his arm, waiting to be put to death. That wait was brought to an end by the grant of a last-minute stay permitting him time to vindicate his constitutional

rights. Following today's decision, however, he will again have to undergo the same indignity and psychological anguish, knowing that this time will probably be the last. Faced with such circumstances, I for one refuse to accept the notion implicit in today's decision that we have kept faith with the dual promise of the Eighth Amendment that the State's power to punish is "exercised within the limits of civilized standards," and that we keep pace with the "evolving standards of decency that mark the progress of a maturing society" in carrying out criminal punishments. *Id.*, at 100–101.

8. Robert Alton Harris, who was convicted of capital murder and sentenced to death on March 6, 1979, was not executed until April 21, 1992. Notwithstanding the thirteen-year gap between the crime and punishment, note the feverish pace of litigation, particularly during the last week of Harris' life.

March 17, 1992 Harris applies for clemency hearing before Governor Pete Wilson.

April 15, 1992 Governor Wilson holds clemency hearing.

April 16, 1992 Governor Wilson denies Harris' clemency petition.

April 16, 1992 (6:00 p.m.) Harris files petition for writ of habeas corpus in California Supreme Court—Ninth State Habeas No. S026177 (Cal.)

April 17, 1992 (10:00 a.m.) Harris's attorneys file a civil rights class action in U.S. District Court for the Northern District of California and request a ten-day temporary restraining order prohibiting use of lethal gas, *Fierro v. Gomez.* No. 92-1482-MHP (N.D. Cal.)

April 17, 1992 (4:30 p.m.) California Supreme Court denies ninth state habeas, 1992 Cal. LEXIS 1830 (Cal. 1992). No. CR S026177 (Cal.)

April 18, 1992 (8:55 a.m.) Harris files petition for writ of habeas corpus in U.S. District Court for the Southern District of California—Fourth Federal Habeas. No. 92-0588-T (S.D. Cal.)

April 18, 1992 (9:00 a.m.) U.S. District Judge Howard Turrentine holds hearing on fourth habeas petition. No. 92-0588-T (S.D. Cal.)

April 18, 1992 (11:15 a.m.) U.S. District Judge Howard Turrentine rejects fourth federal habeas petition, denies a request for stay of execution, and denies a certificate of probable cause for an appeal on the merits. No. 92-0588-T (S.D. Cal.)

April 18, 1992 (4:30 p.m.) Harris files application to recall the mandate in the third federal habeas petition (Harris III) in the Ninth Circuit. No. 90-55402 (9th Cir.)

April 18, 1992 (6:00 p.m.) Judge Turrentine signs written order denying fourth federal habeas. No. 92-0588-T (S.D. Cal.)

April 18, 1992 (8:00 p.m.) After a 6:00 p.m. hearing, U.S. District Court Judge Marilyn Hall Patel issues a ten-day temporary restraining order prohibiting the use of lethal gas, *Fierro v. Gomez*, 790 F. Supp. 966 (N.D. Cal. 1992). No. 92-1482-MHP (N.D. Cal.)

April 18, 1992 (8:30 p.m.) Attorney General files application for a writ of mandamus in the Ninth Circuit to overturn the temporary restraining order. No. 92-70237 (9th Cir.)

April 19, 1992 (11:00 a.m.) Harris files a request for stay of execution and application for certificate of probable cause in Ninth Circuit to appeal denial of fourth federal habeas. No. 92-55426 (9th Cir.)

April 19, 1992 (6:00 p.m.) Ninth Circuit panel conducts telephonic oral argument on all issues relating to civil rights action and fourth federal habeas petition. No. 90-55402 (9th Cir.); 92-55426 (9th Cir.); 92-70237 (9th Cir.)

April 19, 1992 (11:30 p.m.) Ninth Circuit panel grants Attorney General's petition for writ of mandamus on lethal gas case, opinions to follow. 1992 U.S. App. LEXIS 7931, 92 D.A.R. 5330 (9th Cir. 1992) No. 92-70237 (9th Cir.)

April 20, 1992 (10:00 a.m.) Ninth Circuit panel denies Harris' application to recall mandate in third federal habeas in *Harris v. Vasquez*, 961 F.2d 1449 (9th Cir. 1992). No. 92-55402 (9th Cir.)

April 20, 1992 (10:00 a.m.) Ninth Circuit panel unanimously denies Harris' application for stay of execution and certificate of probable cause in fourth federal habeas in *Harris v. Vasquez*, 961 F.2d 1450 (9th Cir. 1992). No. 92-55426 (9th Cir.)

April 20, 1992 (3:00 p.m.) Majority opinion of Ninth Circuit panel granting writ of mandate in civil rights case issues in *Gomez v. United States District Court*, 966 F.2d 460 (9th Cir. 1992). No. 92-70237 (9th Cir.)

April 20, 1992 (5:15 p.m.) Harris files petition for rehearing, suggestion for rehearing en banc, and request for stay of execution on fourth federal habeas. No. 92-55426 (9th Cir.)

April 20, 1992 (6:25 p.m.) A single Ninth Circuit judge issues stay for seven days under Ninth Circuit Rule 22-5—First Stay. No. 92-55426 (9th Cir.)

April 20, 1992 (6:30 p.m.) Attorney General files application in U.S. Supreme Court to vacate the first stay. No. A-766 (U.S.)

April 20, 1992 (7:00 p.m.) Ninth Circuit Judge Noonan issues dissenting opinion on lethal gas case issues in *Gomez v. United States District Court*, 966 F.2d 460–63 (9th Cir. 1992) (Noonan, J., dissenting). No. 92-70237 (9th Cir.)

April 20, 1992 (8:30 p.m.) Harris files opposition to application to vacate first stay. No. A-766 (U.S.)

April 20, 1992 (10:00 p.m.) Ten Ninth Circuit judges issue order staying execution in lethal gas case—Second Stay. 92-70237 (9th Cir.)

April 20, 1992 (10:15 p.m.) Attorney General files application to vacate second stay. No. A-767 (U.S.)

April 20, 1992 (11:20 p.m.) U.S. Supreme Court vacates first stay in *Harris v. Vasquez*, 503 U.S. 1000 (1992). No. A-766 (U.S.)

April 20, 1992 (midnight) Harris files federal habeas corpus petition in U.S. District Court for the Northern District of California—Fifth Federal Habeas. No. 92-1504-RMW (N.D. Cal.)

April 21, 1992 (12:05 a.m.) A single Ninth Circuit judge issues third stay of execution under Ninth Circuit Rule 22-5 in *Gomez v. Fierro* (9th Cir. 1992). No. 92-70237 (9th Cir.)—Third Stay.

April 21, 1992 (12:30 a.m.) Attorney General files application to vacate third stay in conjunction with application to vacate second stay. No. A-767 (U.S.)

April 21, 1992 (12:30 a.m.) U.S. District Court Judge Ron Whyte dismisses fifth federal habeas petition and transfers case to the U.S. District Court for the Southern District of California, under established venue rules. No. 92-1504-RMW (N.D. Cal.)

April 21, 1992 (12:45 a.m.) Fifth federal habeas petition is transferred and filed in San Diego in the U.S. District Court for the Southern District of California. No. 92-615-T (S.D. Cal.)

April 21, 1992 (1:00 a.m.) Harris' attorneys withdraw the fifth federal habeas petition. No. 92-615-T (S.D. Cal.)

April 21, 1992 (2:47 a.m.) U.S. District Judge Patel sends order to San Quentin and Attorney General requiring the prison to permit the execution to be videotaped.

April 21, 1992 (3:00 a.m.) U.S. Supreme Court vacates second and third stays in *Gomez v. United States District Court*, 503 U.S. 653 (1992). No. A-767 (U.S.)

April 21, 1992 (3:40 a.m.) Harris asks the U.S. District Court for the Northern District of California and the Ninth Circuit to consider his civil rights action to be a sixth federal habeas petition and to grant a stay of execution to exhaust state remedies. No. C-92-1482-MHP (N.D. Cal.); No. 92-70237 (9th Cir.)

April 21, 1992 (3:51 a.m.) Telephone call from Ninth Circuit Judge Harry Pregerson to San Quentin issuing stay telephonically upon the sixth federal habeas petition, received while Harris is sealed in the gas chamber—Fourth Stay.

April 21, 1992 (4:05 a.m.) Attorney General files application in United States Supreme Court to vacate fourth stay of execution. No. A-768 (U.S.)

April 21, 1992 (4:39 a.m.) Written order of Ninth Circuit Judge Pregerson received, granting one-day stay.

April 21, 1992 (5:20 a.m.) Harris files petition for writ of habeas corpus in California Supreme Court—Tenth State Habeas. No. S026235 (Cal.)

April 21, 1992 (5:45 a.m.) U.S. Supreme Court grants application to vacate fourth stay and orders no further stays from federal courts in *Vasquez v. Harris*, 503 U.S. 1000 (1992). No. A-768 (U.S.)

April 21, 1992 (6:00 a.m.) California Supreme Court denies tenth state habeas. No.S026235 (Cal.); Harris returns to the gas chamber at 6:01 a.m. and is pronounced dead at 6:21 a.m.

April 22, 1992 Ninth Circuit panel recalls and vacates writ of mandamus as moot and withdraws opinion filed on April 20, 1992 in *Gomez v. United States District Court*, 966 F.2d 463 (9th Cir. 1992). No. 92-70237 (9th Cir.).

When Harris died in California's gas chamber on April 21, 1992, he became the first person executed in that state since 1967. His case, set forth as an example of the need for federal habeas corpus reform, is chronicled in Lungren & Krotoski, "Public Policy Lessons From the Robert Alton Harris Case," 40 U.C.L.A. L. Rev. 295, 322–26 (1992). One of the last opinions rendered in the *Harris* case follows.

Gomez v. United States District Court
503 U.S. 653 (1992)

PER CURIAM.

Harris claims that his execution by lethal gas is cruel and unusual in violation of the Eighth Amendment. This case is an obvious attempt to avoid the application of *McCleskey v. Zant*, 499 U.S. 467 (1991), to bar this successive claim for relief. Harris has now filed four prior federal habeas petitions. He has made no convincing showing of cause for his failure to raise this claim in his prior petitions.

Even if we were to assume, however, that Harris could avoid the application of *Mc-Cleskey* to bar his claim, we would not consider it on the merits. Whether his claim is framed as a habeas petition or §1983 action, Harris seeks an equitable remedy. Equity must take into consideration the State's strong interest in proceeding with its judgment and Harris' obvious attempt at manipulation. See *In re Blodgett*, 502 U.S. 236 (1992); *Delo v. Stokes*, 495 U.S. 320 (1990) (Kennedy, J., concurring). This claim could have been brought more than a decade ago. There is no good reason for this abusive delay, which has been compounded by last-minute attempts to manipulate the judicial process. A court may consider the last-minute nature of an application to stay execution in deciding whether to grant equitable relief.

The application to vacate the stay of execution of death is granted, and it is ordered that the orders staying the execution of Robert Alton Harris entered by the United States Court of Appeals for the Ninth Circuit in No. 92-70237 on April 20, 1992, are vacated.

Notes on Judicial Impatience

1. The frenzied *Harris* litigation ended when the United States Supreme Court issued the following order:

> April 21, 1992. The application to vacate the stay of execution of sentence of death presented to Justice O'Connor and by her referred to the Court is granted, and it is ordered that the order staying the execution entered by the United States Court of Appeals for the Ninth Circuit on April 21, 1992 is vacated. No further stays of Robert Alton Harris' execution shall be entered by the federal courts except upon order of this court.

Vasquez v. Harris, 503 U.S. 1000 (1992).

Justices Blackmun and Stevens voted against vacating Harris' stay of execution.

2. Judges' impatience can adversely impact a stay application. In *Dobbert v. Wainwright*, 468 U.S. 1231, 1238 (1984), Justice Brennan, dissenting from a denial of a stay of execution, attributed its denial—which would have permitted a possibly innocent defendant to litigate his witness perjury claim—to a lower court's impatience. Specifically, Justice Brennan was troubled by a lower court judge whose opinion denying a stay noted that "[t]his case has been pending for a longer period of time than this nation was involved in World War II and the Korean War combined."

Note: Lonchar v. Thomas, 517 U.S. 314 (1996)

In *Lonchar v. Thomas*, 517 U.S. 314 (1996), the Eleventh Circuit, relying primarily upon the equitable principles discussed in *Gomez v. United States*, 503 U.S. 653 (1992), vacated a lower federal court's stay of execution and dismissed the petitioner's first habeas petition, which was filed on the day of his scheduled execution six years after his conviction and death sentence had become final. The Supreme Court reversed.

Lonchar was convicted and sentenced to death in 1987. Lonchar originally declined to authorize any appeals of his conviction and death sentence other than the mandatory appeal required in his case. Although over the years two of his siblings separately filed federal habeas petitions challenging his competency, Lonchar opposed those petitions and the federal court dismissed them. However in 1995, days before his scheduled execution, Lonchar filed a state habeas petition raising twenty-two claims, including one claim challenging the method of execution. Lonchar advised the state court "that he wished to pursue each of the 22 claims, but was litigating them only to delay his execution, with the hope that the State would change the execution method to lethal injection so he could donate his organs." The state courts briefly stayed the execution and then dismissed the petition. Lonchar then filed a federal habeas corpus petition. The State requested that the petition be denied because of "what it called Lonchar's 'inequitable conduct' in waiting almost six years, and until the last minute, to file a federal habeas petition." Although the federal district court issued a stay of execution, the Eleventh Circuit, relying solely on equitable principles, dismissed the petition and vacated the district court's stay of execution. Significantly, the Eleventh Circuit did not refer to federal Habeas Corpus Rule 9 in reaching its decision. At the time of Lonchar's petition, Rule 9 allowed federal courts to dismiss a habeas petition when "it appears that the state ... has been prejudiced in its ability to respond ... by delay in its filing." The question before the Supreme Court was "whether a federal court may ... dismiss a valid first habeas petition for 'equitable reasons' other than reasons listed in federal statutes or Rules, or well established in this Court's precedents." The Court concluded that, in first federal habeas petitions, Rule 9 controls and federal courts could not rely on equitable principles outside the rules to dismiss the petition.

At the outset, Justice Breyer writing for a five-member majority stated:

> When a district court is faced with a request for a stay in a first federal habeas case: if the district court cannot dismiss the petition on the merits before the scheduled execution, it is obligated to address the merits and must issue a stay to prevent the case from becoming moot. That is, if the district court lacks authority to directly dispose of the petition on the merits, it would abuse its discretion by attempting to achieve the same result indirectly by denying a stay. Of course, a district court is authorized to dismiss a petition summarily when "it appears from the face of the petition and any exhibits annexed to it that the petitioner is not entitled to relief in the district court," just as a court of appeals is not required to address an appeal that fails to meet the certificate of probable cause standard of a "substantial showing of the denial of a federal right." And, as is also true of consideration of appeals, a district court may, within the constraints of due process, expedite proceedings on the merits.

The Court observed that the equitable principles underlying habeas corpus review had evolved into a system of formalized rules and noted that Federal Habeas Rule 9(a) specifically addressed delayed petitions like the one in this case. Rule 9 represents a balance of interests between the equitable interests at stake and the strong interest in review of a first federal habeas petition. Writing for the Court, Justice Breyer stated, "to try to devise some sensible way of supplementing *first* federal habeas petition rules with ad hoc equitable devices would prove difficult. As we discussed above, the interest in permitting federal habeas review of a first petition is quite strong." The Court further stated, "the language of ... Rule [9] requires as a condition of dismissal, a finding of 'prejudice.'" In Lonchar's case, the lower courts did not make a finding of prejudice. The Court distinguished *Gomez, Sawyer v. Whitley*, 505 U.S. 333 (1992), and *Herrera v. Collins*, 506 U.S. 390 (1993), because those cases dealt with second or successive petitions. The Court concluded that Lonchar's first federal habeas petition "should have been examined within the framework of the Habeas Corpus Rules and settled precedents, not according to generalized equitable considerations *outside* that framework."

Four members of the Court concurred in the Court's judgment to reverse the lower court's order vacating of the stay of execution. However, Chief Justice Rehnquist and Justices Scalia, Kennedy and Thomas concluded that, even in first habeas petitions, courts may take into consideration equitable principles when deciding to issue a stay of execution.

Note

In *Anderson v. Buell*, 516 U.S. 1100 (1996), the Supreme Court denied a state's application to vacate a stay of execution entered by the Sixth Circuit. Chief Justice Rehnquist and Justices Scalia, Kennedy and Thomas dissented to the Court's refusal to vacate the stay. Writing for the dissenters, Justice Scalia stated that he would vacate the stay due to the defendant's dilatory delay and inequitable conduct in waiting until just shortly before his scheduled execution before filing his first federal habeas petition. For a discussion of the statute of limitations in federal habeas corpus proceedings under the Antiterrorism and Effective Death Penalty Act, see chapter 13 *infra*.

B. State Post-Conviction Proceedings

1. Introduction

If a capital defendant convicted in state court is denied relief on direct appeal and the United States Supreme Court denies certiorari, usually the next course of action is to seek relief in state post-conviction proceedings. In general, a defendant first seeks state post-conviction relief in the state trial court on all available and not yet fully litigated state and federal claims. If denied relief by the trial court, the defendant must appeal to the state appellate courts. Liebman & Hertz, *Federal Habeas Corpus Practice and Procedure* §§6.1–6.4 (Lexis 5th ed. 2005). It is critical that the defendant raise all claims in state court so that a federal court may later hear those claims in a federal habeas corpus proceeding.

2. Stages in the Prosecution of Typical Criminal Cases

Primary System	State Post-Conviction	Federal Post-Conviction
3. Certiorari petition to U.S. Supreme Court	6. Certiorari petition to U.S. Supreme Court	9. Certiorari petition to U.S. Supreme Court
↑	↑	↑
2. Direct appeal to highest state court	5. Post-conviction appeal to highest state court	8. Appeal to United States Circuit Court of Appeals
↑	↑	↑
1. Trial in state court resulting in conviction and sentence	4. Post-conviction application typically filed in trial court	7. Petition for writ of habeas corpus filed in federal district court

Although post-conviction proceedings typically are initiated after a direct appeal is final, some states require a post-conviction application to be filed while the direct appeal is still pending. See selected statutes excerpted below.

Notes

1. A conviction becomes final in step 3 above, when either (a) the United States Supreme Court denies certiorari, *or* (b) the time for filing the petition for certiorari expires, *whichever occurs first*. The date on which a conviction and sentence becomes final is critical for a number of issues, including the determination of when to file state post-conviction proceedings and the deadline for filing a federal habeas petition.

2. Following the doctrine of *Teague v. Lane*, 489 U.S. 288 (1989) (*infra* chapter 15), some states provide the only law available for defendant to argue in post-conviction proceedings is that which existed at the time defendant's conviction became final. *But see* Hon. Laura Stith, "A Contrast of State and Federal Court Authority to Grant Habeas Relief," 38 Val. U. L. Rev. 421 (2004).

3. Unlike at trial, a defendant's guilt or innocence is usually not the determinative issue in state post-conviction and federal habeas proceedings. Rather, post-conviction and habeas challenges focus on whether or not a conviction and sentence has been illegally obtained. However, in recent years, claims of actual innocence based on newly discovered evidence or scientific techniques, such as DNA testing, are frequently raised for the first time in state post-conviction proceedings.

4. The first step in state post-conviction, step 4 above, usually involves an attempt to convince the judge who presided over the trial that serious errors were committed which resulted in an unlawful conviction and/or sentence. Chances of getting relief at this stage are slim. However, in *Terry Williams v. Taylor*, 529 U.S. 362 (2000) (*supra* chapter 11 and *infra* chapter 13), the same judge who had previously presided over Williams's conviction and capital sentencing proceeding presided over Williams's post-conviction proceedings. The state judge held a two-day post-conviction evidentiary hearing on Williams's claims that trial counsel had been constitutionally ineffective. At the conclusion of the hearing, the judge found that Williams's conviction was valid, but ruled that trial counsel had been ineffective during sentencing. The trial judge recommended that Williams be granted a rehearing on sentencing. The United States Supreme Court agreed with the trial judge.

On state post-conviction review, an Oklahoma trial court reversed the conviction and sentence of Abe Munson upon finding that the state had withheld a great deal of exculpatory information in violation of *Brady v. Maryland*, 373 U.S. 83 (1963). The Oklahoma Court of Criminal Appeals affirmed, *State v. Munson*, 886 P.2d 999 (Okla. Crim. App. 1994), and Munson's case was remanded for a new trial. Munson was subsequently acquitted.

5. Federal habeas review becomes available only after a defendant has exhausted his state direct appeals and state post-conviction relief. Federal review is only available for federal claims (those involving violations of federal statutes or treaties or the United States Constitution).

6. The United States Supreme Court will only grant certiorari if a case raises serious issues of federal statutory or federal constitutional law. Due to the substantial likelihood that the United States Supreme Court will refuse to grant certiorari, steps 3, 6, and 9 provide at best a minuscule prospect of relief.

7. States are free to craft their own post-conviction procedures. Below is a sample of post-conviction statutes and case law from Tennessee, Ohio and Oklahoma. The selected case from Tennessee concerns a non-capital post-conviction case; the cases from Ohio and Oklahoma concern post-conviction proceedings in capital cases.

3. Selected Statutes: Tennessee Post-Conviction Procedure Act

40-30-102 Limitations of actions

(a) Except as provided in subsections (b) and (c), a person in custody under a sentence of a court of this state must petition for post-conviction relief under this part within one (1) year of the date of the final action of the highest state appellate court to which an appeal is taken or, if no appeal is taken, within one (1) year of the date on which the judgment became final, or consideration of such petition shall be barred. The statute of limitations shall not be tolled for any reason, including any tolling or saving provision otherwise available at law or equity. Time is of the essence of the right to file a petition for post-conviction relief or motion to reopen established by this chapter, and the one-year limitations period is an element of the right to file such an action and is a condition upon its exercise. Except as specifically provided in subsections (b) and (c), the right to file a petition for post-conviction relief or a motion to reopen under this chapter shall be extinguished upon the expiration of the limitations period.

(b) No court shall have jurisdiction to consider a petition filed after such time unless:

(1) The claim in the petition is based upon a final ruling of an appellate court establishing a constitutional right that was not recognized as existing at the time of trial, if retrospective application of that right is required. Such petition must be filed within one (1) year of the ruling of the highest state appellate court or the United States supreme court establishing a constitutional right that was not recognized as existing at the time of trial;

(2) The claim in the petition is based upon new scientific evidence establishing that such petitioner is actually innocent of the offense or offenses for which the petitioner was convicted; or

(3) The claim asserted in the petition seeks relief from a sentence that was enhanced because of a previous conviction and such conviction in the case in which the claim is asserted was not a guilty plea with an agreed sentence, and the previous conviction has subsequently been held to be invalid, in which case the petition must be filed within one (1) year of the finality of the ruling holding the previous conviction to be invalid.

(c) This part contemplates the filing of only one (1) petition for post-conviction relief. In no event may more than one (1) petition for post-conviction relief be filed attacking a single judgment. If a prior petition has been filed which was resolved on the merits by a court of competent jurisdiction, any second or subsequent petition shall be summarily dismissed. A petitioner may move to reopen a post-conviction proceeding that has been concluded, under the limited circumstances set out in §40-30-117.

§40-30-120. Stays of execution when petitioner is under sentence of death

(a) When affirming a conviction and sentence of death on direct appeal, the Tennessee supreme court shall contemporaneously set a date for an execution. Such date shall be no less than four (4) months from the date of the judgment of the Tennessee supreme court. Upon the filing of a petition for post-conviction relief, the court in which the conviction occurred shall issue a stay of the execution date which shall continue in effect for the duration of any appeals or until the post-conviction action is otherwise final. The execution date shall not be stayed prior to the filing of a petition for post-conviction relief except upon a showing by the petitioner of the petitioner's inability to file a petition prior to the execution date and that such inability is justified by extraordinary circumstances beyond the petitioner's control....

§ 40-30-121. Priority

Post-conviction cases where the petitioner is under the death sentence shall be given priority over all other matters in docketing by the courts having trial and appellate jurisdiction of the cases.

4. Selected Tennessee Case

Seals v. State
23 S.W.3d 272 (Tenn. 2000)

ANDERSON, C.J., delivered the opinion of the court, in which Drowota, Birch, Barker, and Holder, JJ., joined.

We granted review in this consolidated appeal to determine whether mental incompetency tolls the one-year statute of limitations for filing a post-conviction petition under either a savings provision or constitutional due process. The trial court dismissed the petitions for being time-barred. The Court of Criminal Appeals held that constitutional due process requires that the statute of limitations be tolled while a petitioner is mentally incompetent. We conclude that the statute of limitations is not tolled by a savings provision but may be tolled by due process concerns where a petitioner is denied a reasonable opportunity to raise a claim in a meaningful time and manner. We affirm the judgment of the Court of Criminal Appeals.

We granted this consolidated appeal to decide whether under either the general savings statute set forth in Tenn.Code Ann. §§28-1-106 (1980) or constitutional due process a petitioner's mental incompetence will toll the one-year statute of limitations for filing a post-conviction action under the 1995 Post-Conviction Procedure Act.

Each of the appellees, John Paul Seals and Vikki Lynn Spellman, alleged in their separate post-conviction petitions that they were unable to bring their post-conviction claims within one year from the entry of the trial courts' judgments due to their mental incompetence. Each trial court dismissed the petition for being filed after the expiration of the statute of limitations. The Court of Criminal Appeals reversed, concluding that under our decision in *Watkins v. State*, 903 S.W.2d 302 (Tenn.1995), a petitioner's mental incompetence tolls the statute of limitations.

After reviewing the record and applicable authority, we conclude that the savings provision in Tenn.Code Ann. §§28-1-106 does not toll the one-year statute of limitations but that due process may require tolling to ensure that a petitioner has a meaningful opportunity to present claims in a reasonable time and manner. We therefore affirm the judgment of the Court of Criminal Appeals....

ANALYSIS

We begin by reviewing the history of post-conviction statutes in Tennessee. In *Case v. Nebraska*, 381 U.S. 336 (1965), the United States Supreme Court recommended that states enact procedures for addressing alleged constitutional errors occurring during the conviction process to supplement habeas corpus remedies available in federal court. The Tennessee legislature responded by creating the Post-Conviction Procedure Act in 1967.

Under the Act, relief was to be granted "when the conviction or sentence [wa]s void or voidable because of the abridgment in any way of any right guaranteed by the constitution of [Tennessee] or the Constitution of the United States." Tenn.Code Ann. §40-30-105 (1990) (repealed 1995). Under the original Act, there was no statute of limitations, and a petition could be filed "at any time after [a petitioner] ha[d] exhausted his appellate remedies and before the sentence ha[d] expired or ha[d] been fully satisfied." Tenn.Code Ann. §40-30-102 (1982) (repealed 1986).

Statute of Limitations and the Savings Statute

In 1986, the legislature enacted a three-year statute of limitations in which petitioners had to file their claims:

> [a] prisoner in custody under sentence of a court of this state must petition for post-conviction relief under this chapter within three (3) years of the date of the final action of the highest state appellate court to which an appeal is taken or consideration of such petition shall be barred.

Tenn.Code Ann. §§40-30-102 (1990) (repealed 1995). By its terms, the statute provided for no exceptions and contained no specific provisions on tolling.

In *Watkins*, however, we addressed the issue of whether mental incompetence tolled the three-year period pursuant to a general savings provision, which stated:

> If the person entitled to commence an action is, at the time the cause of action accrued ... of unsound mind, such person ... may commence the action, after the removal of such disability, within the time of limitation for the particular cause of action, unless it exceed [sic] three (3) years, and in that case within three (3) years from the removal of such disability.

Tenn.Code Ann. §§28-1-106. We concluded that post-conviction petitions in this context were to be considered civil in nature, and we held that the savings statute applied to toll the three-year statute of limitations in cases where the petitioner was incompetent. *Watkins*, 903 S.W.2d at 305, 307.

Our holding in *Watkins* with respect to the savings statute does not, however, end the analysis in this case. The legislature enacted the Post-Conviction Procedure Act of 1995, which repealed prior post-conviction statutes and contained several substantial changes. It reduced the time for filing a petition from three years to one year of the date of the highest state appellate court action, or, if there was no appeal, one year of the date of final judgment. Tenn.Code Ann. §§40-30-202(a) (Supp.1996).[1] The 1995 Act included an anti-tolling provision stating that "[t]he statute of limitations shall not be tolled for any reason...." *Id.* Moreover, following our decision in *Watkins*, the legislature again amended the statute to add the following italicized language:

---

1. Section 40-30-202 was renumbered as section 40-30-102 in 2003. [Ed.]

The statute of limitations shall not be tolled for any reason, *including any tolling or saving provision otherwise available at law or equity. Time is of the essence of the right to file a petition for post-conviction relief or motion to reopen established by this chapter, and the one-year limitations period is an element of the right to file such an action and is a condition upon its exercise.*

Tenn.Code Ann. §40-30-202(a) (1997) (emphasis added). Accordingly, as the post-conviction statute has evolved, the legislature has limited the time and opportunity to file petitions seeking relief.

A basic principle of statutory construction is to ascertain and give effect to legislative intent without unduly restricting or expanding the intended scope of a statute. This principle requires the Court to examine the language of a statute and, if unambiguous, apply its ordinary and plain meaning. If the legislative intent is expressed in a manner devoid of contradiction and ambiguity, there is no room for interpretation or construction, and courts are not at liberty to depart from the words of the statute. While the issue with which we are confronted is nearly identical to that in *Watkins,* we now face a different statute. In *Watkins,* the post-conviction procedures afforded an unconditional three years in which to file a petition pursuant to Tenn.Code Ann. §40-30-102. The statute neither contained an anti-tolling provision nor included the enumerated exceptions to the statute of limitations for later-arising claims. Thus, we concluded that the savings statute did apply to toll the statute of limitations.

In contrast, we believe that the language of Tenn.Code Ann. §40-30-202(a) is unambiguous and that its meaning and intended effect are clear. The filing time for a petition for post-conviction relief is one year from the date of the final action. It is not to be tolled for any reason except those enumerated in Tenn.Code Ann. §40-30-202(b). The statute specifically states that the no savings provision is applicable. Accordingly, we hold that the statute of limitations is no longer tolled by the savings statute in Tenn.Code Ann. §28-1-106.

Due Process

Our conclusion that the one-year statute of limitations for filing a post-conviction petition is not tolled by the savings provision does not end our analysis. We must also consider whether a petitioner's mental incompetence requires tolling the statute of limitations as a matter of constitutional due process.

The Fifth Amendment to the United States Constitution states in part that "[n]o person shall ... be deprived of life, liberty, or property without due process of law...." The Fourteenth Amendment to the United States Constitution provides that "[n]o state shall ... deprive any person of life, liberty, or property, without due process of law." The corresponding provision found in the Tennessee Constitution states that "no man shall be taken or imprisoned, or disseized of his freehold, liberties or privileges, or outlawed, or exiled, or in any manner destroyed or deprived of his life, liberty or property, but by the judgment of his peers or the law of the land." Tenn. Const. art. I, §8.

The language of the "due process" provisions in the United States Constitution differs from the "law of the land" provision found in the Tennessee Constitution. Although the terms on occasion have been viewed as synonymous, the United States Supreme Court's interpretations of the United States Constitution establish a minimum level of protection while this Court, as final arbiter of the Tennessee Constitution, is always free to extend greater protection to its citizens.

We have previously recognized that a state has no duty to enact post-conviction procedures and that the opportunity to collaterally attack constitutional violations occurring in the conviction process is not a fundamental right during the conviction process. We also have recognized that a state which does enact post-conviction procedures may set up reasonable procedural requirements, such as a statute of limitations, and that a claim may be terminated "for failure to comply with a reasonable procedural rule without violating due process rights." ...

A petitioner's interest in collaterally attacking a conviction is not a fundamental right that deserves heightened due process protection. However, before a state may terminate a claim for failure to comply with procedural requirements such as statutes of limitations, due process requires that a potential litigant be provided an opportunity for the "presentation of claims at a meaningful time and in a meaningful manner." The test is "whether the time period provides an applicant a reasonable opportunity to have the claimed issue heard and determined."

In *Burford* [*v. State*, 845 S.W.2d 204 (Tenn. 1992)], the petitioner contended that the fifty-year persistent offender sentence imposed upon him for his 1985 robbery conviction was excessive because four of the previous robbery convictions used to enhance his sentence were set aside by a trial court in 1988. Burford's post-conviction claim, filed in 1990, arose after the expiration of the statute of limitations. We concluded that the three-year statute of limitations set forth in Tenn.Code Ann. §§40-30-102, on it face, provided a reasonable opportunity for the presentation of post-conviction claims, but that the *application* of the statute to Burford's case violated due process because he did not have a reasonable opportunity to present his claim in a meaningful time and manner. *Burford*, 845 S.W.2d at 208.

We addressed these due process concerns in the *Watkins* decision, holding that "[e]ven in the absence of a statute tolling the statute of limitations, application of the statute of limitations to the facts of this case would violate constitutional due process." *Watkins*, 903 S.W.2d at 305–06. In discussing *Burford*, we concluded that consideration must be given to the petitioner's interest of having an opportunity to attack his conviction based on the deprivation of a constitutional right and the State's legitimate interest in preventing the piecemeal litigation of stale and groundless claims. We concluded that:

> because a petitioner who was incompetent throughout the limitations period would be denied the opportunity to challenge his conviction *in a meaningful manner,* the failure to toll the limitations period would deny such a petitioner a fair and reasonable opportunity for the bringing of the [post-conviction] petition, and thus, would violate due process.

Id. at 307 (emphasis added). In other words, "if the petitioner was mentally incompetent, and therefore legally incapable, he would be denied any opportunity to assert his constitutional rights in a post-conviction petition, *unless the period of limitations was suspended during his mental incompetence." Id.* (emphasis added). Accordingly, due process requires that some reasonable opportunity to assert those rights be afforded.

We recognize that the *Burford* inquiry has been clarified in some circumstances. In *Sands v. State,* 903 S.W.2d 297 (Tenn.1995), we said that consideration must be given to whether the petitioner is raising a claim that has arisen *after* the statute of limitations has begun to run, i.e., a "later-arising" claim. *Id.* at 301. As we later explained in *Wright v. State,* 987 S.W.2d 26, 28 (Tenn. 1999), a court must:

> (1) determine when the limitations period would normally have begun to run;
> (2) determine whether the grounds for relief actually arose after the limitations

period would normally have commenced; and (3) if the grounds are "later-arising," determine if, under the facts of the case, a strict application of the limitations period would effectively deny the petitioner a reasonable opportunity to present the claim. *Id.* at 28.

The "later-arising claim" limitation in *Sands* reflects the concern that a petitioner who fails to assert an existing claim, that is, a claim that is not later-arising, in a timely fashion may not expect due process relief under *Burford*. This concern is not present in a case where a petitioner fails to assert a claim within the statute of limitations due to mental incompetence as in *Watkins*. Significantly, *Watkins* makes no mention of *Sands* and does not limit the due process analysis in cases involving mental incompetency to later-arising grounds.

The petitioner in *Watkins,* like the petitioners in the present case, raised issues challenging guilty pleas and the ineffective assistance of counsel—issues that were not later-arising. We nonetheless concluded that a petitioner who was mentally incompetent could not be denied a reasonable opportunity to raise these claims in a meaningful manner without violating due process. Thus, we concluded that the mental incompetency, if established, tolled the statute of limitations. We adhere to that holding in the present case.

Accordingly, we conclude that while the one-year statute of limitations set forth in Tenn.Code Ann. §40-30-202(a) does not violate due process on its face, application of the statute must not deny a petitioner a reasonable opportunity to raise a claim in a meaningful time and manner. Thus, a petitioner who is mentally incompetent is denied an opportunity to raise a claim in a meaningful manner unless the statute of limitations is tolled during the period of mental incompetence.

CONCLUSION

We have concluded that the one-year statute of limitations in post-conviction actions set out in Tenn.Code Ann. §40-30-202(a) is not tolled due to mental incompetence under the savings provision in Tenn.Code Ann. §28-1-106. We have further concluded, however, under *Watkins,* that due process requires tolling of the statute of limitations where a petitioner is denied the reasonable opportunity to assert a claim in a meaningful time and manner due to mental incompetence. We therefore agree with the Court of Criminal Appeals that because both Seals and Spellman met the threshold burden of raising the issue of mental incompetence, the cases must be remanded for further proceedings.

We affirm the judgments of the Court of Criminal Appeals.

Notes and Questions

1. Note that *Seals* is a noncapital case. Is there any rationale for not applying the rule in *Seals* to capital cases? What happens when a capital defendant becomes incompetent to be executed due to insanity which develops after the one-year statute of limitations? How should the Tennessee courts handle these cases? See *Van Tran v. State,* 6 S.W.3d 257 (Tenn. 1999) (post-conviction not appropriate mechanism for litigating present competency to be executed).

2. As the court in *Seals* points out, over the past decade, the Tennessee legislature has shortened the time in which a post-conviction application can be filed, has eliminated tolling of the statute of limitations, and has allowed only a few, narrow exceptions to

the statute of limitations. It would appear that the purpose of these changes is to expedite post-conviction review. (In chapter 13, the amendments to the federal habeas statutes and congressional efforts to expedite that process are discussed.)

Under §40-30-121 Tennessee courts are to give post-conviction cases of capital defendants priority. Tennessee has also established a Post-Conviction Defender Commission. Section 40-30-202 of the Tennessee Code provides:

> It is the intent of the general assembly to create the post-conviction defender commission and the office of post-conviction defender to provide for the representation of any person convicted and sentenced to death in this state who is unable to secure counsel due to indigence, and that legal proceedings to challenge such conviction and sentence may be commenced in a timely manner and so as to assure the people of this state that the judgments of its courts may be regarded with the finality to which they are entitled in the interests of justice. It is the further intent that the operation of the post-conviction defender commission and office of post-conviction defender shall be consistent with professional standards and shall not compromise independent professional judgment or create a professional or institutional conflict of interest, appearance of impropriety, breach of attorney-client confidence or secret or other violation of the Tennessee Rules of Professional Conduct or the Tennessee Code of Judicial Conduct to provide representation to indigent condemned prisoners.

3. For more information on state post-conviction proceedings generally, see Liebman and Hertz, *Federal Habeas Corpus Practice and Procedure* §§ 6.1–6.4 (Lexis 5th ed. 2005).

4. For a general discussion of the Tennessee criminal justice system, including its post-conviction practices, see Foley, "The Tennessee Court of Criminal Appeals: A Study and Analysis," 66 Tenn. L. Rev. 427 (1999).

5. Selected Statutes: Ohio Post-Conviction Remedies: §2953.21 — Petition for Postconviction Relief

(A)(1)(a) Any person who has been convicted of a criminal offense or adjudicated a delinquent child and who claims that there was such a denial or infringement of the person's rights as to render the judgment void or voidable under the Ohio Constitution or the Constitution of the United States, and any person who has been convicted of a criminal offense that is a felony, who is an inmate, and for whom DNA testing that was performed under sections 2953.71 to 2953.81 of the Revised Code or under section 2953.82 of the Revised Code provided results that establish, by clear and convincing evidence, actual innocence of that felony offense or, if the person was sentenced to death, establish, by clear and convincing evidence, actual innocence of the aggravating circumstance or circumstances the person was found guilty of committing and that is or are the basis of that sentence of death, may file a petition in the court that imposed sentence, stating the grounds for relief relied upon, and asking the court to vacate or set aside the judgment or sentence or to grant other appropriate relief. The petitioner may file a supporting affidavit and other documentary evidence in support of the claim for relief.

(b) As used in division (A)(1)(a) of this section, "actual innocence" means that, had the results of the DNA testing conducted under sections 2953.71 to 2953.81 of the Revised Code or under section 2953.82 of the Revised Code been presented at trial, no reasonable factfinder would have found the petitioner guilty of the offense of which the petitioner was convicted, or, if the person was sentenced to death, no reasonable factfinder would have found the petitioner guilty of the aggravating circumstance or circumstances the petitioner was found guilty of committing and that is or are the basis of that sentence of death.

(2) Except as otherwise provided in section 2953.23 of the Revised Code, a petition under division (A)(1) of this section shall be filed no later than one hundred eighty days after the date on which the trial transcript is filed in the court of appeals in the direct appeal of the judgment of conviction or adjudication or, if the direct appeal involves a sentence of death, the date on which the trial transcript is filed in the supreme court. If no appeal is taken, except as otherwise provided in section 2953.23 of the Revised Code, the petition shall be filed no later than one hundred eighty days after the expiration of the time for filing the appeal.

(3) In a petition filed under division (A) of this section, a person who has been sentenced to death may ask the court to render void or voidable the judgment with respect to the conviction of aggravated murder or the specification of an aggravating circumstance or the sentence of death.

(4) A petitioner shall state in the original or amended petition filed under division (A) of this section all grounds for relief claimed by the petitioner. Except as provided in section 2953.23 of the Revised Code, any ground for relief that is not so stated in the petition is waived.

(5) If the petitioner in a petition filed under division (A) of this section was convicted of or pleaded guilty to a felony, the petition may include a claim that the petitioner was denied the equal protection of the laws in violation of the Ohio Constitution or the United States Constitution because the sentence imposed upon the petitioner for the felony was part of a consistent pattern of disparity in sentencing by the judge who imposed the sentence, with regard to the petitioner's race, gender, ethnic background, or religion. If the supreme court adopts a rule requiring a court of common pleas to maintain information with regard to an offender's race, gender, ethnic background, or religion, the supporting evidence for the petition shall include, but shall not be limited to, a copy of that type of information relative to the petitioner's sentence and copies of that type of information relative to sentences that the same judge imposed upon other persons.

(B) The clerk of the court in which the petition is filed shall docket the petition and bring it promptly to the attention of the court. The clerk of the court in which the petition is filed immediately shall forward a copy of the petition to the prosecuting attorney of that county.

(C) The court shall consider a petition that is timely filed under division (A)(2) of this section even if a direct appeal of the judgment is pending. Before granting a hearing on a petition filed under division (A) of this section, the court shall determine whether there are substantive grounds for relief. In making such a determination, the court shall consider, in addition to the petition, the supporting affidavits, and the documentary evidence, all the files and records pertaining to the proceedings against the petitioner, including, but not limited to, the indictment, the court's journal entries, the journalized records of the clerk of the court, and the court reporter's transcript. The court reporter's transcript, if ordered and certified by the court, shall be taxed as court costs. If the court dismisses the petition, it shall make and file findings of fact and conclusions of law with respect to such dismissal.

(D) Within ten days after the docketing of the petition, or within any further time that the court may fix for good cause shown, the prosecuting attorney shall respond by answer or motion. Within twenty days from the date the issues are raised, either party may move for summary judgment. The right to summary judgment shall appear on the face of the record.

(E) Unless the petition and the files and records of the case show the petitioner is not entitled to relief, the court shall proceed to a prompt hearing on the issues even if a direct appeal of the case is pending. If the court notifies the parties that it has found grounds for granting relief, either party may request an appellate court in which a direct appeal of the judgment is pending to remand the pending case to the court.

(F) At any time before the answer or motion is filed, the petitioner may amend the petition with or without leave or prejudice to the proceedings. The petitioner may amend the petition with leave of court at any time thereafter.

(G) If the court does not find grounds for granting relief, it shall make and file findings of fact and conclusions of law and shall enter judgment denying relief on the petition. If no direct appeal of the case is pending and the court finds grounds for relief or if a pending direct appeal of the case has been remanded to the court pursuant to a request made pursuant to division (E) of this section and the court finds grounds for granting relief, it shall make and file findings of fact and conclusions of law and shall enter a judgment that vacates and sets aside the judgment in question, and, in the case of a petitioner who is a prisoner in custody, shall discharge or resentence the petitioner or grant a new trial as the court determines appropriate. The court also may make supplementary orders to the relief granted, concerning such matters as rearraignment, retrial, custody, and bail. If the trial court's order granting the petition is reversed on appeal and if the direct appeal of the case has been remanded from an appellate court pursuant to a request under division (E) of this section, the appellate court reversing the order granting the petition shall notify the appellate court in which the direct appeal of the case was pending at the time of the remand of the reversal and remand of the trial court's order. Upon the reversal and remand of the trial court's order granting the petition, regardless of whether notice is sent or received, the direct appeal of the case that was remanded is reinstated.

(H) Upon the filing of a petition pursuant to division (A) of this section by a person sentenced to death, only the supreme court may stay execution of the sentence of death.

(I)(1) If a person sentenced to death intends to file a petition under this section, the court shall appoint counsel to represent the person upon a finding that the person is indigent and that the person either accepts the appointment of counsel or is unable to make a competent decision whether to accept or reject the appointment of counsel. The court may decline to appoint counsel for the person only upon a finding, after a hearing if necessary, that the person rejects the appointment of counsel and understands the legal consequences of that decision or upon a finding that the person is not indigent.

(2) The court shall not appoint as counsel under division (I)(1) of this section an attorney who represented the petitioner at trial in the case to which the petition relates unless the person and the attorney expressly request the appointment. The court shall appoint as counsel under division (I)(1) of this section only an attorney who is certified under Rule 20 of the Rules of Superintendence for the Courts of Ohio to represent indigent defendants charged with or convicted of an offense for which the death penalty can be or has been imposed. The ineffectiveness or incompetence of counsel during proceedings under this section does not constitute grounds for relief in a proceeding under this section, in an appeal of any action under this section, or in an application to reopen a direct appeal.

(3) Division (I) of this section does not preclude attorneys who represent the state of Ohio from invoking the provisions of 28 U.S.C. 154 with respect to capital cases that were pending in federal habeas corpus proceedings prior to the effective date of this amendment insofar as the petitioners in those cases were represented in proceedings under this section by one or more counsel appointed by the court under this section or section 120.06, 120.16, 120.26, or 120.33 of the Revised Code and those appointed counsel meet the requirements of division (I)(2) of this section.

(J) Subject to the appeal of a sentence for a felony that is authorized by section 2953.08 of the Revised Code, the remedy set forth in this section is the exclusive remedy by which a person may bring a collateral challenge to the validity of a conviction or sentence in a criminal case or to the validity of an adjudication of a child as a delinquent child for the commission of an act that would be a criminal offense if committed by an adult or the validity of a related order of disposition.

6. Selected Ohio Case

State v. McNeill

738 N.E.2d 23 (Ohio App. 2000)

WHITMORE, Judge.

Appellant, Freddie McNeill, Jr., appeals from a judgment of the Lorain County Court of Common Pleas that denied his petition for post-conviction relief. This court affirms in part and reverses in part.

I

McNeill was convicted of the aggravated murder of Blake Fulton and was sentenced to death. This court affirmed his conviction and sentence on direct appeal. The Ohio Supreme Court also affirmed the conviction and sentence.

On September 20, 1996, while his direct appeal was pending in this court, McNeill filed a petition for post-conviction relief in the trial court. He asserted, among other things, that he was denied the effective assistance of trial counsel. He submitted an appendix of exhibits that allegedly supported his claims. On October 24, 1996, the state responded by motion, asking the court to dismiss McNeill's petition without a hearing.

After this court decided McNeill's appeal, the record was transmitted directly to the Ohio Supreme Court because McNeill had an appeal as of right. On January 27, 1998, before the record had returned to the Lorain County Court of Common Pleas from the Ohio Supreme Court, the trial court dismissed McNeill's petition for post-conviction relief without a hearing. McNeill appeals and raises eight assignments of error.

II

McNeill's first assignment of error is that the trial court erred in ruling on his petition while the record was in the possession of the Ohio Supreme Court. The record supports McNeill's assertion that the case file was at the Ohio Supreme Court until after the trial court ruled on his petition and there is nothing to indicate that a duplicate record was made.[2] The state does not dispute that the trial court did not have the case file at the time it ruled on McNeill's petition. Thus, the question posed by this assigned error is whether the trial court could properly rule on McNeill's petition without reviewing the case file.

R.C. 2953.21 provides:

"(C) ... Before granting a hearing on a petition filed under division (A) of this section, the court shall determine whether there are substantive grounds for relief. In making such a determination, *the court shall consider,* in addition to the petition, the supporting affidavits, and the documentary evidence, all the files and records pertaining to the proceedings against the petitioner, *including, but not limited to, the indictment, the court's journal entries, the journalized records of the clerk of the court, and the court reporter's transcript....*

..."(E) Unless the petition and the files and records of the case show the petitioner is not entitled to relief, the court shall proceed to a prompt hearing on the issues even if a direct appeal of the case is pending." (Emphasis added.)

The state asserts that, although the trial court is required to "consider" the record, it need not possess the record or actually review it. It cites no authority for this proposition, however. Although some cases have held that R.C. 2953.21(c) does not require the trial court to review the record before dismissing a petition for post-conviction relief, those cases have based their reasoning on a misinterpretation of *State v. Ishmail* (1978), 54 Ohio St.2d 402, 8 Ohio 3d 405, 377 N.E.2d 500.

Other than those cases that have misapplied *Ishmail,* Ohio's courts of appeals have consistently interpreted the term "consider," as it is used in R.C. 2953.21(c), to mean "review" or "examine." A failure to conduct such a review denies the petitioner due process. The trial judge cannot rely on personal memory but must actually consider the issues raised in the petition in the context of the official record of the case.

A review of record, however, is not necessitated by the mere filing of a petition for post-conviction relief. If the petition is baseless on its face, the trial court need not review the record to establish that dismissal is warranted. Therefore, if McNeill's claims were baseless on their face, the trial court had no need to review the record before dismissing his petition.

---

2. As the Ohio Supreme Court noted in its decision affirming this court's dismissal of McNeill's application for delayed reopening, the appellate rules and Supreme Court Rules of Practice now require that a duplicate record be made in capital cases, but those rules were not applicable to McNeill's case. *State v. McNeill* (1998), 83 Ohio St.3d 457, 460, 700 N.E.2d 613, 615–616 (Lundberg Stratton, J., concurring).

A petitioner for post-conviction relief has an initial burden of providing evidence of sufficient operative facts to demonstrate a cognizable claim of a constitutional error. Moreover, a defendant is barred by the doctrine of *res judicata* from raising any defense or constitutional claim that was or could have been raised at trial or on direct appeal from his conviction. *State v. Perry* (1967), 10 Ohio St.2d 175, 39 Ohio2d 189, 226 N.E.2d 104, paragraph nine of the syllabus. McNeill asserted eighteen claims for relief in his petition for post-conviction relief. A review of the claims and the evidence McNeill submitted reveals that most of his claims were baseless on their face.

Because an appeal from the judgment of conviction is limited to the trial court record, a petition for post-conviction relief may defeat the *res judicata* bar only if its claims are based on evidence *de hors* the record. McNeill did attempt to support most of his claims by attaching evidence that he alleged was not in the record. This evidence was not sufficient to defeat the *res judicata* bar, however.

New evidence attached to the petition for post-conviction relief must meet "some threshold standard of cogency; otherwise it would be too easy to defeat the holding of *Perry* by simply attaching as exhibits evidence which is only marginally significant and does not advance the petitioner's claim[.]" Evidence *de hors* the record must demonstrate that these claims could not have been raised on appeal based on the information in the original record. The claim must depend on factual allegations that cannot be determined by an examination of the files and records of the case.

McNeill submitted no evidentiary support for his tenth and fifteenth claims. No further evaluation of those claims is necessary to determine that they were facially barred by the doctrine of *res judicata*.

McNeill attempted to support his fifth and eleventh claims with newspaper articles that referred to events that happened during the trial. This evidence failed to add anything to the substance of these claims, nor did it establish that the claims could not have been fully litigated on the original record. Thus, claims five and eleven were likewise baseless on their face.

The evidence McNeill submitted to support his second, third, eighth, and fourteenth claims failed to even support his allegations. In claims two and three, McNeill alleged improper conduct by the state, but none of his evidence even suggested that the state did anything improper. Moreover, he failed to demonstrate that he could not have raised this issue at trial or on appeal.

McNeill's eighth and fourteenth claims, alleging ineffective assistance of trial counsel, are likewise unsubstantiated. His evidence merely referred to isolated incidents of conduct, but failed to even suggest that these incidents impacted trial counsel's performance, or the effectiveness of his defense, in any way. His eighth claim was that his trial counsel was ineffective for failing to disclose that the attorney-client relationship had broken down. McNeill's evidence indicated that there had been a physical altercation between McNeill and one of his trial counsel. This evidence of one incident between the two falls far short of demonstrating that there had been a complete breakdown in the attorney-client relationship. His evidence supporting claim fourteen also involved isolated incidents in which a defense investigator was allegedly intoxicated. This evidence failed to demonstrate that the defense investigation had been impacted in any way.

Through claim twelve, McNeill asserted that he was prejudiced by the sentencing judge viewing him in "shackles." The evidence he attached indicated, at best, that McNeill wore an electronic immobilization belt during sentencing. This evidence does not demonstrate that the device was even visible to the sentencing judge. Moreover, there is no evidence to establish that this issue could not have been raised at the sentencing hearing, and consequently put on the record, thus preserving the issue for appellate review.

Several of McNeill's other claims, even if arguably supported by the evidence he submitted, fail to make the requisite showing that these issues could not have been raised at trial or on appeal. McNeill's seventeenth claim alleges that the state deprived him of a fair trial because it prevented him from speaking to one of the state's key witnesses prior to trial. The evidence he attached, a hearsay statement of the witness, fails to demonstrate that this argument could not have been raised by trial counsel prior to trial. Certainly, if the allegation was true, trial counsel was aware of the problem prior to trial and could have raised the issue then.

McNeill's first, sixth, seventh, thirteenth and sixteenth claims for relief are general constitutional claims that are not fact-specific to this case. They allege challenges to the death penalty as it is imposed in Ohio and the nation, to Lorain County's jury selection process, and to Ohio's appellate review process in capital cases. Although he attached stacks of documentation to support these claims, none of this evidence established that McNeill was prevented from raising these challenges at trial or on appeal. Although he attaches evidence that is arguably relevant to these challenges, he did not establish that these challenges could not have been raised without this evidence. Moreover, even if this evidence was necessary to support McNeill's challenges, he failed to establish that he was prevented from gaining access to it or was otherwise prevented from presenting it during trial.

Two of McNeill's claims, however, are not baseless on their face. Claims four and nine alleged ineffective assistance of counsel for trial counsel's failure to present certain mitigating evidence during the penalty phase of the trial. McNeill attached the affidavits of several potential witnesses whom he contended should have been, but were not, called to give mitigating testimony. The witnesses included two licensed psychologists and several friends and family members. One of the psychologists diagnosed McNeill with attention deficit hyperactivity disorder and included an extensive report to support the diagnosis. The other psychologist indicated that McNeill's upbringing was impacted by his cultural background and that this evidence should have been offered in mitigation. The potential lay witnesses indicated that they could have testified to specific mitigating aspects of McNeill's behavior and his upbringing, but they were not contacted by McNeill's trial counsel.

Although McNeill's evidence did not necessarily warrant a hearing on McNeill's petition, and may not have even been sufficient to defeat the *res judicata* bar, it is virtually impossible to evaluate the potential merit of these claims without a review of the record. To evaluate whether trial counsel erred by failing to present certain evidence in mitigation, this court will typically review the evidence that was presented. Although trial counsel's decisions regarding the presentation of mitigating evidence are largely a matter of trial strategy, it is impossible to justify counsel's decisions as a matter of sound trial strategy without any review of the record. Because the trial court could not determine from the face of McNeill's petition that claims four and nine were without merit, it should have reviewed the penalty phase of the trial transcript. Because the trial court did not conduct such a review, the case must be remanded on those two claims. McNeill's first assignment of error is sustained solely as to claims four and nine....

The judgment of the trial court is affirmed in part and reversed in part and the cause is remanded for proceedings not inconsistent with this opinion.

Note and Questions

1. Why does Ohio provide for the filing of a post-conviction application prior to a ruling on direct appeal?

2. Most of McNeill's claims were barred by the doctrine of *res judicata*, and the court of appeals refused to hear claims that could have been, but were not, raised at trial or on direct appeal. What claims can be successfully raised on post-conviction?

7. Selected Statutes: Okla. Stat. §1089. Post-Conviction Procedure Act—Capital cases—Post-conviction relief—Grounds for appeal

A. The application for post-conviction relief of a defendant who is under the sentence of death in one or more counts and whose death sentence has been affirmed or is being reviewed by the Court of Criminal Appeals in accordance with the provisions of Section 701.13 of Title 21 of the Oklahoma Statutes shall be expedited as provided in this section. The provisions of this section also apply to noncapital sentences in a case in which the defendant has received one or more sentences of death.

B. The Oklahoma Indigent Defense System shall represent all indigent defendants in capital cases seeking post-conviction relief upon appointment by the appropriate district court after a hearing determining the indigency of any such defendant. When the Oklahoma Indigent Defense System or another attorney has been appointed to represent an indigent defendant in an application for post-conviction relief, the Clerk of the Court of Criminal Appeals shall include in its notice to the district court clerk, as required by Section 1054 of this title, that an additional certified copy of the appeal record is to be transmitted to the Oklahoma Indigent Defense System or the other attorney.

C. The only issues that may be raised in an application for post-conviction relief are those that:

1. Were not and could not have been raised in a direct appeal; and

2. Support a conclusion either that the outcome of the trial would have been different but for the errors or that the defendant is factually innocent.

The applicant shall state in the application specific facts explaining as to each claim why it was not or could not have been raised in a direct appeal and how it supports a conclusion that the outcome of the trial would have been different but for the errors or that the defendant is factually innocent.

D. 1. The application for post-conviction relief shall be filed in the Court of Criminal Appeals within ninety (90) days from the date the appellee's brief on direct appeal is filed or, if a reply brief is filed, ninety (90) days from the filing of that reply brief with the Court of Criminal Appeals on the direct appeal. Where the appellant's original brief on direct appeal has been filed prior to November 1, 1995, and no application for post-conviction relief has been filed, any application for post-conviction relief must be filed in the Court of Criminal Appeals within one hundred eighty (180) days of November 1, 1995. The Court of Criminal Appeals may issue orders establishing briefing schedules or enter any other orders necessary to extend the time limits under this section in cases where the original brief on direct appeal has been filed prior to November 1, 1995.

2. All grounds for relief that were available to the applicant before the last date on which an application could be timely filed not included in a timely application shall be deemed waived.

No application may be amended or supplemented after the time specified under this section. Any amended or supplemental application filed after the time specified under this section shall be treated by the Court of Criminal Appeals as a subsequent application.

3. Subject to the specific limitations of this section, the Court of Criminal Appeals may issue any orders as to discovery or any other orders necessary to facilitate post-conviction review.

4. a. The Court of Criminal Appeals shall review the application to determine:

(1) whether controverted, previously unresolved factual issues material to the legality of the applicant's confinement exist,

(2) whether the applicant's grounds were or could have been previously raised, and

(3) whether relief may be granted under this act.

b. For purposes of this subsection, a ground could not have been previously raised if:

(1) it is a claim of ineffective assistance of trial counsel involving a factual basis that was not ascertainable through the exercise of reasonable diligence on or before the time of the direct appeal, or

(2) it is a claim contained in an original timely application for post-conviction relief relating to ineffective assistance of appellate counsel.

All claims of ineffective assistance of counsel shall be governed by clearly established law as determined by the United States Supreme Court.

If the Court of Criminal Appeals determines that controverted, previously unresolved factual issues material to the legality of the applicant's confinement do not exist, or that the claims were or could have been previously raised, or that relief may not be granted under this act and enters an order to that effect, the Court shall make findings of fact and conclusions of law or may order the parties to file proposed findings of fact and conclusions of law for the Court to consider on or before a date set by the Court that is not later than thirty (30) days after the date the order is issued. The Court of Criminal Appeals shall make appropriate written findings of fact and conclusions of law not later than fifteen (15) days after the date the parties filed proposed findings.

5. If the Court of Criminal Appeals determines that controverted, previously unresolved factual issues material to the legality of the applicant's confinement do exist, and that the application meets the other requirements of paragraph 4 of this subsection, the Court shall enter an order to the district court that imposed the sentence designating the issues of fact to be resolved and the method by which the issues shall be resolved.

The district court shall not permit any amendments or supplements to the issues remanded by the Court of Criminal Appeals except upon motion to and order of the Court of Criminal Appeals subject to the limitations of this section.

The Court of Criminal Appeals shall retain jurisdiction of all cases remanded pursuant to this act.

6. The district attorney's office shall have twenty (20) days after the issues are remanded to the district court within which to file a response. The district court may grant one extension of twenty (20) days for good cause shown and may issue any orders necessary to facilitate post-conviction review pursuant to the remand order of the Court of Criminal Appeals. Any applications for extension beyond the twenty (20) days shall be presented to the Court of Criminal Appeals. If the district court determines that an evidentiary hearing should be held, that hearing shall be held within thirty (30) days from the date that the state filed its response. The district court shall file its decision together with findings of fact and conclusions of law with the Court of Criminal Appeals within forty-five (45) days from the date that the state filed its response or within forty-five (45) days from the date of the conclusion of the evidentiary hearing.

7. Either party may seek review by the Court of Criminal Appeals of the district court's determination of the issues remanded by the Court of Criminal Appeals within ten (10) days from the entry of judgment. Such party shall file a notice of intent to seek review and a designation of record in the district court within (10) days from the entry of judgment. A copy of the notice of intent to seek review and the designation of the record shall be served on the court reporter, the petitioner, the district attorney, and the Attorney General, and shall be filed with the Court of Criminal Appeals. A petition in error shall be filed with the Court of Criminal Appeals by the party seeking review within thirty (30) days from the entry of judgment. If an evidentiary hearing was held, the court reporter shall prepare and file all transcripts necessary for the appeal within sixty (60) days from the date the notice and designation of record are filed. The petitioner's brief-in-chief shall be filed within forty-five (45) days from the date the transcript is filed in the Court of Criminal Appeals or, if no evidentiary hearing was held, within forty-five (45) days from the date of the filing of the notice. The respondent shall have twenty (20) days thereafter to file a response brief. The district court clerk shall file the records on appeal with the Court of Criminal Appeals on or before the date the petitioner's brief-in-chief is due. The Court of Criminal Appeals shall issue an opinion in the case within one hundred twenty (120) days of the filing of the response brief or at the time the direct appeal is decided. If no review is sought within the time specified in this section, the Court of Criminal Appeals may adopt the findings of the district court and enter an order within fifteen (15) days of the time specified for seeking review or may order additional briefing by the parties.

8. If an original application for post-conviction relief is untimely or if a subsequent application for post-conviction relief is filed after filing an original application, the Court of Criminal Appeals may not consider the merits of or grant relief based on the subsequent or untimely original application unless:

   a. the application contains claims and issues that have not been and could not have been presented previously in a timely original application or in a previously considered application filed under this section, because the legal basis for the claim was unavailable, or

   b. (1) the application contains sufficient specific facts establishing that the current claims and issues have not and could not have been presented previously in a timely original application or in a previously considered application filed under this section, because the factual basis for the claim was unavailable as it was not ascertainable through the exercise of reasonable diligence on or before that date, and

(2) the facts underlying the claim, if proven and viewed in light of the evidence as a whole, would be sufficient to establish by clear and convincing evidence that, but for the alleged error, no reasonable factfinder would have found the applicant guilty of the underlying offense or would have rendered the penalty of death.

9. For purposes of this act, a legal basis of a claim is unavailable on or before a date described by this subsection if the legal basis:

a. was not recognized by or could not have been reasonably formulated from a final decision of the United States Supreme Court, a court of appeals of the United States, or a court of appellate jurisdiction of this state on or before that date, or

b. is a new rule of constitutional law that was given retroactive effect by the United States Supreme Court or a court of appellate jurisdiction of this state and had not been announced on or before that date.

E. All matters not specifically governed by the provisions of this section shall be subject to the provisions of the Post-Conviction Procedure Act. If the provisions of this act conflict with the provisions of the Post-Conviction Procedure Act, the provisions of this act shall govern.

8. Selected Oklahoma Case

Patton v. State

989 P.2d 983 (Okla. Crim. App. 1999)

LUMPKIN, Vice-Presiding Judge:

Petitioner Eric Allen Patton was convicted of First Degree Murder (Count I) and First Degree Burglary (Count II), Case No. CF-95-55, in the District Court of Oklahoma County. In Count I, the jury found the existence of three (3) aggravating circumstances and recommended the punishment of death. In Count II, Petitioner was sentenced to one thousand one hundred and twenty (1,120) years imprisonment. This Court affirmed the judgments and sentences in *Patton v. State*. Petitioner filed his Original Application for Post-Conviction Relief in this Court on September 3, 1998, in accordance with 22 O.S.Supp.1998, §1089.

Before considering Petitioner's claims, we must again consider the narrow scope of review available under the amended Post-Conviction Procedure Act. As we have said numerous times: "[T]he Post-Conviction Procedure Act was neither designed nor intended to provide applicants another direct appeal." The Act has always provided petitioners with very limited grounds upon which to base a collateral attack on their judgments. Accordingly, claims which could have been raised in previous appeals but were not are generally waived; and claims raised on direct appeal are *res judicata*. These procedural bars still apply under the amended Act. We have noted the new Act makes it even more difficult for capital post-conviction applicants to avoid procedural bars. Under 22 O.S.Supp.1998, §§1089(C)(1), the only claims which will be considered on post-conviction are those which "[w]ere not and could not have been raised" on direct appeal and which "support a conclusion either that the outcome of the trial would have been different but for the errors or that the defendant is factually innocent." A capital post-conviction claim could not have been raised on direct appeal if (1) it is an ineffective assistance of trial or appellate counsel claim which meets the statute's definition of ineffective counsel; or (2) the legal basis of the claim was not recognized or could not have been reasonably formulated from a decision of the United States Supreme Court, a federal appellate court or an appellate court of this State, or is a new rule of constitutional law given retroactive effect by the Supreme Court or an appellate court of this State. 22 O.S.Supp.1998, §§1089(D)(4)(b), 1089(D)(9). Should a Petitioner meet this burden, this Court shall consider the claim only if it "[s]upports a conclusion either that the outcome of the trial would have been different but for the errors or that the defendant is factually innocent." 22 O.S.Supp.1995, §§1089(C)(2). As we said in *Walker v. State*, 933 P.2d 327 (Okla. Crim. App. 1997), the amendments to the capital post-conviction review statute reflect the legislature's intent to honor and preserve the legal principle of finality of judgment, and we will narrowly construe these amendments to effectuate that intent. Given the newly refined and limited review afforded capital post-conviction applicants, we must also emphasize the importance of the direct appeal as the mechanism for raising all potentially meritorious claims. Because the direct appeal provides appellants their only opportunity to have this Court fully review all claims of error which might arguably warrant relief, we urge them to raise all such claims at that juncture. *Walker*, 933 P.2d at 331. We now turn to Petitioner's claims.

In Propositions I, II and III, Petitioner asserts he was denied the effective assistance of appellate counsel. Specifically, he finds appellate counsel ineffective for failing to: 1) investigate extra-record material on appeal (Proposition I); 2) present mitigating evidence, *i.e.*, evidence of his good behavior while incarcerated and on parole in California, and while hospitalized at Eastern State Hospital in Vinita, Oklahoma, (Proposition II, which also includes an allegation of trial counsel ineffective assistance); and 3) supplement the direct appeal brief with *Darks v. State*, 954 P.2d 152 (Okla. Crim. App. 1998) to challenge the playing of tape recorded statements containing prejudicial comments and opinions made by the interviewing police officers (Proposition III).

    . . . .

While appellate counsel has a duty to raise relevant issues for this Court's consideration, there is no obligation to raise all available non-frivolous issues. *Walker*, 933 P.2d at 334. The mere failure to raise even a meritorious claim does not, in itself, constitute deficient performance. Appellate counsel filed a well written, thoroughly researched brief raising numerous claims at least equally meritorious to that which was omitted and is at issue here. We cannot find that appellate counsel's failure to raise the claim at issue here rendered his performance unreasonable under prevailing professional norms. It has not been shown that appellate counsel breached a duty owed to Petitioner, or that appellate counsel's judgment was "unreasonable under the circumstances or did not fall within the wide range of professional assistance" owed to a client by an attorney. Further, Petitioner has failed to show any external impediment which precluded counsel from raising the issue. In addition, direct appeal counsel did raise this issue in his Petition for Rehearing and this Court found the issue was non-meritorious. Therefore, as Petitioner has not established that appellate counsel's performance was deficient, his claim of ineffective assistance of appellate counsel has no merit and his substantive claims remain procedurally barred.

In Propositions II, V, VI, Petitioner raises claims of ineffective assistance of trial counsel. Specifically, he claims trial counsel was ineffective for failing to present mitigating evidence, i.e., evidence of his good behavior while incarcerated in and on parole in California, and while hospitalized at Eastern State Hospital in Vinita, Oklahoma, (Proposition II); for stipulating in closing argument that the aggravating circumstances outweighed the mitigating evidence (Proposition V); and for alluding to the appellate process during closing argument (Proposition VI). The issue of ineffective assistance of counsel was raised and addressed on direct appeal. Therefore, further consideration of the issue is barred by *res judicata*.

Despite the procedural bar of *res judicata,* a claim of ineffective assistance of trial counsel can be brought for the first time on post-conviction, but only if it requires fact-finding outside of the direct appeal record. 22 O.S.Supp.1998, §§1089(D)(4)(b)(1). "The statutory phrase 'fact-finding outside the direct appeal record' was never meant to negate the principle of waiver." This Court may not review post-conviction claims of ineffective assistance of trial counsel if the facts generating those claims were available to the direct appeal attorney and thus either were or could have been used in the direct appeal. The mere absence of a claim from the direct appeal record is not sufficient: the claim is still waived if the facts contained in it were available to the direct appeal attorney and could have been raised on direct appeal.

Having reviewed Petitioner's arguments, we find the facts upon which his claims of ineffective assistance of trial counsel are based were contained in the record or could have been available to direct appeal counsel such that the arguments could have been raised in the direct appeal. Because Petitioner's claims of trial counsel ineffectiveness do not turn on facts unknown or unavailable at the time of his direct appeal, he has failed to meet the conditions for review of those claims on the merits and therefore review of the claims is barred....

In his tenth and final proposition of error, Petitioner asserts that he has presented sufficient evidence of controverted, previously unresolved factual issues concerning appellate counsel's deficient representation to require an evidentiary hearing. Petitioner directs us to 22 O.S.Supp.1998, §1089(D)(5) and argues that "if this Court determines upon review of the application that 'previously unresolved factual issues material to the legality of the applicant's confinement exist,' and the claim is one which meets the other prerequisites for post-conviction review, an evidentiary hearing is mandatory." He contends that as the claim of ineffective assistance of appellate counsel could not have been raised earlier, this case should be remanded for a full and fair evidentiary hearing to address the question of ineffective representation on direct appeal.

The requirements for evidentiary hearings in post-conviction proceedings are set forth in Rule 9.7(D)(5), *Rules of the Oklahoma Court of Criminal Appeals,* Title 22, Ch.18, App. (1998):

> A request for an evidentiary hearing is commenced by filing an application for an evidentiary hearing, together with affidavits setting out those items alleged to be necessary for disposition of the issue petitioner is advancing. The application for hearing and affidavits submitted by the petitioner shall be cross-referenced to support the statement of specific facts required in the application for post-conviction relief.

See Section 1089(C)(2) of Title 22. The application for an evidentiary hearing shall be filed together with the application for post-conviction relief. See Section 1089(D)(2) of Title 22. **The application for hearing and affidavits must contain sufficient information** to show this Court by clear and convincing evidence the materials sought to be introduced have or are likely to have support in law and fact to be relevant to an allegation raised in the application for post-conviction relief.(Emphasis added.)

Here, Petitioner has not set forth sufficient information to show this Court by clear and convincing evidence the materials concerning direct appeal counsel's representation have or are likely to have support in law and fact to be relevant to an allegation raised in the application for post-conviction relief. He has not set forth any evidence which has been discovered and is now presented to the Court for consideration as to whether it meets the threshold requirements for an evidentiary hearing. He merely presents allegations which are nothing more than unsupported conclusions. Such allegations are merely speculation as to what might be discovered at a later date rather than evidence which has already been developed and needs to be included in the record on appeal to adjudicate the issues raised. Therefore, this proposition is denied.

DECISION

After carefully reviewing Petitioner's Application for post-conviction relief, we conclude (1) there exists no controverted, previously unresolved factual issues material to the legality of Petitioner's confinement; (2) Petitioner could have previously raised collaterally asserted grounds for review; (3) grounds for review which are properly presented have no merit; and (4) the current post-conviction statutes warrant no relief. 22 O.S.Supp.1998, §§1089(D)(4)(a)(1), (2) & (3). Accordingly, Petitioner's Application for Post-Conviction Relief is denied.

Notes

1. In 1995, the Oklahoma Legislature amended and narrowed the post-conviction procedures governing capital criminal defendants. In *Le v. State*, 953 P.2d 52, 54–55 (Okla. Crim. App. 1998), the Oklahoma Court of Criminal Appeals considered the constitutionality of the amendments:

> Le correctly describes the post-conviction statute as a law limiting and defining the type of claim which may be presented and considered on post-conviction. However, that limitation neither usurps nor diminishes this Court's authority and responsibility to exercise independent judgment on the merits of constitutional claims in post-conviction proceedings. As Le admits, Oklahoma is not obliged to provide capital post-conviction procedures. The Legislature has afforded this statutory protection to capital defendants, and may limit the scope of the procedures to ensure finality of judgment. Without the statute, this Court would have no jurisdiction at all in capital post-conviction cases. The fact that the statute is limited in scope does not limit this Court's ability to judge the merits of the claims which are appropriate under the statute: limitation of jurisdiction does not equal limitation of judgment.
>
> Le also claims in Proposition I that the Legislature's "abridgment" of this Court's jurisdiction violates various constitutional limitations. As this Court fully retains the ability to judge the merits of propositions appropriately raised, these claims must fail. Le first argues the statute does not afford him the reasonably adequate opportunity to present his claims. The use of the three-tiered procedural scheme does not in itself deny Le a reasonably adequate opportunity to present claims; it merely limits the scope of the claims he may

present. Le again claims the statute has usurped this Court's obligation and authority to address capital post-conviction claims; as we discuss above, the statute does not limit this Court's ability to consider appropriately raised claims. Le argues the statute violates the Supremacy Clause, but nothing in the statute contradicts the requirement that this Court is bound by the Constitution as the supreme law of the land, and this Court has not allowed the post-conviction statutes to preclude us from deferring to the Constitution in individual cases.

2. What claims can be raised in post-conviction under Oklahoma law? How would you raise these claims? How can post-conviction counsel raise ineffective assistance of appellate counsel claims?

Note on Right to Counsel in State Post-Conviction Proceedings

As noted in chapter 11, there is no constitutional right to the assistance of counsel in state post-conviction proceedings. Most death penalty states, however, provide death row inmates with counsel in state post-conviction proceedings.

> [N]obody in his right mind would expect the average inmate to be capable of proceeding pro se in a capital case—researching the most complex legal issues known to the law, investigating the facts from his narrow death row cell, and providing himself with meaningful representation. Yet a plurality of the Supreme Court has indicated that an equitable justice system may deny legal representation to those on death row. See *Murray v. Giarratano*, 492 U.S. 1, 12 (1989) (plurality opinion) (holding that under the specific conditions in Virginia, where all death row inmates had legal counsel, states are not required to provide counsel to indigent death row prisoners seeking state post-conviction relief). "If the law says that," as Mr. Bumble might bellow, "then the law is a[n] ass, a[n] idiot."
>
> Fortunately, with the recent conversion of the Mississippi Supreme Court, now thirty-three of the thirty-eight states with the death penalty on the books agree with Mr. Bumble and automatically provide for counsel in state post-conviction proceedings. By statute or by practice, all but two states provide counsel, with Georgia and Louisiana standing in unhappy isolation.

Stafford Smith & Starns, "Folly by Fiat: Pretending that Death Row Inmates Can Represent Themselves in State Capital Post-Conviction Proceedings," 45 Loy. L. Rev. 55, 56 (1999).

The following law review article illustrates creative advocacy in favor of the right to counsel in state post-conviction proceedings.

Folly by Fiat: Pretending that Death Row Inmates Can Represent Themselves in State Capital Post-Conviction Proceedings

Clive Stafford Smith & Remy Voisin Starns, 45 Loy. L. Rev. 55, 56 (1999)

In Mississippi, until very recently, the state supreme court had flatly refused to provide counsel, and had refused to stay the execution dates of those who had no lawyer. One man, Willie Russell, came within forty-five minutes of his execution without a lawyer, and it was only the intervention of the United States Court of Appeals for the Fifth Circuit that prevented his death.

In an effort to compel a solution to this problem, Mr. Russell sued the State of Mississippi in federal court. His lawsuit focused heavily on practical facts. Mr. Russell had tested in the range of mental retardation while in school. His lawyers planned to present a full scale evaluation of the other men on death row, commissioned by the Southern Poverty Law Center and conducted by two independent psychologists, Dr. Mark Cunningham and Dr. Mark Vigan. They determined that twenty-seven percent of the other inmates might also fall within the range of mental retardation. A battery of tests also established that the men had very limited reading comprehension abilities. Another test was specifically designed to determine the educational level that would be required merely to understand the Mississippi Post-Conviction Relief Statute. Ultimately, based on the logic that a person who could not get into law school should not be required to act as a lawyer, the inmates were asked to attempt the Law School Admission Test (LSAT).

Perhaps it is not surprising that the results of these tests proved what most sensible people would automatically assume—that indigent, under-educated men who had been sentenced to death are ill-equipped to understand, much less perform, the task of self-representation in post-conviction. However, this only answered a part of the practical question. The researchers and lawyers also tested the hypothesis that the state of mind of a person condemned to death could have an effect on his ability to prepare and present his own defense. Again, the strong findings of hopelessness and depression suggested that the emotional state of those on death row would further reduce their capacity to act as their own attorneys.

Finally, even a highly intelligent and well-educated individual would be challenged if he were asked to seek out and present the evidence that is so crucial to a successful post-conviction petition while confined to his cell for more than twenty-three hours every day. Mr. Russell's attorneys therefore explored the practical realities of his day-to-day existence in an effort to gauge the avenues left open to his self-representation. This focused not only on the obvious fact that Mr. Russell would not be allowed to leave the penitentiary to perform his own investigation, but also on the extremely limited—and rapidly diminishing—legal assistance provided to inmates by the Mississippi State Penitentiary.

The State was not keen to see how far the federal courts would be willing to stretch the rationale of *Giarratano* and sought settlement discussions before discovery could even begin. In the meantime, Mr. Russell added the individual justices of the Supreme Court of Mississippi as defendants to the lawsuit and indicated his intention to take their depositions early in the discovery process.

Fortunately, the judicial system was spared the embarrassing spectacle of the justices under oath trying to explain how, on the one hand, they could speak of the incredible complexity of capital litigation, and yet on the other hand, leave a mentally retarded person like Mr. Russell to represent himself. All of a sudden, in *Jackson v. State*, 732 So.2d 287 (Miss. 1999), the court decided that it could "no longer sit idly by and wait for state legislatures to provide a remedy." The court noted that the "writ of habeas corpus has been a hallmark in the protection of our individual freedoms since being brought to this country by our forefathers from England." While it may once have been viewed as a discretionary appeal, "[t]he reality is that post-conviction efforts, though collateral, have become an appendage, or part, of the death penalty appeal process at the state level." This significance is emphasized, the court continued, by the fact that no federal relief could be sought without first exhausting the state avenues for relief.

The court recognized the reality that "[a]pplications for post-conviction relief often raise issues which require investigation, analysis, and presentation of facts outside the appellate record. The inmate is confined, unable to investigate, and often without training in the law or the mental ability to comprehend the requirements of [the post-conviction statute]." Given that the United States Supreme Court had recently told Mississippi that it may not "bolt the door to equal justice," even in cases involving parental rights, the state court held that "[a]ccess to equal justice is an even greater interest where the State seeks to impose the penalty of death."

Turning to *Giarratano*, the Mississippi court discounted the plurality opinion, which flatly held there was no right to counsel, in favor of Justice Kennedy's concurrence, which emphasized that no Virginia inmate had actually been forced to proceed without counsel. In contrast, "[i]n Mississippi, repeatedly, since 1995, death row inmates have been unable to obtain counsel or requisite help from institutional lawyers."

Mississippi therefore tentatively recognized that the State should not make a fool of itself by making death row inmates represent themselves. This was a notable opinion, for skeptics often suggest that Mississippi ranks fifty-first among the States in its recognition of civil rights. Such is not the case on this occasion. There are, unfortunately, other states that now lag behind Mississippi.

Chapter 13

Introduction to Federal Habeas Corpus Review

A. Historical Overview

Article I, section 9 of the United States Constitution reads: "The privilege of the Writ of Habeas Corpus shall not be suspended, unless when in Cases of Rebellion or Invasion the public safety may require it." U.S. Const. art. I, §9 cl. 2. Habeas corpus derives its name from Latin and means "have the body." The writ of habeas corpus traces its roots to England.

> As initially developed sometime before the thirteenth century, the writ was a form of mesne process by which courts compelled the attendance of parties whose presence would facilitate their proceedings. It was not until the mid-fourteenth century that it came to be used as an independent proceeding designed to challenge illegal detention. The subsequent characterization of habeas corpus as the Great Writ of Liberty—the alleged procedural underpinning of the guarantees of the Magna Carta—stemmed primarily from battles fought in establishing its effectiveness against imprisonment by the Crown without judicial authorization.

LaFave & Israel, *Criminal Procedure* 1178 (2d ed.) (West Pub. Co. 1992).

In the United States, the writ of habeas corpus, explicitly recognized in the federal constitution, was included in the first Judiciary Act, passed in 1789. According to that Act:

> the several courts of the United States, and the several justices and judges of such courts ... shall have power to grant writs of habeas corpus in all cases where any person may be restrained of his or her liberty in violation of the constitution, or of any treaty or law of the United States.

Originally, the writ extended to federal prisoners in custody "under or by colour of the authority of the United States." In *Ex Parte Dorr*, 44 U.S. (3 How.) 103 (1845), the Supreme Court held that the common law writ of habeas corpus did not extend to state prisoners. However, in 1867—the year the Fourteenth Amendment was adopted—Congress passed a new Judiciary Act. Its provisions allowed state prisoners "in custody in violation of the Constitution or laws of the United States" to challenge their confinement in federal court. 28 U.S.C. §2254(a). *Ex Parte Dorr* was thus overruled. For interesting and thought-provoking discussions on the early history of the writ, see Randy Hertz & James Liebman, *Federal Habeas Corpus Practice and Procedure* (5th ed. 2006); Eric Freedman, *Habeas Corpus: Rethinking the Great Writ of Liberty* (New University Press 2001); Freedman, "Milestones in Habeas Corpus: Just Because John Marshall Said It Doesn't Make It So: *Ex Parte Bollman* and the Illusory Prohibition on the Writ of Habeas Corpus for State Prisoners in the Judiciary Act of 1789," 51 Ala. L. Rev. 531 (Winter 2000).

In the early twentieth century, as reflected in *Frank v. Magnum*, 237 U.S. 309 (1915), and in *Moore v. Dempsey*, 261 U.S. 86 (1923), the Court grappled with the scope of habeas review in relation to the state criminal process. *Frank v. Magnum*, the Supreme Court's first major twentieth century habeas corpus decision, held that the habeas remedy should be provided whenever the state, "supplying the corrective process, ... deprives the accused of life or liberty without due process of law." If the state did not provide an effective remedy to vindicate federal constitutional rights, the federal courts had jurisdiction to hear habeas petitions. Whitebread & Slobogin, *Criminal Procedure: An Analysis of Cases and Concepts* 972–973 (4th ed.) (Foundation Press 2001); *see also* Randy Hertz & James Liebman, *Federal Habeas Corpus Practice and Procedure* (5th ed. 2006).

For further reading on the *Frank* case and a more in-depth discussion of the historical roots of habeas corpus, see Freedman, "Milestones in Habeas Corpus: Leo Frank Lives: Untangling the Historical Roots of Meaningful Federal Habeas Review of State Convictions," 51 Ala. L. Rev. 1467 (Summer 2000).

In the early 1950s, nearly forty years after the Court in *Frank* indicated a willingness to open the door for state prisoners seeking review of the federal constitutional claims in federal habeas, the Court again embraced an expansive view of federal habeas review.

> [I]n *Brown v. Allen*, 344 U.S. 443 (1953), the Court made an even more significant pronouncement, holding that, assuming state remedies have been exhausted, a state prisoner can petition a federal court for adjudication of a constitutional claim even when the state corrective process is adequate.
>
> From *Brown* until the 1970s, the Court continued to support an expansive view of the writ, to the point where it became available to virtually any state prisoner with a constitutional claim who had not deliberately bypassed the state corrective process. But since the mid-1970s, the Court, while not overturning *Brown*, has moved from heavy reliance on habeas corpus as a means of reviewing state court decisions to a preference for state resolution of most constitutional conflicts arising in criminal cases....

Whitebread & Slobogin, *Criminal Procedure: An Analysis of Cases and Concepts* 831–832 (2d ed.) (Foundation Press 1986). For further discussion on *Brown v. Allen*, see Freedman, "Milestones in Habeas Corpus: *Brown v. Allen*: The Habeas Corpus Revolution that Wasn't," 51 Ala. L. Rev. 1541 (Summer 2000).

The conflict between the *Brown* and *Frank* cases and those cases in which the Court has retreated from an expansive view of the writ has been hotly debated for a number of years. As a practical matter, the struggle between these two viewpoints emerges in two areas: first, the type of substantive claim a state criminal defendant may bring in federal court; and second, the extent to which habeas relief may be foreclosed due to a criminal defendant's failure to litigate adequately his claims in state court or comply with other procedural requirements.

The retreat from an expansive view of the writ is a result of at least three factors. First, federal courts have greater faith in the capabilities of their state counterparts to resolve state criminal matters. Second, the Supreme Court hopes to promote comity between the federal and state systems by showing greater respect for (and thus increased deference to) the decisions of state courts. Finally, and perhaps most important, the Court repeatedly emphasizes the need for finality in the judicial process and the burden that habeas petitions place on federal courts. Whitebread & Slobogin, *Criminal Procedure: An Analysis of Cases and Concepts* 903 *et seq.* (3d ed.) (Foundation Press 1993). This last point clearly influenced Justice Jackson's concurring opinion in *Brown v. Allen*:

[T]his Court has sanctioned progressive trivialization of the writ until floods of stale, frivolous and repetitious petitions inundate the docket of the lower courts and swell our own. Judged by our own disposition of habeas corpus matters, they have, as a class, become peculiarly undeserving. It must prejudice the occasional meritorious application to be buried in a flood of worthless ones. He who must search a haystack for a needle is likely to end up with the attitude that the needle is not worth the search. Nor is it any answer to say that few of these petitions in any court really result in the discharge of the petitioner. This is the condemnation of the procedure which has encouraged frivolous cases. In this multiplicity of worthless cases, states are compelled to default or to defend the integrity of their judges and their official records, sometimes concerning trials or pleas that were closed many years ago.

Brown, 344 U.S. at 536–537.

Justice Jackson expressed doubt as to the merits of the relatively few cases where the writ was granted. "There is no doubt that if there were a super-Supreme Court, a substantial proportion of our reversals of state courts would also be reversed. We are not final because we are infallible, but we are infallible only because we are final." *Id.* at 540.

At the time Justice Jackson complained about the "flood" of habeas petitions, state inmates filed 541 petitions in federal court. By 1961, there were 1,020 such petitions filed; and by 1970 there were 9,063. In 1991, state prisoners filed 10,325 habeas petitions. 1991 Director of the Admin. Office of the United States Courts Ann. Rep. 191. In 1995, the number of filed habeas petitions had risen to 63,550 habeas petitions, and in 2000, 58,251 habeas petitions were filed. 1999 Annual Report of the Director, Judicial Business of the United States Courts; Administrative Office of the U.S. Courts, Judicial Facts and Figures, Table 2.2.

Note

State prisoners whose rights have been violated may sue for relief in federal court under two separate statutes. First, they may petition for a writ of habeas corpus under 28 U.S.C. §2254. Relief sought under §2254 typically includes a reduction of sentence or a reversal of conviction. In addition, state prisoners challenging the conditions of their imprisonment may bring a civil rights action under 42 U.S.C. §1983. Prisoners suing under §1983 normally seek money damages or declaratory relief. Habeas petitioners, unlike civil rights plaintiffs, may not recover money damages. *Preiser v. Rodriguez*, 411 U.S. 475, 493 (1973).

B. Policy Considerations

Federal Habeas Corpus Practice and Procedure
James S. Liebman, (Michie Company 1988) (Volume 1)

§2.2. The modern debate.

a. *Introduction.* Much has been written about the history and policy of habeas corpus.... [T]o help orient readers to the modern judicial understanding of the writ, this section introduces and poses answers to the three policy questions that have framed recent Supreme Court debate about habeas corpus—whether the courts have so expanded the writ over the past quarter century as to distort its function; whether the writ's only or preeminent rationale should be to protect people against false criminal conviction; and whether the writ has any special role to play in capital cases.

b. *Has the remedy expanded?* As Ronald Sokol noted almost 20 years ago, "[i]t has become fashionable to point out that the scope of the writ today is considerably different from what it was at common law." This same assertion continues to adorn the opinions of Supreme Court justices and others who advocate cutting back the writ. Fashionable as it is, this view is wrong. What is remarkable about the writ is its constancy.

Consider, for example, the 17th century English view of the writ as assuring that "[n]o freeman shall be imprisoned without due process of law" and that "the cause of ... commitment be just or legal." And consider Blackstone's 18th century description of the writ as "efficacious ... in *all manners* of illegal confinement." Consider also the Supreme Court's 1830 understanding of the statutory remedy available in this country as "in the nature of a writ of error, to examine the legality of the commitment" and "to liberate an individual from unlawful imprisonment;" the lower federal courts ante-bellum interpretation of habeas corpus as a privilege designed to ensure that no "arbitrary authority might act without warrant, or 'due process of law'" as the latter words were used in the 5th amendment; and the Supreme Court's various post-bellum characterizations of the writ as a judicial remedy "for every possible case of privation of liberty contrary to the National Constitution, treaties or laws," whose scope "is impossible to widen" (1867); a remedy available whenever a state prisoner "is held in custody in violation of the Fourteenth Amendment ... in that the State thereby deprives him of liberty without due process of law ... [or abridges] his privileges and immunities as a citizen of the United States, ... [or denies him] the equal protection of the laws" (1890); an assurance that the petitioner "was not deprived of his liberty without due process of law, ... so as to violate the provisions of the Fourteenth Amendment to the Federal Constitution" (1906); a procedure for "securing to the petitioners their constitutional rights" (1923); the means "by which the legality of the detention of one in the custody of another [court] could be tested judicially" (1934); a mechanism "to test the constitutional validity of a conviction for crime" (1942); a remedy giving "the final say" to the federal courts as to whether or not "State Supreme Courts have denied rights guaranteed by the United States Constitution" (1953); and a federal judicial authority "conferred by the allegation of an unconstitutional restraint [that] is not defeated by anything that may occur in the state court proceedings" (1963). Consider, finally, that the Court continues today to treat habeas corpus as a forum "for litigating constitutional claims generally" and a procedure in which "a state prisoner's challenge to the trial court's resolution of dispositive federal issues is always fair game [for] federal [review]."

The Supreme Court has deviated only once from the view that Congress intended the federal habeas corpus remedy to be as broad as the rights conferred by the federal Constitution. "The case is tragic and instructive, very much to the point today. For this single lapse in the protective function of the federal habeas corpus jurisdiction is the historical model" for the writ-gutting proposals advanced not only by the currently fashionable revisionist historians of habeas corpus but also in legislation pending before Congress.

In *Frank v. Mangum* in 1915, the Supreme Court denied habeas corpus relief to Leo M. Frank, a Jewish man convicted and sentenced to die for raping and killing a young Christian woman in Atlanta, Georgia. The record before the Supreme Court left it no choice but to assume, as Justice Holmes wrote in dissent, that Frank's trial in the local Georgia court was "dominated" by an anti-semitic "mob", which had forced the trial judge to order "not only the petitioner [Frank] but his counsel to be absent from

Court" when the jury announced the verdict in order to avoid the "probable danger of violence."

Because Georgia had accorded Frank the "corrective process" of an appeal, a majority of the court denied him federal habeas corpus relief. The majority held that he was not even entitled to a federal hearing at which he might have proved that he had been falsely convicted without due process, under what amounted to "lynch law ... practiced by a regularly drawn jury." Finding that Frank had the opportunity to, and did, appeal his "mob domination" claim to the Supreme Court of Georgia, and that the Georgia court, "upon a full review, decided appellant's allegations of fact ... to be unfounded," the Supreme Court majority concluded that Frank's constitutional claim could not be relitigated in habeas corpus proceedings, regardless of its merit.

Justice Holmes dissented, arguing that, as always previously understood, the federal courts' "power to secure fundamental rights" through the writ of habeas corpus "becomes a duty" once "resort to the local appellate tribunal ... has been had in vain." Eight years later, in *Moore v. Dempsey*, 261 U.S. 86 (1923), the full Court restored Justice Holmes' interpretation. As Justice Frankfurter subsequently interpreted *Moore*, "the prior State determination of a claim under the United States Constitution cannot foreclose [federal habeas corpus] consideration of such a claim, else the State court would have the final say which the Congress, by the Act of 1867, provided it should not have." Thus the law has stood until today, fashionable revisionism notwithstanding.

What this glimpse of the last 350 years of the writ's history suggests, and what others convincingly have demonstrated, is that the vessel of habeas corpus has not changed over that period; only its constitutional cargo has changed, as "standards of decency" and due process have "evolved" and become more "enlightened by a humane justice." Accordingly, even while the prevailing standards of due process have altered dramatically over the years—and seem on the verge of altering again—the writ itself only rarely has deviated from its ever-ready function as a federal remedy for all violations of those standards whatever they may be.

Chief among the confusions that have prompted commentators, led by Professor Bator, to mistake the due process clause's protean past for the writ's remarkably constant career stems from the Supreme Court's frequent pre-1920s practice of upholding state and federal convictions upon habeas corpus review on the basis that those convictions were rendered by courts with "jurisdiction both of the offense charged and of the accused." Professor Bator and others erroneously have read such references to jurisdiction as reflecting a limitation of *habeas corpus* to jurisdictional challenges. As Professor Peller has demonstrated, however, it was black letter *due process* law—at least for the 60 years following the Civil War—that criminal defendants got all the process due them so long as the convicting courts "ha[d] jurisdiction of the case and the parties." Thus—as the Supreme Court repeatedly held in direct review decisions during that period as well as in habeas corpus cases—it was the due process protection, not the writ, that "did not extend beyond an examination of the power of the courts ... to proceed at all."

In sum, habeas corpus for centuries has served the same essential function, at essentially the same intergovernmental and intercourt junctions in the Anglo-American system of criminal justice, of judicially ferrying persons whom the government, through restraints, has separated from their rights under the fundamental Law of the Land to the safe harbor afforded by that Law. It simply is not accurate, then, to say that the same ferry boat, traversing the same constitutional crossing, somehow used not to be a ferry boat—because the amount of its cargo and frequency of its trips have increased over time....

d. *A special role in capital cases?* The policies favoring a meaningful federal habeas corpus remedy for state prisoners apply with particular force in capital cases. If the adverse "custodial" consequences of any misdemeanor or felony conviction, including the consequences accompanying parole, probation, and release on recognizance are sufficient to justify federal habeas corpus review as of right, then such review is of infinitely greater importance when the adverse consequence is death.

This is not simply a logical proposition. The Supreme Court frequently has recognized that imposition of the death penalty is such a uniquely final and draconian step from the viewpoint both of society and of the condemned individual that it must be attended with a special set of procedural protections designed to assure both that the courts have reliably identified those defendants who are guilty of a capital crime and for whom execution is an appropriate sanction, and that "the death sentence [is] '..., and appear[s] to be, based on reason rather than caprice or emotion.'" Because habeas corpus review is designed to assure that the state courts have provided due process and that the guilt and sentencing decisions of those courts are reliable, it follows that the habeas corpus remedy is especially critical in capital cases because of the high constitutional standard of due process and the particular need for reliability in such cases.

Less obviously, but equally to the point, capital cases present the situation in which the clash in the state courts between parochial interests and emotions and national constitutional law and liberties is most likely to favor the former and demean the latter— precisely the situation, that is, in which the Framers foresaw a need for a federal appellate check on "a local spirit" and on a state judicial system "too little independent" of that spirit "to be relied upon for the inflexible execution of the national laws." Consider the profile of a "typical" capital case: An outsider only recently arrived in a community—often a rural or small-town community in the South—is charged with taking the life of a local citizen. Typically, the outsider is young, poor, urban, male, and black; if he is white, he is probably a drifter and probably has a criminal record in another State. The victim, on the other hand, is almost assuredly white, a respected member of the community, most usually a local merchant or law enforcement officer. The accused and the victim do not know each other; the latter had no particular reason to expect that the crime would occur as and when it did; in all likelihood, the homicide occurred in the course of some other serious felony, usually a robbery. The evidence against the accused seems overwhelming.

Certainly, such an offense will shock, frighten, and enrage the community. Presumedly, that is why the community reserves its most shocking, frightening, and enraging punishment for such offenses. But inherent in the "local spirit" aroused by just such egregious crimes against the community at the hands, apparently, of someone so thoroughly outside the community is the temptation—indeed, at times, the compulsion—for the legal arm of that community to move more swiftly and directly toward that punishment than "an inflexible execution of the national laws" permits. It is particularly for such cases, therefore, that a postconviction system of appeals to the federal courts needs exist.

The Writ of Habeas Corpus: A Complex Procedure for a Simple Process

Donald P. Lay, 77 Minn. L. Rev. 1015 (1993)

THE POWELL COMMITTEE REPORT

While the Supreme Court was erecting the procedural hurdles in federal habeas corpus, Chief Justice William H. Rehnquist formed an Ad Hoc Committee On Federal Habeas Corpus in Capital Cases. In June 1988, he asked the Committee "to inquire into 'the necessity and desirability of legislation directed toward avoiding delay and the lack of finality' in capital cases." The Chief Justice appointed members of the Committee from the Fifth and Eleventh Circuits because the greatest number of prisoners subject to capital sentences are from those circuits. Retired Associate Justice Lewis F. Powell chaired the Committee, and Professor Albert M. Pierson of the University of Georgia Law School, who had experience representing defendants in capital cases, served as the reporter.

The Committee observed that current habeas corpus procedures dispense justice ineffectively. In particular, the Committee noted three problems with the current system. The first was delay and repetition. Because of the multi-layered state and federal appeal and collateral review processes, piecemeal litigation caused years of delay between sentencing and final judicial resolution. The Committee asserted that the lack of finality undermined public confidence in the criminal justice system. It found, for example, that the average length of proceedings in five of the states within the Fifth and Eleventh Circuits was eight years and two months.[189] Further, eighty percent of the time spent collaterally litigating death penalty cases occurred outside of the state collateral proceedings. The Committee concluded that the present system of collateral review frustrated the law of the thirty-seven states that then had the death penalty. Moreover, the lack of finality in these cases undermined the public's confidence in the criminal justice system.

Second, the Committee noted a serious problem in satisfying the need for qualified counsel to represent inmates in collateral review. Capital habeas litigation is difficult and complicated, and prisoners often fail promptly and properly to exhaust their state remedies. If counsel enters the case when execution is imminent, the prisoner may have already waived serious constitutional claims. The Committee therefore recognized that death-row prisoners need competent counsel in both state and federal collateral review.

Finally, the Committee stressed the fact that habeas corpus petitions are often filed at the last minute, when there is an impending execution. Courts must expend valuable judicial resources as the prisoner seeks a stay of execution. To address this problem, the Committee recommended that the merits of capital cases be reviewed carefully and not

---

189. The longest case the Committee studied covered a period of 14 years and six months. Public concern over the delay in executing death row prisoners cannot be attributed solely to federal habeas corpus proceedings. Critics frequently point to serial killer Ted Bundy's decade on death row as an example of the undue delays that habeas corpus causes in executing state prisoners. *See, e.g., Graham Urges Time Limit on Death Appeals*, L.A. Times, Jan. 26, 1988, §1, at 18 (quoting Sen. Bob Graham's condemnation of Bundy's case as a "typical abuse" of habeas corpus). Most of the delay in Bundy's execution, however, occurred while on direct appeal....

under time pressure. Once this thorough review has been done, last minute litigation should not be permitted.

To resolve these problems, the Committee proposed a new statutory scheme for capital cases. Under the current system, capital litigants have an incentive to delay the judicial proceedings, whereas prisoners sentenced to a term of years tend to assert their claims as soon as possible in order to gain release. Thus, the Committee's proposal was to subject capital cases "to one complete and fair course of collateral review in the state and federal system, free from the time pressure of impending execution, and with the assistance of competent counsel for the defendant."

To accomplish this goal, the Committee drafted proposed legislation. At their option, states could bring capital litigation by prisoners within the statute by providing competent counsel on state collateral review. States that did so would benefit because the proposal contained a six-month statute of limitations period for federal habeas petitions. The Committee noted that although the six-month period seemed short, it is longer than the time provided for appeals in the state and federal systems, or the period for seeking certiorari review in the Supreme Court. Second, the Committee's proposal provided an automatic stay of execution to last until federal habeas corpus proceedings are completed, or until the prisoner fails to file a petition within the limitation period. Finally, although the proposed statute generally includes only claims exhausted in state court, it permits immediate presentation of new claims in federal court in extraordinary circumstances, a practice different than current law. If no relief is granted in the counseled state and federal collateral processes, later federal habeas petitions cannot be the basis of a stay of execution, absent extraordinary circumstances and a colorable showing of factual innocence.

Notes and Questions

1. In *Sanders v. United States*, 373 U.S. 1, 8 (1963), Justice Brennan wrote: "Conventional notions of finality of litigation have no place where life or liberty is at stake and infringement of constitutional rights is alleged." Do you agree?

2. Note Chief Justice Warren Burger's objection to collateral attacks:

> In some of these multiple trial and appeal cases the accused continued his warfare with society for eight, nine, ten years and more. In one case more than sixty jurors and alternates were involved in five trials, a dozen trial judges heard an array of motions and presided over these trials; more than thirty different lawyers participated either as court-appointed counsel or prosecutors and in all more than fifty appellate judges reviewed the case on appeals.
>
> I tried to calculate the costs of all this for one criminal act and the ultimate conviction. The best estimates could not be very accurate, but they added up to a *quarter of a million dollars*. The tragic aspect was the waste and futility, since every lawyer, every judge and every juror was fully convinced of defendant's guilt from the beginning to the end.

Address before the Association of the Bar of the City of New York, N.Y.L.J., Feb. 19, 1970, at 1.

How would Chief Justice Burger respond to Alain René Lesage's suggestion that "Justice is such a fine thing that we cannot pay too dearly for it"? The cost of capital punishment is considered in chapter 1, *supra*.

C. The Antiterrorism and Effective Death Penalty Act of 1996

On April 24, 1996, Congress, responding in part to the April 19, 1995 terrorist attack on the Murrah Federal Building in Oklahoma City and to the perceived inefficiency in the federal habeas review process, passed the Antiterrorism and Effective Death Penalty Act (AEDPA), which was designed to curtail and expedite federal habeas review of state and federal prisoner claims. The AEDPA amended then-existing procedural and substantive rules governing habeas corpus in a number of significant ways. Included in the amendments is 28 U.S.C. §2261, which provides an opt-in, expedited review process for capital cases, which is discussed *infra*. The AEDPA, along with the pre-AEDPA rules, are set forth in full in Coyne & Entzeroth, Supplement to Capital Punishment and the Judicial Process. As Justice Souter observed, "in a world of silk purses and pigs' ears, [the AEDPA] is not a silk purse of the art of statutory drafting." *Lindh v. Murphy*, 521 U.S. 320, 336 (1997).

A key provision—28 U.S.C. §2254—underwent significant changes when the AEDPA was enacted. A comparison of 28 U.S.C. §2254 prior to the AEDPA and as revised by the AEDPA is set out below:

28 U.S.C. §2254 (prior to the AEDPA)—*State custody; remedies in Federal courts*

(a) The Supreme Court, a Justice thereof, a circuit judge, or a district court shall entertain an application for a writ of habeas corpus in behalf of a person in custody pursuant to the judgment of a State court only on the ground that he is in custody in violation of the Constitution or laws or treaties of the United States.

(b) An application for a writ of habeas corpus in behalf of a person in custody pursuant to the judgment of a State court shall not be granted unless it appears that the applicant has exhausted the remedies available in the courts of the State, or that there is either an absence of available State corrective process or the existence of circumstances rendering such process ineffective to protect the rights of the prisoner.

(c) An applicant shall not be deemed to have exhausted the remedies available in the courts of the State, within the meaning of this section, if he has the right under the law of the State to raise, by any available procedure, the question presented.

(d) In any proceeding instituted in a Federal court by an application for a writ of habeas corpus by a person in custody pursuant to the judgment of a State court, a determination after a hearing on the merits of a factual issue, made by a State court of competent jurisdiction in a proceeding to which the applicant for the writ and the State or an officer or agent thereof were parties, evidenced by a written finding, written opinion, or other reliable and adequate written indicia, shall be presumed to be correct, unless the applicant shall establish or it shall otherwise appear, or the respondent shall admit—

(1) that the merits of the factual dispute were not resolved in the State court hearing;

(2) that the factfinding procedure employed by the State court was not adequate to afford a full and fair hearing;

(3) that the material facts were not adequately developed at the State court hearing;

(4) that the State court lacked jurisdiction of the subject matter or over the person of the applicant in the State court proceeding;

(5) that the applicant was an indigent and the State court, in deprivation of his constitutional right, failed to appoint counsel to represent him in the State court proceeding;

(6) that the applicant did not receive a full, fair, and adequate hearing in the State court proceeding; or

(7) that the applicant was otherwise denied due process of law in the State court proceeding;

(8) or unless the part of the record of the State court proceeding in which the determination of such factual issue was made, pertinent to a determination of the sufficiency of the evidence to support such factual determination, is produced as provided for hereinafter, and the Federal court on a consideration of such part of the record as a whole concludes that such factual determination is not fairly supported by the record.

And in an evidentiary hearing in the proceeding in the Federal court, when due proof of such factual determination has been made, unless the evidence of one or more of the circumstances respectively set forth in paragraphs numbered (1) to (7), inclusive, is shown by the applicant, otherwise appears, or is admitted by the respondent, or unless the court concludes pursuant to the provisions of paragraph numbered (8) that the record in the State court proceeding, considered as a whole, does not fairly support such factual determination, the burden shall rest upon the applicant to establish by convincing evidence that the factual determination by the State court was erroneous.

(e) If the applicant challenges the sufficiency of the evidence adduced in such State court proceeding to support the State court's determination of a factual issue made therein, the applicant, if able, shall produce that part of the record pertinent to a determination of the sufficiency of the evidence to support such determination. If the applicant, because of indigency or other reason is unable to produce such part of the record, then the State shall produce such part of the record and the Federal court shall direct the State to do so by order directed to an appropriate State official. If the State cannot provide such pertinent part of the record, then the court shall determine under the existing facts and circumstances what weight shall be given to the State court's factual determination.

(f) A copy of the official records of the State court, duly certified by the clerk of such court to be a true and correct copy of a finding, judicial opinion, or other reliable written indicia showing such a factual determination by the State court shall be admissible in the Federal court proceeding.

28 U.S.C. §2254 (current statute under AEDPA)—*State custody; remedies in Federal courts*

(a)   The Supreme Court, a Justice thereof, a circuit judge, or a district court shall entertain an application for a writ of habeas corpus in behalf of a person in custody pursuant to the judgment of a State court only on the ground that he is in custody in violation of the Constitution or laws or treaties of the United States.

(b)(1) An application for a writ of habeas corpus on behalf of a person in custody pursuant to the judgment of a State court shall not be granted unless it appears that—

(A) the application has exhausted the remedies available in the courts of the State; or

(B)(i) there is an absence of available State corrective process; or

(ii) circumstances exist that render such process ineffective to protect the rights of the applicant.

(2) An applicant for a writ of habeas corpus may be denied on the merits, notwithstanding the failure of the applicant to exhaust the remedies available in the courts of the State.

(3) A State shall not be deemed to have waived the exhaustion requirement or be estopped from reliance upon the requirement unless the State, through counsel, expressly waives the requirement.

(c) An applicant shall not be deemed to have exhausted the remedies available in the courts of the State, within the meaning of this section, if he has the right under the law of the State to raise, by any available procedure, the question presented.

(d) An application for a writ of habeas corpus on behalf of a person in custody pursuant to the judgment of a State court shall not be granted with respect to any claim that was adjudicated on the merits in State court proceedings unless the adjudication of the claim—

(1) resulted in a decision that was contrary to, or involved an unreasonable application of, clearly established Federal law, as determined by the Supreme Court of the United States; or

(2) resulted in a decision that was based on an unreasonable determination of the facts in light of the evidence presented in the State court proceeding.

(e)(1) In a proceeding instituted by an application for a writ of habeas corpus by a person in custody pursuant to the judgment of a State court, a determination of a factual issue made by a State court shall be presumed to be correct. The application shall have the burden of rebutting the presumption of correctness by clear and convincing evidence.

(2) If the applicant has failed to develop the factual basis of a claim in State court proceedings, the court shall not hold an evidentiary hearing on the claim unless the applicant shows that—

(A) the claim relies on—

(i) a new rule of constitutional law, made retroactive to cases on collateral review by the Supreme Court, that was previously unavailable; or

(ii) a factual predicate that could not have been previously discovered through the exercise of due diligence; and

(B) the fact underlying the claim would be sufficient to establish by clear and convincing evidence that but for constitutional error, no reasonable factfinder would have found the applicant guilty of the underlying offense.

(f) If the applicant challenges the sufficiency of the evidence adduced in such State court proceeding to support the State court's determination of a factual issue made therein, the applicant, if able, shall produce that part of the record pertinent to a determination of the sufficiency of the evidence to support such determination. If the applicant, because of indigency or other reason is unable to produce such part of the record, then the State shall produce such part of the record and the Federal court shall direct the State to do so by order directed to an appropriate State official. If the State cannot provide such pertinent part of the record, then the court shall determine under the existing facts and circumstances what weight shall be given to the State court's factual determination.

(g)   A copy of the official records of the State court, duly certified by the clerk of such court to be a true and correct copy of a finding, judicial opinion, or other reliable written indicia showing such a factual determination by the State court shall be admissible in the Federal court proceeding.

(h)   Except as provided in section 408 of the Controlled Substances Act, in all proceedings brought under this section, and any subsequent proceedings on review, the court may appoint counsel for an applicant who is or becomes financially unable to afford counsel, except as provided by a rule promulgated by the Supreme Court pursuant to statutory authority. Appointment of counsel under this section shall be governed by section 3006A of title 18.

(i)   The effectiveness or incompetence of counsel during Federal or State collateral post-conviction proceedings shall not be a ground for relief in a proceeding arising under section 2254.

Notes and Questions

1. What are some of the significant differences between the current §2254 and the pre-AEDPA §2254? What impact do you think the changes will have for state prisoners seeking to litigate claims in federal court that the state court has ruled on previously?

2. In addition to the revision in §2254, the AEDPA modified other federal habeas statutes, including 28 U.S.C. §2244, which governs a prisoner's ability to file a second or successive habeas petition, 28 U.S.C. §2255, which sets out the procedures for federal prisoners filing habeas petitions, and 28 U.S.C. §2253, which controls habeas appeals by federal and state prisoners. Further, the AEDPA sets out a number of special "opt-in" procedures for capital cases, which did not exist prior to 1996. 28 U.S.C. §§2261–2266.

Overview of Federal Habeas Corpus Process under AEDPA

James S. Liebman & Randy Hertz, Federal Habeas Corpus Practice
and Procedure (5th ed. 2005) (Lexis Law Publishing)

§3.2   Overview of AEDPA.

On April 24, 1996, President Clinton signed into law the Antiterrorism and Effective Death Penalty Act of 1996 (AEDPA). Title I of the Act made important changes in the statutes governing federal habeas corpus practice for state prisoners and section 2255 practice for federal prisoners, enacted a new set of statutes to govern federal habeas corpus procedures in capital cases in "opt-in" States, and amended Rule 22 of the Federal Rules of Appellate Procedure and the statutory provisions for appointment and compensation of counsel for indigent habeas corpus petitioners and section 2255 movants.

The Conference Committee report (there are no committee reports) described AEDPA's effects in the following manner:

This title incorporates reforms to curb the abuse of the statutory writ of habeas corpus, and to address the acute problems of unnecessary delay and abuse in capital cases. It sets a one year limitation on an application for a habeas writ and revises the procedures for consideration of a writ in federal court. It provides for the exhaustion of state remedies and requires deference to the determinations of state courts that are neither "contrary to," nor an "unreasonable application of," clearly established federal law.

The revision in capital habeas practice also sets a time limit within which the district court must act on a writ, and provides the government with the right to seek a writ of mandamus if the district court refuses to act within the allotted time period. Successive petitions must be approved by a panel of the court of appeals and are limited to those petitions that contain newly discovered evidence that would seriously undermine the jury's verdict or that involve new constitutional rights that have been retroactively applied by the Supreme Court.

In capital cases, procedures are established for the appointment of counsel, conduct of evidentiary hearings, and the application of the procedures to state unitary review systems. Courts are directed to give habeas petitions in capital cases priority status and to decide those petitions. within specified time periods. These procedures apply both to state and federal capital cases.

Upon signing the bill, the President issued a Statement declaring that AEDPA was intended to "streamline Federal appeals for convicted criminals sentenced to the death penalty" but not to make substantive changes in the standards for granting the writ. The President stated that he would not have "signed this bill" if he thought the federal courts would "interpret[] [it] in a manner that would undercut meaningful Federal habeas corpus review." He called upon "the Federal courts ... [to] interpret these provisions to preserve independent review of Federal legal claims and the bedrock constitutional principle of an independent judiciary."

Part of AEDPA is devoted to amending provisions of the preexisting habeas corpus statute, which have long been codified in Chapter 153 of the Judicial Code and govern habeas corpus actions filed by state prisoners (including, at least on one theory, state capital prisoners subject to the "special procedures" discussed just below) as well as section 2255 motions filed by federal prisoners. AEDPA also, however, created a new Chapter 154 of the Judicial Code containing a set of "Special Habeas Corpus Procedures in Capital Cases." These special procedures and standards (which tend to restrict access to habeas corpus relief and include, among other things, accelerated deadlines for the filing and resolution of federal habeas corpus petitions) apply only to habeas corpus petitions filed by capital prisoners in the custody of States that "opt in" to the special provisions by establishing, in a statutorily specified way, a "mechanism for the appointment, compensation, and reimbursement of [state postconviction] counsel" that satisfies certain statutory standards. In essence, States that "opt in" receive certain advantages in the way of restricted federal habeas corpus review of their capital prisoners as a *quid pro quo* for their having provided the affected capital prisoners with certain procedural advantages during state postconviction proceedings. Until recently, no State had been held to have qualified for opt-in, status, and a number of States have acknowledged that they do not qualify for that status or have been held not to qualify by the courts.

. . . .

AEDPA changed the longstanding provisions of the federal habeas corpus statute — i.e., those long codified in Chapter 153 of the Judicial Code — in the following ways:

- *Statute of limitations:* AEDPA established a one-year period of limitations for the filing of habeas corpus petitions. In many cases, the petition's limitations period runs from the date on which the judgment of conviction and sentence became final upon the completion of direct review. In other cases, the petition's limitations period runs from some later date — e.g., the date on which an unconstitutional impediment to filing a claim in the petition was removed, or the date on which the legal or factual bases for a claim in the petition first became discoverable through the exercise of due diligence. The statute of limitations is tolled while properly filed state postconviction proceedings are pending.

- *Provision of counsel and support resources:* AEDPA set a maximum hourly fee for counsel appointed to represent indigent petitioners in federal habeas corpus proceedings in capital cases. AEDPA also amended the procedures that indigent capital and noncapital prisoners must use to secure leave to hire and to secure compensation for court-funded investigators, expert witnesses, and other providers of support services by (1) requiring that lawyers who wish to make an *ex parte* request for funding for support services first make a "proper showing" of the "need for confidentiality"; and (2) setting a general limit on the amount of funds available for such support services in each case, while providing procedures for obtaining additional funds in appropriate cases.

- *Exhaustion of state remedies:* AEDPA amended the preexisting rules governing exhaustion of state remedies in two modest respects: (1) If a federal habeas corpus petition contains an unexhausted claim that otherwise would require dismissal for nonexhaustion, and if the court ascertains that all the claims in the petition are without merit, the court may deny the petition on the merits rather than dismissing for nonexhaustion. (2) The federal courts' authority to consider unexhausted claims when the state waives the exhaustion requirement is limited to express waivers by the state.

- *Effect of state court factfindings; federal hearing standards:* AEDPA simplified but did not substantially alter the preexisting provisions governing the effect in federal habeas corpus proceedings of state court findings of fact. AEDPA did substantially alter the standard for obtaining a federal evidentiary hearing when the petitioner's default was responsible for the state courts' failure to develop the material facts. Under the new standard, a petitioner who defaulted on the facts in the state courts may not obtain a federal evidentiary hearing to develop those facts except upon a showing of "cause" and "innocence."

- *Federal court treatment of legal claims previously adjudicated by a state court:* AEDPA regulates a federal habeas corpus court's resolution of federal claims that previously were adjudicated by a state court. If the state court fairly adjudicated the legal merits of the federal claim and adequately explained its decision, the federal court may not grant relief unless the state court's adjudication of the claim was "contrary to clearly established [Supreme Court] law" or "involved an unreasonable application of clearly established [Supreme Court] law" or "resulted in a decision that was based on an unreasonable determination of the facts in light of the evidence presented in the State court proceeding."

- *Successive petitions:* AEDPA altered both the procedures and standards for filing successive habeas corpus petitions. (1) Procedurally, the statute requires the petitioner to apply to a circuit panel for authorization to file a successive petition in the district court. The circuit panel may authorize the filing of a successive petition only upon the petitioner's *prima facie* showing that the petition satisfies AEDPA's new successive petition standards. The circuit panel has a limited time frame in which to act on the motion for leave to file the petition in the district court, and rehearing and *certiorari* review of the panel's determination are barred, although certain other forms of review are not barred. (2) AEDPA's new successive petition standards prohibit same-claim successive petitions and limit new-claim successive petitions to cases in which the petitioner can make an adequate showing either that the legal rule on which she relies is new and retroactively applicable to her case or that the facts on which she relies previously were unavailable and that she probably is innocent.

• *Appeals:* AEDPA conditions appeals by petitioners on their obtaining a "certificate of appealability." The procedures and standards for seeking such a certificate are roughly equivalent to the preexisting rules for obtaining "certificates of probable cause to appeal" except in the following respects. (1) The certificate must indicate not only that the case as a whole, but also that a specific "issue or. issues," satisfy the requisite standard (a "substantial showing of the denial of a constitutional right"). Although the relevant provision does not say so, a number of courts have read it to limit the claims the court of appeals may address on appeal to those that the certificate identifies as having satisfied the standard. (2) One provision of AEDPA seems to require a circuit judge or Supreme Court Justice—and thus to forbid a district court judge—to issue a certificate of appealability, although a neighboring provision seems to preserve pre-AEDPA practice by empowering district judges to rule on requests for certificates and to require that they generally do so in the first instance. Although some district court judges initially took the position that AEDPA deprives them of the authority to issue a certificate of appealability, every circuit court that has addressed the subject has held that district courts may, and should, rule on certificates of appealability in the first instance.

Notes

1. The constitutionality of the AEDPA was attacked initially on the ground that the provisions of the statute curtailing second and successive petitions constituted an impermissible limitation of the Supreme Court's jurisdiction in violation of Article III, section 2 of the United States Constitution. The Court addressed this issue in *Felker v. Turpin*, 518 U.S. 651 (1996), a unanimous decision authored by Chief Justice Rehnquist. The Court held in *Felker* that (1) the AEDPA did not preclude the Court from entertaining an original application for habeas corpus relief, although the various provisions of the AEDPA did affect the standards governing the granting of such relief, (2) the "gatekeeping" provisions under the AEDPA for applications seeking a successive habeas petition did not render the Act unconstitutional, and (3) although the Act did place a restraint on the "abuse of the writ" doctrine, the AEDPA did not violate the Constitution's Suspension Clause, Art. I, §9, cl. 2, which provides, "[t]he Privilege of the Writ of Habeas Corpus shall not be suspended." For further discussion on the abuse of the writ doctrine and successive habeas petitions see chapter 17. Justices Souter, Stevens and Breyer filed separate concurrences in *Felker*.

2. In *Lindh v. Murphy*, 521 U.S. 320 (1997), the Court held that all habeas petitions which were filed before April 24, 1996 and which did not qualify under the AEDPA's Chapter 154 capital opt-in provisions, would be controlled by the pre-AEDPA proce-

dural and substantive law and would not be subject to the more restrictive provisions of the AEDPA. Although *Lindh* dealt with the habeas petition of a non-capital state criminal defendant, it is evident that under *Lindh*, a capital state criminal defendant who has filed his federal habeas petition prior to April 24, 1996, and whose state has not opted-in to the AEDPA special procedures for capital defendants, will have his federal habeas case reviewed and analyzed under pre-AEDPA standards. Chief Justice Rehnquist filed a dissent in *Lindh* in which Justices Scalia, Kennedy and Thomas joined. It was the opinion of these four justices that the AEDPA applied to all pending federal habeas cases.

3. Although the AEDPA does not apply to habeas petitions filed before April 24, 1996, it is applicable to all habeas petitions filed thereafter, including cases in which the prisoner's state court conviction occurred before the effective date of the AEDPA. Thus, a prisoner whose conviction occurred in 1992 would nonetheless be subject to the limitations of the AEDPA if he filed his habeas petition after April 24, 1996.

4. Even if a petitioner's habeas petition was filed in district court prior to April 24, 1996, if his habeas appeal is filed after the effective date of the AEDPA, then the appeal provisions of the AEDPA will apply to the petitioner's appeal of his denial of habeas relief. In *Slack v. McDaniel*, 529 U.S. 473 (2000) (*infra* chapter 17), the Court held that "when a habeas corpus petitioner seeks to initiate an appeal of the dismissal of a habeas corpus petition after April 24, 1996 (the effective date of AEDPA), the right to appeal is governed by the certificate of appealability (COA) requirements now found at 28 U.S.C. §2253(c). This is true whether the habeas corpus petition was filed in the district court before or after AEDPA's effective date."

5. Prior to the AEDPA, there was generally no statutory time limit for filing a petition for habeas corpus relief. In a dramatic departure from that practice, §2244(d) of the AEDPA provides a complicated one-year statute of limitations for federal habeas petitions filed by state prisoners. This one-year statute of limitations may be tolled only under certain limited conditions as set out in §2254(d)(2) of the AEDPA.

6. In *Miller-El v. Cockrell*, 537 U.S. 322 (2003), the Court examined the appeals process for a habeas petitioner:

> As mandated by federal statute, a state prisoner seeking a writ of habeas corpus has no absolute entitlement to appeal a district court's denial of his petition. 28 U.S.C. §2253. Before an appeal may be entertained, a prisoner who was denied habeas relief in the district court must first seek and obtain a COA from a circuit justice or judge. This is a jurisdictional prerequisite because the COA statute mandates that "[u]nless a circuit justice or judge issues a certificate of appealability, an appeal may not be taken to the court of appeals...." §2253(c)(1). As a result, until a COA has been issued federal courts of appeals lack jurisdiction to rule on the merits of appeals from habeas petitioners.
>
> A COA will issue only if the requirements of §2253 have been satisfied. "The COA statute establishes procedural rules and requires a threshold inquiry into whether the circuit court may entertain an appeal." *Slack*, 529 U.S. at 482. As the Court of Appeals observed in this case, §2253(c) permits the issuance of a COA only where a petitioner has made a "substantial showing of the denial of a constitutional right." In *Slack, supra*, at 483, we recognized that Congress codified our standard, announced in *Barefoot v. Estelle*, 463 U.S. 880 (1983), for determining what constitutes the requisite showing. Under the controlling standard, a petitioner must "sho[w] that reasonable jurists could debate whether (or, for that matter, agree that) the petition should have been resolved

in a different manner or that the issues presented were 'adequate to deserve encouragement to proceed further.'" 529 U.S. at 484.

The COA determination under §2253(c) requires an overview of the claims in the habeas petition and a general assessment of their merits. We look to the District Court's application of AEDPA to petitioner's constitutional claims and ask whether that resolution was debatable amongst jurists of reason. This threshold inquiry does not require full consideration of the factual or legal bases adduced in support of the claims. In fact, the statute forbids it. When a court of appeals side steps this process by first deciding the merits of an appeal, and then justifying its denial of a COA based on its adjudication of the actual merits, it is in essence deciding an appeal without jurisdiction.

To that end, our opinion in *Slack* held that a COA does not require a showing that the appeal will succeed. Accordingly, a court of appeals should not decline the application for a COA merely because it believes the applicant will not demonstrate an entitlement to relief. The holding in *Slack* would mean very little if appellate review were denied because the prisoner did not convince a judge, or, for that matter, three judges, that he or she would prevail. It is consistent with §2253 that a COA will issue in some instances where there is no certainty of ultimate relief. After all, when a COA is sought, the whole premise is that the prisoner "'has already failed in that endeavor.'" *Barefoot, supra,* at 893, n. 4.

Our holding should not be misconstrued as directing that a COA always must issue. Statutes such as AEDPA have placed more, rather than fewer, restrictions on the power of federal courts to grant writs of habeas corpus to state prisoners. *Duncan v. Walker,* 533 U.S. 167, 178 (2001) ("'AEDPA's purpose [is] to further the principles of comity, finality, and federalism'") (quoting *Williams v. Taylor,* 529 U.S. 420, 436 (2000)); *Williams v. Taylor,* 529 U.S. 362, 399 (2000) (opinion of O'Connor, J.). The concept of a threshold, or gateway, test was not the innovation of AEDPA. Congress established a threshold prerequisite to appealability in 1908, in large part because it was "concerned with the increasing number of frivolous habeas corpus petitions challenging capital sentences which delayed execution pending completion of the appellate process...." *Barefoot, supra,* at 892. By enacting AEDPA, using the specific standards the Court had elaborated earlier for the threshold test, Congress confirmed the necessity and the requirement of differential treatment for those appeals deserving of attention from those that plainly do not. It follows that issuance of a COA must not be *pro forma* or a matter of course.

A prisoner seeking a COA must prove "something more than the absence of frivolity" or the existence of mere "good faith" on his or her part. *Barefoot, supra,* at 893. We do not require petitioner to prove, before the issuance of a COA, that some jurists would grant the petition for habeas corpus. Indeed, a claim can be debatable even though every jurist of reason might agree, after the COA has been granted and the case has received full consideration, that petitioner will not prevail. As we stated in *Slack,* "[w]here a district court has rejected the constitutional claims on the merits, the showing required to satisfy §2253(c) is straightforward: The petitioner must demonstrate that reasonable jurists would find the district court's assessment of the constitutional claims debatable or wrong."

7. Section 2254(d) sets out the standard of review that a federal court must apply when reviewing state court decisions. Specifically, §2254 provides that a writ of habeas

corpus shall not be granted unless the state court proceeding "(1) resulted in a decision that was contrary to, or involved an unreasonable application of, clearly established Federal law, as determined by the Supreme Court of the United States; or (2) resulted in a decision that was based on an unreasonable determination of the facts in light of the evidence presented in the State court proceeding." In applying this language, the various circuit courts of appeals employed different standards of review. The Fourth and Fifth Circuits took a very narrow view of this language. The Fifth Circuit concluded that a federal court could "grant habeas relief only if a state court decision [was] so clearly incorrect that it would not be debatable among reasonable jurists," or, stated another way, "an application of law to facts is *unreasonable* only when it can be said that reasonable jurists considering the question would be of one view that the state court ruling was incorrect." *Drinkard v. Johnson*, 97 F.3d 751, 767–68 (5th Cir. 1996). Similarly, the Fourth Circuit found that unless a state court decision is in "square conflict" with a Supreme Court precedent that is controlling as to law and fact, a writ of habeas corpus should issue "only when the state courts have decided the question by interpreting or applying the relevant precedent in a manner that reasonable jurists would all agree is unreasonable." *Green v. French*, 143 F.3d 865, 870 (4th Cir. 1998). In the following decision, the Supreme Court made clear the standard of review applicable under the AEDPA.

Terry Williams v. Taylor
529 U.S. 362 (2000)

[This case is also excerpted and discussed in chapter 11. The earlier excerpt provides a more detailed discussion on the underlying facts of the case and the Court's analysis of the petitioner's ineffective assistance of counsel claim.]

Justice STEVENS announced the judgment of the Court and delivered the opinion of the Court with respect to Parts, I, III, and IV, and an opinion with respect to Parts II and V. Justice Souter, Justice Ginsburg, and Justice Breyer join Justice Stevens' opinion in its entirety. Justice O'Connor and Justice Kennedy joined Parts I, III, and IV of this opinion.

The questions presented are whether Terry Williams' constitutional right to the effective assistance of counsel as defined in *Strickland v. Washington*, 466 U.S. 668 (1984), was violated, and whether the judgment of the Virginia Supreme Court refusing to set aside his death sentence "was contrary to, or involved an unreasonable application of, clearly established Federal law, as determined by the Supreme Court of the United States," within the meaning of 28 U.S.C. §2254(d)(1). We answer both questions affirmatively.

I

[This section details the facts of the case and is reprinted in chapter 11. In sum, after convicting Terry Williams of robbery and capital murder, a jury found a probability of future dangerousness and sentenced Williams to death. The Virginia Supreme Court affirmed. Williams then sought state collateral relief arguing in part that trial counsel was ineffective and that he had been prejudiced by counsel's deficient performance.] ...

State Habeas Corpus Proceedings

In 1988 Williams filed for state collateral relief in the Danville Circuit Court. The petition was subsequently amended, and the Circuit Court (the same judge who had presided over Williams' trial and sentencing) held an evidentiary hearing on Williams' claim that trial counsel had been ineffective. Based on the evidence adduced after two days of hearings, Judge Ingram found that Williams' conviction was valid, but that his trial attorneys had been ineffective during sentencing.

... Judge Ingram therefore recommended that Williams be granted a rehearing on the sentencing phase of his trial.

The Virginia Supreme Court did not accept that recommendation. Although it assumed, without deciding, that trial counsel had been ineffective, it disagreed with the trial judge's conclusion that Williams had suffered sufficient prejudice to warrant relief. [T]he court concluded that there was no reasonable possibility that the omitted evidence would have affected the jury's sentencing recommendation, and that Williams had failed to demonstrate that his sentencing proceeding was fundamentally unfair.

Federal Habeas Corpus Proceedings

Having exhausted his state remedies, Williams sought a federal writ of habeas corpus pursuant to 28 U.S.C. §2254. After reviewing the state habeas hearing transcript and the state courts' findings of fact and conclusions of law, the federal trial judge agreed with the Virginia trial judge: The death sentence was constitutionally infirm.

... [In reaching this conclusion, the federal district judge] found that the Virginia Supreme Court had erroneously assumed that *Lockhart*[*v. Fretwell*, 506 U.S. 364 (1993)], had modified the *Strickland* standard for determining prejudice, and that it had made an important error of fact in discussing its finding of no prejudice. Having introduced his analysis of Williams' claim with the standard of review applicable on habeas appeals provided by 28 U.S.C. §2254(d), the judge concluded that those errors established that the Virginia Supreme Court's decision "was contrary to, or involved an unreasonable application of, clearly established Federal law" within the meaning of §2254(d)(1).

The Federal Court of Appeals reversed. It construed §2254(d)(1) as prohibiting the grant of habeas corpus relief unless the state court "'decided the question by interpreting or applying the relevant precedent in a manner that reasonable jurists would all agree is unreasonable.'" [163 F.3d 860, 865] (quoting *Green v. French,* 143 F.3d 865, 870 (C.A.4 1998)). Applying that standard, it could not say that the Virginia Supreme Court's decision on the prejudice issue was an unreasonable application of the tests developed in either *Strickland* or *Lockhart.* It explained that the evidence that Williams presented a future danger to society was "simply overwhelming," it endorsed the Virginia Supreme Court's interpretation of *Lockhart,* and it characterized the state court's understanding of the facts in this case as "reasonable."

We granted certiorari, and now reverse.

II

In 1867, Congress enacted a statute providing that federal courts "shall have power to grant writs of habeas corpus in all cases where any person may be restrained of his or her liberty in violation of the constitution, or of any treaty or law of the United States." Over the years, the federal habeas corpus statute has been repeatedly amended, but the scope of that jurisdictional grant remains the same. It is, of course, well settled that the fact that constitutional error occurred in the proceedings that led to a state-court conviction may not alone be sufficient reason for concluding that a prisoner is entitled to the remedy of habeas. On the other hand, errors that undermine confidence in the fundamental fairness of the state adjudication certainly justify the issuance of the federal writ. The deprivation of the right to the effective assistance of counsel recognized in *Strickland* is such an error.

The warden here contends that federal habeas corpus relief is prohibited by the amendment to 28 U.S.C. §2254, enacted as a part of the Antiterrorism and Effective Death Penalty Act of 1996 (AEDPA). The relevant portion of that amendment provides:

> (d) An application for a writ of habeas corpus on behalf of a person in custody pursuant to the judgment of a State court shall not be granted with respect to any claim that was adjudicated on the merits in State court proceedings unless the adjudication of the claim—
>
> > (1) resulted in a decision that was contrary to, or involved an unreasonable application of, clearly established Federal law, as determined by the Supreme Court of the United States....

In this case, the Court of Appeals applied the construction of the amendment that it had adopted in its earlier opinion in *Green v. French.* Accordingly, it held that a federal court may issue habeas relief only if "the state courts have decided the question by interpreting or applying the relevant precedent in a manner that reasonable jurists would all agree is unreasonable."

We are convinced that that interpretation of the amendment is incorrect. It would impose a test for determining when a legal rule is clearly established that simply cannot be squared with the real practice of decisional law. It would apply a standard for determining the "reasonableness" of state-court decisions that is not contained in the statute itself, and that Congress surely did not intend. And it would wrongly require the federal courts, including this Court, to defer to state judges' interpretations of federal law.

... The inquiry mandated by the amendment relates to the way in which a federal habeas court exercises its duty to decide constitutional questions; the amendment does not alter the underlying grant of jurisdiction in §2254(a). When federal judges exercise their federal-question jurisdiction under the "judicial Power" of Article III of the Constitution, it is "emphatically the province and duty" of those judges to "say what the law is." At the core of this power is the federal courts' independent responsibility—independent from its coequal branches in the Federal Government, and independent from the separate authority of the several States—to interpret federal law. A construction of AEDPA that would require the federal courts to cede this authority to the courts of the States would be inconsistent with the practice that federal judges have traditionally followed in discharging their duties under Article III of the Constitution. If Congress had intended to require such an important change in the exercise of our jurisdiction, we believe it would have spoken with much greater clarity than is found in the text of AEDPA.

This basic premise informs our interpretation of both parts of §2254(d)(1): first, the requirement that the determinations of state courts be tested only against "clearly established Federal law, as determined by the Supreme Court of the United States," and second, the prohibition on the issuance of the writ unless the state court's decision is "contrary to, or involved an unreasonable application of," that clearly established law. We address each part in turn.

The "clearly established law" requirement

In *Teague v. Lane,* 489 U.S. 288 (1989) [*infra* chapter 15], we held that the petitioner was not entitled to federal habeas relief because he was relying on a rule of federal law that had not been announced until after his state conviction became final. The antiretroactivity rule recognized in *Teague,* which prohibits reliance on "new rules," is the functional equivalent of a statutory provision commanding exclusive reliance on "clearly established law." Because there is no reason to believe that Congress intended to require federal courts to ask both whether a rule sought on habeas is "new" under *Teague*—which remains the law— and also whether it is "clearly established" under AEDPA, it seems safe to assume that Congress had congruent concepts in mind. It is perfectly clear that AEDPA codifies *Teague* to the extent that *Teague* requires federal habeas courts to deny relief that is contingent upon a rule of law not clearly established at the time the state conviction became final....

The "contrary to, or an unreasonable application of," requirement

The message that Congress intended to convey by using the phrases, "contrary to" and "unreasonable application of" is not entirely clear. The prevailing view in the Circuits is that the former phrase requires *de novo* review of 'pure' questions of law and the latter requires some sort of "reasonability" review of so-called mixed questions of law and fact.

We are not persuaded that the phrases define two mutually exclusive categories of questions. Most constitutional questions that arise in habeas corpus proceedings—and therefore most "decisions" to be made—require the federal judge to apply a rule of law to a set of facts, some of which may be disputed and some undisputed.... In constitutional adjudication, as in the common law, rules of law often develop incrementally as earlier decisions are applied to new factual situations. But rules that depend upon such elaboration are hardly less lawlike than those that establish a bright-line test.

Indeed, our pre-AEDPA efforts to distinguish questions of fact, questions of law, and "mixed questions," and to create an appropriate standard of habeas review for each, generated some not insubstantial differences of opinion as to which issues of law fell into which category of question, and as to which standard of review applied to each. We thus think the Fourth Circuit was correct when it attributed the lack of clarity in the statute, in part, to the overlapping meanings of the phrases "contrary to" and "unreasonable application of." See *Green,* 143 F.3d, at 870.

The statutory text likewise does not obviously prescribe a specific, recognizable standard of review for dealing with either phrase. Significantly, it does not use any term, such as"*de novo*" or "plain error," that would easily identify a familiar standard of review. Rather, the text is fairly read simply as a command that a federal court not issue the habeas writ unless the state court was wrong as a matter of law or unreasonable in its application of law in a given case. The suggestion that a wrong state-court "decision"—a legal judgment rendered "after consideration of *facts, and ... law*"—may no longer be redressed through habeas (because it is unreachable under the "unreasonable application" phrase) is based on a mistaken insistence that the §2254(d)(1) phrases have not only independent, but mutually exclusive, meanings. Whether or not a federal court can issue the writ "under [the] 'unreasonable application' clause," the statute is clear that habeas may issue under §2254(d)(1) if a state court "decision" is "contrary to ... clearly established Federal law." We thus anticipate that there will be a variety of cases, like this one, in which both phrases may be implicated.

Even though we cannot conclude that the phrases establish "a body of rigid rules," they do express a "mood" that the federal judiciary must respect. In this respect, it seems clear that Congress intended federal judges to attend with the utmost care to state-court decisions, including all of the reasons supporting their decisions, before concluding that those proceedings were infected by constitutional error sufficiently serious to warrant the issuance of the writ....

... Our disagreement with Justice O'Connor about the precise meaning of the phrase "contrary to," and the word "unreasonable," is, of course, important, but should affect only a narrow category of cases. The simplest and first definition of "contrary to" as a phrase is "in conflict with." In this sense, we think the phrase surely capacious enough to include a finding that the state-court "decision" is simply "erroneous" or wrong. (We hasten to add that even "diametrically different" from, or "opposite" to, an established federal law would seem to include "decisions" that are wrong in light of that law.) And there is nothing in the phrase "contrary to"—as Justice O'Connor appears to agree— that implies anything less than independent review by the federal courts. Moreover, state-court decisions that do not "conflict" with federal law will rarely be "unreasonable" under either her reading of the statute or ours. We all agree that state-court judgments must be upheld unless, after the closest examination of the state-court judgment, a federal court is firmly convinced that a federal constitutional right has been violated. Our difference is as to the cases in which, at first-blush, a state-court judgment seems entirely reasonable, but thorough analysis by a federal court produces a firm conviction that that judgment is infected by constitutional error. In our view, such an erroneous judgment is "unreasonable" within the meaning of the act even though that conclusion was not immediately apparent.

In sum, the statute directs federal courts to attend to every state-court judgment with utmost care, but it does not require them to defer to the opinion of every reasonable state-court judge on the content of federal law. If, after carefully weighing all the reasons for accepting a state court's judgment, a federal court is convinced that a prisoner's custody—or, as in this case, his sentence of death—violates the Constitution, that independent judgment should prevail. Otherwise the federal "law as determined by the Supreme Court of the United States" might be applied by the federal courts one way in Virginia and another way in California. In light of the well-recognized interest in ensuring that federal courts interpret federal law in a uniform way, we are convinced that Congress did not intend the statute to produce such a result.

III

In this case, Williams contends that he was denied his constitutionally guaranteed right to the effective assistance of counsel when his trial lawyers failed to investigate and to present substantial mitigating evidence to the sentencing jury. The threshold question under AEDPA is whether Williams seeks to apply a rule of law that was clearly established at the time his state-court conviction became final. That question is easily answered because the merits of his claim are squarely governed by our holding in *Strickland v. Washington*.

... It is past question that the rule set forth in *Strickland* qualifies as "clearly established Federal law, as determined by the Supreme Court of the United States." ... This Court's precedent "dictated" that the Virginia Supreme Court apply the *Strickland* test at the time that court entertained Williams' ineffective-assistance claim.... Williams is therefore entitled to relief if the Virginia Supreme Court's decision rejecting his ineffective-assistance claim was either "contrary to, or involved an unreasonable application of," that established law. It was both.

IV

The Virginia Supreme Court erred in holding that our decision in *Lockhart v. Fretwell,* modified or in some way supplanted the rule set down in *Strickland.*

… Unlike the Virginia Supreme Court, the state trial judge omitted any reference to *Lockhart* and simply relied on our opinion in *Strickland* as stating the correct standard for judging ineffective-assistance claims.

… The trial judge analyzed the ineffective-assistance claim under the correct standard; the Virginia Supreme Court did not.

… [I]t is evident to us that the [Virginia's Supreme] court's contrary decision turned on its erroneous view that a "mere" difference in outcome is not sufficient to establish constitutionally ineffective assistance of counsel. Its analysis in this respect was thus not only "contrary to," but also, inasmuch as the Virginia Supreme Court relied on the inapplicable exception recognized in *Lockhart,* an "unreasonable application of" the clear law as established by this Court.

Second, the State Supreme Court's prejudice determination was unreasonable insofar as it failed to evaluate the totality of the available mitigation evidence—both that adduced at trial, and the evidence adduced in the habeas proceeding—in reweighing it against the evidence in aggravation.… It thus failed to accord appropriate weight to the body of mitigation evidence available to trial counsel.

V

In our judgment, the state trial judge was correct both in his recognition of the established legal standard for determining counsel's effectiveness, and in his conclusion that the entire postconviction record, viewed as a whole and cumulative of mitigation evidence presented originally, raised "a reasonable probability that the result of the sentencing proceeding would have been different" if competent counsel had presented and explained the significance of all the available evidence. It follows that the Virginia Supreme Court rendered a "decision that was contrary to, or involved an unreasonable application of, clearly established Federal law." Williams' constitutional right to the effective assistance of counsel as defined in *Strickland v. Washington* was violated.

Accordingly, the judgment of the Court of Appeals is reversed, and the case is remanded for further proceedings consistent with this opinion.

Justice O'CONNOR delivered the opinion of the Court with respect to Part II (except as to the footnote), concurred in part, and concurred in the judgment. Justice Kennedy joins this opinion in its entirety. The Chief Justice and Justice Thomas join this opinion with respect to Part II. Justice Scalia joins this opinion with respect to Part II, except as to the footnote. Chief Justice Rehnquist, and Justices Scalia and Thomas dissent as to Parts I, III, and IV, in which the Court finds petitioner was denied effective assistance of counsel during sentencing and that he was entitled to habeas relief.

In 1996, Congress enacted the Antiterrorism and Effective Death Penalty Act (AEDPA). In that Act, Congress placed a new restriction on the power of federal courts to grant writs of habeas corpus to state prisoners. The relevant provision, 28 U.S.C. §2254(d)(1), prohibits a federal court from granting an application for a writ of habeas corpus with respect to a claim adjudicated on the merits in state court unless that adjudication "resulted in a decision that was contrary to, or involved an unreasonable application of, clearly established Federal law, as determined by the Supreme Court of the United States." The Court holds today that the Virginia Supreme Court's adjudication of Terry Williams' application for state habeas corpus relief resulted in just such a decision.

I agree with that determination and join Parts I, III, and IV of the Court's opinion. Because I disagree, however, with the interpretation of §2254(d)(1) set forth in Part II of Justice Stevens' opinion, I write separately to explain my views.

I

Before 1996, this Court held that a federal court entertaining a state prisoner's application for habeas relief must exercise its independent judgment when deciding both questions of constitutional law and mixed constitutional questions (*i.e.,* application of constitutional law to fact). In other words, a federal habeas court owed no deference to a state court's resolution of such questions of law or mixed questions.... Under the federal habeas statute as it stood in 1992 ... our precedents dictated that a federal court should grant a state prisoner's petition for habeas relief if that court were to conclude in its independent judgment that the relevant state court had erred on a question of constitutional law or on a mixed constitutional question.

If today's case were governed by the federal habeas statute prior to Congress' enactment of AEDPA in 1996, I would agree with Justice Stevens that Williams' petition for habeas relief must be granted if we, in our independent judgment, were to conclude that his Sixth Amendment right to effective assistance of counsel was violated.

II

A

Williams' case is *not* governed by the pre-1996 version of the habeas statute.... Accordingly, for Williams to obtain federal habeas relief, he must first demonstrate that his case satisfies the condition set by §2254(d)(1). That provision modifies the role of federal habeas courts in reviewing petitions filed by state prisoners.

Justice Stevens' opinion in Part II essentially contends that §2254(d)(1) does not alter the previously settled rule of independent review. Indeed, the opinion concludes its statutory inquiry with the somewhat empty finding that §2254(d)(1) does no more than express a " 'mood' that the federal judiciary must respect." For Justice Stevens, the congressionally enacted "mood" has two important qualities. First, "federal courts [must] attend to every state-court judgment with utmost care" by "carefully weighing all the reasons for accepting a state court's judgment." Second, if a federal court undertakes that careful review and yet remains convinced that a prisoner's custody violates the Constitution, "that independent judgment should prevail."

... Justice Stevens arrives at his erroneous interpretation by means of one critical misstep. He fails to give independent meaning to both the "contrary to" and "unreasonable application" clauses of the statute. By reading §2254(d)(1) as one general restriction on the power of the federal habeas court, Justice Stevens manages to avoid confronting the specific meaning of the statute's "unreasonable application" clause and its ramifications for the independent-review rule. It is, however, a cardinal principle of statutory construction that we must " 'give effect, if possible, to every clause and word of a statute.' " Section 2254(d)(1) defines two categories of cases in which a state prisoner may obtain federal habeas relief with respect to a claim adjudicated on the merits in state court. Under the statute, a federal court may grant a writ of habeas corpus if the relevant state-court decision was either (1) "*contrary to* ... clearly established Federal law, as determined by the Supreme Court of the United States," or (2) "*involved an unreasonable application of* ... clearly established Federal law, as determined by the Supreme Court of the United States." (Emphases added.)

The Court of Appeals for the Fourth Circuit properly accorded both the "contrary to" and "unreasonable application" clauses independent meaning. The Fourth Circuit's interpretation of §2254(d)(1) in Williams' case relied, in turn, on that court's previous decision in *Green v. French*. With respect to the first of the two statutory clauses, the Fourth Circuit held in *Green* that a state-court decision can be "contrary to" this Court's clearly established precedent in two ways. First, a state-court decision is contrary to this Court's precedent if the state court arrives at a conclusion opposite to that reached by this Court on a question of law. Second, a state-court decision is also contrary to this Court's precedent if the state court confronts facts that are materially indistinguishable from a relevant Supreme Court precedent and arrives at a result opposite to ours.

The word "contrary" is commonly understood to mean "diametrically different," "opposite in character or nature," or "mutually opposed." The text of §2254(d)(1) therefore suggests that the state court's decision must be substantially different from the relevant precedent of this Court. The Fourth Circuit's interpretation of the "contrary to" clause accurately reflects this textual meaning. A state-court decision will certainly be contrary to our clearly established precedent if the state court applies a rule that contradicts the governing law set forth in our cases....

On the other hand, a run-of-the-mill state-court decision applying the correct legal rule from our cases to the facts of a prisoner's case would not fit comfortably within §2254(d)(1)'s "contrary to" clause. Assume, for example, that a state-court decision on a prisoner's ineffective-assistance claim correctly identifies *Strickland* as the controlling legal authority and, applying that framework, rejects the prisoner's claim. Quite clearly, the state-court decision would be in accord with our decision in *Strickland* as to the legal prerequisites for establishing an ineffective-assistance claim, even assuming the federal court considering the prisoner's habeas application might reach a different result applying the *Strickland* framework itself. It is difficult, however, to describe such a run-of-the-mill state-court decision as "diametrically different" from, "opposite in character or nature" from, or "mutually opposed" to *Strickland,* our clearly established precedent. Although the state-court decision may be contrary to the federal court's conception of how *Strickland* ought to be applied in that particular case, the decision is not "mutually opposed" to *Strickland* itself.

Justice Stevens would instead construe §2254(d)(1)'s " contrary to" clause to encompass such a routine state-court decision. That construction, however, saps the "unreasonable application" clause of any meaning. If a federal habeas court can, under the "contrary to" clause, issue the writ whenever it concludes that the state court's *application* of clearly established federal law was incorrect, the "unreasonable application" clause becomes a nullity. We must, however, if possible, give meaning to every clause of the statute. Justice Stevens not only makes no attempt to do so, but also construes the "contrary to" clause in a manner that ensures that the "unreasonable application" clause will have no independent meaning. We reject that expansive interpretation of the statute. Reading §2254(d)(1)'s "contrary to" clause to permit a federal court to grant relief in cases where a state court's error is limited to the manner in which it *applies* Supreme Court precedent is suspect given the logical and natural fit of the neighboring "unreasonable application" clause to such cases.

... [A] state-court decision involves an unreasonable application of this Court's precedent if the state court identifies the correct governing legal rule from this Court's cases but unreasonably applies it to the facts of the particular state prisoner's case. Second, a state-court decision also involves an unreasonable application of this Court's precedent if the state court either unreasonably extends a legal principle from our precedent to a new context where it should not apply or unreasonably refuses to extend that principle to a new context where it should apply.

A state-court decision that correctly identifies the governing legal rule but applies it unreasonably to the facts of a particular prisoner's case certainly would qualify as a decision "involv[ing] an unreasonable application of ... clearly established Federal law." Indeed, we used the almost identical phrase "application of law" to describe a state court's application of law to fact in the certiorari question we posed to the parties in *Wright* [*v. West*, 505 U.S. 277 (1992)].*

... [I]t is sufficient to hold that when a state-court decision unreasonably applies the law of this Court to the facts of a prisoner's case, a federal court applying §2254(d)(1) may conclude that the state-court decision falls within that provision's "unreasonable application" clause.

B

There remains the task of defining what exactly qualifies as an "unreasonable application" of law under §2254(d)(1). The Fourth Circuit held in *Green* that a state-court decision involves an "unreasonable application of ... clearly established Federal law" only if the state court has applied federal law "in a manner that reasonable jurists would all agree is unreasonable." The placement of this additional overlay on the "unreasonable application" clause was erroneous....

Defining an "unreasonable application" by reference to a "reasonable jurist," ... is of little assistance to the courts that must apply §2254(d)(1) and, in fact, may be misleading. Stated simply, a federal habeas court making the "unreasonable application" inquiry should ask whether the state court's application of clearly established federal law was objectively unreasonable. The federal habeas court should not transform the inquiry into a subjective one by resting its determination instead on the simple fact that at least one of the Nation's jurists has applied the relevant federal law in the same manner the state court did in the habeas petitioner's case. The "all reasonable jurists" standard would tend to mislead federal habeas courts by focusing their attention on a subjective inquiry rather than on an objective one. For example, the Fifth Circuit appears to have applied its "reasonable jurist" standard in just such a subjective manner. See *Drinkard v. Johnson*, 97 F.3d 751, 769 (1996). As I explained in *Wright* with respect to the "reasonable jurist" standard in the *Teague* context, "[e]ven though we have characterized the new rule inquiry as whether 'reasonable jurists' could disagree as to whether a result is dictated by precedent, the standard for determining when a case establishes a new rule is 'objective,' and the mere existence of conflicting authority does not necessarily mean a rule is new."

The term "unreasonable" is no doubt difficult to define. That said, it is a common term in the legal world and, accordingly, federal judges are familiar with its meaning.

---

* The legislative history of §2254(d)(1) also supports this interpretation. See, *e.g.,* 142 Cong. Rec. 7799 (1996) (remarks of Sen. Specter) ("[U]nder the bill deference will be owed to State courts' decisions on the application of Federal law to the facts. Unless it is unreasonable, a State court's decision applying the law to the facts will be upheld"); 141 Cong. Rec. 14666 (1995) (remarks of Sen. Hatch) ("[W]e allow a Federal court to overturn a State court decision only if it is contrary to clearly established Federal law or if it involves an 'unreasonable application' of clearly established Federal law to the facts").

For purposes of today's opinion, the most important point is that an *unreasonable* application of federal law is different from an *incorrect* application of federal law.... In my separate opinion in *Wright* [*v. West*, 505 U.S. 277 (1992)], I made the same distinction, maintaining that "a state court's *incorrect* legal determination has [never] been allowed to stand because it was *reasonable*. We have always held that federal courts, even on habeas, have an independent obligation to say what the law is." In §2254(d)(1), Congress specifically used the word "unreasonable," and not a term like "erroneous" or "incorrect." Under §2254(d)(1)'s "unreasonable application" clause, then, a federal habeas court may not issue the writ simply because that court concludes in its independent judgment that the relevant state-court decision applied clearly established federal law erroneously or incorrectly. Rather, that application must also be unreasonable.

... Throughout this discussion the meaning of the phrase "clearly established Federal law, as determined by the Supreme Court of the United States" has been put to the side. That statutory phrase refers to the holdings, as opposed to the dicta, of this Court's decisions as of the time of the relevant state-court decision. In this respect, the "clearly established Federal law" phrase bears only a slight connection to our *Teague* jurisprudence. With one caveat, whatever would qualify as an old rule under our *Teague* jurisprudence will constitute "clearly established Federal law, as determined by the Supreme Court of the United States" under §2254(d)(1). The one caveat, as the statutory language makes clear, is that §2254(d)(1) restricts the source of clearly established law to this Court's jurisprudence.

In sum, §2254(d)(1) places a new constraint on the power of a federal habeas court to grant a state prisoner's application for a writ of habeas corpus with respect to claims adjudicated on the merits in state court. Under §2254(d)(1), the writ may issue only if one of the following two conditions is satisfied—the state-court adjudication resulted in a decision that (1) "was contrary to ... clearly established Federal law, as determined by the Supreme Court of the United States," or (2) "involved an unreasonable application of ... clearly established Federal law, as determined by the Supreme Court of the United States." Under the "contrary to" clause, a federal habeas court may grant the writ if the state court arrives at a conclusion opposite to that reached by this Court on a question of law or if the state court decides a case differently than this Court has on a set of materially indistinguishable facts. Under the "unreasonable application" clause, a federal habeas court may grant the writ if the state court identifies the correct governing legal principle from this Court's decisions but unreasonably applies that principle to the facts of the prisoner's case.

III

Although I disagree with Justice Stevens concerning the standard we must apply under §2254(d)(1) in evaluating Terry Williams' claims on habeas, I agree with the Court that the Virginia Supreme Court's adjudication of Williams' claim of ineffective assistance of counsel resulted in a decision that was both contrary to and involved an unreasonable application of this Court's clearly established precedent. Specifically, I believe that the Court's discussion in Parts III and IV is correct and that it demonstrates the reasons that the Virginia Supreme Court's decision in Williams' case, even under the interpretation of §2254(d)(1) I have set forth above, was both contrary to and involved an unreasonable application of our precedent....

Accordingly, although I disagree with the interpretation of §2254(d)(1) set forth in Part II of Justice Stevens' opinion, I join Parts I, III, and IV of the Court's opinion and concur in the judgment of reversal.

Notes on Standard of Review Under § 2254(d) of the AEDPA

1. Part II of Justice O'Connor's concurring opinion was joined by a majority of the Court. Thus, the standard of review set forth in Part II of Justice O'Connor's opinion is the applicable standard.

2. Since *Williams*, the Supreme Court has had several opportunities to further expound on the standard of review that federal courts are to employ under § 2254(d) of the AEDPA. In *Wiggins v. Smith*, 539 U.S. 510 (2003), the Supreme Court reversed a decision by the Fourth Circuit Court of Appeals which denied habeas relief to a capital defendant. Like *Williams*, the Court in *Wiggins* found that Wiggins was entitled to habeas relief on the ground that trial counsel's mitigation investigation and performance during capital sentencing proceedings fell below a constitutionally acceptable level of legal representation. Previously, the Maryland Court of Appeals had reviewed Wiggins' conviction and death sentence—both on direct appeal and in state post-conviction—and applying *Strickland v. Washington*, 466 U.S. 668 (1984), found counsel's performance constitutionally acceptable. On habeas review, the Supreme Court determined that the Maryland Court of Appeals' analysis and holding were objectively unreasonable. In reaching this conclusion, the Supreme Court found that the state court had made a "clear factual error" in its review of the trial court record. The Supreme Court then conducted a *de novo* review of the record and concluded, in fact, that trial counsel's mitigation investigation was inadequate and prejudicial. Although acknowledging that the state court applied the correct Supreme Court law, the Court nonetheless decided that the state court applied this rule of law in an unreasonable manner. Accordingly, the Supreme Court found Wiggins was entitled to habeas relief with respect to his death sentence.

In other cases, the Supreme Court has stressed the limits of habeas review under 28 U.S.C. § 2254(d). For example, in *Woodford v. Visciotti*, 537 U.S. 19 (2003) (per curiam), the California Supreme Court affirmed Visciotti's conviction and death sentence finding that although trial counsel's representation during sentencing was inadequate, counsel's performance was not prejudicial and was, therefore, constitutionally sufficient. On habeas review, the Ninth Circuit disagreed with the California Supreme Court, concluded that counsel's performance was constitutionally deficient, and granted habeas relief with respect to Visciotti's death sentence. The Supreme Court reversed the Ninth Circuit's grant of the writ, finding that the California Supreme Court applied the correct law in a manner that was not unreasonable. In reaching this conclusion, the Supreme Court emphasized that an unreasonable application of the law is different from an incorrect application of the law. In the view of the Supreme Court, the Ninth Circuit had substituted its judgment of the case for the state court's judgment of the case; under the AEDPA, a federal court does not have that discretion.

In *Mitchell v. Esparza*, 124 S.Ct. 7 (2003) (per curiam), the Sixth Circuit granted habeas relief with respect to Esparza's death sentence on the grounds that the Ohio courts had improperly and unreasonably applied federal law with respect to Esparza's capital sentencing proceedings. In reversing the Sixth Circuit, the Supreme Court stated, "'a federal court may not overrule a state court for simply holding a view different from its own, when the precedent from this Court is, at best, ambiguous. As the Ohio Court of Appeals' decision does not conflict with the reasoning or the holdings of our precedent, it is not 'contrary to ... clearly established Federal law.'" 124 S.Ct. at 11.

Finally, in *Yarborough v. Alvarado*, 124 S.Ct. 2140 (2004), a non-capital case, the Supreme Court in a five-to-four decision reversed the Ninth Circuit's grant of habeas relief. The Ninth Circuit had concluded that the California Supreme Court had erroneously found that a 17-year-old suspect was not in custody and not entitled to *Miranda* warnings during a police interrogation. In finding that the state court had not unreasonably applied the law or an extension of the law, Justice Kennedy, writing for the majority, stated:

> The term "unreasonable" is "a common term in the legal world and, accordingly, federal judges are familiar with its meaning." At the same time, the range of reasonable judgment can depend in part on the nature of the relevant rule. If a legal rule is specific, the range may be narrow. Applications of the rule may be plainly correct or incorrect. Other rules are more general, and their meaning must emerge in application over the course of time. Applying a general standard to a specific case can demand a substantial element of judgment. As a result, evaluating whether a rule application was unreasonable requires considering the rule's specificity. The more general the rule, the more leeway courts have in reaching outcomes in case by case determinations.

124 S.Ct. at 2149.

3. In *Brown v. Payton*, 125 S.Ct. 1432 (2005), the prosecutor during the sentencing phase of William Payton's capital murder trial misstated the law and incorrectly argued to the jury that it could not consider Payton's post-crime religious conversion as mitigation evidence. The trial court did not correct the prosecution's misstatement of the law, but rather, advised the jury that counsels' arguments were not evidence. In his direct appeal to the California Supreme Court, Payton sought relief, in part, based on an ambiguity in the California mitigation instructions and the prosecutor's incorrect argument regarding his post-crime mitigation evidence and the capital sentencing process. The California Supreme Court denied relief, and the United States Supreme Court denied certiorari review of Payton's direct appeal. On a petition for habeas corpus, the Ninth Circuit Court of Appeals granted habeas relief, and the United States Supreme Court granted certiorari review. The Supreme Court reversed the Ninth Circuit. Although the Supreme Court agreed that the prosecutor misstated the law concerning mitigation and that the trial court did not correct that error, *id.* at 1440–1442, the Court nonetheless concluded that under § 2254(d)(1) of the AEDPA, the California Supreme Court's decision denying relief to Payton was not an unreasonable application of federal law. *Id.* at 1442.

In his concurring opinion, Justice Breyer stated:

> In my view, this is a case in which Congress' instruction to defer to the reasonable conclusions of state-court judges makes a critical difference. See 28 U.S.C. § 2254(d)(1). Were I a California state judge, I would likely hold that Payton's penalty-phase proceedings violated the Eighth Amendment. In a death case, the Constitution requires sentencing juries to consider all mitigating evidence. See, e.g., *Penry v. Lynaugh*, 492 U.S. 302, 319 (1989). And here, there might well have been a "reasonable likelihood" that Payton's jury interpreted factor (k), 1 Cal. Jury Instr., Crim., No. 8.84.1(k) (4th rev. ed. 1979), "in a way that prevent[ed]" it from considering "constitutionally relevant" mitigating evidence—namely, evidence of his postcrime religious conversion. *Boyde v. California*, 494 U.S. 370, 380 (1990).
>
> Unlike *Boyde*, the prosecutor here told the jury repeatedly—and incorrectly—that factor (k) did not permit it to take account of Payton's postcrime religious conversion. See post, at 1438–1439, 1448–1449 (Souter, J., dissenting). Moreover, the trial judge—also incorrectly—did nothing to correct the record, likely leaving the jury with the impression that it could not do that which the Constitution says it must. Finally, factor (k) is ambiguous as to

whether it encompassed Payton's mitigation case. Factor (k)'s text focuses on evidence that reduces a defendant's moral culpability for committing the offense. And evidence of postcrime conversion is less obviously related to moral culpability than is evidence of precrime background and character. For all these reasons, one could conclude that the jury here might have thought factor (k) barred its consideration of mitigating evidence, even if the jury in *Boyde* would not there have reached a similar conclusion.

Nonetheless, in circumstances like the present, a federal judge must leave in place a state-court decision unless the federal judge believes that it is "contrary to, or involved an unreasonable application of, clearly established Federal law, as determined by the Supreme Court of the United States." § 2254(d)(1). For the reasons that the Court discusses, I cannot say that the California Supreme Court decision fails this deferential test. I therefore join the Court's opinion.

Id. at 1442–1443.

4. In *Bell v. Cone*, 125 S.Ct. 847 (2005) (per curiam), the Court considered the Sixth Circuit's granting of a writ of habeas corpus to Gary Cone on the grounds that the "especially heinous, atrocious, or cruel" aggravating factor was unconstitutionally vague and that the Tennessee Supreme Court failed to cure this constitutional problem by applying a narrowed construction to the aggravating factor. The Supreme Court reversed the Sixth Circuit finding that:

> In sum, even assuming that the Court of Appeals was correct to conclude that the State's statutory aggravating circumstance was facially vague, the court erred in presuming that the State Supreme Court failed to cure this vagueness by applying a narrowing construction on direct appeal. The state court did apply such a narrowing construction, and that construction satisfied constitutional demands by ensuring that respondent was not sentenced to death in an arbitrary or capricious manner. See *Godfrey*, 446 U.S., at 428. The state court's affirmance of respondent's sentence on this ground was therefore not "contrary to ... clearly established Federal law," 28 U.S.C. § 2254(d)(1), and the Court of Appeals was without power to issue a writ of habeas corpus. We reverse the judgment of the Sixth Circuit and remand the case for further proceedings consistent with this opinion.

Id. at 855–856.

AEDPA Chapter 154 — "Opt-In" Procedures Governing Capital Defendants

Clearly, one impetus for the AEDPA was the delay between the imposition of a death sentence on a state criminal defendant and the actual execution of that individual. This delay in death penalty cases was perceived to be caused in part by federal habeas process. In an effort to expedite that process Congress added a new chapter—Chapter 154, 28 U.S.C. § 2261—to its federal habeas statute specifically designed to govern habeas petitions filed by state prisoners under a sentence of death. Chapter 154 is made applicable to a state prisoner only if the state wherein the prisoner was convicted and sentenced to death specifically "opts in" to Chapter 154 by complying with certain standards and procedures. To date, no state has opted-in. Chapter 154, 28 U.S.C. § 2261, is reprinted below.

28 U.S.C. §2261

(a) This chapter shall apply to cases arising under section 2254 brought by prisoners in State custody who are subject to a capital sentence. It shall apply only if the provisions of subsections (b) and (c) are satisfied.

(b) This chapter is applicable if a State establishes by statute, rule of its court of last resort, or by another agency authorized by State law, a mechanism for the appointment, compensation, and payment of reasonable litigation expenses of competent counsel in State post-conviction proceedings brought by indigent prisoners whose capital convictions and sentences have been upheld on direct appeal to the court of last resort in the State or have otherwise become final for State law purposes. The rule of court or statute must provide standards of competency for the appointment of such counsel.

(c) Any mechanism for the appointment, compensation, and reimbursement of counsel as provided in subsection (b) must offer counsel to all State prisoners under capital sentence and must provide for the entry of an order by a court of record–

> (1) **appointing one or more counsels to represent the prisoner upon a finding that the prisoner is indigent and accepted the offer or is unable competently to decide whether to accept or reject the offer;**

> (2) **finding, after a hearing if necessary, that the prisoner rejected the offer of counsel and made the decision with an understanding of its legal consequences; or**

> (3) **denying the appointment of counsel upon a finding that the prisoner is not indigent.**

(d) No counsel appointed pursuant to subsections (b) and (c) to represent a State prisoner under capital sentence shall have previously represented the prisoner at trial or on direct appeal in the case for which the appointment is made unless the prisoner and counsel expressly request continued representation.

(e) The ineffectiveness or incompetence of counsel during State or Federal post-conviction proceedings in a capital case shall not be a ground for relief in a proceeding arising under section 2254. This limitation shall not preclude the appointment of different counsel, on the court's own motion or at the request of the prisoner, at any phase of State or Federal post-conviction proceedings on the basis of the ineffectiveness or incompetence of counsel in such proceedings.

AEDPA's "Opt-In" Provisions

James S. Liebman & Randy Hertz, *Federal Habeas Corpus Practice and Procedure* (5th ed. 2005) (Lexis Law Publishing)

§3.3 AEDPA's "opt-in" provisions.

a. *Introduction; qualifying States.*

… AEDPA's "opt-in" provisions—which establish a set of "special habeas corpus procedures in capital cases" including an accelerated schedule for the filing and consideration of petitions—apply only to capital cases from States that "opt in" by providing certain procedural advantages to capital prisoners pursuing state postconviction remedies. A number of States have acknowledged that they do not qualify for opt-in status, and, until recently, none of the States that had claimed to have opted in had been found to have satisfied the statutory prerequisites for doing so. Subsection b describes those prerequisites. Subsection c explains the special procedures that apply to States that do qualify.

b. Prerequisites for opting in.

To qualify for the opt-in provisions, a State must "establish[] by statute, rule of its court of last resort, or by another agency authorized by State law" two types of protections for indigent capital prisoners in state postconviction proceedings:

- The State's statute or rule must create "a mechanism for the appointment, compensation, and payment of reasonable litigation expenses of competent counsel in State post-conviction proceedings brought by indigent prisoners whose capital convictions and sentences have been upheld on direct appeal to the court of last resort in the State or have otherwise become final for State law purposes."

- The statute or rule must "provide standards of competency for the appointment of such counsel."

Additionally, the "mechanism for the appointment, compensation, and reimbursement of [postconviction] counsel" must satisfy three conditions:

- It must "offer counsel to all State prisoners under capital sentence."

- The State must "provide for the entry of an order by a court of record—(1) appointing one or more counsels to represent the prisoner upon a finding that the prisoner is indigent and accepted the offer or is unable competently to decide whether to accept or reject the offer; (2) finding, after a hearing if necessary, that the prisoner rejected the offer of counsel and made the decision with an understanding of its legal consequences; or (3) denying the appointment of counsel upon a finding that the prisoner is not indigent."

- The mechanism must ensure that "[n]o counsel appointed ... to represent a State prisoner under capital sentence shall have previously represented the petitioner at trial or on direct appeal in the case for which the appointment is made unless the prisoner and counsel expressly request continued representation."

Although AEDPA preserves the preexisting rule that "[t]he ineffectiveness of counsel during State or Federal post-conviction proceedings in a capital case shall not be a ground for [habeas corpus] relief," it makes clear that "[t]his limitation shall not preclude the appointment of a different counsel, on the court's own motion or at the request of the prisoner, at any phase of State or Federal postconviction proceedings on the basis of the ineffectiveness or incompetence of counsel in such proceedings."

Recognizing that some States have replaced the traditional state postconviction procedure with a procedure that consolidates the direct review and postconviction stages, the federal legislation also sets forth the prerequisites such a State would have to satisfy in order to qualify for the opt-in provisions. The statute provides that States with "a 'unitary review' procedure" (which the statute defines as "a State procedure that authorizes a person under sentence of death to raise, in the course of direct review of the judgment, such claims as could be raised on collateral attack") may qualify for the opt-in provisions if:

- "[T]he State establishes by rule of its court of last resort or by statute a mechanism for the appointment, compensation, and payment of reasonable litigation expenses of competent counsel in the unitary review proceedings, including expenses relating to the litigation of collateral claims in the proceedings."

- "The rule of court or statute ... provide[s] standards of competency for the appointment of such counsel."

- The "procedure ... include[s] an offer of counsel following trial for the purpose of representation on unitary review, and entry of an order, as provided in section 2261(c), concerning appointment of counsel or waiver or denial of appointment of counsel for that purpose."

- The procedure ensures that "[n]o counsel appointed to represent the prisoner in the unitary review proceedings [has] ... previously represented the prisoner at trial in the case for which the appointment is made unless the prisoner and counsel expressly, request continued representation."

A State that fails to satisfy any of the statutory prerequisites. is categorically prohibited from obtaining the benefits of the opt-in provisions. For example, a district court in California found (in a decision subsequently reversed on procedural grounds) that the State does not qualify for opt-in status, notwithstanding the existence of a state mechanism for appointing and compensating counsel in state postconviction proceedings, because the mechanism was not contained in a "rule of court or statute," it fails to "impose any binding or mandatory standards" for the appointment of counsel, and it does not "require counsel to have any experience or competence in bringing [state] habeas petitions.".…

c. Procedures in qualifying opt-in States.

If a State makes an adequate showing of its compliance with the statutory prerequisites for opting in, then the "special habeas corpus procedures" in Chapter 154 apply to federal habeas corpus petitions filed by capital prisoners from that State (or, at least, those prisoners who received the benefit of the state postconviction procedures needed to enable the State to opt in).….

Chapter 154's "special procedures" either supplement or replace the procedures applicable in other cases in regard to: (1) the time frames for filing and resolving the petition at the district court and appellate levels; (2) the standards and procedures for stays of execution; (3) the rules governing the amendment of a petition; and (4) the treatment of claims that were not raised and decided on the merits in state court. Each set of "special procedures" is discussed in turn below.

1. The opt-in provisions accelerate capital habeas corpus proceedings in the following respects:

- The deadline for the filing of a federal habeas corpus petition by capital prisoners in qualifying opt-in States is 180 days—in contrast to the one-year limitations period that applies to all noncapital habeas corpus petitions, capital habeas corpus petitions from nonopt-in States, and section 2255 motions. The opt-in statute of limitations begins running on the date of the "final State court affirmance of the conviction and sentence on direct review or the expiration of the time for seeking such review." The statute of limitations is tolled during the period when the United States Supreme Court is considering a petition for certiorari from the final state court judgment on direct review and during the period when the state courts are considering the prisoner's "first petition for post-conviction review or other collateral relief." The legislation also provides for an additional tolling period of up to 30 days upon a showing of "good cause."

- The district court must "render a final determination and enter a final judgment ... not later than 180 days after the date on which the application [for a writ of habeas corpus] is filed." The statute permits the district court to extend this period for up to 30 days upon a finding that "the ends of justice that would be served by allowing the delay outweigh the best interests of the public and the applicant in a speedy disposition of the application." The state can enforce these timing requirements by petitioning the court of appeals for a writ of mandamus; if a mandamus petition is filed, it must be resolved by the court of appeals within 30 days of filing.

- If the federal district court's final order is appealed, the court of appeals must "render a final determination" of the appeal within 120 days of the filing of the reply brief (or, if no reply brief is filed, within 120 days of the filing of the answering brief). A subsequent petition for rehearing or rehearing *en banc* must be decided within 30 days of its filing (or, in cases in which a responsive pleading is filed, within 30 days of the filing of the latter pleading). If rehearing or rehearing *en banc* is granted, a final determination must be rendered within 120 days. The state can enforce these timing requirements by applying to the Supreme Court for a writ of mandamus.

The timing requirements for action by the district court and the court of appeals apply not only to an initial federal habeas corpus petition but also to successive petitions and redeterminations following reversal and remand by a higher court. AEDPA specifies that the timing requirement. for judicial action are not an independent basis for a stay of execution, and that a violation of the timing rules is not a basis for habeas corpus relief.

The foregoing AEDPA-imposed time limits present a significant constitutional question. Because the exercise of judgment is at the core of the judicial function, a Congressionally-imposed time limit that requires resolution of a case at a pace that is inconsistent with the measured exercise of the court's judgment unconstitutionally encroaches upon an Article III court's judicial powers and responsibilities. Accordingly, the AEDPA time limits would appear to have an unconstitutional effect in any case in which the issues cannot be adequately resolved in the short time frames afforded by AEDPA....

2. An opt-in provision narrowly restricts a capital habeas corpus petitioner's ability to amend a petition after the state answers it. Until the state files its answer, the existing (liberal) rules for amendment continue to apply. After the state answers, the statute forbids amendments unless they raise a "new claim" of the narrowly circumscribed sort that one of AEDPA's nonopt-in provisions permits a habeas corpus petitioner to raise in a second or successive petition. As section 28.3e *infra* explains, a claim satisfies AEDPA's successive petition rules only if the claim could not previously have been raised because it depends upon either (1) a "new rule of constitutional law, made retroactive to cases on collateral review by the Supreme Court," or (2) newly acquired facts that "could not have been discovered previously through the exercise of due diligence" and that "if proven and viewed in light of the evidence as a whole, would be sufficient to establish by clear and convincing evidence that, but for constitutional error, no reasonable factfinder would have found the applicant guilty of the underlying offense."

3. Finally, under section 2264(a), federal courts in opt-in cases "shall only consider a claim or claims that have been raised and decided on the merits in State courts" except in three exceptional circumstances....

Notes and Questions

1. Shortly after the passage of the AEDPA, state officials in California began making public statements that California met the opt-in requirements of Chapter 154 and that the

state intended to avail itself of the benefits of that chapter. In response to these statements, capital defendants filed an action in federal court seeking declaratory and injunctive relief. The federal district court issued a declaratory judgment that California did not qualify under Chapter 154 and enjoined the state from seeking benefits under that chapter. The Ninth Circuit affirmed and state officials filed a petition for certiorari with the United States Supreme Court. The Court, in *Calderon v. Ashmus*, 523 U.S. 740 (1998), granted certiorari and reversed. Writing for a unanimous court, Chief Justice Rehnquist found that this declaratory action did not present a case or controversy under Article III of the Constitution. The Court found that the capital prisoners could raise the issue of the applicability of Chapter 154 during the course of the habeas proceedings and that the Declaratory Judgment Act could not be used as a collateral means for answering this question. The Court did not rule on whether or not California met the opt-in requirements of Chapter 154.

2. Recall that under Chapter 154, a petition is subject to a 180-day statute of limitations, as opposed to the one-year statute of limitations under Chapter 153. What would happen to a petitioner who files her petition after the expiration of the 180-day statute of limitations but before the expiration of the one-year statute of limitations, and thereafter a federal court determines that the state meets the opt-in provisions of Chapter 154. Should the petitioner's petition be dismissed as untimely? Must a capital petitioner who suspects that a state may seek to invoke Chapter 154, file within 180 days to avoid this dilemma? What are the advantages and disadvantages of this approach? It was, in part, this dilemma that prompted capital defendants to seek declaratory relief in *Calderon v. Ashmus*.

3. For further discussion of the opt-in provisions under the AEDPA see Eric M. Freedman, "Add Resources and Apply them Systemically: Governments' Responsibilities Under the Revised ABA Capital Defense Representation Guidelines," 31 Hofstra L. Rev. 1097 (2003); Note, "The Option Not Taken: A Progressive Report on Chapter 154 of the Anti-Terrorism and Effective Death Penalty Act," 9 Cornell J.L. & Pub. Pol'y 607 (2000).

4. In *Ashmus v. Woodford*, 202 F.3d 1160 (9th Cir. 2000), the Ninth Circuit found that at least as of 1998, California had not met the opt-in requirements of Chapter 154 and the state was not entitled to invoke the benefits of Chapter 154 as to the petitioner. See also *Baker v. Corcoran*, 229 F.3d 276 (4th Cir. 2000), *cert. denied*, 121 S.Ct. 1194 (2001) (finding Maryland did not meet opt-in requirements); *Kreutzer v. Bowersox*, 231 F.3d 460 (8th Cir. 2000) (finding Missouri did not meet opt-in requirements); *Lucas v. Johnson*, 132 F.3d 1069 (5th Cir. 1998) (finding Texas did not meet opt-in requirements); *Smith v. Anderson*, 104 F. Supp.2d 773 (S.D. Ohio 2000) (finding Ohio did not meet opt-in requirements).

D. Other Limitations on Federal Habeas Review

1. Harmless Error: Brecht v. Abrahamson, 507 U.S. 619 (1993)

At his first degree murder trial in Wisconsin state court, Brecht admitted shooting the victim, but claimed that it was an accident. To impeach Brecht's testimony, the state, *inter alia*, made several references to the fact that, before he was given his *Miranda* warnings at an arraignment, Brecht failed to tell anyone with whom he came in contact that the shooting was accidental. In addition, the state made several references to Brecht's post-*Miranda*-warning silence. After finding Brecht guilty, the jury sentenced him to life in prison.

The state court of appeals set the conviction aside on the ground that the state's references to Brecht's post-*Miranda* silence violated due process under *Doyle v. Ohio*, 426 U.S. 610 (1976). That court found the *Doyle* error sufficiently prejudicial to require reversal.

The Wisconsin Supreme Court reinstated the conviction, holding that the error was "harmless beyond a reasonable doubt" under the standard set forth in *Chapman v. California*, 386 U.S. 18, 24 (1967). On habeas review, the federal district court disagreed and set aside the conviction. The United States Court of Appeals for the Seventh Circuit held that the proper standard of harmless-error review was that set forth in *Kotteakos v. United States*, 328 U.S. 750, 766 (1946). Under that standard, the court must ask whether the *Doyle* violation "had substantial and injurious effect or influence in determining the jury's verdict." Applying this standard, the court concluded that Brecht was not entitled to relief.

The United States Supreme Court agreed. Writing for the Court in *Brecht v. Abrahamson*, 507 U.S. 619 (1993), Chief Justice Rehnquist distinguished between types of constitutional error. At one end of the spectrum are "structural defects in the constitution of the trial mechanism, which defy analysis by 'harmless error' standards." The mere existence of such defects—for example, deprivation of the right to counsel—requires automatic reversal because they infect the entire trial process.

At the other end of the spectrum of constitutional error is "trial error." These occur "during the presentation of the case to the jury" and are amenable to harmless error analysis because they "may … be quantitatively assessed in the context of other evidence presented in order to determine [the effect they had on the trial]." According to the Court, a *Doyle* error fits squarely into the category of trial error. As such, it is amenable to harmless error analysis. Also, on federal habeas corpus review, the appropriate harmless error standard is that announced in *Kotteakos*: whether the error had substantial and injurious effect or influence in determining the jury's verdict. According to the Court:

> Under this standard, habeas petitioners may obtain plenary review of their constitutional claims, but they are not entitled to habeas relief based on trial error unless they can establish that it resulted in "actual prejudice." The *Kotteakos* standard is thus better tailored to the nature and purpose of collateral review, and more likely to promote the considerations underlying our recent habeas cases. Moreover, because the *Kotteakos* standard is grounded in the federal harmless-error rule (28 U.S.C. §2111), federal courts may turn to an existing body of case law in applying it.

Notes and Questions

1. Recall that under the *Chapman* harmless error standard (*supra* chapter 10), which applies to cases on direct appeal, the beneficiary of the constitutional error (usually the government) is required to prove beyond a reasonable doubt that the error complained of did not contribute to the verdict. Under *Brecht*, which party in federal habeas bears the burden on the harmless error issue?

2. Under *Brecht*, the correct harmless error standard in habeas corpus cases is whether the error had a "substantial and injurious effect on influence in determining the jury's verdict." What if the harmless error question was never addressed by the state court? In *Orndorf v. Lockhart*, 998 F.2d 1246 (8th Cir. 1993), the court held that *Brecht* does not apply and that the *Chapman* harmless error standard is the appropriate test.

2. Full and Fair Hearing

In *Stone v. Powell*, 428 U.S. 465 (1976), the Court held that where a state has provided a defendant with an opportunity for full and fair litigation of a claim that evidence used against her was obtained through an unlawful search or seizure in violation of the Fourth Amendment, she may not relitigate that claim on federal habeas. The Court noted, however, that "Fourth Amendment violations are different in kind from denials of Fifth or Sixth Amendment rights." According to the majority, its decision was "not concerned with the scope of the habeas corpus statute as authority for litigating constitutional claims generally," in substantial part because "the exclusionary rule is a judicially created remedy rather than a personal constitutional right."

In *Rose v. Mitchell*, 443 U.S. 545 (1979), the Court rejected the argument that *Stone v. Powell* should be extended to preclude federal habeas review of claims of racial discrimination in the selection of members of a state grand jury, notwithstanding the fact that the selection of petit jurors was free from constitutional infirmity and that guilt was established beyond a reasonable doubt at a trial devoid of constitutional error. That same year, the Court denied a request to apply *Stone* to bar habeas consideration of a Fourteenth Amendment due process claim of insufficient evidence to support a state conviction. *Jackson v. Virginia*, 443 U.S. 307 (1979).

In *Kimmelman v. Morrison*, 477 U.S. 365 (1986), the Court for the third time declined to extend the rule in *Stone* beyond its original boundaries. The *Kimmelman* majority refused to apply *Stone* to bar habeas review of certain claims of ineffective assistance of counsel under the Sixth Amendment.

Likewise, the Court in *Withrow v. Williams*, 507 U.S. 680 (1993), held that *Stone*'s restriction on the exercise of federal habeas jurisdiction does not extend to a state prisoner's claim that his conviction rests on statements obtained in violation of the *Miranda* safeguards. According to Justice Souter's majority opinion in *Withrow*, the *Stone* rule was not jurisdictional in nature, but was based on prudential concerns counseling against applying the Fourth Amendment exclusionary rule of *Mapp v. Ohio*, 367 U.S. 643 (1961), on collateral review. In contrast to *Mapp*, *Miranda* safeguards a fundamental trial right by protecting a defendant's Fifth Amendment privilege against self-incrimination. Also, *Miranda* facilitates the correct ascertainment of guilt by preventing the use of unreliable statements at trial. Finally, eliminating review of *Miranda* claims in federal habeas would not relieve the burdens placed on federal courts. The Court found it "reasonable to suppose that virtually [every barred] *Miranda* claim[] would simply be recast" as a due process claim that the conviction rested on an involuntary confession.

From time to time, reform efforts are directed at extending the *Stone* rule through legislation which would preclude federal habeas court jurisdiction over claims which have received a "full and fair hearing" in state court. One such legislative proposal prompted this letter from retired Justice William J. Brennan to United States Representative Jack Brooks.

> The Great Writ of habeas corpus is the principal means by which federal courts can protect the Bill of Rights in state criminal cases. The crime bill recently passed by the Senate, however, contains proposals that would effectively strip federal courts of their habeas corpus jurisdiction.
>
> According to that bill, when state courts "fully and fairly adjudicate" a federal constitutional claim, federal courts are barred from reviewing the

claim. "Full and fair adjudication" is a legal term of art, both in habeas corpus and other contexts. Under the "full and fair adjudication" standard, the state courts need only hold a procedurally regular hearing; even cases in which the state court has overlooked serious constitutional violations would be immune from federal courts' review. This prospect is particularly troubling in state capital cases: an American Bar Association study reveals that in forty percent of such cases, habeas courts have, until now, granted relief. For these reasons, I must agree with the recent decision by the Judicial Conference of the United States to "oppose the inclusion of language relating to full and fair adjudication."

The Senate crime bill is of course intended to reduce unnecessary delays in carrying out valid sentences. The bill, however, addresses these delays simply by making relief for constitutional violations impossible. It is unwise, I think, to purchase greater speed in criminal proceedings at the price of our constitutional liberties. Moreover, the Senate bill fails to address one important cause of delay in state criminal, particularly capital, proceedings — the inadequacy of trial counsel who in many cases fail to identify and raise constitutional issues in timely fashion. I note in this connection the recommendation of the American Bar Association and the Judicial Conference of the United States that a mandatory system of specific attorney competency standards be established in every state that imposes the death penalty.

This is a complex issue, not easily understood. I hope you will take the time to study it carefully because it is vital to this country's constitutional protections and longstanding legal traditions.

Does the AEDPA extend *Stone v. Powell* to any other context, or does it appear that Congress declined to expand this doctrine in enacting the AEDPA?

E. The Role of Innocence in Federal Habeas Corpus

Is Innocence Irrelevant? Collateral Attack on Criminal Judgments

Henry J. Friendly, 38 U. Chi. L. Rev. 142 (1970)

For many reasons, collateral attack on criminal convictions carries a serious burden of justification.

First, as Professor Bator has written, "it is essential to the educational and deterrent functions of the criminal law that we be able to say that one violating that law will swiftly and certainly become subject to punishment, just punishment." It is not an answer that a convicted defendant generally remains in prison while collateral attack is pending. Unbounded willingness to entertain attacks on convictions must interfere with at least one aim of punishment — "a realization by the convict that he is justly subject to sanction, that he stands in need of rehabilitation." This process can hardly begin "if society continuously tells the convict that he may not be justly subject to reeducation and treatment in the first place."

... A second set of difficulties arises from the fact that under our present system collateral attack may be long delayed—in *habeas corpus* as long as the custody endures, in federal *coram nobis* forever. The longer the delay, the less the reliability of the determination of any factual issue giving rise to the attack.... Inability to try the prisoner is even more likely in the case of collateral attack on convictions after guilty pleas, since there will be no transcript of testimony of witnesses who are no longer available....

A remedy that produces no result in the overwhelming majority of cases, an unjust one to the state in much of the exceedingly small minority, and a truly good one only rarely, would seem to need reconsideration with a view to caring for the unusual case of the innocent man without being burdened by so much dross in the process.

Indeed, the most serious single evil with today's proliferation of collateral attack is its drain upon the resources of the community—judges, prosecutors, and attorneys appointed to aid the accused, and even of that oft overlooked necessity, courtrooms. Today of all times we should be conscious of the falsity of the bland assumption that these are in endless supply.... [O]ur greatest single problem is the long delay in bringing accused persons to trial. The time of judges, prosecutors, and lawyers now devoted to collateral attacks, most of them frivolous, would be much better spent in trying cases. To say we must provide fully for both has a virtuous sound but ignores the finite amount of funds available in the face of competing demands.

A fourth consideration is Justice Jackson's never refuted observation that "[i]t must prejudice the occasional meritorious application to be buried in a flood of worthless ones." The thought may be distasteful but no judge can honestly deny it is real.

Finally, there is ... the human desire that things must sometime come to an end. Mr. Justice Harlan has put it as well as anyone:

> Both the individual criminal defendant and society have an interest in insuring that there will at some point be the certainty that comes with an end to litigation, and that attention will ultimately be focused not on whether a conviction was free from error but rather on whether the prisoner can be restored to a useful place in the community.

These five objections are not at all answered by the Supreme Court's conclusory pronouncement: "Conventional notions of finality of litigation have no place where life or liberty is at stake and infringement of constitutional rights is alleged." Why do they have *no* place? One will readily agree that "where life or liberty is at stake," different rules should govern the determination of guilt than when only property is at issue: The prosecution must establish guilt beyond a reasonable doubt, the jury must be unanimous, the defendant need not testify, and so on. The defendant must also have a full and fair opportunity to show an infringement of constitutional rights by the prosecution even though his guilt is clear. I would agree that even when he has had all this at trial and on appeal,"[t]he policy against incarcerating or executing an innocent man ... should far outweigh the desired termination of litigation."

... [C]ollateral attack may have become so much a way of prison life as to have created its own self-generating force: it may now be considered merely something done as a matter of course during long incarceration. Today's growing number of prisoner petitions despite the minute percentage granted points that way.... [A] requirement that, with certain exceptions, an applicant for habeas corpus must make a colorable showing of innocence would enable courts of first instance to screen out rather rapidly a great multitude of applications not deserving their attention and devote their time to those few where injustice may have been done, and would effect an even greater reduction in the burden on appellate courts....

... In such cases the criminal process itself has broken down; the defendant has not had the kind of trial the Constitution guarantees. To be sure, there remains a question why, if the issue could have been raised on appeal and either was not or was decided adversely, the defendant should have a further opportunity to air it. Still, in these cases where the attack concerns the very basis of the criminal process, few would object to allowing collateral attack regardless of the defendant's probable guilt. These cases would include all those in which the defendant claims he was without counsel to whom he was constitutionally entitled...."Of all the rights that an accused person has, the right to be represented by counsel is by far the most pervasive, for it affects his ability to assert any other rights he may have."

Another area in which collateral attack is readily justified irrespective of any question of innocence is where a denial of constitutional rights is claimed on the basis of facts which "are *dehors* the record and their effect on the judgment was not open to consideration and review on appeal." The original judgment is claimed to have been perverted, and collateral attack is the only avenue for the defendant to vindicate his rights. Examples are convictions on pleas of guilty obtained by improper means, or on evidence known to the prosecution to be perjured, or where it later appears that the defendant was incompetent to stand trial.

A third justifiable area for collateral attack irrespective of innocence is where the state has failed to provide proper procedure for making a defense at trial and on appeal.... [O]ne can hardly quarrel with the proposition that if a state does not afford a proper way of raising a constitutional defense at trial, it must afford one thereafter, and this without a colorable showing of innocence by the defendant.

New constitutional developments relating to criminal procedure are another special case.... But here the Supreme Court itself has given us the lead. In only a few instances has it determined that its decisions shall be fully retroactive—the right to counsel, *Jackson v. Denno*, equal protection claims, the sixth amendment right to confrontation, and double jeopardy. In most cases the Court has ruled that its new constitutional decisions concerning criminal procedure need not be made available for collateral attack on earlier convictions. These include the extension to the states of the exclusionary rule with respect to illegally seized evidence, the prohibition of comment on a defendant's failure to take the stand, the rules concerning interrogation of persons in custody, the right to a jury trial in state criminal cases, the requirement of counsel at line-ups, and the application of the fourth amendment to non-trespassory wiretapping. While neither a state nor the United States is bound to limit collateral attack on the basis of a new constitutional rule of criminal procedure to what the Supreme Court holds to be demanded, I see no occasion to be holier than the pope.

Federal Habeas Corpus Practice and Procedure
James S. Liebman, (Michie Company 1988) (Volume 1)

c. *Is innocence irrelevant?* In his famous article by the same name, the late Judge Henry Friendly asked: "Is Innocence Irrelevant" in habeas corpus? There are two historically unassailable answers to Judge Friendly's question.

The first answer is that, "yes," innocence is indeed irrelevant. As Justice Powell has stated—albeit in arguing that history should be contravened in this instance—"history reveals no exact tie of the writ of habeas corpus to a constitutional claim relating to innocence or guilt." Justice Powell might have left out the word "exact," for the history of the Court's efforts over the years to preserve a boundary around an already broad remedy is a history of holdings that, whatever else it is, habeas corpus is not a writ of error designed to cure factually erroneous convictions. In Justice Holmes' words, "what we have to deal with is not the petitioners' innocence or guilt but solely the question whether their constitutional rights have been preserved." The Supreme Court accordingly has not hesitated to grant habeas corpus relief when there was little question that the constitutionally wronged petitioner was guilty, or to deny such relief when there was good reason to believe the petitioner was innocent but when no constitutional error was found in the process by which conviction came to pass.

The point here is ... : Habeas corpus is—and in this country always has been—a remedy for unlawful detention, not for detention of the innocent. It is in fact arguable that a habeas corpus petitioner's apparent guilt should *heighten*, not cut off or diminish the scrutiny of the procedures by which he was convicted and sentenced. Consider, first, that habeas corpus—particularly its use in this country since the Civil War—is one means by which the availability of federal judicial and quasi-appellate remedies serve as a check on "the prevalency of a local spirit" and on the ill effects of granting "jurisdiction of national causes" to "state judges, holding their office during pleasure, or from year to year [who are] too little independent" of the local spirit "to be relied upon for the inflexible execution of the national laws." Consider, second, that the Bill of Rights—among the most fundamental of the "national laws" and the principle source of habeas corpus claims—was added to the Constitution (simultaneously with Congress' adoption of the first habeas corpus statute), then extended 75 years later to the States (simultaneously with the extension of the habeas corpus remedy to state prisoners), in part at least to protect unpopular persons, causes, and classes, from just this "prevalency of a local spirit." Consider, finally, the principle that "[i]n proportion to the grounds of ... distrust of the [local] tribunals ought to be the facility ... of appeals"—and, accordingly, the facility of habeas corpus review, which has been understood in this country at least since 1807 as a "clearly appellate" remedy when the actions of another court are at issue.

... The second historically correct answer to Judge Friendly's question is that, "no," innocence is of course not "irrelevant." The fear that an innocent person's liberty or, worse, his life may be forfeited because of unfair proceedings has long been recognized as one, among other, circumstances that makes issuance of the writ most felicitous. Indeed, it would not be surprising to learn (if we somehow could learn) that the subset of habeas corpus cases in which relief actually is granted includes more than its proportionate share of the cases in which innocent persons have been convicted.

Nor can this second answer be passed off entirely as reflecting a lawless willingness to find constitutional violations in cases involving the apparently innocent, when no violations would be found were the petitioners more obviously guilty. The courts properly ought to take the fact that an innocent person may have been convicted (or that a blameworthy person has been convicted of an offense other than the one for which he is to blame) as one, among other, indicators that some unconstitutional breakdown in the procedures has occurred. Accordingly, as a matter of fact and probably of law, the petitioner's possible innocence is clearly "relevant" and counsel for a probably innocent client properly may take zealous steps to make that fact plain to the habeas corpus court, whatever the claims being advanced.

… Although the absence of an affirmative showing of innocence does not bar federal habeas corpus review, a couple of recent Supreme Court decisions authored by Justice O'Connor have identified limited circumstances in which such a showing will *remove* otherwise preclusive obstacles to such review. [*Murray v. Carrier*, 477 U.S. 478 (1986); *Smith v. Murray*, 477 U.S. 527 (1986), *infra*, chapter 14.] Most particularly, the Court has held that, in those situations in which some procedural miscue by petitioner or counsel in the state courts has created an adequate and independent "waiver" or "procedural default" ground for denying a meritorious constitutional claim, a showing that the "constitutional violation has probably resulted in the conviction of one who is actually innocent" will enable "a federal habeas court [to] grant the writ."

… The answer, then, to Judge Friendly's question remains something of a paradox. Given, however, the Supreme Court's recent reliance on a "showing of innocence" as a way *to* relief that otherwise would be barred, and a minority's continuing flirtation with more preclusive uses of the concept, the question for the coming years is likely to be — "*How* Relevant Is Innocence?"

Herrera v. Collins

506 U.S. 390 (1993)

Chief Justice REHNQUIST delivered the opinion of the Court.

Petitioner Leonel Torres Herrera was convicted of capital murder and sentenced to death in January 1982. He unsuccessfully challenged the conviction on direct appeal and state collateral proceedings in the Texas state courts, and in a federal habeas petition. In February 1992 — 10 years after his conviction — he urged in a second federal habeas petition that he was "actually innocent" of the murder for which he was sentenced to death, and that the Eighth Amendment's prohibition against cruel and unusual punishment and the Fourteenth Amendment's guarantee of due process of law therefore forbid his execution. He supported this claim with affidavits tending to show that his now-dead brother, rather than he, had been the perpetrator of the crime. Petitioner urges us to hold that this showing of innocence entitles him to relief in this federal habeas proceeding. We hold that it does not.

[One night in late September 1981, Officer David Rucker was found dead beside his patrol car shortly before 11 p.m. Around this same time Officers Enrique Carrisalez and Enrique Hernandez encountered a vehicle speeding away from the area where Rucker's body had been found. Carrisalez pulled the car over. The driver and Carrisalez exchanged words and then the driver fatally shot Carrisalez.

Herrera was arrested for the murder of Carrisalez and Rucker. Hernandez identified Herrera as the driver of the car. Prior to his death, Carrisalez also identified Herrera. The speeding car was registered to Herrera's live-in girlfriend. Herrera's social security card was found alongside Rucker's patrol car. Blood splatters on Rucker's car matched Herrera. A letter implicating Herrera in the murder of Rucker was also found on Herrera's person when he was arrested.]

[After Herrera unsuccessfully sought relief in state court and in federal court on a writ of habeas corpus], [p]etitioner … returned to state court and filed a second habeas petition, raising, among other things, a claim of "actual innocence" based on newly discovered evidence. In support of this claim petitioner presented the affidavits of Hector Villarreal, an attorney who had represented petitioner's brother, Raul Herrera, Sr., and of Juan Franco Palacious, one of Raul Sr.'s former cellmates. Both individuals claimed that Raul Sr., who died in 1984, had told them that he—and not petitioner—had killed Officers Rucker and Carrisalez. The State District Court denied this application, finding that "no evidence at trial remotely suggest[ed] that anyone other than [petitioner] committed the offense." The Texas Court of Criminal Appeals affirmed and we denied certiorari.

In February 1992, petitioner lodged the instant habeas petition—his second—in federal court, alleging, among other things, that he is innocent of the murders of Rucker and Carrisalez, and that his execution would thus violate the Eighth and Fourteenth Amendments. In addition to proffering the above affidavits, petitioner presented the affidavits of Raul Herrera, Jr., Raul Sr.'s son, and Jose Ybarra, Jr., a schoolmate of the Herrera brothers. Raul Jr. averred that he had witnessed his father shoot Officers Rucker and Carrisalez and petitioner was not present. Raul Jr. was nine years old at the time of the killings. Ybarra alleged that Raul Sr. told him one summer night in 1983 that he had shot the two police officers. Petitioner alleged that law enforcement officials were aware of this evidence, and had withheld it in violation of *Brady v. Maryland*, 373 U.S. 83 (1963).

The District Court dismissed most of petitioner's claims as an abuse of the writ. However, "in order to ensure that Petitioner can assert his constitutional claims and out of a sense of fairness and due process," the District Court granted petitioner's request for a stay of execution so that he could present his claim of actual innocence, along with the Raul Jr. and Ybarra affidavits, in state court. Although it initially dismissed petitioner's *Brady* claim on the ground that petitioner had failed to present "any evidence of withholding exculpatory material by the prosecution," the District Court also granted an evidentiary hearing on this claim after reconsideration.

The Court of Appeals vacated the stay of execution.... We granted certiorari and the Texas Court of Criminal Appeals stayed petitioner's execution. We now affirm.

Petitioner asserts that the Eighth and Fourteenth Amendments to the United States Constitution prohibit the execution of a person who is innocent of the crime for which he was convicted. This proposition has an elemental appeal, as would the similar proposition that the Constitution prohibits the imprisonment of one who is innocent of the crime for which he was convicted. After all, the central purpose of any system of criminal justice is to convict the guilty and free the innocent. But the evidence upon which petitioner's claim of innocence rests was not produced at his trial, but rather eight years later. In any system of criminal justice, "innocence" or "guilt" must be determined in some sort of a judicial proceeding. Petitioner's showing of innocence, and indeed his constitutional claim for relief based upon that showing, must be evaluated in the light of the previous proceedings in this case, which have stretched over a span of 10 years.

A person when first charged with a crime is entitled to a presumption of innocence, and may insist that his guilt be established beyond a reasonable doubt. Other constitutional provisions also have the effect of ensuring against the risk of convicting an innocent person [including the right to confront adverse witnesses, the right to effective assistance of counsel, the right to proof beyond a reasonable doubt, the right to exculpatory evidence, and the right to a fair trial]. In capital cases, we have required additional protections because of the nature of the penalty at stake. All of these constitutional safeguards, of course, make it more difficult for the State to rebut and finally overturn the presumption of innocence which attaches to every criminal defendant. But we have also observed that "[d]ue process does not require that every conceivable step be taken, at whatever cost, to eliminate the possibility of convicting an innocent person." To conclude otherwise would all but paralyze our system for enforcement of the criminal law.

Once a defendant has been afforded a fair trial and convicted of the offense for which he was charged, the presumption of innocence disappears. Here, it is not disputed that the State met its burden of proving at trial that petitioner was guilty of the capital murder of Officer Carrisalez beyond a reasonable doubt. Thus, in the eyes of the law, petitioner does not come before the Court as one who is "innocent," but on the contrary as one who has been convicted by due process of law of two brutal murders....

Claims of actual innocence based on newly discovered evidence have never been held to state a ground for federal habeas relief absent an independent constitutional violation occurring in the underlying state criminal proceeding.... This rule is grounded in the principle that federal habeas courts sit to ensure that individuals are not imprisoned in violation of the Constitution—not to correct errors of fact.

More recent authority construing federal habeas statutes speaks in a similar vein. "Federal courts are not forums in which to relitigate state trials." The guilt or innocence determination in state criminal trials is "a decisive and portentous event." "Society's resources have been concentrated at that time and place in order to decide, within the limits of human fallibility, the question of guilt or innocence of one of its citizens." Few rulings would be more disruptive of our federal system than to provide for federal habeas review of free-standing claims of actual innocence.

... In his brief [petitioner] states that the federal habeas court should have "an important initial opportunity to hear the evidence and resolve the merits of Petitioner's claim." Acceptance of this view would presumably require the habeas court to hear testimony from the witnesses who testified at trial as well as those who made the statements in the affidavits which petitioner has presented, and to determine anew whether or not petitioner is guilty of the murder of Officer Carrisalez. Indeed, the dissent's approach differs little from that hypothesized here.

The dissent would place the burden on petitioner to show that he is "probably" innocent. Although petitioner would not be entitled to discovery "as a matter of right," the District Court would retain its "discretion to order discovery ... when it would help the court make a reliable determination with respect to the prisoner's claim." And although the District Court would not be required to hear testimony from the witnesses who testified at trial or the affiants upon whom petitioner relies, it would allow the District Court to do so "if the petition warrants a hearing." At the end of the day, the dissent would have the District Court "make a case-by-case determination about the reliability of newly discovered evidence under the circumstances," and then "weigh the evidence in favor of the prisoner against the evidence of his guilt." ...

Yet there is no guarantee that the guilt or innocence determination would be any more exact. To the contrary, the passage of time only diminishes the reliability of criminal adjudications. Under the dissent's approach, the District Court would be placed in the even more difficult position of having to weigh the probative value of "hot" and "cold" evidence on petitioner's guilt or innocence....

... [Petitioner contends that the Fourteenth Amendment entitles him to a new trial or a vacation of his sentence of death, but] we cannot say that Texas' refusal to entertain petitioner's newly discovered evidence eight years after his conviction transgresses a principle of fundamental fairness "rooted in the traditions and conscience of our people." This is not to say, however, that petitioner is left without a forum to raise his actual innocence claim. For under Texas law, petitioner may file a request for executive clemency. Clemency is deeply rooted in our Anglo-American tradition of law, and is the historic remedy for preventing miscarriages of justice where judicial process has been exhausted....

Executive clemency has provided the "fail safe" in our criminal justice system. It is an unalterable fact that our judicial system, like the human beings who administer it, is fallible. But history is replete with examples of wrongfully convicted persons who have been pardoned in the wake of after-discovered evidence establishing their innocence. In his classic work, Professor Edwin Borchard compiled 65 cases in which it was later determined that individuals had been wrongfully convicted of crimes. Clemency provided the relief mechanism in 47 of these cases; the remaining cases ended in judgments of acquittals after new trials. E. Borchard, *Convicting the Innocent* (1932). Recent authority confirms that over the past century clemency has been exercised frequently in capital cases in which demonstrations of "actual innocence" have been made.

... [I]n state criminal proceedings the trial is the paramount event for determining the guilt or innocence of the defendant. Federal habeas review of state convictions has traditionally been limited to claims of constitutional violations occurring in the course of the underlying state criminal proceedings. Our federal habeas cases have treated claims of "actual innocence," not as an independent constitutional claim, but as a basis upon which a habeas petitioner may have an independent constitutional claim considered on the merits, even though his habeas petition would otherwise be regarded as successive or abusive. History shows that the traditional remedy for claims of innocence based on new evidence, discovered too late in the day to file a new trial motion, has been executive clemency.

We may assume, for the sake of argument in deciding this case, that in a capital case a truly persuasive demonstration of "actual innocence" made after trial would render the execution of a defendant unconstitutional, and warrant federal habeas relief if there were no state avenue open to process such a claim. But because of the very disruptive effect that entertaining claims of actual innocence would have on the need for finality in capital cases, and the enormous burden that having to retry cases based on often stale evidence would place on the States, the threshold showing for such an assumed right would necessarily be extraordinarily high. The showing made by petitioner in this case falls far short of any such threshold....

The affidavits filed in this habeas proceeding were given over eight years after petitioner's trial. No satisfactory explanation has been given as to why the affiants waited until the 11th hour—and, indeed, until after the alleged perpetrator of the murders himself was dead—to make their statements. Equally troubling, no explanation has been offered as to why petitioner, by hypothesis an innocent man, pleaded guilty to the murder of Rucker.

Moreover, the affidavits themselves contain inconsistencies, and therefore fail to provide a convincing account of what took place on the night Officers Rucker and Carrisalez were killed. For instance, the affidavit of Raul Jr., who was nine years old at the time, indicates that there were three people in the speeding car from which the murderer emerged, whereas Hector Villarreal attested that Raul Sr. told him that there were two people in the car that night. Of course, Hernandez testified at petitioner's trial that the murderer was the only occupant of the car. The affidavits also conflict as to the direction in which the vehicle was heading when the murders took place, and petitioner's whereabouts on the night of the killings.

Finally, the affidavits must be considered in light of the proof of petitioner's guilt at trial—proof which included two eyewitness identifications, numerous pieces of circumstantial evidence, and a handwritten letter in which petitioner apologized for killing the officers and offered to turn himself in under certain conditions. That proof, even when considered alongside petitioner's belated affidavits, points strongly to petitioner's guilt.

This is not to say that petitioner's affidavits are without probative value. Had this sort of testimony been offered at trial, it could have been weighed by the jury, along with the evidence offered by the State and petitioner, in deliberating upon its verdict. Since the statements in the affidavits contradict the evidence received at trial, the jury would have had to decide important issues of credibility. But coming 10 years after petitioner's trial, this showing of innocence falls far short of that which would have to be made in order to trigger the sort of constitutional claim which we have assumed, *arguendo*, to exist.

The judgment of the Court of Appeals is affirmed.

Justice SCALIA, with whom Justice Thomas joins, concurring.

We granted certiorari on the question whether it violates due process or constitutes cruel and unusual punishment for a State to execute a person who, having been convicted of murder after a full and fair trial, later alleges that newly discovered evidence shows him to be "actually innocent." I would have preferred to decide that question, particularly since, as the Court's discussion shows, it is perfectly clear what the answer is: There is no basis in text, tradition, or even in contemporary practice (if that were enough), for finding in the Constitution a right to demand judicial consideration of newly discovered evidence of innocence brought forward after conviction. In saying that such a right exists, the dissenters apply nothing but their personal opinions to invalidate the rules of more than two-thirds of the States, and a Federal Rule of Criminal Procedure for which this Court itself is responsible. If the system that has been in place for 200 years (and remains widely approved) "shocks" the dissenters' consciences, perhaps they should doubt the calibration of their consciences, or, better still, the usefulness of "conscience-shocking" as a legal test.

I nonetheless join the entirety of the Court's opinion, including the final portion—because there is no legal error in deciding a case by assuming *arguendo* that an asserted constitutional right exists, and because I can understand, or at least am accustomed to, the reluctance of the present Court to admit publicly that Our Perfect Constitution lets stand any injustice, much less the execution of an innocent man who has received, though to no avail, all the process that our society has traditionally deemed adequate. With any luck, we shall avoid ever having to face this embarrassing question again, since it is improbable that evidence of innocence as convincing as today's opinion requires would fail to produce an executive pardon....

Justice BLACKMUN, with whom Justice Stevens and Justice Souter join [except as to the last paragraph], dissenting.

Nothing could be more contrary to contemporary standards of decency, or more shocking to the conscience, than to execute a person who is actually innocent....

I

The Court's enumeration of the constitutional rights of criminal defendants surely is entirely beside the point. These protections sometimes fail.[1] We really are being asked to

---

1. One impressive study has concluded that 23 innocent people have been executed in the United States in this century, including one as recently as 1984. Bedau & Radelet, "Miscarriages of Justice in Potentially Capital Cases," 40 Stan. L. Rev. 21, 36, 173–179 (1987); M. Radelet, H. Bedau, & C. Putnam, *In Spite of Innocence* 282–356 (1992). The majority cites this study to show that clemency has been exercised frequently in capital cases when showings of actual innocence have

decide whether the Constitution forbids the execution of a person who has been validly convicted and sentenced but who, nonetheless, can prove his innocence with newly discovered evidence. Despite the State of Texas' astonishing protestation to the contrary, I do not see how the answer can be anything but "yes."

A

The Eighth Amendment prohibits "cruel and unusual punishments." This proscription is not static but rather reflects evolving standards of decency. I think it is crystal clear that the execution of an innocent person is "at odds with contemporary standards of fairness and decency." Indeed, it is at odds with any standard of decency that I can imagine....

I believe it contrary to any standard of decency to execute someone who is actually innocent. Because the Eighth Amendment applies to questions of guilt or innocence, *Beck v. Alabama*, 447 U.S. 625, 638 (1980), and to persons upon whom a valid sentence of death has been imposed, *Johnson v. Mississippi*, 486 U.S. 578, 590 (1988), I also believe that petitioner may raise an Eighth Amendment challenge to his punishment on the ground that he is actually innocent....

B

Petitioner's claim [also] falls within our [Fourteenth Amendment] due process precedents. In *Rochin v. California*, 342 U.S. 165 (1952), deputy sheriffs investigating narcotics sales broke into Rochin's room and observed him put two capsules in his mouth. The deputies attempted to remove the capsules from his mouth and, having failed, took Rochin to a hospital and had his stomach pumped. The capsules were found to contain morphine. The Court held that the deputies' conduct "shock[ed] the conscience" and violated due process. "Illegally breaking into the privacy of the petitioner, the struggle to open his mouth and remove what was there, the forcible extraction of his stomach's contents—this course of proceeding by agents of government to obtain evidence is bound to offend even hardened sensibilities. They are methods too close to the rack and the screw to permit of constitutional differentiation." The lethal injection that petitioner faces as an allegedly innocent person is certainly closer to the rack and the screw than the stomach pump condemned in *Rochin*. Execution of an innocent person is the ultimate "'arbitrary impositio[n].'" It is an imposition from which one never recovers and for which one can never be compensated. Thus, I also believe that petitioner may raise a substantive due process challenge to his punishment on the ground that he is actually innocent.

III

A

... The possibility of executive clemency is *not* sufficient to satisfy the requirements of the Eighth and Fourteenth Amendments. The majority correctly points out: "A pardon is an act of grace." The vindication of rights guaranteed by the Constitution has never been made to turn on the unreviewable discretion of an executive official or ad-

---

been made. But the study also shows that requests for clemency by persons the authors believe were innocent have been refused. See, e.g., Bedau & Radelet, 40 Stan. L. Rev., at 91 (discussing James Adams who was executed in Florida on May 10, 1984); M. Radelet, H. Bedau, & C. Putnam, *In Spite of Innocence*, at 5–10 (same).

ministrative tribunal. Indeed, in *Ford v. Wainwright*, 477 U.S. 399 (1986), we explicitly rejected the argument that executive clemency was adequate to vindicate the Eighth Amendment right not to be executed if one is insane. The possibility of executive clemency "exists in every case in which a defendant challenges his sentence under the Eighth Amendment. Recognition of such a bare possibility would make judicial review under the Eighth Amendment meaningless."

"The government of the United States has been emphatically termed a government of laws, and not of men. It will certainly cease to deserve this high appellation, if the laws furnish no remedy for the violation of a vested legal right." If the exercise of a legal right turns on "an act of grace," then we no longer live under a government of laws. "The very purpose of a Bill of Rights was to withdraw certain subjects from the vicissitudes of political controversy, to place them beyond the reach of majorities and officials and to establish them as legal principles to be applied by the courts." It is understandable, therefore, that the majority does not say that the vindication of petitioner's constitutional rights may be left to executive clemency....

C

The question that remains is what showing should be required to obtain relief on the merits of an Eighth or Fourteenth Amendment claim of actual innocence. I agree with the majority that "in state criminal proceedings the trial is the paramount event for determining the guilt or innocence of the defendant." I also think that "a truly persuasive demonstration of 'actual innocence' made after trial would render the execution of a defendant unconstitutional." The question is what "a truly persuasive demonstration" entails, a question the majority's disposition of this case leaves open.

... I would hold that, to obtain relief on a claim of actual innocence, the petitioner must show that he probably is innocent. This standard is supported by several considerations. First, new evidence of innocence may be discovered long after the defendant's conviction. Given the passage of time, it may be difficult for the State to retry a defendant who obtains relief from his conviction or sentence on an actual-innocence claim. The actual-innocence proceeding thus may constitute the final word on whether the defendant may be punished. In light of this fact, an otherwise constitutionally valid conviction or sentence should not be set aside lightly. Second, conviction after a constitutionally adequate trial strips the defendant of the presumption of innocence. The government bears the burden of proving the defendant's guilt beyond a reasonable doubt, but once the government has done so, the burden of proving innocence must shift to the convicted defendant.... When a defendant seeks to challenge the determination of guilt after he has been validly convicted and sentenced, it is fair to place on him the burden of proving his innocence, not just raising doubt about his guilt.

... I believe that if a prisoner can show that he is probably actually innocent, in light of all the evidence, then he has made "a truly persuasive demonstration" and his execution would violate the Constitution. I would so hold....

V

I have voiced disappointment over this Court's obvious eagerness to do away with any restriction on the States' power to execute whomever and however they please. I have also expressed doubts about whether, in the absence of such restrictions, capital punishment remains constitutional at all. *Sawyer v. Whitley*, 112 S. Ct. 2514,

2529–2530 (1992) (opinion concurring in the judgment). Of one thing, however, I am certain. Just as an execution without adequate safeguards is unacceptable, so too is an execution when the condemned prisoner can prove that he is innocent. The execution of a person who can show that he is innocent comes perilously close to simple murder.

Notes

1. Leonel Herrera was executed by lethal injection on May 12, 1993. He maintained his innocence even as he was strapped to the death chamber gurney. In his last statement, Herrera said

> I am innocent, innocent, innocent. And make no mistake about this. I owe society nothing. I would like to encourage all those who stood by me to continue the struggle for human rights and continue to help those who are innocent.... I am an innocent man. And something very wrong is taking place tonight.

Graczyk, *Man Executed for Killing Police Officer*, Dallas Morning News, May 13, 1993.

2. The Court in *Herrera* never actually resolved the question of whether the Eighth Amendment prohibits the execution of a defendant who makes an adequate showing — based upon newly discovered evidence — that he is "actually innocent." Six justices concluded that no matter what standard was used to define "adequate showing of actual innocence," Herrera could not possibly satisfy it. Nonetheless, a careful reading of the *Herrera* opinions suggests that, if the issue were properly raised, at least five justices would require at least *some* federal substantive review of a defendant's claim of actual innocence. The three dissenting justices would require review whenever a defendant could show that he is "probably actually innocent." 506 U.S. at 443–44 (Blackmun, J., dissenting, joined in part by Stevens and Souter, JJ.). And Justice O'Connor's concurrence, which was joined by Justice Kennedy, stated: "I cannot disagree with the fundamental legal principle that executing the innocent is inconsistent with the Constitution. Regardless of the verbal formula employed ... the execution of a legally and factually innocent person would be a constitutionally intolerable event." *Id.* at 419. For a discussion of alternative proposals for handling innocence claims in federal habeas, see Freedman, "Innocence, Federalism and the Capital Jury: Two Legislative Proposals for Evaluating Post-Trial Evidence of Innocence in Death Penalty Cases," 18 N.Y.U. Rev. L. & Soc. Change 315 (1990–1991).

3. In *Schlup v. Delo*, 513 U.S. 298 (1995), the Supreme Court addressed the question of actual innocence not as a free-standing claim on which habeas relief could be based, but rather in the context of an ineffective assistance of counsel claim and as grounds sufficiently excusing a petitioner's failure to raise the issue in state court proceedings so that that issue could be reviewed on the merits in federal habeas. Justice Stevens wrote the majority opinion in *Schlup*, in which Justices O'Connor, Souter, Ginsburg, and Breyer joined. On the issue of actual innocence, Justice Stevens wrote in pertinent part:

> As a preliminary matter, it is important to explain the difference between Schlup's claim of actual innocence and the claim of actual innocence asserted in *Herrera v. Collins*. In *Herrera*, the petitioner advanced his claim of innocence to support a novel substantive constitutional claim, namely that the execution of an innocent person would violate the Eighth Amendment. Under petitioner's theory in *Herrera*, even if the proceedings that had resulted in his con-

viction and sentence were entirely fair and error-free, his innocence would render his execution a "constitutionally intolerable event."

Schlup's claim of innocence, on the other hand, is procedural, rather than substantive. His constitutional claims are based not on his innocence, but rather on his contention that the ineffectiveness of his counsel, and the withholding of evidence by the prosecution, denied him the full panoply of protections afforded to criminal defendants by the Constitution. Schlup, however, faces procedural obstacles that he must overcome before a federal court may address the merits of those constitutional claims. Because Schlup has been unable to establish "cause and prejudice" sufficient to excuse his failure to present his evidence in support of his first federal petition, Schlup may obtain review of his constitutional claims only if he falls within the "narrow class of cases ... implicating a fundamental miscarriage of justice." Schlup's claim of innocence is offered only to bring him within this "narrow class of cases." Schlup's claim thus differs in at least two important ways from that presented in *Herrera*. First, Schlup's claim of innocence does not by itself provide a basis for relief. Instead, his claim for relief depends critically on the validity of his *Strickland* and *Brady* claims. Schlup's claim of innocence is thus "not itself a constitutional claim, but instead a gateway through which a habeas petitioner must pass to have his otherwise barred constitutional claim considered on the merits."

More importantly, a court's assumptions about the validity of the proceedings that resulted in conviction are fundamentally different in Schlup's case than in Herrera's. In *Herrera*, petitioner's claim was evaluated on the assumption that the trial that resulted in his conviction had been error-free. In such a case, when a petitioner has been "tried before a jury of his peers, with the full panoply of protections that our Constitution affords criminal defendants," it is appropriate to apply an "extraordinarily high" standard of review.

Schlup, in contrast, accompanies his claim of innocence with an assertion of constitutional error at trial. For that reason, Schlup's conviction may not be entitled to the same degree of respect as one, such as Herrera's, that is the product of an error-free trial. Without any new evidence of innocence, even the existence of a concededly meritorious constitutional violation is not in itself sufficient to establish a miscarriage of justice that would allow a habeas court to reach the merits of a barred claim. However, if a petitioner such as Schlup presents evidence of innocence so strong that a court cannot have confidence in the outcome of the trial unless the court is also satisfied that the trial was free of nonharmless constitutional error, the petitioner should be allowed to pass through the gateway and argue the merits of his underlying claims.

Consequently, Schlup's evidence of innocence need carry less of a burden. In *Herrera* (on the assumption that petitioner's claim was, in principle, legally well founded), the evidence of innocence would have had to be strong enough to make his execution "constitutionally intolerable" even if his conviction was the product of a fair trial. For Schlup, the evidence must establish sufficient doubt about his guilt to justify the conclusion that his execution would be a miscarriage of justice unless his conviction was the product of a fair trial.

... If there were no question about the fairness of the criminal trial, a *Herrera*-type claim would have to fail unless the federal habeas court is itself convinced that those new facts unquestionably establish Schlup's innocence. On the other hand, if the habeas court were merely convinced that those new facts raised sufficient doubt about Schlup's guilt to undermine confidence in the result of the trial without the assurance that that trial was untainted by constitutional error, Schlup's threshold showing of innocence would justify a review of the merits of the constitutional claims.

4. Consider John Adams' final argument in defense of British soldiers accused of murder at the Boston Massacre. See *Legal Papers of John Adams*, L. Kinvin Wroth and Hiller B. Zobel, editors (Cambridge, Mass.: Harvard University Press, 1965) volume 3, p. 242.

We find in the rules laid down by the greatest English judges, who have been the brightest of mankind, [that] we are to look upon it as more beneficial that many guilty persons should escape unpunished than one innocent person should suffer. The reason is because it is of more importance to [the] community that innocence should be protected than it is that guilt should be punished, for guilt and crimes are so frequent in the world that all of them cannot be punished, and many times they happen in such a manner that it is not of much consequence to the public whether they are punished or not. But when innocence itself is brought to the bar and condemned, especially to die, the subject will exclaim, "It is immaterial to me whether I behave well or ill, for virtue itself is no security." And if such a sentiment as this should take place in the mind of the subject there would be an end to all security whatsoever.

Chapter 14

State Barriers to Federal Habeas Review

A. Exhaustion of State Remedies

In *Ex Parte Royall*, 117 U.S. 241 (1886), the Supreme Court held that state prisoners must exhaust, that is fully pursue, state court remedies for their federal claims before seeking federal habeas relief for such claims. This exhaustion rule—which has proved to be only the first of many procedural hurdles placed in the path of state prisoners seeking relief from unlawful confinement—thus began as a judicially crafted limitation on the ability of federal courts to hear certain claims raised by state prisoners. This requirement was first codified in 1948. Prior to the enactment of the AEDPA, 28 U.S.C. §2254(b) provided:

> An application for a writ of habeas corpus in behalf of a person in custody pursuant to the judgment of a State court shall not be granted unless it appears that the applicant has exhausted the remedies available in the courts of the State, or that there is either an absence of available State corrective process or the existence of circumstances rendering such process ineffective to protect the rights of the prisoner.

When Congress enacted the AEDPA, it elaborated on the exhaustion requirements governing habeas petitions. The exhaustion provisions of the AEDPA provide in §2254:

> (b) (1) An application for a writ of habeas corpus on behalf of a person in custody pursuant to the judgment of a State court shall not be granted unless it appears that—
>
> (A) the applicant has exhausted the remedies available in the courts of the State; or
>
> (B)(i) there is an absence of available State corrective process; or
>
> (ii) circumstances exist that render such process ineffective to protect the rights of the applicant.
>
> (2) An applicant for a writ of habeas corpus may be denied on the merits, notwithstanding the failure of the applicant to exhaust the remedies available in the courts of the State.
>
> (3) A State shall not be deemed to have waived the exhaustion requirement or be estopped from reliance upon the requirement unless the State, through counsel, expressly waives the requirement.
>
> (c) An applicant shall not be deemed to have exhausted the remedies available in the courts of the State, within the meaning of this section, if he has the

right under the law of the State to raise, by any available procedure, the question presented.

28 U.S.C. § 2254(b),(c).

Before Congress modified the exhaustion requirements through the AEDPA, the Court held that the exhaustion doctrine required total exhaustion of all claims raised in habeas petitions, including "mixed" habeas petitions, *i.e.*, those petitions which contain both exhausted and unexhausted claims.

Rose v. Lundy
455 U.S. 509 (1982)

Justice O'CONNOR delivered the opinion of the Court except as to Part III-C.

In this case we consider whether the exhaustion rule in 28 U.S.C. §2254(b), (c) requires a federal district court to dismiss a petition for a writ of habeas corpus containing any claims that have not been exhausted in the state courts. Because a rule requiring exhaustion of all claims furthers the purposes underlying the habeas statute, we hold that a district court must dismiss such "mixed petitions," leaving the prisoner with the choice of returning to state court to exhaust his claims or of amending or resubmitting the habeas petition to present only exhausted claims to the district court.

I

Following a jury trial, respondent Noah Lundy was convicted on charges of rape and crime against nature, and sentenced to the Tennessee State Penitentiary. After the Tennessee Court of Criminal Appeals affirmed the convictions and the Tennessee Supreme Court denied review, the respondent filed an unsuccessful petition for post-conviction relief in the Knox County Criminal Court.

The respondent subsequently filed a petition in Federal District Court for a writ of habeas corpus under 28 U.S.C. §2254, alleging four grounds for relief: (1) that he had been denied the right to confrontation because the trial court limited the defense counsel's questioning of the victim; (2) that he had been denied the right to a fair trial because the prosecuting attorney stated that the respondent had a violent character; (3) that he had been denied the right to a fair trial because the prosecutor improperly remarked in his closing argument that the State's evidence was uncontradicted; and (4) that the trial judge improperly instructed the jury that every witness is presumed to swear the truth. After reviewing the state court records, however, the District Court concluded that it could not consider claims three and four "in the constitutional framework" because the respondent had not exhausted his state remedies for those grounds. The court nevertheless stated that "in assessing the atmosphere of the cause taken as a whole these items may be referred to collaterally."[1]

Apparently in an effort to assess the "atmosphere" of the trial, the District Court reviewed the state trial transcript and identified 10 instances of prosecutorial misconduct, only five of which the respondent had raised before the state courts. In addition, although purportedly not ruling on the respondent's fourth ground for relief—that the

---

1. The Tennessee Criminal Court of Appeals had ruled specifically on grounds one and two, holding that although the trial court erred in restricting cross-examination of the victim and the prosecuting attorney improperly alluded to the respondent's violent nature, the respondent was not prejudiced by these errors.

state trial judge improperly charged that "every witness is presumed to swear the truth"—the court nonetheless held that the jury instruction, coupled with both the restriction of counsel's cross-examination of the victim and the prosecutor's "personal testimony" on the weight of the State's evidence, violated the respondent's right to a fair trial and ordered that petitioner be released from prison or granted a new trial.... In short, the District Court considered several instances of prosecutorial misconduct never challenged in the state trial or appellate courts, or even raised in the respondent's habeas petition.

The Sixth Circuit affirmed the judgment of the District Court.... The court specifically rejected the State's argument that the District Court should have dismissed the petition because it included both exhausted and unexhausted claims.

II

The petitioner urges this Court to apply a "total exhaustion" rule requiring district courts to dismiss every habeas corpus petition that contains both exhausted and unexhausted claims. The petitioner argues at length that such a rule furthers the policy of comity underlying the exhaustion doctrine because it gives the state courts the first opportunity to correct federal constitutional errors and minimizes federal interference and disruption of state judicial proceedings. The petitioner also believes that uniform adherence to a total exhaustion rule reduces the amount of piecemeal habeas litigation.

III

A

The exhaustion doctrine existed long before its codification by Congress in 1948. In *Ex parte Royall*, 117 U.S. 241, 251 (1886), this Court wrote that as a matter of comity, federal courts should not consider a claim in a habeas corpus petition until after the state courts have had an opportunity to act....

Subsequent cases refined the principle that state remedies must be exhausted except in unusual circumstances. In *Ex parte Hawk*, 321 U.S. 114, 117 (1944), this Court reiterated that comity was the basis for the exhaustion doctrine: "it is a principle controlling all habeas corpus petitions to the federal courts, that those courts will interfere with the administration of justice in the state courts only 'in rare cases where exceptional circumstances of peculiar urgency are shown to exist.'"[7] None of these cases, however, specifically applied the exhaustion doctrine to habeas petitions containing both exhausted and unexhausted claims.

In 1948, Congress codified the exhaustion doctrine in 28 U.S.C. §2254, citing *Ex parte Hawk* as correctly stating the principle of exhaustion. Section 2254, however, does not directly address the problem of mixed petitions. To be sure, the provision states that a remedy is not exhausted if there exists a state procedure to raise "the question presented," but we believe this phrase to be too ambiguous to sustain the conclusion that Congress intended to either permit or prohibit review of mixed petitions. Because the legislative history of §2254, as well as the pre-1948 cases, contains no reference to the problem of mixed petitions, in all likelihood Congress never thought of the problem.

---

7. The Court also made clear, however, that the exhaustion doctrine does not bar relief where the state remedies are inadequate or fail to "afford a full and fair adjudication of the federal contentions raised."

Consequently, we must analyze the policies underlying the statutory provision to determine its proper scope.

B

The exhaustion doctrine is principally designed to protect the state courts' role in the enforcement of federal law and prevent disruption of state judicial proceedings. Under our federal system, the federal and state "courts [are] equally bound to guard and protect rights secured by the Constitution." Because "it would be unseemly in our dual system of government for a federal district court to upset a state court conviction without an opportunity to the state courts to correct a constitutional violation," federal courts apply the doctrine of comity, which "teaches that one court should defer action on causes properly within its jurisdiction until the courts of another sovereignty with concurrent powers, and already cognizant of the litigation, have had an opportunity to pass upon the matter."

A rigorously enforced total exhaustion rule will encourage state prisoners to seek full relief first from the state courts, thus giving those courts the first opportunity to review all claims of constitutional error. As the number of prisoners who exhaust all of their federal claims increases, state courts may become increasingly familiar with and hospitable toward federal constitutional issues. Equally as important, federal claims that have been fully exhausted in state courts will more often be accompanied by a complete factual record to aid the federal courts in their review.

The facts of the present case underscore the need for a rule encouraging exhaustion of all federal claims. In his opinion, the District Court Judge wrote that "there is such mixture of violations that one cannot be separated from and considered independently of the others." Because the two unexhausted claims for relief were intertwined with the exhausted ones, the judge apparently considered all of the claims in ruling on the petition. Requiring dismissal of petitions containing both exhausted and unexhausted claims will relieve the district courts of the difficult if not impossible task of deciding when claims are related, and will reduce the temptation to consider unexhausted claims....

Rather than an "adventure in unnecessary lawmaking," our holdings today reflect our interpretation of a federal statute on the basis of its language and legislative history, and consistent with its underlying policies. There is no basis to believe that today's holdings will "complicate and delay" the resolution of habeas petitions, or will serve to "trap the unwary *pro se* prisoner." On the contrary, our interpretation of §2254(b), (c) provides a simple and clear instruction to potential litigants: before you bring any claims to federal court, be sure that you first have taken each one to state court. Just as *pro se* petitioners have managed to use the federal habeas machinery, so too should they be able to master this straightforward exhaustion requirement. Those prisoners who misunderstand this requirement and submit mixed petitions nevertheless are entitled to resubmit a petition with only exhausted claims or to exhaust the remainder of their claims....

Rather than increasing the burden on federal courts, strict enforcement of the exhaustion requirement will encourage habeas petitioners to exhaust all of their claims in state court and to present the federal court with a single habeas petition. To the extent that the exhaustion requirement reduces piecemeal litigation, both the courts and the prisoners should benefit, for as a result the district court will be more likely to review all of the prisoner's claims in a single proceeding, thus providing for a more focused and thorough review....

IV

In sum, because a total exhaustion rule promotes comity and does not unreasonably impair the prisoner's right to relief, we hold that a district court must dismiss habeas petitions containing both unexhausted and exhausted claims. Accordingly, the judgment of the Court of Appeals is reversed, and the case is remanded for proceedings consistent with this opinion.

Justice BLACKMUN, concurring in the judgment.

... The Court's interest in efficient administration of the federal courts ... does not require dismissal of mixed habeas petitions. In fact, that concern militates against the approach taken by the Court today. In order to comply with the Court's ruling, a federal court now will have to review the record in a §2254 proceeding at least summarily in order to determine whether all claims have been exhausted. In many cases a decision on the merits will involve only negligible additional effort. And in other cases the court may not realize that one of a number of claims is unexhausted until after substantial work has been done. If the district court must nevertheless dismiss the entire petition until all grounds for relief have been exhausted, the prisoner will likely return to federal court eventually, thereby necessitating duplicative examination of the record and consideration of the exhausted claims — perhaps by another district judge. Moreover, when the §2254 petition does find its way back to federal court, the record on the exhausted grounds for relief may well be stale and resolution of the merits more difficult.

The interest of the prisoner and of society in "preserv[ing] the writ of habeas corpus as a 'swift and imperative remedy in all cases of illegal restraint or confinement,'" is the final policy consideration to be weighed in the balance. Compelling the habeas petitioner to repeat his journey through the entire state and federal legal process before receiving a ruling on his exhausted claims obviously entails substantial delay. And if the prisoner must choose between undergoing that delay and forfeiting unexhausted claims, society is likewise forced to sacrifice either the swiftness of habeas or its availability to remedy all unconstitutional imprisonments. Dismissing only unexhausted grounds for habeas relief, while ruling on the merits of all unrelated exhausted claims, will diminish neither the promptness nor the efficacy of the remedy and, at the same time, will serve the state and federal interests described by the Court....

Notes and Questions

1. The AEDPA incorporates the holding in *Rose v. Lundy*. Accordingly, under the current habeas statute an inmate who files a mixed petition will be subject to dismissal of her petition without prejudice pending exhaustion of state remedies.

2. Observe that under §2254(b)(2) of the AEDPA, habeas relief may be denied even if a petitioner has failed to exhaust all his claims in state court. This denial of relief would include both exhausted and unexhausted claims. What is the rationale for this provision? Should a federal court grant relief if a petition contains both exhausted and unexhausted claims?

3. The one-year statute of limitations under 28 U.S.C. §2244(d)(1) of the AEDPA presents additional concerns when considering dismissal of habeas petitions for failure to exhaust. Section 2244(d)(1) provides:

A 1-year period of limitation shall apply to an application for a writ of habeas corpus by a person in custody pursuant to the judgment of a State court. The limitation period shall run from the latest of—

(A) the date on which the judgment became final by the conclusion of direct review or the expiration of the time for seeking such review;

(B) the date on which the impediment to filing an application created by State action in violation of the Constitution or laws of the United States is removed, if the applicant was prevented from filing by such State action;

(C) the date on which the constitutional right asserted was initially recognized by the Supreme Court, if the right has been newly recognized by the Supreme Court and made retroactively applicable to cases on collateral review; or

(D) the date on which the factual predicate of the claim or claims presented could have been discovered through the exercise of due diligence.

Now, not only must a prisoner exhaust his state remedies, but also she must assure that her federal habeas petition is filed within the one-year statute of limitations.

Somewhat ameliorating this situation, Congress provided a tolling of the statute of limitations in §2244(d)(2) as follows: "The time during which a properly filed application for State post-conviction or other collateral review with respect to the pertinent judgment or claim is pending shall not be counted toward any period of limitation under this subsection." The Supreme Court addressed what constitutes a properly filed state court postconviction application in *Artuz v. Bennet*, 531 U.S. 4 (2000). In *Artuz*, the Court held:

An application is "filed," as that term is commonly understood, when it is delivered to, and accepted by, the appropriate court officer for placement into the official record. And an application is "properly filed" when its delivery and acceptance are in compliance with the applicable laws and rules governing filings. These usually prescribe, for example, the form of the document, the time limits upon its delivery, the court and office in which it must be lodged, and the requisite filing fee. In some jurisdictions the filing requirements also include, for example, preconditions imposed on particular abusive filers, or on all filers generally.

What happens, however, if a state prisoner files a state post-conviction application in the wrong state court or fails to comply with the state procedural rules so as to invoke jurisdiction of the proper state court? Under such circumstances, should the post-conviction application be deemed "properly filed" so as to toll the statute of limitations?

Suppose a prisoner files a mixed petition in federal court and after four months the district court dismisses the petition without prejudice so that the petitioner may seek state review of his claims first. Should the time that the petitioner's habeas petition was pending in federal court count towards the tolling of the statute of limitations? What should a federal court do if it finds it must dismiss a mixed petition, but also finds that the statute of limitations would expire before the petitioner would be able to re-file after exhaustion of his state remedies?

4. In Part III, subsection C of *Rose v. Lundy*, Justice O'Connor wrote:

The prisoner's principal interest, of course, is in obtaining speedy federal relief on his claims. A total exhaustion rule will not impair that interest since he can always amend the petition to delete the unexhausted claims, rather than returning to state court to exhaust all of his claims. By invoking this procedure, however, the prisoner would risk forfeiting consideration of his unexhausted claims in federal court. Under 28 U.S.C. §2254 Rule 9(b), a district court may dismiss subsequent petitions if it finds that "the failure of the petitioner to assert those [new] grounds in a prior petition constituted an abuse of the writ."

For further discussion of the abuse of the writ doctrine and habeas petitions see *infra* chapter 17.

Anderson v. Harless
459 U.S. 4 (1982)

PER CURIAM.

Respondent was convicted of two counts of first degree murder and was sentenced to life imprisonment. The Michigan Court of Appeals affirmed respondent's conviction, and the Michigan Supreme Court, on review of the record, denied respondent's request for relief.

Respondent then filed a petition for writ of habeas corpus, pursuant to 28 U.S.C. §2254, in the United States District Court for the Eastern District of Michigan. He alleged, *inter alia*, that the trial court's instruction on "malice"—a crucial element in distinguishing between second degree murder and manslaughter under Michigan law—was unconstitutional....

Relying primarily on *Sandstrom v. Montana*, 442 U.S. 510 (1979), the District Court held that this instruction unconstitutionally shifted the burden of proof to respondent and was inconsistent with the presumption of innocence. The court also held that respondent had exhausted available state-court remedies, as required by 28 U.S.C. §§2254(b) and (c), since his conviction had been reviewed by both the Michigan Court of Appeals and the Michigan Supreme Court. The District Court ordered that the application for writ of habeas corpus be granted unless respondent was retried within 90 days.

The United States Court of Appeals for the Sixth Circuit affirmed. The court held that respondent's claim had been properly exhausted in the state courts, because respondent had presented to the Michigan Court of Appeals the facts on which he based his federal claim and had argued that the malice instruction was "reversible error." The court also emphasized that respondent, in his brief to the Michigan Court of Appeals, had cited *People v. Martin*, 392 Mich. 553, 221 N.W.2d 336 (1974)—a decision predicated solely on state law in which no federal issues were decided, but in which the defendant had argued broadly that failure to properly instruct a jury violates the Sixth and Fourteenth Amendments. In the view of the United States Court of Appeals, respondent's assertion before the Michigan Court of Appeals that the trial court's malice instruction was erroneous, coupled with his citation of *People v. Martin*, provided the Michigan courts with sufficient opportunity to consider the issue encompassed by respondent's subsequent federal habeas petition.

We reverse. In *Picard v. Connor*, 404 U.S. 270 (1971), we made clear that 28 U.S.C. §2254 requires a federal habeas petitioner to provide the state courts with a "fair opportunity" to apply controlling legal principles to the facts bearing upon his constitutional claim. It is not enough that all the facts necessary to support the federal claim were before the state courts, or that a somewhat similar state-law claim was made. In addition, the habeas petitioner must have "fairly presented" to the state courts the "substance" of his federal habeas corpus claim.

In this case respondent argued on appeal that the trial court's instruction on the element of malice was "erroneous." He offered no support for this conclusion other than a citation to, and three excerpts from, *People v. Martin*,—a case which held that, under Michigan law, malice should not be implied from the fact that a weapon is used. Not surprisingly, the Michigan Court of Appeals interpreted respondent's claim as being predicated on the state-law rule of *Martin*, and analyzed it accordingly.

The United States Court of Appeals concluded that "the due process ramifications" of respondent's argument to the Michigan court "were self-evident," and that respondent's "reliance on *Martin* was sufficient to present the state courts with the substance of his due process challenge to the malice instruction for habeas exhaustion purposes." We disagree. The District Court based its grant of habeas relief in this case on the doctrine that certain sorts of "mandatory presumptions" may undermine the prosecution's burden to prove guilt beyond a reasonable doubt and thus deprive a criminal defendant of due process. The Court of Appeals affirmed on the same rationale. However, it is plain from the record that this constitutional argument was never presented to, or considered by, the Michigan courts. Nor is this claim even the same as the constitutional claim advanced in *Martin*—the defendant there asserted a broad federal due process right to jury instructions that "properly explain" state law, and did not rely on the more particular analysis developed in cases such as *Sandstrom*.

Since it appears that respondent is still free to present his *Sandstrom* claim to Michigan Court of Appeals, we conclude that he has not exhausted his available state-court remedies as required by 28 U.S.C. §2254. Accordingly, the petition for certiorari and respondent's motion for leave to proceed *in forma pauperis* are granted, the judgment of the United States Court of Appeals for the Sixth Circuit is reversed, and the case is remanded to that court for further proceedings consistent with this opinion.

Justice STEVENS, with whom Justice Brennan, and Justice Marshall join, dissenting.

Few issues consume as much of the scarce time of federal judges as the question whether a state prisoner adequately exhausted his state remedies before filing a petition for a federal writ of habeas corpus. Distressingly, the Court seems oblivious of this fact and takes action in this case that can only exacerbate that problem....

I agree with the sensible approach to the exhaustion issue that was followed by the District Court and the Court of Appeals. I also believe that approach was entirely faithful to *Picard v. Connor*, which requires only that the "substance" of the federal claim (not the form) be "fairly presented" to the state courts. In this case the only arguable justification for dismissing the petition for failure to exhaust is a possibility that the state court might decide the instruction issue differently if phrased in terms of *Sandstrom v. United States* rather than in terms of *People v. Martin*. That possibility is virtually nonexistent. The Court apparently perceives this case as a simple application of *Picard*; I think it can only be explained as an expansion of *Picard*. Such an expansion should be accompanied by a more careful analysis than the Court provides in this case, and it should not be undertaken without full briefing and argument.

But even if I shared the Court's analysis of the exhaustion question in this particular case, I would nevertheless take issue with its decision to grant certiorari for the sole purpose of correcting what it considers to be a technical, procedural error. It is not appropriate for this Court to expend its scarce resources crafting opinions that correct technical errors in cases of only local importance where the correction in no way promotes the development of the law....

Notes and Question

1. Notions of comity undergird the exhaustion requirement. Comity dictates that the state should have an opportunity to correct errors within its judicial system before being subject to the scrutiny of federal courts. As the Supreme Court has noted, the exhaustion requirement reflects the policies of comity and federalism between the state and federal governments and expresses the recognition that "'it would be unseemly in our dual system of government for a federal district court to upset a state court conviction without an opportunity to the state courts to correct a constitutional violation.'" *Picard v. Connor*, 404 U.S. 270, 275 (1971) (quoting *Darr v. Burford*, 339 U.S. 200, 204 (1950)).

2. What happens if the state fails to raise the issue of nonexhaustion? Prior to the enactment of the AEDPA, the issue could be considered waived unless comity and judicial efficiency dictated otherwise. *Granberry v. Greer*, 481 U.S. 129 (1987). Under the AEDPA, however, "[a] State shall not be deemed to have waived the exhaustion requirement or be estopped from reliance upon the requirement unless the State, through counsel, expressly waives the requirement." 28 U.S.C. §2254(b)(3).

B. Procedural Bar—Introduction

Most states have procedural bars that prevent defendants from raising claims either on appeal or in state post-conviction proceedings if the claims were not raised when the error occurred, or soon thereafter. State procedural defaults, whether at trial, on appeal, or in state post-conviction proceedings, may also bar federal habeas corpus review of a claim. The question of whether a procedural bar precludes federal habeas review of a claims is a threshold issue that a federal court must address when reviewing a habeas petition. *Lambrix v. Singletary*, 520 U.S. 518 (1997).

In *Fay v. Noia*, 372 U.S. 391, 438 (1963), the United States Supreme Court addressed whether an accused, whose failure to raise a confession issue on direct appeal barred state post-conviction relief, was also barred from raising the confession issue on a writ of federal habeas corpus. Justice Brennan's majority opinion established the "deliberate bypass" rule which allowed the petitioner to seek federal habeas relief, even if he procedurally defaulted his state court remedies, provided that the petitioner had not deliberately bypassed the state procedures. The Court stated:

> Although we hold that the jurisdiction of the federal courts on habeas corpus is not affected by procedural defaults incurred by the applicant during the state court proceedings, we recognize a limited discretion in the federal judge to deny relief to an applicant under certain circumstances. Discretion is implicit in the statutory command that the judge, after granting the writ and holding a hearing of appropriate scope, "dispose of the matter as law and justice requires;" and discretion was the flexible concept employed by the federal courts in developing the exhaustion rule. Furthermore, habeas corpus has traditionally been regarded as governed by equitable principles. Among them is the principle that a suitor's conduct in relation to the matter at hand may disentitle him to the relief he seeks. Narrowly circumscribed, in conformity to the historical role of the writ of habeas corpus as an effective and impera-

tive remedy for detentions contrary to fundamental law, the principle is unexceptionable. We therefore hold that the federal habeas judge may in his discretion deny relief to an applicant who has deliberately bypassed the orderly procedure of the state courts and in so doing has forfeited his state court remedies.

The decision in *Fay* was controversial and the post-Warren Court set about dismantling the deliberate bypass rule. For an excellent discussion on the history of the effect of state procedural default on federal habeas corpus review see Whitebread & Slobogin, *Criminal Procedure, An Analysis of Cases and Concepts*, §33.03 (3d edition) (Foundation Press 1992). In *Wainwright v. Sykes*, 433 U.S. 72 (1977) (below), the Court revisited the deliberate bypass standard and established a new standard for federal habeas review for petitioners raising claims which had been defaulted under state procedural rules.

C. Cause and Prejudice Requirement

Wainwright v. Sykes
433 U.S. 72 (1977)

Mr. Justice REHNQUIST delivered the opinion of the Court.

We granted certiorari to consider the availability of federal habeas to review a state convict's claim that testimony was admitted at his trial in violation of his *Miranda* rights, a claim which the Florida courts have previously refused to consider on the merits because of noncompliance with a state contemporaneous objection rule. Petitioner Wainwright, on behalf of the State of Florida, here challenges a decision of the Court of Appeals for the Fifth Circuit ordering a hearing in state court on the merits of respondent's contention.

[John Sykes was convicted of third degree murder. At trial, two police officers testified that after Sykes had been read his *Miranda* rights and declined counsel, Sykes told the officers that he had shot the victim. Sykes' lawyer did not object to the admissibility of the officers' statements at trial. Likewise, on direct appeal Sykes did not challenge the admissibility of the statements. The state appellate court affirmed Sykes' conviction. Sykes then sought state post-conviction relief claiming, for the first time, that his statements to the police were involuntary and thus inadmissible. The state courts denied relief.

Sykes next sought a writ of habeas corpus in federal court. The Fifth Circuit Court of Appeals found that Sykes was not barred from seeking relief in federal court because "[t]he failure to object in this case cannot be dismissed as a trial tactic, and thus a deliberate by-pass." The Fifth Circuit upheld the federal district court's order requiring that the state hold a hearing on the voluntariness of Sykes' statements. The United States Supreme Court granted certiorari "to consider the availability of federal habeas corpus to review a state convict's claim that testimony was admitted at trial in violation of his rights under *Miranda v. Arizona*, a claim which the Florida courts have previously refused to consider on the merits because of noncompliance with a state contemporaneous-objection rule." Under that state procedural rule, Sykes' attorney's failure to object to the *Miranda* violation at trial prevented further review of Sykes' confession.]

The simple legal question before the Court calls for a construction of the language of 28 U.S.C. §2254(a), which provides that the federal courts shall entertain an application for a writ of habeas corpus "in behalf of a person in custody pursuant to the judgment of a state court only on the ground that he is in custody in violation of the Constitution or laws or treaties of the United States." But, to put it mildly, we do not write on a clean slate in construing this statutory provision.

... Where the habeas petitioner challenges a final judgment of conviction rendered by a state court, this Court has been called upon to decide no fewer than four different questions, all to a degree interrelated with one another: (1) What types of federal claims may a federal habeas court properly consider? (2) Where a federal claim is cognizable by a federal habeas court, to what extent must that court defer to a resolution of the claim in prior state proceedings? (3) To what extent must the petitioner who seeks federal habeas exhaust state remedies before resorting to the federal court? (4) In what instances will an adequate and independent state ground bar consideration of otherwise cognizable federal issues on federal habeas review? [After discussing the first three questions, the Court addressed the fourth.]

As to the role of adequate and independent state grounds, it is a well-established principle of federalism that a state decision resting on an adequate foundation of state substantive law is immune from review in the federal courts. The application of this principle in the context of a federal habeas proceeding has therefore excluded from consideration any questions of state substantive law, and thus effectively barred federal habeas review where questions of that sort are either the only ones raised by a petitioner or are in themselves dispositive of his case. The area of controversy which has developed has concerned the reviewability of federal claims which the state court has declined to pass on because not presented in the manner prescribed by its *procedural* rules. The adequacy of such an independent state procedural ground to prevent federal habeas review of the underlying federal issue has been treated very differently than where the state-law ground is substantive. The pertinent decisions marking the Court's somewhat tortuous efforts to deal with this problem are: *Ex parte Spencer*, 228 U.S. 652 (1913); *Brown v. Allen*, 344 U.S. 443 (1953); *Fay v. Noia*, 372 U.S. 391 (1963); *Davis v. United States*, 411 U.S. 233 (1973); and *Francis v. Henderson*, 425 U.S. 536 (1976).

In *Brown*, petitioner Daniels' lawyer had failed to mail the appeal papers to the State Supreme Court on the last day provided by law for filing, and hand delivered them one day after that date. Citing the state rule requiring timely filing, the Supreme Court of North Carolina refused to hear the appeal. This Court, relying in part on its earlier decision in *Ex parte Spencer*, held that federal habeas was not available to review a constitutional claim which could not have been reviewed on direct appeal here because it rested on an independent and adequate state procedural ground.

In *Fay v. Noia*, respondent Noia sought federal habeas to review a claim that his state-court conviction had resulted from the introduction of a coerced confession in violation of the Fifth Amendment to the United States Constitution. While the convictions of his two codefendants were reversed on that ground in collateral proceedings following their appeals, Noia did not appeal and the New York courts ruled that his subsequent *coram nobis* action was barred on account of that failure. This Court held that petitioner was nonetheless entitled to raise the claim in federal habeas, and thereby overruled its decision 10 years earlier in *Brown v. Allen*....

As a matter of comity but not of federal power, the Court acknowledged [in *Fay v. Noia*] "a limited discretion in the federal judge to deny relief ... to an applicant who had deliberately by-passed the orderly procedure of the state courts and in so doing has forfeited his state court remedies." In so stating, the Court made clear that the waiver must be knowing and actual, "an intentional relinquishment or abandonment of a known right or privilege." Noting petitioner's "grisly choice" between acceptance of his life sentence and pursuit of an appeal which might culminate in a sentence of death, the Court concluded that there had been no deliberate bypass of the right to have the federal issues reviewed through a state appeal.

A decade later we decided *Davis v. United States*, in which a federal prisoner's application under 28 U.S.C. §2255 sought for the first time to challenge the makeup of the grand jury which indicted him. The Government contended that he was barred by the requirement of Fed. Rule Crim. Proc. 12(b)(2) providing that such challenges must be raised "by motion before trial." The Rule further provides that failure to so object constitutes a waiver of the objection, but that "the court for cause shown may grant relief from the waiver." We noted that the Rule "promulgated by this Court and, pursuant to 18 U.S.C. §3771, 'adopted' by Congress, governs by its terms the manner in which the claims of defects in the institution of criminal proceedings may be waived," and held that this standard contained in the Rule, rather than the *Fay v. Noia* concept of waiver, should pertain in federal habeas as on direct review. Referring to previous constructions of Rule 12(b)(2), we concluded that review of the claim should be barred on habeas, as on direct appeal, absent a showing of cause for the noncompliance and some showing of actual prejudice resulting from the alleged constitutional violation.

Last Term, in *Francis v. Henderson*, the rule of *Davis* was applied to the parallel case of a state procedural requirement that challenges to grand jury composition be raised before trial. The Court noted that there was power in the federal courts to entertain an application in such a case, but rested its holding on "considerations of comity and concerns for the orderly administration of criminal justice...." While there was no counterpart provision of the state rule which allowed an exception upon some showing of cause, the Court concluded that the standard derived from the Federal Rule should nonetheless be applied in that context since "'(t)here is no reason to ... give greater preclusive effect to procedural defaults by federal defendants than to similar defaults by state defendants.'" As applied to the federal petitions of state convicts, the *Davis* cause-and-prejudice standard was thus incorporated directly into the body of law governing the availability of federal habeas corpus review.

To the extent that the dicta of *Fay v. Noia* may be thought to have laid down an all-inclusive rule rendering state timely objection rules ineffective to bar review of underlying federal claims in federal habeas proceedings—absent a "knowing waiver" or a "deliberate bypass" of the right to so object—its effect was limited by *Francis*, which applied a different rule and barred a habeas challenge to the makeup of a grand jury. Petitioner Wainwright in this case urges that we further confine its effect by applying the principle enunciated in *Francis* to a claimed error in the admission of a defendant's confession....

We ... conclude that Florida procedure did, consistently with the United States Constitution, require that petitioner's confession be challenged at trial or not at all, and thus his failure to timely object to its admission amounted to an independent and adequate state procedural ground which would prevent direct review here.

We thus come to the crux of this case. Shall the rule of *Francis v. Henderson*, barring federal habeas review absent a showing of "cause" and "prejudice" attendant to a state procedural waiver, be applied to a waived objection to the admission of a confession at trial? We answer that question in the affirmative.

As earlier noted in the opinion, since *Brown v. Allen*, it has been the rule that the federal habeas petitioner who claims he is detained pursuant to a final judgment of a state court in violation of the United States Constitution is entitled to have the federal habeas court make its own independent determination of his federal claim, without being bound by the determination on the merits of that claim reached in the state proceedings. This rule of *Brown v. Allen* is in no way changed by our holding today. Rather, we deal only with contentions of federal law which were not resolved on the merits in the state proceeding due to respondent's failure to raise them there as required by state procedure. We leave open for resolution in future decisions the precise definition of the "cause"-and-"prejudice" standard, and note here only that it is narrower than the standard set forth in dicta in *Fay v. Noia*, which would make federal habeas review generally available to state convicts absent a knowing and deliberate waiver of the federal constitutional contention. It is the sweeping language of *Fay v. Noia*, going far beyond the facts of the case eliciting it, which we today reject.

The reasons for our rejection of it are several. The contemporaneous-objection rule itself is by no means peculiar to Florida, and deserves greater respect than *Fay* gives it, both for the fact that it is employed by a coordinate jurisdiction within the federal system and for the many interests which it serves in its own right. A contemporaneous objection enables the record to be made with respect to the constitutional claim when the recollections of witnesses are freshest, not years later in a federal habeas proceeding. It enables the judge who observed the demeanor of those witnesses to make the factual determinations necessary for properly deciding the federal constitutional question. While the 1966 amendment to §2254 requires deference to be given to such determinations made by state courts, the determinations themselves are less apt to be made in the first instance if there is no contemporaneous objection to the admission of the evidence on federal constitutional grounds.

A contemporaneous-objection rule may lead to the exclusion of the evidence objected to, thereby making a major contribution to finality in criminal litigation. Without the evidence claimed to be vulnerable on federal constitutional grounds, the jury may acquit the defendant, and that will be the end of the case; or it may nonetheless convict the defendant, and he will have one less federal constitutional claim to assert in his federal habeas petition. If the state trial judge admits the evidence in question after a full hearing, the federal habeas court pursuant to the 1966 amendment to §2254 will gain significant guidance from the state ruling in this regard. Subtler considerations as well militate in favor of honoring a state contemporaneous-objection rule. An objection on the spot may force the prosecution to take a hard look at its whole card, and even if the prosecutor thinks that the state trial judge will admit the evidence he must contemplate the possibility of reversal by the state appellate courts or the ultimate issuance of a federal writ of habeas corpus based on the impropriety of the state court's rejection of the federal constitutional claim.

We think that the rule of *Fay v. Noia*, broadly stated, may encourage "sandbagging" on the part of defense lawyers, who may take their chances on a verdict of not guilty in a state trial court with the intent to raise their constitutional claims in a federal habeas court if their initial gamble does not pay off. The refusal of federal habeas courts to honor contemporaneous-objection rules may also make state courts themselves less stringent in their enforcement. Under the rule of *Fay v. Noia*, state appellate courts know that a federal constitutional issue raised for the first time in the proceeding before them may well be decided in any event by a federal habeas tribunal. Thus, their choice is between addressing the issue notwithstanding the petitioner's failure to timely object, or else face the prospect that the federal habeas court will decide the question without the benefit of their views.

The failure of the federal habeas courts generally to require compliance with a contemporaneous-objection rule tends to detract from the perception of the trial of a criminal case in state court as a decisive and portentous event. A defendant has been accused of a serious crime, and this is the time and place set for him to be tried by a jury of his peers and found either guilty or not guilty by that jury. To the greatest extent possible all issues which bear on this charge should be determined in this proceeding: the accused is in the court-room, the jury is in the box, the judge is on the bench, and the witnesses, having been subpoenaed and duly sworn, await their turn to testify. Society's resources have been concentrated at that time and place in order to decide, within the limits of human fallibility, the question of guilt or innocence of one of its citizens. Any procedural rule which encourages the result that those proceedings be as free of error as possible is thoroughly desirable, and the contemporaneous-objection rule surely falls within this classification.

We believe the adoption of the *Francis* rule in this situation will have the salutary effect of making the state trial on the merits the "main event," so to speak, rather than a "tryout on the road" for what will later be the determinative federal habeas hearing. There is nothing in the Constitution or in the language of §2254 which requires that the state trial on the issue of guilt or innocence be devoted largely to the testimony of fact witnesses directed to the elements of the state crime, while only later will there occur in a federal habeas hearing a full airing of the federal constitutional claims which were not raised in the state proceedings. If a criminal defendant thinks that an action of the state trial court is about to deprive him of a federal constitutional right there is every reason for his following state procedure in making known his objection.

The "cause"-and-"prejudice" exception of the *Francis* rule will afford an adequate guarantee, we think, that the rule will not prevent a federal habeas court from adjudicating for the first time the federal constitutional claim of a defendant who in the absence of such an adjudication will be the victim of a miscarriage of justice. Whatever precise content may be given those terms by later cases, we feel confident in holding without further elaboration that they do not exist here. Respondent has advanced no explanation whatever for his failure to object at trial, and, as the proceeding unfolded, the trial judge is certainly not to be faulted for failing to question the admission of the confession himself. The other evidence of guilt presented at trial, moreover, was substantial to a degree that would negate any possibility of actual prejudice resulting to the respondent from the admission of his inculpatory statement.

We accordingly conclude that the judgment of the Court of Appeals for the Fifth Circuit must be reversed, and the cause remanded to the United States District Court for the Middle District of Florida with instructions to dismiss respondent's petition for a writ of habeas corpus.

Death by Lottery—Procedural Bar of Constitutional Claims in Capital Cases Due to Inadequate Representation of Indigent Defendants

Stephen B. Bright, 92 W. Va. L. Rev. 679 (1990)

A. The Rationale For Sykes *Is at Odds with the Reality of Representation of the Poor in Capital Cases*

The majority in *Sykes* concluded that its procedural default rule would encourage the presentation of constitutional claims at the state criminal trial, thereby resulting in a trial "as free of error as possible." This assumes a defense counsel who is aware of the constitutional claim and is capable of preserving it. Where this critical ingredient to the adversary process is missing, an onerous procedural bar does nothing to remove a constitutional deficiency from the trial; it simply sweeps it under the rug.

Sykes does not encourage the states to provide competent counsel. Instead, *Sykes* and *Strickland v. Washington*, 466 U.S. 668 (1984), reward them for providing inadequate counsel. The state obtains two benefits from the poor representation the defendant receives: the likelihood of obtaining the death sentence is increased and any constitutional deficiencies that occur in the process may be insulated from review. Ironically, the result of *Sykes* and *Strickland* is that, so long as counsel is not so bad as to fall below the *Strickland* standard, the poorest level of representation at trial receives the least scrutiny in post-conviction review.

Sykes overlooks which side controls the selection of counsel in cases of indigent defendants. Its rationale may apply in the case of knowledgeable, sophisticated defendants who can afford to hire their own lawyers to protect their rights. However, the poor person accused of a crime does not select his attorney; one is appointed for him. A local community, outraged over the murder of one of its members, usually has no incentive to protect the constitutional rights of the one accused of the killing. Often court-appointed counsel do not welcome the assignment or empathize with the plight of their clients. Counsel may have greater loyalty to the community from where future business will come than to the defendant he is appointed to represent. Not infrequently, these court-appointed lawyers are less than zealous in their representation and do not serve the interests of their clients.

The strict procedural default rule adopted in *Sykes* also rests upon the Court's undocumented fear of "sandbagging"—the withholding of meritorious claims by lawyers who somehow know that an appellate court will surely sustain them on appeal. However, the dismal history of representation by court-appointed attorneys in capital cases indicates that most of them lack the sophistication required to "sandbag." An attorney whose total knowledge of criminal law is "*Miranda* and *Dred Scott*" is hardly in a position to recognize and hide many constitutional issues.

But beyond these obvious limitations upon those who defend the poor in capital trials for as little as $1,000 to $2,500, almost any lawyer is going to try to prevail in the forum where the case is tried, not "save" an issue for an uncertain later day in a court whose composition and receptiveness to the issue cannot possibly be calculated at the time of trial.

Notes and Questions

1. The *Sykes* Court stated four reasons for adopting the cause and prejudice standard. First, a contemporaneous objection is preferred because it clarifies the record when recollections of witnesses are freshest. Second, finality in criminal litigation is enhanced by precluding federal review. Third, a stricter standard than *Fay*'s deliberate bypass test will discourage "sandbagging" by defense lawyers "who may take their chances on a verdict of not guilty in a state trial court with the intent to raise their constitutional claims in a federal habeas court if their initial gamble does not pay off." Finally, federal habeas review should be restricted because it detracts from the state trial as a "decisive and portentous event." Do you find these reasons persuasive?

2. Justices Brennan and Marshall dissented from the majority's abandonment of the deliberate bypass rule of *Fay v. Noia*. The dissenters observed that failure to raise an objection at trial often is not the result of conscious decisionmaking on the part of the de-

fendant; rather, it is frequently the result of inadvertence, ignorance, negligence, inexperience or incompetence of trial counsel. According to the dissenters, the *Fay* deliberate bypass rule recognizes this reality while simultaneously protecting the state's interest in strictly applying state procedural bars where the defendant deliberately fails to raise a claim. Moreover, the *Fay* bypass test is superior to the newly-adopted cause and prejudice test because "the bypass test simply refuses to credit what is essentially a lawyer's mistake as a forfeiture of constitutional rights."

3. In his concurrence in *Sykes*, Justice Stevens doubted whether the cause and prejudice standard will assure that defendants will be able to vindicate fundamental miscarriages of justice in federal court. Do you think Justice Stevens' concerns are legitimate? For further discussion of this issue, see Justice Stevens' concurrence in *Murray v. Carrier*, 477 U.S. 478 (1986) (*infra* this chapter) and Justice Stevens' dissent in *Smith v. Murray*, 477 U.S. 527 (1986) (*infra* this chapter).

4. Before *Sykes*, a defendant's failure to preserve a constitutional claim in the state courts would not prevent review in federal court providing the defendant had not deliberately bypassed state procedure. After *Sykes*, defense counsel's failure to comply with a contemporaneous objection rule at trial precluded federal habeas corpus review of a constitutional claim. According to Stephen B. Bright, Director of the Southern Center for Human Rights in Atlanta, the *Sykes* decision significantly increased the burdens of capital attorneys seeking to provide effective assistance of counsel.

> Cases decided after *Sykes* have established virtually impossible requirements that defense counsel must be errorless and capable of anticipating changes in the law. A mistake or negligence on the part of counsel does not excuse a default. Ignorance on the part of counsel of an emerging constitutional theory that is being litigated in other jurisdictions is no excuse for failing to raise an issue. And failure to raise and preserve an issue that is completely without merit under existing case law will bar relief if the right is later recognized.

> For an attorney to provide the representation anticipated by *Sykes* and subsequent cases, he or she must be completely conversant with federal constitutional decisions of the state and federal courts throughout the nation. The lawyer must also keep abreast of developments in all of the federal circuits, the state appellate courts and the writings of commentators. This is necessary so that counsel will be aware of all issues "percolating" in those courts, recognize the "tools to construct [the] constitutional claim" and then raise and present all issues long before they achieve general acceptance in the courts.

> Moreover, the lawyer must be aware of the necessity of raising all of these "percolating" issues even though they may be foreclosed by existing case law of the state and federal courts that have jurisdiction over the case. Otherwise, if the law changes due to a new United States Supreme Court decision, the defendant will be barred from obtaining relief because of his failure to assert an objection when it was meritless.

See Bright, "Death By Lottery—Procedural Bar of Constitutional Claims in Capital Cases Due to Inadequate Representation of Indigent Defendants," 92 W. Va. L. Rev. 679, 687–688 (1990). For further discussion of ineffective assistance of counsel, see *supra* chapter 11.

5. The Court in *Murray v. Carrier*, 477 U.S. 478 (1986) (*infra* this chapter), rejected the claim that a different standard for procedural default should govern when the default occurs on appeal rather than at trial. The Court found that:

[a] State's procedural rules serve vital purposes at trial, on appeal, and on state collateral attack. The important role of appellate procedural rules is aptly captured by the Court's description in *Reed v. Ross*, 468 U.S. 1 (1984) [*infra* this chapter], of the purposes served by the procedural rule at issue there, which required the defendant initially to raise his legal claims on appeal rather than on postconviction review: "It affords the state courts the opportunity to resolve the issue shortly after trial, while evidence is still available both to assess the defendant's claim and to retry the defendant effectively if he prevails in his appeal. This type of rule promotes not only the accuracy and efficiency of judicial decisions, but also the finality of those decisions, by forcing the defendant to litigate all of his claims together, as quickly after trial as the docket will allow, and while the attention of the appellate court is focused on his case." These legitimate state interests, which are manifestly furthered by the comparable procedural rule at issue in this case, warrant our adherence to the conclusion to which they led the Court in *Reed v. Ross*—that the cause and prejudice test applies to defaults on appeal as to those at trial....

The real thrust of respondent's arguments appears to be that on appeal it is inappropriate to hold defendants to the errors of their attorneys. Were we to accept that proposition, defaults on appeal would presumably be governed by a rule equivalent to *Fay v. Noia*'s "deliberate bypass" standard, under which only personal waiver by the defendant would require enforcement of a procedural default. We express no opinion as to whether counsel's decision not to take an appeal at all might require treatment under such a standard, but, for the reasons already given, we hold that counsel's failure to raise a particular claim on appeal is to be scrutinized under the cause and prejudice standard when that failure is treated as a procedural default by the state courts. Attorney error short of ineffective assistance of counsel does not constitute cause for a procedural default even when that default occurs on appeal rather than at trial. To the contrary, cause for a procedural default on appeal ordinarily requires a showing of some external impediment preventing counsel from constructing or raising the claim.

6. Judge Donald P. Lay has argued that the cause and prejudice test does not achieve its intended goals:

First it is very time consuming. The federal district courts must undertake lengthy and excessive analyses to determine first, whether there was a procedural bypass; second, whether there was cause; third, whether there was prejudice; and fourth, whether either the conviction or the death penalty represents a miscarriage of justice. Second, this exacting analysis creates inevitable delay at each level of the federal system—magistrate, district court, appellate court and Supreme Court. Undoubtedly, the Court feels these factors do not override the demands of federalism. However, I find this balance especially difficult to reconcile in light of the more important trade-off—denying prisoners a review of convictions or death sentences that states may have imposed in violation of federal constitutional fairness....

The cause and prejudice standard conflicts with the very purpose of federal habeas corpus. As a court-made rule, the cause and prejudice requirement is designed to artificially provide great deference to state trial and appellate proceedings, thus lending greater integrity to the finality of state court judgements.

… Any rule that protects an unconstitutional state court judgment is hardly worth promoting. Federal habeas corpus was not designed to give deference and comity to state finality rules, but to serve as a vehicle for attacking state convictions that rest upon unconstitutional process.

Lay, "The Writ of Habeas Corpus: A Complex Procedure for a Simple Process," 77 Minn. L. Rev. 1015, 1037–1038 (1993).

7. Section 2254 of the AEDPA does not speak directly to the *Wainwright v. Sykes* cause and prejudice standard although §2254(e)(2) does address the consequences for failure to fully develop the factual basis of a claim in state court.

In contrast, the opt-in provisions of the AEDPA specifically provide that only claims that were actually litigated in state court are amenable to review in federal habeas. Under Chapter 154, claims not raised in state court are foreclosed from review unless the petitioner can show that he falls within one of three exceptions: (1) his failure to raise the claim was the result of state action in violation of the Constitution or federal laws, (2) the failure to raise the claim was the result of the Supreme Court's recognition of a new federal right that is given retroactive effect, or (3) the failure to raise the claim is based on a factual predicate that could not have been discovered through the exercise of due diligence.

D. What Constitutes Cause

In *Wainwright v. Sykes*, the Court adopted a rule requiring petitioners to show cause and prejudice for procedurally defaulting issues during their state trials. This standard requires both that a petitioner show cause for not complying with the state procedural rule and actual prejudice resulting from the alleged constitutional violation. The Court left open, however, the precise scope and nature of what constitutes "cause" for failing to comply with state procedural rules. The definition of "cause" has become a thorny and important question for petitioners seeking federal habeas relief. In *Engle v. Isaac* and *Reed v. Ross*, the Court struggled with the definition and parameters of the "cause" prong of the cause and prejudice standard.

Engle v. Isaac
456 U.S. 107 (1982)

Justice O'CONNOR delivered the opinion of the Court.

[The Court heard *Engle v. Isaac* along with two other cases raising similar issues, *Perini v. Bell* and *Engle v. Hughes*. Isaac was convicted of aggravated assault in Ohio state court in September 1975; Bell was convicted of murder in Ohio state court in April 1975; and Hughes was convicted of voluntary manslaughter in Ohio state court in January 1975. These three cases were unrelated except that each defendant raised self-defense as an affirmative defense to the charges against him. In each case, the trial court instructed the jury that the defendant bore the burden of proving self-defense by a preponderance of the evidence. Neither Isaac, Bell nor Hughes objected to the jury instruction on self-defense. Ohio imposed a contemporaneous objection rule on all criminal defendants which provided, "No person may assign as error any portion of the charge or omission therefrom unless he objects thereto before the jury retires…."

In 1976, the Ohio Supreme Court in *State v. Robinson*, 351 N.E. 2d 88 (1976), ruled that under Ohio law, the defendant only needs to produce *some* evidence of self-defense. Once the defendant makes such a showing, the prosecution bears the burden of disproving self-defense beyond a reasonable doubt. *Robinson* thus presented grounds on which to challenge the self-defense instruction used at the defendants' trials.

Almost five years before the trials of Isaac, Bell and Hughes, the United States Supreme Court in *In re Winship*, 397 U.S. 358 (1970), held that the Due Process Clause of the Fourteenth Amendment requires that the state prove each element of a charged offense beyond a reasonable doubt. In 1975, three months before Isaac's trial, but after the trials of Bell and Hughes, the United States Supreme Court in *Mullaney v. Wilbur*, 421 U.S. 684 (1975), invalidated a state rule requiring a criminal defendant to negate the malice element of the offense of murder by proving that he acted in the heat of passion.

Even though they did not object to the self-defense instruction at trial, Isaac, Bell and Hughes each sought a writ of federal habeas corpus on the ground that the instruction on self-defense violated state law under *Robinson*, and violated the Due Process Clause of the Fourteenth Amendment by shifting the burden of proof on the issue of self-defense to the defendants.

The United States Supreme Court held that a writ of federal habeas corpus could not be used to provide relief for state law errors. The Court then examined whether the potential due process error in the self-defense instruction was barred from review under a writ of habeas corpus because of the defendants' failure to object to the instruction at trial.]

III

B

Respondents seek cause for their defaults in two circumstances. First, they urge that they could not have known at the time of their trials that the Due Process Clause addresses the burden of proving affirmative defenses. Second, they contend that any objection to Ohio's self-defense instruction would have been futile since Ohio had long required criminal defendants to bear the burden of proving this affirmative defense.

We note at the outset that the futility of presenting an objection to the state courts cannot alone constitute cause for a failure to object at trial. If a defendant perceives a constitutional claim and believes it may find favor in the federal courts, he may not bypass the state courts simply because he thinks they will be unsympathetic to the claim. Even a state court that has previously rejected a constitutional argument may decide, upon reflection, that the contention is valid. Allowing criminal defendants to deprive the state courts of this opportunity would contradict the principles supporting *Sykes*.

Respondents' claim, however, is not simply one of futility. They further allege that, at the time they were tried, they could not know that Ohio's self-defense instructions raised constitutional questions. A criminal defendant, they urge, may not waive constitutional objections unknown at the time of trial.

We need not decide whether the novelty of a constitutional claim ever establishes cause for a failure to object. We might hesitate to adopt a rule that would require trial counsel either to exercise extraordinary vision or to object to every aspect of the proceedings in the hope that some aspect might mask a latent constitutional claim. On the other hand, later discovery of a constitutional defect unknown at the time of trial does not invariably render the original trial fundamentally unfair. These concerns, however, need not detain us here since respondents' claims were far from unknown at the time of their trials.

In re Winship, 397 U.S. 358, 364 (1970), decided four and one-half years before the first of respondents' trials, laid the basis for their constitutional claim. In *Winship* we held that "the Due Process Clause protects the accused against conviction except upon proof beyond a reasonable doubt of every fact necessary to constitute the crime with which he is charged." During the five years following this decision, dozens of defendants relied upon this language to challenge the constitutionality of rules requiring them to bear a burden of proof. In most of these cases, the defendants' claims countered well-established principles of law. Nevertheless, numerous courts agreed that the Due Process Clause requires the prosecution to bear the burden of disproving certain affirmative defenses. In light of this activity, we cannot say that respondents lacked the tools to construct their constitutional claim.

We do not suggest that every astute counsel would have relied upon *Winship* to assert the unconstitutionality of a rule saddling criminal defendants with the burden of proving an affirmative defense. Every trial presents a myriad of possible claims. Counsel might have overlooked or chosen to omit respondents' due process argument while pursuing other avenues of defense. We have long recognized, however, that the Constitution guarantees criminal defendants only a fair trial and a competent attorney. It does not insure that defense counsel will recognize and raise every conceivable constitutional claim. Where the basis of a constitutional claim is available, and other defense counsel have perceived and litigated that claim, the demands of comity and finality counsel against labeling alleged unawareness of the objection as cause for a procedural default....

Close analysis of respondents' habeas petitions reveals only one colorable constitutional claim. Because respondents failed to comply with Ohio's procedures for raising that contention, and because they have not demonstrated cause for the default, they are barred from asserting that claim under 28 U.S.C. §2254. The judgments of the Court of Appeals are reversed, and these cases are remanded for proceedings consistent with this opinion.

Reed v. Ross
468 U.S. 1 (1984)

Justice BRENNAN delivered the opinion of the Court.

In March 1969, respondent Daniel Ross was convicted of first-degree murder in North Carolina and sentenced to life imprisonment. At trial, Ross had claimed lack of malice and self-defense. In accordance with well-settled North Carolina law, the trial judge instructed the jury that Ross, the defendant, had the burden of proving each of these defenses. Six years later, this Court decided *Mullaney v. Wilbur*, 421 U.S. 684 (1975), which struck down, as violative of due process, the requirement that the defendant bear the burden of proving the element of malice. Two years later, *Hankerson v. North Carolina*, 432 U.S. 233 (1977), held that *Mullaney* was to have retroactive application. The question presented in this case is whether Ross' attorney forfeited Ross' right to relief under *Mullaney* and *Hankerson* by failing, several years before those cases were decided, to raise on appeal the unconstitutionality of the jury instruction on the burden of proof....

Engle v. Isaac left open the question whether the novelty of a constitutional issue at the time of a state-court proceeding could, as a general matter, give rise to cause for defense counsel's failure to raise the issue in accordance with applicable state procedures. Today, we answer that question in the affirmative.

Because of the broad range of potential reasons for an attorney's failure to comply with a procedural rule, and the virtually limitless array of contexts in which a procedural default can occur, this Court has not given the term "cause" precise content. Nor do we attempt to do so here. Underlying the concept of cause, however, is at least the dual notion that, absent exceptional circumstances, a defendant is bound by the tactical decisions of competent counsel, and that defense counsel may not flout state procedures and then turn around and seek refuge in federal court from the consequences of such conduct. A defense attorney, therefore, may not ignore a State's procedural rules in the expectation that his client's constitutional claims can be raised at a later date in federal court. Similarly, he may not use the prospect of federal habeas corpus relief as a hedge against the strategic risks he takes in his client's defense in state court. In general, therefore, defense counsel may not make a tactical decision to forgo a procedural opportunity—for instance, an opportunity to object at trial or to raise an issue on appeal—and then, when he discovers that the tactic has been unsuccessful, pursue an alternative strategy in federal court. The encouragement of such conduct by a federal court on habeas corpus review would not only offend generally accepted principles of comity, but would also undermine the accuracy and efficiency of the state judicial systems to the detriment of all concerned. Procedural defaults of this nature are, therefore, "inexcusable," and cannot qualify as "cause" for purposes of federal habeas corpus review.

On the other hand, the cause requirement may be satisfied under certain circumstances when a procedural failure is not attributable to an intentional decision by counsel made in pursuit of his client's interests. And the failure of counsel to raise a constitutional issue reasonably unknown to him is one situation in which the requirement is met. If counsel has no reasonable basis upon which to formulate a constitutional question, setting aside for the moment exactly what is meant by "reasonable basis," it is safe to assume that he is sufficiently unaware of the question's latent existence that we cannot attribute to him strategic motives of any sort.

Counsel's failure to raise a claim for which there was no reasonable basis in existing law does not seriously implicate any of the concerns that might otherwise require deference to a State's procedural bar. Just as it is reasonable to assume that a competent lawyer will fail to perceive the possibility of raising such a claim, it is also reasonable to assume that a court will similarly fail to appreciate the claim. It is in the nature of our legal system that legal concepts, including constitutional concepts, develop slowly, finding partial acceptance in some courts while meeting rejection in others. Despite the fact that a constitutional concept may ultimately enjoy general acceptance, as the *Mullaney* issue currently does, when the concept is in its embryonic stage, it will, by hypothesis, be rejected by most courts. Consequently, a rule requiring a defendant to raise a truly novel issue is not likely to serve any functional purpose. Although there is a remote possibility that a given state court will be the first to discover a latent constitutional issue and to order redress if the issue is properly raised, it is far more likely that the court will fail to appreciate the claim and reject it out of hand. Raising such a claim in state court, therefore, would not promote either the fairness or the efficiency of the state criminal justice system. It is true that finality will be disserved if the federal courts reopen a state prisoner's case, even to review claims that were so novel when the cases were in state court that no one would have recognized them. This Court has never held, however, that finality, standing alone, provides a sufficient reason for federal courts to compromise their protection of constitutional rights under §2254.

In addition, if we were to hold that the novelty of a constitutional question does not give rise to cause for counsel's failure to raise it, we might actually disrupt state-court proceedings by encouraging defense counsel to include any and all remotely plausible constitutional claims that could, some day, gain recognition. Particularly disturbed by this prospect, Judge Haynsworth, writing for the Court of Appeals in this case, stated:

> "If novelty were never cause, counsel on appeal would be obliged to raise and argue every conceivable constitutional claim, no matter haw far fetched, in order to preserve a right for post-conviction relief upon some future, unforeseen development in the law. Appellate courts are already overburdened with meritless and frivolous cases and contentions, and an effective appellate lawyer does not dilute meritorious claims with frivolous ones. Lawyers representing appellants should be encouraged to limit their contentions on appeal at least to those which may be legitimately regarded as debatable."

Accordingly, we hold that where a constitutional claim is so novel that its legal basis is not reasonably available to counsel, a defendant has cause for his failure to raise the claim in accordance with applicable state procedures. We therefore turn to the question whether the *Mullaney* issue, which respondent Ross has raised in this action, was sufficiently novel at the time of the appeal from his conviction to excuse his attorney's failure to raise it at that time.

As stated above, the [federal] Court of Appeals found that the state of the law at the time of Ross' appeal did not offer a "reasonable basis" upon which to challenge the jury instructions on the burden of proof. We agree and therefore conclude that Ross had cause for failing to raise the issue at that time. Although the question whether an attorney has a "reasonable basis" upon which to develop a legal theory may arise in a variety of contexts, we confine our attention to the specific situation presented here: one in which this Court has articulated a constitutional principle that had not been previously recognized but which is held to have retroactive application. In *United States v. Johnson*, 457 U.S. 537 (1982), we identified three situations in which a "new" constitutional rule, representing "a clear break with the past," might emerge from this Court. First, a decision of this Court may explicitly overrule one of our precedents. Second, a decision may "overtur[n] a longstanding and widespread practice to which this Court has not spoken, but which a near-unanimous body of lower court authority has expressly approved." And, finally, a decision may "disapprov[e] a practice this Court arguably has sanctioned in prior cases." By definition, when a case falling into one of the first two categories is given retroactive application, there will almost certainly have been no reasonable basis upon which an attorney previously could have urged a state court to adopt the position that this Court has ultimately adopted. Consequently, the failure of a defendant's attorney to have pressed such a claim before a state court is sufficiently excusable to satisfy the cause requirement. Cases falling into the third category, however, present a more difficult question. Whether an attorney had a reasonable basis for pressing a claim challenging a practice that this Court has arguably sanctioned depends on how direct this Court's sanction of the prevailing practice had been, how well entrenched the practice was in the relevant jurisdiction at the time of defense counsel's failure to challenge it, and how strong the available support is from sources opposing the prevailing practice.

This case is covered by the third category. At the time of Ross' appeal, *Leland v. Oregon*, 343 U.S. 790 (1952), was the primary authority addressing the due process constraints upon the imposition of the burden of proof on a defendant in a criminal trial.... *Leland* ... confirmed "the long-accepted rule ... that it was constitutionally permissible to provide that various affirmative defenses were to be proved by the defendant," and arguably sanctioned the practice by which a State crafts an affirmative defense to shift to the defendant the burden of disproving an essential element of a crime.

As stated above, North Carolina had consistently engaged in this practice with respect to the defenses of lack of malice and self-defense for over a century. Indeed, it was not until five years after Ross' appeal that the issue first surfaced in the North Carolina courts, and even then it was rejected out of hand.

Moreover, prior to Ross' appeal, only one Federal Court of Appeals had held that it was unconstitutional to require a defendant to disprove an essential element of a crime for which he is charged. Even that case, however, involved the burden of proving an alibi, which the Court of Appeals described as the "den[ial of] the possibility of [the defendant's] having committed the crime by reason of being elsewhere." The court thus contrasted the alibi defense with "an affirmative defense [which] generally applies to justification for his admitted participation in the act itself," and distinguished *Leland* on that basis. In addition, at the time of Ross' appeal, the Superior Court of Connecticut had struck down, as violative of due process, a statute making it unlawful for an individual to possess burglary tools "without lawful excuse, the proof of which excuse shall be upon him." Because these cases provided only indirect support for Ross' claim, and because they were the only cases that would have supported Ross' claim at all, we cannot conclude that they provided a reasonable basis upon which Ross could have realistically appealed his conviction.

In *Engle v. Isaac*, this Court reached the opposite conclusion with respect to the failure of a group of defendants to raise the *Mullaney* issue in 1975. That case differs from this one, however, in two crucial respects. First, the procedural defaults at issue there occurred five years after we decided *Winship*, which held that "the Due Process Clause protects the accused against conviction except upon proof beyond a reasonable doubt of every fact necessary to constitute the crime with which he is charged." As the Court in *Engle v. Isaac* stated, *Winship* "laid the basis for [the habeas petitioners'] constitutional claim." Second, during those five years, "numerous courts agreed that the Due Process Clause requires the prosecution to bear the burden of disproving certain affirmative defenses." Moreover, as evidence of the reasonableness of the legal basis for raising the *Mullaney* issue in 1975, *Engle v. Isaac* emphasized that "dozens of defendants relied upon [*Winship*] to challenge the constitutionality of rules requiring them to bear a burden of proof." None of these bases of decision relied upon in *Engle v. Isaac* is present in this case.

We therefore conclude that Ross' claim was sufficiently novel in 1969 to excuse his attorney's failure to raise the *Mullaney* issue at that time. Accordingly, we affirm the decision of the Court of Appeals with respect to the question of "cause."

Justice REHNQUIST, with whom the Chief Justice, Justice Blackmun and Justice O'Connor join, dissenting.

Today's decision will make less sense to laymen than it does to lawyers. Respondent Ross was convicted of first degree murder in a North Carolina trial court in 1969. In 1977, eight years later, he instituted the present federal habeas action seeking to have his conviction set aside on the ground that an instruction given by the trial judge improperly placed upon him, rather than on the State, the burden of proving the defenses of "lack of malice" and "self defense." Today, fifteen years after the trial, the Court holds that Ross's conviction must be nullified on federal constitutional grounds. Responding to the State's contention that Ross never raised any objection to the instruction given by the trial judge, and that North Carolina law requires such an objection, the Court blandly states that no competent lawyer in 1969 could have been expected that such an objection would have been sustained, because the law was to the contrary. Consequently, we have the anomalous situation of a jury verdict in a case tried properly by then-prevailing constitutional standards being set aside because of legal developments that occurred long after the North Carolina conviction became final.

Note

Since *Reed* the Supreme Court has reformulated the standards for giving retroactive effect to new rules of law. See chapter 15, *infra*.

E. Inadvertent Error Does Not Constitute Cause

Murray v. Carrier
477 U.S. 478 (1986)

Justice O'CONNOR delivered the opinion of the Court.

[In 1977, a Virginia jury convicted respondent Clifford Carrier of rape and abduction. Before trial, the trial court denied Carrier's discovery request to examine the victim's statements to the police. On appeal, trial counsel initially raised, in his notice of appeal, that the trial court erred in denying Carrier's discovery request. However, in the final petition for appeal, appellate counsel, without consulting Carrier, omitted this claimed error. The Virginia Supreme Court refused the appeal.

Subsequently, Carrier, proceeding *pro se*, raised the discovery issue in his state habeas corpus petition. The state objected to the claim because Carrier did not raise it on direct appeal. The state habeas court dismissed the habeas petition and the Virginia Supreme Court denied certiorari.

Carrier then sought relief in federal court. The district court denied relief citing procedural default and failure to exhaust state remedies. The federal court of appeals found that Carrier need only show that counsel's "failure to object or to appeal his claim was the product of his attorney's ignorance or oversight, not a deliberate tactic," and remanded the case to the district court to apply this standard to the procedural default. The United States Supreme Court granted certiorari "to consider whether a federal habeas petitioner can show cause for a procedural default by establishing that competent defense counsel inadvertently failed to raise the substantive claim of error rather than deliberately withholding it for tactical reasons."]

II

Wainwright v. Sykes held that a federal habeas petitioner who has failed to comply with a State's contemporaneous-objection rule at trial must show cause for the procedural default and prejudice attributable thereto in order to obtain review of his defaulted constitutional claim. In so holding, the Court explicitly rejected the standard described in *Fay v. Noia*, under which a federal habeas court could refuse to review a defaulted claim only if "an applicant ha[d] deliberately by-passed the orderly procedure of the state courts," by personal waiver of the claim amounting to " 'an intentional relinquishment or abandonment of a known right or privilege.' " At a minimum, then, *Wainwright v. Sykes* plainly implied that default of a constitutional claim by counsel pursuant to a trial strategy or tactical decision would, absent extraordinary circumstances, bind the habeas petitioner even if he had not personally waived that claim. Beyond that, the Court left open "for resolution in future decisions the precise definition of the 'cause'-and-'prejudice' standard."

We revisited the cause and prejudice test in *Engle v. Isaac*, 456 U.S. 107 (1982)....

The thrust of ... our decision in *Engle* is unmistakable: the mere fact that counsel failed to recognize the factual or legal basis for a claim, or failed to raise the claim despite recognizing it, does not constitute cause for a procedural default....

We think, then, that the question of cause for a procedural default does not turn on whether counsel erred or on the kind of error counsel may have made. So long as a defendant is represented by counsel whose performance is not constitutionally ineffective under the standard established in *Strickland v. Washington*, 466 U.S. 668 (1984), we discern no inequity in requiring him to bear the risk of attorney error that results in a procedural default. Instead, we think that the existence of cause for a procedural default must ordinarily turn on whether the prisoner can show that some objective factor external to the defense impeded counsel's efforts to comply with the State's procedural rule. Without attempting an exhaustive catalog of such objective impediments to compliance with a procedural rule, we note that a showing that the factual or legal basis for a claim was not reasonably available to counsel, or that "some interference by officials" made compliance impracticable, would constitute cause under this standard.

Similarly, if the procedural default is the result of ineffective assistance of counsel, the Sixth Amendment itself requires that responsibility for the default be imputed to the State, which may not "conduc[t] trials at which persons who face incarceration must defend themselves without adequate legal assistance." *Cuyler v. Sullivan*, 446 U.S. 335, 344 (1980). Ineffective assistance of counsel, then, is cause for a procedural default. However, we think that the exhaustion doctrine, which is "principally designed to protect the state courts' role in the enforcement of federal law and prevent disruption of state judicial proceedings," generally requires that a claim of ineffective assistance be presented to the state courts as an independent claim before it may be used to establish cause for a procedural default. The question whether there is cause for a procedural default does not pose any occasion for applying the exhaustion doctrine when the federal habeas court can adjudicate the question of cause—a question of federal law—without deciding an independent and unexhausted constitutional claim on the merits. But if a petitioner could raise his ineffective assistance claim for the first time on federal habeas in order to show cause for a procedural default, the federal habeas court would find itself in the anomalous position of adjudicating an unexhausted constitutional claim for which state court review might still be available. The principle of comity that underlies the exhaustion doctrine would be ill served by a rule that allowed a federal district court "to upset a state court conviction without an opportunity to the state courts to correct a constitutional violation," and that holds true whether an ineffective assistance claim is asserted as cause for a procedural default or denominated as an independent ground for habeas relief....

III

However, as we also noted in *Engle*, "[i]n appropriate cases" the principles of comity and finality that inform the concepts of cause and prejudice "must yield to the imperative of correcting a fundamentally unjust incarceration." We remain confident that, for the most part, "victims of a fundamental miscarriage of justice will meet the cause-and-prejudice standard." But we do not pretend that this will always be true. Accordingly, we think that in an extraordinary case, where a constitutional violation has probably resulted in the conviction of one who is actually innocent, a federal habeas court may grant the writ even in the absence of a showing of cause for the procedural default.

There is an additional safeguard against miscarriages of justice in criminal cases, and one not yet recognized in state criminal trials when many of the opinions on which the concurrence relies were written. That safeguard is the right to effective assistance of counsel, which, as this Court has indicated, may in a particular case be violated by even an isolated error of counsel if that error is sufficiently egregious and prejudicial. The presence of such a safeguard may properly inform this Court's judgment in determining "[w]hat standards should govern the exercise of the habeas court's equitable discretion" with respect to procedurally defaulted claims. The ability to raise ineffective assistance claims based in whole or in part on counsel's procedural defaults substantially undercuts any predictions of unremedied manifest injustices. We therefore remain of the view that adherence to the cause and prejudice test "in the conjunctive" will not prevent federal habeas courts from ensuring the "fundamental fairness [that] is the central concern of the writ of habeas corpus."

The cause and prejudice test may lack a perfect historical pedigree. But the Court acknowledged as much in *Wainwright v. Sykes*, noting its "historic willingness to overturn or modify its earlier views of the scope of the writ, even where the statutory language authorizing judicial action has remained unchanged." The cause and prejudice test as interpreted in *Engle* and in our decision today is, we think, a sound and workable means of channeling the discretion of federal habeas courts

IV

Respondent has never alleged any external impediment that might have prevented counsel from raising his discovery claim in his petition for review, and has disavowed any claim that counsel's performance on appeal was so deficient as to make out an ineffective assistance claim. Respondent's petition for federal habeas review of his procedurally defaulted discovery claim must therefore be dismissed for failure to establish cause for the default, unless it is determined on remand that the victim's statements contain material that would establish respondent's actual innocence. The judgment of the Court of Appeals is reversed, and the case is remanded for further proceedings consistent with this opinion.

Justice STEVENS, with whom Justice Blackmun joins, concurring in the judgment.

The heart of this case is a prisoner's claim that he was denied access to material that might have established his innocence. The significance of such a claim can easily be lost in a procedural maze of enormous complexity....

I

The character of respondent's constitutional claim should be central to an evaluation of his habeas corpus petition. Before and during his trial on charges of rape and abduction, his counsel made timely motions for discovery of the statements made by the victim to the police. By denying those motions, the trial court significantly curtailed the defendant's ability to cross-examine the prosecution's most important witness, and may well have violated the defendant's right to review "evidence favorable to an accused upon request ... where the evidence is material either to guilt or to punishment." *Brady v. Maryland*, 373 U.S. 83, 87 (1963). That right is unquestionably protected by the Due Process Clause. Indeed, the Court has repeatedly emphasized the fundamental importance of that federal right.

The constitutional claim advanced by respondent calls into question the accuracy of the determination of his guilt. On the record before us, however, we cannot determine whether or not he is the victim of a miscarriage of justice. Respondent argues that the trial court's analysis was severely flawed. Even if the trial judge applied the correct standard, the conclusion that there was no "exculpatory" material in the victim's statements does not foreclose the possibility that inconsistencies between the statements and the direct testimony would have enabled an effective cross-examination to demonstrate that respondent is actually innocent. On the other hand, it is possible that other evidence of guilt in the record is so overwhelming that the trial judge's decision was clearly not prejudicial to the defendant. The important point is that we cannot evaluate the possibility that respondent may be the victim of a fundamental miscarriage of justice without any knowledge about the contents of the victim's statements....

II

In my opinion, the "cause and prejudice" formula that the Court explicates in such detail today is not dispositive when the fundamental fairness of a prisoner's conviction is at issue. That formula is of recent vintage, particularly in comparison to the writ for which it is invoked. It is, at most, part of a broader inquiry into the demands of justice....

In a recent exposition of the "cause and prejudice" standard, moreover, the Court again emphasized that "cause and prejudice" must be considered within an overall inquiry into justice. In *Engle v. Isaac*, 456 U.S. 107 (1982), the Court closed its opinion with the assurance that it would not allow its judge-made "cause" and "actual prejudice" standard to become so rigid that it would foreclose a claim of this kind:

> The terms "cause" and "actual prejudice" are not rigid concepts; they take their meaning from the principles of comity and finality discussed above. In appropriate cases those principles must yield to the imperative of correcting a fundamentally unjust incarceration. Since we are confident that victims of a fundamental miscarriage of justice will meet the cause-and-prejudice standard, we decline to adopt the more vague inquiry suggested by the words "plain error."

In order to be faithful to that promise, we must recognize that cause and prejudice are merely components of a broader inquiry which, in this case, cannot be performed without an examination of the victim's statements....

IV

Procedural default that is adequate to foreclose appellate review of a claim of constitutional error in a state criminal trial should ordinarily also bar collateral review of such a claim in a federal district court. But the history of the Court's jurisprudence interpreting the Acts of Congress authorizing the issuance of the writ of habeas corpus unambiguously requires that we carefully preserve the exception which enables the federal writ to grant relief in cases of manifest injustice. That exception cannot be adequately defined by a simply stated rule. The procedural default is always an important factor to be carefully reviewed; as Justice Frankfurter explained: "All that has gone before is not to be ignored as irrelevant." But it is equally clear that the prisoner must always have some opportunity to reopen his case if he can make a sufficient showing that he is the victim of a fundamental miscarriage of justice. Whether the inquiry is channeled by the use of the terms "cause" and "prejudice"—or by the statutory duty to "dispose of the matter as law and justice require," 28 U.S.C. §2243—it is clear to me that appellate procedural default should not foreclose habeas corpus review of a meritorious constitutional claim that may establish the prisoner's innocence.

The Court is therefore entirely correct in its decision to remand the case for further proceedings on the substance of respondent's claim. Because we did not grant certiorari to consider the proper standard that should govern the further proceedings in the District Court, and because we have not had the benefit of briefs or argument concerning that standard, I express no opinion on the Court's suggestion that the absence of "cause" for his procedural default requires respondent to prove that the "constitutional violation has probably resulted in the conviction of one who is actually innocent," or on the relationship of that standard to the principles explicated in [cases governing the suppression of evidence]. There will be time enough to consider the proper standard after the District Court has examined the victim's statements and made whatever findings may be appropriate to determine whether "law and justice require" the issuance of the Great Writ in this case.

Accordingly, I concur in the judgment but not in the Court's opinion.

Note and Question

The Court in *Murray v. Carrier*, 477 U.S. 478 (1986), concluded that ineffective assistance of counsel constitutes cause for procedural default. However, the Court further found that the exhaustion doctrine requires that a claim of ineffective assistance of counsel must first be raised in state court before it may be used to show cause for a procedural default. If the ineffective assistance of counsel occurs during direct appeal, how, as a practical matter, will the issue of ineffective assistance of counsel be presented to the state courts?

F. Procedural Default as Ineffective Assistance

Smith v. Murray
477 U.S. 527 (1986)

Justice O'CONNOR delivered the opinion of the Court.

[Petitioner Michael Marnell Smith was convicted of the rape and murder of Audry Weiler. Prior to trial, petitioner's court-appointed attorney, David Pugh, requested the appointment of a psychiatrist, Dr. Wendell Pile, to examine Smith. Although counsel generally advised Smith not to discuss prior criminal episodes with anyone, he did not specifically advise Smith not to tell Dr. Pile about prior offenses. During the examination, Dr. Pile questioned Smith about the crime and prior incidents of deviate sexual behavior. After initially declining to answer, Smith told Dr. Pile that "he had once torn the clothes off a girl on a school bus before deciding not to carry out his original plan to rape her." In accordance with Virginia law, Dr. Pile's report and diagnosis, along with this statement, was forwarded to Smith, the district attorney, and the trial court.

During the sentencing phase the district attorney, over Smith's objections, called Dr. Pile to testify about the school bus incident and his diagnosis of petitioner. The jury, after lengthy deliberations, recommended that Smith be sentenced to death. Smith appealed his conviction raising thirteen separate claims. However, he did not raise as an error on appeal the admission of Dr. Pile's testimony because he believed that Virginia case law would not support the claim. An *amicus curiae* brief filed by the University of Virginia Law School Post-Conviction Assistance Project did raise the Pile issue. The state supreme court affirmed Smith's conviction and sentence and refused to address claims in the *amicus* brief that were not raised in Smith's brief.

Smith then sought state habeas relief raising for the first time since trial the claim that Pile's testimony violated the Fifth and Fourteenth Amendments. The state habeas court found that Smith had forfeited this claim by failing to raise it on direct appeal and, at a subsequent hearing, determined that Smith's lawyer was not ineffective. Smith's conviction and sentence were again affirmed.

Smith next sought federal habeas relief. The federal district court denied the petition and the court of appeals affirmed. The United States Supreme Court granted certiorari.

The Court initially "granted certiorari to decide whether and, if so, under what circumstances, a prosecutor may elicit testimony from a mental health professional concerning the content of an interview conducted to explore the possibility of presenting psychiatric defenses at trial," and "to review the Court of Appeals' determination that any error in the admission of the psychiatrist's evidence in this case was irrelevant under the holding of *Zant v. Stephens*, 462 U.S. 862 (1983)." However, the Court, on examination, concluded that Smith defaulted his underlying constitutional claim by failing to press it before the Supreme Court of Virginia on direct appeal. Accordingly, the Court declined to address the merits of Smith's claims and affirmed the judgment dismissing the petition for a writ of habeas corpus.]

II

... We need not determine whether petitioner has carried his burden of showing actual prejudice from the allegedly improper admission of Dr. Pile's testimony, for we think it self-evident that he has failed to demonstrate cause for his noncompliance with Virginia's procedures. We have declined in the past to essay a comprehensive catalog of the circumstances that would justify a finding of cause. Our cases, however, leave no doubt that a deliberate, tactical decision not to pursue a particular claim is the very antithesis of the kind of circumstance that would warrant excusing a defendant's failure to adhere to a State's legitimate rules for the fair and orderly disposition of its criminal cases....

Here the record unambiguously reveals that petitioner's counsel objected to the admission of Dr. Pile's testimony at trial and then consciously elected not to pursue that claim before the Supreme Court of Virginia. The basis for that decision was counsel's perception that the claim had little chance of success in the Virginia courts. With the benefit of hindsight, petitioner's counsel in this Court now contends that this perception proved to be incorrect. Even assuming that to be the case, however, a State's subsequent acceptance of an argument deliberately abandoned on direct appeal is irrelevant to the question whether the default should be excused on federal habeas. Indeed, it is the very prospect that a state court "may decide, upon reflection, that the contention is valid" that undergirds the established rule that "perceived futility alone cannot constitute cause," for "[a]llowing criminal defendants to deprive the state courts of [the] opportunity" to reconsider previously rejected constitutional claims is fundamentally at odds with the principles of comity that animate *Sykes* and its progeny.

Notwithstanding the deliberate nature of the decision not to pursue his objection to Dr. Pile's testimony on appeal—a course of conduct virtually dispositive of any effort to satisfy *Sykes'* "cause" requirement—petitioner contends that the default should be excused because Mr. Pugh's decision, though deliberate, was made in ignorance. Had he investigated the claim more fully, petitioner maintains, "it is inconceivable that he would have concluded that the claim was without merit or that he would have failed to raise it."

The argument is squarely foreclosed by our decision in *Murray v. Carrier,* which holds that "the mere fact that counsel failed to recognize the factual or legal basis for a claim, or failed to raise the claim despite recognizing it, does not constitute cause for a procedural default." Nor can it seriously be maintained that the decision not to press the claim on appeal was an error of such magnitude that it rendered counsel's performance constitutionally deficient under the test of *Strickland v. Washington. Carrier* reaffirmed that "the right to effective assistance of counsel ... may in a particular case be violated by even an isolated error ... if that error is sufficiently egregious and prejudicial." But counsel's deliberate decision not to pursue his objection to the admission of Dr. Pile's testimony falls far short of meeting that rigorous standard. After conducting a vigorous defense at both the guilt and sentencing phases of the trial, counsel surveyed the extensive transcript, researched a number of claims, and decided that, under the current state of the law, 13 were worth pursuing on direct appeal. This process of "winnowing out weaker arguments on appeal and focusing on" those more likely to prevail, far from being evidence of incompetence, is the hallmark of effective appellate advocacy. It will often be the case that even the most informed counsel will fail to anticipate a state appellate court's willingness to reconsider a prior holding or will underestimate the likelihood that a federal habeas court will repudiate an established state rule. But, as *Strickland v. Washington* made clear, "[a] fair assessment of attorney performance requires that every effort be made to eliminate the distorting effects of hindsight, to reconstruct the circumstances of counsel's challenged conduct, and to evaluate the conduct from counsel's perspective at the time." Viewed in light of Virginia law at the time Mr. Pugh submitted his opening brief to the Supreme Court of Virginia, the decision not to pursue his objection to the admission of Dr. Pile's testimony fell well within the "wide range of professionally competent assistance" required under the Sixth Amendment to the Federal Constitution.

Nor can petitioner rely on the novelty of his legal claim as "cause" for noncompliance with Virginia's rules. Petitioner contends that this Court's decisions in *Estelle v. Smith,* 451 U.S. 454 (1981), and *Ake v. Oklahoma,* 470 U.S. 68 (1985), which were decided well after the affirmance of his conviction and sentence on direct appeal, lend support to his position that Dr. Pile's testimony should have been excluded. But ... the question is not whether subsequent legal developments have made counsel's task easier, but whether at the time of the default the claim was "available" at all. As petitioner has candidly conceded, various forms of the claim he now advances had been percolating in the lower courts for years at the time of his original appeal. Moreover, in this very case, an *amicus* before the Supreme Court of Virginia specifically argued that admission of Dr. Pile's testimony violated petitioner's rights under the Fifth and Sixth Amendments. Under these circumstances, it simply is not open to argument that the legal basis of the claim petitioner now presses on federal habeas was unavailable to counsel at the time of the direct appeal.

We conclude, therefore, that petitioner has not carried his burden of showing cause for noncompliance with Virginia's rules of procedure. That determination, however, does not end our inquiry. As we noted in *Engle* and reaffirmed in *Carrier,* "'[i]n appropriate cases' the principles of comity and finality that inform the concepts of cause and prejudice 'must yield to the imperative of correcting a fundamentally unjust incarceration.' " Accordingly, "where a constitutional violation has probably resulted in the conviction of one who is actually innocent, a federal habeas court may grant the writ even in the absence of a showing of cause for the procedural default."

We acknowledge that the concept of "actual," as distinct from "legal," innocence does not translate easily into the context of an alleged error at the sentencing phase of a trial on a capital offense. Nonetheless, we think it clear on this record that application of the cause and prejudice test will not result in a "fundamental miscarriage of justice." ... [T]he alleged constitutional error [in this case] neither precluded the development of true facts nor resulted in the admission of false ones. Thus, even assuming that, as a legal matter, Dr. Pile's testimony should not have been presented to the jury, its admission did not serve to pervert the jury's deliberations concerning the ultimate question whether in fact petitioner constituted a continuing threat to society. Under these circumstances, we do not believe that refusal to consider the defaulted claim on federal habeas carries with it the risk of a manifest miscarriage of justice.

Nor can we concur in Justice Stevens' suggestion that we displace established procedural default principles with an amorphous "fundamental fairness" inquiry. Precisely which parts of the Constitution are "fundamental" and which are not is left for future elaboration. But, for Justice Stevens, when a defendant in a capital case raises a "substantial, colorable" constitutional claim, a federal court should entertain it no matter how egregious the violation of state procedural rules, and regardless of the fairness of the opportunity to raise that claim in the course of his trial and appeal. We reject the suggestion that the principles of *Wainwright v. Sykes* apply differently depending on the nature of the penalty a State imposes for the violation of its criminal laws. We similarly reject the suggestion that there is anything "fundamentally unfair" about enforcing procedural default rules in cases devoid of any substantial claim that the alleged error undermined the accuracy of the guilt or sentencing determination. In view of the profound societal costs that attend the exercise of habeas jurisdiction, such exercise "carries a serious burden of justification." When the alleged error is unrelated to innocence, and when the defendant was represented by competent counsel, had a full and fair opportunity to press his claim in the state system, and yet failed to do so in violation of a legitimate rule of procedure, that burden has not been carried.

Accordingly, we affirm the judgment of the Court of Appeals upholding the dismissal of petitioner's application for a writ of habeas corpus.

Justice STEVENS, with whom Justice Marshall and Justice Blackmun join ... dissenting.

The record in this case unquestionably demonstrates that petitioner's constitutional claim is meritorious, and that there is a significant risk that he will be put to death *because* his constitutional rights were violated.

The Court does not take issue with this conclusion. It is willing to assume that (1) petitioner's Fifth Amendment right against compelled self-incrimination was violated; (2) his Eighth Amendment right to a fair, constitutionally sound sentencing proceeding was violated by the introduction of the evidence from that Fifth Amendment violation; and (3) those constitutional violations made the difference between life and death in the jury's consideration of his fate. Although the constitutional violations and issues were sufficiently serious that this Court decided to grant certiorari, this Court concludes that petitioner's presumably meritorious constitutional claim is procedurally barred and that petitioner must therefore be executed.

In my opinion, the Court should reach the merits of petitioner's argument. To the extent that there has been a procedural "default," it is exceedingly minor—perhaps a kind of "harmless" error. Petitioner's counsel raised a timely objection to the introduction of the evidence obtained in violation of the Fifth Amendment. A respected friend of the Court—the University of Virginia Law School's Post-Conviction Assistance Project—brought the issue to the attention of the Virginia Supreme Court in an extensive *amicus curiae* brief. Smith's counsel also raised the issue in state and federal habeas corpus proceedings, and, as noted, the Court of Appeals decided the case on the merits. Consistent with the well-established principle that appellate arguments should be carefully winnowed, however, Smith's counsel did not raise the Fifth Amendment issue in his original appeal to the Virginia Supreme Court—an unsurprising decision in view of the fact that a governing Virginia Supreme Court precedent, which was then entirely valid and only two years old, decisively barred the claim.

Nevertheless, the Court finds the lawyer's decision not to include the constitutional claim "virtually dispositive." The Court offers the remarkable explanation that "[u]nder these circumstances"—in which petitioner's death penalty will stand despite serious Fifth and Eighth Amendment violations that played a critical role in the determination that death is an appropriate penalty—"we do not believe that refusal to consider the defaulted claim on federal habeas carries with it the risk of a manifest miscarriage of justice." ...

II

The introduction of petitioner's comments to the court-appointed psychiatrist clearly violated the Fifth Amendment. As the majority points out, psychiatric reports by court-appointed psychiatrists "were routinely forwarded to the court and ... were then admissible under Virginia law." However, "[a]t no point prior to or during the interview did Dr. Pile inform petitioner that his statements might later be used against him or that he had the right to remain silent and to have counsel present if he so desired." Moreover, the court-appointed psychiatrist related petitioner's description of an earlier sexual assault in a letter to the court and to the prosecution, as well as to the defense, and testified about the description, at the State's request, at petitioner's capital sentencing hearing. The State thus relied on Dr. Pile's testimony as evidence of "future dangerousness," one of the two aggravating circumstances found by the jury to justify a sentence of death....

Given the historic importance of the Fifth Amendment, and the fact that the violation of this right made a significant difference in the jury's evaluation of petitioner's "future dangerousness" (and consequent death sentence), it is not only proper, but imperative, that the federal courts entertain petitioner's entirely meritorious argument that the introduction of the psychiatrist's testimony at his sentencing hearing violated that fundamental protection.

III

It is also quite clear that the introduction of the evidence violated his Eighth Amendment right to a fair sentencing proceeding....

IV

Thus, I would not only reach the merits of petitioner's constitutional claim but also would conclude that it has merit. The question that remains is the one the Court addresses in the last two paragraphs of its opinion—whether the constitutional error warrants the conclusion that the death penalty should be set aside in this habeas corpus proceeding. I think that question should be answered by reference to the language of the governing statute—the writ should issue "as law and justice require." To hold, as the Court does today, that petitioner's death sentence must stand despite the fact that blatant constitutional violations presumably made the difference between the jury's recommendation of life or death, violates not only "law," but, quite clearly, "justice" as well.

I respectfully dissent.

Notes and Question

1. For a review of the psychiatric issues raised in *Smith v. Murray*, see *supra* chapter 10.

2. *Coleman v. Thompson*, 501 U.S. 722 (1991) (*infra* this chapter), also addresses attorney error as cause to excuse default in federal habeas. After Coleman's conviction and sentence were affirmed on direct appeal in state court, Coleman filed a petition for post-conviction relief in state court. The lower state court again affirmed his conviction and sentence. Coleman next sought relief in the state supreme court. Unfortunately, counsel filed the notice of appeal three days after the notice was required to be filed. The State of Virginia filed a motion to dismiss on the ground that the appeal was not filed in a timely manner and the state supreme court granted the motion. Coleman next filed a petition for habeas corpus in federal court but was denied relief because he had procedurally defaulted in state court.

Coleman argued that the attorney error in failing to timely file the state appeal constituted sufficient cause to excuse default in federal habeas. The Supreme Court disagreed.

> ... There is no constitutional right to an attorney in state post-conviction proceedings. Consequently, a petitioner cannot claim constitutionally ineffective assistance of counsel in such proceedings. Coleman contends that it was his attorney's error that led to the late filing of his state habeas appeal. This error cannot be constitutionally ineffective, therefore Coleman must "bear the risk of attorney error that results in a procedural default." ...
>
> Because Coleman had no right to counsel to pursue his appeal in state habeas, any attorney error that led to the default of Coleman's claims in state court cannot constitute cause to excuse the default in federal habeas. As Coleman does not argue in this Court that federal review of his claims is necessary to prevent a fundamental miscarriage of justice, he is barred from bringing these claims in federal habeas. Accordingly, the judgment of the Court of Appeals is affirmed.

3. Was Coleman's federal habeas attorney ineffective for failing to allege that federal review of Coleman's claims was necessary to prevent a fundamental miscarriage of justice?

4. Section 2254(i) of the AEDPA provides, "The effectiveness or incompetence of counsel during Federal or State collateral post-conviction proceedings shall not be a ground for relief in a proceeding arising under section 2254."

5. In remarks made at the Judicial Conference of the Second Circuit, Justice Thurgood Marshall addressed the problem of procedural default and ineffective assistance of counsel.

> Pressing against the capital defendant from the other side is the Supreme Court's restrictive definition of what constitutes unconstitutional ineffective assistance of counsel at trial. The severe rules the Court has adopted to assure that the trial is the "main event" have been unaccompanied by measures to ensure the fairness and accuracy of that event. The Court has not yet recognized that the right of effective assistance must encompass a right to counsel familiar

with death penalty jurisprudence at the trial stage. Instead, in all but the most egregious case, a court cannot or will not make a finding of ineffective assistance of counsel because counsel has met what the Supreme Court has defined as a minimal standard of competence for criminal lawyers. As a consequence, many capital defendants find that errors by their lawyers preclude presentation of substantial constitutional claims, but that such errors—with the resulting forfeitures of rights—are not sufficient in themselves to constitute ineffective assistance.

Marshall, "Remarks on the Death Penalty Made at the Judicial Conference of the Second Circuit," 86 Colum. L. Rev. 1 (1986).

G. Adequate and Independent State Grounds

As demonstrated by *Wainwright v. Sykes*, a petitioner who fails to present a federal constitutional claim to the state court—in the manner prescribed by the state court's procedural rules—runs the risk that the state will refuse to address the merits of the claim on the basis of procedural default. Most frequently, procedural default occurs when a defendant fails to follow the state's rules requiring the defendant to make a contemporaneous objection to improprieties which occur at trial. Federal courts' jurisdiction extends only to issues of federal law. As both pre-AEDPA law and the current §2254(a) state, "The Supreme Court, a Justice thereof, a circuit judge, or a district court shall entertain an application for a writ of habeas corpus in behalf of a person in custody pursuant to the judgment of a State court only on the ground that he is in custody in violation of the Constitution or laws or treaties of the United States." Thus, as the Court made clear in *Michigan v. Long* (below), if the state court decision refusing to address the merits of the defendant's claim rests upon "adequate and independent state grounds," the federal courts lack jurisdiction over the dispute.

Michigan v. Long
463 U.S. 1032 (1983)

Justice O'CONNOR delivered the opinion of the Court.

[David Kerk Long was convicted of possessing marijuana which the police found in the passenger compartment and trunk of the car he was driving. The Supreme Court of Michigan reversed Long's conviction because "the sole justification of the ... search, protection of police officers and others nearby, cannot justify the search in this case."]

II

Before reaching the merits [of Long's search and seizure claim], we must consider Long's argument that we are without jurisdiction to decide this case because the decision [of the state Supreme Court] ... rests on an adequate and independent state ground. The court below referred twice to the state constitution in its opinion, but otherwise relied exclusively on federal law. Long argues that the Michigan courts have provided greater protection from searches and seizures under the state constitution than is afforded under the Fourth Amendment, and the references to the state constitution therefore establish an adequate and independent ground for the decision below.

It is, of course, "incumbent upon this Court ... to ascertain for itself ... whether the asserted non-federal ground independently and adequately supports the judgment." Although we have announced a number of principles in order to help us determine whether various forms of references to state law constitute adequate and independent state grounds, we openly admit that we have thus far not developed a satisfying and consistent approach for resolving this vexing issue. In some instances, we have taken the strict view that if the ground of decision was at all unclear, we would dismiss the case. In other instances, we have vacated or continued a case in order to obtain clarification about the nature of a state court decision. In more recent cases, we have ourselves examined state law to determine whether state courts have used federal law to guide their application of state law or to provide the actual basis for the decision that was reached....

This ad hoc method of dealing with cases that involve possible adequate and independent state grounds is antithetical to the doctrinal consistency that is required when sensitive issues of federal-state relations are involved. Moreover, none of the various methods of disposition that we have employed thus far recommends itself as the preferred method that we should apply to the exclusion of others, and we therefore determine that it is appropriate to reexamine our treatment of this jurisdictional issue in order to achieve the consistency that is necessary.

The process of examining state law is unsatisfactory because it requires us to interpret state laws with which we are generally unfamiliar, and which often, as in this case, have not been discussed at length by the parties. Vacation and continuance for clarification have also been unsatisfactory both because of the delay and decrease in efficiency of judicial administration and, more important, because these methods of disposition place significant burdens on state courts to demonstrate the presence or absence of our jurisdiction. Finally, outright dismissal of cases is clearly not a panacea because it cannot be doubted that there is an important need for uniformity in federal law, and that this need goes unsatisfied when we fail to review an opinion that rests primarily upon federal grounds and where the *independence* of an alleged state ground is not apparent from the four corners of the opinion. We have long recognized that dismissal is inappropriate "where there is strong indication ... that the federal constitution as judicially construed controlled the decision below."

Respect for the independence of state courts, as well as avoidance of rendering advisory opinions, have been the cornerstones of this Court's refusal to decide cases where there is an adequate and independent state ground. It is precisely because of this respect for state courts, and this desire to avoid advisory opinions, that we do not wish to continue to decide issues of state law that go beyond the opinion that we review, or to require state courts to reconsider cases to clarify the grounds of their decisions. Accordingly, when, as in this case, a state court decision fairly appears to rest primarily on federal law, or to be interwoven with the federal law, and when the adequacy and independence of any possible state law ground is not clear from the face of the opinion, we will accept as the most reasonable explanation that the state court decided the case the way it did because it believed that federal law required it to do so. If a state court chooses merely to rely on federal precedents as it would on the precedents of all other jurisdictions, then it need only make clear by a plain statement in its judgment or opinion that the federal cases are being used only for the purpose of guidance, and do not themselves compel the result that the court has reached. In this way, both justice and judicial administration will be greatly improved. If the state court decision indicates clearly and expressly that it is alternatively based on bona fide separate, adequate, and independent grounds, we, of course, will not undertake to review the decision.

This approach obviates in most instances the need to examine state law in order to decide the nature of the state court decision, and will at the same time avoid the danger of our rendering advisory opinions. It also avoids the unsatisfactory and intrusive practice of requiring state courts to clarify their decisions to the satisfaction of this Court. We believe that such an approach will provide state judges with a clearer opportunity to develop state jurisprudence unimpeded by federal interference, and yet will preserve the integrity of federal law. "It is fundamental that state courts be left free and unfettered by us in interpreting their state constitutions. But it is equally important that ambiguous or obscure adjudications by state courts do not stand as barriers to a determination by this Court of the validity under the federal constitution of state action."

The principle that we will not review judgments of state courts that rest on adequate and independent state grounds is based, in part, on "the limitations of our own jurisdiction."[7] The jurisdictional concern is that we not "render an advisory opinion, and if the same judgment would be rendered by the state court after we corrected its views of federal laws, our review could amount to nothing more than an advisory opinion." Our requirement of a "plain statement" that a decision rests upon adequate and independent state grounds does not in any way authorize the rendering of advisory opinions. Rather, in determining, as we must, whether we have jurisdiction to review a case that is alleged to rest on adequate and independent state grounds, we merely assume that there are no such grounds when it is not clear from the opinion itself that the state court relied upon an adequate and independent state ground and when it fairly appears that the state court rested its decision primarily on federal law.

Our review of the decision below under this framework leaves us unconvinced that it rests upon an independent state ground. Apart from its two citations to the state constitution, the court below relied exclusively on its understanding of *Terry v. Ohio*, 392 U.S. 1 (1968), and other federal cases. Not a single state case was cited to support the state court's holding that the search of the passenger compartment was unconstitutional.... The references to the state constitution in no way indicate that the decision below rested on grounds in any way independent from the state court's interpretation of federal law. Even if we accept that the Michigan constitution has been interpreted to provide independent protection for certain rights also secured under the Fourth Amendment, it fairly appears in this case that the Michigan Supreme Court rested its decision primarily on federal law.

Rather than dismissing the case, or requiring that the state court reconsider its decision on our behalf solely because of a mere possibility that an adequate and independent ground supports the judgment, we find that we have jurisdiction in the absence of a plain statement that the decision below rested on an adequate and independent state ground. It appears to us that the state court "felt compelled by what it understood to be federal constitutional considerations to construe ... its own law in the manner it did."

---

7. In *Herb v. Pitcairn*, 324 U.S. 117, 128 (1945), the Court also wrote that it was desirable that state courts "be asked rather than told what they have intended." It is clear that we have already departed from that view in those cases in which we have examined state law to determine whether a particular result was guided or compelled by federal law. Our decision today departs further from *Herb* insofar as we disfavor further requests to state courts for clarification, and we require a clear and express statement that a decision rests on adequate and independent state grounds. However, the "plain statement" rule protects the integrity of state courts for the reasons discussed above. The preference for clarification expressed in *Herb* has failed to be a completely satisfactory means of protecting the state and federal interests that are involved.

[After concluding that the search of respondent's car was proper under federal law, the Court reversed the Michigan Supreme Court, and remanded for further proceedings.]

Harris v. Reed

489 U.S. 255 (1989)

Justice BLACKMUN delivered the opinion of the Court.

In this case, we consider whether the "plain statement rule" of *Michigan v. Long,* 463 U.S. 1032, (1983), applies in a case on federal habeas review as well as in a case on direct review in this Court. We hold that it does.

I

Petitioner Warren Lee Harris was convicted in the Circuit Court of Cook County, Ill., of murder. On direct appeal, petitioner challenged only the sufficiency of the evidence. The Appellate Court of Illinois, by an unpublished order, affirmed the conviction.

Petitioner then returned to the Circuit Court of Cook County and filed a petition for postconviction relief, alleging that his trial counsel had rendered ineffective assistance in several respects, including his failure to call alibi witnesses. The court dismissed the petition without an evidentiary hearing. The Appellate Court of Illinois, in another unpublished order, again affirmed.

In its order, the Appellate Court referred to the "well-settled" principle of Illinois law that "those [issues] which could have been presented [on direct appeal], but were not, are considered waived." The court found that, "except for the alibi witnesses," petitioner's ineffective-assistance allegations "could have been raised in [his] direct appeal." The court, however, went on to consider and reject petitioner's ineffective-assistance claim on its merits.

Petitioner did not seek review in the Supreme Court of Illinois. Instead, he pursued his ineffective-assistance-of-counsel claim in federal court by a petition for a writ of habeas corpus under 28 U.S.C. §2254. The District Court recognized that if the Illinois Appellate Court had held this claim to be waived under Illinois law, this Court's decision in *Wainwright v. Sykes* would bar a federal court's consideration of the claim unless petitioner was able to show either "cause and prejudice" or a "miscarriage of justice."

The District Court, however, determined that the Illinois Appellate Court had not held any portion of the ineffective-assistance claim to have been waived. First, the District Court observed, the state court had "made clear" that the waiver did not apply to the issue of alibi witnesses. Second, the court never clearly held any other issue waived. The state court "did not appear to make two rulings in the alternative, but rather to note a procedural default and then ignore it, reaching the merits instead." Based on this determination, the District Court concluded that it was permitted to consider the ineffective-assistance claim in its entirety and ordered an evidentiary hearing. After that hearing, the court, in an unpublished memorandum and order, dismissed the claim on the merits, although it characterized the case as "a close and difficult" one.

The Court of Appeals affirmed the dismissal but did not reach the merits because, in disagreement with the District Court, it believed the ineffective-assistance claim to be procedurally barred. Considering the Illinois Appellate Court's order "ambiguous" because it contained "neither an explicit finding of waiver nor an expression of an intention to ignore waiver," the Court of Appeals nonetheless asserted that a reviewing court "should try to assess the state court's intention to the extent that this is possible." Undertaking this effort, the Court of Appeals concluded that the order "suggest[ed]" an intention "to find all grounds waived except that pertaining to the alibi witnesses." Based on this interpretation of the order, the Court of Appeals concluded that the merits of petitioner's federal claim had been reached only "as an alternate holding," and considered itself precluded from reviewing the merits of the claim....

II

A

This Court long has held that it will not consider an issue of federal law on direct review from a judgment of a state court if that judgment rests on a state-law ground that is both "independent" of the merits of the federal claim and an "adequate" basis for the court's decision. Although this doctrine originated in the context of state-court judgments for which the alternative state and federal grounds were both "substantive" in nature, the doctrine "has been applied routinely to state decisions forfeiting federal claims for violation of state procedural rules."

The question whether a state court's reference to state law constitutes an adequate and independent state ground for its judgment may be rendered difficult by ambiguity in the state court's opinion. In *Michigan v. Long*, this Court laid down a rule to avoid the difficulties associated with such ambiguity. Under *Long*, if "it fairly appears that the state court rested its decision primarily on federal law," this Court may reach the federal question on review unless the state court's opinion contains a "'plain statement' that [its] decision rests upon adequate and independent state grounds."

The *Long* "plain statement" rule applies regardless of whether the disputed state-law ground is substantive (as it was in *Long*) or procedural, as in *Caldwell v. Mississippi*, 472 U.S. 320 (1985). Thus, the mere fact that a federal claimant failed to abide by a state procedural rule does not, in and of itself, prevent this Court from reaching the federal claim: "[T]he state court must actually have relied on the procedural bar as an independent basis for its disposition of the case." Furthermore, ambiguities in that regard must be resolved by application of the *Long* standard.

B

The adequate and independent state ground doctrine, and the problem of ambiguity resolved by *Long*, is of concern not only in cases on direct review pursuant to 28 U.S.C. §§1257, but also in federal habeas corpus proceedings pursuant to 28 U.S.C. §§2254. *Wainwright v. Sykes* made clear that the adequate and independent state-ground doctrine applies on federal habeas. Under *Sykes* and its progeny, an adequate and independent finding of procedural default will bar federal habeas review of the federal claim, unless the habeas petitioner can show "cause" for the default and "prejudice attributable thereto," or demonstrate that failure to consider the federal claim will result in a "'fundamental miscarriage of justice.'"

Conversely, a federal claimant's procedural default precludes federal habeas review, like direct review, only if the last state court rendering a judgment in the case rests its judgment on the procedural default. Moreover, the question whether the state court indeed has done so is sometimes as difficult to answer on habeas review as on direct review

Habeas review thus presents the same problem of ambiguity that this Court resolved in *Michigan v. Long*. We held in *Long* that unless the state court clearly expressed its reliance on an adequate and independent state-law ground, this Court may address a federal issue considered by the state court. We applied that rule in *Caldwell v. Mississippi*, 472 U.S., at 327, to a "somewhat cryptic" reference to procedural default in a state-court opinion. Although *Long* and *Caldwell* arose on direct review, the principles underlying those decisions are not limited to direct review. Indeed, our opinion in *Caldwell* relied heavily upon our earlier application of the adequate and independent state ground doctrine to habeas review in *Ulster County*. See *Caldwell*, 472 U.S., at 327–328. *Caldwell* thus indicates that the problem of ambiguous state-court references to state law, which led to the adoption of the *Long* "plain statement" rule, is common to both direct and habeas review. Faced with a common problem, we adopt a common solution: a procedural default does not bar consideration of a federal claim on either direct or habeas review unless the last state court rendering a judgment in the case "clearly and expressly" states that its judgment rests on a state procedural bar.[9]

C

Respondents [the state of Illinois], however, urge us to adopt a different rule for habeas cases, arguing that if a state-court decision is ambiguous as to whether the judgment rests on a procedural bar, the federal court should presume that it does. Respondents claim that applying the *Long* "plain statement" requirement to habeas cases would harm the interests of finality, federalism, and comity. This Court has been alert in recognizing that federal habeas review touches upon these significant state interests. *Wainwright v. Sykes* itself reveals this. We believe, however, that applying *Long* to habeas burdens those interests only minimally, if at all. The benefits, in contrast, are substantial.

A state court remains free under the *Long* rule to rely on a state procedural bar and thereby to foreclose federal habeas review to the extent permitted by *Sykes*. Requiring a state court to be explicit in its reliance on a procedural default does not interfere unduly with state judicial decisionmaking. As *Long* itself recognized, it would be more intrusive for a federal court to second-guess a state court's determination of state law. Moreover, state courts have become familiar with the "plain statement" requirement under *Long* and *Caldwell*. Under our decision today, a state court need do nothing more to preclude habeas review than it must do to preclude direct review.

In contrast, respondents' proposed rule would impose substantial burdens on the federal courts. At oral argument, counsel for respondents conceded that in some circumstances, under their proposal, the federal habeas court would be forced to examine the state-court record to determine whether procedural default was argued to the state court, or would be required to undertake an extensive analysis of state law to determine whether a procedural bar was potentially applicable to the particular case. Much time would be lost in reviewing legal and factual issues that the state court, familiar with state law and the record before it, is better suited to address expeditiously. The "plain

---

9. This rule necessarily applies only when a state court has been presented with the federal claim, as will usually be true given the requirement that a federal claimant exhaust state court remedies before raising the claim in a federal habeas petition. Of course, a federal habeas court need not require that a federal claim be presented to a state court if it is clear that the state court would hold the claim procedurally barred. This case, however, does not involve an application of this exhaustion principle because petitioner did raise his ineffective-assistance claim in state court.

statement" requirement achieves the important objective of permitting the federal court rapidly to identify whether federal issues are properly presented before it. Respondents' proposed rule would not do that.

Thus, we are not persuaded that we should depart from *Long* ... simply because this is a habeas case. Having extended the adequate and independent state ground doctrine to habeas cases, we now extend to habeas review the "plain statement" rule for determining whether a state court has relied on an adequate and independent state ground.

III

Applying the "plain statement" requirement in this case, we conclude that the Illinois Appellate Court did not "clearly and expressly" rely on waiver as a ground for rejecting any aspect of petitioner's ineffective-assistance-of-counsel claim. To be sure, the state court perhaps laid the foundation for such a holding by stating that most of petitioner's allegations "could have been raised [on] direct appeal." Nonetheless, as the Court of Appeals recognized, this statement falls short of an explicit reliance on a state-law ground. Accordingly, this reference to state law would not have precluded our addressing petitioner's claim had it arisen on direct review. As is now established, it also does not preclude habeas review by the District Court.

The judgment of the Court of Appeals is reversed and the case is remanded for further proceedings consistent with this opinion.

Coleman v. Thompson
501 U.S. 722 (1991)

Justice O'CONNOR delivered the opinion of the Court.

This is a case about federalism. It concerns the respect that federal courts owe the States and the States' procedural rules when reviewing the claims of state prisoners in federal habeas corpus.

I

A Buchanan County, Virginia, jury convicted Roger Keith Coleman of rape and capital murder and fixed the sentence at death for the murder. The trial court imposed the death sentence, and the Virginia Supreme Court affirmed both the convictions and the sentence. This Court denied certiorari.

Coleman then filed a petition for a writ of habeas corpus in the Circuit Court for Buchanan County, raising numerous federal constitutional claims that he had not raised on direct appeal. After a two-day evidentiary hearing, the Circuit Court ruled against Coleman on all claims. The court entered its final judgment on September 4, 1986.

Coleman filed his notice of appeal with the Circuit Court on October 7, 1986, 33 days after the entry of final judgment. Coleman subsequently filed a petition for appeal in the Virginia Supreme Court. The Commonwealth of Virginia, as appellant, filed a motion to dismiss the appeal. The sole ground for dismissal urged in the motion was that Coleman's notice of appeal had been filed late. Virginia Supreme Court Rule 5:9(a) provides that no appeal shall be allowed unless a notice of appeal is filed with the trial court within 30 days of final judgment.

The Virginia Supreme Court did not act immediately on the Commonwealth's motion, and both parties filed several briefs on the subject of the motion to dismiss and on the merits of the claims in Coleman's petition. On May 19, 1987, the Virginia Supreme Court issued the following order, dismissing Coleman's appeal:

> On December 4, 1986 came the appellant, by counsel, and filed a petition for appeal in the above-styled case.
>
> Thereupon came the appellee, by the Attorney General of Virginia, and filed a motion to dismiss the petition for appeal; on December 19, 1986 the appellant filed a memorandum in opposition to the motion to dismiss; on December 19, 1986 the appellee filed a reply to the appellant's memorandum; on December 23, 1986 the appellee filed a brief in opposition to the petition for appeal; on December 23, 1986 the appellant filed a surreply in opposition to the appellee's motion to dismiss; and on January 6, 1987 the appellant filed a reply brief.
>
> Upon consideration whereof, the motion to dismiss is granted and the petition for appeal is dismissed.

This Court again denied certiorari.

Coleman next filed a petition for writ of habeas corpus in the United States District Court for the Western District of Virginia. In his petition, Coleman presented four federal constitutional claims he had raised on direct appeal in the Virginia Supreme Court and seven claims he had raised for the first time in state habeas. The District Court concluded that, by virtue of the dismissal of his appeal by the Virginia Supreme Court in state habeas, Coleman had procedurally defaulted the seven claims. The District Court nonetheless went on to address the merits of all 11 of Coleman's claims. The court ruled against Coleman on all of the claims and denied the petition.

The United States Court of Appeals for the Fourth Circuit affirmed. The court held that Coleman had defaulted all of the claims that he had presented for the first time in state habeas.... [The Fourth Circuit also] concluded that the Virginia Supreme Court had met the "plain statement" requirement of *Harris* by granting a motion to dismiss that was based solely on procedural grounds. The Fourth Circuit held that the Virginia Supreme Court's decision rested on independent and adequate state grounds and that Coleman had not shown cause to excuse the default. As a consequence, federal review of the claims Coleman presented only in the state habeas proceeding was barred. We granted certiorari, to resolve several issues concerning the relationship between state procedural defaults and federal habeas review, and now affirm....

III

A

Coleman contends that the presumption of *Michigan v. Long*, 463 U.S. 1032 (1983), and *Harris v. Reed*, 489 U.S. 255 (1989) — that the Court will presume no independent and adequate state ground for a state court decision when the decision "fairly appears to rest primarily on federal law, or to be interwoven with federal law, and when the adequacy and independence of any possible state law ground is not clear from the face of the opinion" — applies in this case, and precludes a bar to habeas, because the Virginia Supreme Court's order dismissing Coleman's appeal did not "clearly and expressly" state that it was based on state procedural grounds. Coleman reads *Harris* too broadly. A predicate to the application of the *Harris* presumption is that the decision of the last state court to which the petitioner presented his federal claims must fairly appear to rest primarily on federal law or to be interwoven with federal law.

Coleman relies on other language in *Harris.* That opinion announces that "a procedural default does not bar consideration of a federal claim on either direct or habeas review unless the last state court rendering a judgment in the case clearly and expressly states that its judgment rests on a state procedural bar." Coleman contends that this rule, by its terms, applies to all state court judgments, not just those that fairly appear to rest primarily on federal law.

Coleman has read the rule out of context. It is unmistakably clear that *Harris* applies the same presumption in habeas that *Long* and *Caldwell* adopted in direct review cases in this Court. Indeed, the quoted passage purports to state the rule "on either direct or habeas review." *Harris,* being a federal habeas case, could not change the rule for direct review; the reference to both direct and habeas review makes plain that *Harris* applies precisely the same rule as *Long. Harris* describes the *Long* presumption, and hence its own, as applying only in those cases in which "'it fairly appears that the state court rested its decision primarily on federal law.'" That in one particular exposition of its rule *Harris* does not mention the predicate to application of the presumption does not change the holding of the opinion.

Coleman urges a broader rule: that the presumption applies in all cases in which a habeas petitioner presented his federal claims to the state court. This rule makes little sense. In direct review cases, "[i]t is ... incumbent upon this Court ... to ascertain for itself ... whether the asserted non-federal ground independently and adequately supports the [state court] judgment." Similarly, federal habeas courts must ascertain for themselves if the petitioner is in custody pursuant to a state court judgment that rests on independent and adequate state grounds. In cases in which the *Long* and *Harris* presumption applies, federal courts will conclude that the relevant state court judgment does not rest on an independent and adequate state ground. The presumption, like all conclusive presumptions, is designed to avoid the costs of excessive inquiry where a *per se* rule will achieve the correct result in almost all cases....

Per se rules should not be applied, however, in situations where the generalization is incorrect as an empirical matter; the justification for a conclusive presumption disappears when application of the presumption will not reach the correct result most of the time. The *Long* and *Harris* presumption works because in the majority of cases in which a state court decision fairly appears to rest primarily on federal law or to be interwoven with such law, and the state court does not plainly state that it is relying on an independent and adequate state ground, the state court decision did not in fact rest on an independent and adequate state ground. We accept errors in those small number of cases where there was nonetheless an independent and adequate state ground in exchange for a significant reduction in the costs of inquiry.

The tradeoff is very different when the factual predicate does not exist. In those cases in which it does not fairly appear that the state court rested its decision primarily on federal grounds, it is simply not true that the "most reasonable explanation" is that the state judgment rested on federal grounds. Yet Coleman would have the federal courts apply a conclusive presumption of no independent and adequate state grounds in every case in which a state prisoner presented his federal claims to a state court, regardless of whether it fairly appears that the state court addressed those claims. We cannot accept such a rule, for it would greatly and unacceptably expand the risk that federal courts will review the federal claims of prisoners in custody pursuant to judgments resting on independent and adequate state grounds. Any efficiency gained by applying a conclusive presumption, and thereby avoiding inquiry into state law, is simply not worth the cost in the loss of respect for the State that such a rule would entail.

It may be argued that a broadly applicable presumption is not counterfactual after it is announced: once state courts know that their decisions resting on independent and adequate state procedural grounds will be honored in federal habeas only if there is a clear and express statement of the default, these courts will provide such a statement in all relevant cases. This argument does not help Coleman. Even assuming that *Harris* can be read as establishing a presumption in all cases, the Virginia Supreme Court issued its order dismissing Coleman's appeal before this Court decided *Harris*. As to this state court order, the absence of an express statement of procedural default is not very informative.

In any event, we decline to establish such a rule here, for it would place burdens on the States and state courts in exchange for very little benefit to the federal courts. We are, as an initial matter, far from confident that the empirical assumption of the argument for such a rule is correct. It is not necessarily the case that state courts will take pains to provide a clear and express statement of procedural default in all cases, even after announcement of the rule. State courts presumably have a dignitary interest in seeing that their state law decisions are not ignored by a federal habeas court, but most of the price paid for federal review of state prisoner claims is paid by the State. When a federal habeas court considers the federal claims of a prisoner in state custody for independent and adequate state law reasons, it is the State that must respond. It is the State that pays the price in terms of the uncertainty and delay added to the enforcement of its criminal laws. It is the State that must retry the petitioner if the federal courts reverse his conviction. If a state court, in the course of disposing of cases on its overcrowded docket, neglects to provide a clear and express statement of procedural default, or is insufficiently motivated to do so, there is little the State can do about it. Yet it is primarily respect for the State's interests that underlies the application of the independent and adequate state ground doctrine in federal habeas.

A broad presumption would also put too great a burden on the state courts. It remains the duty of the federal courts, whether this Court on direct review, or lower federal courts in habeas, to determine the scope of the relevant state court judgment. We can establish a *per se* rule that eases the burden of inquiry on the federal courts in those cases where there are few costs to doing so, but we have no power to tell state courts how they must write their opinions. We encourage state courts to express plainly, in every decision potentially subject to federal review, the grounds upon which its judgment rests, but we will not impose on state courts the responsibility for using particular language in every case in which a state prisoner presents a federal claim—every state appeal, every denial of state collateral review—in order that federal courts might not be bothered with reviewing state law and the record in the case.

Nor do we believe that the federal courts will save much work by applying the *Harris* presumption in all cases. The presumption at present applies only when it fairly appears that a state court judgment rested primarily on federal law or was interwoven with federal law, that is, in those cases where a federal court has good reason to question whether there is an independent and adequate state ground for the decision. In the rest of the cases, there is little need for a conclusive presumption. In the absence of a clear indication that a state court rested its decision on federal law, a federal court's task will not be difficult.

There is, in sum, little that the federal courts will gain by applying a presumption of federal review in those cases where the relevant state court decision does not fairly appear to rest primarily on federal law or to be interwoven with such law, and much that the States and state courts will lose. We decline to so expand the *Harris* presumption.

B

The *Harris* presumption does not apply here. Coleman does not argue, nor could he, that it "fairly appears" that the Virginia Supreme Court's decision rested primarily on federal law or was interwoven with such law. The Virginia Supreme Court stated plainly that it was granting the Commonwealth's motion to dismiss the petition for appeal. That motion was based solely on Coleman's failure to meet the Supreme Court's time requirements. There is no mention of federal law in the Virginia Supreme Court's three-sentence dismissal order. It "fairly appears" to rest primarily on state law.

Coleman concedes that the Virginia Supreme Court dismissed his state habeas appeal as untimely, applying a state procedural rule. He argues instead that the court's application of this procedural rule was not independent of federal law.

Virginia Supreme Court Rule 5:5(a) declares that the 30-day requirement for filing a notice of appeal is "mandatory." The Virginia Supreme Court has reiterated the unwaivable nature of this requirement. Despite these forthright pronouncements, Coleman contends that in this case the Virginia Supreme Court did not automatically apply its time requirement. Rather, Coleman asserts, the Court first considered the merits of his federal claims, and applied the procedural bar only after determining that doing so would not abridge one of Coleman's constitutional rights....

Coleman cites *Tharp v. Commonwealth*, 211 Va. 1, 175 S.E.2d 277 (1970). In that case, the Virginia Supreme Court announced that it was ending its practice of allowing extensions of time for petitions of writs of error in criminal and state habeas cases:

> Henceforth we will extend the time for filing a petition for a writ of error only
> if it is found that to deny the extension would abridge a constitutional right.

Coleman contends that the Virginia Supreme Court's exception for constitutional claims demonstrates that the court will conduct at least a cursory review of a petitioner's constitutional claims on the merits before dismissing an appeal.

We are not convinced that *Tharp* stands for the rule that Coleman believes it does. Coleman reads that case as establishing a practice in the Virginia Supreme Court of examining the merits of all underlying constitutional claims before denying a petition for appeal or writ of error as time barred. A more natural reading is that the Virginia Supreme Court will only grant an extension of time if the denial itself would abridge a constitutional right. That is, the Virginia Supreme Court will extend its time requirement only in those cases in which the petitioner has a constitutional right to have the appeal heard.

This was the case, for example, in *Cabaniss v. Cunningham*, 206 Va. 330, 143 S.E.2d 911 (1965). *Cabaniss* had defaulted the direct appeal of his criminal conviction because the trial court had failed to honor his request for appointed counsel on appeal, a request the court was required to honor under the Constitution. The Virginia Supreme Court, on state collateral review, ordered that *Cabaniss* be given counsel and allowed to file a new appeal, although grossly out of time. Enforcing the time requirements for appeal in that case would have abridged *Cabaniss'* constitutional right to counsel on appeal. Such a rule would be of no help to Coleman. He does not contend that the failure of the Virginia Supreme Court to hear his untimely state habeas appeal violated one of his constitutional rights.

Even if we accept Coleman's reading of *Tharp*, however, it is clear that the Virginia Supreme Court did not apply the *Tharp* rule here. *Tharp* concerns the filing requirement for petitions. Here, it was not Coleman's petition for appeal that was late, but his notice of appeal. A petition for appeal to the Virginia Supreme Court is a document filed with that court in which the petitioner describes the alleged errors in the decision below. It need only be filed within three months of the final judgment of a trial court. By contrast, the notice of appeal is a document filed with the trial court that notifies that court and the Virginia Supreme Court, as well as the parties, that there will be an appeal; it is a purely ministerial document. The notice of the appeal must be filed within 30 days of the final judgment of the trial court. Coleman has cited no authority indicating that the Virginia Supreme Court has recognized an exception to the time requirement for filing a notice of appeal. . . .

Finally, Coleman argues that the Virginia Supreme Court's dismissal order in this case is at least ambiguous because it was issued "[u]pon consideration" of all the filed papers, including Coleman's petition for appeal and the Commonwealth's brief in opposition, both of which discussed the merits of Coleman's federal claims. There is no doubt that the Virginia Supreme Court's "consideration" of all filed papers adds some ambiguity, but we simply cannot read it as overriding the court's explicit grant of a dismissal motion based solely on procedural grounds. Those grounds are independent of federal law. . . .

IV

. . . We now make it explicit: In all cases in which a state prisoner has defaulted his federal claims in state court pursuant to an independent and adequate state procedural rule, federal habeas review of the claims is barred unless the prisoner can demonstrate cause for the default and actual prejudice as a result of the alleged violation of federal law, or demonstrate that failure to consider the claims will result in a fundamental miscarriage of justice. *Fay v. Noia* was based on a conception of federal/state relations that undervalued the importance of state procedural rules. The several cases after *Fay* that applied the cause and prejudice standard to a variety of state procedural defaults represent a different view. We now recognize the important interest in finality served by state procedural rules, and the significant harm to the States that results from the failure of federal courts to respect them.

Murray v. Carrier applied the cause and prejudice standard to the failure to raise a particular claim on appeal. There is no reason that the same standard should not apply to a failure to appeal at all. All of the State's interests—in channeling the resolution of claims to the most appropriate forum, in finality, and in having an opportunity to correct its own errors—are implicated whether a prisoner defaults one claim or all of them. A federal court generally should not interfere in either case. By applying the cause and prejudice standard uniformly to all independent and adequate state procedural defaults, we eliminate the irrational distinction between *Fay* and the rule of cases like *Francis v. Henderson*, 425 U.S. 536 (1976), *Sykes*, 433 U.S. 72 (1976), *Engle*, 456 U.S. 107 (1982) and *Carrier*, 477 U.S. 478 (1986).

We also eliminate inconsistency between the respect federal courts show for state procedural rules and the respect they show for their own. This Court has long understood the vital interest served by federal procedural rules, even when they serve to bar federal review of constitutional claims. . . . No less respect should be given to state rules of procedure.

V

A

Coleman maintains that there was cause for his default. The late filing was, he contends, the result of attorney error of sufficient magnitude to excuse the default in federal habeas.

Murray v. Carrier considered the circumstances under which attorney error constitutes cause. Carrier argued that his attorney's inadvertence in failing to raise certain claims in his state appeal constituted cause for the default sufficient to allow federal habeas review. We rejected this claim, explaining that the costs associated with an ignorant or inadvertent procedural default are no less than where the failure to raise a claim is a deliberate strategy: It deprives the state courts of the opportunity to review trial errors. When a federal habeas court hears such a claim, it undercuts the State's ability to enforce its procedural rules just as surely as when the default was deliberate. We concluded: "So long as a defendant is represented by counsel whose performance is not constitutionally ineffective under the standard established in *Strickland v. Washington*, we discern no inequity in requiring him to bear the risk of attorney error that results in a procedural default."

Applying the *Carrier* rule as stated, this case is at an end. There is no constitutional right to an attorney in state post-conviction proceedings. Consequently, a petitioner cannot claim constitutionally ineffective assistance of counsel in such proceedings. Coleman contends that it was his attorney's error that led to the late filing of his state habeas appeal. This error cannot be constitutionally ineffective; therefore Coleman must "bear the risk of attorney error that results in a procedural default." ...

B

... Because Coleman had no right to counsel to pursue his appeal in state habeas, any attorney error that led to the default of Coleman's claims in state court cannot constitute cause to excuse the default in federal habeas. As Coleman does not argue in this Court that federal review of his claims is necessary to prevent a fundamental miscarriage of justice, he is barred from bringing these claims in federal habeas. Accordingly, the judgment of the Court of Appeals is affirmed.

Justice BLACKMUN, with whom Justice Marshall and Justice Stevens join, dissenting.

Federalism; comity; state sovereignty; preservation of state resources; certainty: the majority methodically inventories these multifarious state interests before concluding that the plain-statement rule of *Michigan v. Long* does not apply to a summary order. One searches the majority's opinion in vain, however, for any mention of petitioner Coleman's right to a criminal proceeding free from constitutional defect or his interest in finding a forum for his constitutional challenge to his conviction and sentence of death. Nor does the majority even allude to the "important need for uniformity in federal law," which justified this Court's adoption of the plain-statement rule in the first place. Rather, displaying obvious exasperation with the breadth of substantive federal habeas doctrine and the expansive protection afforded by the Fourteenth Amendment's guarantee of fundamental fairness in state criminal proceedings, the Court today continues its crusade to erect petty procedural barriers in the path of any state prisoner seeking review of his federal constitutional claims. Because I believe that the Court is creating a Byzantine morass of arbitrary, unnecessary, and unjustifiable impediments to the vindication of federal rights, I dissent....

II

B

... It is well settled that the existence of a state procedural default does not divest a federal court of jurisdiction on collateral review. Rather, the important office of the federal courts in vindicating federal rights gives way to the States' enforcement of their procedural rules to protect the States' interest in being an equal partner in safeguarding federal rights. This accommodation furthers the values underlying federalism in two ways. First, encouraging a defendant to assert his federal rights in the appropriate state forum makes it possible for transgressions to be arrested sooner and before they influence an erroneous deprivation of liberty. Second, thorough examination of a prisoner's federal claims in state court permits more effective review of those claims in federal court, honing the accuracy of the writ as an implement to eradicate unlawful detention. The majority ignores these purposes in concluding that a State need not bear the burden of making clear its intent to rely on such a rule. When it is uncertain whether a state court judgment denying relief from federal claims rests on a procedural bar, it is inconsistent with federalism principles for a federal court to exercise discretion to decline to review those federal claims.

In justifying its new rule, the majority first announces that, as a practical matter, the application of the *Long* presumption to a summary order entered in a case where a state prisoner presented federal constitutional claims to a state court is unwarranted, because "it is simply not true that the 'most reasonable explanation' is that the state judgment rested on federal grounds." The majority provides no support for this flat assertion. In fact, the assertion finds no support in reality. "Under our federal system, the federal and state 'courts [are] equally bound to guard and protect the rights secured by the Constitution.'" Accordingly, state prisoners are required to present their federal claims to state tribunals before proceeding to federal habeas, "to protect the state courts' role in the enforcement of federal law and prevent disruption of state judicial proceedings." See 28 U.S.C. §2254. Respect for the States' responsible assumption of this solemn trust compels the conclusion that state courts presented with federal constitutional claims actually resolve those claims unless they indicate to the contrary.

The majority claims that applying the plain-statement rule to summary orders "would place burdens on the States and state courts," suggesting that these burdens are borne independently by the States and their courts. The State, according to the majority, "pays the price" for federal review of state prisoner claims "in terms of uncertainty and delay" as well as in the cost of a retrial. The majority is less clear about the precise contours of the burden this rule is said to place on state courts, merely asserting that it "would also put too great a burden on the state courts."

The majority's attempt to distinguish between the interests of state courts and the interests of the States in this context is inexplicable. States do not exist independent of their officers, agents, and citizens. Rather, "[t]hrough the structure of its government, and the character of those who exercise government authority, a State defines itself as a sovereign." The majority's novel conception of dichotomous interests is entirely unprecedented. Moreover, it admits of no readily apparent limiting principle. For instance, should a federal habeas court decline to review claims that the state judge committed constitutional error at trial simply because the costs of a retrial will be borne by the State? After all, as the majority asserts, "there is little the State can do about" constitutional errors made by its trial judges.

Even if the majority correctly attributed the relevant state interests, they are, nonetheless, misconceived. The majority appears most concerned with the financial burden that a retrial places on the States. Of course, if the initial trial conformed to the mandate of the Federal Constitution, not even the most probing federal review would necessitate a retrial. Thus, to the extent the State must "pay the price" of retrying a state prisoner, that price is incurred as a direct result of the State's failure scrupulously to honor his federal rights, not as a consequence of unwelcome federal review.

The majority also contends without elaboration that a "broad presumption [of federal jurisdiction] would ... put too great a burden on the state courts." This assertion not only finds no support in *Long*, where the burden of the presumption on state courts is not even mentioned, but also is premised on the misconception that the plain-statement rule serves only to relieve the federal court of the "bother" of determining the basis of the relevant state-court judgment. Viewed responsibly, the plain-statement rule provides a simple mechanism by which a state court may invoke the discretionary deference of the federal habeas court and virtually insulate its judgment from federal review. While state courts may choose to draw their orders as they wish, the right of a state prisoner, particularly one sentenced to death, to have his federal claim heard by a federal habeas court is simply too fundamental to yield to the State's incidental interest in issuing ambiguous summary orders....

Notes and Questions

1. *Coleman* holds that the adequate and independent state ground doctrine bars federal habeas review when a state court's refusal to address petitioner's federal claims is based on procedural default. The Court feared that without the adequate and independent state ground doctrine, "habeas petitioners would be able to avoid the exhaustion requirement by defaulting their federal claims in state court." In light of the earlier discussion on exhaustion, to what extent do you find this fear justified? Does the AEDPA have any impact on this concern?

2. According to *Harris v. Reed*, 489 U.S. 255, 264 n.10 (1989), "[t]he adequate and independent state ground doctrine requires the federal court to honor a state holding that is a sufficient basis for the state court's judgment, even when the state court also relies on federal law." Nonetheless, a state procedural ground is not "adequate" unless it is "strictly or regularly followed." *Johnson v. Mississippi*, 486 U.S. 578, 587 (1988).

3. In *Ylst v. Nunnemaker*, 501 U.S. 797, 803 (1991), the Court considered "whether the unexplained denial of a petition for habeas corpus by a state court lifts a state procedural bar imposed on direct appeal, so that a state prisoner may then have his claim heard on the merits in a federal habeas proceeding." In answering this question in the negative, the Court adopted the following presumption:

> [W]here there has been one reasoned state judgment rejecting a federal claim, later unexplained orders upholding that judgment or rejecting the same claim rest upon the same ground. If an earlier opinion "fairly appear[s] to rest primarily upon federal law," we will presume that no procedural default has been invoked by a subsequent unexplained order that leaves the judgment or its consequences in place. Similarly where, as here, the last reasoned opinion on the claim explicitly imposes a procedural default, we will presume that a later decision rejecting the claim did not silently disregard that bar and consider the merits.

4. The Court in *Caldwell v. Mississippi*, 472 U.S. 320 (1985), made clear that the mere existence of a state procedural bar is not sufficient to deprive the Court of jurisdiction. The Court stated:

> Respondent first argues that this Court lacks jurisdiction to decide this issue because the decision of the Mississippi Supreme Court rests on adequate and

independent state grounds. Although petitioner interposed a contemporaneous objection to the prosecutor's argument, he did not initially assign the issue as error on appeal. Under Mississippi rules, "[n]o error not distinctly assigned shall be argued by counsel, except upon request of the Court, but the Court may, at its option, notice a plain error not assigned or distinctly specified." In this case, the State Supreme Court raised the issue of the prosecutor's comments *sua sponte*. It was discussed at oral argument, in postargument briefs submitted by both sides, and in the opinion of the State Supreme Court. Respondent nevertheless argues that the decision below rests on the state-law ground of failure to comply with Rule 6.

The mere existence of a basis for a state procedural bar does not deprive this Court of jurisdiction; the state court must actually have relied on the procedural bar as an independent basis for it disposition of the case. Moreover, we will not assume that a state-court decision rests on adequate and independent state grounds when the "state court decision fairly appears to rest primarily on federal law, or to be interwoven with the federal law, and when the adequacy and independence of any possible state law ground is not clear from the face of the opinion." "If the state court decision indicates clearly and expressly that it is alternatively based on bona fide separate, adequate, and independent grounds, we, of course, will not undertake to review the decision."

An examination of the decision below reveals that it contains no clear or express indication that "separate, adequate, and independent" state-law grounds were the basis for the court's judgment. Indeed, the reference to the waiver issue in the prevailing opinion below, although somewhat cryptic, argues against the position urged by respondent.

This conclusion is substantially bolstered by the fact that the Mississippi court discussed the challenge to the prosecutor's argument at some length, evaluating it as a matter of both federal and state law before rejecting it as unmeritorious. Moreover, this conclusion is consistent with the Mississippi Supreme Court's behavior in other capital cases, where it has a number of times declined to invoke procedural bars. Given the standards of *Michigan v. Long*, 463 U.S. 1032 (1983), and *Ulster County Court v. Allen*, 442 U.S. 140 (1979), it is apparent that we have jurisdiction.

5. What happens when, in seeking to bar federal habeas review of a conviction, the state relies on the petitioner's default of a state procedural rule which the state courts do not consistently enforce? The United States Supreme Court addressed this issue in *Johnson v. Mississippi*, 486 U.S. 578, 587–589 (1988):

Finally, we are not persuaded that the state court's conclusion that under state law petitioner is procedurally barred from raising this claim because he failed to attack the validity of the New York conviction on direct appeal bars our consideration of his claim. In its brief before this Court, the State does not rely on the argument that petitioner's claim is procedurally barred because he failed to raise it on direct appeal. Because the State Supreme Court asserted this bar as a ground for its decision, however, we consider whether that bar provides an adequate and independent state ground for the refusal to vacate petitioner's sentence. "[W]e have consistently held that the question of when and how defaults in compliance with state procedural rules can preclude our consideration of a federal question is itself a federal question." "[A] state procedural ground is not 'adequate' unless the procedural rule is 'strictly or regularly followed.' We find no evidence that the procedural bar relied on by the Mississippi Supreme Court here has been consistently or regularly applied. Rather, the weight of Mississippi law is to the contrary. In *Phillips v. State*, the Mississippi Supreme Court considered whether defendant could properly attack in a sentencing hearing a prior conviction which the State sought to use to enhance his sentence. The court made it clear that the sentencing hearing was not the appropriate forum of such an attack:

[T]he trial court is not required to go beyond the face of the prior convictions sought to be used in establishing the defendant's status as an habitual offender. If, on its face, the conviction makes a proper showing that a defendant's prior plea of guilty was both knowing and voluntary, that conviction may be used for the enhancement of the defendant's punishment under the Mississippi habitual offender act....

[A]ny such frontal assault upon the constitutionality of a prior conviction should be conducted in the form of an entirely separate procedure solely concerned with attacking that conviction. This role is neither the function nor the duty of the trial judge in a hearing to determine habitual offender status. Likewise, any such proceeding should be brought in the state in which such conviction occurred, pursuant to that state's established procedures. Should such proceeding in the foreign state succeed in overturning the conviction, then relief should be sought in Mississippi by petition for writ of error *coram nobis*.

The reasoning of *Phillips* suggests that the direct appeal of a subsequent conviction and concomitant enhanced sentence is not the appropriate forum for challenging a prior conviction that on its face appears valid. In directing that evidence of invalidation of such a conviction in another proceeding could be brought to the court's attention in a collateral attack of the subsequent conviction, the court did not suggest that the failure previously to raise the issue in the inappropriate forum would bar its consideration on collateral attack.

The Mississippi Supreme Court has applied its reasoning in *Phillips* to facts substantially similar to those presented in this case. In *Nixon v. State*, the court held that the reasoning of *Phillips* applied when a defendant in a capital case sought to attack the validity of a prior conviction introduced to support the finding of an aggravating circumstance at sentencing. In light of the Mississippi Supreme Court's decisions in *Phillips* and *Nixon*, we cannot conclude that the procedural bar relied on by the Mississippi Supreme Court in this case has been consistently or regularly applied. Consequently, under federal law it is not an adequate and independent state ground for affirming petitioner's conviction.

H. Evidentiary Hearings in Federal Habeas Corpus

During the same year that the Court decided *Fay v. Noia*, the Court in *Townsend v. Sain*, 372 U.S. 293 (1963), addressed an accused's right to a plenary hearing in a federal habeas corpus proceeding. According to Chief Justice Warren's majority opinion, "where an applicant for a writ of habeas corpus alleges facts which, if proved, would entitle him to relief, the federal court to which the application is made has the power to receive evidence and try the facts anew." Moreover, the habeas court must hold an evidentiary hearing if:

(1) the merits of the factual dispute were not resolved in the state hearing; (2) the state factual determination is not fairly supported by the record as a whole; (3) the fact-finding procedure employed by the state court was not adequate to afford a full and fair hearing; (4) there is a substantial allegation of newly discovered evidence; (5) the material facts were not adequately developed at the state-court hearing; or (6) for any reason it appears that the state trier of fact did not afford the habeas applicant a full and fair fact hearing.

Townsend "substantially increased the availability of evidentiary hearings in habeas corpus proceedings and made mandatory much of what had previously been within the broad discretion of the District Court." *Smith v. Yeager*, 393 U.S. 122, 125 (1968). Nonetheless, an evidentiary hearing was not mandatory, even though the petitioner met one of the six criteria, where the petitioner had "deliberately bypassed" the opportunity to develop the factual issues in state proceedings. In *Keeney v. Tamayo-Reyes*, 504 U.S. 1 (1992), the Court reexamined *Fay*'s "deliberate bypass" standard with respect to evidentiary hearings and a petitioner's failure to raise factual issues in state proceedings.

Keeney v. Tamayo-Reyes
504 U.S. 1 (1992)

Justice WHITE delivered the opinion of the Court.

Respondent is a Cuban immigrant with little education and almost no knowledge of English. In 1984, he was charged with murder arising from the stabbing death of a man who had allegedly attempted to intervene in a confrontation between respondent and his girlfriend in a bar.

Respondent was provided with a defense attorney and interpreter. The attorney recommended to respondent that he plead *nolo contendere* to first-degree manslaughter. Respondent signed a plea form that explained in English the rights he was waiving by entering the plea. The state court held a plea hearing, at which petitioner was represented by counsel and his interpreter. The judge asked the attorney and interpreter if they had explained to respondent the rights in the plea form and the consequences of his plea; they responded in the affirmative. The judge then explained to respondent, in English, the rights he would waive by his plea, and asked the interpreter to translate. Respondent indicated that he understood his rights and still wished to plead *nolo contendere*. The judge accepted his plea.

Later, respondent brought a collateral attack on the plea in a state-court proceeding. He alleged his plea had not been knowing and intelligent and therefore was invalid because his translator had not translated accurately and completely for him the *mens rea* element of manslaughter. He also contended that he did not understand the purposes of the plea form or the plea hearing. He contended that he did not know he was pleading no contest to manslaughter, but rather that he thought he was agreeing to be tried for manslaughter.

After a hearing, the state court dismissed respondent's petition, finding that respondent was properly served by his trial interpreter and that the interpreter correctly, fully, and accurately translated the communications between respondent and his attorney. The State Court of Appeals affirmed, and the State Supreme Court denied review.

Respondent then entered Federal District Court seeking a writ of habeas corpus. Respondent contended that the material facts concerning the translation were not adequately developed at the state-court hearing, implicating the fifth circumstance of *Townsend v. Sain*, 372 U.S. 293, 313 (1963), and sought a federal evidentiary hearing on whether his *nolo contendere* plea was unconstitutional. The District Court found that the failure to develop the critical facts relevant to his federal claim was attributable to inexcusable neglect and that no evidentiary hearing was required. Respondent appealed.

The Court of Appeals for the Ninth Circuit recognized that the alleged failure to translate the *mens rea* element of first-degree manslaughter, if proved, would be a basis for overturning respondent's plea, and determined that material facts had not been adequately developed in the state postconviction court, apparently due to the negligence of postconviction counsel. The court held that *Townsend v. Sain* and *Fay v. Noia* required an evidentiary hearing in the District Court unless respondent had deliberately bypassed the orderly procedure of the state courts. Because counsel's negligent failure to develop the facts did not constitute a deliberate bypass, the Court of Appeals ruled that respondent was entitled to an evidentiary hearing on the question whether the *mens rea* element of first-degree manslaughter was properly explained to him.

We granted certiorari to decide whether the deliberate bypass standard is the correct standard for excusing a habeas petitioner's failure to develop a material fact in state-court proceedings. We reverse....

In *Wainwright v. Sykes*, 433 U.S. 72 (1977), we rejected the application of *Fay*'s standard of "knowing waiver" or "deliberate bypass" to excuse a petitioner's failure to comply with a state contemporaneous-objection rule, stating that the state rule deserved more respect than the *Fay* standard accorded it. We observed that procedural rules that contribute to error-free state trial proceedings are thoroughly desirable. We applied a cause-and-prejudice standard to a petitioner's failure to object at trial and limited *Fay* to its facts. We have consistently reaffirmed that the "cause and prejudice" standard embodies the correct accommodation between the competing concerns implicated in a federal court's habeas power....

The concerns that motivated the rejection of the deliberate bypass standard in *Wainwright*, *Coleman*, and other cases are equally applicable to this case. As in cases of state procedural default, application of the cause-and-prejudice standard to excuse a state prisoner's failure to develop material facts in state court will appropriately accommodate concerns of finality, comity, judicial economy, and channeling the resolution of claims into the most appropriate forum.

Applying the cause-and-prejudice standard in cases like this will obviously contribute to the finality of convictions, for requiring a federal evidentiary hearing solely on the basis of a habeas petitioner's negligent failure to develop facts in state-court proceedings dramatically increases the opportunities to relitigate a conviction.

Similarly, encouraging the full factual development in state court of a claim that state courts committed constitutional error advances comity by allowing a coordinate jurisdiction to correct its own errors in the first instance. It reduces the "inevitable friction" that results when a federal habeas court "overturn[s] either the factual or legal conclusions reached by the state-court system."

Also, by ensuring that full factual development takes place in the earlier, state-court proceedings, the cause-and-prejudice standard plainly serves the interest of judicial economy. It is hardly a good use of scarce judicial resources to duplicate factfinding in federal court merely because a petitioner has negligently failed to take advantage of opportunities in state-court proceedings.

Furthermore, ensuring that full factual development of a claim takes place in state court channels the resolution of the claim to the most appropriate forum. The state court is the appropriate forum for resolution of factual issues in the first instance, and creating incentives for the deferral of factfinding to later federal-court proceedings can only degrade the accuracy and efficiency of judicial proceedings. This is fully consistent with and gives meaning to the requirement of exhaustion....

Finally, it is worth noting that applying the cause-and-prejudice standard in this case also advances uniformity in the law of habeas corpus. There is no good reason to maintain in one area of habeas law a standard that has been rejected in the area in which it was principally enunciated. And little can be said for holding a habeas petitioner to one standard for failing to bring a claim in state court and excusing the petitioner under another, lower standard for failing to develop the factual basis of that claim in the same forum. A different rule could mean that a habeas petitioner would not be excused for negligent failure to object to the introduction of the prosecution's evidence, but nonetheless would be excused for negligent failure to introduce any evidence of his own to support a constitutional claim.

Respondent Tamayo-Reyes is entitled to an evidentiary hearing if he can show cause for his failure to develop the facts in state-court proceedings and actual prejudice resulting from that failure. We also adopt the narrow exception to the cause-and-prejudice requirement: A habeas petitioner's failure to develop a claim in state-court proceedings will be excused and a hearing mandated if he can show that a fundamental miscarriage of justice would result from failure to hold a federal evidentiary hearing.

The State concedes that a remand to the District Court is appropriate in order to afford respondent the opportunity to bring forward evidence establishing cause and prejudice, and we agree that the respondent should have that opportunity. Accordingly, the decision of the Court of Appeals is reversed, and the cause is remanded to the District Court for further proceedings consistent with this opinion.

Note

Under *Townsend v. Sain*, 372 U.S. 293, 312 (1963), a federal court generally must hold an evidentiary hearing if the state court failed to afford petitioner a full and fair hearing. Before *Keeney*, petitioner's failure to adequately develop material facts at a state court hearing would not disentitle him to an evidentiary hearing in federal court—providing the failure to develop the facts was a result of excusable neglect and not an attempt to deliberately bypass state court procedures. In *Keeney*, the Court rejected the argument that the *Fay* deliberate bypass standard is the correct standard for excusing a federal habeas petitioner's failure to develop a material fact in state court proceedings. Instead, under *Keeney*, petitioners who fail to adequately develop material facts in state court are required to show cause and prejudice. Absent a showing of cause and prejudice, a hearing will be mandated only if petitioner can show that "a fundamental miscarriage of justice" would result from failure to hold a federal evidentiary hearing. *Keeney*, 504 U.S. 1, 7–12 (1992). According to *McCleskey v. Zant*, to demonstrate a fundamental miscarriage of justice a federal habeas petitioner must show that he is innocent. *McCleskey*, 449 U.S. 467, 493–496, 502–503 (1991). The role of innocence in federal habeas is considered more fully in chapters 13 and 17.

I. Evidentiary Hearings under the AEDPA — Section 2254(e)

The AEDPA was enacted four years after *Keeney v. Tamayo-Reyes*, and the new habeas statute was seen as essentially codifying *Keeney*. Section 2254(e) provides:

(e)(1) In a proceeding instituted by an application for a writ of habeas corpus by a person in custody pursuant to the judgment of a State court, a determination of a factual issue made by a State court shall be presumed to be correct. The application shall have the burden of rebutting the presumption of correctness by clear and convincing evidence.

(2) If the applicant has failed to develop the factual basis of a claim in State court proceedings, the court shall not hold an evidentiary hearing on the claim unless the applicant shows that—

(A) the claim relies on—

(i) a new rule of constitutional law, made retroactive to cases on collateral review by the Supreme Court, that was previously unavailable; or

(ii) a factual predicate that could not have been previously discovered through the exercise of due diligence; and

(B) the fact underlying the claim would be sufficient to establish by clear and convincing evidence that but for constitutional error, no reasonable factfinder would have found the applicant guilty of the underlying offense.

This provision of the AEDPA rejects the *Townsend v. Sain* relitigation-of-the-facts approach to federal habeas evidentiary hearings, and embraces the *Keeney* approach to evidentiary hearings. Furthermore, the statute defines cause and prejudice in the context of developing the factual record in state court. "Cause" exists under §2254(e) only where "the claim relies on (i) a new rule of constitutional law, made retroactive to cases on collateral review by the Supreme Court, that was previously unavailable; or (ii) a factual predicate that could not have been previously discovered through the exercise of due diligence." "Prejudice" can be found only where "the fact underlying the claim would be sufficient to establish by clear and convincing evidence that but for constitutional error, no reasonable factfinder would have found the applicant guilty of the underlying offense."

Michael Williams v. Taylor
529 U.S. 420 (2000)

Justice KENNEDY, delivered the opinion for a unanimous Court.

Petitioner Michael Wayne Williams received a capital sentence for the murders of Morris Keller, Jr., and Keller's wife, Mary Elizabeth. Petitioner later sought a writ of habeas corpus in federal court. Accompanying his petition was a request for an evidentiary hearing on constitutional claims which, he alleged, he had been unable to develop in state-court proceedings. The question in this case is whether 28 U.S.C. §2254(e)(2), as amended by the Antiterrorism and Effective Death Penalty Act of 1996 (AEDPA), bars the evidentiary hearing petitioner seeks. If petitioner "has failed to develop the factual basis of [his] claim[s] in State court proceedings," his case is subject to §2254(e)(2), and he may not receive a hearing because he concedes his inability to satisfy the statute's further stringent conditions for excusing the deficiency.

I

On the evening of February 27, 1993, Verena Lozano James dropped off petitioner and his friend Jeffrey Alan Cruse near a local store in a rural area of Cumberland County, Virginia. The pair planned to rob the store's employees and customers using a .357 revolver petitioner had stolen in the course of a quadruple murder and robbery he had committed two months earlier. Finding the store closed, petitioner and Cruse walked to the Kellers' home. Petitioner was familiar with the couple, having grown up down the road from where they lived. He told Cruse they would have "a couple thousand dollars." Cruse, who had been holding the .357, handed the gun to petitioner and knocked on the door. When Mr. Keller opened the door, petitioner pointed the gun at him as the two intruders forced their way inside. Petitioner and Cruse forced Mr. Keller to the kitchen, where they discovered Mrs. Keller. Petitioner ordered the captives to remove their clothing. While petitioner kept guard on the Kellers, Cruse searched the house for money and other valuables. He found a .38-caliber handgun and bullets. Upon Cruse's return to the kitchen, petitioner had Cruse tie their captives with telephone cords. The Kellers were confined to separate closets while the intruders continued ransacking the house.

When they gathered all they wanted, petitioner and Cruse decided to rape Mrs. Keller. With Mrs. Keller pleading with them not to hurt her or her husband, petitioner raped her. Cruse did the same. Petitioner then ordered the Kellers to shower and dress and "take a walk" with him and Cruse. As they were leaving, petitioner told Mrs. Keller he and Cruse were going to burn down the house. Mrs. Keller begged to be allowed to retrieve her marriage license, which she did, guarded by petitioner.

As the prosecution later presented the case, details of the murders were as follows. Petitioner, now carrying the .38, and Cruse, carrying the .357, took the Kellers to a thicket down a dirt road from the house. With petitioner standing behind Mr. Keller and Cruse behind Mrs. Keller, petitioner told Cruse, "We'll shoot at the count of three." At the third count, petitioner shot Mr. Keller in the head, and Mr. Keller collapsed to the ground. Cruse did not shoot Mrs. Keller at the same moment. Saying "he didn't want to leave no witnesses," petitioner urged Cruse to shoot Mrs. Keller. Cruse fired one shot into her head. Despite his wound, Mr. Keller stood up, but petitioner shot him a second time. To ensure the Kellers were dead, petitioner shot each of them two or three more times.

After returning to the house and loading the stolen property into the Kellers' jeep, petitioner and Cruse set fire to the house and drove the jeep to Fredericksburg, Virginia, where they sold some of the property. They threw the remaining property and the .357 revolver into the Rappahannock River and set fire to the jeep....

Petitioner was arrested and charged with robbery, abduction, rape, and the capital murders of the Kellers. At trial in January 1994, Cruse was the Commonwealth's main witness. He recounted the murders as we have just described.... He also described petitioner as the mastermind of the murders.... Testifying on his own behalf, petitioner admitted he was the first to shoot Mr. Keller and it was his idea to rob the store and set fire to the house. He denied, however, raping or shooting Mrs. Keller, and claimed to have shot Mr. Keller only once. Petitioner blamed Cruse for the remaining shots and disputed some other parts of Cruse's testimony.

The jury convicted petitioner on all counts. After considering the aggravating and mitigating evidence presented during the sentencing phase, the jury found the aggravating circumstances of future dangerousness and vileness of the crimes and recommended a death sentence. The trial court imposed the recommended sentence. The Supreme Court of Virginia affirmed petitioner's convictions and sentence, and we denied certiorari....

Petitioner filed a habeas petition in state court alleging, in relevant part, that the Commonwealth failed to disclose a second agreement it had reached with Cruse.... Finding no merit to petitioner's claims, the Virginia Supreme Court dismissed the habeas petition, and we again denied certiorari.

Petitioner filed a habeas petition in the United States District Court for the Eastern District of Virginia on November 20, 1996. In addition to his claim regarding the alleged undisclosed agreement between the Commonwealth and Cruse, the petition raised three claims relevant to questions now before us. First, petitioner claimed the prosecution had violated *Brady v. Maryland*, [373 U.S. 83 (1963)], in failing to disclose a report of a confidential pre-trial psychiatric examination of Cruse. Second, petitioner alleged his trial was rendered unfair by the seating of a juror who at voir dire had not revealed possible sources of bias. Finally, petitioner alleged one of the prosecutors committed misconduct in failing to reveal his knowledge of the juror's possible bias.

The District Court granted an evidentiary hearing on the undisclosed agreement and the allegations of juror bias and prosecutorial misconduct but denied a hearing on the psychiatric report. Before the evidentiary hearing could be held, the Commonwealth filed an application for an emergency stay and a petition for a writ of mandamus and prohibition in the Court of Appeals. The Commonwealth argued that petitioner's evidentiary hearing was prohibited by 28 U.S.C. §2254(e)(2). A divided panel of the Court of Appeals granted the emergency stay and remanded for the District Court to apply the statute to petitioner's request for an evidentiary hearing. On remand, the District Court vacated its order granting an evidentiary hearing and dismissed the petition, having determined petitioner could not satisfy §2254(e)(2)'s requirements.

The Court of Appeals affirmed....

On October 18, 1999, petitioner filed an application for stay of execution and a petition for a writ of certiorari. On October 28, we stayed petitioner's execution and granted certiorari to decide whether §2254(e)(2) precludes him from receiving an evidentiary hearing on his claims. We now affirm in part and reverse in part.

II

A

Petitioner filed his federal habeas petition after AEDPA's effective date, so the statute applies to his case. The Commonwealth argues AEDPA bars petitioner from receiving an evidentiary hearing on any claim whose factual basis was not developed in state court, absent narrow circumstances not applicable here. Petitioner did not develop, or raise, his claims of juror bias, prosecutorial misconduct, or the prosecution's alleged *Brady* violation regarding Cruse's psychiatric report until he filed his federal habeas petition. Petitioner explains he could not have developed the claims earlier because he was unaware, through no fault of his own, of the underlying facts. As a consequence, petitioner contends, AEDPA erects no barrier to an evidentiary hearing in federal court.

Section 2254(e)(2), the provision which controls whether petitioner may receive an evidentiary hearing in federal district court on the claims that were not developed in the Virginia courts, becomes the central point of our analysis....

By the terms of its opening clause the statute applies only to prisoners who have "failed to develop the factual basis of a claim in State court proceedings." If the prisoner has failed to develop the facts, an evidentiary hearing cannot be granted unless the prisoner's case meets the other conditions of §2254(e)(2). Here, petitioner concedes his case does not comply with §2254(e)(2)(B), so he may receive an evidentiary hearing only if his claims fall outside the opening clause....

B

We start, as always, with the language of the statute. Section 2254(e)(2) begins with a conditional clause, "[i]f the applicant has failed to develop the factual basis of a claim in State court proceedings," which directs attention to the prisoner's efforts in state court. We ask first whether the factual basis was indeed developed in state court, a question susceptible, in the normal course, of a simple yes or no answer. Here the answer is no.

The Commonwealth would have the analysis begin and end there. Under its no-fault reading of the statute, if there is no factual development in the state court, the federal habeas court may not inquire into the reasons for the default when determining whether the opening clause of §2254(e)(2) applies. We do not agree with the Commonwealth's interpretation of the word "failed." ...

We give the words of a statute their "ordinary, contemporary, common meaning," absent an indication Congress intended them to bear some different import. In its customary and preferred sense, "fail" connotes some omission, fault, or negligence on the part of the person who has failed to do something. To say a person has failed in a duty implies he did not take the necessary steps to fulfill it. He is, as a consequence, at fault and bears responsibility for the failure. In this sense, a person is not at fault when his diligent efforts to perform an act are thwarted, for example, by the conduct of another or by happenstance. Fault lies, in those circumstances, either with the person who interfered with the accomplishment of the act or with no one at all. We conclude Congress used the word "failed" in the sense just described. Had Congress intended a no-fault standard, it would have had no difficulty in making its intent plain. It would have had to do no more than use, in lieu of the phrase "has failed to," the phrase "did not." ...

Our interpretation of §2254(e)(2)'s opening clause has support in *Keeney v. Tamayo-Reyes*, 504 U.S. 1, a case decided four years before AEDPA's enactment. In *Keeney*, a prisoner with little knowledge of English sought an evidentiary hearing in federal court, alleging his *nolo contendere* plea to a manslaughter charge was not knowing and voluntary because of inaccuracies in the translation of the plea proceedings. The prisoner had not developed the facts of his claim in state collateral proceedings, an omission caused by the negligence of his state post conviction counsel. The Court characterized this as the "prisoner's failure to develop material facts in state court." We required the prisoner to demonstrate cause and prejudice excusing the default before he could receive a hearing on his claim, unless the prisoner could "show that a fundamental miscarriage of justice would result from failure to hold a federal evidentiary hearing."

... [T]he opening clause of §2254(e)(2) codifies *Keeney*'s threshold standard of diligence, so that prisoners who would have had to satisfy *Keeney*'s test for excusing the deficiency in the state-court record prior to AEDPA are now controlled by §2254(e)(2).

When the words of the Court are used in a later statute governing the same subject matter, it is respectful of Congress and of the Court's own processes to give the words the same meaning in the absence of specific direction to the contrary....

The Commonwealth argues a reading of "failed to develop" premised on fault empties §2254(e)(2)(A)(ii) of its meaning. To treat the prisoner's lack of diligence in state court as a prerequisite for application of §2254(e)(2), the Commonwealth contends, renders a nullity of the statute's own diligence provision requiring the prisoner to show "a factual predicate [of his claim] could not have been previously discovered through the exercise of due diligence." §2254(e)(2)(A)(ii). We disagree....

We are not persuaded by the Commonwealth's further argument that anything less than a no-fault understanding of the opening clause is contrary to AEDPA's purpose to further the principles of comity, finality, and federalism. There is no doubt Congress intended AEDPA to advance these doctrines. Federal habeas corpus principles must inform and shape the historic and still vital relation of mutual respect and common purpose existing between the States and the federal courts. In keeping this delicate balance we have been careful to limit the scope of federal intrusion into state criminal adjudications and to safeguard the States' interest in the integrity of their criminal and collateral proceedings....

... For state courts to have their rightful opportunity to adjudicate federal rights, the prisoner must be diligent in developing the record and presenting, if possible, all claims of constitutional error. If the prisoner fails to do so, himself or herself contributing to the absence of a full and fair adjudication in state court, §2254(e)(2) prohibits an evidentiary hearing to develop the relevant claims in federal court, unless the statute's other stringent requirements are met. Federal courts sitting in habeas are not an alternative forum for trying facts and issues which a prisoner made insufficient effort to pursue in state proceedings. Yet comity is not served by saying a prisoner "has failed to develop the factual basis of a claim" where he was unable to develop his claim in state court despite diligent effort. In that circumstance, an evidentiary hearing is not barred by §2254(e)(2).

III

Now we apply the statutory test. If there has been no lack of diligence at the relevant stages in the state proceedings, the prisoner has not "failed to develop" the facts under §2254(e)(2)'s opening clause, and he will be excused from showing compliance with the balance of the subsection's requirements. We find lack of diligence as to one of the three claims but not as to the other two.

A

Petitioner did not exercise the diligence required to preserve the claim that nondisclosure of Cruse's psychiatric report was in contravention of *Brady v. Maryland*, 373 U.S. 83 (1963). The report concluded Cruse "ha[d] little recollection of the [murders of the Kellers], other than vague memories, as he was intoxicated with alcohol and marijuana at the time." The report had been prepared in September 1993, before petitioner was tried; yet it was not mentioned by petitioner until he filed his federal habeas petition and attached a copy of the report. Petitioner explained that an investigator for his federal habeas counsel discovered the report in Cruse's court file but state habeas counsel had not seen it when he had reviewed the same file....

[Nonetheless,] [t]here are repeated references to a "psychiatric" or "mental health" report in a transcript of Cruse's sentencing proceeding, a copy of which petitioner's own state habeas counsel attached to the state habeas petition he filed with the Virginia

Supreme Court. The transcript reveals that Cruse's attorney described the report with details that should have alerted counsel to a possible *Brady* claim....

The transcript put petitioner's state habeas counsel on notice of the report's existence and possible materiality. The sole indication that counsel made some effort to investigate the report is an October 30, 1995, letter to the prosecutor in which counsel requested "[a]ll reports of physical and mental examinations, scientific tests, or experiments conducted in connection with the investigation of the offense, including but not limited to: ... [a]ll psychological test or polygraph examinations performed upon any prosecution witness and all documents referring or relating to such tests...." After the prosecution declined the requests absent a court order, it appears counsel made no further efforts to find the specific report mentioned by Cruse's attorney. Given knowledge of the report's existence and potential importance, a diligent attorney would have done more. Counsel's failure to investigate these references in anything but a cursory manner triggers the opening clause of §2254(e)(2).

As we hold there was a failure to develop the factual basis of this *Brady* claim in state court, we must determine if the requirements in the balance of §2254(e)(2) are satisfied so that petitioner's failure is excused. Subparagraph (B) of §2254(e)(2) conditions a hearing upon a showing, by clear and convincing evidence, that no reasonable factfinder would have found petitioner guilty of capital murder but for the alleged constitutional error. Petitioner concedes he cannot make this showing, and the case has been presented to us on that premise. For these reasons, we affirm the Court of Appeals' judgment barring an evidentiary hearing on this claim.

B

We conclude petitioner has met the burden of showing he was diligent in efforts to develop the facts supporting his juror bias and prosecutorial misconduct claims in collateral proceedings before the Virginia Supreme Court.

Petitioner's claims are based on two of the questions posed to the jurors by the trial judge at voir dire. First, the judge asked prospective jurors, "Are any of you related to the following people who may be called as witnesses?" Then he read the jurors a list of names, one of which was "Deputy Sheriff Claude Meinhard." Bonnie Stinnett, who would later become the jury foreperson, had divorced Meinhard in 1979, after a 17-year marriage with four children. Stinnett remained silent, indicating the answer was "no." Meinhard, as the officer who investigated the crime scene and interrogated Cruse, would later become the prosecution's lead-off witness at trial.

After reading the names of the attorneys involved in the case, including one of the prosecutors, Robert Woodson, Jr., the judge asked, "Have you or any member of your immediate family ever been represented by any of the aforementioned attorneys?" Stinnett again said nothing, despite the fact Woodson had represented her during her divorce from Meinhard....

Woodson provided an affidavit in which he admitted "[he] was aware that Juror Bonnie Stinnett was the ex-wife of then Deputy Sheriff Claude Meinhard and [he] was aware that they had been divorced for some time." Woodson stated, however, "[t]o [his] mind, people who are related only by marriage are no longer 'related' once the marriage ends in divorce." Woodson also "had no recollection of having been involved as a private attorney in the divorce proceedings between Claude Meinhard and Bonnie Stinnett." He explained that "[w]hatever [his] involvement was in the 1979 divorce, by the time of trial in 1994 [he] had completely forgotten about it."

Even if Stinnett had been correct in her technical or literal interpretation of the question relating to Meinhard, her silence after the first question was asked could suggest to the finder of fact an unwillingness to be forthcoming; this in turn could bear on the veracity of her explanation for not disclosing that Woodson had been her attorney. Stinnett's failure to divulge material information in response to the second question was misleading as a matter of fact because, under any interpretation, Woodson had acted as counsel to her and Meinhard in their divorce. Coupled with Woodson's own reticence, these omissions as a whole disclose the need for an evidentiary hearing. It may be that petitioner could establish that Stinnett was not impartial, or that Woodson's silence so infected the trial as to deny due process.

... The trial record contains no evidence which would have put a reasonable attorney on notice that Stinnett's non-response was a deliberate omission of material information. State habeas counsel did attempt to investigate petitioner's jury, though prompted by concerns about a different juror. Counsel filed a motion for expert services with the Virginia Supreme Court, alleging "irregularities, improprieties and omissions exist[ed] with respect to the empaneling [sic] of the jury." Based on these suspicions, counsel requested funding for an investigator "to examine all circumstances relating to the empanelment of the jury and the jury's consideration of the case." The Commonwealth opposed the motion, and the Virginia Supreme Court denied it and dismissed the habeas petition, depriving petitioner of a further opportunity to investigate. The Virginia Supreme Court's denial of the motion is understandable in light of petitioner's vague allegations, but the vagueness was not the fault of petitioner. Counsel had no reason to believe Stinnett had been married to Meinhard or been represented by Woodson. The underdevelopment of these matters was attributable to Stinnett and Woodson, if anyone. We do not suggest the State has an obligation to pay for investigation of as yet undeveloped claims; but if the prisoner has made a reasonable effort to discover the claims to commence or continue state proceedings, §2254(e)(2) will not bar him from developing them in federal court.

The Court of Appeals held state habeas counsel was not diligent because petitioner's investigator on federal habeas discovered the relationships upon interviewing two jurors who referred in passing to Stinnett as "Bonnie Meinhard." The investigator later confirmed Stinnett's prior marriage to Meinhard by checking Cumberland County's public records. ("The documents supporting [petitioner's] Sixth Amendment claims have been a matter of public record since Stinnett's divorce became final in 1979. Indeed, because [petitioner's] federal habeas counsel located those documents, there is little reason to think that his state habeas counsel could not have done so as well"). We should be surprised, to say the least, if a district court familiar with the standards of trial practice were to hold that in all cases diligent counsel must check public records containing personal information pertaining to each and every juror. Because of Stinnett and Woodson's silence, there was no basis for an investigation into Stinnett's marriage history. Section 2254(e)(2) does not apply to petitioner's related claims of juror bias and prosecutorial misconduct.

We further note the Commonwealth has not argued that petitioner could have sought relief in state court once he discovered the factual bases of these claims some time between appointment of federal habeas counsel on July 2, 1996, and the filing of his federal habeas petition on November 20, 1996. As an indigent, petitioner had 120 days following appointment of state habeas counsel to file a petition with the Virginia Supreme Court. State habeas counsel was appointed on August 10, 1995, about a year before petitioner's investigator on federal habeas uncovered the information regarding Stinnett and Woodson. As state postconviction relief was no longer available at the time the facts came to light, it would have been futile for petitioner to return to the Virginia courts. In these circumstances, though the state courts did not have an opportunity to consider the new claims, petitioner cannot be said to have failed to develop them in state court by reason of having neglected to pursue remedies available under Virginia law.

Our analysis should suffice to establish cause for any procedural default petitioner may have committed in not presenting these claims to the Virginia courts in the first instance. Questions regarding the standard for determining the prejudice that petitioner must establish to obtain relief on these claims can be addressed by the Court of Appeals or the District Court in the course of further proceedings. These courts ... will take due account of the District Court's earlier decision to grant an evidentiary hearing based in part on its belief that "Juror Stinnett deliberately failed to tell the truth on voir dire."

The decision of the Court of Appeals is affirmed in part and reversed in part. The case is remanded for further proceedings consistent with this opinion.

Chapter 15

Retroactivity

Introduction

In *Brown v. Allen*, 344 U.S. 443 (1953), the Supreme Court instructed federal habeas courts to "independently apply the correct constitutional standards" to a petitioner's claim, "no matter how fair and completely the claim had been litigated in the state courts." Federal habeas courts, in other words, were to have the "final say" on the merits of a state prisoner's federal constitutional claim. Thirty-six years after *Brown*, the Court in *Teague v. Lane*, 489 U.S. 288 (1989), "substantially altered the nature of that 'final say' given to the federal habeas courts." LaFave and Israel, *Criminal Procedure* 1227 (2d ed.) (West Pub. Co. 1992). Under the *Brown* standard, the federal habeas court was required to ask how it would interpret the Constitution. How does *Teague*, immediately below, alter the federal habeas court's duty?

Teague v. Lane
489 U.S. 288 (1989)

Justice O'CONNOR announced the judgment of the Court and delivered the opinion of the Court with respect to Parts I, II, and III, and an opinion with respect to Parts IV and V, in which Chief Justice Rehnquist, Justice Scalia, and Justice Kennedy join.

In *Taylor v. Louisiana*, 419 U.S. 522 (1975), this Court held that the Sixth Amendment required that the jury venire be drawn from a fair cross section of the community. The Court stated, however, that "in holding that petit juries must be drawn from a source fairly representative of the community we impose no requirement that petit juries actually chosen must mirror the community and reflect the various distinctive groups in the population. Defendants are not entitled to a jury of any particular composition." *Id.* at 538. The principal question presented in this case is whether the Sixth Amendment's fair cross section requirement should now be extended to the petit jury. Because we adopt Justice Harlan's approach to retroactivity for cases on collateral review, we leave the resolution of that question for another day.

I

Petitioner Frank Dean Teague, a black man, was convicted by an all-white Illinois jury of three counts of attempted murder, two counts of armed robbery, and one count of aggravated battery. During jury selection for petitioner's trial, the prosecutor used all 10 of his peremptory challenges to exclude blacks.... After the prosecutor had struck six blacks, petitioner's counsel moved for a mistrial. The trial court denied the motion. When the prosecutor struck four more blacks, petitioner's counsel again moved for a mistrial, arguing that petitioner was "entitled to a jury of his peers." The prosecutor defended the challenges by stating that he was trying to achieve a balance of men and women on the jury. The trial court denied the motion, reasoning that the jury "appear[ed] to be a fair [one]."

On appeal, petitioner argued that the prosecutor's use of peremptory challenges denied him the right to be tried by a jury that was representative of the community. The Illinois Appellate Court rejected petitioner's fair cross section claim. The Illinois Supreme Court denied leave to appeal, and we denied certiorari.

Petitioner then filed a petition for a writ of habeas corpus in the United States District Court for the Northern District of Illinois. Petitioner repeated his fair cross section claim.... He also argued, for the first time, that under *Swain v. Alabama*, 380 U.S. 202 (1965), a prosecutor could be questioned about his use of peremptory challenges once he volunteered an explanation. The District Court, though sympathetic to petitioner's arguments, held that it was bound by *Swain* and Circuit precedent.

[While Teague's case was pending in federal court on appeal from a denial of federal habeas relief, we decided] *Batson v. Kentucky*, 476 U.S. 79 (1986) [*supra* chapter 6], which overruled a portion of *Swain*. After *Batson* was decided, the Court of Appeals held that petitioner could not benefit from the rule in that case because *Allen v. Hardy*, 478 U.S. 255 (1986) (per curiam), had held that *Batson* would not be applied retroactively to cases on collateral review. The Court of Appeals also held that petitioner's *Swain* claim was procedurally barred and in any event meritless. The Court of Appeals rejected petitioner's fair cross section claim, holding that the fair cross section requirement was limited to the jury venire....

IV

Petitioner[] [contends that] the Sixth Amendment's fair cross section requirement applies to the petit jury. As we noted at the outset, *Taylor* expressly stated that the fair cross section requirement does not apply to the petit jury. Petitioner nevertheless contends that the *ratio decidendi* of *Taylor* cannot be limited to the jury venire, and he urges adoption of a new rule. Because we hold that the rule urged by petitioner should not be applied retroactively to cases on collateral review, we decline to address petitioner's contention.

A

In the past, the Court has, without discussion, often applied a new constitutional rule of criminal procedure to the defendant in the case announcing the new rule, and has confronted the question of retroactivity later when a different defendant sought the benefit of that rule. In several cases, however, the Court has addressed the retroactivity question in the very case announcing the new rule. These two lines of cases do not have a unifying theme, and we think it is time to clarify how the question of retroactivity should be resolved for cases on collateral review....

In our view, the question "whether a decision [announcing a new rule should] be given prospective or retroactive effect should be faced at the time of [that] decision." Retroactivity is properly treated as a threshold question, for, once a new rule is applied to the defendant in the case announcing the rule, evenhanded justice requires that it be applied retroactively to all who are similarly situated. Thus, before deciding whether the fair cross section requirement should be extended to the petit jury, we should ask whether such a rule would be applied retroactively to the case at issue. This retroactivity determination would normally entail application of the *Linkletter v. Walker*, 381 U.S. 618 (1965), standard, but we believe that our approach to retroactivity for cases on collateral review requires modification.

It is admittedly often difficult to determine when a case announces a new rule, and we do not attempt to define the spectrum of what may or may not constitute a new rule for retroactivity purposes. In general, however, a case announces a new rule when it breaks new ground or imposes a new obligation on the States or the Federal Government. To put it differently, a case announces a new rule if the result was not *dictated* by precedent existing at the time the defendant's conviction became final. Given the strong language in *Taylor* and our statement in *Akins v. Texas*, 325 U.S. 398, 403 (1945), that "[f]airness in [jury] selection has never been held to require proportional representation of races upon a jury," application of the fair cross section requirement to the petit jury would be a new rule.

Not all new rules have been uniformly treated for retroactivity purposes. Nearly a quarter of a century ago, in *Linkletter*, the Court attempted to set some standards by which to determine the retroactivity of new rules. The question in *Linkletter* was whether *Mapp v. Ohio*, which made the exclusionary rule applicable to the States, should be applied retroactively to cases on collateral review. The Court determined that the retroactivity of *Mapp* should be determined by examining the purpose of the exclusionary rule, the reliance of the States on prior law, and the effect on the administration of justice of a retroactive application of the exclusionary rule. Using that standard, the Court held that *Mapp* would only apply to trials commencing after that case was decided. The *Linkletter* retroactivity standard has not led to consistent results. Instead, it has been used to limit application of certain new rules to cases on direct review, other new rules only to the defendants in the cases announcing such rules, and still other new rules to cases in which trials have not yet commenced. Not surprisingly, commentators have "had a veritable field day" with the *Linkletter* standard, with much of the discussion being "more than mildly negative."

Dissatisfied with the *Linkletter* standard, Justice Harlan advocated a different approach to retroactivity. He argued that new rules should always be applied retroactively to cases on direct review, but that generally they should not be applied retroactively to criminal cases on collateral review.

In *Griffith v. Kentucky*, 479 U.S. 314 (1987), we rejected as unprincipled and inequitable the *Linkletter* standard for cases pending on direct review at the time a new rule is announced, and adopted the first part of the retroactivity approach advocated by Justice Harlan. We agreed with Justice Harlan that "failure to apply a newly declared constitutional rule to criminal cases pending on direct review violates basic norms of constitutional adjudication."

... [Because] "selective application of new rules violates the principle of treating similarly situated defendants the same," we refused to continue to tolerate the inequity that resulted from not applying new rules retroactively to defendants whose cases had not yet become final. [W]e held that "a new rule for the conduct of criminal prosecutions is to be applied retroactively to all cases, state or federal, pending on direct review or not yet final...."

B

Justice Harlan believed that new rules generally should not be applied retroactively to cases on collateral review. He argued that retroactivity for cases on collateral review could "be responsibly [determined] only by focusing, in the first instance, on the nature, function, and scope of the adjudicatory process in which such cases arise...." With regard to the nature of habeas corpus, Justice Harlan wrote:

> Habeas corpus always has been a *collateral* remedy, providing an avenue for upsetting judgments that have become otherwise final. It is not designed as a substitute for direct review. The interest in leaving concluded litigation in a state of repose, that is, reducing the controversy to a final judgment not subject to further judicial revision, may quite legitimately be found by those responsible for defining the scope of the writ to outweigh in some, many, or most instances the competing interest in readjudicating convictions according to all legal standards in effect when a habeas petition is filed.

Given the "broad scope of constitutional issues cognizable on habeas," Justice Harlan argued that it is "sounder, in adjudicating habeas petitions, generally to apply the law prevailing at the time a conviction became final than it is to seek to dispose of [habeas] cases on the basis of intervening changes in constitutional interpretation." As he had explained in *Desist v. United States*, 394 U.S. 244 (1969) (Harlan, J., dissenting),

> the threat of habeas serves as a necessary additional incentive for trial and appellate courts throughout the land to conduct their proceedings in a manner consistent with established constitutional principles. In order to perform this deterrence function, ... the habeas court need only apply the constitutional standards that prevailed at the time the original proceedings took place.

Justice Harlan identified only two exceptions to his general rule of nonretroactivity for cases on collateral review. First, a new rule should be applied retroactively if it places "certain kinds of primary, private individual conduct beyond the power of the criminal law-making authority to proscribe." Second, a new rule should be applied retroactively if it requires the observance of "those procedures that ... are 'implicit in the concept of ordered liberty.'"

We agree with Justice Harlan's description of the function of habeas corpus. "[T]he Court never has defined the scope of the writ simply by reference to a perceived need to assure that an individual accused of [a] crime is afforded a trial free of constitutional error." Rather, we have recognized that interests of comity and finality must also be considered in determining the proper scope of habeas review. Thus, if a defendant fails to comply with state procedural rules and is barred from litigating a particular constitutional claim in state court, the claim can be considered on federal habeas only if the defendant shows cause for the default and actual prejudice resulting therefrom. We have declined to make the application of the procedural default rule dependent on the magnitude of the constitutional claim at issue, or on the State's interest in the enforcement of its procedural rule.

This Court has not "always followed an unwavering line in its conclusions as to the availability of the Great Writ. Our development of the law of federal habeas corpus has been attended, seemingly, with some backing and filling." Nevertheless, it has long been established that a final civil judgment entered under a given rule of law may withstand subsequent judicial change in that rule. In *Chicot County Drainage District v. Baxter State Bank*, 308 U.S. 371 (1940), the Court held that a judgment based on a jurisdictional statute later found to be unconstitutional could have *res judicata* effect. The Court based its decision in large part on finality concerns. "The actual existence of a statute, prior to such a determination [of unconstitutionality], is an operative fact and may have consequences which cannot justly be ignored. The past cannot always be erased by a new judicial declaration.... Questions of ... prior determinations deemed to have finality and acted upon accordingly ... demand examination."

These underlying considerations of finality find significant and compelling parallels in the criminal context. Application of constitutional rules not in existence at the time a conviction became final seriously undermines the principle of finality which is essential to the operation of our criminal justice system. Without finality, the criminal law is deprived of much of its deterrent effect. The fact that life and liberty are at stake in criminal prosecutions "shows only that 'conventional notions of finality' should not have *as much* place in criminal as in civil litigation, not that they should have *none*." "[I]f a criminal judgment is ever to be final, the notion of legality must at some point include the assignment of final competence to determine legality." As explained by Professor Mishkin:

> From this aspect, the *Linkletter* problem becomes not so much one of prospectivity or retroactivity of the rule but rather of the availability of collateral attack—in [that] case federal habeas corpus—to go behind the otherwise final judgment of conviction.... For the potential availability of collateral attack is what created the "retroactivity" problem of *Linkletter* in the first place; there seems little doubt that without that possibility the Court would have given short shrift to any arguments for "prospective limitation" of the *Mapp* rule.

The "costs imposed upon the State[s] by retroactive application of new rules of constitutional law on habeas corpus ... generally far outweigh the benefits of this application." In many ways the application of new rules to cases on collateral review may be more intrusive than the enjoining of criminal prosecutions, for it continually forces the States to marshal resources in order to keep in prison defendants whose trials and appeals conformed to then-existing constitutional standards. Furthermore, as we recognized in *Engle v. Isaac*, "[s]tate courts are understandably frustrated when they faithfully apply existing constitutional law only to have a federal court discover, during a [habeas] proceeding, new constitutional commands."

We find these criticisms to be persuasive, and we now adopt Justice Harlan's view of retroactivity for cases on collateral review. Unless they fall within an exception to the general rule, new constitutional rules of criminal procedure will not be applicable to those cases which have become final before the new rules are announced.

V

Petitioner's conviction became final in 1983. As a result, the rule petitioner urges would not be applicable to this case, which is on collateral review, unless it would fall within an exception.

The first exception suggested by Justice Harlan—that a new rule should be applied retroactively if it places "certain kinds of primary, private individual conduct beyond the power of the criminal law-making authority to proscribe,"—is not relevant here. Application of the fair cross section requirement to the petit jury would not accord constitutional protection to any primary activity whatsoever.

The second exception suggested by Justice Harlan—that a new rule should be applied retroactively if it requires the observance of "those procedures that ... are 'implicit in the concept of ordered liberty,'"—we apply with a modification. The language used by Justice Harlan in *Mackey v. United States*, 401 U.S. 667, 693-694 (1971), leaves no doubt that he meant the second exception to be reserved for watershed rules of criminal procedure:

Typically, it should be the case that any conviction free from federal constitutional error at the time it became final, will be found, upon reflection, to have been fundamentally fair and conducted under those procedures essential to the substance of a full hearing. However, in some situations it might be that time and growth in social capacity, as well as judicial perceptions of what we can rightly demand of the adjudicatory process, will properly alter our understanding of the *bedrock procedural elements* that must be found to vitiate the fairness of a particular conviction. For example, such, in my view, is the case with the right to counsel at trial now held a necessary condition precedent to any conviction for a serious crime.

In *Desist*, Justice Harlan had reasoned that one of the two principal functions of habeas corpus was "to assure that no man has been incarcerated under a procedure which creates an impermissibly large risk that the innocent will be convicted," and concluded "from this that all 'new' constitutional rules which significantly improve the pre-existing fact-finding procedures are to be retroactively applied on habeas." In *Mackey*, Justice Harlan gave three reasons for shifting to the less defined *Palko v. Connecticut*, 302 U.S. 319 (1969), approach. First, he observed that recent precedent, particularly *Kaufman v. United States*, 394 U.S. 217 (1969) (permitting Fourth Amendment claims to be raised on collateral review), led "ineluctably ... to the conclusion that it is not a principal purpose of the writ to inquire whether a criminal convict did in fact commit the deed alleged." Second, he noted that cases such as *Coleman v. Alabama*, 399 U.S. 1 (1970) (invalidating lineup procedures in the absence of counsel), gave him reason to doubt the marginal effectiveness of claimed improvements in factfinding. Third, he found "inherently intractable the purported distinction between those new rules that are designed to improve the factfinding process and those designed principally to further other values."

We believe it desirable to combine the accuracy element of the *Desist* version of the second exception with the *Mackey* requirement that the procedure at issue must implicate the fundamental fairness of the trial. Were we to employ the *Palko* test without more, we would be doing little more than importing into a very different context the terms of the debate over incorporation. Reviving the *Palko* test now, in this area of law, would be unnecessarily anachronistic. Moreover, since *Mackey* was decided, our cases have moved in the direction of reaffirming the relevance of the likely accuracy of convictions in determining the available scope of habeas review. Finally, we believe that Justice Harlan's concerns about the difficulty in identifying both the existence and the value of accuracy-enhancing procedural rules can be addressed by limiting the scope of the second exception to those new procedures without which the likelihood of an accurate conviction is seriously diminished.

Because we operate from the premise that such procedures would be so central to an accurate determination of innocence or guilt, we believe it unlikely that many such components of basic due process have yet to emerge. We are also of the view that such rules are "best illustrated by recalling the classic grounds for the issuance of a writ of habeas corpus — that the proceeding was dominated by mob violence; that the prosecutor knowingly made use of perjured testimony; or that the conviction was based on a confession extorted from the defendant by brutal methods."[3]

---

3. Because petitioner is not under sentence of death, we need not, and do not, express any views as to how the retroactivity approach we adopt today is to be applied in the capital sentencing context....

An examination of our decision in *Taylor* applying the fair cross section requirement to the jury venire leads inexorably to the conclusion that adoption of the rule petitioner urges would be a far cry from the kind of absolute prerequisite to fundamental fairness that is "implicit in the concept of ordered liberty." The requirement that the jury venire be composed of a fair cross section of the community is based on the role of the jury in our system. Because the purpose of the jury is to guard against arbitrary abuses of power by interposing the commonsense judgment of the community between the State and the defendant, the jury venire cannot be composed only of special segments of the population. "Community participation in the administration of the criminal law ... is not only consistent with our democratic heritage but is also critical to public confidence in the fairness of the criminal justice system." But as we stated in *Daniel v. Louisiana*, 420 U.S. 31, 32 (1975), which held that *Taylor* was not to be given retroactive effect, the fair cross section requirement "[does] not rest on the premise that every criminal trial, or any particular trial, [is] necessarily unfair because it [is] not conducted in accordance with what we determined to be the requirements of the Sixth Amendment." Because the absence of a fair cross section on the jury venire does not undermine the fundamental fairness that must underlie a conviction or seriously diminish the likelihood of obtaining an accurate conviction, we conclude that a rule requiring that petit juries be composed of a fair cross section of the community would not be a "bedrock procedural element" that would be retroactively applied under the second exception we have articulated....

For the reasons set forth above, the judgment of the Court of Appeals is affirmed.

Justice BRENNAN, with whom Justice Marshall joins, dissenting.

Today a plurality of this Court, without benefit of briefing and oral argument, adopts a novel threshold test for federal review of state criminal convictions on habeas corpus....

II

C

... [F]rom the plurality's exposition of its new rule, one might infer that its novel fabrication will work no great change in the availability of federal collateral review of state convictions. Nothing could be further from the truth. Although the plurality declines to "define the spectrum of what may or may not constitute a new rule for retroactivity purposes," it does say that generally "a case announces a new rule when it breaks new ground or imposes a new obligation on the States or the Federal Government." Otherwise phrased, "a case announces a new rule if the result was not *dictated* by precedent existing at the time the defendant's conviction became final." This account is extremely broad. Few decisions on appeal or collateral review are "*dictated*" by what came before. Most such cases involve a question of law that is at least debatable, permitting a rational judge to resolve the case in more than one way. Virtually no case that prompts a dissent on the relevant legal point, for example, could be said to be "*dictated*" by prior decisions. By the plurality's test, therefore, a great many cases could only be heard on habeas if the rule urged by the petitioner fell within one of the two exceptions the plurality has sketched. Those exceptions, however, are narrow. Rules that place "'certain kinds of primary, private individual conduct beyond the power of the criminal law-making authority to proscribe,'" are rare. And rules that would require "new procedures without which the likelihood of an accurate conviction is seriously diminished" are not appreciably more common. The plurality admits, in fact, that it "believe[s] it unlikely that many such components of basic due process have yet to emerge." The plurality's approach today can thus be expected to contract substantially the Great Writ's sweep.

Its impact is perhaps best illustrated by noting the abundance and variety of habeas cases we have decided in recent years that could never have been adjudicated had the plurality's new rule been in effect....

For example, in *Nix v. Whiteside*, 475 U.S. 157 (1986), the Court ruled that a defendant's right to counsel under the Sixth Amendment is not violated when a defense attorney refuses to cooperate with him in presenting perjured testimony at trial. Clearly, the opposite result sought by the petitioner could not have been dictated by prior cases, nor would the introduction of perjured testimony have improved the accuracy of factfinding at trial. The claim presented on habeas was therefore novel yet well outside the plurality's exceptions. Were the claim raised tomorrow on federal collateral review, a court could not reach the merits, as did we. The same is true of numerous right-to-counsel and representation claims we have decided where the wrong alleged by the habeas petitioner was unlikely to have produced an erroneous conviction.

Likewise, because "the Fifth Amendment's privilege against self-incrimination is not an adjunct to the ascertainment of truth," claims that a petitioner's right to remain silent was violated would, if not dictated by earlier decisions, ordinarily fail to qualify under the plurality's second exception. In *Estelle v. Smith*, 451 U.S. 454 (1981) [*supra* chapter 10], for example, we held that a psychiatrist who examined the defendant before trial without warning him that what he said could be used against him in a capital sentencing proceeding could not testify against him at such a proceeding. Under the plurality's newly fashioned rule, however, we could not have decided that case on the merits. The result can hardly be said to have been compelled by existing case law, and the exclusion of such testimony at sentencing cannot have influenced the jury's determination of the defendant's guilt or enhanced the likely accuracy of his sentence.[5]

Habeas claims under the Double Jeopardy Clause will also be barred under the plurality's approach if the rules they seek to establish would "brea[k] new ground or impos[e] a new obligation on the States or the Federal Government," because they bear no relation to the petitioner's guilt or innocence. So, too, will miscellaneous due process and Sixth Amendment claims that relate only tangentially to a defendant's guilt or innocence. And of course cases closely related to Teague's, such as *Lockhart v. McCree*, 476 U.S. 162 (1986), where we held that the removal for cause of so-called "*Witherspoon*-excludables" does not violate the Sixth Amendment's fair cross section requirement, would be beyond the purview of this Court when they arrived on habeas.

D

These are massive changes, unsupported by precedent. They also lack a reasonable foundation. By exaggerating the importance of treating like cases alike and granting relief to all identically positioned habeas petitioners or none, "the Court acts as if it has no choice but to follow a mechanical notion of fairness without pausing to consider 'sound principles of decisionmaking.'" Certainly it is desirable, in the interest of fair-

---

5. In "limiting the scope of the second exception to those new procedures without which the likelihood of an accurate conviction is seriously diminished," the plurality presumably intends the exception to cover claims that involve the accuracy of the defendant's sentence as well as the accuracy of a court's determination of his guilt. Thus, the plurality's new rule apparently would not prevent capital defendants, for example, from raising Eighth Amendment, due process, and equal protection challenges to capital sentencing procedures on habeas corpus.

ness, to accord the same treatment to all habeas petitioners with the same claims. Given a choice between deciding an issue on direct or collateral review that might result in a new rule of law that would not warrant retroactive application to persons on collateral review other than the petitioner who brought the claim, we should ordinarily grant certiorari and decide the question on direct review.…

… Sometimes a claim which, if successful, would create a new rule not appropriate for retroactive application on collateral review is better presented by a habeas case than by one on direct review. In fact, sometimes the claim is only presented on collateral review. In that case, while we could forgo deciding the issue in the hope that it would eventually be presented squarely on direct review, that hope might be misplaced, and even if it were in time fulfilled, the opportunity to check constitutional violations and to further the evolution of our thinking in some area of the law would in the meanwhile have been lost.…

… Permitting the federal courts to decide novel habeas claims not substantially related to guilt or innocence has profited our society immensely. Congress has not seen fit to withdraw those benefits by amending the statute that provides for them. And although a favorable decision for a petitioner might not extend to another prisoner whose identical claim has become final, it is at least arguably better that the wrong done to one person be righted than that none of the injuries inflicted on those whose convictions have become final be redressed, despite the resulting inequality in treatment.…

III

Even if one accepts the plurality's account of the appropriate limits to habeas relief, its conclusion that Teague's claim may not be heard is dubious.… Teague's claim is simply that the Sixth Amendment's command that no distinctive groups be systematically excluded from jury pools, or from venires drawn from them, applies with equal force to the selection of petit juries. He maintains that this firmly established principle prohibits the prosecution from using its peremptory challenges discriminatorily to prevent venirepersons from sitting on the jury merely because they belong to some racial, ethnic, or other group cognizable for Sixth Amendment purposes. Teague's claim is therefore closely akin to that which prevailed in *Batson v. Kentucky*, 476 U.S. 79 (1986), where we held that the Equal Protection Clause forbids the prosecution from using its peremptory challenges to exclude venirepersons from the jury solely because they share the defendant's race. The only potentially significant difference is that Teague's claim, if valid, would bar the prosecution from excluding venirepersons from the petit jury on account of their membership in some cognizable group even when the defendant is not himself a member of that group, whereas the Equal Protection Clause might not provide a basis for relief unless the defendant himself belonged to the group whose members were improperly excluded.

Once Teague's claim is characterized correctly, the plurality's assertions that on its new standard his claim is too novel to be recognized on habeas corpus, and that the right he invokes is "a far cry from the kind of absolute prerequisite to fundamental fairness that is 'implicit in the concept of ordered liberty,'" are dubious. The requirement Teague asks us to impose does not go far beyond our mandates in *Taylor*, *Duren*, and *Batson*; indeed, it flows quite naturally from those decisions.…

The plurality's assertion that Teague's claim fails to fit within Justice Harlan's second exception is also questionable.…

[R]ecently, in *Vasquez v. Hillery*, 474 U.S. at 263, we expressly rejected the claim that "discrimination in the grand jury has no effect on the fairness of the criminal trials that result from that grand jury's actions." Because "intentional discrimination in the selection of grand jurors is a grave constitutional trespass, possible only under color of state authority, and wholly within the power of the State to prevent," we reaffirmed our decision in *Rose v. Mitchell*, 443 U.S. 545 (1979), and held that a prisoner may seek relief on federal habeas for racial discrimination in the selection of the grand jury that indicted him and that such claims are not subject to harmless-error review. Compelling the State to indict and try him a second time, we said, despite the heavy burdens it imposes, "is not disproportionate to the evil that it seeks to deter." The plurality's assertion that an allegation, like Teague's, of discrimination in the selection of the petit jury—with far graver impact on the fundamental fairness of a petitioner's trial than the discrimination we condemned in *Hillery*—is too tangentially connected with truth finding to warrant retroactive application on habeas corpus under its new approach therefore strains credibility.

IV

A majority of this Court's Members now share the view that cases on direct and collateral review should be handled differently for retroactivity purposes. In *Griffith v. Kentucky*, 479 U.S. 314 (1987), the Court adopted Justice Harlan's proposal that a new rule be applied retroactively to all convictions not yet final when the rule was announced. If we had adhered to our precedents, reached Teague's Sixth Amendment claim, and ruled in his favor, we would ultimately have had to decide whether we should continue to apply to habeas cases the three-factor approach outlined in *Stovall v. Denno*, or whether we should embrace most of the other half of Justice Harlan's proposal and ordinarily refuse to apply new rules retroactively to cases on collateral review, except in the cases where they are announced.

In my view, that is not a question we should decide here.... Certainly it is not one the Court need decide before it considers the merits of Teague's claim because, as the plurality mistakenly contends, its resolution properly determines whether the merits should be reached. By repudiating our familiar approach without regard for the doctrine of *stare decisis*, the plurality would deprive us of the manifold advantages of deciding important constitutional questions when they come to us first or most cleanly on collateral review. I dissent.

Notes and Questions

1. As the *Teague* majority makes clear, a "new rule" may be defined as one that "was not *dictated* by precedent existing at the time the defendant's conviction became final." In *Butler v. McKellar*, 494 U.S. 407 (1990), the Court said that if a rule "was susceptible to debate among reasonable minds," it could not have been dictated by precedent, and was properly classified as a new rule. Thus, the new role of a federal habeas court is simply "to ask whether the state court's interpretation of the United States Constitution was a reasonably debatable reading of the Supreme Court precedent prevailing at that point in time when the opportunity for direct review of the prisoner's conviction ended." LaFave & Israel, *Criminal Procedure* 1228 (2d ed.) (West Pub. Co. 1992). If the answer is "yes," petitioner is seeking a new rule and *Teague* prevents the federal habeas court from examining the merits. Put differently, unless the rule which the habeas petitioner seeks is dictated by precedent existing at the time her conviction became final, federal court review is barred.

2. As the Court explained in *Lambrix v. Singletary*, 520 U.S. 518, 527 (1997), it employs a three-step analysis to determine whether a constitutional rule is "new" for the purposes of *Teague*.

In *Teague* we held that, in general, "new constitutional rules of criminal procedure will not be applicable to those cases which have become final before the new rules are announced." To apply *Teague*, a federal court engages in a three-step process. First, it determines the date upon which the defendant's conviction became final. Second, it must "[s]urve[y] the legal landscape as it then existed,' and 'determine whether a state court considering [the defendant's] claim at the time his conviction became final would have felt compelled by existing precedent to conclude that the rule [he] seeks was required by the Constitution." Finally, if the court determines that the habeas petitioner seeks the benefit of a new rule, the court must consider whether the relief sought falls within one of the two narrow exceptions to nonretroactivity.

The determination that a decision constitutes a "new rule" for purposes of retroactivity is discussed in Randy Hertz & James Liebman, FEDERAL HABEAS CORPUS PRACTICE AND PROCEDURE § 25.5 (5th ed. 2005).

3. Recall that under the AEDPA, §2254(d)(1) provides, "An application for a writ of habeas corpus on behalf of a person in custody pursuant to the judgment of a State court shall not be granted with respect to any claim that was adjudicated on the merits in State court proceedings unless the adjudication of the claim resulted in a decision that was contrary to, or involved an unreasonable application of, *clearly established Federal law, as determined by the Supreme Court of the United States.*" (Emphasis added.) Arguably this provision extends *Teague* so that a petitioner not only is limited to precedent existing at the time of her conviction became final, but also she is limited to only Supreme Court precedent. A federal habeas court could not apply its own circuit's jurisprudence in addition to the Supreme Court's rulings in reviewing a habeas petition. Do you find this to be a reasonable interpretation of §2254? What other interpretation might one give this provision?

4. In *Terry Williams v. Taylor*, 529 U.S. 362 (2000), Justice O'Connor stated:

That statutory phrase [in §2254(d)] refers to the holdings, as opposed to the dicta, of this Court's decisions as of the time of the relevant state-court decision. In this respect, the "clearly established Federal law" phrase bears only a slight connection to our *Teague* jurisprudence. With one caveat, whatever would qualify as an old rule under our *Teague* jurisprudence will constitute "clearly established Federal law, as determined by the Supreme Court of the United States" under §2254(d)(1). The one caveat, as the statutory language makes clear, is that §2254(d)(1) restricts the source of clearly established law to this Court's jurisprudence.

5. In describing the relationship between *Teague* and 28 U.S.C. § 2254, the Court in *Horn v. Banks*, 536 U.S. 266 (2002) (per curiam), stated:

While it is of course a necessary prerequisite to federal habeas relief that a prisoner satisfy the AEDPA standard of review set forth in 28 U.S.C. §§ 2254(d) ("[a]n application ... shall not be granted ... *unless*" the AEDPA standard of review is satisfied (emphasis added)), none of our post-AEDPA cases have suggested that a writ of habeas corpus should automatically issue if a prisoner satisfies the AEDPA standard, or that AEDPA relieves courts from the responsibility of addressing properly raised *Teague* arguments. To the contrary, if our post-AEDPA cases suggest anything about AEDPA's relationship to *Teague*, it is that the AEDPA and *Teague* inquiries are distinct. Thus, in addition to performing any analysis required by AEDPA, a federal court considering a habeas petition must conduct a threshold *Teague* analysis when the issue is properly raised by the state.

6. Generally, a conviction becomes final for *Teague* purposes when the defendant has exhausted all direct appeals and when either the time for filing a petition for certiorari on direct review has elapsed, or the Supreme Court has denied a petition for certiorari on direct review. *Teague*, 489 U.S. at 295. However, once the Supreme Court denies certiorari on direct review of a criminal conviction, the petitioner may file a motion for reconsideration of the Court's denial of the certiorari petition. If this step is taken, the conviction arguably becomes final at the time the Court denies the motion for reconsideration.

7. Does the distinction drawn in *Teague* between cases on collateral review and those on direct appeal promote fairness? What about the prisoner whose appeal becomes final two days before the Supreme Court hands down a decision which would have provided the prisoner relief had his appeal still been pending?

Justice White recognized that mere fortuity often makes the difference between whether a case proceeds quickly to collateral review or languishes on direct review.

> Let us assume that X and Y are accomplices in a murder and that they are tried separately in the state courts. For any one of several reasons, including reversal and retrial or consensual delay, X's case proceeds slowly through direct review while Y's conviction is quickly affirmed. Assume further that after X's conviction is affirmed by the State's highest court, this Court holds that a practice employed in both the X and Y trials violates the Constitution. Both X and Y come before this Court at the same time seeking to have the new rule applied to their cases—X on direct review and Y by way of collateral attack.

Williams v. United States, 401 U.S. 646 (1971). Of course, under *Teague*, although X and Y were convicted of the same crime in the same state court system, X would receive the benefit of the new rule, but Y would not.

7. What result under *Teague* if the federal habeas petitioner argues for the reversal of a prior decision?

8. How does *Teague* and/or 28 U.S.C. § 2254(d)(1) comport with *Trop v. Dulles*, 356 U.S. 86, 101 (1958)—a case which suggests that "evolving standards of decency" prohibit the execution of someone whose death sentence, according to later-developed standards, was returned as a result of unreliable procedures?

9. *Teague* was not a capital case and the plurality expressly reserved the question whether *Teague*'s retroactivity rules would apply in the capital sentencing context. The Court answered that question affirmatively in *Penry v. Lynaugh*, 492 U.S. 302 (1989) (below).

Penry v. Lynaugh
492 U.S. 302 (1989)

Justice O'CONNOR announced the judgment of the Court and delivered the opinion for a unanimous Court with respect to Parts I and IV-A, the opinion of the Court with respect to Parts II-B and III, in which Brennan, Marshall, Blackmun, and Stevens, JJ., joined, the opinion of the Court with respect to Parts II-A and IV-B, in which Rehnquist, C.J., and White, Scalia, and Kennedy, JJ., joined, and an opinion with respect to Part IV-C.

[For a discussion of the merits of Penry's Eighth Amendment and mental retardation claims, see *supra* chapter 5.]

II

A

Penry is currently before the Court on his petition in federal court for a writ of habeas corpus. Because Penry is before us on collateral review, we must determine, as a threshold matter, whether granting him the relief he seeks would create a "new rule." *Teague v. Lane*, 489 U.S. 288, 301. Under *Teague*, new rules will not be applied or announced in cases on collateral review unless they fall into one of two exceptions.

Teague was not a capital case, and the plurality opinion expressed no views regarding how the retroactivity approach adopted in *Teague* would be applied in the capital sentencing context. The plurality noted, however, that a criminal judgment necessarily includes the sentence imposed, and that collateral challenges to sentences "delay the enforcement of the judgment at issue and decrease the possibility that 'there will at some point be the certainty that comes with an end to litigation.'" In our view, the finality concerns underlying Justice Harlan's approach to retroactivity are applicable in the capital sentencing context, as are the two exceptions to his general rule of nonretroactivity.

B

As we indicated in *Teague*, "[i]n general … a case announces a new rule when it breaks new ground or imposes a new obligation on the States or the Federal Government." Or, "[t]o put it differently, a case announces a new rule if the result was not dictated by precedent existing at the time the defendant's conviction became final." *Teague* noted that "[i]t is admittedly often difficult to determine when a case announces a new rule." Justice Harlan recognized "the inevitable difficulties that will arise in attempting 'to determine whether a particular decision has really announced a "new" rule at all or whether it has simply applied a well-established constitutional principle to govern a case which is closely analogous to those which have been previously considered in the prior case law.'"

Penry's conviction became final on January 13, 1986, when this Court denied his petition for certiorari on direct review of his conviction and sentence. This Court's decisions in *Lockett v. Ohio*, 438 U.S. 586 (1978) [*supra* chapter 8], and *Eddings v. Oklahoma*, 455 U.S. 104 (1982) [*supra* chapter 8], were rendered before his conviction became final. Under the retroactivity principles adopted in *Griffith v. Kentucky*, 479 U.S. 314 (1987), Penry is entitled to the benefit of those decisions. Citing *Lockett* and *Eddings*, Penry argues that he was sentenced to death in violation of the Eighth Amendment because, in light of the jury instructions given, the jury was unable to fully consider and give effect to the mitigating evidence of his mental retardation and abused background, which he offered as the basis for a sentence less than death. Penry thus seeks a rule that when such mitigating evidence is presented, Texas juries must, upon request, be given jury instructions that make it possible for them to give effect to that mitigating evidence in determining whether a defendant should be sentenced to death. We conclude, for the reasons discussed below, that the rule Penry seeks is not a "new rule" under *Teague*.

Penry does not challenge the facial validity of the Texas death penalty statute, which was upheld against an Eighth Amendment challenge in *Jurek v. Texas*. Nor does he dispute that some types of mitigating evidence can be fully considered by the sentencer in the absence of special jury instructions. Instead, Penry argues that, on the facts of this case, the jury was unable to fully consider and give effect to the mitigating evidence of his mental retardation and abused background in answering the three special issues. In our view, the relief Penry seeks does not "impos[e] a new obligation" on the State of Texas. Rather, Penry simply asks the State to fulfill the assurance upon which *Jurek* was based: namely, that the special issues would be interpreted broadly enough to permit the sentencer to consider all of the relevant mitigating evidence a defendant might present in imposing sentence.

In *Jurek*, the joint opinion of Justices Stewart, Powell, and Stevens noted that the Texas statute narrowed the circumstances in which the death penalty could be imposed to five categories of murders. Thus, although Texas had not adopted a list of statutory aggravating factors that the jury must find before imposing the death penalty, "its action in narrowing the categories of murders for which a death sentence may ever be imposed serves much the same purpose," and effectively "requires the sentencing authority to focus on the particularized nature of the crime." To provide the individualized sentencing determination required by the Eighth Amendment, however, the sentencer must be allowed to consider mitigating evidence. Indeed, as *Woodson v. North Carolina* made clear, "in capital cases the fundamental respect for humanity underlying the Eighth Amendment ... requires consideration of the character and record of the individual offender and the circumstances of the particular offense as a constitutionally indispensable part of the process of inflicting the penalty of death.". . .

Thus, at the time Penry's conviction became final, it was clear from *Lockett* and *Eddings* that a State could not, consistent with the Eighth and Fourteenth Amendments, prevent the sentencer from considering and giving effect to evidence relevant to the defendant's background or character or to the circumstances of the offense that mitigates against imposing the death penalty. Moreover, the facial validity of the Texas death penalty statute had been upheld in *Jurek* on the basis of assurances that the special issues would be interpreted broadly enough to enable sentencing juries to consider all of the relevant mitigating evidence a defendant might present. Penry argues that those assurances were not fulfilled in his particular case because, without appropriate instructions, the jury could not fully consider and give effect to the mitigating evidence of his mental retardation and abused childhood in rendering its sentencing decision. The rule Penry seeks—that when such mitigating evidence is presented, Texas juries must, upon request, be given jury instructions that make it possible for them to give effect to that mitigating evidence in determining whether the death penalty should be imposed—is not a "new rule" under *Teague* because it is dictated by *Eddings* and *Lockett*. Moreover, in light of the assurances upon which *Jurek* was based, we conclude that the relief Penry seeks does not "impos[e] a new obligation" on the State of Texas.... [Therefore, the Court remanded Penry's case for resentencing so that the jury could adequately consider all mitigating evidence, including Penry's mental retardation and life history.]

IV

A

[Penry also claimed that the Eighth Amendment precludes the execution of the mentally retarded.] Under *Teague*, we address the retroactivity issue as a threshold matter because Penry is before us on collateral review. If we were to hold that the Eighth Amendment prohibits the execution of mentally retarded persons such as Penry, we would be announcing a "new rule." Such a rule is not dictated by precedent existing at the time Penry's conviction became final. Moreover, such a rule would "brea[k] new ground" and would impose a new obligation on the States and the Federal Government.

In *Teague*, we concluded that a new rule will not be applied retroactively to defendants on collateral review unless it falls within one of two exceptions. Under the first exception articulated by Justice Harlan, a new rule will be retroactive if it places "'certain kinds of primary, private individual conduct beyond the power of the criminal lawmaking authority to proscribe.'" Although *Teague* read this exception as focusing solely on new rules according constitutional protection to an actor's primary conduct, Justice Harlan did speak in terms of substantive categorical guarantees accorded by the Constitution, regardless of the procedures followed. This Court subsequently held that the Eighth Amendment, as a substantive matter, prohibits imposing the death penalty on a certain class of defendants because of their status, or because of the nature of their offense. In our view, a new rule placing a certain class of individuals beyond the State's power to punish by death is analogous to a new rule placing certain conduct beyond the State's power to punish at all. In both cases, the Constitution itself deprives the State of the power to impose a certain penalty, and the finality and comity concerns underlying Justice Harlan's view of retroactivity have little force. As Justice Harlan wrote: "There is little societal interest in permitting the criminal process to rest at a point where it ought properly never to repose." Therefore, the first exception set forth in *Teague* should be understood to cover not only rules forbidding criminal punishment of certain primary conduct but also rules prohibiting a certain category of punishment for a class of defendants because of their status or offense. Thus, if we held, as a substantive matter, that the Eighth Amendment prohibits the execution of mentally retarded persons such as Penry regardless of the procedures followed, such a rule would fall under the first exception to the general rule of nonretroactivity and would be applicable to defendants on collateral review. Accordingly, we address the merits of Penry's claim.... [The Court ultimately rejected Penry's claim that the execution of a mentally retarded criminal defendant violated the Eighth Amendment.]

Justice BRENNAN, with whom Justice Marshall joins, concurring in part and dissenting in part.

I

I dissented in *Teague v. Lane* and I continue to believe that the plurality's unprecedented curtailment of the reach of the Great Writ in that case was without foundation. The *Teague* plurality adopted for no adequate reason a novel threshold test for federal review of state criminal convictions that, subject to narrow exceptions, precludes federal courts from considering a vast array of important federal questions on collateral review, and thereby both prevents the vindication of personal constitutional rights and deprives our society of a significant safeguard against future violations. In this case, the Court compounds its error by extending *Teague's* notion that new rules will not generally be announced on collateral review to cases in which a habeas petitioner challenges the constitutionality of a capital sentencing procedure. This extension means that a person may be killed although he or she has a sound constitutional claim that would have barred his or her execution had this Court only announced the constitutional rule before his or her conviction and sentence became final. It is intolerable that the difference between life and death should turn on such a fortuity of timing, and beyond my comprehension that a majority of this Court will so blithely allow a State to take a human life though the method by which sentence was determined violates our Constitution.

I say the Court takes this step "blithely" advisedly. The Court extends *Teague* without the benefit of briefing or oral argument. *Teague*, indeed, was decided only after we had heard argument in this case. Rather than postponing decision on the important issue whether *Teague* should be extended to capital cases until it is presented in a case in which it may be briefed and argued, the Court rushes to decide *Teague*'s applicability in such circumstances here. It does so in two sentences, saying merely that not to apply *Teague* would result in delay in killing the prisoner and in a lack of finality. There is not the least hint that the Court has even considered whether different rules might be called for in capital cases, let alone any sign of reasoning justifying the extension. Such peremptory treatment of the issue is facilitated, of course, by the Court's decision to reach the *Teague* question without allowing counsel to set out the opposing arguments.

Though I believe *Teague* was wrongly decided, and the Court's precipitous decision to extend *Teague* to capital cases an error, nevertheless if these mistakes are to be made law I agree that the Court's discussion of the question whether the jury had an opportunity to consider Penry's mitigating evidence in answering Texas' three "special issues" does not establish a "new rule." ... I also agree that there is an exception to *Teague* so that new rules "prohibiting a certain category of punishment for a class of defendants because of their status or offense" may be announced in, and applied to, cases on collateral review.

Notes

1. In *Penry* (decided the same term as *Teague*), the Court was required to determine whether the rule Penry sought—that the Constitution demanded additional jury instructions to permit full consideration of Penry's mitigating evidence of mental retardation and child abuse under Texas law—was a "new rule," prohibited by *Teague* from being announced in federal habeas proceedings. Even though numerous state and federal courts had rejected precisely the claim that Penry urged, the Court held that Penry's result was "dictated" by precedent existing at the time Penry's conviction and sentence became final. The Court reached the merits of Penry's claim and ultimately granted relief.

The Court granted certiorari in *Graham v. Collins*, 506 U.S. 461 (1993), to review the United States Court of Appeals for the Fifth Circuit's application of *Penry* to various types of mitigating evidence including youth, unstable family background, and positive character traits. According to the Court, the *Teague* inquiry was whether "reasonable jurists hearing [Graham's] claim at the time his conviction became final 'would have felt compelled by existing precedent' to rule in his favor." Applying this standard, the Court denied relief.

Graham's mitigating evidence was distinguishable from Penry's evidence of mental retardation in that Graham's evidence could have compelled a jury to answer "no" to the future dangerousness special issue. Conversely, Penry's evidence "compelled an affirmative answer" to the future dangerousness inquiry.

2. For further discussion of the application of *Teague* to capital cases, see David R. Dow, "*Teague* and Death: The Impact of Current Retroactivity Doctrine on Capital Defendants," 19 Hastings Const. L. Q. 23 (1992); Paul J. Heald, "Retroactivity, Capital Sentencing, and the Jurisdictional Contours of Habeas Corpus," 42 Ala. L. Rev. 1273 (1991).

Gray v. Netherland

518 U.S. 152 (1996)

Chief Justice REHNQUIST delivered the opinion of the Court.

Petitioner, convicted of capital murder, complains that his right to due process of law under the Fourteenth Amendment was violated because he was not given adequate notice of some of the evidence the Commonwealth intended to use against him at the penalty hearing of his trial. We hold that this claim would necessitate a "new rule," and that therefore it does not provide a basis on which he may seek federal habeas relief....

I

B

On Monday, December 2, 1985, petitioner's trial began. [Prior to trial,] petitioner's counsel moved that the trial court order the prosecution to disclose the evidence it planned to introduce in the penalty phase. The prosecutor acknowledged that "in the event [petitioner] is found guilty we do intend to introduce evidence of statements he has made to other people about other crimes he has committed of which he has not been convicted." In particular, the prosecution intended to show that petitioner had admitted to a notorious double-murder in Chesapeake, a city adjacent to Suffolk. Lisa Sorrell and her 3-year-old daughter, Shanta, had been murdered five months before McClelland [the victim in this case] was killed. The prosecutor told petitioner's counsel in court that the only evidence he would introduce would be statements by petitioner to Tucker or fellow inmates that he committed these murders.

On Thursday, December 5, 1985, the jury convicted petitioner on all counts. That evening, the prosecution informed petitioner's counsel that the Commonwealth would introduce evidence, beyond petitioner's own admissions, linking petitioner to the Sorrell murders. The additional evidence included photographs of the crime scene and testimony by the police detective who investigated the murders and by the state medical examiner who performed autopsies on the Sorrells' bodies. The testimony was meant to show that the manner in which Lisa and Shanta Sorrell had been killed resembled the manner in which McClelland was killed. The next morning, petitioner's counsel made two motions "to have excluded from evidence during [the] penalty trial any evidence pertaining to any ... felony for which the defendant has not yet been charged." Counsel argued that the additional evidence exceeded the scope of unadjudicated-crime evidence admissible for sentencing under Virginia law, because "[i]n essence, what [the prosecutor is] doing is trying [the Sorrell] case in the minds of the jurors." Although counsel also complained that he was not "prepared for any of this [additional evidence], other than [that petitioner] may have made some incriminating statements," and that the "[d]efense was taken by surprise," he never requested a continuance. The trial court denied the motions to exclude....

The jury fixed petitioner's sentence for McClelland's murder at death. The trial court entered judgment on the verdicts for all the charges against petitioner and sentenced him to death. The Virginia Supreme Court affirmed, and denied certiorari. The Suffolk Circuit Court dismissed petitioner's state petition for a writ of habeas corpus. The Virginia Supreme Court affirmed the dismissal, and we denied certiorari.

C

Petitioner then sought a writ of habeas corpus from the United States District Court for the Eastern District of Virginia. With respect to the Sorrell murders, he argued, inter alia, that he had "never been convicted of any of these crimes nor was he awaiting trial for these crimes," that the Commonwealth "did not disclose its intentions to use the Sorrell murders as evidence against [him] until such a late date that it was impossible for [his] defense counsel reasonably to prepare or defend against such evidence at trial," and that Tucker "'sold' his testimony to the Commonwealth for ... less than a life sentence...."

[The District Court granted a writ of habeas corpus. The Fourth Circuit, however, reversed the judgment granting the writ.] [T]he Commonwealth scheduled petitioner's execution for December 14, 1995. Petitioner applied for a stay of execution and petitioned for a writ of certiorari from this Court. We granted his stay application on December 13, 1995. On January 5, 1996, we granted certiorari, limited to the questions whether petitioner's notice-of-evidence claim stated a new rule and whether the Commonwealth violated petitioner's due process rights under *Brady* by withholding evidence exculpating him from responsibility for the Sorrell murders....

Petitioner makes a separate due process challenge to the manner in which the prosecution introduced evidence about the Sorrell murders. We perceive two separate claims in this challenge. As we will explain in greater detail below, petitioner raises a "notice-of-evidence" claim, which alleges that the Commonwealth deprived petitioner of due process by failing to give him adequate notice of the evidence the Commonwealth would introduce in the sentencing phase of his trial. He raises a separate "misrepresentation" claim, which alleges that the Commonwealth violated due process by misleading petitioner about the evidence it intended to use at sentencing....

III

C

We turn to the notice-of-evidence claim, and consider whether the Court of Appeals correctly concluded that this claim sought the retroactive application of a new rule of federal constitutional law. We have concluded that the writ's purpose may be fulfilled with the least intrusion necessary on States' interest of the finality of criminal proceedings by applying constitutional standards contemporaneous with the habeas petitioner's conviction to review his petition. Thus, habeas relief is appropriate only if "a state court considering [the petitioner's] claim at the time his conviction became final would have felt compelled by existing precedent to conclude that the rule [he] seeks was required by the Constitution."

At the latest, petitioner knew at the start of trial that the prosecutor intended to introduce evidence tending to show that he committed the Sorrell murders. He knew then that the Commonwealth would call Tucker to the stand to repeat his statement that petitioner had admitted to committing the murders. He nonetheless contends that he was deprived of adequate notice of the other witnesses, the police officer and the medical examiner who had investigated the Sorrell murders, whom he was advised that the prosecutor would call only on the evening before the sentencing hearing. But petitioner did not attempt to cure this inadequacy of notice by requesting more time to respond to this evidence. He instead moved "to have excluded from evidence during this penalty trial any evidence pertaining to any other—any felony for which the defendant has not yet been charged."

On these facts, for petitioner to prevail on his notice-of-evidence claim, he must establish that due process requires that he receive more than a day's notice of the Commonwealth's evidence. He must also establish that due process required a continuance whether or not he sought one, or that, if he chose not to seek a continuance, exclusion was the only appropriate remedy for the inadequate notice. We conclude that only the adoption of a new constitutional rule could establish these propositions....

We therefore hold that petitioner's notice-of-evidence claim would require the adoption of a new constitutional rule.

D

Petitioner argues that relief should be granted nonetheless, because the new rule he proposes falls within one of *Teague*'s two exceptions. "The first exception permits the retroactive application of a new rule if the rule places a class of private conduct beyond the power of the State to proscribe." This exception is not at issue here. "The second exception is for 'watershed rules of criminal procedure' implicating the fundamental fairness and accuracy of the criminal proceeding." Petitioner argues that his notice-of-evidence new rule is "mandated by long-recognized principles of fundamental fairness critical to accuracy in capital sentencing determinations."

We observed in *Saffle v. Parks* that the paradigmatic example of a watershed rule of criminal procedure is the requirement that counsel be provided in all criminal trials for serious offenses. "Whatever one may think of the importance of [petitioner's] proposed rule, it has none of the primacy and centrality of the rule adopted in *Gideon* or other rules which may be thought to be within the exception." The rule in *Teague* therefore applies, and petitioner may not obtain habeas relief on his notice-of-evidence claim.

We hold that petitioner's *Brady* claim is procedurally defaulted and that his notice-of-evidence claim seeks retroactive application of a new rule. Neither claim states a ground upon which relief may be granted in federal habeas corpus proceedings. However, we vacate the judgment of the Court of Appeals, and remand the case for consideration of petitioner's misrepresentation claim in proceedings consistent with this opinion.

Justice GINSBURG, with whom Justice Stevens, Justice Souter, and Justice Breyer join, dissenting.

Basic to due process in criminal proceedings is the right to a full, fair, potentially effective opportunity to defend against the State's charges. Petitioner Gray was not accorded that fundamental right at the penalty phase of his trial for capital murder. I therefore conclude that no "new rule" is implicated in his petition for habeas corpus, and dissent from the Court's decision, which denies Gray the resentencing proceeding he seeks....

II

A case announces a "new rule" under *Teague* "if the result was not dictated by precedent existing at the time the defendant's conviction became final." Gray's conviction became final in 1987, when we denied certiorari to review the Virginia Supreme Court's decision on direct appeal. As explained below, precedent decided well before 1987 "dictates" the conclusion that Gray was not accorded due process at the penalty phase of his trial.

Gray's claim is encompassing, but it is fundamental. Under the Due Process Clause, he contends, a capital defendant must be afforded a meaningful opportunity to explain or deny the evidence introduced against him at sentencing. The District Court concluded that Gray was stripped of any meaningful opportunity to explain or deny the Sorrell murders evidence, for his lawyers were unfairly "ambushed"—clearly surprised and devastatingly disarmed by the prosecutor's decision, announced on the eve of the penalty trial, to introduce extensive evidence other than Gray's statements. Gray's counsel reasonably relied on the prosecutor's unequivocal "statements only" pledge, made at the outset of trial; based on the prosecutor's assurances, defense counsel spent no resources tracking down information in police records on the Sorrell murders. The prosecutor's switch, altogether unanticipated by defense counsel, left them with no chance to uncover, through their own investigation, information that could have defused the prosecutor's case, in short, without time to prepare an effective defense.

The Fourth Circuit recast Gray's claim, transforming it into an assertion of a broad constitutional right to discovery in capital cases. This Court also restates and reshapes Gray's claim. The Court first slices Gray's whole claim into pieces; it then deals discretely with each segment it "perceive[s]," a "misrepresentation" claim, and a supposed "notice-of-evidence" claim. Gray, himself, however, has "never claimed a constitutional right to advance discovery of the Commonwealth's evidence." His own claim is more basic and should not succumb to artificial endeavors to divide and conquer it.

There is nothing "new" in a rule that capital defendants must be afforded a meaningful opportunity to defend against the State's penalty phase evidence. As this Court affirmed more than a century ago: "Common justice requires that no man shall be condemned in his person or property without … an opportunity to make his defence." A pro forma opportunity will not do. Due process demands an opportunity to be heard "at a meaningful time and in a meaningful manner."

Teague is not the straightjacket the Commonwealth misunderstands it to be. *Teague* requires federal courts to decide a habeas petitioner's constitutional claims according to the "law prevailing at the time [his] conviction became final." But *Teague* does not bar federal habeas courts from applying, in "a myriad of factual contexts," law that is settled—here, the right to a meaningful chance to defend against or explain charges pressed by the State.

The District Court did not "forg[e] a new rule," by holding, on the facts of this case, that Gray was denied a meaningful opportunity to challenge the Sorrell murders evidence. Ordinarily, it is incumbent upon defense counsel, after receiving adequate notice of the triable issues, to pursue whatever investigation is needed to rebut relevant evidence the State may introduce. Here, however, in keeping with the practice approved by Virginia's highest court, the prosecutor expressly delineated the scope and character of the evidence he would introduce with respect to the Sorrell murders: nothing other than statements Gray himself allegedly made. Gray's lawyers reasonably relied on the prosecutor's "statements only" assurance by forgoing inquiry into the details of the Sorrell crimes. Resource-consuming investigation, they responsibly determined, was unnecessary to cast doubt on the veracity of inmate "snitch" testimony, the only evidence the prosecutor initially said he would offer.

Gray's lawyers were undeniably caught short by the prosecutor's startling announcement, the night before the penalty phase was to begin, that he would in effect put on a "mini-trial" of the Sorrell murders. At that point, Gray's lawyers could not possibly conduct the investigation and preparation necessary to counter the prosecutor's newly announced evidence. Thus, at the penalty trial, defense counsel were reduced nearly to the role of spectators. Lacking proof, later uncovered, that "strongly suggested" Timothy Sorrell, not Gray, was the actual killer, Gray's lawyers could mount only a feeble cross-examination of Detective Slezak; counsel simply inquired of the detective whether highly-publicized crimes could prompt "copycat" crimes. Gray's lawyers had no questions at all for Doctor Presswalla, the medical examiner who testified about the Sorrell autopsies.

In sum, the record shows, beyond genuine debate, that Gray was not afforded a "meaningful" opportunity to defend against the additional Sorrell murders evidence. The fatal infection present in Gardner infects this case as well: defense counsel were effectively deprived of an opportunity to challenge the "accuracy or materiality" of information relied on in imposing the death sentence. Unexposed to adversary testing, the Sorrell murders evidence "carrie[d] no assurance of reliability." The "debate between adversaries," valued in our system of justice for its contribution "to the truth-seeking function of trials," was precluded here by the prosecutor's eve-of-sentencing shift, and the trial court's tolerance of it. To hold otherwise "would simply be to ignore actualities."

… For the reasons stated, I conclude that the District Court's decision vacating Gray's death sentence did not rest on a "new rule" of constitutional law. I would therefore reverse the judgment of the Court of Appeals, and respectfully dissent from this Court's decision.

Stringer v. Black
503 U.S. 222 (1992)

Justice KENNEDY delivered the opinion of the Court.

The death sentence of the petitioner in this case was decreed by a judgment that became final before we decided either *Maynard v. Cartwright*, 486 U.S. 356 (1988) [*supra* chapter 7], or *Clemons v. Mississippi*, 494 U.S. 738 (1990) [*supra* chapter 8]. The petitioner, James R. Stringer, argues that the State of Mississippi committed the same error in his case as it did in *Clemons*, and that under both *Maynard* and *Clemons* his sentence is unconstitutional. The question presented is whether in a federal habeas corpus proceeding a petitioner is foreclosed from relying on *Maynard* and *Clemons* because either or both announced a new rule as defined in *Teague v. Lane*, 489 U.S. 288 (1989).

I

… Under Mississippi law the death sentence may be imposed for murders designated by statute as "capital murder." Miss. Code Ann. §97-3-19(2) (Supp. 1991). A killing in the course of a burglary or robbery is included within that category. Following a capital murder conviction, the jury in the Mississippi system proceeds to the sentencing phase of the case. For a defendant who has been convicted of capital murder to receive the death sentence, the jury must find at least one of eight statutory aggravating factors, and then it must determine that the aggravating factor or factors are not outweighed by the mitigating circumstances, if any.

The jury found petitioner guilty of capital murder in the course of a robbery. In the sentencing phase the jury found that there were three statutory aggravating factors. The aggravating factors as defined in the jury instructions, and for the most part following the statutory wording, were:

1. The Defendant contemplated that life would be taken and/or the capital murder was intentionally committed and that the Defendant was engaged in an attempt to commit a robbery; and was committed for pecuniary gain.

2. The capital murder was committed for the purpose of avoiding or preventing the detection and lawful arrest of James R. Stringer, the Defendant.

3. The capital murder was especially heinous, atrocious or cruel.

The trial court in its instructions did not further define the meaning of the third factor.

On direct review the Mississippi Supreme Court affirmed. With respect to the sentence the court found it was not "imposed under the influence of passion, prejudice or any other arbitrary factor;" "the evidence fully support[ed] the jury's finding of statutorily required aggravating circumstances;" and the death sentence was not disproportionate to sentences imposed in other cases. Petitioner's conviction became final when we denied certiorari on February 19, 1985. Postconviction relief was denied in the state courts.

This case comes to us from proceedings begun when petitioner filed his first federal habeas petition in the United States District Court.... The relevant claim is petitioner's contention that the third aggravating factor found by the jury and considered in the sentencing proceeding, the "heinous, atrocious or cruel" aggravating factor, was so vague as to render the sentence arbitrary, in violation of the Eighth Amendment's proscription of cruel and unusual punishment. The District Court found the claim subject to a procedural bar and, in the alternative, ruled it had no merit. Without consideration of the procedural bar question, the Court of Appeals affirmed on the merits, finding no constitutional infirmity in the jury's consideration of the third aggravating factor because two other aggravating factors were unchallenged. When the Court of Appeals affirmed, we had not decided *Clemons v. Mississippi,* and we later vacated its opinion for further consideration. On remand the Court of Appeals held that petitioner was not entitled to rely on *Clemons* or the related case of *Maynard v. Cartwright* in his habeas corpus proceeding because those decisions announced a new rule after his sentence was final. The court relied upon its earlier analysis in *Smith v. Black,* 904 F.2d 950 (1990), a case that had also presented the question whether *Clemons* and *Maynard* announced a new rule. We granted certiorari, and now reverse.

II

Subject to two exceptions, a case decided after a petitioner's conviction and sentence became final may not be the predicate for federal habeas corpus relief unless the decision was dictated by precedent existing when the judgment in question became final. *Butler v. McKellar,* 494 U.S. 407 (1990); *Penry v. Lynaugh,* 492 U.S. 302 (1989); *Teague v. Lane,* 489 U.S. 288 (1989). As we explained in *Butler,* "[t]he 'new rule' principle ... validates reasonable, good-faith interpretations of existing precedents made by state courts even though they are shown to be contrary to later decisions." Neither one of the exceptions is at issue here, so our inquiry is confined to the question whether *Clemons, Maynard,* or both announced a new rule.

When a petitioner seeks federal habeas relief based upon a principle announced after a final judgment, *Teague* and our subsequent decisions interpreting it require a federal court to answer an initial question, and in some cases a second. First, it must be determined whether the decision relied upon announced a new rule. If the answer is yes and neither exception applies, the decision is not available to the petitioner. If, however, the decision did not announce a new rule, it is necessary to inquire whether granting the relief sought would create a new rule because the prior decision is applied in a novel setting, thereby extending the precedent. The interests in finality, predictability, and comity underlying our new rule jurisprudence may be undermined to an equal degree by the invocation of a rule that was not dictated by precedent as by the application of an old rule in a manner that was not dictated by precedent.

A

A determination whether *Maynard* and *Clemons* announced a new rule must begin with *Godfrey v. Georgia*, 446 U.S. 420 (1980) [*supra* chapter 7]. In *Godfrey* we invalidated a death sentence based upon the aggravating circumstance that the killing was "outrageously or wantonly vile, horrible and inhuman." The formulation was deemed vague and imprecise, inviting arbitrary and capricious application of the death penalty in violation of the Eighth Amendment. We later applied the same analysis and reasoning in *Maynard*. In *Maynard* the aggravating circumstance under an Oklahoma statute applied to a killing that was "especially heinous, atrocious, or cruel." We found the language gave no more guidance than did the statute in *Godfrey*, and we invalidated the Oklahoma formulation.

In the case now before us Mississippi does not argue that *Maynard* itself announced a new rule. To us this appears a wise concession. *Godfrey* and *Maynard* did indeed involve somewhat different language. But it would be a mistake to conclude that the vagueness ruling of *Godfrey* was limited to the precise language before us in that case. In applying *Godfrey* to the language before us in *Maynard*, we did not "brea[k] new ground." *Maynard* was, therefore, for purposes of *Teague*, controlled by *Godfrey*, and it did not announce a new rule.

B

Of more substance is the State's contention that it was a new rule to apply the *Godfrey* and *Maynard* holdings to the Mississippi sentencing process. The State argues this must have been an open question when petitioner's sentence became final, with *Clemons* yet undecided. We acknowledge there are differences in the use of aggravating factors under the Mississippi capital sentencing system and their use in the Georgia system in *Godfrey*. In our view, however, those differences could not have been considered a basis for denying relief in light of precedent existing at the time petitioner's sentence became final. Indeed, to the extent that the differences are significant, they suggest that application of the *Godfrey* principle to the Mississippi sentencing process follows, *a fortiori*, from its application to the Georgia system.

1

The principal difference between the sentencing schemes in Georgia and Mississippi is that Mississippi is what we have termed a "weighing" State, while Georgia is not. Under Mississippi law, after a jury has found a defendant guilty of capital murder and found the existence of at least one statutory aggravating factor, it must weigh the aggravating factor or factors against the mitigating evidence. By contrast, in Georgia the jury must find the existence of one aggravating factor before imposing the death penalty, but aggravating factors as such have no specific function in the jury's decision whether a defendant who has been found to be eligible for the death penalty should receive it under all the circumstances of the case. Instead, under the Georgia scheme, "'[i]n making the decision as to the penalty, the factfinder takes into consideration all circumstances before it from both the guilt-innocence and the sentence phases of the trial. These circumstances relate both to the offense and the defendant.'"

That Mississippi is a weighing State only gives emphasis to the requirement that aggravating factors be defined with some degree of precision. By express language in *Zant v. Stephens*, 462 U.S. 862 (1983) [*supra* chapter 8], we left open the possibility that in a weighing State infection of the process with an invalid aggravating factor might require invalidation of the death sentence. Although we later held in *Clemons v. Mississippi* that under such circumstances a state appellate court could reweigh the aggravating and mitigating circumstances or undertake harmless-error analysis, we have not suggested that the Eighth Amendment permits the state appellate court in a weighing State to affirm a death sentence without a thorough analysis of the role an invalid aggravating factor played in the sentencing process.

We require close appellate scrutiny of the import and effect of invalid aggravating factors to implement the well-established Eighth Amendment requirement of individualized sentencing determinations in death penalty cases. In order for a state appellate court to affirm a death sentence after the sentencer was instructed to consider an invalid factor, the court must determine what the sentencer would have done absent the factor. Otherwise, the defendant is deprived of the precision that individualized consideration demands under the *Godfrey* and *Maynard* line of cases....

In view of the well-established general requirement of individualized sentencing and the more specific requirement that a sentence based on an improper factor be reassessed with care to assure that proper consideration was given, there was no arguable basis to support the view of the Court of Appeals that at the time petitioner's sentence became final the Mississippi Supreme Court was permitted to apply a rule of automatic affirmance to any death sentence supported by multiple aggravating factors, when one is invalid.

With respect to the function of a state reviewing court in determining whether or not the sentence can be upheld despite the use of an improper aggravating factor, the difference between a weighing State and a nonweighing State is not one of "semantics," as the Court of Appeals thought, but of critical importance. In a nonweighing State, so long as the sentencing body finds at least one valid aggravating factor, the fact that it also finds an invalid aggravating factor does not infect the formal process of deciding whether death is an appropriate penalty. Assuming a determination by the state appellate court that the invalid factor would not have made a difference to the jury's determination, there is no constitutional violation resulting from the introduction of the invalid factor in an earlier stage of the proceedings. But when the sentencing body is told to weigh an invalid factor in its decision, a reviewing court may not assume it would have made no difference if the thumb had been removed from death's side of the scale. When the weighing process itself has been skewed, only constitutional harmless-error analysis or reweighing at the trial or appellate level suffices to guarantee that the defendant received an individualized sentence. This clear principle emerges not from any single case, as the dissent would require, but from our long line of authority setting forth the dual constitutional criteria of precise and individualized sentencing. Thus, the principal difference between the sentencing systems of Mississippi and Georgia: the different role played by aggravating factors in the two States, underscores the applicability of *Godfrey* and *Maynard* to the Mississippi system.

2

Although it made no similar argument in *Clemons* itself, the State contends now that before *Clemons* it was reasonable to believe there was no constitutional requirement to define aggravating factors with precision in the Mississippi system. It points to the fact that in order for a jury to find a defendant guilty of capital murder it must find that the crime fits within the narrow and precise statutory definition of that offense. Any additional consideration of aggravating factors during the sentencing phase, under this view, is of no constitutional significance because the requisite differentiation among defendants for death penalty purposes has taken place during the jury's deliberation with respect to guilt....

The State's premise ... is in error.... [The] dispositive ... fact [is] that the Mississippi Supreme Court, which is the final authority on the meaning of Mississippi law, has at all times viewed its sentencing scheme as one in which aggravating factors are critical in the jury's determination whether to impose the death penalty. It would be a strange rule of federalism that ignores the view of the highest court of a State as to the meaning of its own law.

As a matter of federal law, moreover, the view of the Mississippi Supreme Court that *Godfrey*'s dictates apply to its capital sentencing procedure is correct. Indeed, it is so evident that the issue was not even mentioned in *Clemons*. There we took for granted, and the State did not challenge, the proposition that if a State uses aggravating factors in deciding who shall be eligible for the death penalty or who shall receive the death penalty, it cannot use factors which as a practical matter fail to guide the sentencer's discretion....

The State next argues that *Clemons*' application of *Godfrey* to Mississippi could not have been dictated by precedent because prior to *Clemons* the Fifth Circuit concluded that *Godfrey* did not apply to Mississippi. Before addressing the merits of this argument we reiterate that the rationale of the Fifth Circuit has not been adopted by the Mississippi Supreme Court, which, as a state court, is the primary beneficiary of the *Teague* doctrine. The Mississippi Supreme Court has recognized that it is bound by *Godfrey*.

The Fifth Circuit's pre-*Clemons* views are relevant to our inquiry, but not dispositive. The purpose of the new rule doctrine is to validate reasonable interpretations of existing precedents. Reasonableness, in this as in many other contexts, is an objective standard, and the ultimate decision whether *Clemons* was dictated by precedent is based on an objective reading of the relevant cases. The short answer to the State's argument is that the Fifth Circuit made a serious mistake in *Evans v. Thigpen*, 809 F.2d 239 (1987), and *Johnson v. Thigpen*, 806 F.2d 1243 (1986). The Fifth Circuit ignored the Mississippi Supreme Court's own characterization of its law and accorded no significance to the fact that in Mississippi aggravating factors are central in the weighing phase of a capital sentencing proceeding. As we have explained, when these facts are accorded their proper significance, the precedents even before *Maynard* and *Clemons* yield a well-settled principle: use of a vague or imprecise aggravating factor in the weighing process invalidates the sentence and at the very least requires constitutional harmless-error analysis or reweighing in the state judicial system.

We reverse the decision of the Court of Appeals and remand the case for further proceedings consistent with this opinion.

Notes and Questions

1. Justice Souter, joined by Justice Scalia and Justice Thomas, dissented in *Stringer*: "I do not think that precedent in 1985 dictated the rule that weighing a vague aggravating circumstance necessarily violates the Eighth Amendment even when there is a finding of at least one other, unobjectionable, aggravating circumstance." Justice Souter observed that *Stringer*'s "conviction became final for *Teague* purposes on February 19, 1985."

2. How important is the determination that a case announces a "new rule." In *Beard v. Banks*, 542 U.S. 406 (2004), the Court, by a 5-to-4 vote, refused to give retroactive effect to *Mills v. Maryland*, 486 U.S. 367 (1988) (*supra* chapter 8), in which the Court held that capital sentencing schemes could not require juror unanimity with respect to mitigating factors. Although *Mills* arguably replied on prior precedent for its holding, Justice Thomas, writing for the majority, found *Mills* announced a new rule of procedural law that was not entitled to retroactive application. As a result Mr. Banks, whose conviction and sentence became final in 1987 and who had been convicted by a jury that erroneously believed it had to unanimously agree on mitigating evidence, did not get the benefit of *Mills*. In reaching this conclusion, Justice Thomas noted:

> The generalized *Lockett* rule (that the sentencer must be allowed to consider any mitigating evidence) could be thought to support the Court's conclusion in *Mills* and *McKoy*. But what is essential here is that it does not mandate the *Mills* rule. Each of the cases relied on by *Mills* (and *McKoy*) specifically considered only obstructions to the *sentencer's* ability to consider mitigating evidence. *Mills'* innovation rests with its shift in focus to individual jurors. We think it clear that reasonable jurists could have differed as to whether the *Lockett* principle compelled Mills.
>
> But there is no need to guess. In *Mills*, four justices dissented, reasoning that because nothing prevented the jurors from hearing any mitigating evidence that the defendant proffered, the *Lockett* principle did not control. In *McKoy*, three justices dissented, explaining that " 'the principle established in *Lockett*' does not remotely support" the new focus on individual jurors. The dissent in *McKoy* stressed the Court's move from jury to juror. Indeed, prior to Mills, *none* of the Court's relevant cases addressed individual jurors, a trend that continued even after *Mills*.
>
> ....
>
> Thus, although the *Lockett* principle—conceived of at a high level of generality—could be thought to support the *Mills* rule, reasonable jurists differed even as to this point. It follows *a fortiori* that reasonable jurists could have concluded that the *Lockett* line of cases did not compel *Mills*.

542 U.S. at 414-416. The dissent disagreed, stating that *Mills* did not establish a new rule of procedural law, but instead was a "straightforward application of longstanding" case law, and thus not subject to *Teague* restrictions.

Lockhart v. Fretwell
506 U.S. 364 (1993)

Chief Justice REHNQUIST delivered the opinion of the Court.

[At the time of petitioner's trial, the Eighth Circuit had found that it was unconstitutional for the State to use an aggravating factor that duplicated an element of the underlying felony of the felony-murder charge. In fact, the State had used such an aggravating circumstance at petitioner's trial and had counsel objected to the use of that aggravating factor, his objection would have been sustained. While petitioner's case was pending on review, the decision of the Eighth Circuit on duplicative aggravating circumstances was overruled. The Supreme Court held that counsel's failure to make an objection in petitioner's sentencing proceeding did not constitute "prejudice" within the meaning of *Strickland v. Washington*, 466 U.S. 668 (1984), because of the subsequent reversal of the Eighth

Circuit precedent; therefore, the petitioner did not get the benefit of the law that was in effect at the time of his trial because that law was subsequently overturned. See *supra* chapter 11.]

... The dissent contends that this holding is inconsistent with the retroactivity rule announced in *Teague v. Lane*, 489 U.S. 288, 310 (1989), but we think otherwise. *Teague* stands for the proposition that new constitutional rules of criminal procedure will not be announced or applied on collateral review. As the dissent acknowledges, this retroactivity rule was motivated by a respect for the States' strong interest in the finality of criminal convictions, and the recognition that a State should not be penalized for relying on "the constitutional standards that prevailed at the time the original proceedings took place." "The 'new rule' principle therefore validates reasonable, good-faith interpretations of existing precedents made by state courts even though they are shown to be contrary to later decisions." *Butler v. McKellar*, 494 U.S. 407, 414 (1990).

A federal habeas petitioner has no interest in the finality of the state court judgment under which he is incarcerated: indeed, the very purpose of his habeas petition is to overturn that judgment. Nor does such a petitioner ordinarily have any claim of reliance on past judicial precedent as a basis for his actions that corresponds to the State's interest described in the quotation from *Butler, supra*. The result of these differences is that the State will benefit from our *Teague* decision in some federal habeas cases, while the habeas petitioner will not. This result is not, as the dissent would have it, a "windfall" for the State, but instead is a perfectly logical limitation of *Teague* to the circumstances which gave rise to it. *Cessante ratione legis, cessat et ipsa lex.*

Justice STEVENS, with whom Justice Blackmun joins, dissenting.

Changes in the law are characteristic of constitutional adjudication. Prior to 1985, most of those changes were in the direction of increasing the protection afforded an individual accused of crime. To vindicate the legitimate reliance interests of state law enforcement authorities, however, and in recognition of the state interest in preserving the outcome of trials adhering to contemporaneous standards, the Court often refused to apply its new rules retroactively. In *Teague v. Lane*, the Court gave full expression to its general policy of allowing States "to keep in prison defendants whose trials and appeals conformed to then-existing constitutional standards," holding that the claims of federal habeas petitioners will, in all but exceptional cases, be judged under the standards prevailing at the time of trial.

Since 1985, relevant changes in the law often have been in a different direction, affording less rather than more protection to individual defendants.[11] An even-handed approach to retroactivity would seem to require that we continue to evaluate defendants' claims under the law as it stood at the time of trial. If, under *Teague*, a defendant may not take advantage of subsequent changes in the law when they are favorable to

---

11. See, e.g., *Payne v. Tennessee*, 111 S. Ct. 2597 (1991) (Eighth Amendment does not preclude use of victim impact evidence against capital defendant at sentencing; overruling *Booth v. Maryland*, 482 U.S. 496 (1987), and *South Carolina v. Gathers*, 490 U.S. 805 (1989)); *Arizona v. Fulminante*, 111 S. Ct. 1246 (1991) (harmless error rule applicable to admission of involuntary confessions); *Duckworth v. Eagan*, 492 U.S. 195 (1989) (*Miranda* warnings adequate despite suggestion that lawyer will not be appointed until after interrogation); *Florida v. Riley*, 488 U.S. 445 (1989) (police may search greenhouse from helicopter at altitude of 400 feet without warrant).

him, then there is no self-evident reason why a State should be able to take advantage of subsequent changes in the law when they are adverse to his interests.

The Court, however, takes a directly contrary approach here. Today's decision rests critically on the proposition that respondent's ineffective assistance claim is to be judged under the law as it exists today, rather than the law as it existed at the time of trial and sentencing. In other words, respondent must make his case under *Perry v. Lockhart*, 871 F.2d 1384 (8th Cir. 1989), decided four years after his sentencing; unlike the State, he is not entitled to rely on "then-existing constitutional standards" which rendered him ineligible for the death penalty at the time that sentence was imposed.

I have already explained why the Court's reliance on hindsight is incompatible with our right to counsel jurisprudence. It is also, in my judgment, inconsistent with case law that insists on contemporaneous constitutional standards as the benchmark against which defendants' claims are to be measured. A rule that generally precludes defendants from taking advantage of post-conviction changes in the law, but allows the State to do so, cannot be reconciled with this Court's duty to administer justice impartially. Elementary fairness dictates that the Court should evaluate respondent's ineffective assistance claim under the law as it stood when he was convicted and sentenced—under *Collins*, and also under *Strickland* as it was understood until today.

As I see it, the only windfall at issue here is the one conferred upon the State by the Court's decision. Had respondent's counsel rendered effective assistance, the State would have been required to justify respondent's execution under a legal regime that included *Collins*. It is highly unlikely that it could have met this burden in the Arkansas courts, and it almost certainly could not have done so in the federal courts on habeas review. Now, however, the State is permitted to exploit the ineffective assistance of respondent's counsel, and the lapse in time it provided, by capitalizing on post-sentencing changes in the law to justify an execution. Because this windfall is one the Sixth Amendment prevents us from bestowing, I respectfully dissent.

The Two Teague *Exceptions*

Teague's general rule—that new rules of criminal procedure do not apply retroactively to cases which had become final on direct review at the time the new rule was decided—admits of two exceptions. First, a new rule will be applied retroactively "if it places certain kinds of primary, private individual conduct beyond the power of the criminal law-making authority to proscribe." *Teague*, 489 U.S. at 307. For example, a ruling that a trial court lacked authority to convict or punish a criminal defendant in the first place will be given full retroactive effect. This exception was extended in *Penry* to include "rules prohibiting a certain category of punishment for a class of defendants because of their status or offense." *Penry*, 492 U.S. at 330. Thus, if a habeas petitioner sought a rule that the Eighth Amendment categorically prohibits the execution of a class of individuals, it would be a new rule that arguably would apply retroactively because it would prohibit a certain category of punishment due to the defendant's status.

Teague's second exception to nonretroactivity embraces new rules which "require[] the observance of 'those procedures that ... are implicit in the concept of ordered liberty.'" *Teague*, 489 U.S. at 307. In *Sawyer v. Smith*, 497 U.S. 227, 242 (1990), the Court held that a rule qualifying under this exception must "not only improve accuracy, but also alter our understanding of the *bedrock procedural elements* essential to the fairness of a proceeding." *Teague* itself concluded that this type of new procedure was "so central to an accurate determination of innocence or guilt [that] ... it [is] unlikely that many such components of basic due process have yet to emerge." *Teague*, 489 U.S. at 313. To date, the Court has not found a single case to fall within this second exception.

Notes

1. In *Schriro v. Summerlin*, 542 U.S. 348 (2004), the Supreme Court, by a 5-to-4 vote, refused to apply *Ring v. Arizona*, 536 U.S. 584 (2004) (*supra* chapter 9), retroactively. In refusing to apply *Ring* retroactively, Justice Scalia, writing for the majority, found: (1) *Ring* was a new rule of procedural law, (2) it did not change the class of persons or range of conduct subject to the death penalty, and (3) it was not entitled to the *Teague* exception that watershed rules of criminal procedure implicating the fairness and accuracy of the proceeding may be applied retroactively. Writing for the dissent, Justice Breyer listed several factors and reasons showing that *Ring* is not only a watershed rule but also a rule that enhances the accuracy and reliability of the capital sentencing process.

2. For further discussion on the Court's retroactivity doctrine see Lyn Entzeroth, "Reflections on Fifteen Years of the *Teague v. Lane* Retroactivity Paradigm: A Study of the Persistence, the Pervasiveness, the Perversity of the Court's Doctrine," 35 N. M. L. Rev. 161 (2005); A. Christopher Bryant, "Retroactive Application of 'New Rules' and the Antiterrorism and Effective Death Penalty Act," 70 Go. Wash. L. Rev. 1 (2002); Paul J. Heald, "Retroactivity, Capital Sentencing, and the Jurisdictional Contours of Habeas Corpus," 42 Ala. L. Rev. 1273 (1991); Richard Falcon & Daniel Meltzer, "New Law, Non-Retroactivity, and Constitutional Remedies," 104 Harv. Law Rev. 1731, 1759 (1991). For an interesting discussion of the difference of retroactivity in state and federal proceedings see Hon. Laura Stith, "A Contrast of State and Federal Court Authority to Grant Habeas Relief," 38 Val. U. L. Rev. 421 (2004).

Chapter 16

Presumption of Correctness

A. State Court Findings of Fact: 28 U.S.C. Section 2254(d)

How far should a federal habeas court inquire into the merits of a capital conviction? Should the scope of review of a federal habeas court depend upon whether the federal habeas court is reviewing questions of fact, questions of law, or mixed questions of law and fact? Under §2254(d) of the pre-AEDPA habeas statute, the following standard of review applied to state findings of fact:

(d) In any proceeding instituted in a Federal court by an application for a writ of habeas corpus by a person in custody pursuant to the judgment of a State court, a determination after a hearing on the merits of a factual issue, made by a State court of competent jurisdiction in a proceeding to which the applicant for the writ and the State or an officer or agent thereof were parties, evidenced by a written finding, written opinion, or other reliable and adequate written indicia, shall be presumed to be correct, unless the applicant shall establish or it shall otherwise appear, or the respondent shall admit—

(1) that the merits of the factual dispute were not resolved in the State court hearing;

(2) that the factfinding procedure employed by the State court was not adequate to afford a full and fair hearing:

(3) that the material facts were not adequately developed at the State court hearing;

(4) that the State court lacked jurisdiction of the subject matter or over the person of the applicant in the State court proceeding;

(5) that the applicant was an indigent and the State court, in deprivation of his constitutional right, failed to appoint counsel to represent him in the State court proceeding;

(6) that the applicant did not receive a full, fair, and adequate hearing in the State court proceeding; or

(7) that the applicant was otherwise denied due process of law in the State court proceeding;

(8) or unless the part of the record of the State court proceeding in which the determination of such factual issue was made, pertinent to a determination of the sufficiency of the evidence to support such factual determination, is produced as provided for hereinafter, and the Federal court on a consideration of

such part of the record as a whole concludes that such factual determination is not fairly supported by the record.

In contrast, § 2254(e)(1) simply provides:

> In a proceeding instituted by an application for a writ of habeas corpus by a person in custody pursuant to the judgment of a State court, a determination of a factual issue made by a State court shall be presumed to be correct. The application shall have the burden of rebutting the presumption of correctness by clear and convincing evidence.

The following case discusses the presumption of correctness and the pre-AEDPA § 2254(d).

Sumner v. Mata

455 U.S. 591 (1982)

PER CURIAM.

This is the second time that this matter has come before us. In *Sumner v. Mata*, 449 U.S. 539 (1981), decided last Term, we held that 28 U.S.C. §2254(d) requires federal courts in habeas proceedings to accord a presumption of correctness to state-court findings of fact. This requirement could not be plainer. The statute explicitly provides that "a determination after a hearing on the merits of a factual issue, made by a State court of competent jurisdiction..., shall be presumed to be correct." Only when one of seven specified factors is present or the federal court determines that the state-court finding of fact "is not fairly supported by the record" may the presumption properly be viewed as inapplicable or rebutted.

We held further that the presumption of correctness is equally applicable when a state appellate court, as opposed to a state trial court, makes the finding of fact, and we held that if a federal court concludes that the presumption of correctness does not control, it must provide a written explanation of the reasoning that led it to conclude that one or more of the first seven factors listed in §2254(d) were present, or the "reasoning which led it to conclude that the state finding was 'not fairly supported by the record.'"

Applying these general principles to the case at hand, we found in our decision last Term that the Court of Appeals for the Ninth Circuit had neither applied the presumption of correctness nor explained why it had not. Instead, the court had made findings of fact that were "considerably at odds" with the findings made by the California Court of Appeal without any mention whatsoever of §2254(d).

In reaching the conclusion that the Court of Appeals had not followed §2254(d), we rejected the argument, advanced by respondent Robert Mata, that the findings of fact made by the Court of Appeals and the California court were not in conflict. Mata was convicted in 1973 in state trial court of the first-degree murder of a fellow inmate. There were three witnesses to the murder, each of whom identified Mata as a participant in the killing. On appeal to the California Court of Appeal, Mata argued for the first time that the photographic lineup procedure used by the state police was so impermissibly suggestive as to deprive him of due process. After examining the evidence, the California Court of Appeal rejected this assertion. It concluded that the pretrial procedures had not been unfair under the test stated by this Court in *Simmons v. United States*, 390 U.S. 377 (1968) [which set forth the standards for determining whether a pretrial identification procedure comports with due process.]

The Court of Appeals for the Ninth Circuit reached a different conclusion [than the state court of appeals],[5] and did so on the basis of factfindings that were clearly in conflict with those made by the state court. We noted that the Court of Appeals had relied, *inter alia*, on its own conflicting findings that "(1) the circumstances surrounding the witnesses' observation of the crime were such that there was a grave likelihood of misidentification; (2) the witnesses had failed to give sufficiently detailed descriptions of the assailant; and (3) considerable pressure from both prison officials and prison factions had been brought to bear on the witnesses."[6] We concluded that the "findings made by the Court of Appeals for the Ninth Circuit are considerably at odds with the findings made by the California Court of Appeal. We remanded so that the Court of Appeals could review its determination of the issue and either apply the statutory presumption or explain why the presumption did not apply in light of the factors listed in §2254(d). We expressed no view as to whether the procedures had been impermissibly suggestive. That was a question for the Court of Appeals to decide in the first instance after complying with §2254(d).

On remand, the Court of Appeals found that it was not necessary for it to apply the presumption of correctness or explain why the presumption should not be applied. Rather, agreeing with the argument advanced by Mata and the dissenting opinion in *Sumner v. Mata*, 449 U.S. 539 (1981), the court concluded that §2254(d) was simply irrelevant in this case because its factfindings in no way differed from those of the state court. It argued that its disagreement with the state court was "over the legal and constitutional significance of certain facts" and not over the facts themselves. It found that whether or not the pretrial photographic identification procedure used in this case was impermissibly suggestive was a mixed question of law and fact as to which the presumption of correctness did not apply. And it reinstated its conclusion that the pretrial procedures had been impermissibly suggestive and that Mata therefore was entitled to release or a new trial.

We have again reviewed this case and conclude that the [Ninth Circuit] Court of Appeals apparently misunderstood the terms of our remand. Nor did it comply with the requirements of §2254(d). We agree with the Court of Appeals that the ultimate question as to the constitutionality of the pretrial identification procedures used in this case is a mixed question of law and fact that is not governed by §2254(d). In deciding this question, the federal court may give different weight to the facts as found by the state court and may reach a different conclusion in light of the legal standard. But the questions of fact that underlie this ultimate conclusion are governed by the statutory presumption as our earlier opinion made clear. Thus, whether the witnesses in this case had an opportunity to observe the crime or were too distracted; whether the witnesses gave a detailed, accurate description; and whether the witnesses were under pressure from prison officials or others are all questions of fact as to which the statutory presumption applies.

---

5. The decision of the Court of Appeals for the Ninth Circuit differed not only with that of the California Court of Appeal on direct appeal but also with the decision of three levels of state courts in state habeas proceedings and with the decision of the Federal District Court in federal habeas proceedings.

6. In dissent Justice Brennan argued that there was no conflict between the facts as found by the state court and as found by the Court of Appeals. He argued that the California court's finding that the witnesses had an opportunity to view the killing was not in conflict with a finding by the Court of Appeals that the witnesses were "quite likely" distracted at the time of the killing. He argued further that the California court's finding that the descriptions given by the witnesses were "accurate" was not in conflict with a finding that these descriptions were not detailed. Finally, the dissent appears to have considered that the existence of influence by prison officials was not a question of fact but of law. It is obvious that a majority of the Court did not find this reasoning persuasive. On our remand, the Court of Appeals apparently adopted Justice Brennan's dissenting views.

Of course, the federal courts are not necessarily bound by the state court's findings. Section 2254(d) permits a federal court to conclude, for example, that a state finding was "not fairly supported by the record." But the statute does require the federal courts to face up to any disagreement as to the facts and to defer to the state court unless one of the factors listed in §2254(d) is found. Although the distinction between law and fact is not always easily drawn, we deal here with a statute that requires the federal courts to show a high measure of deference to the factfindings made by the state courts. To adopt the [federal] Court of Appeals' view would be to deprive this statutory command of its important significance.

Our remand directed the Court of Appeals to re-examine its findings in light of the statutory presumption. We pointed the way by identifying certain of its findings that we considered to be at odds with the findings of the California Court of Appeal. We asked the [federal] Court of Appeals to apply the statutory presumption or explain why the presumption was not applicable in view of the factors listed in the statute. The Court of Appeals did neither. Accordingly, we again must remand. Again we note that "we are not to be understood as agreeing or disagreeing with the majority of the Court of Appeals on the merits of the issue of impermissibly suggestive identification procedures."

The motion of respondent for leave to proceed *in forma pauperis* is granted. The petition for writ of certiorari is granted, the judgment of the Court of Appeals for the Ninth Circuit is vacated, and the case is remanded for further proceedings consistent with this opinion.

Justice BRENNAN, with whom Justice Marshall joins, dissenting.

In my view, the opinion of the Court of Appeals for the Ninth Circuit not only accords with the views I expressed last Term, which, as the Court points out did not prevail, but also with the principles expressed in the Court's opinion last Term and restated by the Court today. It is on this basis that I dissent from the Court's second, and in this instance summary, vacation.

When this case was before us last Term, I expressed the view that it was unnecessary for the Court of Appeals to explain its failure to consider the restrictions of §2254(d), because "the difference between the Court of Appeals for the Ninth Circuit and the California Court of Appeal was over the applicable legal standard, and not over the particular facts of the case," rendering §2254(d) obviously inapplicable. The Court disagreed, holding that in all cases federal courts must apply §2254(d) or explain why it was inapplicable: "No court reviewing the grant of an application for habeas corpus should be left to guess as to the habeas court's reasons for granting relief notwithstanding the provisions of §2254(d)." But I thought then, and the Court today agrees, that §2254(d) is inapplicable to the ultimate question whether pretrial identification procedures are "impermissibly suggestive."

The Court's explicit recognition that §2254(d) does not govern the ultimate question as to the constitutionality of the pretrial identification procedures used in this case renders all the more confounding the Court's present disposition. Following this Court's directive on remand, the Court of Appeals clarified the basis for its original opinion: Section 2254(d) was inapplicable because the federal court "substantially agree[d] with the 'historical' or 'basic' facts adduced by the California Court of Appeal," but disagreed with "the legal and constitutional significance of certain facts," and thus the "legal conclusion" of the state court.

I can only interpret this second vacation as evincing either the suspicion that the Court of Appeals, despite its protestations to the contrary, actually relied on factual findings inconsistent with those of the state court or that the Court of Appeals failed to distinguish its ultimate conclusion from subsidiary questions of fact. The unfairness of such suspicion is manifest. There is no reason to think, borrowing from this Court's declaration to the Court of Appeals last Term, that, despite this Court's difference of opinion, the judges of the Ninth Circuit are "not doing their mortal best to discharge their oath of office."

There is no basis for disbelieving the Court of Appeals' assurance that it has accepted the factual findings of the California Court of Appeal and that it granted relief only because it concluded that the pretrial identification procedures employed in this case were, as a matter of law, unconstitutional. Accordingly, I dissent and would affirm the judgment of the Court of Appeals.

Notes and Questions

1. What are the obvious differences between the pre-AEDPA presumption of correctness and the AEDPA standard? What are the more subtle differences and similarities? To what extent does §2254 (e) follow the Court's views in *Sumner v. Mata*? To what extent is it different?

2. In addition to the presumption of correctness standard set out in §2254(e) of the AEDPA, §2254(d)(2) provides: "[a]n application for a writ of habeas corpus on behalf of a person in custody pursuant to the judgment of a State court shall not be granted with respect to any claim that was adjudicated on the merits in State court proceedings unless the adjudication of the claim ... resulted in a decision that was based on an unreasonable determination of the facts in light of the evidence presented in the State court proceeding." How does this provision affect the presumption of correctness standard in §2254(e)?

Note on Mixed Questions of Law and Fact

According to the *Mata* Court, "whether the witnesses in this case had an opportunity to observe the crime or were too distracted; whether the witnesses gave a detailed, accurate description; and whether the witnesses were under pressure from prison officials or others are all questions of fact as to which the statutory presumption [of correctness] applies." However, the "ultimate conclusion as to whether the facts as found state a constitutional violation is a mixed question of law and fact."

In *Miller v. Fenton*, 474 U.S. 104 (1985), the Court stated that mixed constitutional questions are "subject to plenary review" on habeas. Petitioners in *Wright v. West*, 505 U.S. 277 (1992), urged the Court to overrule *Miller v. Fenton* and apply the presumption of correctness to mixed claims in addition to factual claims.

B. Federal Court Review of State Court's Application of Law to Specific Facts

Wright v. West
505 U.S. 277 (1992)

Justice THOMAS announced the judgment of the Court and delivered an opinion, in which the Chief Justice and Justice Scalia joined.

In this case, we must determine whether the Court of Appeals for the Fourth Circuit correctly applied our decision in *Jackson v. Virginia*, 443 U.S. 307 (1979), in concluding that the evidence against respondent Frank West was insufficient, as a matter of due process, to support his state-court conviction for grand larceny.

I

Between December 13 and December 26, 1978, someone broke into the Westmoreland County, Virginia, home of Angelo Cardova and stole items valued at approximately $3,500. On January 10, 1979, police conducted a lawful search of the Gloucester County, Virginia, home of West and his wife. They discovered several of the items stolen from the Cardova home, including various electronic equipment (two television sets and a record player); articles of clothing (an imitation mink coat with the name "Esther" embroidered in it, a silk jacket emblazoned "Korea 1970," and a pair of shoes); decorations (several wood carvings and a mounted lobster); and miscellaneous household objects (a mirror framed with seashells, a coffee table, a bar, a sleeping bag and some silverware). These items were valued at approximately $800, and the police recovered other, unspecified items of Cardova's property with an approximate value of $300.

West was charged with grand larceny. Testifying at trial on his own behalf, he admitted to a prior felony conviction, but denied having taken anything from Cardova's house. He explained that he had bought and sold "a lot of ... merchandise" from "several guys" at "flea bargain places" where, according to West, "a lot of times you buy things ... that are stolen" although "you never know it." On cross-examination, West said that he had bought many of the stolen items from a Ronnie Elkins, whom West claimed to have known for years. West testified that he purchased one of the wood carvings, the jacket, mounted lobster, mirror and bar from Elkins for about $500. West initially guessed, and then twice positively asserted, that this sale occurred before January 1, 1979. In addition, West claimed to have purchased the coat from Elkins for $5 around January 1, 1979. His testimony did not make clear whether he was describing one transaction or two, whether there were any other transactions between himself and Elkins, where the transactions occurred, and whether the transactions occurred at flea markets. West testified further that he had purchased one of the television sets in an entirely separate transaction in Goochland County, from an individual whose name he had forgotten. Finally, West testified that he did not remember how he had acquired the second television, the coffee table, and the silverware.

[The jury found West guilty and sentenced him to ten years in prison. The Supreme Court of Virginia denied West's petition for appeal in which West alleged, among other claims, that the evidence was insufficient. Seven years later, West filed a writ of habeas corpus claiming the evidence was insufficient and presenting an affidavit corroborating his innocence. Again, the Virginia Supreme Court rejected his appeal. West then sought a writ of habeas corpus in federal court, but the federal district court denied relief. The Fourth Circuit Court of Appeals, however, concluded that the evidence was insufficient and granted relief.] [T]he State Attorney General sought review in this Court on, among other questions, whether the Court of Appeals had applied *Jackson v. Virginia* correctly in this case. We granted certiorari, and requested additional briefing on the question whether a federal habeas court should afford deference to state-court determinations applying law to the specific facts of a case. We now reverse.

II

The habeas corpus statute permits a federal court to entertain a petition from a state prisoner "only on the ground that he is in custody in violation of the Constitution or laws or treaties of the United States." The court must "dispose of the matter as law and justice require." For much of our history, we interpreted these bare guidelines and their predecessors to reflect the common-law principle that a prisoner seeking a writ of habeas corpus could challenge only the jurisdiction of the court that had rendered the judgment under which he was in custody. Gradually, we began to expand the category of claims deemed to be jurisdictional for habeas purposes. Next, we began to recognize federal claims by state prisoners if no state court had provided a full and fair opportunity to litigate those claims. Before 1953, however, the inverse of this rule also remained true: absent an alleged jurisdictional defect, "habeas corpus would not lie for a [state] prisoner ... if he had been given an adequate opportunity to obtain full and fair consideration of his federal claim in the state courts." In other words, the state-court judgment was entitled to "*absolute* respect," *Kuhlmann v. Wilson*, 477 U.S. 436, 446 (1986) (opinion of Powell, J.), and a federal habeas court could not review it even for reasonableness.

We rejected the principle of absolute deference in our landmark decision in *Brown v. Allen*, 344 U.S. 443 (1953). There, we held that a state-court judgment of conviction "is not *res judicata*" on federal habeas with respect to federal constitutional claims, even if the state court has rejected all such claims after a full and fair hearing. Instead, we held, a district court must determine whether the state-court adjudication "has resulted in a satisfactory conclusion." We had no occasion to explore in detail the question whether a "satisfactory" conclusion was one that the habeas court considered *correct*, as opposed to merely *reasonable*, because we concluded that the constitutional claims advanced in *Brown* itself would fail even if the state courts' rejection of them were reconsidered *de novo*. Nonetheless, we indicated that the federal courts enjoy at least the discretion to take into consideration the fact that a state court has previously rejected the federal claims asserted on habeas.

In an influential separate opinion [in *Brown*] endorsed by a majority of the Court, Justice Frankfurter also rejected the principle of absolute deference to fairly-litigated state-court judgments. He emphasized that a state-court determination of federal constitutional law is not "binding" on federal habeas, regardless of whether the determination involves a pure question of law, or a "so-called mixed questio[n]" requiring the application of law to fact. Nonetheless, he stated quite explicitly that a "prior State determination may guide [the] discretion [of the district court] in deciding upon the appropriate course to be followed in disposing of the application." Discussing mixed questions specifically, he noted further that "there is no need for the federal judge, if he could, to shut his eyes to the State consideration."

Despite our apparent adherence to a standard of *de novo* habeas review with respect to mixed constitutional questions, we have implicitly questioned that standard, at least with respect to pure legal questions, in our recent retroactivity precedents. In

Penry v. Lynaugh, 492 U.S. 302, 313–314 (1989), a majority of this Court endorsed the retroactivity analysis advanced by Justice O'Connor for a plurality in *Teague v. Lane*, 489 U.S. 288 (1989). Under *Teague*, a habeas petitioner generally cannot benefit from a new rule of criminal procedure announced after his conviction has become final on direct appeal. *Teague* defined a "new" rule as one that was "not dictated by precedent existing at the time the defendant's conviction became final." In *Butler v. McKellar*, 494 U.S. 407, 415 (1990), we explained that the definition includes all rules "susceptible to debate among reasonable minds." Thus, if a state court has reasonably rejected the legal claim asserted by a habeas petitioner under existing law, then the claim seeks the benefit of a "new" rule under *Butler*, and is therefore not cognizable on habeas under *Teague*. In other words, a federal habeas court "must defer to the state court's decision rejecting the claim unless that decision is patently unreasonable."

[P]etitioners ask that we reconsider our statement ... that mixed constitutional questions are "subject to plenary federal review" on habeas. By its terms, *Teague* itself is not directly controlling, because West sought federal habeas relief under *Jackson v. Virginia*, which was decided a year before his conviction became final on direct review. Nonetheless, petitioners contend, the logic of *Teague* makes our statement [on plenary federal review] untenable. Petitioners argue that if deferential review for reasonableness strikes an appropriate balance with respect to purely legal claims, then it must strike an appropriate balance with respect to mixed questions as well. Moreover, they note that under the habeas statute itself, a state-court determination of a purely factual question must be "presumed correct," and can be overcome only by "convincing evidence," unless one of eight statutorily enumerated exceptions is present. It makes no sense, petitioners assert, for a habeas court generally to review factual determinations and legal determinations deferentially, but to review applications of law to fact *de novo*. Finally, petitioners find the prospect of deferential review for mixed questions at least implicit in our recent statement that *Teague* concerns are fully implicated "by the application of an old rule in a manner that was not dictated by precedent." For these reasons, petitioners invite us to reaffirm that a habeas judge need not—and indeed may not— "shut his eyes" entirely to state-court applications of law to fact. West develops two principal counterarguments: first, that Congress implicitly codified a *de novo* standard with respect to mixed constitutional questions when it amended the habeas statute in 1966; and second, that *de novo* federal review is necessary to vindicate federal constitutional rights.

We need not decide such far-reaching issues in this case. As in both *Brown v. Allen* and *Jackson v. Virginia*, the claim advanced by the habeas petitioner must fail even assuming that the state court's rejection of it should be reconsidered *de novo*. Whatever the appropriate standard of review, we conclude that there was more than enough evidence to support West's conviction....

In *Jackson*, we emphasized repeatedly the deference owed to the trier of fact and, correspondingly, the sharply limited nature of constitutional sufficiency review. We said that "all of the evidence is to be considered in the light most favorable to the prosecution;" that the prosecution need not affirmatively "rule out every hypothesis except that of guilt;" and that a reviewing court "faced with a record of historical facts that supports conflicting inferences must presume—even if it does not affirmatively appear in the record—that the trier of fact resolved any such conflicts in favor of the prosecution, and must defer to that resolution." Under these standards, we think it clear that the trial record contained sufficient evidence to support West's conviction.

Having granted relief on West's *Jackson* claim, the Court of Appeals declined to address West's additional claim that he was entitled to a new trial, as a matter of due process, on the basis of newly-discovered evidence. As that claim is not properly before us, we decline to address it here. The judgment of the Court of Appeals is reversed, and the case is remanded for further proceedings consistent with this opinion.

Justice O'CONNOR, with whom Justice Blackmun and Justice Stevens join, concurring in the judgment.

I agree that the evidence sufficiently supported respondent's conviction. I write separately only to express disagreement with certain statements in Justice Thomas' extended discussion of this Court's habeas corpus jurisprudence.

First, Justice Thomas errs in describing the pre-1953 law of habeas corpus. While it is true that a state prisoner could not obtain the writ if he had been provided a full and fair hearing in the state courts, this rule governed the merits of a claim under the Due Process Clause. It was not a threshold bar to the consideration of other federal claims, because, with rare exceptions, there were no other federal claims available at the time. During the period Justice Thomas discusses, the guarantees of the Bill of Rights were not yet understood to apply in state criminal prosecutions. The only protections the Constitution afforded to state prisoners were those for which the text of the Constitution explicitly limited the authority of the States, most notably the Due Process Clause of the Fourteenth Amendment. And in the area of criminal procedure, the Due Process Clause was understood to guarantee no more than a full and fair hearing in the state courts....

Second, Justice Thomas quotes Justice Powell's opinion in *Kuhlmann v. Wilson* out of context. Justice Powell said only that the judgment of a committing court of competent jurisdiction was accorded "absolute respect" on habeas in the 19th century, when the habeas inquiry was limited to the jurisdiction of the court. Justice Powell was not expressing the erroneous view which Justice Thomas today ascribes to him, that state court judgments were entitled to complete deference before 1953.

Third, Justice Thomas errs in implying that *Brown v. Allen* was the first case in which the Court held that the doctrine of *res judicata* is not strictly followed on federal habeas. In fact, the Court explicitly reached this holding for the first time in *Salinger v. Loisel*, 265 U.S. 224, 230 (1924). Even *Salinger* did not break new ground: The *Salinger* Court observed that such had been the rule at common law, and that the Court had implicitly followed it in *Carter v. McClaughry*, 183 U.S. 365, 378 (1902), and *Ex parte Spencer*, 228 U.S. 652, 658 (1913). The Court reached the same conclusion in at least two other cases between *Salinger* and *Brown*....

Fourth, Justice Thomas understates the certainty with which *Brown v. Allen* rejected a deferential standard of review of issues of law. The passages in which the *Brown* Court stated that a district court should determine whether the state adjudication had resulted in a "satisfactory conclusion," and that the federal courts had discretion to give some weight to state court determinations, were passages in which the Court was discussing how federal courts should resolve questions of fact, not issues of law. This becomes apparent from a reading of the relevant section of *Brown*, a section entitled "Right to a Plenary Hearing." When the Court then turned to the primary legal question presented—whether the Fourteenth Amendment permitted the restriction of jury service to taxpayers—the Court answered that question in the affirmative without any hint of deference to the state courts. The proper standard of review of issues of law was also discussed in Justice Frankfurter's opinion, which a majority of the Court endorsed. After recognizing that state court factfinding need not always be repeated in federal court, Justice Frankfurter turned to the quite different question of determining the law. He wrote: "Where the ascertainment of the historical facts does not dispose of the claim but calls for interpretation of the legal significance of such facts, *the District Judge must exercise his own judgment* on this blend of facts and their legal values. Thus, so-called mixed questions or the application of constitutional principles to the facts as found leave the duty of adjudication with the federal judge." Justice Frankfurter concluded: "The State court cannot have the last say when it, though on fair consideration and what procedurally may be deemed fairness, may have misconceived a federal constitutional right." *Id.* at 507–508.

Fifth, Justice Thomas incorrectly states that we have never considered the standard of review to apply to mixed questions of law and fact raised on federal habeas. On the contrary, we did so in the very cases cited by Justice Thomas. [See *Townsend v. Sain*, 372 U.S. 293 (1963); *Neil v. Biggers*, 409 U.S. 188 (1972); *Brewer v. Williams*, 430 U.S. 387 (1977); *Cuyler v. Sullivan*, 446 U.S. 335 (1980); *Strickland v. Washington*, 466 U.S. 668 (1984); *Miller v. Fenton*, 474 U.S. 104 (1985).] In *Irvin v. Dowd*, 366 U.S. 717 (1961), we stated quite clearly that "'mixed questions or the application of constitutional principles to the facts as found leave the duty of adjudication with the federal judge.' It was, therefore, the duty of the Court of Appeals to independently evaluate [the issue of jury prejudice]." We then proceeded to employ precisely the same legal analysis as in cases on direct appeal....

To this list of cases cited by Justice Thomas, one could add the following, all of which applied a standard of *de novo* review. *Leyra v. Denno*, 347 U.S. 556, 558–561 (1954); *United States ex rel. Jennings v. Ragen*, 358 U.S. 276, 277 (1959); *Rogers v. Richmond*, 365 U.S. 534, 546 (1961); *Gideon v. Wainwright*, 372 U.S. 335, 339–345 (1963); *Pate v. Robinson*, 383 U.S. 375, 384–386 (1966); *Sheppard v. Maxwell*, 384 U.S. 333, 349–363, (1966); *McMann v. Richardson*, 397 U.S. 759, 766–774 (1970); *Barker v. Wingo*, 407 U.S. 514, 522–536 (1972); *Lego v. Twomey*, 404 U.S. 477, 482–490 (1972); *Morrissey v. Brewer*, 408 U.S. 471, 480–490 (1972); *Gagnon v. Scarpelli*, 411 U.S. 778, 781–791 (1973); *Schneckloth v. Busta- monte*, 412 U.S. 218, 222–249 (1973); *Manson v. Brathwaite*, 432 U.S. 98, 109–117 (1977); *Watkins v. Sowders*, 449 U.S. 341, 345–349 (1981); *Jones v. Barnes*, 463 U.S. 745, 750–754 (1983); *Berkemer v. McCarty*, 468 U.S. 420, 435–442 (1984); *Moran v. Burbine*, 475 U.S. 412, 420–434 (1986); *Kimmelman v. Morrison*, 477 U.S. 365, 383–387 (1986); *Maynard v. Cartwright*, 486 U.S. 356, 360–365 (1988); *Duckworth v. Eagan*, 492 U.S. 195, 201–205 (1989); *Estelle v. McGuire*, 112 S. Ct. 475, 480–481, (1991). There have been many others.

Sixth, Justice Thomas misdescribes *Jackson v. Virginia*. In *Jackson*, the respondents proposed a deferential standard of review, very much like the one Justice Thomas discusses today, that they thought appropriate for addressing constitutional claims of insufficient evidence. We expressly rejected this proposal. Instead, we adhered to the general rule of *de novo* review of constitutional claims on habeas.

Seventh, Justice Thomas mischaracterizes *Teague v. Lane* and *Penry v. Lynaugh* as "question[ing] th[e] standard [of *de novo* review] with respect to pure legal questions." *Teague* did not establish a "deferential" standard of review of state court determinations of federal law. It did not establish a standard of review at all. Instead, *Teague* simply requires that a state conviction on federal habeas be judged according to the law in existence when the conviction became final. In *Teague*, we refused to give state prisoners the retroactive benefit of new rules of law, but we did *not* create any deferential standard of review with regard to old rules....

Eighth, though Justice Thomas suggests otherwise, *de novo* review is not incompatible with the maxim that federal courts should "give great weight to the considered conclusions of a coequal state judiciary," just as they do to persuasive, well-reasoned authority from district or circuit courts in other jurisdictions. A state court opinion concerning the legal implications of precisely the same set of facts is the closest one can get to a "case on point," and is especially valuable for that reason. But this does not mean that we have held in the past that federal courts must presume the correctness of a state court's legal conclusions on habeas, or that a state court's incorrect legal determination has ever been allowed to stand because it was reasonable. We have always held that federal courts, even on habeas, have an independent obligation to say what the law is.

Finally, in his one-sentence summary of respondent's arguments, Justice Thomas fails to mention that Congress has considered habeas corpus legislation during 27 of the past 37 years, and on 13 occasions has considered adopting a deferential standard of review along the lines suggested by Justice Thomas. Congress has rejected each proposal. In light of the case law and Congress' position, a move away from *de novo* review of mixed questions of law and fact would be a substantial change in our construction of the authority conferred by the habeas corpus statute. As Justice Thomas acknowledges, to change the standard of review would indeed be "far-reaching," and we need not decide whether to do so in order to resolve this case.

Notes and Questions

1. Although the Supreme Court in *Wright v. West* asked the parties to brief the issue of whether mixed questions of law and fact should be reviewed under a deferential standard or *de novo*, the Court ducked the issue and concluded that, regardless of the proper standard of review, West's claim of insufficiency of the evidence would fail.

2. *Wright v. West* was decided prior to the AEDPA and, as has been noted throughout the last few chapters, the AEDPA significantly changes the ways in which a habeas petition may be presented and reviewed in federal court. Among these changes is the standard of review applicable to legal questions. Section 2254(d)(1) provides that a federal court may grant a writ only where the state court's legal determination was "contrary to" or an "unreasonable application" of federal law as determined by the Supreme Court. Does this language change the analysis in *Wright v. West*? How does §2254(d)(1) affect a federal court's analysis of a mixed question of law and fact?

3. Consider Justice O'Connor's concurring opinion in *Williams v. Taylor* (*supra* chapter 13). Does she believe that the AEDPA simply codifies *Wright v. West*, or does she find that the statute goes further?

Chapter 17

Successive Habeas Corpus Petitions, Abuse of the Writ, and Clemency

A. Successive Petitions and Abusing the Writ (Pre-AEDPA)

After failing to get relief in state court or on federal habeas, a capital defendant may wish to file an additional habeas petition seeking relief from his conviction or sentence. Prior to the enactment of the AEDPA, a petitioner could file a successive habeas petition to litigate claims that were omitted from a first habeas petition. However, claims raised in a successive petition would have been subject to the abuse of the writ doctrine, which permits a federal court to reject a claim raised in a second or successive habeas corpus petition if the court determines that the claim should have been brought in the first federal habeas petition. A petitioner may be allowed to litigate claims that had been previously raised and denied on the merits if the ends of justice would be served by considering a successive petition. A discussion of the pre-AEDPA successive petition rules and the abuse of the writ doctrine follows.

In *Sanders v. United States*, 373 U.S. 1 (1963), the Court held that successive petitions based on claims previously raised in a first habeas petition may be dismissed if three conditions exist: (1) the same ground presented in the subsequent petition was determined adversely to the petitioner on the prior petition; (2) the prior determination was on the merits; and (3) the "ends of justice" would not be served by reconsideration of the claim. The Court concluded that a new claim brought in a successive habeas petition may be dismissed:

> if a prisoner deliberately withholds one of two grounds for federal collateral relief at the time of filing his first application, in the hope of being granted two hearings rather than one or for some other such reason; [in those circumstances] he may be deemed to have waived his right to a hearing on a second application presenting the withheld ground. The same may be true if ... the prisoner deliberately abandons one of his grounds at the first hearing. Nothing in the traditions of habeas corpus requires the federal courts to tolerate needless piecemeal litigation, to entertain collateral proceedings whose only purpose is to vex, harass, or delay.

Sanders v. United States, 373 U.S. at 18.

In 1966, Congress amended the habeas corpus statute and codified the rule of *Sanders*, forbidding successive petitions raising new claims deliberately withheld from a

911

previous petition. Specifically, §2244(b) provided, "a subsequent application for a writ of habeas corpus ... need not be entertained by a court of the United States ... unless the application alleges and is predicated on a factual or other ground not adjudicated on the hearing of the earlier application for the writ, and unless the court ... is satisfied that the applicant has not on the earlier application deliberately withheld the newly asserted ground or otherwise abused the writ." In 1976, Congress drafted Rule 9(b) of the Rules Governing §2254 Cases:

> *Successive Petitions.* A second or successive petition may be dismissed if the judge finds that it fails to allege new or different grounds for relief and the prior determination was on the merits or, if new and different grounds are alleged, the judge finds that the failure of the petitioner to assert those grounds in a prior petition constituted an abuse of the writ.

Although neither of these statutes specifically uses the "ends of justice" language in *Sanders*, the Court in *Kuhlmann v. Wilson*, 477 U.S. 436 (1986), considered this language in the context of a successive petition raising a previously litigated claim and added its understanding of the "ends of justice." Writing for the Court, Justice Powell stated:

> In the light of the historic purpose of habeas corpus and the interests implicated by successive petitions for federal habeas relief from a state conviction, we conclude that the "ends of justice" require federal courts to entertain such petitions only where the prisoner supplements his constitutional claim with a colorable showing of factual innocence. This standard was proposed by Judge Friendly more than a decade ago as a prerequisite for federal habeas review generally. [See Friendly, "Is Innocence Irrelevant?," *supra* chapter 13.] As Judge Friendly persuasively argued then, a requirement that the prisoner come forward with a colorable showing of innocence identifies those habeas petitioners who are justified in again seeking relief from their incarceration. We adopt this standard now to effectuate the clear intent of Congress that successive federal habeas review should be granted only in rare cases, but that it should be available when the ends of justice so require. The prisoner may make the requisite showing by establishing that under the probative evidence he has a colorable claim of factual innocence. The prisoner must make his evidentiary showing even though—as argued in this case—the evidence of guilt may have been unlawfully admitted.

The Court observed in a footnote that:

> As Judge Friendly explained, a prisoner does not make a colorable showing of innocence "by showing that he might not, or even would not, have been convicted in the absence of evidence claimed to have been unconstitutionally obtained." Rather the prisoner must "show a fair probability that, in light of all the evidence, including that alleged to have been illegally admitted (but with due regard to any unreliability of it) and evidence tenably claimed to have been wrongly excluded or to have become available only after the trial, the trier of the facts would have entertained a reasonable doubt of his guilt." Thus, the question whether the prisoner can make the requisite showing must be determined by reference to all probative evidence of guilt or innocence.

For further discussion on successive petitions and abuse of the writ prior to 1996 see Liebman and Hertz, *Federal Habeas Corpus Practice and Procedure* §§28.2–28.3 (5th ed. 2005).

In the following pre-AEDPA case, the Court applied the "cause and prejudice" standard to successive habeas petitions involving claims not previously presented in a first habeas petition.

McCleskey v. Zant
499 U.S. 467 (1991)

Justice KENNEDY delivered the opinion of the Court.

[For an earlier Supreme Court decision involving Warren McCleskey, see *McCleskey v. Kemp*, 481 U.S. 279 (1987) (*supra* chapter 4).]

The doctrine of abuse of the writ defines the circumstances in which federal courts decline to entertain a claim presented for the first time in a second or subsequent petition for a writ of habeas corpus. Petitioner Warren McCleskey in a second federal habeas petition presented a claim under *Massiah v. United States*, 377 U.S. 201 (1964) [regarding the admissibility of jailhouse confessions], that he failed to include in his first federal petition. The Court of Appeals for the Eleventh Circuit held that assertion of the *Massiah* claim in this manner abused the writ. Though our analysis differs from that of the Court of Appeals, we agree that the petitioner here abused the writ, and we affirm the judgment.

I

[In 1978, Warren McCleskey and three others robbed a furniture store in Georgia. During the course of the robbery, a police officer was shot and killed. Although McCleskey virtually confessed to the killing, he renounced the confession at trial. To counter McCleskey's testimony, the state called Offie Evans who had occupied a cell next to McCleskey. Evans claimed McCleskey admitted to killing the officer. Other direct and circumstantial evidence implicated McCleskey. McCleskey was found guilty and was sentenced to death.

On direct appeal, McCleskey raised six grounds for relief including a claim that the state improperly withheld evidence regarding McCleskey's alleged jailhouse confession to Evans. The state court affirmed McCleskey's conviction. McCleskey then initiated state post-conviction proceedings raising twenty-three challenges to his conviction and sentence, including three challenges to Evans' testimony. One of these three challenges alleged that admission of Evans' testimony violated McCleskey's right to counsel as established in *Massiah v. United States*. The state courts denied McCleskey relief.

In 1981, McCleskey filed his first petition for federal habeas relief asserting eighteen grounds for relief. The *Massiah* claim was not raised. McCleskey was denied relief.

In 1987, McCleskey filed his second habeas petition. This second petition resurrected the *Massiah* claim based on new evidence. This new evidence consisted of a 21-page document which the police had withheld from McCleskey until 1987 and which, according to McCleskey, showed Evans acted in concert with the police. McCleskey argued that this new evidence supported his claim that admission of Evans' testimony violated *Massiah*. The district court reversed McCleskey's conviction based on the *Massiah* claim. The appellate court reversed the district court's order and held that McCleskey had abused the writ by failing to raise the *Massiah* claim in his first federal habeas petition. The Supreme Court granted certiorari.]

II

The parties agree that the government has the burden of pleading abuse of the writ, and that once the government makes a proper submission, the petitioner must show that he has not abused the writ in seeking habeas relief. Much confusion exists though, on the standard for determining when a petitioner abuses the writ.

III

For reasons we explain below, a review of our habeas corpus precedents leads us to decide that the same standard used to determine whether to excuse state procedural defaults should govern the determination of inexcusable neglect in the abuse of the writ context.

The prohibition against adjudication in federal habeas corpus of claims defaulted in state court is similar in purpose and design to the abuse of the writ doctrine, which in general prohibits subsequent habeas consideration of claims not raised, and thus defaulted, in the first federal habeas proceeding. The terms "abuse of the writ" and "inexcusable neglect," on the one hand, and "procedural default," on the other, imply a background norm of procedural regularity binding on the petitioner. This explains the presumption against habeas adjudication both of claims defaulted in state court and of claims defaulted in the first round of federal habeas. A federal habeas court's power to excuse these types of defaulted claims derives from the court's equitable discretion. In habeas, equity recognizes that "a suitor's conduct in relation to the matter at hand may disentitle him to the relief he seeks." *Sanders,* 373 U.S. at 17. For these reasons, both the abuse of the writ doctrine and our procedural default jurisprudence concentrate on a petitioner's acts to determine whether he has a legitimate excuse for failing to raise a claim at the appropriate time.

The doctrines of procedural default and abuse of the writ implicate nearly identical concerns flowing from the significant costs of federal habeas corpus review. To begin with, the writ strikes at finality. One of the law's very objects is the finality of its judgments. Neither innocence nor just punishment can be vindicated until the final judgment is known. "Without finality, the criminal law is deprived of much of its deterrent effect." And when a habeas petitioner succeeds in obtaining a new trial, the "'erosion of memory' and 'dispersion of witnesses' that occur with the passage of time" prejudice the government and diminish the chances of a reliable criminal adjudication.…

Finality has special importance in the context of a federal attack on a state conviction. Reexamination of state convictions on federal habeas "frustrate[s] … 'both the States' sovereign power to punish offenders and their good-faith attempts to honor constitutional rights.'" Our federal system recognizes the independent power of a State to articulate societal norms through criminal law; but the power of a State to pass laws means little if the State cannot enforce them.

Habeas review extracts further costs. Federal collateral litigation places a heavy burden on scarce federal judicial resources, and threatens the capacity of the system to resolve primary disputes. Finally, habeas corpus review may give litigants incentives to withhold claims for manipulative purposes and may establish disincentives to present claims when evidence is fresh.

Far more severe are the disruptions when a claim is presented for the first time in a second or subsequent federal habeas petition. If "[c]ollateral review of a conviction extends the ordeal of trial for both society and the accused," the ordeal worsens during subsequent collateral proceedings. Perpetual disrespect for the finality of convictions disparages the entire criminal justice system.... If re-examination of a conviction in the first round of federal habeas stretches resources, examination of new claims raised in a second or subsequent petition spreads them thinner still. These later petitions deplete the resources needed for federal litigants in the first instance, including litigants commencing their first federal habeas action. The phenomenon calls to mind Justice Jackson's admonition that "[i]t must prejudice the occasional meritorious application to be buried in a flood of worthless ones." And if reexamination of convictions in the first round of habeas offends federalism and comity, the offense increases when a State must defend its conviction in a second or subsequent habeas proceeding on grounds not even raised in the first petition.

The federal writ of habeas corpus overrides all these considerations, essential as they are to the rule of law, when a petitioner raises a meritorious constitutional claim in a proper manner in a habeas petition. Our procedural default jurisprudence and abuse of the writ jurisprudence help define this dimension of procedural regularity. Both doctrines impose on petitioners a burden of reasonable compliance with procedures designed to discourage baseless claims and to keep the system open for valid ones; both recognize the law's interest in finality; and both invoke equitable principles to define the court's discretion to excuse pleading and procedural requirements for petitioners who could not comply with them in the exercise of reasonable care and diligence. It is true that a habeas court's concern to honor state procedural default rules rests in part on respect for the integrity of procedures "employed by a coordinate jurisdiction within the federal system," and that such respect is not implicated when a petitioner defaults a claim by failing to raise it in the first round of federal habeas review. Nonetheless, the doctrines of procedural default and abuse of the writ are both designed to lessen the injury to a State that results through reexamination of a state conviction on a ground that the State did not have the opportunity to address at a prior, appropriate time; and both doctrines seek to vindicate the State's interest in the finality of its criminal judgments.

We conclude from the unity of structure and purpose in the jurisprudence of state procedural defaults and abuse of the writ that the standard for excusing a failure to raise a claim at the appropriate time should be the same in both contexts. We have held that a procedural default will be excused upon a showing of cause and prejudice. We now hold that the same standard applies to determine if there has been an abuse of the writ through inexcusable neglect....

... When a prisoner files a second or subsequent application, the government bears the burden of pleading abuse of the writ. The government satisfies this burden if, with clarity and particularity, it notes petitioner's prior writ history, identifies the claims that appear for the first time, and alleges that petitioner has abused the writ. The burden to disprove abuse then becomes petitioner's. To excuse his failure to raise the claim earlier, he must show cause for failing to raise it and prejudice therefrom as those concepts have been defined in our procedural default decisions. The petitioner's opportunity to meet the burden of cause and prejudice will not include an evidentiary hearing if the district court determines as a matter of law that petitioner cannot satisfy the standard. If petitioner cannot show cause, the failure to raise the claim in an earlier petition may nonetheless be excused if he or she can show that a fundamental miscarriage of justice would result from a failure to entertain the claim. Application of the cause and prejudice standard in the abuse of the writ context does not mitigate the force of *Teague v. Lane*, which prohibits, with certain exceptions, the retroactive application of new law to claims raised in federal habeas. Nor does it imply that there is a constitutional right to counsel in federal habeas corpus....

Considerations of certainty and stability in our discharge of the judicial function support adoption of the cause and prejudice standard in the abuse of the writ context. Well-defined in the case law, the standard will be familiar to federal courts. Its application clarifies the imprecise contours of the term "inexcusable neglect." The standard is an objective one, and can be applied in a manner that comports with the threshold nature of the abuse of the writ inquiry. Finally, the standard provides "a sound and workable means of channeling the discretion of federal habeas courts." "[I]t is important, in order to preclude individualized enforcement of the Constitution in different parts of the Nation, to lay down as specifically as the nature of the problem permits the standards or directions that should govern the District Judges in the disposition of applications for habeas corpus by prisoners under sentence of State Courts."

The cause and prejudice standard should curtail the abusive petitions that in recent years have threatened to undermine the integrity of the habeas corpus process. "Federal courts should not continue to tolerate—even in capital cases—this type of abuse of the writ of habeas corpus." The writ of habeas corpus is one of the centerpieces of our liberties. "But the writ has potentialities for evil as well as for good. Abuse of the writ may undermine the orderly administration of justice and therefore weaken the forces of authority that are essential for civilization." Adoption of the cause and prejudice standard acknowledges the historic purpose and function of the writ in our constitutional system, and, by preventing its abuse, assures its continued efficacy.

[Applying these principles to the facts in McCleskey's case, the Court found that Mc-Cleskey abused the writ and denied relief.]

Justice MARSHALL, with whom Justice Blackmun and Justice Stevens join, dissenting.

Today's decision departs drastically from the norms that inform the proper judicial function. Without even the most casual admission that it is discarding longstanding legal principles, the Court radically redefines the content of the "abuse of the writ" doctrine, substituting the strict-liability "cause and prejudice" standard of *Wainwright v. Sykes* for the good-faith "deliberate abandonment" standard of *Sanders v. United States.* This doctrinal innovation, which repudiates a line of judicial decisions codified by Congress in the governing statute and procedural rules, was by no means foreseeable when the petitioner in this case filed his first federal habeas application. Indeed, the new rule announced and applied today was not even requested by respondent at any point in this litigation. Finally, rather than remand this case for reconsideration in light of its new standard, the majority performs an independent reconstruction of the record, disregarding the factual findings of the District Court and applying its new rule in a manner that encourages state officials to conceal evidence that would likely prompt a petitioner to raise a particular claim on habeas. Because I cannot acquiesce in this unjustifiable assault on the Great Writ, I dissent....

I

In *Sanders v. United States*, 373 U.S. 1 (1963), the Court crystallized the various factors bearing on a district court's discretion to entertain a successive petition.[1] The Court in *Sanders* distinguished successive petitions raising previously asserted grounds from those raising previously unasserted grounds. With regard to the former class of peti-

---

1. Although *Sanders* examined the abuse-of-the-writ question in the context of a motion for collateral review filed under 28 U.S.C. §2255, the Court made it clear that the same principles apply in the context of a petition for habeas corpus filed under 28 U.S.C. §2254.

tions, the Court explained, the district court may give "[c]ontrolling weight ... to [the] denial of a prior application" unless "the ends of justice would ... be served by reaching the merits of the subsequent application." With regard to the latter, however, the district court must reach the merits of the petition unless "there has been an abuse of the writ...." In determining whether the omission of the claim from the previous petition constitutes an abuse of the writ, the judgment of the district court is to be guided chiefly by the "'[equitable] principle that a suitor's conduct in relation to the matter at hand may disentitle him to the relief he seeks.'"

What emerges from *Sanders* and its predecessors is essentially a good-faith standard.... [T]he principal form of bad faith that the "abuse of the writ" doctrine is intended to deter is the deliberate abandonment of a claim the factual and legal basis of which are known to the petitioner (or his counsel) when he files his first petition. The Court in *Sanders* stressed this point by equating its analysis with that of *Fay v. Noia*, which established the then-prevailing "deliberate bypass" test for the cognizability of claims on which a petitioner procedurally defaulted in state proceedings. A petitioner also abuses the writ under *Sanders* when he uses the writ to achieve some end other than expeditious relief from unlawful confinement—such as "to vex, harass, or delay." However, so long as the petitioner's previous application was based on a good-faith assessment of the claims available to him, the denial of the application does not bar the petitioner from availing himself of "new or additional information" in support of a claim not previously raised.

"Cause and prejudice"—the standard currently applicable to procedural defaults in state proceedings—imposes a much stricter test. As this Court's precedents make clear, a petitioner has cause for failing effectively to present his federal claim in state proceedings only when "some objective factor external to the defense impeded counsel's efforts to comply with the State's procedural rule...." *Murray v. Carrier, 477 U.S. 478, 488* (1986). Under this test, the state of mind of counsel is largely irrelevant. Indeed, this Court has held that even counsel's reasonable perception that a particular claim is without factual or legal foundation does not excuse the failure to raise that claim in the absence of an objective, external impediment to counsel's efforts. In this sense, the cause component of the *Wainwright v. Sykes* test establishes a strict-liability standard.

Equally foreign to our abuse-of-the-writ jurisprudence is the requirement that a petitioner show "prejudice." Under *Sanders*, a petitioner who articulates a justifiable reason for failing to present a claim in a previous habeas application is not required in addition to demonstrate any particular degree of prejudice before the habeas court must consider his claim. If the petitioner demonstrates that his claim has merit, it is the State that must show that the resulting constitutional error was harmless beyond a reasonable doubt....

II

B

... By design, the cause-and-prejudice standard creates a near-irrebuttable presumption that omitted claims are permanently barred. This outcome not only conflicts with Congress' intent that a petitioner be free to avail himself of newly discovered evidence or intervening changes in law, but also subverts the statutory disincentive to the assertion of frivolous claims. Rather than face the cause-and-prejudice bar, a petitioner will assert all conceivable claims, whether or not these claims reasonably appear to have merit. The possibility that these claims will be adversely adjudicated and thereafter be barred from relitigation under the successive-petition doctrine will not effectively discourage the petitioner from asserting them, for the petitioner will have virtually no expectation that any withheld claim could be revived should his assessment of its merit later prove mistaken. Far from promoting efficiency, the majority's rule thus invites the very type of "baseless claims" that the majority seeks to avert.

The majority's adoption of the cause-and-prejudice test is not only unwise, but also manifestly unfair. The proclaimed purpose of the majority's new strict-liability standard is to increase to the maximum extent a petitioner's incentive to investigate all conceivable claims before filing his first petition. Whatever its merits, this was not the rule when the petitioner in this case filed his first petition. From the legislative history of §2244(b) and Rule 9(b) and from the universal agreement of courts and commentators, McCleskey's counsel could have reached no other conclusion but that his investigatory efforts in preparing his client's petition would be measured against the *Sanders* good-faith standard. There can be little question that his efforts satisfied that test; indeed, the District Court expressly concluded that McCleskey's counsel on his first habeas conducted a reasonable and competent investigation before concluding that a claim based on *Massiah* would be without factual foundation. Before today, that would have been enough. The Court's utter indifference to the injustice of retroactively applying its new, strict-liability standard to this habeas petitioner stands in marked contrast to this Court's eagerness to protect States from the unfair surprise of "new rules" that enforce the constitutional rights of citizens charged with criminal wrongdoing.

This injustice is compounded by the Court's activism in fashioning its new rule. The applicability of *Sykes'* cause-and-prejudice test was not litigated in either the District Court or the Court of Appeals. The additional question that we requested the parties to address reasonably could have been read to relate merely to the burden of proof under the abuse-of-the-writ doctrine; it evidently did not put the parties on notice that this Court was contemplating a change in the governing legal standard, since respondent did not even mention *Sykes* or cause-and-prejudice in its brief or at oral argument, much less request the Court to adopt this standard. In this respect, too, today's decision departs from norms that inform the proper judicial function. It cannot be said that McCleskey had a fair opportunity to challenge the reasoning that the majority today invokes to strip him of his *Massiah* claim....

IV

Ironically, the majority seeks to defend its doctrinal innovation on the ground that it will promote respect for the "rule of law." Obviously, respect for the rule of law must start with those who are responsible for pronouncing the law. The majority's invocation of "'the orderly administration of justice'" rings hollow when the majority itself tosses aside established precedents without explanation, disregards the will of Congress, fashions rules that defy the reasonable expectations of the persons who must conform their conduct to the law's dictates, and applies those rules in a way that rewards state misconduct and deceit. Whatever "abuse of the writ" today's decision is designed to avert pales in comparison with the majority's own abuse of the norms that inform the proper judicial function.

I dissent.

Notes

1. Although *McCleskey* addressed successive habeas petitions raising new habeas claims as opposed to previously litigated habeas claims, the Court also has applied the

cause and prejudice standard to previously litigated claims raised in successive habeas petitions. See *Schlup v. Delo*, 513 U.S. 298, 318 (1995); *Sawyer v. Whitley*, 505 U.S. 333, 338 (1992).

2. McCleskey claimed that he met the cause and prejudice standard because the police withheld critical evidence regarding his *Massiah* claim until after McCleskey's first habeas petition had been rejected. In rejecting this argument, the Court reasoned:

> That McCleskey did not possess or could not reasonably have obtained certain evidence fails to establish cause if other known or discoverable evidence could have supported the claim in any event. "[C]ause ... requires a showing of some external impediment preventing counsel from constructing or raising a claim." For cause to exist, the external impediment, whether it be government interference or the reasonable unavailability of the factual basis for the claim, must have prevented petitioner from raising the claim. Abuse of the writ doctrine examines petitioner's conduct: the question is whether petitioner possessed, or by reasonable means could have obtained, a sufficient basis to allege a claim in the first petition and pursue the matter through the habeas process. The requirement of cause in the abuse of the writ context is based on the principle that petitioner must conduct a reasonable and diligent investigation aimed at including all relevant claims and grounds for relief in the first federal habeas petition. If what petitioner knows or could discover upon reasonable investigation supports a claim for relief in a federal habeas petition, what he does not know is irrelevant. Omission of the claim will not be excused merely because evidence discovered later might also have supported or strengthened the claim....
>
> ... McCleskey has had at least constructive knowledge all along of the facts he now claims to have learned only from the [recently discovered evidence which consisted of a 21-page document]. The unavailability of the document did not prevent McCleskey from raising the *Massiah* claim in the first federal petition and is not cause for his failure to do so. And of course, McCleskey cannot contend that his false representations at trial constitute cause for the omission of a claim from the first federal petition....
>
> McCleskey nonetheless seeks to hold the State responsible for his omission of the *Massiah* claim in the first petition. His current strategy is to allege that the State engaged in wrongful conduct in withholding the 21-page document. This argument need not detain us long. When all is said and done, the issue is not presented in the case, despite all the emphasis upon it in McCleskey's brief and oral argument. The Atlanta police turned over the 21-page document upon request in 1987. The District Court found no misrepresentation or wrongful conduct by the State in failing to hand over the document earlier, and our discussion of the evidence in the record concerning the existence of the statement, as well as the fact that at least four courts have considered and rejected petitioner's *Brady* claim, belies McCleskey's characterization of the case. And as we have taken care to explain, the document is not critical to McCleskey's notice of a *Massiah* claim anyway.

In contrast to the majority's views, Justice Marshall in his dissent concluded:

> To appreciate the hollowness [of the majority's analysis] — and the dangerousness — of this reasoning, it is necessary to recall the District Court's central finding: that the State *did* covertly plant Evans in an adjoining cell for the pur-

pose of eliciting incriminating statements that could be used against McCleskey at trial. Once this finding is credited, it follows that the State affirmatively misled McCleskey and his counsel throughout their unsuccessful pursuit of the *Massiah* claim in state collateral proceedings and their investigation of that claim in preparing for McCleskey's first federal habeas proceeding. McCleskey's counsel deposed or interviewed the assistant district attorney, various jailers, and other government officials responsible for Evans' confinement, all of whom denied any knowledge of an agreement between Evans and the State.

Against this background of deceit, the State's withholding of Evans' 21-page statement assumes critical importance. The majority overstates McCleskey's and his counsel's awareness of the statement's contents.... But in any event, the importance of the statement lay much less in what the statement said than in its simple *existence*. Without the statement, McCleskey's counsel had nothing more than his client's testimony to back up counsel's own suspicion of a possible *Massiah* violation; given the state officials' adamant denials of any arrangement with Evans, and given the state habeas court's rejection of the *Massiah* claim, counsel quite reasonably concluded that raising this claim in McCleskey's first habeas petition would be futile. All this changed once counsel finally obtained the statement, for at that point, there was credible, independent corroboration of counsel's suspicion. This additional evidence not only gave counsel the reasonable expectation of success that had previously been lacking, but also gave him a basis for conducting further investigation into the underlying claim. Indeed, it was by piecing together the circumstances under which the statement had been transcribed that McCleskey's counsel was able to find Worthy, a state official who was finally willing to admit that Evans had been planted in the cell adjoining McCleskey's.[12]

The majority's analysis of this case is dangerous precisely because it treats as irrelevant the effect that the State's disinformation strategy had on counsel's assessment of the reasonableness of pursuing the *Massiah* claim. For the majority, all that matters is that no external obstacle barred McCleskey from finding Worthy. But obviously, counsel's decision even to look for evidence in support of a particular claim has to be informed by what counsel reasonably perceives to be the prospect that the claim may have merit; in this case, by withholding the 21-page statement and by affirmatively misleading counsel as to the State's involvement with Evans, state officials created a climate in which McCleskey's first habeas counsel was perfectly justified in focusing his attentions elsewhere. The sum and substance of the majority's analysis is that McCleskey had no "cause" for failing to assert the *Massiah* claim because he did not try hard enough to pierce the State's veil of deception. Because the majority excludes from its conception of cause any recognition of how state officials can distort a petitioner's reasonable perception of whether pursuit of a particular claim is worthwhile, the majority's conception of "cause" creates an incentive for state officials to engage in this very type of misconduct.

3. *McCleskey v. Zant*, 499 U.S. 467 (1991), extended both the cause and prejudice exception and the actual innocence exception to cases involving abuse of the writ. Al-

---

12. The majority gratuitously characterizes Worthy's testimony as being contradictory on the facts essential to McCleskey's *Massiah* claim. According to the District Court—which is obviously in a better position to know than is the majority—"Worthy never wavered from the fact that someone, at some point, requested his permission to move Evans to be near McCleskey."

though the Court stated that the actual innocence exception provides "an additional safeguard against compelling an innocent man to suffer an unconstitutional loss of liberty," the Court denied relief. McCleskey lost because his claimed constitutional error "resulted in the admission at trial of truthful inculpatory evidence which did not affect the reliability of the guilty determination." Warren McCleskey was executed on September 25, 1991.

Sawyer v. Whitley
505 U.S. 333 (1992)

Chief Justice REHNQUIST delivered the opinion of the Court.

The issue before the Court is the standard for determining whether a petitioner bringing a successive, abusive, or defaulted federal habeas claim has shown he is "actually innocent" of the death penalty to which he has been sentenced so that the court may reach the merits of the claim. Robert Wayne Sawyer, the petitioner in this case, filed a second federal habeas petition containing successive and abusive claims. The Court of Appeals for the Fifth Circuit refused to examine the merits of Sawyer's claims. It held that Sawyer had not shown cause for failure to raise these claims in his earlier petition, and that he had not shown that he was "actually innocent" of the crime of which he was convicted or the penalty which was imposed. We affirm the Court of Appeals and hold that to show "actual innocence" one must show by clear and convincing evidence that but for a constitutional error, no reasonable juror would have found the petitioner eligible for the death penalty under the applicable state law....

[A jury convicted Sawyer of the brutal murder of Frances Arwood and sentenced him to death.] Sawyer's conviction and sentence were affirmed on appeal by the Louisiana Supreme Court. We granted certiorari, and vacated and remanded with instructions to reconsider in light of *Zant v. Stephens*, 462 U.S. 862 (1983). On remand, the Louisiana Supreme Court reaffirmed the sentence. Petitioner's first petition for state postconviction relief was denied. In 1986, Sawyer filed his first federal habeas petition, raising 18 claims, all of which were denied on the merits. We again granted certiorari and affirmed the Court of Appeals' denial of relief. Petitioner next filed a second motion for state postconviction relief. The state trial court summarily denied this petition as repetitive and without merit, and the Louisiana Supreme Court denied discretionary review.

The present petition before this Court arises out of Sawyer's second petition for federal habeas relief. After granting a stay and holding an evidentiary hearing, the District Court denied one of Sawyer's claims on the merits and held that the others were barred as either abusive or successive. The Court of Appeals granted a certificate of probable cause on the issue whether petitioner had shown that he is actually "innocent of the death penalty" such that a court should reach the merits of the claims contained in this successive petition. The Court of Appeals held that petitioner had failed to show that he was actually innocent of the death penalty because the evidence he argued had been unconstitutionally kept from the jury failed to show that Sawyer was ineligible for the death penalty under Louisiana law. For the third time we granted Sawyer's petition for certiorari, and we now affirm.

Unless a habeas petitioner shows cause and prejudice, a court may not reach the merits of: (a) *successive claims* that raise grounds identical to grounds heard and decided on the merits in a previous petition, *Kuhlmann v. Wilson*, 477 U.S. 436 (1986);

(b) new claims, not previously raised, which constitute an *abuse of the writ, McCleskey v. Zant,* 499 U.S. 467 (1991); or (c) *procedurally defaulted claims* in which the petitioner failed to follow applicable state procedural rules in raising the claims, *Murray v. Carrier,* 477 U.S. 478 (1986). These cases are premised on our concerns for the finality of state judgments of conviction and the "significant costs of federal habeas review."

We have previously held that even if a state prisoner cannot meet the cause and prejudice standard, a federal court may hear the merits of the successive claims if the failure to hear the claims would constitute a "miscarriage of justice." In a trio of 1986 decisions, we elaborated on the miscarriage of justice, or "actual innocence," exception. As we explained in *Kuhlmann v. Wilson,* the exception developed from the language of the federal habeas statute, which, prior to 1966, allowed successive claims to be denied without a hearing if the judge were "satisfied that the ends of justice will not be served by such inquiry." We held that despite the removal of this statutory language from 28 U.S.C. §2244(b) in 1966, the miscarriage of justice exception would allow successive claims to be heard if the petitioner "establish[es] that under the probative evidence he has a colorable claim of factual innocence." *Kuhlmann, supra,* at 454.[5] In the second of these cases we held that the actual innocence exception also applies to procedurally defaulted claims.

In *Smith v. Murray,* 477 U.S. 527 (1986), we found no miscarriage of justice in the failure to examine the merits of procedurally defaulted claims in the capital sentencing context. We emphasized that the miscarriage of justice exception is concerned with actual as compared to legal innocence, and acknowledged that actual innocence "does not translate easily into the context of an alleged error at the sentencing phase of a trial on a capital offense." We decided that the habeas petitioner in that case had failed to show actual innocence of the death penalty because the "alleged constitutional error neither precluded the development of true facts nor resulted in the admission of false ones."

In subsequent cases, we have emphasized the narrow scope of the fundamental miscarriage of justice exception. In *Dugger v. Adams,* 489 U.S. 401 (1989), we rejected the petitioner's claim that his procedural default should be excused because he had shown that he was actually innocent. Without endeavoring to define what it meant to be actually innocent of the death penalty, we stated that "[d]emonstrating that an error is by its nature the kind of error that might have affected the accuracy of a death sentence is far from demonstrating that an individual defendant probably is 'actually innocent' of the sentence he or she received." Just last Term in *McCleskey v. Zant,* we held that the "narrow exception" for miscarriage of justice was of no avail to the petitioner because the constitutional violation, if it occurred, "resulted in the admission at trial of truthful inculpatory evidence which did not affect the reliability of the guilt determination."

. . . .

---

5. Our standard for determining actual innocence was articulated in *Kuhlmann* as: "[T]he prisoner must 'show a fair probability that, in light of all the evidence, including that alleged to have been illegally admitted (but with due regard to any unreliability of it) and evidence tenably claimed to have been wrongly excluded or to have become available only after the trial, the trier of the facts would have entertained a reasonable doubt of his guilt.'" 477 U.S., at 455, n. 17 quoting Friendly, Is Innocence Irrelevant? Collateral Attack on Criminal Judgments, 38 U.Chi.L.Rev. 142, 160 (1970).

... [After discussing standards to apply in determining whether an individual is innocent of the death penalty and reviewing petitioner's claims,] [w]e hold that petitioner has failed to show by clear and convincing evidence that but for constitutional error at his sentencing hearing, no reasonable juror would have found him eligible for the death penalty under Louisiana law. The judgment of the Court of Appeals is therefore affirmed.

Justice BLACKMUN, concurring in the judgment.

I cannot agree with the majority that a federal court is absolutely barred from reviewing a capital defendant's abusive, successive, or procedurally defaulted claim unless the defendant can show "by clear and convincing evidence that but for a constitutional error, no reasonable juror would have found the petitioner eligible for the death penalty under the applicable state law." For the reasons stated by Justice Stevens in his separate opinion, which I join, I believe that the Court today adopts an unduly cramped view of "actual innocence." I write separately not to discuss the specifics of the Court's standard, but instead to reemphasize my opposition to an implicit premise underlying the Court's decision: that the only "fundamental miscarriage of justice" in a capital proceeding that warrants redress is one where the petitioner can make out a claim of "actual innocence." I also write separately to express my ever-growing skepticism that, with each new decision from this Court constricting the ability of the federal courts to remedy constitutional errors, the death penalty really can be imposed fairly and in accordance with the requirements of the Eighth Amendment....

When I was on the United States Court of Appeals for the Eighth Circuit, I once observed, in the course of reviewing a death sentence on a writ of habeas corpus, that the decisional process in a capital case is "particularly excruciating" for someone "who is not personally convinced of the rightness of capital punishment and who questions it as an effective deterrent." *Maxwell v. Bishop*, 398 F.2d 138, 153–154 (1968), *vacated*, 398 U.S. 262 (1970). At the same time, however, I stated my then belief that "the advisability of capital punishment is a policy matter ordinarily to be resolved by the legislature." Four years later, as a member of this Court, I echoed those sentiments in my separate dissenting opinion in *Furman*. Although I reiterated my personal distaste for the death penalty and my doubt that it performs any meaningful deterrent function, I declined to join my Brethren in declaring the state statutes at issue in those cases unconstitutional.

My ability in *Maxwell v. Bishop*, 398 F.2d 138 (1968), *Furman v. Georgia*, 408 U.S. 238, 405 (1972), and the many other capital cases I have reviewed during my tenure on the federal bench to enforce, notwithstanding my own deep moral reservations, a legislature's considered judgment that capital punishment is an appropriate sanction, has always rested on an understanding that certain procedural safeguards, chief among them the federal judiciary's power to reach and correct claims of constitutional error on federal habeas review, would ensure that death sentences are fairly imposed. Today, more than 20 years later, I wonder what is left of that premise underlying my acceptance of the death penalty.

Only last Term I had occasion to lament the Court's continuing "crusade to erect petty procedural barriers in the path of any state prisoner seeking review of his federal constitutional claims" and its transformation of "the duty to protect federal rights into a self-fashioned abdication." [*Coleman v. Thompson, supra* chapter 14]. This Term has witnessed the continued narrowing of the avenues of relief available to federal habeas petitioners seeking redress of their constitutional claims. It has witnessed, as well, the execution of two victims of the "new habeas," Warren McCleskey and Roger Keith Coleman.

Warren McCleskey's case seemed the archetypal "fundamental miscarriage of justice" that the federal courts are charged with remedying.... McCleskey demonstrated that state officials deliberately had elicited inculpatory admissions from him in violation of his Sixth Amendment rights and had withheld information he needed to present his claim for relief. In addition, McCleskey argued convincingly in his final hours that he could not even obtain an impartial clemency hearing because of threats by state officials against the pardons and parole board. That the Court permitted McCleskey to be executed without ever hearing the merits of his claims starkly reveals the Court's skewed value system, in which finality of judgments, conservation of state resources, and expediency of executions seem to receive greater solicitude than justice and human life.

The execution of Roger Keith Coleman is no less an affront to principles of fundamental fairness. Last Term, the Court refused to review the merits of Coleman's claims by effectively overruling, at Coleman's expense, precedents holding that state court decisions are presumed to be based on the merits (and therefore, are subject to federal habeas review) unless they explicitly reveal that they were based on state procedural grounds. Moreover, the Court's refusal last month to grant a temporary stay of execution so that the lower courts could conduct a hearing into Coleman's well-supported claim that he was innocent of the underlying offense demonstrates the resounding hollowness of the Court's professed commitment to employ the "fundamental miscarriage of justice exception" as a "safeguard against compelling an innocent man to suffer an unconstitutional loss of liberty."

As I review the state of this Court's capital jurisprudence, I thus am left to wonder how the ever-shrinking authority of the federal courts to reach and redress constitutional errors affects the legitimacy of the death penalty itself. Since *Gregg v. Georgia*, the Court has upheld the constitutionality of the death penalty where sufficient procedural safeguards exist to ensure that the State's administration of the penalty is neither arbitrary nor capricious. At the time those decisions issued, federal courts possessed much broader authority than they do today to address claims of constitutional error on habeas review and, therefore, to examine the adequacy of a State's capital scheme and the fairness and reliability of its decision to impose the death penalty in a particular case. The more the Court constrains the federal courts' power to reach the constitutional claims of those sentenced to death, the more the Court undermines the very legitimacy of capital punishment itself.

Notes and Questions

1. In *Sawyer v. Whitley*, 505 U.S. 333 (1992), the Court articulated the standard it intended to apply in determining whether a capital defendant was innocent of death:

> The present case requires us to further amplify the meaning of "actual innocence" in the setting of capital punishment. A prototypical example of "actual innocence" in a colloquial sense is the case where the State has convicted the wrong person of the crime. Such claims are of course regularly made on motions for new trial after conviction in both state and federal courts, and quite regularly denied because the evidence adduced in support of them fails to meet the rigorous standards for granting such motions. But in rare instances it may turn out later, for example, that another person has credibly confessed to the

crime, and it is evident that the law has made a mistake. In the context of a noncapital case, the concept of "actual innocence" is easy to grasp.

It is more difficult to develop an analogous framework when dealing with a defendant who has been sentenced to death. The phrase "innocent of death" is not a natural usage of those words, but we must strive to construct an analog to the simpler situation represented by the case of a noncapital defendant. In defining this analog, we bear in mind that the exception for "actual innocence" is a very narrow exception, and that to make it workable it must be subject to determination by relatively objective standards. In the every day context of capital penalty proceedings, a federal district judge typically will be presented with a successive or abusive habeas petition a few days before, or even on the day of, a scheduled execution, and will have only a limited time to determine whether a petitioner has shown that his case falls within the "actual innocence" exception if such a claim is made.

Since our decision in *Furman v. Georgia,* 408 U.S. 238 (1972), our Eighth Amendment jurisprudence has required those States imposing capital punishment to adopt procedural safeguards protecting against arbitrary and capricious impositions of the death sentence. In response, the States have adopted various narrowing factors which limit the class of offenders upon which the sentencer is authorized to impose the death penalty. For example, the Louisiana statute under which petitioner was convicted defines first-degree murder, a capital offense, as something more than intentional killing. In addition, after a defendant is found guilty in Louisiana of capital murder, the jury must also find at the sentencing phase beyond a reasonable doubt at least one of a list of statutory aggravating factors before it may recommend that the death penalty be imposed.

But once eligibility for the death penalty has been established to the satisfaction of the jury, its deliberations assume a different tenor. In a series of cases beginning with *Lockett v. Ohio,* 438 U.S. 586, 604 (1978), we have held that the defendant must be permitted to introduce a wide variety of mitigating evidence pertaining to his character and background. The emphasis shifts from narrowing the class of eligible defendants by objective factors to individualized consideration of a particular defendant. Consideration of aggravating factors together with mitigating factors, in various combinations and methods dependent upon state law, results in the jury's or judge's ultimate decision as to what penalty shall be imposed.

Considering Louisiana law as an example, then, there are three possible ways in which "actual innocence" might be defined. The strictest definition would be to limit any showing to the elements of the crime which the State has made a capital offense. The showing would have to negate an essential element of that offense. The Solicitor General, filing as *amicus curiae* in support of respondent, urges the Court to adopt this standard. We reject this submission as too narrow, because it is contrary to the statement in *Smith v. Murray,* 477 U.S. 527, 537 (1986), that the concept of "actual innocence" could be applied to mean "innocent" of the death penalty. This statement suggested a more expansive meaning to the term of "actual innocence" in a capital case than simply innocence of the capital offense itself.

The most lenient of the three possibilities would be to allow the showing of "actual innocence" to extend not only to the elements of the crime, but also to the existence of aggravating factors, and to mitigating evidence which bore, not on the defendant's eligibility to receive the death penalty, but only on the ultimate discretionary decision between the death penalty and life imprisonment. This, in effect is what petitioner urges upon us. He contends that actual innocence of the death penalty exists where "there is a 'fair probability' that the admission of false evidence, or the preclusion of true mitigating evidence [caused by a constitutional error], resulted in a sentence of death." Although petitioner describes his standard as narrower than that adopted by the Eighth and Ninth Circuit Courts of Appeals, in reality it is only more closely related to the facts of his case in which he alleges that constitutional error kept true mitigating evidence from the jury. The crucial consideration according to petitioner, is whether due to constitutional error the sentencer was presented with "'a factually inaccurate sentencing profile'" of the petitioner.

Insofar as petitioner's standard would include not merely the elements of the crime itself, but the existence of aggravating circumstances, it broadens the extent of the inquiry but not the type of inquiry. Both the elements of the crime and statutory aggravating circumstances in Louisiana are used to narrow the class of defendants eligible for the death penalty. And proof or disproof of aggravating circumstances, like proof of the elements of the crime, is confined by the statutory definitions to a relatively obvious class of relevant evidence. Sensible meaning is given to the term "innocent of the death penalty" by allowing a showing in addition to innocence of the capital crime itself a showing that there was no aggravating circumstance or that some other condition of eligibility had not been met.

But we reject petitioner's submission that the showing should extend beyond these elements of the capital sentence to the existence of additional mitigating evidence. In the first place, such an extension would mean that "actual innocence" amounts to little more than what is already required to show "prejudice," a necessary showing for habeas relief for many constitutional errors. If federal habeas review of capital sentences is to be at all rational, petitioner must show something more in order for a court to reach the merits of his claims on a successive habeas petition than he would have had to show to obtain relief on his first habeas petition.

But, more importantly, petitioner's standard would so broaden the inquiry as to make it anything but a "narrow" exception to the principle of finality which we have previously described it to be. A federal district judge confronted with a claim of actual innocence may with relative ease determine whether a submission, for example, that a killing was not intentional, consists of credible, noncumulative and admissible evidence negating the element of intent. But it is a far more difficult task to assess how jurors would have reacted to additional showings of mitigating factors, particularly considering the breadth of those factors that a jury under our decisions must be allowed to consider.

The Court of Appeals in this case took the middle ground among these three possibilities for defining "actual innocence" of the death penalty, and adopted this test:

> [W]e must require the petitioner to show, based on the evidence proffered plus all record evidence, a fair probability that a rational trier of fact would have entertained a reasonable doubt as to the existence of

those facts which are prerequisites under state or federal law for the imposition of the death penalty.

The Court of Appeals standard therefore hones in on the objective factors or conditions which must be shown to exist before a defendant is eligible to have the death penalty imposed. The Eleventh Circuit Court of Appeals has adopted a similar "eligibility" test for determining actual innocence. We agree with the Courts of Appeals for the Fifth and Eleventh Circuits that the "actual innocence" requirement must focus on those elements which render a defendant eligible for the death penalty, and not on additional mitigating evidence which was prevented from being introduced as a result of a claimed constitutional error.

2. Demonstrating "actual innocence" under *Sawyer* requires a showing by clear and convincing evidence that, but for a constitutional error, no reasonable juror would have found the petitioner eligible for the death penalty under the governing law. In addition, the *Sawyer* Court adopted an approach which focuses solely on the aggravating circumstances that rendered the defendant death-eligible. Consequently, the existence of additional mitigating evidence becomes irrelevant. Does this seem consistent with modern death penalty jurisprudence? Is it fair?

B. Successive Petitions and Abuse of the Writ under the AEDPA

The previous section set out the law on successive petitions and abuse of the writ prior to 1996. In passing the AEDPA in April 1996, Congress effected significant procedural and substantive changes to this area of habeas law. For a discussion of these changes and their ramifications see Liebman and Hertz, *Federal Habeas Corpus Practice and Procedure* §§28.3–28.4 (5th ed. 2005). Also, for a comprehensive overview of successive petitions and abuse of the writ under the AEDPA, see Jeffrey, "Successive Habeas Corpus Petitions and Section 2255 Motions after the Anti-Terrorism and Effective Death Penalty Act of 1996: Emerging Procedural and Substantive Issues," 84 Marq. L. Rev. 43 (2000).

In contrast to the 1966 version of §2244, which essentially codified *Sanders*, §2244(b) of the AEDPA provides:

(b)(1) A claim presented in a second or successive habeas corpus application under section 2254 that was presented in a prior application shall be dismissed.

(2) A claim presented in a second or successive habeas corpus application under section 2254 that was not presented in a prior application shall be dismissed unless—

(A) the applicant shows that the claim relies on a new rule of constitutional law, made retroactive to cases on collateral review by the Supreme Court, that was previously unavailable; or

(B)(i) the factual predicate for the claim could not have been discovered previously through the exercise of due diligence; and (ii) the facts underlying the claim, if proven and viewed in light of the evidence as a whole, would be sufficient to establish by clear and convincing evidence that, but for constitutional error, no reasonable factfinder would have found the applicant guilty of the underlying offense.

(3)(A) Before a second or successive application permitted by this section is filed in the district court, the applicant shall move in the appropriate court of appeals for an order authorizing the district court to consider the application.

(B) A motion in the court of appeals for an order authorizing the district court to consider a second or successive application shall be determined by a three-judge panel of the court of appeals.

(C) The court of appeals may authorize the filing of a second or successive application only if it determines that the application makes a prima facie showing that the application satisfies the requirements of this subsection.

(D) The court of appeals shall grant or deny the authorization to file a second or successive application not later than 30 days after the filing of the motion.

(E) The grant or denial of an authorization by a court of appeals to file a second or successive application shall not be appealable and shall not be the subject of a petition for rehearing or for a writ of certiorari.

(4) A district court shall dismiss any claim presented in a second or successive application that the court of appeals has authorized to be filed unless the applicant shows that the claim satisfies the requirements of this section.

This statute adds a new procedural layer placing courts of appeals in a "gatekeeping" role in which the appellate court must determine as a threshold matter whether a petitioner can even file a successive petition in district court. Substantively, the AEDPA significantly restricts those cases in which a successive petition can be filed.

Stewart v. Martinez-Villareal

523 U.S. 637 (1998)

Chief Justice REHNQUIST delivered the opinion of the Court.

In *Ford v. Wainwright,* 477 U.S. 399, 410 (1986) [*supra* chapter 5], we held that "the Eighth Amendment prohibits a State from inflicting the penalty of death upon a prisoner who is insane." In this case, we must decide whether respondent Martinez-Villareal's *Ford* claim is subject to the restrictions on "second or successive" applications for federal habeas relief found in the newly revised 28 U.S.C. §§2244. We conclude that it is not.

Respondent was convicted on two counts of first-degree murder and sentenced to death. He unsuccessfully challenged his conviction and sentence on direct appeal in the Arizona state courts. He then filed a series of petitions for habeas relief in state court, all of which were denied. He also filed three petitions for habeas relief in federal court, all of which were dismissed on the ground that they contained claims on which the state remedies had not yet been exhausted.

In March 1993, respondent filed a fourth habeas petition in federal court. In addition to raising other claims, respondent asserted that he was incompetent to be executed. Counsel for the State urged the District Court to dismiss respondent's *Ford* claim as premature. The court did so but granted the writ on other grounds. The Court of Appeals for the Ninth Circuit reversed the District Court's granting of the writ but explained that its instruction to enter judgment denying the petition was not intended to affect any later litigation of the *Ford* claim.

On remand to the District Court, respondent, fearing that the newly enacted Antiterrorism and Effective Death Penalty Act (AEDPA) might foreclose review of his *Ford* claim, moved the court to reopen his earlier petition. In March 1997, the District Court denied the motion and reassured respondent that it had "'no intention of treating the [*Ford*] claim as a successive petition.'" Shortly thereafter, the State obtained a warrant for respondent's execution. Proceedings were then held in the Arizona Superior Court on respondent's mental condition. That court concluded that respondent was fit to be executed. The Arizona Supreme Court rejected his appeal of that decision.

Respondent then moved in the Federal District Court to reopen his *Ford* claim. He challenged both the conclusions reached and the procedures employed by the Arizona state courts. Petitioners responded that under AEDPA, the court lacked jurisdiction. The District Court agreed with petitioners, ruling on May 16, 1997, that it did not have jurisdiction over the claim. Respondent then moved in the Court of Appeals for permission to file a successive habeas corpus application. The Court of Appeals stayed respondent's execution so that it could consider his request. It later held that §2244(b) did not apply to a petition that raises only a competency to be executed claim and that respondent did not, therefore, need authorization to file the petition in the District Court. It accordingly transferred the petition that had been presented to a member of that court back to the District Court.

We granted certiorari, to resolve an apparent conflict between the Ninth Circuit and the Eleventh Circuit on this important question of federal law. See, *e.g., In re Medina,* 109 F.3d 1556 (C.A.11 1997).

Before reaching the question presented, however, we must first decide whether we have jurisdiction over this case. In AEDPA, Congress established a "gatekeeping" mechanism for the consideration of "second or successive habeas corpus applications" in the federal courts. An individual seeking to file a "second or successive" application must move in the appropriate court of appeals for an order directing the district court to consider his application. §2244(b)(3)(A). The court of appeals then has 30 days to decide whether to grant the authorization to file. A court of appeals' decision whether to grant authorization "to file a second or successive application shall not be appealable and shall not be the subject of a petition for rehearing or for a writ of certiorari."

If the Court of Appeals in this case had granted respondent leave to file a second or successive application, then we would be without jurisdiction to consider petitioners' petition and would have to dismiss the writ. This is not, however, what the Court of Appeals did. The Court of Appeals held that the §2244(b) restrictions simply do not apply to respondent's *Ford* claim, and that there was accordingly no need for him to apply for authorization to file a second or successive petition. We conclude today that the Court of Appeals reached the correct result in this case, and that we therefore have jurisdiction to consider petitioners' petition.

Section 2244(b) provides:

"(b)(1) A claim presented in a second or successive habeas corpus application under section 2254 that was presented in a prior application shall be dismissed.

"(2) A claim presented in a second or successive habeas corpus application under section 2254 that was not presented in a prior application shall be dismissed unless—

"(A) the applicant shows that the claim relies on a new rule of constitutional law, made retroactive to cases on collateral review by the Supreme Court, that was previously unavailable; or

"(B)(i) the factual predicate for the claim could not have been discovered previously through the exercise of due diligence; and

"(ii) the facts underlying the claim, if proven and viewed in light of the evidence as a whole, would be sufficient to establish by clear and convincing evidence that, but for constitutional error, no reasonable factfinder would have found the applicant guilty of the underlying offense."

If respondent's current request for relief is a "second or successive" application, then it plainly should have been dismissed. The *Ford* claim had previously been presented in the 1993 petition, and would therefore be subject to dismissal under subsection (b)(1). Even if we were to consider the *Ford* claim to be newly presented in the 1997 petition, it does not fit within either of subsection (b)(2)'s exceptions, and dismissal would still be required.

Petitioners contend that because respondent has already had one "fully-litigated" habeas petition, the plain meaning of §2244(b) as amended requires his new petition to be treated as successive." Under that reading of the statute, respondent is entitled to only one merits judgment on his federal habeas claims. Because respondent has already presented a petition to the District Court, and the District Court and the Court of Appeals have acted on that petition, §2244(b) must apply to any subsequent request for federal habeas relief.

But the only claim on which respondent now seeks relief is the *Ford* claim that he presented to the District Court, along with a series of other claims, in 1993. The District Court, acting for the first time on the merits of any of respondent's claims for federal habeas relief, dismissed the *Ford* claim as premature, but resolved all of respondent's other claims, granting relief on one. The Court of Appeals subsequently reversed the District Court's grant of relief. At that point it became clear that respondent would have no federal habeas relief for his conviction or his death sentence, and the Arizona Supreme Court issued a warrant for his execution. His claim then unquestionably ripe, respondent moved in the state courts for a determination of his competency to be executed. Those courts concluded that he was competent, and respondent moved in the Federal District Court for review of the state court's determination.

This may have been the second time that respondent had asked the federal courts to provide relief on his *Ford* claim, but this does not mean that there were two separate applications, the second of which was necessarily subject to §2244(b). There was only one application for habeas relief, and the District Court ruled (or should have ruled) on each claim at the time it became ripe. Respondent was entitled to an adjudication of all of the claims presented in his earlier, undoubtedly reviewable, application for federal habeas relief. The Court of Appeals was therefore correct in holding that respondent was not required to get authorization to file a "second or successive" application before his *Ford* claim could be heard.

If petitioners' interpretation of "second or successive" were correct, the implications for habeas practice would be far reaching and seemingly perverse. In *Picard v. Connor,* 404 U.S. 270, 275 (1971), we said:

"It has been settled since *Ex parte Royall,* 117 U.S. 241 (1886), that a state prisoner must normally exhaust available state judicial remedies before a federal court will entertain his petition for *habeas corpus*.... The exhaustion-of-state-remedies doctrine, now codified in the federal habeas statute, 28 U.S.C. §§2254(b) and (c), reflects a policy of federal state comity.... It follows, of course, that once the federal claim has been fairly presented to the state courts, the exhaustion requirement is satisfied."

Later, in *Rose v. Lundy*, 455 U.S. 509, 522 (1982), we went further and held that "a district court must dismiss habeas petitions containing both unexhausted and exhausted claims." But none of our cases expounding this doctrine have ever suggested that a prisoner whose habeas petition was dismissed for failure to exhaust state remedies, and who then did exhaust those remedies and returned to federal court, was by such action filing a successive petition. A court where such a petition was filed could adjudicate these claims under the same standard as would govern those made in any other first petition.

We believe that respondent's *Ford* claim here—previously dismissed as premature—should be treated in the same manner as the claim of a petitioner who returns to a federal habeas court after exhausting state remedies. True, the cases are not identical; respondent's *Ford* claim was dismissed as premature, not because he had not exhausted state remedies, but because his execution was not imminent and therefore his competency to be executed could not be determined at that time. But in both situations, the habeas petitioner does not receive an adjudication of his claim. To hold otherwise would mean that a dismissal of a first habeas petition for technical procedural reasons would bar the prisoner from ever obtaining federal habeas review.

Petitioners place great reliance on our decision in *Felker v. Turpin*, 518 U.S. 651 (1996), but we think that reliance is misplaced. In *Felker* we stated that the "new restrictions on successive petitions constitute a modified res judicata rule, a restraint on what used to be called in habeas corpus practice 'abuse of the writ.' " It is certain that respondent's *Ford* claim would not be barred under any form of res judicata. Respondent brought his claim in a timely fashion, and it has not been ripe for resolution until now.

Thus, respondent's *Ford* claim was not a "second or successive" petition under §2244(b) and we have jurisdiction to review the judgment of the Court of Appeals on petitioners' petition for certiorari. But for the same reasons that we find we have jurisdiction, we hold that the Court of Appeals was correct in deciding that respondent was entitled to a hearing on the merits of his *Ford* claim in the District Court. The judgment of the Court of Appeals is therefore affirmed.

Slack v. McDaniel

529 U.S. 473 (2000)

KENNEDY, J., delivered the opinion of the Court, Part I of which was unanimous, Part II of which was joined by Chief Justice Rehnquist, and Justices O'Connor, Scalia, Thomas, and Ginsburg, and Parts III and IV of which were joined by Chief Justice Rehnquist and Justices Stevens, O'Connor, Souter, Ginsburg, and Breyer. Justice SCALIA filed an opinion concurring in part and dissenting in part, in which Justice Thomas joined.

Justice KENNEDY delivered the opinion of the Court.

We are called upon to resolve a series of issues regarding the law of habeas corpus, including questions of the proper application of the Antiterrorism and Effective Death Penalty Act of 1996 (AEDPA). We hold as follows:

... [A] habeas petition which is filed after an initial petition was dismissed without adjudication on the merits for failure to exhaust state remedies is not a "second or successive" petition as that term is understood in the habeas corpus context. Federal courts do, however, retain broad powers to prevent duplicative or unnecessary litigation.

I

Petitioner Antonio Slack was convicted of second-degree murder in Nevada state court in 1990. His direct appeal was unsuccessful. On November 27, 1991, Slack filed a petition for writ of habeas corpus in federal court under 28 U.S.C. §2254. Early in the federal proceeding, Slack decided to litigate claims he had not yet presented to the Nevada courts. He could not raise the claims in federal court because, under the exhaustion of remedies rule explained in *Rose v. Lundy*, 455 U.S. 509 (1982), a federal court was required to dismiss a petition presenting claims not yet litigated in state court. Accordingly, Slack filed a motion seeking to hold his federal petition in abeyance while he returned to state court to exhaust the new claims. Without objection by the State, the District Court ordered the habeas petition dismissed "without prejudice." The order, dated February 19, 1992, further stated, "Petitioner is granted leave to file an application to renew upon exhaustion of all State remedies."

After an unsuccessful round of state postconviction proceedings, Slack filed a new federal habeas petition on May 30, 1995. The District Court later appointed counsel, directing him to file an amended petition or a notice of intention to proceed with the current petition. On December 24, 1997, counsel filed an amended petition presenting 14 claims for relief. The State moved to dismiss the petition. As its first ground, the State argued that Slack's petition must be dismissed because it was a mixed petition, that is to say a petition raising some claims which had been presented to the state courts and some which had not. As its second ground, the State cited *Farmer v. McDaniel*, 98 F.3d 1548 (C.A.9 1996), and contended that, under the established rule in the Ninth Circuit, claims Slack had not raised in his 1991 federal habeas petition must be dismissed as an abuse of the writ.

The District Court granted the State's motion. First, the court relied on *Farmer* to hold that Slack's 1995 petition was "[a] second or successive petition," even though his 1991 petition had been dismissed without prejudice for a failure to exhaust state remedies. The court then invoked the abuse of the writ doctrine to dismiss with prejudice the claims Slack had not raised in the 1991 petition. This left Slack with four claims, each having been raised in the 1991 petition; but one of these, the court concluded, had not yet been presented to the state courts. The court therefore dismissed Slack's remaining claims because they were in a mixed petition. Here, Slack seeks to challenge the dismissal of claims as abusive; he does not contend that all claims presented in the amended petition were exhausted.

The District Court's dismissal order was filed March 30, 1998. On April 29, 1998, Slack filed in the District Court a pleading captioned "Notice of Appeal." Consistent with Circuit practice, the court treated the notice as an application for a certificate of probable cause (CPC) under the pre-AEDPA version of 28 U.S.C. §2253; and it denied a CPC, concluding the appeal would raise no substantial issue. The Court of Appeals likewise denied a CPC. As a result, Slack was not permitted to take an appeal of the order dismissing his petition. We granted certiorari. Slack contends that he is entitled to an appeal of the dismissal of his petition, arguing that the District Court was wrong to hold that his 1995 petition was "second or successive." We agree that Slack's 1995 petition was not second or successive....

III

... The District Court dismissed claims Slack failed to raise in his 1991 petition based on its conclusion that Slack's 1995 petition was a second or successive habeas petition. This conclusion was wrong. A habeas petition filed in the district court after an initial habeas petition was unadjudicated on its merits and dismissed for failure to exhaust state remedies is not a second or successive petition.

Slack commenced this habeas proceeding in the District Court in 1995, before AEDPA's effective date. Because the question whether Slack's petition was second or successive implicates his right to relief in the trial court, pre-AEDPA law governs, see *Lindh v. Murphy*, 521 U.S. 320 (1997), though we do not suggest the definition of second or successive would be different under AEDPA. See *Stewart v. Martinez-Villareal*, 523 U.S. 637 (1998) (using pre-AEDPA law to interpret AEDPA's provision governing "second or successive habeas applications"). The parties point us to Rule 9(b) of the Rules Governing Section 2254 Cases in the United States District Courts as controlling the issue. The Rule incorporates our prior decisions regarding successive petitions and abuse of the writ, *McCleskey v. Zant*, 499 U.S. 467, 487 (1991), and states: "A second or successive petition [alleging new and different grounds] may be dismissed if ... the judge finds that the failure of the petitioner to assert those grounds in a prior petition constituted an abuse of the writ." As the text demonstrates, Rule 9(b) applies only to "a second or successive petition."

The phrase "second or successive petition" is a term of art given substance in our prior habeas corpus cases. The Court's decision in *Rose v. Lundy*, instructs us in reaching our understanding of the term. *Rose v. Lundy* held that a federal district court must dismiss habeas corpus petitions containing both exhausted and unexhausted claims. The opinion, however, contemplated that the prisoner could return to federal court after the requisite exhaustion. ("Those prisoners who ... submit mixed petitions nevertheless are entitled to resubmit a petition with only exhausted claims or to exhaust the remainder of their claims"). It was only if a prisoner declined to return to state court and decided to proceed with his exhausted claims in federal court that the possibility arose that a subsequent petition would be considered second or successive and subject to dismissal as an abuse of the writ. ("[A] prisoner who decides to proceed only with his exhausted claims and deliberately sets aside his unexhausted claims risks dismissal of subsequent federal petitions").

This understanding of the second or successive rule was confirmed two Terms ago when we wrote as follows: "[None] of our cases ... have ever suggested that a prisoner whose habeas petition was dismissed for failure to exhaust state remedies, and who then did exhaust those remedies and returned to federal court, was by such action filing a successive petition. A court where such a petition was filed could adjudicate these claims under the same standard as would govern those made in any other first petition." *Stewart v. Martinez-Villareal*. We adhere to this analysis. A petition filed after a mixed petition has been dismissed under *Rose v. Lundy* before the district court adjudicated any claims is to be treated as "any other first petition" and is not a second or successive petition.

The State contends that the prisoner, upon his return to federal court, should be restricted to the claims made in his initial petition. Neither *Rose v. Lundy* nor *Martinez-Villareal* require this result, which would limit a prisoner to claims made in a pleading that is often uncounseled, hand-written, and pending in federal court only until the state identifies one unexhausted claim. The proposed rule would bar the prisoner from raising nonfrivolous claims developed in the subsequent state exhaustion proceedings contemplated by the *Rose* dismissal, even though a federal court had yet to review a single constitutional claim. This result would be contrary to our admonition that the complete exhaustion rule is not to "trap the unwary pro se prisoner." It is instead more appropriate to treat the initial mixed petition as though it had not been filed, subject to whatever conditions the court attaches to the dismissal. *Rose v. Lundy* dictated that, whatever particular claims the petition contained, none could be considered by the federal court.

Slack's 1991 petition was dismissed under the procedure established in *Rose v. Lundy*. No claim made in Slack's 1991 petition was adjudicated during the three months it was pending in federal court. As such, the 1995 petition should not have been dismissed on the grounds that it was second or successive. Reasoning to the contrary found in the Court of Appeals' *Farmer* decision, rendered before *Martinez-Villareal*, is incorrect. Our view that established practice demonstrates that Slack's 1995 petition is not second or successive is confirmed as well by opinions of the Courts of Appeals which have addressed the point under similar circumstances.

The State complains that this rule is unfair. The filing of a mixed petition in federal court requires it to appear and to plead failure to exhaust. The petition is then dismissed without prejudice, allowing the prisoner to make a return trip through the state courts to exhaust new claims. The State expresses concern that, upon exhaustion, the prisoner would return to federal court but again file a mixed petition, causing the process to repeat itself. In this manner, the State contends, a vexatious litigant could inject undue delay into the collateral review process. To the extent the tactic would become a problem, however, it can be countered without upsetting the established meaning of a second or successive petition.

First, the State remains free to impose proper procedural bars to restrict repeated returns to state court for postconviction proceedings. Second, provisions of AEDPA may bear upon the question in cases to which the Act applies. AEDPA itself demonstrates that Congress may address matters relating to exhaustion and mixed petitions through means other than rules governing "second or successive" petitions. Third, the Rules of Civil Procedure, applicable as a general matter to habeas cases, vest the federal courts with due flexibility to prevent vexatious litigation. As Slack concedes, in the habeas corpus context it would be appropriate for an order dismissing a mixed petition to instruct an applicant that upon his return to federal court he is to bring only exhausted claims. Once the petitioner is made aware of the exhaustion requirement, no reason exists for him not to exhaust all potential claims before returning to federal court. The failure to comply with an order of the court is grounds for dismissal with prejudice. In this case, however, the initial petition was dismissed without condition and without prejudice. We reject the State's argument that refusing to give a new meaning to the established term "second or successive" opens the door to the abuses described.

IV

Slack has demonstrated that reasonable jurists could conclude that the District Court's abuse of the writ holding was wrong, for we have determined that a habeas petition filed after an initial petition was dismissed under *Rose v. Lundy* without an adjudication on the merits is not a "second or successive" petition. Whether Slack is otherwise entitled to the issuance of a [certificate of appealability] is a question to be resolved first upon remand. The decision of the Court of Appeals is reversed, and the case is remanded for further proceedings consistent with this opinion.

Justice SCALIA, with whom Justice Thomas joins, concurring in part and dissenting in part.

I join the opinion of the Court, except for its discussion in Parts III and IV of whether Slack's postexhaustion petition was second or successive. I believe that the Court produces here, as it produced in a different respect in *Stewart v. Martinez-Villareal*, 523 U.S. 637 (1998), a distortion of the natural meaning of the term "second or successive."

The opinion relies on *Martinez-Villareal*, together with *Rose v. Lundy*, 455 U.S. 509 (1982), to conclude that a prisoner whose federal petition is dismissed to allow exhaustion may return to federal court without having his later petition treated as second or successive, regardless of what claims it contains. Neither the holdings nor even the language of those opinions suggest that proposition. As for holdings: *Martinez-Villareal* did not even involve the issue of exhaustion, and so has no bearing upon the present case. The narrow holding of *Rose v. Lundy* was that a habeas petition containing both exhausted and unexhausted claims must be dismissed, but it can be fairly said to have embraced the proposition that the petitioner could return with the same claims after they all had been exhausted. This latter proposition could be thought to rest upon the theory that a petition dismissed for lack of exhaustion is a petition that never existed, so that any other later petition would not be second or successive. Or it could be thought to rest upon the theory that the later refiling of the original claims, all of them now exhausted, is just a renewal of the first petition, implicitly authorized by the dismissal to permit exhaustion. The former theory is counterfactual; the latter is quite plausible.

The language the Court quotes from *Rose* and *Martinez-Villareal* also does not justify the Court's mixed-petitions-don't-count theory. The quotation from *Rose* says only that "prisoners who ... submit mixed petitions ... are entitled to ... exhaust the remainder of their claims." This does not suggest that they are entitled to add new claims, or to return, once again, without accomplishing the exhaustion that the court dismissed the petition to allow. And the quotation from *Martinez-Villareal* indicates only that when a prisoner whose habeas petition was dismissed for failure to exhaust state remedies "then did exhaust those remedies" and refile in federal court, the court "could adjudicate these claims under the same standard as would govern those made in any other first petition." This does not require treating the later filed petition as a "first" petition regardless of whether it bears any resemblance to the petition initially filed. In fact, *Martinez-Villareal* clearly recognized the potential significance of raising a new claim rather than merely renewing an old one: It held that a petition raising a claim of incompetence to be executed previously dismissed as premature was not second or successive, but expressly distinguished, and left open, the situation where the claim had not been raised in the earlier petition....

Because I believe petitioner's inclusion of new and unexhausted claims in his postexhaustion petition rendered it second or successive, he is not entitled to a certificate of appealability, and I would affirm the decision of the Court of Appeals.

Notes and Questions

1. Section 2244 does not define what constitutes a "successive" petition. The Court has turned to its pre-AEDPA case law to determine whether a state criminal defendant has in fact filed a successive petition. Do you think it appropriate for the Court to apply

pre-AEDPA case law to determine the meaning of a statute clearly intended to change that law? Justice Scalia certainly did not find it appropriate. Dissenting in *Martinez-Villareal*, he wrote:

> It is axiomatic that "the power to award the writ [of habeas corpus] by any of the courts of the United States, must be given by written law." And it is impossible to conceive of language that more clearly precludes respondent's renewed competency-to-be-executed claim than the written law before us here: a "claim *presented* in a second or successive habeas corpus application ... that was *presented* in a prior application shall be dismissed." 28 U.S.C. §2244(b)(1) (emphasis added). The Court today flouts the unmistakable language of the statute to avoid what it calls a "perverse" result. There is nothing "perverse" about the result that the statute commands, except that it contradicts pre-existing judge-made law, which it was precisely the purpose of the statute to change.
>
> Respondent received a full hearing on his competency-to-be-executed claim in state court. The state court appointed experts and held a 4-day evidentiary hearing, after which it found respondent "aware that he is to be punished for the crime of murder and ... aware that the impending punishment for that crime is death...." Respondent appealed this determination to the Supreme Court of Arizona, which accepted jurisdiction and denied relief. He sought certiorari of that denial in this Court, which also denied relief. To say that it is "perverse" to deny respondent a second round of time-consuming lower-federal-court review of his conviction and sentence—because that means forgoing lower-federal-court review of a competency-to-be-executed claim that arises only after he has already sought federal habeas on other issues—is to say that state-court determinations must always be reviewable, not merely by this Court, but by federal district courts. That is indeed the principle that this Court's imaginative habeas-corpus jurisprudence had established, but it is not a principle of natural law. Lest we forget, Congress did not even have to create inferior federal courts, let alone invest them with plenary habeas jurisdiction over state convictions. And for much of our history, as Justice Thomas points out, prisoners convicted by validly constituted courts of general criminal jurisdiction had no recourse to habeas corpus relief *at all*. See *Wright v. West*, 505 U.S. 277, 285–286 (1992) (opinion of Thomas, J.)....
>
> Today's opinion resembles nothing so much as the cases of the 1920's that effectively decided that the Clayton Act, designed to eliminate federal-court injunctions against union strikes and picketing, "restrained the federal courts from nothing that was previously proper." T. Powell, The Supreme Court's Control Over the Issue of Injunctions in Labor Disputes, 13 Acad. Pol. Sci. Proc. 37, 74 (1928). In criticizing those cases as examples of *Gefuhlsjurisprudenz* (and in insisting upon "the necessity of preferring ... the *Gefuhl* of the legislator to the *Gefuhl* of the judge"), Dean Landis recalled Dicey's trenchant observation that "judge-made law occasionally represents the opinion of the day before yesterday." Landis, "A Note on Statutory Interpretation," 43 Harv. L.Rev. 886, 888 (1930), quoting A. Dicey, Law and Opinion in England 369 (1926). As hard as it may be for this Court to swallow, in yesterday's enactment of AEDPA Congress curbed our prodigality with the Great Writ. The words that Landis applied to the Clayton Act fit very nicely the statute that

emerges from the Court's decision in the present case: "The mutilated [AEDPA] bears ample testimony to the 'day before yesterday' that judges insist is today." I dissent.

Do you agree with Justice Scalia's criticism of the Court?

2. The Court in *Slack v. McDaniel*, 529 U.S. 473 (2000), also discussed the manner in which a court of appeal is to issue a certificate of appealability, or COA, after a district court denies a habeas petition. Prior to the AEDPA, appellate review of the dismissal of a habeas petition was governed by 28 U.S.C. §2253, which provided that no appeal could be taken from the final order in a habeas corpus proceeding "unless the justice or judge who rendered the order or a circuit justice or judge issues a certificate of probable cause [or CPC]." Section 2253 did not explain the standards for the issuance of a CPC, but in *Barefoot v. Estelle*, 463 U.S. 880, 893 (1983), the Court found that in order for a court of appeal to issue a certificate of probable cause, a prisoner must make "a substantial showing of the denial of a federal right."

The AEDPA amended §2253, by adding subsection (c), which provides:

(1) Unless a circuit justice or judge issues a certificate of appealability [COA], an appeal may not be taken to the court of appeals from—

   (A) the final order in a habeas corpus proceeding in which the detention complained of arises out of process issued by a State court; or

   (B) the final order in a proceeding under section 2255.

(2) A certificate of appealability may issue under paragraph (1) only if the applicant has made a substantial showing of the denial of a constitutional right.

(3) The certificate of appealability under paragraph (1) shall indicate which specific issue or issues satisfy the showing required by paragraph (2).

In *Slack*, the Court, after finding that the AEDPA version of §2253 was applicable to the petitioner, held that "when the district court denies a habeas petition on procedural grounds without reaching the prisoner's underlying constitutional claim, a COA should issue (and an appeal of the district court's order may be taken) if the prisoner shows, at least, that jurists of reason would find it debatable whether the petition states a valid claim of the denial of a constitutional right, and that jurists of reason would find it debatable whether the district court was correct in its procedural ruling." In reaching this conclusion, the Court expounded on the meaning and effect of §2253 as amended under the AEDPA. The Court stated:

> Under AEDPA, a COA may not issue unless "the applicant has made a substantial showing of the denial of a constitutional right." Except for substituting the word "constitutional" for the word "federal," §2253 is a codification of the CPC standard announced in *Barefoot v. Estelle*, 463 U.S., at 894. Congress had before it the meaning *Barefoot* had given to the words it selected; and we give the language found in §2253(c) the meaning ascribed it in *Barefoot*, with due note for the substitution of the word "constitutional." To obtain a COA under §2253(c), a habeas prisoner must make a substantial showing of the denial of a constitutional right, a demonstration that, under *Barefoot*, includes showing that reasonable jurists could debate whether (or, for that matter, agree that) the petition should have been resolved in a different manner or that the issues presented were "adequate to deserve encouragement to proceed further."

Where a district court has rejected the constitutional claims on the merits, the showing required to satisfy §2253(c) is straightforward: The petitioner must demonstrate that reasonable jurists would find the district court's assessment of the constitutional claims debatable or wrong. The issue becomes somewhat more complicated where, as here, the district court dismisses the petition based on procedural grounds. We hold as follows: When the district court denies a habeas petition on procedural grounds without reaching the prisoner's underlying constitutional claim, a COA should issue when the prisoner shows, at least, that jurists of reason would find it debatable whether the petition states a valid claim of the denial of a constitutional right and that jurists of reason would find it debatable whether the district court was correct in its procedural ruling. This construction gives meaning to Congress' requirement that a prisoner demonstrate substantial underlying constitutional claims and is in conformity with the meaning of the "substantial showing" standard provided in *Barefoot*, and adopted by Congress in AEDPA. Where a plain procedural bar is present and the district court is correct to invoke it to dispose of the case, a reasonable jurist could not conclude either that the district court erred in dismissing the petition or that the petitioner should be allowed to proceed further. In such a circumstance, no appeal would be warranted.

Determining whether a COA should issue where the petition was dismissed on procedural grounds has two components, one directed at the underlying constitutional claims and one directed at the district court's procedural holding. Section 2253 mandates that both showings be made before the court of appeals may entertain the appeal. Each component of the §2253(c) showing is part of a threshold inquiry, and a court may find that it can dispose of the application in a fair and prompt manner if it proceeds first to resolve the issue whose answer is more apparent from the record and arguments.

3. Although Slack's appeal of his denial of habeas relief was governed by the AEDPA, his habeas petition, which was filed in 1995, was controlled by pre-AEDPA law. Nonetheless, the Court stated, "We do not suggest that the definition of second or successive would be different under AEDPA." 529 U.S. at 486.

4. Note that 28 U.S.C. §2244(b)(3)(E) provides: "The grant or denial of an authorization by a court of appeals to file a second or successive application shall not be appealable and shall not be the subject of a petition for rehearing or for a writ of certiorari." In *Felker v. Turpin*, 518 U.S. 651 (1996) (*supra* chapter 13), the Court addressed the effect of curtailing Supreme Court review of decisions by the lower courts to deny an individual a second or successive application. Although the AEDPA apparently precludes Supreme Court appellate review of denials of second and successive petitions, the Court held "that the Act does not preclude this Court from entertaining an application for habeas corpus relief, although it does affect the standards governing the granting of such relief. We also conclude that the availability of such relief in this Court obviates any claim by petitioner under the Exceptions Clause of Article III, §2, of the Constitution, and that the operative provisions of the Act do not violate the Suspension Clause of the Constitution, Art. I, §9." 518 U.S at 654. In particular, the Court found "that although the Act does impose new conditions on our authority to grant relief, it does not deprive this Court of jurisdiction to entertain original habeas petitions." 518 U.S. at 658. It is well-recognized that the modern Supreme Court rarely hears original habeas petitions. Liebman and Hertz, *Federal Habeas Corpus Practice and Procedure* §40.3 (5th ed. 2005). However, in *Castro v. United States*, 540 US 375 (2003), where the

petitioner was challenging the circuit court's characterization of his habeas petition, the Court refused to apply § 2244(b)(3)(E) to preclude the Court from reviewing whether the petitioner's petition was, in fact, his first or second habeas petition.

5. In *Tyler v. Cain*, 533 U.S. 656 (2001), the Court considered 28 U.S.C. § 2244(b)(2)(A), which provides that a applicant may obtain a second or successive habeas review of a claim if "the applicant shows that the claim relies on a new rule of constitutional law, made retroactive to cases on collateral review by the Supreme Court, that was previously unavailable," and whether the applicant could obtain a second habeas hearing based on the Court's decision in *Cage v. Louisiana*, 498 U.S. 39 (1990) (per curiam). The Court concluded:

II

AEDPA greatly restricts the power of federal courts to award relief to state prisoners who file second or successive habeas corpus applications. If the prisoner asserts a claim that he has already presented in a previous federal habeas petition, the claim must be dismissed in all cases. § 2244(b)(1). And if the prisoner asserts a claim that was *not* presented in a previous petition, the claim must be dismissed unless it falls within one of two narrow exceptions. One of these exceptions is for claims predicated on newly discovered facts that call into question the accuracy of a guilty verdict. § 2244(b)(2)(B). The other is for certain claims relying on new rules of constitutional law. § 2244(b)(2)(A).

It is the latter exception that concerns us today. Specifically, § 2244(b)(2)(A) covers claims that "rel[y] on a new rule of constitutional law, made retroactive to cases on collateral review by the Supreme Court, that was previously unavailable." This provision establishes three prerequisites to obtaining relief in a second or successive petition: First, the rule on which the claim relies must be a "new rule" of constitutional law; second, the rule must have been "made retroactive to cases on collateral review by the Supreme Court"; and third, the claim must have been "previously unavailable." In this case, the parties ask us to interpret only the second requirement; respondent does not dispute that *Cage* created a "new rule" that was "previously unavailable." Based on the plain meaning of the text read as a whole, we conclude that "made" means "held" and, thus, the requirement is satisfied only if this Court has held that the new rule is retroactively applicable to cases on collateral review.

A

... Quite significantly, under this provision [28 U.S.C. § 2244(b)(2)(A)], the Supreme Court is the only entity that can "ma[k]e" a new rule retroactive. The new rule becomes retroactive, not by the decisions of the lower court or by the combined action of the Supreme Court and the lower courts, but simply by the action of the Supreme Court.

The only way the Supreme Court can, by itself, "lay out and construct" a rule's retroactive effect, or "cause" that effect "to exist, occur, or appear," is through a holding. The Supreme Court does not "ma[k]e" a rule retroactive when it merely establishes principles of retroactivity and leaves the application of those principles to lower courts. In such an event, any legal conclusion that is derived from the principles is developed by the lower court (or perhaps by a combination of courts), not by the Supreme Court. We thus conclude that a new rule is not "made retroactive to cases on collateral review" unless the Supreme Court holds it to be retroactive.

533 U.S. 661–663. For further discussion of the retroactivity doctrine see chapter 15.

6. For further discussion of successive petitions see Entzeroth, "Struggling for Federal Judicial Review of Successive Claims of Innocence: A Study of How Federal Courts Wrestled with the AEDPA to Provide Individuals Convicted of Non-Existent Crimes with Habeas Review," 60 Miami L. Rev. 75 (2005); Stevenson, "The Politics of Fear and Death: Successive Problems in Capital Habeas Corpus Cases," 77 N.Y.U. L. Rev. 699 (2002); Jeffrey, "Successive Habeas Corpus Petitions and Section 2255 Motions After Antiterrorism and Effective Death Penalty Act of 1996: Emerging Procedural and Substantive Issues," 84 Marq. L. Rev. 43 (2000).

C. Clemency

After exhausting her state and federal avenues of relief, a capital defendant has one last place she can turn for relief: executive clemency from either the governor or (for persons sentenced to die for federal offenses) the president. Executive clemency for persons convicted of capital offenses has been recognized historically as a final avenue for relief and mercy. Ridolfi, "Not Just An Act of Mercy: The Demise of Post-Conviction Relief and A Rightful Claim to Clemency," 24 N.Y.U. Rev. L. & Soc. Change 43 (1998) (in the American colonies, executive pardon was originally seen as a royal prerogative of forgiveness for an offense against the crown) [hereinafter "Rightful Claim to Clemency"]; Korengold, Noteboom & Gurwitch, "And Justice for Few: The Collapse of the Capital Clemency System in the United States," 20 Hamline L. Rev. 349, 353 (1996) ("[b]y the time of the Norman Conquest in 1055, the throne's exclusive prerogative to grant mercy was firmly established") [hereinafter "And Justice for Few"]; Bedau, "The Decline of Clemency in Capital Cases," 18 Rev. L. & Soc. Change 255 (1990–91) (executive clemency dates back to biblical times; Pilate, at the urging of the mob, granted clemency to Barabbas but not to Jesus); Kobil, "Do The Paperwork or Die: Clemency, Ohio Style?," 52 Ohio St. L.J. 655 (1991) [hereinafter "Clemency, Ohio Style?"] (King Henry VIII granted a pardon to Sir Thomas More by commuting his sentence—from being "drawn on a hurdle through London, after which he was to be hanged until he was 'half dead,' and then cut down alive to have 'his privy parts cut off, his belly ripped, his bowels burnt, his four quarters set up over four gates of the city, and his head upon London-Bridge'"—to "simple beheading"); Kobil, "The Quality of Mercy Strained: Wresting the Pardoning Power from the King," 69 Tex. L. Rev. 569 (1991) [hereinafter "The Quality of Mercy"] (providing an interesting discussion of clemency from the ancient Greeks to modern America).[6] Since clemency remains a route through which

---

6. See Note, "A Matter of Life and Death: Due Process Protection in Capital Clemency Proceedings," 90 Yale L.J. 889, 896 (1981) [hereinafter "A Matter of Life and Death"] (history of clemency reveals royal grants of clemency were granted in a substantial number of capital cases); Abramowitz & Paget, "Executive Clemency in Capital Cases," 39 N.Y.U. L. Rev. 136, 136–149 (1964) (discussion of the history of clemency).

modern-day death row inmates may seek relief,[7] a brief discussion of the clemency process follows.[8]

Executive clemency encompasses pardons, amnesty, commutations, reprieves, and remissions of fines and forfeitures. "The Quality of Mercy Strained," *supra*; Abramowitz & Paget, *supra* at 137–138. A pardon "is that facet of executive clemency which, when invoked, entirely abrogates legal punishment." Abramowitz & Paget, *supra*, at 138. A full pardon freely absolves the person pardoned of all legal ramifications; a partial pardon relieves a person of only some punishment or absolves only a portion of the offense. In addition, a pardon may be unconditional, freeing the defendant of all criminal liability; or it may be conditional, taking effect only upon the performance of certain conditions. Lavinsky, "Executive Clemency: Study of a Decisional Problem Arising in the Terminal Stages of the Criminal Process," 42 Chi.-Kent L. Rev. 13, 17 (1965).

Amnesty is generally granted to groups of individuals. Amnesty does not eradicate the offense; it simply constitutes a forgiveness of the offense. "The Quality of Mercy," *supra*. Commutation, on the other hand, is "the mitigation of criminal punishment through the substitution of a lesser sentence for a greater one." Abramowitz & Paget, *supra*, at 138. A reprieve merely suspends execution of the death sentence, but it does not change or reduce the punishment. Lavinsky, *supra*, at 18.

Several rationales have been advanced supporting grants of executive clemency. Bedau, *supra*, at 257. The first, and most traditional view, is that clemency is "an act of grace.... It is the private, though official, act of the executive magistrate." *United States v. Wilson*, 32 U.S. (7 Pet.) 150 (1833). In this regard, clemency may be used by the executive as an act of power, and the granting or denying of clemency often has more to do with political interests and expediency than with justice and mercy. "The Quality of Mercy," *supra*, at 585–589.

A second view is that clemency provides the executive, or other properly appointed body, with the quasi-judicial authority to provide a final review of a case in which factors ordinarily not considered by the courts may be taken into account. Rockefeller, "Executive Clemency and the Death Penalty," 21 Cath. U.L. Rev. 94, 96 (1971) (Arkansas Governor Winthrop Rockefeller demonstrated his opposition to the death penalty when, in 1970, he commuted the sentences of all 15 death row inmates in Arkansas); see "A Matter of Life and Death," *supra*, at 897.

A third view is that clemency "exists to afford relief from undue harshness or evident mistake in the operation of the criminal law. The administration of justice by the courts is not necessarily always wise or certainly considerate of circumstances which properly mitigate guilt." *Ex parte Grossman*, 267 U.S. 87, 120–121 (1925). See "Rightful Claim to Clemency," *supra* (arguing that the governor of California abdicated his constitutional mandate and redefined the pardoning power by restricting clemency to cases of actual

---

7. See *United States v. Wilson*, 32 U.S. (7 Pet.) 150, 161 (1833) (discussing important role of clemency in the justice system); M. Koosed, "Some Perspectives on the Possible Impact of Diminished Federal Review of Ohio Death Sentences," 19 Cap. U.L. Rev. 695, 756–758 (1990) (discussion of history, justification and evolution of clemency process in United States); "A Matter of Life and Death," *supra*, at 896 (clemency has long been recognized as an integral part of the criminal justice system).

8. Some commentators have questioned whether clemency remains a viable alternative to those condemned to death. Bedau, *supra*; Koosed, *supra*, at 755.

innocence or appealing mitigating circumstances, and refusing to grant clemency in cases of legal error); Note, "Reviving Mercy in the Structure of Capital Punishment," 99 Yale L.J. 389 (1989) (arguing that mercy should play a greater role in granting clemency in cases where justified and warning that the current "death penalty bureaucracy" of lawyers, juries and judges is ill-equipped to dispense mercy).

Regardless of the rationale underlying a grant of clemency, the clemency process is an important mechanism which may be used to grant relief in situations where the courts can not, or will not, grant appropriate relief. As Professor Hugo Adam Bedau has noted:

> First, the appellate courts can be counted on to define narrowly what will count as legally reversible error and what suffices to secure relief on this ground. The result is that not every error will be remedied by the courts, and these errors will go unremedied unless the executive steps in. Second, the legislature knows or should know that its criminal statutes are not self-enforcing any more than they are self-interpreting. As in the past, there will be inequities and inconsistencies in application of the laws. These can be remedied, if at all, only after they have occurred, and not all such remedies will be forthcoming from the appellate courts. Third, society should want some branch of government to have the power to reduce sentences where the punishment is inappropriately severe or excessive in a particular case. This concern should be especially strong where the failure to reduce a sentence entails the death of a prisoner by lawful execution. The natural place to lodge such power is with the executive, whose responsibility it is in any case to carry out legislatively authorized and judicially imposed sentences.

Bedau, *supra* at 259.

While all states provide for some form of clemency, diverse laws govern the various clemency processes.[9] Despite the diversity among jurisdictions, all clemency decisions "are standardless in procedure, discretionary in exercise, and unreviewable in result." Bedau, *supra*, at 257. A governor or other appointed body may act with complete discretion and arbitrariness in granting or denying clemency. The standardless nature and the lack of review over clemency decisions has prompted criticism and concern particularly given the inevitable political nature of the clemency process. See "The Quality of Mercy Strained," *supra* (noting the limited controls over and review of clemency decisions throughout history); "A Matter of Life and Death," *supra*, at 891 (arguing that procedural safeguards and protections should be installed in the clemency process for capital cases and suggesting that their absence permits "uncontrolled discretion detract[ing] from the value of clemency as the state's final opportunity to assess the appropriateness of the death penalty").

---

9. Alaska, Arkansas, California, Colorado, Hawaii, Illinois, Iowa, Kansas, Kentucky, Louisiana, Maryland, Michigan, Mississippi, Missouri, New Hampshire, New Jersey, New Mexico, New York, North Carolina, Ohio, Oregon, South Dakota, Tennessee, Vermont, Virginia, Washington, West Virginia, Wisconsin and Wyoming place the clemency power in the governor alone, although an advisory body may make non-binding recommendations to the governor in many of these states. "The Quality of Mercy Strained," *supra*, at 605 n.232 (1991), *citing, Nat'l Governors' Ass'n Center for Policy Research, Guide to Executive Clemency Among the American States* 15 (1988). Arizona, Delaware, Florida, Indiana, Maine, Massachusetts, Minnesota, Montana, Nebraska, Nevada, North Dakota, Oklahoma, Pennsylvania, Rhode Island, Texas and Utah provide that the governor share clemency decisions with an administrative panel or board. *Id.* at 605 n.233. Finally, in Alabama, Connecticut, Georgia, Idaho and South Carolina, an administrative panel has the principal authority to make clemency decisions. *Id.* at 605 n.234.

In addition, since the Supreme Court's decisions in *Furman* and *Gregg*, pardons or commutations of death sentences have dropped significantly. Bedau, *supra*, at 264; Koosed, *supra*, at 759–763. For example, between 1960 and 1970, for every ten capital defendants executed, eight capital defendants were granted clemency. "And Justice for Few," *supra* at 357. From 1976 to 1996, the rate of clemency dropped to one grant of clemency for every five executions. *Id.* The proportionate decline of commutations in the States of Florida and Texas was even greater. *Id.* "Various reasons have been offered to explain the decline in grants of clemency in capital cases. First, many observers believe that a governor would commit "political suicide" by granting clemency in a capital case. "And Justice for few," *supra*, at 363–65; Bedau, *supra*, at 268; Koosed, *supra*, at 775–788; "The Quality of Mercy Strained," *supra*, at 607–610. Second, others believe that, due to the procedural safeguards that have been implemented in capital cases since *Furman* and *Gregg*, death sentences are meted out with as much fairness as is possible. "And Justice for Few," *supra*, at 365–66; Bedau, *supra*, at 268–269; Koosed, *supra*, at 763. And, third, still others contend that appellate review of death sentences provides adequate protection to the capital defendant. Bedau, *supra*, at 269; Koosed, *supra*, at 763–773. Regardless of the reasons, the decline in grants of clemency has led some observers to conclude that, in certain states, clemency is a not a viable option for death row inmates. Bedau, *supra*, at 266. See Rappaport, "Symposium on Law, Psychology and the Emotions: Retribution and Redemption in the Operation of Executive Clemency," 74 Chi.-Kent L. Rev. 1501 (2001) (discussing the retributive nature inherent in the current decline in grants of clemency and arguing for the redemptive value of executive commutations).

Some notable exceptions to the recent decline in clemency in death penalty cases exist. For example, in 1986, Governor Tony Anaya of New Mexico granted commutations to all six persons on death row in his state. See Koosed, *supra*, at 757 n.279. In 1991, Governor Richard Celeste of Ohio granted clemency to sixty-eight individuals, including eight individuals on death row. "Clemency, Ohio Style?," *supra*, at 656.[10] More recently, Illinois Governor George Ryan pardoned four innocent death row inmates on January 10, 2003, and he commuted the sentences of all 167 inmates on Illinois' death row on January 11, 2003. Three inmates' sentences were commuted to forty years imprisonment; 164 inmates' sentences were commuted to life without the possibility of parole. "Clemency," located at www.deathpenaltyinfo.org, citing Chicago Tribune, Jan. 12 & 15, 2003. All three governors were serving their final terms in office.

Political and international pressure occasionally factor into a grant of clemency. For example, in 1999, Missouri Governor Mel Carnahan granted clemency to death row inmate Darrel Mease at the urging of Pope John Paul II during the pontiff's visit to Missouri. Virginia Governor L. Douglas Wilder commuted the death sentence of Joe Giarratano in 1991 after much political pressure and media attention was brought to bear on that case, but in 1992, refused to commute the sentence of Roger Keith Coleman, despite international publicity and impassioned claims of innocence, after Coleman failed an eleventh-hour lie detector test. In 1998, then-Governor George W. Bush granted clemency to the notorious serial killer Henry Lee Lucas, who confessed to killing over 600 people, but who appeared innocent of the crime for which he sat on Texas' death row. However, Governor Bush refused clemency to Karla Faye Tucker, an admitted murderer who converted to Christianity and underwent such a remarkable

---

10. The actions of Governor Celeste led to widespread outrage and efforts to undo his grants of clemency and to change the clemency process. "Clemency, Ohio Style?," *supra*.

personal transformation in prison that many people, including the Reverend Pat Robertson, asked Governor Bush to commute her death sentence. For a discussion and comparison of the Lucas and Tucker cases, see Notes & Comments, "Clemency in Texas — A Question of Mercy?" 6 Tex. Wesleyan L. Rev. 131 (1999). In 2001, President Bill Clinton, without explanation, commuted the federal death sentence of Ronald David Chandler. Also in 2001, Clinton's successor, George W. Bush, Jr., ignored Pope John Paul II's request for clemency for convicted terrorist Timothy McVeigh. In 2004, Oklahoma Governor Brad Henry commuted the death sentence of Osbaldo Torres to life without the possibility of parole noting (1) that Torres' co-defendant was the shooter, and (2) the violation of Torres' Vienna Convention rights may have contributed to an unreliable trial result. "Clemency," located at www.deathpenaltyinfo.org, citing The Oklahoman, May 14, 2004.

Modern clemency procedures have been criticized for lacking the means and ability to provide relief in appropriate cases. Whether this criticism is justified or not, condemned inmates will continue to avail themselves of the process in hopes — however slender — that the executive will grant relief that has not been forthcoming from other quarters.

Notes and Questions

1. In *Ohio Adult Parole Authority v. Woodard*, 523 U.S. 272, 281–82 (1998), the Court concluded that no more process is due in capital clemency proceedings than the minimal amount that suffices in noncapital cases.

2. For an interesting perspective on California Governor Pete Wilson's decision not to grant clemency to Robert Alton Harris, who was executed on April 20, 1992, see J.R. Brown, "The Quality of Mercy," 40 U.C.L.A. L. Rev. 327 (1992). Further, M.B. Lavinsky, "Executive Clemency: Study of a Decisional Problem Arising in the Terminal Stages of the Criminal Process," 42 Chi.-Kent L. Rev. 13 (1965), provides an account of Illinois Governor Otto Kerner's clemency decisions and examines why clemency was granted in one case but not another.

3. Recall *Herrera v. Collins*, 506 U.S. 390 (1993) [*supra* chapter 13]. In that case, the Court denied habeas corpus relief to a Texas death row inmate who claimed new evidence proved his innocence. The Court noted that Herrera could seek relief through executive clemency. Ultimately, Governor Ann Richards and the Texas Board of Pardons and Paroles refused to issue reprieves and Herrera was executed by lethal injection on May 12, 1993.

4. Grants of clemency have long been used for political rather than merciful reasons. Professor Kobil observed in his article, "The Quality of Mercy Strained: Wresting the Pardoning Power from the King," 69 Tex. L. Rev. 569 (1991), that Presidents Abraham Lincoln and Andrew Johnson granted amnesties conditioned on pledging allegiance to the United States Constitution to persons who supported the Confederacy during the Civil War. This grant of amnesty was politically motivated and helped stabilize the country during reconstruction. George Washington, John Adams and Thomas Jefferson likewise used the presidential pardoning power for political purposes. More recent examples include Richard Nixon's conditional pardon of Jimmy Hoffa, Gerald Ford's pardon of Richard Nixon, the pardons George Bush, Sr., issued to persons involved in the Iran-Contra scandal (including defense secretary Caspar Weinberger), and Bill Clinton's pardon of Marc Rich.

5. The political calculations that enter into the decision to grant clemency to a death row inmate were powerfully and candidly described by former California Governor Ed-

mund "Pat" Brown in his book *Public Justice, Private Mercy* (Weidenfeld & Nicolson 1989). Governor Brown, who was personally opposed to the death penalty, had to decide the fate of a man facing execution for the murder of a young girl. The condemned man had suffered an injury as a child rendering him mentally defective and the Governor viewed executing this man as an act of vengeance rather than justice. According to Brown, one state legislator, who strongly supported the execution, held a key vote in a piece of migrant farm worker's legislation, which would benefit the parents of the victim who were farm laborers. Brown described his dilemma:

> Rose Marie Riddle was dead, and nothing I could do would bring her back. By letting Richard Lindsey go to the gas chamber, I was giving her parents and people like them a chance at a living wage. The scales tipped. I picked up my pen and on the first page of the clemency file wrote these words: "I will take no action." Four days later, Lindsey was dead. That same week, the farm labor bill passed through committee and a few months later was signed into law.

Brown & Adler, *Public Justice, Private Mercy* at 84. For further discussion of Governor Brown's decision in this case, see Kobil, "The Quality of Mercy Strained: Wresting the Pardoning Power from the King," 69 Tex. L. Rev. 569, 608 (1991).

6. During the 1992 presidential campaign, Bill Clinton, then governor of Arkansas, refused to grant clemency to Rickey Ray Rector, a mentally impaired death row inmate who arguably could not comprehend the consequences of his death sentence. Clinton's decision to allow the execution to proceed occurred during the height of allegations that he had engaged in an extra-marital affair with Gennifer Flowers. For an excellent discussion of the political motivations in the Rector case and Clinton's decision, see Frady, "Death in Arkansas," The New Yorker at 105–133 (Feb. 22, 1993).

7. Some authors have suggested introducing procedural safeguards into the clemency process. Proposals include creating clemency panels that are completely insulated from political pressures. *See* "And Justice for Few," *supra*; "The Quality of Mercy Strained," *supra*; Note, "A Matter of Life and Death: Due Process Protection in Capital Clemency Proceedings," 90 Yale L.J. 889 (1981). In late 2003, Kentucky Governor Paul Patton commuted Kevin Stanford (*supra* chapter 5) from death to life without the possibility of parol based on Stanford's age at the time of the commission of his crime. "Clemency," located at www.deathpenaltyinfo.org. What types of safeguards or protections, if any, would be effective or useful? How should members of the clemency panels be selected? What standards should guide the clemency panels?

Some standards that might be used to guide the clemency process include: whether a substantial doubt of guilt exists; whether the defendant is very young or suffered from diminished mental capacity, mental retardation, or intoxication at the time of the offense; whether the sentence is disproportionate to punishments meted out in other cases; whether special circumstances indicate that the sentence is disproportionate based on factors such as age or mental capacity; whether race or gender affected the sentencing process; and, whether the crime was committed out of necessity, coercion or adherence to moral principles. Kobil, "The Quality of Mercy Strained: Wresting the Pardoning Power from the King," 69 Tex. L. Rev. 569, 624–633 (1991). What other factors or considerations should enter into the clemency process? What about the interests of the victims' families or law enforcement personnel?

8. On January 29, 1991, the Ohio Attorney General sued to invalidate former Ohio Governor Richard Celeste's lame duck exercise of clemency. Among those named as defendants in the complaint for declaratory judgment were eleven recipients of clemency,

including seven of the eight death penalty commutees. See Kobil, "Clemency, Ohio Style?," 52 Ohio St. L.J. 655, 686 (1991). What is the proper scope of judicial review of executive clemency decisions?

9. Should clemency systems be revised? Consider the wholesale grants of clemency issued by former New Mexico Governor Tony Anaya just before he left office and Governor Ryan's decision to commute the death sentences of 167 death row inmates. Should rules be implemented so that governors may not broadly commute the sentences of all death row inmates based on individual personal beliefs?

10. Not all grants of executive clemency are warmly received. For example, King Henry VIII used his pardoning power to change Sir Thomas More's method of execution from being hung until half dead, disemboweled while alive, and then quartered, to simple beheading. When More learned of the king's act of mercy, he reportedly said, "God forbid the king should use any more such mercy to any of my friends, and God bless all my posterity from such pardons." Howell, *Trial of Sir Thomas More*, in *State Trials* 385, 394 (1535).

11. Consider the following reasons proffered in support of a clemency petition filed on behalf of William Witherspoon (the petitioner in *Witherspoon v. Illinois*, 391 U.S. 510 (1968) (*supra* chapter 6). Do you find any persuasive?

(A) The supreme, irrevocable penalty of death, if invoked at all, should be reserved for the vicious and depraved. Petitioner is neither vicious or depraved; there is abundant and irrefutable evidence that he is a person of great potentiality for social usefulness. His intimate knowledge of crime, his powers of observation, his articulateness and his desire to be of public service should be utilized in the study of ways and means of preventing crime and rehabilitating prisoners.

(B) This community, like the rest of the nation, is divided on the subject of capital punishment; more persons being opposed to it than in favor. Yet all those opposed to capital punishment were excluded from the jury. Thus, there was not a representative jury, but one slanted in favor of the death penalty.

(C) Informed men and women in all walks of life have urged executive clemency. These include many leaders of the community.

(D) In the opinions of those best acquainted with the petitioner—the Sheriff and the County Jail personnel and those who have been in close contact with him since his conviction—petitioner has demonstrated qualities that justify the extending of mercy to him.

(E) Petitioner is so completely rehabilitated that his execution at this time would outrage the public conscience and discourage the principle of rehabilitation generally.

(F) There is pending in the United States District Court a new habeas corpus proceeding. In any event, petitioner's life should be spared pending the final determination of that proceeding.

Lavinsky, "Executive Clemency: Study of a Decisional Problem Arising in the Terminal Stages of the Criminal Process," 42 Chi.-Kent L. Rev. 13, 49–50 (1965).

Chapter 18

The Federal Death Penalty

A. Historical Summary of the Federal Death Penalty

The English common law, from which American law originally derived, embraced capital punishment. According to one early English law:

> "Let the man who slayeth another wilfully perish by death. Let him who slayeth another of necessity or unwillingly, or unwilfully, as God may have sent him into his hands and for whom he has not lain in wait be worthy of his life and of lawful bot if he seek an asylum."

3 J. Stephen, *History of the Criminal Law of England* 24 (1883).

Nowhere in the Constitution is explicit mention made of the death penalty. Nonetheless, the Fifth Amendment contemplates that the federal government may deprive citizens of life after giving due process. Also, the Fifth Amendment requires the use of grand juries in federal capital prosecutions. Thus, it is not surprising that capital punishment has long been a penalty available to federal prosecutors enforcing federal laws.

In 1790, the first Congress crafted the first federal criminal code by passing an "Act for the Punishment of Certain Crimes Against the United States." This law mandated the death penalty for several offenses including treason, willful murder on federal property, forgery, piracy, counterfeiting, and several crimes on the high seas. According to the statute, those convicted "shall suffer death." 1 Stat. 112, sec. 1, 3, 8 (1790); 1 Stat. 115 sec. 14 (1790); 1 Stat. 117 sec. 23 (1790). See Little, "The Federal Death Penalty: History and Some Thoughts About the Department of Justice's Role," 26 Fordham Urb. L. J. 347 (1999).

By 1894, the number of offenses punishable by death under the United States Code had greatly expanded. These included rape, insurrection, rebellion, murder, and accessory before the fact to murder. A majority of capital offenses at that time were related to the military or national security. Separate military codes governing the army and the navy included death penalty provisions. Other capital offenses included spying; murder or piracy upon the high seas; treason; arson of a dwelling house within a fort; destruction of a vessel at sea; robbery on the high seas; seaman laying violent hands on his commander; and acts of hostility against the United States committed on the high seas. The slave trade also provided an impetus for capital statutes. Piracy in confining or detaining Africans on board a vessel and piracy in landing and seizing Africans on foreign shores were both capital crimes. Finally, last minute attempts to cheat the executioner were punishable by death. Rescuing a "person guilty of a capital crime while going to or during execution" rendered the rescuer death-eligible. See generally Curtis, *Capital*

Crimes: Punishments Prescribed Therefor by Federal and State Laws and Those of Foreign Countries 6 (1894).

In 1897, Congress passed an "Act to Reduce the Cases in Which the Death Penalty May Be Inflicted," reducing the number of potential federal capital offenses to five. This statute also eliminated the mandatory death sentence which automatically flowed from conviction of a given capital offense and replaced it with a system giving jurors discretion to determine if a particular defendant should be put to death.

From 1927 to 1963, the federal government executed thirty-four people. While most were put to death for murder, several individuals were executed for sabotage, espionage and kidnapping. Methods of execution in federal cases included hanging, electrocution and the gas chamber. The final federal execution of the twentieth century occurred in Iowa in 1963, when Victor Feguer was hanged for kidnapping and murdering a doctor.

From 1972, the year of the Supreme Court's *Furman* decision, until the late 1980's, the death penalty had been almost exclusively a state prerogative and federal capital prosecutions were rare.

As the next case demonstrates, even before *Furman*, the federal death penalty was vulnerable to constitutional attack.

United States v. Jackson
390 U.S. 570 (1968)

Mr. Justice STEWART delivered the opinion of the Court.

The Federal Kidnaping Act, 18 U.S.C. section 1201(a), provides:

> "Whoever knowingly transports in interstate ... commerce, any person who has been unlawfully ... kidnaped ... and held for ransom ... or otherwise ... shall be punished (1) by death if the kidnaped person has not been liberated unharmed, and if the verdict of the jury shall so recommend, or (2) by imprisonment for any term of years or for life, if the death penalty is not imposed."

This statute thus creates an offense punishable by death "if the verdict of the jury shall so recommend." The statute sets forth no procedure for imposing the death penalty upon a defendant who waives the right to jury trial or upon one who pleads guilty.

On October 10, 1966, a federal grand jury in Connecticut returned an indictment charging in count one that three named defendants, the appellees in this case, had transported from Connecticut to New Jersey a person who had been kidnaped and held for ransom and who had been harmed when liberated. The District Court dismissed this count of the indictment, holding the Federal Kidnaping Act unconstitutional because it makes "the risk of death" the price for asserting the right to jury trial, and thereby "impairs ... free exercise" of that constitutional right. The Government appealed directly to this Court, and we noted probable jurisdiction. We reverse.

We agree with the District Court that the death penalty provision of the Federal Kidnaping Act imposes an impermissible burden upon the exercise of a constitutional right, but we think that provision is severable from the remainder of the statute. There is no reason to invalidate the law in its entirety simply because its capital punishment clause violates the Constitution. The District Court therefore erred in dismissing the kidnaping count of the indictment.

I

One fact at least is obvious from the face of the statute itself: In an interstate kidnaping case where the victim has not been liberated unharmed, the defendant's assertion of the right to jury trial may cost him his life, for the federal statute authorizes the jury—and only the jury—to return a verdict of death. The Government does not dispute this proposition. What it disputes is the conclusion that the statute thereby subjects the defendant who seeks a jury trial to an increased hazard of capital punishment. As the Government construes the statute, a defendant who elects to be tried by a jury cannot be put to death even if the jury so recommends—unless the trial judge agrees that capital punishment should be imposed. Moreover, the argument goes, a defendant cannot avoid the risk of death by attempting to plead guilty or waive jury trial. For even if the trial judge accepts a guilty plea or approves a jury waiver, the judge remains free, in the Government's view of the statute, to convene a special jury for the limited purpose of deciding whether to recommend the death penalty. The Government thus contends that, whether or not the defendant chooses to submit to a jury the question of his guilt, the death penalty may be imposed if and only if both judge and jury concur in its imposition. On this understanding of the statute, the Government concludes that the death penalty provision of the Kidnaping Act does not operate to penalize the defendant who chooses to contest his guilt before a jury. It is unnecessary to decide here whether this conclusion would follow from the statutory scheme the Government envisions, for it is not in fact the scheme that Congress enacted.

At the outset, we reject the Government's argument that the Federal Kidnaping Act gives the trial judge discretion to set aside a jury recommendation of death. So far as we are aware, not once in the entire 34-year history of the Act has a jury's recommendation of death been discarded by a trial judge. The Government would apparently have us assume either that trial judges have always agreed with jury recommendations of capital punishment under the statute—an unrealistic assumption at best—or that they have abdicated their statutory duty to exercise independent judgment on the issue of penalty. In fact, the explanation is a far simpler one. The statute unequivocally states that, "if the verdict of the jury shall so recommend," the defendant "shall be punished ... by death...." The word is "shall," not "may." In acceding without exception to jury recommendations of death, trial judges have simply carried out the mandate of the statute.

Nothing in the language or history of the Federal Kidnaping Act points to any such result. On the contrary, an examination of the death penalty provision in its original form demonstrates that Congress could not have intended the meaning the Government now seeks to attribute to it. For the statute as it stood in 1934 provided that the offender

> "shall, upon conviction, be punished (1) by death if the verdict of the jury shall so recommend, provided that the sentence of death shall not be imposed by the court if, prior to its imposition, the kidnaped person has been liberated unharmed, or (2) if the death penalty shall not apply nor be imposed the convicted person shall be punished by imprisonment in the penitentiary for such term of years as the court in its discretion shall determine...."

48 Stat. 781.

In this form, the statutory language simply will not support the interpretation that the offender "shall be punished by death or by imprisonment" if the jury recommends the death penalty. For the statute in this form makes unmistakably clear that, if the death penalty applies—i.e., if the jury has recommended death—then the punishment shall be death unless, before the judge has imposed sentence, the victim has been liberated unharmed. There is absolutely no reason to think that the purely formal transformations through which the statute has passed since 1934 were intended to alter this basic penalty structure.

The Government nonetheless urges that we overlook Congress' choice of the imperative. Whatever might have been assumed in the past, we are now asked to construe the statute so as to eliminate the jury's power to fix the death penalty without the approval of the presiding judge. "(T)his reading," it is said, would conform "to the long tradition that makes the trial judge in the federal courts the arbiter of the sentence." And so it would. The difficulty is that Congress intentionally discarded that tradition when it passed the Federal Kidnaping Act. Over the forcefully articulated objection that jury sentencing would represent an unwarranted departure from settled federal practice, Congress rejected a version of the Kidnaping Act that would have left punishment to the court's discretion and instead chose an alternative that shifted from a single judge to a jury of 12 the onus of inflicting the penalty of death. To accept the Government's suggestion that the jury's sentencing role be treated as merely advisory would return to the judge the ultimate duty that Congress deliberately placed in other hands.

The thrust of the clause in question was clearly expressed by the House Judiciary Committee that drafted it: Its purpose was, quite simply, "to permit the jury to designate a death penalty for the kidnaper." The fact that Congress chose the word "recommend" to describe what the jury would do in designating punishment cannot obscure the basic congressional objective of making the jury rather than the judge the arbiter of the death sentence. The Government's contrary contention cannot stand.

Equally untenable is the Government's argument that the Kidnaping Act authorizes a procedure unique in the federal system — that of convening a special jury, without the defendant's consent, for the sole purpose of deciding whether he should be put to death. We are told initially that the Federal Kidnaping Act authorizes this procedure by implication. The Government's reasoning runs as follows: The Kidnaping Act permits the infliction of capital punishment whenever a jury so recommends. The Act does not state in so many words that the jury recommending capital punishment must be a jury impaneled to determine guilt as well. Therefore the Act authorizes infliction of the death penalty on the recommendation of a jury specially convened to determine punishment. The Government finds support for this analysis in a Seventh Circuit decision construing the Federal Kidnaping Act to mean that the death penalty may be imposed whenever "an affirmative recommendation (is) made by a jury," including a jury convened solely for that purpose after the court has accepted a guilty plea. *Seadlund v. United States*, 7 Cir., 97 F.2d 742, 748. Accord, *Robinson v. United States*, D.C., 264 F.Supp. 146, 153. But the statute does not say "a jury." It says "the jury." At least when the defendant demands trial by jury on the issue of guilt, the Government concedes that "the verdict of the jury" means what those words naturally suggest: the general verdict of conviction or acquittal returned by the jury that passes upon guilt or innocence. Thus, when such a jury has been convened, the statutory reference is to that jury alone, not to a jury impaneled after conviction for the limited purpose of determining punishment. Yet the Government argues that, when the issue of guilt has been tried to a judge or has been eliminated altogether by a plea of guilty, "the verdict of the jury" at once assumes a completely new meaning. In such a case, it is said, "the verdict of the jury" means the recommendation of a jury convened for the sole purpose of deciding whether the accused should live or die.

The Government would have us give the statute this strangely bifurcated meaning without the slightest indication that Congress contemplated any such scheme. Not a word in the legislative history so much as hints that a conviction on a plea of guilty or a conviction by a court sitting without a jury might be followed by a separate sentencing proceeding before a penalty jury. If the power to impanel such a jury had been recognized elsewhere in the federal system when Congress enacted the Federal Kidnaping Act, perhaps Congress' total silence on the subject could be viewed as a tacit incorporation of this sentencing practice into the new law. But the background against which Congress legislated was barren of any precedent for the sort of sentencing procedure we are told Congress impliedly authorized.

The Government nonetheless maintains that Congress' failure to provide for the infliction of the death penalty upon those who plead guilty or waive jury trial was no more than an oversight that the courts can and should correct. At least twice, Congress has expressly authorized the infliction of capital punishment upon defendants convicted without a jury, but when on the assumption that the failure of Congress to do so here was wholly inadvertent, it would hardly be the province of the courts to fashion a remedy. Any attempt to do so would be fraught with the gravest difficulties: If a special jury were convened to recommend a sentence, how would the penalty hearing proceed? What would each side be required to show? What standard of proof would govern? To what extent would conventional rules of evidence be abrogated? What privileges would the accused enjoy? Congress, unlike the state legislatures that have authorized jury proceedings to determine the penalty in capital cases, has addressed itself to none of these questions.

It is one thing to fill a minor gap in a statute—to extrapolate from its general design details that were inadvertently omitted. It is quite another thing to create from whole cloth a complex and completely novel procedure and to thrust it upon unwilling defendants for the sole purpose of rescuing a statute from a charge of unconstitutionality. We recognize that trial judges sitting in federal kidnaping cases have on occasion chosen the latter course, attempting to fashion on an ad hoc basis the ground rules for penalty proceedings before a jury. We do not know what kinds of rules particular federal judges have adopted, how widely such rules have varied, or how fairly they have been applied. But one thing at least is clear: Individuals forced to defend their lives in proceedings tailor-made for the occasion must do so without the guidance that defendants ordinarily find in a body of procedural and evidentiary rules spelled out in advance of trial. The Government notes with approval "the decisional trend which has sought ... to place the most humane construction on capital legislation." Yet it asks us to extend the capital punishment provision of the Federal Kidnaping Act in a new and uncharted direction, without the compulsion of a legislative mandate and without the benefit of legislative guidance. That we decline to do.

II

Under the Federal Kidnaping Act, therefore, the defendant who abandons the right to contest his guilt before a jury is assured that he cannot be executed; the defendant ingenuous enough to seek a jury acquittal stands forewarned that, if the jury finds him guilty and does not wish to spare his life, he will die. Our problem is to decide whether the Constitution permits the establishment of such a death penalty, applicable only to those defendants who assert the right to contest their guilt before a jury. The inevitable effect of any such provision, is of course, to discourage assertion of the Fifth Amendment right not to plead guilty and to deter exercise of the Sixth Amendment right to demand a jury trial. If the provision had no other purpose or effect than to chill the assertion of constitutional rights by penalizing those who choose to exercise them, then it would be patently unconstitutional. But, as the Government notes, limiting the death penalty to cases where the jury recommends its imposition does have another objective: It avoids the more drastic alternative of mandatory capital punishment in every case. In this sense, the selective death penalty procedure established by the Federal Kidnaping Act may be viewed as ameliorating the severity of the more extreme punishment that Congress might have wished to provide. The Government suggests that, because the Act thus operates "to mitigate the severity of punishment," it is irrelevant that it "may have the incidental effect of inducing defendants not to contest in full measure." We cannot agree. Whatever might be said of Congress' objectives, they cannot be pursued by means that needlessly chill the exercise of basic constitutional rights. The question is not whether the chilling effect is "incidental" rather than intentional; the question is whether that effect is unnecessary and therefore excessive. In this case the answer to that question is clear. The Congress can of course mitigate the severity of capital punishment. The goal of limiting the death penalty to cases is which a jury recommends it is an entirely legitimate one. But that goal can be achieved without penalizing those defendants who plead not guilty and demand jury trial. In some States, for example, the choice between life imprisonment and capital punishment is left to a jury in every case—regardless of how the defendant's guilt has been determined. Given the availability of this and other alternatives, it is clear that the selective death penalty provision of the Federal Kidnaping Act cannot be justified by its ostensible purpose. Whatever the power of Congress to impose a death penalty for violation of the Federal Kidnaping Act, Congress cannot impose such a penalty in a manner that needlessly penalizes the assertion of a constitutional right. See *Griffin v. State of California*, 380 U.S. 609. It is no answer to urge, as does the Government, that federal trial judges may be relied upon to reject coerced pleas of guilty and involuntary waivers of jury trial. For the evil in the federal statute is not that it necessarily coerces guilty pleas and jury waivers but simply that it needlessly encourages them. A procedure need not be inherently coercive in order that it be held to impose an impermissible burden upon the assertion of a constitutional right. Thus the fact that the Federal Kidnaping Act tends to discourage defendants from insisting upon their innocence and demanding trial by jury hardly implies that every defendant who enters a guilty plea to a charge under the Act does so involuntarily. The power to reject coerced guilty pleas and involuntary jury waivers might alleviate, but it cannot totally eliminate, the constitutional infirmity in the capital punishment provision of the Federal Kidnaping Act.

The Government alternatively proposes that this Court, in the exercise of its supervisory powers, should simply instruct federal judges sitting in kidnaping cases to reject all attempts to waive jury trial and all efforts to plead guilty, however voluntary and well-informed such attempted waivers and pleas might be. In that way, we could assure that every defendant charged in a federal court with aggravated kidnaping would face a possible death penalty, and that no defendant tried under the federal statute would be induced to forgo a constitutional right. But of course the inevitable consequence of this "solution" would be to force all defendants to submit to trial, however clear their guilt and however strong their desire to acknowledge it in order to spare themselves and their families the spectacle and expense of protracted courtroom proceedings.

It is true that a defendant has no constitutional right to insist that he be tried by a judge rather than a jury, *Singer v. United States*, 380 U.S. 24, and it is also true "that a criminal defendant has (no) absolute right to have his guilty plea accepted by the court." *Lynch v. Overholser*, 369 U.S. 705, 719. But the fact that jury waivers and guilty pleas may occasionally be rejected hardly implies that all defendants may be required to submit to a full-dress jury trial as a matter of course. Quite apart from the cruel impact of such a requirement upon those defendants who would greatly prefer not to contest their guilt, it is clear—as even the Government recognizes—that the automatic rejection of all guilty pleas "would rob the criminal process of much of its flexibility." As one federal court has observed: "The power of a court to accept a plea of guilty is traditional and fundamental. Its existence is necessary for the ... practical ... administration of the criminal law. Consequently, it should require an unambiguous expression on the part of the Congress to withhold this authority in specified cases." If any such approach should be inaugurated in the administration of a federal criminal statute, we conclude that the impetus must come from Congress, not from this Court. The capital punishment provision of the Federal Kidnaping Act cannot be saved by judicial reconstruction.

Mr. Justice WHITE, with whom Mr. Justice Black joins, dissenting.

The Court strikes down a provision of the Federal Kidnaping Act which authorizes only the jury to impose the death penalty. No question is raised about the death penalty itself or about the propriety of jury participation in its imposition, but confining the power to impose the death penalty to the jury alone is held to burden impermissibly the right to a jury trial because it may either coerce or encourage persons to plead guilty or to waive a jury and be tried by the judge. In my view, however, if the vice of the provision is that it may interfere with the free choice of the defendant to have his guilt or innocence determined by a jury, the Court needlessly invalidates a major portion of an Act of Congress. The Court itself says that not every plea of guilty or waiver of jury trial would be influenced by the power of the jury to impose the death penalty. If this is so, I would not hold the provision unconstitutional but would reverse the judgment, making it clear that pleas of guilty and waivers of jury trial should be carefully examined before they are accepted, in order to make sure that they have been neither coerced nor encouraged by the death penalty power in the jury.

Because this statute may be properly interpreted so as to avoid constitutional questions, I would not take the first step toward invalidation of statutes on their face because they arguably burden the right to jury trial.

Note

Title 18 of the federal criminal code has capital punishment provisions in the following sections: 18 U.S.C. §34 (1982) (aircraft or motor vehicle destruction); §351 (assassination of high ranking government personnel); §794 (espionage); §844(d)(f) (using explosives that result in a death); §111(b) (general federal murder statute); §1751 (assassination of the President and the President's staff); §1992 (train wrecking); and §2381 (treason). Of comparatively recent vintage, the so-called "drug kingpin" statute, codified at 21 U.S.C. §848, is considered immediately below.

B. Selected Statutes and Cases

Note on the Anti-Drug Abuse Act, 21 U.S.C. Section 848 et seq.

In 1988, President Reagan signed into law the Anti-Drug Abuse Act, 21 U.S.C. §848 et seq., also known as the "drug kingpin statute." The law created the first enforceable federal death penalty statute adopted after *Furman* for murders committed by persons involved in certain drug trafficking activities. The death penalty provisions were added to the "continuing criminal enterprise" statute, first enacted in 1984. The drug trafficking enterprise can consist of as few as 5 individuals. Even a low-ranking "foot soldier" in the organization can be subjected to the death penalty if involved in a killing.

1. Drug Offenses

United States v. Pitera

795 F. Supp. 546 (E.D.N.Y. 1992)

RAGGI, District Judge:

Thomas Pitera stands before the court charged in a twenty count indictment with racketeering, drug trafficking, and various firearms violations. Count Three of the indictment accuses Mr. Pitera of killing two persons, Richard Leone and Solomon Stern, while engaging in or working in furtherance of a continuing criminal enterprise. Such conduct carries a possible sentence of death. 21 U.S.C. §848(e)(1)(A). The government has served notice of its intent to seek the death penalty if Mr. Pitera is found guilty of Count Three.

Mr. Pitera challenges the constitutionality of §848(e)(1)(A)'s death penalty provision. Joining in the attack as *amici curiae* are the Association of the Bar of the City of New York, the New York State Defenders Association, the National Association of Criminal Defense Lawyers, the New York State Association of Criminal Defense Lawyers, the National Legal Aid and Defender Association, and the New York Criminal Bar Association....

Statutory Background: The Anti-Drug Abuse Act of 1988

The Anti-Drug Abuse Act of 1988 makes it a capital offense intentionally to kill another person in connection with the commission of serious federal drug crimes....

The Act details procedures to be followed before a defendant can be executed. Initially, the government must serve notice "a reasonable time before trial" of its intent to seek the death penalty. If a defendant is found guilty of violating §848(e)(1)(A), a separate sentencing hearing must be conducted, generally before the same jury that determined guilt. The purpose of the hearing is to permit consideration of any "aggravating" and "mitigating" factors relevant to whether or not the defendant should be sentenced to death. The information adduced need not conform to the Federal Rules of Evidence, so long as the court is convinced that its "probative value is [not] substantially outweighed by the danger of unfair prejudice, confusion of the issues, or misleading the jury."

The process by which a jury is to consider sentencing factors is specific. Preliminarily, the government must prove beyond a reasonable doubt and to the unanimous satisfaction of the jury at least two of the aggravating factors expressly set forth in the statute (hereinafter referred to as "statutory aggravating factors"). Moreover, it must advise the defendant a reasonable time before trial of which statutory aggravating factors it intends to prove. One of these must be from among the four listed in §848(h)(1). The other must be from among those listed in §848(n)(2)–(12). Absent proof of these statutory aggravating factors, a jury cannot vote to impose the death penalty.

If a jury is satisfied that at least two such statutory aggravating factors have been proved, it may then consider any mitigating factors established by the defendant, whether from among those listed in §848(m) or not, and any other aggravating factors of which the government gives notice in advance of trial (hereinafter referred to as "non-statutory aggravating factors"). Although non-statutory aggravating factors must be proved to the jury's unanimous satisfaction beyond a reasonable doubt, mitigating factors need only be established by a preponderance of the evidence. Moreover, any juror persuaded of a mitigating factor may consider it in reaching a sentencing decision; unanimity is not required.

A jury that finds the required statutory aggravating factors proved must consider whether these factors, along with any non-statutory aggravating ones, so outweigh any mitigating factors as to justify a sentence of death in the discrete case. Even absent any mitigating factors, a jury must still be unanimously satisfied beyond a reasonable doubt that the proved aggravating factors are themselves sufficient to justify capital punishment before a sentence of death can be imposed.

Invidious factors cannot influence a jury's determination as to the death penalty. Indeed, each juror must sign a certificate attesting that neither the defendant's nor the victim's "race, color, religious beliefs, national origin, or sex" played any part in the deliberations.

Although a jury cannot vote for the death penalty absent the required findings and certifications just detailed, a jury is never required to impose a death sentence even if it finds sufficient grounds to do so under the applicable law. Indeed, a court must specifically so instruct the jury.

The statute labels a jury's finding in favor of the death penalty a "recommendation." In fact, it is determinative, for upon such a "recommendation" the trial court "shall sentence the defendant to death." Absent a recommendation of death, the court must sentence a defendant to a minimum of 20 years and a maximum of life imprisonment.

Appellate review of a death sentence is expressly provided by the law. Such appeal may be consolidated with a challenge to the judgment of conviction, and the case is to be given priority on the appellate docket.

Discussion

II. Arbitrary and Capricious Sentencing

The majority of the arguments advanced by defendant and *amici* contend that the statute at issue fails to ensure that the death penalty is imposed in a consistently reasoned manner.... [S]tatutes must "genuinely narrow the class of persons eligible for the death penalty and must reasonably justify the imposition of a more severe sentence on the defendant compared to others found guilty of murder." "[R]ational criteria" must be articulated "that narrow the decisionmaker's judgment as to whether the circumstances of a particular defendant's case" meet the "threshold below which the death penalty cannot be imposed." Moreover, when, as in this case, a jury generally inexperienced in sentencing decisions is entrusted with "so grave [a] determination" as "whether a human life should be taken or spared, that discretion must be suitably directed and limited so as to minimize the risk of wholly arbitrary and capricious action."

The means by which sentencing discretion can be narrowed and directed are varied. For example, a legislature can limit the types of murders for which capital punishment may be imposed. Alternatively, it can require proof of specific aggravating factors. In this case, Congress appears to have done both: limiting the type of homicide for which the death penalty can be imposed to intentional murders committed in relation to a serious drug crime, and providing for specific aggravating factors that must be found before a sentence of death can be considered. Nevertheless, Mr. Pitera and *amici* contend that the statutory scheme is constitutionally inadequate. The court addresses in turn the particular cited deficiencies.

A. Vagueness of the Crime

Amici submit that the crime outlined in 21 U.S.C. §848(e)(1)(A) is unconstitutionally vague. Specifically, they argue that the statute, in failing to specify the relationship to be proved between the defendant and the killing, between the enterprise and the killing, and between the defendant and the enterprise, risks arbitrary imposition of the death penalty. *Amici* further suggest that the statute violates due process in singling out certain drug-related murders for capital punishment when other equally or more heinous murders are not so punished. Neither argument has merit.

1. Eighth Amendment Vagueness

Generally, a vagueness challenge to a criminal statute invokes due process and focuses on the adequacy of notice to a defendant that certain conduct is prohibited. An eighth amendment vagueness challenge to a capital punishment statute has a different focus. The critical inquiry is whether the statute so poorly informs the *jury* as to what it "must find to impose the death penalty" that there is a risk that it is left "with the kind of open-ended discretion that was held invalid in *Furman v. Georgia*."

This case presents no such risk. The statute plainly states the relationship that must be established between a defendant and the charged murder: a defendant must have himself "intentionally kill[ed] the victim" or he must have "counsel[ed], command[ed], induce[d], procure[d], or cause[d] the intentional killing." The latter clause, far from being ambiguous, as *amici* argue, parallels 18 U.S.C. §2 and states principles on which juries are routinely instructed. In any event, the court understands the government's position to be that Mr. Pitera himself committed the two murders charged in Count Three. Thus, no jury confusion about his alleged involvement will arise.

The court further rejects *amici*'s suggestion that §848(e)(1)(A) is fatally vague in failing to define the relationship that must be proved between a defendant's efforts on behalf of a continuing criminal enterprise and the alleged killing. A common sense reading of the statute supports the conclusion that a defendant faces federal prosecution only for homicidal acts committed "[while he was] engaging in or working in furtherance of a continuing criminal enterprise...." *Amici*'s speculation that the statute would permit federal prosecution of a drug kingpin who killed his spouse in a domestic dispute unrelated to his drug dealing is not only fanciful, it is jurisdictionally suspect. As between two possible interpretations of a statute, a court is, quite simply, obliged to adopt that which is not constitutionally defective. The government, moreover, concedes that it must prove a relationship between the murders alleged and Mr. Pitera's involvement in the charged enterprise. The court understands this to be akin to that "vertical" relationship that must be proved between predicate acts and enterprises in racketeering cases. It will charge the jury accordingly.

Finally, the court finds no impermissible vagueness in the statute's description of the involvement a defendant must have in the charged enterprise. The government must prove that defendant was "engaging in or working in furtherance of a continuing criminal enterprise." How one "engages in" a continuing criminal enterprise is expressly defined in §848(c). Moreover, courts routinely consider whether a defendant's actions are "in furtherance" of other criminal activity when applying Fed. R. Evid. 801(d)(2)(E) (co-conspirator hearsay exception).

Amici contend that "working in furtherance of a continuing criminal enterprise" can mean aiding and abetting it. They note that the Second Circuit has rejected aiding and abetting as a basis for finding a defendant guilty of violating 21 U.S.C. §848(a) and (b). This argument ignores the different concerns addressed by §848(a) and (b) on the one hand, and §848(e)(1)(A) on the other. The former sections focus on individuals who head significant continuing drug enterprises. Section 848(e)(1)(A) focuses on individuals who commit murders in connection with the most serious drug crimes, specifically, in connection with continuing drug enterprises or in connection with the importation or distribution of significant quantities of drugs. While ... there is something illogical about convicting an aider and abettor for criminal conduct that focuses directly on the leadership role a defendant plays in a continuing criminal enterprise, that incongruity is not present in Congress's express decision to punish severely anyone who actually kills or who counsels, commands, induces, procures, or causes the intentional killing of a human being in connection with large-scale drug trafficking.

In any event, this case does not require the court to resolve the scope of a defendant's liability under §848(e)(1)(A) for homicides committed while "working in furtherance of a continuing criminal enterprise." The government here contends that Mr. Pitera did, indeed, head the drug enterprise. In short, this case will be presented to the jury on the theory that Mr. Pitera committed the charged homicides while "engaging in" a continuing criminal enterprise. Proper instructions pursuant to §848(c) will ensure that the jury understands this concept.

2. Due Process/Equal Protection

Amici further argue that §848(e)(1)(A) violates the equal protection guarantee implicit in the due process clause of the fifth amendment by irrationally singling out for possible execution a class of persons whose homicidal conduct may be no more, and possibly less, serious than that engaged in by others....

... Drug trafficking is recognized as "one of the greatest problems affecting the health and welfare of our population." To address the concern, Congress has already provided for a potential sentence of life imprisonment for large scale traffickers. The Supreme Court has rejected the argument that such a severe sentence is cruel and unusual. One of the most troubling aspects of drug trafficking is, of course, the frequency with which it spawns crimes of violence, particularly murder. In this context, Congress could reasonably have concluded that, when the risk of drug-related violence translates into the reality of an intentional murder, the death penalty is an appropriate sanction....

B. Statutory Aggravating Factors

The government has advised Mr. Pitera that, if he is convicted of Count Three, it will seek to prove three statutory aggravating factors. To satisfy its requirement under §848(n)(1), it expects to prove that Mr. Pitera "intentionally killed Richard Leone and Solomon Stern." To satisfy its requirement under §848(n)(2)–(12), the government expects to prove that "defendant committed [the Leone/Stern murders] after substantial planning and premeditation," and that he committed these murders "in an especially heinous, cruel, or depraved manner in that [they] involved torture or serious physical abuse to the victims." ...

1. Intentional Killing

This court agrees that the "intentional killing" factor stated in §848(n)(1)(A) mirrors the *mens rea* element of the charged crime. Defendant's suggestion that this duplication mandates a finding of unconstitutionality misperceives the purpose of statutory aggravating factors in a capital sentencing scheme. In *Lowenfield v. Phelps* [*supra* chapter 7], the Court explained that "[t]he use of aggravating circumstances is not an end in itself, but a means of genuinely narrowing the class of death eligible persons and thereby channeling the jury's discretion." In that case, the only aggravating factor proved, defendant's specific intent to kill or inflict great bodily harm upon more than one person, also duplicated an element of the charged homicide. Because the element itself narrowed the class of murderers that could be sentenced to death, the Court upheld imposition of the death penalty, noting that such narrowing could be achieved "by jury findings at either the sentencing phase of the trial or the guilt phase."

As with the statute in *Lowenfield*, §848(e)(1)(A) significantly narrows the class of murderers eligible for the death penalty at the guilt phase. A jury must be persuaded that a defendant intentionally committed homicide and that he did so in connection with large-scale drug trafficking. Moreover, Congress requires the finding of at least one other aggravating factor drawn from the list in §848(n)(2)–(12) before the death penalty can be considered. This further defines and limits the class of persons eligible for capital punishment....

2. Especially Heinous, Cruel or Depraved Manner Involving Torture or Serious Physical Abuse to the Victim

Defendant argues that the statutory factor permitting consideration of whether a defendant committed murder in "an especially heinous, cruel or depraved manner in that it involved torture or serious physical abuse to the victim" is too vague to constitute a real narrowing of the class of persons subject to the death penalty. The court must decide whether the provision adequately informs a jury as to what it must find to impose the death penalty or whether it invites the exercise of open-ended discretion.

By itself, the term "especially heinous, cruel or depraved" is too vague to narrow a jury's discretion in the manner required by the Constitution. Its modification in §848(n)(12) by the phrase "in that it involved torture or serious physical abuse to the victim" does, however, provide sufficient specificity to withstand challenge....

C. Non-Statutory Aggravating Factors

Defendant and *amici* challenge that part of §848(j) permitting the prosecution to select the non-statutory aggravating factors that it will present for jury consideration at the sentencing hearing. *Amici* contend that the use of such factors always injects arbitrariness and capriciousness into the sentencing process. Mr. Pitera submits that, if non-statutory aggravating factors are weighed against mitigating factors, "proportionality review" by an appellate court is constitutionally mandated. He further argues that the discretion here afforded federal prosecutors constitutes an impermissible delegation of Congress's legislative powers and runs afoul of the *ex post facto* clause. The court is unpersuaded by these arguments.

1. Non-Statutory Aggravating Factors Always Arbitrary and Capricious

Amici's contention that any consideration of non-statutory aggravating factors is constitutionally suspect has been squarely rejected by the Supreme Court in *Zant v. Stephens* [*supra* chapter 8]. In that case, the Court held that the invalidation of one of three statutory aggravating factors did not require reversal of a death sentence since the two remaining statutory aggravating factors supported the sentence, and since the information received pursuant to the invalid factor was properly considered as a non-statutory aggravating factor....

The statutory scheme here at issue similarly involves a congressional narrowing of the class of persons eligible for the death penalty, both as a result of the limited homicidal acts that Congress has labeled "capital" and by the required proof of statutory aggravating factors. Non-statutory aggravating factors are considered only after a defendant's membership in this narrow class is established beyond a reasonable doubt and only as a part of the jury's individualized sentencing consideration. Thus, although non-statutory aggravating factors cannot serve both to identify the class of capital defendants and to inform a jury's individualized sentencing decision, where, as in this case, the non-statutory factors perform only the latter task, their consideration does not render a capital sentencing decision arbitrary or capricious.

2. Need for "Proportionality Review"

In capital punishment jurisprudence, "proportionality review" refers to appellate inquiry into whether imposition of the death penalty in a particular case is proportionate to the punishment imposed on others convicted of the same crime. In *Pulley v. Harris*, 465 U.S. 37 (1989), the Supreme Court held that such review, while often useful, is not constitutionally required in all capital cases....

This court is satisfied, for the reasons stated in Part II-F of this memorandum, that Congress has provided for full appellate review of death sentences imposed under §848(e)(1)(A). Indeed, the court is convinced that the scope of this review is broad enough to permit appellate consideration of proportionality in an appropriate case, even though it is not required in every case....

3. Delegation of Legislative Powers

Article I, section 1 of the Constitution provides that "[a]ll legislative Powers herein granted shall be vested in a Congress of the United States." ... Defendant and *amici* submit that Congress has impermissibly delegated a part of its legislative power to fix sentence by permitting the prosecution to select the non-statutory aggravating factors on which it will rely at a capital sentencing hearing. The court finds no impermissible delegation in this case.

In identifying and presenting non-statutory factors for the jury's consideration, the prosecution does not intrude upon the legislative prerogative either to define the capital crime or to narrow the class of persons eligible for the death penalty. As already noted, that constitutionally-mandated narrowing has been achieved by Congress in limiting the types of homicides for which the death penalty may be imposed and in requiring proof of certain statutory aggravating factors. The prosecution's role is limited to that phase of the proceeding wherein the jury makes an individualized sentencing determination as to the defendant on trial. In the course thereof the prosecution engages in advocacy, not legislation....

The court ... rejects defendant's and *amici's* delegation challenge to the statute's provision for consideration of non-statutory aggravating factors finding (1) that if the jury finds [that the prosecutor] proved both the crime of conviction and the statutory aggravating factors, the prosecution's presentation of non-statutory factors is an exercise in advocacy derived from the executive's discretion to prosecute, not the legislature's power to fix sentence, and (2) that, even if this limited exercise of prosecutorial discretion were deemed to constitute a legislative delegation, its exercise is sufficiently circumscribed, both by the statute and by judicial review, to ensure against overbroad application.

4. Ex Post Facto Implications

Article I, section 9 of the Constitution prohibits *ex post facto* laws. The Supreme Court has interpreted the clause to proscribe any legislation (1) making illegal that which was legal at the time of the alleged criminal activity, (2) increasing the punishment for a crime after its commission, or (3) depriving the accused of any legal defense available at the time the crime was committed. Mr. Pitera contends that any government reliance, in aggravation of the homicides charged in Count Three, on other murders he may have committed prior to passage of §848(e)(1)(A) violates the *ex post facto* clause.

The argument is flawed in several respects. First, Count Three does not involve, as Mr. Pitera urges, a "straddle" crime. Such a crime holds a defendant accountable for conduct that occurs in part before and in part after the enactment of the relevant law. In straddle crimes—for example, racketeering charges involving one predicate act occurring prior to passage of the statute, and another after enactment—a defendant must be given clear statutory notice of what continuing conduct can resurrect his past misdeeds, for the earlier acts are themselves elements of the crime of conviction. In this case, the government's reliance on other homicides in aggravation of those charged in Count Three does not make those earlier murders any part of the crime of conviction.

Neither does the government here seek to increase the punishment for any of the earlier homicides, as defendant also suggests. At most, it uses this earlier conduct as evidence of Mr. Pitera's character to assist the jury in determining whether it should impose the maximum sentence of death for Count Three. In *Gryger v. Burke*, 334 U.S. 728 (1948), the Supreme Court upheld, against an *ex post facto* challenge, a statute permitting enhancement of sentence for crimes committed before passage of the crime of conviction. The enhanced penalty was "not to be viewed as either a new jeopardy or additional penalty for the earlier crimes. It is a stiffened penalty for the latest crime, which is considered to be an aggravated offense because a repetitive one." ...

Viewed in this light, a jury's consideration of these prior crimes not only does not implicate the *ex post facto* clause; it comes squarely within the broad review of all relevant facts and circumstances that ideally characterizes individualized sentencing. Indeed, in a non-capital context, the Second Circuit has specifically upheld a sentencing court's consideration of prior criminal conduct to which defendant pleaded guilty but had not yet been formally sentenced. Such conduct was found relevant to a defendant's character, since it suggested he was more likely to commit other crimes. So in this case, a jury is entitled to consider whether Mr. Pitera may not only have intentionally killed Messrs. Leone and

Stern, but also other individuals, which murders may have involved torture or serious physical abuse to the victims. These factors are relevant to his character and his propensity to commit violent crimes. Because such consideration neither exposes him to conviction for criminal conduct of which he was not given fair notice nor subjects him to further punishment for earlier crimes, the court finds no *ex post facto* defect in the statutory scheme.

D. Mitigating Factors

Amici's contention that the enumerated mitigating factors in §848(m) impermissibly limit what a defendant may present at a sentencing hearing merits little discussion. Section 848(j) expressly provides that a defendant may proffer "any ... mitigating factors set forth in [§848(m)] ... *or any other mitigating factor....*" (emphasis added). Thus, Congress has ensured compliance with those Supreme Court cases holding that a capital defendant cannot be precluded from proffering any factors relevant to his character or the circumstances of the crime "which may call for a less severe penalty."

E. Evidentiary Standard

The Federal Rules of Evidence do not apply at a capital sentencing hearing. Mr. Pitera contends that this omission invites an evidentiary "free for all" lacking the heightened reliability essential to a death penalty proceeding. This issue may never surface in this case since the government advises that its proof as to aggravating circumstances will likely duplicate its evidence at trial and, thus, necessarily conform to the Federal Rules. Nevertheless, because it neither concedes the point nor expressly limits its presentation, the court considers defendant's argument....

The Federal Rules of Evidence are critical to the conduct of criminal trials to enable "truth [to] be ascertained and proceedings [to be] justly determined." But the focus of a trial is singular: "whether a defendant is guilty of having engaged in criminal conduct of which he has been specifically accused." An individualized consideration of sentence, by contrast, necessitates a broader inquiry into all aspects of the defendant's life and the crime committed. A simple example best illustrates why the concerns of the two proceedings are not always best served by the Federal Rules of Evidence. At trial, a jury generally cannot consider evidence of a defendant's past criminal conduct in deciding whether he has committed the charged offense. That precise evidence is, however, deemed highly probative at sentencing....

This court expects that in many circumstances reference to the Federal Rules of Evidence will be useful in deciding whether information proffered at a capital sentencing hearing is sufficiently reliable to be more probative than prejudicial. The Rules will not, however, be determinative. For example, they tolerate multiple layers of hearsay, without requiring judicial inquiry into reliability. The heightened standard applicable to capital sentencing proceedings may, however, demand further indicia of reliability before a court can say that the probative value of any such hearsay outweighs its prejudicial potential. Because of this heightened standard, a court's consideration of the probative value of information compared to its prejudicial impact may yield different results under §848(j) than under Fed. R. Evid. 403. By way of contrast, certified judgments of prior convictions are highly reliable evidence and may be admissible at a capital sentencing hearing as probative proof of a defendant's character regardless of the limitations of Fed. R. Evid. 404(b).

The constitutional mandate is for a sentencing proceeding that ensures heightened reliability. The court is convinced that such a standard can adequately be factored into a consideration of whether proffered evidence is more probative than prejudicial. The court accordingly rejects defendant's challenge to the statute's evidentiary standard.

F. Meaningful Appellate Review

... In this case Congress has provided for appellate review. 21 U.S.C. §848(q). The issue is thus whether the scope of that review is so limited as to cause the entire capital scheme to run afoul of the eighth amendment. Mr. Pitera cites a portion of §848(q)(3) as evidence of such impermissible limitation:

> [T]he court shall affirm the sentence if it determines that —
>
> (A) the sentence of death was not imposed under the influence of passion, prejudice, or any other arbitrary factor; and
>
> (B) the information supports the special findings of the existence of every aggravating factor upon which the sentence was based, together with, or the failure to find, any mitigating factors as set forth or allowed in this section.

Not insignificantly, the section further provides that "[i]n all other cases, the court shall remand the case for reconsideration under this section." Nevertheless, Mr. Pitera contends that, since no express provision is made for review of legal errors that may occur at the sentencing hearing, the law impermissibly requires affirmance of a death sentence even in the face of plain errors such as inflammatory prosecutorial remarks, improper jury instructions or unsuitable jury behavior.

Defendant's argument depends on a crabbed reading of the statute that ignores two important points. First, Congress has mandated appellate consideration of whether a capital sentence was infected by "any arbitrary factor." The term "arbitrary" has particular meaning in modern death penalty jurisprudence. As the Supreme Court cases relied on in this memorandum amply demonstrate, although the death penalty, per se, is not violative of the eighth amendment, any imposition that is arbitrary and capricious is impermissibly cruel and unusual. An arbitrary factor must perforce include errors of law that are not harmless, for such errors, particularly in the context of a weighing statute, may impermissibly tip the scales in favor of death. Indeed, amici suggest that this is a reasonable interpretation of the statute and the government concurs.

Second, defendant overlooks the section immediately preceding §848(q)(3), wherein Congress makes plain that appellate review of a capital sentence is to be exhaustive.... This court thus concludes that no aspect of a capital sentencing proceeding is impervious to appellate review. If any feature—whether the vagueness of a factor, or the sufficiency of the information adduced, or a court's instructions, or a prosecutor's remarks, or a jury's conduct—reveals that the sentencing decision may have been arbitrarily arrived at, remand is contemplated....

Because this court finds no basis for thinking that the court of appeals will be limited in its power fully to review any sentence imposed, this court rejects this aspect of defendant's and amici's constitutional challenge....

IV. Failure to Provide Means of Execution

The capital sentencing scheme at issue provides no means for its implementation. This omission is without congressional explanation.[9] The one federal judge who has ac-

---

9. Prior federal death penalty law had provided for a defendant to be executed in whatever local facilities were available in the state where the defendant was convicted. If local law did not permit capital punishment, the court was to designate an alternate forum. See 18 U.S.C. §3566 (repealed

tually pronounced a death sentence pursuant to §848(e)(1)(A) has thus concluded that it cannot presently be implemented. The executive branch, which is traditionally charged with the responsibility for carrying out sentences, is, after all, obliged to do so in accordance with enacted law.

Amici contend that Congress's oversight is more than an embarrassment, it is a constitutional defect because (1) the prospect of an indefinite term of imprisonment, terminable only by some future execution provision, itself constitutes cruel and unusual punishment, and (2) the subsequent enactment of any implementing legislation will violate the *ex post facto* clause. Although this court is perplexed, both by Congress's failure to provide a means of execution, and by the executive's pursuit of a punishment before a means of carrying it out is specified, it must reject *amici*'s contentions because they either lack merit or are premature.

A. Cruel and Unusual Punishment

Amici's claim that the uncertainty inherent in Congress's failure to enact implementing legislation is itself constitutionally cruel and unusual relies on *In re Medley*, 134 U.S. 160 (1890). In that case, the Supreme Court observed that "when a prisoner sentenced by a court to death is confined in the penitentiary awaiting the execution of the sentence, one of the most horrible feelings to which he can be subjected during that time is the uncertainty ... as to the precise time when his execution will take place." At issue in *Medley* was legislation passed after a capital defendant was sentenced permitting the warden to withhold from him the exact date of his execution. The new statute was declared unconstitutional, but not because it was cruel and unusual. Rather, the new level of uncertainty constituted an increased punishment that violated the *ex post facto* clause.

Assuming that *Medley* is pertinent to *amici*'s eighth amendment claim, the challenge is simply premature. Mr. Pitera has been charged with a capital crime. He has not been convicted or sentenced of one. Even if such were to be the outcome of this case, defendant would have the right to appeal. Conceivably, before such events run their course, Congress may pass implementing legislation. Under such circumstances, Mr. Pitera would not be subject to the kind of uncertainty forecast by *amici*.

More troubling to the court is the possibility that Congress will not address the issue in the near future, such that a capital defendant, even after having pursued all appeals, could be incarcerated for several years before implementing legislation is enacted. Double jeopardy, however, proscribes multiple punishments for the same crime. This potential concern is not ripe for consideration before the capital trial is concluded. Whether it ever needs to be addressed will depend both on the outcome of the trial and on Congress.

B. Ex Post Facto

Amici argue that any subsequent implementing legislation will violate the *ex post facto* clause. They contend that, at present, the maximum sentence that can be imposed on Mr. Pitera is life imprisonment. Any change in this situation will constitute an impermissible increase in punishment. The court disagrees. The maximum possible sen-

---

1984). 18 U.S.C. §3596, pending in Congress, provides for similar implementation. See H.R. 3371, 102nd Cong., 1st Sess. (1991), reprinted in H.R. Conf. Rep. No. 405, 102nd Cong., 1st Sess. 9 (1991).

tence that can presently be imposed upon the defendant is death. Indeed, §848(l) requires a court to impose such a sentence if the jury recommends it....

The fact that such a sentence cannot presently be implemented does not mean that subsequently enacted procedures will violate the *ex post facto* clause. Congress, in enacting §848(e)(1)(A), has already served plain notice on those who would commit intentional murders in connection with significant drug dealing that they face a possible sentence of death. Thus, Mr. Pitera had fair warning of the consequences of his conduct at the time he allegedly committed the Leone/Stern homicides.

In *Dobbert v. Florida*, 432 U.S. 282 (1977), the Supreme Court held that such fair warning was sufficient to defeat an *ex post facto* challenge.... The Supreme Court held that the original statute adequately served "fair warning" upon defendant of the state's intent to punish murder with a sentence of death. Thus, statutory changes that do not increase "the quantum of punishment attached to the crime," but that simply specify the methods by which an imposed sentence is effected, do not implicate the *ex post facto* clause.

Amici suggest that subsequent implementing legislation may provide for means of execution that are themselves cruel and unusual. Should any implementing legislation be subject to an eighth amendment challenge, a defendant will be heard. This court cannot, however, engage in a speculative consideration of the issue.

Conclusion

For the reasons stated in this memorandum and order, the court finds (1) that the death penalty does not constitute cruel and unusual punishment in all cases, (2) that the capital statute here at issue does not risk arbitrary and capricious imposition of the death penalty, (3) that defendant was not arbitrarily and vindictively singled out for prosecution, and (4) that the present inability to implement a death sentence does not preclude capital prosecution. The motion challenging constitutionality is, therefore, denied.

Notes and Questions

1. *Pitera* was the first case in the Second Circuit in which the United States sought the death penalty pursuant to §848(e)(1). Ultimately Pitera, a white Mafia contract killer, was convicted of eight murders, three of which qualified as capital offenses. Nonetheless, Pitera received a life sentence from a New York jury. Other early cases brought by the Justice Department under section 848 include:

United States v. Cooper, where separate juries sitting in the Northern District of Illinois found defendants Alexander Cooper and Anthony Davis, two black Chicago gang members, guilty of violating 21 U.S.C. §848(e)(1)(A). Both juries declined to impose the death penalty. The defendants were instead each sentenced to life imprisonment. The trial court's opinion upholding the constitutionality of the death penalty statute is reported at 754 F. Supp. 617 (N.D. Ill. 1990).

United States v. Chandler, 90 CR 266 (1991), where a jury in the Northern District of Alabama found Ronald David Chandler, a white marijuana grower, guilty of violating 21 U.S.C. §848(e)(1)(A) and recommended the death penalty. Chandler ultimately was sentenced to death for the murder for hire of a subordinate in his drug ring.

United States v. Villarreal, 91 CR 004, where a jury sitting in the Eastern District of Texas found Hispanic defendants, Baldemar Villarreal and Reynaldo

Villarreal, guilty of violating 21 U.S.C. §848(e)(1)(B). The jury was not persuaded, however, of the presence of certain statutory aggravating factors required to impose the death penalty. Accordingly, Baldemar Villarreal was sentenced to life imprisonment while Reynaldo Villarreal was sentenced to 40 years imprisonment. Constitutional challenges were denied without opinion. The case was affirmed on appeal. 963 F.2d 725 (5th Cir. 1992).

United States v. Pretlow, where a trial in the District of New Jersey ended without a verdict after Bilal Pretlow, a young, black gang member, killed himself during trial. The trial court's opinion upholding the constitutionality of §848(e)(1)(A) is reported at 779 F. Supp. 758 (D.N.J. 1991).

United States v. Tipton, et al., 3-92-CR-68 (E.D. Va.), where three young, black crack dealers were sentenced to death for their roles in a series of eleven drug-related homicides. Defendants' death sentences were affirmed on appeal. *United States v. Tipton*, 90 F.3d 861 (4th Cir. 1996).

United States v. Hutching, Molina, McCullah et al., No. CR-032-S (E.D. Okla.), where two white and one Hispanic defendant were tried jointly in connection with the drug-related kidnapping and murder of a Muskogee, Oklahoma auto dealership employee. John McCullah, one of the white defendants, was sentenced to death. The other defendants received life sentences. McCullah's conviction was affirmed, but his case was remanded for a new sentencing hearing, *United States v. McCullah*, 76 F.3d 1087 (10th Cir. 1996), and he was resentenced to life in prison.

United States v. Juan Raul Garza, No. CR 93-0009 (S.D. Texas), where a Hispanic drug dealer was sentenced to death by a jury in connection with the murders of three local drug traffickers. Garza's death sentence was affirmed on appeal, *United States v. Garza*, 63 F.3d 1342 (5th Cir. 1995), and he was denied habeas relief which he sought pursuant to 28 U.S.C. §2255. *United States v. Garza*, 165 F.3d 312 (5th Cir. 1999). The Supreme Court denied certiorari in 1999, 528 U.S. 1006. Until convicted Oklahoma City bomber Timothy McVeigh waived his appeals and volunteered to be executed, many expected Garza to become the first federal prisoner executed since 1963. Garza was executed eight days after McVeigh in 2001.

2. As mentioned above, a federal jury in Alabama imposed the death penalty in *United States v. Chandler*. Defendant Ronald David Chandler appealed his conviction and sentence and, in 1993, the Eleventh Circuit considered whether the death penalty as established under the 1988 Anti-Drug Abuse Act, 21 U.S.C. §848, was constitutional. *United States v. Chandler*, 996 F.2d 1073 (11th Cir. 1993). The Eleventh Circuit upheld the constitutionality of the death penalty provisions of the Anti-Drug Abuse Act, concluding—as did Judge Raggi in *Pitera*—that the federal statute adequately narrowed the class of persons eligible for the death penalty even though one of the aggravating circumstances duplicates an element of the crime.

The Eleventh Circuit also addressed the jury's sentencing power under §848(k). Section 848(k) provides that the jury must weigh the aggravating and mitigating evidence to determine whether the death penalty should be imposed rather than a sentence of life imprisonment without the possibility of parole or some other lesser sentence. The Eleventh Circuit concluded that under §848(k), the jury has the sole power to sentence a defendant to death and, if the jury recommends the death sentence, the judge must impose it. If the jury does not recommend death, the judge imposes a sentence other than death. The jury does not have the authority to impose a lesser sentence. The court rejected Chandler's claim that this sentencing scheme violated the Fifth and Eighth Amendments.

In addition, Chandler challenged jury instructions (1) that, in the event that the jury did not recommend a sentence of death, the jury should not be concerned with what sentence he should receive, and (2) that the district judge would decide Chandler's sentence if the jury did not recommend death. Chandler contended that the district court violated §848(k) and the Fifth and Eighth Amendments by failing to specifically advise the jurors that if they did not return a sentence of death, the judge could impose a sentence of life imprisonment without the possibility of parole or some lesser sentence. The court rejected Chandler's argument and found that the judge's instructions were adequate under §848(k).

What do you think of the sentencing scheme under §848(k)? Was the Eleventh Circuit correct in concluding that the judge's instructions were adequate? What would the effect of specifically advising the jury that the defendant could be sentenced to life imprisonment without the possibility of parole be on the jury's decision-making process? Is this information important? Could the potential sentence of life imprisonment without the possibility of parole be construed as a mitigating circumstance that the jury must consider in deciding whether or not to impose a sentence of death? See *Turner v. Mississippi*, 573 So.2d 657 (Miss. 1990), *supra* chapter 9.

In one of his last acts before leaving office on January 20, 2001, President Clinton commuted Chandler's sentence because of doubts about Chandler's guilt.

3. *Pitera* addressed the federal death penalty statute's failure to provide a means for implementing executions. Since the decision in *Pitera*, regulations have been implemented which set out the manner in which one is to be executed under federal law. The execution protocol under 28 C.F.R. §§26.1–26.5 provides that the sentence of death imposed under the federal death penalty statutes shall be executed by a United States Marshal designated by the United States Marshal Service on a date and at a federal penal or correctional institution designated by the Director of the Federal Bureau of Prisons. Execution shall be by lethal injection. In 1999, the federal government opened its own death row facility, the United States Penitentiary at Terre Haute, Indiana. Regulations provide, "No officer or employee of the Department of Justice shall be required to be in attendance at or to participate in any execution if such attendance or participation is contrary to the moral or religious convictions of the officer or employee."

4. Under the federal death penalty statutes and the newly crafted procedures governing the implementation of execution, there exists the possibility that an individual could be convicted and sentenced to death in a state which currently does not provide for the death penalty under state law. Is there a potential conflict between the interests of the state and the federal government? Could a state prohibit the infliction and implementation of the death penalty on its soil?

Note on Race and the Federal Death Penalty

Between November 1988, when President Reagan signed the Anti-Drug Abuse Act into law, and October 21, 1993, the Justice Department authorized federal prosecutors to seek the death penalty under federal law against thirty defendants. Of these, roughly seventy-three percent were black. Half of the remaining twenty-seven percent were Mexican-Americans. Statement of Bryan Stevenson and David Bruck before the U.S. House of Representatives Committee on the Judiciary, Subcommittee on Crime and Criminal Justice, October 21, 1993.

According to a 2000 Justice Department study, of the 682 potential federal death penalty cases United States attorneys forwarded to Justice for review between 1995 and July 2000, 20 percent of the defendants were white and 80 percent were minorities. United States attorneys recommended the death penalty be sought for 183 defendants, 26 percent of them white and 74 percent minorities. The study found that minorities are over-represented in the federal death penalty system, as both victims and defendants, relative to the general population. U.S. Dep't of Justice, "The Federal Death Penalty System: A Statistical Survey 1988–2000" (2000). "Sadly, the same is true of the entire criminal justice system, both state and federal," Attorney General Janet Reno said. "This should be of concern to us all."

Kevin McNally, Federal Death Penalty Resource Counsel, observed that, as of January 26, 2004, Attorney General Ashcroft had approved a capital prosecution for 103 defendants: 26 whites (25%), 56 blacks (54%), 18 Hispanics (17%), 2 Asians (2%), and 1 Native American (1%). Of 312 defendants approved for capital prosecution by three Attorneys General, 233 (75%) are members of minority groups. Of twenty-six prisoners then on federal death row, "nineteen" (73%) "are non-white." "Eighteen (69%) of the twenty-six federal death row inmates are black." McNally, "Race and the Federal Death Penalty: A Non-Existent Problem Gets Worse," 53 DePaul L. Rev. 1615 (2004).

Thus far, the federal government has executed only three prisoners under the revised federal death penalty statutes: Timothy McVeigh (Caucasian) and Juan Garza (Latino) in 2001; and Louis Jones (African American) in 2003.

2. Political Assassinations

18 U.S.C. §1751. Presidential and Presidential staff assassination, kidnaping, and assault; penalties

(a) Whoever kills (1) any individual who is the President of the United States, the President-elect, the Vice President, or, if there is no Vice President, the officer next in the order of succession to the Office of the President of the United States, the Vice President-elect, or any person who is acting as President under the Constitution and laws of the United States, or (2) any person appointed under section 105(a)(2)(A) of title 3 employed in the Executive Office of the President or appointed under section 106(a)(1)(A) of title 3 employed in the Office of the Vice President, shall be punished as provided by sections 1111 and 1112 of this title.

(b) Whoever kidnaps any individual designated in subsection (a) of this section shall be punished (1) by imprisonment for any term of years or for life, or (2) by death or imprisonment for any term of years or for life, if death results to such individual.

(c) Whoever attempts to kill or kidnap any individual designated in subsection (a) of this section shall be punished by imprisonment for any term of years or for life.

(d) If two or more persons conspire to kill or kidnap any individual designated in subsection (a) of this section and one or more of such persons do any act to effect the object of the conspiracy, each shall be punished (1) by imprisonment for any term of years or for life, or (2) by death or imprisonment for any term of years or for life, if death results to such individual.

18 U.S.C. §351. Congressional, Cabinet, and Supreme Court assassination, kidnaping, and assault; penalties

(a) Whoever kills any individual who is a Member of Congress or a Member-of-Congress-elect, a member of the executive branch of the Government who is the head, or a person nominated to be head during the pendency of such nomination, of a department listed in section 101 of title 5 or the second ranking official in such department, the Director (or a person nominated to be Director during the pendency of such nomination) or Deputy Director of Central Intelligence, a major Presidential or Vice Presidential candidate (as defined in section 3056 of this title), or a Justice of the United States, as defined in section 451 of title 28, or a person nominated to be a Justice of the United States, during the pendency of such nomination, shall be punished as provided by sections 1111 and 1112 of this title.

(b) Whoever kidnaps any individual designated in subsection (a) of this section shall be punished (1) by imprisonment for any term of years or for life, or (2) by death or imprisonment for any term of years or for life, if death results to such individual.

(c) Whoever attempts to kill or kidnap any individual designated in subsection (a) of this section shall be punished by imprisonment for any term of years or for life.

(d) If two or more persons conspire to kill or kidnap any individual designated in subsection (a) of this section and one or more of such persons do any act to effect the object of the conspiracy, each shall be punished (1) by imprisonment for any term of years or for life, or (2) by death or imprisonment for any term of years or for life, if death results to such individual.

Note

Would-be presidential assassin John W. Hinckley was charged under §1751(c) for his March 30, 1981 attack on President Ronald Reagan. See *United States v. Hinckley*, 525 F. Supp. 1342 (D.D.C. 1981).

3. Treason and Espionage

18 U.S.C. §2381. Treason

Whoever, owing allegiance to the United States, levies war against them or adheres to their enemies, giving them aid and comfort within the United States or elsewhere, is guilty of treason and shall suffer death, or shall be imprisoned not less than five years and fined not less than $10,000; and shall be incapable of holding any office under the United States.

18 U.S.C. §794. Gathering or delivering defense information to aid foreign government

(a) Whoever, with intent or reason to believe that it is to be used to the injury of the United States or to the advantage of a foreign nation, communicates, delivers, or transmits, or attempts to communicate, deliver, or transmit, to any foreign government, or to any faction or party or military or naval force within a foreign country, whether recognized or unrecognized by the United States, or to any representative, officer, agent, employee, subject, or citizen thereof, either directly or indirectly, any document, writing, code book, signal book, sketch, photograph, photographic negative, blueprint, plan, map, model, note, instrument, appliance, or information relating to the national defense, shall be punished by death or by imprisonment for any term of years or for life, *except that the sentence of death shall not be imposed unless the jury or, if there is no jury, the court, further finds that the offense resulted in the identification by a foreign power (as defined in §101(a) of the Foreign Intelligence Surveillance Act of 1978) of an individual acting as an agent of the United States and consequently in the death of that individual, or directly concerned nuclear weaponry, military spacecraft or satellites, early warning systems, or other means of defense or retaliation against large-scale attack; war plans; communications intelligence or cryptographic information; or any other major weapons system or major element of defense strategy.* (Emphasis added.)

(b) Whoever, in time of war, with intent that the same shall be communicated to the enemy, collects, records, publishes, or communicates, or attempts to elicit any information with respect to the movement, numbers, description, condition, or disposition of any of the Armed Forces, ships, aircraft, or war materials of the United States, or with respect to the plans or conduct, or supposed plans or conduct of any naval or military operations, or with respect to any works or measures undertaken for or connected with, or intended for the fortification or defense of any place, or any other information relating to the public defense, which might be useful to the enemy, shall be punished by death or by imprisonment for any term of years or for life.

Note on 18 U.S.C. §794

The italicized language in §794(a) was added when Congress amended the statute in 1994. As you read *United States v. Harper*, a case decided ten years before the statute was amended, consider whether the language added to §794(a) in 1994 sufficiently addresses the problems identified by the Ninth Circuit Court of Appeals.

United States v. Harper
729 F.2d 1216 (9th Cir. 1984)

REINHARDT, Circuit Judge:

James Durward Harper is charged with obtaining and selling national defense information to Polish agents in violation of United States espionage statutes. In the district court, the government and Harper agreed that the death penalty provision of the espionage statutes involved is unconstitutional. The district judge nevertheless issued a pretrial order in which he held the relevant death penalty provision constitutional. Harper appeals the order, as well as a subsequent amendment to the order, and also seeks a writ of mandamus directing the district court to vacate the order. On appeal, both parties continue to assert that the death penalty provision of the espionage statutes is unconstitutional. However, the government argues that we do not have jurisdiction over the appeals and that this is not an appropriate case in which to issue a writ of mandamus. We conclude that we lack jurisdiction over the appeals because no final judgment is involved. We hold, however, that this is an appropriate case in which to exercise our mandamus jurisdiction. We further hold that the death penalty provision of the Espionage Act is unconstitutional and void. Accordingly, we direct the district court to vacate its pretrial order.

FACTS

Harper is a defendant in a criminal case set for trial before the United States District Court for the Northern District of California a few weeks hence. He is accused of violating 18 U.S.C. §794 (1982) by obtaining secret national defense information and knowingly and wilfully transmitting it to an officer of the Polish Intelligence Service with intent and reason to believe that the information would be used to the injury of the United States and to the advantage of the Polish People's Republic and the Union of Soviet Socialist Republics. He allegedly received $250,000 from the Polish government for the information he conveyed.

The Espionage Act, 18 U.S.C. §§791–99 (1982), provides that a person convicted of violating section 794 "shall be punished by death or by imprisonment for any term of years or for life." However, the Act contains no guidelines to control the sentencing authority's discretion in determining whether the death penalty is to be imposed.

At Harper's arraignment, the district court asked both parties for briefs on the applicability of the death penalty provision. Both parties took the position that section 794's death penalty provision had been rendered unconstitutional by *Furman v. Georgia*, 408 U.S. 238 (1972), and its progeny.

Subsequently, the district court issued an "Order Re Penalty Provision of 18 U.S.C. §794," in which he determined that the death penalty provision was constitutional. His purpose in issuing the order was two-fold: "(1) to provide the defendant with certain knowledge of the penalties which may be imposed upon conviction; and (2) to determine whether the additional procedural safeguards afforded defendants in capital cases are warranted in the case at hand." The court first determined that capital punishment for acts of espionage is not uniformly disproportionate to the severity of the offense and is therefore not unconstitutional *per se*. It then proceeded to determine whether the specific provision in section 794 was valid. The court recognized that the eighth amendment requires that a sentencing authority's discretion to impose the death penalty must be "'suitably directed and limited so as to minimize the risk of wholly arbitrary and capricious action,'" and it acknowledged that "the sentencing discretion afforded it by section 794 necessitates the formulation of sentencing guidelines which will ensure the reliable imposition of punishment." The court, however, found section 794 constitutional by reading the section as delegating to district courts faced with death penalty trials the duty to formulate and apply the necessary guidelines....

III. The Constitutionality of Section 794's Death Penalty Provision

The district court recognized that, after *Furman* and its progeny, a sentencing authority's discretion to impose the death penalty "must be suitably directed and limited so as to minimize the risk of wholly arbitrary and capricious action." *Gregg v. Georgia*, 428 U.S. 153, 189 (1976). The district court believed, however, that the constitutional problems with the statute would be cured if it formulated the necessary guidelines limiting its discretion itself, and it proposed to do so when the sentencing stage was reached. In this regard, the district court clearly erred.

In *Furman*, the Supreme Court struck down a death penalty statute that left the decision whether to impose the death penalty to the unfettered discretion of the sentencing authority. In *Gregg v. Georgia*, 428 U.S. 153 (1976), the Court upheld the constitutionality of the revised Georgia death penalty statute because the discretion of the sentencing authority to impose the death penalty had by then been suitably limited and guided by the legislature. The question presented by this case is whether the guidelines plainly required by *Gregg* and its companion cases must be contained in the statute or may be formulated by the sentencing judge at the time of sentencing. Although this is a question of first impression, the cases cited above leave no room for the argument that the guidelines may be formulated by the judge at the time of sentencing or at any other time.

First, it would certainly be anomalous to hold that the guidelines, which are required in order to limit the discretion of a sentencing authority, may be supplied by the sentencing authority itself. Whenever the judge is the sentencing authority, the guidelines would, under the district court's theory, be no limitation at all. The requirement that the discretion be "suitably limited and directed" clearly requires an *external* limitation.

Moreover, the Court's opinions compel the conclusion that, whether the sentencing authority is the judge or the jury, the guidelines must come from Congress, not from the courts. *Gregg* is replete with references to the peculiarly legislative character of sentencing determinations, and the particularly limited role of judges in this area....

... [I]n finding Georgia's revised procedures constitutional, the Court emphasized that the guidelines were statutory: "[Under the revised Georgia procedures, the jury] must find a *statutory* aggravating circumstance before recommending a sentence of death." The Court has thus plainly required that guidelines be expressly articulated *by the legislature* in the statute authorizing the death penalty.

The conclusion that the Constitution requires legislative guidelines in death penalty cases is thus inescapable. That is the position not only of petitioner, but also of the government, whose brief on this issue in the district court stated that section 794's death penalty provision is "unenforceable and void because it sets forth no *legislated* guidelines to control the fact-finder's discretion...." The Department of Justice has long been of the view that *Furman* rendered section 794's death penalty provision unconstitutional. Moreover, the Senate has recently passed a bill, supported by the Justice Department, that would authorize the imposition of the death penalty for certain crimes, including espionage.

In light of the above, we believe it clear that the death penalty provision of the espionage statutes is unconstitutional. It cannot be saved by judicial formulation of the missing, but essential, statutory guidelines.

... On the merits, we hold that section 794's death penalty provision is unconstitutional and void. Accordingly a writ directing the district court to vacate its "Order re Penalty Provision of 18 U.S.C. §794" should issue. It is so ordered.

Notes and Question

1. As noted above, Congress amended §794(a) in 1994 by adding the following language:

> except that the sentence of death shall not be imposed unless the jury or, if there is no jury, the court, further finds that the offense resulted in the identification by a foreign power (as defined in §101(a) of the Foreign Intelligence Surveillance Act of 1978) of an individual acting as an agent of the United States and consequently in the death of that individual, or directly concerned nuclear weaponry, military spacecraft or satellites, early warning systems, or other means of defense or retaliation against large-scale attack; war plans; communications intelligence or cryptographic information; or any other major weapons system or major element of defense strategy.

Does this language cure to any extent the defect of the statute identified in *Harper*? In addition, 18 U.S.C. §3592 sets out the aggravating factors applicable to espionage.

2. In 1951, Ethel and Julius Rosenberg were convicted and sentenced to death for conspiring to violate 18 U.S.C. §794. In sentencing the Rosenbergs to die in Sing Sing's electric chair, Judge Frank Kaufman remarked: "I consider your crime worse than murder.... I believe your conduct in putting into the hands of the Russians the A-bomb ... has already caused, in my opinion, the Communist aggression in Korea, with the resultant casualties exceeding 50,000, and ... millions more innocent people may pay the price of your treason...." Judge Kaufman later refused to modify the sentence. In so holding, he commented:

> At the time of the imposition of the sentences in this case I pointed out that the crime for which these defendants stood convicted was worse than murder. The distinction is based on reason. The murderer kills only his victim while the traitor violates all members of the group to which he owes his allegiance.

United States v. Rosenberg, 109 F. Supp. 108, 110 (S.D.N.Y. 1953). Julius and Ethel Rosenberg were executed on June 19, 1953, during the height of McCarthyism and mass anti-Communist hysteria. For an interesting discussion of the Rosenbergs' case, see J.H. Sharlitt, *Fatal Error: The Miscarriage of Justice that Sealed the Fate of the Rosenbergs* (1989), in which the author argues that the Rosenbergs were tried, convicted and sentenced under the wrong statute.

2. For other post-*Furman* cases addressing the constitutionality and application of the death penalty provision of §794, see *United States v. Hemlich*, 521 F. Supp. 1246 (M.D. Fla. 1981); *United States v. Pollard*, 959 F.2d 1011 (D.C. Cir. 1992).

3. In 2001, F.B.I. agent Robert Hanssen was indicted on 21 charges of conspiracy and espionage, including 14 charges that could result in his facing the death penalty. Although his crime was described as "the worst intelligence disaster in U.S. history," Hanssen avoided the death penalty by agreeing to cooperate with federal prosecutors and was sentenced in 2002 to life without the possibility of parole.

The Problem of "Zombie Statutes"

Recall that the Court in *Furman v. Georgia*, 408 U.S. 238 (1972), invalidated state death penalty statutes which gave the factfinder unguided discretion to decide whether to impose life or death for capital crimes. Federal capital statutes then in effect suffered from the same constitutional defect. Thus, any federal death penalty statute that was not passed (or amended) since *Furman* was likely to be unconstitutional. For example, the general federal murder statute which provides for the death penalty (18 U.S.C. §1111) was declared unenforceable by the United States Department of Justice. After *Furman*, Congress quickly acted to amend the federal kidnapping statute to delete its death penalty provisions. 18 U.S.C. §1201. Similarly, Congress amended the Air Piracy Statute, 49 U.S.C. §1472, to provide the procedural safeguards mandated by *Furman*.

The United States Attorney's Manual, revised in 1988, acknowledged the problem with pre-*Furman* statutes which had not been amended.

> [T]here are some death penalty provisions which are so broad that no reasonable argument could be made that they would survive an Eighth Amendment challenge. For example ... the general federal murder provision, 18 U.S.C. §1111, [is unconstitutional because it] gives the jury unguided discretion as to which murders will be punished by the death penalty.

U.S. Attorney's Manual, §9-10.010 (1988). Nonetheless, the Manual maintained that "the death penalty may be permissible for certain crimes in addition to aircraft hijacking. There are arguments, never considered by the Supreme Court, that imposition of the death penalty for narrowly drawn offenses against the United States and its officials remain viable under the rationale of *Jurek v. Texas*, 428 U.S. 262 (1976)." The Justice Department's theory was that each federal judge called upon to preside over capital murder prosecutions brought under the pre-*Furman* federal murder statutes may construct his or her own capital sentencing provisions. Using this theory, on March 25, 1991, the Justice Department authorized the capital murder prosecution of a defendant charged with murdering a federal witness. *United States v. Louie and Lebron*, (E.D. Pa. No. 91-00016). A death-qualified jury was empanelled. The case did not reach the sentencing phase because Lebron was acquitted. The Justice Department pressed its theory again in *United States v. Woolard and Bruner*, 981 F.2d 756 (5th Cir. 1993). This time the trial court rejected the government's invitation to fashion constitutional capital sentencing procedures, holding that to do so "would be a usurpation of a legislative function." On appeal, the United States Court of Appeals for the Fifth Circuit agreed. *United States v. Woolard and Bruner*, 981 F.2d 756 (5th Cir. 1993).

Notes and Questions

1. Is there any coherent rationale for exempting the federal death penalty statutes from the requirements of *Furman*?

2. If the federal death penalty statutes were deficient under *Furman*, couldn't they be cured by judicially imposed sentencing guidelines which comport with the Fifth and Eighth Amendments? Or are legislative guidelines constitutionally required? See *United States v. Harper*, *supra* this chapter.

3. For a discussion of the federal death penalty generally, and the drug kingpin statute in particular, see Jordan, "Death For Drug Related Killings: Revival of the Federal Death Penalty," 67 Chi.-Kent L. Rev. 79 (1992); and Acosta, "Imposing the Death Penalty Upon Drug Kingpins," 27 Harv. J. On Legis. 596 (1990).

4. Prior to the resumption of federal executions in 2001, the last federal prisoner executed in the United States was Victor Feguer. Feguer was hanged in Iowa on March 15, 1963 for kidnapping and murder. For an opinion denying relief to Feguer authored by then Circuit Judge Harry Blackmun, see *Feguer v. United States*, 302 F.2d 214 (8th Cir. 1962). An analysis of Justice Blackmun's death penalty jurisprudence is presented in Coyne, "Marking the Progress of a Humane Justice: Harry Blackmun's Death Penalty Epiphany," 43 Kansas L. Rev. 367 (1995).

5. The Federal Death Penalty Act of 1994, discussed immediately below, was designed to bring federal death penalty statutes into conformity with *Furman* and *Gregg*.

The Federal Death Penalty Act of 1994[1]
Randall Coyne

In September 1994, President Clinton signed into law the Violent Crime Control and Law Enforcement Act of 1994. Title VI of this omnibus crime package — the Federal Death Penalty Act of 1994 — dramatically expanded the number of federal of-

---

1. The author gratefully acknowledges the help and encouragement of David Bruck, Federal Death Penalty Resource Counsel.

fenses punishable by death. As demonstrated below, this expansion was accomplished by (1) creating new federal crimes which are punishable by death; (2) adding death as a sentencing option to recently-created federal offenses; and (3) resurrecting dormant, pre-*Furman*[2] federal death penalty statutes by purporting to cure their constitutional deficiencies.

Newly-Created Federal Crimes Punishable by Death

Newly-created federal offenses which are punishable by death include:

*Drive-by shootings which result in death (18 U.S.C. §36);

*Drug trafficking in large quantities, even where no death results (18 U.S.C. §3591(b)(1));

*Attempting, authorizing or advising the killing of any public officer, juror or witness in a case involving a continuing criminal enterprise—regardless of whether such a killing actually occurs (18 U.S.C. §3591(b)(2));

*Murder at a United States international airport (18 U.S.C. §36);

*Murder by an escaped federal prisoner (18 U.S.C. §1120);

*Murder by a federal life-term prisoner (18 U.S.C. §1120);

*Murder by gun during federal crimes of violence and drug trafficking offenses (18 U.S.C. §924(i));

*Murder involving firearm or other dangerous weapon during attack on federal facilities (18 U.S.C. §930(c));

*Murder of federal jurors and court officers (18 U.S.C. §1503(b));

*Murder of a federal witness, victim or informant (18 U.S.C. §1513(a));

*Murder of a state correctional officer by a federal prisoner (18 U.S.C. §1121);

*Murder of state or local officials engaged in assisting federal law enforcement officials (18 U.S.C. §1121);

*Murder of a United States national abroad (18 U.S.C. §1118);

*Murder of United States national abroad by terrorism (18 U.S.C. §2332);

*Murder within the special maritime and territorial jurisdiction of the United States (18 U.S.C. §§2280, 2281);

*Smuggling aliens where death results (8 U.S.C. §1324(a)(B)(iv));

---

2. In *Furman v. Georgia*, 408 U.S. 238 (1972), a majority of the Supreme Court struck down the death penalty laws throughout the United States. According to one estimate, 613 prisoners awaiting execution throughout the country were spared when *Furman* resulted in the commutation of their sentences to life. Marquart & Sorenson, "A National Study of the *Furman*-Commuted Inmates: Assessing the Threat to Society From Capital Offenders," 23 Loyola L.A. L. Rev 5, 11 (1989).

Three members of the *Furman* majority, Justices William Douglas, Potter Stewart and Byron White, concluded that imposing and carrying out the death penalty in the cases before the Court constituted cruel and unusual punishment in violation of the Eighth and Fourteenth Amendments. The two other members of the majority, Justice William Brennan and Justice Thurgood Marshall, ruled that the death penalty was unconstitutional in all cases. All members of the majority agreed that the fatal flaw was the lack of standards to guide jurors in deciding whether a defendant should live or die. As Justice Stewart observed, "These death sentences are cruel and unusual in the way that being struck by lightning is cruel and unusual.... If any basis can be discerned for the selection of these few to be sentenced to die, it is the constitutionally impermissible basis of race."

*Torture resulting in death outside the United States (18 U.S.C. §2340(A));

*Using weapons of mass destruction (for example, biological weapons or poison gas) which results in death (18 U.S.C. §2332a).

Two newly-minted capital statutes—ostensibly aimed at escalating the federal government's war against drugs—raise serious constitutional questions. Both provide death as a sanction for crimes which do not involve homicide.

Continuing criminal enterprise-related trafficking in large quantities of drugs is punishable by death under 18 U.S.C. §3591(b)(1). Given the federal criminal law's disparate treatment of powder and crack cocaine, relatively small amounts of the latter would subject a trafficker to the death penalty. According to David Bruck of the Federal Death Penalty Resource Center, 300 kilograms of powder cocaine would be required before a trafficker faced capital charges. Conversely, a mere three kilograms crack cocaine would justify capital charges against the trafficker.

The second capital offense which does not require a homicide is set forth in 18 U.S.C. §3591(b)(2). That statute authorizes death for a drug kingpin who "directs, advises, authorizes, or assists" another who attempts to kill a public officer, juror, or witness—regardless of whether such a killing actually takes place.

The United States Department of Justice advised Congress that these non-homicidal death penalty laws were likely unconstitutional under *Coker v. Georgia*, 433 U.S. 544 (1977) (death penalty unconstitutional for the rape of an adult woman). Undeterred, both houses of Congress passed these provisions by lopsided margins. Perhaps to forestall invalidation under *Coker*, Congress fashioned a special list of aggravating circumstances which would render a trafficker death-eligible under §3591(b). These include:

(1) previous conviction of an offense for which death or life imprisonment was authorized;
(2) previous conviction of other serious offenses;
(3) previous serious drug felony conviction;
(4) use of a firearm in furthering the enterprise or in committing the offense;
(5) distributing drugs to a person under 21 years old;
(6) distributing drugs near a school;
(7) using minors in trafficking;
(8) adulterating the drug with a lethal substance; or
(9) any other aggravating factor for which notice has been given.

18 U.S.C. §3592(d).

Existing Federal Crimes Made Capital

Existing federal crimes for which death was added as a sentencing option include:

*Carjacking which results in death (18 U.S.C. §2119);

*Child molestation committed within federal territorial jurisdiction which results in death (18 U.S.C. §2245);

*Genocide (18 U.S.C. §1091);

*Hostage taking which results in death (18 U.S.C. §1203);

*Murder for hire involving interstate travel or the use of interstate facilities (18 U.S.C. §1958);

*Murder for the purpose of aiding racketeering activity (18 U.S.C. §1959);

*Sexual abuse committed within federal territorial jurisdiction resulting in death (18 U.S.C. §2245);

*Violating a person's federally-protected rights based on race, religion or national origin, where death results (18 U.S.C. §§241, 242, 245, 247).

Reviving the Zombie Statutes

In addition, the law resurrected the death penalty provisions of several pre-*Furman*[3] federal statutes which, because they were never amended along the lines suggested in *Gregg v. Georgia*, 428 U.S. 153 (1976), were widely believed to be unconstitutional. Congress revived these "zombie"[4] statutes in precisely the same way various states repaired their statutes to conform to the dictates of *Furman* and *Gregg*—by guiding the sentencer's discretion to decide whether to impose life or death. These revitalized statutes include:

*Aircraft hijacking which results in death (49 U.S.C. §1473);

*Assassination of the President or Vice-President (18 U.S.C. §1751(a));

*Assassination of Members of Congress, Cabinet Members, Supreme Court Justices, and major presidential or vice presidential candidates (18 U.S.C. §351);

*Destroying aircraft, motor vehicles or their facilities where death results (18 U.S.C. §34);

*Destroying federal property with explosives or by arson where death results (18 U.S.C. §844(f));

*Destroying property used in interstate commerce with explosives or by arson in a manner resulting in death (18 U.S.C. §844(i));

*Espionage (18 U.S.C. §794);

*First degree murder on federal land or federal property (18 U.S.C. §1111);

*Kidnapping which results in death (18 U.S.C. §1201);

*Mailing harmful articles (for example, explosives) where death results (18 U.S.C. §1716);

*Murder of federal law enforcement officials or employees (18 U.S.C. §1114);

*Murder of foreign officials or internationally-protected people on United States soil (18 U.S.C. §1116);

*Robbery of a federally-insured bank where death results (18 U.S.C. §2113(e));

*Train sabotage which results in death (18 U.S.C. §1992);

*Transporting or receiving explosives with the intent to kill in a manner resulting in death (18 U.S.C. §844(d));

*Treason (18 U.S.C. §2381).

Procedures in Federal Capital Cases

When the Supreme Court in 1972 struck down Georgia's death penalty statute in *Furman v. Georgia*, 408 U.S. 238 (1972), the Court identified a critical flaw in Georgia's law: it vested unfettered discretion in the decisionmaker in choosing whether to sen-

---

3. See *supra* note 2 and accompanying text.

4. David Bruck, Federal Death Penalty Resource Counsel, should be credited with coining the marvelous expression, "zombie statutes." Although technically "dead" after *Furman*, these unconstitutional statutes were, until 1994, never amended nor ever deleted from the United States Code.

tence a defendant to death or to some lesser punishment. Accordingly, the Court invalidated all capital sentencing procedures — state and federal — which created a substantial risk that death would be imposed in an arbitrary or capricious manner. Consequently, *Furman* invalidated the death sentences of all inmates awaiting execution in thirty states and the District of Columbia, regardless of whether the death sentence was imposed under state or federal law.

Screening Protocols

Federal prosecutors who wish to file capital charges are required by Department of Justice regulations to follow protocols established by Attorney General Reno in 1995. "The so-called replacement 'blue sheet' for the United States Attorney's Manual, Section 9-10.000 (Capital Crimes) created a three step bureaucratic process involving: (1) the local decision (sometimes made by a U.S. Attorney upon the recommendation of a local death penalty review committee); (2) review by the Attorney General's Capital Case Review Committee; and finally, (3) the decision by the Attorney General." [5] The Attorney General has the power to seek the death penalty, even though the local U.S. Attorney has recommended otherwise. *United States v. Cooper*, 91 F. Supp.2d 90 (D.D.C. 2000); *United States v. Lee*, 89 F. Supp.2d 1017 (E.D. Ark. 2000).

Race-Blind Case Screening?

The Justice Department claims that it carries out its capital case review process in a "race-blind" manner. The U.S. Attorney's Office "does not provide information about the race or ethnicity of the defendant to review committee members, to attorneys from the criminal division's Capital Case Unit to assist the review committee, or to the Attorney General." [6] Nonetheless, information regarding race is sometimes provided by defense counsel arguing against a death penalty prosecution, and can sometimes be discovered from the paperwork normally provided by the U.S. Attorney's Office as attachments to their submissions. Moreover, as Federal Death Penalty Resource Counsel Kevin McNally points out, "It is not hard to guess the racial or ethnic background of the defendants whose indictments charge members of the 'Bloods' gang, the Cosa Nostra,' or the 'Latin Kings.' As such, DOJ's insistence that the process, or the Attorney General's decision, is 'race blind' seems perhaps more political cover than practical reality." [7] And, of course, the decision at the most important stage — the initial selection of defendants by federal law enforcement and local prosecutors — is not "race blind."

An Improved Right to Counsel

Buried at the very end of the Federal Death Penalty Act of 1994 (FDPA) is a short provision that may dramatically improve the quality of representation available to defendants facing federal capital charges. Section 60026 represents the first substantive amendment to the federal counsel statute since 1790. 18 U.S.C. §3005 is amended in three ways. First, at a minimum two lawyers must be appointed to represent federal capital defendants. Second, at least one lawyer appointed in a federal capital case must

---

5. McNally, "Race and the Federal Death Penalty: A Non-existent Problem Gets Worse," 53 DePaul L. Rev. 1615 (2004) (hereinafter, "A Non-existent Problem"). For a suggestion that the Justice Department decisions endorsing capital charges under the Anti-Drug Abuse Act of 1988 are tainted with racial bias, see *supra* pp. 225–226, 966–967.

6. U.S. Dep't of Justice, The Federal Death Penalty System: Supplementary Data, Analysis, and Revised Protocol for Capital Case Review (2001).

7. McNally, "A Non-existent Problem," at 1619.

have experience in capital defense work. Finally, before making any appointments, the court must consider the Federal Public Defender's recommendation regarding which counsel are qualified for appointment in capital cases.

Notice of Intent to Seek Death

Under §3593(a), the government is required to inform the defendant of its intent to seek death within a reasonable time before trial or before the court accepts defendant's guilty plea. This provision is consistent with *Lankford v. Idaho*, 500 U.S. 110 (1991). After Bryan Lankford was found guilty of two counts of first degree murder, the trial judge required the state to provide notice whether it would seek the death penalty. The prosecutor filed a document indicating that the state would not seek the death penalty. Consequently, during the sentencing hearing defense counsel and the prosecutor argued about the merits of concurrent or consecutive sentences and fixed or indeterminate sentence terms. Nonetheless, the judge sentenced Lankford to death.

In a 5–4 decision, the United States Supreme Court reversed. Due process was violated, according to the Court, because the trial judge's silence, after the state filed its notice not to seek death, concealed from the parties the principal issues to be decided at the hearing. Thus the procedure was tainted by an impermissible risk that the adversary process may have malfunctioned.

Section 3593 of the FDPA goes well beyond *Lankford* in one respect: the statute requires that notice of the state's intent to seek death be provided to the defendant and to the court *before trial or plea. Lankford* can be read narrowly to require only that notice be given before sentencing of the state's intent to seek death. In addition to requiring that the government announce its intent to seek the defendant's death, section 3593 requires the government to list the aggravating factors that it proposes to prove to justify a sentence of death. 18 U.S.C. §3593(a)(2).

Sentencing Procedures

The FDPA encompasses sentencing procedures crafted to eliminate constitutional inadequacies identified in *Furman* and remedied in subsequent statutes passed by Georgia,[8] Florida,[9] and Texas.[10] First and foremost, the federal law was amended to provide enumerated aggravating factors (which may call for a sentence of death) and mitigating factors (which may call for a sentence less than death).[11] Clearly these provisions are intended to channel the sentencer's discretion in choosing among various sentencing alternatives.

Relaxed Evidentiary Standard

The FDPA permits the jury to consider any information relevant to the sentence, subject only to exclusion if the danger of creating unfair prejudice, confusing the issues, or misleading the jury outweighs its probative value. 18 U.S.C. §3593(c). Because the statute speaks in terms of "information" and not "evidence," hearsay statements which would be inadmissible under the Federal Rules of Evidence may be introduced on behalf of—or against—the defendant. This obviously raises due

---

8. Gregg v. Georgia, 428 U.S. 153 (1976).

9. Proffitt v. Florida, 428 U.S. 242 (1976).

10. Jurek v. Texas, 428 U.S. 262 (1976).

11. Compare 18 U.S.C. §3592(a) (mitigating factors) with 18 U.S.C. §3592(b) (aggravating factors for espionage and treason); 18 U.S.C. §3592(c) (aggravating factors for homicide); and 18 U.S.C. §3592(d) (aggravating factors for drug offenses).

process concerns of reliability and implicates the Sixth Amendment rights of confrontation and cross-examination.

Mitigating Evidence

Additional procedural safeguards may be found in 18 U.S.C. §3593. That statute requires a separate sentencing hearing to determine whether death is appropriate and entitles the defendant to a 12-member sentencing jury. 18 U.S.C. §3593(b). The defendant bears the burden of establishing any mitigating factor by a preponderance of the evidence. 18 U.S.C. §3593(d). Mitigating factors set forth in the statute include:

(1) impaired capacity;

(2) duress;

(3) relatively minor participation in the underlying offense;

(4) the existence of equally culpable defendants who will not be sentenced to death;

(5) absence of a significant prior history of other criminal conduct;

(6) the defendant committed the offense under severe mental or emotional disturbance;

(7) the victim consented to the criminal conduct which resulted in the victim's death.

18 U.S.C. §3592(a).

In addition, consistent with *Lockett v. Ohio*, 438 U.S. 586 (1978), the defendant is permitted to offer as mitigating evidence "other factors in the defendant's background, record, or character, or any other circumstance of the offense that mitigate against imposition of the death sentence." 18 U.S.C. §3592(a)(8).

Aggravating Evidence

The government bears the burden of establishing aggravating factors beyond a reasonable doubt. 18 U.S.C. §3593(d). There are three different sets of aggravating circumstances: those for espionage and treason (§3592(b)); those for homicide (§3592(c)); and those for non-homicide drug offenses (§3592(d)). Moreover, "a finding with respect to any aggravating factor must be unanimous. If no aggravating factor set forth in section 3592 is found to exist, the court shall impose a sentence other than death." 18 U.S.C. §3593(d). Conversely, mitigating circumstances need only be found by a single juror in order to be established.

Victim Impact Evidence

Victim impact evidence may affect a federal prosecutor's decision to seek the death penalty. Although the new law stops short of listing victim impact evidence as a category of aggravating evidence, it achieves much the same result in §3593. Section 3593(a) provides that, in deciding whether a sentence of death is justified, the government may consider the effect of the offense on the victim and the victim's family. Oral testimony and victim impact statements are permitted. However, if the government intends to rely on victim impact evidence, it must file with the court and serve on the defendant written notice.

Weighing Required

Once aggravating and mitigating circumstances are established, the sentence is determined by weighing. Section 3593(d) directs the sentencer to:

consider whether all the aggravating factor or factors found to exist sufficiently outweigh all the mitigating factor or factors found to exist to justify a sentence of death.

The United States Constitution does not proscribe a specific method or standard for weighing aggravating and mitigating circumstances. *Zant v. Stephens*, 462 U.S. 862 (1983). Nor does the statute provide one. However, it does provide some guidance. For example, death is not automatically imposed in cases in which one or more aggravating factors are found and no mitigating factors are found. The statute commands the sentencer to consider "whether the aggravating factor or factors alone are sufficient to justify a sentence of death." 18 U.S.C. §3593(e). Sentencing options include death, life without possibility of release or some other lesser sentence. The expression "life without possibility of release" suggests potential constitutional problems. If that language is interpreted to preclude the President from exercising executive clemency by pardoning or commuting sentences, it almost certainly runs afoul of Article 2, Section 2 of the United States Constitution.

When the jury recommends either a sentence of death or of life without possibility of release, the trial court is bound by the recommendation and the defendant "shall [be] sentence[d] ... accordingly." 18 U.S.C. §3594. Otherwise the court retains discretion to impose any lesser sentence authorized by law. There is one remarkable sentencing feature: In the event the maximum sentence authorized by law is life imprisonment (with the possibility of parole), the court may nonetheless impose a sentence of life without the possibility of release.

Certificate of Fair Treatment

An earlier version of the crime bill contained a provision so controversial that many believed it would derail passage of the entire crime package. The Racial Justice Act was designed to remedy racial discrimination in the imposition of the death penalty. In a real sense, the Act was a rather belated legislative response to the Supreme Court's 1987 decision in *McCleskey v. Kemp*, 481 U.S. 279 (1987). Under the Act, a capital defendant would have been allowed to demonstrate through statistically valid studies that there was a pattern of racially discriminatory capital sentencing which included his case. The state would then have the chance to rebut with evidence that the defendant's case was not tainted with impermissible racial bias. Threat of a Republican filibuster convinced supporters to abandon the provision and it was deleted from the final version of the bill.

A curious provision which conservatives claimed would eliminate discriminatory treatment in capital cases did survive. Under §3593(f), federal judges in capital sentencing proceedings must instruct the jury that:

> in considering whether a sentence of death is justified, it shall not consider the race, color, religious beliefs, national origin, or sex of the defendant or of any victim.

Additionally, if a jury recommends a death sentence, it must furnish the court with a certificate signed by each juror swearing that discrimination played no part in the decision and that the same sentencing recommendation would have been made no matter what the race, color, religious beliefs, national origin, or sex of the defendant or any victim. 18 U.S.C. §3593(f).

Right to Appeal

If a death sentence is imposed, the condemned inmate has a right to appeal both conviction and death sentence under §3595. An appeal is initiated by filing a notice of appeal with the appropriate regional circuit court of appeals. 18 U.S.C. §3595(a).

The court of appeals is required to review the entire record in the case, including (1) evidence submitted at trial; (2) information submitted during sentencing; (3) the sentencing procedures; and (4) any special findings regarding aggravating and mitigating circumstances. 18 U.S.C. §3595(b). There are three stated grounds for relief:

(1) the death sentence was imposed under the influence of passion, prejudice or any other arbitrary factor;

(2) the admissible evidence and information adduced does not support the special finding of the existence of the required aggravating factor; or

(3) the proceedings involved any other legal error requiring reversal which was properly preserved for appeal under the rules of criminal procedure.

18 U.S.C. §3595(c).

Federal capital defendants on appeal face two often insurmountable barriers. Procedural default prevents them from raising on appeal issues not properly preserved at trial. 18 U.S.C. §3595(c)(2)(C). Also, no relief may be provided for any error which the government proves to be harmless beyond a reasonable doubt. 18 U.S.C. §3595(c)(2). Accord *Chapman v. California*, 386 U.S. 18 (1967).

Clemency

Federal death row inmates can seek clemency from the President, who alone has pardon power. Guidelines specify that an inmate must be given 120 days notice of an execution date. Once an execution date has been set, the prisoner has 30 days within which to file a clemency petition.

Federal Death Row

Execution protocol under federal law is described in §3596. When an inmate's execution date draws near, the Attorney General is required to release the inmate into the custody of a United States Marshal whose job it is to supervise the inmate's death. In 1999, the United States Penitentiary (USP) Terre Haute, Indiana, opened a Special Confinement Unit to provide "humane, safe, and secure confinement of male offenders who have been sentenced to death" by the federal government. Inmates with federal death sentences were transferred from other federal and state correctional facilities to USP Terre Haute for placement in this Special Confinement Unit.

Based on the increasing number of federal death penalty cases throughout the country, opening the Special Confinement Unit at USP Terre Haute has become necessary to implement federal death sentences under applicable federal statutes and regulations. The staff assigned to the Special Confinement Unit received specialized training for managing this type of special offender.

The physical design of the two-story renovated housing unit includes 50 single-cells, upper tier and lower tier corridors, an industrial work shop, indoor and outdoor recreation areas, a property room, a food preparation area, attorney and family visiting rooms, and a video-teleconferencing area that is used to facilitate inmate access to the courts and their attorneys.

The Special Confinement Unit operations ensure inmates are afforded routine institution services and programs such as work programs, visitation, commissary privileges, telephone access, and law library services.

Persons Exempt from the Federal Death Penalty

The Federal Death Penalty Act of 1994 is not totally devoid of merciful qualities. Several groups are spared the ultimate punishment. These include persons less than 18 years of age at the time of the offense, 18 U.S.C. §3591(a), mentally retarded persons, 18 U.S.C. §3596(c), and insane persons, 18 U.S.C. §3596(c). Pregnant women are also ineligible to be executed, but apparently only while they remain pregnant. 18 U.S.C. §3596(b).

The new law also ensures that government employees who oppose capital punishment are not required to participate in state-sanctioned killing. Government workers who oppose the death penalty on moral or religious grounds can not be required to either attend or participate in executions. 18 U.S.C. §3597(b). This provision applies to state and federal correctional employees, Department of Justice employees, and members of the United States Marshals Service.

Indian Country Option

Of particular importance in states with large Native American populations is a provision which restricts the federal government's ability to seek the death of Native Americans. Section 3598 of the new law prevents the capital prosecution of persons subject to the criminal jurisdiction of an Indian tribal government where federal jurisdiction is based solely on Indian country and where the offense occurred within the boundaries of Indian country. However, the governing body of the Indian tribe can waive its sovereign immunity by opting to apply the new federal death penalty provisions to persons subject to its criminal jurisdiction. Almost all tribes have opted not to use the federal death penalty.

Note on Capital Crimes That Do Not Involve Homicide

Although most of the crimes designated as capital under the Federal Death Penalty Act of 1994 involve murder, several non-homicide crimes such as treason (18 U.S.C. §2381) and espionage (18 U.S.C. §794(b)) are punishable by death. See Eldred, "The New Federal Death Penalties," 22 Am. J. Crim. L. 293, 296 (1994). Can non-homicide crimes result in death sentences since *Coker v. Georgia*, 433 U.S. 584 (1977) (death penalty for rape of an adult woman held unconstitutional) (*supra* chapter 1)? *Coker* did not hold that the death penalty may be imposed only for homicide. Nonetheless, several states have routinely invalidated as disproportionate state laws that imposed death as a punishment for crimes not involving homicide. Even so, in several states non-homicide crimes may still serve as a basis for a death sentence. For example, five states (Arkansas, California, Colorado, Georgia and Louisiana) still prescribe the death penalty for treason. Louisiana permits a death sentence for the aggravated rape of a child under age 12. South Dakota allows the death penalty for aggravated kidnapping. U.S. Dep't of Justice, Bureau of Justice Statistics Bulletin, Capital Punishment 2004. See also Matura, "When Will It Stop? The Use of the Death Penalty for Non-Homicide Crimes," 24 J. Legis. 249 (1998).

In *Jones v. United States*, 527 U.S. 373 (1999), which immediately follows, the Court examined the 1994 Federal Death Penalty Act for the first time.

Jones v. United States

527 U.S. 373 (1999)

Justice THOMAS delivered the opinion of the Court, except as to Part III-A. Justice Scalia joins all but Part III-A of the opinion.

Petitioner was sentenced to death for committing a kidnaping resulting in death to the victim. His sentence was imposed under the Federal Death Penalty Act of 1994, 18

U.S.C. §3591. We are presented with three questions: whether petitioner was entitled to an instruction as to the effect of jury deadlock; whether there is a reasonable likelihood that the jury was led to believe that petitioner would receive a court-imposed sentence less than life imprisonment in the event that they could not reach a unanimous sentence recommendation; and whether the submission to the jury of two allegedly duplicative, vague, and overbroad nonstatutory aggravating factors was harmless error. We answer "no" to the first two questions. As for the third, we are of the view that there was no error in allowing the jury to consider the challenged factors. Assuming error, *arguendo*, we think it clear that such error was harmless.

I

Petitioner Louis Jones, Jr., kidnaped Private Tracie Joy McBride at gunpoint from the Goodfellow Air Force Base in San Angelo, Texas. He brought her to his house and sexually assaulted her. Soon thereafter, petitioner drove Private McBride to a bridge just outside of San Angelo, where he repeatedly struck her in the head with a tire iron until she died. Petitioner administered blows of such severe force that, when the victim's body was found, the medical examiners observed that large pieces of her skull had been driven into her cranial cavity or were missing.

The Government charged petitioner with, *inter alia*, kidnaping with death resulting to the victim, in violation of 18 U.S.C. §1201(a)(2), an offense punishable by life imprisonment or death. Exercising its discretion under the Federal Death Penalty Act of 1994, the Government decided to seek the latter sentencing option. Petitioner was tried in the District Court for the Northern District of Texas and found guilty by the jury.

The District Court then conducted a separate sentencing hearing pursuant to 18 U.S.C. §3593. As an initial matter, the sentencing jury was required to find that petitioner had the requisite intent, see §3591(a)(2); it concluded that petitioner intentionally killed his victim and intentionally inflicted serious bodily injury resulting in her death. Even on a finding of intent, however, a defendant is not death-eligible unless the sentencing jury also finds that the Government has proved beyond a reasonable doubt at least one of the statutory aggravating factors set forth at §3592. See §3593 (e). Because petitioner was charged with committing a homicide, the Government had to prove 1 of the 16 statutory aggravating factors set forth at 18 U.S.C. §3592(c). The jury unanimously found that two such factors had been proved beyond a reasonable doubt—it agreed that petitioner caused the death of his victim during the commission of another crime, see §3592(c)(1), and that he committed the offense in an especially heinous, cruel, and depraved manner, see §3592(c)(6).

Once petitioner became death-eligible, the jury had to decide whether he should receive a death sentence. In making the selection decision, the Act requires that the sentencing jury consider all of the aggravating and mitigating factors and determine whether the former outweigh the latter (or, if there are no mitigating factors, whether the aggravating factors alone are sufficient to warrant a death sentence). §§3591(a), 3592, 3593(e). The Act, however, requires more exacting proof of aggravating factors than mitigating ones—although a jury must unanimously agree that the Government established the existence of an aggravating factor beyond a reasonable doubt, §3593(c), the jury may consider a mitigating factor in its weighing process so long as one juror finds that the defendant established its existence by preponderance of the evidence, §§3593(c), (d). In addition to the two statutory aggravators that established petitioner's death-eligibility, the jury also unanimously found two aggravators of the nonstatutory variety had been proved: one set forth victim impact evidence and the other victim vulnerability evidence.³ As for mitigating factors, at least one juror found 10 of the 11 that petitioner proposed and seven jurors wrote in a factor petitioner had not raised on the Special Findings Form.⁴

After weighing the aggravating and mitigating factors, the jury unanimously recommended that petitioner be sentenced to death. The District Court imposed sentence in accordance with the jury's recommendation pursuant to §3594. The United States Court of Appeals for the Fifth Circuit affirmed the sentence. We granted certiorari and now affirm.

II

A

We first decide the question whether petitioner was entitled to an instruction as to the consequences of jury deadlock. Petitioner requested, in relevant part, the following instruction:

> "In the event, after due deliberation and reflection, the jury is unable to agree on a unanimous decision as to the sentence to be imposed, you should so advise me and I will impose a sentence of life imprisonment without possibility of release. . . .

> "In the event you are unable to agree on [a sentence of] Life Without Possibility of Release or Death, but you are unanimous that the sentence should not be less than Life Without Possibility of Release, you should report that vote to the Court and the Court will sentence the defendant to Life Without the Possibility of Release."

In petitioner's view, the Eighth Amendment requires that the jury be instructed as to the effect of their inability to agree. He alternatively argues that we should invoke

---

3. As phrased on the Special Findings Form, the nonstatutory aggravating factors read:
"3(B). Tracie Joy McBride's young age, her slight stature, her background, and her unfamiliarity with San Angelo, Texas."
"3(C). Tracie Joy McBride's personal characteristics and the effect of the instant offense on Tracie Joy McBride's family constitute an aggravating factor of the offense."
4. The mitigating factors that the jury found as set forth on the Special Findings Form (along with the number of jurors that found for each factor in brackets) are as follows:
"1. That the defendant Louis Jones did not have a significant prior criminal record." [6]
"2. That the defendant Louis Jones' capacity to appreciate the wrongfulness of the defendant's conduct or to conform to the requirements of law was significantly impaired, regardless of whether the capacity was so impaired as to constitute a defense to the charge." [2]
"3. That the defendant Louis Jones committed the offense under severe mental or emotional disturbance." [1]
"4. That the defendant Louis Jones was subjected to physical, sexual, and emotional abuse as a child (and was deprived of sufficient parental protection that he needed)." [4]
"5. That the defendant Louis Jones served his country well in Desert Storm, Grenada, and for 22 years in the United States Army." [8]
"6. That the defendant Louis Jones is likely to be a well-behaved inmate." [3]
"7. That the defendant Louis Jones is remorseful for the crime he committed." [4]
"8. That the defendant Louis Jones' daughter will be harmed by the emotional trauma of her father's execution." [9]
"9. That the defendant Louis Jones was under unusual and substantial internally generated duress and stress at the time of the offense." [3]
"10. That the defendant Louis Jones suffered from numerous neurological or psychological disorders at the time of the offense." [1]
Seven jurors added petitioner's ex-wife as a mitigating factor without further elaboration.

our supervisory power over the federal courts and require that such an instruction be given.

Before we turn to petitioner's Eighth Amendment argument, a question of statutory interpretation calls for our attention. The Fifth Circuit held that the District Court did not err in refusing petitioner's requested instruction because it was not substantively correct. According to the Court of Appeals, §3593(b)(2)(C), which provides that a new jury shall be impaneled for a new sentencing hearing if the guilt phase jury is discharged for "good cause," requires the District Court to impanel a second jury and hold a second sentencing hearing in the event of jury deadlock. The Government interprets the statute the same way (although its reading is more nuanced) and urges that the judgment below be affirmed on this ground.

Petitioner, however, reads the Act differently. In his view, whenever the jury reaches a result other than a unanimous verdict recommending a death sentence or life imprisonment without the possibility of release, the duty of sentencing falls upon the district court pursuant to §3594, which reads:

> "Upon a recommendation under section 3593(e) that the defendant should be sentenced to death or life imprisonment without possibility of release, the court shall sentence the defendant accordingly. Otherwise, the court shall impose any lesser sentence that is authorized by law. Notwithstanding any other law, if the maximum term of imprisonment for the offense is life imprisonment, the court may impose a sentence of life imprisonment without possibility of release."

Petitioner's argument is based on his construction of the term "[o]therwise." He argues that this term means that when the jury, after retiring for deliberations, reports itself as unable to reach unanimous verdict, the sentencing determination passes to the court.

As the dissent also concludes petitioner's view of the statute is the better one. The phrase "good cause" in §3593(b)(2)(C) plainly encompasses events such as juror disqualification, but cannot be read so expansively as to include the jury's failure to reach a unanimous decision. Nevertheless, the Eighth Amendment does not require that the jury be instructed as to the consequences of their failure to agree.

To be sure, we have said that the Eighth Amendment requires that a sentence of death not be imposed arbitrarily. See, *e.g., Buchanan v. Angelone,* 522 U.S. 269, 275 (1998). In order for a capital sentencing scheme to pass constitutional muster, it must perform a narrowing function with respect to the class of persons eligible for the death penalty and must also ensure that capital sentencing decisions rest upon an individualized inquiry. The instruction that petitioner requested has no bearing on what we have called the "eligibility phase" of the capital sentencing process. As for what we have called the "selection phase," our cases have held that in order to satisfy the requirement that capital sentencing decisions rest upon an individualized inquiry, a scheme must allow a "broad inquiry" into all "constitutionally relevant mitigating evidence." Petitioner does not argue, nor could he, that the District Court's failure to give the requested instruction prevented the jury from considering such evidence.

In theory, the District Court's failure to instruct the jury as to the consequences of deadlock could give rise to an Eighth Amendment problem of a different sort: We also have held that a jury cannot be "affirmatively misled regarding its role in the sentencing process." *Romano v. Oklahoma,* 512 U.S. 1, 9 (1994). In no way, however, was the jury affirmatively misled by the District Court's refusal to give petitioner's proposed instruction. The truth of the matter is that the proposed instruction has no bearing on the jury's role in the sentencing process. Rather, it speaks to what happens in the event that the jury is unable to fulfill its role—when deliberations break down and the jury is unable to produce a unanimous sentence recommendation. Petitioner's argument, although less than clear, appears to be that a death sentence is arbitrary within the meaning of the Eighth Amendment if the jury is not given any bit of information that might possibly influence an individual juror's voting behavior. That contention has no merit. We have never suggested, for example, that the Eighth Amendment requires a jury be instructed as to the consequences of a breakdown in the deliberative process. On the contrary, we have long been of the view that "[t]he very object of the jury system is to secure unanimity by a comparison of views, and by arguments among the jurors themselves." *Allen v. United States,* 164 U.S. 492, 501 (1896). We further have recognized that in a capital sentencing proceeding, the Government has "a strong interest in having the jury express the conscience of the community on the ultimate question of life or death." *Lowenfield v. Phelps,* 484 U.S. 231, 238 (1988) (citation omitted). We are of the view that a charge to the jury of the sort proposed by petitioner might well have the effect of undermining this strong governmental interest.[6]

We similarly decline to exercise our supervisory powers to require that an instruction on the consequences of deadlock be given in every capital case. In drafting the Act, Congress chose not to require such an instruction. Cf. §3593(f) (district court "shall instruct the jury that, in considering whether a sentence of death is justified, it shall not consider the race, color, religious beliefs, national origin, or sex of the defendant or of any victim and that the jury is not to recommend a sentence of death unless it has concluded that it would recommend a sentence of death for the crime in question no matter what the race, color, religious beliefs, national origin, or sex of the defendant or of any victim may be"). Petitioner does point us to a decision from the New Jersey Supreme Court requiring, in an exercise of that court's supervisory authority, that the jury be informed of the sentencing consequences of nonunanimity. See *New Jersey v. Ramseur,* 524 A.2d 188, 280–286 (1987). Of course, New Jersey's practice has no more relevance to our decision than the power to persuade. Several other States have declined to require a similar instruction. See, *e.g., North Carolina v. McCarver,* 341 N.C. 364, 394 (1995); *Brogie v. Oklahoma,* 695 P.2d 538, 547 (Okla. Crim. App. 1985); *Calhoun v. Maryland,* 297 Md. 563, 593–595 (1983); *Coulter v. Alabama,* 438 So.2d 336, 346 (Ala. Crim. App. 1982); *Justus v. Virginia,* 220 Va. 971, 979 (1980). We find the reasoning of the Virginia Supreme Court in *Justus* far more persuasive than that of the New Jersey Supreme Court, especially in light of the strong governmental interest that we have recognized in having the jury render a unanimous sentence recommendation: "The court properly refused an instruction offered by the defendant which would have told the jury that if it could not reach agreement as to the appropriate punishment, the court would dismiss it and impose a life sentence. While this was a correct statement of law it concerned a procedural matter and was not one which should have been the subject of an instruction. It would have been an open invitation for the jury to avoid its responsibility and to disagree." In light of the legitimate reasons for not instructing the jury as to the consequences of deadlock, and in light of congressional silence, we will not exercise our supervisory powers to require that an instruction of the sort petitioner sought be given in every case. Cf. *Shannon v. United States,* 512 U.S. 573, 587 (1994).

---

6. It is not insignificant that the Courts of Appeals to have addressed this question, as far as we are aware, are uniform in rejecting the argument that the Constitution requires an instruction as to the consequences of a jury's inability to agree.

B

Petitioner further argues that the jury was led to believe that if it could not reach a unanimous sentence recommendation he would receive a judge-imposed sentence less severe than life imprisonment, and his proposed instruction as to the consequences of deadlock was necessary to correct the jury's erroneous impression. Moreover, he contends that the alleged confusion independently warrants reversal of his sentence under the Due Process Clause, the Eighth Amendment, and the Act itself. He grounds his due process claim in the assertion that sentences may not be based on materially untrue assumptions, his Eighth Amendment claim in his contention that the jury is entitled to accurate sentencing information, and his statutory claim in an argument that jury confusion over the available sentencing options constitutes an "arbitrary factor" under §3595(c)(2)(A).

To put petitioner's claim in the proper context, we must briefly review the jury instructions and sentencing procedures used at trial. After instructing the jury on the aggravating and mitigating factors and explaining the process of weighing those factors, the District Court gave the following instructions pertaining to the jury's sentencing recommendation:

> "Based upon this consideration, you the jury, by unanimous vote, shall recommend whether the defendant should be sentenced to death, sentenced to life imprisonment without the possibility of release, or sentenced to some other lesser sentence. If you unanimously conclude that the aggravating factors found to exist sufficiently outweigh any mitigating factor or factors found to exist, or in the absence of any mitigating factors, that the aggravating factors are themselves sufficient to justify a sentence of death, you may recommend a sentence of death. Keep in mind, however, that regardless of your findings with respect to aggravating and mitigating factors, you are never required to recommend a death sentence. If you recommend the imposition of a death sentence, the court is required to impose that sentence. If you recommend a sentence of life without the possibility of release, the court is required to impose that sentence. If you recommend that some other lesser sentence be imposed, the court is required to impose a sentence that is authorized by the law. In deciding what recommendation to make, you are not to be concerned with the question of what sentence the defendant might receive in the event you determine not to recommend a death sentence or a sentence of life without the possibility of release. That is a matter for the court to decide in the event you conclude that a sentence of death or life without the possibility of release should not be recommended."

The District Court also provided the jury with four decision forms on which to record its recommendation.[7] In its instructions explaining those forms, the District Court told the jury that its choice of form depended on its recommendation:

---

7. The decision forms read as follows:

"*DECISION FORM A.* We the jury have determined that a sentence of death should not be imposed because the government has failed to prove beyond a reasonable doubt the existence of the required intent on the part of the defendant or a required aggravating factor. *DECISION FORM B.* Based upon consideration of whether the aggravating factor or factors found to exist sufficiently outweigh any mitigating factor or factors found to exist, or in the absence of any mitigating factors, whether the aggravating factor or factors are themselves sufficient to justify a sentence of death, we recommend, by unanimous vote, that a sentence of death be imposed. *DECISION FORM C.* We the jury recommend, by unanimous verdict, a sentence of life

"The forms are self-explanatory: Decision Form A should be used if you determine that a sentence of death should not be imposed because the government failed to prove beyond a reasonable doubt the existence of the required intent on the part of the defendant or a required aggravating factor. Decision Form B should be used if you unanimously recommend that a sentence of death should be imposed. Decision Form C or Decision Form D should be used if you determine that a sentence of death should not be imposed because: (1) you do not unanimously find that the aggravating factor or factors found to exist sufficiently outweigh any mitigating factor or factors found to exist; (2) you do not unanimously find that the aggravating factor or factors found to exist are themselves sufficient to justify a sentence of death where no mitigating factor has been found to exist; or (3) regardless of your findings with respect to aggravating and mitigating factors you are not unanimous in recommending that a sentence of death should be imposed. Decision Form C should be used if you unanimously recommend that a sentence of imprisonment for life without the possibility of release should be imposed. Decision Form D should be used if you recommend that some other lesser sentence should be imposed."

Petitioner maintains that the instructions in combination with the Decision Forms led the jury to believe that if it failed to recommend unanimously a sentence of death or life imprisonment without the possibility of release, then it would be required to use Decision Form D and the court would impose a sentence less than life imprisonment. The scope of our review is shaped by whether petitioner properly raised and preserved an objection to the instructions at trial. A party generally may not assign error to a jury instruction if he fails to object before the jury retires or to "stat[e] distinctly the matter to which that party objects and the grounds of the objection." Fed. Rule Crim. Proc. 30. These timeliness and specificity requirements apply during the sentencing phase as well as the trial. They enable a trial court to correct any instructional mistakes before the jury retires and in that way help to avoid the burdens of an unnecessary retrial. While an objection in a directed verdict motion before the jury retires can preserve a claim of error, objections raised after the jury has completed its deliberations do not. See *Singer v. United States*, 380 U.S. 24, 38 (1965). Nor does a request for an instruction before the jury retires preserve an objection to the instruction actually given by the court. Otherwise, district judges would have to speculate on what sorts of objections might be implied through a request for an instruction and issue rulings on "implied" objections that a defendant never intends to raise. Such a rule would contradict Rule 30's mandate that a party state distinctly his grounds for objection.

Petitioner did not voice the objections to the instructions and decision forms that he now raises before the jury retired. While Rule 30 could be read literally to bar any review of petitioner's claim of error, our decisions instead have held that an appellate court may conduct a limited review for plain error. Petitioner, however, contends that the Federal Death Penalty Act creates an exception. He relies on language in the Act providing that an appellate court shall remand a case where it finds that "the sentence of death was imposed under the influence of passion, prejudice, or any other arbitrary factor." §3595(c)(2)(A). According to petitioner, the alleged jury confusion over the avail-

---

imprisonment without the possibility of release.
DECISION FORM D. We the jury recommend some other lesser sentence."

able sentencing options is an arbitrary factor and thus warrants resentencing even if he did not properly preserve the objection.

This argument rests on an untenable reading of the Act. The statute does not explicitly announce an exception to plain-error review, and a congressional intent to create such an exception cannot be inferred from the overall scheme. Statutory language must be read in context and a phrase "gathers meaning from the words around it." Here, the same subsection that petitioner relies upon further provides that reversal is warranted where "the proceedings involved any other legal error requiring reversal of the sentence that was properly preserved for appeal under the rules of criminal procedure." §3595(c)(2)(C). This language makes clear that Congress sought to impose a timely objection requirement at sentencing and did not intend to equate the phrase "arbitrary factor" with legal error. Petitioner's broad interpretation of §3595(c)(2)(A) would drain §3595(c)(2)(C) of any independent meaning.

We review the instructions, then, for plain error. Under that review, relief is not warranted unless there has been (1) error, (2) that is plain, and (3) affects substantial rights. Appellate review under the plain-error doctrine, of course, is circumscribed and we exercise our power under Rule 52(b) sparingly. An appellate court should exercise its discretion to correct plain error only if it "seriously affect[s] the fairness, integrity, or public reputation of judicial proceedings." *United States v. Olano*, 407 U.S. 732.

Petitioner's argument—which depends on the premise that the instructions and decision forms led the jury to believe that it did not have to recommend unanimously a lesser sentence—falls short of satisfying even the first requirement of the plain-error doctrine, for we cannot see that any error occurred. We have considered similar claims that allegedly ambiguous instructions caused jury confusion. The proper standard for reviewing such claims is "whether there is a reasonable likelihood that the jury has applied the challenged instruction in a way that violates the Constitution."

There is no reasonable likelihood that the jury applied the instructions incorrectly. The District Court did not expressly inform the jury that it would impose a lesser sentence in case of deadlock. It simply told the jury that, if they recommended a lesser sentence, the court would impose a sentence "authorized by the law." Nor did the District Court expressly require the jury to select Decision Form D if it could not reach agreement. Instead, it exhorted the jury "to discuss the issue of punishment with one another in an effort to reach agreement, if you can do so."

Notwithstanding the absence of an explicit instruction on the consequences of nonunanimity, petitioner identifies several passages which, he believes, support the inference that the jury was confused on this point. He trains on that portion of the instructions telling the jury that the court would decide the sentence if they did not recommend a sentence of death or life without the possibility of release. Petitioner argues that this statement, coupled with two earlier references to a "lesser sentence" option, caused the jury to infer that the District Court would impose a lesser sentence if they could not unanimously agree on a sentence of death or life without the possibility of release. He maintains that this inference is strengthened by a later instruction: "In order to bring back a verdict recommending the punishment of death or life without the possibility of release, all twelve of you must unanimously vote in favor of such specific penalty." According to petitioner, the failure to mention the "lesser sentence" option in this statement strongly implied that, in contradistinction to the first two options, the "lesser sentence" option did not require jury unanimity.

Petitioner parses these passages too finely. Our decisions repeatedly have cautioned that instructions must be evaluated not in isolation but in the context of the entire charge. See, *e.g., Bryan v. United States*, 524 U.S. 184, 199 (1998). We agree with the Fifth Circuit that when these passages are viewed in the context of the entire instructions, they lack ambiguity and cannot be given the reading that petitioner advances. We previously have held that instructions that might be ambiguous in the abstract can be cured when read in conjunction with other instructions. Petitioner's claim is far weaker than those we evaluated in *Bryan*, because the jury in this case received an explicit instruction that it had to be unanimous. Just prior to its admonition that the jury should not concern itself with the ultimate sentence if it does not recommend death or life without the possibility of release, the trial court expressly instructed the jury in unambiguous language that any sentencing recommendation had to be by a unanimous vote. Specifically, it stated that "you the jury, by unanimous vote, shall recommend whether the defendant should be sentenced to death, sentenced to life imprisonment without the possibility of release, or sentenced to some other lesser sentence." Other instructions, by contrast, specified when the jury did not have to act unanimously. For example, the District Court explicitly told the jury that its findings on the mitigating circumstances, unlike those on the aggravating circumstances, did not have to be unanimous.[10] To be sure, the District Court could have used the phrase "unanimously" more frequently. But when read alongside an unambiguous charge that any sentencing recommendation be unanimous and other instructions explicitly identifying when the jury need not be unanimous, the passages identified by petitioner do not create a reasonable likelihood that the jury believed that deadlock would cause the District Court to impose a lesser sentence.

Petitioner also relies on alleged ambiguities in the decision forms and the explanatory instructions. He stresses the fact that Decision Form D (lesser sentence recommendation), unlike Decision Forms B (death sentence) and C (life without the possibility of release), did not contain the phrase "by unanimous vote" and required only the foreperson's signature. These features of Decision Form D, according to petitioner, led the jury to conclude that nonunanimity would result in a lesser sentence. According to petitioner, the instructions accompanying Decision Form D, unlike those respecting Decision Forms B and C, did not mention unanimity, thereby increasing the likelihood of confusion. With respect to this aspect of petitioner's argument, we agree with the Fifth Circuit that "[a]lthough the verdict forms standing alone could have persuaded a jury to conclude that unanimity was not required for the lesser sentence option, any confusion created by the verdict forms was clarified when considered in light of the entire jury instruction." The District Court's explicit instruction that the jury had to be unanimous and its exhortation to the jury to discuss the punishment and attempt to reach agreement make it doubtful that the jury thought it was compelled to employ Decision Form D in the event of disagreement....

Even assuming, *arguendo,* that an error occurred (and that it was plain), petitioner cannot show that it affected his substantial rights. Any confusion among the jurors over the effect of a lesser sentence recommendation was allayed by the District Court's admonition that the jury should not concern itself with the effect of such a recommenda-

---

10. The relevant portion of the instruction read: "You will also recall that I previously told you that all twelve of you had to unanimously agree that a particular aggravating circumstance was proved beyond a reasonable doubt before you consider it. Quite the opposite is true with regard to mitigating factors. A finding with respect to a mitigating factor may be made by any one or more of the members of the jury, and any member who finds by a preponderance of the evidence the existence of a mitigating factor may consider such factor established for his or her weighing of aggravating and mitigating factors regardless of the number of other jurors who agree that such mitigating factor has been established."

tion. The jurors are presumed to have followed these instructions. See *Shannon*, 512 U.S., at 585. Even if the jurors had some lingering doubts about the effect of deadlock, therefore, the instructions made clear that they should set aside their concerns and either report that they were unable to reach agreement or recommend a lesser sentence if they believed that this was the only option.

Moreover, even assuming that the jurors were confused over the consequences of deadlock, petitioner cannot show the confusion necessarily worked to his detriment. It is just as likely that the jurors, loathe to recommend a lesser sentence, would have compromised on a sentence of life imprisonment as on a death sentence. Where the effect of an alleged error is so uncertain, a defendant cannot meet his burden of showing that the error actually affected his substantial rights. Cf. *Romano*, 512 U.S., at 14. In *Romano*, we considered a similar argument, namely, that jurors had disregarded a trial judge's instructions and given undue weight to certain evidence. In rejecting that argument, we noted that, even assuming that the jury disregarded the trial judge's instructions, "[i]t seems equally plausible that the evidence could have made the jurors more inclined to impose a death sentence, or it could have made them less inclined to do so." Any speculation on the effect of a lesser sentence recommendation, like the evidence in *Romano*, would have had such an indeterminate effect on the outcome of the proceeding that we cannot conclude that any alleged error in the District Court's instructions affected petitioner's substantial rights.

III

A

Apart from the claimed instructional error, petitioner argues that the nonstatutory aggravating factors found and considered by the jury, were vague, overbroad, and duplicative in violation of the Eighth Amendment, and that the District Court's error in allowing the jury to consider them was not harmless beyond a reasonable doubt. The Eighth Amendment, as the Court of Appeals correctly recognized, permits capital sentencing juries to consider evidence relating to the victim's personal characteristics and the emotional impact of the murder on the victim's family in deciding whether an eligible defendant should receive a death sentence. See *Payne v. Tennessee*, 501 U.S. 808, 827 (1991) ("A State may legitimately conclude that evidence about the victim and about the impact of the murder on the victim's family is relevant to the jury's decision as to whether or not the death penalty should be imposed. There is no reason to treat such evidence differently than other relevant evidence is treated"). Petitioner does not dispute that, as a general matter, such evidence is appropriate for the sentencing jury's consideration. His objection is that the two nonstatutory aggravating factors were duplicative, vague, and overbroad so as to render their use in this case unconstitutional, a point with which the Fifth Circuit agreed, although it ultimately ruled in the Government's favor on the ground that the alleged error was harmless beyond a reasonable doubt.

The Government here renews its argument that the nonstatutory aggravators in this case were constitutionally valid. At oral argument, however, it was suggested that this case comes to us on the assumption that the nonstatutory aggravating factors were invalid because the Government did not cross-appeal on the question. As the prevailing party, the Government is entitled to defend the judgment on any ground that it properly raised below. It further was suggested that because we granted certiorari on the Government's rephrasing of petitioner's questions and because the third question— "whether the court of appeals correctly held that the submission of invalid nonstatutory aggravating factors was harmless beyond a reasonable doubt"—presumes error, we must assume the nonstatutory aggravating factors were erroneous. We are not convinced that the reformulated question presumes error. The question whether the nonstatutory aggravating factors were constitutional is fairly included within the third question presented—we might answer "no" to the question "[w]hether the Court of Appeals correctly held that the submission of invalid nonstatutory aggravating factors was harmless beyond a reasonable doubt," 525 U.S. 809 (1998), by explaining that the Fifth Circuit was incorrect in holding that there was error. Without a doubt, the Government would have done better to call our attention to the fact that it planned to argue that the nonstatutory aggravating factors were valid at the petitioning stage. But it did not affirmatively concede that the nonstatutory aggravators were invalid, and absent such a concession, we think that the Government's argument is properly presented.

We first address petitioner's contention that the two nonstatutory aggravating factors were impermissibly duplicative. The Fifth Circuit reasoned that "[t]he plain meaning of the term 'personal characteristics,' used in [nonstatutory aggravator] 3(C), necessarily includes 'young age, slight stature, background, and unfamiliarity,' which the jury was asked to consider in 3(B)." The problem, the court thought, was that this duplication led to "double counting" of aggravating factors. Following a Tenth Circuit decision, *United States v. McCullah*, 76 F.3d 1087, 1111 (1996), the Fifth Circuit was of the view that in a weighing scheme, "double counting" has a tendency to skew the process so as to give rise to the risk of an arbitrary, and thus unconstitutional, death sentence. In the Fifth Circuit's words, there may be a thumb on the scale in favor of death "[i]f the jury has been asked to weigh the same aggravating factor twice." We have never before held that aggravating factors could be duplicative so as to render them constitutionally invalid, nor have we passed on the "double counting" theory that the Tenth Circuit advanced in *McCullah* and the Fifth Circuit appears to have followed here. What we have said is that the weighing process may be impermissibly skewed if the sentencing jury considers an invalid factor. See *Stringer v. Black*, 503 U.S. 222, 232 (1992). Petitioner's argument (and the reasoning of the Fifth and Tenth Circuits) would have us reach a quite different proposition—that if two aggravating factors are "duplicative," then the weighing process necessarily is skewed, and the factors are therefore invalid.

1

Even accepting, for the sake of argument, petitioner's "double counting" theory, there are nevertheless several problems with the Fifth Circuit's application of the theory in this case. The phrase "personal characteristics" as used in factor 3(C) does not obviously include the specific personal characteristics listed in 3(B)—"young age, her slight stature, her background, and her unfamiliarity with San Angelo"—especially in light of the fact that 3(C) went on to refer to the impact of the crime on the victim's family. In the context of considering the effect of the crime on the victim's family, it would be more natural to understand "personal characteristics" to refer to those aspects of the victim's character and personality that her family would miss the most. More important, to the extent that there was any ambiguity arising from how the factors were drafted, the Government's argument to the jury made clear that 3(B) and 3(C) went to entirely different areas of aggravation—the former clearly went to victim vulnerability while the latter captured the victim's individual uniqueness and the effect of the crime on her family. See, *e.g.*, 25 Record 2733–2734 ("[Y]ou can consider [the victim's] young age, her slight stature, her background, her unfamiliarity with the San Angelo area. She is barely five feet tall [and] weighs approximately 100 pounds. [She is] the ideal victim"); ("[Y]ou can consider [the victim's] personal characteristics and the effects of the instant offense on her family. You heard about this young woman, you heard about her from her mother, you heard about her from her friends that knew her. She was special, she was unique, she was loving, she was caring, she had a lot to offer this world"). As such, even if the phrase "personal characteristics" as used in factor 3(C) *was* understood to include the specific personal characteristics listed in 3(B), the factors as a whole were not duplicative — at best, certain evidence was relevant to two different aggravating factors. Moreover, any risk that the weighing process would be skewed was eliminated by the District Court's instruction that the jury "should not simply count the number of aggravating and mitigating factors and reach a decision based on which number is greater [but rather] should consider the weight and value of each factor."

2

We also are of the view that the Fifth Circuit incorrectly concluded that factors 3(B) and 3(C) were unconstitutionally vague. In that court's view, the nonstatutory aggravating factors challenged here "fail[ed] to guide the jury's discretion, or [to] distinguish this murder from any other murder." The Court of Appeals, relying on our decision in *Maynard v. Cartwright*, 486 U.S. 356, 361–362 (1988), also was of the opinion that "[t]he use of the terms 'background,' 'personal characteristics,' and 'unfamiliarity' without further definition or instruction left the jury with open-ended discretion." Ensuring that a sentence of death is not so infected with bias or caprice is our "controlling objective when we examine eligibility and selection factors for vagueness." *Tuilaepa v. California*, 512 U.S. 967, 973 (1994). Our vagueness review, however, is "quite deferential." As long as an aggravating factor has a core meaning that criminal juries should be capable of understanding, it will pass constitutional muster. Assessed under this deferential standard, the factors challenged here surely are not vague. The jury should have had no difficulty understanding that factor 3(B) was designed to ask it to consider whether the victim was especially vulnerable to petitioner's attack. Nor should it have had difficulty comprehending that factor 3(C) asked it to consider the victim's personal traits and the effect of the crime on her family.[14] Even if the factors as written were somewhat vague, the Fifth Circuit was wrong to conclude that the factors were not given further definition. As we have explained, the Government's argument made absolutely clear what each nonstatutory factor meant.

3

Finally, we turn to petitioner's contention that the challenged nonstatutory factors were overbroad. An aggravating factor can be overbroad if the sentencing jury "fairly could conclude that an aggravating circumstance applies to *every* defendant eligible for the death penalty." *Arave v. Creech*, 507 U.S. 463, 474 (1993). We have not, however, specifically considered what it means for a factor to be overbroad when it is important only for selection purposes and especially when it sets forth victim vulnerability or vic-

---

14. Petitioner argues that the term "personal characteristics" was so vague that the jury may have thought it could consider the victim's race and the petitioner's race under factor 3(C). In light of the remainder of the factor and the Government's argument with respect to the factor, we fail to see that possibility. In any event, in accordance with the Death Penalty Act's explicit command in §3593(f), the District Court instructed the jury not to consider race at all in reaching its decision. Jurors are presumed to have followed their instructions. See *Richardson v. Marsh*, 481 U.S. 200, 206 (1987).

tim impact evidence. Of course, every murder will have an impact on the victim's family and friends and victims are often chosen because of their vulnerability. It might seem, then, that the factors 3(B) and 3(C) apply to every eligible defendant and thus fall within the Eighth Amendment's proscription against overbroad factors. But that cannot be correct; if it were, we would not have decided *Payne* as we did. Even though the *concepts* of victim impact and victim vulnerability may well be relevant in every case, *evidence* of victim vulnerability and victim impact in a particular case is inherently individualized. And such evidence is surely relevant to the selection phase decision, given that the sentencer should consider all of the circumstances of the crime in deciding whether to impose the death penalty. See *Tuilaepa*, 512 U.S., at 976.

What is of common importance at the eligibility and selection stages is that "the process is neutral and principled so as to guard against bias or caprice in the sentencing decision." So long as victim vulnerability and victim impact factors are used to direct the jury to the individual circumstances of the case, we do not think that principle will be disturbed. Because factors 3(B) and 3(C) directed the jury to the evidence specific to this case, we do not think that they were overbroad in a way that offended the Constitution.

B

The error in this case, if any, rests in loose drafting of the nonstatutory aggravating factors; as we have made clear, victim vulnerability and victim impact evidence are appropriate subjects for the capital sentencer's consideration. Assuming that use of these loosely drafted factors was indeed error, we conclude that the error was harmless.

Harmless-error review of a death sentence may be performed in at least two different ways. An appellate court may choose to consider whether absent an invalid factor, the jury would have reached the same verdict or it may choose instead to consider whether the result would have been the same had the invalid aggravating factor been precisely defined. See *Clemons v. Mississippi*, 494 U.S. 738, 753–754 (1990). The Fifth Circuit chose to perform the first sort of analysis, and ultimately concluded that the jury would have returned a recommendation of death even had it not considered the two supposedly invalid non-statutory aggravating factors:

> "After removing the offensive non-statutory aggravating factors from the balance, we are left with two statutory aggravating factors and eleven mitigating factors to consider when deciding whether, beyond a reasonable doubt, the death sentence would have been imposed had the invalid aggravating factors never been submitted to the jury. At the sentencing hearing, the government placed great emphasis on the two statutory aggravating factors found unanimously by the jury—Jones caused the death of the victim during the commission of the offense of kidnapping; and the offense was committed in an especially heinous, cruel, and depraved manner in that it involved torture or serious physical abuse of the victim. Under part two of the Special Findings Form, if the jury had failed to find that the government proved at least one of the statutory aggravating factors beyond a reasonable doubt, then the deliberations would have ceased leaving the jury powerless to recommend the death penalty. Therefore, the ability of the jury to recommend the death penalty hinged on a finding of a least one statutory aggravating factor. Conversely, jury findings regarding the non-statutory aggravating factors were not required before the jury could recommend the death penalty. After removing the two non-statutory aggravating factors from the mix, we conclude that the two remaining statutory aggravating factors unanimously found by

the jury support the sentence of death, even after considering the eleven mitigating factors found by one or more jurors. Consequently, the error was harmless because the death sentence would have been imposed beyond a reasonable doubt had the invalid aggravating factors never been submitted to the jury."

Petitioner claims that the court's analysis was so perfunctory as to be infirm. His argument is largely based on the following passage from *Clemons*: "*Under these circumstances,* it would require a detailed explanation based on the record for us possibly to agree that the error in giving the invalid 'especially heinous' instruction was harmless." 494 U.S., at 753–754. *Clemons*, however, involved quite different facts. There, an "especially heinous" aggravating factor was determined to be unconstitutionally vague. The only remaining aggravating factor was that the murder was committed during a robbery for pecuniary gain. The State had repeatedly emphasized the invalid factor and said little about the valid aggravator. Despite this, all that the Mississippi Supreme Court said was: "We likewise are of the opinion beyond a reasonable doubt that the jury's verdict would have been the same with or without the 'especially heinous, atrocious or cruel' aggravating circumstance." We quite understandably required a "detailed explanation based on the record" in those circumstances.

The same "detailed explanation on the record" that we required in *Clemons* may not have been necessary in this case. But even if the Fifth Circuit's harmless-error analysis was too perfunctory, we think it plain, under the alternative mode of harmless-error analysis, that the error indeed was harmless beyond a reasonable doubt. See §3595(c)(2) (federal death sentences are not to be set aside on the basis of errors that are harmless beyond a reasonable doubt). Had factors 3(B) and 3(C) been precisely defined in writing, the jury surely would have reached the same recommendation as it did. The Government's argument to the jury cured the nonstatutory factors of any infirmity as written. We are satisfied that the jury in this case actually understood what each factor was designed to put before it, and therefore have no doubt that the jury would have reached the same conclusion had the aggravators been precisely defined in writing.

For the foregoing reasons, the judgment of the Court of Appeals is affirmed.

Justice GINSBURG, with whom Justice Stevens and Justice Souter join, and with whom Justice Breyer joins as to Parts I, II, III, and V, dissenting.

The Federal Death Penalty Act of 1994 (FDPA), 18 U.S.C. §§3591–3598, establishes a complex regime applicable when the Government seeks the ultimate penalty for a defendant found guilty of an offense potentially punishable by death. This case is pathmarking, for it is the first application of the FDPA. Two questions, as I comprehend petitioner's core objections, warrant prime attention.

First, when Congress specifies only two sentencing options for an offense, death or life without possibility of release, must the jury be told exactly that? Or, can a death decision stand despite misleading trial court "lesser sentence" instructions, specifically, instructions open to the construction that lack of a unanimous jury vote for either life or death would allow the judge to impose a sentence less severe than life in prison? Second, when the jury is unable to agree on a unanimous recommendation in a case in which death or life without possibility of release are the only sentencing options, must the judge then impose the life sentence? Or, is the judge required or permitted to impanel a second jury to make the life or death decision?

The Court of Appeals for the Fifth Circuit confronted these two questions and resolved both for the prosecution. The Fifth Circuit also tolerated the trial court's submission of two nonstatutory aggravating factors to the jury, although the appeals court found those factors duplicative and vague. The lower courts' disposition for death, despite the flawed trial proceedings, and this Court's tolerance of the flaws, disregard a most basic guide: "[A]ccurate sentencing information is an indispensable prerequisite to a [jury's] determination of whether a defendant shall live or die." *Gregg v. Georgia*, 428 U.S. 153, 190 (1976) (joint opinion of Stewart, Powell, and Stevens, JJ.). That "indispensable prerequisite" was not satisfied in this case. I would reverse and remand so that the life or death decision may be made by an accurately informed trier.

I

After authorizing the federal death penalty for a small category of cases in 1988,[2] Congress enacted comprehensive death penalty legislation in 1994. See FDPA, 108 Stat.1959. Applicable to over 40 existing and newly declared death eligible offenses, see 18 U.S.C. §3591; the FDPA prescribes penalty-phase procedures; principally, it provides for a separate sentencing hearing whenever the Government seeks the death penalty for defendants found guilty of a covered offense.

In death-eligible homicide cases, the Act instructs, the jury must respond sequentially to three inquiries; imposition of the death penalty requires unanimity on each of the three. First, the jury determines whether there was a killing or death resulting from the defendant's intentional engagement in life-threatening activity. See 18 U.S.C. §3591(a)(2).[6] Second, the jury decides which, if any, of the Government-proposed aggravating factors, statutory and nonstatutory, were proved beyond a reasonable doubt. See §3593(d).[7] Third, if the jury finds at least one of the statutory aggravators proposed by the Government, the jury then determines whether the aggravating factors "sufficiently outweigh" the mitigating factors to warrant a death sentence, or, absent mitigating factors, whether the aggravators alone warrant that sentence. §3593(e). The mitigating factors, seven statutory and any others tending against the death sentence, are individually determined by each juror; unlike aggravating factors, on which the jury must unanimously agree under a "beyond a reasonable doubt" standard, a mitigating factor may be considered in the jury's weighing process if any one juror finds the factor proved by a "preponderance of the evidence." See §§3592(a), (c), 3593(d). The weigh-

---

2. The predecessor Anti-Drug Abuse Act of 1988 authorized the death penalty for murder resulting from certain drug-related offenses. See 21 U.S.C. §848(e). The FDPA states that its procedures apply to "any [federal] offense for which a sentence of death is provided," 18 U.S.C. §3591(a)(2), but does not repeal the 1988 Act, which differs in some respects. See, *e.g.,* 21 U.S.C. §§848(q)(4)–(9) (mandatory appointment of habeas counsel and provision of investigative and expert services).

6. Section 3591(a)(2) allows the death penalty for a defendant found guilty of a death-eligible homicide "if the defendant, as determined beyond a reasonable doubt at the [sentencing] hearing":

"(A) intentionally killed the victim;

"(B) intentionally inflicted serious bodily injury that resulted in the death of the victim;

"(C) intentionally participated in an act, contemplating that the life of a person would be taken or intending that lethal force would be used in connection with a person, other than one of the participants in the offense, and the victim died as a direct result of the act; or

"(D) intentionally and specifically engaged in an act of violence, knowing that the act created a grave risk of death to a person, other than one of the participants in the offense, such that participation in the act constituted a reckless disregard for human life and the victim died as a direct result of the act."

7. The FDPA lists 16 aggravating factors for homicide and allows the jury to "consider whether any other aggravating factor for which notice has been given [by the Government] exists." 18 U.S.C. §3592(c). Nonstatutory aggravators "may include factors concerning the effect of the offense on the victim and the victim's family." §3593(a).

ing is not numeric; the perceived significance, not the number, of aggravating and mitigating factors determines the decision.

II

Louis Jones, Jr.'s crime was atrocious; its commission followed Jones's precipitous decline in fortune and self-governance on termination of his 22-year Army career. On February 18, 1995, Jones forcibly abducted Private Tracie Joy McBride at gunpoint from the Goodfellow Air Force Base in San Angelo, Texas. In the course of the abduction, Jones struck Private Michael Alan Peacock with a handgun, leaving him unconscious. Thereafter, Jones sexually assaulted and killed McBride, leaving her body under a bridge located 20 miles outside of San Angelo.

In the fall of 1995, Jones was tried before a jury and convicted of kidnaping with death resulting, in violation of 18 U.S.C. §1201(a)(2). A separate sentencing hearing followed to determine whether Jones would be punished by death.

At the close of the sentencing hearing, Jones submitted proposed jury instructions. Jones's instruction no. 4 would have advised the jury that it must sentence Jones to life without possibility of release rather than death "[i]f any one of you is not persuaded that justice demands Mr. Jones's execution." Jones's instruction no. 5 would have advised that, if "the jury is unable to agree on a unanimous decision as to the sentence to be imposed," the jury should so inform the judge, who would then "impose a sentence of life imprisonment without possibility of release." Proposed instructions nos. 4 and 5, although inartfully drawn, unquestionably sought to convey this core information: If the jurors did not agree on death, then the only sentencing option, for jury or judge, would be life without possibility of release. Jones also objected, on vagueness grounds, to two of the three nonstatutory aggravators proposed by the Government.

The District Court rejected Jones's proposed instructions nos. 4 and 5 and refused to strike or modify the nonstatutory aggravators to which Jones had objected. The trial court instructed the jury that it could recommend death, life without possibility of release, or a lesser sentence, in which event the court would decide what the lesser sentence would be.

The jury apparently found the case close. It rejected three of the seven aggravators the Government urged.[11] And one or more jurors found each of the specific mitigating factors submitted by Jones. The jury deliberated for a day and a half before returning a verdict recommending death.

Jones moved for a new trial on the ground, supported by postsentence juror statements, that the court's instructions had misled the jurors. Specifically, Jones urged that the charge led jurors to believe that a deadlock would result in a court-imposed lesser sentence; to avoid such an outcome, Jones asserted, jurors who favored life without possibility of release changed their votes to approve the death verdict. The vote change, Jones maintained, was not hypothetical; it was backed up by juror statements. The District Court denied the new trial motion.

---

11. The jury rejected the following aggravators: (1) the crime involved substantial planning and premeditation, see 18 U.S.C. §3592(c)(9); (2) the crime created a grave risk to a person other than the victim, see §3592(c)(5); and (3) Jones posed a future danger to the lives and safety of other persons. It found as aggravators: (1) Jones killed the victim during the commission of kidnaping, see §3592(c)(1); (2) the crime was especially heinous, cruel, and depraved, see §3592(c)6; (3) the victim's young age, slight stature, background, and unfamiliarity with San Angelo, Texas; and (4) the victim's personal characteristics and the effect of the offense on her family.

The Court of Appeals for the Fifth Circuit affirmed the death sentence. The appeals court ruled first that the District Court correctly refused to instruct that a jury deadlock would yield a court-imposed sentence of life imprisonment without possibility of release. Jury deadlock under the FDPA, the Fifth Circuit stated, would not occasion an automatic life sentence; instead, that court declared, deadlock would necessitate a second sentencing hearing before a newly impaneled jury. The Court of Appeals further observed that, "[a]lthough the use of instructions to inform the jury of the consequences of a hung jury ha[s] been affirmed, federal courts have never been affirmatively required to give such instructions."

Next, the appeals court determined that the instructions, read in their entirety, "could not have led a reasonable jury to conclude that non-unanimity would result in the imposition of a lesser sentence." Jones could not rely on juror statements, the Fifth Circuit held, to show that the jury, in fact, was so misled when it sentenced him to death.

Nor, in the Court of Appeals' view, did the District Court err *plainly* by conveying to the jury the misinformation that three sentencing options were available—death, life imprisonment without release, or some other lesser sentence. Noting that the FDPA takes account of all three possibilities, while the kidnaping statute authorizes only two sentences, death or life imprisonment the Fifth Circuit acknowledged that the District Court had erred in giving the jury a lesser sentence option: "[T]he substantive [kidnaping] statute takes precedence over the death penalty sentencing provisions" and limits the options to death or life imprisonment without release. The appeals court nevertheless concluded that the District Court's error was not "plain" because the FDPA was new and no prior opinion had addressed the question; hence, no "clearly established law" was in place at the time of Jones's sentencing hearing.

The Fifth Circuit also considered Jones's challenge to the nonstatutory aggravators presented to the jury at the Government's request. The court held that the two found by the jury—the victim's "young age, her slight stature, her background, and her unfamiliarity with San Angelo, Texas," and her "personal characteristics and the effect of the offense on [her] family"—were "duplicative" of each other, and also impermissibly "vague and overbroad." The court declined to upset the death verdict, however, because it believed "the death sentence would have been imposed beyond a reasonable doubt had the invalid aggravating factors never been submitted to the jury."

III

The governing law gave Jones's jury at the sentencing phase a life (without release) or death choice. The District Court, however, introduced, erroneously, a third prospect, "some other lesser sentence." App. 44.[13] Moreover, the court told the jury "not to be concerned" with what that lesser sentence might be, for "[t]hat [was] a matter for the court to decide." The jury's choice was clouded by that misinformation. I set out below my reasons for concluding that the misinformation rendered the jury's death verdict unreliable.

A

The District Court instructed the jury:

---

13. The problem was not, as the Court describes it, a failure to give the jury "[a] bit of information that might possibly influence an individual juror's voting behavior," rather, the jury was "affirmatively misled," by the repeated misinformation the charge and decision forms conveyed.

"[Y]ou the jury, by unanimous vote, shall recommend whether the defendant should be sentenced to death, sentenced to life imprisonment without the possibility of release, or sentenced to some other lesser sentence.

"If you recommend that some other lesser sentence be imposed, the court is required to impose a sentence that is authorized by the law. In deciding what recommendation to make, you are not to be concerned with the question of what sentence the defendant might receive in the event you determine not to recommend a death sentence or a sentence of life without the possibility of release. That is a matter for the court to decide in the event you conclude that a sentence of death or life without the possibility of release should not be recommended.

"In order to bring back a verdict recommending the punishment of death or life without the possibility of release, all twelve of you must unanimously vote in favor of such specific penalty."

Those instructions misinformed the jury in two intertwined respects: First, they wrongly identified a "lesser sentence" option;[14] second, the instructions were open to the reading that, absent juror unanimity on death or life without release, the District Court could impose a lesser sentence.

The Fifth Circuit, and the United States in its submission to this Court, acknowledged the charge error. Section 1201, which defines the crime, governs. It calls for death or life imprisonment, nothing less, and neither parole nor good-time credits could reduce the life sentence. See Brief for United States 13–14, n. 2 ("[W]e agree with petitioner that the only sentences that could have been imposed are death and life without release (because the kidnapping statute, 18 U.S.C. [§]1201, authorizes only death and life imprisonment, and neither parole nor good-time credits could reduce the life sentence)."). The third option listed in the FDPA provision, "some other lesser sentence," §3593(e), is available only when the substantive statute does not confine the sentence to life or death. The Fifth Circuit found the error "not so obvious, clear, readily apparent, or conspicuous." I disagree and would rank the District Court's misconstruction "plain error," because the FDPA unquestionably is a procedural statute that does not alter substantive prescriptions. No serious doubt should have existed on that score.

The flawed charge did not simply include a nonexistent option. It could have been understood to convey that, absent juror unanimity, some "lesser sentence" might be imposed by the court. That message came from instructions that the jury must be unanimous to "bring back a verdict recommending the punishment of death or life without the possibility of release," that "some other lesser sentence" was possible, and that the jury should not "be concerned with the sentence the defendant might receive in the event [it] determine[d] not to recommend a death sentence or a sentence of life without the possibility of release," Jones's proposed instructions—that he would be sentenced to life without possibility of release if the jury did not agree on death—should have made it apparent that he sought to close the door the flawed charge left open.

---

14. The verdict forms compounded the error by allowing the jurors to return as their decision the statement: "We the jury recommend some other lesser sentence." Jones does not press the District Court's identification of a lesser sentence option as an independent ground for reversal. That error, however, is an essential component of his argument that the misinformation conveyed by District Court led the jury to believe that deadlock could result in a less-than-life sentence.

There is, at least, a reasonable likelihood that the flawed charge tainted the jury deliberations. See *Boyde v. California*, 494 U.S. 370, 380 (1990) (where "[t]he claim is that the instruction is subject to an erroneous interpretation," the "proper inquiry is whether there is a reasonable likelihood that the jury has applied the challenged instruction" erroneously). As recently noted, a jury may be swayed toward death if it believes the defendant otherwise may serve less than life in prison. See *Simmons v. South Carolina*, 512 U.S. 154, 163 (1994) (plurality opinion) ("[I]t is entirely reasonable for a sentencing jury to view a defendant who is eligible for parole as a greater threat to society than a defendant who is not."). Jurors may have been persuaded to switch from life to death to ward off what no juror wanted, *i.e.*, any chance of a lesser sentence by the judge.

The Court, in common with the Fifth Circuit and the Solicitor General, insists it was just as likely that jurors not supporting death could have persuaded death-prone jurors to give way and vote for a life sentence. I would demur (say so what) to that position. It should suffice that the potential to confuse existed, *i.e.*, that the instructions could have tilted the jury toward death. The instructions "introduce[d] a level of uncertainty and unreliability into the factfinding process that cannot be tolerated in a capital case." *Beck v. Alabama*, 447 U.S. 625, 643 (1980). "Capital sentencing should not be a game of 'chicken,' in which life or death turns on the happenstance of whether the particular 'life' jurors or 'death' jurors in each case will be the first to give in, in order to avoid a perceived third sentencing outcome unacceptable to either set of jurors."

B

The Fifth Circuit held that the District Court was not obliged to tell the jury that Jones's default penalty was life without possibility of release in part because the appeals court viewed that instruction as "substantively [in]correct." As the Fifth Circuit comprehended the law, if the jury deadlocked, "a second sentencing hearing would have to be held in front of a second jury impaneled for that purpose." But the FDPA, it seems to me clear, does not provide for a second shot at death. The dispositive provision, as I read the Act, is §3594, which first states that the court shall sentence the defendant to death or life imprisonment without possibility of release if the jury so recommends, and then continues:

> "Otherwise, the court shall impose any lesser sentence that is authorized by law. Notwithstanding any other law, if the maximum term of imprisonment for the offense is life imprisonment, the court may impose a sentence of life imprisonment without possibility of release." 18 U.S.C. §3594.

The "[o]therwise" clause, requiring judge sentencing, becomes operative when a jury fails to make a unanimous recommendation at the close of deliberations. The Fifth Circuit's attention was deflected from the §3594 path by §3593(b)(2)(C), which provides for a sentencing hearing "before a jury impaneled for the purpose of the hearing if the jury that determined the defendant's guilt was discharged for good cause." Discharge for "good cause" under §3593(b)(2)(C), however, is most reasonably read to cover guilt-phase (and, by extension, penalty-phase) juror disqualification due to, *e.g.*, exposure to prejudicial extrinsic information or illness. The provision should not be read expansively to encompass failure to reach a unanimous life or death decision.

The Government refers to a "background rule" allowing retrial if the jury is unable to reach a verdict, and urges that the FDPA should be read in light of that rule. But retrial is not the prevailing rule for capital penalty-phase proceedings. As the Government's own survey of state laws shows, in life or death cases, most States require judge sentencing once a jury has deadlocked. App. to Brief for United States 1a–6a (identifying 25 States in which the court imposes sentence upon deadlock and three States in which a new sentencing hearing is possible); see also Acker & Lanier, Law, Discretion, and the Capital Jury: Death Penalty Statutes and Proposals for Reform, 32 Crim. L. Bull. 134, 169 (1996) ("In twenty-five of the twenty-nine states in which capital juries have final sentencing authority, a deadlocked sentencing jury is transformed into a 'lifelocked' jury. That is, the jury's inability to produce a unanimous penalty-phase verdict results in the defendant's being sentenced to life imprisonment or life imprisonment without parole."

Furthermore, at the time Congress adopted the FDPA, identical language in the predecessor Anti-Drug Abuse and Death Penalty Act of 1988 had been construed to mandate court sentencing upon jury deadlock. See *United States v. Chandler*, 996 F.2d 1073, 1086 (C.A.11 1993) ("If the jury does not [recommend death], the district court sentences the defendant."); *United States v. Pitera*, 795 F.Supp. 546, 552 (E.D.N.Y.1992) ("Absent a recommendation of death, the court must sentence a defendant.").[22] The House Report suggests that Congress understood and approved that construction. See H.R.Rep. No. 103-467, p. 9 (1994) ("If the jury is not unanimous, the judge shall impose the sentence pursuant to Section 3594.").

IV

Piled on the key instructional error, the trial court presented the jury with duplicative, vague nonstatutory aggravating factors. The court told the jury to consider as aggravators, if established beyond a reasonable doubt, factors 3(B)—the victim's "young age, her slight stature, her background, and her unfamiliarity with San Angelo, Texas"—and 3(C)—the victim's "personal characteristics and the effect of the instant offense on [her] family." The jury found both.

The District Court did not clarify the meaning of the terms "background" and "personal characteristics." Notably, the term "personal characteristics" in aggravator 3(C) necessarily included "young age," "slight stature," "background," and "unfamiliarity," factors the jury was told to consider in aggravator 3(B). I would not attribute to the Court genuine disagreement with that proposition. Double counting of aggravators "creates the risk of an arbitrary death sentence." 132 F.3d, at 251; see also *United States v. McCullah*, 76 F.3d 1087, 1111 (C.A.10 1996) ("Such double counting of aggravating factors, especially under a weighing scheme, has a tendency to skew the weighing process and creates the risk that the death sentence will be imposed arbitrarily."). The Fifth Circuit considered the District Court's lapse inconsequential, concluding that "the two remaining statutory aggravating factors support the sentence of death, even after considering the eleven mitigating factors."

Appellate courts should hesitate to assert confidence that "elimination of improperly considered aggravating circumstances could not possibly affect the balance." *Barclay v. Florida*, 463 U.S. 939, 958 (1983). Adding the overlapping aggravators to the more disturbing misinformation conveyed in the charge, I see no basis for concluding

---

22. Like the FDPA, the Anti-Drug Abuse Act provides for a new sentencing jury if the guilt-phase jury "has been discharged for good cause," 21 U.S.C. §848(i)(1)(B)(iii), and states, immediately after providing for the death sentence upon jury recommendation, that "[o]therwise the court shall impose a sentence, other than death, authorized by law," §848(l). Under the Anti-Drug Abuse Act, unlike the FDPA, the only binding recommendation the jury can make is for death.

"it would have made no difference if the thumb had been removed from death's side of the scale."

V

The Fifth Circuit's tolerance of error in this case, and this Court's refusal to face up to it, cannot be reconciled with the recognition in *Woodson v. North Carolina*, 428 U.S. 280, 305 (1976) (plurality opinion), that "death is qualitatively different." If the jury's weighing process is infected by the trial court's misperceptions of the law, the legitimacy of an ensuing death sentence should not hinge on defense counsel's shortfalls or the reviewing court's speculation about the decision the jury would have made absent the infection. I would vacate the jury's sentencing decision and remand the case for a new sentencing hearing, one that would proceed with the accuracy that superintendents of the FDPA should demand.

Note on the Reinstatement of the Federal Death Penalty

Those interested in the reinstatement of the death penalty on the federal level, and the *Jones* case in particular, should see Comment, "Testing the Federal Death Penalty Act of 1994," 29 Tex. Tech L. Rev. 1043 (1998), and Cutler, "Death Resurrected: The Reimplementation of the Federal Death Penalty," 23 Seattle U.L. Rev. 1189 (2000). See also Kannar, "Federalizing Death," 44 Buff. L. Rev. 325 (1996) and Little, "The Federal Death Penalty: History and Some Thoughts About the Department of Justice's Role," 26 Fordham Urb. L.J. 347 (1999).

Note on the Resurgence of Due Process Challenges to the Federal Death Penalty

In 2002, within a span of three months, two district courts struck down the Federal Death Penalty Act (FDPA) as unconstitutional. *United States v. Quinones*, 205 F. Supp. 2d 256 (S.D.N.Y.), *rev'd*, 313 F.3d 49 (2d Cir. 2002), and *United States v. Fell*, 217 F. Supp. 2d 469 (D. Vt.), *rev'd*, 360 F.3d 135 (2d Cir. 2004), each held that the FDPA failed to protect the due process rights of federal capital defendants. Although the two courts employed differing rationales, both cases applied the Due Process Clause of the Fifth Amendment, rather than the Eighth Amendment's Cruel and Unusual Punishment Clause.

Applying a substantive due process analysis, the *Quinones* court found the FDPA to be unconstitutional in light of persuasive evidence of a substantial risk of wrongful convictions in capital cases. The court noted that more than 100 death row inmates had been shown to have been wrongfully convicted, some of whom came within hours of wrongful execution.

The *Fell* court focused on whether the FDPA's relaxed evidentiary standard at sentencing—permitting the introduction of "information," including hearsay, that would be inadmissible under the Federal Rules of Evidence—violated procedural due process. In *Fell*, the government sought to introduce a statement allegedly made by Fell's deceased co-defendant in order to establish Fell's eligibility for a death sentence. Because the Sixth Amendment rights to confront and cross-examine witnesses have long been recognized as essential to due process, the court struck down the FDPA provision.

Although both *Quinones* and *Fell* were ultimately reversed by the Second Circuit, both district court rulings were based on an overriding concern for heightened reliability in capital cases. *See* Herman, "Death Penalty Due Process: Evaluating Due Process Challenges to the Federal Death Penalty Act," 53 DePaul L. Rev. 1777 (2004) (observing that "*Quinones* and *Fell* provide substance to the language of death penalty jurisprudence that is too often aspirational rhetoric").

Note and Question on the Oklahoma City Bombing Cases

On April 19, 1995, a truck bomb exploded in front of the Alfred P. Murrah federal building in downtown Oklahoma City. One hundred sixty-eight people died of bomb-related injuries and one rescue worker died from injuries sustained during the rescue effort. Hundreds of others were injured. The United States Department of Justice filed federal capital charges against Timothy McVeigh and Terry Nichols, the suspected bombers, under 18 U.S.C. §§844(f) and 2332a. Is there any prohibition against the Oklahoma County District Attorney filing capital charges under Oklahoma state law? United States Chief District Judge Richard Matsch's exhaustive treatment of defense challenges to the federal capital charges follows.

United States v. McVeigh and Nichols
944 F. Supp. 1478 (D. Colo. 1996)

MATSCH, Chief Judge

On October 20, 1995, the government filed a Notice of Intention to Seek the Death Penalty as to defendant Timothy James McVeigh, and an identical notice as to defendant Terry Lynn Nichols. These notices, under 18 U.S.C. §3593(a), invoke the provisions of the Federal Death Penalty Act, ("Act") 18 U.S.C. §§3591–3596.

Before the notices were filed, defendant Timothy McVeigh moved to disqualify the Attorney General and all other officers and employees of the Department of Justice from any participation in the process of deciding whether to seek the death penalty in this case. That motion, filed July 25, 1995, was fully briefed but not decided before the reassignment of this case and the change of venue. The defendant Terry Nichols joined in the motion. The particular relief sought in the motion to disqualify is now moot because the notices have been filed. The contentions made must be considered, however, because they also affect the validity of these notices as challenged by the defendants' motions to strike.

Mr. Nichols filed a separate civil action in the Western District of Oklahoma, *Terry Lynn Nichols v. Janet Reno*, Civil Action No. 96-M-606, (formerly CIV-95-1824W), which was transferred to this court. The complaint in that case, brought under the Administrative Procedures Act, made some of the same contentions contained in Mr. McVeigh's motion to disqualify. This court granted the defendants' motion to dismiss the civil action in a memorandum opinion and order entered on May 29, 1996. *Nichols v. Reno*, 931 F. Supp. 748 (D. Colo. 1996). Although the dismissal resulted from the conclusion that the complaint did not state a claim for relief within the court's jurisdiction, the reasoning is applicable here on the merits of Mr. McVeigh's motion to disqualify.

The premise of the motion is that the Attorney General made the decision to seek the death penalty before any suspect was even identified. On April 19, 1995, shortly after the explosion in Oklahoma City giving rise to the charges in this case, General Reno publicly announced that the death penalty would be sought in any prosecution for bombing the Murrah Building. The President repeated that public pledge two days later, shortly after Timothy McVeigh was identified as a suspect. Later on that day, April 21, when Mr. McVeigh appeared before Magistrate Judge Ronald L. Howland in Oklahoma City, an Assistant United States Attorney advised the court that the maximum penalty on the charge of violation of 18 U.S.C. §844(f) was death.

In the memorandum opinion and order deciding the civil case, the court reviewed the "Death Penalty Protocol" published in the United States Attorneys' Manual, prescribing a procedure for prosecutors to follow to obtain authority to seek the death penalty in any criminal case. Patrick Ryan, United States Attorney for the Western District of Oklahoma, wrote a letter to Timothy McVeigh's attorney, Stephen Jones, inviting his participation in the Protocol process. Mr. Jones refused any participation, claiming that it would be futile because these public statements showed that the decision had already been made. Despite the refusal, the Department of Justice procedure was followed and the formal notices of intention to seek the death penalty were approved according to the Protocol. Counsel for Terry Nichols did submit statements pursuant to the Protocol, as described in the civil case opinion. Counsel for both defendants have asked for discovery of the Department of Justice internal documents relevant to the notices to support their motions. That request is denied. Such documents are not pertinent to the McVeigh motion to disqualify or to the defendants' motions to strike the death penalty notices because the administrative decision to file them is not judicially reviewable.

As this court ruled in the civil action, the decision to seek the death penalty under the Act is a matter of prosecutorial discretion. The Protocol did not create any individual right or entitlement subject to the due process protections applicable to an adjudicative or quasi-adjudicative governmental action. The Act expressly provides that the attorney for the government shall file and serve the death penalty notice if he believes that the "circumstances of the offense" are such that a sentence of death is justified. §3593(a). There is no requirement that the prosecutor consider any other matters, including any mitigating factors concerning the offense or the character and circumstances of a particular defendant. The decision of a jury whether to recommend a sentence of death is made only after a full hearing and consideration of aggravating and mitigating factors provided by information submitted pursuant to the adversary process. §3593(b)-(e). The constitutional protections of the life and liberty of a defendant are provided by the sentencing hearing following trial of the charges in the indictment. The issuance of these notices is essentially a prosecutor's charging decision. The McVeigh motion to disqualify the Attorney General and Department of Justice officials is denied on the merits.

In their motions to strike the death penalty notices the defendants assert that the notices filed on October 20, 1995, violate the Fifth and Eighth Amendments. The defendants claim that the prosecution has exposed them to the possibility of capital punishment as a result of arbitrary and irrational decisions. Nothing has been submitted to show or suggest that the notices were filed because of any discriminatory motive, invidious classification or improper motivation as to either defendant. Those are the only grounds warranting judicial interdiction of such action by an officer of the executive branch of government. Accordingly, there is no merit to this contention.

Additionally, the defendants suggest that Fed. R. Crim. P. 7 is applicable to these notices and that they fail to include adequate statements of the essential facts relied on as required by subsection (c) of the rule. Assuming that the rule fairly states the requirement of adequate notice for procedural due process and is, therefore, applicable to the notices, there is no violation when the notices are read in conjunction with the allegations of the indictment. The indictment contains such detailed statements of what the prosecution intends to prove that these defendants previously challenged its language as being inflammatory and containing prejudicial surplusage. Taken together, the indictment and notices give the defendants adequate information as to what the government will rely on at trial and sentencing. Additional notice has been given in the extensive discovery provided by the prosecutors.

The defense motions claim that the Act is facially unconstitutional in several aspects. The broadest argument is that under all circumstances the death penalty is cruel and unusual punishment prohibited by the Eighth Amendment. That argument is foreclosed by the decisions of the Supreme Court. *McCleskey v. Kemp*, 481 U.S. 279, 300–303 (1987).

The defendants claim that the government's notice violates the Fifth Amendment grand jury requirement. This position was rejected in the Memorandum Opinion and Order filed on September 9, 1996. *United States v. McVeigh and Nichols*, 940 F. Supp. 1571 (D. Colo. 1996).

The defendants argue that the Act does not permit meaningful appellate review because Congress provided in §3595 that a sentence of death will be reviewed upon appeal only if the defendant files a notice of appeal within the time specified for filing any other notice of appeal. There is no automatic appellate review as in some of the state statutes which have been validated by the Supreme Court since *Furman v. Georgia*, 408 U.S. 238 (1972). The defendants say that conditioning sentence review upon a request by the defendant is an invalid limitation, suggesting that a defendant may be unable to decide to appeal because of depression or other mental or emotional infirmity after the sentencing. That contention is highly speculative. While the decision to appeal a conviction and sentence must be made by a defendant, the court has the duty to provide the assistance of counsel who must also be given the authority and means to employ such consultants and advisors, including psychiatrists, upon an appropriate *ex parte* showing of need under 21 U.S.C. §848(q). Conjecture about a particular defendant's ability to make an informed and rational decision to appeal a sentence is not a basis for invalidating the Act. Adequate resources are ensured to protect against the possibility of the loss of an appeal resulting from such circumstances. Moreover, §3595 of the Act provides for consolidation of the appeal of the sentence with an appeal of the judgment of conviction and directs that the case be given priority over all other cases in the appellate court. The full record of pretrial, trial and sentencing proceedings may be presented to the court of appeals.

The defendants also assert that the Act improperly imposes a legislative limitation on the scope of review of a death sentence in 18 U.S.C. §3595(c). That subsection directs the court of appeals to address all substantive and procedural issues raised on the sentence appeal and to consider whether the death sentence "was imposed under the influence of passion, prejudice or any other arbitrary factor and whether the evidence supports the special finding of the existence of an aggravating factor required to be considered under §3592." It further provides that upon such a determination or upon a conclusion that the proceedings involved any other legal error requiring reversal that was adequately preserved for appeal under the Federal Rules of Criminal Procedure, the case shall be remanded for reconsideration under §3593 or imposition of a sentence other than death. Section 3595(c)(2)(C) adds the following direction:

> The court of appeals shall not reverse or vacate a sentence of death on account of any error which can be harmless, including any erroneous special findings of an aggravating factor, where the Government establishes beyond a reasonable doubt that the error was harmless.

It is presumed that such a showing by the government would be based on the record for review under §3595(b).

The defendants claim that because of these restrictions, those who are sentenced to death under this Act are denied equal protection of the law as compared with persons sentenced under other statutes.

The general jurisdiction of the court of appeals is granted in 28 U.S.C. §1291, providing for appeals from all final decisions of the district courts. Review of sentences other than for the death penalty is under 18 U.S.C. §3742(a), providing that a defendant may file a notice of appeal for review of a sentence imposed in violation of law, resulting from an incorrect application of the sentencing guidelines, a sentence greater than provided under the applicable guideline range, or, when imposed for an offense for which there is no sentencing guideline, "is plainly unreasonable." Thus, the review provided for a death sentence is actually broader in scope than that for any other sentence.

The harmless error restriction on reversal of any decision is well established. *United States v. Tipton*, 90 F.3d 861, 899–901 (4th Cir. 1996). As already noted, a consolidated appeal of conviction and sentence is contemplated by the statute so the court of appeals will have before it any issues which are asserted as error in the trial resulting in the conviction. Additionally, this court is unwilling to speculate as to the approach that the Tenth Circuit Court of Appeals may take with respect to the possible application of the "plain error" doctrine and the scope of appellate review under the Constitution, in spite of any purported limitations in the statute. Reading this statute as an interference with the authority of the court of appeals to correct a fundamental error in a particular type of case would construe it in contradiction of the constitutional doctrine of separation of powers. Cf. *United States v. Bradley*, 880 F. Supp. 271, 283 (M.D .Pa. 1994) (construing the Act to avoid constitutional infirmity by reading its provision for appellate review of "arbitrary finding[s]" to allow reversal of a sentence if reversible errors occurred at trial).

Defense counsel argue that the death penalty notices are invalid because they include aggravating factors not listed in the statute. The defendants note an inconsistency in the Act in that §3592(c) lists specific aggravating factors which may be included in the government's notice for homicide crimes under §3591(a)(2) and then provides that the jury may consider "whether any other aggravating factor for which notice has been given exists." Yet, in §3591, Congress provided for a sentence of death if "after consideration of the factors set forth in §3592 ..." it is determined that imposition of a sentence of death is justified. Thus, §3591 appears to limit the jury to consideration of such of the 15 specific statutory aggravating factors in §3592(c) as may be listed in the government's notice. Additionally, under §3593(e), to recommend death, all jurors must determine that at least one aggravating factor required to be considered under §3592(c) has been proved beyond a reasonable doubt and then consider whether all the aggravating factors so proved sufficiently outweigh all the mitigating factors found to exist by a preponderance of the evidence to justify a sentence of death. There is no specific mention of non-statutory aggravating factors in that section. Noteworthy, however, in §3593(a), the factors for which notice is provided "may include the effect of the offense on the victim and the victim's family," a factor not among those specified in §3592(c).

Other courts have read the other death penalty statute, 21 U.S.C. §848(e), to permit inclusion of non-statutory aggravating factors. *United States v. McCullah*, 76 F.3d 1087, 1106–07 (10th Cir. 1996). In a recent case, the District Court of Kansas reached the same result under this Act. *United States v. Nguyen*, 928 F. Supp. 1525, 1536–37 (D. Kan. 1996). The reasoning of these cases is persuasive on this issue.

The defendants assert that if the Act is interpreted to permit non-statutory aggravating factors, it is unconstitutional as a delegation of legislative authority to officers of the executive branch without any guiding policy limiting what the prosecutors may choose to include in their notice. There is some merit to the argument as an abstraction. Both sides cite *Mistretta v. United States*, 488 U.S. 361 (1989), in support of their respective positions concerning this delegation argument. As noted in an earlier opinion, *United States v. McVeigh and Nichols*, 940 F. Supp. 1571 (D. Colo. 1996), the court should not address abstract constitutional questions. There is no merit to the defendants' arguments in the context of a sentencing hearing under §3593.

While it is true that Congress did not impose policy limitations or give clear guidance to prosecuting attorneys as to what may be included as non-statutory aggravating factors, the sentencing hearing is governed by the court within the adversary process. Accordingly, the validity of particular non-statutory aggravating factors may be litigated and adjudicated before the court, just as is being done in the present motions. It is then the judicial authority of the court within the factual context of particular cases that controls the scope of the sentencing hearing. The guiding principles for judicial determination of the validity of particular non-statutory aggravators is the death penalty jurisprudence developed by the Supreme Court. Thus, the aggravating factors must serve the purpose of selection of the defendant for the special penalty with individual consideration to his character and particular conduct in the offense. See *McCullah*, 76 F.3d at 1106 (noting that non-statutory aggravating factors are guided by the principle of individualized sentencing).

Mr. McVeigh also asserts that the addition of non-statutory aggravating factors is barred by the Ex Post Facto clause in Art. I, Sec. 9, of the Constitution. The answer to that argument is that the enactment of this statute was a change in sentencing procedure, not a change in the definition of a crime or an increase in the punishment. *Dobbert v. Florida*, 432 U.S. 282, 293–94 (1977); *Hatch v. Oklahoma*, 58 F.3d 1447, 1463–65 (10th Cir. 1995).

The Act does not require an appellate review of the proportionality of a death sentence compared with others convicted of the same crime. Recognizing that the Supreme Court held that a proportionality review is not required by the Eighth Amendment in *Pulley v. Harris*, 465 U.S. 37, 43–44 (1984), the defendants attempt to distinguish that ruling on the ground that the California statute involved in that case did not permit the use of non-statutory aggravating factors. Thus, a proportionality review is urged to be an indispensable requirement to check against the arbitrary imposition of the death penalty if non-statutory aggravating factors are included. This attempted distinction is not persuasive. As discussed later in this opinion, the function of aggravating factors, whether or not statutorily required, is to provide assurance that the jury arrives at a rational decision, after following an assessment process adequately designed to measure the variables involved in the crime and the circumstances of the perpetrator, to select him as deserving the maximum punishment.

Another general challenge to the constitutionality of the Act made by the defendants is directed to §3593(c) providing for proof of mitigating and aggravating factors by "information" regardless of admissibility under the Federal Rules of Evidence, "except that information may be excluded if its probative value is outweighed by the danger of creating unfair prejudice, confusing the issues, or misleading the jury." Thus, the only explicit standard for exclusion is an adaptation from Fed. R. Evid. 403. The court's discretion is broader in the penalty hearing, however, because under

Rule 403 the court may exclude relevant evidence only if its probative value is substantially outweighed by such dangers whereas the statute has no such quantitative limitation. Read literally, the substitution of information for evidence in §3593(c) raises the specter of violations of the Confrontation Clause and other fundamental protections contained in the Fifth and Sixth Amendments. What saves the statute is the fact that the hearing is governed by the trial judge who has considerable discretion in controlling the presentation of the "information" to the jury in both content and form. Congress has no authority to prevent the court from protecting the life and liberty of a defendant by the exercise of its Article III authority to conduct all hearings before it.

The defendants have made the general objection to most of the statutory and non-statutory aggravating factors in the notices that they are vague and overbroad. Analysis of the merits of this challenge requires some reflection on the purpose and function of aggravating factors in the sentencing scheme established by the Act. That, in turn, requires some restatement of the Court-dictated imperatives for a constitutionally valid sentence to death.

The Court was unable to form a plurality to support a single opinion stating why the imposition and carrying out of the death penalty in Georgia and Texas before 1972 constituted cruel and unusual punishment in violation of the Eighth and Fourteenth Amendments in *Furman v. Georgia*, 408 U.S. 238 (1972). Four separate opinions were filed in support of the judgment in *Gregg v. Georgia*, 428 U.S. 153 (1976), that a sentence to death for murder under a new sentencing scheme adopted by the Georgia legislature was not an unconstitutional punishment. Individual justices have continued to struggle with attempts to articulate their views about the imperatives of a valid procedure in the many subsequent decisions approving and disapproving variations in state laws governing the extreme punishment of death. They have been more clear in stating what is prohibited than what is required. Thus, the penalty of death may not be ordered automatically, arbitrarily, irregularly, randomly, capriciously, wantonly, freakishly, disproportionately or under any procedure that permits discrimination by race, religion, wealth, social position or economic class.

To be valid, the procedure must protect against a decision motivated by passion and prejudice. It must guide the jurors to individualized consideration of each defendant. The aggravating factors considered must be objectively provable and rationally related to the criminal conduct in the offenses proven at trial. There can be no limitation on the ability of individual jurors to consider mitigating factors. The jurors must be unanimous if their finding is that death is justified, and the jury must articulate the reasons in a manner enabling meaningful appellate review. What must be clear in the end is that the jury has performed its task of acting as the conscience of the community in making a moral judgment about the worth of a specific life balanced against the societal value of a deserved punishment for a particular crime. See *Arave v. Creech*, 507 U.S. 463, 470–71 (1993); *McCleskey v. Kemp*, 481 U.S. 279, 302–03 (1986); *Godfrey v. Georgia*, 446 U.S. 420, 428 (1980).

Congress has attempted to meet these requirements in two death penalty statutes. The first, the Anti-Drug Abuse Act of 1988, now codified at 21 U.S.C. §848(e)(g), provides for the possibility of the death penalty for killings committed while the perpetrators are engaged in certain drug crimes. The second is the Death Penalty Act, applicable to all other offenses for which death has been legislatively prescribed as a possible punishment. §§3591–3596. Both statutes require a separate penalty phase hearing to consider aggravating factors identified in a pretrial notice and such mitigating factors as the defendant may introduce at the hearing.

If there are convictions in this case requiring a penalty phase hearing, the jury will proceed in a sequential manner, first determining whether the government proved one of the four intentions described in §3591(a)(2)(A) through (D). If the jurors are not unanimous in finding that one of these intentions existed, their task is complete and the court will sentence according to the Sentencing Guidelines. If such an intention is found, the jury will then consider whether they are unanimously agreed that at least one of the statutory aggravating factors identified in the government's notice has been proved beyond a reasonable doubt. If such a factor is found, the jury may then consider any other aggravating factors submitted to them, if also proved beyond a reasonable doubt, and each juror will then weigh those factors so proven against such mitigating factors as each individual juror may find to exist by a preponderance of the information presented at the hearing. §3593(d) & (e). Unanimous specific findings must be made as to aggravating factors and the jury may not return a recommendation that a defendant be sentenced to death unless the jurors are unanimously agreed that such aggravating factor or factors sufficiently outweigh all the mitigating factors found to exist to justify a sentence of death.

In effect, a sentence of death may not be imposed for anything other than an intentional killing as defined in §3591(a)(2), and then only after careful consideration of aggravating and mitigating factors particularized as to each defendant.

The aggravating factors function to focus the jury's attention on the particular facts and circumstances pertinent to each defendant found guilty of an offense punishable by death in the context of mitigating factors unique to him as an individual human being. They serve to assist the jury in distinguishing "those who deserve capital punishment from those who do not...." *Arave v. Creech*, 507 U.S. 463, 474 (1993). The notice filed by the government gives the defendants the opportunity to prepare for the hearing and provides the court with some frame of reference for ruling on objections to the information offered at the hearing. It describes how the prosecution intends to "channel the sentencer's discretion by 'clear and objective standards' that provide specific and detailed guidance and make rationally reviewable the death sentencing process."

The Supreme Court has held that aggravating factors must be in sufficiently clear language to be understandable by the jury. *Tuilaepa v. California*, 512 U.S. 967 (1994). In considering this issue at this time, it must be recognized that the notices will be given to a jury with additional instructions to assist in further narrowing and defining the terms used and the concepts communicated.

With these general principles in mind, the particular aggravating factors identified in the notices must be considered. The government has given notice of five factors listed as statutory factors under §3592(c)(1). Each must be examined.

 1. That the deaths or injuries resulting in death occurred during the commission of an offense under 18 U.S.C. 33 (destruction of a motor vehicle or a motor vehicle facility), 18 U.S.C. 844(d) (transportation of explosives in interstate commerce for certain purposes), 18 U.S.C. 844(f) (destruction of government property by explosives), 18 U.S.C. 844(i) (destruction of property affecting interstate commerce by explosives), and 18 U.S.C. 2332a (use of a weapon of mass destruction). See Section 3592(c)(1).

Of the five crimes listed, three have not been charged in the indictment. Two— §844(f) and §2332a—are charged in the indictment, although the reference to §2332a is indefinite in that there are subsections to that section and two of those subsections are charges in counts one and two of the indictment. The defendants correctly observe that §2332a is not one of the crimes listed in §3592(c)(1). As the government notes, it is obvious that the reference to §2339 in the statute with the parenthetical identifier "(use of weapons of mass destruction)" shows a typographical error. The court accepts that position.

The defendants object to this factor because the introduction of multiple predicate offenses to support it could confuse the jury and lead it to consider each of the enumerated predicate offenses as being separate aggravating factors, thereby unfairly weighting this factor and the calculus. There are appropriate procedural answers to that objection. First, the jury instructions can clearly advise that these offenses are simply multiple means for determining that this single aggravating factor, a killing in the course of another offense, is shown to exist. Second, the jury can be required by a special interrogatory to show unanimity in finding which of the underlying offenses they rely on if an affirmative finding is made with respect to this first aggravating factor.

Additionally, the defendants object to this factor because two of the offenses referred to entirely duplicate counts of the indictment, while others duplicate various elements of the charged crimes. The government counters that the commission of these enumerated felony offenses narrows the class of death-eligible defendants and fulfills the principle of selectivity. The government correctly asserts that the Supreme Court's opinion in *Lowenfield v. Phelps*, 484 U.S. 231 (1988), prevents this factor from being stricken on the ground that it fails to narrow the class of defendants that are eligible for the death penalty. The Tenth Circuit applied *Lowenfield* in *United States v. McCullah*, 76 F.3d 1087 (10th Cir. 1996), to uphold the use of an aggravating factor that duplicated charges in the indictment against a narrowing challenge. The court ruled that because the federal death penalty statute in that case, 21 U.S.C. §848(e), had already narrowed the field of death-eligible defendants, the aggravating factor was not invalid because it failed to further narrow that category. Similarly, the intent requirement of the Act operates in this case to narrow the category of death eligibility for the charged crimes, and thus, this first aggravating factor does not fall under this challenge.

However, with respect to those offenses that entirely repeat a charge in the indictment, there is a problem of duplication that was not raised in either *Lowenfield* or *McCullah*. This problem must be viewed in the context of the weighing procedure required by the Act. In *Stringer v. Black*, 503 U.S. 222, 117 (1992), the Supreme Court discussed the severe effect that inappropriate aggravating factors have in a weighing scheme:

> The difference between a weighing State and a non-weighing State is not one of "semantics" ... but of critical importance. In a nonweighing State, so long as the sentencing body finds at least one valid aggravating factor, the fact that it also finds an invalid aggravating factor does not infect the formal process of deciding whether death is an appropriate penalty.... But when the sentencing body is told to weigh an invalid factor in its decision, a reviewing court may not assume it would have made no difference if the thumb had been removed from death's side of the scale.

503 U.S. at 231–32 (citation omitted).

Because the Court has held that the weighing process is highly sensitive to the influence of aggravating factors that might unfairly tip the scales in favor of death, the government may not introduce those offenses as aggravating factors that duplicate the crimes charged in the indictment. To allow the jury to weigh as an aggravating factor a crime already proved in a guilty verdict would unfairly skew the weighing process in favor of death. Accordingly, the offenses under §844(f) and §2332a are stricken. As to any charged offense for which a verdict of not guilty is returned, that offense must then be stricken from the notice because permitting the jury to find it as an aggravating factor in a penalty hearing would result in an inconsistent verdict. Those offenses that merely have overlapping elements with the crimes charged in the indictment may be introduced because the penalty jury will not have predetermined the defendant's guilt with respect to all elements of those crimes.

The defendants also challenge the inclusion of those offenses under §3592(c)(1) that are not charged in the indictment. This challenge presents the same issue that is raised in the defendants' objections to the third non-statutory aggravating factor—the commission of the crimes of burglary, robbery and theft to finance and facilitate the underlying crimes charged. The defendants' argument is that due process requires consideration of these other crimes only upon conviction of them. The court agrees and the problem is solved by instructing the jury that they must find each of the essential elements of those uncharged offenses as a part of their finding of the existence of this aggravating factor beyond a reasonable doubt. Adequate instructions will also answer the defendants' objection that this statutory factor violates the Fifth Amendment because it is too vague.

2. That the defendant, in the commission of the offense(s), knowingly created a grave risk of death to one or more persons in addition to the victim(s) of the offense(s). See Section 3592(c)(5).

The defendants in their vagueness objection to this factor point out that no details are alleged and that there is uncertainty with respect to whether an intent to place others at grave risk must be shown. Read in the context of the factual allegations of the indictment, there is no problem here. The government intends to prove that the truck bomb was of such force as to create a risk to persons who were not physically affected by the explosion. The issue is one of scope and a clarifying instruction may validate this factor.

3. That the defendant committed the offense(s) after substantial planning and premeditation to cause the death of one or more persons and to commit an act of terrorism. See Section 3592(c)(9).

The defendants criticize the word "substantial" as having no definite meaning. In this court's view, substantial is one of those everyday words having a common sense core meaning that jurors will be able to understand. *Tuilaepa*, 114 S. Ct. at 2636.

4. That various victims were particularly vulnerable due to old age, youth, and infirmity. See Section 3592(c)(11).

There is considerable uncertainty with respect to this factor. In the government's response to these motions, the prosecutors have not identified which of the categories will be relied on to support the allegation. Obviously, from the ages given for the victims listed in count one of the indictment, the children killed in this explosion might be considered vulnerable because of their youth. To rule out this aggravator for vagueness at this time would be a premature determination of its validity. The court must await the evidence, at least at the trial of the counts of the indictment, before determining whether and to what extent a penalty phase jury will be allowed to consider this factor.

5. That the defendant committed the offense(s) against one or more federal public servants who were law enforcement officers, (a) while such victim(s) were engaged in the performance of official duties, (b) because of such victim(s)' performance of official duties, and (c) because of such victim(s)' status as public servants. See Section 3592(c)(14)(D).

Although the defendants again challenge this as vague and overbroad with overlapping categories, the court's principal concern here is with duplication of the crimes charged in the eight murder counts. As noted in the court's previous memorandum opinion and order relating to the facial validity of the indictment, *United States v. McVeigh and Nichols*, 940 F. Supp. 1571 (D. Colo. 1996), the government has made clear that for conviction on these counts it will rely on the fact that the victims named in them were law enforcement officers who were killed while engaged in the performance of official duties. To that extent, there is an unwarranted duplication. The notice, however, includes the assertion that these and perhaps other persons were killed because of the performance of their official duties and because of their status as public servants. Because this factor differs from the crime in the indictment, it is not duplicative. Whether there will be adequate "information" to support this contention will be a matter to be addressed after a penalty phase hearing.

The government has included four non-statutory aggravating factors in the notices.

1. That the offense(s) committed by the defendant resulted in multiple deaths of 169 persons.

The defendants object that this duplicates counts one and two in the indictment. While that is true with respect to the allegations that deaths resulted, the government will not be required to prove the specific number of persons whose deaths resulted from criminal acts to obtain convictions. Thus, this non-statutory factor does not duplicate the proof at trial, but simply permits the jury to consider the number of persons killed and weigh that fact in determining the penalty.

2. That, in committing the offense(s) charged in the indictment, the defendant caused serious physical and emotional injury, including maiming, disfigurement, and permanent disability, to numerous individuals.

This is objected to as duplication but the same analysis made in approving the previous aggravating factor is appropriate. It is not only that some persons were maimed, disfigured and injured. The number of such persons warrants consideration by the jury in the selection process.

3. That the defendant committed, caused, and aided and abetted acts of burglary, robbery, and theft to finance and otherwise facilitate the commission of the capital offense(s) charged in the indictment.

Again, the defendants assert that there must be convictions of such crimes to warrant their consideration. As previously noted, the court will require, by its instructions, that the jury find beyond a reasonable doubt that all of the essential elements of these crimes have been proved and that the motivation for them was to finance and facilitate the crimes of conviction.

4. Victim impact evidence concerning the effect of the defendant's offense(s) on the victims and the victims' families, as evidenced by oral testimony and victim impact statements that identify the victims of the offense(s) and the extent and scope of injury and loss suffered by the victims and the victims' families.

This is the most problematical of all of the aggravating factors and may present the greatest difficulty in determining the nature and scope of the "information" to be considered. Congress expressly provided for victim impact consideration in the Death Penalty Statute but it did not put any limits on what can be considered. §3593(a). That is a matter for the court's discretion and must be determined with consideration for the constitutional limitation that the jury must not be influenced by passion or prejudice. *Payne v. Tennessee*, 501 U.S. 808, 825 (1991). However, because victim impact evidence is relevant only to demonstrate the specific harm caused by a particular crime, *id.*, it seems clear that the victims' testimony must reflect the harm caused by the criminal conduct, rather than the impact of the trial proceedings. This point supports the court's ruling that Rule 615 applies to exclude from the trial proceedings those persons who may testify as victims giving evidence to support this factor at the penalty hearing.

Upon the foregoing, it is ordered that with the exception of the deletions necessary to avoid invalid duplication in the aggravating factors, the defendants' motions are denied.

Note on Federal Execution Protocols

The Justice Department instituted an elaborate process to handle any last-minute legal interruptions which might prevent or delay the execution of Timothy McVeigh, the first inmate executed by the federal government since 1963. According to anonymous sources within the Justice Department, two hours before the execution, prison officials planned to cut off visits by family members and attorneys to give McVeigh one final opportunity to seek a stay from the courts or from President Bush.

The execution protocol required prison officials at the execution command center in the Terre Haute, Indiana, federal prison to make last minute phone calls to the White House and to check with the courts to see if McVeigh's lawyers filed any requests to stop the execution. Forty-five minutes before the execution—and again, 10 minutes before the execution—the White House was contacted by telephone. In the event of a delay, officials conducting the execution could be reached up to the moment the executioner begins administering the lethal injection. According to the U.S. Bureau of Prisons' "Execution Protocol" manual, in the event of a delay, a U.S. marshal assigned to the execution room "will instruct the Executioner[s] to step away from the execution equipment and will notify the condemned individual and all present that the execution has been stayed or delayed."

Note on Resumption of Federal Executions

In 2001, following a 38-year hiatus, the federal government resumed executions at the federal penitentiary in Terre Haute, Indiana. On June 11, 2001, Timothy James McVeigh—sentenced to death in June 1997 for the bombing of the Oklahoma City federal building in 1995—was killed by lethal injection. McVeigh became the first federal inmate executed since 1963, when Victor Feguer was hanged for kidnaping and murdering a doctor. (Opinions issued in the *McVeigh* case are reproduced *supra* at pages 446–448 and 1003–1013.)

Eight days later, Juan Raul Garza, sentenced to death in August 1993 in Texas for the murders of three other drug traffickers, was lethally injected. (Garza's case is referenced in the casebook at the end of Note 1, page 965.)

Louis Jones, Jr., sentenced to death in November 1995 in Texas for the murder and kidnapping of a young, white, female soldier, Tracy Joy McBride, died by lethal injection on March 18, 2003. Jones' case was reviewed by the Supreme Court (*supra* pages 982–1002) which affirmed Jones' conviction and death sentence. Jones, like McVeigh, a decorated Gulf War veteran with no prior criminal record, claimed that his exposure to nerve gas in Iraq and post-traumatic stress from his combat tours contributed to the murder. Unlike McVeigh, Jones sought clemency from President Bush.

4. Military Death Penalty

Note on the History of the Military Death Penalty

In *Loving v. United States*, 517 U.S. 748 (1996) (*infra* this chapter), the Court briefly described the history of the death penalty within the American military:

> Although American courts-martial from their inception have had the power to decree capital punishment, they have not long had the authority to try and to sentence members of the armed forces for capital murder committed in the United States in peacetime. In the early days of the Republic the powers of courts-martial were fixed in the Articles of War. Congress enacted the first Articles in 1789 by adopting in full the Articles promulgated in 1775 (and revised in 1776) by the Continental Congress. The Articles adopted by the First Congress placed significant restrictions on court-martial jurisdiction over capital offenses. Although the death penalty was authorized for 14 military offenses, the Articles followed the British example of ensuring the supremacy of civil court jurisdiction over ordinary capital offenses that were punishable by the law of the land and were not special military offenses. That provision was deemed protection enough for soldiers, and in 1806 Congress debated and rejected a proposal to remove the death penalty from court-martial jurisdiction.
>
> Over the next two centuries, Congress expanded court-martial jurisdiction. In 1863, concerned that civil courts could not function in all places during hostilities, Congress granted courts-martial jurisdiction of common-law capital crimes and the authority to impose the death penalty in wartime. In 1916, Congress granted to the military courts a general jurisdiction over common-law felonies committed by service members, except for murder and rape committed within the continental United States during peacetime. Persons accused of the latter two crimes were to be turned over to the civilian authorities. In 1950, with the passage of the UCMJ [Uniform Code of Military Justice], Congress lifted even this restriction. Article 118 of the UCMJ ... [sets out] four types of murder subject to court-martial jurisdiction, two of which are punishable by death....
>
> So matters stood until 1983, when the CMA [Court of Military Appeals] confronted a challenge to the constitutionality of the military capital punishment scheme in light of *Furman v. Georgia*, 408 U.S. 238 (1972), and our ensuing death penalty jurisprudence. Although it held valid most of the death penalty procedures followed in courts-martial, the court found one fundamental defect: the failure of either the UCMJ or the RCM [Rules for Courts-Martial] to require that court-martial members "specifically identify the aggravating factors upon which they have relied in choosing to impose the death penalty." *United States v. Matthews*, 16 M.J. 354, 379. The Court reversed Matthews' death sentence, but ruled that either Congress or the President could remedy the defect and that the new procedures could be applied retroactively.
>
> The President responded to *Matthews* in 1984 with an Executive Order promulgating RCM 1004, which set out categories of aggravating factors for use in military courts-martial.

The *Matthews* case, cited above in the excerpt from *Loving v. United States*, is reprinted below, immediately following the federal murder statute under which Matthews was charged.

10 U.S.C. §918. Art. 118. Murder

Any person subject to this chapter who, without justification or excuse, unlawfully kills a human being, when he—

(1) has a premeditated design to kill;

(2) intends to kill or inflict great bodily harm;

(3) is engaged in an act which is inherently dangerous to others and evinces a wanton disregard of human life; or

(4) is engaged in the perpetration or attempted perpetration of burglary, sodomy, rape, robbery, or aggravated arson; is guilty of murder, and shall suffer such punishment as a court-martial may direct, except that if found guilty under clause (1) or (4), he shall suffer death or imprisonment for life as a court-martial may direct.

United States v. Matthews

16 M.J. 354 (CMA 1983)

EVERETT, Chief Judge:

This is a capital case—the first to reach our Court in many years. Having reviewed the record pursuant to Article 67(b)(1), Uniform Code of Military Justice, 10 U.S.C. §867(b)(1), we conclude that no prejudicial error was committed which affects the findings. However, under present circumstances, the death sentence cannot be imposed, but we authorize a rehearing where the death sentence may be imposed if certain conditions are met.

I
Statement of Facts

On March 2, 1979, charges were preferred against appellant for the premeditated murder and rape of Phyllis Jean Villanueva three days earlier at an American military installation in the Federal Republic of Germany, in violation of Articles 118 and 120, UCMJ, 10 U.S.C. §§918 and 920, respectively. [Appellant was found guilty on all counts and sentenced to death.] ...

V

B. Application of These Principles in the Military Justice System

Although the military justice system established by the Uniform Code of Military Justice and implemented by the Manual for Courts-Martial is over 30 years old, it already contains most of the procedural safeguards now mandated by the Supreme Court when the death penalty is to be imposed.

1. A bifurcated sentencing procedure is employed and, during the presentencing proceedings, the court-martial members are instructed by the military judge as to their duties.

2. Certain aggravating circumstances, such as premeditation, specific intent, and murder during commission of specified felonies, must be found by the court

members—although by only a two-thirds vote. These findings identify the instances in which an accused is eligible for the death penalty. After the findings, evidence may be submitted to identify other aggravating circumstances for the members.

3. The accused has unlimited opportunity to present mitigating and extenuating evidence; and in his instructions the military judge must identify such evidence to the court members for their deliberations on sentence.

4. Mandatory review of the facts, the law, and the appropriateness of the sentence in terms of other similar cases—both jurisdiction-wide and service-wide—is provided by the convening authority and by the Courts of Military Review. Mandatory review by this Court is required as to all matters of law. Finally, the President must approve all death sentences; and he may approve any part or amount, commute the sentence as he sees fit, or suspend all or any part of the sentence except the death sentence.

Moreover, the military justice system goes even further in providing safeguards in the area of appellate review.[12] Indeed, appellate government counsel—as well as the Department of Justice and other *amici curiae* supporting appellee's position—argued before this Court that the Uniform Code presently complies with Supreme Court precedents.

C. Defects in the Military Justice System

Unfortunately, neither the Code nor the Manual requires that the court members specifically identify the aggravating factors upon which they have relied in choosing to impose the death penalty. Since they provide no insight into their sentencing deliberations, it is impossible upon review to determine whether they have made "an *individualized* determination on the basis of the character of the individual and the circumstances of the crime," and whether they have "adequately differentiate[d] this case in an objective, evenhanded, and substantively rational way" from the other murder cases in which the death penalty was not imposed.

The Government contends that the court members' finding that the murder of Mrs. Villaneuva was premeditated narrows the class of murders subject to capital punishment to whatever extent may be required by *Zant v. Stephens*, 462 U.S. 862 (1983). We disagree. As the Air Force Court of Military Review has observed, Article 118(1) of the Code, which proscribes premeditated murder, "parallels numerous statutes struck down in *Furman* and its companions."

It is especially difficult to justify use of premeditation as the sole aggravating factor which allows a court-martial to impose a death sentence, because in military justice evidence is sufficient to establish premeditation which in some jurisdictions would not suffice for that purpose. Under the military definition,

---

12. The military justice system also provides other safeguards against the "arbitrary or capricious" imposition of the death penalty. The circumstances of the offense are investigated by an officer appointed under the authority of Article 32, Uniform Code of Military Justice, 10 U.S.C. §832, who must make recommendations as to the level of court-martial to try the case and as to possible punishment levels. The staff judge advocate to the convening authority prepares a pretrial advice giving his recommendations in the same area. The convening authority exercises his discretion in referring the case to a particular level of court-martial and to the maximum punishment it may impose. All of these steps are to insure that, at least on the basis of evidence available at that point, the accused is within a narrowed class of persons eligible for the imposition of the death penalty and that there is reasonable justification for that classification. After the case is referred to trial, the court members, the convening authority, the Court of Military Review, this Court, and the President, must also affirmatively find that the sentence is appropriate for imposition on the accused.

[p]remeditated murder is murder committed after the formation of a specific intent to kill someone and consideration of the act intended. It is not necessary that the intention to kill shall have been entertained for any particular or considerable length of time. When a fixed purpose to kill has been deliberately formed, it is immaterial how soon afterwards it is put into execution. The existence of premeditation may be inferred from the circumstances surrounding the killing.

Certainly premeditation as thus interpreted falls far short of "deliberation," which in several state capital punishment statutes is used as an "aggravating circumstance" that limits the class of those subject to capital punishment.

The Air Force Court of Military Review was also concerned that the finding of premeditation as an element of the crime did not require a unanimous vote of the court members. As they pointed out:

Initially, only two-thirds of the members need concur in findings of guilty. There is no *guarantee* of unanimity at this stage since no procedure exists to discover if any member voted for a finding other than premeditated murder.

Later, however, it becomes the duty of each member to vote for a proper sentence for premeditated murder; this is so, regardless of his or her possible earlier vote on findings that the accused is either innocent or guilty of some lesser offense not requiring the forced choice of death or life imprisonment. At this point, a death penalty sentence must be unanimous. A "hold out" member who voted during findings for other than premeditated murder is compelled to vote the appropriate sentence for a premeditated murderer — without regard to his or her earlier opinion that the accused is not guilty of that specific crime.

It follows that — even assuming that premeditation somehow becomes the military statutory aggravating/narrowing factor — *there is no guarantee that the members found premeditation unanimously.*

The evidence of record in this case provides ample aggravating circumstances to distinguish it from other murder cases and to justify the imposition of the sentence imposed. However, the lack of specific findings of identified aggravating circumstances makes meaningful appellate review, at any level, impossible, and we cannot be sure that the sentence was correctly imposed....

VI

Presidential Power to Remedy Defects in Sentencing Procedure

Congress obviously intended that in cases where an accused servicemember is convicted of premeditated murder, certain types of felony murder, or rape, the court-martial members should have the option to adjudge a death sentence. Probably this intent cannot be constitutionally effectuated in a case where the rape of an adult female is involved, at least, where there is no purpose unique to the military mission that would be served by allowing the death penalty for this offense. *Coker v. Georgia*, 433 U.S. 584 (1977). Similarly, the imposition of capital punishment in a felony-murder case, where the accused has only aided and abetted the felony may be constitutionally proscribed. *Enmund v. Florida*, 458 U.S. 782 (1982). However, a conviction of premeditated murder can sustain a death sentence if proper sentencing procedures are employed.

We have held that the sentencing procedure in appellant's case was defective because of the failure to require that the court members make specific findings as to individualized aggravating circumstances—findings which can, in turn, be reviewed factually and legally. Congress can take action to remedy this defect that now exists in the sentencing procedure employed by courts-martial in capital cases. However, corrective action also can be taken by the President in the exercise of his responsibilities as commander-in-chief under Article II, Section 2, and of powers expressly delegated to him by Congress.

The congressional delegation of powers to the President has traditionally been quite broad in the field of military justice. Pursuant to Article 36 of the Uniform Code, the President promulgates rules to govern pretrial, trial, and post-trial procedures of courts-martial. Unlike other Federal criminal statutes, the punitive articles of the Uniform Code for the most part authorize punishment "as a court-martial may direct"; no maximum or minimum sentence is specified. However, as contemplated by Article 56 of the Uniform Code, 10 U.S.C. §856, the President prescribes maximum punishments for the various offenses.

The great breadth of the delegation of power to the President by Congress with respect to court-martial procedures and sentences grants him the authority to remedy the present defect in the court-martial sentencing procedure for capital cases. Indeed, a proposed revision of the Manual for Courts-Martial, which has been circulated for public comment, contains a rule—R.C.M. 1004—which prescribes special procedures for sentencing in capital cases.

VII

A
Applicability of New Procedures to a Rehearing

As we interpret *Dobbert v. Florida*, 432 U.S. 282 (1977), if the President—or the Congress, if it should choose—provides a constitutionally adequate procedure for imposing the death penalty in trials by courts-martial, that procedure could be used in the trial of persons who theretofore had committed premeditated or felony murders. In *Dobbert* the Supreme Court—rejecting a defense claim that a change in the Florida method of adjudging a death sentence could not be applied to Dobbert because of the *ex post facto* limitation—ruled that such a change was only "procedural" in nature. We perceive no distinction between Dobbert's situation and that of a servicemember who commits a premeditated murder and is tried under constitutionally valid procedures prescribed by the President after the date of the crime.

Similarly, we can make no meaningful distinction between the situation of a civilian or military defendant who is validly sentenced under procedures not in effect when he committed a capital crime, and that of an accused who, upon conviction of a capital offense, is sentenced to death under unconstitutional procedures but is then resentenced under constitutionally valid procedures which have been established in the interval. In both instances, the accused knew at the time of the crime that it authorized capital punishment, and that he ran the risk of this penalty.

Thus, if adequate procedures for adjudging death sentences now existed in the military system, Matthews could be resentenced under those procedures, even though they had not existed at the time of his original trial. He could not complain that the punishment was *ex post facto* since, from the outset, Article 118 of the Uniform Code had given him notice of the penalty to which he might be subjecting himself....

B

Allowance of Time to Issue New Procedures

... [I]f Congress or the President acts promptly to remedy the defect in court-martial sentencing procedure for capital offenses, the Government should be allowed to subject appellant to the death penalty in resentence proceedings that meet the standards of Article 55 and of the Eighth Amendment....

IX

Decision

Accordingly, we hold that the death sentence against Matthews was improperly adjudged.

The decision of the United States Army Court of Military Review is reversed as to sentence and the record of trial is returned to the Judge Advocate General of the Army. He may either submit the record to the Court of Military Review which may substitute a sentence of life imprisonment and accessory penalties, or he may return the record to an appropriate convening authority for referral to a general court-martial for a rehearing on sentence if constitutionally valid procedures are provided by the President or Congress within 90 days of the date on which the mandate in this case is issued.

Notes and Questions

1. Shortly after the *Matthews* decision, an extensive overhaul of the Manual for Courts-Martial cured the constitutional defect identified in Chief Judge Everett's opinion. See Analysis, Rule 1004, Manual for Courts-Martial, United States (1984).

2. The Uniform Code of Military Justice identifies fourteen potentially capital offenses. These include premeditated murder (art. 118), felony murder (art. 118(4)) and rape (art. 120a). See UCMJ arts. 1–140, 10 U.S.C. §§801–940. The remaining eleven are purely military offenses. They are:

(1) desertion in time of war (art. 85);

(2) assaulting or willfully disobeying a superior commissioned officer in time of war (art. 90);

(3) mutiny or sedition (art. 95);

(4) misbehavior before the enemy (art. 99);

(5) subordinate compelling surrender (art. 100);

(6) improper use of a countersign in time of war (art. 101);

(7) forcing a safeguard (art. 102);

(8) aiding the enemy (art. 104);

(9) spying in time of war (art. 106);

(10) espionage (art. 106); and

(11) misbehavior of a sentinel in time of war (art. 113).

3. Is article 120a, which provides the death penalty for rape, constitutional after *Coker v. Georgia*, 433 U.S. 584 (1977)? Recall that *Coker* (*supra* chapter 2) held that the death penalty for the rape of an adult woman, without more, is unconstitutional. Rule

for Courts-Martial 1004 limits imposition of death for rape to cases where the victim is under the age of twelve or where the rapist maimed or attempted to kill his victim. R.C.M. 1004 (c)(9)(A), (B).

4. Article 106 makes spying in time of war an offense for which death is the mandatory penalty. Is article 106 constitutional? Recall the Court's decisions in *Woodson v. North Carolina*, 428 U.S. 280 (1976), and *Sumner v. Shuman*, 483 U.S. 66 (1987) (*supra* chapter 3). In 1985, Congress passed a new spying statute, article 106a, reproduced below:

10 U.S.C. §906a. Art. 106a. Espionage

(a)(1) Any person subject to this chapter who, with intent or reason to believe that it is to be used to the injury of the United States or to the advantage of a foreign nation, communicates, delivers, or transmits, or attempts to communicate, deliver, or transmit, to any entity described in paragraph (2), either directly or indirectly, anything described in paragraph (3) shall be punished as a court-martial may direct, except that if the accused is found guilty of an offense that directly concerns (A) nuclear weaponry, military spacecraft or satellites, early warning systems, or other means of defense or retaliation against large scale attack, (B) war plans, (C) communications intelligence or cryptographic information, or (D) any other major weapons system or major element of defense strategy, the accused shall be punished by death or such other punishment as a court-martial may direct....

(3) The accused shall be given broad latitude to present matters in extenuation and mitigation.

(c) A sentence of death may be adjudged by a court-martial for an offense under this section (article) only if the members unanimously find, beyond a reasonable doubt, one or more of the following aggravating factors:

(1) The accused has been convicted of another offense involving espionage or treason for which either a sentence of death or imprisonment for life was authorized by statute.

(2) In the commission of the offense, the accused knowingly created a grave risk of substantial damage to the national security.

(3) In the commission of the offense, the accused knowingly created a grave risk of death to another person.

5. On January 31, 1945, Private Eddie D. Slovik was executed by firing squad in the European theater of operations. Slovik was the only United States soldier put to death for desertion (art. 85) during World War II. Does Slovik's unique status suggest any argument that article 85 may be unconstitutional? Since 1916, 135 people have been executed by the Army. Nat'l L. J., Apr. 5, 1999. The last military execution occurred on April 13, 1961, when U.S. Army Private John A. Bennett was hanged for rape and attempted murder. Serrano, *Last Soldier to Die at Leavenworth Hanged in an April Storm*," L.A. Times, July 12, 1994. The military has since adopted lethal injection as its execution method.

6. The Manual for Courts-Martial (MCM) provides the military procedures for capital cases. Unlike most state and federal capital statutes, the MCM prohibits guilty pleas where death may be imposed. UCMJ, art. 45(b). Rules for Court Martial (R.C.M.) require trial before members, rather than a single judge. R.C.M. 501(a)(1)(B). Unless the

vote on guilt is unanimous, death may not be imposed during the sentencing phase. UCMJ, art. 52(b)(1).

During sentencing, the defense is given "broad latitude" to introduce mitigating evidence. R.C.M. 1004(b)(3). Mitigating factors are not set forth in the statute. Statutory aggravating circumstances, however, are specified. The court must find one or more aggravating circumstances present before the defendant becomes death eligible. Even then, death may be imposed only if "[a]ll members concur that any extenuating or mitigating circumstances are substantially outweighed by any aggravating circumstances admissible." R.C.M. 1004(b). The vote for death must be unanimous. R.C.M. 1004(d)(4)(A). The revised Manual for Courts Martial cures the *Matthews* defect through R.C.M. 1004(b)(8) which provides that, in announcing a sentence of death, the president of the court is required to list those statutory aggravating circumstances found by the members.

When a death sentence is imposed, the record is reviewed by the convening authority—a high ranking commanding officer who decided to bring the case to trial and to seek a death sentence. The convening authority has the power to reduce—but not increase—sentences. Next, the record is transmitted to one of four intermediate appellate courts: the Army, Navy-Marine Corps, Air Force, or Coast Guard Court of Criminal Appeals. If the death sentence is affirmed, the case goes before the Court of Appeals for the Armed Services (formerly the Court of Military Appeals), a 5-member Article 1 court. If the Court of Appeals for the Armed Services affirms the sentence, the case is eligible for review by the Supreme Court on certiorari. Following Supreme Court review, the case is sent to the President. (No service member can be executed unless the President personally approves of the death penalty.) Once presidential review is completed, the condemned prisoner can apply for federal habeas relief. Sullivan, "A Matter of Life and Death: Examining the Military Death Penalty's Fairness," Fed. Lawyer, June 1998.

Loving v. United States
517 U.S. 748 (1996)

KENNEDY, J., delivered the opinion of the Court, in which Rehnquist, C. J., and Stevens, Souter, Ginsburg, and Breyer, JJ., joined, and in which O'Connor and Scalia, JJ., joined as to Parts I, II, III, IV-B, and IV-C. Stevens, J., filed a concurring opinion, in which Souter, Ginsburg, and Breyer, JJ., joined. Scalia, J., filed an opinion concurring in part and concurring in the judgment, in which O'Connor, J., joined. Thomas, J., filed an opinion concurring in the judgment.

The case before us concerns the authority of the President, in our system of separated powers, to prescribe aggravating factors that permit a court-martial to impose the death penalty upon a member of the Armed Forces convicted of murder.

I

On December 12, 1988, petitioner Dwight Loving, an Army private stationed at Fort Hood, Texas, murdered two taxicab drivers from the nearby town of Killeen. He attempted to murder a third, but the driver disarmed him and escaped. Civilian and Army authorities arrested Loving the next afternoon. He confessed.

After a trial, an eight-member general court-martial found Loving guilty of, among other offenses, premeditated murder and felony murder under Article 118 of the Uniform Code of Military Justice (UCMJ), 10 U.S.C. §§918(1), (4).

In the sentencing phase of the trial, the court-martial found three aggravating factors:

(1) that the premeditated murder of the second driver was committed during the course of a robbery, Rule for Courts-Martial (RCM) 1004(c)(7)(B);

(2) that Loving acted as the triggerman in the felony murder of the first driver, RCM 1004(c)(8); and

(3) that Loving, having been found guilty of the premeditated murder, had committed a second murder, also proved at the single trial, RCM 1004(c)(7)(J).

The court-martial sentenced Loving to death. The commander who convened the court-martial approved the findings and sentence. The United States Army Court of Military Review and the United States Court of Appeals for the Armed Forces (formerly the United States Court of Military Appeals (CMA)) affirmed, ... reject[ing] Loving's claims that the President lacked authority to promulgate the aggravating factors that enabled the court-martial to sentence him to death. We granted certiorari.

II

... Article 118 of the UCMJ describes four types of murder subject to court-martial jurisdiction, two of which are punishable by death: "Any person subject to this chapter who, without justification or excuse, unlawfully kills a human being, when he—

(1) has a premeditated design to kill;

(2) intends to kill or inflict great bodily harm;

(3) is engaged in an act which is inherently dangerous to another and evinces a wanton disregard of human life; or

(4) is engaged in the perpetration or attempted perpetration of burglary, sodomy, rape, robbery, or aggravated arson;

is guilty of murder, and shall suffer such punishment as a court-martial may direct, except that if found guilty under clause (1) or (4), he shall suffer death or imprisonment for life as a court-martial may direct." 10 U.S.C. §918.

So matters stood until 1983, when the CMA confronted a challenge to the constitutionality of the military capital punishment scheme in light of *Furman v. Georgia*, 408 U.S. 238 (1972), and our ensuing death penalty jurisprudence. Although it held valid most of the death penalty procedures followed in courts-martial, the court found one fundamental defect: the failure of either the UCMJ or the RCM to require that court-martial members "specifically identify the aggravating factors upon which they have relied in choosing to impose the death penalty." *United States v. Matthews*, 16 M.J. 354, 379. The court reversed Matthews' death sentence, but ruled that either Congress or the President could remedy the defect and that the new procedures could be applied retroactively.

The President responded to *Matthews* in 1984 with an Executive Order promulgating RCM 1004. In conformity with 10 U.S.C. §852(a)(1), the Rule, as amended, requires a unanimous finding that the accused was guilty of a capital offense before a death sentence may be imposed, RCM 1004(a)(2). The Rule also requires unanimous findings (1) that at least one aggravating factor is present and (2) that any extenuating or mitigating circumstances are substantially outweighed by any admissible aggravating circumstances, 1004(b). RCM 1004(c) enumerates 11 categories of aggravating factors sufficient for imposition of the death penalty. The Rule also provides that the accused is to have "broad latitude to present evidence in extenuation and mitigation," 1004(b)(3), and is entitled to have the members of the court-martial instructed to consider all such evidence before deciding upon a death sentence, 1004(b)(6).

This is the scheme Loving attacks as unconstitutional. He contends that the Eighth Amendment and the doctrine of separation of powers require that Congress, and not the President, make the fundamental policy determination respecting the factors that warrant the death penalty.

III

A preliminary question in this case is whether the Constitution requires the aggravating factors that Loving challenges. The Government does not contest the application of our death penalty jurisprudence to courts-martial, at least in the context of a conviction under Article 118 for murder committed in peacetime within the United States, and we shall assume that *Furman* and the case law resulting from it are applicable to the crime and sentence in question. Cf. *Trop v. Dulles*, 356 U.S. 86 (1958) (analyzing court-martial punishments under the Eighth Amendment). The Eighth Amendment requires, among other things, that "a capital sentencing scheme must 'genuinely narrow the class of persons eligible for the death penalty and must reasonably justify the imposition of a more severe sentence on the defendant compared to others found guilty of murder.'" *Lowenfield v. Phelps*, 484 U.S. 231, 244 (1988) (quoting *Zant v. Stephens*, 462 U.S. 862, 877 (1983)). Some schemes accomplish that narrowing by requiring that the sentencers find at least one aggravating circumstance. The narrowing may also be achieved, however, in the definition of the capital offense, in which circumstance the requirement that the sentencer "find the existence of an aggravating circumstance in addition is no part of the constitutionally required narrowing process."

Although the Government suggests the contrary, we agree with Loving, on the assumption that *Furman* applies to this case, that aggravating factors are necessary to the constitutional validity of the military capital punishment scheme as now enacted. Article 118 authorizes the death penalty for but two of the four types of murder specified: premeditated and felony murder are punishable by death, 10 U.S.C. §§918(1), (4), whereas intentional murder without premeditation and murder resulting from wanton and dangerous conduct are not, §§918(2), (3). The statute's selection of the two types of murder for the death penalty, however, does not narrow the death-eligible class in a way consistent with our cases. Article 118(4) by its terms permits death to be imposed for felony murder even if the accused had no intent to kill and even if he did not do the killing himself. The Eighth Amendment does not permit the death penalty to be imposed in those circumstances. *Enmund v. Florida*, 458 U.S. 782, 801 (1982). As a result, additional aggravating factors establishing a higher culpability are necessary to save Article 118. We turn to the question whether it violated the principle of separation of powers for the President to prescribe the aggravating factors required by the Eighth Amendment.

IV

Even before the birth of this country, separation of powers was known to be a defense against tyranny. Though faithful to the precept that freedom is imperiled if the whole of legislative, executive, and judicial power is in the same hands, The Federalist No. 47, pp. 325–326 (J. Madison) (J. Cooke ed. 1961), the Framers understood that a "hermetic sealing off of the three branches of Government from one another would preclude the establishment of a Nation capable of governing itself effectively," *Buckley v. Valeo*, 424 U.S. 1, 120–121 (1976) (per curiam). "While the Constitution diffuses power the better to secure liberty, it also contemplates that practice will integrate the dispersed powers into a workable government. It enjoins upon its branches separateness but interdependence, autonomy but reciprocity." Although separation of powers "'d[oes] not mean that these [three] departments ought to have no partial agency in, or no controul over the acts of each other,'" *Mistretta v. United States*, 488 U.S. 361, 380–381 (1989) (quoting The Federalist No. 47, supra, at 325–326 (emphasis deleted)), it remains a basic principle of our constitutional scheme that one branch of the Government may not intrude upon the central prerogatives of another. Even when a branch does not arrogate power to itself, moreover, the separation-of-powers doctrine requires that a branch not impair another in the performance of its constitutional duties.

Deterrence of arbitrary or tyrannical rule is not the sole reason for dispersing the federal power among three branches, however. By allocating specific powers and responsibilities to a branch fitted to the task, the Framers created a National Government that is both effective and accountable. Article I's precise rules of representation, member qualifications, bicameralism, and voting procedure make Congress the branch most capable of responsive and deliberative lawmaking. Ill suited to that task are the Presidency, designed for the prompt and faithful execution of the laws and its own legitimate powers, and the Judiciary, a branch with tenure and authority independent of direct electoral control. The clear assignment of power to a branch, furthermore, allows the citizen to know who may be called to answer for making, or not making, those delicate and necessary decisions essential to governance.

Another strand of our separation-of-powers jurisprudence, the delegation doctrine, has developed to prevent Congress from forsaking its duties. Loving invokes this doctrine to question the authority of the President to promulgate RCM 1004. The fundamental precept of the delegation doctrine is that the lawmaking function belongs to Congress, U.S. Const., Art. I, §1, and may not be conveyed to another branch or entity. This principle does not mean, however, that only Congress can make a rule of prospective force. To burden Congress with all federal rulemaking would divert that branch from more pressing issues, and defeat the Framers' design of a workable National Government. Thomas Jefferson observed: "Nothing is so embarrassing nor so mischievous in a great assembly as the details of execution." 5 Works of Thomas Jefferson 319 (P. Ford ed. 1904) (letter to E. Carrington, Aug. 4, 1787).

"'The true distinction ... is between the delegation of power to make the law, which necessarily involves a discretion as to what it shall be, and conferring authority or discretion as to its execution, to be exercised under and in pursuance of the law. The first cannot be done; to the latter no valid objection can be made.'"

Loving contends that the military death penalty scheme of Article 118 and RCM 1004 does not observe the limits of the delegation doctrine. He presses his constitutional challenge on three fronts. First, he argues that Congress cannot delegate to the President the authority to prescribe aggravating factors in capital murder cases. Second, he contends that, even if it can, Congress did not delegate the authority by implicit or explicit action. Third, Loving believes that even if certain statutory provisions can be construed as delegations, they lack an intelligible principle to guide the President's discretion. Were Loving's premises to be accepted, the President would lack authority to prescribe aggravating factors in RCM 1004, and the death sentence imposed upon him would be unconstitutional.

A

Loving's first argument is that Congress lacks power to allow the President to prescribe aggravating factors in military capital cases because any delegation would be inconsistent with the Framers' decision to vest in Congress the power "To make Rules for the Government and Regulation of the land and naval Forces." U.S. Const., Art. I, §8, cl. 14. At least in the context of capital punishment for peacetime crimes, which implicates the Eighth Amendment, this power must be deemed exclusive, Loving contends. In his view, not only is the determination of aggravating factors a quintessential policy judgment for the Legislature, but the history of military capital punishment in England and America refutes a contrary interpretation. He asserts that his offense was not tried in a military court throughout most of English and American history. It is this historical exclusion of common-law capital crimes from military jurisdiction, he urges, that must inform our understanding of whether Clause 14 reserves to Congress the power to prescribe what conduct warrants a death sentence, even if it permits Congress to authorize courts-martial to try such crimes. Mindful of the historical dangers of autocratic military justice and of the limits Parliament set on the peacetime jurisdiction of courts-martial over capital crimes in the first Mutiny Act, 1 Wm. & Mary, ch. 5 (1689), and having experienced the military excesses of the Crown in colonial America, the Framers harbored a deep distrust of executive military power and military tribunals. It follows, Loving says, that the Framers intended that Congress alone should possess the power to decide what aggravating factors justify sentencing a member of the Armed Forces to death.

We have undertaken before, in resolving other issues, the difficult task of interpreting Clause 14 by drawing upon English constitutional history. Doing so here, we find that, although there is a grain of truth in Loving's historical arguments, the struggle of Parliament to control military tribunals and the lessons the Framers drew from it are more complex than he suggests. The history does not require us to read Clause 14 as granting to Congress an exclusive, non-delegable power to determine military punishments. If anything, it appears that England found security in divided authority, with Parliament at times ceding to the Crown the task of fixing military punishments. From the English experience the Framers understood the necessity of balancing efficient military discipline, popular control of a standing army, and the rights of soldiers; they perceived the risks inherent in assigning the task to one part of the Government to the exclusion of another; and they knew the resulting parliamentary practice of delegation. The Framers' choice in Clause 14 was to give Congress the same flexibility to exercise or share power as times might demand.

In England after the Norman Conquest, military justice was a matter of royal prerogative. The rudiments of law in English military justice can first be seen in the written orders issued by the King for various expeditions. For example, in 1190 Richard I issued an ordinance outlining six offenses to which the crusaders would be subject, including two punishable by death: "Whoever shall slay a man on ship-board, he shall be bound to the dead man and thrown into the sea. If he shall slay him on land he shall be bound to the dead man and buried in the earth." Ordinance of Richard I—A. D. 1190. The first comprehensive articles of war were those declared by Richard II at Durham in 1385 and Henry V at Mantes in 1419, which decreed capital offenses that not only served military discipline but also protected foreign noncombatants from the ravages of war. T. Meron, Henry's Wars and Shakespeare's Laws: Perspectives on the Law of War in the Later Middle Ages 91–93 (1993). Articles of War, sometimes issued by military commanders acting under royal commission in the ensuing centuries, were not fixed codes, at least through the 17th century; rather, "each war, each expedition, had its own edict," which lost force after the cessation of hostilities and the disbanding of the army that had been formed.

Thus, royal ordinances governed the conduct of war, but the common law did not countenance the enforcement of military law in times of peace "when the king's courts [were] open for all persons to receive justice according to the laws of the land."

"The Common Law made no distinction between the crimes of soldiers and those of civilians in time of peace. All subjects were tried alike by the same civil courts, so 'if a life-guardsman deserted, he could only be sued for breach of contract, and if he struck his officer he was only liable to an indictment or action of battery.'" Reid, supra, at 24, n. 44 (quoting 2 J. Campbell, Lives of the Chief Justices of England 91 (1849)).

See also 1 T. Macaulay, History of England 272 (n. d.) (hereinafter Macaulay).

The triumph of civil jurisdiction was not absolute, however. The political disorders of the 17th century ushered in periods of harsh military justice, with soldiers and at times civilian rebels punished, even put to death, under the summary decrees of courts-martial. Military justice was brought under the rule of parliamentary law in 1689, when William and Mary accepted the Bill of Rights requiring Parliament's consent to the raising and keeping of armies. In the Mutiny Act of 1689, Parliament declared the general principle that "noe Man may be forejudged of Life or Limbe or subjected to any kinde of punishment by Martiall Law or in any other manner then by the Judgement of his Peeres and according to the knowne and Established Laws of this Realme," but decreed that "Soldiers who shall Mutiny or stirr up Sedition or shall desert Their Majestyes Service be brought to a more Exemplary and speedy Punishment than the usuall Forms of Law will allow," and "shall suffer Death or such other Punishment as by a Court-Martiall shall be Inflicted."

In one sense, as Loving wants to suggest, the Mutiny Act was a sparing exercise of parliamentary authority, since only the most serious domestic offenses of soldiers were made capital, and the militia was exempted. He misunderstands the Mutiny Act of 1689, however, in arguing that it bespeaks a special solicitude for the rights of soldiers and a desire of Parliament to exclude Executive power over military capital punishment.

The Mutiny Act, as its name suggests, came on the heels of the mutiny of Scottish troops loyal to James II. The mutiny occurred at a watershed time. Menaced by great continental powers, England had come to a grudging recognition that a standing army, long decried as an instrument of despotism, had to be maintained on its soil. The mutiny cast in high relief the dangers to the polity of a standing army turned bad. Macaulay describes the sentiment of the time:

"There must then be regular soldiers; and, if there were to be regular soldiers, it must be indispensable, both to their efficiency, and to the security of every other class, that they should be kept under a strict discipline. An ill disciplined army ... [is] formidable only to the country which it is paid to defend. A strong line of demarcation must therefore be drawn between the soldiers and the rest of the community. For the sake of public freedom, they must, in the midst of freedom, be placed under a despotic rule. They must be subject to a sharper penal code, and to a more stringent code of procedure, than are administered by the ordinary tribunals."

The Mutiny Act, then, was no measure of leniency for soldiers. With its passage, "the Army of William III was governed under a severer Code than that made by his predecessors under the Prerogative authority of the Crown. The Mutiny Act, without displacing the Articles of War and those Military Tribunals under which the Army had hitherto been governed, gave statutory sanction to the infliction of Capital Punishments for offences rather Political than Military, and which had rarely been so punished under Prerogative authority." Indeed, it was the Crown that later tempered the excesses of courts-martial wielding the power of capital punishment. It did so by stipulating in the Articles of War (which remained a matter of royal prerogative) that all capital sentences be sent to it for revision or approval.

Popular suspicion of the standing army persisted, and Parliament authorized the Mutiny Acts only for periods of six months and then a year. But renewed they were time and again, and Parliament would alter the power of courts-martial to impose the death penalty for peacetime offenses throughout the next century. It withdrew the power altogether in 1713, only to regret the absence of the penalty during the rebellion of 1715. The third of the Mutiny Acts of 1715 subjected the soldier to capital punishment for a wide array of peacetime offenses related to political disorder and troop discipline. And, for a short time in the 18th century, Parliament allowed the Crown to invest courts-martial with a general criminal jurisdiction over soldiers even at home, placing no substantive limit on the penalties that could be imposed; until 1718, that jurisdiction was superior to civil courts. The propriety of that general jurisdiction within the kingdom was questioned, and the jurisdiction was withdrawn in 1749. Nevertheless, even as it continued to adjust the scope of military jurisdiction at home, Parliament entrusted broad powers to the Crown to define and punish military crimes abroad. In 1713, it gave statutory sanction to the Crown's longstanding practice of issuing Articles of War without limiting the kind of punishments that might be imposed; and, in the same Act, it delegated the power to "erect and constitute Courts Martial with Power to try hear and determine any Crime or Offence by such Articles of War and inflict Penalties by Sentence or Judgement of the same in any of Her Majesties Dominions beyond the Seas or elsewhere beyond the Seas (except in the Kingdom of Ireland) ... as might have been done by Her Majesties Authority beyond the Seas in Time of War."

As Loving contends, and as we have explained elsewhere, the Framers well knew this history, and had encountered firsthand the abuses of military law in the colonies. See *Reid*, 354 U.S. at 27–28. As many were themselves veterans of the Revolutionary War, however, they also knew the imperatives of military discipline. What they distrusted were not courts-martial per se, but military justice dispensed by a commander unchecked by the civil power in proceedings so summary as to be lawless. The latter was the evil that caused Blackstone to declare that "martial law"— by which he, not observing the modern distinction between military and martial law, meant decrees of courts-martial disciplining soldiers in wartime—"is built upon no settled principles, but is entirely arbitrary in its decisions, [and] is, as Sir Matthew Hale observes, in truth and reality no law, but something indulged rather than allowed as a law." The partial security Englishmen won against such abuse in 1689 was to give Parliament, preeminent guardian of the British constitution, primacy in matters of military law. This fact does not suggest, however, that a legislature's power must be exclusive. It was for Parliament, as it did in the various Mutiny Acts, to designate as the times required what peacetime offenses by soldiers deserved the punishment of death; and it was for Parliament, as it did in 1713, to delegate the authority to define wartime offenses and devise their punishments, including death. The Crown received the delegated power and the concomitant responsibility for its prudent exercise. The lesson from the English constitutional experience was that Parliament must have the primary power to regulate the Armed Forces and to determine the punishments that could be imposed upon soldiers by courts-martial. That was not inconsistent, however, with the further power to divide authority between it and the Crown as conditions might warrant.

Far from attempting to replicate the English system, of course, the Framers separated the powers of the Federal Government into three branches to avoid dangers they thought latent or inevitable in the parliamentary structure. The historical necessities and events of the English constitutional experience, though, were familiar to them and inform our understanding of the purpose and meaning of constitutional provisions. As we have observed before, with this experience to consult they elected not to "freeze court-martial usage at a particular time" for all ages following, nor did they deprive Congress of the services of the Executive in establishing rules for the governance of the military, including rules for capital punishment. In the words of Alexander Hamilton, the power to regulate the Armed Forces, like other powers related to the common defense, was given to Congress

> "without limitation: Because it is impossible to foresee or define the extent and variety of national exigencies, or the corresponding extent & variety of the means which may be necessary to satisfy them. The circumstances that endanger the safety of nations are infinite, and for this reason no constitutional shackles can wisely be imposed on the power to which the care of it is committed. This power ought to be co-extensive with all the possible combinations of such circumstances; and ought to be under the direction of the same councils, which are appointed to preside over the common defence."

The Federalist No. 23, at 147 (emphasis deleted).

The later-added Bill of Rights limited this power to some degree, but did not alter the allocation to Congress of the "primary responsibility for the delicate task of balancing the rights of servicemen against the needs of the military."

Under Clause 14, Congress, like Parliament, exercises a power of precedence over, not exclusion of, Executive authority. This power is no less plenary than other Article I powers, and we discern no reasons why Congress should have less capacity to make measured and appropriate delegations of this power than of any other. Indeed, it would be contrary to precedent and tradition for us to impose a special limitation on this particular Article I power, for we give Congress the highest deference in ordering military affairs. *Rostker v. Goldberg*, 453 U.S. 57, 64–65 (1981). And it would be contrary to the respect owed the President as Commander in Chief to hold that he may not be given wide discretion and authority. We decline to import into Clause 14 a restrictive nondelegation principle that the Framers left out.

There is no absolute rule, furthermore, against Congress' delegation of authority to define criminal punishments. We have upheld delegations whereby the Executive or an independent agency defines by regulation what conduct will be criminal, so long as Congress makes the violation of regulations a criminal offense and fixes the punishment, and the regulations "confin[e] themselves within the field covered by the statute." The exercise of a delegated authority to define crimes may be sufficient in certain circumstances to supply the notice to defendants the Constitution requires. In the circumstances presented here, so too may Congress delegate authority to the President to define the aggravating factors that permit imposition of a statutory penalty, with the regulations providing the narrowing of the death-eligible class that the Eighth Amendment requires.

In 1950, Congress confronted the problem of what criminal jurisdiction would be appropriate for Armed Forces of colossal size, stationed on bases that in many instances were small societies unto themselves. Congress, confident in the procedural protections of the UCMJ, gave to courts-martial jurisdiction of the crime of murder. It further declared the law that service members who commit premeditated and felony murder may be sentenced to death by a court-martial. There is nothing in the constitutional scheme or our traditions to prohibit Congress from delegating the prudent and proper implementation of the capital murder statute to the President acting as Commander in Chief.

B

Having held that Congress has the power of delegation, we further hold that it exercised the power in Articles 18 and 56 of the UCMJ. Article 56 specifies that "the punishment which a court-martial may direct for an offense may not exceed such limits as the President may prescribe for that offense." 10 U.S.C. §856. Article 18 states that a court-martial "may, under such limitations as the President may prescribe, adjudge any punishment not forbidden by [the UCMJ], including the penalty of death when specifically authorized by" the Code. §818. As the Court of Military Appeals pointed out in *Curtis*, for some decades the President has used his authority under these Articles to increase the penalties for certain noncapital offenses if aggravating circumstances are present. For example, by regulation, deserters who are apprehended are punished more severely than those who surrender; drunk drivers suffer a harsher fate if they cause an accident resulting in the death of a victim; and the punishment of thieves is graded by the value of the stolen goods. See *Curtis*, 32 M.J. at 261. The President has thus provided more precision in sentencing than is provided by the statute, while remaining within statutory bounds. This past practice suggests that Articles 18 and 56 support as well an authority in the President to restrict the death sentence to murders in which certain aggravating circumstances have been established.

There is yet a third provision of the UCMJ indicative of congressional intent to delegate this authority to the President. Article 36 of the UCMJ, which gives the President the power to make procedural rules for courts-martial, provides:

> "Pretrial, trial, and post-trial procedures, including modes of proof, for [courts martial] ... may be prescribed by the President by regulations which shall, so far as he considers practicable, apply the principles of law and the rules of evidence generally recognized in the trial of criminal cases in the United States district courts, but which may not be contrary to or inconsistent with this chapter."

10 U.S.C. §836(a).

Although the language of Article 36 seems further afield from capital aggravating factors than that of Article 18 or 56, it is the provision that a later Congress identified as the source of Presidential authority to prescribe these factors. In 1985, Congress enacted Article 106a of the UCMJ, 10 U.S.C. §906a, which authorized the death penalty for espionage. The Article requires a finding of an aggravating factor if the accused is to be sentenced to death; it enumerates three such factors, but allows death to be decreed on "any other factor that may be prescribed by the President by regulations under section 836 of this title (article 36)." §906a(c)(4). Article 106a itself, then, is premised on the President's having authority under Article 36 to prescribe capital aggravating factors, and "subsequent legislation declaring the intent of an earlier statute is entitled to great weight in statutory construction." Whether or not Article 36 would stand on its own as the source of the delegated power, we hold that Articles 18, 36, and 56 together give clear authority to the President for the promulgation of RCM 1004.

Loving points out that the three Articles were enacted as part of the UCMJ in 1950, well before the need for eliminating absolute discretion in capital sentencing was established in *Furman v. Georgia*, 408 U.S. 238 (1972), and the cases that followed. (Slight amendments to the Articles have been made since but are not relevant here.) In 1950, he argues, Congress could not have understood that it was giving the President the authority to bring an otherwise invalid capital murder statute in line with Eighth Amendment strictures. Perhaps so, but *Furman* did not somehow undo the prior delegation.

What would have been an act of leniency by the President prior to *Furman* may have become a constitutional necessity thereafter, but the fact remains the power to prescribe aggravating circumstances has resided with the President since 1950.

C

It does not suffice to say that Congress announced its will to delegate certain authority. Congress as a general rule must also "lay down by legislative act an intelligible principle to which the person or body authorized to [act] is directed to conform." The intelligible-principle rule seeks to enforce the understanding that Congress may not delegate the power to make laws and so may delegate no more than the authority to make policies and rules that implement its statutes. Though in 1935 we struck down two delegations for lack of an intelligible principle, *A. L. A. Schechter Poultry Corp. v. United States*, 295 U.S. 495 (1935), and *Panama Refining Co. v. Ryan*, 293 U.S. 388 (1935), we have since upheld, without exception, delegations under standards phrased in sweeping terms. See, *e.g.*, *National Broadcasting Co. v. United States*, 319 U.S. 190, 216–217, 225–226 (1943) (upholding delegation to the Federal Communications Commission to regulate radio broadcasting according to "public interest, convenience, or necessity"). Had the delegations here called for the exercise of judgment or discretion that lies beyond the traditional authority of the President, Loving's last argument that Congress failed to provide guiding principles to the President might have more weight. We find no fault, however, with the delegation in this case.

In *United States v. Curtis*, the Court of Military Appeals discerned a principle limiting the President's discretion to define aggravating factors for capital crimes in Article 36: namely, the directive that regulations the President prescribes must "apply the principles of law ... generally recognized in the trial of criminal cases in the United States district courts, but which may not be contrary to or inconsistent with this chapter," 10 U.S.C. §836(a). We think, however, that the question to be asked is not whether there was any explicit principle telling the President how to select aggravating factors, but whether any such guidance was needed, given the nature of the delegation and the officer who is to exercise the delegated authority. First, the delegation is set within boundaries the President may not exceed. Second, the delegation here was to the President in his role as Commander in Chief. Perhaps more explicit guidance as to how to select aggravating factors would be necessary if delegation were made to a newly created entity without independent authority in the area. The President's duties as Commander in Chief, however, require him to take responsible and continuing action to superintend the military, including the courts-martial. The delegated duty, then, is interlinked with duties already assigned to the President by express terms of the Constitution, and the same limitations on delegation do not apply "where the entity exercising the delegated authority itself possesses independent authority over the subject matter." Like the Court of Military Appeals, *Curtis*, 32 M.J. at 263, n. 9, we need not decide whether the President would have inherent power as Commander in Chief to prescribe aggravating factors in capital cases. Once delegated that power by Congress, the President, acting in his constitutional office of Commander in Chief, had undoubted competency to prescribe those factors without further guidance. "The military constitutes a specialized community governed by a separate discipline from that of the civilian," and the President can be entrusted to determine what limitations and conditions on punishments are best suited to preserve that special discipline.

It is hard to deem lawless a delegation giving the President broad discretion to prescribe rules on this subject. From the early days of the Republic, the President has had congressional authorization to intervene in cases where courts-martial decreed death.

American Articles of War of 1806, Art. 65. It would be contradictory to say that Congress cannot further empower him to limit by prospective regulation the circumstances in which courts-martial can impose a death sentence. Specific authority to make rules for the limitation of capital punishment contributes more toward principled and uniform military sentencing regimes than does case-by-case intervention, and it provides greater opportunity for congressional oversight and revision.

Separation-of-powers principles are vindicated, not disserved, by measured cooperation between the two political branches of the Government, each contributing to a lawful objective through its own processes. The delegation to the President as Commander in Chief of the authority to prescribe aggravating factors was in all respects consistent with these precepts, and the promulgation of RCM 1004 was well within the delegated authority. Loving's sentence was lawful, and the judgment of the Court of Appeals for the Armed Forces is affirmed.

Justice STEVENS, with whom Justice Souter, Justice Ginsburg, and Justice Breyer join, concurring.

As Justice Scalia correctly points out, petitioner has not challenged the power of the tribunal to try him for a capital offense. It is important to add to this observation that petitioner's first victim was a member of the Armed Forces on active duty and that the second was a retired serviceman who gave petitioner a ride from the barracks on the same night as the first killing. On these facts, this does not appear to be a case in which petitioner could appropriately have raised the question whether the holding in *Solorio v. United States*, 483 U.S. 435 (1987), should be extended to reach the imposition of the death penalty for an offense that did not have the "service connection" required prior to the change in the law effected in that case.

The question whether a "service connection" requirement should obtain in capital cases is an open one both because *Solorio* was not a capital case, and because *Solorio's* review of the historical materials would seem to undermine any contention that a military tribunal's power to try capital offenses must be as broad as its power to try noncapital ones. Moreover, the question is a substantial one because, when the punishment may be death, there are particular reasons to ensure that the men and women of the Armed Forces do not by reason of serving their country receive less protection than the Constitution provides for civilians.

As a consequence of my conclusion that the "service connection" requirement has been satisfied here, I join not only the Court's analysis of the delegation issue, but also its disposition of the case. By joining in the Court's opinion, however, I do not thereby accept the proposition that our decision in *Solorio* must be understood to apply to capital offenses. Nor do I understand the Court's decision to do so. That question, as I have explained, remains to be decided.

Justice THOMAS, concurring in the judgment.

It is not clear to me that the extensive rules we have developed under the Eighth Amendment for the prosecution of civilian capital cases, including the requirement of proof of aggravating factors, necessarily apply to capital prosecutions in the military, cf. *Chappell v. Wallace*, 462 U.S. 296, 300–302 (1983), and this Court has never so held, see *Schick v. Reed*, 419 U.S. 256, 260 (1974). I am therefore not certain that this case even raises a delegation question, for if Loving can constitutionally be sentenced to death without proof of aggravating factors, he surely cannot claim that the President violated the Constitution by promulgating aggravating factors that afforded more protection than that to which Loving is constitutionally entitled.

Like the majority, I conclude that the Government prevails even if we assume, without deciding, that aggravating factors are required in this context. There is abundant authority for according Congress and the President sufficient deference in the regulation of military affairs to uphold the delegation here, and I see no need to resort to our nonmilitary separation-of-powers and "delegation doctrine" cases in reaching this conclusion. I write separately to explain that by concurring in the judgment in this case, I take no position with respect to Congress' power to delegate authority or otherwise alter the traditional separation of powers outside the military context....

Note on the Variable Size of Court-Martial Panels in Capital Cases

Although no state provides for a panel of less than 12 jurors in a capital case, military panels can consist of as few as five members. *United States v. Curtins*, 32 M.J. 252 (C.M.A.). Also, the number of panelists in a capital court-martial can vary from case to case. Jurors who are removed from a court-martial panel are usually not replaced as long as a quorum remains. This poses a dilemma to defense counsel: whether to remove biased panel members—thereby reducing the statistical chance of finding the one vote necessary to avoid a death sentence. See Sullivan, "Playing the Numbers: Court-Martial Panel Size and the Military Death Penalty," 158 Mil. L. Rev. 1 (1998) (suggesting that until the problem of variable panel size in death penalty cases is eliminated, capital courts-martial will remain a numbers game fixed in the prosecution's favor).

Note on Life Without Parole Option

For crimes that occurred on or after November 17, 1997, a sentence of life without the possibility of parole is a possible alternative to death. Before the military adopted the LWOP option, a service member serving a life sentence would become eligible for parole after serving ten years.

Chapter 19

International Law and the Death Penalty

A. International Restrictions on Capital Punishment

Most Western nations have abolished the death penalty for ordinary offenses, either through constitutional amendment or legislation. The nations that have abolished the death penalty include: Great Britain[1], Canada, France, the Netherlands, Norway, Mexico, Italy, Austria, Denmark, Luxembourg, Germany, Spain, Iceland and Switzerland. South Africa, which had consistently applied the death penalty for many years, abolished capital punishment for all crimes in 1997.[2] Nations which join the United States in imposing the death penalty include China, Egypt, Iraq, Iran, Japan and Singapore.

The crimes for which one may receive the death penalty vary greatly. Algeria and Tunisia have executed dozens of Islamic militants, and Egypt announced in 1993 that it intended to carry out the first of many executions of militants convicted of terrorism. In Bosnia-Herzegovina, two Serb soldiers were sentenced to death for war crimes, which included massacring civilians and murdering and raping captive women. In Romania, deposed dictator Nicolae Ceausescu and his wife were executed by an eighty-man firing squad. In Malaysia, a mandatory death penalty is imposed in drug trafficking cases.

In China, even mundane offenses may result in the imposition of death. For example, two Chinese farmers were sentenced to death and immediately executed for selling the skins of three endangered giant pandas. China also executed five men convicted of stealing power transformers that caused power outages and crop failures. A guilty verdict for counterrevolutionary activity may also result in the penalty of death.

In one notorious 1990 case, Iraq sentenced a British journalist to death for spying. Under Iraqi law, no appeal was allowed for the Iranian-born British journalist. Despite

---

1. In Great Britain, the death penalty was abolished in 1956 partly in response to the execution of Derek Bentley, a mentally disabled teenager who was convicted of killing a police officer. The British Home Secretary acknowledged possible government wrongdoing in the case. Bentley's sister continues to press for a full pardon and a ruling absolving her brother of any wrongdoing. N.Y. Times, Aug. 1, 1993. Bentley's case was the subject of a 1991 film entitled, "Let Him Have It," and the Elvis Costello song, "Let Him Dangle" (Spike 1989). Do you think that a single case, like Bentley's, could spark abolition of the death penalty in the United States?

2. For an excellent but chilling discussion of the death penalty in South Africa, see D. Bruck, *On Death Row in Pretoria Central*, The New Republic (July 13 & 20, 1987). See also *State v. Makwanyane and Mchunu*, Case. No. CCT/3/94 (1995) (*infra* this chapter).

pleas from Great Britain and other European nations, Iraq executed the journalist within days of his conviction and sentence. In response, then-Prime Minister Margaret Thatcher recalled the British Ambassador to Iraq. The Bush administration refused to join the worldwide protest against the execution.

Historically, some of the most monstrous crimes known to humanity have been perpetrated by heads of state. Adolph Hitler, Benito Mussolini, Idi Amin, Jean Claude Duvalier and Moammar Gadhafi are believed to be personally responsible for hundreds of thousands of murders, mutilations and sundry atrocities. Nonetheless, it is extremely rare for a sitting head of state to be criminally prosecuted or punished by another state for crimes against humanity, genocide or state-sponsored torture.

In 1999, the British House of Lords held that former Chilean General, Senator, and Head of State Augusto Pinochet was not immune as a former head of state from prosecution for crimes of alleged torture during the 1980s. *Regina v. Bartle and the Commissioner of Police for the Metropolis and Others, Ex Parte Pinochet* (U.K. House of Lords Mar. 24, 1999). The Chilean Supreme Court appeared to clear the way for Pinochet's prosecution for human rights violations in Chile by voting that Pinochet's self-serving "immunity for life" designation did not prevent his being brought to trial. Pinochet was prosecuted, but the court dismissed the charges for medical reasons (Pinochet was found to be suffering from vascular dementia.) As one international law expert noted, "[i]nternational law is a limited system constrained on one end by voluntary compliance of consenting sovereign states and on the other by the political deadlock of the moment. Until some radical change occurs in international law or the politics of the moment, it is still good to be the king." Penrose, "It's Good To Be King!: Prosecuting Heads of State and Former Heads of State Under International Law," 39 Colum. J. Transnat'l L. 193, 197, 202–03 (2000).

Note on Capital Punishment in Japan

Contrast the capital punishment system in the United States with the system operating in Japan. Japan's Code of Criminal Procedure lists eighteen offenses punishable by death: (1) leading an insurrection; (2) inciting foreign aggression; (3) assisting an enemy; (4) arson of an inhabited structure; (5) damaging an inhabited structure; (6) destruction by explosives; (7) causing death by derailing a train or capsizing a ship; (8) vehicular manslaughter; (9) causing death by poisoning the water supply; (10) domestic murder; (11) murder; (12) murder during the course of a robbery; (13) rape during a robbery which results in death; (14) unlawful use of explosives; (15) killing by duel; (16) manslaughter by causing an airplane crash; (17) manslaughter caused by seizing an aircraft; and (18) killing a hostage.

In practice, since the end of World War II, Japan has reserved the death penalty for crimes involving homicide. The death penalty is reserved "for murders where cruelty and disregard for human life have been paramount, where the murderer has shown little repentance and the victim's family little forgiveness." Reasons for exercising clemency and voiding a death sentence include illness, old age, repentance and forgiveness by the murder victim's family members.

In 2002, human rights experts estimated that 56 inmates faced execution by hanging in Japan. Only five or six prisoners are executed each year. (By comparison, China, which considers executions to be state secrets, kills between 3,500 and 15,000 prisoners each year. Many of these executions are by a single pistol shot to the head following mass trials and public humiliation.)

A typical death row inmate in Japan spends years waiting in permanent solitary confinement. His cell is furnished with three floor mats and a toilet bucket. Constantly under surveillance by video cameras, the inmate has no access to radio, television or news media. Recreation consists of a thirty minute period for exercise outdoors with other death row inmates. No communication is permitted ever. The remaining ten hours of the day are spent sitting motionless on the cell floor. Only two activities are permitted: reading books approved by a prison official and thinking. Inmates may receive thirty minute visits from family members and lawyers. Once the death sentence is confirmed, however, lawyers are not allowed to visit unless the prison director has granted the inmate's request to apply for a retrial.

Like China, Japan's Death Row is surrounded by a shroud of secrecy. The Ministry of Justice insists that it has no duty to confirm or deny that executions have taken place. According to a senior government official, "The authorities are not legally obligated to notify relatives or lawyers of an impending execution." As a result, frequently no one is told when an execution occurs.

After years of languishing on death row, the inmate himself learns of his imminent death only moments before his execution. Justice Ministry officials insist that their system of secret executions is the most humane form of capital punishment because the prisoners "would lose themselves to despair" if they knew that they were to die on a certain day. "They might even try to commit suicide or escape."

Prisoners learn of their execution moments before they are hung. They are given only enough time to clean their cell, write a final letter and receive last rites. A guard escorts the condemned inmate to a room with a small Buddhist altar. There, the prisoner is offered a last meal and is given some time to prepare for death. Next, he is blindfolded and handcuffed and is taken to the nearby gallows. The only witnesses are representatives from the prosecutor's office. To spare the conscience of the executioner, Japan has five executioners, each of whom simultaneously presses a button. Only one of these buttons actually springs the trap door open, sending the executee to his death.

After the execution, government officials notify family members who are given 24 hours to collect the dead prisoner. Because of the intense shame felt by relatives of executed prisoners, the remains of most of the executed prisoners go unclaimed.

Ministry of Justice annual statistics indicate the number of prisoners executed during the previous year. Names, dates, and method of execution are not provided. The policy of secrecy is designed, according to a Ministry spokesperson, "to protect the family of the prisoner from the shame of having it known that their relative has been executed."

Families of murder victims are compensated by the government and may receive up to 9.2 million yen. (Up to 30 million yen is awarded to families of citizens killed by traffic accidents.)

Japan may have been the first country to abolish the death penalty. In A.D. 724, Emperor Shomu banned executions, citing the sanctity of human life. Shomu's ban on capital punishment in Japan did not last long. However, a ban was reinstated in 810 and there were no executions in Japan until 1156.

From the late 12th century until the early 19th century, tens of thousands of people were put to death in Japan. Execution methods included burning at the stake, burying alive, crucifixion, drawing and quartering, dunking in boiling water, sawing in half, skewering and strangulation. See generally, Yardley, *In Worker's Death, View of China's*

Harsh Justice, The New York Times (Dec. 31, 2005); French, *Secrecy of Japan's Executions is Criticized as Unduly Cruel*, The New York Times, (June 30, 2002); Kristoff, *Death Penalty Popular in Japan*, The New York Times (May 29, 1995); The Tokyo Journal (Mar. 1994); Foreign Policy, May/June 2005.

Note on Capital Punishment in China

China's capital punishment protocol differs dramatically from Japan's. Not surprising, China, the world's most populous country, has the largest death row population. Approximately 65 crimes are punishable by death in China. Many of these are nonviolent, economic offenses. Capital crimes include trading in cultural relics, sabotaging dikes, prostitution, embezzlement and organizing secret religious societies. On one occasion, a businessman was executed for trademark infringement after being convicted for making and selling a Chinese liquor called Maotai.

Eckholm's article, *Judicial Caprice in China*, The New York Times (Sept. 10, 2000), is illustrative:

> As described in an article in the Washington Post, executions in China are commonplace.... Details of China's relentless quest to execute four men suspected of killing two taxi drivers in 1994 raise troubling questions about that nation's criminal justice system. Three times since 1996, the same local court has convicted the four men of murder, and sentenced all of them to death. And three times those convictions were overturned on appeal by the same three-judge panel. In reversing the convictions, the Hebei provincial high court cited credible evidence that the confessions were extracted by torture, potential witnesses were threatened by the police, exonerating records were suppressed and key forensic tests were crudely doctored.

> Nonetheless, the four defendants—two farmers, a truck driver and a factory welder whose ages range from 28 to 35—remained imprisoned as of September 2000 in Chengde, a major tourist center. Chinese prosecutors planned to retry the men, and again seek their deaths.

> The defendants have so far escaped execution only because their families—all farmers and workers—were willing to bear official persecution and severe financial strains to mount repeated legal appeals. Three family members were jailed for months at a time, for "protecting criminals."

> "Violent or grossly unfair practices by the police, prosecutors and local courts are common in China, especially outside major cities. Cases of torture and wrongful imprisonment are increasingly reported in the controlled Chinese press, a sign that the central leadership feels it must acknowledge and attack a problem that for most Chinese is a more immediate human rights concern than any grand issue of democracy."

> The continued prosecution in Chengde is "out of step with the demands of a society under the rule of law," a prominent Beijing attorney, Jiang Xiaoming, wrote in a Beijing newspaper in August. "Although the case in Chengde appears to be extreme, similar ones are quite common in China, and I don't mean just a handful of them," said Hu Yunteng, an expert on criminal procedure and the death penalty with the Chinese Academy of Social Sciences in Beijing as well as a practicing defense attorney.

Despite major improvements in the criminal procedure code that took effect in 1997, important shortcomings remain, such as a lack of protection from double jeopardy. More common threats to fairness include a traditional, widely shared assumption in China that "if evidence points toward an individual, he must be guilty," Mr. Hu said. And in many localities, legal experts say, Communist Party officials, the police and prosecutors hold sway over the courts. "The public security organs can be very powerful," Mr. Hu said, "and to their way of thinking, once they've expended so much time and energy on a case, if a verdict of innocence comes in, they find this very hard to accept."

The torture of defendants is not rare, many lawyers say, and is often ignored by judges. In the Chengde case, interrogators applied an electric prod to one man's genitals, inserted an electrified wire into the anus of another and beat one of the men with an iron rod, according to relatives and defense attorneys and the testimony of cellmates. Reached by telephone, two different Chengde police officials refused to comment on the torture charges.

An unusual aspect of this case is the critical scrutiny it has received in newspapers outside of Hebei Province. The August 10, 2000 issue of Southern Weekend, a nationally circulated newspaper published in Guangzhou, printed a detailed expose, including excerpts from the appeals court's description of glaring inconsistencies in the forensic evidence and of the alleged torture. Key tests of blood samples used to tie defendants to the killing, for example, were dated days before the men had even been detained, according to the court record. But few residents of Chengde have heard any of this: local media have not reported on the legal reversals and charges of official misconduct.

Defending the prosecutions, an administrator of the Chengde intermediate court, where the convictions occurred, told Southern Weekend, "This case can't be wrong." Investigators had sometimes been careless with evidence, admitted the official, Miao Hongqing, but all the defendants had confessed, and the circumstantial evidence and blood tests all matched up. He accused the families of colluding to make up alibis.

The four men only became suspects some three months after the killings of the taxi drivers, which to the embarrassment of the police had gone unsolved. According to the families, the police first picked up Chen Guoqing on an unrelated matter. "It all started when the police accused Chen Guoqing of raping a girl from a street stall," said his mother, Ms. Wang. "They fined him [the equivalent of $36] but he refused to pay, saying he was innocent. A few days later, he was taken away and tortured."

In police hands, Mr. Chen not only confessed to a role in the killings but implicated more than a dozen of his fellow villagers. Some have fled the area, and others were not prosecuted for unknown reasons.

The relatives insist that the men have strong alibis. His family swears that Chen Guoqing, for example, was on duty at a local boiler plant during one of the killings. A defense attorney said that factory records proving Mr. Chen's claim had been introduced at trial, but ignored by the judges. On one of the nights he is accused of committing murder, Zhu Yangqiang was at home in bed with an intravenous drip, on his second day of recovery from a street fight, according to his mother and neighbors. Ms. Wang said that clinic records of his medical treatment were seized by investigators, mentioned in the first trial to no effect and have not been produced since.

Fu Yiru, the mother of another defendant, He Guoqiang, 28, said that once they heard their son was a suspect they urged him to turn himself in to clear his name, and he agreed. "How we regret it now," she said.

In repeatedly overturning the convictions, the Hebei provincial high court declared, "The facts are unclear and the evidence is insufficient." In principle, this should lead to a presumption of innocence and the appeals court could have ordered the men released rather than giving local officials the option of a retrial. But, because of ingrained assumptions about guilt, personal and political ties between the courts and even concern about the lower court's possible financial liability for wrongful imprisonment, flawed cases are often sent back in this manner to the original venue, said Mr. Hu, the legal authority. "We have a lot of criminal cases like this one, going back and forth like a Ping-Pong match," he said.

China executes more people every year than the rest of the world combined. In 2004, a high-level delegate to the National People's Congress publicly estimated that China's annual execution rate was "nearly 10,000." Outside scholars have put the annual number as high as 15,000.

Perhaps because the American presumption of innocence is entirely absent from China's criminal justice system, those charged are almost always convicted. Sentences are rarely reversed. This is due in part to the fact that the same judges who hear the condemned prisoner's appeal also handle mandatory final review of the case. This means that the judges are reviewing their own ruling, a practice that provides virtually no meaningful oversight.

Executions frequently take place immediately after sentencing. More common, however, is for executions to be scheduled before major holidays. The morning of execution, the condemned inmate is photographed, seated and shackled to the floor. Then, if officials desire and regardless of the inmate's wishes, he is injected with an anticoagulant to facilitate harvesting of his organs.

Although executions often are shrouded in secrecy as in Japan, Chinese prisoners sometimes are transported to "death sentencing rallies" just before they are killed. The rallies, held "to educate the living," take place in sports stadiums before throngs of office and factory workers who have received free tickets at work. This attempt at deterrence is known as "killing the chicken to scare the monkey."

After the rally, the condemned is taken to Beijing Supreme People's Court Project 86, the execution ground. Three soldiers escort the inmate to his death. Two hold the inmate's arms while the third forces him to kneel. The executioner, armed with a large caliber carbine rifle, stands behind the inmate. When the squad leader shouts "Get ready," the soldiers release their grip on the inmate and the executioner fires. Most often, the inmate is shot in the head. However, if the inmate's corneas are to be harvested, the inmate will be shot in the chest. A doctor checks for a pulse and orders a second bullet if necessary. To complete the process, a photographer takes post-mortem pictures.

If organs are to be harvested, the inmate's body is immediately transported by ambulance to a hospital. Regulations published by the Chinese government—"On the Use of Dead Bodies or Organs From Condemned Criminals"—state that for a prisoner to be a donor, prior consent must be given by that person or surviving family, unless the body is unclaimed. Human rights activists point out that because prisoners are often prevented from communicating with family members, there is no one to claim the body, which is harvested and cremated almost immediately. The government also insists that the medical teams assigned to harvest the organs act stealthily: "Surgical vans must not display hospital logos; surgeons must not wear hospital uniforms when at the execution site; guards must be present until the organ is removed; and the corpses should be promptly cremated following the removal of the organs." With more than 75,000 people on waiting lists for organs in the United States, there is a robust demand for the organs pilfered from prisoners. These are sold on the black market for up to $10,000.

If organs are not to be harvested, the body is taken directly to a crematorium. Sometimes, before the ashes are released, family members are required to pay a bill for the cost of the bullet (approximately 6 cents). In addition, family members must pay for cremation and the cost of transportation to the crematorium.

During the 1970s, China broadcast executions on prime-time television. Several reasons prompted a return to secrecy. Perhaps foremost, China sought to improve its reputation throughout the world. Also, unrepentant dissidents were fond of yelling anti-government slogans before death. Just before an execution (usually at 10:00 a.m.), a curfew takes effect and teams of soldiers guard the execution area.

China's decision to discontinue the prime-time broadcast of executions may have been prompted by a botched execution. The Associated Press reported a mass execution of 13 criminals before a crowd of 10,000 in a sports stadium at the end of 1995. One woman, after having been shot twice, turned her head toward her executioner and begged to be shot a third time. See generally, Yardley, *In Worker's Death, View of China's Harsh Justice*, The New York Times (Dec. 31, 2005); Baard & Cooney, *The People's Republic Has Long Been Suspected of Selling Organs from Prisoners*, The Village Voice (2001); Owen, "Death Row Inmates or Organ Donors: China's Source of Body Organs for Medical Transplantation," 5 Ind. Int'l & Comp. J. 495 (1995); *China Executes 13 Criminals Before Crowd of 10,000*, San Jose Mercury (Dec. 16, 1995); Wong, *Death Sentence Rallies, Prisoner Executions Held to Educate Living*, The Detroit News (Apr. 10, 1994); Sun, *China's Executed Convicts Donate Organs Unwittingly*, The Washington Post (Mar. 27, 1994); Sun, *China's Executioners: A Punishing Schedule*, The Washington Post (Mar. 27, 1994); Sun, *China Increases Use of the Death Penalty Amid Societal Turmoil*, The Courier-Journal (Mar. 27, 1994).

International Law as a Limitation on the Imposition of the Death Penalty

In 1993, Texas executed Ramon Montoya, a citizen of Mexico, and Carlos Santana, a citizen of the Dominican Republic. Neither Mexico nor the Dominican Republic have the death penalty. Both countries unsuccessfully tried to intervene to save the lives of their countrymen. Similarly, the Canadian government attempted to intervene on behalf of a Canadian national awaiting execution in Texas. In an *amicus curiae* brief filed in the United States District Court for the Eastern District of Texas, the Canadian government argued that Joseph Faulder, a Canadian citizen, was not notified of his right to inform the Canadian consulate of his arrest and receive the assistance of the consulate, as required by an international treaty. Canada claimed that this deprivation violated the Fifth, Sixth and Fourteenth Amendments of the United States Constitution. *Faulder v. Johnson*, 81 F.3d 515 (5th Cir. 1996).

With increasing frequency, countries which do not have the death penalty rely on international law to prevent the extradition of an American citizen to the United States to face capital charges. For example, in 1993, the Dallas Morning News reported that France—which outlawed capital punishment in 1981—agreed to extradite to Texas Joy Aylor, after receiving adequate assurances that Aylor would not face the death penalty for her role in the murder of her husband's girlfriend. Similarly, in 2001, the International Herald Tribune noted that United States authorities faced a significant legal hurdle before they would be able to bring to trial James Kopp, a man accused of murdering a Buffalo, New York doctor who provided abortions. Kopp was arrested in Dinan, a port in Brittany, France. Because French law forbids the extradition of anyone who could face the death penalty, French officials said that Kopp would not be turned over to the United States unless they were given assurances that Kopp would not be executed. *French May Oppose Extradition to U.S.*, Int'l Herald Trib. (Apr. 2, 2001).

While American and French authorities wrangled over Kopp's extradition, French President Jacques Chirac, speaking at the March, 2001 U.N. Human Rights Commission in Geneva, called for the "universal abolition of the death penalty, with the first step being a general moratorium." International and political ramifications of such conflicts are discussed below.

For further discussion on this topic, see Uribe, "Consuls at Work: Universal Instruments of Human Rights and Consular Protection in the Context of Criminal Justice," 19 Hous. J. Int'l L. 375 (1997); Aceves, "The Vienna Convention on Consular Relations: A Study of Rights, Wrongs, and Remedies," 31 Vand. J. Transnat'l L. 257 (1998); Brown & Muirhead, "Extradition: Divergent Trends in International Cooperation," 33 Harv. Int'l L.J. 223 (1992).

B. Selected Cases

The European System

In the international community, regional systems exist to protect human rights. The European system provides comprehensive protection of human rights and effective service to its member nations, making it one of the most successful guardians of basic liberties. Human rights protection is accomplished in the European system through "fact finding missions" related to human rights violations, annual reporting of human rights conditions in member nations, and enforcement of human rights norms through a regional court.

The European system has three branches: the European Commission of Human Rights, the European Court of Human Rights, and the Committee of Ministers of the Council of Europe. The European system centers around the Convention for the Protection of Human Rights and Fundamental Freedoms, Nov. 4, 1950, 213 U.N.T.S. 222, *entered into force* Sept. 3, 1953. Twenty-one European nations, forming the Council of Europe, are parties to this convention. As parties to the Convention, members of the Council of Europe submit to the jurisdiction of the Court of Human Rights. The Court of Human Rights, in turn, acts as a "Super-Supreme Court" on human rights issues and may overrule the highest courts of its member nations.

Before the Court of Human Rights assumes jurisdiction over a case, however, all domestic remedies available in the nation where an action was first brought must be exhausted. In addition, the Commission on Human Rights acts as a screening body. Only when the Commission agrees that a case should be submitted to the Court of Human Rights may the Court rule on the merits.

The case of *Soering v. United Kingdom*, 11 EHRR 439 (1989), reprinted below, provides an example of how the Court of Human Rights handles allegations of human rights violations in the context of capital punishment. *Soering* also illustrates how international law has influenced the application of the death penalty in the United States.

Jens Soering, a German national, came to the United States at the age of eleven with his parents. Soering remained in the United States and attended college at the University of Virginia. While in school, Soering met and befriended a Canadian national, Elizabeth Haysom. Elizabeth's parents, William and Nancy Haysom, vigorously opposed Soering's relationship with their daughter. Elizabeth Haysom and Soering eventually decided to murder Haysom's parents. To establish an alibi, Soering and Haysom rented a car and drove from Virginia to Washington D.C. Soering then drove back to the Haysom home in Virginia and stabbed Haysom's parents to death. Both victims' throats were slit. Following the murders, Soering and Haysom left the United States.

In April of 1986, Soering and Haysom were arrested in England for check fraud. In June a grand jury of the Circuit Court of Bedford County, Virginia, indicted Soering and Haysom on charges of murdering Haysom's parents. That August, the United States requested the extradition of Soering, pursuant to the Extradition Treaty of 1972 between the United States and the United Kingdom. In October, the British Embassy in Washington requested an assurance by the United States that Soering would not be given the death penalty. Although the United States provided the requested assurance, it was later made clear to the United Kingdom that the ultimate decision regarding the death penalty rested with the prosecutor of Bedford County, Virginia, and that the death penalty would most likely be sought. Subsequently, after a number of appeals by Soering, the Secretary of State of the United Kingdom signed a warrant ordering Soering's surrender to the United States.

In July 1988, Soering filed an application with the European Commission on Human Rights. The following month, the President of the Commission instructed the United Kingdom that Soering should not be extradited until the Commission had an opportunity to review the case. After reviewing the case, the Commission determined that Soering could be extradited to the United States. However, the Commission also concluded that the case should be submitted to the Court of Human Rights for final adjudication.

The following excerpt summarizes the Court of Human Rights' decision and its analysis of Article III of the Convention for the Protection of Human Rights and Fundamental Freedoms. Article III of the Convention provides, "No one shall be subjected to torture or to inhuman or degrading treatment or punishment."

Soering v. United Kingdom

(Series A, No. 161; Application No. 14038/88) (7 July 1989) 11 EHRR 439

... Article III makes no provision for exceptions and no derogation from it is permissible under Article XV in time of war or other national emergency. This absolute prohibition on torture and on inhuman or degrading treatment or punishment under the terms of the Convention shows that Article III enshrines one of the fundamental values of the democratic societies making up the Council of Europe....

The question remains whether the extradition of a fugitive to another State where he would be subjected or be likely to be subjected to torture or to inhuman or degrading treatment or punishment would itself engage the responsibility of a Contracting State under Article III.... Extradition in such circumstances, while not explicitly referred to in the brief and general wording of Article III, would plainly be contrary to the spirit and intendment of the Article, and in the Court's view this inherent obligation not to extradite also extends to cases in which the fugitive would be faced in the receiving State by a real risk of exposure to inhuman or degrading treatment or punishment proscribed by that Article.

What amounts to "inhuman or degrading treatment or punishment" depends on all the circumstances of the case. Furthermore, inherent in the whole of the convention is a search for a fair balance between the demands of the general interest of the community and the requirements of the protection of the individual's fundamental rights. As movement about the world becomes easier and crime takes on a larger international dimension, it is increasingly in the interest of all nations that suspected offenders who flee abroad should be brought to justice. Conversely, the establishment of safe havens for fugitives would not only result in danger for the State obliged to harbor the protected person but also tend to undermine the foundations of extradition. These considerations must also be included among the factors to be taken into account in the interpretation and application of the notions of inhuman and degrading treatment or punishment in extradition cases....

[T]he decision by a Contracting State to extradite a fugitive may give rise to an issue under Article III, and hence engage the responsibility of that State under the Convention, where substantial grounds have been shown for believing that the person concerned, if extradited, faces a real risk of being subjected to torture or to inhuman or degrading treatment or punishment in the requesting country. The establishment of such responsibility inevitably involves an assessment of conditions in the requesting country against the standards of Article III of the Convention. Nonetheless, there is no question of adjudicating on or establishing the responsibility of the receiving country, whether under general international law, under the Convention or otherwise. Insofar as any liability under the Convention is or may be incurred, it is liability incurred by the extraditing Contracting State by reason of its having taken action which has as a direct consequence the exposure of an individual to proscribed ill-treatment.

B. Application of Article III in the Particular Circumstances of the Present Case

The extradition procedure against the applicant in the United Kingdom has been completed, the Secretary of State having signed a warrant ordering his surrender to the United States' authorities; this decision, albeit as yet not implemented, directly affects him. It therefore has to be determined on the above principles whether the foreseeable consequences of Mr. Soering's return to the United States are such as to attract the application of Article III. This inquiry must concentrate firstly on whether Mr. Soering runs a real risk of being sentenced to death in Virginia, since the source of the alleged inhuman and degrading treatment or punishment, namely the "death row phenomenon," lies in the imposition of the death penalty.

[The Court concluded that there were grounds to believe that Soering faced a risk of being sentenced to death and being subjected to the "death row phenomenon." "The Court's conclusion is therefore that the likelihood of the feared exposure of the applicant to the 'death row phenomenon' has been shown to be such as to bring Article III into play."] ...

2. Whether in the circumstances the risk of exposure to the "death row phenomenon" would make extradition a breach of Article III.

(a) General considerations

As is established in the Court's case law, ill-treatment, including punishment, must attain a minimum level of severity if it is to fall within the scope of Article III. The assessment of this minimum is, in the nature of things, relative; it depends on all the circumstances of the case, such as the nature and context of the treatment or punishment, the manner and method if its execution, its duration, its physical or mental effects and, in some instances, the sex, age and state of health of the victim.

Treatment has been held by the Court to be both "inhuman" because it was premeditated, was applied for hours at a stretch and "caused, if not actual bodily injury, at least intense physical and mental suffering," and also "degrading" because it was "such as to arouse in [its] victims feelings of fear, anguish and inferiority capable of humiliating and debasing them and possibly breaking their physical or moral resistance." In order for a punishment or treatment associated with it to be "inhuman" or "degrading," the suffering or humiliation involved must in any event go beyond that inevitable element of suffering or humiliation connected with a given form of legitimate punishment. In this connection, account is to be taken not only of the physical pain experienced but also, where there is a considerable delay before execution of the punishment, of the sentenced person's mental anguish of anticipating the violence he is to have inflicted on him.

Capital punishment is permitted under certain conditions by Article II, Section 1 of the Convention, which reads:

> Everyone's right to life shall be protected by law. No one shall be deprived of his life intentionally save in the execution of a sentence of a court following his conviction of a crime for which this penalty is provided by law.

In view of this wording, the applicant did not suggest that the death penalty *per se* violated Article III. He, like the two Government Parties, agreed with the Commission that the extradition of a person to a country where he risks the death penalty does not in itself raise an issue under either Article II or Article III. On the other hand, Amnesty International in their written comments argued that the evolving standards in Western Europe regarding the existence and use of the death penalty required that the death penalty should now be considered as an inhuman and degrading punishment within the meaning of Article III.

Certainly, "the Convention is a living instrument which … must be interpreted in the light of present-day conditions;" and, in assessing whether a given treatment or punishment is to be regarded as inhuman or degrading for the purposes of Article III, "the Court cannot but be influenced by the developments and commonly accepted standards in the penal policy of the member States of the Council of Europe in this field." *De facto* the death penalty no longer exists in time of peace in the contracting States to the Convention. In the few Contracting States which retain the death penalty in law for some peacetime offenses, death sentences, if ever imposed, are nowadays not carried out….

Whether these marked changes have the effect of bringing the death penalty *per se* within the prohibition of ill-treatment under Article III must be determined on the principles governing the interpretation of the Convention.

The Convention is to be read as a whole and Article III should therefore be construed in harmony with the provisions of Article II. On this basis Article III evidently cannot have been intended by the drafters of the Convention to include a general prohibition of the death penalty since that would nullify the clear wording of Article II, Section 1.

Subsequent practice in national penal policy, in the form of a generalized abolition of capital punishment, could be taken as establishing the agreement of the Contracting States to abrogate the exception provided for under Article II, Section 1 and hence to remove a textual limit on the scope for evolutive interpretation of Article III. However, Protocol No 6, as a subsequent written agreement, shows that the intention of the Contracting Parties as recently as 1983 was to adopt the normal method of amendment of the text in order to introduce a new obligation to abolish capital punishment in time of peace and, what is more, to do so by an optional instrument allowing each State to choose the moment when to undertake such an engagement. In these conditions, notwithstanding the special character of the Convention, Article III cannot be interpreted as generally prohibiting the death penalty.

That does not mean however that circumstances relating to a death sentence can never give rise to an issue under Article III. The manner in which it is imposed or executed, the personal circumstances of the condemned person and a disproportionality to the gravity of the crime committed, as well as the conditions of detention awaiting execution, are examples of factors capable of bringing the treatment or punishment received by the condemned person with the proscription under Article III. Present-day attitudes in the contracting States to capital punishment are relevant for the assessment whether the acceptable threshold of suffering or degradation has been exceeded.

(b) The particular circumstances

The applicant submitted that the circumstances to which he would be exposed as a consequence of the implementation of the Secretary of State's decision to return him to the United States, namely the "death row phenomenon," cumulatively constitute such serious treatment that his extradition would be contrary to Article III. He cited in particular the delays in the appeal and review procedures following a death sentence, during which time he would be subject to increasing tension and psychological trauma; the fact, so he said, that the judge or jury in determining sentence is not obliged to take into account the defendant's age and mental state at the time of the offense; the extreme conditions of his future detention on "death row" in Mecklenburg Correctional Center, where he expects to be the victim of violence and sexual abuse because of his age, color and nationality; and the constant spectre of the execution itself, including the ritual of execution. He also relied on the possibility of extradition or deportation, which he would not oppose, to the Federal Republic of Germany as accentuating the disproportionality of the Secretary of State's decision....

[T]he conclusion expressed by the Commission was that the degree of severity contemplated by Article III would not be attained. The United Kingdom Government shared this opinion. In particular, it disputed many of the applicant's factual allegations as to the conditions on death row in Mecklenburg and his expected fate there.

(i) Length of detention prior to execution.

[J]ust as some lapse of time between sentence and execution is inevitable if appeal safeguards are to be provided to the condemned person, so it is equally part of human nature that the person will cling to life by exploiting those safeguards to the full. However well-intentioned and even potentially beneficial is the provision of the complex of post-sentence procedures in Virginia, the consequence is that the condemned prisoner has to endure for many years the conditions on death row and the anguish and mounting tension of living in the ever-present shadow of death.

(ii) Conditions on death row.

As to conditions in Mecklenburg Correctional Center, where the applicant could expect to be held if sentenced to death, the court bases itself on the facts which were uncontested by the United Kingdom Government, without finding it necessary to determine the reliability of the additional evidence adduced by the applicant, notably as to the risk of homosexual abuse and physical attack undergone by prisoners on death row.

The stringency of the custodial regime in Mecklenburg, as well as the services (medical, legal and social) and the controls (legislative, judicial and administrative) provided for inmates, are described in some detail above. In this connection, the United Kingdom Government drew attention to the necessary requirement of extra security for the safe custody of prisoners condemned to death for murder. Whilst it might thus well be justifiable in principle, the severity of a special regime such as that operated on death row in Mecklenburg is compounded by the fact of inmates being subject to it for a protracted period lasting on average six to eight years.

(iii) The applicant's age and mental state.

At the time of the killings, the applicant was only 18 years old and there is some psychiatric evidence, which was not contested as such, that he "was suffering from [such] an abnormality of mind … as substantially impaired his mental responsibility for his acts."

Unlike Article II of the Convention, Article VI of the 1966 International Covenant on Civil and Political Rights and Article IV of the 1969 American Convention on Human Rights expressly prohibit the death penalty from being imposed on persons aged less than 18 at the time of commission of the offense. Whether or not such a prohibition be inherent in the brief and general language of Article II of the European Convention, its explicit enunciation in other, later international instruments, the former of which has been ratified by a large number of States party to the European Convention, at the very least indicates that as a general principle the youth of the person concerned is a circumstance which is liable, with others, to put in question the compatibility with Article III of measures connected with a death sentence.

It is in line with the Court's case law to treat disturbed mental health as having the same effect for the application of Article III.

Virginia law, as the United Kingdom Government and the Commission emphasized, certainly does not ignore these two factors. Under the Virginia Code account has to be taken of mental disturbance in a defendant, either as an absolute bar to conviction if it is judged to be sufficient to amount to insanity or, like age, as a fact in mitigation at the sentencing stage. Additionally, indigent capital murder defendants are entitled to the appointment of a qualified mental health expert to assist in the preparation of their submissions at the separate sentencing proceedings. These provisions in the Virginia Code undoubtedly serve, as the American courts have stated, to prevent the arbitrary or capricious imposition of the death penalty and narrowly to channel the sentencer's discretion. They do not however remove the relevance of age and mental condition in relation to the acceptability, under Article III, of the "death row phenomenon" for a given individual once condemned to death.

Although it is not for this Court to prejudge issues of criminal responsibility and appropriate sentence, the applicant's youth at the time of the offense and his then mental state, on the psychiatric evidence as it stands, are therefore to be taken into consideration as contributory factors tending, in his case, to bring the treatment on death row within the terms of Article III.

(iv) Possibility of extradition to the Federal Republic of Germany.

The purpose for which [Soering's] removal to the United States was sought, in accordance with the Extradition Treaty between the United Kingdom and the United States, is undoubtedly a legitimate one. However, sending Mr. Soering to be tried in his own country would remove the danger of a fugitive criminal going unpunished as well as the risk of intense and protracted suffering on death row. It is therefore a circumstances of relevance for the overall assessment under Article III in that it goes to the search for the requisite fair balance of interests and to the proportionality of the contested extradition decision in the particular case.

(c) Conclusion

For any prisoner condemned to death, some element of delay, between imposition and execution of the sentence and the experience of severe stress in conditions necessary for strict incarceration are inevitable. The democratic character of the Virginia legal system in general and the positive features of Virginia trial, sentencing and appeal procedures in particular are beyond doubt. The Court agrees with the Commission that the machinery of justice to which the applicant would be subject in the United States is in itself neither arbitrary nor unreasonable, but, rather, respects the rule of law and affords not inconsiderable procedural safeguards to the defendant in a capital trial. Facilities are available on death row for the assistance of inmates, notably through provision of psychological and psychiatric services.

However, in the Court's view, having regard to the very long period of time spent on death row in such extreme conditions, with the ever-present and mounting anguish of awaiting execution of the death penalty, and to the personal circumstances of the applicant, especially his age and mental state at the time of the offense, the applicant's extradition to the United States would expose him to a real risk of treatment going beyond the threshold set by Article III. A further consideration of relevance is that in the particular instance the legitimate purpose of extradition could be achieved by another means which would not involve suffering of such exceptional intensity or duration.

Accordingly, the Secretary of State's decision to extradite the applicant to the United States would, if implemented, give rise to a breach of Article III.

Note on the Death Row Phenomenon

The time spent on death row while awaiting execution concerned the European Court of Human Rights in *Soering*. The evidence was that if Soering were to be sentenced to death under Virginia law he would face an average of six to eight years on death row. The European Court commented on the serious human rights consequences of holding a convict under the threat of death for a prolonged length of time:

"However well-intentioned and even potentially beneficial is the provision of the complex of post-sentence procedures in Virginia, the consequence is that the condemned prisoner has to endure for many years the conditions on death row and the anguish and mounting tension in the ever-present shadow of death."

In *Pratt v. Attorney General for Jamaica, infra*, pp. 1056–1057, note 4, the Judicial Committee of the Privy Council ruled against the decision of the Jamaican government which sought to carry out death sentences against two appellants who had been on death row for over 14 years. Lord Griffiths for the Committee stated:

> "In their Lordships' view a State that wishes to retain capital punishment must accept the responsibility of ensuring that execution follows as swiftly as practicable after sentence, allowing a reasonable time for appeal and consideration of reprieve. *It is part of the human condition that a condemned man will take every opportunity to save his life through use of the appellate procedure. If the appellate procedure enables the prisoner to prolong the appellate hearings over a period of years, the fault is to be attributed to the appellate system that permits such delay and not to the prisoner who takes advantage of it. Appellate procedures that echo down the years are not compatible with capital punishment. The death row phenomenon must not become established as a part of our jurisprudence.*" [Emphasis added.]

The role of the death row phenomenon in extradition proceedings was not conclusively determined by the Canadian Supreme Court in *Kindler v. Canada*, 2 S.C.R. 779 (1991). Justice Cory, with whom Chief Justice Lamer concurred, was of the view that it would be wrong to extradite someone who would face the death row phenomenon. Justice Sopinka did not deal with the question while Justice McLachlin alluded to "the complexity of the issue." Justice La Forest was critical of the concept. He said:

> "While the psychological stress inherent in the death row phenomenon cannot be dismissed lightly, it ultimately pales in comparison to the death penalty. Besides, the fact remains that a defendant is never forced to undergo the full appeal procedure, but the vast majority choose to do so. It would be ironic if delay caused by the appellant's taking advantage of the full and generous avenue of the appeals available to him should be viewed as a violation of fundamental justice."

Notes

1. One commentator predicted that "the Court's rulings on the death penalty [in the *Soering* case] will have little, if any, direct impact either inside or outside the countries belonging to the Council of Europe. However, the Court's reliance upon the death penalty to undergird the 'death row phenomenon' may well lead to the eventual reduction in the use of capital punishment in other countries. It is reasonable to assume that this possibility was one of the major factors motivating the *Soering* judgment." Comment, "The *Soering* Case," 85 Am. J. Int'l L. 128, 143 (1991).

2. The *Soering* decision has been characterized as demonstrating the willingness of the European Court of Human Rights "not only to react after a problem of human rights had occurred, but also its competence of jurisdiction in special categories of cases with imminent risks of infringements upon the Convention and, therefore, its ability to *prevent* a violation of human rights." Breitenmoser & Wilms, "Human Rights v. Extradition: The *Soering* Case," 11 Mich. J. Int'l L. 845, 872–873 (1990).

In addition to the "growing movement towards the abolition of the death penalty among the European states, the United Nations also opened for signature and ratification a new human rights instrument aimed at the abolition of capital punishment. On December 15, 1989, the General Assembly adopted this new instrument, which is contained in the Second Optional Protocol to the International Covenant on Civil and Political Rights, by a recorded vote of fifty-nine in favor to twenty-six against, with forty-eight abstentions." *Id.*

3. Is it more accurate to describe an American death sentence as "life in prison without the possibility of parole but with the uncertain and unpredictable possibility of execution many years later"? The psychological agony of such a sentence is of course highly retributive. However, under accepted human rights norms, the penalty is the equivalent of torture. See, *e.g., Pratt v. Attorney General of Jamaica*, 4 All E.R. 769, 770–71 (P.C. 1993).

4. The "death row phenomenon" may be one reason why there appears to be an increase in capital volunteers—those capital defendants and death row inmates who waive their rights to trial, appeal and post-conviction proceedings in hopes of expediting their executions. For example, while serving a 20-year sentence for second degree murder in New York state, Thomas Grasso was extradited to Oklahoma to face capital murder charges in an unrelated killing. Grasso confessed to the Oklahoma murder, waived all of his rights, pleaded guilty and asked for a death sentence. After receiving an Oklahoma death sentence, Grasso vigorously challenged New York's right to force him to serve his New York sentence before being returned to Oklahoma for execution. According to Grasso, "I did it. The state says I deserve [to be executed]. Why prolong it? I don't want to spend the rest of my life in prison waiting for it to happen." Aug. 1993 A.B.A. Journal at 32. See *supra* chapter 9 for further discussion of the *Grasso* case and volunteers.

There is, however, a widening acceptance amongst those closely associated with the administration of justice in retentionist states that the finality of the death penalty, combined with the determination of the criminal justice system to satisfy itself fully that the conviction is not wrongful, seems inevitably to provide lengthy delays, and the associated psychological trauma. It is apposite to recall in this connection the observation of Justice Frankfurter of the United States Supreme Court, dissenting, in *Solesbee v. Balkcom*, 339 U.S. 9, 14 (1950), that the "onset of insanity while awaiting execution of a death sentence is not a rare phenomenon." As one death row inmate described the intolerable stress of awaiting execution:

> I go to sleep and I dream of me sitting down in that chair. I mean it's such a fearful thought. Me walking down the tier, sitting down in it, them hooking it up and turning it on.... I can wake up, my heart's beating fast, I'm sweating like hell, just like I'd rinsed my head in water.... I feel like I'm going to have a heart attack.

Inciardi, *Criminal Justice* 509 (3d ed. 1990).

Related concerns have been expressed by Justice Breyer, dissenting from decisions not to issue writs of certiorari in *Elledge v. Florida*, 525 U.S. 944 (1998), and *Knight v. Florida*, 528 U.S. 990 (1999). In the latter case, Justice Breyer cited a Florida study of inmates which showed that 35 percent of those committed to death row attempted suicide.

The Short Decision

In *Soering*, the European Court of Human Rights held that Jens Soering could not be extradited to the United States due to the possibility that Soering would experience the "death row phenomenon" if he were sentenced to death. The Court reasoned that although the Convention on Human Rights did not specifically prohibit the death penalty, allowing Soering to be exposed to the "death row phenomenon" would be a violation of the Convention's prohibition, in Article III, against inhuman or degrading treatment or punishment. International law experts immediately recognized the potential effect of the *Soering* decision on diplomatic relations between the United States and members of the Council of Europe. *Soering* and the *Short* decision (discussed below) have been sharply criticized for posing significant threats to the United States military's jurisdiction over military personnel in Western Europe. See Parkerson & Stoehr, "The U.S. Military Death Penalty in Europe: Threats From Recent European Human Rights Developments," 129 Military L. Rev. 41 (1990).

The year following the *Soering* decision, the Supreme Court of the Netherlands confronted similar issues and rendered an equally important decision. Staff Sergeant Charles Short of the United States Air Force was stationed at Soesterberg Air Base in the Netherlands. Short's wife, Esin Hasturk, lived with him at the base. On March 30, 1988, the Dutch Royal Marechaussee (the military police) arrested Short as a suspect in the murder of his wife. During interrogation by Dutch authorities, Short admitted to killing his wife, dismembering her body, placing the body parts in plastic bags, and putting the bags near a dike in Amsterdam.

As a member of the United States military, Short faced prosecution under the Uniform Code of Military Justice (UCMJ). Because penalties under the UCMJ included a possible death sentence (see *supra* chapter 18), the Dutch government refused to relinquish Short to the United States authorities for prosecution.

The procedural history of Short's case in the Dutch courts is complex. However, the ultimate issue decided by the Supreme Court of the Netherlands was straightforward: how to balance the interests of the United States under the NATO Status Treaty with the interests of the Netherlands under the European Convention on Human Rights, Protocol 6. The NATO Status Treaty gives the United States military jurisdiction over its members stationed abroad. The European Convention's Protocol 6 specifically prohibits imposition of the death penalty.[1]

The following passage is excerpted from the Opinion of the Advocate General of the Netherlands. The Supreme Court of the Netherlands relied heavily upon this Opinion in reaching its decision.

Short v. Kingdom of the Netherlands
Nos. 13.949, 13.95029 ILM 1388 (1990)

Article VII of the NATO Status Treaty

The first three paragraphs of Article VII of the NATO Status Treaty read:

1. Subject to the provisions of this Article,

     (a) the military authorities of the sending State shall have the right to exercise within the receiving State all criminal and disciplinary juris-

---

1. The Sixth Protocol was adopted on April 28, 1893. It was the first instrument in international law to obligate its signatories to abolish the death penalty during peacetime.

diction conferred on them by the law of the sending State over all persons subject to the military law of that State;

(b) the authorities of the receiving State shall have jurisdiction over the members of a force or civilian component and their dependents with respect to offenses committed within the territory of the receiving State and punishable by the law of that State.

2.   (a) The military authorities of the sending State shall have the right to exercise exclusive jurisdiction over persons subject to the military law of that State with respect to offenses, including offenses relating to its security, punishable by the law of the sending State, but not by the law of the receiving State.

(b) The authorities of the receiving State shall have the right to exercise exclusive jurisdiction over members of a force or civilian component and their dependents with respect to offenses, including offenses relating to the security of that State, punishable by its law but not by the law of the sending State.

(c) For the purposes of this paragraph and of paragraph 3 of this Article a security offense against a State shall include

(i) treason against the State;

(ii) sabotage, espionage or violation of any law relating to official secrets of that State, or secrets relating to the national defence of that State.

3. In cases where the right to exercise jurisdiction is concurrent the following rules shall apply:

(a) The military authorities of the sending State shall have the primary right to exercise jurisdiction over a member of a force or of a civilian component in relation to

(i) offenses solely against the property or security of that State, or offenses solely against the person or property of another member of the force or civilian component of that State or of a dependent;

(ii) offenses arising out of any act or omission done in the performance of official duty.

(b) In the case of any other offense the authorities of the receiving State shall have the primary right to exercise jurisdiction.

(c) If the State having the primary right decides not to exercise jurisdiction, it shall notify the authorities of the other State as soon as practicable. The authorities of the State having the primary right shall give sympathetic consideration to a request from the authorities of the other State for a waiver of its right in cases where that other State considers such waiver to be of particular importance.

In view of the fact that the act of which Short is suspected is punishable under the laws of both the sending State, the United States, and the receiving State, The Netherlands, in the present case the provisions of paragraph 2 involving cases of exclusive jurisdiction of the sending State or the receiving State are not applicable, while the provisions of the third paragraph are: both States have jurisdiction. Under paragraph 3 (a)(i), however, the United States as the sending State has "the primary right to exercise jurisdiction" over Short, because the crime of which he is suspected is exclusively directed against the person of a member of the family of a member of the armed forces, his wife. The exception mentioned in paragraph 3 (c) is not applicable, because the United States, the State which has the primary right to exercise jurisdiction, has made it clear that it intends to do so and has rejected the request by The Netherlands to refrain from invoking this primary right. Therefore, The Netherlands, on the basis of Article VII, paragraph 5 (a), which provides:

> [t]he authorities of the receiving and sending States shall assist each other in the arrest of members of a force or civilian component or their dependents in the territory of the receiving State and in handing them over to the authority which is to exercise jurisdiction in accordance with the above provisions,

is bound to extradite ("to hand over") Short to the U.S. authorities. This is not changed by Article VII, paragraph 7 (a) which forbids the sending State to execute a death penalty in the State of residence if the legislation of this State does not provide for such a penalty in a similar case. It does not follow that the sending State is prohibited from executing the death penalty outside the territory of the State of residence and (as a consequence) likewise that the obligation to extradite does not exist in case of a crime for which the legislation of the sending State imposes the death penalty. It follows that the provisions of Article VII of the NATO Status Treaty obligate The Netherlands to hand Short over to the military authorities of the U.S.

Article VII of the Extradition Treaty with the U.S.

The first paragraph of Article VII of the Extradition Treaty between the Kingdom and the U.S. provides:

> If on the deed for which extradition is requested the death penalty may be imposed under the law of the requesting State and the law of the requested State does not permit such penalty for that deed, extradition may be refused unless the requesting State offers sufficient guarantees in the opinion of the requested State that the death penalty will not be imposed or if it is imposed, will not be executed.

Should the State refuse the extradition of Short to the U.S. on the basis of this rule, now that the U.S. has not given a guarantee that the death penalty which might be imposed will not be executed? This may only be answered in the affirmative if the concept of extradition within the meaning of the Extradition Treaty includes the concept of handing over within the meaning of Article V, paragraph 5, sub (a) of the NATO Status Treaty, and only if the Extradition Treaty takes precedence over the NATO Status Treaty.

I conclude from this discussion that the Ministers concerned consider "handing over" and "extradition" to be two separate legal concepts and that as far as the constitutional guarantees are concerned, the handing over pursuant to Article VII of the NATO Status Treaty is not to be considered as a species of the genus extradition. The Extradition Act (Act of 9 March 1967, Stb. 139) also makes an express distinction between extradition and handing over and states that it is not applicable to handing over. The Extradition Treaty with the U.S. does not contain a provision concerning the relationship between the obligation to extradite under that Treaty and the obligation to hand over under Article VII of the NATO Status Treaty. The parliamentary history of the Act to approve the treaty is silent on this question. Considering the [foregoing discussion] and in view of Article III of the Extradition Treaty, which provides: "When a treaty conflicting with this Act is submitted for approval to parliament, we will also make a proposal for adjustment of this Act," in my view one may deduce from this silence that the Extradition Treaty with the U.S. does not concern handing over within the meaning of Article VII, paragraph 5, sub (a), of the NATO Status Treaty. The Extradition Treaty and the NATO Status Treaty therefore do not deal with the same subject, so that the rule *lex posterior derogat legi priori* is not applicable. It follows that the exception of Article VII, paragraph 1, of the Extradition Treaty with the U.S. cannot on the basis of Article VII of the NATO Status Treaty be invoked against the handing over of Short to the authorities of the U.S. as intended by the State.

Article I of the European Convention

Article I of the European Convention reads: "The High Contracting Parties shall secure to everyone within their jurisdiction the right and freedoms defined in Section I of this Convention."

Given the fact that the U.S. has "the primary right to exercise jurisdiction" under Article VII, paragraph 3, sub (a)(1) of the NATO Status Treaty, and has indicated that it wishes to avail itself thereof, does Short find himself "within the jurisdiction" (French text: "relevant de leur jurisdiction") of The Netherlands in the sense of Article I of the European Convention? The history of the treaty shows that the words "within their jurisdiction" have replaced the words "residing in" in the original draft. The purpose of this change was "to widen as far as possible the categories of persons who are to benefit by the guarantee contained in the Convention." The European Commission for Human Rights habitually interprets the words "within their jurisdiction" broadly.

It may be deduced from the foregoing that Short finds himself "within the jurisdiction" of The Netherlands within the meaning of Article I European Convention, simply by his being on Dutch territory, unless The Netherlands was to have no "actual authority and responsibility" at all concerning Short in view of the rules of the NATO Status Treaty. This is not the case. Article VII of the NATO Status Treaty distributes the authority to exercise jurisdiction over criminal offenses committed by members of the military force of the sending State and the State of residence. The member of the military force sent is pursuant thereto immune from jurisdiction by the State of residence for a certain number of offenses. For remaining offenses the rules of Article VII leave the criminal and general jurisdiction of the State of residence, based on the principle of territoriality, intact. The circumstance that in the present case the authority to exercise jurisdiction over Short has been attributed to the U.S. does not at all mean that The Netherlands loses its general jurisdiction founded on the principle of territoriality. The Netherlands retains for the major part "actual authority and responsibility" over Short as long as he finds himself on Dutch territory and is thus bound in the exercise thereof to respect the rights and freedoms guaranteed by the European Convention.

The Sixth Protocol to the European Convention

The Sixth Protocol to the European Convention concerning the abolition of the death penalty was approved by State Act of 5 February 1986, and entered into force for the Kingdom on 1 May 1986. Article I of this Protocol provides: "The death penalty shall be abolished. No one shall be condemned to such penalty or executed."

Does this rule entail that the State is obligated to refrain from handing over Short to the military authorities of the U.S., now that Short may be condemned to death when subjected to adjudication under U.S. legislation, and it is not excluded that the death penalty will be executed?

The European Court for Human Rights in its judgment of 7 July 1989 (1/1989/161/217), the *Soering*-judgment, has considered *inter alia* with respect to the question whether and in how far Article III of the European Convention ("No one shall be subjected to torture or to inhuman or degrading treatment or punishment") is applicable in extradition cases.

[E]xtradition may result in a violation of Article III of the European Convention, if it can be assumed on valid grounds that the requested person runs a real chance to be subjected to torture or to inhuman or humiliating treatment or punishment after extradition. The responsibility of the extraditing State rests in such a case on the circumstance that its acts have the direct result that the requested person will be subjected to said acts. In view of Article II, paragraph 1, of the European Convention, the death penalty as such is not incompatible with Article III of the European Convention.[3] Extradition on the basis of an act which is punishable by death under the legislation of the requesting State, therefore, does not in itself result in a violation of Article III of the European Convention.

The question arises whether this is also the case if the extraditing State has ratified the Sixth Protocol to the European Convention. The Court did not rule on this question in the *Soering* judgment. It is to be assumed that by ratifying the Sixth Protocol the ratifying State considers imposition and execution of the death penalty inhuman treatment which Article III of the European Convention forbids. Moreover, the exception contained in the second part of the second sentence of the first paragraph of Article II of the European Convention loses its validity for States which become party to the Protocol. In my view it follows that a State which is a party to the Sixth Protocol and proceeds with extradition for an act which is subject to the death penalty under the legislation of the requesting State, acts in conflict with Article II as well as Article III of the European Convention, if it can be assumed on valid grounds that the requested person after extradition runs a real chance of being condemned to death and the possibility that the death penalty will be executed on him is not excluded. (Remember that Article I of the Protocol forbids not only the execution of the death penalty but also the imposition thereof.) This is because the extradition has as an immediate result that the requested person is subjected to an inhuman treatment, the imposition of and the possible execution of the death penalty.

In this context is it necessary to make a distinction between extradition and handing over in the sense of Article VII of the NATO Status Treaty? I would not think so. It follows from the *Soering* judgment that the responsibility of the State rests on the fact that by its actions it exposes the person concerned to treatment forbidden by Article III of

---

3. Recall that in *Soering* it was not the death penalty *per se* but the death row phenomenon which the court held would be a violation of the European Convention's prohibition against cruel and unusual punishment.

the European Convention. The essential point is whether the conduct of the State will have as a result that the person concerned will be exposed to the forbidden treatment, irrespective of the juridical qualification of the act of transmission. In my view, it follows that The Netherlands violates Article II and III of the European Convention, combined with Article I Sixth Protocol, by handing Short over to the military authorities of the U.S., now that it can be assumed on valid grounds that Short, after being handed over, runs a real chance of being condemned to death and the possibility that the death penalty will be executed on him is not excluded.

Incompatible treaty obligations?

The foregoing leads to the conclusion that in the present case the State faces indeed two incompatible treaty obligations. Based on Article VII of the NATO Status Treaty the State is obligated to hand over Short to the military authorities of the U.S., while the European Convention and the Sixth Protocol related thereto obligate the State to refrain from handing him over. As the U.S. have refused to give a guarantee that a death penalty to which Short may be condemned will not be executed, the obligations resting on the State are incompatible. Whichever choice the State makes, performance of one of the obligations entails violation of the other.

[After a discussion on which treaty should apply, the advocate general concluded that] [t]he rule of Article VII, paragraph 5, sub (a), under which The Netherlands is obliged to hand over Short to the military authorities of the U.S. is in my view not to be considered a directly applicable rule, whereas the rules of Article II and III European Convention combined with Article I of the Sixth Protocol are undoubtedly directly applicable rules. The court is therefore permitted to judge whether the State by honoring its obligation under the NATO Status Treaty to hand Short over violates the rights which Short derives from Article II and III of the European Convention, combined with Article I Sixth Protocol and whether the State thereby commits a tort vis-à-vis Short.

Does the State commit a tort vis-à-vis Short by handing him over?

Above, … I argued that handing Short over under the given circumstances violates Article II and III of the European Convention, combined with Article I of the Sixth Protocol. Does it follow that the State therefore commits a tort against Short and that the injunction requested by Short should be granted? Or should it first be investigated whether the circumstance that the State is obliged vis-à-vis the United States to hand Short over may justify the conduct of the State, or whether the State given its interest by honoring its obligation vis-à-vis the United States is not bound to safeguard the interest of Short? [I] would think that the conclusion that the State by handing Short over violates its duty vis-à-vis Short under Article II and III of the European Convention combined with Article I Sixth Protocol leads directly to the conclusion that the State commits a tort against Short. The mere fact that for a certain action of the State the form of a treaty has been chosen or that the State has assumed such obligation by treaty, makes such conduct for the evaluation of a directly applicable treaty (in this case the European Convention) indistinguishable from conduct of the State which does not rest on a treaty obligation. It is as difficult for the State to justify violation of the European Convention by invoking its internal legislation as to justify such violation by invoking treaties it has concluded with other States. My conclusion is that the State commits a tort against Short by giving precedence to its obligation under the NATO Status Treaty above its obligation which cannot be reconciled therewith, flowing from the European Convention and the Sixth Protocol. The injunction against handing over requested by Short against the State in my opinion is lawful and well grounded.

Concluding remark

Now that the outcome of this case in my opinion must be that the State under the given circumstances shall not proceed to hand over Short to the military authorities of the U.S., there does not arise a negative conflict of jurisdiction but, in view of the serious nature of the offense of which Short is accused, a decidedly undesirable situation. The Netherlands does not have jurisdiction to judge Short. The U.S. does have jurisdiction but can judge Short only by default. I mention in this connection that the written memorials show that the Court of Appeal in Amsterdam on May 29, 1989 declared itself incompetent to deal with the criminal proceedings against Short. Meanwhile, Short has filed an appeal to the Supreme Court against this decision. However undesirable the situation may be, in my view this is no reason to judge otherwise about the legality of handing Short over as intended by the State. Perhaps the situation that will arise will induce the U.S. to offer after all a guarantee that a death penalty to which Short may be subjected will not be executed, in which case handing over would be possible after all. The conclusion is that your Court shall set aside the decisions of the Court of Appeal, shall itself dispose of the matter and shall confirm the decisions rendered in the first instance by the President of the District Court at The Hague.

Notes and Questions

1. After the *Short* decision, the United States military prosecutor elected not to seek the death penalty against Short because Short did not meet the death penalty criteria under United States military law. When that decision was conveyed to the Dutch government, Short was turned over to American officials for prosecution. See Parkerson & Lepper, "*Short v. Kingdom of the Netherlands*," 85 Am. J. Int'l L. 698, 702 (1991) (authors express concern that, even though the decision not to charge Short with a capital offense was independent of the Netherlands' opposition to turning Short over to the United States, the prosecutor's decision may be seen "as the weakening of an otherwise staunch American resolve to stand on American rights under the NATO SOFA").

2. Peacetime offenses subject to the death penalty under the United States military justice system are generally offenses in which both the United States and a European nation have concurrent jurisdiction. The NATO Status of Forces Agreement (SOFA) provides that each state may waive jurisdiction to allow the other state jurisdiction over the case. The decision to waive jurisdiction is an executive decision and cannot be challenged in the United States courts. Parkerson & Stoehr, "The U.S. Military Death Penalty in Europe: Threats from Recent European Human Rights Developments," 129 Military L. Rev. 41, 46–48 n.29 (1990). See *Wilson v. Girard*, 354 U.S. 524 (1957); *Holmes v. Laird*, 459 F.2d 1211 (D.C. Cir. 1972). Relying on a United States Senate resolution, United States military authorities seek to maximize United States jurisdiction over such cases. Under this policy, requests by the European nations, or host nations, to assume jurisdiction will be denied. As a practical matter, this policy leaves open only the possibility of host nations issuing waivers in response to United States requests to assume jurisdiction.

Until relatively recently, European nations did not oppose the imposition of the death penalty by the United States military upon United States military personnel provided the execution was not carried out on European soil. However, this attitude is changing, and waivers of jurisdiction in capital cases increasingly are viewed as politically unacceptable. With greater frequency, European host nations are asserting national interests in capital cases and are refusing to grant waivers of jurisdiction.

3. The growing conflict between the European NATO members and the United States presents a dilemma for American foreign policy. As opposition to the death penalty increasingly becomes to Europeans an aspect of their fundamental sovereign interests, the United States will be forced to make some policy choices. Will the United States continue to regard its current policy of strict application to capital cases of the exercise of jurisdiction provisions of the NATO SOFA as something that is essential to the activities of United States military forces in Europe—and particularly to overall U.S. administration of military justice? Or is this an area where some flexibility in United States policy may be required in view of the need to respect a matter of particular host nation sensitivity in the interests of maintaining friendly cooperation within the alliance?

If the United States adopts a more "flexible approach" to capital crimes committed on European soil, what are the domestic ramifications of that policy? Should capital offenses committed on United States soil be treated differently from those committed on foreign soil? How should this potential unequal treatment affect morale and discipline? Should United States military justice be subject to the changing views of the world community? Should United States policy fluctuate depending on the host nation's policy on the death penalty? And how would adaptation to the growing world dissatisfaction with the death penalty affect the constitutionality of the United States military death penalty scheme?

4. On November 2, 1993, the Judicial Committee of the Privy Council—the highest court of appeals for member countries of the British Commonwealth—ruled that it is inhuman punishment to hold a prisoner on death row for several years after he has been sentenced to death, even if the delay is caused by the prisoner himself pursuing all available lines of appeal. According to the Privy Council, whose members are drawn from the House of Lords, a country which retains the death penalty must ensure that execution follows the sentence reasonably promptly, while giving adequate time for appeal and possible reprieve. The Council ruled that cases which take more than five years to proceed to execution will be commuted to life imprisonment in the future. The Guardian, Nov. 3, 1993, at p. 4.

The landmark decision involved the case of two Jamaican prisoners, Earl Pratt and Ivan Morgan. Pratt and Morgan were sentenced to death on January 15, 1979 for a murder committed on October 6, 1977. Each man received three last minute stays of execution. The Privy Council agreed that to hang them after more than fourteen years of delay would violate §17(1) of the Jamaica Constitution. That section provides: "No person shall be subjected to ... inhuman or degrading punishment." The Council commuted both death sentences to life imprisonment. The Guardian, Nov. 11, 1993, at p. 10. In addition, 105 Jamaican death row inmates who had spent more than five years waiting to be executed received reprieves. Moreover, the ruling resulted in reprieves to more than 100 death row inmates in Trinidad, Mauritius and Belize. Sixteen other Commonwealth countries then considered the Privy Council to be their final court of appeal and were also directly affected by the decision. Commentators speculated that, under the principle of "persuasive authority," courts in India, Malawi, Malaysia, Nigeria and South Africa would likely follow the decision. The Guardian, Nov. 3, 1993, at page 4. The Privy Council decision is reported as *Pratt & Morgan v. Attorney General for Jamaica*, 3 SLR 995, 2 AC 1, 4 All ER 769 (Privy Council 1993) (en banc).

In 2001, 11 Caribbean countries that want to use the death penalty to fight rising crime rates signed an agreement to replace Britain's Privy Council with a regional supreme court. Caribbean leaders have accused the Privy Council—the region's highest court—of hindering local efforts to enforce the death penalty. The island governments expect that executions will curb violent crime, much of it tied to drug-trafficking.

Signatories to the agreement include Barbados, Guyana, Antigua and Barbuda, Dominica, Grenada, Jamaica, Trinidad and Tobago, St. Lucia, St. Kitts and Nevis. (Suriname also signed on to use the new Caribbean Court of Justice because it is a member of the Caribbean Community trade bloc, though, as a former Dutch colony, it never used the Privy Council.)

Members of the community that did not sign the agreement included the Bahamas, Grenadines, Haiti, Montserrat and St. Vincent. It was expected that if the agreement is ratified, judges could be selected to sit on the court, which will be based in Trinidad, before early 2003. Human rights groups fear that the new Caribbean Court of Justice will be a "hanging court."

It should surprise no one that creative defense lawyers have argued that the "death row phenomenon" and the rationale of the *Pratt & Morgan* decision raise serious Eighth Amendment issues regarding the execution of inmates who have languished in American prisons for years while awaiting execution. Although the Supreme Court has not directly addressed the issue, lower federal courts have been reluctant to grant relief. In *Lackey v. Texas*, 514 U.S. 1045 (1995), the Court denied a petition for certiorari and ducked an opportunity to tackle the issue in a case involving a Texas prisoner who had spent 17 years on death row. In a separate memorandum opinion, Justice Stevens argued that Lackey's case should be reviewed. Justice Stevens suggested that in cases of long delays that were not attributable to the prisoner's abuse of the judicial system by repetitive and frivolous filings, the purpose of retribution may already have been satisfied by the severe punishment inflicted. According to Justice Stevens, "the additional deterrent effect from an actual execution now, on the one hand, as compared to 17 years on death row followed by the prisoner's continued incarceration for life, on the other hand, seems minimal." Citing *Pratt v. Attorney General of Jamaica*, Justice Stevens noted that "the highest courts in other countries have found arguments such as [Lackey's] to be persuasive." Lackey's claim, although "novel," was "not without foundation."

The Court also denied certiorari in *Knight v. Florida*, 528 U.S. 990 (1999). Concurring in the denial, Justice Thomas stated that he was "unaware of any support in the American constitutional tradition" for the proposition that a defendant invoking judicial procedures to overturn a death sentence could complain when the execution was delayed. Lack of support in American law, according to Justice Thomas, forced the petitioners to "rely" on decisions of the European Court of Human Rights, the Supreme Court of Zimbabwe, the Supreme Court of India, and the Privy Council. "It is incongruous," Justice Thomas wrote, "to arm capital defendants with an arsenal of 'constitutional' claims which may delay their executions, and simultaneously to complain when executions are inevitably delayed."

Justice Breyer dissented from the denial of certiorari. He emphasized that the long delays in these cases (about 20 years) resulted in significant part from constitutionally defective death penalty procedures. In those circumstances, "the claim that time has rendered the execution inhumane is a particularly strong one." Justice Breyer defended petitioners' reliance on the decisions of courts outside the United States:

> "Obviously this foreign authority does not bind us. After all, we are interpreting a 'Constitution for the United States of America.' [T]his Court has long considered as relevant and informative the way in which foreign courts have

applied standards, roughly comparable to our own constitutional standards in roughly comparable circumstances. In doing so, the Court has found particularly instructive opinions of former Commonwealth nations insofar as those opinions reflect a legal tradition that also underlies our own Eighth Amendment.... Willingness to consider foreign judicial views in comparable cases is not surprising in a Nation that from its birth has given a 'decent respect to the opinions of mankind.' "

For an argument that, under the Supreme Court's objective criteria, the Eighth Amendment is violated by an "inordinate delay between the imposition of a sentence and the actual execution of a capital defendant," see Aarons, "Can Inordinate Delay Between a Death Sentence and Execution Constitute Cruel and Unusual Punishment?," 29 Seton Hall L. Rev. 147, 211 (1998).

5. Amnesty International, an organization staunchly opposed to the use of the death penalty worldwide, has been harshly critical of the United States' position on capital punishment. According to Amnesty International, "there is a serious conflict between retention of the death penalty and the United States' formal pledges and commitments to international human rights standards." This position is more fully described below.

> The resumption and increase in executions under U.S. state laws, as well as proposals to extend the use of the death penalty under U.S. federal law, are clearly contrary to the principles contained in international treaties and standards. In a general comment on Article 6 of the International Covenant on Civil and Political Rights (ICCPR), the United Nations Human Rights Committee said in 1982 that "... all measures of abolition should be considered as progress in the enjoyment of the right to life." This makes clear that the intent of the article was to encourage abolition, not extension of the death penalty.

> The U.S. government ratified the ICCPR in June 1992. However, it entered a large number of reservations to non-derogable articles including Article 6 on the right to life. The protections enshrined in this article are so fundamental to the enjoyment of all the other rights contained in the ICCPR that Amnesty International strongly believes the reservations should be considered null and void. The attitude of the U.S. Government in its ratification of international human rights treaties has become that of ratifying only after making reservations that seek to ensure that no change in existing U.S. practice is required. If all nations were to act in this spirit the international framework of human rights protection would become meaningless.

> A number of individual executions carried out in the U.S.A. in recent years have violated minimum international standards. Many cases have violated the specific standards applying to the death penalty, including the United Nations ECOSOC guidelines.[2] The U.S. government has described these standards as

---

2. Safeguards Guaranteeing Protection of the Rights of Those Facing the Death Penalty, adopted by the United Nations Economic and Social Council (ECOSOC) in 1984 (Resolution 1984/50). These, among other things, prohibit the execution of offenders aged under 18 at the time of the crime. A further resolution (1989/64), adopted in May 1989 by ECOSOC, recommends "eliminating the death penalty for persons suffering from mental retardation or extremely limited mental competence."

"nonbinding;" however, they are an important measure of a country's compliance with minimum international standards. In some cases the U.S. state laws directly conflict with minimum international standards, for example in the cases of under-18-year-old offenders sentenced to death and the execution of prisoners who are severely mentally impaired.

"Open Letter to the President on the Death Penalty," 3 (Amnesty International Jan. 1994) AI Index: AMR 51/01/94.

6. The following opinion from the Canadian Supreme Court provides an extensive analysis of that country's refusal to extradite capital defendants to the United States without assurances that the death penalty will not be imposed.

United States v. Burns

2001 SCC 7. File No.: 26129

APPEAL from a judgment of the British Columbia Court of Appeal (1997), 94 B.C.A.C. 59, 152 W.A.C. 59, 116 C.C.C. (3d) 524, 8 C.R. (5th) 393, 45 C.R.R. (2d) 30, [1997] B.C.J. No. 1558 (QL), finding that the unconditional extradition order was unconstitutional. Appeal dismissed.

THE COURT—

Legal systems have to live with the possibility of error. The unique feature of capital punishment is that it puts beyond recall the possibility of correction. In recent years, aided by the advances in the forensic sciences, including DNA testing, the courts and governments in this country and elsewhere have come to acknowledge a number of instances of wrongful convictions for murder despite all of the careful safeguards put in place for the protection of the innocent. The instances in Canada are few, but if capital punishment had been carried out, the result could have been the killing by the government of innocent individuals. The names of Marshall, Milgaard, Morin, Sophonow and Parsons signal prudence and caution in a murder case. Other countries have also experienced revelations of wrongful convictions, including states of the United States where the death penalty is still imposed and carried into execution.

The possibility of a miscarriage of justice is but one of many factors in the balancing process which governs the decision by the Minister of Justice to extradite two Canadian citizens, Glen Sebastian Burns and Atif Ahmad Rafay, to the United States. A competing principle of fundamental justice is that Canadians who are accused of crimes in the United States can ordinarily expect to be dealt with under the law which the citizens of that jurisdiction have collectively determined to apply to offences committed within their territory, including the set punishment.

Awareness of the potential for miscarriages of justice, together with broader public concerns about the taking of life by the state, as well as doubts about the effectiveness of the death penalty as a deterrent to murder in comparison with life in prison without parole for 25 years, led Canada to abolish the death penalty for all but a handful of military offences in 1976, and subsequently to abolish the death penalty for all offences in 1998.

The abolitionist view is shared by some, but not a majority, of the United States. Michigan, Rhode Island and Wisconsin in fact abolished the death penalty for murder in the 1840s and 1850s, years before the first European state, Portugal, did so, and over a century before Canada did. At present, 12 states are abolitionist while 38 states retain the death penalty. The State of Washington, in which the respondents are wanted for trial on charges of aggravated first degree murder, is a retentionist state.

The extradition of the respondents is sought pursuant to the *Extradition Treaty between Canada and the United States of America*, Can. T.S. 1976 No. 3 (the "treaty" or the "extradition treaty") which permits the requested state (in this case Canada) to refuse extradition of fugitives unless provided with assurances that if extradited and convicted they will not suffer the death penalty. The Minister declined to seek such assurances because of his policy that assurances should only be sought in exceptional circumstances, which he decided did not exist in this case.

The respondents contend that Canada's principled abolition of the death penalty at home, and its spirited advocacy of abolition internationally, confirm Canadian acceptance of abolition as a fundamental principle of our criminal justice system. This principle, they say, combined with the respondents' Canadian citizenship and the fact that they were 18 years old at the time of the alleged offences, constitutionally prohibits the Minister from extraditing them to a foreign jurisdiction without assurances that they will not face a penalty which Canada, as a society, does not permit within its own borders.

The Minister contends, on the other hand, that persons who are found to commit crimes in foreign countries forfeit the benefit of Canada's abolitionist policy. The Constitution does not require Canada, on this view, to project its internal values onto the world stage, and to insist as a condition of extradition that a requesting state view capital punishment in the same light as our domestic legal system does.

We agree that the *Canadian Charter of Rights and Freedoms* does not lay down a constitutional prohibition in all cases against extradition unless assurances are given that the death penalty will not be imposed. The Minister is required (as he did here) to balance on a case-by-case basis those factors that favour extradition with assurances against competing factors that favour extradition without assurances. We hold, however, for the reasons which follow, that such assurances are constitutionally required in all but exceptional cases. We further hold that this case does not present the exceptional circumstances that must be shown before the Minister could constitutionally extradite without assurances. By insisting on assurances, Canada would not be acting in disregard of international extradition obligations undertaken by the Canadian government, but rather exercising a treaty right explicitly agreed to by the United States. We thus agree with the result, though not the reasons, reached by a majority of the judges of the British Columbia Court of Appeal in this case. The Minister's appeal must therefore be dismissed.

I. Facts

The crimes alleged against the respondents were, as the Minister contends, "brutal and shocking coldblooded murder[s]". The father, mother and sister of the respondent Rafay were found bludgeoned to death in their home in Bellevue, Washington, in July 1994. Both Burns and Rafay, who had been friends at high school in British Columbia, admit that they were at the Rafay home on the night of the murders. They claim to have gone out on the evening of July 12, 1994 and when they returned, they say, they found the bodies of the three murdered Rafay family members. The house, they say, appeared to have been burgled.

However, if the confessions allegedly made by the respondents to undercover RCMP officers are to be believed, the three members of the Rafay family were bludgeoned to death by the respondent Burns while the respondent Rafay watched. Burns allegedly told an undercover RCMP officer that he had killed the three victims with a baseball bat while wearing only underwear so as not to get blood on his clothes. Rafay's father, Tariq Rafay, and mother, Sultana Rafay, were beaten to death in their bedroom. The force used was so violent that blood was spattered on all four walls and the ceiling of the room. The respondent Rafay's sister, Basma Rafay, was beaten about the head and left for dead in the lower level of the house. She later died in hospital. Burns allegedly explained that following the attacks, he had a shower at the Rafay home to clean off the victims' blood. The discovery of hairs with Caucasian characteristics in the shower near the master bedroom, where the two parents were killed, supports this story. There is also evidence of dilute blood covering large sections of the shower stall. The respondents allegedly told the police that they drove around the municipality disposing of various items used in the killings as well as some of the parents' electronic devices, apparently to feign a burglary. The respondent Rafay is also alleged to have told the officer the killings were "a necessary sacrifice in order that he could get what he wanted in life". With the death of all other members of his family, Rafay stood to inherit his parents' assets and the proceeds of their life insurance. Burns, it is alleged, participated in exchange for a share in the proceeds under an agreement with Rafay. He was, the prosecution alleges, a contract killer.

The Bellevue police suspected both of the respondents but did not have enough evidence to charge them. When the respondents returned to Canada, the Bellevue police sought the cooperation of the RCMP in their investigation of the murders. The RCMP initiated an elaborate and in the end, they say, productive undercover operation. An RCMP officer posed as a crime boss and subsequently testified that, after gaining the confidence of the respondents, he repeatedly challenged them to put to rest his professed scepticism about their stomach for serious violence. The respondents are alleged to have tried to reassure him by bragging about their respective roles in the Bellevue murders.

The respondents assert their innocence. They claim that in making their alleged confessions to the police they were play-acting as much as the undercover policeman to whom they confessed. At this stage of the criminal process in Washington, they are entitled to the presumption of innocence. What to make of it all will be up to a jury in the State of Washington.

The respondents were arrested in British Columbia and a committal order was issued for their extradition pending the decision of the Minister of Justice on surrender. The then Minister, Allan Rock, signed an unconditional Order for Surrender to have both of the respondents extradited to the State of Washington to stand trial without assurances in respect of the death penalty. If found guilty, the respondents will face either life in prison without the possibility of parole or the death penalty. Washington State provides for execution by lethal injection unless the condemned individual elects execution by hanging (Revised Code of Washington §§10.95.180(1)).

II. The Minister's Decision

An extradition matter does not reach the Minister until an extradition judge has determined that the offence falls within the scope of the treaty and there is a *prima facie* case that the fugitive has committed the crime with which he or she has been charged in the foreign jurisdiction (*Argentina v. Mellino*, [1987] 1 S.C.R. 536, at p. 553). At that stage, the Minister, after hearing representations, makes a decision under §25(1) of the *Extradition Act*, R.S.C. 1985, c. E-23, whether or not to surrender the fugitive, and if so on what terms.

Here, the Minister proceeded on the assumption that the death penalty would be sought by the prosecutors in the State of Washington.

The respondents submitted to the Minister that §6(1) of the *Charter* grants them the right to stay in Canada and that as a result, he was required to consider whether the respondents could be prosecuted in Canada rather than extradited, as permitted by Article 17 *bis* of the extradition treaty and as contemplated as a possible option by this Court in *United States of America v. Cotroni* [1989] 1 S.C.R. 1469. Although there was some evidence that the murders were planned in Canada, no killings occurred here. Canadian prosecutors concluded that Canada could only prosecute the respondents for conspiracy to commit murder. The decision to lay charges in Canada was within the exclusive jurisdiction of the Attorney General of British Columbia, who had decided, prior to this matter going to the federal Minister, that there was insufficient evidence to support a conspiracy charge.

The respondents also submitted to the Minister that he was required by §§6(1), 7 and 12 of the *Charter* to seek assurances that the death penalty would not be imposed. They argued that their unconditional extradition to face the death penalty would "shock the Canadian conscience" because of their age (18 years at the time of the offence) and their nationality (Canadian). The respondents sought to distinguish *Kindler v. Canada (Minister of Justice)*, [1991] 2 S.C.R. 779, and *Reference Re Ng Extradition (Can.)*, [1991] 2 S.C.R. 858, primarily on the basis that, unlike the fugitives in those cases, the respondents have the benefit of §6(1) of the *Charter* by virtue of being Canadian citizens. They were not foreigners seeking to use Canada as a "safe haven". Canada instead is their country of origin and the Canadian government does not, according to the respondents, have the right to expel them when they face the risk of never returning. This, they maintained, would amount to exile and banishment contrary to §6(1) of the *Charter: Canada v. Schmidt*, [1987] 1 S.C.R. 500, and *Cotroni, supra.*

The Minister stated that assurances should be sought only in circumstances where the particular facts of the case warrant a special exercise of discretion and that assurances should not be sought routinely pursuant to Article 6 of the treaty in every case in which the death penalty is applicable. The Minister found that the factors outlined in *Kindler* did not mandate that assurances be sought here. The age of the respondents, although "youthful", qualified them as adults in the Canadian criminal system. The Minister thought Canadian citizenship was not itself a "special circumstance" to allow the respondents to escape from the full weight of the sentencing process in the United States where the murders were committed.

The Minister also rejected the respondents' claim that extradition without assurances would constitute exile and banishment. Extradition to face the death penalty does not amount to banishment since the underlying purpose of extradition is simply to face criminal prosecution. The Minister felt that Canada should not permit itself to become a safe haven for persons seeking to escape justice, even Canadians. Furthermore, there would be no exile because the respondents, once the criminal matters had been dealt with fully, would not be prevented by the Canadian government from returning to this country. In the end, Canadian nationality was simply one of several factors that the Minister considered, but it was not determinative. As stated, the Minister signed the extradition order without seeking or obtaining assurances.

III. British Columbia Court of Appeal

The British Columbia Court of Appeal set aside the Minister's decision and directed the Minister to seek the assurances described in Article 6 of the extradition treaty as a condition of surrender....

IV. Relevant Constitutional and Statutory Provisions

Canadian Charter of Rights and Freedoms

1. The *Canadian Charter of Rights and Freedoms* guarantees the rights and freedoms set out in it subject only to such reasonable limits prescribed by law as can be demonstrably justified in a free and democratic society.

6. (1) Every citizen of Canada has the right to enter, remain in and leave Canada.

7. Everyone has the right to life, liberty and security of the person and the right not to be deprived thereof except in accordance with the principles of fundamental justice.

12. Everyone has the right not to be subjected to any cruel and unusual treatment or punishment.

(1) This Charter applies

(*a*) to the Parliament and government of Canada in respect of all matters within the authority of Parliament including all matters relating to the Yukon Territory and Northwest Territories; and

(*b*) to the legislature and government of each province in respect of all matters within the authority of the legislature of each province.

Constitution Act, 1982

(1) The Constitution of Canada is the supreme law of Canada, and any law that is inconsistent with the provisions of the Constitution is, to the extent of the inconsistency, of no force or effect.

Extradition Act, R.S.C. 1985, c. E-23 (as am. by S.C. 1992, c. 13)

(1) Subject to this Part, the Minister of Justice, on the requisition of a foreign state, may, within a period of ninety days after the date of a fugitive's committal for surrender, under the hand and seal of the Minister, order the fugitive to be surrendered to the person or persons who are, in the Minister's opinion, duly authorized to receive the fugitive in the name and on behalf of the foreign state, and the fugitive shall be so surrendered accordingly.

V. Relevant Provisions from International Documents

Extradition Treaty between Canada and the Government of the United States of America (amended by an Exchange of Notes), Can. T.S. 1976 No. 3, in force March 22, 1976
Article 6

When the offense for which extradition is requested is punishable by death under the laws of the requesting State and the laws of the requested State do not permit such punishment for that offense, extradition may be refused unless the requesting State provides such assurances as the requested State considers sufficient that the death penalty shall not be imposed, or, if imposed, shall not be executed.

Protocol amending the Treaty on Extradition between the Government of Canada and the Government of the United States of America, Can. T.S. 1991 No. 37 (in force November 26, 1991)
Article VII

Article 17 bis If both contracting Parties have jurisdiction to prosecute the person for the offense for which extradition is sought, the executive authority of the requested State, after consulting with the executive authority of the requesting State, shall decide whether to extradite the person or to submit the case to its competent authorities for the purpose of prosecution. In making its decision, the requested State shall consider all relevant factors, including but not limited to:

(i) the place where the act was committed or intended to be committed or the injury occurred or was intended to occur;

(ii) the respective interests of the Contracting Parties;

(iii) the nationality of the victim or the intended victim; and

(iv) the availability and location of the evidence.

VI. Revised Code of Washington

2710.95.030. Sentences for aggravated first degree murder

(1) Except as provided in subsection (2) of this section, any person convicted of the crime of aggravated first degree murder shall be sentenced to life imprisonment without possibility of release or parole. A person sentenced to life imprisonment under this section shall not have that sentence suspended, deferred, or commuted by any judicial officer and the indeterminate sentence review board or its successor may not parole such prisoner nor reduce the period of confinement in any manner whatsoever including but not limited to any sort of good-time calculation. The department of social and health services or its successor or any executive official may not permit such prisoner to participate in any sort of release or furlough program.

(2) If, pursuant to a special sentencing proceeding held under RCW 10.95.050, the trier of fact finds that there are not sufficient mitigating circumstances to merit leniency, the sentence shall be death.

10.95.040. Special sentencing proceeding — Notice — Filing — Service

(1) If a person is charged with aggravated first degree murder as defined by RCW 10.95.020, the prosecuting attorney shall file written notice of a special sentencing proceeding to determine whether or not the death penalty should be imposed when there is reason to believe that there are not sufficient mitigating circumstances to merit leniency.

(2) The notice of special sentencing proceeding shall be filed and served on the defendant or the defendant's attorney within thirty days after the defendant's arraignment upon the charge of aggravated first degree murder unless the court, for good cause shown, extends or reopens the period for filing and service of the notice. Except with the consent of the prosecuting attorney, during the period in which the prosecuting attorney may file the notice of special sentencing proceeding, the defendant may not tender a plea of guilty to the charge of aggravated first degree murder nor may the court accept a plea of guilty to the charge of aggravated first degree murder or any lesser included offense.

(3) If a notice of special sentencing proceeding is not filed and served as provided in this section, the prosecuting attorney may not request the death penalty.

10.95.180. Death Penalty — How executed

(1) The punishment of death shall be supervised by the superintendent of the penitentiary and shall be inflicted by intravenous injection of a substance or substances in a

lethal quantity sufficient to cause death and until the defendant is dead, or, at the election of the defendant, by hanging by the neck until the defendant is dead. In any case, death shall be pronounced by a licensed physician.

VII. Analysis

The evidence amply justifies the extradition of the respondents to Washington State to stand trial on charges of aggravated first degree murder. Under the law of that state, a conviction would carry a minimum sentence of imprisonment for life without the possibility of release or parole. If the prosecutors were to seek the death penalty, they would have the burden of persuading the jury that "there are not sufficient mitigating circumstances" in favour of the respondents. If the jury is so satisfied, the death penalty would be administered by lethal injection or (at the option of the convicted individual), by hanging. If the jury is not so satisfied, the convicted murderer is locked up for life without any possibility of release or parole. An individual convicted of aggravated first degree murder in Washington State thus will either die in prison by execution or will die in prison eventually by other causes. Those are the possibilities. Apart from executive clemency, the State of Washington does not hold out the possibility (or even the "faint hope") of eventual freedom.

The respondents' position is that the death penalty is so horrific, the chances of error are so high, the death row phenomenon is so repugnant, and the impossibility of correction is so draconian, that it is simply unacceptable that Canada should participate, however indirectly, in its imposition. While the government of Canada would not itself administer the lethal injection or erect the gallows, no executions can or will occur without the act of extradition by the Canadian government. The Minister's decision is a prior and essential step in a process that may lead to death by execution.

The root questions here are whether the Constitution supports the Minister's position that assurances need only be sought in exceptional cases, or whether the Constitution supports the respondents' position that assurances must *always* be sought barring exceptional circumstances, and if so, whether such exceptional circumstances are present in this case.

In order to get to the heart of the argument on this appeal, it will be useful to deal initially with the Minister's powers and responsibilities under the *Extradition Act*, and then move to the *Charter* issue (§6 mobility rights) on which the respondents succeeded in the British Columbia Court of Appeal. We reject the §6 argument, for reasons to be discussed. We will then consider the other grounds on which the respondents constructed their constitutional argument against extradition without assurances, namely §12 ("cruel and unusual treatment or punishment") and §7 ("life, liberty and security of the person"). In the end, we conclude that the respondents are entitled to succeed on the sole ground that their extradition to face the death penalty would, in the present circumstances, violate their rights guaranteed by §7 of the *Charter*.

The Extradition Act Confers a Broad Statutory Discretion on the Minister.

The appeal reaches this Court by way of a judicial review of the exercise by the Minister of his discretion under §25(1) of the *Extradition Act* which we reproduce for ease of reference:

25. (1) Subject to this Part, the Minister of Justice, on the requisition of a foreign state, may, within a period of ninety days after the date of a fugitive's com-

mittal for surrender, under the hand and seal of the Minister, order the fugitive to be surrendered to the person or persons who are, in the Minister's opinion, duly authorized to receive the fugitive in the name and on behalf of the foreign state, and the fugitive shall be so surrendered accordingly.

Section 25 creates a broad discretion which the Minister must exercise in accordance with the dictates of the *Charter*: *Kindler*, *supra*, at p. 846; *Schmidt*, *supra*, at pp. 520–21.

We affirm that it is generally for the Minister, not the Court, to assess the weight of competing considerations in extradition policy, but the availability of the death penalty, like death itself, opens up a different dimension. The difficulties and occasional miscarriages of the criminal law are located in an area of human experience that falls squarely within "the inherent domain of the judiciary as guardian of the justice system": *Re B.C. Motor Vehicle Act*, *supra*, at p. 503. It is from this perspective, recognizing the unique finality and irreversibility of the death penalty, that the constitutionality of the Minister's decision falls to be decided.

Section 6(1) ("Mobility Rights") of the Charter Does Not Invalidate an Extradition Without Assurances.

The present Minister contends that, from a policy as well as a legal perspective, the nationality of the fugitive ought to remain an irrelevant consideration. Otherwise, she argues, it could mean that if Burns were a Canadian citizen and Rafay were not, only the latter would be extradited to face the death penalty, despite the allegation that it was Burns who did the actual killing.

We affirm that extradition is a *prima facie* infringement of the §6(1) right of every Canadian citizen to "remain in" Canada: *Cotroni*, *supra*, at pp. 1480–81. The respondents will not, on this occasion, leave their homeland willingly. Their forcible removal must be justified under §1 of the *Charter*.

[LaForest, J., writing for the five-member majority in *Catroni*, found that a *prima facie* violation of §6 of the *Charter* could be saved under §1]. "As against this somewhat peripheral *Charter* infringement must be weighed the importance of the objectives sought by extradition—the investigation, prosecution, repression and punishment of both national and transnational crimes for the protection of the public. These objectives, we saw, are of pressing and substantial concern. They are, in fact, essential to the maintenance of a free and democratic society. In my view, they warrant the limited interference with the right guaranteed by §6(1) to remain in Canada. That right, it seems to me, is infringed as little as possible, or at the very least as little as reasonably possible."

[I]n *Kindler*, La Forest J. expressed the concern that if Canada did not have the "right and duty" to extradite or expel undesirable aliens, "Canada could become a haven for criminals and others whom we legitimately do not wish to have among us" (p. 834). While expressed in connection with aliens, the concern could also apply to citizens, even though citizens, unlike aliens, enjoy the added protection of §6. We accept that when the respondents are in British Columbia they are "at home". They are also using "home" as a safe haven. A murderer who flees the scene of a crime across an international boundary is seeking a "safe haven" irrespective of whether he or she holds citizenship in the state from which flight commenced, or in the destination state, or in neither. In all cases, the international boundary is to some extent an obstacle to law enforcement. Equally, to the extent the "safe haven" argument seeks to make Canada a safer place by returning to face justice in a foreign country fugitives who are considered dangerous, citizenship is irrelevant because the objective is advanced by extraditing Canadian fugitives as much as it is by extraditing persons of other nationalities.

The respondents contend that to satisfy the *Charter* requirement that their §6 mobility rights be impaired "as minimally as possible" the Minister is obliged to seek assurances. Extradition without assurances, they say, is not minimal impairment. Such assurances, however, would not uphold a "right to remain". Extradition with assurances would result in the forcible removal of the respondents from Canada as much as extradition without assurances.

The respondents, unless acquitted, will be subject to life in prison without possibility of release or parole. The Revised Code of Washington §§10.95.030 could scarcely be more emphatic:

> (1) Except as provided in subsection (2) of this section [the death penalty], any person convicted of the crime of aggravated first degree murder *shall be sentenced to life imprisonment without possibility of release or parole.* A person sentenced to life imprisonment under this section shall not have that sentence suspended, deferred, or commuted by any judicial officer and the indeterminate sentence review board or its successor may not parole such prisoner nor reduce the period of confinement in any manner whatsoever including but not limited to any sort of good-time calculation. The department of social and health services or its successor or any executive official may not permit such prisoner to participate in any sort of release or furlough program. [Emphasis added.]

The evidence is that the practice in Washington State conforms to the statutory provision. Thus, the relevant law contemplates that whether assurances are obtained or not, the fugitive, if convicted, will equally be unable to return to or "enter" Canada. In neither case would the bar to return be imposed by the Government of Canada.

Donald J.A. considered that prisoner exchange programs or possible legislative change in Washington State do at least create "a faint hope" of return because, as he says, "where there is life there is hope" (at para. 27). He also refers to the possibility of delayed executive clemency. The possible eventuality of legislative change or other exceptional relief in a foreign jurisdiction from a punishment that may never be imposed are events that are also remote from the making of an extradition order. In our view, with respect, efforts to stretch mobility rights to cover the death penalty controversy are misplaced. The real issue here is the death penalty. The death penalty is overwhelmingly a justice issue and only marginally a mobility rights issue. The death penalty issue should be confronted directly and it should be confronted under §7 of the *Charter*.

Section 12 ("Cruel and Unusual Treatment or Punishment") is not Directly Engaged in this Appeal Except as a Value to be Considered in the Section 7 Balance.

Section 12 of the *Charter* guarantees the respondents "the right not to be subjected to any cruel and unusual treatment or punishment". Concerns about the death penalty raise the question of whether its imposition would offend this provision. A threshold question, however, is whether in the circumstances of this case §12 can even apply, since it would be the State of Washington and not the government of Canada that would impose and carry out the death sentence.

The *Charter* only guarantees certain rights and freedoms from infringement by "the Parliament and government of Canada" (§32(1)(*a*)) and "the legislature and government of each province" (§32(1)(*b*)).

Nevertheless, counsel for the respondents suggest that Canada cannot avoid shouldering responsibility for the imposition of the death penalty just because it would be a foreign government, if anyone, that puts the respondents to death. The French text of §12 guarantees to the respondents *"la protection contre tous traitements ou peines cruels et inusitées".* The guarantee of "protection", it could be argued, imposes an affirmative obligation on the Canadian state to protect against infliction of the death penalty whether by Canada or by any other government.

There is some support for this view in the decision of the European Court of Human Rights in *Soering* (Eur. Court H.R., *Soering* case, judgment of 7 July 1989, Series A No. 161, at para. 91):

> In sum, the decision by a Contracting State to extradite a fugitive may give rise to an issue under Article 3 [of the *European Convention for the Protection of Human Rights and Fundamental Freedoms*, which is equivalent to section 12 of our *Charter*], and hence engage the responsibility of that State under the Convention, where substantial grounds have been shown for believing that the person concerned, if extradited, faces a real risk of being subjected to torture or to inhuman or degrading treatment or punishment in the requesting country.

The "responsibility of th[e] State" is certainly engaged under the *Charter* by a ministerial decision to extradite without assurances. While the Canadian government would not itself inflict capital punishment, its decision to extradite without assurances would be a necessary link in the chain of causation to that *potential* result. The question is whether the linkage is strong enough and direct enough to invoke §12 in an extradition proceeding, especially where, as here, there are many potential outcomes other than capital punishment.

The view previously taken by this Court is that the proper place for the "state responsibility" debate is under §7. We affirm the correctness of that approach.

This issue was extensively canvassed in *Kindler* and *Ng*. The Court concluded that extradition by the Canadian government did not violate the guarantee against cruel and unusual punishment because the only action by the Canadian government was to hand the fugitives over to law enforcement authorities in the United States, not to impose the death penalty. La Forest J., concurring, stated in *Kindler, supra*, at p. 831:

> "The Minister's actions do not constitute cruel and unusual punishment. The execution, if it ultimately takes place, will be in the United States under American law against an American citizen in respect of an offence that took place in the United States. It does not result from any initiative taken by the Canadian Government. Canada's connection with the matter results from the fact that the fugitive came here of his own free will, and the question to be determined is whether the action of the Canadian Government in returning him to his own country infringes his liberty and security in an impermissible way."

And further, McLachlin J. stated at pp. 845–46:

> "[T]his Court has emphasized that we must avoid extraterritorial application of the guarantees in our *Charter* under the guise of ruling extradition procedures unconstitutional. The punishment, if any, to which the fugitive is ultimately subject will be punishment imposed, not by the Government of Canada, but by the foreign state. *To put it another way, the effect of any Cana-*

dian law or government act is too remote from the possible imposition of the penalty complained of to attract the attention of §12. To apply §12 directly to the act of surrender to a foreign country where a particular penalty may be imposed, is to overshoot the purpose of the guarantee and to cast the net of the Charter broadly in extraterritorial waters." [Emphasis added.]

In our view, the degree of causal remoteness between the extradition order to face trial and the *potential* imposition of capital punishment as one of many possible outcomes to this prosecution make this a case more appropriately reviewed under §7 than under §12. It must be kept in mind that the values underlying various sections of the Charter, including §12, form part of the balancing process engaged in under §7. In *Kindler, supra,* both McLachlin J. and La Forest J. specifically recognized that §12 informs the interpretation of §7: *Kindler, supra,* at pp. 831 and 847; *Schmidt, supra,* at p. 522; *Re B.C. Motor Vehicle Act, supra*; R. v. Hebert, [1990] 2 S.C.R. 151.

The Outcome of this Appeal is Governed by Section 7 of the Charter ("Fundamental Justice").

58 Section 7 of the Charter *provides that:*

> "Everyone has the right to life, liberty and security of the person and the right not to be deprived thereof except in accordance with the principles of fundamental justice."

It is evident that the respondents are deprived of their liberty and security of the person by the extradition order: *Kindler, supra,* at p. 831. Their lives are potentially at risk. The issue is whether the threatened deprivation is in accordance with the principles of fundamental justice.

This Court has recognized from the outset that the punishment or treatment reasonably anticipated in the requesting country is clearly relevant. Section 7 is concerned not only with the act of extraditing, but also the *potential* consequences of the act of extradition. This principle was recognized in the extradition context by La Forest J. in *Schmidt, supra,* at p. 522:

> "I have no doubt either that in some circumstances the manner in which the foreign state will deal with the fugitive on surrender, whether that course of conduct is justifiable or not under the law of that country, may be such that it would violate the principles of fundamental justice to surrender an accused under those circumstances. To make the point, I need only refer to a case that arose before the European Commission on Human Rights, *Altun v. Germany* (1983), 5 E.H.R.R. 611, where it was established that prosecution in the requesting country might involve the infliction of torture. *Situations falling far short of this may well arise where the nature of the criminal procedures or penalties in a foreign country sufficiently shocks the conscience as to make a decision to surrender a fugitive for trial there one that breaches the principles of fundamental justice enshrined in §7."*

[Emphasis added.]

In their submissions on whether extradition without assurances is contrary to the principles of fundamental justice, the parties drew heavily on the decisions in *Kindler* and *Ng.* [In both cases,] the Minister was held to have the power, though not the duty, to extradite without assurances.

The respondents submit that even if the analytical framework developed in *Kindler* and *Ng* is accepted (i.e., balancing "the conflicting considerations" or "factors": *Kindler*, at p. 850), the result of those cases should not determine the outcome here. *Kindler* and *Ng* should either be distinguished on the facts or revisited on the weight to be given to the "factor" of capital punishment because of changed circumstances in the 10 years since those cases were decided.

The Proper Analytical Approach (the "Balancing Process") Was Set Out by this Court in its decisions in Kindler and Ng.

It is important to recognize that neither *Kindler* nor *Ng* provides a blanket approval to extraditions to face the death penalty. In *Kindler*, La Forest J., at p. 833, referred to a §7 "balancing process" in which "the global context must be kept squarely in mind". At p. 835, he acknowledged the possible existence of circumstances that "may constitutionally vitiate an order for surrender".

It is inherent in the *Kindler* and *Ng* balancing process that the outcome may well vary from case to case depending on the mix of contextual factors put into the balance. Some of these factors will be very specific, such as the mental condition of a particular fugitive. Other factors will be more general, such as the difficulties, both practical and philosophic, associated with the death penalty. Some of these factors will be unchanging; others will evolve over time. The outcome of this appeal turns more on the practical and philosophic difficulties associated with the death penalty that have increasingly preoccupied the courts and legislators in Canada, the United States and elsewhere rather than on the specific circumstances of the respondents in this case. Our analysis will lead to the conclusion that in the absence of exceptional circumstances, which we refrain from trying to anticipate, assurances in death penalty cases are always constitutionally required.

The Minister approached this extradition decision on the basis of the law laid down in *Kindler* and *Ng* and related cases. Having regard to some of the expressions used in the case law, he concluded that the *possibility* of the death penalty does not pose a situation that is "simply unacceptable" (*Allard, supra*, at p. 572), nor would surrender of the respondents without assurances "shock the conscience of Canadians" (*Schmidt, supra*, at p. 522; *Kindler, supra*, and *Ng, supra*) or violate "the Canadian sense of what is fair and right" (*per* McLachlin J. in *Kindler, supra*, at p. 850). A similar pre-*Charter* formulation was applied in a death penalty case under the *Canadian Bill of Rights*, S.C. 1960, c. 44, where Laskin C.J. asked "whether the punishment prescribed is so excessive as to outrage standards of decency" in *Miller v. The Queen*, [1977] 2 S.C.R. 680, at p. 688.

While we affirm that the "balancing process" set out in *Kindler* and *Ng* is the correct approach, the phrase "shocks the conscience" and equivalent expressions are not to be taken out of context or equated to opinion polls. The words were intended to underline the very exceptional nature of circumstances that would constitutionally limit the Minister's decision in extradition cases. The words were not intended to signal an abdication by judges of their constitutional responsibilities in matters involving fundamental principles of justice. In this respect, Canadian courts share the duty described by President Arthur Chaskalson of the Constitutional Court of South Africa in declaring unconstitutional the death penalty in that country:

> Public opinion may have some relevance to the enquiry, but, in itself, it is no substitute for the duty vested in the Courts to interpret the Constitution and to uphold its provisions without fear or favour. If public opinion were to be deci-

sive, there would be no need for constitutional adjudication. The protection of rights could then be left to Parliament, which has a mandate from the public, and is answerable to the public for the way its mandate is exercised.... The very reason for establishing the new legal order, and for vesting the power of judicial review of all legislation in the courts, was to protect the rights of minorities and others who cannot protect their rights adequately through the democratic process. Those who are entitled to claim this protection include the social outcasts and marginalised people of our society. It is only if there is a willingness to protect the worst and weakest amongst us that all of us can be secure that our own rights will be protected.

(*S. v. Makwanyane* (1995), (3) S.A. 391, at para. 88)

Use of the "shocks the conscience" terminology was intended to convey the exceptional weight of a factor such as the youth, insanity, mental retardation or pregnancy of a fugitive which, because of its paramount importance, may control the outcome of the *Kindler* balancing test on the facts of a particular case. The terminology should not be allowed to obscure the ultimate assessment that is required: namely whether or not the extradition is in accordance with the principles of fundamental justice. The rule is *not* that departures from fundamental justice are to be tolerated unless in a particular case it shocks the conscience. An extradition that violates the principles of fundamental justice will *always* shock the conscience. The important inquiry is to determine what constitutes the applicable principles of fundamental justice in the extradition context.

The "shocks the conscience" language signals the possibility that even though the rights of the fugitive are to be considered in the context of other applicable principles of fundamental justice, which are normally of sufficient importance to uphold the extradition, a particular treatment or punishment may sufficiently violate our sense of fundamental justice as to tilt the balance against extradition. Examples might include stoning to death individuals taken in adultery, or lopping off the hands of a thief. The punishment is so extreme that it becomes the controlling issue in the extradition and overwhelms the rest of the analysis. The respondents contend that now, unlike perhaps in 1991 when *Kindler* and *Ng* were decided, capital punishment is *the* issue.

Factors that Arguably Favour Extradition Without Assurances

Within this overall approach, a number of the "basic tenets of our legal system" relevant to this appeal may be found in previous extradition cases:

—that individuals accused of a crime should be brought to trial to determine the truth of the charges (see *Cotroni, supra,* at pp. 1487 and 1495), the concern in this case being that if assurances are sought and refused, the Canadian government could face the possibility that the respondents might avoid a trial altogether;

—that justice is best served by a trial in the jurisdiction where the crime was allegedly committed and the harmful impact felt (*Mellino, supra,* at pp. 555 and 558; *Idziak, supra,* at p. 662; and see *Cotroni, supra,* at p. 1488);

—that individuals who choose to leave Canada leave behind Canadian law and procedures and must generally accept the local law, procedure and punishments which the foreign state applies to its own residents. As Wilson J., dissenting in the result in *Cotroni, supra,* stated at p. 1510: "A Canadian citizen who leaves Canada for another state must expect that he will be answerable to the justice system of that state in respect of his conduct there;"

—that extradition is based on the principles of comity and fairness to other cooperating states in rendering mutual assistance in bringing fugitives to justice (*Mellino, supra*, at p. 551; and see *Idziak, supra*, at p. 663); subject to the principle that the fugitive must be able to receive a fair trial in the requesting state (*Mellino, supra*, at p. 558; *Allard, supra*, at p. 571).

A state seeking Canadian cooperation today may be asked to yield up a fugitive tomorrow. The extradition treaty is part of an international network of mutual assistance that enables states to deal both with crimes in their own jurisdiction and transnational crimes with elements that occur in more than one jurisdiction. Given the ease of movement of people and things from state to state, Canada needs the help of the international community to fight serious crime within our own borders. Some of the states from whom we seek cooperation may not share our constitutional values. Their cooperation is nevertheless important. The Minister points out that Canada satisfies itself that certain minimum standards of criminal justice exist in the foreign state before it makes an extradition treaty in the first place.

The Minister argues, very fairly, that expressions of judicial deference to ministerial extradition decisions extend in an unbroken line from *Schmidt* to *Kindler*. Such deference, taken together with the proposition that an individual (including a Canadian) who commits crimes in another state "must expect [to be] answerable to the justice system of that state in respect of his conduct there" (*Cotroni, supra*, p. 1510), provides a sufficient basis, the Minister says, for upholding the extradition without assurances.

Countervailing Factors that Arguably Favour Extradition Only with Assurances

We now turn to the factors that appear to weigh against extradition without assurances that the death penalty will not be imposed.

(a) *Principles of Criminal Justice as Applied in Canada*

The death penalty has been rejected as an acceptable element of criminal justice by the Canadian people, speaking through their elected federal representatives, after years of protracted debate. Canada has not executed anyone since 1962. Parliament abolished the last legal vestiges of the death penalty in 1998 (*An Act to Amend the National Defence Act*, S.C. 1998, c. 35) some seven years after the decisions of this Court in *Kindler* and *Ng*. In his letter to the respondents, the Minister of Justice emphasized that "in Canada, Parliament has decided that capital punishment is not an appropriate penalty for crimes committed here, and I am firmly committed to that position."

While government policy at any particular moment may or may not be consistent with principles of fundamental justice, the fact that successive governments and Parliaments over a period of almost 40 years have refused to inflict the death penalty reflects, we believe, a fundamental Canadian principle about the appropriate limits of the criminal justice system.

We are not called upon in this appeal to determine whether capital punishment would, if authorised by the Canadian Parliament, violate §12 of the *Charter* ("cruel and unusual treatment or punishment"), and if so in what circumstances. It is, however, incontestable that capital punishment, whether or not it violates §12 of the *Charter*, and whether or not it could be upheld under §1, engages the underlying values of the prohibition against cruel and unusual punishment. It is final. It is irreversible. Its imposition has been described as arbitrary. Its deterrent value has been doubted. Its implementation necessarily causes psychological and physical suffering. It has been rejected by the Canadian Parliament for offences committed within Canada. Its potential imposition in this case is thus a factor that weighs against extradition without assurances.

(b) *The Abolition of the Death Penalty Has Emerged as a Major Canadian Initiative at the International Level, and Reflects a Concern Increasingly Shared by Most of the World's Democracies.*

In *Re B.C. Motor Vehicle Act, supra,* Lamer J. expressly recognized that international law and opinion is of use to the courts in elucidating the scope of fundamental justice, at p. 512:

> [Principles of fundamental justice] represent principles which have been recognized by the common law, the international conventions and by the very fact of entrenchment in the *Charter,* as essential elements of a system for the administration of justice which is founded upon the belief in the dignity and worth of the human person and the rule of law.

Dickson C.J. made a similar observation in *Slaight Communications, supra,* at pp. 1056–57:

> ... Canada's *international human rights obligations* should inform not only the *interpretation of the content of the rights* guaranteed by the *Charter* but also the interpretation of what can constitute pressing and substantial §1 objectives which may justify restrictions upon those rights. [Emphasis added.]

Further in *Reference re Public Service Employee Relations Act (Alta.),* [1987] 1 S.C.R. 313, at p. 348, Dickson C.J. stated:

> The various sources of international human rights law—declarations, covenants, conventions, judicial and quasi-judicial decisions of international tribunals, customary norms—must, in my opinion, be relevant and persuasive sources for the interpretation of the *Charter's* provisions.

See also *R. v. Keegstra,* [1990] 3 S.C.R. 697, at pp. 750 and 791.

Although this particular appeal arises in the context of Canada's bilateral extradition arrangements with the United States, it is properly considered in the broader context of international relations generally, including Canada's multilateral efforts to bring about change in extradition arrangements where fugitives may face the death penalty, and Canada's advocacy at the international level of the abolition of the death penalty itself.

(i) *International Initiatives Opposing Extradition Without Assurances*

A provision for assurances is found in the extradition arrangements of countries other than Canada and the United States. Article 11 of the Council of Europe's *European Convention on Extradition,* signed December 13, 1957 (E.T.S. No. 24) is virtually identical to Article 6 of the Canada-U.S. treaty. To the same effect is Article 4(d) of the *Model Treaty on Extradition* passed by the General Assembly of the United Nations in December 1990 which states that extradition may be refused:

> (d) If the offence for which extradition is requested carries the death penalty under the law of the requesting State, unless that State gives such assurance as the requested State considers sufficient that the death penalty will not be imposed or, if imposed, will not be carried out;

We are told that from 1991 onwards Article 4(d) has gained increasing acceptance in state practice. Amnesty International submitted that Canada currently is the only country in the world, to its knowledge, that has abolished the death penalty at home but continues to extradite without assurances to face the death penalty abroad. Counsel for the Minister, while not conceding the point, did not refer us to any evidence of state practice to contradict this assertion.

The United Nations Commission on Human Rights Resolutions 1999/61 (adopted April 28, 1999) and 2000/65 (adopted April 27, 2000) call for the abolition of the death penalty, and in terms of extradition state that the Commission

> "[r]equests States that have received a request for extradition on a capital charge to reserve explicitly the right to refuse extradition in the absence of effective assurances from relevant authorities of the requesting State that capital punishment will not be carried out."

Canada supported these initiatives. When they are combined with other examples of Canada's international advocacy of the abolition of the death penalty itself ... it is difficult to avoid the conclusion that in the Canadian view of fundamental justice, capital punishment is unjust and it should be stopped.

(d) *Other Factors*

Other factors that weigh against extradition without assurances include the growing awareness of the rate of wrongful convictions in murder cases, and concerns about the "death row phenomenon", aptly described by Lord Griffiths in *Pratt v. Attorney General for Jamaica*, [1993] 4 All E.R. 769 (J.P.C.), at p. 783:

> "There is an instinctive revulsion against the prospect of hanging a man after he has been held under sentence of death for many years. What gives rise to this instinctive revulsion? The answer can only be our humanity: we regard it as an inhuman act to keep a man facing the agony of execution over a long extended period of time."

An Accelerating Concern about Potential Wrongful Convictions is a Factor of Increased Weight Since Kindler and Ng Were Decided.

The avoidance of conviction and punishment of the innocent has long been in the forefront of "the basic tenets of our legal system". It is reflected in the presumption of innocence under §11(d) of the *Charter* and in the elaborate rules governing the collection and presentation of evidence, fair trial procedures, and the availability of appeals. The possibility of miscarriages of justice in murder cases has long been recognized as a legitimate objection to the death penalty, but our state of knowledge of the scope of this potential problem has grown to unanticipated and unprecedented proportions in the years since *Kindler* and *Ng* were decided. This expanding awareness compels increased recognition of the fact that the extradition decision of a Canadian Minister could pave the way, however unintentionally, to sending an innocent individual to his or her death in a foreign jurisdiction.

(a) *The Canadian Experience*

Our concern begins at home. There have been well-publicized recent instances of miscarriages of justice in murder cases in Canada. Fortunately, because of the abolition of the death penalty, meaningful remedies for wrongful conviction are still possible in this country. [The Court summarized wrongful murder cases involving, *inter alia*, (1)

Donald Marshall, Jr., who served 11 years before being exonerated; Marshall was awarded in excess of $1,000,000 in compensation; and David Milgaard, who served 23 years in jail; Milgaard received $10,000,000 in compensation.]

These miscarriages of justice of course represent a tiny and wholly exceptional fraction of the workload of Canadian courts in murder cases. Still, where capital punishment is sought, the state's execution of even one innocent person is one too many.

In all of these cases, had capital punishment been imposed, there would have been no one to whom an apology and compensation *could* be paid in respect of the miscarriage of justice (apart, possibly, from surviving family members), and no way in which Canadian society with the benefit of hindsight could have justified to itself the deprivation of human life in violation of the principles of fundamental justice.

Accordingly, when Canada looks south to the present controversies in the United States associated with the investigation, defence, conviction, appeal and punishment in murder cases, it is with a sense of appreciation that many of the underlying criminal justice problems are similar. The difference is that imposition of the death penalty in the retentionist states inevitably deprives the legal system of the possibility of redress to wrongfully convicted individuals.

[The Court next examined the problems of miscarriages of justice in the United States and the increasing vigor of the American moratorium movement. This portion of the Court's opinion is reproduced *supra* chapter 1.]

[After surveying examples of recent wrongful executions in the United Kingdom, the Court noted]:

> The U.K. experience is relevant for the obvious reason that these men might be free today if the state had not taken their lives. But there is more. These convictions were quashed not on the basis of sophisticated DNA evidence but on the basis of frailties that perhaps may never be eliminated from our system of criminal justice.... These cases demonstrate that the concern about wrongful convictions is unlikely to be resolved by advances in the forensic sciences, welcome as those advances are from the perspective of protecting the innocent and punishing the guilty.

(d) *Conclusion*

The recent and continuing disclosures of wrongful convictions for murder in Canada, the United States and the United Kingdom provide tragic testimony to the fallibility of the legal system, despite its elaborate safeguards for the protection of the innocent. When fugitives are sought to be tried for murder by a retentionist state, however similar in other respects to our own legal system, this history weighs powerfully in the balance against extradition without assurances.

The "Death Row Phenomenon" is of Increasing Concern Even to Retentionists.

The evidence filed on this appeal includes a report by Chief Justice Richard P. Guy, Chief Justice of the State of Washington, dated March 2000 entitled "Status Report on the Death Penalty in Washington State". In the report the Chief Justice notes the following statistics relevant to the present discussion:

—Since 1981, 25 men have been convicted and sentenced to death. Four have had their judgments reversed by the federal courts, 2 have had their sentences reversed by the Washington State Supreme Court, and 3 have been executed.

— The case of one defendant who was sentenced to be executed 18 years ago is still pending.

— Two of the three executed defendants chose not to pursue appeals to the federal courts.

— For cases completed in the federal courts, state and federal review has taken an average of 11.2 years.

— State review after conviction has averaged 5.5 years.

In his introduction to the Status Report, the Chief Justice made the following observations (at p. 2):

> Because a death sentence is irreversible, opportunities for proving innocence in addition to those furnished in other felony cases are offered to the defendant in order to avoid erroneous executions. The importance of the review system is illustrated by the current situation in Illinois, a state in which 12 men have been executed since the 1980s but another 13 men sentenced to death have been exonerated. Appellate review of their cases resulted in reversal of their judgments after they were able to prove their innocence through the use of newly discovered DNA techniques or for other reasons.

The death row phenomenon is not a controlling factor in the §7 balance, but even many of those who regard its horrors as self-inflicted concede that it is a relevant consideration. To that extent, it is a factor that weighs in the balance against extradition without assurances.

The Balance of Factors in This Case Renders Extradition of the Respondents Without Assurances a Prima facie Infringement of their Section 7 Rights.

Reviewing the factors for and against unconditional extradition, we conclude that to order extradition of the respondents without obtaining assurances that the death penalty will not be imposed would violate the principles of fundamental justice.

The Minister has not pointed to any public purpose that would be served by extradition *without* assurances that is not substantially served by extradition *with* assurances, carrying as it does in this case the prospect on conviction of life imprisonment without release or parole. With assurances, the respondents will be extradited and be made answerable to the legal system where the murders took place. The evidence shows that on previous occasions when assurances have been requested of foreign states they have been forthcoming without exception. (See, for example, Ministerial Decision in the Matter of the Extradition of Lee Robert O'Bomsawin, December 9, 1991; Ministerial Decision in the Matter of the Extradition of Rodolfo Pacificador, October 19, 1996.) There is no basis in the record to support the hypothesis, and counsel for the Minister did not advance it, that the United States would prefer no extradition at all to extradition with assurances. Under Washington State law it by no means follows that the prosecutor will seek the death penalty if the respondents are extradited to face charges of aggravated first degree murder.

It is true that if assurances are requested, the respondents will not face the same punishment regime that is generally applicable to crimes committed in Washington State, but the reality is that Washington requires the assistance of Canada to bring the respondents to justice. Assurances are not sought out of regard for the respondents, but out of regard for the principles that have historically guided this country's criminal justice system and are presently reflected in its international stance on capital punishment.

International experience, particularly in the past decade, has shown the death penalty to raise many complex problems of both a philosophic and pragmatic nature. While there remains the fundamental issue of whether the state can ever be justified in taking the life of a human being within its power, the present debate goes beyond arguments over the effectiveness of deterrence and the appropriateness of vengeance and retribution. It strikes at the very ability of the criminal justice system to obtain a uniformly correct result even where death hangs in the balance.

International experience thus confirms the validity of concerns expressed in the Canadian Parliament about capital punishment. It also shows that a rule requiring that assurances be obtained prior to extradition in death penalty cases not only accords with Canada's principled advocacy on the international level, but is also consistent with the practice of other countries with whom Canada generally invites comparison, apart from the retentionist jurisdictions in the United States.

The "balancing process" mandated by *Kindler* and *Ng* remains a flexible instrument. The difficulty in this case is that the Minister proposes to send the respondents without assurances into the death penalty controversy at a time when the legal system of the requesting country is under such sustained and authoritative *internal* attack. Although rumblings of this controversy in Canada, the United States and the United Kingdom pre-dated *Kindler* and *Ng*, the concern has grown greatly in depth and detailed proof in the intervening years. The imposition of a moratorium (*de facto* or otherwise) in some of the retentionist states of the United States attests to this concern, but a moratorium itself is not conclusive, any more than the lifting of a moratorium would be. What is important is the recognition that despite the best efforts of all concerned, the judicial system is and will remain fallible and reversible whereas the death penalty will forever remain final and irreversible.

The arguments in favour of extradition without assurances would be as well served by extradition with assurances. There was no convincing argument that exposure of the respondents to death in prison by execution advances Canada's public interest in a way that the alternative, eventual death in prison by natural causes, would not. This is perhaps corroborated by the fact that other abolitionist countries do not, in general, extradite without assurances.

The arguments against extradition without assurances have grown stronger since this Court decided *Kindler* and *Ng* in 1991. Canada is now abolitionist for all crimes, even those in the military field. The international trend against the death penalty has become clearer. The death penalty controversies in the requesting State—the United States—are based on pragmatic, hard-headed concerns about wrongful convictions. None of these factors is conclusive, but taken together they tilt the §7 balance against extradition without assurances.

Accordingly, we find that the Minister's decision to decline to request the assurances of the State of Washington that the death penalty will not be imposed on the respondents as a condition of their extradition, violates their rights under §7 of the *Charter*.

Extradition of the Respondents Without Assurances Cannot Be Justified Under Section 1 of the Charter.

The final issue is whether the Minister has shown that the violation of the respondents' §7 rights that would occur if they were extradited to face the death penalty can be upheld under §1 of the *Charter* as reasonable and demonstrably justifiable in a free and democratic society. The Court has previously noted that it would be rare for a violation of the fundamental principles of justice to be justifiable under §1: *Re B.C. Motor Vehicle Act, supra*, at p. 518. Nevertheless, we do not foreclose the possibility that there may be situations where the Minister's objectives are so pressing, and where there is no other way to achieve those objectives other than through extradition without assurances, that a violation might be justified. In this case, we find no such justification.

The Minister must show that the refusal to ask for assurances serves a pressing and substantial purpose; that the refusal is likely to achieve that purpose and does not go further than necessary; and that the effect of unconditional extradition does not outweigh the importance of the objective: *R. v. Oakes*, [1986] 1 S.C.R. 103. In our opinion, while the government objective of advancing mutual assistance in the fight against crime is entirely legitimate, the Minister has not shown that extraditing the respondents to face the death penalty without assurances is necessary to achieve that objective.

The Minister cites two important policies that are integral to Canada's mutual assistance objectives, namely, (1) maintenance of comity with cooperating states; and (2) avoiding an influx to Canada of persons charged with murder in retentionist states for the purpose of avoiding the death penalty.

With respect to the argument on comity, there is no doubt that it is important for Canada to maintain good relations with other states. However, the Minister has not shown that the means chosen to further that objective in this case—the refusal to ask for assurances that the death penalty will not be exacted—is necessary to further that objective. There is no suggestion in the evidence that asking for assurances would undermine Canada's international obligations or good relations with neighbouring states. The extradition treaty between Canada and the United States explicitly provides for a request for assurances and Canada would be in full compliance with its international obligations by making it. More and more states are becoming abolitionist and reserving to themselves the right to refuse to extradite unconditionally, as already mentioned.

In *Soering, supra*, the European Court of Human Rights held that, in the circumstances of that case, extradition of a West German national from the United Kingdom to face possible execution in the United States would violate the European Convention on Human Rights. West Germany was willing to try Soering in Germany on the basis of his nationality. The European Court ruled that the option of a trial of Soering in West Germany was a "circumstance of relevance for the overall assessment under Article 3 in that it goes to the search for the requisite fair balance of interests and to the proportionality of the contested extradition decision in the particular case" (para. 110) and that "[a] further consideration of relevance is that in the particular instance the legitimate purpose of extradition could be achieved by another means which would not involve suffering of such exceptional intensity or duration" (para. 111). By "another means", the court had in mind the trial of Soering in West Germany. In the present appeal as well, "the legitimate purpose of extradition could be achieved by another means", namely extradition *with* assurances, in perfect conformity with Canada's commitment to international comity.

We have already addressed the speculative argument that an American government might prefer to let accused persons go without trial by refusing to give assurances. As European states now routinely request assurances that the death penalty will not be imposed on an extradited person, there is little indication that U.S. governments would ever refuse such guarantees. A state seeking to prosecute a serious crime is unlikely to decide that if it cannot impose the ultimate sanction—the death penalty—it will not prosecute at all. Seeking assurances that the death penalty will not be imposed does not amount to asking for lawlessness.

An issue could also arise where a treaty did not contain an assurance clause equivalent to Article 6 of the Canada-U.S. treaty. The argument would then be raised that the Canadian government violated the §7 rights of fugitives by failing to insist on such a provision. That issue is not raised by the facts of this case and we leave consideration of the point to an appeal where it is fully argued.

As noted, the Minister's second argument is that it is necessary to refuse to ask for assurances in order to prevent an influx to Canada of persons who commit crimes sanctioned by the death penalty in other states. This in turn would make Canada an attractive haven for persons committing murders in retentionist states. The "safe haven" argument might qualify as a pressing and substantial objective. Indeed, it was accepted as such in *Kindler*, *supra*, by both La Forest J. (at p. 836) and McLachlin J. (at p. 853).

International criminal law enforcement including the need to ensure that Canada does not become a "safe haven" for dangerous fugitives is a very legitimate objective, but there is no evidence whatsoever that extradition to face life in prison without release or parole provides a lesser deterrent to those seeking a "safe haven" than the death penalty, or even that fugitives approach their choice of refuge with such an informed appreciation of tactics. If Canada suffers the prospect of being a haven from time to time for fugitives from the United States, it likely has more to do with geographic proximity than the Minister's policy on treaty assurances. The evidence as stated is that Ministers of Justice have on at least two occasions (since *Kindler* and *Ng*) refused to extradite without assurances, and no adverse consequences to Canada from those decisions were brought to our attention. The respondents pointed out that "[s]ince the execution by the United States of two Mexican nationals in 1997, Mexican authorities have consistently refused to extradite anyone, nationals or non-nationals, in capital cases without first seeking assurances" (respondents' factum, at para. 63).

The fact is, however, that whether fugitives are returned to a foreign country to face the death penalty or to face eventual death in prison from natural causes, they are equally prevented from using Canada as a safe haven. Elimination of a "safe haven" depends on vigorous law enforcement rather than on infliction of the death penalty once the fugitive has been removed from the country.

We conclude that the infringement of the respondents' rights under §7 of the *Charter* cannot be justified under §1 in this case. The Minister is constitutionally bound to ask for and obtain an assurance that the death penalty will not be imposed as a condition of extradition.

VIII. Conclusion

The outcome of this appeal turns on an appreciation of the principles of fundamental justice, which in turn are derived from the basic tenets of our legal system. These basic tenets have not changed since 1991 when *Kindler* and *Ng* were decided, but their application in particular cases (the "balancing process") must take note of factual developments in Canada and in relevant foreign jurisdictions. When principles of fundamental justice as established and understood in Canada are applied to these factual developments, many of which are of far-reaching importance in death penalty cases, a balance which tilted in favour of extradition without assurances in *Kindler* and *Ng* now tilts against the constitutionality of such an outcome. For these reasons, the appeal is dismissed.

Notes

1. In their submissions on whether extradition without assurances is contrary to the principles of fundamental justice, the parties drew heavily on the decisions in *Kindler* and *Ng*. Joseph Kindler was an American citizen who had escaped to Canada after being convicted in Pennsylvania for the brutal murder of an 18-year old who was scheduled to testify against him in a burglary case. The jury which convicted Kindler had recommended that he face the death penalty. Prior to being sentenced, he escaped to Canada. After seven months as a fugitive in Quebec, Kindler was captured and escaped again. After remaining at large for nearly two years, Kindler was recaptured. Judicial review of Kindler's surrender order was dismissed by the Canadian Supreme Court even though the death penalty was no longer simply a possibility. It had already been recommended by the jury. Nevertheless, the Canadian Supreme Court held that the Minister was entitled to extradite without assurances.

In the companion appeal, the respondent Charles Ng was a British subject born in Hong Kong and subsequently resident in the United States. He had been arrested in Calgary after shooting at two department store security guards who tried to apprehend him for shoplifting. Once his identity was established, he was extradited to the State of California to face numerous charges of murder. He was subsequently convicted and sentenced to death for murdering 11 people—six men, three women and two baby boys—during what one newspaper described as a "spree of sexual torture and murder in rural California." In that case, as well, the Canadian Minister was held to have the power, though not the duty, to extradite without assurances.

2. The *Burns* Court's discussion of the American experience with wrongful capital convictions and the American Bar Association's call for a death penalty moratorium is excerpted *supra*, chapter 1.

Notes and Questions on Duty to Advise Foreign Citizens of Their Consular Rights

According to the Death Penalty Information Center, 120 foreign nationals were on death row in the United States as of May 24, 2006. Under the Vienna Convention on Consular Relations (VCCR), authorities must inform a detained foreign national that, if requested, his or her consulate will be notified. The detained foreign national is entitled to this information "without delay" and the consulate must be notified "without delay." The purpose of the VCCR is to allow foreign nationals arrested outside their country to obtain the assistance of their government. Consular assistance can include explanations of differences in the legal systems, interpreters, help in locating witnesses, contact with family members, *amicus* briefs, and diplomatic appeals. The United States aggressively demands that American citizens detained abroad be accorded their consular rights. See Carter, "The Rights of Foreign Nationals Under the Vienna Convention on Consular Relations," CACJ/CPDA Def. Sem. (2001); see also Sims & Carter, "Representing Foreign Nationals: Emerging Importance of the Vienna Convention on Consular Relations as a Defense Tool," The Champion (Sept./Oct. 1998).

According to the Mexican government, Miguel Angel Flores, a Mexican citizen sentenced to die for the 1989 rape and murder of a 20-year-old video store employee in Texas, was deprived of due process because he was not advised of his right to contact the Mexican embassy. Mexico filed a formal protest with the United States State Department, claiming that it first learned of the charges against Flores nearly one year after he had been sentenced to death. Flores, 20 years old at the time of the murder, had no criminal record or history of violence. His court-appointed lawyer, who did not speak Spanish, put on no character witnesses or mitigating evidence. The Mexican government said that had it been notified it would have helped Flores hire a lawyer and would have ensured that members of Flores' family—who also did not speak English—would have been available to testify at Flores' sentencing hearing. Bonner, *U.S. Bid to Execute Mexican Draws Fire*, The New York Times (Oct. 30, 2000).

Angel Breard, a Paraguayan citizen was put to death in Virginia in 1998, despite requests from the United States State Department, the International Court of Justice and the Paraguayan government. The ICJ voted unanimously that Breard had been denied his consular rights and urged that the United States "should take all measures at its disposal" to prevent his execution. Neither the United States Supreme Court nor Virginia Governor Gilmore acted to halt the execution. In a per curiam opinion denying relief (and by a vote of 6–3, refusing to stay Breard's execution), the Court held that: (1) by not asserting his Vienna Convention claim in state court, Breard procedurally defaulted on this claim; (2) state authorities' violation of consular notification provisions of the Vienna Convention had no continuing consequences of a kind which would permit Paraguay to bring suit against state under Eleventh Amendment exemption; and (3) the Paraguayan Consul General, in bringing suit to set aside Breard's conviction, was acting only in his official capacity, and had no greater ability to proceed under federal civil rights statute than did the country he represented. *Breard v. Greene*, 523 U.S. 371 (1998).

Seven months after Breard's execution, the United States issued a formal apology to Paraguay over the failure of U.S. authorities to notify Breard of his consular rights. The United States' apology noted that

> "such notification was required by the Vienna Convention on Consular Relations and would have been made by competent U.S. authorities. This failure to notify Mr. Breard was unquestionably a violation of an obligation owed to the Government of Paraguay. We fully appreciate that the United States must see to it that foreign nationals in the United States receive the same treatment that we expect for our citizens overseas. We cannot have a double standard."

One day after receiving the apology, Paraguay withdrew its case against the U.S. at the International Court of Justice. The Paraguayan government announced that its concerns had been met, and praised "the courage of the U.S. government in admitting an error." Within days of that announcement, the U.S. government withdrew threatened trade sanctions against Paraguay for condoning the widespread copying of trademarked goods.

Not all foreign governments have been so easily mollified. Denial of consular rights to two German nationals led Germany to file suit against the United States in the World Court in 2000. Germany's lawsuit marked only the fourth time in nearly half a century that an ally sued the United States in the international court. Germany's suit sought reparations for Arizona's 1999 executions of two brothers, Karl and Walter LaGrand. Arizona officials admitted, many years after the LaGrand brothers were arrested, that they never notified the LaGrands of their consular rights.

What would an appropriate remedy be in such a suit? Is the foreign government the injured party when consular rights are ignored? If damages were to be awarded, how would they be measured? For an earlier decision of the International Court of Justice in the *LaGrand* case, see *Germany v. United States*, 1999 I.C.J. 9 (Mar. 3, 1999).

Note on Germany v. United States of America (The LaGrand Case), ICJ, 27 June 2001

Consider the following report from the International Court of Justice.

The Court finds that the United States has breached its obligations to Germany and to the LaGrand brothers under the Vienna Convention on Consular Relations. The Court finds, for the first time in its history, that orders indicating provisional measures are legally binding.

THE HAGUE, 27 June 2001. Today the International Court of Justice (ICJ), principal judicial organ of the United Nations, delivered its Judgment in the *LaGrand Case (Germany v. United States of America)*. In its Judgment, which is final, without appeal and binding for the Parties, the Court, with regard to the merits of the dispute:

– *finds* by fourteen votes to one that, by not informing Karl and Walter LaGrand without delay following their arrest of their rights under Article 36, paragraph 1 (b), of the Vienna Convention on Consular Relations, and by thereby depriving Germany of the possibility, in a timely fashion, to render the assistance provided for by the Convention to the individuals concerned, the United States breached its obligations to Germany and to the LaGrand brothers under Article 36, paragraph 1, of the Convention;

– *finds* by fourteen votes to one that, by not permitting the review & reconsideration, in the light of the rights set forth in the Convention, of the convictions and sentences of the LaGrand brothers after the violations referred to in paragraph (3) above had been established, the United States breached its obligation to Germany and to the LaGrand brothers under Article 36, paragraph 2, of the Convention;

– *finds* by thirteen votes to two that, by failing to take all measures at its disposal to ensure that Walter LaGrand was not executed pending the final decision of the International Court of Justice in the case, the United States breached the obligation incumbent upon it under the Order indicating provisional measures issued by the Court on 3 March 1999;

– *takes note* unanimously of the commitment undertaken by the United States to ensure implementation of the specific measures adopted in performance of its obligations under Article 36, paragraph 1(b), of the Convention;

– and *finds* that this commitment must be regarded as meeting Germany's request for a general assurance of non-repetition;

– *finds* by fourteen votes to one that should nationals of Germany nonetheless be sentenced to severe penalties, without their rights under Article 36, paragraph 1(b), of the Convention having been respected, the United States, by means of its own choosing, shall allow the review and reconsideration of the conviction and sentence by taking account of the violation of the rights set forth in that Convention.

Reasoning of the Court

In its Judgment, the Court begins by outlining the history of the dispute. It recalls that the brothers Karl and Walter LaGrand—German nationals who had been permanently residing in the United States since childhood—were arrested in 1982 in Arizona for their involvement in an attempted bank robbery, in the course of which the bank manager was murdered and another bank employee seriously injured. In 1984, an Arizona court convicted both of murder in the first degree and other crimes, and sentenced them to death. The LaGrands being German nationals, the Vienna Convention on Consular Relations required the competent authorities of the United States to inform them without delay of their right to communicate with the consulate of Germany. The United States acknowledged that this did not occur. In fact, the consulate was only made aware of the case in 1992 by the LaGrands themselves, who had learnt of their rights from other sources. By that stage, the LaGrands were precluded because of the doctrine of "procedural default" in United States law from challenging their convictions and sentences by claiming that their rights under the Vienna Convention had been violated. Karl LaGrand was executed on 24 February 1999. On 2 March 1999, the day before the scheduled date of execution of Walter LaGrand, Germany brought the case to the International Court of Justice.

On 3 March 1999, the Court made an Order indicating provisional measures (a kind of interim injunction), stating inter alia that the United States should take all measures at its disposal to ensure that Walter LaGrand was not executed pending a final decision of the Court. On that same day, Walter LaGrand was executed.

The Court then examines certain objections of the United States to the Court's jurisdiction and to the admissibility of Germany's submissions. It finds that it has jurisdiction to deal with all Germany's submissions and that they are admissible.

Ruling on the merits of the case, the Court observes that the United States does not deny that it violated, in relation to Germany, Article 36, paragraph 1 (b), of the Convention, which required the competent authorities of the United States to inform the LaGrands of their right to have the consulate of Germany notified of their arrest. It adds that in the present case this breach led to the violation of paragraph 1 (a) and paragraph 1 (c) of that Article, which deal respectively with mutual rights of communication and access of consular officers and their nationals, and the right of consular officers to visit their nationals in prison and to arrange for their legal representation. The Court further states that the United States not only breached its obligations to Germany as a State party to the Convention, but also that there had been a violation of the individual rights of the LaGrand brothers under Article 36, paragraph 1, which rights can be invoked in the Court by their national State.

The Court then turns to Germany's submission that the United States, by applying rules of its domestic law, in particular the doctrine of "procedural default," violated Article 36, paragraph 2, of the Convention. This provision requires the United States to "enable full effect to be given to the purposes for which the rights accorded [under Article 36] are intended." The Court states that, in itself, the rule does not violate Article 36. The problem arises, according to the Court, when the rule in question does not allow the detained individual to challenge a conviction and sentence by invoking the failure of the competent national authorities to comply with their obligations under Article 36, paragraph 1. The Court concludes that in the present case, the procedural default rule had the effect of preventing Germany, in a timely fashion, from assisting the LaGrands as provided for by the Convention. Under those circumstances, the Court holds that in the present case the above-mentioned rule violated paragraph 2 of Article 36.

With regard to the alleged violation by the United States of the Court's Order of 3 March 1999 indicating provisional measures, the Court points out that it is the first time that it is called upon to determine the legal effects of orders made under Article 41 of its Statute—the interpretation of which has been the subject of extensive controversy in the literature. After interpreting Article 41, the Court finds that such orders do have binding effect. In the present case, the Court concludes that its Order of 3 March 1999 "was not a mere exhortation" but "created a legal obligation for the United States." The Court goes on to consider the measures taken by the United States to implement the Order. It observes that the mere transmission of its Order to the Governor of Arizona without any comment was "certainly less than could have been done even in the short time available." It finds the same to be true of the United States Solicitor General's categorical statement in his brief letter to the United States Supreme Court that "an order of the International Court of Justice indicating provisional measures is not binding."

The Court further notes that the Governor of Arizona decided not to give effect to the Order, even though the Arizona Clemency Board had recommended a stay of execution for Walter LaGrand. It observes that the United States Supreme Court rejected an application by Germany for a stay of execution, "[g]iven the tardiness of the pleas and the jurisdictional barriers they implicate," while it would have been open to it, as one of its members urged, to grant a preliminary stay, which would have given it "time to consider … the jurisdictional and international legal issues involved."

The Court concludes that the United States did not comply with the Order of 3 March 1999. In respect of Germany's request seeking an assurance that the United States will not repeat its unlawful acts, the Court takes note of the fact that the latter repeatedly stated in all phases of these proceedings that it is carrying out a vast and detailed programme in order to ensure compliance by its competent authorities with Article 36 of the Convention.

The Court considers that this commitment to ensure implementation of specific measures must be regarded as meeting the request made by Germany. The Court finds, nevertheless, that if the United States, notwithstanding this commitment, should fail in its obligation of consular notification to the detriment of German nationals, an apology would not suffice in cases where the individuals concerned have been subjected to prolonged detention or convicted and sentenced to severe penalties; in the case of such a conviction and sentence it would be incumbent upon the United States to allow the review and reconsideration of the conviction and sentence by taking account of the violation of the rights set forth in the Convention.

Torres v. Mullin

124 S.Ct. 919 (2003) (Mem.)

Petition for a writ of certiorari denied.

Opinion of Justice STEVENS, respecting the denial of the petition for certiorari.

My dissent from the hastily crafted opinion in *Breard v. Greene*, 523 U.S. 371 (1998) (*per curiam*), rested on procedural grounds: The Court's departure from its normal rules governing the processing of certiorari petitions deprived us of the briefing and argument necessary for the careful consideration of important issues. *Id.,* at 379–380. I am now persuaded that my dissent should have been directed at the merits of the Court's holding.

In *Breard* the Court refused to stay the imminent execution of a citizen of Paraguay. Breard's federal habeas corpus application alleged that the Virginia authorities failed to advise Breard of his right under Article 36 of the Vienna Convention on Consular Relations to have the Paraguayan Consulate notified of his arrest and trial. This Court held that Breard procedurally defaulted his claim by failing to raise it in the Virginia state courts. *Id.,* at 375–376. The opinion did not discuss the possibility that Breard may have failed to assert the treaty claim because he knew nothing about the treaty until after the state proceedings were concluded. It surely is reasonable to presume that most foreign nationals were unaware of the provisions of the Vienna Convention (as are, it seems, many local prosecutors). That is precisely why the Convention places the notice obligation on the governmental authorities.

There is obvious tension between the holding in *Breard* and the purpose of Article 36 of the Vienna Convention. In its authoritative interpretation of Article 36 in the *LaGrand Case (F.R.G. v. U.S.)*, 2001 I.C.J. No. 104, ¶¶90–91 (Judgment of June 27), http://www.icj-cij.org/icwww/idocket/ igus/igusframe.htm (as visited Oct. 24, 2003, and available in Clerk of Court's case file), the International Court of Justice (ICJ) explained:***

> "The problem arises when the procedural default rule does not allow the detained individual to challenge a conviction and sentence by claiming, in reliance on Article 36, paragraph 1, of the Convention, that the competent national authorities failed to comply with their obligation to provide the requisite consular information 'without delay', thus preventing the person from seeking and obtaining consular assistance from the sending State.

> … Under these circumstances, the procedural default rule had the effect of preventing 'full effect [from being] given to the purposes for which the rights accorded under this article are intended,' and thus violated paragraph 2 of Article 36."

Applying the procedural default rule to Article 36 claims is not only in direct violation of the Vienna Convention, but it is also manifestly unfair. The ICJ's decision in *LaGrand* underscores that a foreign national who is presumptively ignorant of his right to notification should not be deemed to have waived the Article 36 protections simply because he failed to assert that right in a state criminal proceeding.

Article VI, cl. 2, of our Constitution provides that the "Laws of the United States," expressly including "all Treaties made … under the Authority of the United States, shall be the supreme Law of the Land." The Court was unfaithful to that command when it held that Congress may not require county employees to check the background of prospective handgun purchasers, *Printz v. United States*, 521 U.S. 898 (1997), that Congress may not exercise its Article I powers to abrogate a State's common-law immunity from suit, *Seminole Tribe of Fla. v. Florida*, 517 U.S. 44 (1996), and that a State may not be required to provide its citizens with a remedy for its violation of their federal rights, *Alden v. Maine*, 527 U.S. 706 (1999). The Court is equally unfaithful to that command when it permits state courts to disregard the Nation's treaty obligations.

Note on Mexico v. United States of America (Avena and Other Mexican Nationals), ICJ, 31 March 2004

In early 2003, the government of Mexico, in a direct challenge to the Bush administration, petitioned the International Court of Justice to block the execution of 51 Mexicans on death rows scattered throughout the United States. The 1963 Vienna Convention signed by the United States, Mexico and most other nations, requires governments to inform foreign prisoners of their rights to communicate with their consulates. Mexico's petition claimed that American officials, both state and local, have ignored that treaty. Mexico's petition sought a ruling ordering new trials for the condemned Mexican prisoners.

*** The United States has consented to the compulsory jurisdiction of the International Court of Justice over Convention-related disputes. Optional Protocol Concerning the Compulsory Settlement of Disputes, Apr. 24, 1963, Art. 1, [1970] 21 U.S.T. 326, T.I.A.S. No. 6820.

The ICJ is the highest tribunal of the United Nations, but lacks enforcement powers. The ICJ decision is summarized in the following ICJ press release. (The full text of the *LaGrand* and *Avena* opinions and orders are available on the International Court of Justice's website, located at www.icj-cij.org).

Avena and Other Mexican Nationals (Mexico v. United States of America)

The Court finds that the United States of America has breached its obligations to Mr. Avena and 50 other Mexican nationals and to Mexico under the Vienna Convention on Consular Relations

THE HAGUE, 31 March 2004. Today the International Court of Justice, the principal judicial organ of the United Nations, delivered its Judgment in the case concerning *Avena and Other Mexican Nationals (Mexico v. United States of America)*.

In its Judgment, which is final, without appeal and binding on the Parties, the Court, with regard to the merits of the dispute,

– "*finds* by fourteen votes to one that, by not informing, without delay upon their detention, the 51 Mexican nationals referred to in paragraph 106 (1) above of their rights under Article 36, paragraph 1 *(b)*, of the Vienna Convention on Consular Relations of 24 April 1963, the United States of America breached the obligations incumbent upon it under that subparagraph;

– *finds* by fourteen votes to one that, by not notifying the appropriate Mexican consular post without delay of the detention of the 49 Mexican nationals referred to in paragraph 106 (2) above and thereby depriving the United Mexican States of the right, in a timely fashion, to render the assistance provided for by the Vienna Convention to the individuals concerned, the United States of America breached the obligations incumbent upon it under Article 36, paragraph 1 *(b)*;

– *finds* by fourteen votes to one that, in relation to the 49 Mexican nationals referred to in paragraph 106 (3) above, the United States of America deprived the United Mexican States of the right, in a timely fashion, to communicate with and have access to those nationals and to visit them in detention, and thereby breached the obligations incumbent upon it under Article 36, paragraph 1 *(a)* and *(c)*, of the Convention;

– *finds* by fourteen votes to one that, in relation to the 34 Mexican nationals referred to in paragraph 106 (4) above, the United States of America deprived the United Mexican States of the right, in a timely fashion, to arrange for legal representation of those nationals, and thereby breached the obligations incumbent upon it under Article 36, paragraph 1 (c)), of the Convention;

– *finds* by fourteen votes to one that, by not permitting the review and reconsideration, in the light of the rights set forth in the Convention, of the conviction and sentences of Mr. César Roberto Fierro Reyna, Mr. Roberto Moreno Ramos and Mr. Osvaldo Torres Aguilera, after the violations referred to in subparagraph (4) above had been established in respect of those individuals, the United States of America breached the obligations incumbent upon it under Article 36, paragraph 2, of the Convention;

– *finds* by fourteen votes to one that the appropriate reparation in this case consists in the obligation of the United States of America to provide, by means of its own choosing, review and reconsideration of the convictions and sentences of the Mexican nationals referred to in subparagraphs (4), (5), (6) and (7) above, by taking account both of the violation of the rights set forth in Article 36 of the Convention and of paragraphs 138 to 141 of this Judgment;

– unanimously *takes note* of the commitment undertaken by the United States of America to ensure implementation of the specific measures adopted in performance of its obligations under Article 36, paragraph 1 *(b)*, of the Vienna Convention; and finds that this commitment must be regarded as meeting the request by the United Mexican States for guarantees and assurances of non-repetition;

– unanimously *finds* that, should Mexican nationals nonetheless be sentenced to severe penalties, without their rights under Article 36, paragraph 1 *(b)*, of the Convention having been respected, the United States of America shall provide, by means of its own choosing, review and reconsideration of the conviction and sentence, so as to allow full weight to be given to the violation of the rights set forth in the Convention, taking account of paragraphs 138 to 141 of this Judgment."

Reasoning of the Court

In its Judgment the Court begins by outlining the history of the case. It recalls that on 9 January 2003 Mexico instituted proceedings against the United States of America in a dispute concerning alleged breaches of Articles 5 and 36 of the Vienna Convention on Consular Relations of 24 April 1963 in relation to the treatment of a number of Mexican nationals who had been tried, convicted and sentenced to death in criminal proceedings in the United States. The original claim related to 54 such persons, but as a result of subsequent adjustments by Mexico, only 52 individual cases are involved. On 9 January 2003 Mexico also asked the Court to indicate provisional measures, and in particular to order the United States to take all measures necessary to ensure that no Mexican national was executed pending a final decision of the Court. On 5 February 2003 the Court unanimously adopted an Order indicating such measures, stating *inter alia* that the "United States of America shall take all measures necessary to ensure that Mr. César Roberto Fierro Reyna, Mr. Roberto Moreno Ramos and Mr. Osvaldo Torres Aguilera ... are not executed pending final judgment in these proceedings."

The Court then examines four objections of the United States to the Court's jurisdiction and five to the admissibility of the claims of Mexico. It rejects those objections after first having rejected the objection of Mexico to the admissibility of the United States objections.

Ruling on the merits of the case, the Court first addresses the question of whether the 52 individuals concerned had Mexican nationality only, or whether some of them were also United States nationals, as claimed by that State. Concluding that the United States has not proved that claim, the Court finds that the United States did have obligations (to provide consular information) under Article 36, paragraph 1 (b), of the Vienna Convention towards the 52 Mexican nationals.

The Court then examines the meaning of the expression "without delay" used in paragraph 1 *(b)* of Article 36. It finds that the duty to provide consular information exists once it is realized that the person is a foreign national, or once there are grounds to think so, but considers that, in the light *inter alia* of the Convention's *travaux préparatoires* the term "without delay" is not necessarily to be interpreted as meaning "immediately upon arrest". The Court then concludes that, on the basis of this interpretation, the United States has nonetheless violated its obligation to provide consular notification in all of the cases save one.

The Court then takes note of the interrelated nature of the three subparagraphs *(a)*, *(b)* and *(c)* of paragraph 1 of Article 36 of the Vienna Convention and finds, in 49 of the cases, that the United States has also violated its obligation under subparagraph *(a)* to enable Mexican consular officers to communicate with, have access to and visit their nationals; while, in 34 cases, it finds that the United States has also, in addition, violated its obligation under subparagraph *(c)* to enable Mexican consular officers to arrange for legal representation of their nationals.

The Court then turns to Mexico's submission in relation to paragraph 2 of Article 36, whereby it claims that the United States violated its obligations under that paragraph by failing to provide "meaningful and effective review and reconsideration of convictions and sentences impaired by a violation of Article 36 (1)," *inter alia* as a result of the operation of the "procedural default" rule. The Court begins by observing that the procedural default rule has not been revised since it drew attention in its Judgment in the *LaGrand* case to the problems which its application could cause for defendants who sought to rely on violations of the Vienna Convention in appeal proceedings. The Court finds that in three cases paragraph 2 of Article 36 has been violated by the United States, but that the possibility of judicial re-examination is still open in 49 of the cases.

Turning to the legal consequences of the above-found breaches and to what legal remedies should be considered, the Court notes that Mexico seeks reparation in the form of *"restitutio in integrum,"* that is to say partial or total annulment of conviction and sentence, as the "necessary and sole remedy." The Court, citing the decision of its predecessor, the Permanent Court of International Justice, in the *Chorzów Factory* case, points out that what is required to make good the breach of an obligation under international law is "reparation in an adequate form." Following its Judgment in the *La-Grand* case the Court finds that in the present case adequate reparation for violations of Article 36 should be provided by review and reconsideration of the convictions and sentences of the Mexican nationals by United States courts.

The Court considers that the choice of means for review and reconsideration should be left to the United States, but that it is to be carried out by taking account of the violation of rights under the Vienna Convention.

The Court then addresses the function of executive clemency. Having found that it is the judicial process that is suited for the task of review and reconsideration, the Court finds that the clemency process, as currently practised within the United States criminal justice system, is not sufficient in itself to serve that purpose, although appropriate clemency procedures can supplement judicial review and reconsideration.

Finally, with regard to Mexico's request for the cessation of wrongful acts by the United States, the Court finds no evidence of a "regular and continuing" pattern of breaches by the United States of Article 36 of the Vienna Convention. And as to its request for guarantees and assurances of non-repetition the Court recognizes the United States efforts to encourage implementation of its obligations under the Vienna Convention and considers that that commitment by the United States meets Mexico's request.

At the end of its reasoning, the Court emphasizes that, in the present case, it has been addressing issues of principle from the viewpoint of the general application of the Vienna Convention. It observes that, while the present case concerns only Mexicans, its Judgment cannot be taken to imply that the Court's conclusions do not apply to other foreign nationals finding themselves in similar situations in the United States.

The Court finally points out that its Order of 5 February 2003 indicating provisional measures mentioned above, according to its terms and to Article 41 of the Statute, was effective pending final judgment, and that the obligations of the United States in that respect are, with effect from the date of the Judgment, replaced by those declared in this Judgment. The Court observes that it has found in relation to the three persons concerned in the Order (among others), that the United States has committed breaches of its obligations under Article 36, paragraph 1, of the Vienna Convention; and that moreover, in respect of those three persons alone, the United States has also committed breaches of Article 36, paragraph 2. The review and reconsideration of conviction and sentence required by Article 36, paragraph 2, which is the appropriate remedy for breaches of Article 36, paragraph 1, has not been carried out. The Court considers that in these three cases it is for the United States to find an appropriate remedy having the nature of review and reconsideration according to the criteria indicated in the Judgment.

Note on the Aftermath of the Avena Decision: Osbaldo Torres and Jose Medellin

Six weeks after the International Court of Justice's sweeping ruling in *Mexico v. United States*, the Oklahoma Court of Criminal Appeals halted the execution of Mexican national Osbaldo Torres just five days shy of his scheduled execution. Hours later, Oklahoma Governor Brad Henry commuted Torres' death sentence to life without parole. Both the Court of Criminal Appeals and Governor Henry cited the ICJ ruling and agreed that Torres had been denied his right under the Vienna Convention on Consular Relations to contact the Mexican consulate upon his arrest for capital murder.

The 3–2 decision of the Oklahoma Court of Criminal Appeals appears to be the first application of *Mexico v. United States* to an American capital case. According to Judge Charles Chapel's concurrence, the Court of Criminal Appeals was bound by the ICJ ruling given the United States treaty obligations. *State v. Torres* (unpublished). In Judge Chapel's view, Torres' trial might have come out differently had the Mexican government been notified of his arrest. Judge Chapel noted that the Mexican government routinely helps its citizens secure qualified capital counsel, investigators, expert witnesses and translators.

In dissent, Judge Gary Lumpkin wrote that the ICJ decision in *Mexico v. United States* was not binding on Oklahoma. Further, even though the Mexican government's assistance in obtaining qualified capital counsel, investigators, experts and translators might be laudable, it was "not the legal standard." *See generally* Liptak, *Execution of Mexican is Halted*, The New York Times, May 14, 2004.

Like Torres, Jose Medellin, a Mexican national, was convicted of murder and sentenced to death without being advised of his right to consular access as required by the Vienna Convention. *Medellin v. Dretke*, 125 S.Ct. 2088, 2089 (2005) (per curiam). After being denied relief by state courts on his claim that Texas deprived him of his right to consular access, Medellin sought federal habeas relief; however, the district court denied relief and the Fifth Circuit Court of Appeals denied Medellin's application for a certificate of appealability. 125 S.Ct. at 2089–2090. The Supreme Court granted certiorari in *Medellin v. Dretke*, 125 S.Ct. 2088 (2005), to decide (1) "whether a federal court is bound be the International Court of Justice's (ICJ) ruling that United States courts must reconsider petitioner Jose Medellín's claim for relief under the Vienna Convention on Consular Relations … without regard to procedural default doctrines," 125 S.Ct. at 2089, and (2) "whether a federal court should give effect, as a matter of judicial comity and uniform treaty interpretation, to the ICJ's judgment." 125 S.Ct. at 2089.

While Medellin's case was pending before the U.S. Supreme Court, the White House issued the following:

> **MEMORANDUM FOR THE ATTORNEY GENERAL SUBJECT:** Compliance with the Decision of the International Court of Justice in *Avena* the United States is a party to the Vienna convention on Consular Relations (the "Convention") and the Convention's Optional Protocol Concerning the Compulsory Settlement of Disputes (Optional Protocol), which gives the International Court of Justice (ICJ) jurisdiction to decide disputes concerning the "interpretation and application" of the Convention. I have determined, pursuant to the authority vested in me as President by the Constitution and the laws of the United States of America, that the United States will discharge its international obligation under the decision of the International Court of Justice in the Case Concerning Avena and Other Mexican Nationals *(Mexico v. United States of America) (Avena)*, 2004 ICJ 128 (Mar. 31), by having State courts give affect to the decision in accordance with general principles of comity in cases filed by the 51 Mexican nationals addressed in that decision.

George W. Bush, Memorandum for the Attorney General (Feb. 28, 2005), App. 2 to Brief for United States as *Amicus Curiae*, 2005 WL 504990, at 1aa (Feb. 28, 2005).

In reaction to this memorandum from the White House, the Supreme Court in *Medellin v. Dretke*, concluded:

> More than two months after we granted certiorari, and a month before oral argument in this case, President Bush issued a memorandum that stated the United States would discharge its international obligations under the *Avena* judgment by "having State courts give effect to the [ICJ] decision in accordance with general principles of comity in cases filed by the 51 Mexican nationals addressed in that decision." George W. Bush, Memorandum for the Attorney General (Feb. 28, 2005), App. 2 to Brief for United States as *Amicus Curiae* 9a. Relying on this memorandum and the *Avena* judgment as separate bases for relief that were not available at the time of his first state habeas corpus action, Medellíin filed a successive state application for a writ of habeas corpus just four days before oral argument here. That state proceeding may provide Medellíin with the review and reconsideration of his Vienna Convention claim that the ICJ required, and that Medellíin now seeks in this proceeding. This new development, as well as the factors discussed below, leads us to dismiss the writ of certiorari as improvidently granted. …
>
> In light of the possibility that the Texas courts will provide Medellíin with the review he seeks pursuant to the *Avena* judgment and the President's memorandum, and the potential for review in this Court once the Texas courts have heard and decided Medellíin's pending action, we think it would be unwise to

reach and resolve the multiple hindrances to dispositive answers to the questions here presented. Accordingly, we dismiss the writ as improvidently granted.

125 S.Ct. at 2090, 2092.

The Court also noted in footnote 1 of its Order, "Of course Medellín, or the State of Texas, can seek certiorari in this Court from the Texas courts' disposition of the state habeas corpus application. In that instance, this Court would in all likelihood have an opportunity to review the Texas courts' treatment of the President's memorandum and *Case Concerning Avena and other Mexican Nationals (Mex. v. U.S.)*, 2004 I.C.J. No. 128 (Judgment of Mar. 31), unencumbered by the issues that arise from the procedural posture of this action."

Four justices dissented from the dismissal of the case. Justice O'Connor, with whom Justices Stevens, Souter, and Breyer joined, stated:

> I would vacate the Court of Appeals' decision to deny Medellín a COA with which to proceed, and remand for further proceedings. After we granted certiorari in this case, the President informed his Attorney General that the United States would discharge its obligations under the *Avena* judgment "by having State courts give effect to the decision." George W. Bush, Memorandum for the Attorney General (Feb. 28, 2005), App. 2 to Brief for United States as *Amicus Curiae* 9a. Medellín has since filed a successive petition in state court. It is possible that the Texas court will grant him relief on the basis of the President's memorandum. On remand, the Court of Appeals for the Fifth Circuit may have wished to consider that possibility when scheduling further federal proceedings, and to hold the case on its docket until Medellín's successive petition was resolved in state court.

125 S.Ct. at 2105.

Note on Treaty Reservations

Occasionally, a party to a treaty may wish to accept most, but not all, of its obligations. A party may not agree with a particular provision in the treaty or may lack power to accept a particular provision. In those circumstances, the party may seek to enter into a "reservation" to the treaty. The following case illustrates an example in which a juvenile sentenced to death sought to persuade a state court to overturn his death sentence based on United States' treaty obligations.

Domingues v. State
961 P.2d 1279 (Nev. 1998)

YOUNG, Justice.

This case raises the single issue of whether NRS [Nevada Revised Statutes] 176.025 is superseded by an international treaty ratified by the United States, which prohibits the execution of individuals who committed capital offenses while under the age of eighteen. NRS 176.025 allows imposition of the death penalty on a defendant who was sixteen years old or older at the time that the capital offense was committed.

On October 22, 1993, sixteen-year-old Michael Domingues murdered a woman and her four-year-old son in the victims' home. In August 1994, a jury found Domingues guilty of one count of burglary, one count of robbery with the use of a deadly weapon, one count of first degree murder, and one count of first degree murder with the use of a deadly weapon. At seventeen years of age, Domingues was sentenced to death for each of the two murder convictions. On May 30, 1996, this court upheld Domingues' convictions and sentence. *Domingues v. State*, 917 P.2d 1364 (1996).

On November 7, 1996, Domingues filed a motion for correction of illegal sentence, arguing that "execution of a juvenile offender violates an international treaty ratified by the United States and violates customary international law." Article 6, paragraph 5 of the International Covenant on Civil and Political Rights (ICCPR) provides that: "Sentence of death shall not be imposed for crimes committed by persons below eighteen years of age and shall not be carried out on pregnant women." ICCPR, Dec. 19, 1966, art. 6, S. Treaty Doc. No. 95-2, 999 U.N.T.S. 171, 175.

In 1992, the United States Senate ratified the ICCPR, with the following pertinent reservation and declaration:

> That the United States reserves the right, subject to its Constitutional constraints, to impose capital punishment on any person (other than a pregnant woman) duly convicted under existing or future laws permitting the imposition of capital punishment, *including such punishment for crimes committed by persons below eighteen years of age.*

> That the United States declares that the provisions of Articles 1 through 27 of the [ICCPR] *are not self-executing.* 138 Cong.Rec. S4781-01, S4783-84 (daily ed. April 2, 1992) (emphasis added).

At a hearing on Domingues' motion to correct the illegal sentence, the district court concluded that the sentence was not facially illegal and, thus, it lacked jurisdiction to correct the sentence; on March 7, 1997, the district court issued an order denying Domingues' motion. Domingues appeals from this order.

Domingues contends that pursuant to the ICCPR, imposition of the death sentence on one who committed a capital offense while under the age of eighteen is illegal. ICCPR, 999 U.N.T.S. at 175. Although the United States Senate ratified the ICCPR with a reservation allowing juvenile offenders to be sentenced to death, Domingues asserts that this reservation was invalid and thus this capital sentencing prohibition set forth in the treaty is the supreme law of the land. See 138 Cong. Rec. S4781-01, S4783-84 (daily ed. April 2, 1992). Domingues contends that his death sentence, imposed for crimes he committed when he was sixteen years old, is thereby facially illegal. See *Edwards v. State*, 918 P.2d 321, 324 (1996) (recognizing the inherent power of the district court to correct a facially illegal sentence); *Anderson v. State*, 528 P.2d 1023 (1974). We disagree.

We conclude that the Senate's express reservation of the United States' right to impose a penalty of death on juvenile offenders negates Domingues' claim that he was illegally sentenced. Many of our sister jurisdictions have laws authorizing the death penalty for criminal offenders under the age of eighteen, and such laws have withstood Constitutional scrutiny. See *Stanford v. Kentucky*, 492 U.S. 361 (1989) [*supra* chapter 5]; Nanda, "The United States Reservation to the Ban on the Death Penalty for Juvenile Offenders: An Appraisal Under the International Covenant on Civil and Political Rights," 42 DePaul L. Rev. 1311, 1312–13 (1995).

NRS 176.025 provides that the death penalty shall not be imposed upon individuals who were under sixteen years of age at the time that the offense was committed. Because Domingues was sixteen at the time he committed a capital offense, we conclude that the death penalty was legally imposed upon him. Accordingly, we affirm the decision of the district court denying Domingues' motion to correct the sentence.

SPRINGER, Chief Justice, dissenting.

The International Covenant on Civil and Political Rights, to which the United States is a "party," forbids imposing the death penalty on children under the age of eighteen. International treaties of this kind ordinarily become the "supreme law of the land." Under the majority's interpretation of the treaty, the United States, at least with regard to executing children, is a "party" to the treaty, while at the same time rejecting one of its most vital terms. Under Nevada's interpretation of the treaty, the United States will be joining hands with such countries as Iran, Iraq, Bangladesh, Nigeria and Pakistan in approving death sentences for children. I withhold my approval of the court's judgment in this regard.

ROSE, Justice, dissenting.

Following a brief hearing, the district court summarily concluded that the death sentence was facially valid in spite of an international treaty signed by the United States which prohibits the execution of individuals who were under eighteen years of age when the crime was committed. I believe this complicated issue deserved a full hearing, evidentiary if necessary, on the effect of our nation's ratification of the ICCPR and the reservation by the United States Senate to that treaty's provision prohibiting the execution of anyone who committed a capital crime while under eighteen years of age.

The penultimate issue that the district court should have considered is whether the Senate's reservation was valid. Article 4(2) of the treaty states that there shall be no derogation from Article 6 which includes the prohibition on the execution of juvenile offenders. ICCPR, 999 U.N.T.S. at 174. Furthermore, there is authority to support the proposition that the Senate's reservation was invalid. See, *e.g.*, Restatement (Third) of the Foreign Relations Law of the United States §313 (1987); Nanda, "The United States Reservation to the Ban on the Death Penalty for Juvenile Offenders: An Appraisal Under the International Covenant on Civil and Political Rights," 42 DePaul L. Rev. 1311, 1331–32 (1993).

If the reservation was not valid, then the district court should determine whether the United States is still a party to the treaty. If the reservation was a "sine qua non" of the acceptance of the whole treaty by the United States, then the United State's ratification of the treaty could be considered a nullity. See Schabas, "Invalid Reservations to the International Covenant on Civil and Political Rights: Is the United States Still a Party?," 21 Brook. J. Int'l. L. 277, 318–19 (1995). But, if the United States has shown an intent to accept the treaty as a whole, the result could be that the United States is bound by all of the provisions of the treaty, notwithstanding the reservation.

These are not easy questions and testimony about the international conduct of the United States concerning the subjects contained in the treaty, in addition to expert testimony on the effect of the Senate's reservation may be necessary. A federal court that deals with federal law on a daily basis might be better equipped to address these issues; however, the motion is before the state court and it should do its best to resolve the matter. Accordingly, I would reverse the district court's denial of Domingues' motion and remand the case for a full hearing on the effect of the ICCPR on Domingues' sentence.

Questions

Do you think the Nevada Supreme Court was wise in avoiding a hearing on whether the United States' reservation to the ban on the death penalty for juvenile offenders was valid? Would such an inquiry intrude too closely on questions best left to the federal courts? How, if ever, could Domingues present his claim to a federal court?

C. Abolitionist and Retentionist Countries

Note on the International Abolition Movement

The Canadian Supreme Court, in *Burns* (*supra* this chapter), discussed the international abolition movement:

International Initiatives to Abolish the Death Penalty

[There have been important initiatives within the international community denouncing the death penalty. These include: *Extrajudicial, summary or arbitrary executions: Report by the Special Rapporteur*, U.N. Doc. E/CN.4/1997/60, at para. 79; *Extrajudicial, summary or arbitrary executions: Note by the Secretary-General*, U.N. Doc. A/51/457, at para. 145; United Nations Commission on Human Rights Resolutions 1997/12, 1998/8, 1999/61, and 2000/65.]

In this connection, Canada's representative is reported as stating as follows:

"Suggestions that national legal systems needed merely to take into account international law was inconsistent with international legal principles. National legal systems should make sure they were in compliance with international laws and rights, in particular when it came to the right to life."(Press Release HR/CN/788 (April 7, 1997)) See also resolutions adopted by the Parliamentary Assembly of the Council of Europe (Resolution 1044 (1994)) and the European Parliament (resolutions B4-0468, 0487, 0497, 0513 and 0542/97 (1997)) calling on all countries to abolish the death penalty, and the declaration of June 29, 1998 of the European Union's General Affairs Council stating that: "The [European Union] will work towards the universal abolition of the death penalty as a strongly held policy now agreed by all [European Union] Member States."

Abolition is also the policy of the *Second Optional Protocol to the International Covenant on Civil and Political Rights*, GA Res. 44/128 (December 15, 1989) (in force in 1991); U.N. Doc. A/46/40, at paras. 64–65, and see generally W. A. Schabas, *The Abolition of the Death Penalty in International Law* (2nd ed. 1997), at p. 176), the *Protocol to the American Convention on Human Rights to Abolish the Death Penalty*, [1990] 29 I.L.M. 1447 (the Organization of American States), and *Protocol No. 6 to the Convention for the Protection of Human Rights and Fundamental Freedoms Concerning the Abolition of the Death Penalty*(the Council of Europe) which contain similar prohibitions on state parties to those Protocols. A significant number of countries have signed or ratified the latter Protocol since *Kindler* and *Ng* were decided: see Council of Europe, *The Death Penalty: Abolition in Europe* (May 1999), at pp. 169–84.

It is noteworthy that the United Nations Security Council excluded the death penalty from the punishments available to the International Criminal Tribunals for the former

Yugoslavia (Resolution 827, May 25, 1993) and for Rwanda (Resolution 955, November 8, 1994), despite the heinous nature of the crimes alleged against the accused individuals. This exclusion was affirmed in the Rome Statute of the International Criminal Court, signed on December 18, 1998.

This evidence does not establish an international law norm against the death penalty, or against extradition to face the death penalty. It does show, however, significant movement towards acceptance internationally of a principle of fundamental justice ... namely the abolition of capital punishment.

State Practice Increasingly Favors Abolition of the Death Penalty

... [S]ince *Kindler* and *Ng* (discussed *supra*, this chapter, in *United States v. Burns*) were decided in 1991, a greater number of countries have become abolitionist.

Amnesty International reports that in 1948, the year in which the Universal Declaration of Human Rights was adopted, only eight countries were abolitionist. In January 1998, the Secretary-General of the United Nations, in a report submitted to the Commission on Human Rights (U.N. Doc. E/CN.4/1998/82), noted that 90 countries retained the death penalty, while 61 were totally abolitionist, 14 ... were classified as abolitionist for ordinary crimes and 27 were considered to be abolitionist *de facto* (no executions for the past 10 years) for a total of 102 abolitionist countries. At the present time, it appears that the death penalty is now abolished (apart from exceptional offences such as treason) in 108 countries. These general statistics mask the important point that abolitionist states include all of the major democracies except some of the United States, India and Japan ("Dead Man Walking Out," *The Economist*, June 10–16, 2000, at p. 21). According to statistics filed by Amnesty International, 85 percent of the world's executions in 1999 were accounted for by only five countries: the United States, China, the Congo, Saudi Arabia and Iran.

The existence of an international trend against the death penalty is useful in testing our values against those of comparable jurisdictions. This trend against the death penalty supports some relevant conclusions. First, criminal justice, according to international standards, is moving in the direction of abolition of the death penalty. Second, the trend is more pronounced among democratic states with systems of criminal justice comparable to our own. The United States (or those parts of it that have retained the death penalty) is the exception, although of course it is an important exception. Third, the trend to abolition in the democracies, particularly the Western democracies, mirrors and perhaps corroborates the principles of fundamental justice that led to the rejection of the death penalty in Canada.

Note on United Nations Commission on Human Rights Death Penalty Resolution

In April 2005, 53 countries attending the 61st annual meeting of the United Nations Commission on Human Rights met in Geneva, Switzerland. The Commission on Human Rights, which makes recommendations to the U.N. General Assembly, considered whether to pass a resolution condemning the death penalty and urging abolition.

The resolution passed 26–17, with 10 abstentions. The United States voted against it.

Abolitionist and Retentionist Countries
Amnesty International (2005)
www.web.amnesty.org

More than half the countries in the world have now abolished the death penalty in law or practice. The numbers are as follows:

Abolitionist for All Crimes: 84
Abolitionist for Ordinary Crimes Only: 12
Abolitionist in Practice: 24
Retentionist Countries: 76
Total Abolitionist in Law or Practice: 120

Andorra	East Timor	Marshall Islands	Sao Tome and
Angola	Ecuador	Mauritius	Principe
Armenia	Estonia	Micronesia (Feder-	Senegal
Australia	Finland	ated States)	Serbia and Mon-
Austria	France	Moldova	tenegro
Azerbaijan	Georgia	Monaco	Seychelles
Belgium	Germany	Mozambique	Slovak Republic
Bhutan	Guinea-Bissau	Namibia	Slovenia
Bosnia-Herzegovina	Haiti	Nepal	Solomon Islands
Bulgaria	Honduras	Netherlands	South Africa
Cambodia	Hungary	New Zealand	Spain
Canada	Iceland	Nicaragua	Sweden
Cape Verde	Ireland	Nicue	Switzerland
Colombia	Italy	Norway	Turkmenistan
Costa Rica	Kiribati	Palau	Turkey
Cote D'ivoire	Liechtenstein	Panama	Tuvalu
Croatia	Lithuania	Paraguay	Ukraine
Cyprus	Luxembourg	Poland	United Kingdom
Czech Republic	Macedonia (Former	Portugal	Uruguay
Denmark	Yugoslav Repub-	Romania	Vanuatu
Djibouti	lic)	Samoa	Vatican City State
Dominican Rep.	Malta	San Marino	Venezuela

2. Abolitionist for Ordinary Crimes Only

Countries whose laws provide for the death penalty only for exceptional crimes such as crimes under military law or crimes committed in exceptional circumstances:

Albania	Chile	Greece	Peru
Argentina	Cook Islands	Israel	
Bolivia	El Salvador	Latvia	
Brazil	Fiji	Mexico	

3. Abolitionist in Practice

Countries which retain the death penalty for ordinary crimes such as murder but can be considered abolitionist in practice in that they have not executed anyone during the past 10 years and are believed to have a policy or established practice of not carrying out executions. The list also includes countries which have made an international commitment not to use the death penalty:

Algeria	Congo (Republic)	Mali	Sri Lanka
Benin	Gambia	Mauritania	Suriname
Brunei Darussalam	Grenada	Nauru	Togo
Burkina Faso	Kenya	Niger	Tonga
Central African	Madagascar	Papua New Guinea	Tunisia
Republic	Maldives	Russian Federation	

4. Retentionist

Countries Which Retain the Death Penalty for Ordinary Crimes*

Afghanistan	Ethiopia	Libya	Sudan
Antigua and Bar-	Gabon	Malawi	Swaziland
buda	Ghana	Malaysia	Syria
Bahamas	Guatemala	Mongolia	Taiwan (Republic
Bahrain	Guinea	Morocco	of China)
Bangladesh	Guyana	Myanmar	Tajikistan
Barbados	India	Nigeria	Tanzania
Belarus	Indonesia	Oman	Thailand
Belize	Iran	Pakistan	Trinidad and To-
Botswana	Iraq	Palestinian	bago
Cameroon	Jamaica	Authority	Turkmenistan
Chad	Japan	Qatar	Uganda
Chile	Jordan	Rwanda	United Arab
China (People's	Kazakstan	St. Christopher &	Emirates
Republic)	Korea (North)	Nevis	United States of
Comoros	Korea (South)	St. Lucia	America
Congo (Dem. Rep.)	Kuwait	St. Vincent & The	Uzbekistan
Cuba	Kyrgyzstan	Grenadines	Viet Nam
Dominica	Laos	Saudi Arabia	Yemen
Egypt	Lebanon	Sierra Leone	Zambia
Equatorial Guinea	Lesotho	Singapore	Zimbabwe
Eritrea	Liberia	Somalia	

* Most of these countries and territories are known to have carried out executions during the past 10 years. On some countries Amnesty International has no record of executions but is unable to ascertain whether or not executions have in fact been carried out. Several countries have carried out executions in the past 10 years but have since instituted moratoria on executions.

Countries Which Have Abolished the Death Penalty since 1976

1976: Portugal abolished the death penalty for all crimes.

1978: Denmark abolished the death penalty for all crimes.

1979: Luxembourg, Nicaragua and Norway abolished the death penalty for all crimes. Brazil, Fiji and Peru abolished the death penalty for ordinary crimes.

1981: France and Cape Verde abolished the death penalty for all crimes.

1982: The Netherlands abolished the death penalty for all crimes.

1983: Cyprus and El Salvador abolished the death penalty for ordinary crimes.

1984: Argentina abolished the death penalty for ordinary crimes.

1985: Australia abolished the death penalty for all crimes.

1987: Haiti, Liechtenstein and the German Democratic Republic (1) abolished the death penalty for all crimes.

1989: Cambodia, New Zealand, Romania and Slovenia (2) abolished the death penalty for all crimes.

1990: Andorra, Croatia (2), the Czech and Slovak Federal Republic (3), Hungary, Ireland, Mozambique, Namibia and Sao Tome and Principe abolished the death penalty for all crimes.

1992: Angola, Paraguay and Switzerland abolished the death penalty for all crimes.

1993: Greece, Guinea-Bissau, Hong Kong (4) and Seychelles abolished the death penalty for all crimes.

1994: Italy abolished the death penalty for all crimes.

1995: Djibouti, Mauritius, Moldova and Spain abolished the death penalty for all crimes.

1996: Belgium abolished the death penalty for all crimes.

1997: Georgia, Nepal, Poland and South Africa abolished the death penalty for all crimes. Bolivia and Bosnia-Herzegovina abolished the death penalty for ordinary crimes.

1998: Azerbaijan, Bulgaria, Canada, Estonia, Lithuania and the United Kingdom abolished the death penalty for all crimes.

1999: East Timor, Turkmenistan and Ukraine abolished the death penalty for all crimes. Latvia abolished the death penalty for ordinary crimes.

2000: Albania, abolished the death penalty for ordinary crimes. Malta and Cote D'ivoire abolished the death penalty for all crimes.

2001: Chile, abolished the death penalty for ordinary crimes.

2002: Turkey, and The Federal Republic of Yugoslavia and Cyprus, abolished the death penalty for ordinary crimes.

2003: Armenia abolished the death penalty for ordinary crimes.

2004: Bhutan, Samoa, Senegal and Turkey, abolished the death penalty for all crimes.

Notes:

(1) In 1990 the German Democratic Republic became unified with the Federal Republic of Germany, where the death penalty had been abolished in 1949.

(2) Slovenia and Croatia abolished the death penalty while they were still republics of the Socialist Federal Republic of Yugoslavia. The two republics became independent in 1991.

(3) In 1993 the Czech and Slovak Federal Republic divided into two states, the Czech Republic and Slovakia.

(4) In 1997 Hong Kong was returned to Chinese rule as a special administrative region of China. Amnesty International understands that Hong Kong will remain abolitionist.

(5) In 1999 the Latvian parliament voted to ratify Protocol No. 6 to the European Convention on Human Rights, abolishing the death penalty for peacetime offences.

(6) In 2000 Albania ratified Protocol No. 6 to the European Convention on Human Rights, abolishing the death penalty for peacetime offences.

Note on Capital Commutations in Russia

In 1992, Russian President Boris Yeltsin established a Death Penalty Review Panel, which was staffed by a number of liberals including Anatoly Pristavkin, a novelist and chairman of the review panel. During the first few years of its existence, the panel recommended commuting the death sentences of 365 men on Russia's death row. Yeltsin commuted 340 of those sentences. But in 1995 Yeltsin's attitude changed dramatically. He commuted only five sentences and ordered 132 executions. Observers noted that this change of heart may have been due to a number of political factors, including popular support for the death penalty during an election year. However, this change of heart also put Yeltsin at odds with Western European nations that have outlawed the death penalty. Elimination of the death penalty is a requirement for admission to the Council of Europe. In an effort to be accepted by the European nations, Yeltsin promised to abolish the death penalty within three years. Kraft, *Executions Accelerate in Russia*, Los Angeles Times (May 1, 1996); Clark, *Boris the Merciless Raises Execution Quota*, The Observer (Mar. 17, 1996). Yeltsin made good on his promise in June 1999, when he signed a decree commuting the death sentences of all convicts on Russia's death row.

Note on Abolition in South Africa

South Africa, formerly considered one of the most repressive regimes in the world, abolished capital punishment in 1995. Excerpts from the South African Constitutional Court's opinion follow.

State v. Makwanyane and Mchunu
Case No. CCT/3/94 (June 6, 1995)

By a unanimous vote of its 11-member Constitutional Court, South Africa, a country which once led the world in executions, outlawed the death penalty on June 6, 1995. Announcing the decision, Arthur Chaskalson, president of the Constitutional Court, said, "Everyone, including the most abominable of human beings, has a right to life, and capital punishment is therefore unconstitutional." "Retribution can not be accorded the same weight under our Constitution as the right to life and dignity. It has not been shown that the death sentence would be materially more effective to deter or prevent murder than the alternative sentence of life imprisonment would be."

The Constitutional Court of the Republic of South Africa struck down the death penalty on the ground that capital punishment violated the newly-enacted Republic of South Africa Constitution. *State v. Makwanyane and Mchunu*, Case No. CCT/3/94 (June 6, 1995). Prior to the decision in *Makwanyane*, South Africa's use of the death penalty was notorious. It is estimated that between 1981 and 1990 approximately 1,100 people were executed in South Africa, including Transkei, Ciskei, Bophuthatswana and Venda. In 1989, South Africa imposed a moratorium on executions, although the sentence of death continued to be imposed. At the time of the Court's decision in *Makwanyane*, between 300 and 400 people were on death row in South Africa.

In 1993, a new Constitution of South Africa took effect. This Constitution was designed to promote human rights and democracy and to provide a transition from the culture and system of apartheid to a new system of government aimed at embracing all people of South Africa. While the South African Constitution did not explicitly ban the penalty of death for serious offenses, several key provisions in Chapter 3 of the Constitution led the Court to conclude that the death penalty could not stand.

Chapter 3 of Constitution sets out the fundamental rights guaranteed to all South Africans. In particular, Chapter 3, section 8 provides, "every person shall have the right to equality before the law and to equal protection of the law": Chapter 3, section 9 provides, "every person shall have the right to life"; Chapter 3, section 10 provides, "every person shall have the right to respect for and protection of his or her dignity"; and Chapter 3, section 11(2) prohibits "cruel, inhuman or degrading punishment." In addition, section 33 of Chapter 3, provides, in part, "The rights entrenched in this Chapter may be limited by law of general application, provided that such limitation — (a) shall be permissible only to the extent that it is — (i) reasonable; and (ii) justifiable in an open and democratic society based on freedom and equality; and (b) shall not negate the essential content of the right in question."

Writing for a unanimous court, Judge Chaskalson concluded that section 11(2) and the other relevant provisions of the South African Constitution prohibited the death penalty. Judge Chaskalson wrote:

> The carrying out of the death sentence destroys life, which is protected without reservation under section 9 of our Constitution, it annihilates human dignity which is protected under section 10, elements of arbitrariness are present in its enforcement and it is irremediable. Taking these factors into account, as well as the assumption that I have made in regard to public opinion in South Africa, and giving the words of section 11(2) the broader meaning to which they are entitled at this stage of the enquiry, rather than a narrow meaning, I am satisfied that in the context of our Constitution the death penalty is indeed a cruel, inhuman and degrading punishment.

Id. at para. 95 (footnote omitted).

After concluding that the death penalty generally constituted a cruel, inhuman and degrading punishment, the Court considered whether, under section 33 of Chapter 3, the prohibition against cruel, inhuman and degrading punishment could be limited so as to allow the implementation of the death penalty in cases of serious criminal violations. The Court concluded that it could not. Judge Chaskalson wrote:

> The rights to life and dignity are the most important of all human rights, and the source of all other personal rights in Chapter Three. By committing ourselves to a society founded on the recognition of human rights we are required to value these two rights above all others. And this must be demonstrated by the State in everything it does, including the way it punishes criminals. This is not achieved by objectifying murderers and putting them to death to serve as an example to others in the expectation that they might possibly be deterred thereby.
>
> In the balancing process the principal factors that have to be weighed are on the one hand the destruction of life and dignity that is a consequence of the implementation of the death sentence, the elements of arbitrariness and the possibility of error in the enforcement of capital punishment, and the existence of a severe alternative punishment (life imprisonment) and, on the other, the claim that the death sentence is a greater deterrent to murder, and will more ef-

fectively prevent its commission, than would a sentence of life imprisonment, and that there is a public demand for retributive justice to be imposed on murderers, which only the death sentence can meet.

Retribution cannot be accorded the same weight under our Constitution as the rights to life and dignity, which are the most important of all the rights in Chapter Three. It has not been shown that the death sentence would be materially more effective to deter or prevent murder than the alternative sentence of life imprisonment would be. Taking these factors into account, as well as the elements of arbitrariness and the possibility of error in enforcing the death penalty, the clear and convincing case that is required to justify the death sentence as a penalty for murder, has not been made out. The requirements of section 33(1) have accordingly not been satisfied, and it follows that the provisions of section 277(1)(a) of the Criminal Procedure Act, 1977 [which codifies the death penalty as a form of punishment in certain cases] must be held to be inconsistent with section 11(2) of the Constitution. In the circumstances, it is not necessary for me to consider whether the section would also be inconsistent with sections 8, 9 or 10 of the Constitution if they had been dealt with separately and not treated together as giving meaning to section 11(2).

Many factors and considerations appear to have contributed to Judge Chaskalson's conclusion that the death penalty constitutes a cruel, inhuman and degrading punishment in violation of South Africa's Constitution. Among these factors were the effects that race, poverty, language barriers, the experience of trial counsel and the temperament of the trial judge often play a role in determining who is sentenced to death. Judge Chaskalson stated "[w]e have to accept these differences in the ordinary criminal cases that come before the courts, even to the extent that some may go to gaol when others similarly placed may be acquitted or receive non-custodial sentences. But death is different, and the question is, whether this acceptable when the difference is between life and death. Unjust imprisonment is a great wrong, but if it is discovered, the prisoner can be released and compensated; but the killing of an innocent person is irremediable." Judge Chaskalson also found to be an important factor the lack of evidence showing that the death penalty was a more effective deterrent than life imprisonment.

Judge Chaskalson considered the treatment of the death penalty in other countries and emphasized the decision of the Hungarian Constitutional Court which held the death penalty unconstitutional under the newly-enacted Hungarian Constitution. *Id.* at para. 83–85. Judge Chaskalson discussed the death penalty as applied under the United States Constitution. He observed that the attempt to apply the death penalty in a constitutional manner in the United States had resulted in lengthy and costly litigation and concluded "we should not follow [the American] route."

Judge Chaskalson drew on the textual differences between the constitutions of the United States and South Africa. In particular, Judge Chaskalson noted that section 33 of South Africa's Constitution compelled a different conclusion on the question of capital punishment than that reached by the United States Supreme Court. Judge Chaskalson wrote, "In this [the South African Constitution] differs from the Constitution of the United States, which does not contain a limitation clause, as a result of which courts in that country have been obliged to find limits to constitutional rights through a narrow interpretation of the rights themselves." Under South Africa's Constitution

the position is different. It is not whether the decision of the State has been shown to be clearly wrong; it is whether the decision of the State is justifiable according to the criteria prescribed by section 33. It is not whether the infliction of death as a punishment for murder is not without justification, it is whether the infliction of death as punishment for murder has been shown to be both reasonable and necessary, and to be consistent with other requirements of section 33.

Id. at para. 102.

While all Constitutional Court judges concurred in the conclusions and result reached in Judge Chaskalson's majority opinion, several wrote separately to emphasize specific factors which compelled their decision or to highlight salient features of the South African experience with the death penalty. In his concurrence, Judge Ackermann wrote,

> The conclusion which I reach is that the imposition of the death penalty is inevitably arbitrary and unequal. Whatever the scope of the right to life in section 9 of the Constitution may be, it unquestionably encompasses the right not to be deliberately put to death by the state in a way which is arbitrary and unequal. I would therefore hold that section 277(1)(a) of the Criminal Procedure Act is inconsistent with the section 9 right to life. I would moreover also hold that it is inconsistent with section 11(2). Where the arbitrary and unequal infliction of punishment occurs at the level of a punishment so unique as the death penalty, it strikes me as being cruel and inhuman.

Id. at para. 166.

Judge Didcott similarly found that the death penalty violated sections 9 and 11(2), and agreed with much of Judge Chaskalson's analysis. Judge Didcott also gave voice to South Africa's unique history and with the country's current efforts to put into place democratic institutions. Judge Didcott wrote:

> South Africa has experienced too much savagery. The wanton killing must stop before it makes a mockery of the civilised, humane and compassionate society to which the nation aspires and has constitutionally pledged itself. And the state must set the example by demonstrating the priceless value it places on the lives of all its subjects, even the worst.

Id. at para. 190.

Judge Kentridge agreed with Judges Chaskalson and Didcott, adding "the striking down of the death penalty entails no sympathy whatsoever for the murderer, nor any condonation of his crime. What our decision does entail is a recognition that even the worst and most vicious criminals are not excluded from the protections of the Constitution." *Id.* at para. 204.

Judge Kriegler agreed with the conclusions of Judge Chaskalson, but focused on the right to life guaranteed in section 9 of Chapter 3. He found that the death penalty ran afoul of section 9 and could not be saved by the limitations provision in section 33. Similarly, Judge Sachs focused on the right to life clause and found it to be the jumping off point in analyzing the death penalty. Judge Langa also focused on section 9 stating,

> The emphasis I place on the right to life is, in part, influenced by the recent experiences of our people in this country. The history of the past decades has been such that the value of life and human dignity have been demeaned. Political, social and other factors created a climate of violence resulting in a culture of retaliation and vengeance. In the process, respect for life and for the inherent dignity of every person became the main casualties. The State has been part

of this degeneration, not only because of its role in the conflicts of the past, but also by retaining punishments which did not testify to a high regard for the dignity of the person and the value of every human life.

Id. at para. 218. Likewise, Judge O'Regan found the death penalty ran afoul of the right to life and the right to dignity.

In separate opinions, Judges Madala, Mahomed and Mokgoro discussed the concept of "ubantu" which is embodied in the postamble to the South Africa Constitution. Ubantu was described as:

> the ethos of an instinctive capacity for and enjoyment of love towards our fellow men and women; the joy and the fulfillment involved in recognizing their innate humanity; the reciprocity this generates in interaction within the collective community; the richness of the creative emotions which it engenders and moral energies which it releases both in the givers and the society which they serve and are served by.

Id. at para. 263.

Ubantu was further described as denoting humanity and morality. *Id.* at para. 308. These three judges emphasized that, while they agreed with the opinion of the Court, they also found the death penalty inconsistent with "ubantu" as embraced by the new South Africa.

Index